A
ENGLISH-SWAHILI
DICTIONARY

A ENGLISH-SWAHILI DICTIONARY

FOUNDED ON

A. C. MADAN'S

A ENGLISH-SWAHILI DICTIONARY

REVISED BY

FREDERICK JOHNSON

GYAN

Published by

GYAN

Gyan Publishing House
5, Ansari Road
Daryaganj, New Delhi-110002
Phone: 011-47034999, 9811692060
E-mail: books@gyanbooks.com

Distribution Network
gyanbooks.com
India, USA, Canada, UK, Australia, France

ISBN : 978-81-212-4569-2 (HB)
First Published, 1939

2nd Impression 2020

Printed at: Gyan Press, Delhi.

A
English-Swahili Dictionary
Author: A. C. Madan

AN ENGLISH-SWAHILI DICTIONARY

A

A ni neno lisilofasirika kwa Kiswahili isipokuwa pengine maana yake ni -moja, -o -ote, -mojawapo. Mfano: *Tell a man, to go,* mwambie mtu mmoja (ye yote, mmojawapo) kuenda. Kwa kawaida hutangulia kila jina (*noun*) la umoja au la jumla isipokuwa ni mojawapo maalum. Mfano: *a man,* mtu (mmoja, ye yote, mmojawapo), *a score,* korija (moja, yo yote, mojawapo), lakini mtu yule, *the* (*that*) *man*; korija ile, *the* (*that*) *score*. Pengine **an** hutumika badala ya **a,** ndiyo kutangulia (1) vokali zote isipokuwa *eu* na matamko mengine ya *u,* na (2) kutangulia *h* isyotamkwa, mfano: *an hour, an addict, an egg, an idiot, an orange, an ulcer,* lakini, *a horse, a eulogy, a unit.* **a** hutumika kutangulia *one,* mfano: *a one.* Pengine huweza kufasirika, kama 'kwa' mfano: *a shilling a hundred,* mia kwa shilingi moja.

aback, *adv.* kwa nyuma. *Be taken aback,* shtuka, fadhaika, staajabu, staajabika, shangaa, tekewa, duwaa, tunduwaa.

abaft, *adv. and prep.* kwa (katika) shetri, nyuma ya chombo (kibaharia).

abandon, *v.t.* (*desert*) tupa, acha, toka katika, gea, jitenga na; (*resign*) toa, acha. *Abandon oneself to,* jitia kabisa (*e.g.* huzuni, furaha, dhambi, tamaa &c.). —, *n.* kujitia kwa moyo, hali ya kutojizuia. **abandoned,** *a.* (*deserted*) -lioachwa, -liotupwa, -kiwa, -tupu; (*profligate*) -ovu, -potovu, fisadi, fasiki, -asherati. *An abandoned village,* mahame, ganjo, tongo. **abandonment,** *n.* tendo la kutupa au kuacha, kutupa, kutupwa; hali ya kutupwa au kuachwa, kuacha, kuachwa, ukiwa, kupotea, kukata tamaa; (*carelessness*) ulegevu, uzembe; (*complete surrender*) kujitia (kushiriki) kabisa katika jambo.

abase, *v.t.* tweza, tusha, dhili, fedhehesha, hakiri, vunja heshima au cheo. **abasement,** *n.* utwezo, unyonge, udhilifu, unyenyekeo, unyenyekevu.

abash, *v.t.* tia haya, tahayarisha, aibisha, fedhehesha, fadhaisha. **abashment,** *n.* fadhaa, haya, soni, tahayuri, fedheha.

abate, *v.t.* punguza, komesha; — *v.i.* pungua, punguka, koma. **abatement,** *n.* kipunguo, upunguo, upunguzo.

abattoir, *n.* machinjoni, mahali mjini pa kuchinjia ng'ombe, mbuzi &c.

abbacy, abbess, *n.* **abbey,** *n.* taz. *abbot.*

abbot, *n.* mkuu wa nyumba ya watawa waliojitenga kwa ajili ya dini. **abbacy,** *n.* kazi (cheo) ya *abbot.* **abbess,** *n.* *abbot* wa kike. **abbey,** *n.* nyumba ya *abbot* na watawa walio chini yake.

abbreviate, *v.t.* kata, fupisha, punguza, kusuru. **abbreviation,** *n.* mfupisho, ufupisho, mkato, mkato wa neno wa maneno *e.g.* k.w.k. badala ya kadha wa kadha; taz. badala ya tazama.

abdicate, *v.t.* jiuzulu, jitoa (hasa katika cheo kikubwa kama cha ufalme, usultani &c.). **abdication,** *n.* tendo la kujiuzulu.

abdomen, *n.* tumbo, uvungu wa tumbo. **abdominal,** *a.* -a tumbo. *Abdominal pains,* maumivu ya (msokoto wa) tumbo.

abduct, *v.t.* chukua (iba) kwa hila au kwa nguvu isiyo halali (hasa mwanamke), nyang'anya. **abduction,** *n.* tendo la kuiba (kuchukua) kwa hila au nguvu isiyo halali, hasa mwanamke, mtoto au mtu.

abeam, *adv.* kwa (katika) katikati ya chombo, kwa kukingama na chombo (kibaharia).

abed, *adv.* kitandani.

aberrant, *a.* -potovu, -liopotoka. **aberration,** *n.* upotoe, upotovu; (*of mind*) upungufu wa akili, wazimu, kichaa, mafuu.

abet, *v.t.* saidia, sukumiza, shirikiana na, -wa shauri moja na (hasa kwa mabaya). **abetment,** *n.* msaada, usukumizi, ushirika, shawishi. **abettor,** *n.* mshiriki, msaidizi, mshawishi (hasa kwa mabaya), mbuya.

abeyance, *n.* hali ya kutotumika kwa muda, ya kufifia (lakini huenda kutumika au kufufuliwa tena). *This rule is in abeyance,* amri hii haina nguvu siku hizi (lakini labda itafufuliwa tena).

abhor, *v.t.* chukia sana, chukizwa sana na, kirihi, zia, zira. **abhorrence,** *n.* machukio makuu, karaha, kirahi. **abhorrent,** *a.* -a kuchukiza sana, makuruhi.

abide, *v.t.* (*p.t. and pf.t.* **abode**) ngoja, ngojea; (*endure, tolerate*) stahimili, vumilia; — *v.i.* (*remain in a place*) kaa mahali, shinda mahali; (*remain*) dumu. *Abide by,* shika, fuata (ahadi, kusudi, amri *&c.*). **abiding,** *a.* -a kudumu, -a milele. **abode,** *n.* makao, nyumba, makazi, maskani, kitende, mastakimu, watani.

ability, *n.* akili, nguvu, uwezo, ustadi, umahiri. **abilities,** *n. pl.* nguvu au ustadi wa akili za mtu. **able,** *a.* -stadi, -a akili, -a nguvu, hodari. *Able-bodied,* -enye nguvu na afya ya mwili. *Be able,* weza, -wa na nguvu, -wa stadi. **ably,** *adv.* kwa ustadi.

abject, *a.* -nyonge kabisa, duni, hafifu. *Abject poverty,* ufukara, umaskini kabisa. **abjection,** *n.* **abjectness,** *n.* unyonge, uhafifu, udhilifu, ukata.

abjure, *v.t.* kana kwa kiapo, apiza; jikania (kitu au jambo kwa kiapo); jitenga kabisa na kitu (jambo, mahali) kwa kiapo.

ablaze, *adv. and a.* -a kuwaka, -a kung'aa, -a kumeka kama kwa moto au jua. *He was ablaze with anger,* moyo wake uliwaka kwa hasira. *The house is ablaze,* nyumba inawaka moto, inaungua.

able, *a.* taz. *ability.*

ablution, *n.* mwosho, mwogo. *Perform ablutions,* oga, nawa; (*ceremonial*) tawadha, fanya tohara.

ably, *adv.* taz. *ability.*

abnegate, *v.t.* jihini, jinyima; kana, katalia. **abnegation,** *n.* tendo la kujikatalia (la kukana, la kujihini, la kujinyima).

abnormal, *a.* -geni, -siyo ya kawaida au desturi; -a kupita kiasi (yaani kwa udogo au ukubwa) cha kawaida. **abnormality,** *n.* kioja, dubwana, kitu kisicho cha kawaida, kipitacho kiasi cha kawaida.

aboard, *adv. and prep.* chomboni, merikebuni, melini. *Go aboard,* panda chomboni. *Put aboard,* pakia.

abode, *n.* taz. *abide.*

abolish, *v.t.* ondoa kabisa, ondolea mbali, tangua, futa, batili. **abolition,** *n.* tanguo, ondoleo, tendo la kutangua.

abominate, *v.t.* chukia mno, kirihi. **abominable,** *a.* -a kuchukiza mno, makuruhi, -ovu kabisa. **abomination,** *n.* chukizo, machukio makuu, cho chote kinachochukiza mno, kirahi.

aboriginal, *a.* -a asili, -a kwanza. **aborigines,** *n.* watu wa asili wa nchi.

abort, *v.i.* haribu (avya) mimba; (*come to nothing*) via, dumaa, kundaa dumu katika hali isiyopevuka. **abortion,** *n.* mimba iliyoharibika, tendo la kuharibu (kuavya) mimba, cho chote kisichokomaa, kiumbe, chenye umbo lililoharibika hata kuchukiza mno, dubwana, kioja, chukizo; kazi ya bure. **abortive,** *a.* -liyozaliwa (-liyotokea) kabla ya wakati ufaao, -a bure, -siyofaa, -liopooza.

abound, *v.i.* -wa -ingi, jaa tele. *Abound in* (*with*), -wa na wingi wa, jaa sana. **abundance,** *n.* wingi, tele, maridhawa, halaiki, ujazo, uneemefu;

(*of harvest*), neema, baraka, usitawi. **abundant,** *a.* -ingi, tele, maridhawa. **abundantly,** *adv.* kwa wingi, chekwa-chekwa, kochokocho.

about, *prep.* (*around*) kuzunguka, *e.g. he went about the city,* alizunguka mjini; (*on the outside*) *e.g. the city had a wall about it,* mji ulizungukwa na ukuta; (*near to*) karibu, kama, kadiri ya, *e.g. about such and such o'clock,* karibu (kama, kadiri ya) saa fulani; (*concerning*) juu ya, habari za, *e.g. tell me about him,* niambie habari yake (juu yake). *Go about your business,* shika shughuli (kazi) yako. — *adv.* huko na huko, kuzunguka, pande zote, *e.g. go about the city,* nenda huko na huko mjini, zunguka mjini; *build a wall about the city,* jenga ukuta kuzunguka mji (pande zote za mji; (*nearly*) *e.g. I am about to go,* nakwenda sasa hivi. *He was about to die,* alitaka kufa. *What are you about?* unafanya nini? *Come about,* fanyika, -wa, tukia, pata kuwa. *Bring about,* fanya, fanyika. *Turn and turn about,* kwa zamu.

above, *adv. and prep.* juu (ya); (*more*) zaidi (ya); (*excelling*) kupita. *Above-board,* wazi, dhahiri, -nyofu, -adilifu.

abrade, *v.t.* chubua, kwaruza. **abrasion,** *n.* mchubuo, chubuko, kwaruzo.

abreast, *adv.* sambamba, kwa hali ya kuwa na sehemu za mbele katika mstari ulio sawa, bila kutangulia wala kuwa nyuma. *Keep abreast of the times,* jijulisha siku zote habari za kisasa.

abridge, *v.t.* kata, punguza, fupisha. **abridgement,** *n.* fupisho, muhtasari; (*reduction*) upunguzo, mkato.

abroad, *adv.* (*outside*) nje; (*everywhere*) kote kote; (*in foreign parts*) ugenini. *Be abroad, go abroad,* safiri, tembea ugenini. *Be all abroad,* -wa na wasiwasi, fadhaika, hangaika, potewa akili. *Get abroad,* toka nje, tangaa, julika, vuma. *Scatter abroad,* tawanya, eneza kila mahali. *Spread abroad,* eneza, tangaza, vumisha.

abrogate, *v.t.* tangua, ondoa, vunja, batili, futa. **abrogation,** *n.* tanguo, mtanguo, kutangua.

abrupt, *a.* -a ghafula, kama kwamba imekatika, -a haraka, -siotazamiwa; (*steep*) -a kutelemka (kupanda) ghafula; (*of manners*) -a haraka, -a harara. **abruptness,** *n.* hamaki, harara, haraka; kuwa *abrupt.*

abscess, *n.* jipu; (*in throat*) halula.

abscond, *v.i.* jificha, toroka, kimbia (hasa kuepuka sheria). **absconder,** *n.* mtoro.

absence, *n.* kutokuwapo, ughaibu; (*lack*) ukosefu, ukosekano, utovu. *There is an absence of food,* chakula hakipo (kimeadimika). *In my absence,* wakati ambao mimi sipo.

absent, *a. Be absent,* tokuwapo, adimika. *He is absent,* hako. *He absents himself,* hako, ameacha kuja makusudi. *He is absent-minded,* yu msahaulifu, ana tabia ya kusahau mambo, amechukuliwa na chechele. **absentee,** *n.* asiyekuwapo mahali palipohusu. **absently,** *adv.* bila kuwaza, bila kuangalia.

absolute, *a.* (*perfect*) kamili, halisi; (*independent*) -tupu, safi, peke yake (yaani bila kuchanganyika na kitu kingine); (*despotic*) -enye amri zote peke yake; (*infinite*) isiyo na kiasi wala mipaka, ipitayo akili. **absolutely,** *adv.* pia, hasa, kabisa, bila shaka, hakika.

absolution, *n.* ondoleo la dhambi, masamaha, ghofira. **absolve,** *v.t.* ghofiri, samehe, achilia, ondoa hatiani.

absorb, *v.t.* -la, sharabu, -nywa, meza, tumia -ote kabisa; (*occupy*) shughulisha sana, vuta macho (akili, mawazo, fikira). *Be absorbed,* mezwa kabisa, nywewa kabisa; (*in thought &c.*) -wa katika fikira, shughulika sana hata kutofikiri vingine. **absorbent,** *a.* -a kunywa, -a kunywea, -a kumeza. — *n.* kitu kinachosharabu au kunywa au kumeza. **absorbing,** *a.* -a kuvuta moyo sana, -a kusahaulisha vingine. **absorption,**

n. tendo la kunywa (la kunywea, la kusharabu, la kumeza); (*engrossment*) hali ya kushughulika au kuvutwa mno na jambo hata kusahau mengine yote.

abstain, *v.i.* (*from*) epukana (na kitu), jihinisha, jinyima; (*for reasons of religion, health, taboo, totem*) gunga, zia, zira. *Abstain from food,* funga. **abstainer,** *n.* ajinyimaye (hasa ulevi). **abstention,** *n.* tendo la kuepukana na au kujinyima; (*on religious grounds, for health reasons &c.*) mwiko, mzio. **abstinent,** *a.* -a kuepukana na, -a kujinyima, -a kiasi, tawasufi. **abstinence,** *n.* kiasi katika kula na kunywa *&c.*, hali ya kufunga (kujihinisha, kutokula, kuzia, kuzira, kushika mwiko, kugunga). **abstemious,** *a.* -a kiasi, -a kujinyima (hasa kula na kunywa na vitu vya anasa).

abstract, *v.t.* toa katika, chukua kwa hila, iba, tenga; (*oneself, mind, attention*) jitenga (ufahamu, moyo, akili). — *a.* -a kuwazika tu, *e.g.* rangi ya ua na tabia za mtu *&c.* huwazika tu, haziwezi kushikika, ni mawazo ya *abstract*; (*abstruse*) -gumu, -a fumbo. — *n.* muhtasari, fupisho; (*essence*) kitu kilichotolewa katika kingine, *e.g.* alwaridi ni *abstract* ya ua fulani. **abstracted,** *a. Be abstracted,* tolewa katika, ondolewa katika; (*engrossed*) -wa katika hali ya kutoangalia, -wa katika fikira. **abstraction,** *n.* usahaulifu, hali ya kuwaza mengine, hali ya kushughulika na jambo hata kutoangalia mengine; tendo la kutoa katika (la kuiba).

abstruse, *a,* -a fumbo, -gumu kufahamika.

absurd, *a.* -a upuzi, -pumbavu, -a kuchekesha; (*false*) -a dhahiri kuwa si kweli wala haielekei kuwa; (*unreasonable*) muhali. **absurdity,** *n.* upumbavu, ubishi, upuzi.

abundance, *n.,* **abundant,** *a.,* **abundantly,** *adv.* taz *abound.*

abuse, *v.t.* tumia vibaya, tendea vibaya, dhulumu; (*by word*) amba, tukana, shutumu. — *n.* matumizi mabaya, kutendea vibaya; (*bad words*) matukano, matusi, shutumu; (*bad practice*) desturi mbaya, jambo lisilo haki, mazoea mabaya. **abusive,** *a,* -enye kutumia (kutendea) vibaya, -a kutukana.

abut, *v.i.* pakana na, -wa jirani na, -wa mwisho wa, egemea. **abutment,** *n.,* nguzo, tegemeo, egemeo.

abyss, *n.* shimo kubwa, shimo la kwenda chini sana. **abysmal,** *a.* bila mwisho kwa kwenda chini. *Abysmal ignorance,* upeo wa ujinga.

Abyssinia, *n.* Habeshi, Uhabeshi. **Abyssinian,** *n.* Mhabeshi.

acacia, *n.* namna ya mti, jamii ya mkakaya.

academy, *n.* skuli, shule, chuo (hasa mnamofundishwa elimu kubwa). **academic, academical,** *a.* -a kuhusu elimu ya skuli, -a chuoni, -a elimu.

accede, *v.i.* fikia mahali (cheo, hali); (*assent*) kubali, ridhia, toa idhini.

accelerate, *v.t.* zidisha mbio au mwendo, himiza; — *v.i.* zidi mwendo. **acceleration,** *n.* ongezo la mwendo. **accelerator,** *n.* mtu au kitu kinachoongeza mwendo.

accent, *n.* tamko la sauti, tamko la nguvu, mkazo wa sauti, alama ya mkazo, tamko la kawaida la jamii ya watu (la watu wakaao katika nchi fulani, la mtu fulani), lafudhi. — *v.t.* kazia sauti, tokeza. **accented,** *a.* -enye kutamkwa kwa nguvu, -enye mkazo wa sauti. **accentuate,** *v.t.* kaza sauti, tia mkazo wa tamko; (*enforce*) tia nguvu, zidisha, kaza, onyesha hasa, tokeza.

accept, *v.t.* pokea, kubali. **acceptable,** *a.* -a kupendeza, -a kukubalika. **acceptance,** *n.* ukubali, kibali; (*agreement*) sharti, maagano. **acceptation,** *n.* kibali; (*meaning*) maana.

access, *n.* (*liberty*) ruhusa ya kukaribia (ya kuingia); (*means of*) mlango, njia ya kufikia; (*increase*) maongezo, mazidio; (*sudden burst*) kipindi, mshindo. **accessible,** *a.* -a kuweza kukaribiwa, kufikika. *An accessible person,* mtu mpole awezaye kujiwa (kuendewa, kuambilika), mjibu. **accession,** *n.,* kuingia ufalme, kutawazwa; (*arrival*) majilio; (*increase*) maongezo. **accessory,** *a.* -a zaidi, -a kusaidia, -a msaada. — *n.* ongezo, ongezo la zana au vyombo; msaidizi, mshiriki, ashirikiye katika shauri kama la wizi *&c.* kwa kusaidia au kukubali.

accident, *n.* tukio, bahati, nasibu, ajali; (*disaster*) tukio baya, msiba. **accidental,** *a.* -a bahati, -a ajali, si makusudi, si ya lazima. — *n.* cho chote kisicho cha lazima. **accidentally,** *adv.* kwa ajali, bila kukusudiwa.

acclaim, *v.t.* tangaza kwa ukelele, sifu kwa ukelele, pokea kwa shangwe na vifijo. **acclamation,** *n.* vifijo, ukelele au vigelegele vya kusifu (vya kufurahia).

acclimatize, *v.t.* zoeza tabia za ugenini. *Sickness of acclimatization,* mkunguru.

acclivity, *n.* mwinuko, kilima, kiduta.

accolade, *n.* tendo la mfalme kumpa mtu heshima au cheo cha *knighthood,* kwa kumgusa begani kwa ubapa wa upanga na kutaja maneno yahusuyo.

accommodate, *v.t.* (*adapt*) tengeneza, ratibu, ratibisha, rekebisha (ili kufaa mambo yalivyo); (*oblige*) fadhili, nafisi, nafisisha, ridhisha; (*entertain*) karibisha, weka vizuri. *The house was built to accommodate ten people,* nyumba ilijengwa kuweka watu kumi. **accommodating,** *a.* -enye hisani, -a kuridhia, -pole, -a kupatana, -suluhifu; (*pliable &c.*) -a kuweza kutengenezwa (kurekebishwa) kwa urahisi. **accommodation,** *n.* matengenezo, mapatano; (*kindness*) fadhili, hisani, upendeleo, tajamala; (*board &c.*) mahali pa kukaa, makao.

accompaniment, *n.* ufuaso, fuatano, mwandamano; (*of music*) sauti linganifu. **accompany.** *v.t.* enda na, fuatana na; (*part of the way*) sindikiza, adi; (*of music*) fuata mwimbaji kwa kupiga muziki.

accomplice, *n.* msaidizi, mwenzi, mshirika, msiri (hasa katika mabaya).

accomplish, *v.t.* fanya, maliza, timiliza, tekeleza, fikiliza, faulu, isha, pata, weza; (*by great effort, or self denial*) kusuru. **accomplished,** *a.* (*complete*) -timilifu, kamili; (*educated*) -enye maarifa mengi (elimu nyingi, malezi mema, mafao mengi). **accomplishment,** *n.* (*end*) mwisho, tendo, ukomo; (*acquirement*) malezi mema, adili, adabu, matendo na mazungumzo yafaayo mbele ya watu.

accord, *v.t.* (*to*) jalia, tolea, -pa; — *v.i.*(*with*) patana, afikiana, lingana. **accordance,** *n.* upatano, umoja wa shauri. *With one accord,* kwa umoja. *It is in accordance with his wish,* ndivyo apendavyo. *Of his own accord,* kwa hiari yake, bila kuamrishwa. **accordant,** *a,* -enye kupatana au kulingana na. **accordingly,** *adv.* basi, kwa sababu hiyo, kwa hiyo. **according to,** *prep.* kwa kupatana na, kwa namna ya, kwa, kwa kadiri ya.

accordion, *n.* kinandą cha mkono (cha mivukuto).

accost, *v.t.* amkia, anza kusema na, salimu.

accouchement, *n.* tendo la mwanamke kuzaa mtoto, uzazi.

account, *v.t.* hesabu, kadiri, dhani, thamini; — *v.i.* (*for*) toa hesabu ya, eleza sababu (maana, kisa) ya, -wa sababu ya, jua maana ya. — *n.* (*reckoning*) hesabu, idadi; (*value*) thamani; (*statement*) habari, taarifa; (*reason*) sababu, kisa, hoja, ajili. *On account of,* kwa ajili ya, kwa sababu ya. *On no account,* sivyo, hapana kabisa, hasha. *On any account,* iwayo yote. *Render account,* toa hesabu. *Call to account,* taka hesabu (sababu, kisa) kwa. *Make up account,* fanya hesabu. *Include* *in account*, tia (andika) katika hesabu (au habari). *Give an account of*, simulia, hadithia, eleza habari ya; (*advance*) karadha. *Turn to account*, tumia vyema (kwa faida au nafuu). *Take into account*, kumbuka, hesabu. **accountable,** *a.* *Be accountable*, diriki. *Be made accountable for*, pasishwa. *He is accountable*, ni juu yake, amepasiwa. **accountancy,** *n.* kazi ya (mahali pa) kutunza au kufanya hesabu. **accountant,** *n.* karani (mwenye kazi ya kutunza hesabu). **account-book,** *n.* daftari ya hesabu.

accoutre, *v.t.* vika (hasa mavazi ya askari). **accoutrements,** *n.* mavazi (hasa ya askari pamoja na ukanda, mabeti &c.); matandiko ya farasi &c.

accredit, *v.t.* aminisha, sadikisha, pasha heshima; (*depute*) agiza, -pa daraka. **accredited,** *a.* -a kukubaliwa, -a kuaminiwa.

accretion, *n.* maongezo, lakini hasa yaliyozidi polepole kama utando juu ya maji, *e.g.* ukoga, ugozi.

accrue, *v.i.* zidi; (*result*) tokea, patikana, fuata. *The profits which accrue from work*, faida zinazotokea au kupatikana kwa kufanya kazi.

accumulate, *v.t.* kusanya, fanya chungu, chuma, weka akiba, limbika, lundika, dunduliza; — *v.i.* (*become increased*) ongezeka, zidi, kusanyika. **accumulation,** *n.* chungu, limbiko, lundiko, mkusanyo, akiba; (*quantity*) wingi. **accumulative,** *a.* -enye kuzidi, -enye kuongezeka, -enye kuweka, -wekevu, bahili. **accumulator,** *n.* mtu au kitu kinachokusanya wingi, chombo kinachotiwa na kuweka wingi wa nguvu za elektrisiti au umeme.

accurate, *a.* sahihi, barabara, isiyo na hitilafu, -enye kufanyika kwa uangalifu sana. **accuracy,** *n.* usahihi, usawa. **accurately,** *adv.* sahihi, barabara, sawasawa.

accursed, *a.* -liolaaniwa, -ovu kabisa, maleuni.

accuse, *v.t.* shtaki, laumu, suta, kengemeka. **accusation,** *n.* lawama, masuto, mashtaka. **accused,** *n.* mshtakiwa. **accuser,** *n.* mshtaki.

accustom, *v.t.* zoeza, tendekeza. *I am accustomed*, nimozoea. *Accustom oneself*, jizoeza. **accustomed,** *a.* -a desturi, -a kawaida, -zoevu. *He is accustomed to work*, mzoevu wa kazi.

ace, *n.* ree, yaani karata ya kuchezea yenye ng'anda moja, au dadu yenye alama moja; kipeo, kilicho bora; mtu hodari wa eropleni aliyepiga eropleni nyingi za adui.

acerbity, *n.* ukali, uchungu (wa kitu au moyo).

acetic, *a.* -enye asili ya ukali wa siki, -kali.

acetylene, *n.* hewa inayotoka *carbide of calcium* ikitiwa maji, iwakapo hutoa nuru kali. Hutumika katika taa nyingine za baisikeli na karabai.

ache, *n.* maumivu yanayoendelea, umizo. **ache,** *v.i.* uma, umiza (kwa maumivu yanayoendelea), changa.

achieve, *v.t.* maliza, isha fanya, faulu, pata, fikiliza. **achievement,** *n.* tendo (hasa tendo kuu), kazi bora.

acid, *a.* -kali, -chungu. — *n.* namna ya dawa kali katika kuonja; nyingine ni kali sana kama *hydrochloric acid*; hula madini; huungana na *alkali* kuwa *salts*. Siki ni *acid* isiyo kali sana. *Acid test*, jaribio la kuhakikisha kabisa (namna, tabia, thamani &c. ya kitu au mtu). **acidity,** *n.* ukali, uchungu (kama wa siki).

acidulate, *v.t.* tia uchungu (ukali) wa ladha.

acknowledge, *v.t.* kiri, ungama, kubali; (*receipt of*) julisha habari kama kitu kimewasili, stakabadhi; (*thank for*) toa asante ya. **acknowledgement,** *n.* ungamo; (*thanks*) asante, mashukuru; (*receipt*) stakabadhi, risiti.

acme, *n.* (*highest point*) kikomo, kipeo; (*perfection*) ukamilifu, usitawi.

acne, *n.* kinusi, chunusi.

acolyte, *n.* msaidizi, mhudumu, hasa katika ibada za kanisa.

acorn, *n.* tunda au mbegu za mti uitwao *oak*.

acoustic, *a.* -a kuhusu uwezo wa kusikia kwa masikio; -enye kutumika katika kusikia kwa masikio; -a kuhusu elimu ya sauti. **acoustics,** *n.* elimu ihusuyo usikizi wa sauti.

acquaint, *v.t.* julisha, pasha habari, fahamisha, bashiri, arifu, hadithia, aridhia. **acquaintance,** *n.* ujuzi, maarifa; (*person*) mtu umjuaye (si rafiki hasa). **acquainted,** *a. be acquainted with,* jua habari za, tambua, fahamu.

acquiesce, *v.i.* kubali, toa idhini, ridhika, ridhia. **acquiescence,** *n.* ukubali, uradhi, idhini, ridhaa. **acquiescent,** *a.* -enye kuridhika, -enye kukubali, -tiifu, -sikivu.

acquire, *v.t.* pata, jipatia (hasa kwa kujifunza au kujizoeza au kwa jitihadi). **acquirement,** *n.* upataji, akili au elimu iliyopatikana kwa kujifunza au kwa jitihadi. **acquisition,** *n.* tendo la kupata; pato, yaliyopatikana, mali; (*rarity*) tunu. **acquisitive,** *a.* -enye nia ya kupata. **acquisitiveness,** *n.* tabia ya kuwa na nia ya kupata.

acquit, *v.t.* fanya huru, achilia; (*judicially*) hukumu kuwa mtu hana hatia katika jambo aliloshtakiwa; (*settle*) lipa (kama deni). *He acquitted himself well,* alitenda kwa uhodari, alijipatia sifa. **acquittal,** *n.* ondoleo la hatia la sheria. **acquittance,** *n.* mlipo wa deni, tendo la kusamehe deni au ahadi &c., hati ya kushuhudia tendo hilo, stakabadhi.

acre, *n.* kipimo cha eneo chenye yadi za eneo 4,840. **acreage,** *n.* jumla ya hesabu ya *acre* zilizo katika shamba, kiwanja &c.

acrid, *a.* -chungu, -kali (hasa kwa kuonja). **acridity, acridness,** *n.* uchungu, ukali.

acrimony, *n.* uchungu (ukali) wa moyo (wa maneno). **acrimonious,** *a.* -kali, -chungu.

acrobat, *n.* mfanyaji michezo ya ustadi ya kutumia viungo vya mwili, kama ile ya kucheza juu ya kamba iliyonyoshwa juu kati ya miti miwili &c. **acrobatic,** *a.* -enye tabia ya *acrobat.*

across, *adv. and prep.* toka upande huu mpaka upande wa pili (wa), ng'ambo (ya.). *Go across* (*water*), vuka; (*land*) pita kati ya, pitia. *Draw a line across,* (piga) andika mstari katikati. *Lie across,* kingama. *Lie across each other,* pandana.

acrostic, *n.* shairi ambalo herufi ya kwanza au ya mwisho ya kila mstari zikipangwa taratibu, hufanya neno au maneno.

act, *v.t. and i.* tenda, fanya; (*be effective*) tenda kazi, toa nguvu, enda, pata njia; (*feign*) cheza, jifanya, igiza. *Act up to* (*a promise &c.*) timiza, tekeleza, fikiliza, (ahadi &c.). *Act for,* -wa badala ya, mahali pa, -wa wakili wa, -wa katika makamu ya, -wa niaba ya. *Act upon* (*affect*), vuta, geuza, endesha; (*follow*) fuata. *He is acting,* anaiga, ajifanya tu. *In the act,* katika kutenda, pale pale, mara hiyo. — *n.* kitendo, amali, feli; (*law*) sheria; (*part of play &c.*) sehemu ya mchezo wa kuigiza mambo ya hadithi (ya utenzi &c.). *Act of God,* tukio la nguvu ya asili lisiloweza kujulikana mbele, wala kuzuilika kwa nguvu ya kibinadamu. *Act of grace,* fadhili, hasa achilio au samaha la adhabu linalotolewa na mfalme. **acting,** *n.* kutenda, utendaji; (*pretence*) kujisingizia, kujifanya, hila, uwongo; (*play*) mchezo, unyago. — *a.* (*acting for*) badala ya, makamu ya, niaba ya. **action,** *n.* kitendo, amali, utendaji; (*gesticulation*) ishara ya kupunga au kutikisa mkono, konyezo &c.; (*fighting*) pigano, vita; (*prosecution*) daawa, mashtaka, madai; (*in play or story &c.*) maendeleo ya mambo katika mchezo (hadithi &c.). **active,** *a.* -enye kutenda, -a amali, -enye kufanya, -enye juhudi, -tendaji, -epesi (hodari) katika kutenda. *Be active,* biabia, tenda kazi, enda. **activity,** *n.* wepesi wa kutenda, bidii, juhudi, shughuli, utendaji.

actor, *n.* mtenda; (*player*) mcheza; (*personator*) mwigaji. **actress**, *n.*, *actor* wa kike. **actual**, *a.* hasa, kweli, hakika, halisi, -a kuwapo kweli na sasa. **actually**, *adv.* hasa, kweli. **actuary**, *n.* karani afanyaye hesabu zihusuzo bima. **actuate**, *v.t.* anzisha, endesha, vuta, ongoza, chochea, tia shonga, tia chonjo, shawishi.

acumen, *n.* akili, utambuzi, werevu, welekevu, wepesi wa kufahamu, busara.

acute, *a.* -enye ncha kali; (*of mind*) -a akili, -erevu; (*severe*) -kali. *Acute angle*, pembekali (yaani pungufu ya pembemraba). **acutely**, *adv.* vikali, sana, kwa nguvu. **acuteness**, *n.* akili, werevu; (*intensity*) ukali.

adage, *n.* mithali, fumbo la maneno (la zamani).

adamant, *n.* namna ya jiwe gumu mno, kama almasi. *Be adamant*, -wa imara kabisa, kataa kabisa neno lililoombwa. **adamantine**, *a.* kisichoweza kuvunjika wala kupenyezeka, imara; (*of character*) -shupavu, -gumu.

Adam's apple, *n.* kikoromeo, zoloto, kongomeo.

adapt, *v.t.* tengeneza, rekebisha, geuza, badili, vuta (ili kufaa kusudi fulani); linga, linganisha, fanyiza. **adaptableness**, **adaptability**, *n.* hali au tabia ya kuweza kujifanya (au kufanywa) kufaa. **adaptable**, *a.* -a kuweza kufanya (au kufanywa) kufaa. **adaptation**, *n.* tendo la kutengeneza (kubadili, kugeuza) ili kufaa kusudi fulani; kilichokwisha kugeuzwa ili kufaa.

add, *v.t.* jumlisha, ongeza, hesabu, pakiza. *Add to*, tia zaidi, ongeza, kithiri. *Add up*, jumlisha. **addendum**, *n.* ongezo. **addition**, *n.* tendo la kujumlisha &c.; kitu kilichotiwa zaidi, ziada, ongezo, jazi, jazo; (*in arithmetic*) hesabu, jumla. *In addition to*, juu ya, zaidi ya, tena. **additional**, *a.* -ingine, zaidi.

adder, *n.* namna ya nyoka mdogo mwenye sumu. *Puff adder*, fira, swila.

addict, *v.t.* *Be addicted to*, jitoa kwa, jifunga kwa, shiriki, zoea; shindwa na zoea; pendelea (hasa ubaya, *e.g.* ulevi). — *n.* mzoevu (hasa wa ulevi, desturi mbaya). **addictedness**, **addiction**, *n.* uzoevu, upendelevu (wa kunywa ulevi &c.).

addition, *n.*, **additional**, *a.* taz. *add.*

addle, *v.t.* ozesha, chafua, vuruga, tia fujo. **addled**, *a.* -bovu, viza. *Addle-headed*, *Addle-pated*, -enye akili zilizochafuka, -siyeweza kufikiri taratibu, -enye wasiwasi.

address, *v.t.* ambia, sema na, hubiria, hadithia, hutubia, simulia; (*letter*) andikia, tia anwani. — *n.* (*speech*) hotuba, hadithi, mahubiri, simulizi; (*cleverness*) akili, ubingwa, ustadi, umahiri, wepesi, welekevu; (*of a letter*) anwani; (*written*) hati, barua; (*manners*) adabu, malezi, makini. *Address oneself*, jitia, jifanya tayari, jishughulisha na, shika; (*speak*) sema. *Pay addresses to*, jipendekeza kwa, bembeleza, taka uchumba, posa. **addressee**, *n.* mtu ambaye anwani yake imeandikwa katika bahasha ya barua, apelekewaye barua.

adduce, *v.t.* taja, leta (hoja au neno la kuthibitisha).

adenoid, *n.* tezi la nyuma ya pua.

adept, *a.* -stadi, -bingwa, hodari, mahiri. — *n.* mstadi, mbingwa, fundi, mwelekevu, mweledi.

adequate, *a.* sawa, -a kutosha, -toshelevu, -a kukifu, -a kufaa kwa kusudi fulani. **adequacy**, **adequateness**, *n.* hali ya kutosha au kufaa, kefu, utoshelevu.

adhere, *v.i.* (*to*) ambata, nata, shikamana, gandamana; (*be consistent*) shika (fuata) kawaida (mashauri &c.), lingana, patana. **adherence**, *n.* ufuasi, uaminifu. **adherent**, *a.* -enye kuambata &c. — *n.* mfuasi, mwaminifu. **adhesion**, *n.* wambiso, tendo au hali ya kuambata; ufuasi, ukubali. **adhesive**, *a.* -a kuambata, -a kunata, -a kugandamana na.

ad hoc, kwa kusudi hili maalum.
adieu, *n.* kwa heri, Mungu akuweke (neno la kuaga). *Bid adieu to,* aga, agana na; (*finally*) aga buriani.
adipose, *a.* -enye mafuta, -nene, -nono.
adit, *n.* mlango, mahali pa kuingilia (hasa katika shimo la kuchimba makaa &c.).
adjacent, *a.* -a karibu, -a jirani, -a kupakana. *Be adjacent,* tangamana, pakana.
adjective, *n.* neno liongezalo maana ya jina (*noun*).
adjoin, *v.i.* pakana na, tangamana na. **adjoining,** *a.* -a kupakana na, -a pili, -a karibu, -a jirani.
adjourn, *v.t.* ahirisha, chelewesha, weka mpaka siku nyingine. **adjournment,** *n.* tendo la kuahiri; muda katikati ya kuahiriwa na tendo kufanyika.
adjudge, *v.t.* hukumu; (*assign*) patisha kitu kwa hukumu; (*settle*) kata maneno au shauri, amua. **adjudicate,** *v.i.* toa hukumu. **adjudication,** *n.* hukumu. **adjudicator,** *n.* hakimu, ahukumuye, mwamuzi, akataye maneno au shauri.
adjunct, *n.* ongezo, kiungo, kilichounganishwa au kutiwa; kifaa, kiongezacho manufaa. **adjunctive,** *a.* -a kuongeza manufaa. **adjunctively,** *adv.* pamoja na.
adjure, *v.t.* apisha; (*implore*) sihi kwa moyo au bidii. **adjuration,** *n.* tendo la kuapisha, kiapo; kusihi kwa moyo.
adjust, *v.t.* panga, tengeneza, rekebisha, zatiti, ratibisha, linganisha; (*a quarrel*) amua, patanisha, suluhisha. **adjustment,** *n.* linganisho, patanisho, suluhu, rekebisho, siasa.
adjutant, *n.* afisa wa kiaskari mwenye daraja ya kumsaidia mkuu wa jeshi (*bird*) namna ya ndege kama korongo.
ad libitum (ad lib.), kadiri upendavyo.
administer, *v.t.* (*govern*) tawala, simamia, amuru; (*supply*) -pa, toa; (*medicine*) tia, nywesha; (*punishment*) tia, pasisha (adhabu). **administration,** *n.* utawala, usimamizi &c.; (*government*) serikali. **administrative,** *a.* -enye kutawala, -enye kuhusu utawala. **administrator,** *n.* mtawala, mkuu; (*of an estate*) mrithishi, asimamiaye na kugawanya mali ya marehemu.
admirable, *a.*, **admirably,** *adv.* taz. *admire.*
admiral, *n.* mkuu wa kundi la manowari, admeli. **admiralty,** *n.* jamii ya wakuu wa serikali isimamiayo mambo yahusuyo manowari zote.
admiration, *n.* taz, *admire.*
admire, *v.t.* (*approve*) penda, stahi, heshimu, sifu; (*wonder at*) staajabia, shangaa. **admirable,** *a.* -zuri, -a kusifiwa, -a kupendwa, -a ajabu, -stahifu. **admirably,** *adv.* vizuri, barabara, kufaa sana, kwa jinsi inayostahili kusifiwa &c. **admiration,** *n.* tendo la kupenda (kustahi, kusifu, kustaajabu); mshangao, ajabu, sifa. **admirer,** *n.* mpenda, msifu, astahiye, aheshimuye, mfuasi.
admit, *v.t.* ruhusu kuingia, karibisha, achia kuingia; (*acknowledge*) kiri, ungama; (*concede*) kubali, ridhia. **admissible,** *a.* -a kukubali, -a kufaa, halali. **admission,** *n.* ruhusa ya kuingia; (neno) lililokiriwa (kuungamwa, kukubaliwa). **admittance,** *n.* ruhusa ya kuingia.
admix, *v.t.* changanya na. **admixture,** *n.* kilichotiwa na kuchanganywa, mchanganyiko.
admonish, *v.t.* onya, gombeza, rudi, karipia, kemea (kwa upole), taradhia. **admonishment, admonition,** *n.* onyo la upole, marudi. **admonitory,** *a.* -enye onyo la upole.
ado, *n.* udhia, shida, fujo, ghasia, zahama, sumbuko, matata.
adolescence, *n.* ujana, miaka toka kubalehe mpaka kupevuka. **adolescent,** *a.* -a katika kubalehe. — *n.,* mbalehe, kijana.
Adonis, *n.* mtu mzuri sana (wa sura na maungo).

adopt, *v.t.* chagua, kubali, tumia, ingiza. *To adopt a child,* kumlea mtoto na kumfanya mwana. **adoption,** *n.* mchaguo, uchaguo, mwingizo, uingizo; hali ya kuchaguliwa (ya kuingizwa *&c.*).
adorable, *a.,* **adoration,** *n.* taz. *adore.*
adore, *v.t.* sujudu, abudu, penda mno. **adorable,** *a.* -liyostahili kuabudiwa, -a kupendwa mno. **adoration,** *n.* tendo la kusujudu (la kusifu, la kupenda mno). **adorer,** *n.* aabuduye, apendaye au kuheshimu mno.
adorn, *v.t.* pamba, vika, remba, rembesha. **adornment,** *n.* pambo, urembo, uzuri.
adrift, *a. and adv.* (*be*) potea, legea, chukuliwa (au kwenda) huko na huko (kama kwa upepo, mawimbi *&c.*). *Cut adrift,* tenga, katia kamba (ya chombo).
adroit, *a.* -stadi, -bingwa, -erevu, hodari, mahiri. **adroitly,** *adv.* kwa uhodari, kwa wepesi, kwa werevu, kwa ustadi. **adroitness,** *n* ustadi, werevu, welekevu, ubingwa, ufundi, wepesi, umahiri.
adulation, *n.* taz. *adulate.*
adulate, *v.t.* sifu mno (pengine kwa sifa zisizostahili ili kujipendekeza). **adulation,** *n.* sifio kubwa mno, sifa nyingi (pengine hutumika kwa jinsi iliyo nzuri; pengine kwa sifa zisizostahili ili kujipendekeza).
adult, *a.* -zima, -pevu. — *n.* mtu mzima (kwa umri), ngumbaru.
adulterate, *v.t.* ghoshi, changanya na kitu duni, haribu. **adulteration,** *n.* kughoshi, mchanganyo, mchanganyiko. **adulterer,** *n.* mzinzi mwanamume, mgoni. **adulteress,** *n.* mzinzi mwanamke. **adulterous,** *a.* -zinifu, -zinzi, -a uzinzi. **adultery,** *n.* uzinzi, zinaa, uasherati, ugoni.
ad valorem, *a. and adv.* kwa kadiri ya thamani ilivyo.
advance, *v.t.* sogeza, jongeza, leta, endesha mbele; (*promote*) pandisha cheo; (*encourage progress*) endesha (kuza) hali; (*advance an opinion &c.*) toa kauli, shauri; (*of money*) kopesha, toa karadha, lipa mbele; — *v.i.* (*go ahead*) enda, zidi, endelea mbele. — *n.* maendeleo, maondokeo; (*of money*) karadha; (*friendship*) urafiki, mapatano. *He made advances,* alitaka urafiki. *In advance,* kabla, mbele (ya wakati uliopasiwa). **advancement,** *n.* endeleo, maondokeo, ongezo la cheo (la hali); (*of money*) karadha.
advantage, *n.* faida, nafuu, heri, baraka, manufaa, mafao. *Be an advantage,* faa. *Have the advantage,* pita, shinda, -wa bora. *Take advantage of* (*use*), tumia, faidi, chumia; (*cheat*) punja, ghilibu, laghai, karamkia.
advantageous, *a.* -a kufaa, -enye faida, -ema. **advantageously,** *adv.* kwa jinsi ya kufaa (kuleta nafuu au faida).
advent, *n.* majilio, mjio; (*season*) muda (wenye Jumapili nne) unaotangulia sikukuu ya Kuzaliwa Yesu Kristo.
adventitious, *a.* -a bahati, -a nasibu, -a kigeni.
adventure, *n.* jambo la hatari (la ujasiri, la ajabu, la kubahatisha). *He related his adventures,* alisimulia mambo yaliyompata. — *v.t. and i.* jasiri *&c.* taz. *venture.* **adventurer,** *n.* mjasiri, atendaye mambo ya kubahatisha *&c.,* mpitaji njia (ajiingizaye katika mambo kwa hila ili ajipatie sifa au faida). **adventuress,** *n.* *adventurer* wa kike. **adventurous,** *a.* -jasiri, -a kubahatisha, -enye tabia ya kujihatirisha.
adverb, *n.* neno liongezalo maana ya *verb, adjective,* au *adverb.* **adverbial,** *a,* -a kuhusu *adverb.*
adversary, *n.* taz. *adverse.*
adverse, *a.* -a uadui, -a kupinga, -baya, -zuilifu, -a bahati mbaya, -a kudhuru, -enye kisirani. **adversary,** *n.* adui, hasimu, mtesi, mshindani; (*Satan*) shetani. **adversely,** *adv.* kwa uadui, kwa kupinga (kuzuia, kudhuru *&c.*). **adversity,**

n. jambo baya, shari, taabu, msiba, mateso, shida, hasara, dhiki, maafa, masaibu.

advert, *v.i.* (*to*) (*mention*) nena, taja; (*attend to*) angalia. **advertise,** *v.t.* tangaza, vumisha habari za, tembeza, eneza sifa za. **advertisement,** *n.* tangazo. **advertiser,** *n.* mtangazi, mvumisha habari.

advice, *n.* shauri, onyo, kauli; (*information*) taarifa. **advisable,** *a.* afadhali, heri, -ema, bora. **advise,** *v.t.* onya, shauri, nasihi, asa, shawishi; (*inform*) arifu, julisha. **advisedly,** *adv.* kwa kusudi. **adviser,** *n.* mshauri, mwonyi.

advocate, *n.* mdai, mwombeaji, mteti, mteteaji, wakili. — *v.t.* tetea, shindania, nenea; (*recommend*) shauri. **advocacy,** *n.* uwakili, ombeo, uombezi, teteo, uteteaji.

adze, *n.* tezo.

aegis, *n.* himaya, ulinzi, utunzaji.

aeon (eon), *n.* kipindi kirefu cha wakati; kipindi cha wakati kisichoweza kupimika; milele.

aerate, *v.t.* tia hewa ya *carbonic acid*, au ya namna nyingine. *Aerated waters*, maji yaliyotiwa hewa, kama vile *soda*. **aeration,** *n.* tendo la kutia hewa (la kuanika ili hewa iingie). **aerial,** *a.* -a angani, -a kwenda juu sana, -epesi kama hewa. — *n.* uzi wa simu ulionyoshwa ili kupokea simu za hewani. **aerodrome,** *n.* kituo au kambi ya eropleni. **aerogram,** *n.* simu ya hewani. **aerograph,** *v.t.* peleka simu ya hewani. **aerolite,** *n.* kimwondo, jiwe lililoanguka kutoka juu angani. **aeronaut,** *n.* fundi arukaye kwa eropleni. **aeroplane,** *n.* eropleni, mashine kama motakaa irukayo juu na kwenda hewani. **aerostatics,** *n.* elimu ya hewa na sehemu na tabia yake, na vitu vilivyomo; elimu inayohusu eropleni.

aerie, *n.* tundu la ndege kama tai, walao vinyama.

aerodrome, *n.*, **aerogram,** *n.*, **aerograph,** *n.*, **aerolite,** *n.*, **aeronaut,** *n.*, **aeroplane,** *n.*, **aerostatics,** *n.*, taz. *aerate*.

aesthetic, aesthetical, *a.* -a kupatana na kanuni za uzuri, -sanifu. **aesthetics,** *n.* maarifa ya kupambanua yaliyo mazuri kwa kanuni za usanifu na uzuri.

afar, *adv.* mbali. *From afar*, kwa mbali.

affable, *a.* -pole, -kunjufu, -enye utu mwema, -latifu, -a kuambilika, -enye tabia hata watu huweza kusema naye bila shida. *An affable person*, mjibu, mkunjufu, mwanana. **affability, affableness,** *n.* upole, ukunjufu, jamala, uanana.

affair, *n.* jambo, shughuli, kazi, neno, kadhia, kitu, kigambo. **affairs,** *n.* mambo, malimwengu, kazi. *Public affairs*, mambo ya serikali. *A grand affair*, tamasha. *Urgent affair*, amara, jambo muhimu.

affect, *v.t.* (*change*) badili, geuza; (*act on feelings*) kulia, sikitisha, huzunisha, choma moyo, tia huruma; (*make a show or pretence of*) jifanya, jiona, jisingizia, jitendekeza; (*having a liking for*) penda, fuata desturi (mazoea, mwendo &c.); (*of dress*) vaa (mavazi ya namna fulani); (*affect with*) tia, pasha, ambukiza. *Be affected* (*by*), geuzwa, vutwa; (*feelings*) sikitishwa, huzunishwa, tiwa hofu (furaha, ajabu) &c.); dhurika. **affectation,** *n.* kujifanya, kujisingizia usivyo, kujiona, kiburi; (*display*) ulimbwende, ushaufu, umalidadi, madaha, makuu, mkogo. **affected,** *a.* -liogeuzwa; (*pretended*) -a kujisingizia, -a kujifanya, -a kujitendekeza, -a uwongo; (*diseased, injured*) -lioshikwa na ugonjwa (au maumivu), -lioumia. **affecting,** *a.* -enye kuhuzunisha, -a kusikitisha, -a kustaajabisha, -a kuchoma moyo. **affection,** *n.* (*love*) upendo, huba, shauku; (*ailment*) ugonjwa, uele, maradhi. *Mutual affection*, upendano, urafiki. **affectionate,** *a.* -enye moyo wa kupenda (wa shauku, huba), muhebi. **affectionately,** *adv.* kwa upendo.

affiance, *n.* ahadi ya kuoa (kuoza, kuolewa); (*trust*) imani. — *v.t.* posa, ahidi kuoa (kuoza, kuolewa). **affianced,** *a.* (*be affianced*) poswa.

affidavit, *n.* maneno au hati yenye maneno ambayo mtu ameapa kuwa ni kweli mbele ya mtu mwenye amri ya kuapisha.

affiliate, *v.t.* pokea kuwa mshirika au mwana katika jamaa, au jamii ya watu au chama (chuo &c.). **affiliation,** *n.* upokeo wa mtu kuwa mshirika au mwana chama &c.

affinity, *n.* udugu, ujamaa, ukoo; (*likeness*) mfano, ufananaji, kufanana na, hali ya kuwa na tabia au kanuni zilizofanana.

affirm, *v.t.* sema kwa uthabiti (kwa hakika), thibitisha, sema ndiyo, yakinisha. **affirmation,** *n.* thibitisho, tendo la kuthibitisha; maneno yaliyosemwa kwa uthabiti. **affirmative,** *a.* -enye kuthibitisha, -a kuyakinisha. *He answered in the affirmative,* alijibu ndiyo, alikubali.

affix, *v.t.* kaza, tia, bandika. — *n.* sehemu ya neno iliyotiwa mbele yake au nyuma yake ili kuongeza maana yake; bandiko, pakizo, nyongeza.

afflatus, *n.* mawazo yamjiayo mtu (hasa ya dini), *e.g.* yamjiayo nabii (mtunga mashairi &c.).

afflict, *v.t.* tesa, dhuru, umiza, huzunisha, sibu, onea, dhulumu, sumbua, udhi, adhibu. **affliction,** *n.* taabu, huzuni, mateso, msiba, dhiki, ugonjwa, adhabu, dhuluma.

affluent, *a.* -enye wingi wa. — *n.* mto mdogo uingiao mto mwingine au ziwani. **affluence,** *n.* wingi, utajiri, mali nyingi, neema, usitawi.

afford, *v.t.* toa, fanya, fanyiza; (*be able*) weza, stahili, toshelea. *He can afford to pay,* aweza kulipa. *He afforded me no chance of,* hakunipa nafasi (wasaa) ya.

afforest, *v.t.* panda miti mahali ili kufanya msitu. **afforestation,** *n.* upanzi wa miti ili kufanya mwitu.

affranchise, *v.t.* toa katika utumwa au katika mambo yaliyopasiwa.

affray, *n.* pigano, vita, ugomvi.

affright, *v.t.* ogofya, tisha, shtusha, gutusha. — *n.* hofu ya ghafula, mshtuko, tisho, gutusho.

affront, *v.t.* (*insult*) chukiza, udhi, tukana kwa wazi. — *n.* (*outrage*) ufidhuli, jeuri; (*abuse*) matukano; (*disgrace*) aibu. **affronted,** *a.* (*be*) chukizwa, tukanwa, udhika.

afire, *adv.* katika hali ya kuwaka (moto, moyo, hasira &c.).

aflame, *adv.* katika hali ya kuwaka (ya kumeka).

afloat, *adv. and a.* (*be afloat*) elea majini; (*begin*) anza; (*unfixed*) -wa -mefunguliwa, -siyokazwa. *Set afloat,* eleza, shua; (*begin*) anzisha, zindua.

afoot, *adv.* kwa miguu. *To be afoot,* kuwa inaendelea, kuwa tayari.

afore, *prep. and adv.* mbele (ya), kabla (ya).

aforehand, *adv.* kabla ya wakati uliopasa.

aforementioned, aforesaid, *a.* -liokwisha tajwa.

aforethought, *a.* -liofikiriwa mbele.

aforetime, *adv.* zamani, wakati uliopita.

afraid, *a.* (*be*) ogopa, hofu, -wa na woga.

afresh, *adv.* tena, upya.

African, *a.* -a nchi ya *Africa.* — *n.* mwenyeji, mzalia wa *Africa.* **Africander,** *n.* mzalia wa Wazungu wa *South Africa.*

aft, *a. and adv.* (-a) nyuma, (-a) karibu na au kuiendea shetri ya chombo.

after, *a.* -a baadaye, -a nyuma, -a kufuata. — *adv. and prep.* baada (ya), nyuma (ya). *To go after,* fuata, (*search for*) tafuta. *After the manner of, or in imitation of,* kwa kuiga, kwa kufuatisha. *After the name of,* kwa jina la. *After all,* ijapokuwa, hata hivi, iwayo yote. *Take after,* iga, fuatisha, fanana na, landa. *After his own heart,* -a kumpendeza. *After he had gone away,* alipokwisha kwenda.

afterbirth, *n.* kondo ya nyuma.
aftercrop, *n.* vuno la pili la shamba la mwaka ule mmoja.
afterglow, *n.* ukungu wa jioni, mwangaza uonekanao mbinguni pengine jua liishapo kuchwa.
aftermath, *n.* matokeo ya vita, matata *&c.*
afternoon, *a.* alasiri, muda katikati ya saa sita na jioni.
afterpains, *n.* zingizi; maumivu yafuatayo baada ya uzazi, kondo ya nyuma iishapo kutoka.
afterthought, *n.* lililowazwa baadaye, wazo la baadaye.
afterwards, *adv.* baadaye, halafu, hatimaye, mwishowe.
again, *adv.* tena, mara ya pili.
against, *prep.* (*in opposition to*) juu ya, kushindana na, mbalimbali na; (*opposite to, facing*) kuelekea, kukabili; (*in contact*) karibu na, kugusana; (*in collision with*) kupambana na; (*in provision for*) kwa ajili ya, kwa.
agape, *a. and adv.* -a (kwa) kufunua midomo (kuachama) kwa kuona ajabu, (kwa kutazamia, kwa kushangaa, kwa kuangalia sana).
agate, *n.* namna ya kito cha thamani.
age, *n.* (*duration of life*) maisha, aushi; (*number of years of age*) umri; (*period*) zamani, muda, siku. *To be of age,* kuwa na miaka ishirini na moja. *Old age,* uzee, ukongwe. *Of same age,* hirimu, hirimu moja, marika. *He was twenty years of age,* alikuwa miaka ishirini, alikuwa na umri wa miaka ishirini. *Past ages,* zamani za kale. **aged,** *a.* (*of persons*) -zee, -kongwe; (*of things*) -kuukuu, -a kale. **ageless,** *a.* -a. milele, -a kudumu mpaka mwisho.
agency, *n.* taz. *agent.*
agenda, *n.* orodha ya mambo yaliyokusudiwa kufanywa au kufikiriwa katika mkutano.
agent, *n.* (*person or thing acting or exerting power*) mfanyi, mtendi, mtendaji, -enye kutenda; (*in business*) wakili, karani; (*political*) mjumbe, balozi. **agency,** *n.* (*means, force*) nguvu, njia, kazi; (*office*) kazi (nyumba) ya wakili; uwakili, ukarani.
agglomerate, *v.t.* kusanya; — *v.i.* zidi hata kuwa chungu, kusanyika. **agglomeration,** *n.* kusanyo (ongezo) hata kuwa chungu; kusanyiko, chungu.
agglutinate, *v.t.* ambatisha. **agglutination,** *n.* ambatisho, wambiso wa sehemu, vitu vilivyoambatishwa pamoja.
aggrandise, *v.t.* kusa, zidisha cheo, tukuza. **aggrandisement,** *n.* ongezo la cheo (hali *&c.*).
aggravate, *v.t.* kuliza, ongeza ubaya (wa kosa, wa umivu, wa jambo, wa taabu *&c.*); (*provoke*) kasirisha, chokoza, chosha, udhi. **aggravation,** *n.* ukulifu, uchokozi, kichocho, jambo litialo hasira, uchungu, liongezalo ubaya wa jambo. **aggravating,** *a.* -a kukasirisha, -a kuudhi.
aggregate, *v.t.* kusanya kufanya chungu (kundi *&c.*). — *n.* kusanyiko, jamii; (*sum, total*) jumla. — *a.* -enye kufanyika kwa sehemu zilizokusanywa pamoja. **aggregation,** *n.* mkusanyiko (watu, vitu).
aggression, *n.* jeuri, shambulio, chanzo cha vita (ugomvi, kudhuru *&c.*); chokochoko ya vita. **aggressive,** *a.* -enye tabia ya kuanzisha ugomvi (ya kuleta vita), -gomvi, -a shari, -a jeuri. **aggressor,** *n.* adui, mleta vita au ugomvi, ashambuliaye kwanza, mgomvi, mshari, mjeuri.
aggrieve, *v.t.* lemea, dhuru, umiza, udhi, tia uchungu, sikitisha.
aghast, *a.* (*be*) pagawa (kwa fadhaa au hofu), tishwa mno (hata kupigwa na bumbuazi).
agile, *a.* -epesi (wa mwendo). **agility,** *n.* wepesi (wa mwendo).
agitate, *v.t.* (*stir violently*) tikisatikisa, tukusa, shtua, shtusha, koroga, sukasuka, chafua; (*excite, disturb*) harakisha, fadhaisha, washa, chochea; (*discuss*) bishania. **agitation,** *n.* (*commotion, excitement*) haraka,

ghasia, zahama, msukosuko, machafuko; (*perturbation of mind*) hangaiko, fadhaa, wasiwasi; (*discussion*) fitina, mabishano, machocheo. **agitator**, *n.* mfitini, achocheaye fitina katika watu.

aglow, *a. and adv.* -enye kumeka, -enye kuwaka. *Be aglow*, waka, ng'aa, meka.

agnate, *a.* -a kuumeni, -a upande wa baba. — *n.* ndugu wa kuumeni.

agnostic, *n.* asadikiye kuwa hatuna habari za Mungu wala hatuwezi kuzipata. **agnosticism**, *n.* hali ya kusadiki kama *agnostic*.

ago, *adv.* zamani. *Long ago*, zamani sana, hapo kale. *A little while ago*, punde hivi. *Ten days ago*, tangu siku kumi. *How long ago?* tangu lini?

agog, *a. and adv.* kwa kutazamia sana.

agonize, *v.t.* umiza vibaya sana, tesa; — *v.i.* umia vibaya, -wa na maumivu makali. **agony**, *n.* maumivu makuu &c.; kipeo cha maumivu.

agrarian, *a.* -a kuhusu ardhi (mashamba, nchi) na kugawanywa kwake, -a mashamba.

agree, *v.i.* -wa na umoja, patana, agana, chukuana, ridhiana, afiki, afikana; (*consent*) kubali; (*harmonize*) lingana, elekea, fanana, chukuana, faa. **agreeable**, *a.* -a kufaa, -a kupendeza, -a kupendekeza, -zuri, -tamu, -kunjufu, latifu, -a kukubali, -a kuridhika. *Agreeable* (*with*), kwa jinsi ya, kwa namna ya, kama. **agreement**, *n.* (*contract*) mapatano, katibu, mkataba, sharti, mwafaka, maafikano, agano, maagano, kiaga, miadi; (*harmony*) hali ya kufanana (ya kuchukuana, ya kupendeleana), ulinganifu, itifaki.

agriculture, *n.* kilimo, mlimo, ukulima, elimu ya kilimo, zaraa. **agricultural**, *a.* -a kuhusu kilimo, -a mashamba. **agriculturist**, *n.* mkulima, mlimaji, mwenye elimu ya kilimo.

aground, *adv.* *Be aground*, pwelewa. *Run aground*, kwama mwambani, pwelea, panda pwani.

ague, *n.* homa ya kutetemesha, baridi; hali ya kutetemeka kwa homa au baridi.

ah, *int.* sauti ya kustaajabu (ya furaha, ya kuhurumia, ya kunung'unika, kadiri ya hali au tamko la sauti lilivyo): Salale! masalale! lo!

aha, *int.* sauti ya kustaajabu (ya furaha, ya kudharau &c. kadiri ya tamko la sauti lilivyo): salale! masalale! sefule! kefule!

ahead, *adv.* mbele, kwa kutangulia.

ahoy, *int.* sauti ya kuita, hasa ya kibaharia.

aid, *v.t.* saidia, auni, nafidhi. —*n.* msaada, shime, amara.

aide-de-camp, *n.* afisa aliyechaguliwa na mkuu wa jeshi la kiaskari kumtumikia kwa namna nyinginezo maalum.

aigrette, *n.* yangeyange, ndege mwenye kishungi mweupe kama korongo mdogo.

ail, *v.i.* ugua, umia, taabika. *What ails you?* una nini? unaumwa nini?

ailment, *n.* ugonjwa, uele, maradhi, umivu, udhaifu.

aim, *v.t.* (*gun* &c.) piga shabaha, linga; — *v.i.* (*at*) pigia shabaha, elekezea bunduki; (*desire, intend*) taka, tamani, kusudia, nuia, azimu. — *n.* shabaha; (*purpose*) kusudi, nia, azimio, gharadhi.

air, *n.* hewa, anga, upepo mwepesi; (*tune*) wimbo; (*appearance*) umbo, sura, kikao; (*airs, affected manner*) madaha, kiburi, matuko, makuu, fahari. *Give oneself airs*, takabari, deka, jiona, jifaharisha; — *v.t.* anika; (*display*) onyesha, tangaza. **airily**, *adv.* kwa wepesi, kwa furaha. **airiness**, *n.* (*lightness*) wepesi; (*unreality*) uhafifu; (*openness*) uwazi, hali ya kuwa wazi, penye hewa nyingi. **airing**, *n.* tendo la kupunga hewa (la kutembea nje, la kuanika juani au mbele ya moto). **airless**, *a.* bila hewa, hali ya kutokuwapo upepo kabisa, shwari. **airship**, *n.*

namna ya eropleni. **airtight,** *a.* -a kuzibwa kabisa hata hewa haiwezi kuingia; (*of an argument &c.*) neno lisilokanika. **airy,** *a.* -enye wingi wa hewa, -a juu; (*trifling*) -epesi, -tupu, hafifu; (*open to air*) wazi, -enye wingi wa hewa, baridi. *To take air,* kujulikana wazi. *Be in the air,* vumika, julikana pote, enea pote; (*of visionary*) ndoto.

aisle, *n.* sehemu ya kanisa kwa marefu; upande mmoja wa marefu ya kanisa.

ajar, *adv.* kufunguliwa kidogo. *Leave the door ajar,* acha mlango wazi kidogo, sindua mlango kidogo.

akimbo, *adv.* kwa kuweka mkono kiunoni na kiko kutokeza.

akin, *a.* -a damu moja, -a jamaa moja; -a namna ile ile, -enye tabia zilizofanana sana.

alabaster, *n.* namna ya jiwe jeupe lililofanana na marmar.

alack, alack-a-day, *int.* ole! (neno la kuonyesha masikitiko, la majonzi, la majuto).

alacrity, *n.* wepesi, bidii, utayari, uwahi.

alarm, *n.* kamsa, habari za hatari; hofu, mshtuko wa hofu; (*alarm, alarum clock*) saa yenye kengele inayoweza kurekebishwa hata ilie saa inayotakiwa (ya kumwamshia mtu usingizini wakati atakapo). —*v.t.* piga kamsa, julisha hatari, shtua, ogofya. **alarming,** *a.* -a kutia hofu, -a kutisha, -a kuogofya. **alarmist,** *n.* atoaye habari za hatari; azoeaye kubashiri hatari.

alas, *int.* ole! (sauti ya kuonyesha huzuni, majuto).

alb, *n.* vazi la kasisi kama kanzu.

albatross, *n.* ndege mkubwa wa baharini.

albeit, *conj.* ingawa, ijapokuwa. —*adv.* walakini.

albino, *n.* zeru, zeruzeru; mtu au mnyama ambaye ngozi na nywele zake ni nyeupe si za kawaida, na mboni za macho yake ni nyekundu kidogo.

album, *n.* kitabu cha kutilia picha (majina ya watu, mashairi, tikiti za posta &c.).

albumen, *n.* ute wa yai; kitu kama ute wa yai kilichomo katika nyama na mboga. **albuminoid,** *a.* -a kama *albumen.*

alchemy, *n.* elimu ya alkimia, ndiyo asili ya elimu ya dawa. **alchemist,** *n.* mwenye elimu ya alkimia (zamani, kazi ya watu hao hasa ilikuwa kujaribu kuvumbua dawa iwezayo kugeuza madini nyingine ziwe dhahabu, na ya kuzidisha urefu wa maisha).

alcohol, *n.* dawa iliyo nguvu ya pombe, tembo na ulevi; hutokana na sukari na vitu vyenye asili ya sukari vichachapo. **alcoholic,** *a.* -a vileo, -a *alcohol.* **alcoholism,** *n.* dalili na hali ya ugonjwa uletwao na *alcohol* au ulevi.

Alcoran, *n.* taz. *Koran.*

alcove, *n.* shubaka; mahali pa kupumzikia penye uvuli.

alder, *n.* namna ya mti.

alderman, *n.* mzee wa baraza ya mji.

ale, *n.* namna ya pombe. **ale-house,** *n.* nyumba ya pombe.

alert, *a.* -epesi, -a tayari, bila kusita wala kukawia, -a macho. *On the alert,* tayari, -epesi, -wa macho.

algae, *n.* (*plur.*) majani madogo yaotayo juu ya maji yaliyo juani, huliwa na viluwiluwi vya mbu.

algebra, *n.* hesabu inayotumia herufi badala ya tarakimu.

alias, *n.* jina la kujipa lisilo la kweli (hasa la mwizi, au mkosaji wa sheria).

alibi, *n.* udhuru kudai ya kuwa mtu aliyeshtakiwa jambo hakuwako pale jambo lilipotendeka.

alien, *a.* -geni, -enye tabia zisizo sawa na, -a namna mbali, -siopatana na. —*n.* mgeni. **alienate,** *v.t.* (*persons*) farakisha, tengea mbali, fitini; (*property*) sihia, acha, toa. **alienation,** *n.* mfarakisho, ufarakisho.

alienist, *n.* mtu agangaye wagonjwa wa wazimu au kichaa.

alight (1), *v.i.* shuka, telemka, tua.

alight (2), *a.* (*be*) waka, ng'aa, meka.
align, aline, *v.t.* weka (panga) katika mstari au mistari iliyo sawa. **alignment, alinement,** *n.* mpango wa mstari au mistari iliyo sawa.
alike, *a.* sawasawa, -enye kufanana, -a kulanda, -a namna ile moja. — *adv.* kwa jinsi ya namna iliyo sawasawa.
aliment, *n.* chakula, maakuli, mlo, lukuma, riziki. **alimentary,** *a* -a kuhusu chakula (riziki); -a chakula. *Alimentary canal,* viungo vya mwili vihusuvyo chakula, yaani umio, tumbo na matumbo. **alimony,** *n.* malipo alipayo mume kumpa mkewe hali wameachana kwa sheria.
alive, *a.* -zima, hai. *Be alive to a thing,* ona, tambua, angalia, jua. *Look alive!* haya! amka!
alkali, *n.* namna ya dawa ziunganazo na *acid* na kufanya namna ya chumvi; hutumika kuchanganywa na mafuta kutengenezea sabuni. **alkaline,** *a.* -enye tabia za *alkali.* **alkaloid,** *n.* namna ya dawa kali iliyo asili ya dawa nyingine za miti, kama *morphine, strychnine &c.*
all, *a.* -ote, -zima, kila -moja -a, -o -ote. *All the thing,* kitu chote, kitu kizima. *All the men,* watu wote, kila mmoja wa watu, watu wo wote; (*only*) -tupu. — *adv.* pia, kabisa. *It is all sugar,* sukari tupu. *All in all. He is all in all to him,* ni kama moyo (nafsi) wake. *At all,* hata kidogo. *Not at all good,* si jema hata kidogo. *If it is at all good,* ikiwa njema kidogo tu. *If he goes at all,* hata akienda. *Not at all,* sivyo kabisa, hasha, mbalimbali. *All but, All along* (*all the time*) siku zote; (*at the same time*) papo hapo, pale pale, sawia. *All the same, all one,* mamoja, haidhuru, iwayo yote, hata hivi, lakini. *All right,* vyema, basi, haidhuru. *After all,* hata hivi, ingawa hii, ijapokuwa. *All there,* macho, tayari, -enye akili timamu. *On all fours,* kwa miguu yote minne, kwa miguu na mikono; (*appropriate*) sawasawa, barabara. *For good and all,* mwisho kabisa. *Once for all,* mara moja tu.
allay, *v.t.* tuliza, punguza (ukali au uzito wa maumivu *&c.*), lainisha, nyamazisha.
allege, *v.t.* toa hoja, toa neno, nena, taja. **allegation,** *n.* neno, hoja, ushuhuda.
allegiance, *n.* utii umpasao raia kwa mkubwa (mfalme, sultani) wake.
allegory, *n.* fumbo la maneno, kisa chenye maana iliyofichwa, mfano, mithali. **allegorical,** *a.* -a mfano, -a fumbo. **allegorize,** *v.t.* sema kwa mafumbo.
alleviate, *v.t.* tuliza, punguza (ukali au uzito wa maumivu *&c.*), tuliza, nyamazisha, lainisha. **alleviation,** *n.* faraja, lipunguzalo (ukali *&c.*), kitulizo.
alley, *n.* njia ndogo (katika mji), kichochoro.
alliance, *n.* taz. *ally.*
alligator, *n.* namna ya mamba wa *America.*
alliteration, *n.* mpango wa maneno mawili au zaidi yenye herufi za kwanza zilizo na tamko lile lile. Kiswahili kina *alliteration* nyingi, *e.g. ki*tu *ki*kubwa *ki*kali *ki*lichoanguka *ki*likatika. **alliterative,** *a.* -enye *alliteration.*
allocate, *v.t.* gawanyia (ili kila mtu au jambo apewe au lipewe sehemu iliyopasa). **allocation,** *n.* mgawo, mgawanyo; sehemu iliyotolewa katika ugawanyo.
allot, *v.t.* gawanya, awadha. **allotment,** *n.* mgawo, mgawanyo; (*ground*) shamba, kipande cha shamba, konde.
allow, *v.t.* (*permit*) acha, ruhusu, toa ruhusa; (*acknowledge*) kubali (maneno), kiri; (*give money*) toa (fedha), lipa; (*remit*) punguza bei. *Allow for,* (*take account of*) kumbuka na kuhesabu mambo yawezayo kupunguza uzito wa jambo; (*let pass*) achilia, samehe; (*give time for*) limbika, ngojea, kalia. *Allow me to pass,* nipishe. **allowable,** *a.* halali, -enye

kuruhusiwa, -a kujuzu. **allowance,** *n.* liloruhusiwa; (*fixed amount*) posho, haki, sehemu. *Make allowance for,* kumbuka na kuhesabu mambo yawezayo kupunguza uzito wa jambo. *Make an allowance,* tolea posho (fedha badala ya posho).

alloy, *v.t.* changanya madini; punguza thamani au ubora. — *n.* mchanganyiko wa madini; mabaya yaliyochanganyika na mema.

allude, *v.i.* taja katika kusema au kuandika; taja juujuu tu, kama kwa werevu. **allusion,** *n.* neno juu ya jambo, litajwalo katika kutaja mengine; mtajo.

allure, *v.t.* vuta kwa werevu, tamanisha, shawishi, bilisi, bembeleza; (*entice women*) tongoza. **allurement,** *n.* kitu kivutacho, cha kutamanisha, mvuto, ushawishi, ubilisi; (*of women*) utongozi. **alluring,** *a.* -a kuvuta, -a kutamanisha.

allusion, *n.* taz. *allude.*

alluvial, *a.* -a matope ya mito; (*country*) nchi iliyokuwa matope ya mito ikakauka maji. **alluvium,** *n.* matope yaliyoachwa na maji ya mto.

ally, *v.t.* ungana, hasa kwa kufanya udugu, utani, urafiki, kwa kuoana au kwa sababu ya kufanana. *Be allied,* patana, -wa na urafiki; (*of connexion or resemblance*) -wa kama, fanana na, -wa namna ya. *Allied armies,* majeshi ya marafiki. *These matters are closely allied,* mambo haya yamefanana sana, ni ya namna ile moja. — *n.* rafiki, mtani, mshirika, msaidizi; (*of states*) taifa lililofanya urafiki na jingine kwa mapatano. **alliance,** *n.* mwungano kwa mapatano (ndoa, urafiki &c.); (*family*) ahali, utani, udugu; (*marriage*) ndoa, arusi, nikaha.

almanac, *n.* kalenda, takwimu; orodha yenye utaratibu wa siku, majuma na miezi ya mwaka.

almighty, *a.* -enye nguvu zote, -enye enzi (ezi), -enye kuweza vyote. *The Almighty,* Mwenyezi Mungu.

almond, *n.* (*tree*) mlozi; (*fruit*) lozi.

almost, *adv.* karibu sana lakini si kabisa, nusura.

alms, *n.* sadaka, zaka, bakshishi. **alms-house,** *n.* nyumba ya kukaa maskini bila kulipa upangaji.

aloe, *n.* jamii ya mimea kama msubili; udi.

aloft, *adv.* juu.

alone, *a.* pekee, bila kuwapo -ingine. *I* (*you, he &c.*) *alone,* peke yangu (yako, yake &c.); (*deserted*) -a ukiwa; (*only*) -tupu, tu, bila kitu kingine. *Leave me alone,* usiniudhi, usinisumbue.

along, *adv. and prep.* kwa mbele, katika. *Along with,* pamoja na. *Come along!* Haya! njoo! Twende zetu! *All along,* siku zote, wakati wote. *Go along,* nenda, toka. *Pass or steer along the shore,* ambaza (ambaa) pwani. **alongside,** *adv. and prep.* mbavuni, kando, karibu. *Go alongside* (*of ship, jetty &c.*), karibia, ambaa. *Lay alongside,* lala (laza) karibu, kaa ubavuni.

aloof, *adv.* mbali. **aloofness,** *n.* hali ya kujitenga na shughuli za wengine, ya kutoangalia wafikiriyo wengine.

aloud, *adv.* kwa sauti kubwa.

alp, *n.* mlima mrefu. **alps,** *n.* safu za milima mirefu katika nchi ya *Switzerland, France,* na *Italy.* **alpen, alpine,** *a.* -a kuhusu *Alps* au milima mirefu. *Alpenstock,* mkongojo mrefu watumiao watu wapandao milima mirefu.

alpaca, *n.* mnyama kama kondoo wa nchi ya *Peru*; (*material*) namna ya nguo ifumwayo kwa manyoya ya mnyama huyo.

alpha, *n.* herufi ya kwanza ya alfabeti ya Kiyunani.

alphabet, *n.* herufi za lugha zilizopangwa katika taratibu ya kawaida, yaani **a, b, ch, d** &c., alfabeti. **alphabetical,** *a.* -a kufuata taratibu ya mpango wa alfabeti.

alpine, *a.* taz. *alp.*

already, *adv.* kabla ya wakati upasao, zamani. *It is done already,* imekwisha fanyika.

also, *adv.* na, tena, vilevile, aidha, vile, pia.

altar, *n.* madhabahu, namna ya meza panapotolewa dhabihu au kafara.

alter, *v.t.* badili, geuza, geuza namna; — *v.i.* badilika, geuka. **alteration**, *n.* badilisho, ugeuzi, geuzo; ubadili, badiliko, mageuko.

altercate, *v.i.* gombana, bishana kwa maneno makali, zozana. **altercation**, *n.* ugomvi, ubishano wa maneno makali, mzozo.

alternate, *v.t.* fanya kwa zamu, fanya kufuatana zamu kwa zamu (moja baada ya moja), badiliana; — *v.i.* fuata zamu kwa zamu (moja baada ya moja); fuata kila ya pili. — *a.* -a moja baada ya moja, -a kila -a pili. *Take the alternate loads*, chukua mzigo huu, acha, huu, chukua huu &c. yaani chukua kila mzigo wa pili.

alternately, *adv.* kwa zamu. *Carry alternately*, pokezana. **alternative**, *a.* -enye hiari ya mambo mwaili, -ingine, -a pili. — *n.* hiari ya mambo mawili, shauri la pili. *I have no alternative*, sina budi, sina hiari. *There are two alternatives for you*, una hiari ya mambo mawili. *Is there no alternative?* hakuna shauri jingine?

although, *conj.* ijapokuwa, ijapo, ingawa, angao, kwamba, juu ya hayo.

altitude, *n.* urefu (wa kwenda juu), kimo.

alto, *n.* namna ya sauti iliyo ya juu ya kinaume, ya chini ni *bass*, ya pili, *baritone*, ya tatu, *tenor*, na ya juu *alto*.

altogether, *adv.* pamoja, kwa jamii; hasa, kabisa, pia, kwa jumla, bila kuacha moja au sehemu.

altruism, *n.* tabia ya kupenda wengine kuliko nafsi (ya kuishi na kutenda mambo kwa ajili ya nafuu ya wengine). **altruistic**, *a.* -enye tabia ya *altruism*. **altruistically**, *adv.* kwa moyo wa kupenda wengine kuliko nafsi yako.

alum, *n.* shabu (namna ya chumvi), hutumika kutengenezea rangi ya kutilia kili, na kufanya taka zizame chini katika maji machafu &c.

aluminium, *n.* namna ya madini nyepesi sana, nyeupe kama fedha.

always, *adv.* sikuzote, daima, kwa kawaida, kila mara, abadi.

am, *v.* -wa, -li- (katika *verbs*, -na-, -me-, yenye habari ya mimi). Taz. **be** (*p.t.* **was**, *pf.t.* **been**). *I am* (*exist*) nipo. *I am*, ni, niko, nili. *Whoever I am*, niwaye yote. *I am a man*, mimi mtu. *I who am strong shall go*, mimi niliye hodari nitakwenda. *I am going*, ninakwenda. *I am tired*, nimechoka. *I am to go*, nina sharti (lazima, sina budi) kwenda. *What am I to do?* nifanyeje? *Are you going? Yes, I am going.* Unakwenda? Ndiyo, nakwenda.

amalgam, *n.* changanyiko la zebaki na madini nyingine. **amalgamate**, *v.t.* changanya zebaki pamoja na madini; changanya au unganisha vitu; — *v.i.* ungana, ungamana.

amalgamation, *n.* changanyo (ungamano) la vitu, au watu.

amanuensis, *n.* karani, mwandishi, hasa aandikaye maneno yanayosemwa; katibu, hasa wa imla.

amaranthine, *a.* -siofifia.

amass, *v.t.* kusanya, pata, chuma (mali, vitu vingi &c.), fanya chungu ya.

amateur, *n.* mtu atendaye kazi ya ufundi au sanaa kwa kuipenda (si kwa uchumi), mchezaji michezo bila kutazamia pato. **amateurish**, *a.* si kamili, si stadi sana, kama kazi ya *amateur* (si ya fundi hasa).

amatory, *a.* -a shauku, -a ashiki, -a kutia shauku (upendo, huba, ashiki).

amaze, *v.t.* staajabisha, shangaza, fadhaisha, shtusha. *Be amazed*, staajabu, staajabika, tosheka, shangaa. **amazement**, *n.* ushangao, mshangao, fadhaa. *Blank amazement*, bumbuazi, hali ya kutunduwaa. **amazing**, *a.* -enye kushangaza, -a kutunduwaza, -a kustaajabisha.

Amazon, *n.* mwanamke mwenye nguvu na tabia kama za mwanamume (neno hili limetokana na jina la askari wa kike wa hadithi za zamani).

ambassador, *n.* mjumbe, balozi mkuu apelekwaye katika nchi za mataifa mengine na mfalme wa nchi yake. **ambassadorial,** *a.* -a kuhusu *Ambassador.* **ambassadorship,** *n.* kazi ya *ambassador.*

amber, *n.* kaharabu, namna ya gundi iliyogeuka hata ikawa kama jiwe, yenye rangi ya manjano; hutumika kufanyizia ushanga na mapambo.

ambergris, *n.* ambari; kitu kama nta chenye rangi ya majivu kinukiacho vizuri; huonekana pengine baharini, na pengine katika matumbo ya nyangumi.

ambidexter, *a.* *and* *n.* -enye kuweza kutumia mikono miwili kwa ustadi ulio sawa. **ambidexterity,** *n.* ustadi (uhodari) wa kufanya kwa mikono yote miwili sawa.

ambient, *a.* -a kuzunguka, -a pande zote. — *n.* kizungukacho pande zote (kama hewa, anga, mbingu).

ambiguous, *a.* -enye maana isiyo dhahiri au inayofahamika kuwili, -a fumbo. **ambiguity,** *n.* shaka la maana ya maneno.

ambition, *n.* tamaa ya nguvu (cheo, heshima, ubora, fahari &c.). **ambitious,** *a.* -enye nia au tamaa ya kuendelea (ya kukuza hali &c.), -a kutaka makuu. **ambitiously,** *adv.* kwa tamaa ya nguvu (cheo, hali bora &c.).

amble, *v.i.* enda dalji, enda mwendo wa farasi (kuinua miguu yote miwili ya upande mmoja, kisha kuinua ile miwili ya upande wa pili); enda polepole kwa madaha. — *n.* mwendo wa *amble*; mwendo wa dalji, mwendo wa polepole unaozidi ule wa kutembea lakini haupati mbio za shoti.

ambrosia, *n.* kinywaji kitamu; kitu kitamu cha kupendeza mno; (katika hadithi za zamani za Kiyunani; chakula cha miungu).

ambulance, *n.* gari au namna ya machela ya kuchukulia wagonjwa; gari au vikosi vya magari vya kuchukulia wagonjwa na zana za madaktari vitani. **ambulatory,** *a.* -enye nguvu ya (uwezo wa) kuenda (kuhama).

ambuscade, *n.* maoteo, maficho; kikosi cha askari waliojificha ili kuwaotea adui. — *v.t.* *and* *i.* otea njiani; vizia kwa siri, ficha (askari) katika maoteo; shambulia kutoka mafichoni (maoteoni).

ambush, *v.* *and* *n.* sawasawa na *ambuscade.*

ameliorate, *v.t.* kuza (hali), tengeneza, fanya -zuri zaidi; — *v.i.* endelea, tengenea, ondokea. **amelioration,** *n.* kuendeleza hali neema, heri, tengeneo, maondokeo.

amen, *int.* amin, na iwe.

amenable, *a.* -tiifu, -sikivu, -epesi kuongozwa au kutawalwa.

amend, *v.t.* sahihisha, fanya -zuri zaidi, tengeneza; — *v.i.* pona (kwa mambo na hali). *Make amends,* ridhisha, lipa (kwa ajili ya jambo baya au upungufu). **amendment,** *n.* linalosahihisha, tengenezo badilisho au badiliko (la sheria &c.).

amenity, *n.* uzuri wa mahali (mambo au tabia); hali na mambo yapendezayo, mapendezi.

American, *a.* -a Amerika. — *n.* mwenyeji wa Amerika.

amethyst, *n.* kito chenye thamani chenye rangi ya samawi.

amiable, *a.* -pole, -ema. -a kupendeza, latifu, -kunjufu, -enye tabia nzuri, -enye kustahili kupendwa. **amiability,** *n.* ukunjufu, upole, tabia nzuri.

amicable, *a.* -a amani, -a urafiki, -a upole.

amid, amidst, *prep.* kati ya, katikati ya, katika, miongoni mwa, baina ya.

amiss, *a.* *and* *adv.* -siyo barabara, -siyo sahihi; vibaya. *What is amiss?* kuna nini? *Take amiss,* kosa kufahamu vyema, onea chuki (uchungu), chukizwa na.

amity, *n.* urafiki, nia njema.

ammonia, *n.* namna ya dawa yenye harufu kali sana hata mtu akiinusa huumia puani.

ammunition, *n.* zana za vita (hasa risasi na baruti).

amnesty, *n.* msamaha wa watu walioikosa serikali.

amoeba, *n.* jamii ya vijidudu vidogo sana visivyoonekana kwa macho, hukaa katika maji ya maziwa na udongo.

amok, *adv.* taz. *amuck.*

among, **amongst**, *prep.* miongoni mwa, katikati ya, baina ya.

amorous, *a.* -epesi kupenda wanawake, -enye shauku (ashiki) ya wanawake, -a shauku (ashiki) nyingi; -a kuhusu upendo. **amour**, *n.* uasherati, uzinzi.

amorphous, *a.* -siyo na umbo wala sura maalum.

amount, *v.i.* pata kiasi (cha) au kadiri ya, -wa sawa (na). *It amounts to this,* maana yake ni hii. — *n.* jumla, yote pamoja; (*quantity*) kiasi, kadiri; (*large quantity*) wingi.

amour, *n.* taz. *amorous.*

ampere, *n.* kipimo cha nguvu ya umeme (elektrisiti).

amphibia, *n. pl.* wanyama wanaoweza kuishi nchi kavu na majini pia. **amphibious**, *a.* -enye kuweza kuishi nchi kavu na majini pia.

amphitheatre, *n.* uwanda wa duara wenye viti vingi kuizunguka wakaapo watu kutazama michezo.

ample, *a.* -kubwa, -a kutosha, -ingi, tele, maridhawa. **amplification**, *n.* ziada, ongezo. **amplifier**, *n.* kitu kinachozidisha au kukuza. **amplify**, *v.t.* zidisha, kuza, ongeza. **amplitude**, *n.* ukubwa, upana, wingi.

amputate, *v.t.* kata (mguu, mkono au kiungo kingine). **amputation**, *n.* mkato (wa mguu, mkono &c.).

amuck, *adv.* *run amuck,* shikwa na wazimu na kupiga mbio huku na huku na kudhuru watu.

amulet, *n.* talasimu, hirizi, kago, sihiri, fingo.

amuse, *v.t.* zungumza, pendeza, furahisha, chekesha. **amusement**, *n.* mazungumzo, maongezi, mchezo; (*pleasure*), tafrija, furaha. **amusing**, *a.* -cheshi, -a kufurahisha &c.

an, taz. *a.*

anachronism, *n.* kosa la kuhesabu wakati, kosa la tarehe ya jambo lililotokea; jambo lisilopatana na mambo ya wakati unaotajwa au kufikiriwa.

anaconda, *n.* chatu (wa Amerika ya kusini).

anaemia, *n.* ugonjwa uletwao na upungufu wa damu (au wa chembe nyekundu zilizo katika damu). **anaemic**, *a.* -enye upungufu wa damu.

anaesthetic, *n.* dawa ya kumfanya mtu asione maumivu.

anagram, *n.* neno au sentensi iliyotungwa kwa kubadili taratibu za herufi za neno jingine, au sentensi nyingine, *e.g.* 'nina' 'nani', 'tabora' 'robota' &c.

analogy, *n.* usawa wa tabia au kazi ya vitu ambavyo tabia au kazi zake nyingine zinahitilafiana kabisa; ulinganifu wa tabia au kazi &c., *e.g.* vidole vya kipofu ni kama macho ya mtu awezaye kuona; kadiri ya ulinganifu; mfano; mithali. **analogical**, *a.* -a kufanana. **analogous**, *a.* -a kulinganika, -a kufanana, -a mfano. **analogue**, *n.* mfano.

analyse, *v.t.* changanua, tenga mbalimbali sehemu za kitu kizima. **analysis**, *n.* mchanganuo, mtengo wa kitu katika sehemu zake mbalimbali; utafiti wa asili ya vitu ili kuvumbua sheria zinazotawala nguvu zake mbalimbali. **analyst**, *n.* mwenye kazi ya kufanya *analysis.*

anarchy, *n.* ukosekano wa serikali katika nchi; machafuko ya mambo ya utawala. **anarchist**, *n.* mfitini katika mambo ya serikali, achocheaye fitina au uasi juu ya serikali.

anathema, *n.* laana. **anathematize**, *v.t.* laani.

anatomy, *n.* elimu ya mwili na viungo vyake jinsi vilivyo (iliyopatikana kwa kutenga sehemu zake).

anatta, *n.* (*tree*) mzingefuri, (*pulp*) zingefuri.

ancestor, *n.* mzazi (*wa kiume*), babu, jadi. **ancestress**, *n.* mzazi (wa kike) bibi. **ancestral**, *a.* -a wazazi, -a babu, -a nasaba. **ancestry**, *n.* wazazi, ukoo, nasaba, jadi.

anchor, *n.* nanga, baura; tegemeo. *Weigh anchor*, ng'oa nanga. — *v.t.* tia (puliza) nanga; (*fasten*) funga, kaza. **anchorage**, *n.* bandari au mahali vyombo vinapoweza kutia nanga; mahali pafaapo kukaa salama na kwa raha; ushuru au gharama inayotozwa vyombo vitiavyo nanga bandarini.

anchorite, *n.* mtu aliyejitenga na malimwengu, hasa kwa ajili ya dini, mtawa.

ancient, *a.* -a kale, -a zamani. — *n.* mzee sana.

ancillary, *a.* -dogo kwa cheo (kwa daraka); -a chini (kwa cheo, daraka &c.).

and, *conj.* na, -ka- *This and that*, hii na hii. *He went and bought*, alikwenda akanunua.

anecdote, *n.* hadithi ndogo, kisa, hekaya, ngano.

anele, *v.t.* paka mafuta.

anent, *adv.* and *prep.* kwa, juu ya habari ya.

aneroid, *n.* chombo cha kupimia uzito wa hewa kisicho na zebaki wala maji ndani yake.

anew, *adv.* tena, upya.

angel, *n.* malaika, mjumbe wa Mungu. **angelic**, *a.* -a malaika, -ema sana, takatifu.

anger, *n.* hasira, ghadhabu, chuki, uchungu, ukali, kasirani, virugu, ghaidi, kani. — *v.t.* kasirisha, ghadhibisha, chukiza. **angrily**, *adv.* kwa hasira (ghadhabu, chuki, uchungu). **angry**, *a.* -enye hasira, -a ghadhabu, -a chuki, -enye uchungu. *Be angry*, kasirika, ghadhibika, udhika.

angle, (1) *n.* pembe, nukta ikutanapo mistari miwili. **angular**, *a.* -enye pembe; (*of persons*) mwembamba sana hata hutokeza mifupa.

angle, (2) *v.t.* vua samaki kwa mwanzi na mshipi; bembeleza, jaribu kupata kitu kwa hila au werevu. **angler**, *n.* mvuvi avuaye kwa mwanzi na mshipi.

Anglican, *a.* -a kiingereza, hasa -a Kanisa la kiingereza. **Anglo**, *pfx.* -a kiingereza.

angrily, *adv.* **angry**, *a.* taz. *anger*

anguish, *n.* maumivu makuu ya mwili au roho; uchungu.

angular, *a.* taz. *angle*, (1).

anil, *n.* mmea uitwao mnili ambao majani na vikonyo vyake hutumika kufanyizia rangi. **aniline**, *n.* dawa inayopatikana katika mnili, pia katika makaa ya mawe; hutumika kufanyizia rangi.

animadvert, *v.i.* (*upon*) nenea, karipia, laumu.

animal, *n.* mnyama, nyama, hayawani; kiumbe chenye uhai kisicho mmea; (*small*) mdudu. — *a.* -a nyama, -a kinyama; -enye tamaa nyingi za mwili. *Animal spirits*, wingi wa afya na uzima; moyo wa kuchangamka. **animalcule**, *n.* kijinyama, kijidudu (hasa kisichoonekana). **animalism**, *n.* hali ya kuvutwa kwa tamaa za mwili tu, anasa za mwili; unyama, uhayawani.

animate, *v.t.* huisha, tia uzima (afya, nguvu &c.); (*cheer*) amsha, tia moyo. — *a.* hai, -enye uhai, -zima. **animated**, *a.* -epesi, -a nguvu. **animation**, *n.* wepesi, bidii, utendaji, moyo wa nguvu.

animus, *n.* moyo, nia; (*intention*) maana, kusudi; (*grudge*) chuki, undani.

ankle, *n.* kifundo cha mguu. **anklet**. *n.* mtali, furungu.

ankylostoma, *n.* kichango kidogo sana kiletacho ugonjwa wa safura kikikaa tumboni. **ankylostomiasis**, *n.* ugonjwa wa safura.

anna, *n.* sehemu kumi na sita kwa moja ya rupia.

annals, *n.* tarehe, habari za miaka zilizotungwa kwa taratibu ya tarehe.
anneal, *v.t.* tia matiko; tia ugumu chuma (madini, kioo) kwa kukiyeyusha na kukiacha kipoe kwa taratibu.
annex, *v.t.* unga, tia, jitwalia, nyang'anya (nchi au shamba &c). **annex, annexe**, *n.* kilichotiwa mwishoni, ongezo (hasa jengo lililounganishwa).
annihilate, *v.t.* haribu kabisa, angamiza; tangua, towesha. **annihilation**, *n.* angamizo, tanguo, mvunjo, maangamizi; hali ya kutokuwa (ya kutoweka).
anniversary, *n.* sikukuu ya ukumbusho wa jambo kila mwaka.
anno domini, *adv.* katika miaka ya Bwana Wetu (Yesu Kristo). Hufupishwa na kuandikwa A.D.
annotate, *v.t.* tia maelezo (mafafanusi), eleza. **annotation**, *n.* maelezo, mafafanusi.
announce, *v.t.* tangaza, bashiri, hubiri wazi, piga mbiu juu ya, vumisha habari ya. **announcement**, *n.* tangazo, habari wazi, mbiu. **annunciation**, *n.* mtangazo, bashiri, habari, tangazo. *The Annunciation*, Bikira Mariamu kuhubiriwa na malaika.
annoy, *v.t.* sumbua, udhi, chokoza, kefyakefya, sunza, nyanyasa, kera, tashtiti. **annoyance**, *n.* sumbuo, kero, sumbuko, udhia, gubu, janga, makeke, kasirani. **annoying**, *a.* -a kusumbua, -a kuudhi &c. **annoyingly**, *adv.* kwa kusumbua, kuudhi.
annual, *a.* -a kila mwaka, -a mwaka mmoja tu. **annually**, *adv.* kila mwaka. **annuity**, *n.* fedha ilipwayo kila mwaka.
annul, *v.t.* tangua, batili, futa. **annulment**, *n.* mtanguo, tanguo, mfuto.
annular, *a.* -a mviringo kama pete, -liopetemana.
annunciation, *n.* taz. *announce*.
anodyne, *n.* dawa itulizayo maumivu; kitulizo.
anoint, *v.t.* paka mafuta au dawa ya mafuta; weka wakfu (bariki) kwa kupaka mafuta.
anomalous, *a.* -geni, -peke yake, siyofuata kawaida. **anomaly**, *n.* kitu kisicho cha desturi au kawaida, kigeni.
anon, *adv.* halafu kidogo, mara.
anonymous, *a.* bila jina, -siyotiwa jina, -a siri.
anopheles, *n.* aina moja ya mbu; wa kike huleta homa ya *malaria*, Viluwiluwi vyake hupenda zaidi maji safi; hukaa sawasawa juu ya maji. Waliopevuka huwa na madoadoa juu ya mabawa yao.
another, *a.* -ingine, -a pili, -ingine ya namna ile ile, -a mbalimbali. *Take one with another*, fikiri yote pamoja; chagua -a wastani.
answer, *v.t.* jibu, itika; (*satisfy*) ridhisha, tosha; (*solve*) leta jawabu, fumbua; (*repay*) lipa; — *v.i.* jibu, itika; (*answer for*) diriki, ahidi, dhaminia; (*be useful*) faa; (*correspond*) lingana. *Answer for, i.e. suffer the consequences of* (*action, crime &c.*) pata adhabu (maumivu &c.), iliyostahili. *Answer to, i.e. act in conformity with*) vutwa na, fuata. — *n.* jibu, itiko, jawabu, fumbo.
answerable, *a.* -a kuweza kujibiwa; -enye kudhamini, -enye daraka, -a kufaa, -a kulingana. *He is answerable for his son's actions*, matendo ya mwanawe ni juu yake.
ant, *n.* (*soldier*) chungu; (*white*) mchwa; (*brown*) siafu; (*red*) maji moto; (*small black*) sisimizi, nyenyere. **ant-hill**, *n.* kichuguu.
antacid, *n.* *and a.* dawa izimuayo ukali (kama ule wa siki &c.).
antagonism, *n.* ushindani, uadui, upingamizi, husuma. **antagonist**, *n.* mshindani, adui, hasimu, mpinga. **antagonistic**, *a.* -a uadui, -a kupinga, -a kushindana na.
antarctic, *a.* -a ncha ya kusini ya dunia.
antecedent, *a.* -a kutangulia (kwa wakati si mahali) -a zamani. — *n.*

litangulialo (kwa wakati). **antecedents,** *n. pl.* matendo, tabia, desturi na habari zilizokwisha pita za mtu.

antechamber, *n.* chumba cha kuingilia chumba kikuu, ukumbi.

antedate, *n.* tarehe iliyotangulia ile iliyopasa. — *v.t.* tia tarehe iliyotangulia iliyo ya kweli; badili tarehe ya jambo na kuifanya iwe kabla ya tarehe iliyotajwa kwanza; harakisha tarehe.

antediluvian, *a.* -a zamani sana, -a kale; -enye kufanana na mambo yaliyokuwa kabla ya gharika ya Nuhu. — *n.* aliyeishi kabla ya gharika; mzee sana; ashikaye sana desturi za zamani.

antelope, *n.* mnyama ye yote wa jamii ya paa, pofu, kulungu *&c.*; (*sable*) palahala.

antemeridian, *a.* -a kabla ya saa sita ya mchana.

antennae, *n. pl.* viungo vya wadudu kama pembe watumiavyo kupapasia; (*aerial*) nyuzi za simu zinazotumika kupokea simu za hewani.

antenuptial, *a.* -a kabla ya ndoa.

anterior, *a.* -a kutangulia, -a kabla.

anteroom, *n.* taz. *antechamber.*

anthem, *n.* wimbo wa dini; wimbo wa furaha (wa kusifu).

ant-hill, *n.* taz. *ant.*

anthology, *n.* kusanyiko la mashairi au masomo mazuri.

anthracite, *n.* namna ya makaa ya mawe yawakayo bila kutoa ndimi nyingi za moto, wala moshi, wala harufu.

anthrax, *n.* namna ya maradhi ya wanyama, hasa ng'ombe na kondoo; huambukiza wanadamu pia.

anthropoid, *a.* -enye umbo la au kufanana na wanadamu. **anthropology,** *n.* elimu ihusuyo habari zote za binadamu; lakini hasa ya mapokeo, dini na desturi za watu wasiostaarabika.

anti-, *pfx.* kinyume cha, kutopatana na, kushindana na, kuiga, -a uwongo, *e.g.* *antichrist,* mshindani mkuu wa Kristo na dini ya kikristo; *anti-christian,* -a kushindana na dini ya kikristo.

antic, *n.* kichezo, mkogo, tendo la kurukaruka (la kutapatapa, la kuranda).

anticipate, *v.t.* twaa (onja, fanya, zuia, fikiri, ogopa *&c.*) kabla ya wakati upasao; (*expect*) tazamia mbele, tumaini, dhani. **anticipation,** *n.* onjo la mbele, tendo au hali ya kutwaa kabla ya wakati wake; tendo la kutukia kabla ya wakati wake; fikiri juu ya jambo kabla halijatokea.

anticlimax, *n.* (katika hotuba) maneno hafifu (ya upuzi, ya ovyo) kufuata maneno mazito (ya maana, ya akili) na kwa hiyo kuharibu nguvu ya hotuba.

antidote, *n.* kizuiacho dhara ya kitu kilicholiwa au mambo yaliyotendwa, *e.g.* dawa inayoharibu nguvu ya sumu *&c.*

antimony, *n.* wanja wa manga.

antipathy, *n.* chuki, machukio, uadui, machukiano.

antiphon, *n.* wimbo wa kuitikiana au wa kupokezana.

antipodes, *n.* upande wa pili wa dunia; watu wakaao upande wa pili wa dunia; mtu au kitu kinachohitilafiana kabisa na kingine.

antiquary, *n.* achunguaye habari za vitu (hasa sanamu na sanaa) vya zamani au kuvikusanya na kuviweka. **antiquated,** *a.* -a kikale, -a kuukuu, -liyotanguka kwa vitu au mambo mapya. **antique,** *a.* -a kikale. **antiquity,** *n.* zamani za kale; watu wa zamani.

antiseptic, *a. and n.* dawa izuiayo vidonda visioze; izuiayo vijidudu (*bacteria*) visizaliane; izuiayo vyakula visioze.

antithesis, *n.* ushindani; kilicho mbalimbali; kinyume.

antitoxin, *n.* dawa iliyo katika damu ipiganayo na sumu ya ugonjwa.

antitype, *n.* kilicho asili ya mfano.

antler, *n.* pembe ya *antelope.*

antonym, *n.* neno lililo kinyume cha neno jingine.

anus, *n.* mkundu.

anvil, *n.* fuawe.

anxiety, *n.* mashaka, wasiwasi, hangaiko, kiherehere, fadhaa, haraka. **anxious**, *a.* -a mashaka, -a hofu ya hatari. *Be anxious*, ona mashaka, taharuki, shughulika, fadhaika, hamanika, hangaika. *Be anxious* (*for*) kumbuka, hofia, taka, tamani; (*about*), hofia, sikitikia. **anxiously**, *adv.* kwa mashaka, kwa kutazamia sana, kwa shaka au hofu.

any, *a.* -o ote. *Any one, anybody*, ye yote, awaye, yote. *Anything*, kitu cho chote. *In any case, at any rate*, kwa kila hali, kwa vyo vyote. *There is not any*, hapana hata kidogo. **anyhow, anyways**, *adv.* kwa vyo vyote, kwa namna yo yote, kwa kila hali. *Anywhere*, po pote. *Anywise*, kwa kadiri yo yote, kwa namna yo yote. *If anything*, ikiwapo (kwa kadiri yo yote).

aorta, *n.* mshipa mkubwa (*artery*) wa damu wa upande wa kushoto wa moyo; umegawanyika kufanya mishipa midogo ya kupelekea damu safi yenye nguvu kila mahali mwilini.

apace, *adv.* mbio, kwa kasi, kwa haraka, hima.

apart, *adv.* mbali, kwa faragha; (*separately*) moja moja; (*asunder, parted*) mbalimbali; (*out of consideration, apart from*) isipokuwa. *Set apart*, weka mbali, tenga, bagua, baidisha. *Force* (*draw*) *apart*, nanua, mamanua.

apartment, *n.* chumba, mkato wa nyumba. *Let apartments*, pangisha vyumba.

apathy, *n.* utepetevu, ubaridi. **apathetic**, *a.* -tepetevu, baridi.

ape, *n.* nyani. — *v.t.* iga mambo na matendo. **apish**, *a.* -a kinyani, kama nyani.

aperient, *n.* dawa ya kuharisha, msahala, haluli.

aperitive, *n.* kinywaji kizuri kichungu cha kunywa kabla ya kula ili kuamsha tamaa ya kula; taz. *aperient.*

aperture, *n.* tundu, kipenyo, mwangaza, dirisha.

apex, *n.* kilele, ncha, kipeo, kilembwa, kileleta.

aphasia, *n.* hali ya kutoweza kusema kwa sababu ya ugonjwa wa ubongo.

aphorism, *n.* msemo mfupi wa maana sana, mithali ya maneno.

aphrodisiac, *a. and n.* dawa &c. -a kuamsha tamaa ya kiume au kike, mkuyati.

apiary, *n.* mahali pa kufugia nyuki, mzinga wa nyuki.

apiece, *adv.* kwa kila -moja -moja; kwa kila -mojawapo.

apish, *a.* taz. *ape.*

aplomb, *n.* uwima; hali ya kujitumainia (ya kujitoshelea, ya kujikinai), ukinaifu, ukavu wa macho, ubaridi.

apocalypse, *n.* kitabu cha mwisho wa Agano Jipya; Ufunuo.

apocrypha, *n.* baadhi ya vitabu vya Maandiko Matakatifu visivyokubaliwa na Wayahudi wala kwa kanuni za Kanisa la kiingereza. **apocryphal**, *a.* -a *apocrypha*; isiyothibitishwa; -a kubunika, -a uwongo.

apodosis, *n.* kwa elimu ya sarufi: sehemu ya pili ya nia yenye masharti ya kiarifa, *e.g.* angefanya kazi, ningefurahi. Sehemu ya kwanza, yaani 'angefanya kazi', huitwa *protasis*, sehemu ya pili, yaani ile itakayotokea ikiwa ya kwanza hufanyika, huitwa *apodosis.*

apologetic, *a.* (*exercising*) -a kutoa udhuru, -a kukiri kwa majuto; (*defending*) -a kujitetea, -a kujikania kosa; (*acknowledging*) -a kujutia kosa. **apologetically**, *adv.* kwa majuto &c. **apologize**, *v.i.* toa udhuru, omba radhi, kiri kosa, jitetea. *I beg to apologize*, kunradhi; niwie radhi. **apology**, *n.* udhuru, maneno ya kujitetea (ya kuomba radhi, ya kutoa udhuru, ya kukiri kosa).

apoplexy, *n.* kiharusi, ugonjwa wa ghafula wa ubongo umfanyao mtu asiweze kumudu viungo vyake, wala kuona kwa kugusa.

apostasy, *n.* ukafiri, tendo la mtu kukana dini yake. **apostate,** *n.* kafiri akanaye dini yake; mkufuru. — *a.* -a uwongo, -a hiana. **apostatize,** *v.i.* kufuru, ritadi.

apostle, *n.* mtume, mmojawapo wa mitume kumi na wawili wa Yesu Kristo. **apostolic,** *a.* -a mitume, -a zamani za mitume. *Apostles' Creed,* Imani ya Mitume.

apostrophe, *n.* alama katika maandishi (') kujulisha ya kuwa herufi moja haipo; alama ya -a kwa Kiingereza, *e.g. John's book,* kitabu cha John. Katika maandishi ya Kiswahili hutumika kubainisha tofauti ya sauti ya ng, *e.g.* ng'ombe na ngao.

apothecary, *n.* atengenezaye na kuuza dawa.

appal, *v.t.* tisha, ogofya, shangaza, fadhaisha. **appalling,** *a.* -a kutisha, -a kuogofya mno. -a kushangaza, -a kufadhaisha, -a bumbuazi.

apparatus, *n.* vyombo vya kufanyia kazi, zana za kazi, samani, ala, vifaa.

apparel, *n.* mavazi, nguo. — *v.t.* vika, visha.

apparent, *a.* dhahiri, wazi, -a kuonekana, -a kutambulikana; (*seeming, uncertain, not real*) -a kuonekana kama kwamba. **apparently,** *adv.* labda; kwa kadiri ionekanavyo.

apparition, *n.* tukio, kivuli, mzuka, kioja, njozi.

appeal, *v.i.* (*call on*) ita, omba, taja, sihi; (*for mercy, help*) lalama, piga kiyowe, taka msaada; (*for judgement*) taka hukumu, kimbilia; (*to superior court or authority*) taka rufani. *It appeals to the eye,* inavuta macho, inatazamisha. — *n.* (*petition*) haja, maombi; (*for mercy*) lalamiko; (*to higher court*) rufani. **appealingly,** *adv.* kwa kusihi, kwa maombi &c. **appellant,** *n.* atakaye rufani; mwombaji.

appear, *v.i.* onekana, tokea; (*suddenly*) zuka; (*look like*) -wa kama; (*present oneself formally*) enda mbele ya, hudhuria, -ja mbele ya, wajihi, simamia katika; (*appear, act for another*) simamia shaurini kwa. *It appears so to me,* naona ndivyo. *It appears* (*impersonally*) huonekana kama kwamba. **appearance,** *n.* tendo la kuonekana (la kusimamia &c); (*aspect*) sura, wajihi, umbo; (*apparition*) tokeo, kivuli, mzuka, njozi; (*resemblance*) mfano. *To all appearances,* kadiri ionekanavyo. *To keep up appearances,* kujisingizia kama ndivyo mambo yalivyo, kumbe sivyo; kufanya ili kuepuka haya au aibu. *To put in an appearance,* fika mwenyewe, hudhuria.

appease, *v.t.* tuliza, ridhisha, nyamazisha, suluhisha. **appeasement,** *n.* kitulizo, utulizo, suluhu.

appellant, *n.* taz. *appeal.*

appellation, *n.* jina.

append, *v.t.* tia mwishoni (juu, nyuma, baadaye). **appendage,** *n.* kilichotiwa mwishoni. **appendicitis,** *n.* ugonjwa wa *appendix* kufanya jipu. **appendix,** *n.* mwisho wa hati au kitabu &c. uliotiwa baadaye; nyongeza; kifuko kidogo kinachotokeza katika chango ya tumbo.

appertain, *v.i.* pasa, husu; fungamana, -wa -enye habari ya; -wa mali (haki, tabia) ya. **appertaining** (*to*), *a.* -a kupasa -a kuhusu, -a kufaa, -a kustahili, -a kufungamana (na).

appetence, appetency, *n.* tamaa, shauku (hasa ya kike na kiume).

appetite, *n.* tamaa, uchu, roho, shauku, njaa (ya chakula, kinywaji, kike, kiume &c.). **appetize,** *v.t.* amsha tamaa ya chakula, tamanisha chakula. **appetizing,** *a.* -a kutamanisha; (*of food*) -a kuchapukia.

applaud, *v.t.* sifu kwa kupiga makofi (vifijo, ukelele, sauti kubwa); pigia ukelele wa sifa, tukuza, shangilia. **applause,** *n.* vifijo, tendo la kusifu kwa makofi &c.

apple, *n.* tofaa, tunda la kizungu kama pera; (*tree*) mtofaa. *Apple of the eye,* mboni ya jicho. *Adam's apple,* kikoromeo, zoloto. *Apple-pie order,* taratibu kabisa, barabara, siasa.

appliance, *n.*, **applicable,** *a.*, **applicant,** *n.*, **application,** *n.* taz. *apply.*

apply, *v.t.* tia, tumia; (*medicine*) paka, bandika; (*for*) taka, omba; — *v.i.* (*suit*) faa, lingana. *Apply for,* omba, taka. *Apply to* (*ask*) tolea haja, kimbilia; (*suit*) pasa, faa; (*refer to*) husika na, nenea, -wa na habari ya. *Apply oneself to,* jitia katika, shiriki. **appliance,** *n.* kitu cha kutumika, kifaacho kwa kazi, zana, samani, chombo, ala. **applicable,** *a.* -a kufaa, -a kutumika, -a kupasa, -a kuhusu. **applicant,** *n.* mdai, mwombaji, mletaji haja. **application,** *n.* tendo la kutia (la kutumia); mpako, mbandiko; (*request*) haja, maombi; (*use*) matumizi; (*diligence*) bidii, welekevu; (*of something in regard to something else*) matumizi ya jambo kwa ajili ya kueleza au kudhihirisha jambo jingine.

appoint, *v.t.* weka, amuru, agiza, fanya. **appointment,** *n.* miadi, ahadi ya kuonana wakati maalum; tendo la kuweka mtu katika kazi; amri, maagizo, maafikano; (*situation*) kazi; (*arrangement*) tengenezo. *They made an appointment for six o'clock,* waliwekeana saa thenashara wakutane. **appointments,** *n. pl.* vyombo, zana, manufaa. vikorokoro, vifaa.

apportion, *v.t.* gawanya, gawia sehemu zilizo za haki. **apportionment,** *n.* mgawo, mgawanyo.

apposite, *a.* -enye maana, -a kufaa, -elekevu, -a njia, -a bahati, -a kuhusu.

appraise, *v.t.* tia bei, kadiri, pima thamani au kadiri ya ubora wa kitu. **appraisement,** *n.* kisio la thamani (la kadiri au ubora).

appreciable, *a.*, **appreciably,** *adv.*, taz. *appreciate.*

appreciate, *v.t.* (*understand*) fahamu, tambua vyema uzuri wa manufaa ya kitu au jambo; (*enjoy*) furahia, pendezwa na, ona vyema; (*estimate highly*) thamini; — *v.i.* (*of value*) zidi thamani. **appreciable,** *a.* -a kadiri iwezayo kuonekana, -a kutambulikana, -a kupimikana. *It is hardly appreciable,* ni kidogo tu hata ni kama kwamba hapana. **appreciably,** *adv.* kwa kadiri iwezayo kuonekana au kutambulikana. **appreciation,** *n.* tendo au hali ya kuthamini (ya kufahamu vyema uzuri wa manufaa, ya kufurahia), shukrani; (*in value*) zidio la thamani, kuzidi kwa thamani.

apprehend, *v.t.* kamata, shika, bamba; (*understand*) fahamu, tambua; (*fear*) hofu, ogopa. **apprehensible,** *a.* -a kufahamika, -a kutambulika &c. **apprehension,** *n.* tendo la kukamatwa (la kushikwa); (*understanding*) ufahamu, akili, ujuzi; (*fear*) hofu. **apprehensive,** *a.* -enye kufahamu vyema, -enye akili, -elekevu; -enye hofu, -a kutazamia kwa hofu, -a kuchelea.

apprentice, *n.* mwanafunzi wa kazi. — *v.t.* tia kwa fundi, fanya mwanafunzi. **apprenticeship,** *n.* uanafunzi, muda wa kujifunza au kufundishwa kazi.

apprise, *v.t.* ambia, arifu, pasha habari, bashiri.

approach, *v.t.* karibia, sogea karibu, jongea karibu, jongelea, jia, endea; (*resemble*) fanana, lingana, landa. — *n.* mjio, majilio; (*means of*) njia, mlango; (*resemblance*) mfano. **approachable,** *a.* (*be*) fikika, patika; (*of persons*) ambilika.

approbation, *n.* idhini, ukubali, kibali; sifa nzuri.

appropriate, *v.t.* jitwalia, iba; (*set apart*) weka kwa kusudi fulani. — *a.* -a kufaa, -a kuhusu. **appropriately,** *adv.* kwa jinsi ya kufaa. **appropriation,** *n.* tendo la kujitwalia (la kuiba); sehemu (ya fedha &c.) iliyowekwa kwa kusudi fulani.

approve, *v.t.* sifu, penda, pendezwa na; (*sanction*) toa idhini, kubali. **approval,** *n.* kibali, idhini. *Goods on approval,* bidhaa za mrejaa.

approximate, *a.* -a karibu sawa. — *v.i.* karibia sana, -wa karibu sawasawa (na). **approximately,** *adv.* karibu sana, kwa kadiri iliyo karibu kuwa sawasawa. **approximation,** *n.* kisicho sawasawa kabisa ila ni karibu sana, kisio.

appurtenance, *n.* zana, kitu kinachohusu kitu kingine.

apricot, *n.* tunda la kizungu kama embe dodo.

April, *n.* mwezi wa nne wa mwaka wa kizungu; Aprili.

apron, *n.* vazi au kipande cha kitambaa cha kuvalia mbele (hasa kufunika mavazi yasichafuke wakati wa kufanya kazi).

apropos, *adv.* kwa kufaa (kusudi, habari *&c.*); juu ya (kusudi, habari *&c.*). — *a.* -a kufaa, -a bahati.

apse, *n.* sehemu ya mwisho ya kanisa lenye umbo la mviringo; (*of mosque*) mhirabu.

apt, *a.* -epesi, -elekevu, hodari, -zoevu, -a tayari, -a kuelekea. *He is apt to forget,* huelekea kusahau. **aptitude,** *n.*, **aptness,** *n.* wepesi, welekevu, utayari, tabia ya kufaa (ya kuelekea), ustadi. **aptly,** *adv.* vizuri, vyema, kwa wakati au namna ifaayo.

aquarium, *n.* kisiwa au tangi la maji la kuwekea mimea, samaki, na wanyama wa majini. **aquatic,** *a.* -a maji, -a majini, -a kuishi majini. Bata ni *aquatic. Aquatic sports,* michezo ya majini. **aqueduct,** *n.* mfereji wa maji. **aqueous,** *a.* -a maji.

aquiline, *a.* -a tai, -a kama mdomo wa tai. *Aquiline nose,* pua kali iliyopindika kama ile ya tai.

Arab, *n.* Mwarabu. **Arabia,** *n.* Uarabu, Bara Arabu, Arabuni, Manga. **Arabic, Arabian,** *a.* -a kiarabu, -a Manga.

arable, *a.* -a kulimika. *Arable land,* nchi inayolimika.

arbiter, arbitrator, *n.* mwamuzi, mpatanishi, msuluhishi; mtu achaguliwaye au mwenye amri kukata shauri. **arbitrament,** *n.* hukumu ya *arbitrator.* **arbitrate,** *v.i.* hukumu, amua, patanisha, suluhisha. **arbitration,** *n.* maamuzi, hukumu, suluhu. **arbitrary,** *a.* -siyo na sheria wala kanuni; -geugeu, -a kubadilibadili; (*despotic*) -dhalimu, -jeuri, -a kuhukumu kwa peke yake (kwa nguvu bila sheria wala shauri). *He is arbitrary,* hashauriani na mtu.

arboriculture, *n.* ukulima wa miti.

arbour, *n.* mahali pa kukaa pa kupumzika penye uvuli katika bustani.

arc, *n.* mkato au sehemu ya kizingo cha duara.

arcade, *n.* njia yenye maduka iliyoikizwa dari; njia yenye safu za nguzo zenye matao juu yake.

arch, (1) *n.* tao. —*v.t.* fanya tao, jenga tao juu. **archway,** *n.* njia inayopita chini ya tao.

arch, (2) *a.* -erevu, -enye hila, -janja.

arch, (3) *pfx. a.* -kuu, *e.g.* **archangel,** *n.* malaika mkuu. **archbishop,** askofu mkuu. **archdeacon,** kasisi mkuu.

archaeology, *n.* maarifa ya mambo ya kale. **archaic,** *a.* -a kale isiyotumika sasa. **archaism,** *n.* neno la kikale, hasa lisilotumika sasa.

archangel, *n.*, **archbishop,** *n.*, **archdeacon,** *n.* taz. *arch,* (3).

archer, *n.* mpigaji upindi. **archery,** *n.* ufundi wa kupiga upindi.

archetype, *n.* kielelezo cha kwanza, namna ya asili.

archipelago, *n.* bahari yenye visiwa vidogo vingi; jamii ya visiwa vidogo.

architect, *n.* mwandishi wa ramani za majengo; mjenzi mwenye maarifa mengi ya ujenzi. **architecture,** *n.* maarifa ya ujenzi; ujenzi.

archives, *n.* mahali pawekwapo hati na tarehe.

archway, *n.* taz. *arch,* (1).

arctic, *a.* -a kaskazini sana; baridi sana.

ardent, *a.* -a kuwaka, -kali, -enye bidii, -a juhudi, -enye shauku. **ardently,** *adv.* kwa nguvu, kwa bidii, kwa juhudi, kwa shauku nyingi. **ardour,** *n.* bidii, nguvu ya shauku &c. *Ardent spirits,* vileo vyenye *alcohol* nyingi, vyenye kulevya sana.

arduous, *a.* -gumu, -a taabu, -enye kuhitaji bidii au nguvu nyingi hata kufaulu; -a kuchosha kwa ajili ya nguvu au bidii inayotakiwa. *An arduous task,* kazi ngumu isiyowezekana ila kwa taabu.

are, *v.* kama *am,* ila hueleza habari za wewe, sisi, ninyi na wao.

area, *n.* eneo, uwanja.

areca, *n.* (*tree*) mpopoo; (*fruit*) popoo.

arena, *n.* uwanja (wa katikati ya (*amphitheatre*) wa kuchezea; mahali pa kushindania.

argue, *v.t.* toa hoja (sababu, maneno) ya kuthibitisha au ya kukanusha, jadili, shindana kwa maneno, hojiana, tetana, bishana, jadiliana, babaka. *To argue* (*a person*) *into or out of,* vuta, shawishi (mtu) hata afanye (au asifanye) jambo fulani. **argument,** *n.* sababu, hoja, kisa, maneno; majadiliano, mabishano; habari za hotuba; muhtasari ya habari zilizo katika kitabu. **argumentative,** *a.* -hoji, -a maneno mengi, -kaidi, -a kubishana &c.

aria, *n.* wimbo (hasa wa sauti au ala moja).

Arianism, *n.* mafundisho ya uzushi wa Arius aliyeishi panapo A.D. 300, ambaye alikana Uungu wa Kristo.

arid, *a.* -kavu sana, yabisi, -kame. **aridity, aridness,** *n.* ukavu, ukame, uyabisi.

aright, *adv.* kwa jinsi iliyopasa, sahihi, sawasawa, barabara.

arise, *v.i. p.t.* **arose,** *pf.t.* **arisen.** (*get up*) ondoka, inuka, panda; (*stand*) ondoka, simama; (*occur*) tokea, tukia.

aristocracy, *n.* (*government*) utawala kwa watu wa koo zilizo bora (kwa watu wenye hali zilizo bora); (*class*) jamii ya watu wa koo zilizo bora (ya wakuu wa nchi, watoto wa watu). **aristocrat,** *n.* mtoto wa watu, mwungwana, mtu wa ukoo ulio bora. **aristocratic,** *a.* -a *aristocracy,* -a kiungwana, -a cheo bora, -a kitajiri, -a jamii ya watu wakuu.

arithmetic, *n.* elimu ya hesabu. **arithmetical,** *a.* -a hesabu. **arithmetician,** *a.* mwenye elimu nyingi za hesabu, stadi wa hesabu.

ark, *n.* sanduku kubwa; (*Noah's*) safina, chombo alichounda Nuhu kabla ya gharika.

arm, (1) *n.* mkono; cho chote kitokacho kama mkono; *e.g.* mkono wa bahari ni ghuba au hori. *Armchair,* kiti chenye mikono. *Armhole,* tundu la vazi la kupitishia mkono. *Arm-in-arm,* kwa kushikana mikono, kwa urafiki au kwa kusaidiana sana. *Keep at arm's length,* epusha, epukana na, epuka urafiki na au kuzoeana na. *Right arm,* tegemeo kuu, msaidizi mkuu. *With open arms,* kwa urafiki, kwa upendo. **armless,** *a.* bila mikono. **armlet,** *n.* kikuku, bangili, kitu cha kuvaa mkononi; mkono mdogo. **armpit,** *n.* kwapa.

arm, (2) *n.* silaha. **arms,** *n.pl.* jamii ya silaha, zana za vita. *Firearms,* silaha zitumiazo baruti, *e.g.* bunduki, bastola. *To lay down arms,* kuacha vita. *Under arms,* -enye silaha tayari kwa vita. *Up in arms,* -enye hasira, tayari kugombana, hamaki. **arm,** *v.t.* -pa silaha; — *v.i.* twaa silaha. **armed,** *a.* -enye silaha. **armament,** *n.* (*forces*) jeshi lenye silaha; (*stores*) zana za vita, hasa mizinga ya manowari. **armature,** *n.* sehemu ya mashine ya umeme (elektrisiti) inayozunguka nguvu ya umeme inapoipitia. **armour,** *n.* (*weapons*) silaha; (*dress*) mavazi ya chuma ya vita, yaani deraya; (*ships*) chuma cha mbavuni mwa manowari cha kuzuia risasi za mizinga ya adui. **armourer,** *n.* mfua silaha, mtunzaji silaha za jeshi. **armoury,** *n.* ghala ya silaha. **army,** *n.* jeshi la askari; jeshi lo lote la watu lililo na kusudi lo lote maalum; umati wa watu.

armadillo, *n.* mnyama kama kakakuona.

armament, *n.* taz. *arm*, (2).
armistice, *n.* mapatano ya kuacha vita kwa muda; mapumziko (ya vita); amani.
armlet, *n.* taz. *arm*, (1).
armour, *n.*, **armourer**, *n*, **armoury**, *n.* taz. *arm*, (2).
armpit, *n.* taz. *arm*, (1).
aroma, *n.* harufu nzuri, nukato. **aromatic**, *a.* -a kunukia vizuri.
arose, *v.* taz. *arise*.
around, *adv. and prep.* pande zote (za), kuzunguka, kandokando (za), mzingo (wa).
arouse, *v.t.* amsha, sukuma, washa, harakisha, chochea, tia shonga.
arquebus, *n.* namna ya bunduki ya zamani.
arrack, *n.* araka, namna ya kileo kikali kifanyizwacho kwa sukari na mchele wa mpunga.
arraign, *v.t.* shtaki, tia hukumuni.
arrange, *v.t.* (*put in order*) andika, zatiti, tengeneza, safidi, sabidi, panga, ratibu; (*organize, settle*) fanya shughuli ya, toa shauri la, amuru, tengeneza. *Arrange a quarrel*, amua, tuliza, patanisha wagomvi, suluhisha. **arrangement**, *n.* matengenezo, taratibu, madaraka, amri, shauri, mpango; (*agreement*) mapatano, maagano, maafikano, suluhu.
arrant, *a.* kabisa, -a kupindukia. *An arrant thief*, mwizi wa kupindukia.
arras, *n.* nguo ya kutundika ukutani nyumbani, ni mapambo.
array, *v.t.* panga, zatiti, andika; (*dress*) vika, pamba. — *n.* (*order*) safusafu, taratibu; (*dress*) mavazi, pambo, urembo; (*of people*) jamii nzima.
arrear, **arrears**, *n.* kilicho nyuma (kwa wakati); kisicholipwa; kisichotendwa, deni. *To be in arrears*, -wa na deni, wiwa; -wa na hali ya kazi kuchelewa.
arrest, *v.t.* (*stop*) simamisha, zuia; (*seize*) kamata, shika, funga, dara, bamba; (*catch attention*) vuta macho, tazamisha. — *n.* *He made an arrest*, alimkamata mtu; (*stoppage*) zuio, kizuizi.
arrive, *v.i.* fika, wasili, -ja; (*arrive (at)*), fika, fikia, soza, patia, tekelea. **arrival**, *n.* mfiko, majilio, mjio, kifiko, kikomo.
arrogant, *a.* -enye kiburi (kutakabari, fidhuli), -a kudeka, -a kunyeta, sodawi. **arrogance, arrogancy**, *n.* kiburi, ufidhuli, majivuno, usafihi, unyeti, unyarafu, usodawi. **arrogantly**, *adv.* kwa kiburi (ufidhuli, majivuno, jeuri). **arrogate**, *v.t.* jidai, jitwalia bila haki, jipatia (hasa kwa jeuri).
arrow, *n.* mshale; (*shaft*) wano, uti; (*head*) kigumba, chembe cha mshale; alama ipigwayo chapa katika mali ya serikali ya kiingereza.
arrowroot, *n.* wanga.
arsenal, *n.* ghala kubwa ya kuwekea silaha na zana za vita.
arsenic, *n.* namna moja ya sumu inayotumika katika dawa nyinginezo.
arson, *n.* kuteketeza nyumba (shamba &c.) za watu kwa kusudi.
art, *n.* sanaa, ustadi wa kazi, ufundi, *e.g.* kupiga muziki (kuandika picha, kuchora sanamu &c.); (*cunning*) hila, werevu; (*skill*) akili, elimu, ustadi. *Art of medicine, writing, &c.* utabibu, uandishi &c. *Work of art*, kazi ya sanaa (ya ustadi mwingi, ya ufundi mkuu). *Arts and manufactures*, kazi za akili na za mikono. **artful**, *a.* -stadi, -erevu, -janja (hasa -enye hila). **artfully**, *adv.* kwa ustadi; kwa hila (ujanja, uayari). **artfulness**, *n.* hila, werevu, ujanja. **artifice**, *n.* hila, mtego. **artificer**, *n.* fundi. **artificial**, *a.* -liofanywa na watu, si -a asili, si halisi, -a kubunika, -a uwongo, -a kuiga yasivyo. **artisan**, *n.* fundi, mtu wa kazi. **artist**, *n.* mstadi; fundi, hasa mfanya kazi za sanaa; (*painter*) mwandishi wa picha za rangi. **artiste**, *n.* mtu apataye uchumi kwa kuwaimbia wengine au kuwafurahisha kwa michezo yake. **artistic**, *a.* -a sanaa, -stadi, -sanifu, -zuri

artless, *a.* -jinga, bila hila, -nyofu. **artlessly**, *adv.* kwa unyofu, kwa ujinga.

artery, *n.* mshipa mkubwa upelekao damu moyoni mpaka kila sehemu ya mwili; (*road*) njia kuu, barabara. **arterial**, *a.* -a kufanana na *artery*.

artesian well, *n.* kisima cha kwenda chini sana mpaka kufika penye maji ya chini, na maji huja juu bila kutumia bomba.

artful, *a.*, **artfully**, *adv.*, **artfulness**, *n.* taz. *art.*

arthritis, *n.* ugonjwa wa yabisi kavu.

article, *n.* kitu; (*written*) nakala, sehemu ya andiko, juzuu, su--; (*clause*) sharti. *Article of faith*, sharti ya imani. *Article of commerce*, bidhaa. Maneno *a*, *an*, *the*, huitwa *article* katika elimu ya sarufi.

articulate, *a.* dhahiri, -enye kutamkwa vizuri. — *v.i.* tamka vyema; tamka kwa sauti dhahiri. **articulation**, *n.* tamko.

artifice, *n.*, **artificer**, *n.*, **artificial**, *a.* taz. *art.*

artillery, *n.* silaha za vita, hasa mizinga; jamii ya askari wa mizinga.

artisan, *n.*, **artist**, *n.*, **artiste**, *n.*, **artistic**, *a.*, **artless**, *a.*, **artlessly**, *adv.* taz. *art.*

Aryan, *a.* -a kuhusu lugha za *Sanscrit*, *Kiajemi*, *Kiyunani*, *Kirumi*, *Kiitalia*, *Kiingereza* na *Kidachi*, -a kuhusu mataifa yanayotumia lugha hizo.

as, *conj.* and *adv.* (*in that degree, in like manner*) -vyo, -vyo-: *as a man sows, so shall he reap*, mtu apandavyo ndivyo atakavyovuna; (*such . . . as*) kama: *such things as chairs*, vitu kama viti; (*same . . . as*) kama, -vyo-: *he did the same as so and so*, alifanya kama alivyofanya fulani; *this is the same sort as that*, hiki ni kama kile, (ni sawasawa na kile); (*since, because*) kwa sababu, kwa maana, kwa kuwa; (*when, while*) wakati, pindi, pale, -po- -poki-: *as he was going* (*while or when he was going*) alipokuwa akienda, alipokienda; (*for instance, example*) kwa mfano, methali; (*so as to*) ili, kwa jinsi ya (au kwa kutumia *Subj. Mood*), *e.g. he ran so as to overtake him*, alipiga mbio (kwa jinsi ya) (ili) apate kumfikia. *As long as it is wide*, upana na urefu sawasawa. *Just as*, vivi hivi. *As far as* (*ever*) *I can*, *As much as*, *As long as*, kama (kadiri) niwezavyo. *As soon as I can*, upesi niwezavyo. *As long as*, *As much as*, sawa na. *As far as*, hata, mpaka, hadi. *As if*, kama. *Same as*, sawa na. *Such as*, kama. *This as well as that*, hiki na kile pia, hiki pamoja na kile, hiki na tena kile, hiki sawa na kile. *Men as well as women*, wanaume kwa wanawake. *As well*, pia, sawasawa, vile vile. *As to*, *As for*, kwa juu ya, kwa habari ya, mintarafu ya. *As it were*, kama. *Just as well*, mamoja, haidhuru. *As yet*, bado, hata sasa.

asafoetida, *n.* mvuje.

asbestos, *n.* kitu kama jiwe la nyuzinyuzi (kimefanana sana na pamba au katani iliyogandamizwa pamoja). Huzuia sana moto na joto lisipenye, wala hakiungui. Hutumika kufanyia vigae vya kuzuia ukali wa jua &c.

ascend, *v.i.* panda, inuka, kwea, paa; — *v.t.* panda, kwea. *To be in the ascendant*, panda, zidi, shinda. **ascendancy**, *n.* nguvu, uwezo unaotawala. **ascendant**, *a.* -a kushinda, bora, -a juu ya upeo wa macho. **ascension**, *n.* mpao, mpando. *Ascension Day*, sikukuu ya kupaa mbinguni Yesu Kristo. **ascent**, *n.* mpando, mpao; (*hill*) kilima, mwinuko; (*means of ascent*) pandio. *Line of ascent*, ukoo, jadi, nasaba.

ascertain, *v.t.* hakikia, pata hakika, yakinia, sahihisha, hoji, pata kujua.

ascetic, *n.* ajinyimaye vitu na mambo ya kufurahisha, hata yakiwa halali, kwa ajili ya dhamiri yake; ajaribuye kuwa mwema na kuepukana na maovu, kwa kujinyima anasa za mwili; mtawa. **asceticism**, *n.* hali ya *ascetic*.

ascribe, *v.t.* (*to*) andikia, hesabia, wekea, tolea. *Ascribe wrongly to,* singizia, zulia. **ascription,** *n.* toleo la sifa (heshima &c.), sifa.
aseptic, *a.* -a kutokuoza, -sioelekea kuoza.
asexual, *a.* -siyo -a kiume wala -a kike.
ash, (1) *n.* (*tree*) namna ya mti.
ash, (2) **ashes,** *n.* majivu. *Ash Wednesday,* Jumatano ya Majivu, siku ya kwanza ya Kwaresima.
ashamed, *a.* (*be*) ona haya, tahayari, fadhaika, aibika, fedheheka.
ashore, *adv.* *pwani.* *The ship has gone ashore,* chombo kimekwama pwani, kimepanda pwani, kimepwelewa. *He has gone ashore,* ameshuka pwani.
Asian, Asiatic, *a.* -a nchi ya *Asia.*
aside, *adv.* upande, kando; (*in private*) faraghani, kwa siri. *Go aside,* jitenga. *Speak aside,* sema kwa sauti ndogo ili watu (ila wale walio karibu) wasisikie, nong'ona, nong'onezana. *To set aside (judgement),* futa, tangua (hukumu).
asinine, *a.* taz. *ass.*
ask, *v.t.* (*request*) taka, omba, sihi; (*invite*) alika, karibisha; (*question*) uliza, hoji. *Ask after,* ulizia hali.
askance, askew, aslant, *adv.* upande, mshazari. *Look askance at,* tazama kitongotongo.
asleep, *a.* (*be*) lala, sinzia, (*of limbs, i.e. numbed*) -fa ganzi.
aslope, *a.* *and adv.* -a (kwa) kuinama.
asp, *n.* nyoka mdogo mwenye sumu.
asparagus, *n.* namna ya mboga.
aspect, *n.* (*of persons*) sura, umbo, wajihi, uso, tabia; (*of things*) jinsi, namna, sura, hali, maono; (*view*) mandhari. *Have a (southern) aspect,* elekea, kabili (kusini).
aspen, *n.* namna ya mti wa Ulaya. — *a.* -a *aspen*; -a kutetemeka.
asperity, *n.* ukali, hamaki, harara, uchungu.
asperse, *v.t.* singizia, sengenya, shutumu. **aspersion,** *n.* masingizio, masengenyo, shutumu.
asphalt, *n.* namna ya lami ngumu; huyeyushwa na kuchanganywa na changarawe na kutandazwa juu ya barabara. Ipoapo huwa ngumu sana.
asphyxia, *n.* msongo wa roho, hal ya kuzimia roho kwa kusongwa.
asphyxiate, *v.t.* nyonga (songa) sana hata kuzimia roho. **asphyxiation,** *n.* tendo la kusongwa sana hata kuzimia roho, msongo wa roho.
aspirant, *n.* taz. *aspire.*
aspirate, *v.t.* tamka kwa pumzi nyingi kama kutamka herufi *H.* — *n.* tamko la herufi *H.* **aspiration,** *n.* mvuto wa pumzi; taz. chini ya *aspire.* **aspiratory,** *a.* -a kuhusu kuvuta pumzi.
aspire, *v.i.* (*to*) taka sana, tamani, jitahidi sana kupata (kitu bora &c.). **aspirant,** *n.* atakaye, ajaribuye sana kupata (kitu bora, cheo, heshima, sifa &c.). **aspiration,** *n.* tamaa, jitihadi ya kupata (kitu bora &c.).
ass, *n.* punda; (*fool*) mjinga, mpumbavu, baradhuli. **asinine,** *a.* punda, -a kama punda, -pumbavu sana. *Make oneself an ass,* jipumbaza.
assagai, assegai, *n.* mkuki.
assail, *v.t.* rukia, endea kwa jeuri (shari), shambulia, fanyia jeuri (shari). **assailant,** *n.* mtu arukiaye, ashambuliaye, adui, mshari.
assassin, *n.* mwuaji wa siri (wa hila, wa kutukia ghafula) hasa wa kuajiriwa. **assassinate,** *v.t.* ua kwa siri (hila &c.). **assassination,** *n.* mauaji ya siri.
assault, *v.t.* rukia, shambulia (kama *assail*). — *n.* shambulio la ghafula kama vita; tendo la kupiga mtu (la kumrukia); shambulio lo lote la maneno, maombi &c.
assay, *v.t.* hakikia kiasi cha madini iliyomo katika mawe yenye madini; jaribia, jitahidi. — *n.* tendo la kuhakikia kiasi cha madini iliyomo katika mawe ya madini; jaribu, jaribio, jitihadi.
assemble, *v.t.* kusanya, ita pamoja, kutanisha; — *v.i.* kusanyika, ku,

tana, -ja pamoja. **assemblage,** *n.* kusanyiko, mkutano. **assembly,** *n.* kukusanya; kusanyiko, mkutano.

assent, *v.i.* (*assent to*) kubali, kiri, sema ndiyo, toa idhini, itikia. — *n.* idhini, kibali, ukubali. *Signify assent,* itikia. **assentient,** *a.* -a kukubali. — *n.* akubaliye, atoaye idhini.

assert, *v.t.* dai, simamia, tetea; nena kwa uthabiti, thibitisha kwa maneno. *Assert oneself,* jitokeza, jitanguliza, jidai. **assertion,** *n.* neno thabiti, neno la kuthibitisha; tendo la kudai haki. *Mere assertion,* neno tupu lisilothibitika. **assertive,** *a.* -enye kuthibitisha; -enye kujitokeza kudai haki; -enye kusema ndiyo.

assess, *v.t.* hesabu kadiri ya ushuru au kodi itakayopasa kulipwa; kisia; toza kodi (ushuru). **assessable,** *a.* -enye kuhesabiwa kwa ajili ya ushuru au kodi. **assessment,** *n.* tendo la *assess*; hesabu itakayotozewa ushuru au kodi; kodi au ushuru. **assessor,** *n.* ahesabuye kadiri ya ushuru au kodi itakayotozwa; mshauri wa hakimu au jaji.

assets, *n. pl.* mali, jumla ya mali aliyo nayo mtu.

asseverate, *v.t.* nena kwa uthabiti, taz. *assert.* **asseveration,** *n.* taz. *assertion.*

assiduity, *n.* utendaji, bidii, juhudi, jitihadi. **assiduous,** *a.* -enye bidii nyingi ya kazi, -tendaji. **assiduously,** *adv.* kwa bidii nyingi, kwa juhudi, kwa moyo. **assiduousness,** *n.* ujitahidi, utendaji, bidii.

assign, *v.t.* gawanyia, andikia, hesabia, dhani kuwa -a: *it is assigned to so and so,* hudhaniwa (huhesabiwa) kuwa kazi ya fulani; (*of work*) amrisha, pakiza; (*of date*) weka (tarehe, siku). **assignation,** *n.* tarehe, siku, tendo la kuonana (pengine mwanamume na mwanamke kwa mabaya).

assimilate, *v.t.* fanya sawa (ya jinsi ya kufaa), fananisha; tumia (*e.g.* mwili kutumia chakula kiliwacho). *He could not assimilate* (*of food*), hakikumtulia tumboni; (*of knowledge*) haikumwelea vyema.

assist, *v.t.* saidia, auni, nafidhi, nusuru. **assistance,** *n.* msaada, muawana, amara; (*united labour*) ujima. **assistant,** *n.* msaidizi.

assizes, *n. pl.* baraza au korti za hakimu au jaji azungukapo miji mikubwa Uingereza.

associate, *v.t.* tia pamoja, shirikisha, unganisha; — *v.i.* (*with*) shirikiana na, fanya urafiki na, ungana na, ongea na. *A person to associate with,* mtu wa kuandamana naye. *Be associated with,* changamana na. *I associate this with my home,* nikiona hii nakumbuka kwetu. — *n.* mwenzi, rafiki, mshirika, mwanachama. **association,** *n.* jumuia, bia, tendo la kushirikiana (la kutia pamoja &c.); (*society*) ushirika, umoja, chama, jamaa, kampani; (*meaning*) maana, ukumbusho. *It has many old associations for us,* inatukumbusha mambo mengi yaliyopita. *Form an association,* fanya bia au chama. *Association of ideas,* maunganisho ya mawazo yaliyofanana (yaliyohusiana).

assort, *v.t.* chagua, gawanya jamii (namna) mbalimbali; ainisha; panga namna mbalimbali. **assorted,** *a.* (*arranged in different sorts*) -liyopangwa (liyotengwa-, liyogawanywa) namna mbalimbali; (*variety*) -a namna nyingi mbalimbali. **assortment,** *n.* mchaguo, tendo la kugawanya namna mbalimbali; (*arrangement in classes*) kusanyiko la vitu vilivyopangwa kila namna peke yake; (*variety*) kusanyiko la vitu vya namna nyingi.

assuage, *v.t.* tuliza, nyamazisha, punguza, *e.g. assuage thirst,* tuliza kiu; — *v.i.* tulia, pungua.

assume, *v.t.* (*adopt, take in, take upon one's self*) jitilia, jifanya, jitwalia; (*take for granted*) sadiki, kubali, tumia jambo (neno) lisilothibitika (kama kwamba limethibitika); (*be presumptuous*) takabari, jiona, piga makuu, jitokeza, jitanguliza. *You assumed I was an ignoramus*, ulinifanya sijui mambo (ulidhani, ulikubali, ulisadiki yasiyothibitishwa). **assumed**, *a.* (*appropriated*) -a kutwaliwa; (*pretended*) -a kusingiziwa; (*taken for granted*) -a kukubaliwa (kusadikiwa, kupokewa) kuwa msingi wa (asili ya, maana ya) jambo linalofikiriwa. **assuming**, *a.* -enye kiburi, -a majivuno, -a kujitanguliza. — *conj.* kama, madhali, ikiwa. **assumption**, *n.* wazo tu, dhana tu, neno lisilohakikishwa, taz. *assume*; (*pride*) majivuno, makuu. *The Assumption*, kuchukuliwa mbinguni Bikira Mariamu.

assure, *v.t.* thibitisha, hakikisha; (*guarantee*) ahidi, yakinisha. *I assure you it is so*, nakuambia hakika ndivyo yalivyo. **assurance**, *n.* (*confidence*) matumaini; (*feeling of certainty*) kuona hakika, yakini; (*self reliance*) kujitoshea; (*pride*) kinaya, majivuno; (*guarantee*) dhamana, ushuhuda, mathubutu, ahadi. *Life assurance*, bima. **assured**, *a.* -a hakika, bila shaka. **assuredly**, *adv.* kwa hakika, kwa uthabiti, bila shaka.

asterisk, *n.* alama hii (*) maana yake katika maandiko ni kujulisha habari ya kuwa maelezo yameandikwa kando au chini ya ukurasa.

astern, *adv.* shetrini, kwa (katika) nyuma. *Tow astern*, fungasha.

asthma, *n.* ugonjwa wa pumu. **asthmatic, asthmatical**, *a.* -a pumu.

astigmatism, *n.* ugonjwa wa macho; miali ya nuru iletayo picha ya vitu machoni huwa imepotoka.

astir, *adv. be astir*, isha kuondoka kitandani, -wa macho, shughulika; sukasuka.

astonish, *v.t.* ajabisha, staajabisha, shangaza, bumbuaza, toshea. **astonished**, *a.* (*be*) toshewa, shangaa, staajabu, roja, maka, tunduwaa. **astonishing**, *a.* -a ajabu sana, -a kustaajabisha, -a kushangaza. **astonishingly**, *adv.* kwa jinsi ya ajabu, kwa jinsi ya kushangaza. **astonishment**, *n.* ajabu, mshangao, butaa, mastaajabu, bumbuazi, kimako.

astound, *v.t.* taz. *astonish*. **astounding**, *a.* -a ajabu, -a kushangaza.

astraddle, *adv.* kwa kutagaa, mguu mmoja upande huu na mmoja upande huu, taz. *astride*.

astral, *a.* -enye kuhusu nyota.

astray, *adv. go astray*, potea, kosa, potoka.

astride, *adv.* kwa kutagaa, taz. *astraddle*.

astringent, *a.* -a kukausha (meno, damu, choo). — *n.* dawa ya kufunga choo.

astrologer, *n.* mnajimu. **astrology**, *n.* unajimu, falaki; elimu ya zamani (asili ya elimu) ya nyota; ya sasa huitwa *astronomy*.

astronomer, *n.* mwenye elimu ya nyota. **astronomy**, *n.* elimu ya nyota.

astute, *a.* -erevu, -janja, -enye akili. **astutely**, *adv.* kwa hila, kwa ujanja, kwa akili. **astuteness**, *n.* werevu, ujanja, akili.

asunder, *adv.* mbalimbali, kwa vipande, vipande vipande. *Burst asunder*, rarua, pasua, vunjia mbali; raruka, pasuka &c.

asylum, *n.* (*refuge*) kimbilio; (*house*) nyumba watunzwamo maskini, vipofu, wenye wazimu &c.

at, *prep.* kwa, katika, -ni, penye. *At Abdallah's* kwa Abdallah. *At rest*, katika amani. *At home*, nyumbani. *At the tree*, penye mti. *At once*, mara, mara ile, halahala. *Not at all*, sivyo kabisa, siyo hata kidogo. *At first*, kwanza, mwanzoni. *At any rate*, ikiwa yo yote, iwayo yote, kwa yo yote. *At him!* huyo! mkamate! *Be at, go at* (*attack*) endea, rukia; (*engage in*) fanya, shiriki, -wamo katika. *What are you at?* unafanya nini? *At length* (*finally*) hatima, baadaye; (*fully*) kwa maneno mengi, kwa wingi. *At last,* mwisho, hatimaye.

atavism, *n.* marejeo kwa tabia za babu wazazi (si wazazi hasa) kwa wanyama na mimea; marejeo kwa tabia za asili. **atavistic**, *a.* -enye kurejea kwa tabia za babu (za asili).

ate, *p.t.* ya *eat.*

atheism, *n.* kutosadiki kuwa yuko Mungu. Kusema 'hakuna Mungu', ukani wa Mungu. **atheist**, *n.* asiyesadiki kuwa yuko Mungu. **atheistic**, *a.* -a *atheism.*

athirst, *a.* -enye kiu, -enye shauku, -enye kutamani sana.

athlete, *n.* mshindani wa michezo, mwenye maungo, mshupavu, kakawana, mbeja wa kano. **athletic**, *a.* -a kuhusu mashindano ya michezo (ya ustadi wa michezo). **athletics**, *n. pl.* mashindano ya kujaribia mbio (nguvu, ustadi wa michezo); michezo.

at-home, *n.* makaribisho ya kuzungumza ya saa maalum.

athwart, *prep.* kwa upande, kwa kupinga, kwa kukingama.

Atlantic Ocean, *n.* bahari kuu inayopakana na nchi ya Ulaya, Afrika na Amerika.

atlas, *n.* kitabu cha ramani.

atmosphere, *n.* hewa, upepo; (*upper air*) anga; (*surroundings*) ulimwengu, malimwengu (mambo, tabia &c.) zivutazo mtu kuona raha (fadhaa, wema, ubaya &c.). **atmospheric**, *a.* -a hewa.

atoll, *n.* kisiwa cha matumbawe.

atom, *n.* kipande kidogo mno, chembe, nukta. *Not an atom,* hakuna hata chembe.

atone, *v.i.* lipia, ridhisha, lipia ukosefu (upungufu); (*by offering*) toa kafara kwa ajili ya, fidia, tambikia. **atonement**, *n.* malipo, malipaji, maridhio; (*offering*) kafara, fidio, tambiko. *The Atonement,* upatanisho wa Yesu Kristo kwa kufa kwake.

atrocious, *a.* -baya mno, -ovu mno, -katili, -a kulaumiwa sana, -a kuchukiza, makuruhi, habithi.

atrocity, *n.* jambo baya mno, ukatili.

atrophy, *n.* hali ya kufifia (kupungua, kupotewa na nguvu, kupooza). **atrophied**, *a.* -liyofifia (kupungua, kupooza, kupotewa na nguvu).

attach, *v.t.* fungia, fungasha, ambatisha; (*appoint*) amuru, weka, tia; (*engage, attract*) gandamiza, ambatisha, vuta; (*seize*) shika, twaa. *I attach much importance to this,* naona ina maana sana. **attachable**, *a.* -enye kuweza kufungiwa &c. **attached**, *a.* (*be*) fungiwa, shikwa &c. ambatana, fungamana, gandamana, twaliwa. (*like*) penda, selelea; (*mutual*) pendana. **attachment**, *n.* tendo la serikali kushika mali ya mtu kufidia deni &c.; (*love*) upendo, upendano, huba, shauku, ashiki; (*thing attached*) kifungo, kilichofungiwa; mali iliyoshikwa na serikali sheriani.

attack, *v.t.* endea kwa nguvu (shari, jeuri), rukia, shambulia, kumba, shindana na, leta vita; (*subject*) anzia; (*of illness*) shika, pata; (*accuse*) bisha, shtaki, suta. — *n.* mwendeo wa nguvu (wa shari, wa jeuri), shambulio, vita; (*illness*) (kushikwa (kupatwa) na ugonjwa, kipindi; (*accusation*) mashtaka, masuto; (*beginning of operation*) mwanzo (wa kufanya). *He attacked his food,* alianza kula chakula chake.

attain, *v.t. and i.* pata, fikia, maliza. **attainable**, *a.* (*be*) fikika, patikana. **attainment**, *n.* mpato, pato. **attainments**, *n. pl.* maarifa, malezi.

attar, *n.* uturi, alwaridi, manukato ya maua hasa ya waridi.

attempt, *v.t.* jaribu, jitahidi; (*try to get*) jaribu kutwaa (kupata, kushinda &c.) *He attempted his life,* alijaribu kumwua. — *n.* jaribu, jaribio, bidii, jitihadi.

attend, *v.i.* (*be in attendance*) ngojea, fuatana, hudumu, tumikia; (*pay attention*) angalia, sikiliza, elekeza moyo; (*take care of*) angalia, shughulikia; — *v.t.* (*as doctor*) alika; (*as nurse*) uguza; (*be present*) hudhuria. *Attend school,* enda chuoni, soma.

attendance, *n.* mngojeo, ngojeo, hudhurio; utumishi, huduma. *Be in attendance on,* ngojea, fuatana na.

attendant, *n.* mtumishi, mhudumu, mfuasi, mlinzi. — *a.* -a kungojea, -liofuatana. **attention,** *n.* uhudumu, utumishi, tumikio, ngojeo, bidii, uangalifu, nadhari, usikizi, usikivu, maelekezo ya moyo. *Pay, give attention,* angalia, sikiliza, fanya kwa bidii. *Stand at attention (soldiers),* pangana (simama) sawasawa. *Attract attention,* vuta macho, tazamisha watu. **attentive,** *a.* angalifu, -a bidii, -sikizi, -sikivu.

attest, *v.t.* shuhudia, thibitisha; (*a person*) apisha. **attestation,** *n.* ushuhuda; hati ya kushuhudia, kiapo. **attestor,** *n.* mwapishi.

attic, *n.* orofa ya juu kabisa.

attire, *v.t.* vika visha. — *n.* mavazi, nguo, vao.

attitude, *n.* (*position*) kikao, jinsi ya kusimama; (*condition*) hali, mambo; (*mental*) shauri, nia, moyo.

attorney, *n.* mwanasheria, wakili. *Power of attorney,* wakala, hati ya uwakili.

attract, *v.t.* vuta, karibisha, tazamisha, tamanisha, pendeza, shawishi. **attraction,** *n.* mvuto, mvutano, nguvu ivutayo; kivutacho, kipendezacho. *Personal attraction,* uzuri, madaha, haiba. **attractive,** *a.* -a kupendeza, -a kutamanisha, -a kuvuta, -zuri.

attribute, *v.t.* tolea, hesabia, wekea; sema (ona, dhani) ndiyo sababu ya. *I attribute his illness to the rain,* naona mvua ndiyo sababu ya ugonjwa wake. *Be attributed to,* dhaniwa ni (mali ya, kazi ya, kwa sababu ya, sifa ya &c.). — *n.* jinsi, tabia, sifa.

attrition, *n.* kulika, hali ya kulika (kwa kusuguliwa, kwa kutumika).

attune, *v.t.* rekebisha sauti, linganisha sauti zipatane; linganisha, patanisha. **attunement,** *n.* ulinganifu.

auburn, *a.* -enye rangi kama ya hudhurungi.

auction, *n.* mnada, lilam. *Sell by auction,* nadi. **auctioneer,** *n.* mnadi, dalali.

audacious, *a.* (*daring, bold*) -jasiri, hodari; (*impudent*) -shupavu, -kavu wa macho, -juvi, fidhuli, -safihi.

audacity, *n.* ujasiri, ukavu wa macho, ujuvi, ushupavu, ufidhuli, usafihi.

audible, *a.* -a kusikika, -a kusikilikana. **audibly,** *adv.* kwa jinsi ya kusikika. **audience,** *n.* watu waliopo, wasikizi, jamii ya watu waliohudhuria kusikiliza; (*reception*) baraza. *Have an audience (of)* kwenda barazani (kwa), barizi, amkia (mtu mwenye cheo kikubwa). *Hold an audience,* barizi, fanya baraza. **audit,** *v.t.* kagua hesabu. **audit,** *n.* mkaguo wa hesabu. **audition,** *n.* uwezo wa kusikia, tendo la kusikia. **auditor,** *n.* msikizi; (*of accounts*) mkaguzi wa hesabu. **auditorium,** *n.* mahali wakaapo watu wahudhuriao kusikiliza (hotuba, michezo &c.).

au fait, *a.* -enye kujua habari, *e.g. To put a person au fait,* kumjulisha, kumweleza habari.

auger, *n.* kekee, chombo cha kuzulia (cha kutobolea).

aught, *n.* kitu cho chote, cho chote.

augment, *v.t.* zidisha, ongeza, kuza. **augmentation,** *n.* zidisho, nyongeza.

augur, *v.i.* bashiri, agua. — *n.* mbashiri, mwaguzi. **augury,** *n.* ubashiri; (*omen*) ndege; (*token*) ishara.

august, *a.* -tukufu, adhimu, -a stahifu, -a stahili heshima. **August,** *n.* mwezi wa nane wa mwaka wa kizungu, Agosti.

aunt, *n.* shangazi, ndugu wa kike wa baba au mama.

au revoir, kwa heri ya kuonana.

aureole, *n.* duara inayoandikwa

kuzunguka vichwa vya watakatifu katika picha, maana yake ni kuonyesha utukufu wao, taji ya dhahabu.

auricle, *n.* sehemu ya nje ya sikio; sehemu ya juu katika moyo (ziko mbili). **auricular,** *a.* -a sikio; -a siri, -a faraghani; -a kujulikana kwa kusikia au kwa kuambiwa. **aurist,** *n.* daktari auguzaye magonjwa ya masikio.

auriferous, *a.* (mawe &c.) -enye dhahabu ndani yake.

auspices, *n. pl.* msaada, himaya, fadhili. *Favourable auspices,* ndege njema. **auspicious,** *a.* heri, -a bahati, -ema, -a ndege njema.

austere, *a.* -gumu, -kali; bila vitu vya kupasha raha au anasa. **austerity,** *n.* ugumu, ukali; hali ya kuwa bila vitu viletavyo raha na anasa.

authentic, *a.* halisi, thabiti, kweli, hasa. **authenticate,** *v.t.* thibitisha, shuhudia (ukweli wa); fanya hakika. **authenticity,** *n.* kweli, hakika, usahihi, uhalisi.

author, *n.* Muumba; mbuni vitabu; mtunga nyimbo au mashairi; mwandishi wa habari; mtengenezaji; (*beginning*) asili, mwanzo, sababu. **authoress,** *n.* *author* wa kike. **authoritative,** *a.* -enye nguvu (amri). **authoritatively,** *adv.* kwa nguvu ya kuwa na amri, kwa thabiti. **authority,** *n.* uwezo, amri, nguvu, mamlaka, hukumu; (*officer*) mwenye amri (hukumu); serikali; (*witness, evidence*) shahidi, ushuhuda, mathubutu. *He is an authority on this subject,* yu mtu mwenye maarifa yawezayo kupokewa bila shaka juu ya jambo hili. **authorization,** *n.* ruhusa, amri, idhini, sahihi. **authorize,** *v.t.* (*give leave*) ruhusu, -pa ruhusa, toa idhini; (*order*) amuru, fanya halali, halalisha, sahihisha. **authorship,** *n.* ubuni, utungo, mwanzo.

autobiography, *n.* habari za maisha ya mtu zilizoandikwa na yeye mwenyewe.

autocar, *a.* gari liendalo kwa nguvu za mashine yake ya mvuke wa maji yanayochemka, au ya mvuke wa petroli &c.

autocrat, *n.* mtu (mfalme, mkuu &c.) atawalaye kwa nguvu zake peke yake. **autocracy,** *n.* utawala (mamlaka, hukumu) ya mtu mmoja peke yake. **autocratic,** *a* -a jinsi ya *autocrat.*

autograph, *n.* mwandiko wa mtu mwenyewe; (*signature*) sahihi ya jina.

automatic, *a.* -a kujiendea, -enye uwezo wa kwenda mwenyewe au kufanya kazi peke yake (kwa nguvu zake); -enye kufuata kawaida (mwendo, taratibu &c.) ile ile bila kuibadili; (*mechanically*) -enye kufanya mambo bila akili (bila kufikiri) kama mashine ifanyavyo. **automatically,** *adv.* kwa kujienda, kwa jinsi mashine ifanyavyo, kwa kufuata kawaida (mwendo, taratibu &c.) ile ile bila kubadili. **automaton,** *n.* kitu kiendacho wenyewe, au kwa mashine iliyowekwa ndani yake; mtu afanyaye mambo yake yote bila kufikiri wala kutumia akili, kama kwamba ni mashine tu.

automobile, *n.* motakaa.

autonomy, *a.* utawala wa -enyewe (mji, taifa &c.); uhuru au haki ya kujitawala -enyewe.

autopsy, *n.* uchunguzi wa maiti kuvumbua sababu ya kufa.

autumn, *n.* wakati wa miezi ya Septemba, Oktoba, Novemba Ulaya; ni kama wakati wa masika. **autumnal,** *a.* -a *autumn.*

auxiliary, *a.* -a kusaidia, -a kuongeza nguvu, msaada. — *n.* msaidizi; (*grammar*) kiarifa (*verb*) kisaidiacho kufanya wakati na hali ya kiarifa kingine.

avail, *v.t. and i.* faa, weza, faidi. — *n.* kifaa, manufaa, faida. **available,** *a.* -a kutumikana, -a kupatikana, -wa tayari.

avalanche, *n.* poromoko la theluji mlimani.

avarice, *n.* tamaa ya mali, roho, ubahili, choyo. **avaricious,** *a.* -enye kutamani sana mali, -a choyo, bahili.

avast, *int.* Bas! acha! (kibaharia).

avaunt, *int.* nenda! ondoka! toka!

avenge, *v.t.* lipiza (twaa) kisasi.

avenue, *n.* njia ya kuendea mji au nyumba, mara nyingi huwa safu mbili za miti, huku na huku; njia ya kufikia au kupatia (usitawi, utajiri &c.).

aver, *v.t.* nena kwa uthabiti; sema ni kweli.

average, *n.* wastani, hesabu au kiasi cha kadiri, *e.g.* watu wengine ni warefu, wengine wafupi; kimo cha katikati ni *average*. Mji una watu 300, mwingine una 400, mwingine una 500; wastani (*average*) ya watu wakaao katika miji hiyo ni jumla ya watu wa miji yote ikigawanywa kwa hesabu ya miji, yaani 12,000 kugawanywa na 3, ndiyo 400. **average,** *a.* -a wastani, -a kadiri, -a katikati, -a siku zote, -a kawaida.

averse, *a.* (*be averse to*) topenda, chukia. *He is averse to it*, haipendi. **aversion,** *n.* chukio, kitu kichukizacho, karaha.

avert, *v.t.* kinga, epa, zuia, geuzia mbali, ambaza, pisha.

aviary, *n.* mahali pa kuwekea ndege, kitundu.

aviation, *n.* ufundi au mruko wa hewani katika eropleni. **aviator,** *n.* aongozaye eropleni.

avid, *a.* -a bidii, -a choyo, -a pupa. **avidity,** *n.* tamaa, bidii, pupa, tutuo. *To eat with avidity*, kula kwa pupa. **avidly,** *adv.* kwa pupa (choyo, tutuo).

avocation, *n.* shughuli, kazi, uchumi, maishilio.

avoid, *v.t.* epuka, epa, ambaa, bari. **avoidable,** (*be*) -a kuepukika. **avoidance,** *n.* mwepuko; (*annulling*) mtanguo, utanguo.

avoirdupois weight, *n.* kipimo cha uzito cha Uingereza, cha kutumia ratli zenye wakia 16.

avouch, *v.t. and i.* kiri, ungama, taja (nena) kwa wazi. **avowed,** *a.* wazi, -a dhahiri. *He is an avowed thief*, amejikiri ni mwizi. **avowal,** *n.* neno dhahiri, maneno ya kukiri.

avuncular, *a.* -a mjomba.

await, *v.t.* ngoja, ngojea, tazamia, kalia.

awake, awaken, *v.t.* (*p.t.* **awoke,** *pf.t.* **awaked**), amsha; chochea; — *v.i.* amka, zinduka, zindukana, ondokewa usingizi. *Be awake to*, tanabahi, fahamu. *He is awake*, yu macho. **awakening,** *n.* mwamko, tendo la kuanza kushughulika au kuangalia jambo usilolijali tokea hapo.

award, *v.t.* hukumia; toa zawadi, tuza, jalia. — *n.* hukumu; tuzo, zawadi, tahadhari.

aware, *a.* (*be aware*) jua, tambua, fahamu, -wa macho, tanabahi.

awash, *a.* (*be awash*) wa sawasawa na usawa wa uso wa maji hata kuloweshwa na maji.

away, *adv.* (kwa) mbali; (*onward, along, in the direction of*) mbele, kwa; (*forthwith*) mara, bila kusita; (*continuously*) bila kuacha, mfululizo; (*as intens.*) sana, mno, kabisa. *I saw him some distance away*, nilimwona kwa mbali. *He has gone away*, amekwenda zake. *He is away*, hayuko, hako. *Make away with*, ondoa, tupa, poteza. *Do away with*, komesha, tangua. *Fall away* (*from*), achilia. *Away with him!* mchukue! mwondolee mbali. *Away! Away with you!* nenda! toka! ondoka! potelea mbali. *Fire away*, piga sasa (bila kusita, mfululizo). *Fight away*, piga sana (bila kuacha). *Sing away*, imba sana (bila kuacha). *Away across the horizon*, mbele kupita upeo wa macho. *He has passed away*, amekufa. *He has fainted away*, amezimia kabisa. *Far and away the best*, bora sana kuliko (yote).

awe, *n.* kicho, uchaji, hofu (kwa ajili ya kitisho au heshima &c.). — *v.t.* tisha, ogofya (kwa ajili ya kitisho au cheo kikuu au utukufu). **awe-**

some, *a.* -a kuogofya, -a kutisha. **awestruck,** *a.* (*be*) pagawa kwa hofu (kwa ajili ya kitisho, kwa ajili ya kuona ajabu au utukufu). **awful,** *a.* -a kutisha, -a kuogofya, -a kicho. Pia hutumika kama 'sana' 'mno' '-baya'. *I am in awful pain,* ninaumwa sana. *He is an awful scoundrel,* yeye ni mtu mbaya mno. *He has an awful character,* tabia yake mbaya sana.

awhile, *adv.* kwa muda kidogo, kitambo.

awkward, *a.* (*clumsy*), -jinga; si stadi, si -bingwa, si -elekevu, si -epesi, si -hodari *&c.*; (*difficult*) -gumu, -enye matata (mashaka, hatari); (*of character*) -gumu, -shupavu, -a kinyongo, -a kasirani.

awl, *n.* msharasi, chombo cha kutobolea vitundu vidogo.

awning, *n.* pazia, hema ya kuzuia ukali wa jua, chandalua.

awoke, *v. p.t.* ya awake.

awry, *a. and adv.* (*be awry*) potoka, -wa upande, (*go awry*) -enda pogo (mshazari).

axe, *n.* shoka.

axilla, *n.* kwapa.

axiom, *n.* hakika, neno lisilokanikika kabisa, linalokubaliwa na wote wenye akili. **axiomatic,** *a.* kama *axiom,* hakika, halisi.

axis, *n.* kitu (mti, msumari *&c.*) kipenyacho kitu kinachozunguka (kama pia *&c.*). *Axis* ya dunia, mhimili wa dunia.

axle, *n.* mti au chuma cha katikati ya gurudumu au magurudumu mawili ambacho kwacho gurudumu (au magurudumu) huzunguka.

ay, aye, *adv.* ndiyo, naam; (*always*) daima, sikuzote.

ayah, *n.* yaya, mlezi.

azure, *n. and a.* rangi ya uwingu, samawati, buluu.

B

baa, *n.* mlio wa kondoo. — *v.i.* lia kama kondoo.

babble, *v.i.* payapaya, payuka, puza, puzika, bwata, bwabwaja, toa nje habari za siri; (*of water*) bubujika, fanya sauti kama maji ya kijito. — *n.* maneno ya upuzi, vijineno, mapayo. **babbler,** *n.* apayukaye, mpuzi, atoaye nje habari za siri.

babe, baby, *n.* mtoto mchanga, kitoto, malaika. **babyhood,** *n.* utoto uchanga. **babyish,** *a.* -a kitoto.

babel, *n.* (*confusion*) machafuko, ghasia, makelele, fujo.

baboo, babu, *n.* karani wa kihindi.

baboon, *n.* nyani mkubwa.

baby, *n.,* **babyhood,** *n.,* **babyish,** *a.* taz. *babe.*

baccarat, *n.* mchezo wa karata.

bacchanalian, *a.* -a ngoma ya ulevi.

bachelor, *n.* mvulana, mseja, mwanamume asiyeoa bado, kapera; mtu aliyehitimu katika *University,* na kupewa daraja humo; daraja ya chini ya *knighthood.* **bachelorhood, bachelorship,** *n.* hali ya kuwa *bachelor,* uvulana, ujane, useja, ukapera.

bacillus, *n.* (*pl.* **bacilli**) kijidudu kidogo sana, mfano wa kistari, vingine ni asili ya maradhi ya namna nyinginezo.

back, *n.* mgongo, sehemu ya nyuma ya mwili; (*part behind*) sehemu iliyo nyuma; (*back of book*) kikunjo, kurasa ziliposhonwa au kufungwa pamoja; (*back of knife*) mafutuni, kigongo cha kisu; (*back of the neck*) kikosi, kisogo. — *adv.* nyuma, kinyume, katika hali ya kwanza, kama kwanza, kuko huko. *Some time back*, zamani kidogo. *Six years back*, tangu miaka sita. *Give back, turn back*, rudisha, rejeza. *Go back*, rudi, rejea. — *v.t.* (*help*) saidia; (*bet on*) wekea masharti, pinga thibitisha wazo au neno kwa kubahatisha kitu au fedha; (*force back*) rudisha nyuma, sogeza nyuma, sukuma nyuma; (*back a cheque, bill &c.*) tia sahihi ili kudhamini; — *v.i.* (*go back*) rudi, enda kinyumenyume. *Be on one's back*, (*ill*) lala, -wa mgonjwa; (*as burden*) lemea. *Lie on the back*, lala chali, lala kimgongogongo. *Set the back up*, chukiza, kasirisha. *Break the back of*, maliza sehemu iliyo kubwa au iliyo ngumu ya kazi, karibia kumaliza, karibia kushinda. *Turn the back on*, acha, tupa, -pa mgongo, -pa kisogo. *To the back bone*, kabisa, hasa, halisi. *Back to back*, mgongo kwa mgongo. *To back down*, acha kauli au cheo, ghairi. *To back out*, toa udhuru ili kutotimiza ahadi &c. *To back up*, saidia, tegemeza. **backbite**, *v.t.* amba, singizia, chongea, chongeleza, sengenya. **backbiter**, *n.* mwambi, mwambaji, mchongezi, msengenyi.

backbone, *n.* uti wa mgongo; (*strength, main support*) tegemeo, uthabiti, nguzo, nguvu, ugumu; (*reliableness*) utumainifu, uhodari, bidii, ujitahidi. *He has no backbone*, yu mkulifu, yu mdhaifu, mwepesi kushindwa, hatumainiki. **background**, *n.* mahali pa nyuma, mahali pa kufichia. **backing**, *n.* msaada, tegemezo, wasaidizi. **backside**, *n.* matako. **backslide**, *v.i.* acha dini, kengeua, rudia mazoea mabaya. **backslider**, *n.* aachaye dini yake au kurudia mazoea mabaya. **backward, backwards**, *adv.* -a nyuma, -a kuchelewa; (*dull*) -zito -a akili, si -elekevu; (*not advanced*) -jinga; (*not civilized*) -shenzi. *Backward and forward*, huko na huko. **backwardness**, *n.* uzito wa akili, hali ya kuwa nyuma. **backwash**, *n.* mkondo wa maji unaorudi nyuma, *e.g.* maji yapelekwayo nyuma kwa nguvu ya mashua au chombo kilichokwisha pita. **backwoods**, *n.* mwitu.

bacon, *n.* nyama ya nguruwe iliyotiwa chumvi na kutengenezwa isioze.

bacterium (*pl.* **bacteria**), *n.* vijimea vidogo sana viongezekavyo upesi mno, vingine ni asili ya magonjwa mengineyo; vingine huwaletea wanadamu faida. Elimu ya *bacteria* huitwa *bacteriology*.

bad (1), *v. p.t.* ya *bid*.

bad (2), *a.* (*evil, wicked*) -baya, -ovu; (*hurtful*) -a kudhuru, -a kuumiza, -a hasara, -a shari; (*hateful*) -a kuchukiza, makuruhi; (*incorrect, faulty*) -bovu, hafifu, -ovyo, -a takataka, -nyonge, -pungufu, -enye hitilafu. *Bad blood*, hasira, uadui, shari, chuki. *Bad debts*, deni zisizolipwa. *To go bad*, oza, vunda. *To go to the bad*, potea, potelea mbali, potoa, angamia, potoka. *To the bad*, hasara, upungufu. *With bad grace*, kwa sharti, kwa kushurutishwa, kwa uchungu, bila kutaka. *He is bad* (*sick*) hawezi. *He is an utterly bad man*, yu baa, mtu mwovu kabisa. *It is too bad*, haipendezi, sikubali, sitaki, haifai kabisa. *Be in a bad humour*, deka, kasirika. **baddish**, *a.* -baya kidogo, dhaifu. **badly**, *adv.* vibaya, kwa jinsi ilivyo *bad*. **badness**, *n.* ubaya, ubovu, uovu &c.

badge, *n.* alama, dalili ya kujulisha mtu au kitu; (*medal*) nishani.

badger, *n.* mnyama wa Ulaya ukubwa wake kama mbweha, afukuaye chini. — *v.t.* sumbua, chokoza, udhi, chagiza.

badinage, *n.* dhihaka, ucheshi, mzaha, masihara.

badly, *adv.* **badness,** *n.* taz. *bad* (2).

baffle, *v.t.* zuia, pinga, kinza, fumba, shinda kwa hila, katiza shauri. **baffling,** *a.* -a fumbo, -siofahamika.

bag, *n.* mfuko; (*large*) fuko; (*small*) kifuko; (*various kinds*) mkoba, shanta kibogoshi, gunia, kifumbu, kanda, kapu &c.; (*for books, clothing &c.*) bahasha, kitumba, furushi; (*for sleeping in*) fumba; (*of fishing*) mvuo, numbi jumla ya samaki waliovuliwa na mvuvi mara moja; (*of hunting*) mawindo, jumla ya wanyama waliopigwa au kuuawa na mwindaji katika windo moja. — *v.t.* (*swell*) tokeza, kubaza, benuka; (*hunting*) piga (mawindo); (*take*) twaa. *Bag and baggage,* vikorokoro, (*with*) pamoja na vitu vyote pia. *Bag of bones,* kimbaombao, mtu aliyekonda hata ni mifupa tu. *Let the cat out of bag,* toa siri nje. **baggage,** *n.* vyombo, vikorokoro, mizigo; hema na zana za jeshi la askari. **baggage room,** *n.* chumba cha kuwekea mizigo; (*of dhow*) feuli. **bagging,** *n.* gunia, kitu cha kutengenezea mifuko. **baggy,** *a.* -a kama mfuko, -a kukubaza, -a kupwaya, -liolegea. **bags,** *n.* suruali.

bagatelle, *n.* (*game*) mchezo wa kugonganisha tufe za pembe juu ya meza; (*a trifle*) kitu kidogo cho chote kisicho cha thamani, kitakataka.

baggage, *n.* mwanamke mfidhuli; taz. *bag.*

bagging, *n.,* **baggy,** *a.,* **bags,** *n.* taz. *bag.*

bah, *int.* neno la kuonyesha dharau au chukizo.

bail (1), *n.* mdhamini, dhamana. — *v.t.* dhamini, dhamini mtu ili awekwe huru. *Bail bond,* ahadi atoayo mtu awekwaye huru kwa kudhaminiwa.

bail (2), *v.t.* kumba maji katika chombo, teka, vuta maji.

bail (3), *n.* kijiti cha juu ya *stumps* katika mchezo wa *cricket.*

bailiff, *n.* wakili, msimamizi.

bairn, *n.* mtoto.

bait, *n.* chambo; (*allurement*) ubembe, kitu kimvutacho mtu afanye jambo; (*food for journey*) masurufu ya njiani. — *v.t.* tia chambo, ambika; (*worry*) chokoza, sumbua, udhi, tesa; (*feed*) lisha (punda, farasi &c.) njiani.

bake, *v.t.* kausha, fanya -gumu (kwa joto la jua au kwa moto); (*food*) oka (mkate, nyama &c.). **baker,** *n.* mwokaji mikate. **bakery,** *n.* mahali pa kuokea mikate, jiko, joko. **baking,** *n.* uokaji; mwoko, jumla ya vitu vilivyookwa pamoja.

balance, *n.* (*weighing machine*) mizani, kapani; (*equilibrium*) usawa wa uzito (nguvu &c.); (*settlement of account*) urari; (*remainder*) baki, sazo. *Be in the balance,* -wa hukumuni, -wa katika kuhukumiwa (mashaka, hatari). — *v.i.* (*be in equilibrium*) -wa sawasawa (kwa kadiri ya uzito, nguvu &c.); (*waver*) sita; — *v.t.* (*weigh*) pima katika mizani; (*consider*) fikiri; (*make equal*) sawazisha; (*compare*) linganisha; (*making of account, strike a balance*) jumlisha hesabu, fanya urari wa hesabu, katiana.

balcony, *n.* roshani.

bald, *a.* -enye upara (upaa), bila nywele wala manyoya; (*bare*) -tupu, -siyotengenezwa, bila uzuri, mfuto, bila ufasaha, hafifu. **baldness,** *n.* upara (upaa), kidazi, hali ya kutokuwa na nywele wala manyoya; (*of speech &c.*) uhafifu, uchache. *A shaved or bald place on the head,* kipara, kidazi.

balderdash, *n.* upuzi, maongezi hafifu, mapayo, vijineno.

baldness, *n.* taz. *bald.*

bale (1), *n.* mtumba, mzigo, furushi, robota, bunda. — *v.t.* funga katika mitumba (robota, mzigo &c.).

bale (2), *v.t.* kumba maji, teka, vuta maji; (taz. *bail* (2)).
baleful, *a.* -enye huzuni nyingi, -enye masikitiko mengi; -korofi, -haribifu, -baya, -a shari, -a madhara.
balk, *n.* (*of wood*) boriti kubwa, gogo; (*hindrance*) zuio, mgogoro. — *v.t.* shinda, zuia, pingia njia, katiza shauri; — *v.i.* epa, sita, kataa.
ball, *n.* tufe, mpira (wa kucheza), kitu cho chote kilicho cha mviringo kama chungwa; (*round lump*) donge; (*bullet*) risasi; (*shot*) marisaa; (*dancing party*) ngoma ya watu wengi. *Ball bearings,* gololi. *Ball and socket joint,* kiungo cha tufe na kombe, kama mkono uungwapo na bega. *Ball of eye,* jicho. *Keep the ball rolling,* endelea
ballad, *n.* wimbo usimuliao hadithi, utenzi.
ballast, *n.* farumi. *He has no ballast,* hana uthabiti.
ballet, n. ngoma ya kuigiza hadithi &c.
balloon, *n.* mfuko mkubwa uliojaa namna ya hewa nyepesi wa kurukia juu hewani kwa wepesi wa hewa iliyotiwa ndani yake na kuchukua kitu, kama kapu kubwa la kukalia watu. — *v.t.* ruka juu katika *balloon*; (*swell*) vimba, kubaza, tokeza. **balloonist,** *n.* mtu arukaye juu katika *balloon.*
ballot, *n.* kura, kipande cha karatasi au kibarua kinachotumika kujulishia mtu au jambo lichaguliwalo katika chaguo la siri; chaguo la siri (kujulishia jambo lichaguliwalo kwa kuweka karatasi au kibarua katika sanduku lililowekewa kusudi hilo). — *v.i.* chagua kwa *ballot,* piga kura.
balm, *n.* marhamu ya kutulizia au kuponyeshea, kitulizo, faraja. **balmy,** *a.* -a kunukia, -a kuburudisha, -a kutuliza.
baluster, *n.* kiguzo cha kuchukulia mti au ubao wa kushikia upande wa ngazi (madaraja ya kupandia).
balustrade, *n.* safu ya viguzo vyenye ubao juu ukingoni pa roshani, au pa madaraja ya-kupandia.
bamboo, *n.* mwanzi.
bamboozle, *v.t.* zuzua, danganya, fadhaisha, fumba, pumbaza, laghai, ghilibu.
ban, *n.* tangazo la kurufuku (la kuharimisha); (*curse*) laana. — *v.t.* kataza, rufuku, harimisha; (*curse*) laani.
banal, *a.* hafifu, baridi, duni.
banana, *n.* (*plant*) mgomba; (*fruit*) ndizi; (*bunch of bananas, fruit*) chane. *Fruit stalk of bananas,* mkungu.
band, *n.* kitu cha kufungia au cha kuungia; utepe, ukanda; (*body of persons*) kundi, chama, jamii, kikosi; (*musicians*) jamii ya wapigaji ngoma, tarumbeta &c.; (*stripe*) mstari, mlia, mialamu, mfuo. — *v.i.* (*together*) kutana, fanya kundi, changa, shirikiana; — *v.t.* kutanisha, kusanya.
bandbox, *n.* kasha jepesi la kuwekea kofia.
bandage, *n.* utambaa, kitambaa. — *v.t.* fungia utambaa, funga kwa kitambaa.
bandana, *n.* leso ya rangi.
bandit, *n.* mnyang'anyi, haramia.
bandoleer, bandolier, *n.* ukanda wenye mabeti ya kuwekea risasi za bunduki.
bandy, *v.t.* tupa huko na huko; bishana.
bandy-legged, *a.* -enye matege (machege).
bane, *n.* uharibifu, kifo, madhara, hasara, teso, sumu, liga. **baneful,** *a.* -baya, -a kudhuru, -a shari.
bang (1), *n.* shindo, mshindo, mgoto. — *v.t.* piga sana, pigisha mshindo (kama kufunga mlango kwa nguvu &c.); (*beat*) piga, chapa; — *v.i.* fanya kishindo. — *int.* bomu! sauti ya kuigiza mshindo.
bang (2), *n.* bangi.
bangle, *n.* bangili, kikuku.
banish, *v.t.* hamishia mbali, fukuzia mbali, ondoshea mbali. **banishment,** *n.* uhamisho, hali ya kuhamishwa, ufukuzo.

banister, *n.* safu ya viguzo vyenye ubao juu upande wa ngazi (madaraja ya kupandia); taz. *baluster.*

banjo, *n.* zeze la kizungu, gambusi.

bank, *n.* fungu la mchanga (udongo); (*of river &c.*) ukingo; (*of oars in galley &c.*) safu; (*for money*) nyumba ya kuwekea (ya kubadilia fedha), banki; (*opposite bank*) ng'ambo; (*along the bank*) kando. — *v.t.* fanya fungu (la udongo, la mchanga &c.); (*of fires*) funika kwa makaa na kuyagandamiza ili moto uwake polepole kwa muda mkubwa: *banked fires,* mioto iliyofunikwa hivyo; (*of money*) weka fedha katika *bank;* — *v.i.* kusanyika na kufanya chungu. **bankbook,** *n.* daftari yenye hesabu ya fedha ziwekwazo na kutolewa katika *bank.* **banker,** *n.* atunzaye fedha zilizowekwa na watu; mvunja fedha; mbadili fedha. **banking,** *n.* kazi ya *banker.* **banknote,** *n.* barua ya fedha, noti ya *bank,* hawala, hundi. **bank-cheque,** *n.* karatasi yenye sahihi ya kutwalia fedha katika *bank.*

bankrupt, *n.* mtu aliyefilisika. — *v.t.* filisi. *Be bankrupt,* filisika. **bankruptcy,** *n.* ufilisi, hali ya kufilisika.

banner, *n.* bendera, beramu.

banns, *n.* tangazo la ndoa, tangazo la kuwa watu fulani wamekusudia kuoana.

banquet, *n.* karamu. — *v.t.* fanyia karamu; — *v.i.* -la karamu.

banshee, *n.* kizimwi.

bantam, *n.* kuku mdogo wa aina moja. *Bantam weight,* mpigaji ngumi asiyezidi uzani wa ratli 116.

banter, *v.t.* bishana na kwa ucheshi (dhihaka), fanyia ubishi (mzaha); — *v.i.* cheka, fanya mzaha. — *n.,* mzaha, mabishano (ya ucheshi), masihara.

Bantu, *n.* jina litumikalo katika elimu ihusuyo mataifa na lugha kwa jumla ya makabila ya katikati na ya kusini ya Afrika yaliyotokana na mbegu moja zamani sana. Huitwa Bantu kwa sababu neno kwa 'watu' katika lugha zao nyingi ni 'bantu' (katika nyingine ni 'watu', 'atu', 'andu', 'wandu' &c.); pia ni jamii ya lugha wazitumiazo.

banyan, *n.* Banyani, Mhindi asiye Mwislamu wala Mkristo, ila mfuasi wa Brahma.

baobab, *n.* mbuyu.

baptize, *v.t.* batiza, fanya ibada ya ubatizo, yaani kutia maji mtu au kumtia majini na kumpa jina; dalili ya kuwa ameingizwa katika ushirika wa dini ya kikristo. **baptism,** *n.* ubatizo, tendo la *baptize.* **baptismal,** *a.* -enye kuhusu ubatizo. **Baptist,** *n.* mbatizaji; madhehebu ya Wakristo ambao hutia watu majini kabisa wala hawawanyunyizii maji tu, tena, watu sharti wawe wakubwa wawezao kukubali dini ya kikristo kwa hiari yao.

bar, *n.* pao au ufito wa kitu cho chote, mchi; (*of wood*) mti, nguzo, ufito; (*for door*) kipinga, pingo; (*small*) komeo, kiwi; (*of iron*) ufito wa chuma, pao la chuma; (*of soap*) kinoo; (*of gold, silver &c.*) mkuo; (*obstruction*) kinga, kizuizi, mgogoro; (*of river, harbour*) fungu la mchanga, mwamba, kizingiti, mawimbi (pa kutokea mto); (*place of judgement*) baraza ya hukumu, mahakma; (*lawyers*) jamii ya wanasheria; (*drinking*) pa kuuzia mvinyo, pombe &c., mkahawa; (*of music*) kifungu. *Prisoner at the bar,* mfungwa hukumuni. *Go to the bar,* jitia katika kazi ya uanasheria. — *v.t.* (*obstruct*) pingia njia, kinga, zuia; (*door*) tia kiwi, komea. **barrier,** *n.* kizuio, kizuizi, mgogoro, boma, kinga. **barring,** *prep.* isipokuwa, ila.

barb, *n.* mwiba kama ule wa chembe cha mshale au wa ndoana, jino la mshale. **barbed,** *a.* -enye mwiba au miiba, *e.g. barbed wire,* seng'enge yenye miiba.

barbarian, *a.* -shenzi. — *n.* mshenzi, mkorofi, mtu katili. **barbaric,** *a.* -shenzi, -katili. **barbarism,** *n.* ushenzi, hali ya (desturi za) kishenzi;

(*in language*) neno kosefu, neno lisilo sahihi. **barbarity**, *n.* ushenzi, ukali, ukatili, ukorofi. **barbarous**, *a.* -a kishenzi; (*cruel*) -katili, -karofi, -kali. **barbarously**, *adv.* kwa ushenzi, kwa ukatili, kwa ukorofi.

barbecue, *n.* mnyama (ng'ombe, kondoo &c.) aliyebanikwa bila kuchanguliwa; (*frame*) uchaga.

barbed, *a.* taz. *barb.*

barbel, *n.* kambare.

barber, *n.* kinyozi.

barbet, *n.* (*Zanzibar Golden rumped*) kitororo.

barbican, *n.* mlango au daraja la kulinda mji.

bard, *n.* mtunga mashairi, mshairi.

bare, (1) *v. p.t.* ya *bear.*

bare, (2) *a.* wazi, -tupu, pasipo kitu, -a peke yake, -a kutosha tu bila kuzidi. — *v.t.* toa wazi, funua, ondoa kitu kinachofunika, *e.g.* mavazi, mapambo &c.; (*bare one's head*) vua kofia; (*bare the teeth*) kenua. **barefaced**, *a.* bila haya, -pujufu; -tupu, wazi. *A barefaced lie*, uwongo mtupu (wazi, dhahiri). **bareheaded**, *a.* kichwa wazi. **barely**, *adv.* kwa shida. **bareness**, *n.* hali ya kuwa *bare*, utupu, uwazi,, weupe.

bargain, *n.* maafikano, mapatano, agano, maagano; kitu kilichopatikana kwa bei ya nafuu (kwa bei iliyopungua thamani yake hasa). *Into the bargain*, zaidi, juu, nafuu, faida. *Make a bargain* (*contract*), andikiana mkataba (mapatano), afikiana, agana. — *v.i.* pigania bei, patana. *I did not bargain for that*, sikufikiri (sikuhesabu, sikutazamia) haya (na kwa hiyo nimepata hasara). **bargaining**, *n.* ubazazi, piganio la bei.

barge, *n.* mashua kubwa, mashua kubwa ya mitoni yenye mkuku mfupi kwa kwenda chini, tishari. — *v.i.* (*into*) pambana na, jiingiza kwa nguvu (kwa jeuri, bila kukusudia &c.).

baritone, *n.* sauti ya kinaume ya kuimba, si juu sana (*tenor, alto*), wala chini sana (*bass*), ila katikati; mwanamume aimbaye kwa sauti hiyo.

bark, (1) *n.* (*sound*) mguno, mbweko, mlio kama wa mbwa. — *v.i.* gumia, bweka, lia kama mbwa; sema kwa sauti kali ya ghafula. *His bark is worse than his bite*, maneno yake ni makali kuliko matendo yake, si mkali kama maneno yake.

bark, (2) *n.* namna ya chombo kama jahazi lenye milingoti mitatu.

bark, (3) *n.* (*of tree*) gome; (*soft*) ganda. — *v.t.* ambua gome.

barley, *n.* shayiri.

barm, *n.* chachu, hamira.

barn, *n.* ghala ya nafaka.

barnacle, *n.* kombe za baharini ziambatanazo na miamba na chini ya vyombo; mtu aambatanaye sana na mwingine.

barometer, *n.* kipimo cha kupimia uzito wa hewa ili kujua habari za mvua na upepo.

baron, *n.* jina la heshima la mtu mwenye cheo chini ya *Earl.* **baroness**, *n.* *baron* wa kike. **baronet**, *n.* jina la heshima la *baron* mdogo. **baronetcy**, *n.* cheo cha *baron.* **baronial**, *a.* -a kuhusu *baron.* **barony**, *n.* makazi na cheo cha *baron.*

barque, *n.* taz. *bark* (1).

barracks, *n.* nyumba wakaamo kikosi cha askari.

barracouta, *n.* mzira, sansuri.

barrel, *n.* pipa; (*of gun*) kasiba, mtutu, mwanzi, mdomo (*single barrelled*) -enye mtutu mmoja; (*double barrelled*) -enye mitutu miwili. — *v.t.* tia (miminia) katika pipa.

barren, *a.* (*of female*) tasa; (*of male*) gumba; (*of land*) kame, jangwa; (*unprofitable*) -a bure, bila faida, -tupu.

barricade, *n.* boma. — *v.t.* jenga boma, zunguka kwa boma, zuia kwa boma, linda kwa boma.

barrier, *n.*, **barring**, *prep.* taz. *bar.*

barrister, *n.* mwanasheria, wakili (wa sheria).

barrow, (1) *n.* gari dogo (lenye gurudumu moja au mawili).

barrow, (2) *n.* (*mound*) chungu ya udongo kama chuguu kubwa, kilima.

barter, *v.t.* badilisha (mali, bidhaa &c.), badilishana. — *n.* badilishano la mali au bidhaa katika biashara &c.

basalt, *n.* namna ya mawe, meusi magumu sana.

base, (1) *a.* -baya, -nyonge, dhaifu, -a uwongo, -ovu; (*base metal*) madini yo yote isipokuwa dhahabu. **baseness**, *n.* ubaya, unyonge.

base, (2) *n.* upande wa chini, sehemu ya chini, msingi, tako; (*beginning, principle*) chanzo, chimbuko, asili; (*head-quarters*) mahali pa kuanzia au kusimamia (vita &c.). — *v.t.* weka juu ya msingi, tegemeza. **baseless**, *a.* bila msingi, -siotegemezwa, -siodhihirika. **basement**, *n.* orofa ya chini (ya nyumba). **basic**, *a.* -a msingi, -enye tabia za msingi. **basis**, *n.* msingi &c. sawasawa na *base*.

baseness, *n.* taz. *base* (1)

bash, *v.t.* piga kwa nguvu hata kubonyeza.

bashful, *a.* -enye haya. **bashfully**, *adv.* kwa haya. **bashfulness**, *n.* haya.

basic, *a.* taz. *base* (2).

basil, *n.* mrihani.

basilica *n.* namna ya kanisa.

basilisk, *n.* mnyama wa hadithi, ambaye akimtazama mtu, yule mtu lazima afe.

basin, *n.* bakuli; (*of metal, brass*) tasa, kitasa; (*of earthenware*) bia, kibia; (*dock*) gudi; (*valley*) bonde.

basis, *n.* taz. *base* (2).

bask, *v.i.* ota jua, jiotea jua (moto); (*enjoy oneself*) jifurahisha, jinyosha.

basket, *n.* kikapu, kapu; (*different kinds*) pakacha, tunga, dohani, jamanda &c.

bas-relief, *n.* sanamu za kuchora au kunakshi zisizotokeza sana.

bass, (1) *n.* sauti nene ya kinaume.

bass, (2) *n.* namna ya samaki.

bass, (3) *n.* namna ya pombe.

bassinet, *n.* kigari cha kuchukulia mtoto.

bassoon, *n.* namna ya tarumbeta.

bast, *n.* nyuzinyuzi, *e.g.* ugomba, utembo, utembwe, ufumwale &c.

bastard, *n.* mwana wa haramu. — *a.* -a kuzaliwa haramu; -a uwongo, -a kufanana na jamii fulani ila si -a jamii hasa.

baste, (1) *v.t.* (*beat*) piga sana; (*with fat*) paka mafuta kitu kinachookwa.

baste, (2) *v.t.* (*sew*) shikiza, shona kwa shikizo, shulu, piga-bandi.

bastinado, *v.t.* piga nyayoni pa miguu kwa bakora, piga fimbo miguuni.

bastion, *n.* boma la ngome.

bat, (1) *n.* kibao kama kafi cha kuchezea mipira.

bat, (2) *n.* (*animal*) popo.

batch, *n.* fungu, jamii, kundi.

bath, *n.* maji ya kuoga; birika au chombo cha kuogea; (*bathing*) kiogeo, josho; (*dipping*) mchovyo. *Vapour baths*, mavusho, mavukizo, buhuri. *Public baths*, hamami. *Order of the Bath*, cheo cha heshima kubwa cha kiingereza: ziko daraja tatu: ya chini ni C.B. (mwenzi wa Bath), ya pili K.C.B. (mwenzi mkuu wa Bath), ya juu ni G.C.B. (Msalaba mtukufu wa Bath). **bath**, *v.t.* ogesha (mtoto &c.). **bathe**, *v.t.* ogesha, chovya, tia maji (au cho chote kama maji); osha. — *v.i.* oga. **bather**, *n.* aogaye. **bathing**, *n.* mwogo.

bathos, *n.* usemi au maandiko hafifu sana yanayofuata ya ufasaha.

baton, *n.* kirungu, kifimbo (cha polisi, cha mtu aongozaye watu wapigao *band* &c.

battalion, *n.* jeshi la askari lenye vikosi au kampani kadha wa kadha.

batten, (1) *v.i.* nona, nenepa.

batten, (2) *v.t.* (*fasten*) kaza kwa vipande vya mti. — *n.* kipande cha mti cha kukazia, *e.g.* turubai inayofungwa juu ya ngama ya meli &c.

batter, *v.t.* gongagonga, pigilia, bonyezabonyeza kwa kugonga. — *n.* unga na maji yaliyochanganywa na kufanywa laini kwa kupigwapigwa. **battering-ram,** *n.* gogo la kuvunjia boma vitani. **battery,** *n.* jamii ya mzinga; mahali pawekwapo jamii ya mizinga; chombo cha kutengenezea nguvu ya umeme (elektrisiti). *He was charged with assault and battery,* alishtakiwa kuwa amempiga mtu.

battle, *n.* vita, mapigano. — *v.i.* pigana, shindana. **battle-array,** *n.* mpango wa vita. **battle-cry,** *n.* ukelele upigwao vitani ili kuwapa watu moyo. **battlefield,** *n.* mahali vinapopiganwa vita au vilipopiganwa. **battlement,** *n.* buruji, ukuta wa boma wenye mianya au menomeno ya kupenyezea bunduki au mizinga. **battleship,** *n.* manowari.

bauble, *n.* kipuzi, takataka, kitu kizuri kisicho na thamani.

baulk, *n.* taz. *balk.*

bawl, *v.i.* piga kelele, lia, guta. — *n.* ukelele, mlio, guto.

bay, (1) *n.* ghuba. *Bay window,* dirisha linalotokeza, kama roshani.

bay, (2) *v.i.* gumia, bweka, lia (kama mbwa mkubwa). — *n.* mlio wa mbwa mkubwa. *Keep at bay, hold at bay,* simamisha (adui), zuia, kinga. *Stand at bay,* kita, dinda, simama kama mtu anayeshambuliwa na adui.

bay, (3) *n.* namna ya mti wa Ulaya.

bay, (4) *a.* -a rangi kama ya hudhurungi; hutumika tu kwa farasi wenye rangi hiyo.

bayonet, *n.* singe, upanga wa bunduki. — *v.t.* choma kwa singe.

bazaar, *n.* penye maduka, soko, duka; duka linamouzwa vitakataka; kuuza kwa vitu vilivyochangwa kusaidia kusudi maalum, *e.g.* kanisa, hospitali &c.

be, *v.i.* -wa. *Be loved* (*beaten, eaten* &c.) pendwa (pigwa, liwa &c.). *Be tired* (*broken, vexed* &c.) choka (vunjika, kasirika &c.). *Be quiet!* nyamaza! tulia! *Let be!* acha.

beach, *n.* pwani, ufuko. — *v.t.* pandisha pwani, pweleza. **beach-comber,** *n.* mgaagaa pwani.

beacon, *n.* moto mkubwa wa kujulishia habari (ya hatari, furaha &c.); kitu kilichowekwa kuonya (hatari &c.), *e.g.* chungu ya mawe, mlingoti, nguzo, mnara.

bead, *n.* ushanga; (*drop*) tone. **beads,** *n.* (*rosary*) tasbihi. *Cluster of beads,* shada la ushanga, timba ya ushanga. *Belt of beads,* (*women's*) kondavi, shegele; (*circlet*) utunda, kogo. **beady,** *a.* kama ushanga; (*of eyes*) -dogo, -enye kung'aa sana. **beading,** *n.* upapi wa ubao (au wa udongo) uliopambwa kuigiza ushanga; mapambo ya kuta za nyumba.

beagle, *n.* namna ya mbwa aliyefundishwa kuwinda.

beak, *n.* mdomo wa ndege; kitu kinachotokeza kama mdomo wa ndege; omo la jahazi.

beaker, *n.* kikombe cha kunywea.

beam, *n.* boriti ya mti au chuma; mhimili; (*of light*) mwangaza (kama mshale wa moto), kiangaza, kianga, mwali, kiali; (*breadth*) upana wa jahazi au chombo (meli &c.). *Lay on beam ends,* inika. *Be on one's beam ends,* shindwa, dhikika, taiti. — *v.i.* angaza; (*smile*) kunjua uso, chekelea. **beaming,** *a.* -ng'avu, -angavu; (*smiling*) -kunjufu. *A beaming face,* uso mng'avu (mkunjufu).

bean, *n.* mbegu kama jamii ya kunde, choroko, fiwi, haragwe &c. **bean-feast,** *n.* tafrija, mandari.

bear, (1) *n.* dubu; mtu mkali, mchungu. **bearish,** *a.* kama dubu, -kali; *bear-garden,* fujo, ghasia, machafuko, makelele, zahama.

bear, (2) *v.t.* (*p.t.* **bore, bare,** *pf.t.* **borne** (zaa) **born**) (*carry*) chukua, himili; (*endure*) vumilia, stahimili; (*lean upon*) egemea; (*produce*) zaa. *Bear down* (*strain*) kakamua, jika. *Bear up,* stahimili, jipa moyo. *Bear with,* chukuliana na, stahimili, limbika, subiri. *Bear in mind,* kumbuka, zingatia. *Bear a hand,* saidia, auni, fanya shime. *Bear a likeness to,* fanana na, landa. *Bear a grudge against,* onea chuki. *Bear on (press),* songa, elemea; *(rest on)* tegemea, egemea; *(concern)* pasa, husu, fungamana na; -wa na habari ya; *(be directed to)* elekeana na. *Bring to bear,* toa, tumia, lekeza. *Bear out,* shuhudia, thibitisha (maneno ya). *Bear with me,* niwie radhi. *I cannot bear him,* namchukia sana.

bearable, *a.* -a kuchukulika (kuvumulika *&c.*). **bearer,** *n.* mchukuzi, mpagazi, hamali. **bearing,** *n.* *(carrying)* kuchukua, uchukuzi; *(prop)* tegemeo; *(appearance)* umbo, sura; *(behaviour)* mwenendo; *(patience)* saburi, uvumilivu; *(production)* uzazi; *(meaning)* maana; *(position, condition)* mahali, hali, kikao. *Take bearings,* hakikia mahali. *Bearings (machine),* mahali axle iingiapo katika magurudumu. *Ball-bearings,* gololi. *First-born,* kifungua mimba.

beard, *n.* ndevu. *Long, bushy beard,* madevu, sharafa. — *v.t.* endea pasipo hofu, jasiria, tolea ujuvi.

bearer, *n.*, **bearing,** *n.* taz. *bear* (2).

bearish, *a.* taz. *bear* (1).

beast, *n.* mnyama, nyama, hayawani; mtu mchafu, mkoo, mpujufu. **beastliness,** *n.* uchafu, upujufu. **beastly,** *a.* -chafu, -baya. **bestial,** *a.* kama mnyama, -a kinyama; *(filthy)* -chafu, -pujufu kabisa. **bestiality,** *n.* uchafu; mazoea au desturi chafu kabisa zinazochukiza.

beat, *v.t.* (*p.t.* **beat,** *pf.t.* **beaten**) *(strike)* piga, gonga, chapa; *(with hammer &c.)* fua, *(lightly)* babata, fusa, kong'ota; *(surpass)* shinda, pita, tia fora, kulula; *(throb)* tetema, papa; *(of a ship)* bisha; *(of hunting)* tafuta mawindo, saka. *Be beaten by waves &c.,* fuawa; *(conquered)* shindwa, enda kapa. *Beat down (price),* punguza bei, *(obstruction)* bomoa. *Beat in,* vunja, ponda. *Beat hollow,* shinda kabisa. *Beat off, or back,* fukuza, shinda. *Beat time;* kadirisha kwa kupunga kifimbo, mkono *&c.* gota; *(regularly)* gotagota; *(quickly)* gotagota. *Beat up,* tafuta. *Beat about the bush,* sitasita, tangatanga, hangaika. *Beat the air,* shindana bure. *Beat out (a question),* hakiki, hojihoji. *Be dead beat,* choka sana, shindwa, -wa taabani. — *n.* pigo, shindo; *(station)* kingojo, zamu.

beatitude, *n.* hali ya heri. *The Beatitudes,* sifa za heri (katika Injili). **beatific,** *a.* -a heri, -a kufurahisha mno.

beauteous, beautiful, *a,* -zuri, -a haiba. **beautify,** *v.t.* fanya -zuri, pamba, rembesha. **beauty,** *n.* uzuri, urembo, haiba. *A beauty,* mtu mzuri sana, kizuri.

beaver, *n.* mnyama mdogo wa jamii ya panya akaaye majini na nchi kavu pia.

becalm, *v.t.* tuliza, nyamazisha.

becalmed, *a.* *(be)* ingia shwari.

became, *p.t.* ya *become.*

because, *adv. and conj.* kwa sababu (ya), kwa ajili (ya), minajili (ya), kwa, kuwa, maadam, madhali.

bechance, *v.i.* tukia, tokea, jiri.

bêche-de-mer, *n.*, jongoo wa bahari, kojojo, babaje.

beck, *n.* konyezo, ishara. **beckon,** *v.t.* pungia mkono, ashiria, konyeza. *At one's beck and call,* chini ya amri ya, ngojea amri ya.

becloud, *v.t.* ficha kwa mawingu; tia shaka; fumba, ficha hata maana isionekane wazi.

become, *v.i.* (*p.t.* **became,** *pf.t.* **become**) pata kuwa, geuka, -wa; *(suit)* faa, agia, laiki, fanya uzuri, fanya kupendeza, shamiri, -wa wajibu. *That dress becomes you,* nguo hiyo inakufaa inakupendeza, inakuchukua. *It became a tree,* iligeuka mti. **becoming,** *a.* -zuri, -a kufaa, -a kuagia, -a kulaiki, wajibu, -a kustahili. **becomingly,** *adv.* kwa jinsi inayofaa (inayopendeza, iliyo wajibu, inayopasa).

bed, *n.* kitanda, malalo; (*foundation*) msingi. *Bed of sand,* mahali penye mchanga, fungu la mchanga. *Bed of river,* mto, bonde la mto, mto mkavu, papitapo mto, chini ya mto. *Bed* (*of potatoes &c.*), tuta. *Go to bed,* enda kulala, lala. *Make a bed,* tandika. *Bedchamber,* chumba cha kulala. **bedclothes, bedding,** *n.* matandiko (ya kitanda), malalo (mikeka, nguo, godoro, majani). **bedfast, bedridden,** *a.* -gonjwa kitandani. **bedrock,** *a.* -a chini kabisa. **bedstead,** *n.* kitanda; (*with turned legs*) ulili, (*of foreign make*) samadari. **bed,** *v.t.* weka kitandani; weka msingi; weka imara.

bedaub, *v.t.* paka, rashia.

bedclothes, *n.*, **bedding,** *n.* taz. *bed.*

bedeck, *v.t.* pamba, tia urembo, rembesha.

bedew, *v.t.* tia umande, nyunyizia maji.

bedfast, *a.* taz. *bed.*

bedizen, *v.t.* valisha mapambo mengi.

bedlam, *n.* ghasia, zahama, machafuko, makelele, fujo.

Bedouin, *n.* Bedui.

bedridden, *a.*, **bedrock,** *a.*, **bedstead,** *n.* taz. *bed.*

bee, *n.* nyuki. *He has a bee in his bonnet,* ana fikira ya upuzi juu ya jambo fulani, ana kinyongo. **bee-eaters,** *n.* (*merops*) keremkerem. **bee-hive,** *n.* mzinga wa nyuki. **bee-line,** *n.* njia iliyo fupi kutoka mahali mpaka mahali pengine. **beeswax,** *n.* nta.

beech, *n.* namna ya mti wa Ulaya.

beef, *n.* nyama ya ng'ombe. **beef-steak,** *n.* kipande cha nyama ya ng'ombe. **beef-tea,** *n.* mchuzi wa nyama ya ng'ombe. **beefwood,** *n.* (*tree*) mvinje. **beefy,** *a.* -nene, -enye nguvu.

bee-hive, *n.*, **bee-line,** *n.* taz. *bee.*

Beelzebub, *n.*, shetani.

been, *pf.t.* ya *be.*

beer, *n.* pombe; (*sweet, unfermented*) togwa, malenga. *Other kinds are* kangara, ugimbi, boza *&c.* **beer-house,** *n.* nyumba ya pombe.

beestings, *n.* dang'a.

beeswax, *n.* taz. *bee.*

beet, *n.* taz. *beetroot.*

beetle, (1) *n.* mdudu mwenye mabawa atambaaye wa jamii ya mende *&c.*

beetle, (2) *a. and v.i.* tokeza. *Beetle-browed,* -enye nyushi zinazotokeza. *Beetling cliffs,* magenge yanayotokeza juu.

beetroot, *n.* mboga: ziko namna mbili, moja ina kiazi chekundu sana kinacholiwa kama mboga; nyingine ina kiazi cheupe kinachotumika kufanyizia sukari.

befall, *v.t. and i.* (*p.t.* **befell,** *pf.t.* **befallen**) pata, tukia, jiri, angukia.

befit, *v.t.* stahili, faa, pasa, laiki, agia. **befitting,** *a.* wajibu, -zuri, -ema. **befittingly,** *adv.* kwa jinsi inayofaa (inayopasa), vizuri.

befog, *v.t.* funika kwa ukungu; fumba, tia wasiwasi. *Be befogged,* funikwa na ukungu, -wa na wasiwasi wa akili, fumbwa, tatanishwa, zingwa.

before, *adv. and prep.* kabla (ya), mbele (ya), hadhara (ya): kadamnasi, adv. *in public, before people; he arrived before the time,* alifika kabla ya wakati uliopasa; mbele (ya): *he arrived before the place* (*king, magistrate &c.*), alifika mbele ya *or* hadhara ya (mfalme, kadhi *&c.*); zaidi (ya), pita: *that thing comes before that one,* kitu hiki ni bora zaidi ya kile, chapita kile; zamani, kwanza: *I did that before,* nilifanya vile zamani (kwanza). *Before he dies,* kabla hajafa. *Go before, Be beforehand,* enda mbele, tangulia, takadamu, -wa tayari, tayari, -wa kwanza. **beforehand,** *adv.* mbele, kwanza, kabla.

befriend, *v.t.* fadhili, saidia, fanyia urafiki, tendea hisani, karibisha.

beg, *v.t.* omba, taka, (*persistently*) ng'ang'ania; — *v.i.* omba. *Beg the question,* zungusha maneno, sema maneno yenye vipengee. *Beg for pardon,* lalama. *Beg pardon (apologize),* taka radhi. *I beg your pardon,* kunradhi, niwie radhi. *I beg you,* tafadhali. *To go begging,* kutokuwa na mnunuzi, kutotumika, kudharauliwa. **beggar,** *n.* mwombaji, maskini, mkata, fukara, kibapara. *Be made (become) a beggar, Be beggared,* fukarika, kombeka mali, filisika. **beggar,** *v.t.* fukarisha, filisi. *It beggars description,* haiwezi kuelezwa, haielezeki, hainenekani. **beggarly,** *a.* -a maskini, -nyonge, -baya, duni, isiyo na thamani. **beggary,** *n.* umaskini, ufukara, ukata, hohe hahe. **begging,** *n.* maombi, uombezi, kuomba, kulalama.

began, *p.t.* ya *begin.*

beget, *v.t.* (*p.t.* **begot,** *pf.t.* **begotten**) zaa (kwa kiume); (*cause*) fanya, toa.

beggar, *n. and v.,* **beggarly,** *a.,* **beggary,** *n.,* **begging,** *n.* taz. *beg.*

begin, *v.t.* (*p.t.* **began,** *pf.t.* **begun**) anza, ingia; (*work*) maliki, amiri, shika; (*start*) anzisha; — *v.i.* anza. **beginner,** *n.* mwanafunzi, mjinga, mwenye kuanza. **beginning,** *n.* mwanzo, awali, asili, chanzo, chimbuko.

begone, *int.* ondoka! ondokea mbali! nenda!

begot, *p.t.* ya *beget.*

begotten, *pf.t.* ya *beget.*

begrime, *v.t.* chafua, tia uchafu.

begrudge, *v.t.* sunza, toa kwa unyimivu; (*envy*) onea chuki au kijicho (kwa ajili ya mtu kuwa na mali, kitu &c.); onea wivu, husuda.

beguile, *v.t.* danganya, vuta kwa werevu, punja, ghilibu, bilisi, kalamkia, shawishi, ghuri; (*divert*) changamsha, furahisha, ondoa uchovu, pisha wakati kwa furaha (mazungumzo &c.). **beguilement,** *n.* hila, ushawishi, ibilisi, uchangamshi, mazungumzo &c. ya kupisha wakati. **beguiler,** *n.* mshawishi, mdanganyi, mlaghai, ayari.

begun, *pf.t.* ya *begin.*

behalf, *n. on behalf of, prep.* kwa ajili ya, kwa sababu ya, mahali pa, kuwa niaba ya, badala ya.

behave, *v.i.* tenda, enda, fanya kazi, jiweka. **behaviour,** *n.* mwenendo, tabia, mazoea, silika, desturi za mtu. *Good behaviour,* adabu, adili, mwenendo mzuri, mazoea mazuri, malezi mazuri, matendo mema kwa wengine.

behead, *v.t.* kata kichwa.

beheld, *v. p.t. and pf.t.* ya *behold.*

behest, *n.* amri, agizo.

behind, *adv. and prep.* nyuma (ya); (*of time*) baada (ya); (*inferior*) chini (ya); (*on further side*) mbele (ya). *Remain behind,* baki, salia. *Be behind,* chelewa, kawia, ahiri, usiri; (*backward*) pitiwa, shindwa.

behold, *v.t.* (*p.t. and pf.t.* **beheld**) ona, tazama, angalia. *Lo behold!* tazama, tahamaki, kumbe! **beholden,** *a.* (*be*) wiwa na; onea shukrani. **beholder,** *n.* aonaye, aangaliaye, shahidi.

behoof, *n.* fadhili, faida, nafuu. *On your behoof,* kwa jili ya (faida, nafuu) yako.

behove, *v.t. It behoves us,* yatupasa, tumepaswa, yafaa.

being, *n.* (taz. *exist*) kuwa; (*nature*) asili, hali; (*creature*) kiumbe, kitu chenye uhai; (*thing existing*) -enye kuwa. *Human being,* mtu, binadamu. **being** (*participle* ya *verb* kuwa). *That being the case,* kama ni hivyo.

bejewell, *v.t.* pamba kwa vito.

belabour, *v.t.* piga sana, chapa sana.

belated, *a.* (*be belated*) chelea, chelewa, limatika.

belaud, *v.t.* sifu sana.

belay, *v.t.* funga (kibaharia). *Belay there!* basi!

belch, *v.i.* (*eructate*) ungulia, piga mbweu; — *v.t.* (*eject violently*) kokomoa, bubujisha, toa kwa nguvu. — *n.* (*eructation*) kiungulia, mbweu; (*spurt*) bubujiko.

beldam(e), *n.* kizee (mwanamke) mchafu mkorofi.

beleaguer, *v.t.* vizia, otea, zingia.

belfry, *n.* mnara au chumba mnarani mnamowekwa kengele.

Belgian, *n.* mwenyeji wa nchi ya *Belgium,* Mbelgiji.

belial, *n.* shetani.

belie, *v.t.* singizia, igiza yasiyo kweli; onyesha kwa jinsi isiyostahili (isiyo kweli). *That action belies him,* tendo hilo halionyeshi tabia yake ilivyo, si stahili yake, si laiki yake, halimwagii.

believe, *v.t.* amini, sadiki, itikadi; (*think*) ona, dhani, tumaini. — *v.i.* (*trust to*) tumaini, tegemea. *To make believe,* jisingizia, jifanya. **belief,** *n.* imani, itikadi; (*idea*) dhana, wazo; (*creed*) kanuni za imani, (*Muhammedan*) shahada. **believer,** *n.* mwenye imani, mwamini, asadikiye, mfuasi. **believing,** *a.* -enye imani, amini, -tumainifu.

belike, *adv.* labda, huenda.

belittle, *v.t.* fanya -dogo, rahisisha, vunja jina (cheo, ukubwa, thamani &c.).

bell, *n.* kengele; (*small ornamental*) njuga, kivumanzi, mbugi.

belle, *n.* mwanamke mzuri sana, mwanamke aliye mzuri wa mahali.

bellicose, *a.* -kali, -gomvi, -shari, -enye tabia ya kutaka vita au ugomvi.

belligerent, *a.* -a kufanya vita. — *n.* mfanya vita.

bellow, *v.i.* uga, lia kama ng'ombe, nguruma, vuma. — *n.* kama mlio wa ng'ombe, ngurumo, uvumi, mvumo.

bellows, *n.* mivuo, mivukuto.

belly, *n.* tumbo; cho chote kilicho kama tumbo, au kutokeza kama tumbo. — *v.t.* tokeza, fura; — *v.i.* vimba (kama tanga lililovimba kwa upepo) kubaza.

belong, *v.i.* (*to*) -wa mali ya, -wa mtu wa, -wa kitu cha, -wa chini ya, -wa sehemu ya, pasa, husu. *It belongs to me,* hii ni yangu. **belongings,** *n.* mambo, jamaa, mali na vitu vya mtu, vikorokoro.

beloved, *a.* -penzi, -pendwa. — *n.* mpenzi, kipenzi, tiba, muhebi, halili.

below, *adv. and prep.* chini (ya) (mahali, cheo, thamani &c.). *Be below* (*unworthy of*) si stahili. *Here below,* hapa duniani.

belt, *n.* mshipi, ukanda, masombo, mahazamu; (*women's: of beads*) kondavi; (*strap*) ukanda. *Belt of trees &c.,* safu au mstari wa miti. — *v.t.* zungushia mshipi (ukanda &c.); piga kwa ukanda &c.

bemoan, *v.t.* lilia, sikitikia, huzunikia.

bemuse, *v.t.* pumbaza, duwaza, tia fujo, tia wasiwasi.

bench, *n.* ubao wa kukalia, kiti kirefu (kwa marefu); (*of stone*) ufunga; (*judge's*) kiti cha kadhi (hakimu); (*judges*) jamii ya makadhi (ya mahakimu); (*carpenter's &c.*) meza ndefu ya kufanyia kazi.

bend, *v.t.* (*p.t. and p.t.* **bent**) pinda, kunja; — *v.i.* pindika, nepa, nesa, kunjika; — *v.t.* (*direct*) elekeza; — *v.i.* (*incline*) elekea; — *v.t.* (*make a ring of*) peta, peteza, petamanisha; (*subdue*) tiisha; — *v.i.* (*turn*) geuka; (*stoop*) inama, songa; — *v.t.* (*in submission*) angukia, jiweka chini. **bend,** *n.* pindi, kombo, kigosho; (*winding of streams &c.*) pindo, ghuba, mzingo, kuruba.

beneath, *adv.* & *prep.* chini (ya); duni. *He is beneath contempt,* hastahili hata kudharauliwa.

benediction, *n.* mbaraka, baraka, dua ya kutakia heri.

benefaction, *n.* tendo la wema, tendo jema, tajamala, fadhili, sadaka. **benefactor,** *n.* mfadhili, mtenda mema; atoaye mali kwa ajili ya maskini, chuo, dini, &c. **benefactress,** *n. benefactor* wa kike. **benefice,** *n.* kazi ya kasisi mahali fulani yenye uchumi. **beneficence,** *n.* ukarimu, upaji, wema ufanisi. **beneficent,** *a.* -karimu, -paji, -ema. **beneficial,** *a.* -a kufaa, -a msaada, -enye manufaa. **benefit,** *n.* fadhili, faida, chumo, fanaka, ufanisi, kifaa. — *v.t.* fadhili, nafuisha, faa; — *v.i.* faidi, pata nafuu. **benevolence,** *n.* upaji, ukarimu, wema. **benevolent,** *a.* -paji, -karimu, -ema.

benighted, *a.* -a kuchelewa; (*unenlightened*) -jinga, shenzi, -siojua mambo.

benign, benignant, *a.* -ema, -a upole, -anana.

benison, *n.* baraka.

bent (*p.t. and pf.t.* ya *bend*). — *a.* -liopindika, -enye kombo, -a upinde, (taz. *bend*); (*with age, sickness &c.*) kibiongo. *Be bent on*, taka sana, tamani. *Be easily bent*, pindika kwa urahisi, pindamana. — *n.* tabia (ya mtu), moyo, maelekeo (ya mtu).

benumb, *v.t.* tia ganzi, fifisha, poozesha. **benumbed**, *a.* (*be*) -fa ganzi, fifia, pooza.

benzine, *n.* namna ya dawa igeukayo mvuke upesi sana; hutumika kusafisha nguo.

bequeath, *v.t.* rithisha, usia, achia, halifu. **bequest**, *n.* urithi, usia, hiba.

bereave, *v.t.* ondolea, twalia, tolea; acha katika hali ya ukiwa (ya kufiwa). **bereaved**, *a.* (*be*) twaliwa, ondolewa; (*by death*) fiwa. *The bereaved*, mfiwa. **bereavement**, *n.* tendo au hali ya kufiwa, msiba.

bereft, *a.* *be bereft of*, ondolewa (ondokewa) na, potewa na, nyang'anywa. *Bereft of reason*, potewa na akili. *Bereft of speech* (*sight*), potewa na uwezo wa kusema (wa kuona).

beret, *n.* namna ya kofia ndogo.

berg, *n.* mlima au jabali la barafu.

beriberi, *n.* namna moja ya ugonjwa kama safura au istiska.

berry, *n.* tunda dogo lo lote kama forsadi au fuu. *Coffee-berry*, buni.

berth, *n.* (*anchorage*) mahali pa meli kutia nanga na kukaa gatini; (*accommodation*) kijumba melini, garini *&c.*, kao; (*situation*) kazi. — *v.t.* tia (puliza) nanga, egemeza meli gatini. *To give a wide berth to*, epusha, jiepusha na.

beseech, *v.t.* (*p.t. and pf.t.* **besought**) sihi, omba sana, ng'ang'ania, rongaronga. **beseechingly**, *adv.* kwa kuomba (kusihi) sana.

beseem, *v.t.* faa, stahili, laiki, agia.

beset, *v.t.* (*p.t. and pf.t.* **beset**) vizia, zunguka, songa, sumbua, shambulia, hatirisha. **besetting**, *a.* -a kusonga sikuzote, -enye hatari siku zote, -a kuvizia.

beside, *prep.* (*by side of*) kando ya, mbavuni pa; (*over and above*) zaidi ya, juu ya. *He is beside himself*, amerukwa na akili. *That is beside the question*, hiyo ni mbali, haimo, haihusu. **besides**, *adv. and prep.* tena, zaidi (ya), juu (ya).

besiege, *v.t.* zunguka mji vitani, zingia, fanya mazingiwa, husuru, songa sana, songa pande zote.

besmear, *v.t.* paka, rashia.

besmirch, *v.t.* tia taka, chafua; (*of character*) haribu.

besom, *n.* fagio.

besotted, *a.* (*be*) pumbaa kwa kunywa ulevi mwingi.

besought, *p.t. and pf.t.* ya *beseech*.

bespeak, *v.t.* (*p.t.* **bespoke**, *pf.t.* **bespoken**) omba, agizia, taka mbele (*e.g.* agiza nguo zishonwe ziwe tayari siku fulani *&c.*); (*indicate*) onya, onyesha. *Every room is already bespoken*, kila chumba kimekwisha pangishwa.

best, *a.* afadhali, bora, -ema sana, -zuri kupita yote, aali, kamili. *Best man*, rafiki au mngojezi amsaidiaye bwana arusi siku ya arusi. — *n.* kipeo, kilicho bora. *To put one's best foot foremost*, fanya vizuri iwezekanavyo. *Make the best of*, fanya vizuri iwezekanavyo kwa mambo yalivyo; shukuru. *Make the best of one's way*, enda upesi iwezekanavyo (au kwa njia iliyo bora). *Have the best of*, shinda. *At best*, kwa vyo vyote. *To the best of my memory*, niwezavyo kukumbuka. — *adv.* vizuri iwezekanavyo, kwa jinsi iliyo bora, ifaayo zaidi.

bestial, *a.* **bestiality**, *n.* taz. *beast*.

bestir, *v.t.* shtua, amsha; (*oneself*) jiamsha, jishughulisha.

bestow, *v.t.* (*place*) weka; (*give*) toa, -pa. **bestowal**, *n.* tendo la kupa (la kuweka).

bestride, *v.t.* (*p.t.* **bestrode**, *pf.t.*

bestridden) tagaa, kaa hali miguu imepanuka kama mtu akaavyo juu ya punda.

bet, *n.* sharti ya bahatisho, kitu (fedha *&c.*) kilichowekwa au kutajwa cha kubahatisha, yaani jambo fulani likitukia kama ulivyobashiri au kubahatisha, huwa chako, la sivyo, huwa cha yule unayeshindana naye. — *v.t.* pinga, weka sharti; (*affirm by a bet*) piga masharti kama . . .; (*engage in betting*) wekeana masharti.

betake, *v. reflex.* (*p.t.* **betook**, *pf.t.* **betaken**) (*oneself to*) endea, tegemea, kimbilia.

betel, *n.* (*leaf*) tambuu; (*plant*) mtambuu; (*nut*) popoo; (*palm*) mpopoo; (*prepared for chewing*) uraibu.

bethink, *v. reflex.* (*p.t. and pf.t.* **bethought**) fikiri, kumbuka.

betide, *v.t.* tukia, jiri; — *v.i.* pata. *Woe betide you*, msiba ukupate.

betimes, *adv.* mapema, hima, kwa wakati ufaao.

betoken, *v.t.* onya, bashiri, -wa na maana ya.

betook, *p.t.* ya *betake*.

betray, *v.t.* haini, danganya, saliti, toa kwa hila; (*a secret*) toa nje siri uliyoambiwa; (*indicate*) onyesha dhahiri, onyesha wazi (dalili ya hofu, mshangao, furaha *&c.*); (*abandon*) acha, tupa, toa bila kujitahidi kulihifadhi jambo lililokupasa kulitunza; (*seduce*) shawishi, tendea ubaya mtu mwaminifu asiyefahamu ubaya wa jambo. **betrayal**, *n.* uhaini, tendo la kuhaini, usaliti *&c.* **betrayer**, *n.* mhaini, msaliti; mtongozi wa mwanamke mwaminifu asiyejua ubaya wa jambo.

betroth, *v.t.* fanya uchumba, oza, ahidi kuolewa, funga nikaha. **betrothal**, *n.* uchumba, ahadi ya kuoa. **betrothed**, *n.* mchumba.

better, *a.* zaidi, bora, afadhali, aali, aula, -a kufaa zaidi. *Better than*, zaidi ya, bora kuliko, aali kuliko, afadhali kama, kupita, kushinda. *Be better*, pita, shinda; (*in health*) -wa -jambo, pona, ona ashekali, pata nafuu (ahueni). *You had better go*, afadhali uende. *To think better of*, ghairi, geuza shauri. *Get the better of*, shinda, ghilibu. *Be better off*, -wa na hali njema zaidi; (*richer*) -wa na mali zaidi. *Get better*, pona. *Make better*, kuza, sitawisha, endesha, fanya -wa bora, faidia.

between, **betwixt**, *adv. and prep.* katikati (ya), baina (ya), kati (ya). *Between-whiles*, pengine pengine (wakati si mahali). *Between ourselves*, siri yetu, kati yetu sisi tu. *To go between*, kuamua, kusuluhisha, kupatanisha. *A go between*, kijumbe; (*pimp*) kawadi. *Betwixt and between*, katikati.

bevel, *n.* matemo, kama vile ukingo wa ubao. **bevelled**, *a.* -enye ukingo wa matemo.

beverage, *n.* kinywaji, cha kunywa.

bevy, *n.* kundi la ndege (la wanawake).

bewail, *v.t.* lilia, omboleza, sikitikia, jutia.

beware, *v.t. and i.* angalia, tahadhari, fanya hadhari, -wa na hadhari; shuku hatari. *Beware!* jihadhari! *Beware lest you fall*, angalia (fanya hadhari, jihadhari) usije ukaanguka.

bewilder, *v.t.* fadhaisha, shangaza, zuzua, tia wasiwasi, tunduwaza, potoa, poteza. **bewildered**, *a.* (*be*) fadhaika, potea, ona wasiwasi, taataa. **bewilderment**, *n.* bumbuazi, fadhaa, mshangao, wasiwasi.

bewitch, *v.t.* fanyia uchawi, loga, sihiri, nuizia; (*fascinate*) pagaa, poteza akili, shangaza (kwa uzuri). **bewitching**, *a.* -zuri mno (hata kupoteza akili).

beyond, *adv. and prep.* (*farther side*) ng'ambo ya pili (ya), upande wa pili (wa); (*farther onward*) mbele (ya), kupita; (*superior*) kushinda, kupita. — *n.* pasipojulikana, ahera. *Beyond measure*, kupita kiasi (kadiri). *The back of beyond*, mahali pa mbali sana. *It is beyond me*, imenishinda, siwezi kuifahamu.

bezique, *n.* mchezo wa karata.

bhang, *n.* bangi.

bias, *n.* upendeleo, upendelevu, maelekeo. *Have a bias towards,* inamia, elekea, pendelea. —*v.t.* vuta kupendelea (au kuchukiza) jambo au mtu. **biased,** *a.* -enye upendeleo kwa, au kuelekea upande mmoja (wa shauri *&c.*).

bibber, *n.* mlevi.

Bible, *n.* Msahafu Mtakatifu wa kikristo; Maandiko Matakatifu, yaani Agano la Kale na Agano Jipya. **biblical,** *a.* -a kuhusu Msahafu Mtakatifu, -a Msahafu Mtakatifu. **bibliography,** *n.* elimu ya habari za vitabu, watungaji vitabu, habari zilizomo na wakati vilipoandikwa *&c.*

bicentenary, *a.* -a kuhusu miaka mia mbili. — *n.* siku ya kuadhimisha mwaka wa mia mbili.

biceps, *n.* shavu la (musuli ya) mkono katikati ya kiko na bega; pia lile la nyuma ya paja katikati ya goti na tako.

bicker, *v.i.* bishana, gombana, zozana, nunanuna.

bicycle, *n.* baisikeli. **bicyclist,** *n.* mpanda baisikeli.

bid, *v.t.* (*p.t.* **bad, bade, bid,** *pf.t.* **bidden, bid**) (*at auction*) zabuni, pandisha bei; (*first bid*) rasimu; (*final bid*) shtiri; (*invite*) alika, karibisha; (*command*) amuru, agiza, ambia. *Bid farewell,* aga. *Bid fair to be,* taka kuwa, elekea. — *n.* tajo la bei, kuzabuni; jaribio (hasa la shida au ujasiri). **bidder,** *n.* mzabuni. **bidding,** *n.* amri, neno, aliko.

bide, *v.i.* ngoja. *Bide one's time,* ngojea wakati ufaao.

biennial, *a.* -a kudumu au kuendelea miaka miwili; -a kutukia mara moja tu kila miaka miwili. **biennially,** *adv.* kila mwaka wa pili.

bier, *n.* jeneza.

bifurcate, *v.t. and i.* fanya panda (*e.g.* njia, mti, mto). — *a.* -enye panda. **bifurcation,** *n.* panda.

big, *a.* -kubwa, -kuu, -nene, -kuza; (*pregnant*) -enye mimba, -zito. *A very big man* (*ogre, giant*), jitu, pandikizi la mtu. *Big men,* mapande ya watu. *A big dog,* jibwa.

bigamy, *n.* kosa (kwa sheria ya kiingereza na nchi nyingine kadha wa kadha) la kuwa na wake wawili au waume wawili wakati mmoja. **bigamist,** *n.* mwenye kufanya kosa la *bigamy.*

bight, *n.* pindo; (*bay*) ghuba.

bigot, *n.* mshupavu (wa dini, mambo *&c.*). **bigoted,** *a.* -shupavu wa dini, mambo *&c.* **bigotry,** *n.* ushupavu (wa dini, mambo *&c.*).

bilateral, *a.* -enye pande mbili, kingo mbili. **bilaterally,** *adv.* kwa pande zote mbili.

bile, *n.* nyongo; (*ill-humour*) uchungu, chuki. **bilious,** *a.* -a kuhusu nyongo; -enye ugonjwa uletwao na nyongo. **biliousness,** *n.* ugonjwa uletwao na nyongo.

bilge, *n.* ngama, banduru; (*nonsense*) upuzi.

bilharzia, *n.* wadudu waletao ugonjwa wa kichocho. Wadudu hao huzaliwa katika jamii moja ya konokono wa maji, kisha huwamo katika maji, na watu waingiao humo kuoga huweza kuingiwa nao. **bilharziosis,** *n.* ugonjwa wa kichocho.

bilingual, *a.* -enye kusema lugha mbili, hasa kutoka utotoni.

bilious, *a.*, **biliousness,** *n.* taz. *bile.*

bill, (1) *n.* (*of bird*) mdomo (wa ndege), kitu kilichofanana na mdomo wa ndege; (*chopper*) mundu. **bill-hook,** *n.* mundu.

bill, (2) *n.*(*account*) hati ya fedha, hesabu, jumla; (*proposed law*), hati yenye habari za sheria mpya; (*advertisement &c.*) tangazo lililopigwa chapa. *Bill of sale,* ankra. *Bill of exchange,* hawala, hundi. *Bill of fare,* orodha ya vyakula vya mezani. *Bill of health,* cheti cha kushuhudia afya (ya watu waliomo melini *&c.*). *Bill of lading,* orodha ya shehena ya melini. **billet,** *n.* cheti

cha kugawia nyumba askari. **billet-doux,** n. barua ya mchumba.
billhook, *n.* taz. *bill* (1).
billiards, *n.* mchezo wa kugonganisha tufe za pembe juu ya meza.
billion, *n.* mamilioni milioni, yaani 1,000,000,000,000 (katika nchi ya Amerika na ya Ufaransa ni mamilioni elfu, yaani 1,000,000,000).
billow, *n.* wimbi. —*v.i.* jongea kama wimbi. **billowy,** *a.* -enye mawimbi, -a kama mawimbi.
billy-goat, *n.* mbuzi dume, denge wa mbuzi.
biltong, *n.* nyama iliyolengwa na kukaushwa juani, mtande.
bin, *n.* sanduku ya kuwekea nafaka, divai *&c.*
bind, *v.t.* (*p.t. and pf.t.* **bound**) funga, kaza, baba, boba; (*put restraint on*) fanyia sharti, tia sharti, shurutisha, bidi, pasisha; (*of books*) jalidi; (*hem*) minika; (*bandage*) fungia kitambaa; (*cement*) ambatisha; (*render hard*) gandisha; (*constipate*) funga choo. *Bind oneself,* ahidi. **binder,** *n.* mtu au kitu kifungacho. **binding,** *a.* -a kufunga, -a lazima, -a sharti. — *n.* cho chote kifungacho; (*of books*) jalada. **bounden,** *a.* -a wajibu, -a lazima.
binnacle, *n.* sanduku inamowekwa dira melini.
binocular, *n.* darubini ya macho mawili.
bio-, *pfx.* -a kuhusu uzima (uhai, maisha).
biography, *n.* maandiko ya habari za maisha ya mtu.
biology, *n.* habari za maisha ya watu, wanyama na mimea; elimu ya uzima (uhai) na asili yake. **biological,** *a.* -a kuhusu *biology.* **biologist,** *n.* mwenye elimu ya *biology.*
bioscope, *n.* sinema.
biped, *a.* -enye miguu miwili kama mtu, nyani, ndege *&c.* —*n.* mwenye miguu miwili.
biplane, *n.* eropleni yenye mabawa mawili.
birch, *n.* namna ya mti wa Ulaya; (*of twigs*) fimbo au fito za kutia adhabu. — *v.t.* piga kwa fimbo au kwa fito.
bird, *n.* ndege; (*young*) kinda. *Birds of a feather,* watu wa tabia moja. *Get a bird's-eye view,* tazama toka juu, angalia yote pamoja. *A bird in the hand is worth two in the bush,* heri kenda shika, kama kumi nenda uje, '*Better is nine "Take-it!" than ten "Go-and-come!"*'. **bird-lime,** *n.* ulimbo ulimbolimbo. **bird's-nest,** *n.* kitundu, kiota.
birth, *n.* uzazi, uzaliwa; (*beginning*) mwanzo, chanzo, asili, chimbuko; (*rank*) cheo; (*family*) jamaa, ukoo, nasaba. *A man of high birth,* mtu wa ukoo ulio bora, mtoto wa watu. **birthday,** *n.* maulidi, ukumbusho wa kila mwaka wa siku ya kuzaliwa. **birth-mark,** *n.* baka, ndugu. **birthplace,** *n.* mahali mtu alipozaliwa ni *birthplace* yake. **birth-right,** *n.* urithi. *Birth-rate,* hesabu ya watoto waliozaliwa katika jumla ya watu elfu kwa muda wa mwaka mmoja.
biscuit, *n.* mkate mdogo mkavu, biskuti.
bisect, *v.t.* kata sawa bi sawa, kata sehemu mbili zilizo sawa kabisa.
bishop, *n.* askofu. **bishopric,** *n.* uaskofu; jimbo la askofu.
bishop-bird, *n.* (*fire crowned*) kwechi, chekechea.
bison, *n.* mnyama kama nyati.
bissextile, *n.* mwaka mrefu, yaani wenye siku 366, (kila mwaka wa nne wa kizungu una siku 366).
bit, *n.* sehemu, kipande, chenge; (*of a horse*) lijamu; (*of a brace and bit*) msumari wa kekee. *A bit,* kidogo. *Wait a bit,* ngoja kwanza, ngoja kidogo. *I don't care a bit,* mamoja kwangu, si kitu hata kidogo. *Not a bit of it,* hapana, sivyo kabisa, hasha. *Bit by bit,* haba na haba, punde kwa punde, kidogo kidogo. *Take bit by bit,* chota kidogo kidogo. *To do one's bit,* kufanya kadiri (ya kazi, wajibu *&c.*) ipasayo.
bit, *v. pt.* ya *bite.*

bitch, *n.* mbwa jike; jike la wanyama kama mbwa, mbweha *&c.*

bite, *v.t.* (*p.t.* **bit**, *pf.t.* **bitten**) uma, tafuna, mega kwa meno, guguna, donoa; (*pain*) washa, choma; (*take hold of*) kamatisha, shikiza. *Bite off a piece*, mega. *Bite off more than one can chew*, ahidi kufanya mambo usiyoweza. *Bite the dust*, anguka, kufa (hasa katika pigano). — *n.* tendo la kuuma kwa meno; umo, palipoumwa; (*in fishing*) mdono, tendo la samaki kulisha mshipi mtu anapovua samaki; (*mouthful*) mego. **biting**, *a.* -a kuchoma, -kali, -a kuumiza.

bitten, *pf.t.* ya *bite*.

bitter, *a.* -chungu, -kali, -a kukausha meno, -a kutia ukakasi. **bitterness**, *n.* uchungu, ukali, kasirani, ukakasi, wivu, uhasama.

bittern, *n.* ngojamaliko, namna ya ndege kama korongo, mlio wake huvuma.

bitterness, *n.* taz. *bitter*.

bitumen, *n.* namna ya lami.

bivalve, *n.* mnyama mwenye makombe mawili kama chaza; maganda ya mbegu yaliyofanana na chaza, yaani pande mbili.

bivouac, *v.i.* panga kambi ya usiku bila hema. — *n.* kituo, kambi bila hema.

bizarre, *a.* -a kigeni, -a kutazanisha (kuchekesha) kwa ajili ya kuwa kigeni au kupita kiasi cha kupendeza.

blab, *v.i.* payapaya, payuka, bwabwaja; (*tell tales*) chongea, singizia, kashifu; (*tell secret*) toa nje habari za siri; **blabber**, *n.* mpayapaya, mpayukaji, mchongezi, mkashifu, domo kaya. **blabbing**, *n.* payo, uchongezi, ukashifu.

black, *a.* -eusi; (*dark*) -a giza, -a utusitusi; (*dreadful*) -a tisho, -a msiba, -baya, -a kisirani; (*foul, dirty*) -chafu, -pujufu; (*malignant*) -ovu, -baya, -korofi. — *n.* (*colour*) weusi; (*negro*) mweusi. *Black and blue*, rangi ya damu kuvia katika chubuko. *It is in black and white*, imeandikwa. *The outlook is black*, mambo huonekana kuwa mabaya. *Be in any one's black books*, -wa umechukiza mtu. **black, blacken**, *v.t.* fanya -eusi; (*disparage*) aibisha, tia aibu, singizia, sengenya, umbua, vunjia heshima. **black art**, *n.* uchawi, ulozi, usihiri, uramali. **blackball**, *v.t.* toa ishara (kidonge cheusi) ya kutotaka mtu kuchaguliwa kuwa mwana wa chama. **blackboard**, *n.* ubao wa kuandikia chuoni. **blackguard**, *n.* *and a.* baa, mwovu, mnyonge, ayari, mkorofi. — *v.t.* tukana, fanyia jeuri. **blackguardly**, *adv.* kwa jeuri, kwa ukorofi, kwa uovu, viovu. **blacking**, mafuta meusi, dawa ya viatu vyeusi au ya kupaka ngozi nyeusi. **blackish**, *a.* -eusi kidogo. **blackjack**, *n.* kichoma mguu (nguo); (*flag*) bendera ya haramia. **black-lead**, *n.* kitu kama makaa ya mawe (ndicho kilicho katikati ya kalamu iitwayo *lead pencil*). **blackleg**, *n.* mtu akubaliye kufanya kazi ingawa wenzake wametoka kazini kwa ajili ya kutaka kuzidishiwa mshahara. **black-list**, *n.* orodha ya majina ya wakosaji (ya watu, vitu, kazi *&c.*) walioharimishwa kwa sababu fulani. **blackmail**, *n.* mrungula, malipo (fedha *&c.*) yatozwayo na mtu kwa udhalimu asitoe nje habari za kosa kubwa (za jambo la aibu *&c.*). — *v.t.* toza hongo (mrungula, rushwa, fedha *&c.*) kwa udhalimu ili kuficha au kutotoa nje habari za kosa aibu *&c.*). **blackness**, *n.* weusi, giza, utusitusi; uovu. **black sheep**, *n.* mtu mbaya. **blacksmith**, mhunzi, mfua chuma.

bladder, *n.* kibofu. *Football bladder* mpira wa ndani (ya *football*).

blade, *n.* (*of grass*) jani, kijani; (*of sword*) kengee, ubaba; (*of oar or similar object*) bapa; (*of knife*) bapa; (*dashing fellow*) mmalidadi, mbeja, mshaufu, mtanashati, mfua uji, mlimbwende, mrembo.

blain, *n.* kijipu, kilengelenge, chunusi.

blame, *v.t.* (*scold*) karipia, kemea, janga; (*accuse*) shtaki, kengemeka, laumu, shutumu, tia hatiani, aili, ailisha, atibu; (*visit on*) patiliza. — *n.* mashutumu, lawama, hatia, kosa, uaili. **blameable,** *a.* -enye hatia, -enye kosa, -enye kustahili lawama. **blameless,** *a.* -sio kosa, -sio hatia, safi, -nyofu. **blameworthy,** *a.* taz. *blameable.*

blanch, *v.t.* fanya kuwa -eupe; — *v.i.* geuka -eupe.

bland, *a.* -anana, -pole, -tulivu, laini; -tamu. **blandish,** *v.t.* bembeleza, shawishi, sifusifu, rairai. **blandishment,** *n.* ubembelezi, upendeleo, ushawishi.

blank, *a.* -tupu, -eupe; (*face, look*) -a kufadhaika, -a kushangaa, -a kutunduwaa, -a kuzumbaa; bila dalili ya akili wala fahamu. — *n.* mahali pa wazi, uwazi, nafasi wazi. *Blank cartridge,* kiasi cha bunduki kisicho na risasi, ila baruti tu.

blanket, *n.* blanketi.

blare, *v.i.* lia sana, kama mlio wa tarumbeta &c. — *n.* mlio kama ule wa tarumbeta &c.

blasé, *a.* -kinaifu, -a kutoshewa na anasa &c.

blaspheme, *v.t. and i.* nenea Mungu, mambo matakatifu au dini; kufurisha, nena unajisi, tukana, nenea vibaya, laani, apiza. **blasphemer,** *n.* mkufuru; aneneaye Mungu, dini au mambo matakatifu. **blasphemous,** *a.* -a kutukana Mungu, -a kunenea Mungu, dini &c.; **blasphemously,** *adv.* kwa kutukana, kunenea Mungu au dini. **blasphemy,** *n.* maneno ya kumtukana Mungu, dini; unajisi, ukufuru; matukano.

blast, *n.* (*sound*) uvumi, mlio wa upepo wa ghafula, shindo kama la baruti kulipuka &c.; (*rush of air*) upepo wa mshindo (wa ghafula), dhoruba ya upepo; uvukuto; (*blasting*) mlipuko, mpasuko wa baruti &c. — *v.t.* haribu, angamiza; (*lightning*) piga; (*by explosion*) pasua kwa baruti; (*curse*) laani. **blasted,** *a.* -lioangamizwa, -liolaaniwa. **blasting,** *n.* mpasuo kwa baruti &c.

blatant, *a.* -enye ukelele, -enye kishindo; -a kujitokeza kwa majivuno. **blatantly,** *adv.* kwa ukelele; kwa kujivuna &c.

blather, *v.i.* taz. *blether.*

blaze, (1) *n.* mwako, ndimi za moto, mwangaza wa moto, mng'aro wa nuru (wa moto, wa rangi); (*of trees*) alama inayofanywa mtini kwa kuambua kipande cha gome ili kuonyesha njia au mpaka. — *v.i.* waka, ng'aa, meka; — *v.t.* (*of a tree*) fanya alama mtini kwa kubandua kipande cha gome kuonyesha njia au mpaka. **blazer,** *n.* koti la rangi la kuvaa katika michezo &c.

blaze, (2) *v.t. Blaze* (*blazon*) *abroad,* tangaza, eneza habari.

blazer, *n.* taz. *blaze* (1).

blazon, *v.t.* taz. *blaze* (2).

bleach, *v.t.* fanya -eupe (rangi). **bleaching powder,** *n.* namna ya chokaa yenye harufu kali; hutumika kuua wadudu na vijidudu katika maji, na kutakasa nguo.

bleak, *a.* -a ukiwa, baridi, pasipo raha. *A bleak country,* nchi ya ukiwa. *A bleak wind,* upepo wa baridi.

bleary, *a.* (*eyed*) -enye macho mekundu ya kuwasha.

bleat, *v.i.* lia kama kondoo. — *n.* mlio kama wa kondoo.

bled, *v. p.t. and pf.t.* ya *bleed.*

bleed, *v.i.* (*p.t. and pf.t.* **bled**) toka damu;— *v.t.* (*draw blood*) toza damu; (*cup*) umika; (*extort*) toza fedha kwa udhalimu. *He bled freely,* damu nyingi ilimtoka, alitoa damu chapa. *My heart bleeds for him,* namwonea huruma nyingi.

blemish, *n.* ila, kipunguo, athari, baka, dosari, nakisi, tua, waa, kosa, aibu, hitilafu, tofauti. — *v.t.* umbua, lemaza, athiri, haribu uzuri wa, tia ila &c.

blench, *v.i.* nywea (sita) kwa woga.

blend, *v.t.* changanya; — *v.t.* patana. *These things do not blend,* vitu hivi haviwezi kuchanganywa, havipatani. — *n.* changanyiko.

bless, *v.t.* (*p.t. and pf.t.* **blest**) bariki, tabaruku, neemesha, fanya heri, sitawisha, furahisha; sifu, sujudu, abudu. *God bless you*, Mungu akuweke. **blessed**, *a.* -enye heri, -enye furaha (usitawi, neema *&c.*). **blessedness**, *n.* hali ya kubarikiwa (ya heri, ya raha). **blessing**, *n.* mbaraka, baraka, radhi, kitu cho chote kiletacho furaha (usitawi *&c.*); dua la kumwomba Mungu alete heri au abariki mtu au kitu.

blether, *v.i.* payuka, babaika, bwata, bwabwaja, lopoka, twanga saya.

blew, *v. p.t.* ya *blow*.

blight, *n.* maradhi ya mimea; kutu, koga, kawa; cho chote kiharibucho au kuangamiza au kupoozesha. — *v.t.* haribu, umbua, fisha, poteza, fifisha, poozesha, sibu, angamiza.

blind, *a.* (*sightless*) -pofu; (*dark*) -enye giza; (*ignorant or undiscerning*) -jinga, -zembe, -a haraka, -a harara; (*blind alley*) kichochoro kilichozibwa, kisicho na mahali pa kutokea. *Blind of one eye*, -enye chongo. *A blind man*, kipofu. *Blind rage*, ghadhabu kali mno, kiruu. — *v.t.* pofusha; (*deceive*) danganya, laghai, ghilibu, bilisi, hadaa, rubuni; (*dazzle*) tia kiwi cha macho. — *n.* pazia (ya kukingia jua dirishani); (*deceit*) hila, uwongo, mtego, hadaa, ghiliba, madanganyo. **blindfold**, *v.t.* fungia kitambaa machoni, fungia kidoto. — *a.* bila fikira, bila hadhari. **blindly**, *adv.* kwa ujinga, bila kufikiri kwanza. *Blind-man's buff*, kizuizui, bui. **blindness**, *n.* upofu; (*of one eye*) chongo.

blink, *v.i.* pepesa, kopesa, kupia, metameta; — *v.t.* tojali, kataa kuangalia au kufikiri. **blinker**, *n.* kijamanda kidogo, kinga ya macho, kidoto.

bliss, *n.* kipeo cha furaha, raha mustarehe, hali ya heri kamili, jaha. **blissful**, *a.* -a furaha nyingi, -a raha.

blister, *n.* lengelenge; (*eruptive disease*) uwati; (*plaster*) mpako wa dawa kali wa kufanya lengelenge. *v.t.* tokeza lengelenge.

blithe, *a.* -enye furaha, -kunjufu, -epesi wa moyo. **blithely**, *adv.* kwa furaha, kwa moyo mwepesi.

blizzard, *n* upepo mkali wenye theluji.

bloat, *v.t.* vimbisha; — *v.i.* vimba, fura; — *v.t.* (*cure*) kausha katika moshi (*e.g.* samaki). **bloater**, *n.* namna ya samaki aliyekaushwa katika moshi.

blob, *n.* kidonge cha kitu chororo.

block, *n.* kipande, gogo la mti au jiwe *&c.*; (*of houses*) mpango wa nyumba nyingi pamoja; (*obstruction*) zuio; (*pulley*) kapi, ayari, abedari; (*for caps*) faruma; (*for executions*) gogo la kulazia kichwa tayari kukatwa. — *v.t.* pinga njia ziba, zuia, kingamisha, fungisha. **blockade**, *n.* mazingiwa. — *v.t.* husuru, zunguka kwa vita, zingia, fungisha. **blockhead**, *n.* mjinga, mwenye kichwa kigumu, baradhuli.

blond (*fem.* **blonde**), *n.* mtu mwenye nywele nyeupe rangi ya shaba (ya kimanjano) na sura nyeupe. — *a.* (nywele) -enye rangi ya shaba (ya kimanjano).

blood, *n.* damu; (*race*) asili, mbegu, ukoo; (*family*) jamaa, ndugu; (*dandy*) mbeja, mshaufu, mmalidadi, taz. *blade*. *His blood is up*, amekasirika. *In hot blood*, kwa harara, kwa ghadhabu. *In cold blood*, bila hasira, kwa nia si kwa harara, kwa ukali au ukatili tu. **blood-guiltiness**, *n.* hatia ya kuua. **bloodheat**, *n.* joto la damu. **bloodhound**, *n.* aina ya majibwa wawezao kunusia vikali; hutumika kuwindia wakosaji. **bloodshed**, *n.* uuaji, mauaji, tendo la kumwaga damu. **bloodshot**, *a* (jicho) -ekendu kwa damu. **bloodthirsty**, *a.* -enye hamu ya kumwaga damu, -kali sana, katili. **blood-vessel**, *n.* mshipa wa damu (mishipa inayochukua damu toka moyoni ni arteri (mikubwa), kapilari (midogo);

inayochukua damu mpaka katika moyo ni vena). **bloody**. *a*. -a damu, -enye damu; (*cruel*) -kali, katili, -a kiuaji.

bloom, *v.i.* toa maua, chanua; kuwa na hali kamili, yaani sura nzuri na afya kamili; sitawi. — *n*. ua; rangi nzuri; kipeo cha ukamilifu wa mtu au wa kitu. **blooming**, *a*. -a kung'aa, -enye kusitawi, marini.

blossom, *v.i. and n*. taz. *bloom*.

blot, *n*. waa, ila, kiwaa; (*of ink*) kiwaa, kitone; (*disgrace*) aibu. — *v.t.* tia mawaa; (*spoil*) haribu, umbua; (*disgrace*) fedhehesha, aibisha; (*dry ink*) kausha wino. *Blot out*, futa futia mbali. **blotting-paper**, *n*. karatasi ya kukaushia wino.

blotch, *n. and v*. sawasawa na *blot*.

blotting-paper, *n*. taz. *blot*.

blouse, *n*. vazi la kike, kidogo kama shati fupi.

blow, *n*. pigo, kipigo, shindo, kishindo, dharuba; (*disaster*) msiba, maafa, masaibu; (*sudden act*) tendo la ghafula, tukio. *At a single blow*, kwa dharuba moja. *Come to blows, exchange blows*, anza kupigana, ingia vitani. *Without striking a blow*, bila kushindana. — *v.i.* (*of wind*) vuma; — *v.t.* (*with mouth or breath*) toa pumzi, puzia, pulizia, vivia, vuvia. *Blow a trumpet*, piga panda. *Blow one's own trumpet*, jivuna, jigamba, jisifu. *Blow nose*, penga, futa kamasi. *Blow bellows*, vukuta. *Blow over*, pita, tulia. *Blow up*, vunja (pasua) kwa baruti; (*explode*) vunjika, pasuka; (*of a bladder, football, cycle tyre &c.*) puliza. *Blow about*, peperusha; peperuka. *To blow hot and cold*, kusitasita; pengine kutaka shauri, pengine kutolitaka; ghairighairi.

blubber, *n*. mafuta ya nyangumi na wanyama wengine wa bahari.

bludgeon, *n*. gongo, rungu, kibarango. — *v.t* piga kwa gongo (rungu &c.).

blue, *a. and n*. -a rangi ya samawati, kama majani ya bahari, samawati; buluu; (*dark blue*) nili; (*for washing*) buluu. *Blue blood*, damu ya ukoo ulio bora, ya kifalme. *The blues*, hali ya kuudhika, ya kuwa na moyo mzito. *To look blue*, kuudhika, kuwa na moyo mzito. **bluish**, *a*. -enye rangi kidogo ya buluu. **blue-jacket**, *n*. baharia wa manowari. **blue-peter**, *n*. kibendera cha mraba cha buluu chenye mraba mweupe katikati; hutwekwa melini kuonyesha kuwa meli i tayari kuondoka. **blue-stone**, *n*. mrututu.

bluff, *a*. -nyofu; (*surly*) -kali; (*steep*) -a kuinuka ghafula. — *n*. rasi, kilima, genge (ukingoni pa mto au bahari); madanganyo, ulaghai, ghiliba. — *v.t.* danganya, ghilibu, laghai.

blunder, *v.t.* sitasita, kosa; — *v.i.* fuja, buruga, chafua, purukusha. — *n*. kosa, fujo. **blunderer**, *n*. mburugaji wa kazi (au mambo).

blunderbuss, *n*. bunduki fupi yenye kasiba pana.

blunderer, *n*. taz. *blunder*.

blunt, *a*. -butu, dugi; (*plain spoken*) -nyofu, -a kusema waziwazi, -a kusema kweli mambo yalivyo bila kusifusifu. — *v.t.* fanya butu, seneza; punguza nguvu, ukali &c. *Be blunt*, senea. *This knife is blunt*, kisu hiki hakipati (kimesenea). *To blunt the appetite*, fisha tamaa. **bluntness**, *n*. ubutu, udugi; unyofu &c. **bluntly**, *adv*. waziwazi; bila kusifusifu wala kuficha udhaifu au uhafifu wa mambo yalivyo. **blunt-witted**, *a*. -jinga, -zito wa akili.

blur, *n*. waa, doa, unyenyezi. — *v.t.* tia waa, haribu; fanya hata si dhahiri (kama kiwi cha macho, au kiwaa juu ya maandiko &c.).

blurt (*out*), *v.t.* sema ghafula; sema yaliyopaswa kufichwa; payapaya, foka, boboka, bubujika (maneno).

blush, *v.i.* geuka rangi ya uso kwa haya, iva usoni, tahayari, fadhaika. *Put to blush*, fadhaisha, tahayarisha, ivisha uso, hizi, vunja uso. — *n*. rangi nyekundu ya uso (dalili ya fadhaa, haya, aibu); rangi nyekundu, *e.g.* ya ua, ya jua. *The blush of dawn,* ukungu mwekundu wa mapambazuko.

bluster, *v.i.* piga domo, jigamba, jivuna; pambanya, nena kwa kiburi (kwa ufidhuli), onea, ogofya kwa maneno makali. *A blustering wind,* upepo mkali. — *n.* maneno ya kiburi, ufidhuli, majivuno.

boa, *n.* chatu; (*for wearing*) vazi la shingoni la kike lililofanywa kwa manyoya *&c.*

boar, *n.* nguruwe dume.

board, *n.* ubao; (*council*) baraza, halmashauri; (*food*) chakula, riziki; (*table*) meza; (*stiff paper*) karatasi nene ngumu kama jalada ya kitabu. *On board,* merikebuni, melini, garini *&c.* *Take on board,* pakia. *Board and lodging,* chakula na malazi. *Above board,* wazi, dhahiri. *To go to the board,* potea, haribika, angamia. *Boarding-house,* nyumba ya wageni kukaa na kupikiwa. *Boarding-school,* chuo wanamolala na kula watoto. — *v.t.* funika kwa ubao; (*feed*) pikia, lisha, tolea riziki; (*enter ship, train &c.*) ingia, panda (merikebuni, melini, garini *&c.*). *To be boarded,* kupikiwa, kulishwa; (*by medical board*) kupimwa na daktari. **boarder,** *n.* apangaye chumba na kupewa chakula.

boast, *v.i.* jisifu, jiona, jibodoa, jigamba, takabari. — *n.* majivuno, majisifu,. **boaster,** *n.* mjisifu. **boastful,** *a.* -a kujisifu, -a kujivuna, -a makeke.

boat, *n.* mashua; (*ship*) merikebu, meli. — *v.i.* tembea mashuani, safiri mashuani. **boat-hook,** *n.* pondo yenye ncha ya chuma. *To be in the same boat,* kuwa na hali iliyo sawa. **boatswain,** *n.* serahangi.

bob, (1) *v.i.* rukaruka, ning'inia, tikisika; — *v.t.* (*cut short*) kata, fupisha. *Bob up,* zuka, ibuka. *Bob up and down,* tinga.

bob, (2) *n.* shilingi.

bobbin, *n.* kidonge cha uzi.

bobby, *n.* polisi.

bode, *v.t.* onya, onyesha mbele mambo yajayo; bashiri.

bodice, *n.* vazi la kike, kidogo kama fulana, sidiria, kanchiri.

bodily, *a.* taz. *body.*

bodkin, *n.* shazia, sindano kubwa yenye ncha butu.

body, *n.* mwili; (*trunk*) kiwiliwili (*corpse, human*) maiti, mfu; (*corpse, animal*) mzoga, pinda; (*person*) mtu; (*company*) jamii, shirika; (*of troops*) kikosi, kundi, jeshi; (*strength*) nguvu, uzito, ugumu; (*substance*) kitu; (*of wine*) nguvu, ukali. **body odour,** *n.* gugumu. *Heavenly body,* nyota, jua, mwezi. *Somebody,* mtu fulani, mtu. *Anybody,* mtu ye yote. **bodily,** *a.* -a mwili, -a mfano wa mwili. —*adv.* kwa jumla, kwa hali ilivyo. **body-guard,** *n.* kundi la askari walindao mfalme au mtu mwenye cheo kikubwa; kundi la wafuasi.

Boer, *n.* mzaliwa wa Afrika ya Kusini ambaye wazazi wake ni wenye asili ya nchi ya *Holland.*

bog, *n.* ziwa la matope, bwawa, kinamasi. *Be bogged,* topea. **boggy,** *a.* -a rojorojo, -a matope.

bogey, *n.* zimwi, kizuka, dubwana, bwedu.

boggle, *v.i.* sita.

boggy, *a.* taz. *bog.*

bogie, *n.* gari fupi (kwa kimo, si kwa marefu) lenye magurudumu mawili au zaidi lililofungiwa mbele chini ya gari la moshi au behewa ndefu.

bogus, *a.* -a uwongo.

bogy, *n.* taz. *bogey.*

boil, (1) *n.* jipu.

boil, (2) *v.t.* chemsha; (*food*) tokosa; (*water*) pika; — *v.i.* (*be boiling*) chemka; (*bubble*) tutuma; (*with excitement*) kasirika sana, shikwa na ghadhabu, fura kwa hasira, panda hamaki. *Be boiled,* tokota, tokoseka. *Boil over,* furika. *Boil down,* punguza kadiri ya kitu kwa kukichemsha; (*contents of letter &c.*) fupisha barua (maandiko), fanya muhtasari. **boiler,** *n.* chombo cha kupikia maji (ya kuendeshea mashine *&c.*). **boil-**

ing-point, *n.* joto la maji yaanzapo kuchemka.
boisterous, *a.* -a nguvu, -a tadi, -a jeuri, -enye makelele, -a kuchafuka.
bold, *a.* jasiri, -shujaa, -gumu, -enye moto, -thabiti; (*dangerous*) -a hatari; (*forward*) -tundu, -tukutu, -shupavu, -jeuri, -enye macho makavu. *Make bold*, thubutu. **bold-faced**, *a.* -enye macho makavu, -shupavu, -juvi. **boldly**, *adv.* kwa uthabiti, kwa ujasiri *&c.* **boldness**, *n.* uhodari, ujasiri, ujuvi, ushupavu, ukavu wa macho, ufidhuli.
bole, *n.* shina la mti, yaani sehemu iliyo kati ya mizizi na matawi.
boll, *n.* kitumba, kama cha pamba. *Boll worm, Boll weevil*, namna ya funza waharibuo vitumba vya pamba.
bolster, *n.* mto mrefu wa kulazia kichwa; kitegemezo, egemeo. — *v.t.* tegemeza, kaza kwa egemeo, gadimu, imarisha.
bolt, *n.* komeo, kia; (*lightning*) umeme; (*missile*) mshale, risasi; (*screw*) msumari, parafujo, skrubu. — *v.t.* komea, funga, kaza; (*swallow*) meza, -la kwa pupa; — *v.i.* (*out of*) toka, mbio, kimbia, toroka. *Bolt-upright*, wima kabisa.
bomb, *n.* kombora. **bombard**, *v.t.* piga mizinga, vunja kwa mizinga, tupia makombora. *Bombard with questions*, hoji sana. **bombardment**, *n.* shambulio la mizinga. **bombshell**, *n.* kiasi cha kombora. *Like a bombshell*, ghafula mno, la kushangaza sana.
bombast, *n.* maneno makuu, majivuno, makeke. **bombastic**, *a.* -a majivuno, -a maneno makuu, -a makeke.
Bombay dick, *n.* bumbura.
bombshell, *n.* taz. *bomb.*
bona fide, *a. and adv.* (kwa) kweli, halisi.
bonanza, *n.* bahati njema sana.
bonbon, *n.* peremende.
bond, *n.* fungo, kifungo; cho chote kifungacho (*e.g.* kamba, minyororo, pingu *&c.*); (*written*) sharti, hati, mkataba; (*surety*) dhamana. — *v.t.* weka bidhaa *&c.* zinazoingia katika nchi katika ghala ya serikali mpaka ushuru ulipwe. **bondage**, *n.* hali ya kufungwa; utumwa. **bondsman**, *n.* mtumwa.
bone, *n.* mfupa, fupa; (*of fish*) mwiba wa samaki. *A bone of contention*, kisa cha ugomvi. *Have a bone to pick with*, -wa na neno (shauri) na. *To make no bones of*, toogopa, tosita, tojizuia. **bone-dry**, *a.* -kavu kabisa. **bony**, *a.* -enye mifupa mingi -gofu.
bonfire, *n.* moto mkubwa wa sherehe ya jambo fulani.
bonhomie, *n.* ukunjufu, uchangamfu.
bonnet, *n.* namna ya kofia; funiko la mbele la motakaa la kufunika mashine.
bonny, *a.* -zuri.
bonus, *n.* bakshishi, zawadi, ziada.
bony, *a.* taz. *bone.*
booby, *n.* mjinga, mpumbavu, baradhuli.
book, *n.* kitabu, msahafu, chuo; (*account*) daftari. *Bring to book*, taka hesabu, shtaki, pasisha adhabu kwa kosa. *Take a leaf out of another's book*, fuata mfano wa mtu mwingine. — *v.t.* andika katika daftari. **bookcase**, *n.* kabati ya kuwekea vitabu. **bookish**, *a.* -a kupenda kusoma vitabu, -a kujua maarifa tu yatokayo vitabuni. **book-keeping**, *n.* kazi ya kuandika hesabu (ya mali, fedha *&c.*), ukarani wa hesabu. **book-learning**, *n.* maarifa yapatikanayo katika vitabu (si kwa kuona au kutenda mambo). **booklet**, *n.* kitabu kidogo. **book-mark**, *n.* kipande cha kuweka katika kitabu kuonyesha ukurasa uliofikiwa katika kusoma. **book-worm**, *n.* (*insect*) siridado, mdudu alaye karatasi za vitabu; (*person*) mtu apendaye sana kusoma.
boom, (1) *v.t.* nguruma, vuma; (*commerce*) sitawi ghafula; — *v.t.* (*advertise*) tangaza. — *n.* uvumi, mshindo, ngurumo; (*in commerce*)

usitawi au nafuu ya ghafula (kwa ajili ya bidhaa *&c.* kuvumishwa).
boom, (2) *n.* (*of ship*) foromali ndogo; (*obstruction*) borit., magogo *&c.* katika mlango wa mto kuzuia vyombo visiingie.
boomerang, *n.* gongo lililopindika ambalo likitupwa hurudi lenyewe; (*action which recoils*) rada, marejeo.
boon, (1) *n.* fadhili, baraka, tajamala, haja, nafuu, faida, kifaa, manufaa.
boon, (2) *a. Boon companion*, mwenzi mkunjufu (mwema), mwandani.
boor, *n.* mshenzi, msungo, mtu wa kimashamba, chepe, mtu asiyejua desturi, asiye na adabu. **boorish,** *a.* -a kimashamba *&c.*
boot, (1) *n.* kiatu (kikubwa cha kizungu). — *v.t.* vaa viatu; piga teke. **bootlace,** *n.* gidamu, kamba ya kufungia viatu. *Have one's heart in one's boots*, ogopa mno.
boot, (2) *v.t.* faidi. — *n.* nafuu, faida. **bootless,** *a.* -a bure, bila faida. *To boot*, zaidi.
booth, *n.* kibanda.
bootlace, *n.* taz. *boot* (1).
bootless, *a.* taz. *boot* (2).
booty, *n.* mateka, nyara.
booze, *v.t. and i.* -nywa sana ulevi. — *n.* ulevi.
boracic acid, *n.* dawa nyeupe ya kutia vidondani; pia hutumika ili kufanya maziwa yasioze. **borax,** *n.* namna ya dawa itumikayo katika kazi ya kulehemu na katika dawa nyinginezo.
border, *n.* mpaka, ukingo; (*of cloth*) pindo; (*woven*) tarazo. — *v.t.* (*on*) tangamana (na), pakana (na), karibia; (*resemble*) fanana na, landa, -wa kama, karibiana na.
bore, (1) *p.t.* ya *bear*.
bore, (2) *v.t.* zua, toboa, pekecha; (*annoy*) sumbua, pekecha, chokoza, udhi, kera; (*of insects*) bungua; (*ears, nose, for ornament*) toga, dunga. — *n.* (*calibre*) kipimo cha duara ya kitundu cha mtutu wa bunduki, mzinga *&c.*; (*tidal wave*) wimbi kubwa mtoni; (*troublesome person*) mchoshi, mchokozi, mwudhi; (*of a child*) mtundu, mtukutu; (*troublesome thing*) kero, sumbuo, pekecho, kichokozi. **boredom,** *n.* uchovu. **boring,** *n.* tendo la kuzua (la kutoboa, la kupekecha *&c.*); tundu lililotobolewa *&c. Borings*, chembechembe zitokazo katika tundu linalotobolewa.
boric, *n.* sawasawa na *boracic.*
boring, *n.* taz. *bore* (2).
born (*be*), *v.* zaliwa.
borne (*be*) *p.t.* ya *bear*.
borough, *n.* mji, watu wa mji.
borrow, *v.t.* azima, kopa; (*receive*) pokea; (*imitate*) iga, fuatisha. **borrowed,** *a.* -lioazimwa; (*assumed*) -a kuiga, -a kujipa, -a wengine, -a uwongo. **borrower,** *n.* mkopi.
bosh, *n.* upuzi, maneno hafifu. — *int.* Mawe! Upuzi!
bosom, *n.* kifua, moyo. *A bosom friend*, msiri, sahibu. *Abraham's bosom*, ahera, peponi. *To take to one's bosom*, fanya msiri, pendelea.
boss, (1) *n.* nundu, kama kinundu; pambo (la ukutani, mlangoni *&c.*) lililoinuka, la vinundu.
boss, (2) *n.* (*master*) bwana, msimamizi, mwenyewe. — *v.t.* (*control*) tawala (amuru, simamia, ongoza) hasa kwa nguvu ya kujipa.
botanic, *a.* -a kuhusu miti na mimea. **botanist,** *n.* mwenye elimu ya *botany*. **botany,** *n.* elimu ya miti na mimea.
botch, *n.* uvimbe ngozini; kazi iliyoharibika, fujo, upurukushani. — *v.t.* tengeneza ovyo, haribu kazi, buruga, purukusha.
both, *a.* -ote -wili (mbili). — *conj.* na. *Both that and that*, hii na hii.
bother, *n.* udhia, taabu, huja, kisirani, matata. — *v.t.* sumbua, udhi, chokoza, kera; — *v.i.* hangaika, ona wasiwasi, jikalifu. *Don't bother yourself*, haidhuru, usijikalifu. **botheration,** *n.* sawasawa na *bother*. **bothersome,** *a.* -enye udhia, -a kuchokoza, -chokozi, -a kuudhi.
bottle, *n.* chupa; (*of skin*) kiriba;

(*water cooler*) rishai, gudulia. — *v.t.* tia katika chupa; (*anger &c.*) ficha, weza, zuia.

bottom, *n.* chini, upande wa chini, sehemu ya chini; (*basis, beginning*) msingi, mwanzo, asili; (*bottom part, piece*) tako. *At bottom,* hasa, kwa kweli. *Bottom, Get to the bottom* (*of*), fika chini (ya); (*sift*) hakiki, fahamu kabisa. *Be at the bottom of,* -wa asili (mwanzo, sababu) ya. *Bottom upwards,* kifudifudi. **bottomless,** *a.* -a kwenda chini sana (kama kwamba hakuna kitu kizuiacho chini). *The bottomless pit,* Jehannum.

bou-bou, *n.* (*Zanzibar*) tiva.

boudoir, *n.* chumba cha bibi.

bough, *n.* tawi, kitawi, utanzu.

bought, *p.t. and pf.t.* ya *buy.*

bouillon, *n.* mchuzi.

boulder, *n.* mwamba, jiwe kubwa la mviringo, jabali.

boulevard, *n.* njia pana ya kutembelea (yenye safu ya miti ukingoni).

bounce, *v.i.* ruka (kama mpira), duta; — *v.t.* (*bluff*) laghai, ghilibu. — *n.* pigo la ghafula, mruko; majivuno, makeke. **bouncing,** *a.* -kubwa, -zito, -enye nguvu na afya.

bound, (1) *p.t. and pf.t.* ya *bind. I am bound* (*to go*), lazima ni-(ende) sina budi (kwenda), imenibidi. *The ship is bound for Bombay,* meli inakwenda Bombay. *The book is bound,* kitabu kimetiwa jalada. *He is bound to go,* lazima atakwenda, sharti aende. *The affair is bound up in this one,* jambo hili limefungamana na hili.

bound, (2) *v.i.* ruka. — *n.* mruko. *By leaps and bounds,* kwa mbio sana, upesi sana.

bound, (3) *v.t.* (*surround*) zunguka, -wa pande zote; (*set bounds to*) weka mipaka; (*restrain*) zuia. *Be bounded by,* pakana na, -wa na mpaka. *It is bounded by,* mpaka wake ni, imezungukwa na, imepakana na. — *n.* (*limit*) mpaka, kiasi; (*farthest point*) upeo, kikomo, mwisho. *Break bound,* ruka mpaka, pita kiasi. **boundary,** *n.* mpaka. **bounder,** *n.* mtu asiye na adabu, jeuri, mkorofi. **boundless** *a.* -siyo na mpaka (mwisho, kiasi); -kubwa mno, -ingi sana.

bounden, *a.* taz. *bind.*

bounty, *n.* ukarimu, upaji, baraka; (*gift*) zawadi, zaka; (*premium*) bakshishi, ziada. **bounteous,** *a.* -paji, -karimu, -ingi. **bounteously,** *adv.* kwa ukarimu, kwa wingi. **bountiful,** *a.* sawasawa na *bounteous.* **bountifully,** *adv.* sawasawa na *bounteously.*

bouquet, *n.* shada la maua; (*scent*) harufu, nukato.

bout, *n.* zamu, jaribio, shindano; kipindi, mfululizo; (*drinking bout*) mfululizo wa (kipindi cha) kulewa.

bovine, *a.* -a kuhusu ng'ombe; -a kama ng'ombe.

bow, (1) *v.i.* (*bend down*) inama, yonga; (*greet*) salimu, amkia (kwa kuinama); (*give way to, accept*) tii, kubali; — *v.t.* inamisha; (*subdue*) tiisha; (*worship*) sujudu. *To bow to the inevitable,* shukuru. — *n.* (*gesture of respect*) salamu (ya kuinamia), jiinamizi, inamo la kichwa. *Make a bow to,* inamia kichwa.

bow, (2) *n.* (*archer's*) upindi; (*with arrows*) uta; (*of ribbon*) fundo; (*rainbow*) upindi wa mvua. **bow-legged,** *a.* -enye matege. **bow-string,** *n.* upote. *To draw the long bow,* piga chuku. **bow window,** *n.* dirisha linalotokeza.

bow, (3) *n.* (*of ship*) gubeti, omo.

bowels, *n.* matumbo; (*innermost part*) moyo, batini; (*compassion*) huruma.

bower, *n.* chumba cha bibi; mahali pazuri katika bustani; kibanda cha anasa shambani.

bowl, (1) *n.* bakuli; (*of wood*) fua, chano, hero; (*of pipe*) bori. **bowler,** *n.* (*hat*) namna ya kofia.

bowl, (2) *v.t.* fingirisha; tupa mpira (wa *cricket*); — *v.i.* fingirika. *Bowl along,* enda mbio (kama kwa magurudumu). *To bowl over,* angusha, pindua, fadhaisha. **bowls,** *n.* mchezo wa kufingirisha matufe chini.

bow-legged, *a.* taz. *bow* (2).

bowler, *n.* (*hat*) taz. *bowl* (1).

bowsprit, *n.* mlingoti wa maji, dasturi.

bowstring, *n.*, **bow window,** *n.* taz. *bow* (2).

box, (1) *n.* kasha, bweta, sanduku; (*small metal*) kijaluba; (*small paper*) kibumba; (*seat*) kiti cha mwendeshi katika gari; (*wood*) namna ya mti mweupe mgumu. *Christmas box,* ada ya sikukuu ya *Christmas.*

box, (2) *v.t.* (*the ears*) piga makofi; (*fight with fists*) pigana ngumi. *Box on the ear,* piga kofi. **boxer,** *n.* mstadi wa kupigana ngumi.

boy, *n.* mtoto mwanamume, kivulana, kijana mwanamume; (*servant*) boi, mtumishi. **boyhood,** *n.* utoto, ujana. **boyish,** *a.* -a mtoto mwanamume. *Boy scout,* mwana wa chama fulani cha vijana.

boycott, *v.t.* tengea mbali kabisa; katazia maongezi yo yote; harimisha au katazia ununuzi wa bidhaa *&c.*

boyhood, *n.*, **boyish,** *a.* taz. *boy.*

brace, *n.* kitu cha kufungia au kukazia; (*clamp*) gango; (*brace and bit*) kekee; (*suspender*) ukanda; (*pair*) jozi. — *v t.* burudisha, tia nguvu, kaza, kita, tegemeza. **bracing,** *a.* -a kuburudisha, -a kutia nguvu.

bracelet, *n.* (*round*) kikuku, uzinge; (*with points*) bangili; (*flat*) kekee; (*of beads*) kingaja; (*handcuffs*) pingu.

bracken, *n.* mjimbi.

bracket, *n.* kipande cha kutegemea, kitegemeo, kiweko; (*for lamps*) mwango, kiango; (*in printing*) alama hii ( ), kifungo. —*v.t.* tegemeza kwa *bracket*; tia kifungoni, panga maneno katika alama hii ( ) ; panga maneno au majina pamoja kuonyesha kuwa cheo chake ni kimoja.

brackish, *a.* -a chumvi kidogo.

brad, *n.* msumari mwembamba wenye kichwa kidogo.

bradawl, *n.* maharasi.

brag, *v.i.* jigamba, jivuna, jisifu. — *n.* majivuno, majisifu, makeke.

braggart, *n.* mjigamba, mjisifu, chepe.

braid, *n.* kigwe, utepe, almaria; (*of silver or gold*) zari; (*of hair*) msongo. — *v.t.* sokota, suka. **braiding,** *n.* (*of hair*) msuko, msongo.

braille, *n.* namna ya chapa za kutokeza ziwezazo kusomwa na vipofu kwa kuzipapasa na vidole vyao.

brain, *n.* ubongo wa kichwani; (*sense*) akili. *Use the brain,* tumia akili. — *v.t.* vunja kichwa na kumwaga ubongo. **brain-fag,** *n.* uchovu wa ubongo (wa akili).

brainless, *a.* -pumbavu, -asiye na akili, baradhuli. **brain-pan,** *n.* fuvu la kichwa. **brain-wave,** *n.* wazo la ghafula la kufaa katika shida, shauri *&c.* **brainy,** *a.* -enye akili.

braise, *v.t.* pika nyama katika chungu kilichofunikwa.

brake, (1) *n.* kichaka.

brake, (2) *n.* (*carriage*) namna ya gari kubwa; (*of vehicle*) kizuizo, kipande cha kuzuia magurudumu yasiende, au kupunguza mbio zake.

bramble, *n.* mimea yenye miiba kama mchongoma, mkwamba *&c.*

bran, *n.* makapi ya nafaka, kumvi, wishwa.

branch, *n.* tawi, utanzu; (*part*) sehemu; (*branch roads*) njia panda; (*of river, creek*) mkono wa mto au bahari, hori. — *v.i.* gawika; fanya panda. *Branch off,* enda upande, jitenga. *Branch out,* enea (kama matawi *&c.*), ongeza. **branching,** *a.* -enye matawi, -enye kuenea kama matawi, -enye mikono.

brand, *n.* (*firebrand*) kinga; (*stamp*) alama, chapa (ya chuma yenye moto *&c.*); (*sort*) aina, namna; (*mark o disgrace*) alama ya aibu. — *v.t.* tia alama (chapa *&c.* kwa chuma chenye moto *&c.*); (*disgrace*) tia alama ya aibu, aibisha. **brandish,** *v.t.* punga (*e.g.* kinga cha moto, upanga, silaha *&c.*). **brand-new,** *a.* -pya kabisa.

brandy, *n.* namna ya mvinyo kali ifanyizwayo kwa zabibu.
brass, *n.* shaba nyeupe, yaani shaba nyekundu iliyochanganyika na *zinc*; (*money*) senti, fedha za kutumia, fulusi; (*impudence*) ujuvi, ufidhuli, ushupavu, ukavu wa macho, usafihi. **brass,** *a.* -a shaba. **brass-band,** *n.* jamii ya wapigaji tarumbeta.
brassiere, *n.* sidiria, kanchiri.
brat, *n.* jina la dharau la mtoto, mtundu, mtukutu.
bravado, *n.* majisifu, tendo la ushujaa (la ushupavu, la fahari, la ujasiri). **brave,** *a.* -shujaa, hodari, -gumu, thabiti, -shupavu, -jasiri, -juba. — *n.* shujaa, jabari. — *v.t.* endea kwa uhodari (kwa uthabiti &c.); (*be brave*) -wa hodari &c.; vumilia, stahimili. **bravery,** *n.* ushujaa, uthabiti, ugumu, ujasiri &c. **bravo,** *int.* vyema sana!
brawl, *n.* ugomvi wa kelele (wa ghasia). — *v.i.* gombana kwa kelele (kwa ghasia). **brawler,** *n.* mgomvi.
brawn, *n.* nguvu ya mwili, unene; (*preserved meat*) nyama (hasa ya nguruwe) iliyopikwa na kukolea viungo. **brawny,** *a.* -enye nguvu ya mwili, -nene, -shupavu, kakawana.
bray, (1) *v.i.* lia kama punda. **bray,** *n.* mlio (kama wa punda).
bray, (2) *v.t.* vunjavunja, ponda, twanga, funda, saga.
braze, *v.t.* lehemu kwa shaba iliyochanganyika na *zinc*. **brazen,** *a.* -a shaba nyeupe; (*shameless*) -kavu wa macho, -juvi, bila haya, -pujufu. **brazen** *v.t.* (*out*) endea kwa ufidhuli (ujuvi, ushupavu). **brazenly,** *adv.* kwa ushupavu &c. **brazier,** *n.* fundi afanyizaye vitu vya shaba; seredani, samawari, chombo cha kuwekea makaa ya moto, maziga.
breach, *n.* tundu (kama katika ukuta au boma palipobomoka); (*of law*) uhalifu, uasi (wa sheria); (*of promise*) mvunjo wa ahadi (hasa ya kuoa); (*of peace*) ugomvi, ghasia, pigano, lo lote livunjalo amani ya mahali. **breach,** *v.t.* tomoa, vunja.
bread, *n.* mkate (wa ngano); (*of European make*) mkate wa bofulo; (*food*) chakula, riziki; (*livelihood*) uchumi, maishilio. *Bread-crumbs,* chenga za mkate. *Bread-fruit-tree,* mfenesi wa kizungu, mshelisheli.
breadth, *n.* upana, mapana. *He has breadth of vision,* hupima mambo na matokeo yake pia, hufikiri sana kwa maarifa.
break, *v.t.* (*p.t.* **broke,** *pf.t.* **broken**) vunja, pasua, banja, haribu; (*news*) bashiri, arifu; eleza (hasa jambo kubwa); (*law*) halifu, asi, vunja sheria; (*weaken*) punguza nguvu ya; (*tame, train*) fuga; (*break spirit*) vunja moyo, tiisha; (*make bankrupt*) filisi; (*degrade*) vunja cheo, heshima &c.; (*break down*) angusha, shinda; (*humble*) dhili; (*door, wall &c.*) bomoa, bomosha; (*cause to give way*) angamiza, komesha, shinda, legeza; (*break off*) komesha ghafula, kata, vunja, mega; (*of flowers, twigs &c.*) kwanua, kwanyua, konyoa, kongonyoa, monyoa, goboa, chuma; (*in speaking*) katiza maneno; (*separate*) bagua, tenga; (*break in*) vunja, jitia, ingia kwa nguvu, jidukiza, komesha; (*break ground*) lima; (*floor, concrete &c.*) wekua; (*break with friends &c.*) vunjia urafiki, si andamana na; (*break back of*) maliza sehemu iliyo ngumu au kubwa, shinda; (*break wind*) jamba, shuta; (*break charm*) zingua, sukumiza uchawi, tegua; (*break the ice*) anzisha maneno (juu ya jambo kubwa); — *v.i.* vunjika, pasuka, haribika, bomoka &c.; (*abcess*) tumbuka; (*bank*) filisika; (*dawn*) pambazuka; (*break loose*) toka, jitoa kwa nguvu ruka mpaka; (*break out*) toka kwa nguvu, tokea, onekana; (*of water &c.*) bubujika, foka; (*smoke*) fuka, foka; (*fire*) lipuka; (*of sun*) chomoza; (*anger*) waka; (*disperse*) tawanyika, fumukana; (*grow weak*) legea, fifia, haribika; (*voice, gait*) geuka; (*break down*) vunjikavunjika; (*of door, wall &c.*) bomoka; (*give way*) angamia,

koma, shindwa, legea, poromoka; (*break up*) vunjika, angamia; (*break cover*) toka vichakani, tokea, onekana. — *n.* mvunjo, mpasuo, vunjiko, pasuko; (*cessation, stop*) kikomo; (*space*) peupe, nafasi. *Break of day*, mapambazuko. **breakable**, *a.* -a kuvunjika kwa urahisi. — *n.* kitu kinachovunjika kwa urahisi kama sahani, kikombe, &c. **breakage**, *n.* mvunjo, mvunjiko. **breakdown**, *n.* tukio linalofanya gari (motakaa &c.) lisiweze kwenda; ugonjwa mkali wa mwili au akili. **breakfast**, *n.* chamshakinywa, chakula cha asubuhi, kifungua kinywa. **breaker**, *n.* wimbi lenye povu (livunjikalo mwambani au pwani), wimbi la kuumuka. **breakwater**, *n.* boma la kuzuia mawimbi, boma majini.

bream, *n.* namna ya samaki.

breast, *n.* kifua; (*woman's*) maziwa, dodo; (*animal's*) kidari, moyo. *To make a clean breast of*, ungama yote pia. — *v.t.* egemeza kifua; shindana kwa uhodari, panda. **breast-bone**, *n.* mfupa wa katikati ya kifua zinapoungana mbavu; (*of animal*) kidari.

breath, *n.* pumzi, roho, nafsi; (*instant*) dakika moja, kufumba na kufumbua; (*trifle*) kitu kidogo. *A single breath*, upumzi mmoja. *Take away the breath*, pagaza, shtusha, shangaza. *Under the breath*, kwa kunong'ona, kwa hofu, polepole. *A breath of wind*, upepo kidogo. *Speak with bated breath*, sema kwa sauti ndogo kwa ajili ya hofu (kicho &c.). **breathe**, *v.i.* vuta pumzi, pumua, pumzika, tanafusi; (*live*) ishi; — *v.t.* (*reveal*) toa, onya. *Breathe again*, ondokewa na shida, toka katika taabu &c. *Breathe freely*, -wa na raha (baada ya dhiki, shida &c.). *Breathe hard* kokota roho, tweta, korota, koroma. *Breathe one's last*, kata roho, -fa, fariki. **breather**, *n.* kipumziko, kituo. **breathless**, *a.* -a kutwetatweta; (*precipitate*) -a kukata pumzi, -a haraka, -a kusninda roho.

bred, *p.t. and pf.t.* ya *breed*. **well-bred**, *a.* -liolelewa vyema, -adilifu, -a mbegu njema. **ill-bred, low-bred**, *a.* -nyonge, bila adabu, -baya.

breech, *n.* tako, nyuma. *To load by the breech*, shindilia kwa nyuma. *Breech-loader*, bunduki ya viasi (ya kuvunja, ya korotindo). **breeches**, *n.* suruali.

breed, *v.t.* (*p.t. and pf.t.* **bred**) zaa, zalisha, chunga, anzisha, fuga, lea; — *v.i.* zaa, ongezeka, zaliana. — *n.* zao (cho chote kilichozaliwa); namna, jinsi, mbegu. **breeder**, *n.* mzaa, mfuga, mchunga. **breeding**, *n.* uzazi; ufugo; (*education &c.*) malezi, malezi mema; (*manners*) mwendo, adabu. *A breeding fowl* (*goat &c.*), koo la kuku (mbuzi &c.).

breeze, *n.* (*wind*) upepo; baridi; (*quarrel*) ugomvi; (*rumour*) mnong'ono. **breezy**, *a.* -a upepo, -epesi, -changamfu.

brethren, *n.pl.* ya *brother*.

brevity, *n.* ufupi; (*of speech*) uchache wa maneno.

brew, *v.t.* pika pombe &c.; (*devise*) waza, fikiri, tunga (shauri la hila). **brewer**, *n.* mfanya pombe. **brewery**, *n.* mahali pa kupikia pombe.

briar, *n.* namna ya mti kama mchongoma, mbigili, miiba.

bribe, *n.* rushwa, mlungula, chichiri, hongo, kiinikizo, kitu cha kuvuta mtu kurusha haki &c. *Take bribes*, -la rushwa. — *v.t.* penyeza fedha, -pa rushwa, lisha rushwa, honga, inikiza, vuta kwa fedha au kitu kingine. **bribery**, *n.* upenyezi, rushwa.

bricabrac, *n.* vitu vya kale vya thamani, vitu vyo vyote vya thamani (vya tunu, vya kupamba), vitakataka.

brick, *n.* tofali. — *v.t.* ziba kwa matofali. — *a.* -a matofali. **brickbat**, *n.* kipande cha tofali. **brickkiln**, *n.* tanuu ya kuchomea matofali. **bricklayer**, *n.* mwashi aakaye kwa matofali.

bridal, *n.* arusi. — *a.* -a arusi. **bride**, *n.* bibi arusi. **bridegroom**, *n.* bwana arusi.

bridge, (1) *n.* daraja, kantara, tinge-tinge; (*tree or beam*) mtatago, ulalo; (*of ship*) mahali wakaapo maafisa wanaoangalia habari za meli. — *v.t.* vusha daraja, jenga daraja; faulu (katika shida).

bridge, (2) *n.* mchezo mmojawapo wa karata.

bridle, *n.* (*reins*) hatamu, ugwe, kigwe (cha kuongoza punda, farasi &c.); (*bit*) lijamu; (*gesture of pride &c.*) tendo la kutakabari (la kujiona hamaki. — *v.t.* zuia; — *v.i.* (*of persons*) kasirika, takabari, hamaki, panda hamaki.

brief, *n.* -fupi, -a maneno machache, -a kuendelea muda mfupi tu, -a kupita upesi. — *n.* (*lawyers*) muhtasari ya habari za daawa. *Hold a brief for*, tetea, daia. **briefly**, *adv.* kwa ufupi, kwa maneno machache. *In brief*, kwa ufupi (kama *briefly*). **briefness**, *n.* ufupi, uchache (wa maneno, wakati &c.).

brier, *n.* taz. *briar*.

brig, *n.* namna ya merikebu ya matanga yenye milingoti miwili.

brigade, *n.* sehemu ya jeshi la askari kadiri ya 5,000; kundi, kikosi. **brigadier**, *n.* amiri wa *brigade*.

brigand, *n.* mnyang'anyi, haramia. **brigandage**, *n.* unyang'anyi, jeuri.

bright, *a.* -enye kung'aa, -angavu, -eupe, safi; (*joyful*) -a furaha, -kunjufu, marini, -chekelevu, -chezi, -changamfu; (*intelligent*) -a -akili, -angavu, -elekevu. **brighten**, *v.t.* ng'ariza, takasa (*cheer*) furahisha, changamsha, teremesha; (*polish*) katua; — *v.i.* (*of weather*) anuka, takata; (*improve*) geuka -zuri, -fanikia; (*of looks*) kunjuka, changamka. **brightly**, *adv.* kwa kung'aa, kwa wepesi, kwa furaha &c. **brightness**, *n.* ukunjufu, mng'aro, wangavu; (*of weather, after cloudiness*) kichea, ucheachea.

Bright's disease, *n.* ugonjwa wa mafigo.

brilliant, *a.* -a kung'aa, -a kumeta-meta; (*glorious*) -zuri, -tukufu, adhimu. — *n.* almasi, kito. **brilliance, brilliancy**, *n.* mng'ao, wangavu, ung'avu, weupe, uzuri, adhama, utukufu. **brilliantly**, *adv.* kwa kung'aa, kwa weupe &c.; kwa busara nyingi, kwa ustadi (akili) nyingi.

brim, *n.* (*river &c.*) ukingo; (*of vessel*) mdomo, juu; (*of hat*) ukingo. — *v.i.* jaa mpaka juu. *Up to the brim*, -a kujaa sana, -a kufurika, furifuri, farafara. **brimful**, *a.* -a kujaa mpaka ukingo (mpaka juu). **brimming**, *a.* -a kujaa sana, furi-furi, farafara.

brimstone, *n.* kiberiti.

brindled, *a.* -enye madoa, enye mabaka, -enye milia.

brine, *n.* maji ya chumvi; bahari. **briny**, *a.* -a kuhusu bahari, -a chumvi.

bring, *v.t.* (*p.t. and pf.t.* **brought**) leta; (*induce*) shawishi, vuta, ongoza. *Bring about, or bring to pass*, fanyiza, timiza, amili. *Bring an action against*, shtaki, dai. *Bring down*, shusha, dhili, tweza. *Bring forth*, zaa; leta. *Bring forward*, toa, onya. *Bring home*, thibitisha, dhihirisha, eleza wazi. *Bring in*, anzisha, (*of income*) leta faida. *Bring into play or action*, tendesha kazi, endesha, tumia. *Bring on*, anzisha; endesha, kuza. *Bring over*, geuza moyo, shawishi. *Bring around* (*revive*), fufua, huisha, amsha, ponya; (*persuade*) shawishi. *Bring to bear*, tumia, peleka. *Bring under*, tiisha. *Bring up* (*educate &c.*) lea; (*vomit*) tapika; (*stop*) simamisha.

brink, *n.* ukingo. *To be on the brink of*, kuwa karibu ya.

briny, *a.* taz. *brine*.

brisk, *a.* -epesi, -tendaji. — *v.t.* amsha, burudisha, tia nguvu, changamsha; — *v.i.* amka, changamka. **briskness**, *n.* wepesi.

brisket, *n.* nyama va kidari ya ng'ombe.

bristle, *n.* unywele mfupi mgumu. — *v.t.* simamisha nywele (kwa hofu au kuogofywa); tia maogofyo (hasira, kiburi *&c.*); — *v.i.* kasirika, panda hamaki. *Set up one's bristles,* kasirika, panda hamaki.

Britannic, British, *a.* -a Uingereza, -a kiingereza.

brittle, *a.* dhaifu, -epesi kuvunjika (kama chungu *&c.*).

broach, *v.t.* zibua (pipa); (*begin*) anza, anzisha; (*mention*) taja.

broad, *a.* -pana; (*plain*) wazi; (*vulgar*) -sio na adabu; (*comprehensive*) -a akili, -a maarifa mengi, -a kufaa wote. *Broad daylight,* mchana. **broadcast,** *v.t.* eneza, tawanya. — *a.* -liotawanyika kila mahali, lioenezwa kote kote. **broadcloth,** *n.* namna ya nguo kama joho. **broaden,** *v.t.* panua; — *v.i.* panuka. **broadness,** *n.* upana, mapana. **broadside,** *n.* ubavu wa meli; mizinga yote ya upande mmoja wa manowari; tendo la kupiga mizinga yote ya upande mmoja wa manowari.

brocade, *n.* zari, jamdani, kitambaa cha hariri iliyotiwa nakshi au zari. **brocaded,** *a.* -a zari (kitambaa), -liotiwa nakshi au zari.

brochure, *n.* kitabu kidogo.

brogue, *n.* (*shoe*) namna ya kiatu kizito; (*accent*) namna ya matamko, hasa watu wa nchi ya *Ireland* watamkavyo Kiingereza.

broil, (1) *v.t.* (*grill*) kaanga; — *v.i.* (*be hot*) -wa na joto jingi.

broil, (2) *n.* ugomvi wenye kelele; ghasia, mzozo. **broiler,** *n.* mgomvi.

broke, *p.t.* ya *break.*

broken, *pf.t.* ya *break.* — *a.* -liovunjika; liokatika; (*humbled, crushed*) -nyonge, dhaifu, halifu; (*dispersed, routed*) -lioshindwa, -lioangamia; (*bankrupt*) -liofilisika; (*rough*) si sawa, -sio laini, -a kukwaruza, -a kuparuza. *Broken down,* -dhofu, dhaifu, goigoi, -liochakaa. *Broken-hearted,* -enye huzuni nyingi. *He speaks broken English,* hajui vyema Kiingereza, agoteza maneno.

broker, *n.* wakili, dalali. **brokerage,** *n.* kazi ya *broker,* faida au ushuru wa *broker.*

bromide, *n.* namna ya dawa ya kutuliza.

bronchial, *a.* -a kuhusu umio wa pumzi. **bronchitis,** *n.* (ugonjwa wa) kifua, mkamba.

bronze, *n.* shaba nyeusi (shaba nyekundu iliyochanganyika na bati); rangi ya shaba nyeusi. — *a.* -a shaba nyeusi; -enye rangi ya *bronze.*

brooch, *n.* kifungo, bizimu.

brood, *n.* mazao; (*of birds*) makinda; jumla ya makinda walioanguliwa pamoja; (*children*) watoto; (*collection*) jamii, wingi. — *v.i.* (*over*) (*of birds*) atamia; (*meditate on*) fikiri, tafakari; (*sit and brood*) shika tama.

brook, (1) *n.* kijito.

brook, (2) *v.t.* vumilia, stahimili.

broom, *n.* ufagio.

broth, *n.* mchuzi wa nyama na mboga.

brothel, *n.* nyumba ya makahaba (ya malaya), danguro.

brother, *n.* (*pl.* **brothers and brethren**) ndugu mume, ndugu (wa tumbo moja), ahi; (*one of like condition*) mwenzi, mwenye hali moja. **brotherhood,** *n.* udugu, umoja wa watu. **brother-in-law,** *n.* shemeji, mlamu, mwamu. **foster-brother,** *n.* ndugu wa kunyonya. **husband's brother,** *n.* mwamu. **wife's brother,** *n.* wifi. **brotherly,** *a.* -a kama ndugu, -a kidugu. *Half-brother,* ndugu mama mmoja baba mbalimbali (au baba mmoja na mama mbalimbali).

brought, *p.t. and pf.t.* ya *bring.*

brow, *n.* paji la uso, kipaji, kikomo cha uso; (*of hill*) ukingo (wa kilima). *Knit the brows,* kunja kipaji, kunja uso. **browbeat,** *v.t.* pambanya, onea, ogofya, dhulumu.

brown, *n. and a.* rangi kama ya majani makavu (ya kunde), nyekundu nyeusi; hudhurungi. *Brown paper,* karatasi nyeusi kidogo ya kufungia vitu. *Brown study,* hali ya kufikiri sana hata kusahau vingine. **brown,** *v.t.* tia rangi ya *brown;* — *v.i.* geuka rangi ya *brown.*

browse, *v.i.* jilisha, lisha, tafuna majani; (*read in a desultory way*) soma bila kuangalia sana habari ya masomo.

bruin, *n.* dubu.

bruise, *v.t.* chubua, babua; (*by crushing*) ponda, funda, twanga, fyanda; (*by grinding*) saga; — *v.i.* chubuka, babuka. *He bruises easily,* huchubuka kwa urahisi. — *n.* chubuko, alama ya pigo, walio, alama ya damu kuvia kwa kupigwa, vilio la damu. **bruiser,** *n.* mpigaji kwa ngumi.

bruit, *v.t.* eneza habari.

brunette, *n.* mwanamke mwenye nywele na sura nyeusi kidogo.

brunt, *n.* mshindo, uzito, ukali (wa vita, ugomvi, kazi &c.). *To bear the brunt of,* stahimili, vumilia uzito (ukali) wa vita (ugomvi, matata, kazi &c.).

brush, *n.* (*hair and paint*) burashi; (*for sweeping*) ufagio; (*fight*) vita kidogo. — *v.t.* fagia, pangusa, sugua, gusa kidogo (katika kupitia). **brushwood,** *n.* mikoko, kichaka, msitu. *To brush up,* takasa, katua, amsha, jikumbusha (masomo &c.); jiburudisha, jitengeneza.

brusque, *a.* -a ghafula, -enye maneno machache; -siyo na adabu, -kali.

brute, *n.* mnyama, hayawani; (*like a brute*) mtu mbaya, baa, katili, -chafu; (*stupid, idiotic*) -pumbavu. **brutal,** *a.* -kali, -a kama mnyama, -katili, -korofi, -chafu. **brutality,** *n.* ukali, ukorofi, ukatili. **brutally,** *adv.* kwa ukali, kwa ukatili. **brutish,** *a.* kama *brutal.*

bubble, *n.* povu; (*delusion*) jambo hafifu, shauri la hila, matupu, ubatili. — *v.i.* toa povu, umuka, chemka. *To bubble over,* furika, fura (kwa hasira, furaha &c.).

bubo, *n.* mtoki, uvimbe manenani au kwapani, pengine ni jipu. **bubonic,** *a.* -enye mitoki.

buccaneer, *n.* haramia wa bahari.

buck, *n.* dume (wa jamii ya paa, mbuzi, sungura); mmbeja, mmalidadi, mshaufu. **buck,** *v.i.* rukaruka, *e.g.* punda arukapo hali mgongo umeinuka na miguu yake yote ni pamoja.

bucket, *n.* ndoo.

buckle, *n.* kifungo, bizimu. — *v.t.* funga kwa bizimu; — *v.i.* (*bulge*) bonyea. **buckler,** *n.* kigao, ngao, kikingio.

buckram, *n.* namna ya kitambaa kigumu kinachotumika kwa bitana na katika kujalidi vitabu.

bucolic, *a.* -a mashamba, kimashamba.

bud, *n.* jicho, chipukizi; (*unopened*) tumba. *Nip in the bud,* komesha upesi mwanzoni (mwa shauri &c.). — *v.i.* chipua, mea, chanua.

budge, *v.i.* jongea, sogea, enda, mudu; — *v.t.* jongeza, sogeza, hamisha &c.

budget, *n.* (*bundle*) kipeto (cha nyaraka, hati &c.); (*collection*) jamii; (*news*) habari, taarifa; (*public accounts*) habari za gharama ya serikali. — *v.i.* (*for*) hesabia (wekea) fedha kwa gharama (matumizi), yaani hesabu za fedha zinazopokewa na kulipwa, ya matumizi na mapokea.

buff, *a.* -a rangi ya kimanjano; -tupu (watu), *e.g. stripped to the buff,* hali ya kuwa tupu.

buffalo, *n.* nyati, mbogo.

buffer, *n.* kitu cha kuzuia nguvu ya kipigo.

buffet, (1) *n.* pigo la ngumi (konde), kofi, ngumi. — *v.t.* piga ngumi, konde, kofi; (*struggle with*) shindana na.

buffet, (2) *n.* meza ya kuandalia chakula au ya kulia chakula.

buffoon, *n.* mcheshi, mchekeshaji, mpumbavu, majununi. **buffoonery,** *n.* upuzi, upumbavu, ucheshi.

bug, *n.* aina ya wadudu; kunguni.

bugbear, *n.* tisho, kioja, dubwana, chukizo, maafa, afriti, bwedu.

buggy, *n.* gari la farasi la magurudumu mawili.

bugle, *n.* tarumbeta, buruji, paanda, baragumu. — *v.i.* piga *bugle.* **bugler,** *n.* mpigaji *bugle,* buruji.

build, *v.t.* (*p.t. and pf.t.* **built**) jenga; (*masonry*) aka; (*ships*) unda; (*construct*) buni, fanya, fanyiza. *Build in*, zungusha kwa majengo. *Build up*, ziba (kwa kujengea); (*increase, improve*) kuza, endesha. *Build on*, tegemea, tumainia. **builder**, *n.* mjenzi; (*mason*) mwashi; (*of ships*) mwunzi. **building**, *n.* (*with poles &c.*) ujenzi; (*masonry*) uashi; (*of ships*) uunzi; (*a house*) nyumba. *Building materials*, majengo, maunzi.

bulb, *n.* shina la ua au mboga kama kitunguu; kioo cha taa ya umeme. **bulbous**, *a.* -a kufanana na *bulb*.

bulbul, *n.* (*East-Coast black-capped*) shore, teleka; (*Zanzibar sombre*) kuruwiji.

bulge, *n.* uvimbe, mtoki, mbenuko. — *v.i.* (*outwards*) tokeza, vimba, benuka, kubaza, fanya mgongo; (*inwards*) bonyea, fanya uvungu. **bulgy**, *a.* -a kutokeza; (*inwards*) -a uvungu.

bulk, *n.* (*size*) ukubwa; (*chief part*) sehemu iliyo kubwa; (*cargo*) jumla ya shehena. — *v.i.* -wa kubwa; — *v.t.* weka yote pamoja (*e.g.* shehena ya meli). *Sell by bulk*, uza shelabela, uza kwa jumla. *Break bulk*, toa shehena. **bulkhead**, *n.* kiambaza cha kukingama cha meli. **bulky**, *a.* -kubwa, -nene, -zito.

bull, (1) *n.* fahali, ng'ombe dume; dume la ng'ombe (nyangumi, tembo &c.). — *a.* -a dume, -kubwa. *Bull's eye*, katikati hasa ya shabaha. *Take the bull by the horns*, jasiri; ingia hatarini au jambo gumu, au shida bila kuogopa. **bullock**, *n.* ng'ombe maksai.

bull, (2) *n.* (*papal*) tangazo (la *Pope*, askofu wa *Rome*).

bull, (3) *n.* (*verbal*) kosa la usemi la kuchekesha, lenye maana iliyo kinyume cha ile iliyokusudiwa.

bullet, *n.* risasi ya bunduki. **bullet-proof**, *a.* -siyopenyezeka kwa risasi za bunduki.

bulletin, *n.* taarifa; tangazo la kujulisha hali ya mgonjwa mwenye cheo kikuu, kama mfalme.

bullion, *n.* fedha au dhahabu (isiyofanyizwa sarafu).

bullock, *n.* taz. *bull* (1).

bully, *v.t.* chokoza, onea, dhulumu. — *n.* mchokozi, mtesi, mshari, jeuri, dhalimu; (*pimp*) kawadi (atongozaye wanawake kwa ajili ya wengine).

bully beef, *n.* nyama ya ng'ombe iliyopikwa na kuhifadhiwa katika makopo (makebe).

bulrush, *n.* unyasi. *Bulrush millet*, wimbi, mawele.

bulwark, *n.* boma; (*protection*) kinga, nguzo, msaada; (*of ship*) ukingo wa mbavu za meli utokezao juu.

bumboat, *n.* mashua ya kupelekea mboga melini.

bump, *v.i.* gonga, gongana na, dunda, kumba, kumbana na; fanya vishindo kama gari linalopita katika njia mbaya. *I have bumped my head*, nimejigonga kichwa na kuumia. — *n.* pigo, chubuko, kivimbe, mtoki. **bumper**, *n.* kikombe, bilauri iliyojaa mvinyo; cho chote kilichositawi sana, *e.g. bumper harvest*, mavuno makubwa mno. **bumpy**, *a.* -enye kukwaruzakwaruza, -enye mashimo mashimo kama njia iliyoharibika.

bumpkin, *n.* mjinga, mzuzu, mtu wa kimashamba asiyejua desturi.

bumper, *n.* taz. *bump*.

bumptious, *a.* -enye kiburi, -shupavu, -a kujitokeza kwa majivuno, -a kutakabari, -a makeke, -fidhuli.

bumpy, *a.* taz. *bump*.

bun, *n.* mkate mdogo mtamu.

bunch, *n.* (*of fruit &c.*) kichala, kitawi; (*quantity*) fungu, tita, kicha, kichanga; (*of flowers*) shada. — *v.t.* funga pamoja, *e.g.* shada la maua; fanya tita; — *v.i.* songana, fungamana, kunjamana.

bundle, *n.* peto, kipeto, robota, furushi, kifurushi, bindo, bunda, kibumba, kitumba; (*of sticks, grass*) tita, kicha. — *v.t.* funga matita; (*out*) ondosha kwa haraka (kwa fujo); — *v.i.* ondoka kwa haraka (kwa fujo).

bung, *n.* kizibo cha pipa. — *v.t.* ziba.

bungalow, *n.* nyumba ndogo.
bungle, *n.* fujo, burugoburugo, machafuko, kosakosa. —*v.t.* burugaburuga, boronga, purukusha, kosakosa, fuja, koroweza, tia fujo, chafua, gurugusha. **bungled**, *a.* -liofanywa au kutengenezwa ovyo, vibaya. **bungler**, *n.* mburugaji, mfujaji, aharibuye au kufanya mambo ovyo, vibaya, akosayekosaye.
bunion, *n.* kivimbe, hasa cha kidole gumba cha mguu.
bunk, *n.* kitanda (kilichotengenezwa kama sanduku refu) cha melini au garini. **bunker**, *n.* (*of ship*) mahali melini panapowekwa makaa.
bunkum, *n.* maneno yasiyo na maana, mapayo, upuzi.
bunting, *n.* kitambaa cha bendera; bendera; mapambo ya bendera *&c.*
buoy, *n.* chelezo, mlezo, boya. — *v.t.* weka vyelezo; fanya kuelea; (*up*) changamsha. **buoyancy**, *n.* wepesi; (*cheerfulness*) ukunjufu, matumaini. **bouyant**, *a.* -a kuelea, -epesi; (*joyous, hopeful*) -a furaha, -tumainifu, -changamfu.
bur, *n.* taz. *burr* (1) and (2).
burden, (1) *n.* (*of song*) itikio la wimbo; (*of idea*) kiini, maana hasa ya jambo.
burden, (2) *n.* mzigo; (*cargo*) shehena (*trouble*) udhia, taabu, cho chote kilemeacho, kiinikizo. *Be a burden or burdensome*, lemea, udhi. *Beast of burden*, mnyama wa kuchukua mizigo, farasi, punda, ng'ombe, ngamia *&c.* **burdensome**, *a.* -zito, -a kulemea, -lemevu, -a udhia.
bureau, *n.* dawati; meza yenye vitoto; (*office*) chumba au afisi ya kazi ya serikali; afisi. **bureaucracy**, *n* utawala kwa mabwana wa serikali tu kuamrisha kila tendo na mambo ya watu wa nchi.
burgess, *n.*, **burgher**, *n.* mwenyeji wa mji.
burglar, *n.* mwizi (aingiaye nyumbani usiku kuiba). **burglary**, *n.* uizi (wa kuingia nyumbani usiku).
burgle, *v.i.* iba (nyumbani usiku).
burgundy, *n.* namna ya divai.
burial, *n.* taz. *bury.*
burlesque, *n.* maigizo ya mambo ya kuchekesha. — *v.t.* geuza mambo kwa kuyaiga hata yachekeshe.
burly, *a.* -nene, -enye maungo, -shupavu (-a maungo).
burn, *v.t.* (*p.t. and pf.t.* **burnt**, *and* **burned**) choma, unguza, teketeza, washa; (*make by fire*) fanya kwa moto; — *v.i.* chomeka, ungua, waka, teketea, ona joto jingi. *He burns with anger*, hasira yamwaka. — *n.* umizo la moto, moto, mchomo, mwunguzo. *Burn one's boats*, jitenga kabisa hata usiweze kurudi ulikotoka; bahatisha yote kwa kutumaini kufaulu. *Burn one's fingers*, pata hasara (mashaka *&c.*) kwa kujiingiza katika mambo yasiyokuhusu, jihatarisha bure. **burner**, *n.* kipande cha taa chenye utambi. **burning**, *n.* mwako, mchomo. — *a.* -enye joto jingi, -a moto sana, -a kuwasha, -a nguvu, -a bidii nyingi. *Burning question*, jambo linaloshughulisha sana, ambalo watu wengi wanalifikiri.
burnish, *v.t.* katua, ng'arisha, sugua. — *n.* mng'aro.
burr, (1) *n.* tamko la kukwaruza herufi *r.*
burr, (2) *n.* mbegu zenye miibamiiba, zenye manyoya.
burrow, *v.t. and i.* fukua, ingia (kaa) shimoni; chungua sana. — *n.* kishimo (cha mnyama), kitundu (kipenyacho chini), kipango.
bursar, *n.* mtunza fedha; (*scholar*) mwanafunzi aelemishwaye kwa fedha zilizokabidhiwa chuo kwa kusudi hilo. **bursary**, *n.* gharama zilipwazo kwa ajili ya *bursar.*
burst, *v.t.* (*p.t. and pf.t.* **burst**) pasua, vunja; — *v.i.* pasuka, vunjika, funguka ghafula; (*burst out*) toka kwa nguvu, (*as water*) bubujika, buguika, foka. *Burst in*, jipenyeza kwa nguvu. *Burst through* (*out of*), tumbuza, chimbuka. *Burst into tears*, toka machozi ghafula. *Burst*

on (*appear suddenly*), zukia. — *n.* mshindo, jambo la ghafula (kama la kububujika, kufoka &c.).

bury, *v.t.* zika; (*of animals &c.*) fukia; (*conceal*) ficha, setiri, futia mbali; (*cover, overwhelm*) funikiza, angamiza. **burial,** *n.* maziko; (*requisites for funeral*) mazishi, mazikwa; (*attend burial*) enda mazikoni; (*provide a burial*) zisha. *Burial service*, ibada ya kuzika; (*Muhammedan*) talakim, hitima; (*say burial service*) soma talakim. *Burial-ground*, makaburini, maziara, mava.

bus, *n.* kifupi cha *omnibus*, motakaa ya abiria.

bush, (1) *n.* kijiti chenye matawi au vitawi vingi, koko; (*thicket*) kichaka. *Beat about the bush*, zungusha maneno, semasema mengine na kukawia kutoa habari hasa. **bushes,** *n.* makoko, msitu, magugu. **bushy,** *a.* (*with bushes*) -enye msitu mwingi, -a kichaka; (*like a bush*) -a vitawi vingi, -enye nywele nyingi.

bush, (2) *n.* tabaka ya chuma ndani ya mzinga unamopita mchi wa mashine, au mchi wa gurudumu &c.

bushel, *n.* kipimo kadiri ya pishi kumi na sita.

bushy, *a.* taz. *bush*.

busily, *adv.*, **business,** *n.*, **business-like,** *a.* taz. *busy*.

bust, *n.* kifua cha mtu; maziwa ya mwanamke; sanamu ya kuchonga, ya kichwa na kifua tu.

bustard, *n.* namna ya ndege wa jamii ya korongo.

bustle, *v.i.* jishughulisha kwa ghasia (kwa haraka), taharuki; — *v.t.* harakisha, amsha. — *n.* haraka, shughuli nyingi, ghasia, kikaka, kakara, kiherehere.

busy, *a.* -enye kazi nyingi, -tendaji, -enye bidii, -a amali, -a shughuli. — *v. Busy oneself with*, jishughulisha na. **busily,** *adv.* kwa bidii, kwa nguvu, upesi sana. **business,** *n.* shughuli, kazi amara; (*trade*) biashara, uchumi, maishilio; (*affair*) jambo, kisa; (*a troublesome matter*) jambo lenye matata (lenye visa vingi), huja. *You have no business to*, huna amri ya, si kazi yako. *It is not your business*, si amri yako, humo, haikupasi. *What business had you to do that?* kwa nini ulifanya hivi? ilikupasaje kufanya hivi? *Mind your own business*, shika lako, wewe humo. **business-like,** *a.* -enye taratibu, -a amali, -a bidii.

busybody, *n.* mpekuzi, mdadisi, ajitiaye katika mambo ya wengine.

but, *conj.* lakini, walakini; (*except*) ila, isipokuwa; (*only*) tu. *He all but fell*, karibu alianguka. *But for*, isipokuwa kwa, ila kwa.

butcher, *n.* mchinja nyama; (*murderer*) mwuaji, mkatili. — *v.t.* chinja (mnyama kwa chakula); ua kwa ukatili.

butler, *n.* mtumishi atunzaye vileo na maandalio ya meza &c.

butt, (1) *n.* pipa kubwa.

butt, (2) *n.* (*shooting-target*) shabaha; (*laughing-stock*) baradhuli, mjinga, mzuzu.

butt, (3) *n.* (*butt end*) tako, ncha butu, liwato; (*of rifle &c.*) kisimiko, mti, uti (wa bunduki, mkuki).

butt, (4) *v.t.* piga pembe, kumba. *Butt in*, jiingiza, jidukiza. — *n.* pigo, kumbo.

butter, *n.* siagi, samli. **buttermilk,** *n.* mtindi (wa maziwa). **butterfly,** *n.* kipepeo.

buttock, *n.* tako, kitako.

button, *n.* kifungo. — *v.t.* funga kwa vifungo, fumba; — *v.i.* fungika (kwa vifungo). **button-hole,** *n.* kiua. **button-loop,** *n.* kitanzi.

buttress, *n.* nguzo ya kuegemeza (ya egemezo la) ukuta wa nje, gadi. — *v.t.* egemeza, gadimu.

buxom, *a.* (mwanamke) -zuri -nene.

buy, *v.t.* (*p.t. and pf.t.* **bought**) nunua. *Buy off*, zuia kwa kulipa fedha. **buyer,** *n.* mnunuzi, mshtiri.

buzz, *v.i.* vuma (kama nyuki); (*of flies round filth &c.*) ng'ong'a.

buzz, buzzing, *n.* uvumi (kama wa nyuki).

buzzard, *n.* ndege, jamii ya mwewe na kipanga.

by, *prep.* katika, kando ya, karibu na, -ni; (*of agent*) na; (*instrument*) kwa *By the sea,* kando ya (karibu na) bahari. *By the table, house &c.,* mezani, nyumbani *&c. He was beaten by Ali,* alipigwa na Ali. *It was broken by falling,* kilivunjika kwa kuanguka. *By means of a stick,* kwa fimbo. *By reason of,* kwa ajili (sababu) ya; kwa hiyo. *Day by day,* kila siku, siku kwa siku. *By myself,* bi nafsi yangu. *By night,* usiku. *By noon,* kabla ya adhuhuri. *Come by,* pata. *Stand by,* saidia, auni. *Do well by,* tendea mema. *Put (lay) by,* weka. *By the by,* lakini. *By all means,* inshallah, vyema. — *adv.* karibu; (*aside*) upande, mbali; (*in presence of*) kwa. *By and by,* halafu, baadaye.

bygone, *a.* -a zamani, -liopita. *Let bygones be bygones,* yaliyopita na tuyasahau. **by-product,** *n.* kitu kinachofanyika au kupatikana katika kazi ya kufanya au kupata kitu kingine hasa. *e.g.* makaa yachomwapo ili kupata *gas,* namna ya lami hupatikana pia—lami ni *by-product.* **bystander,** *n.* mwenye kuwapo (kuangalia, kuhudhuria). **by-way,** *n.* njia ndogo. **byword,** *n.* mithali; kitu au jambo linalodharauliwa na watu, *e.g. His action became a byword in the town,* tendo lake lilivuma mjini likadharauliwa na watu.

by-law, bye-law, *n.* amri, sheria au sharti ipasayo watu wa mji au wa sehehmu ya nchi fulani au chama *&c.*

byre, *n.* zizi la ng'ombe.

bystander, *n.*, **by-way,** *n.*, **byword,** *n.* taz. *by.*

C

C, Roman letter = 100.

cab, *n.* gari la namna moja la abiria, kichumba cha mwendeshaji katika gari la moshi.

cabal, *n.* chama cha watu wenye kusudi la siri; kusudi la chama chenyewe. **cabalistic,** *a.* -a fumbo. **caballer,** *n.* mfitini, mwana chama cha siri.

cabaret, *n.* mkahawa; mchezo au ngoma ichezwayo mkahawani.

cabbage, *n.* namna ya mboga yenye majani kama ya mfigili yaliyoviringana kama tufe.

cabin, *n.* kijumba, hasa cha melini; kibanda; kipenu; (*in a dhow*) shetri. **cabinet,** *n.* (*small room*) chumba kidogo; (*case*) kabati la kuwekea vitu vya tunu; (*council*) baraza ya mawaziri, halmashauri ya serikali. **cabinet maker,** *n.* seremala afanyizaye vyombo vya nyumbani kama meza, viti *&c.* **cabinet minister,** *n.* waziri wa halmashauri ya serikali.

cable, *n.* amari, kamba nene ya katani, makumbi au nyuzi za chuma yenye nguvu; (*nautical measure*) kipimo cha futi 600; (*telegraph*) uzi wa simu mnene (hasa wa kwenda chini kwa chini ya nchi au ya bahari); simu. **cablegram,** *n.* simu ipelekwayo kwa *cable.*

cacao, *n.* namna ya mti; mbegu zake hutumika kutengenezea *cocoa*.
cache, *n.* ficho la fedha, vyakula, zana za vita &c. — *v.t.* ficha kitu.
cachinnation, *n.* cheko kubwa lenye ukelele.
cackle, *n.* mteteo wa kuku. — *v.i.* tetea (kwa kuku); semasema au chekacheka kwa sauti nyembamba.
cacophony, *n.* sauti au ukelele wa kuchukiza.
cactus, *n.* jamii ya mimea kama mpungate &c.
cad, *n.* mtu mnyonge; mwenye tabia hafifu ya kufanya mambo manyonge, mkosefu wa adabu.
cadaverous, *a.* -a kama maiti, -a kudhoofu au kukonda sana (mwili au uso).
caddy, *n.* mkebe wa kuwekea majani ya chai.
cadence, *n.* mshuko wa sauti mwisho wa fungu la maneno, sauti tamu ya kupendeza, ulinganifu wa sauti.
cadet, *n.* mwanafunzi (hasa wa kazi ya afisa katika manowari au majeshi ya askari).
cadge, *v.t. and i.* ombaomba vitu, londea, buga, dusa, doya, chungia, pandia.
café, *n.* mkahawa. **caffeine**, *n.* dawa inayopatikana katika buni.
cage, *n.* tundu, kitundu, kizimba. — *v.t.* fungia tunduni.
cairn, *n.* chungu kubwa ya mawe (juu ya kaburi au ya mlima iliyo alama).
caitiff, *n.* mtu mnyonge, mwoga.
cajole, *v.t.* bembeleza, vuta kwa werevu, danganya kwa kusifusifu, rairai. **cajolery**, *n.* ubembe.
cake, *n.* mkate mtamu; (*piece*) donge, bumba, kitumba; (*of soap &c.*) kipande; (*of tobacco*) mkate. — *v.i.* ganda, gandamana.
calabash, *n.* (*tree*) mbuyu; (*fruit*) buyu, dundu, kitoma, tumba, tunguri, mbokora &c.
calamity, *n.* msiba mkubwa, hasara, mateso, janga, maafa, baa. **calamitous**, *a.* -a msiba, -a huzuni, -a taabu, -zito.
calcareous, *n.* -enye chokaa. **calcium**, *n.* namna ya madini iliyo katika chokaa.
calculate, *v.t.* hesabu; (*consider*) dhani, ona, fikiri. *Calculate upon*, tumainia, tegemea; (*intend*) kusudia, azimu. *Calculated for*, -a kufaa kwa, -a kutumika kwa. **calculating**, *a.* -enye kufikiri mambo ya mbele; (*selfish*) -choyo -a kuwazia nafuu yake mwenyewe. **calculation**, *n.* hesabu; (*consideration*) shauri, fikira.
caldron (cauldron), *n.* sufuria kubwa, marigedi, birika.
calendar, *n.* takwimu, kalenda.
calf, (1) *n.* (*pl. calves*) ndama wa ng'ombe. **calve**, *v.i.* zaa (kwa ng'ombe).
calf, (2) *n.* (*of leg*) shavu la mguu.
calibre, *n.* kipimo cha duara ya tundu la mwanzi wa bunduki au mzinga; (*mental*) kadiri ya akili; (*capacity*) ukubwa.
calico, *n.* kitambaa kilichofanyizwa kwa pamba kama amerikani, ulaiti, gamti, bafta, kaniki &c.
Calif (Caliph), *n.* khalifa. **Califate (Caliphate)**, *n.* ukhalifa, au milki ya khalifa.
calipers, *n.* taz. *callipers.*
calix, *n.* taz. *calyx.*
calk, *v.* taz. *caulk.*
call, *v.t.* ita, alika, taja; (*visit*) amkia, enda kutazama, zuru; (*to prayers—Muhammedan*) adhini. *Call at* (*of ships &c.*) tua kwa, simama penye. *Call for* (*need*), taka, hitaji; (*deserve*) stahili. *Call forth* (*bring into action*) amsha, tumisha, toza, dhihirisha. *Call in question*, shindania, bishania. *Call names* (*abuse*), tukana; (*read names*) soma (taja) majina. *Call on*, *Make a call on* (*require*) agiza, shurutisha; sihi, omba msaada. *Call out*, piga kelele, lia, gutia; (*muster*) changa, kusanya. *Call over*, soma wazi (majina &c.) *Call to account*, shtaki, hukumu. *Call to the bar*, fanya mwanasheria. *Call together*, kusanya. *Call up*, *Call to mind* (*recollect*), kumbuka; (*remind*) ku-

mbusha. *It is called . . .*, huitwa jina lake . . . *I call it madness*, naona ni wazimu. — *n.* mwito; (*cry*) kilio; ukelele, ukemi; (*visit*) mwamkio, mzuru, mwonano; (*demand, pressing claim*) jambo la kupasa (la kubidi), huja, lazima; (*divine*) sauti ya Mungu. *Pay* (*make a call*) (*morning*) amkia, sabahi, (*evening*) tuesha, (*general*) enda kutazama (kuamkia, kusalimu). *Make a call* (*demand, request*), leta haja, shurutisha, toza fedha. *Call of nature*, kutaka choo, haja. *It is a heavy call upon him*, yamlemea sana. *Stay within call*, kaa karibu (kadiri ya kusikia ukiitwa). *A call upon the purse*, gharama. *A call on time* (*strength*), kazi kubwa (nzito). **caller**, *n.* mtu ajaye kuamkia (kuzuru). **calling**, *n.* mwito; (*occupation*) kazi, uchumi, maishilio, shughuli.

calligraphy, *n.* mwandiko mzuri.

calling, *n.* taz. *call.*

callipers, *n.* namna ya bikari ya kupimia.

callisthenics, *n.* mazoezi ya viungo vya mwili ya kutia nguvu na uzuri.

callosity, *n.* taz. *callous.*

callous, *a.* -gumu, -enye ganzi, -a sugu; (*unfeeling*) -gumu, -shupavu, -siyeonea huruma, katili. **callosity**, *n.* sugu. **callously**, *adv.* bila kuonea huruma, bila kufikiri hasara (maumivu, taabu &c.) inayoletwa na jambo, kwa ukatili.

callow, *a.* -siyo na manyoya, -siyo na ndevu; -changa. *A callow youth*, kijana asiyejua bado mambo ya ulimwengu.

calm, *v.t.* tuliza, nyamazisha, fariji; — *v.i.* tulia, nyamaza, zizima, tuama. — *n.* (*quiet*) utulivu, amani, raha; (*absence of wind*) shwari. — *a.* -a shwari, -pole, -tulivu, kimya, makini, -nyamavu. **calmly**, *adv.* bila ghasia, bila wasiwasi, kwa utulivu, kwa upole. **calmness**, *n.* utulivu, makini, amani, starehe, unyamavu.

calomel, *n.* namna ya dawa ya kuharisha.

caloric, *n. and a.* joto, -a kuhusu joto. **calorific**, *a.* -enye kupasha joto. **calorie, calory**, *n.* kipimo cha joto.

calumniate, *v.*, **calumniation**, *n.*, **calumnious**, *a.* taz. *calumny.*

calumny, *n.* masingizio, masengenyo, uwongo. **calumniate**, *v.t.* singizia, sengenya. **calumniation**, *n.* masingizio, masengenyo, uwongo. **calumnious**, *a.* -a kusingizia, -a kusengenya, -a uwongo.

Calvary, *n.* mahali aliposulibiwa Yesu Kristo; sanamu ya Kusulibiwa kwake Yesu Kristo.

calve, *v.*, **calves**, *n.* taz. *calf* (1).

calyx, *n.* sehemu ya chini ya ua iliyo mfano wa kikombe kidogo.

cam, *n.* kipande kitokezacho katika gurudumu &c. la mashine cha kubadili mwendo usiwe wa kuzunguka ila kupanda na kushuka &c.

camaraderie, *n.* urafiki, nia njema.

camber, *n.* mwinuko wa katikati ya njia au barabara, ili maji yasisimame.

cambric, *n.* kitambaa cha katani chembamba chepesi sana.

came, *p.t.* ya *come.*

camel, *n.* ngamia.

camelopard, *n.* twiga. (taz. *giraffe*).

cameo, *n.* kito kilichochorwa sanamu.

camera, *n.* chombo kinachotumika kupigia picha; (*room*) chumba chenye dari ya kuba. *In camera*, faraghani, si mbele ya watu.

camisole, *n.* vazi la kike kama fulana.

camouflage, *n.* kidanganya macho. — *v.t.* kudanganya macho.

camp, *n.* kituo, kambi, kigono. — *v.i.* tua safarini, fanya kambi, panga.

campaign, *n.* muda vita vinaoendelea; mashughuli ya kueneza habari fulani, *e.g.* ya ugonjwa mbaya, ubaya wa mambo mengineyo, mambo yanayoelekea kukuza hali &c.

camphor, *n.* kafuri, kafuri maiti au karafuu maiti.

can, (1) *v.i.* (*p.t.* **could**, *neg.* **cannot**), weza, ruhusiwa; (*in composition*) -ika, -ikana. *It can be got*, inapatika, inapatikana. *It cannot be done,* haifanyiki, haifanyikani. *I can but (go), I cannot but (go),* sina budi (kwenda), imenibidi (kwenda). *I can speak,* ninaweza kusema. *I cannot speak,* siwezi kusema.

can, (2) *n.* kopo (la bati), mkebe. — *v.t.* tia koponi (katika mkebe).

Canadian, *a.* -a nchi ya *Canada.* — *n.* mwenyeji wa *Canada.*

canal, *n.* mto, mfereji, njia ya maji (iliyofanywa na watu).

canary, *n.* kirumbizi.

cancel, *v.t.* futia mbali; (*annul*) tangua. **cancellation,** *n.* mfuto, mtanguo, kitanguo.

cancer, *n.* namna ya donda baya sana; jamii moja ya nyota.

candid, *a.* -nyofu, -adilifu, -a kunena kweli bila kuvutwa upande huu wala huu (bila kupendelea). **candour,** *n.* maadili, uadilifu, unyofu, tabia ya kunena bila kupendelea.

candidate, *n.* mtaka, ajaribuye kupata (cheo, kazi, heshima &c.).

candle, *n.* mshumaa, tawafa. **candlestick,** *n.* kinara cha mshumaa, mwango. *Burn the candle at both ends,* poteza kuwili. *Not fit to hold a candle to,* si stahili hata kulinganishwa na (kadiri iliyo duni). *The game is not worth the candle,* hafifu (duni) hata haistahili kushughulika nayo.

candour, *n.* taz. *candid.*

candy, *n.* kitu kitamu kilichotengenezwa kwa sukari, *e.g.* halua, kashata &c.

cane, *n.* henzerani, mwanzi mwembamba. — *v.t.* piga kwa henzerani. — *a.* -a henzerani. *Sugar cane,* muwa. *Cane sugar,* sukari ya muwa. **caning,** *n.* mpigo wa henzerani.

canine, *a.* -a mbwa, kama mbwa. *Canine teeth,* meno machonge.

caning, *n.* taz. *cane.*

canister, *n.* kopo (la bati), mkebe.

canker, *n.* donda baya, donda lililooza; maradhi fulani ya mimea; cho chote kinachoozesha au kula kwa maradhi. — *v.t.* ozesha, haribu, ambukiza; — *v.i.* oza (kwa maradhi &c.). **cankerous,** *a.* -a kuozesha, -a kula kwa maradhi, -haribifu.

cannibal, *n.* mtu mla nyama ya kibinadamu. **cannibalism,** *n.* desturi ya (mtu) kula nyama ya kibinadamu, ulaji wa nyama ya wanadamu.

cannon, *n.* mzinga. **cannonade,** *n.* mpigo wa mizinga mingi. **cannon-ball,** *n.* risasi la mviringo la mzinga.

cannot, *v. neg.* ya *can.*

canoe, *n.* mtumbwi, (*with outriggers*) ngalawa, (*large, planked*) dau. (*for two only*) kiperea.

canon, (1) *n.* sheria, kanuni; (*ecclesiastical*) kanuni ya kanisa; (*member of chapter*) kasisi mwenye kiti katika halmashauri ya kanisa kuu la jimbo la askofu. **canonical,** *a.* -a *canon.* **canonize,** *v.t.* ingiza katika hesabu ya Watakatifu wa kikristo.

canon, (2) *n.* taz. *canyon.*

canopy, *n.* chandalua; kipaa cha juu ya kiti cha kifalme &c.

cant, (1) *n.* usemi wa unafiki (wa kutumia maneno yahusuyo dini bila kuyasadiki, kama kwamba unayasadiki); usemi wa madhehebu fulani; usemi wa ovyo. — *v.i.* sema *cant.*

cant, (2) *v.t.* (*over*) laza upande, pindua, inika; — *v.i.* pinduka, lalia upande. — *n.* mwinamo; msukumo wa ghafula.

cantaloup, *n.* namna ya tikitimaji.

cantankerous, *a.* -kaidi, -tundu, -enye uchungu wa moyo.

cantata, *n.* utenzi wa kuimbwa.

canteen, *n.* duka la vyakula (hasa katika kambi ya askari); (*utensil*) chombo kama ndoo au sanduku lenye vyombo vya kupikia na kulia ndani yake.

canter, *v.i.* enda mghad, enda thelth (mwendo wa taratibu); — *v.t.* endesha farasi mwendo wa taratibu. — *n.* mwendo wa mghad (wa thelth, wa taratibu).

cantonment, *n.* kambi, mahali wakaapo askari.

canvas, *n.* nguo nzito kama ile ya matanga au turubali; (*sacking*) gunia. *Under canvas,* kambini, hemani.

canvass, *v.t. and i.* tazamia, chungua, kagua; hoji; ongea juu ya; (*political or for a special cause*) omba msaada (ili kupata kuchaguliwa kwa cheo fulani; au fedha kwa kusudi fulani).

canyon, *n.* mahali papitapo mto penye magenge marefu kando hii na hii.

caoutchouc, *n.* mpira.

cap, *n.* kofia; cho chote kifunikacho kama kofia, kifuniko; (*of a gun*) fataki. — *v.t.* vika kofia; funika; shinda; pita. -wa bora kuliko. *Cap block,* faruma.

capable, *a.* -enye kuweza, hodari, -stadi, -enye akili. **capability,** *n.* nguvu, akili; (*use*) matumizi. **capacious,** *a.* -enye nafasi nyingi ndani, -kubwa ndani. **capacity,** *n.* uwezo wa kuweka vitu; uwezo wa kufahamu; uwazi, kadiri, nafasi, ukubwa wa ndani (kama vile wa chumba, ndoo, chupa &c.).

caparison, *n.* matandiko; maviko, mapambo. — *v.t.* tandika, vika.

cape, (1) *n.* (*garment*) vazi lisilo na mikono la kuvaa mabegani.

cape, (2) *n.* rasi. *The Cape* (*of Good Hope*), Kepi.

caper, *v.i.* randa, rukaruka, chachawa, cheza, jitapatapa. — *n.* mruko, mchezo.

capillary, *n. and a.* kama unywele (wenye uwazi mwembamba sana); mshipa mdogo wa damu, kapilari. **capillary attraction,** *n.* uwezo wa *capillary* kunywea au kuvuta maji ndani yake.

capital, *a.* -a kuhusu kichwa; bora. -kuu, -zuri sana, -a kufaa sana. *He is a capital shot,* yu mpigaji bora wa shabaha. — *n.* mji mkuu; jambo lililo kuu; (*property*) rasilmali, asili ya mali; (*of a column*) sehemu ya juu ya nguzo; (*large letter*) herufi kubwa (*e.g.* A, B, CH, D &c.). *Capital punishment,* adhabu ya kufa (ya kuuawa). **capitalist,** *n.* tajiri, mwenye mali nyingi. **capitally,** *a.* -kuu, -zuri; -a kufaa sana. **capitation,** *n.* tendo la kuhesabu watu wote (vichwa vyote); kodi ya kichwa.

capitulate, *v.i.* jitoa kwa masharti; andikiana masharti (ya kuacha vita, shauri &c.) **capitulation,** *n.* tendo la kujitoa kwa masharti.

capon, *n.* jogoo aliyehasiwa.

caprice, *n.* mgeuzo wa shauri (wa nia, wa moyo) bila kisa maalum; ubadilifu wa moyo au nia; (*folly*) upuzi; (*desire*) matamanio. **capricious,** *a.* -badilifu wa moyo (wa nia); -geugeu.

capsicum, *n.* (*plant*) mpilipili hoho; (*berry*) pilipili.

capsize, *v.t.* pindua juu chini. — *v.i.* pinduka juu chini.

capstan, *n.* duara; kitu kama gogo la kuzungushia kamba ya nanga &c. na kuivuta.

capsule, *n.* gamba lenye mbegu; gamba lililotiwa dawa kiasi maalum.

captain, *n.* (*of ship*) kapiteni, (*of dhow*) nahodha; (*of army and navy*) afisa mwenye cheo cha kapiteni.

caption, *n.* maelezo mafupi ya habari zinazofuata (katika kitabu, gazeti &c.).

captious, *a.* -epesi kulaumu (kukasirika, kuona chuki); -shindani, -bishi.

captivate, *v.t.* pendeza mno, chunusha, shinda moyo, tiisha; (*bewitch*) loga, fanyia uchawi, tega. **captivating,** *a.* -a kupendeza mno, -zuri sana, -a kushinda moyo. **captive,** *n.* mfungwa; (*in war*) mateka. — *a.* -fungwa, -a kutekwa; -a kutiishwa; -a kuvutwa moyo. **captivity,** *n.* utumwa, kifungo. *Be in captivity,* fungwa, -wa mtumwa, -wa teka la vita. **captor,** *n.* afungaye, akamataye. **capture,** *v.t.* kamata, pata, bamba, shika, twaa, nyang'anya. — *n.* tendo la kukamata (la kuteka); kitu au mtu aliyekamatwa au kutekwa; (*booty*) mateka, nyara.

car, *n.* gari; motakaa &c.

carafe, *n.* chupa ya maji ya kunywa ya mezani.

caramel, *n.* sukari iliyounguzwa; vitu vitamu vilivyotengenezwa kwa sukari na siagi.

carat, *n.* kipimo cha kupimia usafi wa dhahabu (cha kupimia uzito wa vito vya thamani).

caravan, *n.* msafara, safari; (*large car*) gari kubwa kama nyumba ndogo. **caravan-porter**, *n.* mpagazi, mchukuzi.

caraway, *n.* (*seed*) kisibiti.

carbide, *n.* kama jiwe ambalo likitiwa maji hutoa namna ya hewa inayoweza kuwashwa.

carbine, *n.* bunduki fupi.

carbolic acid, *n.* dawa ya sumu itokayo katika makaa ya mawe; hutumika sana kusafishia vidonda na vyombo.

carbon, *n.* kitu kilicho asili ya vitu vingi viwezavyo kuunguzwa. Makaa ni *carbon.* Miti, nyama, makaa ya mawe, karatasi, vyote vina *carbon* ndani yake. *Carbon paper*, karatasi yenye rangi nyeusi ya kutia katikati ya kurasa ili kufanya nakala. **carbonaceous**, **carbonic**, *a.* -a kuhusu au -enye *carbon.* **carbonize**, *v.t.* fanya *carbon.* **carbonic acid**, *n.* namna ya hewa itokayo kama *carbon* ikichanganywa na *oxygen*, ni sumu kali; lakini ikitumika kwa namna nyinginezo ina manufaa mengi.

carbuncle, *n.* namna ya kito chekundu; jipu kubwa.

carburettor, *n.* chombo cha motakaa &c. cha kuchanganya mvuke wa petroli pamoja na hewa.

carcass, *n.* mzoga, pinda.

card, (1) *n.* karatasi nene; (*playing*) karata, (*pack*) jozi, (*pips*) ng'anda *or* nganda, (*hearts*) kopa, (*clubs*) pau, (*spades*) shupaza, (*diamonds*) uru, (*King*) mzungu wa nne, (*Queen*) mzungu wa mbili, (*Jack*) mzungu wa tatu au jaji, ghulamu (*Ace*) ree. **cardboard**, *n.* karatasi nene kama ubao mwembamba.

card, (2) *v.t.* chana, chambua.

cardamom, *n.* iliki.

cardboard, *n.* taz. *card* (1).

cardiac, *a.* -a kuhusu moyo.

cardigan, *n.* namna ya koti fupi lililofumwa la sufi.

cardinal, *a.* -kuu, -a maana, -a kiini cha jambo. *Cardinal numbers*, moja, mbili, tatu, nne &c. (taz. *ordinal*). *Cardinal points*, (*north*) kaskazi, (*south*) kusi, (*east*) mashariki, (*west*) magharibi. — *n.* mmojawapo wa baraza kuu ya *Pope* (askofu wa Rumi).

care, *n.* hadhari, uangalifu, utunzi, utunzo, utunzaji, kabidhi, usimamizi, himaya; (*charge*) kitu cha kutunzwa; (*trouble*) mashaka, taabu. — *v.i.* (*regard*) jali, kumbuka, tia moyoni; (*for something done badly*) sikitikia, ona majuto; (*anxious*) jishughulisha, sumbukia. *Have care of*, wekewa, tunza, angalia. *Care for* (*like*) penda, (*feel sympathy*) hurumia. *Take care of*, angalia. *Take care of yourself* (*to a sick person*), ugua pole, (*in general*) jihadhari. *Take care*, angalia, tanadhari, -wa na hadhari, jihadhari. *I do not care*, haidhuru, mamoja pia. **careful**, *a.* -angalifu, -a bidii, -enye kujali. **carefully**, *adv.* kwa uangalifu, kwa hadhari, siasa. **carefulness**, *n.* uangalifu, hadhari. **careless**, *a.* -zembe, -vivu, -purukushani, -a ovyo ovyo. **carelessly**, *adv.* bila uangalifu, kwa haraka, ovyo ovyo, bila kufikiri, kwa uzembe. **carelessness**, *n.* uzembe, upurukushani. **care-taker**, *n.* mngojezi, mtunzaji, mwangalizi. **care-worn**, *a.* -enye kuchoka au kudhikika kwa mashaka (taabu, uangalifu mwingi &c.).

careen, *v.t.* laza upande (*e.g.* chombo au meli ili itengenezwe chini), inika; — *v.i.* lala upande (ubavuni).

career, *n.* (*course*) mwendo; (*life*) namna ya maisha; (*actions*) matendo. — *v.i.* enda mbio.

careful, *a.*, **carefully**, *adv.*, **carefulness**, *n.*, **carelessly**, *adv.*, **carelessness**, *n.* taz. *care.*

caress, *v.t.* bembeleza, kumbatia,

tendea kwa upendo. — *n.* umbatio, tendo au neno la upendo.

care-taker, *n.* **care-worn,** *a.* taz. *care.*

cargo, *n.* shehena, mizigo.

caricature, *n.* picha ya kugeuza sura ya mtu au ya kuiigiza kwa namna inayochekesha au kumfanyia mzaha. — *v.t.* igiza, fuatisha na kugeuza picha (tendo, jambo) hata lichekeshe.

caries, *n.* kuoza kwa jino.

carillon, *n.* kengele zinazoweza kupigwa kufanya sauti ya wimbo; wimbo unaopigwa na kengele hizo.

carminative, *n.* dawa ya kutuliza tumbo.

carmine, *n.* rangi nyekundu. — *a.* -ekundu.

carnage, *n.* machinjo, mauaji.

carnal, *a.* -a kuhusu mwili, -a mwili; a tamaa za mwili.

carnation, *n.* namna ya ua lenye harufu nzuri.

carnival, *n.* sikukuu kabla ya majira ya Kwaresima; sikukuu au sherehe.

carnivora, *n.* jamii ya wanyama walao nyama, *e.g.* simba, fisi, chui *&c.* **carnivorous,** *a.* -a kula nyama.

carol, *n.* wimbo wa furaha au kusifu, hasa wa sikukuu ya Kuzaliwa Yesu Kristo. — *v.t. and i.* imba kwa furaha.

carousal, *n.*, **carouse,** *n.* karamu ya ulevi. — *v.i.* fanya (-la) karamu ya ulevi.

carp, (1) *v.i.* (*at*) nenea, karipia, zoza, guguna, gombagomba kwa makosa madogodogo.

carp, (2) *n.* namna ya samaki wa maji baridi (mtoni).

carpenter, *n.* seremala. **carpentry,** *n.* useremala.

carpet, *n.* zulia. — *v.t.* tandaza zulia.

carriage, *n.*, **carrier,** *n.* taz. *carry.*

carrion, *n.* mzoga, pinda, nyama iliyooza; cho chote kichukizacho.

carrot, *n.* namna ya mboga ya Ulaya iliyofanana kidogo na figili.

carry, *v.t.* chukua, peleka, ongoza; (*move on, extend*) endesha, pitisha, eneza; (*capture*) twaa kwa nguvu, shinda; (*be closely connected with*) fungamana na, -wa na hali moja na; (*of money*) tosha (kwa kusudi fulani); (*carefully*) rongaronga; — *v.i.* (*reach*) fika. *Carry a law,* simamisha sheria, amri; (*motion, resolution*) thibitisha kauli (shauri, makusudi, azimio *&c.*). *Carry a wall, ditch &c.* fanya, fanyiza ukuta, mfereji *&c.* *Carry all before one,* shinda mapingamizi yote. *Carry away,* chukulia; (*excite feelings*) vuta moyo (sikitisha, huzunisha, furahisha *&c.*). *Carry off,* chukua, (*kill*) ua, fisha, (*succeed*) weza, faulu. *Carry on,* endesha, ongeza, fuliza, fanya; (*behave badly*) fanya yasiyofaa, kosa adabu; (*proceed with*) endelea. *Carry child* (*on back*) beba, (*on hip*) eleka. *Carry out, or through,* maliza, fikiliza, timiza, tekeleza. *Carry the day,* shinda, weza, faulu. *Carry weight,* -wa na nguvu (maana). *He carried his point,* alipata mradi wake, alifaulu katika azimio lake (mradi wake). *It carries nothing,* haina nguvu, haina maana. **carriage,** *n.* gari, behewa la gari la moshi; (*act of carrying*) uchukuzi, upagazi; (*act or cost of carrying*) uchukuzi, upagazi, nauli; (*behaviour, bearing*) mwendo, sura, umbo. **carrier,** *n.* mpagazi, mchukuzi, hamali; (*disease*) mwambukizaji, aenezaye ugonjwa. **carrying pole,** *n.* mpiko, mzegazega.

cart, *n.* gari (la kazi lenye magurudumu mawili). — *v.t. and i.* chukua katika gari. **carter,** *n.* mwendeshaji gari. **cart-horse,** *n.* farasi wa kuvuta gari. **cart-load,** *n.* kadiri inayoweza kuchukuliwa katika gari. *Put the cart before the horse,* pindua mambo, yawe kinyume cha yale ya kawaida.

carte blanche, *n.* *To give a person carte blanche,* kumpa mtu nguvu (amri) afanye apendavyo.

cartilage, *n.* ufupa mwororo, mfupa laini unaoweza kunepa.

cartography, *n.* mwandiko wa ramani.

carton, *n.* kibweta kilichofanyizwa na *cardboard.*

cartoon, *n.* picha kubwa ya mwandiko (hasa ya kuigiza mambo yanayotendeka na watu hata yachekeshe). **cartoonist,** *n.* mwandikaji wa *cartoon.*

cartridge, *n.* kiasi au risasi ya bunduki. **cartridge belt** *n.* ukanda wenye mabeti ya kutilia risasi au viasi vya bunduki. **cartridge-paper,** *n.* namna ya karatasi nzito; hutumika sana kuandikia picha.

carve, *v.t.* chora, nakshi, tia nakshi; (*at table*) kata na kugawia nyama mezani. **carver,** *n.* fundi wa kutia nakshi (wa kuchora); (*knife*) kisu cha kukatia nyama. **carving,** *n.* nakshi, choro.

cascade, *n.* maanguko ya maji, maporomoko ya maji. — *v.i.* anguka, poromoka (kama maji).

case, (1) *n.* (*affair*) jambo, kadhia; (*condition*) hali; (*legal*) daawa, kesi; (*patient*) mgonjwa anayeuguzwa. *In case,* ikiwa, iwapo, kama. *It is the case,* ndiyo, naam, ndivyo vilivyo. *Make out a case,* toa sababu au kisa cha jambo (shauri, haja &c.).

case, (2) *n.* kasha, sanduku, bweta; (*of card &c.*) tumba, kitumba, kibumba; (*covering*) kifuniko; (*exterior*) kilicho nje; (*of knife, scissors &c.*) uo, ala. **casing,** *n.* kifunikacho.

casein, *n.* kitu kilicho katika maziwa (hutumika kufanya jibini).

casement, *n.* dirisha.

cash, *n.* fedha za kutumia, sarafu, fulusi, senti; (*ready money, hard cash, spot cash*) fedha taslimu, fedha mkononi, nakidi. — *v.t.* badili noti (hawala, hati ya fedha) kwa fedha. **cash-book,** *n.* daftari. **cashier,** *n.* karani mtunza fedha au daftari.

cashew nut, *n.* korosho, (*fruit*) kanju, bibo, (*tree*) mbibo, mkanju.

cashier, (1) *n.* taz. *cash.*

cashier, (2) *v.t.* ondosha katika kazi kwa sababu ya tendo baya.

cashmere, *n.* Kashmiri; namna ya shali au kitambaa cha sufu (manyoya) ya mbuzi wa Kashmiri.

casing, *n.* taz. *case* (2).

casino, *n.* kilinge, nyumba ya kuchezea ngoma na karata.

cask, *n.* pipa.

casket, *n.* kibweta, kikasha, kisanduku cha kuwekea vitu vya tunu &c.

cassava, *n.* (*plant and root*) muhogo; (*dried pieces*) kopa; (*leaves*) kisamvu.

casserole, *n.* maziga, chombo chenye kifuniko cha kuokea chakula.

cassia, *n.* namna ya mdalasini.

cassock, *n.* vazi lililofanana na kanzu; huvaliwa na makasisi, wahudumu na waimbaji wa kanisani.

cast, *v.t.* (*p.t. and pf.t.* **cast**) tupa, rusha, vurumisha; (*down*) angua, angusha; (*in a mould*) tia, subu, mimina katika kalibu; (*feathers*) jinyonyoa; (*skin*) jichuna, jiambua ngozi; (*leaves*) pukusa; (*lots*) piga kura; (*anchor*) tia (puliza) nanga. *Cast up accounts,* hesabu, jumlisha. *Be cast down,* huzunika, kata tamaa, shushwa moyo. *Cast about,* tafuta, fikirifikiri. — *n.* (*throw*) mtupo, vurumisho, mrusho; (*range*) umbali wa mtupo; (*mould*) kiwita, kalibu, (*copy*) nakili, mfano; (*of play*) wachezaji waliochaguliwa kucheza mchezo fulani; (*squint*) makengeza. **castaway,** *n.* mtu aliyetupwa; fukara, maskini. — *a.* -liotupwa, -isiyofaa kitu. **casting-vote,** *n.* neno mkataa, neno la kukata shauri iwapo nusu wanataka hivi na nusu hivi. **cast-off,** *a.* (*clothing, skin*) mavulio.

castanet, *n.* kitoazi, namna ya kayamba.

castaway, *n.* taz. *cast.*

caste, *n.* jamii ya watu wenye cheo kile cha maisha, au wa madhehebu ile ile. *Lose caste,* potewa na cheo cha maisha, aibika, shushwa.

castellated, *a.* -enye buruji.

castigate, *v.t.* adhibu, rudi, piga. **castigation,** *n.* adhabu kali, mapigo, marudio makali. **castigator,** *n.* atiaye adhabu, mpiga.

casting-vote, *n.* taz. *cast.*
cast iron, *n.* chuma cha kusubu, yaani kilichoyeyushwa katika mawe ya chuma.
castle, *n.* ngome, gereza, nyumba yenye boma, husuni. *Castle in the air*, mawazo ya kutamani vitu au hali, au kuwaza mambo makuu usiyo na hakika nayo kuyapata.
castor, *n.* kigurudumu cha miguu ya viti, meza *&c.* (*cruets*) (chupa) kikopo chenye kifuniko kilichotobolewa vitundu vidogo sana cha kunyunyizia pilipili, chumvi, sukari *&c.* *Castor sugar*, sukari nyembamba sana (kama vumbi).
castor oil, *n*, mafuta ya mbarika (ya mbono); (*plant*) mbarika, mbono; (*seeds*) nyonyo.
castrate, *v.t.* hasi. **castrated**, *a.* maksai.
casual, *a.* (*accidental*) -a bahati, -a nasibu, -a ajali; (*occasional*) -a kutukia mara kwa mara; (*careless*) -zembe, purukushani. *Casual labourer*, kibarua, mfanya kazi ya siku siku tu, au ya kipande. **casualty**, *n.* tukio, tukio baya, msiba; (*fatal*) mauti. *Casualties in war*, waliojeruhiwa au kuuawa au kupotea au kutoroka *&c.*
casuarina, *n.* mvinje.
casuist, *n.* atafutaye habari za mambo ya dhamiri, yaani ya kupambanua mema na mabaya. Mara nyingi hutumika kwa mtu mdanganyifu afanyaye mabaya kuwa kama kwamba ni mema. **casuistic**, **casuistical**, *a.* -a kuhusu mambo ya dhamiri. **casuistry**, *n.* elimu ya kupambanua mema na mabaya; (*sophistry*) mabaya yaliyoelezwa hata yaonekane kwa juujuu kama kwamba ni mema, udanganyifu.
casus belli, *n.* kisa cha vita (pigano, ugomvi).
cat, *n.* paka; (*town cat semi-wild*) shume la paka, paka shume, paka nunda. *Let the cat out of the bag*, toa nje siri. *Rain cats and dogs*, nyesha mvua kubwa. **catgut**, *n.* uzi wa utumbo wa mnyama, kano, ugwe wa kano. **cat's-cradle**, *n.* tambo, kitanda. **cat's-paw**, *n.* baradhuli, mtu aliye chombo au mchezo wa mtu mwingine, aliyedanganywa hata amtumikie mwingine, mjinga. **cat-o'-nine-tails**, *n.* mjeledi mkubwa.
cataclysm, *n.* gharika, mfuriko wa maji; mapinduko makubwa ya mambo, mapinduzi.
catacomb, *n.* pango la kuzikia watu.
catafalque, *n.* jeneza la sherehe.
catalepsy, *n.* kifafa, hali ya kuzimia roho.
catalogue, *n.* orodha ya majina (vitabu, bidhaa *&c.* — *v.t.* andika orodha ya majina *&c.*
catamite, *n.* shoga, mwanamume mwenye kufirwa.
catapult, *n.* manati; mtambo uliotumika vitani zamani wa kutupia mawe adui.
cataract, *n.* maanguko au maporomoko ya maji; (*of the eye*) mtoto jichoni.
catarrh, *n.* mafua, ugonjwa wa makamasi mengi.
catastrophe, *n.* msiba mkuu, machafuko, maangamizi; (*end*) mwisho, kikomo.
catch, *v.t.* (*p.t. and pf.t.* **caught**) shika, kamata, bamba, dara, koroweza, nasa, daka, guia; (*illness*) patikana; shikwa (na ugonjwa); (*fish*) vua (samaki); (*in a trap*) tega, nasa; (*water*) kinga; (*be in time for*) wahi, diriki; (*surprise*) kuta, chungulia, gundulia; (*in the act of adultery*) fumania; (*understand*) fahamu, tambua, sikia; — *v.i.* (*stick fast*) shika, kwama, nata, kaza. *I catch your meaning*, nafahamu maneno yako. *Catch the eye, ear, attention &c.*, vuta macho, tazamisha. *Catch cold*, shikwa na mafua (makamasi). *Catch fire*, waka, anza kuwaka, lipuka. *Catch a sound*, sikia. *Catch up*, patia; (*interrupt*) katiza (dakiza) maneno. *Be catching*, ambukiza; (*attractive*) vuta. **catchy**, *a.* -a kusikiza, -a kuvuta masikio

(sauti, wimbo *&c.*); (*tricky*) -danganyifu -a hila, -erevu.

catechetical, *a.* maswali na majibu, -a kujibizana. **catechism**, *a.* mtungo wa mafundisho kwa namna ya kuuliza maswali na kutoa majibu, majibizano; kitabu cha maswali na majibu chenye kueleza dini ya kikristo. **catechist**, *n.* mwalimu afundishaye kwa majibizano, afundishaye *catechism.* **catechize**, *v.t.* fundisha kwa maswali na majibu, jibizana; hoji juu ya mambo ya dini; uliza sana. **catechumen**, *n.* mwanafunzi wa dini ya kikristo (asiyebatizwa bado). **catechumenate**, *n.* uanafunzi wa dini.

categorical, *a.* dhahiri, -a hakika, halisi. **categorically**, *adv.* kabisa, hasa, bila tofauti. **category**, *n.* aina, namna, jinsi, jamii.

cater, *v.i.* patia chakula, mazungumzo na kadhalika. **caterer**, *n.* mchuuzi mwenye kuwapatia watu wengine chakula, mazungumzo *&c.*

caterpillar, *n.* mdudu wa namna atambaaye, ni mtoto wa kipepeo au nondo. K'wavi ni namna ya *caterpillar.*

catgut, *n.* taz. *cat.*

cathartic, *n.* dawa ya kuharisha (ya kusafisha tumbo).

cathedral, *n.* kanisa kuu la jimbo la askofu.

catholic, *a.* -a kufaa watu wote mahali pote; -fadhili, -pendevu, -a kuhusu Wakristo wote. — *n.* mfuasi wa dini ya Kanisa Katoliko; (*Roman Catholic*) mfuasi wa Kanisa la Rumi. **catholicism**, *n.* mambo ya kufaa watu wote; dini ya Kanisa Katoliko.

cat-o'-nine-tails, *n.*, **cat's-cradle**, *n.*, **cat's-paw**, *n.* taz. *cat.*

cattle, *n.* mifugo, yaani ng'ombe, mbuzi, kondoo *&c.* *Herd cattle*, chunga. *Drive cattle*, swaga. **cattle-fold, cattle-pen**, *n.* zizi, boma la ng'ombe *&c.*

caudal, *a.* -a mkia, kama mkia.

caught, *v. p.t. and pf.t.* ya *catch.*

caul, cawl, *n.* tandabui, zalio.

cauldron, *n.* sufuria kubwa, marigedi, birika.

cauliflower, *n.* namna ya mboga.

caulk (calk), *v.t.* kalafati.

cause, *n.* mwanzo, tendo, asili, sababu, sabiki, ajili, maana, hoja, kisa *&c.*, cho chote kinachofanya kuanzisha au kilicho sababu ya jambo au hali; (*lawsuit*) daawa, shauri, kesi, madai; (*side, party*) upande, hali. *Final cause*, kusudi. *Material cause*, kitu. *Formal cause*, umbo. *Ultimate cause*, asili, chanzo. *Proximate cause*, sababu. *Efficient cause*, kifanyizacho, kiendeshacho, chanzo. *Make common cause, with*, -wa hali moja na, shirikiana na. *Plead a cause*, dai, tetea. — *v.t.* (*produce effect*) fanya, fanyiza, anzisha, tia, -wa sababu ya; (*induce, compel*) shurutisha, amuru, lazimisha. *In comp.* -eza, -iza, -esha, -sha *&c.*, *e.g. cause to go*, endesha; *cause to hate*, chukiza; *cause fear*, ogofya *&c.* *Cause* (*a person*) *to hear*, fanya asikie. *I caused him to go blind*, nilimpofusha. **causative**, *a.* -a kuleta, -a kufanyiza, -a kutenda. **causeless**, *a.* bila sababu, bure.

causeway, *n.* njia kuu ya mawe, njia iliyoinuka.

caustic, *a.* -enye kuchoma kama moto, -a kuunguza; (*of words*) -kali, -chungu. — *n.* namna ya dawa ichomayo bila moto, *e.g.* magadi.

cauterize, *v.t.* choma kwa chuma cha moto au *caustic*, tia pisho, unguza **cautery**, *n.* mchomo wa chuma cha moto au wa *caustic*, pisho; (*marks of*) mapisho.

caution, *n.* uangalifu, hadhari; (*warning*) onyo, shauri. — *v.t.* onya, shauri. **cautious**, *a.* -enye hadhari, -angalifu.

cavalcade, *n.* andamano la watu wapanda farasi. **cavalier**, *n.* mpanda farasi. **cavalierly**, *adv.* kwa kiburi, kwa kutakabari, kwa jeuri, kwa ufidhuli. **cavalry**, *n.* askari wapanda farasi.

cave, cavern, *n.* pango, shimo. *To*

cave in, poromoka, bomoka; (*surrender*) shindwa, jinyenyekea. **cavernous**, *a.* -enye pango.
caviar, caviare, *n.* mayai ya samaki (*sturgeon*); huliwa.
cavil, *v.i.* kinzana (nenea) kwa sababu ndogondogo (bila kisa cha kutosha). — *n.* kinzano au ubishano hafifu.
cavity, *n.* tundu, shimo, mvungu.
caw, *v.i.* lia kama kunguru. — *n.* mlio wa kunguru.
cayenne, cayenne pepper, *n.* pilipili hoho.
cease, *v.i.* koma, nyamaza, tulia, isha, acha, hulu. **ceaseless**, *a.* -isiyo na mwisho. -a daima, -a sikuzote, bila kikomo.
cedar, *n.* mwerezi.
cede, *v.t.* toa kumpa mtu mwingine, achia mtu mwingine.
ceiling, *n.* upande wa chini ya dari.
celebrant, *n.* taz. *celebrate*.
celebrate, *v.t.* (*honour, extol*) tukuza, sifu; (*observe ceremonially*) fanyia heshima (ibada ya dini), adhimisha, adhimu; (*perform ceremony*) fanya; — *v.i.* (*of Holy Communion*) fanya Ushirika Mtakatifu. **celebrant**, *n.* kasisi afanyaye Ushirika Mtakatifu. **celebrated**, *a.* -enye sifa, adhimu, -a kujulikana, mashuhuri, -bayani. **celebration**, *n.* mtukuzo, mwadhimisho; (*of Holy Communion*) Ushirika Mtakatifu. **celebrity**, *n.* sifa nyingi, utukufu. *A celebrity*, mtu maarufu, mbayani.
celerity, *n.* wepesi, mbio, haraka.
celery, *n.* namna ya mboga.
celestial, *a.* -a mbinguni. — *n.* mkaa mbinguni; mtu wa nchi ya *China*. *The Celestial Empire*, nchi ya *China*.
celibacy, *n.* useja, ujane, hali ya mwanamume asiyeoa. **celibate**, *n.* mwanamume asiyeoa, mjane, mseja.
cell, *n.* kijumba, kitundu, kipango; chembechembe zilizo asili ya kila kitu chenye uhai, kwamba ni cha kinyama ama cha kimmea. Chembechembe hizi zaweza kufananishwa na vijumba vya masega ya nyuki, lakini ni ndogo sana; hazionekani ila kwa darubini (*microscope*). **cellular**, *a.* -enye *cells*, -enye vitundu vidogodogo. **celluloid**, *n.* kitu kigumu kama pembe kilichofanywa kwa kugandamiza sana pamba, kafuri na dawa nyingine. **cellulose**, *a.* -a *cells*. — *n.* kitu kilicho asili ya nyuzinyuzi za mimea, *e.g.* pamba, katani &c.
cellar, *n.* chumba kilichochimbwa chini; ghala ya chini ya nyumba, hasa ya mvinyo &c.
cellular, *a.*, **celluloid**, *n.*, **cellulose**, *a. and n.* taz. *cell*.
cement, *n.* saruji, gundi, udongo ulaya &c. yaani kitu kinachounganisha vitu pamoja. — *v.t.* unganisha kwa *cement*; unganisha kwa imara.
cemetery, *n.* makaburini, mava, maziara.
cenotaph, *n.* namna ya jengo la ukumbusho wa watu waliokufa wakazikwa mahali pengine.
cense, *v.t.* fukiza. **censer**, *n.* chetezo, maziga.
censor, *n.* mkaguzi wa vitabu, michezo, picha &c. kabla hazijatolewa; mchungulizi. **censorious**, *a.* -a kuhusu *censor*, -kali, -a kulaumu bure. **censure**, *n.* lawama, karipio, masuto. — *v.t.* laumu, suta, karipia.
census, *n.* mwandiko wa hesabu, hali, uchumi &c. wa watu wote wa nchi.
cent, *n.* senti, sarafu ya sehemu ya mia kwa moja ya shilingi; (*hundred*) mia. *Five per cent.* mia kwa tano. *Percentage*, faida.
centaur, *n.* mnyama wa hadithi mwenye mwili na miguu ya farasi na kichwa na mikono ya binadamu.
centenarian, *n.* mtu mwenye umri wa miaka mia. **centenary**, *n.* miaka mia; sikukuu ya ukumbusho ya kila mwaka wa mia. **centennial**, *a.* -a kila mwaka wa mia.
centigrade, *a.* -enye digrii (daraja) 100; *e.g.* kipimo cha joto kiitwacho *Centigrade thermometer*, kilichoganyika sehemu 100.

centimetre, *n.* kipimo cha sehemu mia kwa moja ya *metre*, yaani 0·3937 inchi.

centipede, *n.* tandu.

centre, *n.* palipo katikati hasa, katikati; (*attractive object*) kitu kinachovuta au kutazamisha. *Centre piece of door*, mfaa. — *v.t.* weka katikati; — *v.i.* -wa katikati. **central,** *a.* -a katikati hasa, -a katikati; (*principal*) -kuu, -a maana. **centralize,** *v.t.* leta katikati. — *v.i.* -ja katikati, *e.g.* kutawala mambo ya nchi kutoka mji mmoja *&c.*

century, *n.* muda wa miaka mia, karne.

ceramic, *a.* -a kuhusu vyombo vilivyofinyangwa, hasa vya kauri.

cereal, *a.* -a nafaka, -a kama nafaka.

cerebellum, *n.*, **cerebral,** *a.*, **cerebro-spinal,** *a.* taz. *cerebrum.*

cerebrum, *n.* sehemu ya ubongo kwenye paji la uso na utosi. **cerebellum,** *n.* sehemu ya ubongo iliyo nyuma, yaani kwenye kogo. **cerebral,** *a.* -a ubongo. **cerebro-spinal,** -a kuhusu *cerebrum* na ubongo ulio katika uti wa mgongo. *Cerebro-spinal fever* (*meningitis*), homa kali inayoambukizwa kwa kamasi, shingo ya mgonjwa hukaza sana, wala hawezi kuigeuza wala kugeuka.

ceremonial, *n. and a.*, **ceremonious,** *a.* taz. *ceremony.*

ceremony, ceremonial, *n.* kawaida za matendo kama zile za ibada ya dini; uzuri, heshima, sherehe. **ceremonial,** *a.* -a kufuata kawaida maalum. **ceremonious,** *a.* -enye sherehe, -a heshima, -enye kushikilia sana kawaida za sherehe.

cerise, *n. and a.* (-enye) rangi nyekundu.

certain, *a.* yakini, kweli, halisi, thabiti, bila shaka; (*fixed*) maalum, mahsusi; (*inevitable*) hapana budi; (*some*) baadhi ya, -ingine; (*one*) -moja fulani. *A certain place*, mahali fulani. *Certain people*, baadhi ya watu, watu wengine (fulani). *A certain man*, mtu mmoja (fulani). *In a certain degree*, kwa kadiri, lakini si kabisa. *To make certain*, kuhakikisha. *We are certain to go*, hatuna budi kwenda, lazima tuende. *Feel certain*, jua sana, yakini, ona hakika, tumaini. **certainly,** *adv.* naam, ndiyo, inshallah, yakini, hakika, kweli, bila shaka, hapana budi. **certainty,** *n.* yakini, hakika, kweli. *It is a dead certainty*, ni hakika kabisa, hakuna shaka lo lote. *Moral certainty*, jambo linaloelekea kuwa hakika hata mtu aweza kulikubali kama kwamba limekwisha thibitika. **certificate,** *n.* hati ya kuthibitisha jambo, sahihi. **certify,** *v.t.* (*make certain*) thibitisha, yakinisha (*attest*) kiri, thibitisha kwa maneno au maandiko, tia sahihi. **certitude,** *n.* kuona hakika, yakini.

cess, *n.* kodi.

cessation, *n.* ukomo, mwisho, pumziko.

cession, *n.* kutoa, kusalimisha.

cesspit, cesspool, *n.* shimo la kumwagia maji machafu lililoakwa chini na kando kwa udongo ulaya, maji yasivuje wala kupenya; maji lazima yavutwe kwa bomba au kwa ndoo. *Cesspool of iniquity*, mahali (mji *&c.*) palipojaa maovu.

chafe, *v.t.* (*rub*) kanda, chua, sugua, singa; (*bruise*) chubua, kwaruza; (*annoy*) sumbua, washa, udhi, kasirisha; — *v.i.* (*fret, rage*) sumbuka, udhika, kasirika, ona uchungu.

chaff, *n.* kapi (*of rice*) kumvi, wishwa; (*jokes*) ubishi, upuzi, mzaha. — *v.t.* bishana kwa ucheshi, fanyia utani (mzaha).

chagrin, *n.* uchungu wa moyo, chuki, chukio, udhiko.

chain, *n.* mnyororo; (*ornamental*) mkufu; (*of events &c.*) mambo mengi yakifuatana, mafuatano, mfululizo. *Door chain*, liza, tumbuu. *A chain of mountains* (*lakes, villages &c.*) mfululizo wa milima (maziwa, miji *&c.*). — *v.t.* funga, fungia mnyororo; zuia.

chair, *n.* kiti; kiti na kazi ya *Professor* (mwalimu mkubwa). — *v.t.* weka katika cheo chenye amri, *e.g.* cha *professor*; chukua mtu juu mbele ya watu kwa sherehe. **chairman**, *n.* mkuu wa baraza, mkutano *&c.*

chaise, *n.* namna ya gari linalovutwa na farasi.

chalice, *n.* kikombe; kikombe cha Ushirika Mtakatifu.

chalk, *n.* chokaa kabla haijachomwa moto, chaki. — *v.t.* paka chaki; fanya alama kwa chaki.

challenge, *v.t.* ita kuja kushindana (katika michezo au kupigana vita) sai; (*question, deny*) kaidi, kana, bisha. — *n.* mwito wa kuja kushindana (kupigana); neno la kukaidi au kubisha *&c.*

chamber, *n.* chumba; (*cavity*) kitundu, shimo, mvungu; (*council*) mkutano, baraza. **chambering**, *n.* uasherati. **chamberlain**, *n.* msimamizi wa nyumba, mtunza mali.

chameleon, *n.* kinyonga, kigeugeu, lumbwi.

champ, *v.i.* tafunatafuna (hasa kwa kelele); fanya kelele la kutafunatafuna.

champagne, *n.* namna ya divai ya kifaransa.

champion, *n.* apiganaye na mwingine (kwa ajili yake mwenyewe au kwa mwingine), ateteaye (mwenyewe au mwingine); mshindi (wa mashindano ya mbio ngumi *&c.*) shujaa, mjasiri. — *a.* bora -a kwanza, -a kupita -ingine. — *v.t.* tetea, shindania, pigania, saidia. **championship**, *n.* ushindi.

chance, *n*, tukio, bahati, sudi, nasibu, kikuti, ajali; (*opportunity*) nafasi; (*risk of danger*) hatari; (*probability*) elekeo. *There is no chance of it*, haitukii, haitokei, haiwezekani, (*it is not probable*) haielekei, si yamkini. *He lost his chance*, alichelewa, hakutumia nafasi, hakuwahi, hakudiriki. *A happy chance*, bahati ya heri, kikuti chema, ndege njema. *Take one's chance*, tumia nafasi, wahi, bahatisha. *Have a chance*, pata nafasi, jaliwa. *There was great chance of danger*, paliweza kuwa na hatari sana. — *v.i.* tukia, -wa, tokea; (*chance upon*) kuta; — *v.t.* (*risk*) bahatisha.

chancel, *n.* upande wa kanisa palipo madhabahu.

chancellor, *n.* mkuu wa korti; mkuu wa *University* (chuo kikuu); (*of diocese*) mshauri wa askofu juu ya kanuni za Kanisa; (*of exchequer*) mkuu wa mambo yahusuyo fedha za nchi.

chancery, *n.* sehemu ya korti kuu ya Uingereza.

chancre, *n.* kidonda cha kaswende mbeleni.

chandelier, *n.* thurea, mwango wenye vinara vingi vya kuwekea mishumaa. **chandler**, *n.* mfanya (mwuzaji) wa mishumaa, sabuni, mafuta *&c.* *Ship's chandler*, mwuza chakula, kamba, na zana za meli na vyombo vya bahari.

change, *v.t.* geuza, badili, badilisha (*money*) vunja; (*mind*) ghairi, rajua; (*round*) zingatia; — *v.i.* badilika, geuka. *Change colour*, iva uso. *Change one's self*, badili nguo. — *n.* mageuzi, mabadili, mabadiliko; mageuko, mabadilisho; (*coins*) senti, fulusi, kichele. **changeable**, *a.* -a kigeugeu, -geugeu, -badilifu, -a kuelekea kubadilibadili, -a kughairi.

changeability, changeableness, *n.* ugeugeu, ugeuzi, ubadilifu, hali ya kubadilibadili, mageuzi mengi.

changeling, *n.* jini aliyedhaniwa ameachwa badala ya mtoto wa kibinadamu aliyechukuliwa na majini (katika hadithi).

channel, *n.* panapopita mto, mfereji, njia ya maji; mlangobahari; mfumbi; njia.

chant, *v.t. and i.* imba. — *n.* wimbo. **chanter**, *n.* mwimbaji. **chanty**, *n.* wimbo unaoimbwa na mabaharia wanapofanya kazi, kutiana shime.

chanticleer, *n.* jogoo, jimbi.

chanty, *n.* taz. *chant.*
chaos, *n.* kisicho na umbo wala taratibu, machafuko matupu. **chaotic**, *a.* -liochafuka, -liofujika.
chap, (1) *v.t.* pasua; — *v.i.* pasuka. — *n.* mpasuko, mtombo wa buba.
chap, (2) *n.* mtu (mwanamume).
chapel, *n.* kanisa dogo (*e.g.* katika kanisa kubwa); kanisa zisizo za madhehebu ya Kanisa la kiingereza. **chaplain**, *n.* kasisi wa manowari (wa jeshi la askari, wa nyumba ya mtu mkuu *&c.*).
chaperon, *n.* mwanamke afuatanaye na kijana mwanamke mahali asiporuhusiwa kwenda peke yake kwa desturi. — *v.t.* fuatana na (kumsindikiza) kijana mwanamke mahali asiporuhusiwa kwenda peke yake ili kumwangalia.
chaplain, *n.* taz. *chapel.*
chaplet, *n.* taji (ya maua); tasbihi.
chaps, *n.* mataya.
chapter, *n.* (of book) sura, mlango; (*of cathedral*) wakuu wa *cathedral*; (*of a society*) mkutano. *A chapter of accidents*, mfululizo wa mambo yaliyotukia (yasiyofikiriwa). *To the end of the chapter*, mpaka mwisho kabisa, daima.
char, *v.t.* unguza, choma kwa moto; *v.i.* ungua (mpaka kuwa makaa).
character, *n.* sifa, moyo, tabia, silika, jinsi, namna, aina; (*high character*) sifa njema, wema; (*written*) herufi, tarakimu, mchoro, mwandiko, alama; (*stamped*) chapa, muhuri; (*condition*) hali, cheo, kazi; (*testimonial*) barua ya kazi. **characteristic**, *a.* -a tabia (namna, jinsi) ya peke yake; -a namna. *It is characteristic of him*, ndiyo kazi (namna, ibada, sifa) yake hasa. — *n.* jambo (sura *&c.*) lionyeshalo tabia ya mtu (au kitu), hulka. **characterize**, *v.t.* eleza habari ya, wasifu, pambanua, fafanusha, ainisha.
charade, *n.* namna ya tambo au kitendawili ambacho uteguzi wake ni neno; sehemu mbalimbali za neno huelezwa kwa namna ya michezo, na watu hujaribu kuvumbua neno zima.
charcoal, *n.* makaa.
charge, *v.t.* (*command*) agiza, amuru, wekea; (*gun*) shindilia; (*exact*) toza, lipiza; (*accuse*) shtaki, suta, kengemeka (*attack*) shambulia, rukia, endea kwa nguvu; (*fill*) jaza, shindilia, tilia. — *n.* agizo, amri, usia; (*care*) utunzo, uangalizi, kabidhi; (*cost*) kima, bei, thamani, gharama, saari; (*in war*) shambulio, mwendeo: (*of gun*) shindilio, kiasi cha bunduki, risasi; (*accusation*) mashtaka, masuto, msuto, mshtaka; (*trust*) amana, tunu, dhamana. *It is in my charge*, nimewekewa jambo hili; ni juu yangu. *Give in charge*, fungisha, weka mikononi mwa serikali (polisi). *Lay to one's charge*, pakiza, pakilika, wekea, tilia. *Without any charge*, bila kulipa, bila gharama, bure, bilashi. **chargeable**, *a.* -a kupasiwa, -a kupatilizwa, -a kupasiwa lawama (hatia *&c.*) **charger**, *n.* (*horse*) farasi wa vita; (*dish*) sahani kubwa.
chariot, *n.* gari kubwa zuri; (zamani —gari la vita au mashindano). **charioteer**, *n.* mwendeshaji *chariot.*
charity, *n.* upendano, wema, ufadhili, hisani, huruma, tabia ya kupenda wengine na kuwafadhili; (*almsgiving*) upaji wa sadaka. **charitable**, *a.* -paji, -ema, -enye huruma, fadhili, -enye hisani.
charlatan, *n.* mdanganyi, jambazi, mjanja, mlaghai, ajisingiziaye mwenye elimu au nguvu asiyo nayo.
charm, *n.* talasimu, hirizi, kago, zinguo, amali, azima, fingo; (*beauty*) uzuri; (*grace*) madaha, haiba; (*agreeableness*) mapendezi. — *v.t.* fanyia uchawi, loga; (*please*) liwaza, pendeza mno; (*attract*) vuta kwa uzuri (mapendezi *&c.*). **charmer**, *n.* mtu (hasa mwanamke) mzuri, mpendezi.
chart, *n.* ramani, hasa ya bahari na pwani; orodha au mpango wa mambo ya maarifa.

charter, *n.* hati, mkataba. — *v.t.* kodi meli *&c.* imarisha kwa hati au mkataba.

charwoman, *n.* mwanamke kibarua, afanyaye kazi ya kufagia, kupangusa vyombo *&c.* nyumbani.

chary, *a.* -nyimivu, -nyiminyimi, -bahili, -a kutoa kidogo kidogo tu, -sunzaji.

chase, (1) *v.t.* winda, saka; (*drive away*) fukuza, winga. — *n.* mwindo, msako; (*pursuit*) mfukuzo, mfuato; (*game*) mawindo. *Give chase*, winda, fuata. *Wild-goose chase*, fanya bidii bure, *e.g.* bila tumaini la kufaulu; kazi bure.

chase, (2) *v.t.* tia temsi, chora, nakshi (madini).

chasm, *n.* shimo kubwa, ufa mkubwa, genge.

chassis, *n.* majengo, mashine na magurudumu ya motakaa *&c.* bila sehemu ya juu.

chaste, *a.* safi, -takatifu, -zuri, -nyofu. **chasten**, *v.t.* rudi, ongoza; punguza harara. **chastened**, *a.* liotakaswa, -liotulizwa (kwa adhabu, mateso *&c*). **chastise**, *v.t.* adhibu, rudi, piga kwa kusudi la kutiisha, tia adabu. **chastisement**, *n.* adhabu kwa ajili ya kutiisha, rada. **chastity**, *n.* utakatifu, usafi; ubikira; kiasi.

chasuble, *n.* vazi la kasisi la kutolea Misa, lisilo na mikono.

chat, *v.i.* ongea, zungumza juu ya mambo ya hivi hivi tu. — *n.* maongezi, mazungumzo, soga, porojo.

chatter, *v.i.* payapaya, bwabwaja, payuka, ongea, zungumza bila maana; (*sound*) tatarika, *e.g.* meno kwa baridi au hofu. — *n.* mapuo, mapayupayu, maongezi hafifu, vijineno. **chatterbox**, **chatterer**, *n.* mpayupayu, mpayukaji, mlimi.

chateau, *n.* jumba.

chattels, *n.* vyombo, vifaa, mapambo ya nyumba, vikorokoro.

chatter, *v.i.* **chatterbox**, *n.* **chatterer**, *n.* taz. *chat.*

chauffeur, *n.* mwendeshaji wa motakaa, dereva (*Engl. driver*) *is now often used.*

cheap, *a.* rahisi, bahasa, kipatikanacho bila shida (bila kufanya bidii); hafifu, isiyo na thamani, duni. *Dirt cheap*, rahisi mno.

cheapen, *v.i.* shuka thamani, pungua bei; — *v.t.* (*make cheap*) rahisisha, punguza bei; shusha thamani, vunja heshima. **cheapness**, *n.* urahisi.

cheat, *v.t.* danganya, punja, kalamkia, hadaa, kenga, renga, kopa, pata kwa hila au kwa werevu, laghai, ghuri. — *n.* mdanganyi, mjanja, ayari, mwenye hila, mwerevu, mlaghai, jambazi, mdhabidhabina.

check, *v.t.* zuia, simamisha, pinga; (*rebuke*) rudi, kemea, karipia; (*mark off*) tia alama, andika; (*by comparison*) tazama kusudi kusahihisha. — *n.* zuio, kizuio; (*pattern*) mirabaraba; (*money*) taz. *Cheque*; (*mark*) alama ya kutilia orodha *&c.*, ili kusahihisha; (*token*) kitu cho chote, kuthibitisha haki ya kitu kilichowekwa, *e.g.* cheti.

checkmate, *n.* mwisho, pigo la mwisho. — *v.t.* shinda kabisa, au, funga bao.

cheek, *n.* shavu la uso; (*impudence*) ujuvi, ushupavu, ufidhuli, usafihi, ukavu wa macho, kiburi. — *v.t.* sema kwa ushupavu (kwa ujuvi *&c.*). **cheek bone**, *n.* kituguta, kitefute. **cheeky**, *a.* -shupavu, -juvi, -enye kiburi, -fidhuli, safihi, -kavu wa macho. *Cheek by jowl*, hali ya kuwa karibu karibu.

cheep, *v.i.* lia kama makinda ya ndege waliavyo.

cheer, *n.* tabia, hali ya moyo; (*good cheer*) furaha, uchangamshi; (*shout*) vifijo, ukelele wa kuamkia (kusalimu, kufurahia, kushangilia, kusifu, kutia moyo au bidii); (*entertainment*) vyakula na mazungumzo. — *v.t.* fariji, furahisha, changamsha, anisi, teremesha; tia moyo, pa moyo; — *v.i.* (*cheer up*) kunjua uso, changamka, ondoa huzuni; (*shout*) piga ukelele wa kuamkia (kusalimu, kushangilia, kufurahia, kusifu, kutia moyo &c.). **cheerful,** *a.* kunjufu, -a furaha, -changamfu. **cheerfulness,** *n.* uchangamfu, ukunjufu. **cheerless,** *a.* bila furaha, bila raha, -sikitivu, -a kuhuzunisha. **cheery,** *a.* -kunjufu, -a furaha, -changamfu.

cheese, *n.* jibini, namna ya chakula kilichotengenezwa kwa maziwa yaliyogandishwa. **cheese-paring,** *a.* -bahili, -nyimivu, kabidhi.

cheetah, *n.* duma, mnyama kama chui ila si mkali.

chef, *n.* mpishi mkuu.

chemical, *n.* taz. *chemist.*

chemise, *n.* vazi la kike kama shati.

chemist, *n.* mwenye elimu ya *chemistry.* **chemical,** *n.* dawa, lakini hasa ni zile zipatikanazo chini ya ardhi kuliko zile za mitini; tena hutumika zaidi kwa kazi kuliko kunywewa na watu. **chemistry,** *n.* elimu ya namna zote za vitu vya duniani vyenye uzito, kama vile: udongo, mawe, maji, hewa ya namna zote na kadhalika; na ya tabia za asili za vitu hivyo; na ya mabadiliko yanayotokea kama vitu vya namna mbalimbali vikiunganika au kuchanganyika pamoja. (Lakini, si mabadiliko yanayofanyika kwa nguvu za asili za duniani, kama vile: ya joto, ya sauti, ya umeme, ya sumaku, na kadhalika. Taz. *Physics.*); elimu ya kuchunguza namna vitu vyo vyote vinavyobadilika kwa kawaida vikiunganika au kuchanganyika pamoja.

cheque, *n.*, **check,** *n.* hawala, hati ya fedha, hundi.

chequered, *a.* -a mirabaraba; -enye mabadiliko mengi.

cherish, *v.t.* tunza, linda, hifadhi, tendea wema; (*nurture*) lisha, chunga, lea.

cheroot, *n.* tumbako iliyosokotwa, biri.

cherry, *n.* namna ya tunda dogo jekundu la Ulaya.

cherub, *n.* mtoto mzuri; malaika (katika picha ni kama uso wa mtoto mwenye mabawa).

chess, *n.* mchezo wa sataranji.

chest, *n.* kifua; (*of animals*) kidari; (*large box*) sanduku. *Chest complaint, or cold on the chest &c.*, kifua. *Chest of drawers,* almari.

chestnut, *n.* (*tree, fruit*) namna ya mti wa Ulaya na matunda yake; (*colour*) rangi ya hudhurungi nyekundu.

chevron, *n.* utepe wa cheo cha askari.

chew, *v.t. and i.* tafuna, guguna, tikita; (*think over*) fikirifikiri. *Chew the cud,* cheua (kwa mnyama).

chicanery, *n.* hila, werevu, ulaghai.

chick, chicken, *n.* kifaranga (cha kuku), kinda (la ndege). **chicken-hearted,** *a.* -oga. **chicken-pox,** *n.* tetewanga.

chide, *v.t.* (*p.t. and pf.t.* **chid**) karipia, kemea; —*v.i.* nung'unika, nuna, zoza.

chief, *n.* jumbe, mfalme, sultani, mkuu &c. — *a.* -kuu, -kubwa, bora, -a kwanza, -enye maana zaidi. **chiefly,** *adv.* kwanza, zaidi, hasa, aghalabu. **chieftain,** *n.* taz. *chief.* **chieftaincy, chieftainship,** *n.* ujumbe, ufalme, usultani, ukuu, enzi &c.

chiffon, *n.* nguo nyembamba kama shashi.

chigoe, *n.* tekenya, funza.

chilblain, *n.* namna ya jipu, hasa la mikononi au miguuni limpatalo mtu hasa wakati wa baridi kali.

child, *n.* (*pl.* **children**) mtoto, mwana, kijana; (*small child*) kitoto, mtoto mchanga, malaika. *From a child,* tangu utoto. *Have a child,* zaa, jifungua. *Be with child,* chukua mimba, -wa mzito. **child-bearing, child-birth,** *n.* uzazi. **childhood,** *n.* utoto, ujana. *Second childhood,* ukongwe. **childhish,** *a.* kitoto; puzi, -jinga. **childless,** *a.* bila mtoto, gumba, tasa. **childlike,** *a.* -a kama mtoto; -enye tabia (mambo &c.) kama mtoto; bila hatia, -tiifu, -sikivu. **child welfare,** *n.* elimu ya utunzaji wa watoto wachanga.

chill, *n.* baridi, homa ya baridi. — *v.t.* tia baridi; gandisha kwa barafu; (*depress*) legeza, shusha moyo; — *v.i.* (*become cold*) poa, geuka kuwa baridi. **chilled,** *a.* iliyofanywa baridi, -liyogandishwa kwa barafu. **chilly,** *a.* -a baridi.

chilli, *n.* pilipili hoho.

chilly, *a.* taz. *chill.*

chime, *n.* sauti za kengele zikigongwa taratibu; ulinganifu wa sauti. — *v.t. and i.* lia (liza) mtungo wa kengele kwa taratibu, *e.g.* kengele za kanisa; — *v.i.* lingana, patana. *Chime in,* jitia kwa upatanifu. *Chime in with,* patana na, lingana na.

chimera, *n.* mnyama katika hadithi mwenye kichwa cha simba, mwili wa mbuzi na mkia wa nyoka, atoaye moto kinywani; wazo lo lote la upuzi lisiloelekea kuwa kweli, kama la ndoto. **chimerical,** *a.* -a upuzi tu, -a kuwazwa tu, -a ndoto ndoto tu.

chimney, *n.* dohani, bomba la kutokea moshi. (la jiko, joko &c.)

chimpanzee, *n.* sokwe, namna ya nyani mkubwa.

chin, *n.* kidevu.

China, *n.* (*country*) China (Sina); (*article*) vyombo, *e.g.* vikombe, sahani, mabakuli &c. vya udongo mweupe, wa kauri; **china-clay,** *n.* udongo laini mweupe wa mfinyanzi, wa kauri. **Chinaman,** *n.* mwenyeji wa nchi ya (China). **Chinese,** *a.* -a China; -a kichina.

chine, *n.* uti wa mgongo; salala, yaani nyama ya mgongoni; kigongo au kilele.

Chinese, *a.* taz. *China.*

chink, (1) *n.* mwanya mwembamba, ufa mwembamba.

chink, (2) *n.* mlio kama wa fedha zikigongana.

chintz, *n.* namna ya kitambaa kama shiti kilichochapwa rangi.

chip, *v.t.* kata, kata vipande vidogo, buabua, vunja kipande kidogo; — *v.i.* katika kipande kidogo, vunjika kipande kidogo. — *n.* kipande kidogo sana, kibanzi, kigeregenja, kigereng'enza, chenga, chembe.

chirp, chirrup, *n.* mlio mwembamba mkali kama wa ndege au mdudu. — *v.i.* lia kama ndege au mdudu; ongea kwa uchangamfu. **chirpy,** *a.* -changamfu, -a furaha.

chisel, *n.* patasi, balari (*morticing*) juba. — *v.t.* kata, chora (kwa patasi au chembeu); (*cheat*) danganya, laghai, ghilibu.

chit, *n.* cheti, barua.

chit-chat, *n.* porojo, soga, mazungumzo, maongezi.

chivalry, *n.* ushujaa, utu bora, uadilifu. **chivalrous,** *a.* -shujaa, -enye kuheshimu, -enye adabu.

chlorine, *n.* namna ya hewa yenye harufu kali sana itokayo chumvini, rangi yake ni ya chanikiwiti. Hutumika kuharibu vijidudu viletavyo ugonjwa, pia katika makombora ya vita ili kuwaangamiza adui. **chloride of lime,** *n.* dawa kama chokaa yenye harufu ya *chlorine*; hutumika kusafishia maji na kuharibu vijidudu vya ugonjwa.

chloroform, *n.* namna moja ya dawa inayotumika kutia usingizi.

chlorophyll, *n.* kitu kilicho asili ya rangi ya mimea.

chock, *v.t.* kaza kwa kabari au kipande. — *n.* kipande au kabari ya kukazia. *Chock-full,* kujaa kabisa, pomoni.

chocolate, *n.* kitu kitengenezwacho kwa unga wa mbegu za mti uitwao *cacao* ukichanganywa na maji hata kuwa laini; kinywaji kinachotengenezwa kwa unga wa *cacao* na maji ya moto, pengine huitwa *cocoa.* — *a.* -a *chocolate*; -enye rangi ya *chocolate,* yaani ya kunde, hudhurungi.

choice, *n.* taz. *choose.*

choir, *n.* jamii ya waimbaji. **choral,** *a.* -a kuimba, -a kuhusu kuimba au waimbaji. **chorister,** *n.* mwimbaji wa *choir.* **chorus,** *n.* jamii ya watu wakiimba au kusema pamoja; (*re-*

frain) itikio la wimbo. *Sing the chorus*, itikia.

choke, *v.t.* kaba, songa roho, sama, zuia pumzi; (*fill up*) songa, ziba, jaza tele; — *v.i.* songwa roho, zuiwa pumzi, paliwa (na chakula *&c.*). — *n.* tendo la kukaba *&c.* *Choke-full*, jaa kabisa (taz. *chock*). *Choke off*, achisha, komesha, zuia, ziba. *Choke up*, ziba kabisa.

choler, *n.* hasira, chuki, harara, ukali. **choleric**, *a.* -epesi kwa hasira, -enye harara, -kali, -a chuki.

cholera, *n.* kipindupindu, waba; ugonjwa mbaya wa kutapika na kuhara sana.

choleric, *a.* taz. *choler*.

choose, *v.t. and i.* (*p.t.* **chose**, *pf.t.* **chosen**) chagua, pambanua, teua, taka, hiari, hitari, kusudia. *You must choose*, nadhari kwako, hiari yako, chagua wewe. *Not much to choose between*, haviachani sana (na vyote ni vibaya). *Pick and choose*, chagua kwa uangalifu. **choice**, *n.* chaguo, hiari, nadhari; kitu kilichochaguliwa, — *a.* -zuri, bora, -a kuchaguliwa, -teule, -a kufaa. *For choice*, afadhali. *Hobson's choice*, chagua kitu kilichotolewa, ama sivyo hupati kitu. *Take one's choice*, twaa ukipendacho.

chop, *v.t.* kata; (*firewood*) chanja, changa, tema (kuni); — *v.i.* (*about*) badilibadili, geukageuka. *Chop and change*, geukageuka, ghairi, zingazinga. — *n.* kipande cha nyama chenye mfupa wa mbavu. **chopper**, *n.* shoka la (kukatia nyama). **choppy**, *a.* (*of sea*) -enye mawimbi, -a kusukasuka.

chops, *n.pl.* mataya, taz. *chaps*.

choppy, *a.* taz. *chop*.

choral, *a.* taz. *choir*.

chord, *n.* sauti tatu au zaidi zinazolingana zikipigwa pamoja; (*string*) utari, uzi wa kinanda, zeze *&c.*; (*geom.*) mstari unaokata kizingo cha duara sehemu mbili.

chorister, *n.* **chorus**, *n.* taz. *choir*.

chortle, *v.i.* chekelea.

chose, *v. p.t.*, **chosen**, *v. pf. t.* ya *choose*.

chrism, *n.* mafuta matakatifu ya ibada nyingine za kikristo. **Christ**, *n.* Yesu Kristo, Masiya. **christen**, *v.t.* taz. *baptize*. **Christendom**, *n.* jamii ya Wakristo wote; jamii ya mataifa walio Wakristo; umati wa Masihi. **Christian**, *n.* Mkristo, Mmasihi. — *a.* -a kikristo, -a Kristo, -a masihi, -a kimasihiya. **Christianity**, *n.* Ukristo, dini ya kikristo. **Christian era**, *n.* wakati unaoanzia siku aliyozaliwa Kristo. *Christian name*, jina mtu analopewa anapobatizwa. **Christianize**, *v.t.* ongoza kuwa Mkristo, fanya Mkristo.

Christmas, *n.*, *Christmas day*, *Xmas.* sikukuu ya kukumbusha kuzaliwa kwake Kristo, yaani tarehe 25 mwezi wa Desemba. *Christmas box*, ada ya *Christmas*, zawadi ya sikukuu. *Christmas eve*, mkesha wa *Christmas* (kesha la *Christmas*).

chromatic, *a.* -a kuhusu rangi; -a rangi; -a kuhusu mpango wa sauti unaopanda kwa *semitones*.

chronic, *a.* -a kudumu sana, -a kuendelea siku nyingi, -a kusedeka, -a kuselelea (kama ugonjwa au mazoea *&c.*). *Chronic invalid*, mgonjwa wa sikuzote.

chronicle, *n.* taarifa, tarehe, hadithi, mtungo kwa ufupi wa habari ya mambo kwa taratibu ya tarehe yaliyotokea. — *v.t.* andika (au simulia) tarehe, yaani habari za mambo kwa taratibu ya tarehe.

chronology, *n.* elimu ya miaka na mambo yafuatanavyo; wakati; taratibu ya miaka.

chronometer, *n.* kitu cha kupimia sahihi wakati unavyopita, saa inayoshika mwendo sahihi.

chrysalis, *n.* buu, jana (hali ya mdudu katikati ya kuwa funza mpaka kutoka na kuruka).

chubby, *a.* -enye uso wa mviringo, -nene.

chuck, *v.t.* tupa; piga polepole chini ya kidevu kama kwa ncha za vidole.

— *n.* kipigo cha polepole sana; mtupo.
chuckle, *n.* kicheko; mlio wa kuku. — *v.i.* lia kama kuku anapowaita vifaranga vyake; (*laugh quietly*) jichekea, chekelea.
chum, *n.* rafiki, hasa hutumika na vijana wa chuoni.
chump, *n.* kisiki cha gogo; kichwa; mjinga. *He is off his chump,* ana wazimu (kichaa).
chunk, *n.* kipande kinene cha kitu cho chote, *e.g.* cha mkate &c.
church, *n.* kanisa; jamii ya wote walio Wakristo; jamii ya makasisi; jamii ya Wakristo wa mahali pamoja, au ya wenye kupatana kwa imani ya dini. **churchman,** *n.* mfuasi wa kanisa la kiingereza. **church-service,** *n.* kawaida ya ibada ya kanisa. **churchwarden,** *n.* msimamizi wa kanisa. **churchyard,** *n.* uwanja wa kanisa, makaburini, karibu ya kanisa. *Church militant,* jamii ya Wakristo walio duniani wanaopigana na uovu. *Church triumphant,* jamii ya Wakristo waliofariki dunia.
churl, *n.* mtu wa kimashamba, mtu asiye na adabu. **churlish,** *a.* bila adabu, -a kimashamba.
churn, *v.t.* sukasuka maziwa (ili kuyagandisha yawe samli); vurugavuruga (kama upepo unavyovuruga bahari). — *n.* chombo cha kusukia maziwa.
chute, *n.* poromoko la maji; mfereji wa maji unaotelemka; njia ya kutelemkia taka, magogo &c.
chutney, *n.* achali ya embe, pilipili, siki &c.
chyle, *n.* namna ya maji meupe yanayotolewa katika chakula kinachopita matumboni.
chyme, *n.* mchanganyiko wa chakula tumboni.
cicatrice, *n.* kovu.
cicerone, *n.* mwongozi.
cider, *n.* kinywaji kinachotengenezwa kwa kushindika matofaa (*apples*).
cigar, *n.* sigara; majani ya tumbako yaliyoviringishwa ya kuvuta, kama biri. **cigarette,** *n.* sigareti, sigara.
cinchona, *n.* jamii ya miti ambayo magome yake hutumika kutengenezea dawa kama kwinini &c.
cincture, *n.* mshipi, ukumbuu.
cinder, *n.* makaa; kitu kilichounguzwa hata kuwa makaa.
cinema, *n.* sinema, nyumba ya kuonyeshea picha zinazoenda kama kwamba ni watu au vitu vyenye uhai. **cinematograph,** *n.* picha zinazoenda kama kwamba ni watu au vitu vyenye uhai; chombo cha kupigia picha hizo. — *v.t.* piga picha za sinema; — *v.t.* onyesha picha za sinema.
Cingalese, *a.* -a Selani (*Ceylon*).
cinnabar, *n.* zingefuri.
cinnamon, *n.* (*tree and bark*) mdalasini.
cipher (cypher), *n.* (*figure*) tarakimu (o), sifuri, tarakimu ya hesabu; mtu au kitu duni kisicho na thamani; (*secret writing*) mwandiko wa fumbo; (*key*) kifumbuo. — *v.t.* fanya hesabu; andika kwa mwandiko wa fumbo.
circle, *n.* duara; mviringo kama wa sahani; (*ring*) pete; (*group*) jamii ya rafiki; duru; wafuasi; watu wenye cheo kimoja. — *v.t. and i.* zunguka, kwenda mwendo wa duara.
circuit, *n.* mzunguko, njia ya kuzunguka; mzunguko wa watu wenye mashughuli katika miji mingine kama vile majaji wazungukao miji mingine kusikiliza mashauri.
circuitous, *a.* -a kuzungukazunguka, -a kupotoka. **circular,** *a.* -a mviringo, -a duara. — *n.* barua (hati, tangazo) ya kueneza habari katika jamii ya watu. **circulate,** *v.t.* eneza, tangaza, vumisha; — *v.i.* (*go round, spread*) zunguka, enea, vumika. **circulation,** *n.* mzunguko, mwenezo; (*of blood*) mzunguko wa damu mwilini mwote toka moyoni na kurudi tena; (*of books &c.*) jumla ya hesabu ya vitabu, magazeti &c. yanayouzwa; (*money*) fedha, sarafu zinazotumika katika nchi.

circumcise, *v.t.* tahiri. **circumcision,** *n.* tohara. *Circumcision rites for boys,* jando, kumbi.

circumference, *n.* kivimbe, mzingo, mstari wa kuzunguka.

circumlocution, *n.* maneno mengi, usemi wa maneno mengi ya bure; maneno ya kuzungusha au kuzunguka.

circumnavigate, *v.t.* safiri kwa merikebu au meli kuzunguka nchi. **circumnavigation,** *n.* safari ya merikebu, meli *&c.* kuzunguka baharini.

circumscribe, *v.t.* andika (weka, tia) mpaka, zuia, fupisha, punguza.

circumspect, *a.* -a kuangalia kila upande, -enye hadhari, -enye busara katika mwenendo; mkaguo. **circumspectly,** *adv.* kwa hadhari, kwa uangalifu, kwa busara.

circumstance, *n.* jambo, neno, kadhia, tukio, hali ya mambo. **circumstances,** *n. pl.* hali zilivyo, manzili; (*good, easy*) usitawi, neema, utajiri *&c.*; (*bad, poor*) umaskini, uhitaji, dhiki. *In* (*or under*) *the circumstances,* kwa hali mambo yalivyo. *Under no circumstances,* sivyo kabisa. **circumstantial,** *a.* -enye mambo yote yapasayo; (*evidence*) si dhahiri au hakika ila huelekea kuwa kwa mambo na hali zilivyokuwa.

circumvallate, *v.t.* zungushia boma. **circumvallation,** *n.* ukuta au boma la kuzungukia mji au ngome.

circumvent, *v.t.* zungusha mtu; danganya, punja, hadaa, ghilibu.

circus, *n.* kiwanja mfano wa duara cha kuchezea, kilinge; jamii ya wachezaji wazungukao mijini kuonyesha michezo yao; tamasha; (*road &c.*) mpango wa nyumba zinazozunguka mahali mfano wa duara.

cirrus, *n.* mavundevunde; mawingu mepesi mepesi ya juu sana.

cistern, *n.* birika, tangi, hodhi.

citadel, *n.* ngome (ndani ya mji).

cite, *v.t.* ita (mbele ya baraza au korti); ((*quote*) nena, taja; leta maneno au hati au maandiko ya kushuhudia. **citation,** *n.* hati, barua (ya kumwita mtu mbele ya baraza au korti); notisi; (*mention*) maneno yaliyotajwa, mtajo wa maneno.

citizen, *n.*, **citizenship,** *n.* taz. *city.*

citron, *n.* (*tree*) mbalungi, (*fruit*) balungi. **citrate,** *n.* dawa chungu kama ukali wa balungi. **citric acid,** *n.* dawa yenye asili ya ukali wa malimau, ndimu *&c.* **citrus,** *n.* mti wa jamii ya mbalungi, mlimau, mdimu, mchungwa *&c.*

city, *n.* mji mkubwa. **citizen,** *n.* mkaa mjini, mwenyeji, raia. **citizenship,** *n.* mambo yampasayo *citizen,* uraia.

civet, *n.* zabadi; (*civet cat*) ngawa; (*small species*) fungo.

civic, civil, *a.* -a kuhusu mji au wakaao mjini, -a mji na watu wake, -a kuhusu watu; -a serikali (lakini si -a kiaskari); (*polite &c.*) -enye adabu, adibu, -a kiungwana; (*law*) -a kuhusu madaawa (lakini si makosa au uhalifu). *Civil war,* vita vya kindani, yaani raia za nchi moja kupigana wao kwa wao. *Civil service,* utumishi wa serikali. **civics,** *n.* elimu ya (uchunguzi wa) mambo yanayohusu watu na serikali, hasa watu wakaao mijini. **civilian,** *n.* raia, (asiye askari). **civility,** *n.* adabu, heshima, uungwana. *Exchange civilities,* salimiana, amkiana, wekeana heshima. **civilize,** *v.t.* toa katika ushenzi au ujinga wa maisha; fundisha mambo yawapasayo waungwana *&c.* (sanaa, sheria za afya, maarifa *&c.*); tamaduni, staarabisha. **civilization,** *n.* utamaduni, ustaarabu, uungwana, hali bora ya kuishi. **civilized,** *a.* -enye kustaarabika, -staarabu, -ungwana. **civilly,** *adv.* kwa adabu, kwa heshima *&c.*

clack, *v.i.* fanya kishindo, alika. — *n.* kishindo cha ghafula, kishindo cha sauti.

clad, taz. *clothed, p.t. and pf.t.* ya *clothe.*

claim, *v.t.* dai, taka kwa haki;

(*assert oneself*) jinena, jitaja; (*without right*) jidai. — *n.* haki, haja, madai, daawa. **claimant,** *n.* mdai, mdaawa.

clairvoyance, *n.* nguvu inayodaiwa na wengine kuona mambo yasiyo-onekana na wengine, *e.g.* mambo yaliyopita, watu waliokufa, mambo yatakayotokea *&c.* **clairvoyant,** *n.* mtu adaiye kuwa ana nguvu ya *clairvoyance.*

clamber, *v.i.* sombea, panda (kwea) kwa shida (kama vile kwa miguu na mikono), paramia, paraga.

clammy, *a.* -a kunata, -a unyevu na kunata kama jasho baridi *&c.*

clamour, *n.* makelele, ghasia, hoihoi. — *v.i.* fanya makelele (ghasia); (*for*) pigia kelele. **clamorous,** *a.* -a makelele, -a ghasia.

clamp, *n.* gango, kigango. — *v.t.* kaza, funga kwa gango.

clan, *n.* kabila, ukoo, jamii ya watu wa mlango mmoja. **clannish,** *a.* -a kushikamana sana kama watu wa ukoo mmoja wafanyavyo. **clanship,** *n.* udugu, ukoo, utani. **clansman,** *n.* mtu wa ukoo fulani; ndugu, mtani.

clandestine, *a.* -a siri, -a kufichwa, -erevu, -penyezevu. **clandestinely,** *adv.* kwa siri.

clang, clank, *v.t. and i.* fanya kishindo kama vyuma vikigongana, au kuvigonganisha. — *n.* kishindo kama cha vyuma kugongana.

clanship, *n.*, **clansman,** *n.*, **clannish,** *a.* taz. *clan.*

clap, *n.* kishindo cha ghafula (kama radi); (*with hands*) kofi; (*of thunder*) radi, ngurumo. — *v.t.* (*the hands*) piga makofi; (*strike with noise*) pigisha kishindo; (*thrust together or fasten suddenly &c.*) tia (weka, funga, bandika *&c.*) upesi sana; — *v.i.* piga makofi (kushangilia, kufurahia). *To clap one in prison,* kumtia mtu kifungoni. *Clap eyes on,* ona. **clap-trap,** *n.* maneno matupu, mapuo, hasa ya kujipendekeza. **clapper,** *n.* kipande kinachogongagonga katika kengele.

claret, *n.* namna ya divai.

clarification, *n.* taz. *clarify.*

clarify, *v.t.* safisha, dhihirisha, eleza wazi; bainisha; — *v.i.* safika, dhihirika. **clarification,** *n.* tendo la kusafisha au kueleza wazi; mbayana.

clarion, *n.* panda, baragumu, tarumbeta. **clarionet,** *n.* namna ya zomari.

clash, *n.* mshindo mkubwa (kama wa vyuma kugongana); (*opposition*) mapigano, makinzano, mabishano, mapambano. — *v.i.* gongana, pambana; (*oppose*) kinzana, bishana, kaidi; — *v.t.* gonganisha kwa mshindo.

clasp, *v.t.* funga (kwa kifungo au bizimu); (*embrace*) kumbatia; (*hold*) kamata, shika; (*in hand*) fumbata; (*clasp hands*) fyata vidole. — *n.* kifungo, bizimu; (*an embrace*) mkumbatio; (*in the hand*) mfumbato.

clasp-knife, *n.* kisu cha kukunja.

class, *n.* cheo, daraja, daraka; (*students*) darasa; (*kind*) namna, jinsi, aina, babu; (*collection*) jamii (ya vitu vya namna moja). — *v.t.* ainisha, panga kwa namna mbalimbali. **classic,** *a.* bora, -zuri, sana. *A classic,* kitabu kilichokubaliwa na wenye elimu kuwa bora cha namna yake, chenye ufasaha, chenye jumla ya maarifa yaliyo bora juu ya jambo fulani *&c.* *The classics,* waandishi au maandiko bora, hasa ya Wayunani na Warumi wa zamani.

classical, *a.* sawasawa na *classic,* -a *classics.* **classify,** *v.t.* ainisha, panga taratibu kwa aina mbalimbali.

classifiable, *a.* -a kupangika (kuweza kupangwa) aina mbalimbali.

classification, *n.* mpango wa aina mbalimbali; mgawanyo wa aina mbalimbali.

clatter, *n.* vishindo vya vitu vikigongana (*e.g.* sahani *&c.*); makelele; maongezi yenye makelele. — *v.i.* fanya vishindo; — *v.t* gonganisha na kufanya vishindo.

clause, *n.* fungu la maneno lenye maana dhahiri; (*of agreement &c.*) sharti.

clave, *p.t.* ya *cleave.*
clavicle, *n.* mtulinga.
clavichord, *n.* mpango wa vipande vya kupigia (kama vile vya kinanda, vya marimba &c.).
claw, *n.* kucha, ukucha; (*of crab, lobster &c.*) gando, gondi. — *v.t.* papura, piga kucha.
clay, *n.* udongo (mzito unaonata kama wa mfinyanzi), towe; mwili wa mwanadamu; *e.g. We are but clay,* sisi ni udongo tu. *Clay-cold,* baridi sana.
clean, *a.* safi, -eupe, nakawa; bila waa, bila hatia; (*ceremonial*) tohara. *Clean slate,* anza upya. *Have clean hands,* bila kosa wala hatia. *Make a clean breast,* ungama, kiri yote kabisa. *Make a clean sweep,* kumba. *Show a clean pair of heels,* toroka, kimbia. **clean, cleanse,** *v.t.* safisha, takasa; (*ceremonially*) eua; (*grain, corn &c.*) twanga, pwaga, menya; (*cotton, cloves*) chambua; (*coco-nuts*) fua; (*fish, copal, by scraping*) paa, palia; (*out of shell*) komba. *Clean up* (*tidy*) nadhifisha. **clean,** *adv.* kabisa, pia. **cleanliness,** *n.* usafi, unadhifu. **cleanly,** *a.* safi, -enye mazoea safi, nadhifu. — *adv.* kwa unadhifu.
clear, *a.* dhahiri, wazi, -baini, -eupe, nakawa, safi, -angavu; (*free from obstruction*) bila kizuizi wala shida; (*without defect*) bila hitilafu. *Clear gain,* faida tupu. *A clear head,* akili timamu. *Clear style,* (*of writing, composition*) nahau, ufasaha. *A clear case,* jambo wazi, dhahiri. *It is quite clear to me,* imeniclea. *Be clear, of weather,* kumetakata. *Clear of,* pasipo, bila, mbali na. — *v.t.* safisha, takasa; ondolea (vizuizi, shida, mashaka, hatia &c.); *jump over*) kiuka, pita juu; (*make gain*) faidi; (*land*) fyeka, lima shamba; — *v.i.* safika, takata; (*pass over*) ondoka, pita. *Clear out, off,* kumba -ote, (*depart*) ondoka. *Clear up,* (*weather*) takata. *Make clear,* safisha, eleza, dhihirisha, bainisha, kunjua, funua, fumbua. *Speak clearly,* pambanua maneno, tamka vizuri, sema kiada. *Be clear* (*intelligible*), elea, elekea. **clearance,** *n.* ondoleo (la vizuizi, shida &c.); (*certificate*) cheti cha kuruhusu meli kuondoka, yaani kushuhudia kuwa imetimiza masharti yote ya forodha; ruhusa. **clearing,** *n.* mahali peupe, palipofyekwa; (*ready for planting*) uchea, uchoo, tendo la kusafisha &c. **clearly,** *adv.* kwa wazi, kwa dhahiri, bila shaka. **clearness,** *n.* weupe, udhahiri, wangavu.
cleat, *n.* makiri.
cleave, (1) *v.t.* (*p.t.* **cleft, clove**; *pf.t.* **cleft, cloven**). pasua, kata, tenga kwa nguvu; (*penetrate*) penya; (*pierce*) choma; — *v.i.* tenguka, pasuka. **cleavage,** *n.* mpasuo; mpasuko; farakano. **cleft,** *n.* ufa, mwanya. *Cleft-palate,* kaakaa la kinywa lenye mpasuko.
cleave, (2) *v.i.* (*p.t.* **cleaved, au clave,** *pf.t.* **cleaved,** (*to*) ambatana na, shikamana na, ganda.
cleft, *p.t. and pf.t. cleave* (1).
clemency, *n.* taz. *clement.*
clement, *a.* -anana, -pole, -enye huruma, -ema. **clemency,** *n.* huruma, upole, utu wema, usamehevu.
clench, *v.* taz. *clinch.*
clergy, *n. pl.* wenye daraja katika Kanisa la kikristo, ndio maaskofu, mapadre, mashemasi &c. **clergyman,** *n.* mmoja wa *clergy.* **cleric,** = *clergyman.* **clerical,** *a.* -a kuhusu *clergy.*
clerk, *n.* karani. **clerkship,** *n.* ukarani, kazi ya karani. **clerical,** *a.* -a kuhusu karani. *Clerical error,* kosa katika kunakili (kufuatisha).
clever, *a.* -enye akili, hodari, -juzi, -bingwa, stadi, mahiri. *A clever workman, mechanic,* fundi, mbingwa, mstadi, waria. **cleverness,** *n.* akili, ujuzi, ustadi, weledi &c.
clew, *n.* bonge la uzi.
click, *n.* mwaliko, sauti ya kualika kama vile kidoko, mtambo wa bunduki &c. — *v.t.* alisha, fanya sauti ya *click,* piga kidoko.

client, *n.* mtu aajiriye mtu mwingine, hasa wakili au mtu wa kumtetea sheriani au aliyezoea kununua mahitaji kwa mwenye duka fulani, au kwenda kwa daktari fulani; mfuasi, rafiki. **clientele,** *n.* jumla ya watu wote wamtumao mtu fulani awatetee au kuwasaidia sheriani, au waliozoea kununua mahitaji kwa mwenye duka fulani, au waliozoea kwenda kwa daktari fulani *&c.*

cliff, *n.* jabali, mtelemko wa ghafula (wa mlima au mahali palipochongoka), genge.

climate, *n.* tabia ya nchi, yaani joto, baridi, upepo, mvua *&c.* **climatic,** *a.* -a kuhusu tabia ya nchi.

climax, *n.* mwisho, kikomo, kipeo.

climb, *v.t.* panda, kwea; panda kwa shida, *e.g.* kwa miguu na mikono; (*a tree*) paraga; — *v.i.* (*slope upwards*) inuka, panda; (*of plants &c.*) tambaa. *Climbing plant,* mmelea, mtambaazi.

clime, *n.* sawasawa na *climate*; nchi, mahali.

clinch, clench, *v.t.* kaza kwa msumari (kuukunja na kuugandamiza); shika sana; kaza sana (*e.g.* meno), fumba sana (mikono); (*an argument*) thibitisha, kata. *A clinching statement,* neno mkataa.

cling, *v.i.* (*p.t. and pf.t.* **clung**) shika, *e.g.* kwa kuzungushia mikono; (*adhere*) ambata, nata; (*together*) ambatana, fungamana, shikamana; (*to*) shikia, shikamana na, gandamana na. **clingy,** *a.* -a kunata, -a kushikashika.

clinic, *n.* mafundisho ya utabibu yanayotolewa katika hospitali; hospitali. *Clinical thermometer,* kipimo cha kupimia homa.

clink, *n.* sauti kama ile ifanyavyo bilauri ikigongwa. — *v.i.* fanya sauti kama bilauri ikigongwa; — *v.t.* pigisha sauti kama kwa kugonganisha bilauri. **clinker,** *n.* mavi ya chuma.

clip, (1) *v.t.* kata kwa mkasi; (*diminish*) punguza, fupisha. **clipper,** *n.* mkasi, jahazi au namna ya merikebu iendayo kasi sana.

clip, (2) *v.t.* shikiza, bana. — *n.* kishikizo, kibano.

clique, *n.* chama au jamii ndogo ya watu wanaoandamana pamoja au walio rafiki sana.

clitoris, *n.* kisimi, kinembe.

cloak, *n.* vazi kama joho; (*a cover*) kitu kinachosetiri au kuficha; (*pretext*) tendo linaloficha kusudi la kweli, tendo la kudanganya, hila. — *v.t.* setiri, ficha, funika.

clock, *n.* saa (kubwa ya mezani, ukutani, au mnarani (si ya mfukoni wala kuvaa mkononi ambayo ni *watch*). *What o'clock is it?* saa ngapi? *Such and such o'clock,* saa fulani. *Go like clockwork,* endelea vizuri sana, bila pingamizi lo lote. *Know what o'clock it is,* kuwa macho, jua mambo yalivyo.

clod, *n.* pumba, bumba, bonge, donge (hasa la udongo); (*person*) mjinga, baradhuli. **clodhopper,** *n.* mtu wa kimashamba, mjinga.

clog, *v.t.* gandiza; tatanisha; zuia — *v.i.* ganda, zibika, zuilika. — *n.* kizuizi; kiatu cha mti, mtalawanda.

cloister, *n.* njia yenye matao inayozunguka behewa au kiwanja nyumba wanamokaa watawa waliojitenga kwa ajili ya dini, taz. *monks.* *The Cloister,* hali ya maisha ya *monks.*

close, *a.* (*shut, narrow &c.*) -liofungwa, -liokazwa, -liokazana, bila mlango au dirisha, bila hewa, -a kusonga, embamba, -a kufinya; (*miserly*) -bahili, -nyimivu, -a choyo; (*near*) karibu; (*hidden*) -liofichwa; (*reserved*) -a kimya, -nyamavu, baridi (*private*) -a siri, a- faragha. *Close to the house,* karibu ya nyumba. *Be close* (*tight*), saki, kaza. *A close room,* chumba kisichopisha hewa, chenye joto (ufukuto). *A close friend,* msiri. *Close fisted, close handed,* bahili, mchoyo, mnyimivu. *It is close to-day,* jasho leo, kumetanda. *At close quarters,* karibu sana.

A close fight, vita vikali vya kusogeleana. *Come close*, karibu, sogea karibu, karibia, jongelea. *It is a close fit*, inakaza, inasaki. *Cut close*, kata sana. — *adv.* karibu; (*much*) sana. — *n.* (*end*) mwisho, kikomo; (*enclosure*) uwanja. **close**, *v.t.* funga, isha; (*eye, mouth &c.*) fumba; (*fist*) fumbata; (*door*) sindika; (*book*) funika; (*fill up*) ziba; (*finish*) maliza; (*close up, enclose*), funga, zunguka; — *v.i.* fungika, fumbika. *Close with* (*agree*) kubali, patana; (*in strife*) songa, shambulia; (*end*) ishia. *Close up, come close*, songana, karibiana. **closely**, *adv.* karibu, sana, kwa bidii, kwa uangalifu; halisi. **closeness**, *n.* kuwa *close*; (*heat*) joto, jasho, ufukuto. **closet**, *n.* kijumba, chumba cha faragha; (*privy*) choo. *Be closeted together*, kutana faraghani (kwa shauri, kusoma *&c.*). **closure**, *n.* mwisho, neno mkataa, kukatiza maneno (katika baraza).

clot, *n.* kidonge, kitungamo, vilio. *The blood is clotted*, damu imevilia (imegandama, imetungama). — *v.i.* gandama, vilia; — *v.t.* gandamisha.

cloth, *n.* nguo au kitambaa cha namna yo yote; (*woollen*) joho, sufu; (*linen*) kitani, bafta; (*calico*) amerikani, ulaiti, gamti *&c.* (*blue*) kaniki, (*brown*) hudhurungi; (*of gold*) zari; (*loin-cloth*) shuka, kikoi, kitambi, doti *&c.* (*turban cloth*) kilemba, kitambi, (*Indian*) ukumbuu; (*table-cloth*) tandiko la meza, nguo ya meza. **clothe**, *v.t.* vika; (*give clothes to*) visha. *Clothe oneself*, vaa, jivalia, jivisha. **clothes**, *n.* mavazi, nguo; (*bed-clothes*) matandiko ya kitanda. **clothing**, *n.* nguo, mavazi, lebasi *&c.*

cloud, *n.* wingu; (*rain*) ghubari; (*scattered*) mavundevunde; (*crowd*) kundi kubwa; (*fear, sorrow &c.*) jambo la hofu (la huzuni *&c.*), lo lote linalotia giza, au kutisha, au kuondoa raha, au kuficha kama wingu. *Under a cloud*, aibuni. *Rise in clouds* (*as dust*) tifuka. — *v.t.* tia kivuli (giza), ficha mwangaza; (*grieve*) huzunisha; (*defame*) aibisha, tweza. *It has clouded over*, kumetanda. **cloudless**, *a.* bila mawingu; kweupe; bila huzuni wala shaka. *Cloudless sky*, kumetakata. **cloudy**, *a.* -enye mawingu (mavunde, giza *&c.*). *It is cloudy*, kumetanda. **cloudiness**, *n.* mawingu, utusitusi.

clout, *n.* kitambaa (hasa cha kusugulia au kusafishia).

clove, (1) *p.t.* ya *cleave*.

clove, (2) *n.* (*tree*) mkarafuu; (*bud*) karafuu; (*stalk*) kikonyo.

cloven, *a.* (*p.t.* ya *cleave*) -liopasuka, -liogawanyika. *Cloven-footed, cloven-hoofed*, -enye kwato mbili (*e.g.* ng'ombe).

clover, *n.* jamii ya mimea fulani ya Ulaya yenye maua matamu; hupendwa sana na ng'ombe, mbuzi *&c.* *Live in clover*, kaa katika hali ya neema (ya wingi).

clown, *n.* (*boor*) mtu wa kimashamba; mtu asiye na adabu; (*fool*) mpumbavu; (*jester*) mcheshi, mchekeshaji. **clownish**, *a.* -a kimashamba; bila adabu; -pumbavu, -puzi.

cloy, *v.t.* kinaisha, chosha.

club, *n.* rungu, gongo, kibarango; (*cards*) pau (*clique*) chama, kikao, shirika la watu (kwa mazungumzo, michezo *&c.*); (*club-house*) nyumba ya mazungumzo na ya kula ya chama, nyumba ya kufanya (kula) bia. — *v.t.* piga kwa rungu *&c.* *Club together*, patana, shirikiana, changa. *Club-foot*, guu (mguu uliopindika).

cluck, *n.* mlio (kama wa kuku anayewaita vifaranga vyake). — *v.i.* fanya mlio kama kuku; piga kidoko.

clue, clew, *n.* (*ball*) kibonge (*e.g.* cha uzi); (*sign*) alama, dalili (ya kuonyesha njia, maana *&c.*), kifunguo, kionyo, kidokozi *&c.*

clump, *n.* bonge (la udongo); kigogo; (*of trees*) kichaka; (*collection*) fungu, jamii.

clumsy, *a.* -zito, -isiyo na umbo zuri; -a ovyo; -jinga. **clumsily**, *adv.* ovyo ovyo.

clung, *p.t. and pf.t.* ya *cling.*

cluster, *n.* shada, kishada, tawi; (*of bananas*) chane; (*group*) jamii, kundi; (*of stars*) thurea. — *v.i.* ota pamoja (kama kishada); kusanyika jamii &c.

clutch, (1) *v.t. and i.* (*the hand*) fumbata; (*hold firmly*) shika sana, shikilia, kamata imara, shika ghafula. — *n.* mfumbato; kitu kinachoshika imara; (*of motor-car &c.*) mtambo unaounganisha na kutenga mashine na mtambo unaozungusha magurudumu.

clutch, (2) *n.* jumla ya mayai yaliyoatamiwa na kuku safari moja, pia vifaranga vilivyoanguliwa.

clutter, *n.* machafuko, fujo. — *v.t.* chafua, fuja.

co., mkato wa *Company* yaani kampani.

coach, *n.* gari (la magurudumu manne); mwalimu wa kufundisha watu mmoja mmoja peke yake; mfundishaji wa michezo ya mashindano. — *v.t.* chukua katika *coach*; fundisha (hasa kuwa tayari kwa mtihani au kwa michezo ya mashindano). — *v.i.* safiri katika *coach.* **coachman,** *n.* sais; mwendeshaji wa *coach.*

coadjutor, *n.* mshirika katika kazi; msaidizi; mwenzi.

coagulate, *v.t.* gandisha; — *v.i.* ganda, tungama; (*of blood*) vilia.

coal, *n.* makaa ya mawe. *Live coals,* makaa ya moto. *Dead coals,* makaa zimwe. *Carry coals to Newcastle,* fanya kazi bure, *c.f. prov.* amerudisha tende Manga, *he has sent back dates to Arabia.* — *v.t. and i.* pakia makaa melini. **coal-gas,** *n.* namna ya hewa inayotoka makaani; hutiwa katika matangi makubwa na kuchukuliwa katika mabomba membamba mpaka nyumbani; humo hutumika kupashia moto majiko na kuwashia taa. **coal-mine, coal-pit,** *n.* shimo la kuchimbua makaa. **coal-tar,** *n.* namna ya lami inayopatikana wakati wa kutengenezwa *coal-gas. Coaling station,* bandari inamowekwa akiba ya makaa ya kupakia melini. *Call* (*haul*) *over the coals,* kemea, karipia.

coalesce, *v.i.* ungana, changanyikana; shirikiana. **coalescence,** *n.* mwungano. **coalition,** *n.* mwungano, shirika, mapatano (ya watu, mataifa &c.).

coarse, *a.* (*rough*), -a kukwaruza; (*inferior*) duni; -a futo, hafifu, ovyo; (*rude*) -shenzi, bila adabu.

coast, *n.* mwambao, pwani, ukingo wa bahari, nchi iliyo karibu na bahari; (*beach*) pwani, ufuko. — *v.i.* pita pwani kwa pwani, ambaa pwani, sairi; telemka mlima juu ya baisikeli na huku miguu inapumzika. **coastal,** *a.* -a pwani. **coast-guard,** *n.* watu wenye zamu kuangalia pwani na kutoa habari za meli zilizokwama au kuvunjika na kuzuia watu wasipenyeze vitu katika nchi bila kulipa ushuru wa forodhani. **coast-line,** *n.* mpaka wa pwani na bahari, pwani.

coat, *n.* vazi lenye mikono, koti; (*of animals*) ngozi, manyoya; (*outer cover*) funiko, sehemu ya nje; (*of paint*) mpako. — *v.t.* funika, tia nje; (*paint*) paka. **coating,** *n.* funika; kitambaa cha koti; mpako.

coax, *v.t.* bemba, bembeleza, rairai, vuta, shawishi, dekeza, tundua. **coaxing,** *n.* ubembe, ushawishi. — *a.* -bembe.

cob, *n.* (*of maize*) gunzi, bunzi, guguta; (*horse*) farasi mfupi mnene.

cobalt, *n.* namna ya rangi ya buluu.

cobble, *v.t.* tengeneza ovyo tu (*e.g.* viatu &c.). **cobbler,** *n.* mtengenezaji viatu; kinywaji cha divai, sukari na vitu vingine vimechanganyika.

coble, *n.* namna ya mashua ya wavuvi.

cobra, *n.* namna ya nyoka anayeweza kuvimbisha shingo yake; (*spitting*) fira, swila.

cobweb, *n.* utando wa buibui.

coccyx, *n.* kifandugu, kitokono, tokono.

cock, *n.* jogoo, jimbi; (*not yet crowing*) pora, kipora; (*male bird*) ndege dume; (*fighting, game*) kuchi; (*tap*) bilula; (*plucky chap*) mbeja. *Cockscomb,* upanga, kilemba, ushungi, undu. *Cock's wattles,* ndevu. *A cock and bull story,* hadithi ya kutiwa chuku, isiyoweza kusadikika. *Knock into a cocked hat,* shinda kabisa. — *v.t.* simikisha; (*a gun*) paza mtambo; (*turn up at side*) pindua upande; — *v.i.* (*strut*) tambatamba. **cockade,** *n.* kishada cha kofia. **cock-crow,** *n.* alfajiri, saa ya kuwika jogoo. **cockerel,** *n.* kipora. **cock-eyed,** *a.* -enye kitongo, -enye makengeza, -a upogo. **cock-sure,** *a.* hakika kabisa. **cocktail,** *n.* kinywaji kikali cha mchanganyiko wa divai &c. **cocky,** *a.* -juvi, -shupavu, -kavu wa macho. **cockpit,** *n.* kiwanja cha kupiganishia majogoo; (*of aeroplane*) mahali pa kukaa mwendeshaji wa eropleni.

cockatoo, *n.* namna ya kasuku.

cockatrice, *n.* mnyama katika hadithi kama jogoo mwenye mkia wa joka.

cock-crow, *n.,* **cockerel,** *n.,* **cock-eyed,** *a.* taz. *cock.*

cockle, *n.* namna ya kombe ya pwani kidogo kama mwanamizi. *Cockles of the heart,* moyo wenyewe.

cockney, *n.* mzalia wa mtaa fulani mji wa London.

cockpit, *n.* taz. *cock.*

cockroach, *n.* mende, kombamwiko.

cock-sure, *a.,* **cocktail,** *n.,* **cocky,** *a.* taz. *cock.*

cocoa, *n.* mbegu za mti uitwao *cacao* zilizosagwa hata kuwa unga; kinywaji kitengenezwacho kwa kuchanganya unga huo pamoja na maji ya moto.

coco-nut, *n.* (*tree*) mnazi; (*ripe nut*) nazi; (*nut with milk*) dafu. *Leaf,* kuti; (*for thatch*) makuti, makuti ya viungo; (*for screen, enclosure*) makuti ya kumba. *Fibre, coir,* makumbi; (*cleaned*) usumba. *Shell,* kifuu. *Milk,* maji. *Copra,* mbata, nazi kavu. *Oil,* mafuta ya nazi. *Oil juice for cooking,* tui. *Grated nut,* chicha.

cocoon, *n.* kifukofuko, nyumba ya mdudu anayotengeneza kwa kujizungushia nyuzinyuzi.

cod, *n.* namna ya samaki wa Ulaya; (*giant rock-cod*) chewa.

coddle, *v.t.* engaenga, tendekeza, endekeza, tundua.

code, *n.* kitabu chenye muhtasari ya sheria; orodha, mpango wa kanuni, sheria, taratibu &c.; kawaida za maisha (za mwenendo); (*cipher*) mpango wa herufi au tarakimu zinazotumika badala ya maneno mazima au mafungu ya maneno ili kupunguza gharama ya kupeleka simu, na kuficha habari za mambo yanayoarifiwa.

codicil, *n.* ongezo au nyongeza ya usia, yaani ulioandikwa baadaye, usia ulipokwisha tiwa sahihi.

coerce, *v.t.* zuia kwa nguvu; (*compel*) shurutisha, lazimisha, tia nguvu (lazima, sharti), ghusubu. **coercion,** *n.* uzuizi, lazima, sharti, nguvu. **coercive,** *a.* -enye nguvu ya kushurutisha, -a kushurutisha, -a nguvu, -a sharti.

coeval, *n.* -enye umri ule ule, hirimu, rika moja.

coffee, *n.* (*plant*) mbuni; (*berry*) buni; (*drink*) kahawa. *Coffee-pot,* mdila. *Coffee-house,* mkahawani. *Coffee-mill,* kinu cha kusagia kahawa.

coffer, *n.* sanduku, kasha kubwa (hasa la kuwekea fedha).

coffin, *n.* sanduku la kuzikia maiti. — *v.t.* tia maiti katika sanduku.

cog, *n.* jino la gurudumu. **cog-wheel,** *n.* gurudumu lenye meno meno.

cogent, *a.* -a nguvu, -a maana, -a kusadikisha, -enye sharti, -a lazima. **cogency,** *n.* nguvu ya kusadikisha. **cogently,** *adv.* kwa jinsi ya kusadikisha.

cogitate, *v.t.* fikiri sana, waza, kumbuka. **cogitation,** *n.,* fikira, wazo.

cognate, *a.* -a namna (jamii, aina) moja; -enye asili au chanzo kile kile.

cognizance, *n*. habari, utambuo; uhakimu; uwezo wa hakimu. *It was not within his cognizance*, alikuwa hana habari juu yake; (*of judge &c.*) hakuwa na amri juu yake, haliku-tokea katika uhakimu wake (katika wilaya yake). *Have cognizance*, jua, tambua, fahamu; (*of magistrate*) -wa na amri ya kuhoji. **cognition**, *n*. habari hakika; ufahamu, wazo. **cognizable**, *a*. -a kujulikana; -a kufahamika; -a katika amri ya hakimu (jaji) &c.

cohabit, *v.i.* ingiliana; kaa kinyumba au nyumba moja (hasa mwanamume na mwanamke wasiooana). **cohabitation**, *n*. hali ya kukaa kinyumba, kukaa pamoja kama mume na mke.

co-heir, *n*. arithiye pamoja na mwingine.

cohere, *v.i.* ambatana, shikamana, fungamana; (*follow*) fuatana kwa taratibu; tegemeana; (*agree together*) lingana, patana. **coherence**, *n*. shikamano, ambatano; fuatano tegemeano; (*firmness*) ugumu; (*agreement*) ulinganifu, upatanifu. **coherent**, *a*. -a kuambatana, -a kufungamana; -a kutegemeana; (*agreeing with*) -a kulingana, -a kupatana; (*rational*) -a maana, -a akili. **cohesion**, *n*. kama *coherence*.

cohort, *n*. jeshi la askari.

coign, *n*. pembe ya nje, jiwe la pembeni; kabari. *Coign of vantage*, mahali pafaapo (pa kuona au kutenda jambo).

coil, *v.t.* kunja, piga pindi, pindanisha, zonga, zungusha; — *v.i.* zunguka, zongamana. — *n*. kipande cha kamba iliyopindika; pindi (kama la kamba la nyoka, la uzi wa simu &c.); (*difficulty*) matatano, matatizo, mashaka.

coin, *n*. sarafu; fedha ya kutumia (zenye chapa ya serikali), senti, shilingi &c. — *v.i.* fanyiza sarafu; (*invent*) buni, tunga, zua. **coinage**, *n*. sarafu, fedha za kutumia za nchi. **coiner**, *n*. mfanyizaji sarafu; mfanyi sarafu za kubuni, yaani za uwongo. *To pay a man in his own coin*, kumtendea mtu kama alivyokutendea.

coincide, *v.i.* lingana, patana, -wa sawa. **coincidence**, *n*. ulinganifu, upatanifu, usawa; jambo litukialo kulingana na jingine kwa nasibu, ajabu.

coiner, *n*. taz. *coin*.

coir, *n*. makumbi ya mnazi; (*cleaned*) usumba.

coition, **coitus**, *n*. tendo la kujamii.

coke, *n*. makaa mawe zimwe.

colander, *n*. bakuli lililotobolewa vitundu, ni namna ya kung'uto.

cold, *n*. baridi. *Cold* (*in the head*), makamasi, mafua; (*in the chest*) kifua, mkamba. *I have a cold*, siwezi mafua (au kamasi). — *a*. -a baridi, -tepetevu, -legevu, bila bidii (upendo, tamaa, shauku, ashiki, faraja &c.). *Become cold*, poa, pata baridi, zizima. *Catch cold, take cold*, patwa na kamasi au mafua. *Give the cold shoulder*, -pa kisogo. *In cold blood*, kwa makusudi, bila huruma, kwa ukali, kwa ukatili. *Throw cold water on*, fisha moyo, poozesha, haribu. **cold-blooded**, *a*. -enye damu baridi (kama samaki); -gumu, -katili. **cold-chisel**, *n*. tindi. **cold-hearted**, *a*. bila huruma, bila upendo, baridi. **coldish**, *a*. baridi kidogo.

colic, *n*. msokoto (msongo) wa tumbo.

collaborate, *v.i.* shiriki katika kazi (hasa ya kubuni vitabu). **collaborator**, *n*. mshiriki au msaidizi wa kazi (hasa kubuni vitabu au katika kutunga habari za elimu &c.).

collapse, *v.i.* anguka, poromoka; zimia, zirai; angamia; kata tamaa, -fa moyo; (*fold up*) kunjana, kunjamana. — *n*. anguko, poromoko; angamizo; hali ya kuzimia (ya kukata tamaa). **collapsible**, *a* -a kuweza kukunjwa, -a kukunjamana. *A collapsible boat*, mashua inayoweza kukunjwa.

collar, *n.* ukosi (mkufu, ukanda, utepe) wa shingo, kala; (*ring*) pete. — *v.t.* shika, kamata (hasa kwa ukosi wa shingo). **collar-bone**, *n.* mtulinga.

collate, *v.t.* linganisha, pambanisha (hasa maandiko); (*arrange*) panga kwa taratibu (*e.g.* kurasa za vitabu tayari kutiwa jalada). **collation**, *n.* ulinganisho; (*meal*) chakula.

collateral, *a.* (*side by side*) sambamba; ubavu kwa ubavu; bega kwa bega; (*from same ancestor*) -enye asili moja lakini wazazi mbalimbali (*e.g.* watoto wa ndugu wawili).

collation, *n.* taz. *collate.*

colleague, *n.* mwenzi, mshiriki.

collect, *v.t.* kusanya, leta pamoja; (*money &c.*) changa; (*into a heap*) zoa, kokoa; — *v.i.* kusanyika, kutanika, kutana. **collect**, *n.* namna ya sala fupi. **collected**, *a.* -liokusanyika au kukusanywa; (*cool &c.*) -tulivu, thabiti, bila wasiwasi, -enye macho makavu. **collection**, *n.* mkusanyo, mkutano, jamii; halaiki; (*of money at meeting &c.*) mchango wa fedha; (*in church*) sadaka; (*book of selections*) kitabu chenye mpango wa masomo. **collective**, *a.* -ote pamoja; jumla, -a jamii. **collectively**, *adv.* kwa kuhusu wote pamoja. **collector**, *n.* mkusanya vitu, *e.g.* vyeti (vya gari la moshi *&c.*); mchanga fedha; mtoza ushuru, kodi, *&c.*; (*clerk*) karani.

colleen, *n.* kijana mwanamke.

college, *n.* chama au jamii ya watu (hasa ya kufundisha au ya kuvumbua elimu); (*large school*) chuo kikubwa; (*building*) nyumba ya chama au jamii ya chuo kikubwa, yaani ya *college.* **collegiate**, *a.* -a kuhusu *college.*

collide, *v.i.* gongana, pambana. **collision**, *n.* mgongano, mpambano.

collier, *n.* mchimbuaji makaa ya mawe; meli ichukuayo shehena ya makaa ya mawe. **colliery**, *n.* shimo la kuchimbua makaa ya mawe, taz. *coal-mine*, na *coal-pit.*

collision, *n.* taz. *collide.*

collop, *n.* kipande cha nyama.

colloquial, *a.*, **colloquialism**, *n.* taz. *colloquy.*

colloquy, *n.* mazungumzo, maongezi. **colloquial**, *a.* -a usemi tu, -a namna ya usemi isiyofuata kanuni hasa za sarufi (ya ovyo). **colloquialism**, *n.* usemi wa ovyo, usiofuata kanuni hasa za sarufi.

collude, *v.i.* patana, saidiana (hasa katika hila, werevu au udanganyifu). **collusion**, *n.* ushirika, upatano (hasa katika udanganyifu); maafikano ya siri (ya hila, ya ujanja); udanganyifu, hila.

colon, (1) *n.* alama hii (:) yaani nukta mbili, maana yake ni kuonyesha mwisho wa kifungu maalum cha fungu la maneno (*sentence*).

colon, (2) *n.* sehemu ya chini ya tumbo kubwa.

colonel, *n.* mkubwa wa *regiment,* yaani kundi la askari; amiri.

colonial, *n.*, **colonist**, *n.*, **colonize**, *v.* taz. *colony.*

colonnade, *n.* safu ya nguzo; safu (ya miti).

colony, *n.* jamii ya watu waliotoka kwao kwenda kukaa ugenini; nchi walipohamia; nchi iliyo chini ya himaya ya nchi nyingine, *e.g. England and her colonies,* Uingereza na nchi zilizo chini ya himaya yake; (*collection*) jamii, wengi wakaao pamoja; *e.g. A colony of insects,* jamii ya wadudu wengi. **colonial**, *a.* -a *colony.* **colonist**, *n.* mtu wa *colony.* **colonize**, *v.t. and i.* fanya *colony.*

colossus, *n.* sanamu kubwa mno; (*giant*) jitu, pandikizi la mtu. **colossal**, *a.* -kubwa mno.

colour, *n.* rangi; (*healthy*) uso wa afya; (*appearance*) sura, launi, maana; (*flag*) bendera, beramu. *A person of colour,* mtu asiye mweupe, asiye mzungu; mtu mweusi; suriama. *Change colour,* iva uso, geuka uso. *Come off with flying colours,* fanya jambo gumu vizuri sana; toka katika shida kwa heshima nyingi. *He is off colour,* hawezi kidogo. — *v.t.* paka (tia) rangi; (*exaggerate*) piga chuku; (*misrepresent*) singizia; (*alter*) geuza, vuta; — *v.i.* pata rangi; (*blush*) geuka uso, iva uso. **colour-blind,** *n.* -a kutoweza kupambanua rangi nyinginezo. **coloured,** *a.* -enye rangi, -a rangi-rangi; (*altered*) -enye kugeuzwa, si kama kweli. **colourless,** *a.* -siyo na rangi; -a kupenyezeka kwa nuru; -angavu. *A colourless person,* mtu baridi, mzito. **colour-sergeant,** *n.* askari mwenye kazi ya kutunza bendera za jeshi la askari.

colporteur, *n.* mtembezi wa vitabu vya dini.

colt, *n.* mwana farasi; (*youth*) kijana mjinga.

column, nguzo, mhimili, mnara; (*row*) safu; mpango wa vitu kwa safu safu, *e.g.* askari, herufi, tarakimu, maneno katika ukurasa wa kitabu &c.

coma, *n.* usingizi mzito sana, hali ya kuzimia roho (ya kuzirai). **comatose,** *a.* -enye usingizi mzito; -enye kuzimia roho; -enye kusinziasinzia; -lepe.

comb, *n.* (*small*) kitana; (*large*) chanuo, shanuo. *Cockscomb,* upanga, ushungi, undu wa jogoo. *Honeycomb,* mazana, masega ya nyuki. — *v.t.* chana, tana, chambua kwa kitana.

combat, *v.t.* pigana, shindana; (*oppose*) zuia, pinga, kaidi. — *n.* vita, pigano, shindano. **combatant,** *n.* mpigani, mshindani.

combination, *n.* taz. *combine.*

combine, *v.t.* unga, changanya; — *v.i.* (*agree*) ungana, patana, saidiana, shirikiana, -wa na shauri moja. — *n.* unganisho, shirika ya makampani ya biashara &c. *Be combined,* -wa na umoja, ungwa pamoja, unganika. **combination,** *n.* mchanganyo, mtangamano; mchanganyiko; shirika; jamii ya vitu vilivyounganishwa; jamii ya watu wenye kusudi lile lile &c.

combustible, *a. and n.* taz. *combustion.*

combustion, *n.* mwako, hali ya kuwaka, mchomo, mwunguzo. **combustible,** *a.* -a kuweza kuwaka; (*excitable*) -a harara. — *n.* cho chote kiwezacho kuwaka.

come, *v.i.* (*p.t.* **came,** *and pf.t.* **come**); ja; (*to, with, for* &c.) jia, jilia; (*arrive at*) wasili, fika. *Come!* njoo! *Come in!* karibu! *In time to come,* wakati ujao, halafu, baadaye. *Come about,* fanyika, tukia, tokea, jiri. *Come across,* kuta, kutana na. *Come apart,* katika, vunjika, pasuka, tenguka. *Come at,* fika, pata. *Come by,* karibia, jia, pita; pata. *Come down,* shuka, telemka; (*be reduced*) pungua. *Come down upon,* wia ukali. *Come in,* ingia, (*be useful*) faa. *Come in for,* pata. *Come into,* rithi. *Come off,* toka; tukia, fanyika; (*escape*) kimbia, okoka; (*like a stamp, plaster* &c.) banduka, (*like head of axe* &c.) bokoka. *Come on,* endelea; (*find*) kuta, vumbua, gundua. *Come out,* tokea wazi, tangaa, bainika. *Come over* (*change*) geuka, enda upande mwingine. *Come right, true,* tokea (isha) vyema; tokea sawasawa, hongera. *Come round,* zunguka; (*recover*) jirudia, tulia; (*coax*) bembeleza, rairai, danganya. *Come short of,* punguka, -wa na upungufu; tokuweza. *Come to,* pata jirudia (kama mtu aliyezimia). *It comes to this,* maana yake ni hii; jawabu ni hii. *Come to grief,* patwa na ajali (matata &c.) *Come to a head,* iva. *Come to an end,* isha, koma. *Come to be,* pata kuwa. *Come to blows,* pigana. *Come to hand,* wasili. *Come to oneself,* jirudia, tulia. *Come to pass,* fanyika, -wa, tukia, jiri. *Come together,* kutana, kusanyika. *Come under,* -wa chini ya. *Come up,* (*grow*) mea, ota, kua, (*appear*) tokea, zuka, onekana. *Come upon,* kuta; (*surprise*) gundua (*in act of wrongdoing*) fumania; (*attack*) shambulia, rukia. *Come up with,* patia, fikia. *All* *comers,* wo wote watakao. **coming,** *n.* kifiko, ujio, majilio.

comedian, *n.,* **comedienne,** *n.* taz. *comedy.*

comedy, *n.* mchezo wa kuigiza mambo ya kuchekesha. **comedian,** *n.* mtu abuniye au kucheza *comedy.* **comedienne,** *n. comedian* wa kike.

comeliness, *n.* taz. *comely.*

comely, *a.* -zuri; -enye sura au maungo ya kupendeza; -enye madaha. **comeliness,** *n.* uzuri, madaha, hali ya kuwa na sura au maungo ya kupendeza.

comestibles, *n.* vyakula.

comet, *n.* nyota yenye mkia.

comfort, *v.t.* fariji, tuliza roho, liwaza, ondolea huzuni, burudisha. — *n.* faraja, msaada, kiguzo, kitulizo, liwazo, burudisho; (*ease*) raha, buraha, hadhi, starehe, anasa, hali njema, fanaka, ufanisi. **comfortable,** *a.* -a kufariji, -a kuburudisha, -a kutuliza, -a kupendeza; -enye raha, -enye faraja, -enye kufaa. **comfortably,** *adv.* kwa raha, bila shida. **comforter,** *n.* mfariji, mburudishi; kitulizo; (*for neck*) shali ya kuvaa shingoni. *The Comforter,* Roho Mtakatifu. **comfortless,** *a.* -a bila raha, bila starehe, bila msaada, bila faraja.

comic, *a.,* **comical,** *a.* -cheshi, -chekeshaji, -a mzaha.

coming, *n.* taz. *come.*

comma, *n.* alama hii (,) yaani koma, maana yake ni kuonyesha mwisho wa kifungu kilicho kidogo cha fungu la maneno. *Inverted commas,* alama hii (" . . .") au (' . . . ') alama za mtajo, maana yake ni kuonyesha ya kuwa maneno yaliyo katikati ya alama yamenakiliwa kutoka katika kitabu kingine, au ni maneno yaliyosemwa na mtu fulani.

command, *v.t.* amuru, amrisha; (*govern*) tawala; (*be a commander*) -wa na amri (*e.g.* mkuu wa askari, wa vita &c.); (*have influence or control*) -wa na amri juu ya (watu, fedha, mali &c.); (*front, overlook*) -wa na kitu chini au mbele; elekea, kabili; *e.g. The town is commanded by a hill,* mji uko chini ya kilima. *The hill commands a plain,* kilima kina uwanda mbele au chini yake. — *n.* (*order*) agizo, amri; (*authority*) utawala, hukumu, nguvu, uwezo, ukuu, kitu kilicho chini au mbele, *e.g.* watu, askari, nchi &c. **commandant,** *n.* mtu mwenye amri juu ya mahali au ya jeshi la askari. **commandeer,** *v.t.* twaa kwa matumizi ya vita au ya majeshi ya askari, kamata shokoa. **commander,** *n.* mkuu wa askari au wa manowari. **commander-in-chief,** *n.* mtu mwenye amri zote za jeshi la askari au la majeshi yote ya nchi. **commanding,** *a.* -a nguvu, -a juu. **commandment,** *n.* amri, sheria, agizo. *Ten commandments,* amri kumi za Nabii Musa.

comme il faut, *a.* barabara, sahihi.

commemorate, *v.t.* fanya ukumbusho wa, adhimisha sikukuu ya kukumbuka mtu au jambo fulani. **commemoration,** *n.* ukumbusho (kwa sala, heshima, sikukuu, mchezo, karamu &c.). **commemorative,** *a.* -a ukumbusho, -enye kukumbusha.

commence, *v.t.* anza, amiri, anzisha, maliki; — *v.i.* anza. **commencement,** *n.* mwanzo, chanzo, asili, chimbuko.

commend, *v.t.* (*praise*) sifu, tukuza; (*entrust*) weka (katika utunzo wa). *Commend me to so-and-so,* nisalimie fulani. **commendable,** *a.* -stahili sifa, -stahiki, -ema. **commendation,** *n.* sifa. **commendatory,** *a.* -enye sifa.

commensurable, *a.* -a kupimika kwa jinsi moja; -a kulingana; -a kadiri moja. **commensurate,** *a.* kipimo au kadiri iliyo sawa na; -a kulingana na, -a kufaa.

comment, *n.* fasiri, fafanusi, elezo; maneno ya kueleza au kujulisha mawazo ya mtu ya maneno (au matendo) ya mtu mwingine. — *v.t.* eleza, fasiri, sema (au andika) maneno ya kueleza mawazo juu ya maneno (au matendo) ya mtu mwingine. **commentary,** *n.* tafsiri, mafafanusi, maelezo.

commerce, *n.* biashara, uchumi. **commercial,** *a.* -a kuhusu biashara na wafanyi biashara. *The commercial world,* watu wa biashara. *Commercial matters, dealings,* mambo ya biashara. *Commercial traveller,* mtu asafiriye kuonyesha vitu vya biashara na kupokea maagizo juu yake.

commination, *n.* maogofya.

commingle, *v.t.* changanya; — *v.i.* changanyika. **commingled,** *a.* -liochanganywa, iliyochanganyika.

commiserate, *v.t.* sikitikia, hurumia, -pa mtu pole. **commiseration,** *n.* huruma, sikitiko.

commissariat, *n.* watoaji chakula, utoaji chakula; watu wenye kazi ya kuwapatia chakula askari, kutoa masurufu, posho.

commissary, *n.* naibu, mjumbe, wakili.

commission, *n.* (*charge*) agizo, amri; (*doing*) tendo, utenzi, utendaji; (*certificate*) hati au cheti cha kumpa mtu nguvu, cheo au amri fulani; (*brokerage*) faida, ushuru, malipo; (*special council*) jamii ya watu waliopewa amri kufanya mambo fulani; (*in the army or navy*) cheo cha afisa (*officer*). **commissioner,** *n.* mwenye kuagizwa, mwenye amri, wakili, mjumbe. *Provincial commissioner,* mtu wa serikali, mkuu wa *Province,* yaani jimbo.

commit, *v.t.* (*crime &c.*) tenda, fanya; (*entrust*) aminisha, weka; (*imprison*) tia kifungoni; (*engage*) ingiza. *Commit to memory,* jifunza hata uweze kukumbuka. *He has committed himself,* amejipa sharti, ameahidi; amejitia matatani; amejifunga. *Commit suicide,* jiua. *Commit murder,* ua. **commitment,** *n.* tendo; cheti au hati ya kufungisha mtu kifungoni; kifungo; sharti; ahadi. **commital,** *n.* taz. *commitment.* **committee,** *n.* jamii ya watu waliochaguliwa kutenda jambo au kushauriana juu yake, halmashauri.

commodious, *a.* -enye nafasi, -kubwa, -a kufaa.

commodity, *n.* fao, kifaa; bidhaa; kitu, mali.

commodore, *n.* cheo cha manowarini katikati ya *admiral* na *captain.*

common, *a.* -a siku zote, -a kawaida, -a watu wote; (*of little value*) -a mfuto, -a ovyo, rahisi, hafifu, -baya, duni, -nyonge, vivi hivi; (*numerous*) tele, -ingi sana; (*same in all, general*) -moja, -a hali moja, sawa. *Have in common,* shiriki, -wa na . . . sawasawa wote. *I have nothing in common with him,* sina hali moja naye, sina mazoea naye. *Out of the common,* -geni, ajabu, si -a kawaida. — *n.* uwanja wa serikali, mahame. *Short commons,* uchache (upungufu) wa chakula. *House of Commons,* halmashauri kubwa ya serikali Uingereza. **commoner,** *n.* mtu tu (asiye na cheo kikuu.) **commonly,** *adv.* kwa desturi, kwa kawaida, aghalabu, mara nyingi. **commonplace,** *a.* -a kawaida. — *n.* neno la vivi hivi tu. **common-sense,** *n.* akili ya kawaida, busara; mawazo au maneno yanayokubaliwa na watu wote. **commonwealth,** *n.* nafuu au faida ya watu wote; utawala wa nchi pasipo na mfalme; jumla ya watu wote wa nchi; taifa.

commotion, *n.* (*disorder, uproar*) udhia, fitina, ghasia, makelele, kishindo, rabsha; (*violent motion*) msukosuko, machafuko.

commune, *v.i.* ongea, zungumza; fanya shauri pamoja. **communal,** *a.* -a watu wa mtaa au mji. **communicate,** *v.t.* (*share, pass*) toa, gawanya, shirikisha, pisha; (*report*) arifu, eleza, nena, julisha, funua, peleka habari, pelekeana habari; — *v.i.* -wa na njia ya kupishana; (*receive Holy Communion*) pokea Ushirika Mtakatifu; (*have intercourse*) ongea, zungumza. **communication,** *n.* habari; (*means of* *intercourse*) njia za kupelekeana habari, maarifa, barua. **communicative,** *a.* -enye tabia ya kuongea (ya kutoa habari). **communion,** *n.* (*sharing*) ushirika; (*intercourse*) mazungumzo, maongezi; urafiki; shauri moja; (*Holy Communion*) Ushirika Mtakatifu. **communism,** *n.* shauri au hali ya kuwa mtu hawezi kuwa na mali peke yake ila mali yote ni ya watu wote shirika. **communist,** *n.* mtu aaminiye shauri la *communism*. **communistic,** *a.* -a kuhusu *communism*. **community,** *n.* jamii ya watu wakikaa pamoja kwa hali moja; jamii ya watu wakaao pamoja (katika mtaa mmoja, mji mmoja *&c.*); umati, *e.g.* umati wa Wahindi (wa Waswahili, wa Waislamu *&c.*)

commutable, *a.*, **commutation,** *n.*, **commutator,** *n.* taz. *commute.*

commute, *v.t.* badilisha; (*punishment*) punguza adhabu. **commutable,** *a.* -a kuweza kubadilishwa. **commutation,** *n.* badilisho, punguzo la adhabu. **commutator,** *n.* chombo cha motakaa *&c.* cha kubadili namna ya nguvu ya elektrisiti, yaani umeme.

compact, *a.* (*firm*) -gumu, -a kukazana, imara, thabiti; (*close*) -a karibu karibu; (*brief*) -a ufupi. — *v.t.* gandamiza; thibitisha. — *n.* maafikano, mapatano, sharti.

companion, *n.* mwenzi, rafiki, mwandani, mwandamizi; (*of a ship*) dirisha la kupitisha mwangaza chini melini; (*companion ladder, way*) ngazi ya kupandia toka sitahani mpaka vyumba vya melini. **companionship,** *n.*, urafiki.

company, *n.* jamii au kundi la watu (askari, mabaharia *&c.*); (*of merchants*) shirika, washiriki, kampani; (*persons present*) watu waliopo, waliohudhuria; (*guests*) wageni, walioalikwa; (*associate*) rafiki, mwenzi; (*fellowship*) urafiki. *Form (join, go shares in) a company,* fanya (kula) bia. *I want company,* nataka mwenzi.

comparable, *a.*, **comparative,** *a.*, **comparatively,** *adv.* taz. *compare.*

compare, *v.t.* pambanisha, linganisha, fafanisha, mithilisha, enenza, angalia kwamba ni sawa. — *v.i.* fanana, -wa sawa. *Compare statements,* enenza maneno. *This is large compared with that,* hii ni kubwa kuliko ile. *It is beyond compare,* haina kifani, ni bora kabisa. **comparable,** *a.* -a kulinganika, -a kulinganikana, -enye sifa sawa, -a kufanana. **comparative,** *a.* -linganifu; -a kupimika kwa kupambanua na kitu kingine; -siyo sawasawa kabisa ila ni karibu sawasawa. **comparatively,** *adv.* karibu, kwa kupambanua na kitu kingine; kwa jinsi isiyo halisi lakini karibu. **comparison,** *n.* mlingano, mlinganyo; (*likeness*) mfano, mithali, kifani, wenezi. *There is no comparison between them,* havifanani hata kidogo, ni mbalimbali kabisa, vinahitilafiana kabisa.

compartment, *n.* kijumba, sehemu ya nyumba, kataa, mkato; (*of railway carriage*) behewa; (*of box &c.*) mtoto.

compass, *n.* (*circle*) duara; (*extent*) eneo; (*limit*) upeo, kikomo, mpaka; (*girth*) uvimbe, mzingo; (*magnetic*) dira; (*drawing compasses*) bikari. — *v.t.* zunguka, zingia; (*obtain*) pata; (*accomplish*) weza, faulu, jirisha. *Fetch a compass,* zunguka.

compassion, *n.* huruma, masikitiko, kite. **compassionate,** *v.t.* hurumia, sikitikia. — *a.* -enye huruma, -pole, raufu.

compatible, *a.* -a kupatana, -a kuelekeana, -a kutangamana, -a kuweza kuchukuana, -a kufaana. **compatibility,** *n.* upatanifu, ulinganifu, usawa; hali ya kuchukuana (ya kupatana *&c.*).

compatriot, *n.* ndugu, mtu wa nchi (yangu, yako, yake *&c.*).

compel, *v.t.* shuruti, shurutisha, lazimisha, tia nguvu, juburu, ghusubu; (*morally*) juzu, bidi.

compendium, *n.* muhtasari; maandiko fulani kwa ufupi. **compendious,** *a.* -fupi, -dogo, -a maneno machache (lakini -enye habari nyingi).

compensate, *v.t.* lipa, fidia, lipia (maumivu, hasara, uchungu *&c.*); (*make equal*) sawazisha. **compensation,** *n.* fidia, kisasi, ridhaa, malipo (kwa ajili ya hasara *&c.*); (*being suitable or equal*) ulinganifu, usawa.

compete, *v.i.* shindana; (*in commerce*) ghilibu. **competence, competency,** *n.* ufao, nguvu, akili, ustadi; (*moderate means*) riziki, mali si nyingi ila za kutosha, nafuu tele. **competent,** *a.* -enye nguvu (akili, ustadi *&c.*) ya kutosha; -a kufaa; (*legitimate*) halali, -a sheria. **competition,** *n.* shindano, ushindani; (*in trade*) mghalaba. **competitive,** *a.* -a shindano, -a ushindani, -a kushindaniwa. **competitor,** *n.* mshindani.

compile, *v.t.* buni (kitabu kwa kutumia vitabu vingine); tunga, kusanya, okota, maarifa, changamanisha. **compilation,** *n.* mkusanyo, mtungo (wa maandiko, maarifa *&c.*); tendo la kubuni (la kutunga). **compiler,** *n.* mtunga vitabu (maarifa *&c.*).

complacency, *n.* taz. *complacent.*

complacent, *a.* -a kuridhika, -a kupendezwa; (*self-satisfied*) -kinaifu. **complacency,** *n.* utulivu, raha, ridhaa; (*self-satisfaction*) kinaya.

complain, *v.i.* nung'unika, guna, lalamika, janga, nuna; (*accuse*) lilia, shtaki; (*be ill*) ugua. **complainant,** *n.* mshtaki; aletaye au kufanya *complaint.* **complaint,** *n.* (*accusation*) mashtaka; (*lament*) maombolezo, kilio, malalamiko; (*grumbling*) nung'uniko; (*illness*) ugonjwa. *Give a complaint to,* ambukiza.

complaisance, *n.* ridhaa, utulivu, adabu, latifu, makini, utu wema, upole; nia ya kupendeza. **complaisant,** *a.* -enye kutaka kupendeza, -pole, -a adabu, makini.

complement, *n.* kitimizo, ujazo, baki; (*full number*) hesabu kamili, kiasi kamili. — *v.t.* kamilisha, timiza. **complementary,** *a.* -a kutimiza, -a kukamilisha, -a kufanya kamili -ote pamoja.

complete, *v.t.* timiza, maliza, timiliza, kamilisha, hitimisha. *Complete one's education,* hitimu. — *a.* kamili, -kamilifu, timilifu, -zima. **completely,** *adv.* kabisa, halisi, pia. **completeness,** *n.* ukamilifu, utimilifu, uzima. **completion,** *n* mwisho, tendo la kumaliza (la kukamilisha *&c.*); hali ya kuwa timamu (ya kukamilika *&c.*).

complex, *a.* -enye sehemu (vipande, matengenezo, tabia *&c.*) nyingi; -gumu kufahamika; -a fumbo; -enye kinyongo. — *n.* kinyongo. **complexion,** *n.* rangi ya uso, takaso; (*disposition, quality*) sura, namna, tabia. **complexity,** *n.* kitu (au jambo) chenye sehemu (vipande, matengenezo, tabia *&c.*) nyingi; matatizo, mashaka; kinyongo.

compliance, *n.*, **compliant,** *a.* taz. *comply.*

complicate, *v.t.* fanya matata, tatiza, tatanisha, fumba. **complicated,** *a.* -enye mafumbo, -gumu kufahamika; taz. *complex.* **complication,** *n.* matata, mashaka, mafumbo; mchanganyo (wa hali, mambo, tabia *&c.*).

complicity, *n.* ushirika (wa kufanya mabaya) taz. *accomplice.*

compliment, *v.t.* salimu, sifu, tolea maneno ya heshima (ya kustahi). — *n.* salamu, maneno ya heshima (ya kusifu). **complimentary,** *a.* -a kusifu, -a kusalimu, -a kuheshimu. *Give my compliments to so-and-so,* nisalimie fulani. *Complimentary title (in letter),* dibaji.

compline, *n.* sala za mwisho jioni.

comply, *v.t.* kubali, itikia, tii, sikia; (*with*) fanya, timiliza, pokea, tii, fuata. **compliance,** *n.* ukubali, kibali, radhi, ridhaa. *In compliance with,* kwa kukubali, kwa kupatana na, kwa kufuata. **compliant,** *a.* -tii,

-sikivu, -pole, -enye tabia ya kukubali (ya kuridhika).

component, *n.* kitu kilichomo, sehemu. — *a.* -liyo sehemu (ya kitu), -liyomo.

comport, *v.t.* (*with*) patana na, faa; — *v.i.* (*oneself*) jiweka, jichukua. **comportment,** *n.* mwenendo, matendo.

compose, *v.t.* fanyiza, tunga, buni, rekabisha, andika; (*quiet*) tuliza, tengeneza; (*form, make up, i.e. substance*) -wa, -wa na . . . ndani, *e.g. It is composed of rock,* ni jiwe, ina jiwe ndani, asili yake ni jiwe, kitu chake ni jiwe; (*set up type*) panga herufi za chapa. **composed,** *a.* -tulivu, makini. -a taratibu. **composer,** *n.* mwandishi (wa vitabu, hasa vya muziki, nyimbo &c.). **composite,** *a.* -enye sehemu (vitu, tabia) zaidi ya moja. **composition,** *n.* utungo, ubuni; mtungo, insha; kitu kilichotungwa au kubuniwa, *e.g.* kitabu, maandiko, nyimbo &c. (*manner, style*) tabia, ufasaha, nahau; (*compensation*) malipo, (*for murder*) dia; (*agreement*) mapatano; (*mixture*) mchanganyiko; (*ingredients*) sehemu mbalimbali, asili, kitu. **compositor,** *n.* mpangaji herufi za chapa. **compost,** *n.* mchanganyiko, hasa wa vitu kufanya mbolea. **composure,** *n.* utulivu, makini, ukavu wa macho.

compound, (1) *v.t.* (*mix*) changanya; (*make*) fanyiza; (*settle by agreement, come to terms*) patana, maliza (tengeneza) kwa mapatano; (*a subscription &c.*) lipa yote pamoja badala ya ada ya kila mwaka &c. (na kwa hiyo kupunguziwa gharama). *Compound a felony,* saidia (ficha) mkosaji. — *a.* -enye sehemu nyinginezo zilizochanganyikana; -enye sehemu zaidi ya moja; -enye sehemu za namna mbalimbali. *A compound fracture of the leg,* mguu uliovunjika vibaya na kufanya jeraha pia.

compound, (2) *n.* ua, uga, kiwanja cha nyumba; kambi la wafanyi kazi.

comprehend, *v.t.* (*understand*) fahamu, tambua, jua, komanya; (*include*) -wa na, weka. *It comprehends all kinds,* namna zote zimo humo. **comprehensible,** *a.* -a maana, -a kufahamika, -a kuelea. **comprehension,** *n.* uwezo wa kufahamu, ufahamu, ujuzi, akili. **comprehensive,** *n.* -enye uwezo wa kufahamu mengi; -enye vitu vingi (maarifa mengi, mambo mengi). *He took a comprehensive view of the subject,* alichungua habari zote za jambo.

compress, *v.t.* gandamiza, bana, shindilia, shindika, songa, kaza, kamua, punguza kwa kushindilia (kwa kubana &c.). **compressible,** *a.* -a kushindilika, -a kupunguzika kwa kugandamizwa (kwa kushindiliwa &c.). **compression,** *n.* mgandamizo, mbano, msongo, mshindilio. **compressor,** *n.* kisongo, mbano, cho chote kinachokaza kwa kushindilia (kwa kubana, kwa kugandamiza &c.).

comprise, *v.t.* -wa na . . . ndani yake, *e.g. The book comprises all sorts of knowledge,* kitabu hiki kina maarifa ya namna zote ndani yake. **comprising,** *a.* -enye.

compromise, *n.* masikilizano, mapatano (ya kila upande juu ya masharti;) mapatano ya kuridhiana. — *v.t.* patana, ridhiana (kwa kila upande juu ya masharti ya jambo &c.); (*endanger*) tia katika hatari (ya matata, udhia, aibu, haya, mashaka &c.); — *v.i.* patana, ridhiana. *Compromise oneself,* jivutia (jiletea, jiingiza katika) tuhuma (mashaka).

comptroller, *n.* taz. *controller.*

compulsion, *n.* shurutisho, nguvu, lazima, sharti. **compulsory,** *a.* -a lazima, -a sharti.

compunction, *n.* majuto, toba, masikitiko, huruma, uchungu.

compute, *v.t.* hesabu, kadiri. **computation,** *n.* hesabu, kadiri.

comrade, *n.* rafiki, mwenzi, sahibu, msiri, mwandani.

con, *v.t.* soma kwa uangalifu; jifunza sana, angalia (chungua) sana.

concatenation, *n.* mafuatano (ya mambo).

concave, *a.* -a mvungu, -enye shimo, -a kubonyea.

conceal, *v.t.* ficha, setiri. **concealment,** *n.* mficho; maficho.

concede, *v.t.* (*admit*) kubali, kiri; (*grant*) toa ruhusa; (*let pass*) acha, achilia.

conceit, *n.* majivuno, kiburi, makuu, unyeti; (*idea*) wazo la kupendeza (la kuchekesha). **conceited,** *a.* -a kiburi, -enye majivuno, -enye kichwa kikubwa, -a kudeka.

conceive, *v.i.* ona, waza, dhani, fahamu; — *v.t.* (*in womb*) pata (tunga, shika, chukua) mimba. **conceivable,** *a.* -a kuwazika, -a kufahamika, -a kuonekana.

concentrate, *v.t.* kusanya mahali pamoja, leta pamoja, unganisha; (*condense*) fanya -zito (kuwa na nguvu zaidi, kuwa -dogo zaidi) kwa kukausha maji (kushindilia, kugandamiza, kubana &c.); — *v.i.* kusanyika, elekea. *Concentrate attention on,* kaza fikira juu ya, fikiri sana juu ya, chunguza sana. **concentrated,** *a.* -liopunguzwa au kufupishwa; -enye nguvu nyingi katika (nafasi, kitu) kidogo. **concentration,** *n.* mkusanyo pamoja, tendo la kufanya zito &c. (taz. *condense*); mkazo wa fikira.

concept, *n.* wazo. **conception,** *n.* wazo, dhana; (*in womb*) mtungo wa mimba; mimba.

concern, *v.t.* pasa, husu, juzu; (*grieve*) sikitisha, (*trouble*) sumbua, udhi, shughulisha, hangaisha, tia fikira, tia shaka. — *n.* ipasayo, ihusuyo; (*matter*) jambo, shughuli; (*sorrow &c.*). masikitiko; (*anxiety*) shaka; (*interest*) fikira; (*trading firm*) shirika, kampani, uchumi. *It is no concern of mine,* hainipasi, mimi simo. **concerning,** *prep.* kwa, juu ya, kwa habari za, mintarafu.

concert, *v.t.* fanya shauri pamoja, tengeneza kwa mapatano. — *n.* umoja wa shauri; mapatano; (*musical*) mazungumzo (tafrija) ya watu kuimba pamoja au kupiga muziki, tarabu. *Concerted action,* tendo linalofanywa na watu pamoja ambalo lilitangulia kutengenezwa.

concession, *n.* (*leave*) ruhusa, idhini, ukubali, radhi, ridhaa; (*thing conceded*) kitu kilichotolewa, kilichoruhusiwa; fadhili, hisani; (*giving up*) kutoa, kusalimu; (*deed*) mkataba.

conchology, *n.* elimu ya konokono na kombe za pwani.

concierge, *n.* bawabu, mngojea mlango.

conciliate, *v.t.* patanisha, suluhisha, afikanisha, ridhisha, tuliza (hasa mtu asiye rafiki). **conciliation,** *n.* upatanisho, tulizo &c. **conciliatory,** *a.* -a kupatanisha, -suluhifu, -a kutuliza.

concise, *a.* -fupi, -a kukata, -enye habari nyingi katika maneno machache. -dogo. **concisely,** *adv.* kwa ufupi au mkato. **conciseness,** ufupi, uchache wa maneno wenye maana dhahiri.

conclave, *n.* baraza ya siri, njama, mzengwe.

conclude, *v.t.* (*make up an end*) isha, maliza, komesha; (*infer*) dhani, ona, tanabahi; — *v.i.* (*come to an end*) isha, fika mwisho, koma. *Conclude a peace,* fanya amani (mapatano). *Conclude a bargain,* funga biashara, patana. **conclusion,** *n.* mwisho; (*inference*) maana (ya maneno, hoja &c.) iliyofahamika; (*judgement*) hukumu, neno mkataa; (*experiment*) jaribio. *In conclusion,* neno la mwisho, mwisho. *Try conclusions,* jaribu, jaribisha, shindana. **conclusive,** *a.* -a nguvu, -a kuthibitisha, -a kuondoa shaka, -a mwisho, -a kukomesha, mkataa.

concoct, *v.t.* fanyiza (shauri, mchanganyo wa vitu, *e.g.* chakula &c.); buni (shauri, maneno ya uwongo &c.). **concoction,** *n.* (*mixture*) mchanganyiko; (*plan*) shauri;

(*medicine*) dawa; (*story*) maneno ya kubuniwa &c.).

concomitant, *a.* pamoja na, -a kufuatana, na, -a kuandamana na.

concord, *n.* upatano, amani, urafiki, umoja, itifaki. **concordance,** *n.* (*harmony*) upatanifu, umoja; (*book of reference*) kamusi ya maneno makuu ya kitabu, hasa Maandiko Matakatifu. **concordant,** *a.* -enye umoja, -enye kupatana, -a kulingana.

concourse, *n.* mkutano, kundi, umati, jeshi.

concrete, *a.* -a kushikika au kuonekana (wala si -a kuwazika tu), *e.g. a concrete example,* mfano unaoweza kushikika au kuonekana; ni kinyume cha *abstract, e.g. an abstract example,* mfano unaoweza kuwazika tu, haushikiki wala kuonekana. — *n.* saruji, chokaa au udongo wa Ulaya uliochanganywa na maji na kokoto, kama sakafu.

concubine, *n.* mwanamke wa kinyumba, (*if a slave*) suria. **concubinage,** *n.* hali ya mwanamke aliyewekwa kinyumba, (*slavery*) usuria.

concupiscence, *n.* shauku nyingi, ashiki nyingi, tamaa ya mwili, ngoa, uchu mwingi (hasa wa kike au wa kiume).

concur, *v.i.* tokea (tendwa, tendeka) wakati ule mmoja; (*agree*) patana, kubali, ridhika. **concurrence,** *n.* mwungano, umoja wa kutenda; upatano, ukubali. **concurrent,** *a.* -a kukutana pamoja; -a kutoka (kutenda, kuwapo au kufuatana) pamoja, -a kuunganishwa. **concurrently,** *adv.* kwa wakati ule mmoja, pamoja, sawia. **concurring,** *a.* -a kupatana, -a kukubali.

concussion, *n.* (*shock*) kishindo, mtikiso; (*collision*) kipigo, mpambano, mgongano; (*medical*) kuzirai kwa sababu ya kipigo cha kichwa.

condemn, *v.t.* (*convict*) hukumu, pasha hukumu (adhabu, kifungo); (*censure*) patiliza, laumu; (*reject*) kataza, tupa, pima kitu na kusema ni kibovu hakifai tena. **condemnable,** *a.* -a kustahili adhabu (hukumu, lawama &c.). **condemnation,** *n.* lawama, mapatilizo, hukumu, laana. **condemnatory,** *a.* -a kupasisha hukumu, -enye laana. **condemned,** *a.* -a kuhukumiwa kuwa na hatia (kupata adhabu, kulaumiwa); -bovu hata kutofaa tena.

condense, *v.t.* punguza ukubwa kwa kubana (kushindilia, kugandamiza, kukausha maji yake, au kwa namna nyingine); (*thicken*) fanya -zito, *e.g.* kugeuza hewa maji &c.; (*shorten*) *abridge*) punguza, katiza, fanya muhtasari ya; — *v.i.* punguka na kuwa -zito zaidi. **condenser,** *n.* chombo cha kugeuza namna nyingine za hewa kuwa majimaji; chombo cha kukusanyia au kugeuzia namna ya nguvu ya umeme (elektrisiti).

condescend, *v.i.* tendea wema (*hisani*) wenye cheo kidogo; (na pengine kupiga ubwana huku anapotenda) jinyenyekea; (*stoop to unworthy action*) jidhili. **condescension,** *n.* wema kwa wenye cheo kidogo; hisani, ufadhili, adabu, unyenyekevu (kwa wenye cheo kidogo -pengine kwa kupiga ubwana).

condign, *a.* -a kustahiliwa; -a kutosha (adhabu).

condiment, *n.* kiungo cha kukolea chakula, *e.g.* chumvi, pilipili, &c.

condition, *n.* (*state*) hali, tabia, hulka, mambo yalivyo; (*rank*) cheo; (*indispensable*) kanuni; (*terms of agreement*) sharti, mapatano, ahadi; (*health*) afya, siha, rai, uzima. **conditional,** *a.* -enye masharti, -a muda tu, si halisi (yaani huelekea kubadilika baadaye kwa kadiri hali ilivyo). **conditioned,** *a.* -enye masharti; -enye hali fulani (nzuri, mbaya &c.).

condole, *v.i.* (*sympathize*) hurumia, sikitikia; (*grieve with*) hani, -pa mbirambi (pole, makiwa). **condolence,** *n.* mbirambi, maneno ya kuhurumia, ya kusikitikia, liwazo; (*letter of*) barua ya tanzia.

condone, *v.t.* achilia, samehe.

conduce, *v.i.* faa, saidia, elekea kuleta. **conducive,** *a.* (*to*) kufaa kwa, -a kuelekea kuleta.

conduct, *v.t.* (*lead*) ongoza, peleka, chukua; (*manage*) tengeneza, endesha; — *v. reflex.* (*behave*) jiweka, jichukua. — *n.* mwongozo; (*management*) matengenezo, usimamizi, uongozi; (*behaviour*) mwenendo, tabia, matendo, maisha. **conductor,** *n.* (*guide*) mwongozi, kiongozi; (*of train &c.*) mwangalizi; (*in science*) kitu kiwezacho kuongoza au kupitisha joto, nguvu ya umeme &c. *Lightning conductor,* chuma cha kukingia umeme.

conduit, *n.* mfereji.

cone, *n.* kitu cha mviringo chini kilichochongoka juu. **conic,** *a.,* **conical,** *a.* -enye umbo la *cone.*

coney, *n.* taz. *cony.*

confection, confectionery, *n.* mchanganyiko, hasa ni vitu vitamu kama sukari, halua, kashata, maandazi, peremende &c. **confectioner,** *n.* mwuzaji (mfanyizaji) maandazi, halua, peremende &c.

confederate, *n.* rafiki, mwenzi, mwenye shauri lile lile moja; mshirika, msaidizi. **confederacy,** *n.* taz. *confederation.* **confederation,** *n.* (*alliance*) urafiki, utani, umoja wa shauri; (*allied powers*) jamii ya watu (miji, makabila, serikali &c.) wenye shauri moja.

confer, *v.t.* (*give*) toa, -pa, jalia, pasisha, tia; — *v.i.* (*with*) fanya shauri pamoja, semezana, ongea, barizi. **conference,** *n.* mazungumzo; (*council*) mkutano wa watu (kwa ajili ya kusemezana juu ya mashauri, elimu &c.); baraza.

confess, *v.t.* kiri, ungama, kubali; (*of priest*) ungamisha. **confession,** *n.* tendo la kukiri au kukubali; ungamo; maungamo; (*creed*) imani, shuhuda. **confessional,** *n.* mahali pa kuungama dhambi kwa kasisi.

confessor, *n.* kasisi mwenye kuungamisha watu dhambi; (*sufferer for faith*) shahidi, avumiliaye mateso au kufa kwa ajili ya dini yake.

confide, *v.t.* weka, aminisha, ambia, kadhibisha. *Confide in,* amini, tumainia, egemea. **confidant,** *n.* msiri. **confidence,** *n.* matumaini, imani, moyo mwepesi, ujasiri, uthabiti; (*self assertion*) ukinaifu, ushupavu; (*secret*) maneno ya siri. *I tell you in confidence,* nakuambia siri. *Take into confidence,* fanya siri, weka siri. *Have confidence in,* tegemea, tumainia. *Have confidence,* jipa moyo. **confident,** *a.* -tumainifu, -jasiri, -enye imani, -enye hakika; (*be*) tumaini, jua sana. aminisha. **confidential,** *a.* -a siri. *Confidential friend,* msiri. **confidentially,** *adv.* kwa siri. **confider,** *n.* mwenye kumwambia mwingine siri yake. **confiding,** *a.* -enye kutumaini, -tumainifu.

configuration, *n.* namna, umbo, sura, hali, tabia.

confine, *v.t.* funga, zuia, weka, wekea mpaka, shindisha. *She is confined to her room,* amekatazwa asitoke au hawezi kutoka chumbani. *Be confined,* zaa (mke), jifungua; (*refer exclusively to*) husika na (kwa). **confines,** *n.* mipaka. **confined,** *a.* -enye mipaka, -fungwa, -embamba (yaani -enye nafasi haba). **confinement,** *n.* mfungo, kifungo; (*child-bearing*) uzazi.

confirm, *v.t.* (*strengthen*) thibitisha, imarisha, tia nguvu, egemeza, tegemeza; (*ratify*) sahihisha, yakinisha, toa idhini; (*perform confirmation*) tia (bandika) mikono baada ya Ubatizo, tolea Kipa imara. **confirmation,** *n.* uthibitisho, shahada, ushahidi, tegemezo, egemeo, mwega, hakika; (*the rite*) Kipa imara. **confirmative,** *a.* -a kuelekea kuthibitisha, -shahidi.

confirmed, *a.* imara; (*inveterate*) kabisa, -a siku nyingi, *e.g. he is a confirmed drunkard,* yu mlevi kabisa wa siku nyingi.

confiscate, *v.t.* nyang'anya, twaa mali (hasa serikali kuadhibisha mtu kwa kutwaa mali zake). — *a.* -enye kutwaliwa na serikali. **confiscation,** tendo la serikali kutwaa mali.

conflagration, *n.* moto mkubwa, mteketeo mkubwa.

conflict, *v.i.* pambana, shindana, hitilafiana, -wa mbalimbali, pingana, -topatana, kaidi. — *n.* mapigano, vita, shindano, mpambano, ugomvi. **conflicting,** *a.* -enye kupigana (pambana, kaidi); mbalimbali na, -a kinyume.

confluence, *n.* mkutano, mchanganyo, mahali pa kukutana (kama mito miwili *&c.*); **confluent,** *a.* -a kuunganika au kuchanganyika pamoja. **conflux,** *n.* taz. *confluence.*

conform, *v.i.* (*to*) fanana, patana; kubali; fuata, tii; — *v.t.* sawazisha, fananisha. **conformable,** *a.* -a kufanana, -a kupatana; (*suitable*) -a kufaa; (*obedient*) tiifu. **conformation,** *n.* umbo, sura, tabia, hali. **conformity,** *n.* usawa, upatano, ulinganifu, ukubali. *In conformity with,* kwa kupatana na, kwa kufuata.

confound, *v.t.* (*defeat*) angamiza, shinda; (*mix*) changanya, chafua; (*perplex, astonish*) shangaza, staajabisha, tunduwaza, fedhehi, fadhaisha, tia wasiwasi.

confraternity, *n.* chama.

confrère, *n.* mwenzi (wa kazi, wa chama).

confront, *v.t.* (*oppose*) kabili, simama mbele, pinga; (*compare, match*) linganisha, pambanisha, piganisha; (*set opposite, bring before*) kabilisha.

confuse, *v.t.* (*mix*) changanya, fuja, buruga, changanyisha; (*perplex*) hangaisha, chafua, tia wasiwasi, bumbuaza, koroweza, rabishi, zonga; (*fail to distinguish*) topambanua; (*confound*) fadhaisha, fedhehi, tahayarisha, hizi. **confused,** *a.* -a wasiwasi, -a fujo, -liochanganyika; (*abashed*) -enye haya, -enye fadhaa, **confusion,** *n.* chafuko, kikaka, kakara, rabsha, fujo, ghasia, (*of mind*) wasiwasi, mbasuo, bumbuazi, dukuduku, dungudungu, kiwewe; (*shame*) fadhaa, haya.

confutation, *n.* taz. *confute.*

confute, *v.t.* (*a person*) kanusha, shinda kwa maneno, onyesha au baini uwongo; (*an argument*) kanusha, dhihirisha uwongo. **confutation,** *n.* kanusho, bayana ya uwongo (ya kushinda uwongo).

congeal, *v.i.* ganda, tungama, gandamana; — *v.t.* gandisha.

congenial, *a.* -enye tabia ya namna ile ile; -a kupatana, -a kufaa, -a kupendeza.

congenital, *a.* -a kuzaliwa na, *e.g.* kilema, ugonjwa mtu aliozaliwa nao.

conger, *n.* mkunga (samaki kama nyoka mkubwa).

congeries, *n.* chungu, jamii, kusanyiko la vitu.

congest, *v.t.* kusanya, songa, jaza sana, shibisha. **congested,** *a.* -enye mavilio ya damu; (*overcrowded*) -a kusongana mno, -a kujaa sana. **congestion,** *n.* mavilio ya damu; (*state of fullness*) songano, songamano, hali ya kusongwa au kulemewa na vitu vingi (kazi, mashughuli *&c.*).

conglomerate, *a.* -a vitu vingi vilivyokusanyika au kuambatana pamoja. — *v.t. and i.* kusanya (kusanyika) vitu vingi pamoja. **conglomeration,** *n.* chungu, kusanyiko la vitu vingi pamoja, jamii.

congratulate, *v.t.* shangilia, takia heri, bariki, -pa mkono wa heri, pukusa, hongeza, pongeza; (*by a present, i.e. at a birth, after a contest or after performing a mission*) fichua, tunza; (*after a journey, danger or contest*) -pa stahili salama, -pa pole; (*at a festival*) -pa mkono wa baraka (wa heri, wa sikukuu, wa idi). **congratulation,** *n.* mkono, mbaraka, sifa, hongezo, hongera, pongezi, pukuso; (*with a present, i.e. at a birth, after contest &c.*) fichuo, tunzo; (*after a journey, danger or contest*) pole, stahili salama; (*at a festival*) mkono wa baraka (wa heri, wa sikukuu, wa idi).

congregate, *v.t.* kusanya; — *v.i.* kutana, kusanyika, kutanika. **congregation,** *n.* kusanyiko la watu; kutano, kundi; (*body of worshippers*) jamii ya watu waabuduo.

congress, *n.* mkutano wa watu; baraza kuu ya *United States* (*America*).

congruence, congruency, *n.* taz. *congruent.*

congruent, *a.* -a kupatana, -a kulingana, -a kufaa. **congruence, congruency,** *n.* upatano, ulinganifu. **congruity,** *n.* usawa, ulinganifu. **congruous,** *a.* -a kupatana, -a kulingana sawa, -a kufaa.

conic, conical, taz. *cone.*

conjecture, *n.* dhana, kisio, bahatisho, maono. — *v.t. and i.* bahatisha, kisia, dhani, ona.

conjoin, *v.t.* unga, unganisha; — *v.i.* ungana. **conjoint,** *a.* -enye umoja, -a shirika. **conjointly,** *adv.* pamoja, kwa shirika.

conjugal, *a.* -a mume na mkewe.

conjugate, *v.t.* (sarufi) taja (andika, pambanua) mabadilio au sehemu zote za kiarifa (*verb*).

conjunction, *n.* mwungano; (sarufi) kiungo. *In conjunction with,* pamoja na, kwa kuungana na. **conjunctly,** *adv.* pamoja. **conjuncture,** *n.* hali, mambo, wakati.

conjure, *v.t.* omba kwa juhudi, sihi kwa juhudi; — *v.i.* (*do tricks*) fanya kiinimacho (mazingaombwe, mizungu); (*spirits*) punga pepo. *Conjure up,* tunga, buni, fikirisha. **conjurer,** *n.* mfanya kiinimacho (mazingaombwe, mizungu). **conjuring,** *n.* kiinimacho, mazingaombwe, mizungu, mauzauza.

connect, *v.t.* funga pamoja, fungasha, unga pamoja, unganisha; — *v.i.* ungika, unganika, shikana, fungamana, shikamana; (*associate*) husu. *These subjects are connected,* mambo haya yanahusiana, yameungamana. **connectedly,** *adv.* kwa kufuatana, kwa kuhusiana; (*without break or pause*) moja kwa moja, mfululizo, mtawalia. **connection,** *n.,* **connexion,** *n.* mwunganisho; (*coherence*) wiano, uhusiano, *e.g. these affairs have no connection with each other,* mambo haya hayawiani, hayahusiani; (*bond, link*) kiungo; (*relation*) ndugu, jamaa, ahali, mtani; (*sexual*) ngono; (*context*) jambo, hali, habari, *e.g. in this connection, in connection with this,* kwa jambo (habari, hali) hili.

connivance, *n.* taz. *connive.*

connive, *v.i.* achilia, pisha, toangalia, tokataza (kosa, tendo &c.); (*abet*) shiriki tendo kwa siri. **connivance,** *n.* tendo la kuachilia (la kupisha, la kutoangalia kosa, tendo &c.); ushirika (katika kosa, tendo).

connoisseur, *n.* mjuzi, mfahamivu, mwenye maarifa mengi ya jambo (sanaa &c.).

connote, *v.t.* onyesha, -wa na maana ya, pamoja na, maana ya asili.

connubial, *a.* -a mume na mkewe.

conquer, *v.t.* shinda, tiisha, weza, pata kwa nguvu au juhudi; — *v.i.* shinda. **conqueror,** *n.* mshindi, mshindaji. **conquered,** *a.* -lioshindwa; (*person*), *n.* mshinde. **conquest,** *n.* ushindi; (*defeat*) ushinde; (*spoils*) mateka, nyara, nchi zilizotiishwa. *To make a conquest,* shinda.

consanguine, *a.* -a damu (jamaa, udugu, ukoo) mmoja. **consanguinity,** *n.* jamaa, ndugu (wa damu si wa urafiki).

conscience, *n.* dhamiri, yaani akili inayotuonya kama matendo yetu ni mema au mabaya; moyo. *Good* (*or bad*) *conscience,* moyo wenye raha (au wasiwasi) kwa ajili ya matendo yetu. *Conscience money,* malipo yalipwayo na mtu kutuliza moyo wake kwa ajili ya tendo baya, kama vile wizi &c. *To be conscience smitten,* juta, ona vibaya kwa ajili ya tendo baya (kosa &c.). **conscientious,** *a.* -aminifu, -enye bidii (kufanya vyema yote yapasayo). *Conscientious objector*, mtu akataaye kufanya neno kwa sababu moyo wake unamwonya ya kuwa si haki, au kuwa halipatani na dini yake. **conscientiousness,** *n.* uaminifu (na tabia ya kufanya kwa bidii na uangalifu mambo yote yapasayo).

conscious, *a.* -a kujua au kufahamu moyoni (nafsini); -enye kujua (ona, -wa na fahamu *&c.*) *e.g. the man who was hurt was still conscious*, yule mtu aliyeumia alikuwa na fahamu bado, yaani hakuzimia; (*shy*) -enye haya, -enye soni. *Be conscious of*, ona, fahamu, jua, sikia *&c. He was conscious of a smell*, alisikia harufu. **consciously,** *adv.* kwa kujua, kwa kusudi, kusudi. **consciousness,** *n.* ufahamu wa nafsini (moyoni, akilini); (*perception*) akili, ufahamu, ujuzi; (*shyness*) haya, soni. *He lost consciousness*, alizimia, alizirai. *He regained consciousness*, alijirudia, alipata fahamu tena.

conscript, *n.* askari au baharia aliyeandikwa kwa lazima ya serikali. — *v.t.* andika (askari) kwa lazima. **conscription,** *n.* tendo la serikali la kuandika askari au baharia kwa lazima.

consecrate, *v.t.* fanya (weka) wakfu, bariki; toa (tenga) kwa ajili ya dini, Mungu, au kusudi fulani; tukuza, fanya takatifu; (*inaugurate*) zindua, tabaruku. **consecrated,** *a.* -takatifu, wakf. **consecration,** *n.* kufanya au kuweka wakf; (*state*) uwakfu.

consecutive, *a.* -a kufuatana mfulizo; -a kufuata, moja kwa moja, mtawalia, kwa msago.

consensus, *n.* upatano, ukubali, umoja, ridhaa (juu ya shauri *&c.*).

consent, *v.i.* kubali, ridhia, penda, ruhusu, toa idhini. — *n.* ukubali, radhi, ridhaa, ruhusa, idhini.

consequence, *n.* tokeo la jambo jingine; (*importance*) ukubwa, heshima, sifa, umaarufu; (*significance*) nguvu, maana. *A person of consequence*, mtu mwenye cheo kikubwa, mtu maarufu *&c. It is of no consequence*, haina maana, haidhuru, si kitu, basi. **consequent,** *a.* -a kufuata, -a baadaye. **consequential,** *a.* kufuata; (*pompous*) -enye majivuno, -enye makuu, -a fahari; (*casual*) -zembe, -purukushani, -a ovyo ovyo. **consequently,** *adv.* (*in consequence*) kwa sababu hiyo, baadaye.

conservation, *n.*, **conservative,** *a.*, **conservatory,** *n.* taz. *conserve*.

conserve, *v.t.* linda, tunza, hifadhi, weka vizuri. **conservation,** *n.* ulinzi, utunzo. **conservative,** *a.* -a kulinda, -a kutunza; -enye kuhifadhi mambo na desturi za kale, -siyependa kubadili mambo. **conservatory,** *n.* nyumba ya kulinda au kuweka vizuri vitu, hasa ya kuotesha maua yasiyoweza kusitawi penye baridi.

consider, *v.t.* (*deliberate on*) fikiri, dhukuru, angalia; (*take into account*) kumbuka; (*suppose, judge*) dhani, dhania, ona. **considerable,** *a.* (*important*) -a kustahili kufikiriwa, -a kukumbukwa; (*more than a little*) -kubwa kidogo, -ingi kidogo, -a kadiri. **considerably,** *adv.* sana. **considerate,** *a.* -enye huruma, -pole, -angalifu, -enye busara. **considerately,** *adv.* kwa huruma, kwa upole, kwa kufikiri (wengine). **consideration,** *n.* (*deliberation*) fikira, shauri, nadhari; (*importance*) cheo, sifa; (*kindness*) uangalifu, huruma, upole, wema; (*motive or reason*) sababu, kisa, jambo, hoja; (*compensation, reward*) lipo, tuzo. *Take into consideration*, angalia, kumbuka. **considering,** *prep.* kwa kuwa, kwa sababu.

consign, *v.t.* (*give to another*) toa, tolea, -pa; (*sign*) tia sahihi; (*transfer*) tolea, sihia mali; (*entrust*) aminisha, weka, wekea; (*commit*) peleka, weka; (*transmit*) peleka, pelekea. **consignee,** *n.* mpelekewa vitu, aliyepewa au kusihiwa mali. **consignment,** *n.* vitu, bidhaa *&c.* zilizopelekwa; hati ya kupelekea (ya kuwekea, ya kusihia) mali.

consist, *v.i.* -wa, ni. *It consists of (in),* kitu chake ni, asili yake ni. **consistence, consistency,** *n.* uzito, ugumu; (*of persons*) unyofu, uthabiti; (*agreement*) upatano, usawa. **consistent,** *a.* thabiti, -aminifu, -nyofu, -a kushikilia jambo, -a kupatana, -a kulingana sawa. **consistently,** *adv.* kwa uthabiti, kwa jinsi ya kupatana (ya kulingana).

consolation, *n.* taz. *console.*

console, *v.t.* fariji, tuliza. **consolation,** *n.* faraja, kitulizo. **consolatory,** *a.* -enye faraja, -a kufariji. **consoler,** *n.* mfariji.

consolidate, *v.t.* (*make firm*) imarisha, thibitisha, tegemeza; (*make solid*) gandamiza, shindilia; (*unite*) unganisha, fanya umoja; — *v.i.* (*grow solid, firm*) thibitika, ungana, gandamana, imarika. **consolidated,** *a.* imara, thabiti, -gumu, -enye umoja, -lioungwa au kuwekwa pamoja.

consomme, *n.* namna ya mchuzi laini.

consonant, *a.* -a kupatana, -a kulingana sawa, -sawa, -a kufanana. — *n.* herufi isiyo vokali (*vowel*), yaani b, ch, d *&c.*, konsonanti. **consonance, consonancy,** *n.* upatano, ulinganifu.

consort, *n.* mwenzi, rafiki, mwandani; (*husband, wife*) mume, mke, meli inayofuatana na nyingine. — *v.i.* andamia, fuata, ongoa; (*be in keeping with*) patana (na).

conspectus, *n.* muhtasari, habari kwa ufupi.

conspicuous, *a.* -enye kuonekana kwa mbali, wazi, -a kutazamisha; (*prominent*) -a kutokeza, -kubwa, bora, mashuhuri.

conspiracy, *n.*, **conspirator,** *n.* taz. *conspire.*

conspire, *v.i.* (*plot*) fanya shauri pamoja (hasa baya). **conspiracy,** *n.* mapatano au maafikano ya kufanya mabaya; upatano wa shauri. **conspirator,** *n.* mwenzi mfitini; mshirika wa jambo baya.

constable, *n.* polisi. **constabulary,** *n.* jamii ya polisi.

constant, *a.* (*unchangeable*) -siyobadilika; (*firm*) thabiti, imara; (*continual*) -a daima, -a sikuzote, -a kawaida; (*faithful*) amini, aminifu. **constancy,** *n.* uthabiti, uaminifu. **constantly,** *adv.* kwa uthabiti, kwa uaminifu; (*frequently*) mara kwa mara, mara nyingi, daima, kila kipindi.

constellation, *n.* jamii ya nyota yenye jina kwa elimu ya falaki; kundi la nyota.

consternation, *n.* hofu kuu, tisho, ushangao, fadhaa, machugachuga, mang'amung'amu, mang'ang'amu.

constipate, *v.t.* funga choo. **constipation,** *n.* hali ya kufunga choo (ya kutopata choo barabara), uyabisi wa tumbo, ukabidhi wa tumbo.

constitute, *v.t.* (*establish*) simamisha, anzisha; (*form or compose*) fanya, fanyiza, -wa; (*appoint*) weka. **constituency,** *n.* jamii ya watu wenye haki kuchagua mtu kukaa katika baraza kuu ya kiingereza, mahali wakaapo watu hao. **constituent,** *n.* sehemu ya mchanganyiko; mtu mmoja wa *constituency.* — *a.* -enye kuwamo. **constitution,** *n.* tabia asili, hulka, umbo, afya, siha; (hali ya uzima wa jumla ya viungo vya mtu ni *constitution* yake, *e.g.* fulani aliugua sana, lakini alipona kwa sababu alikuwa na *good constitution,* yaani kwa asili, viungo vikuu vya mwili wake vilikuwa vizima vyenye afya au siha); (*system of laws &c.*) sheria, kanuni (za chama, za serikali *&c.*), serikali. *The British constitution,* sheria za kiingereza. **constitutional,** *a.* -a asili, -a afya; (*lawful*) halali, -a kutii sheria. *Take a constitutional,* enda kutembea, nyosha miguu (kwa ajili ya afya). **constitutive,** *a.* -enye nguvu (ya kusimamisha, ya kuanzisha, ya kufanyiza); (*original*) -a asili.

constrain, *v.t.* lazimisha, shurutisha; (*morally*) bidi; (*limit*) zuia. **constrained,** *a.* (*forced*) -a sharti, -a lazima, -liyezuiwa au kusongwa; (*embarrassed*) -enye haya (fadhaa, soni, tahayari &c.). **constraint,** *n.* (*force*) nguvu, sharti; (*repression*) zuio, tabia ya kujiweza (ya kutawala tamaa, hasira &c.); (*embarrassment*) haya, soni.

constrict, *v.t.* bana, songa, finya, minya, nyonga. **constricted,** *a.* -embamba, -finyo, -a kubanwa, -a kusongwa, -a kufinywa &c. **constriction,** *n.* mbano, mkazo, msongo, mfinyo &c. **constrictor,** *n.* mbano, mkazo, kitu kinachokaza au kubana, au kunyonga &c. Chatu huitwa *Boa constrictor*, kwa sababu hunyonganyonga mawindo yake.

constringe, *v.t.* kama *constrict*. **constringency,** *n.* kama *constrictor*. **constringent,** *a.* -a kusonga, -a kufinya.

construct, *v.t.* fanya, fanyiza, unga; (*boat*) unda; (*book*) buni; (*house*) jenga. **construction,** *n.* mjengo, mwundo; ujenzi, uunzi; majengo, nyumba, cho chote kilichojengwa, kuungwa au kuundwa; kazi &c.; (*of sentences* &c.) nahau; (*interpretation*) tafsiri, maana. **constructive,** *a.* -a kufanyiza, -a kujenga; (*criticism*) -a kusaidia; (*amounting to*) -siyo halisi ila ni sawasawa na, kama. **constructor,** *n.* mfanyi, mwunzi, mjenzi &c.

construe, *v.t.* (*translate*) fasiri, tafsiri; (*explain*) eleza maana; (*infer*) fahamu maana.

consubstantial, *a.* -enye asili au tabia ile ile. **consubstantiation,** *n.* imani ya madhehebu fulani ya Wakristo ya kuwa mwili na damu hasa ya Yesu Kristo ni pamoja na mkate na divai katika Ushirika Mtakatifu, iishapo kuwekwa wakf.

consuetudinary, *a.* -a kawaida, -a desturi, -a mazoea.

consul, *n.* balozi, mtu apelekwaye na serikali yake kukaa katika nchi ya kigeni awe wakili wake. **consulate,** *n.* nyumba na kazi ya balozi; muda wa kuwa balozi.

consult, *v.t.* taka shauri kwa, shaurisha; (*look up in book* &c.) tafuta (angalia) habari (katika kitabu &c.); — *v.i.* fanya shauri; (*with another*) shauriana. **consultation,** *n.* shauri, mkutano wa kushauriana (hasa wa madaktari, wana sheria &c.).

consume, *v.t.* -la; (*by fire*) teketeza; (*use up*) tumia, maliza; — *v.i.* (*waste away*) lika, dhoofu, haribika. **consumer,** *n.* mlaji; (*user*) mtu atumiaye kitu; (*buyer*) mnunuzi. **consumption,** *n.* (*of food*) ulaji; (*of goods*) utumizi, upotezo; (*sickness*) kifua kikuu. **consumptive,** *a.* -enye ugonjwa wa kifua kikuu.

consummate, *v.t.* kamilisha, timiliza, maliza, isha; (*marriage*) timiliza ndoa, yaani kuifunga kwa ngono baada ya kuoana. — *a.* kamili, -timilifu, kabisa, bora, -ingi, -kubwa. **consummately,** *adv.* kwa ukamilifu. **consummation,** *n.* mwisho, utimizo, tendo la kumaliza (timiza, kamilisha); (*of marriage*) mfungo wa ndoa kwa ngono baada ya kuoana.

consumption, *n.* **consumptive,** *a.* taz. *consume*.

contact, *n.*, mgusano, mwungano, mkutano, mpambano. *Come in contact* (*have dealings with*), kutana, -wa na shughuli, (*collide*) gongana, dundana, pambana. *Be in contact* (*with*), gusana. *Make contact,* unganisha uzi wa simu ili nguvu ya umeme iweze kupita.

contagion, *n.* ambukizo, mwenezo (wa ugonjwa), wito. **contagious,** *a.* -a kuambukiza, -a kueneza. **contagious disease,** *n.* ugonjwa uambukizwao kwa watu kugusana.

contain, *v.t.* (*things*) -wa na (vitu) ndani, weka ndani, chukua ndani, *e.g. this cup contains water,* kikombe hiki kina maji ndani yake; *it is able to contain such and such a measure,* kinaweza kuweka (kuchukua) kipimo fulani; (*hold, be equal to*) -wa kadiri ya, -wa sawa na; *e.g. it contains one pound,* ina kadiri ya (ni sawa na) ratli moja. *To contain oneself,* jizuia, jiweza (kwa habari za tamaa, hasira, haraka, harara *&c.*). **content,** *n.* kadiri, nafasi; (*meaning*) maana. **contents,** *n. pl.* vitu vya ndani, yaliyomo. *Table of contents,* fahirisi.

contaminate, *v.t.* tia uchafu, najisi, haribu, harimu, ambukiza. **contamination,** *n.* najisi, ambukizo, haramu.

contemn, *v.t.* dharau, tweza, hizi, beza, -toangalia, -tojali.

contemplate, *v.t.* fikiri habari za, angalia sana, tazama sana; (*intend*) kusudia, azimu; nuia. (*look forward to*) tazamia; — *v.i.* tafakari. **contemplation,** *n.* fikira, mawazo, taamuli; hali ya kukaa na kushika tama (ya kufikiri sana juu ya jambo fulani). *It is contemplated,* inafikiriwa, inakusudiwa. **contemplative,** *a.* -enye kufikiri sana, -a kutafakari.

contemporaneous, contemporary, *a.* -a wakati ule ule, -a miaka ile ile, -a zamani zile zile *&c.*; -a kuishi (kutokea au kuwapo) wakati ule ule.

contemporary, *n.* mtu wa hirimu au rika lile lile (la mwingine); gazeti linalotolewa siku ile ile au wakati ule ule wa jingine.

contempt, *n.* (*scorn*) dharau, twezo, bezo; (*disgrace*) aibu, udhilifu, unyonge. *Treat with contempt,* dharau, geua, beua, tweza, hizi, hakiri, beza. **contemptible,** *a.* -a kudharauliwa, -nyonge, -dhilifu, duni, hafifu. **contemptuous,** *a.* -a kudharau, -a kutweza, -a kiburi, sodawi.

contend, *v.i.* fanya juhudi, shindana, pigana; (*dispute*) kaidi, bishana, pingana, jadili, shindana kwa maneno, babaka; (*urge one's course*) shika kusema, shikilia kauli, nena kwa nguvu. *Contend for,* tafuta kwa bidii, shindania, tetea. **contention,** *n.* shindano, ushindani, ugomvi, mateto, ukinzani; (*matter in question*) jambo (la kugombania, la kutetewa) teto, kisa; (*assertion*) neno, shauri, kauli. *The bone of contention,* kisa cha shindano au ugomvi *&c.* **contentious,** *a.* -gomvi, -shindani, -kaidi, -bishi.

content, (1) *n.* taz. *contain.*

content, (2) *v.t.* ridhisha. *Be content* (*contented*), ridhi, ridhika, ridhia, ona radhi, -wa radhi; tulia. *Be self contented,* jikinai. **content,** *n.*, **contentment,** *n.* uradhi, radhi, ridhaa, ukinaifu, kinaya. **contentedly,** *adv.* kwa hali ya kuridhika (ya kuona radhi), kwa utulivu.

contention, *n.*, **contentious,** *a.* taz. *contend.*

contentment, *n.* taz. *content* (2).

contents, *n.* taz. *contain.*

contest, *n.* shindano, vita, (*dispute*) mateto, mabishano, ugomvi, tetesi, kisa. *v.t.* (*dispute*) kana, kaidi, teta, bisha; (*strive for*) shindana, shindania kwa kitendo. **contestant,** *n.* mshindani.

context, *n.* maneno yanayotangulia na kufuata aya, mstari au maneno mengine ambayo hudhihirisha maana yake.

contiguity, *n.* mtangamano, ujirani, hali ya kuwa karibu. **contiguous,** *a.* -a kugusana, -a kupakana, -a karibu, -a jirani, -a kutangamana.

continent, *n.* bara kuu; mojawapo la mafungu matano ya dunia, (yaani *Europe, Asia, Africa, America,* na *Australia*). — *a.* -zuilifu wa tamaa (hasa ya kike na kiume); -kiasi, -safi, -tawa. **continency,** *n.* uzuilifu wa tamaa; kiasi katika tamaa (hasa ya kike na kiume; na pengine maana yake ni kutoitimiza kabisa); (*ascetic*) utawa, usafi.

contingency *n.* taz. *contingent.*

contingent, *a.* yamkini, -a kutegemea jambo jingine; -a kuwezekana (lakini hakuna hakika kwamba itatokea). — *n.* sehemu ya jamii, hasa kundi la askari. **contingency,** *n.* matukio, nasibu, bahati, jambo liwezalo kutokea lakini hakuna hakika kwamba litatokea; tukio.

continual, *n.*, **continually**, *adv.*, **continuance**, *n.*, **continuation**, *n.* taz. *continue.*

continue, *v.t.* (*extend*) ongeza, endesha; (*resume*) chaga, charuka; — *v.i.* (*persist*) endelea, fuliza, zidi, sedeka; (*remain, endure*) dumu, kaa, shinda. **continual**, *a.* -a moja kwa moja, -a mfulizo; -a sikuzote, -a kila siku, -a daima, -a kuendelea. **continually**, *adv.* sikuzote; bila kikomo; mara kwa mara; mtawalia, bila kuacha, abadi. **continuance**, *n.* maisha, aushi, udumifu, ufulizo, uendeleo. **continuation**, *n.* mfulizo, mwandamano, fuatano, kinachofuata. **continued**, *a.* -a kuendelea, -a kufuliza, taz. *continual.* **continuity**, *n.* mwendeleo moja kwa moja, mfululizo, mfulizo, ufungamano. **continuous**, *a.* kama *continual.*

contort, *v.t.* geuzageuza, umbua, potoa, nyonganyonga; (*of face*) kunja, finya. **contortion**, *n.* upotoe, mageuzo, mageuzi, upinduzi; mapindi ya maungo; (*of face*) finyo, kasikasi, kunjo la uso. **contortionist**, *n.* mtu ajipindapindaye viungo vyake.

contour, *n.* umbo, sura, namna; mstari unaozunguka sura au umbo la kitu cho chote. *Contour lines*, mistari iandikwayo katika ramani kuonyesha urefu wa kwenda juu wa sehemu za nchi.

contraband, *a.* haramu, marufuku. — *n.* bidhaa (zana, vitu) zilizokatazwa (kugombezwa, au kupigwa marufuku na sheria).

contract, *v.t.* (*lessen, shorten*) punguza, fupisha, kunjisha; (*get disease &c.*) pata, patwa na, patikana na, shikwa na; (*incur debt &c.*) fanya (deni). — *v.i.* punguka, fupika, kunjika, sinyaa; (*agree*) fanya mkataba (mapatano, maagano, sharti, ahadi, maafikano), afikiana. *Be contracted*, (*drawn together, narrow*) finya, finyana, sinyaa, -wa embamba, kunjamana. — *n.* mapatano, mwafaka, maafikano, maagano, sharti, ahadi. *Make, draw up, enter into a contract*, andikiana mapatano, mkataba *&c.* **contraction**, *n.* mpunguo, mfupisho, mkato, mkazo; (*wrinkle*) mfinyo. **contractor**, *n.* mtu afanyaye *contract*, mtu ajitiaye sharti ya kumaliza kazi fulani kwa fedha fulani katika muda fulani; mfanya kazi kwa mkataba; fundi wa mkataba.

contradict, *v.t.* (*deny, oppose*) kana, kanusha, kinza, dakuliza, dinda, zuma; (*assert the contrary*) nena kinyume (cha neno lililosemwa); (*dispute*) bishana, kaidi, checha; (*be contrary to*) achana hitilafiana, -wa kinyume cha. **contradiction**, *n.* mabishano, ukaidi, ubishi, ukinzani, dakizo udaku; (*disagreement*) hitilafu, tofauti, kinyume, neno lililo mbalimbali (lisilopatana). **contradictory**, *a.* -a kinyume, -a mbalimbali, -a kukana, -siopatana; (*of persons*) -kaidi, -tundu, -bishi.

contrariety, *n.*, **contrariness**, *n.* taz. *contrary.*

contrary, *a.* -a mbalimbali, -a kinyume, -a namna nyingine kabisa; (*of persons*) -kaidi, -tundu, -bishi. — *n.* kinyume. **contrariety**, *n.* ushindani, hitilafu, ukaidi, kinyume. **contrariness**, *n.* ukaidi, ubishi.

contrast, *v.i.* (*be in opposition to*) -wa mbalimbali na, -wa kinyume cha, -wa namna nyingine kabisa; — *v.t.* (*set in opposition*) linganisha, pambanisha, kabilisha, elekeza. — *n.* tofauti, hitilafu, kinyume; kitu kilicho mbalimbali, cha namna nyingine kabisa; mwonyesho wa tofauti (baina ya vitu)

contravene, *v.t.* (*oppose*) shindana na; zuia; (*transgress*) halifu, asi, vunja (sheria, kanuni *&c.*). **contravention**, *n.* uasi, uhalifu; (*obstruction*) ukinzani, ushindani.

contretemps, *n.* kizuizi, kikwazo, mgogoro.

contribute, *v.i.* changa, saidia, toa sehemu (ya chango fulani), shiriki, lipa bia, -wamo; (*to newspaper*) peleka habari kupigwa chapa katika gazeti. **contribution,** *n.* mchango, msaada, bia, sadaka, sehemu, mali ya kuchanga; habari zilizopelekwa kupigwa katika gazeti. **contributor,** *n.* mtu atoaye *contribution*. **contributory,** *a.* -enye kusaidia, -a kuelekea kuleta jambo (hali *&c.*).

contrite, *a.* -enye masikitiko kwa ajili ya makosa; -enye toba, -enye majuto. **contrition,** *n.* majuto, toba, masikitiko kwa ajili ya makosa.

contrivance, *n.* taz. *contrive.*

contrive, *v.t.* (*plan*) tengeneza (shauri, hila, kitu cha kufaa *&c.*); (*invent*) vumbua, tunga, zua; — *v.i.* (*effect*) fanya, weza, tengeneza, faulu, pata kufanya, *e.g. he has contrived to find out,* amepata kujua. **contrivance,** *n.* matengenezo, shauri, hila; (*thing*) kitu, chombo *&c.* (kilichofanywa, au kuvumbuliwa).

control, *n.* (*restraint*) uzuifu; (*authority*) utawala, amri, nguvu, usimamizi. — *v.t.* (*restrain*) zuia, weza; (*govern*) tawala, ongoza, simamia. **controller,** *n.* mwongozi, msimamizi, mtawala.

controversial, *a.,* **controversy,** *n.* taz. *controvert.*

controvert, *v.t.* pinga, bishania, shindania, kanusha, kana, kaidi. **controversial,** *a.* -a kuelekea kuleta mabishano (majadiliano); -a kuweza kubishaniwa (kukanushwa, kukaidiwa *&c.*). **controversy,** *n.* ugomvi, mabishano, majadiliano, shindano la maneno, ubishani.

contumacious, *a.* -a kuasi kwa dharau; -kaidi, -tundu, asi, sodawi. **contumacy,** *n.* ukaidi, utundu, uasi, ukinzani au kinzano la dharau, usodawi. **contumelious,** *a.* -a kudharau kwa kujitakabari (kwa jeuri, kwa ufidhuli). **contumely,** *n.* (*rudeness, insolence*) ufidhuli, ujuvi, (masuto, jeuri; (*contempt*) dharau, mzaha, twezo, cheko, fyonyo.

contuse, *v.t.* chubua, ponda, vilisha damu. **contusion,** *n.* chubuo; chubuko, mavilio ya damu.

conundrum, *n.* kitendawili, fumbo (la maneno).

convalesce, *v.i.* pona na kupata afya na nguvu baada ya ugonjwa, pata ashekali. **convalescence,** *n.* hali ya kuwa katika kupona na kupata afya baada ya kuugua. **convalescent,** *a.* -a katika hali ya kuwa katika kupona *&c.* taz. *convalesce,* — *n.* mtu anayepona na kupata afya *&c.* taz. *convalesce.*

convene, *v.t.* kusanya, kutanisha, ita kwenye mkutano; — *v.i.* kusanyika, kutanika.

convenience, *n.* kifaacho, manufaa; (*ease*) nafasi, nafuu, wasaa, raha, hiari. **convenient,** *a.* -a kufaa, -a kuwapo tayari kutumika.

convent, *n.* nyumba ya watawa. **conventicle,** *n.* mkutano wa siri wa dini; nyumba ndogo ya kusalia watu.

convention, *n.* mkutano; (*agreement*) mapatano, maagano; (*established usage*) jambo la desturi. **conventional,** *a.* -a desturi; -siotokana na moyo ila imekuwa mazoea, desturi au kawaida tu, *e.g. a conventional greeting,* maamkio yasiyo ya heshima halisi ila ni ya desturi tu. **conventionalist,** *n.* mtu ashikaye sana mambo (usemi, mavazi, mwendo *&c*) yaliyokubaliwa kuwa ya desturi.

converge, *v.i.* endea mahali pamoja, karibiana, sogeleana, kutana, elekea kukutana; — *v.t.* leta pamoja. **convergence,** *n.* mwendo wa kukaribiana (wa kusogeleana, wa kuelekea kukutana). **convergent, converging,** *a.* -a kuelekea kukutana *&c.*

conversant, *a.,* **conversation,** *n.,* **conversational,** *a.* taz. *converse* (1).

converse, (1) *v.i.* zungumza, ongea, sema, semezana. — *n.* mazungumzo, maongezi. — *a.* taz. chini ya *convert.* **conversant,** *a.* -zoefu, -enye kujua sana. **conversation,** *n.* mazungumzo, maongezi. **conversational,**

a. -a maongezi, -a mazungumzo; -a jinsi ya kutumika katika maongezi.
converse, (2) *a.*, **conversely,** *adv.*, **conversion,** *n.* taz. *convert.*
convert, *v.t.* (*change*) geuza, badili (hali, dini, matumizi *&c.*); (*from irreligious to holy life*) ongoa, hidi; (*apply*) tumia kwa kazi au kusudi fulani. *Be converted,* ongoka. *Make a convert,* ongoza kuwa (Mkristo, Mwislamu *&c.*). — *n.* mwongofu, mtu aliyebadili dini (maisha mabaya *&c.*). **converse,** *a.* -a kinyume, a-upande wa pili; -liogeuzwa au kubadilika. — *n.* kitu kilicho kinyume cha kingine. **conversely,** *adv.* kwa upande wa pili, kwa kugeuza kabisa, kwa kinyume. **conversion,** *n.* mbadiliko wa hali (dini, maisha mabaya *&c.*); ubadili, ugeuzi; (*of character*) wongofu. **convertible,** *a.* -a kuweza kubadilika, -a kugeuka, -a kugeukana; (*equivalent*) -a sawasawa, -a kubadilikana.
convex, *a.* mviringo wa kutokeza, *e.g.* sahani au bakuli lililofudikizwa; -a mbinu, -a kubinuka, -a kukubaza.
convey, *v.t.* (*carry*) chukua; (*transmit*) peleka; (*communicate*) julisha, ambia, arifu, onya; (*make over*) sihia, kabidhi, salimisha, toa, fikisha, wasilisha. **conveyance,** *n.* uchukuzi; (*vehicle*) gari; (*legal document*) hati ya kubadilisha au kusihia mali.
convict, *v.t.* thibitisha hatia ya kosa, tia hatiani, pasisha; (*convince*) sadikisha. — *n.* mfungwa, mtu aliyethibitishwa ana hatia ya kosa (hasa aliyefungwa na serikali kwa adhabu ya kukosa). **conviction,** *n.* thibitisho la hatia ya kosa; tendo la kusadikisha au la kusadiki sana, hakika; (*judgement*) nia, dhana. *It is my own conviction,* nasadiki sana, ndiyo ninayosadiki. *Carry conviction,* sadikisha kabisa, ondoa shaka.
convince, *v.t.* sadikisha, aminisha, julisha (ukweli au uwongo wa jambo); tuliza au ondoa shaka kwa ushuhuda. **convincing,** *a.* -a kusadikisha, -a kuaminisha, -a kuondoa mashaka, -a kujulisha.
convivial, *a.* -a kufurahisha moyo, -a kuchangamsha, -a furaha, -a kuteremesha; -a karamu. **conviviality,** *n.* karamu, furaha, uchangamshi, mteremesho.
convocation, *n.* taz. *convoke.*
convoke, *v.t.* ita, kusanya. **convocation,** *n.* mkutano; baraza ya wakuu wa kanisa la kiingereza.
convolve, *v.i.* viringana, pindana.
convolute, convoluted, *a.* -liovingana, -a pindana, -kunjana. **convolution,** *n.* pindi, kikunjo, mzingo.
convoy, *v.t.* fuatana (sindikiza) kwa ajili ya kulinda; linda njiani. — *n.* (*protection*) ulinzi, himaya ya njiani; (*guard*) walinzi wa msafara (hasa manowari zinazolinda meli zenye zana *&c.*); (*protected party*) msafara wenye walinzi (hasa meli zinazolindwa na manowari).
convulse, *v.t.* sukasuka, tikisa, tetemesha, shtusha sana. *Convulse with laughter,* chekesha mno. **convulsion,** *n.* kifafa, hali ya kufurukuta mikono na miguu au kujipindapinda na kujinyonganyonga (kwa ugonjwa *&c.*); (*of children*) dege, babu, babewana; (*violent disturbance*) msukosuko, machafuko. **convulsive,** *a.* -a kupindapinda, -a kifafa, -a kutetemeka sana. -a kushtukashtuka.
cony (coney), *n.* kwanga, pelele, wibari.
cook, *v.t.* pika; (*alter*) geuza (hesabu daftarini *&c.*); — *v.i.* pikika. — *n.* mpishi. **cookery,** *n.* upishi. **cooking,** *n.* upishi, mpiko, mapishi. *Cooking utensils,* vyombo vya kupikia. *Cooking place,* meko, jikoni. *Cooking range,* (*stones*) meko, mafiga, mafya, (*iron*) jiko.
cool, *a.* -a baridi kidogo, -a vuguvugu, fufutende, -a baridi; (*calm*) -tulivu; (*slack, indifferent*) legevu, tepetevu, -zembe, -vivu; (*unperturbed*) -enye macho makavu; (*impudent*) -shupavu, -fidhuli, -safihi, -juvi. — *v.t.* (*allay or moderate* (*heat*), poza, tia

baridi, baridisha; (*of excitement, passion &c.*). — *v.i.* tulia; — *v.t.* tuliza; (*of water*). — *v.t.* zimua; — *v.i.* poa, pata baridi, burudika, zizima. **coolness,** *n.* baridi kidogo; (*slackness*) ulegevu, utepetevu, uvivu; (*imperturbability*) ukavu wa macho; (*impudence*) ushupavu, ujuvi ujeuri, ufidhuli, usafihi.

coolie, *n.* mtu apakiaye na kupakua mizigo melini, kuli.

coolness, *n.* taz. *cool.*

coop, *n.* kitundu, kizimba (cha kuku &c.), mzinga, zizi. — *v.t.* funga, zuia (zizini &c.). **cooper,** *n.* mfanyiza mapipa.

co-operate, *v.i.* fanya kazi pamoja, saidia, saidiana, shirikiana, fanya bia; (*in cultivation &c. in return for similar help*) fanya ujima. **co-operation,** *n.* shirika (ya watu ili waweze kununua vitu kwa nafuu, kwa urahisi, au kwa kusudi lo lote), bia (*in return for similar help*) ujima. **co-operative,** *a.* -a kusaidiana, -a ushirika, -a kufanya kazi pamoja.

co-opt, *v.t.* karibisha mtu mkutanoni kwa uchaguo wa mkutano. **co-option,** *n.* karibisho la mtu mkutanoni kwa kuchaguliwa na mkutano.

co-ordinate, *a.* -a namna, kadiri au cheo kile kile; -a kulingana sawa. — *v.t.* linganisha, patanisha, sawazisha (kufanya kuwa namna, kadiri au cheo hata kufaana). **co-ordination,** *n.* ulinganifu, usawa; hali ya kuwa namna, kadiri au cheo ya kufaana.

copal, *n.* sandarusi.

cope, (1) *n.* vazi la sherehe la kasisi.

cope, (2) *v.i.* (*with*) weza, faulu, shindana na (hasa kwa kuweza na kushinda).

coping, *n.* kigongo cha ukuta.

copious, *a.* -ingi, furufuru, tele, maridhawa, -a kufurika. **copiously,** *adv.* kwa wingi sana.

copper, *n.* shaba nyekundu; (*vessel*) sufuria; (*coin*) senti, fulusi; (*wire*) uzi wa shaba, masoka, masango, udodi. — *a.* -a shaba nyekundu, -a rangi ya shaba nyekundu. **copper sulphate,** *n.* mrututu.

copra, *n.* mbata, nazi kavu.

copse, *n.* kichaka.

copula, *n.* neno la kuunga mafungu (*sentensi*) mawili ya maneno au maneno mawili katika sentensi moja; kiungo. **copulate,** *v.t. and i.* (*sexually*) jamii, jamiiana; (*vulgar and of animal*) tomba, tombana. **copulation,** *n.* ngono, tendo la *copulate.* **copulative,** *a.* -a kuunga, -a kuunganisha.

copy, *v.t.* nakili, fuatisha; (*imitate*) iga, igiza, fuatisha. — *n.* nakili, nakala, mfano, mwandiko sawa; mwigo. **copier,** *n.* mtu anakiliye; mwigaji. **copy-book,** *n.* kitabu chenye mwandiko wa kufuatishwa. **copyright,** *n.* haki ya mtu aliyebuni kitabu ya kuzuia wengine wasikifuatishe.

coquet, *v.t.* (mwanamke) piga ubembe (umalidadi, madaha) tamanisha, vuta upendo au tia ashiki kwa kuchezacheza, au kubembeleza kwa mahaba &c. **coquetry,** *n.* ubembe, umalidadi, mabembelezi, madaha, mahaba. **coquette,** *n.* (mwanamke) mbembe, mmalidadi, mbembelezi, mpuzi, mwenye mahaba ya hadaa. **coquettish,** *a.* -bembe, -shaufu.

coracle, *n.* mashua ndogo ya fito na ngozi.

coral, *n.* (*red*) marijani, marijani ya fedhaluka; (*rag*) matumbawe. **coral, coralline,** *a.* -a marijani, -a matumbawe.

Coran, *n.* Kurani, Furkani, msahafu mtakatifu wa Waislamu.

cord, *n.* kamba nyembamba, ugwe, kigwe; (*spinal*) uti wa mgongo; (*umbilical*) kitovu. — *v.t.* funga kamba. **cordage,** *n.* kamba. **cordite,** *n.* namna ya baruti ifananayo kidogo na ugwe.

cordial, *a.* -kunjufu, -changamfu, -teremeshi, -ema. *Give a cordial welcome,* pokea kwa furaha, karibisha vizuri. — *n.* kitu (dawa, kinywaji &c.) kifurahishacho moyo, kiburudisho.

cordite, *n.* taz. *cord.*

cordon, *n.* kipande cha kigwe, alama ya heshima fulani; safu (mstari) ya askari (polisi) ya kulinda mahali &c.

core, *n.* moyo, kiini, sehemu ya katikati, maana hasa.

co-respondent, *n.* mwanamume aliyeshtakiwa uzinzi katika daawa ya kutaliki mwanamke.

coriander, *n.* giligilani.

cork, *n.* gome la jamii ya miti fulani; (*of bottle*) kizibo. — *v.t.* ziba. **corkscrew,** *n.* kizibuo, kitu cha kuzibulia.

cormorant, *n.* mnandi, ndege wa bahari alaye samaki.

corn, (1) *n.* (*grain*) nafaka; (*maize*) mahindi; (*wheat*) ngano; (*grain of*) punje. **corn-cob,** *n.* gunzi, bunzi. **corned,** *a.* -a chembe chembe; -a kukolewa au kutiwa chumvi—sioze, *e.g. Corned beef,* nyama ya ng'ombe iliyokolea chumvi isioze upesi, na kuhifadhiwa katika makopo. **corn-field,** *n.* konde au shamba la nafaka. **corn-flour,** *n.* unga mwepesi sana wa mahindi.

corn, (2) *n.* (*on foot*) sugu; (*on forehead*) sijida.

cornea, *n.* chamba, ngozi ngumu inayopenya nuru ya katikati mbele ya macho, kioo cha macho.

cornelian, *n.* akiki, namna ya kito.

corn-cob, *n.*, **corned,** *a.* taz. *corn* (1).

corner, *n.* pembe, ncha mistari (kuta &c.) inapokutana; (*end*) mwisho, ncha; (*of cloth*) tamvua; (*difficulty*) shida, matata, hali mbaya; (*of merchandise* &c.) tendo la kununua bidhaa (mali &c.) yote ya namna moja ili watu waitakao lazima walipe bei aitakayo yule aliyeinunua; (*football*) nafuu ya teke moja la mpira wapewayo wachezaji ikiwa mtu wa upande wa adui ametoa mwenyewe mpira nje ya mstari wa mlango wa upande wake. — *v.t.* tia shidani, weka pembeni, songa, dhiisha, shinda; nunua bidhaa yote ya namna moja. **cornered,** *a.* -enye pembe; -enye kutiwa shidani, -a kushindwa. *Done in a corner,* fanywa (fanyika) faraghani, kwa siri. *Drive into a corner,* tia mashakani (shidani); songa, dhiisha, shinda.

cornet, *n.* namna ya tarumbeta.

corn-field, *n.*, **corn-flour,** *n.* taz. *corn* (1).

cornice, *n.* ushi (wa ukuta).

cornucopia, *n.* hali ya kuwa na wingi (ya neema, ya usitawi).

corollary, *n.* lililofahamika kwa maneno yaliyosemwa (au matendo yaliyofanyika); lifuatalo (jambo), matokeo (ya jambo).

coronation, *n.* tendo la kutia mfalme taji anapotawazwa.

coroner, *n.* mtu mwenye amri ya serikali kuhojihoji sababu ya kifo cha watu wafao ghafula au kwa namna iwezayo kudhaniwa wameuawa &c.

coronet, *n.* kitaji, taji ndogo, pambo la kichwa.

corporal, (1) *n.* cheo cha askari kilicho chini ya *sergeant.*

corporal, (2) *a.* -a mwili, -a kuhusu mwili; -enye mwili (si pepo wala mzuka wala koma tu). *Corporal punishment,* adhabu ya kupigwa (mwilini). — *n.* kitambaa kinachotumika katika ibada ya Ushirika Mtakatifu. **corporate,** *a.* -a umoja wa jamii ya watu; -a jamii ya watu, -a shirika au chama, -a umoja, **corporation,** *n.* umoja wa jamii ya watu, shirika, chama, unene wa tumbo, tumbo kubwa. **corporeal,** *a.* -enye mwili (si pepo tu); -a mwili. **corpse,** *n.* maiti; (*carcass*) mzoga, pindi, pinda. **corpulence,** *n.* unene wa kiwiliwili. **corpulent,** *a.* -nene. **corpuscle,** *n.* kitu kidogo sana, chembe, kama chembechembe zilizomo katika damu zionekanazo kwa darubini. **corps,** *n.* jeshi la askari.

corpulence, *n.*, **corpulent,** *a.*, **corpuscle,** *n.* taz. *corporal* (2).

corral, *n.* zizi la ng'ombe. — *v.t.* tia ng'ombe zizini.

correct, *v.t.* sahihisha, toa makosa, safidi; (*punish*) rudi, adhibisha, tia adabu; (*counterbalance*) sawazisha; (*reform*) ongoza tabia, tengeneza maisha; (*watch, clock &c.*) rekebisha. — *a.* sahihi, fasihi, bila kosa, safi, -zuri, halisi, barabara. *Correct* (*clear style*), nahau, ufasaha. **correction**, *n.* kusahihisha, kutoa makosa, kurekebisha; (*punishment*) adhabu, maonyo, rada, marudio; (*improvement*) matengenezo. **corrective**, *a.* kusahihisha, -a kutengeneza &c.; (*punitive*) kurudi, -a kuadhibisha; (*remedial*) -a kuponya, -a kuzuia (makosa, ugonjwa &c.). **correctly**, *adv.* barabara, sawasawa, sahihi, vizuri, vyema. **correctness**, *n.* usahihi, usafi, ufasaha, uzuri.

correlate, *v.i.* wiana; — *v.t.* elekeza, elekezanya. **correlation**, *n.* maelekeano, wiano, uhusiano.

correspond, *v.i.* (*resemble*) lingana, fanana, afiki, afikiana, elekeana, -wa sawasawa; (*by letters*) andikiana barua. **correspondence**, *n.* ulinganifu, usawasawa, maelekeano, maafikano, mwafaka; (*letters*) barua. **correspondent**, *a.* -a kulingana na, -a sawasawa na. — *n.* mwenzi; mleta habari kwa barua. **corresponding**, *a.* sawa, -linganifu.

corridor, *n.* ujia nyumbani unaounganisha vyumba; ukumbi.

corrigendum, *n.* (*pl.* **corrigenda**) lihitajialo kusahihishwa, *e.g.* makosa katika kitabu.

corroborate, *v.t.* thibitisha, hakikisha, shuhudia. **corroboration**, *n.* thibitisho, ushuhuda. **corroborative**, *a.* -a kuthibitisha, -a kuelekea kuthibitisha.

corrode, *v.t.* -la, haribu, ozesha (kama kwa kutu); — *v.i.* haribika (kama kwa kutu). **corrosion**, *n.* uharibifu kwa kuliwa (kulika) kama kwa kutu. **corrosive**, *a.* -kali, -enye ukali wa kula kuharibu kama kwa kutu &c.

corrugate, *v.t.* kunjakunja kama migongogongo midogo; — *v.i.* kunjamana. **corrugated**, *a.* -enye makunjo au migongogongo midogo. *Corrugated iron* (*sheets*) mabati ya kuezekea. **corrugation**, *n.* migongogongo, mikunjokunjo, makunyanzi.

corrupt, *v.t.* (*make putrid*) ozesha; (*defile*) chafua; (*mar*) haribu, (*deprave*) pevusha, komaza, fisidi; (*alter*) badili, geuza; (*bribe*) tolea, lisha rushwa, penyezea fedha; — *v.i.* oza, haribika. — *a.* (*putrid*) -bovu, -liooza; (*depraved*) -potovu, -chafu, -fisadi, -fasiki, -ovu, habithi, -baya; (*false*) -liobadilika au kugeuzwa. **corruptible**, *a.* -a kuozekana, -a kuelekea kuoza au kuharibika; (*open to bribery*) -a kupokea rushwa &c. **corruption**, *n.* uozi, ubovu, uchafu; (*bribery*) rushwa, upenyezi; (*alteration*) mageuzi, makosa.

corsair, *n.* haramia wa baharini.

corset, *n.* vazi la kike, namna ya mkaja.

cortège, *n.* mwandamano (hasa wa watu kwenda kuzika).

cortex, *n.* gamba, ganda.

coruscate, *v.i.* metameta, memeteka, ng'aa. **coruscation**, *n.* mng'aro, kimetameta.

corvée, *n.* shokoa, kazi ya lazima bila mshahara.

corvette, *n.* manowari ndogo.

cosmetic, *n.* uzuri wanaotumia wanawake, *e.g.* dalia, yasi, liwa &c.

cosmos, *n.* ulimwengu mzima na matengenezo na taratibu zake. **cosmology**, *n.* elimu ya ulimwengu mzima na matengenezo na taratibu zake. **cosmic, cosmical**, *a.* -a kuhusu ulimwengu mzima. **cosmopolitan**, *n.* asiyependelea taifa lo lote ila amejifanya raia wa dunia nzima, yaani wa kila taifa. — *a.* -a kuhusu sehemu zote za ulimwengu; -siyependelea taifa moja tu ila hukumbuka ulimwengu wote.

cosset, *v.t.* engaenga, endekeza, dekeza.

cost, *v.t.* leta bei fulani, wakifu, simama bei fulani, uzwa kwa bei fulani, gharamisha; (*require*) taka, toza, lipiza. *What does it cost?* wauzaje? chauzwaje? kiasi gani? — *n.* bei, kima, thamani, gharama, hasara; (*legal*) gharama ya meza (ya hukumu, ya daawa &c.). *Cost price,* bei ilipwayo na wafanya biashara. *Cost free,* bure, bila gharama. *At all costs,* kwa vyo vyote. **costly,** *a.* ghali, -a gharama kubwa, -a thamani nyingi, -a tunu.

coster, costermonger, *n.* mchuuzi, mtembezi wa matunda, mboga &c.

costive, *a.* -enye kufunga tumbo, -a kufunga choo. **costiveness,** uyabisi wa tumbo.

costly, *a.* taz. *cost.*

costume, *n.* mavazi ya kawaida.

cosy, *a.* raha nyingi, -a anasa.

cot, *n.* nyumba ndogo; (*child's bed*) kitanda cha mtoto mdogo; (*sailor's hammock*) susu.

coterie, *n.* chama, shirika, jamii, jumuiya.

cottage, *n.* nyumba ndogo. **cottager,** *n.* mkulima, kibarua.

cotter, *n.* namna ya msumari au kabari ya kukazia.

cotton, *n.* pamba. *Cotton wool,* pamba.

cotyledon, *n.* jani la kwanza (au majani ya kwanza) linalochipua katika mbegu.

coucal, *n.* (*white browed*) tipitipi, kwembe, hondo, gude; (*green*) ukiki.

couch, *v.i.* jikunyata, jificha, jilaza; (*express*) — *v.t.* eleza kwa maneno. — *n.* kitanda, malalo, malazi.

cough, *v.i.* kohoa; (*to draw attention*) jikohoza. — *n.* kikohozi.

could, *v. p.t.* ya *can.*

council, *n.* baraza, diwani, mkutano, halmashauri. *Hold a council,* barizi, fanya baraza. **councillor,** *n.* diwani, mtu wa baraza, mshauri, msiri.

counsel, *n.* (*advice*) shauri, maonyo, mauidha, mausia; (*plan, purpose*) kusudi, nia; (*lawyer*) mwanasheria, wakili. *Keep one's own counsel*), setiri neno, ficha kusudi (nia, shauri &c.). *Give counsel,* shauri, onya, usia. *Take counsel,* taka shauri, shauriana. — *v.t.* shauri, onya, nasihi. **counsellor,** *n.* mshauri. mwongozi, mwonya; (*friend*) msiri.

count, (1) *n.* jina la heshima la mtu mwenye cheo fulani (la Ufaransa, Udachi na nchi nyinginezo) kama sheik. **countess,** *n.* mke wa *count.*

count, (2) *v.t.* (*reckon*) hesabu, fanya idadi; (*consider*) dhania, ona; — *v.i.* (*depend on*) tegemea, tumainia, kimbilia, amini. *He does not count,* hana maana. *May I count on you?* naweza kukutumaini? — *n.* tendo la kuhesabu; hesabu; (*charge*) jambo la mashtaka. **counter,** *n.* mtu ahesabuye, *e.g. hut counter,* ni mtu mwenye kazi ya kuhesabu nyumba; (*token*) kipande, sarafu &c. ya kuhesabia katika michezo fulani; (*in shop*) meza (ya kuhesabia fedha dukani, au kuwekea vitu vya kuuza). **counting,** *n.* hesabu, idadi. *Counting-house, counting-room*), chumba mnamofanywa hesabu ya wafanya biashara. **countless,** *a.* -a wingi mno hata haiwezi kuhesabika, bila idadi, -ingi mno.

countenance, *n.* (*face*) uso, wajihi; (*favour*) ufadhili, upendeleo, msaada, hisani. *Put out of countenance,* fadhaisha, tahayarisha, vunja uso. *Keep one's countenance,* toonyesha maono, kaza uso kuzuia kicheko &c. *Keep in countenance,* pendelea, fadhili, saidia. *v.t. I cannot countenance it,* siipendi, siipendelei.

counter, (1) *n.* taz. *count* (2).

counter, (2) *adv.* kinyume, kwa jinsi ya kukabili (ya kupinga, ya kuzuia, ya kukinza, ya kushinda, ya kubatili, ya kutangua &c.). — *a.* -a mbalimbali, -a kukinga, -a kinyume, -a kukabili, -a kuzuia, -a kushinda. — *v.t.* zuia, kinga, shinda, batili, tangua. *Run counter to,* shindana na, pinga &c. **counteract,** *v.t.* kinza, batilisha, tangua, zuia, shinda. **counteraction,** *n.* kinzano, pingamizi, kizuizi, tendo la kukabili (la kushinda, la kubatilisha *&c.*). **counter-attraction,** *n.* kivutacho upande mwingine; kinachovuta na kushindana na kingine kinachovuta hata kupunguza mvuto wake. **counterbalance,** *v.t.* sawazisha (kwa kuweka uzito, nguvu, mvuto *&c.* kwa upande ulio mwepesi). **counterblast,** *n.* tendo la kubatilisha (la kurudisha) tendo jingine. **counterfoil,** *n.* kipande (kilicho nakili) cha stakabadhi (barua ya fedha, hawala *&c.*) kinachobaki kwa mkabidhi. **counterfeit,** *v.t.* iga, jifanya, jigeuza; fanya mfano wa. — *n.* mfano, mwigo, kitu kilichotengenezwa kuiga kingine ili kudanganya. — *a.* -a mfano, -a kuiga, -a uwongo. **countermand,** *v.t.* tangua amri, rudia amri ya kwanza. **counterpart,** *n.* kifani, mfano, nakili; sehemu au kitu kimoja cha viwili au zaidi kilicho sawasawa kabisa (na sehemu au kitu kile kingine). **counterpoise,** *v.t.* sawazisha, tia uzito upande ulio mwepesi ili kusawazisha pande zote mbili. — *n.* jiwe la mizani; uzito ulio sawa na ule wa upande mwingine (wa mizani *&c.*). **countersign,** *v.t.* tia sahihi (hati *&c.* iliyokwisha tiwa sahihi na mwingine); thibitisha kwa kutia sahihi. — *n.* neno au ishara ya siri ya kupishwa askari walindao zamu *&c.*

counterpane, *n.* tandiko la juu la kitanda.

counterpart, *n.*, **counterpoise,** *v. and n.*, **countersign,** *v. and n.* taz. *counter* (2).

counting, *n.*, **countless,** *a.* taz. *count* (2).

countrified, *a.* taz. *country.*

country, *n.* nchi; (*district*) jimbo, wilaya; (*as distinct from town*) mashamba. (*Note: names of countries, as a rule prefix U- to the stem of the noun indicating the inhabitants, e.g.* Mwingereza = *An Englishman*; Uingereza = *England.* Mwunguja = *A Zanzibari*; Unguja = *Zanzibar &c.*). **countrified,** *a.* -a kimashamba. **countryman,** *n.* mkulima; (*of the same country*) mtu wa kwetu (kwenu, kwao); ndugu wa kabila moja.

county, *n.* jimbo au wilaya ya Uingereza.

coup, *n.* kipigo, dharuba; kipigo au tendo lifaalo (kwa kusudi fulani).

coupé, *n.* behewa au motakaa *&c.* yenye kiti cha upande mmoja tu cha watu wawili.

couple, *n.* kiungo; (*pair*) jozi, watu (au vitu) wawili wa namna moja au pamoja; (*married*) mume na mke. — *v.t.* (*of agent*) unga, fungasha, tia pamoja; (*of instrument, e.g. rope, chain &c.*) funganisha, unganisha; — *v.i.* (*come together*) ungana, unganika. **couplet,** *n.* mistari miwili ya wimbo au mashairi (hasa yenye tamko lile lile mwishoni). **coupling,** *n.* kiungo.

coupon, *n.* cheti.

courage, *n.* uhodari, ushujaa, uthabiti, ujasiri, ushupavu. *Take courage,* jipa moyo. **courageous,** *a.* hodari, -shujaa, -jasiri, thabiti, -shupavu.

courier, *n.* mjumbe, tarishi; (*guide, dragoman*) kiongozi, msimamizi, mnyapara wa safari.

course, *n.* mwendo, maendeleo, njia, kipito; (*conduct*) mwenendo, maisha, matendo ya kawaida; (*order*) zamu, taratibu, kawaida; (*part of meal &c.*) sehemu (aina ya vyakula vya wakaa moja); (*of ship*) majira; (*series of lectures &c.*) mfulizo, mfululizo; (*race course*) uwanja (wa kushindania mbio *&c.*); (*of bricks*) safu, tabaka, mstari; (*of events*) mambo, mambo yafuatanayo. *Take a different course,* fanya vingine (shauri jingine). *Of course,* ndiyo, naam, hasa, taibu, hakuna budi. *In due course,* kwa taratibu, kwa kawaida. *In course of time,* halafu, baadaye. *In course of conversation,* katika kuongea. — *v.i.* piga mbio, enda kasi; — *v.t.* (*hunt*) winda, windisha mbwa. **courser,** *n.* mpiga mbio; faras mwenye mbio. **coursing,** *n.* shindano la mbwa wa kuwinda.

court, *n.* uwanja, behewa, ua, kitalu; (*palace*) jumba la mfalme; (*suite*) wafuasi wa mfalme; (*law*) baraza ya hukumu; (*judges*) jamii ya mahakimu (ya majaji); (*respect*) heshima, ustahiki, ustahifu. *Pay court to,* heshimu, stahi; (*woo*) posa, bembeleza. — *v.t.* jipendekeza kwa, heshimu; (*woo*) bembeleza, posa, takia uchumba; (*seek*) tafuta, jaribu kupata. **courteous,** *a.* -a adabu, -a heshima, stahifu, -a jamala. **courteousness,** *n.* ustahifu, heshima, adabu, jamala. **courtesan,** *n.* malaya, kahaba. **courtesy,** *n.* adabu, heshima, ustahifu, uungwana, jamala; (*gesture of*) mkunjo wa goti kwa heshima. *Treat with courtesy,* stahi, heshimu. **courtier,** *n.* mfuasi wa mfalme. **courtliness,** *n.* ustahifu, jamala, adabu *&c.* **courtly,** *a.* -a adabu, -a heshima, stahifu *&c.* **court-martial,** *n.* baraza ya wakubwa wa askari au manowarini ya kuhukumu makosa ya watu wao, baraza ya kuhukumu ya vita. **courtship,** *n.* ubembelezi, maposo, uchumba. **courtyard,** *n.* ua, uga, kitalu, uwanja; (*in a house*) behewa.

cousin, mtoto wa ndugu (wa kiume au wa kike) wa baba au mama. binamu.

cove, *n.* ghuba ndogo.

covenant, *n.* maagano, ahadi; (*written*) mkataba, hati ya maagano. — *v.i.* agana, patana, ahidi.

cover, *v.t.* funika, funikiza, gubika, tanda, tandika; (*hide*) setiri, ficha; (*extend over*) enea, tanda; (*be sufficient for, include*) tosha, faa, weka, chukua; (*protect*) linda, hifadhi; (*copulate, of animals*) panda, kwea, tomba, (*of fowls, birds*) kanyaga; (*with rifle &c.*) elekezea shabaha, linga shabaha. **cover, covering,** *n.* kifuniko, kisetiri; (*table*) nguo ya (kitambaa cha) meza; (*of dish*) kawa; (*of a book*) jalada; (*case*) kitumba, uo, ala; (*in hunting &c.*) msitu, kichaka, magugu, maficho. **coverlet,** *n.* tandiko la kitanda la juu. **covert,** *a.* -a siri, -a hila. — *n.* maficho, maoteo. **covertly,** *adv.* kwa siri, kwa hila, kwa werevu.

covet, *v.t.* tamani, taka sana, ona shauku ya (kitu kisicho halali au kisicho chako). **covetous,** *a.* -a choyo, bahili, -enye tamaa (shauku, uchu). **covetousness,** *n.* tamaa, ubahili, choyo, roho.

covey, *n.* kundi (la ndege).

cow, (1) *n.* ng'ombe jike; jike la mnyama kama tembo, kiboko *&c.* *Cow that has calved,* mbuguma. **cowherd,** *n.* mchunga ng'ombe, mchungaji wa ng'ombe. **cowhide,** *n.* ngozi ya ng'ombe.

cow, (2) *v.t.* ogofya, tia hofu, tiisha, vunja moyo. **cowed,** *a.* -enye hofu, -nyonge, -oga.

coward, *n.* mwoga. **cowardice, cowardliness,** *n.* woga. **cowardly,** *a.* -oga, -enye hofu, -nyonge.

cowed, *a.* taz. *cow* (2).

cower, *v.i.* nywea, jikunyata (jikunja) ili kujificha au kwa hofu, tetemeka, gwaya.

cowherd, *n.* **cowhide,** *n.* taz. *cow* (1).

cowl, *n.* namna ya kofia wavaayo *monk*; kifuniko cha bomba la moshi.

cowrie, cowry, *n.* kauri, kete; (*tiger—which is considered of no value*) kululu. Fulani amepata kululu, *i.e.* amepata kitu kisicho na thamani.

coxcomb, *n.* mmalidadi, mpiga madaha, mshaufu, (*slang*) mfua uji.

coxswain, *n.* mwongoza mashua, serehangi, mkuu wa mashua.

coy, *a.* -enye haya, -enye soni, -a hofu, -nyamavu.

cozen, *v.t.* sifusifu, rairai; kopa, punja, danganya, laghai, ghilibu, karamkia.

crab, *n.* kaa (wa pwani); (*small*) kaa koko. *Other kinds*; kaa ungo, kaa chago, chanje, kururu, ngadu, kisagaunga *&c.* **crabbed,** *a.* -kali, -korofi; (*difficult*) -gumu, -baya; (*undecipherable writing*) -a kuchorachora.

crab-plover, *n.* ndoero.
crack, (*joints of fingers*) — *v.t.* alisha; — *v.i.* alika; (*split*) — *v.t.* tia ufa, pasua, atua, vunja; — *v.i.* fanya ufa, pasuka, atuka, vunjika; — *v.t.* (*nuts, shells &c.*) banja; (*of a whip*) alisha, chapa; (*a joke*) fanya mzaha; (*boast about*) vumisha, sifu mno; — *v.i.* (*chat*) zungumza kirafiki. *Crackjaw,* neno lililo gumu kutamkika. *Crack up,* (*praise*) sifu; (*go to pieces*) haribika ghafula, vunjikavunjika. — *n.* ufa, mwatuko; (*sound*) kishindo, mwaliko; (*of thunder*) radi; (*smack*) kipigo cha ghafula; (*chat*) mazungumzo ya kirafiki, porojo, soga. **cracked,** *a.* -enye ufa; (*person—crack brained*) -enye kichaa (wazimu). **cracker,** *n.* namna ya mkate mwembamba mgumu; (*firework*) fataki ya kuchezea. **crackle,** *v.i.* lia, data, tatarika, chakarisha, alikaalika (kama fito zikipasuka au kuchomwa moto). — *n.* mlio wa kualikaalika.
cradle, *n.* kitanda kidogo cha mtoto, mlezi, susu; cho chote kilichofanana na kitanda kidogo, au cha kuwekea kitu, *e.g.* magango ya kuwekea mkono au mguu uliovunjika. — *v.t.* laza (*e.g.* katika kitanda &c.); (*rear*) lea.
craft, *n.* (*cunning*) hila, werevu, udanganyifu; (*dexterity*) ufundi, ustadi, ubingwa, umahiri; (*handicraft*) kazi, uchumi; (*ship*) mashua, vyombo, jahazi, meli &c. *Arts and crafts,* sanaa na kazi za mkono. **craftiness,** *n.* werevu, ujanja, hila, udanganyifu. **craftsman,** *n.* fundi. **crafty,** *a.* -a hila, -erevu.
crag, *n.* mwamba uliochongoka, jabali. **craggy,** *a.* -a kuchongoka, -enye mawe mawe, -a miamba.
cram, *v.t.* jaza sana, shindilia, songa; (*with food*) vimbisha, shibisha; (*teach for examination*) fundisha tayari kwa mtihani, mambo yale yaipasayo tu; — *v.i.* (*eat greedily*) -la kwa pupa, lafua.
cramp, *n.* kiharusi; (*clamp*) gango. — *v.t.* tia kiharusi; (*clamp*) tia gangoni; (*hinder*) zuia, pinga.
crane, *n.* (*bird*) korongo; (*for hoisting*) slingi, winchi, mtambo wa kuinulia vitu vizito. — *v.i.* nyosha shingo. (*e.g.* ili kuona vizuri zaidi).
cranium, *n.* fuvu (bupuru) la kichwa.
crank, *n.* kombo; chuma cha mashine (*e.g.* cha motakaa) cha kuianzisha au kubadili namna ya mwendo wake. — *v.t.* anzisha mashine kwa kuzungusha mpini wake. **cranky,** *a.* kombokombo, -a kikombo; (*eccentric*) -enye kinyongo; (*weak*) dhaifu, goigoi, hafifu.
cranny, *n.* ufa mdogo, mwanya, kitundu.
crape, *n.* kitambaa chepesi cheusi cha msiba, dalili ya mfiwa.
crash, (1) *v.i.* vunjika vipande kwa kishindo; (*move with noise*) enda kwa kishindo; (*fall*) anguka kwa kishindo; (*crash into*) dunda, piga. — *n.* kishindo (cha vitu vinavyoanguka na kuvunjika au kupambana); (*failure of business enterprise*) kampani au tajiri kufilisika, au biashara kuharibika kabisa.
crash, (2) *n.* namna ya kitambaa kizito cha kitani.
crass, *a.* -gumu, sana, kabisa. *Crass ignorance* (*stupidity*), kipeo cha ujinga (upumbavu).
crate, *n.* mzinga, kitundu, zizi la kuchukulia kuku; kitu kama mzinga au pakacha la matete au fito la kuchukulia vitu; sanduku (kasha) la mbao nyepesi lenye nafasi kati ya mbao.
crater, *n.* shimo la katikati ya volkeno, yaani mlima wa moshi.
cravat, *n.* utepe wa kuvaa shingoni.
crave, *v.t.* (*beg*) sihi, omba; (*long for*) tamani sana, taka sana, onea shauku (uchu); (*need*) hitaji. **craving,** *n.* tamaa nyingi, shauku, uchu, kwiu.
craven, *n.* mwongo, mnyonge. — *a.* -oga sana, -nyonge.
crawl, *v.i.* tambaa, jikokota.
crayfish, crawfish, *n.* kamba wa mtoni.

crayon, *n*. chaki yenye rangi, kalamu ya namna ya udongo yenye rangi.

craze, *v.t.* tia kichaa, tia wasiwasi, rusha akili. — *n*. wazimu, kichaa, kinyongo. **crazy**, *a*. (*frail*) -dhaifu; (*demented*) -enye wazimu (kichaa, mafuu).

creak, *v.i.* lia (kama vyuma vinavyokwaruzana) — *n*. mlio wa *creak*.

cream, *n*. maziwa ya mtindi, yaani mafuta ya juu (yakisukwasukwa hugeuka siagi); cho chote kifananacho na mtindi; (*best part*) sehemu iliyo bora. — *v.t.* engua mtindi; — *v.i.* fanya mtindi. — *a*. -a rangi ya mtindi, yaani ya manjano meupe. **creamy**, *a*. -a mtindi au kama mtindi. *Cream of tartar*, namna ya dawa inayotumika katika upishi.

crease, *n*. kunjo, finyo, kunyanzi; (*line*) mfuo, mstari. — *v.t.* kunja, finya, pinda; (*crumple*) vungavunga. — *v.i.* kunjamana, finyana.

create, *v.t.* umba, huluku; (*make*) fanya, fanyiza, buni; (*invent*) vumbua, tunga, zua. **creation**, *n*. muumbo; (*universe*) ulimwengu, viumbe vyote, vitu vyote; (*act or time of*) kuumbwa (kuhulukiwa) kwa ulimwengu. **creator**, *n*. (*The Creator*) Mungu Mwenyezi; (*a creator*) muumba, mfanyiza. **creature**, *n*. kiumbe, cho chote kilichoumbwa, hasa mwanadamu na mnyama; (*living*) kiumbe chenye uhai, *e.g.* mwanadamu, mnyama, ndege, mdudu, samaki; (*inanimate*) kitu; (*as a term of contempt*) nyonge, duni, maskini; (*of endearment*) mpenzi, kipenzi; (*dependant*) mfuasi, mtu; (*puppet*) baradhuli.

crèche, *n*. nyumba wanamotunzwa watoto wadogo wakati mama zao wanapofanya kazi.

credence, *n*. usadiki, imani; (*church furniture*) meza ndogo upande wa madhabahu. *Give credence to*, amini, sadiki. **credentials**, *n*. barua au hati ya kusadikisha au kuthibitisha amri au cheo kinachodaiwa na mtu, hasa katika wageni. **credibility**, *n*. ustahilifu wa kusadikika (wa kuaminika). **credible**, *a*. -a kustahili kusadikika, -a kuaminika, -a kusadikika. **credit**, *n*. (*trust*) tumaini, imani, itibari; (*trustworthiness*) uaminifu; (*good character*) sifa njema; (*honour*) heshima; (*time for payment*) muda (wa kulipa deni); (*credit column*) upande wa daftari wa kuandikia fedha zilizopokewa; (*in bank*) fedha alizo nazo mtu katika banki; (*money on credit*) karadha. *Give credit to* (*praise*) sifu; (*goods, money*) kopesha. *Take on credit*, sadiki (amini) bila ushuhuda. *Allow credit*, kopesha, (*give time*) achia muda, weka muda. *Have the credit of*, sifiwa kwa. *Do credit to*, patia sifa, pendeza; (*work &c.*) tumia (fanya) vizuri iwezekanavyo. *Letter of credit*, barua au hati ya sifa; hati ya fedha. *Give* (*goods*) *on credit*, kopesha. *Receive on credit*, kopa. — *v.t.* amini, sadiki; (*lend*) kopesha, (*money*) karidhi. *Credit a person with*, andikia, wekea, aminia. **creditable**, *a*. -enye kuleta heshima (sifa). **creditor**, *n*. (*claimant*) mdai, mwia. *He is my creditor*, aniwia, nawiwa naye, mimi ni mdeni wake. **credulity**, *n*. wepesi wa kuamini (kusadiki) bila ushuhuda, ujinga. **credulous**, *a*. -epesi kuamini (kusadiki) bila ushuhuda, -jinga. **creed**, *n*. imani, kanuni za imani; (*Muhammadan*) shahada, fatiha.

creek, *n*. hori, ghuba ndogo, wangwa.

creel, *n*. kikapu cha kuchukulia samaki.

creep, *v.i.* (*p.t. & pf.t.* **crept**) tambaa, enda polepole, nyapa, jikokota. *Creep up to*, nyatia, nyemelea, nyendea. *The creeps*, hali ya damu kusisimka, msisimko. **creeper**, *n*. mnyama (mmea) anayetambaa, mtambaazi. **creepy**, **creeping**, *a*. -tambaazi. *A creepy feeling, sensation*, mnyeo, kusisimka kwa damu, msisimko.

cremate, *v.t.* unguza, choma maiti badala ya kuzika. **cremation**, *n*.

mchomo, mwunguzo (hasa wa maiti).

crematorium, crematory, cremation ground, *n.* mahali pachomwapo maiti.

creole, *n.* mtu aliyezaliwa *West Indies, Mauritius* au Amerika ya Kusini; (2) mtu ambaye wazazi wake ni mmoja mweupe na mwingine mweusi.

creosote, *n.* namna ya dawa nyekundu yenye harufu kali; asili yake ni lami.

crept, *p.t. and pf.t.* ya *creep.*

crescent, *n.* mwezi mwandamo, mwezi kongo; sura ya mwezi mwandamo, hilali (ni alama ya serikali ya Maturuki); jamii ya nyumba zilizopangwa sura ya *crescent.*

cress, *n.* namna ya majani yanayoliwa; yana uchungu kidogo kama pilipili.

crest, *n.* (*tuft*) shungi, kishungi, kilemba, kishada, bwenzi; (*top*) kilele, ncha ya juu; (*of cock*) upanga wa jogoo, undu; (*heraldic*) alama ya kuonyesha nasaba na ukoo, kama chapa ya nishani. **crested,** *a.* -enye kishungi. **crestfallen,** *a.* kushushwa moyo, -a majonzi, -a kushindwa, -a kukata tamaa, -a kuudhika.

cretin, *n.* mtu ambaye mwili na akili zake zimevia. **cretinism,** *n.* hali ya mwili na akili ya mtu kuvia.

cretonne, *n.* namna ya kitambaa kilichochapwa sura na rangi; hutumika kufanyia mapazia na kufunika viti *&c.*

crevasse, *n.* shimo, mwanya, ufa mkubwa (hasa katika mto wa barafu).

crevice, *n.* ufa mdogo, mwanya, mwatuko.

crew, (1) *n.* jamii ya mabaharia; kundi la watu (hutumika pengine kwa dharau, pengine kwa watu waovu).

crew, (2) *p.t.* ya *crow.*

crib, *n.* kitanda kidogo cha mtoto; hori (ya kuwekea chakula cha punda, na ng'ombe *&c.*). — *v.t.* (*cramp*) songa; (*appropriate*) iba; fuatisha (kwa kusudi kudanganya).

cribbage, *n.* namna ya mchezo wa karata.

crick, *n.* kiharusi (hasa cha shingoni).

cricket, (1) *n.* nyenje, chenene, panzi, mdudu kama nzige.

cricket, (2) *n.* (*game*) mchezo wa jamii mbili za watu; hutumia mpira, bao la kupigia mpira, na vijiti vitatu upande huu na huu kuonyesha mpaka wa kukimbilia.

cried, *p.t.* ya *cry.* **crier,** *n.* (*public*) mpiga mbiu.

crime, *n.* tendo la kuvunja (kuasi, kuhalifu) sheria, jinaya, dhambi, taksiri, manza. **criminal,** *a.* -a kuvunja (kuasi, kuhalifu sheria); -ovu, -baya. jinai. — *n.* mtu mhalifu, mwasi wa sheria, mvunja sheria *&c.*

crimp, *v.t.* tia mikunjo (viwimbiwimbi, marinda).

crimson, *n.* nyekundu kama damu. — *a.* -a rangi nyekundu.

cringe, *v.i.* nywea, jinyenyekea, jiinamisha, jikunyata, jipendekeza, jifanya kama mtumwa.

crinkle, *v.t.* vungavunga, kunjakunja, nyonganyonga; — *v.i.* nyongoka, potoka, finyana, kunjamana.

cripple, *n.* kiwete, kilema. — *a.* -a kiwete, -a kwenda chopi. — *v.t.* fanya kiwete, lemaza; (*impair*) hasiri, vunja, haribu au punguza manufaa ya kitu.

crisis, *n.* kipeo, upeo (wa hatari, ugonjwa, shida *&c.*); wakati hasa wa kugeuza au kufanya jambo, ama sivyo, laelekea kuharibika (kuleta hatari *&c.*).

crisp, *a.* (*close curled*) -a pilipili (kama nywele); (*brittle*) -kavu hata kuweza kufikichika; (*fresh, bracing, as of air*) -a baridi, -a kuburudisha; (*firm*) -gumu kidogo, -bichi (kama majani mabichi).

criterion, *n.* (*means or standard of judging*) jinsi au tabia ya kupima (ya kukadiria, ya kupambanua) kitu; (*test*) hakika; (*rule, standard*) kanuni, kawaida.

critic, *n.* (*judge*) mjuzi, mstadi wa kupima uzuri (ufasaha, ukweli, uhafifu *&c.*) wa vitabu (kazi, sanaa, matendo *&c.*); mtaka yaliyo bora, mhakiki; (*fault finder*) mteuzi, mchaguzi, mtetaji, mkinzani, mvumbua makosakosa; mchunguzi. **critical,** *a.* (*discerning*) -juzi, -fahamivu, -a kupambanua au kupima (uzuri au uhafifu wa mambo); (*captious*) -epesi kuvumbua na kutoa makosa madogodogo; -a kigomvi; (*discriminating*) -chaguzi. -teuzi, -a kuchagua, -a kuhakikisha; (*decisive*) -a hatari, -a shida. **criticism,** *n.* (*judgement*) ujuzi, uteuzi, utambuzi, upimaji wa uzuri au uhafifu wa vitabu (sanaa, kazi, matendo *&c.*); (*opinion*) maneno (maandiko) ya kuonyesha au kueleza uzuri na uhafifu wa kitabu (kazi, matendo *&c.*); (*fault finding*) lawama, upekuzi, mateto. **criticize,** *v.t.* (*judge*) hukumu au pima (uzuri au uhafifu wa mambo); (*find fault*) laumu, rahisisha, dadisidadisi, chunguachungua, chambua.

croak, *v.i.* lia (kama chura au kunguru); (*grumble*) nuna, nung'unika, guna, teta; (*forebode evil*) bashiri mabaya.

crochet, *n.* kazi ya kusuka kwa nyuzi za kitani, au za hariri *&c.* — *v.t.* suka nyuzi za hariri *&c.*

crockery, *n.* vyombo vya udongo, *e.g.* sahani, vikombe *&c.*

crocodile, *n.* mamba, ngwena.

crone, *n.* kizee. **crony,** *n.* msiri au rafiki wa siku nyingi.

crook, *n.* (*staff*) kingoe, fimbo ndefu iliyopindika mwishoni; (*hook*) kota, kulabu; (*bend*) kombo, pindi, kigosho, matege; (*trick*) hila, werevu. — *v.t.* pinda, tia kombo, potoa; — *v.i.* pindika, potoka. **crooked,** *a.* -enye kombo, -a kombokombo, -a mshazari, -enye matege, -liopotoka. **crookedness,** *n.* kombo, kota, matege, upotofu.

croon, *v.i.* imba bila kutamka maneno (au kwa sauti ndogo).

crop, *n.* (*produce*) mavuno, mazao, matunda; (*of bird*) umio, kibofu cha kooni, gole; (*riding whip*) mchapo; (*of hair*) mkato mfupi wa nywele; (*quantity*) wingi. — *v.t.* kata fupi, (kama nywele); (*of animals*) -la (majani *&c.*). *Crop out,* tokeza juu ya ardhi. *Crop up,* tokea, onekana, zuka. **cropper,** *n.* mwanguko. *Come a cropper,* anguka, shindwa.

croquet, *n.* mchezo wa kupiga tufe chini kwa namna ya nyundo ya mti.

crosier, crozier, *n.* fimbo ya Askofu.

cross, *n.* miti miwili ya mkingamo, msalaba; (*trial*) jaribu, taabu, kinga. — *v.t.* (*each other*) pandana, pitana; (*river*) vuka, enda ng'ambo ya pili; (*by tree &c.*) tataga; (*pass*) pita; (*obstruct, interfere with*) zuia, kingama, pinga, sumbua, udhi, chokoza, tia matata; (*be athwart*) kata, kingamiza; (*pass each other*) pitana; (*mix breeds*) changanya mbegu; (*arms, legs*) pachika, tekanya, pakata (mikono, miguu); (*threads*) rudufu; (*cheque*) andika jina la *Bank,* au *& Co.* kati ya mistari miwili katika *cheque* ili fedha zisipatikane isipokuwa kwa idhini ya *Bank*; (*cross oneself*) jitia alama ya msalaba; — *v.i.* vuka, pita. *Cross the path* (*of any one*), pinga (mtu). *Cross one's mind,* ingia ghafula katika fikira. — *a.* (*ill-tempered*) -kali, -a hasira, -a chuki, -a kuchacha, -a kukimwa; (*athwart*) -a kwenda upande, -a mshazari, -a kukingamiza; (*opposite*) -a kukabili, -a kuelekea; (*lying across*) -a kukingama, -a kupandana. *Be cross* (*hard to please*), deka, fanya chuki. **crossbow,** *n.* upindi. **cross-examine,** *v.t.* hojihoji, ulizauliza, chambua. taz. *cross-question.* **cross-grained,** *a.* -enye nyuzi zinazopitana; (*persons*) -kaidi, -tundu, -a chuki. **crossing,** *n.* (*going over*) mvuko, mpito, kivuko; (*being athwart*) mkingamo, panda; (*cross* *breeding*) mchanganyo wa mbegu. *Crossing place*, kivuko. **cross-patch**, *n.* mkaidi, mtundu, mchukiaji. **cross-purpose**, *n.* kusudi la kinyume, lisilopatana; ukaidi, utundu. **cross-question**, *v.t.* hojihoji, dodosa, ulizauliza, jadili, susuika, taradhia. **cross-reference**, *n.* mtajo wa ukurasa katika kitabu au sehemu nyingine ya kitabu. **cross-road**, *n.* njia panda. **cross-way**, *n.* njia ya kukingama, njia panda. **cross-wise**, *adv.* kwa kukingama.

crotch, *n.* (*of legs*) kitako katikati ya miguu.

crotchety, *a.* -a kombokombo, -kaidi, -a kasirani, -a kufuata nia yake, -enye kinyongo.

crouch, *v.t.* jikunyata, jikunja, inama, chutama.

croup, *n.* ugonjwa wa kooni, hasa wa watoto.

crow, *n.* (*pied*) kunguru. *As the crow flies*, kwa mwendo moja kwa moja, njia iliyo fupi sawasawa kabisa. — *v.i.* (*of cock*) wika; (*of child*) lia kwa furaha; (*crow over*) cheka, simanga, shangilia, jivunia. **crowbar**, *n.* mtaimbo. **crow's-nest**, *n.* kingojo cha juu katika mlingoti wa chombo.

crowd, *n.* kundi, makutano, matangamano, msongano, halaiki, umati, kaumu, ghasia; (*the common people*) watu, akina yahe. — *v.i.* songana, songamana, -ja kwa wingi, jaa; — *v.t.* songa, jaza sana. *Crowd round*, songa.

crown, *n.* taji; (*of head*) utosi; (*sovereign*) mfalme, serikali; (*perfection*) uzuri, sifa, upeo, sehemu iliyo bora, ukamilifu, utimilifu; (*top*) sehemu ya juu, kichwa, kilele, kileleta. — *v.t.* tia taji, tawaza; (*be at top of*) -wa juu ya; (*reward*) tuza, sitawisha; (*complete*) kamilisha, timiliza. **crown colony**, *n.* nchi ambayo serikali yake ni chini ya serikali ya kiingereza. **crown prosecutor**, *n.* wakili wa serikali katika mashtaka. **crowned**, *a.* -enye kuvaa taji, -a kutawazwa; (*rewarded*) -a kutuzwa; (*consumated*) kamili, -timilifu. **crown prince**, *n.* mtoto mwanamume wa mfalme atakayerithi ufalme. **crown-land**, *n.* ardhi ya serikali. **crown witness**, *n.* shahidi wa serikali katika mashtaka.

crow's-nest, *n.* taz. *crow*.

crucial, *a.* -a maana, -a kuonya, -a kuhakikisha, -a kuthibitisha.

crucible, *n.* kalibu, chungu cha kuyeyushia madini.

crucifix, *n.* sanamu ya Yesu Kristo amepigiliwa msalabani. **crucifixion**, *n.* kufa kwa kuwambwa mtini, kusulibiwa. **cruciform**, *a.* -enye sura ya (umbo la) msalaba.

crucify, *v.t.* sulibisha, sulubu, fisha kwa kuwamba mtini; (*subdue completely*) tiisha kabisa (*e.g.* tamaa mbaya &c.); (*torment*) tesa.

crude, *a.* (*immature, raw*) -bichi, -changa; (*of taste*) -chungu; (*unfinished*) -siotengenezwa; (*uninstructed*) -siofundishwa; (*rude*) -isiyo adabu; (*foolish*) -jinga. **crudeness, crudity**, *n.* ubichi, ujinga.

cruel, *a.* -katili, -kali, bila rehema, jahili, -baya, -dhalimu, -jeuri, -korofi, -habithi. **cruelty**, *n.* ukatili, ukali, jeuri, ukorofi, udhalimu, jefule.

cruet, *n.* kichupa cha kuwekea viungo, *e.g.* pilipili, chumvi &c. **cruet-stand**, *n.* kiweko chenye vichupa vya kuwekea viungo.

cruise, *v.i.* vinjari; (meli) enda huko na huko, zunguka. — *n.* kutembea huko na huko kwa meli, kuvinjari. **cruiser**, *n.* manowari ya kuvinjari.

crumb, *n.* chembe, chenga, kidogo, (*leavings*) kombo. *The crumb of a loaf*, nyama ya mkate. **crumble**, *v.t.* fikicha, fikinya, finyafinya; — *v.i.* fikichika, vurugika, geuka mavumbi, chakaa, -wa mavumbi; (*of masonry*) mumunyika. **crumbly**, *a.* -a kuelekea kufikichika, -tifu, -tifutifu.

crumple, *v.t.* kunjakunja, vungavunga; — *v.i.* kunjamana, vungikavungika; (*collapse*) anguka, poromoka; (*morally*) fadhaika.

crunch, *v.t. and i.* saga kwa meno, chakacha, tafuna kwa kelele au kishindo, saga kwa miguu, *e.g.* changarawe.

crupper, *n.* mtafara, kitanzi cha mkiani cha tandiko la punda, farasi *&c.*

crusade, *n.* pigano juu ya maovu (au kwa kusudi fulani, *e.g. a crusade against consumption,* pigano juu ya ugonjwa wa kifua kikuu, yaani kuuondoa ugonjwa huo; vita vya dini, vita vitakatifu. (katika habari za zamani, ni vita vya Wakristo juu ya Maturuki). **crusader,** *n.* mpigani katika *crusade.*

cruse, *n.* kikombe, chupa ndogo.

crush, *v.t.* seta, ponda, vyoga, fyanda, bana, kamua, gandamiza; (*crumple*) vungavunga ; (*subdue*) tiisha, vunja nguvu ya; (*ruin*) angamiza, lemeza, lemea sana; — *v.i.* vungika, kunjika. — *n.* gandamizo, msongo; (*crowd*) msongano, ghasia, udhai.

crust, *n.* (*bread*) ganda la mkate; (*on rice &c.*) ukoko; (*on teeth*) ukoga; (*on water*) ukoga, gaga, ukungu, ugozi; (*as rust &c.*) kuvu, kutu; (*covering*) utando, utando mgumu; (*of the earth*) uso wa dunia, ardhi, mawe *&c.* (*salt encrusted*) chunyu. **crustated,** *a.* -a kufunikwa na *crust.* **crusty,** *a.* kama ganda (ukoko, ukoga, kuvu, utandu, utando *&c.*); (*bad tempered*) -kali, -a chuki, -a kasirani.

rustacea, *n.* jamii ya wanyama na cwadudu wenye magamba, *e.g.* kaa, kamba *&c.*

rustated, *a.*, **crusty,** *n.* taz. *crust.*

crutch, *n.* (*for oar*) kileti; (*support*) cegemeo; (*for walking*) mkongojo, mkongojo wa kwapani; (*of legs*) kitako katikati ya miguu.

crux, *n.* jambo linaletalo shida, fumbo, tatizo.

cry, *v.i.* (*p.t. and pf.t.* **cried**) lia, gutia, sema kwa sauti kubwa, paliza sauti, omboleza; (*for help*) piga yowe; (*for mercy*) lalama, lalamika; (*shed tears*) lia, toka machozi. *Cry out at,* pigia kelele. *Cry against,* teta, bisha. *Cry down,* laumu; shusha heshima; rahisisha, punguza thamani. *Cry off,* jitoa (katika jambo uliloahidi au kupatana juu yake). *Cry quits,* ridhiana, patana; sema ya kuwa mambo ni sawasawa, hapana tofauti. *Cry up,* sifu. — *n.* kilio, mlio, ukelele, ukemi; (*for help*) yowe, unyende; (*of joy*) kigelegele, hoihoi, hoya; (*for combined effort*) shiine; (*for mercy*) lalamo. *A far cry,* mbali sana, mwendo mrefu. *Within cry of,* katika mwendo wa kuweza kusikia au kusikika.

crypt, *n.* chumba kilichofukuliwa chini ya kanisa (hasa pa kuzikia maiti). **cryptic,** *a.* kufichwa, -a siri, -a fumbo. **cryptogram, cryptograph,** *n.* maandiko ya fumbo (ya siri).

crystal, *n.* jiwe kama kioo. *As clear as crystal,* angavu kabisa, dhahiri kabisa. **crystalline,** *a.* -a kama jiwe, -angavu, -a kung'aa. **crystallization,** *n.* kugeuka kwa maji au vitu kuwa kama *crystal,* kuganda au kukauka kwa vitu vya majimaji. **crystallize,** *v.t.* gandisha; (*clarify*) dhihirisha; — *v.i.* ganda, fanya (fanyika) kitu kama kioo; (*become clear*) dhihirika.

cub, *n.* mtoto (wa wanyama wa mwitu kama simba, chui, mbweha *&c.*); mtoto wa mbwa. Pia ni jina la dharau la mtoto.

cube, *n.* kitu cha miraba sita iliyo sawasawa; hesabu fulani mara hesabu ile ile mara hesabu ile ile tena, *e.g. cube* ya 3 ni $3 \times 3 \times 3$, ndiyo 27.

cubicle, *n.* mkato wa nyumba, au kichumba cha kulala.

cubit, *n.* dhiraa, mkono.

cuckoo, *n.* (*Didric*) tama la bibi,

mtombo, mtomboro, mlembe, ndege wa asali.

cucumber, *n.* tango, *Cucumber tree*, mbilimbi.

cud, *n.* cheuo. *Chew the cud*, cheua, tafunatafuna kama ng'ombe, mbuzi *&c. Chew the cud*, (pengine hutumika kwa kufikirifikiri).

cuddle, *v.t.* sogeza kifuani, kumbatia, beba, bembeleza, pakata; — *v.i.* (*nestle*) songamana; jikunja, *e.g.* katika kitanda usiku wa baridi.

cudgel, *n.* gongo, rungu. *Take up the cudgels for*, pigania, tetea. — *v.t.* piga kwa gongo. *Cudgel one's brains*, fikiri sana, tafuta sana shauri la kufaa, jisumbua akili.

cue, *n.* fimbo ya kuchezea *billiards*; (*hint*) kionyo, ishara, konyeza, shauri. *Give a cue to*, onya, ashiria, konyeza.

cuff, (1) *n.* (*of a coat &c.*) sijafu.

cuff, (2) *n.* (*buffet*) konzi, mdukuo, kofi. — *v.t.* (*ears*) piga kofi; (*buffet*) piga konde (konzi, mdukuo).

cuirass, *n.* vazi la kiaskari kama kisibau cha ngozi ngumu au chuma.

cuisine, *n.* upishi.

cul-de-sac, *n.* njia iliyozibwa upande mmoja; (*fig.*) mgogoro.

culex, *n.* jamii moja ya mbu; huambukiza ugonjwa wa matende.

culinary, *a.* -a kuhusu jikoni au upishi, -a kupika.

cull, *v.t.* chuma, chagua, teua, kusanya.

culminate, *v.i.* fika juu, fika upeo, isha; (*reach perfection*) iva, kamilika, timilika. **culmination**, *n.* ncha ya juu, upeo, kipeo, mwisho, ukamilifu, utimilifu.

culpable, *a.* -enye hatia, -a kupasiwa hukumu, -a kustahili adhabu, -a kukosa. **culpability**, *n.* hali ya kuwa na hatia, ustahilifu wa adhabu.

culprit, *n.* mkosaji, mwenye hatia.

cult, *n.* madhehebu (ya dini, ibada, mazoea, heshima *&c.*).

cultivate, *v.t.* lima, panda mbegu, otesha; (*increase*) sitawisha, ongeza; (*improve*) tengeneza, fundisha, ongoza, endesha, kuza, staarabisha. **cultivated**, *a.* (*land &c.*) -liolimwa, -liotengenezwa; (*mind*) -a elimu, -a adili, -a utamaduni, -staarabu, -enye malezi mema. **cultivation**, *n.* mlimo, kilimo, ukulima; (*civilization, refinement*) malezi mema, mafundisho, adili, ujuzi, utamaduni, ustaarabu. **cultivator**, *n.* mkulima, mlimaji; chombo cha kulimia na kupalilia. **culture**, *n.* mlimo, kilimo, ukulima; (*education*) malezi, malezi mema, elimu; (*manners*) adabu, utamaduni, ustaarabu, uungwana. **cultured**, *a.* -liolimwa; -enye kulelewa vizuri, -a adabu, -enye elimu, -a utamaduni, -a ustaarabu.

culvert, *n.* mfereji wa chini chini wa kuchukulia maji toka upande mmoja wa njia mpaka upande wa pili.

cumber, *v.t.* zuia, pinga, sumbua.

cumbersome, cumbrous, *a.* -zito, -a kulemea, -a udhia, -zuifu, -sumbufu, -a kuzidi kuwa kubwa.

cummerbund, *n.* mahazamu, masombo, ukumbuu, mshipi.

cumulative, *a.* -a kuzidizidi, -a kupakiza.

cumulus, *n.* mawingu mfano wa mlima yenye weusi chini yake.

cunning, *n.* werevu, ujanja, hila, ujuzi, leba; (*skill*) ustadi, ubingwa, ufundi, umahiri, weledi. — *a.* -erevu, -janja, -a hila, -kakamavu, kalamzi; (*skilful*) -stadi, -bingwa, mahiri.

cup, *n.* kikombe; (*metal*) kopo. — *v.t.* (*bleed*) umika, tia chuku. *In his cups*, wakati alipolewa. *Many a slip betwixt the cup and the lip*, ni methali, maana yake, Hakuna hakika ya mambo ya mbele, huweza kutokea jambo baya hata karibu na mwisho, ni kama kusema: Jambo usilolijua ni usiku wa giza.

cupboard, *n.* kabati, sanduku au kichumba cha kuwekea vyombo, *e.g.* sahani, vikombe *&c.* **cupper**, *n.* mwumika, mtia chuku. **cupping**, *n.* mwumiko, umiko.

cupid, *n.* mungu wa mapenzi, katika

hadithi za zamani za Kiyunani.
cupidity, *n.* shauku, uchu, roho, tamaa (hasa ya mali).
cupping, *n.* taz. *cup.*
cupola, *n.* kuba, zege, dari ya tao kama bakuli kubwa lililofudikizwa.
cur, *n.* mbwa wa mbegu duni, kijibwa; mtu mnyonge.
curable, *a.* taz. *cure.*
curate, *n.* padre au kasisi msaidizi. **curacy**, *n.* kazi au makao ya *curate.*
curative, *a.* taz. *cure.*
curator, *n.* mwangalizi, hasa wa nyumba ya kuonyesha vitu vya tunu na vya zamani.
curb, *v.t.* tiisha, zuia, kinza; (*with bridle*) zuia kwa hatamu. — *n.* kizuizi; (*of harness*) lijamu; (*of hearth*) ukingo wa chuma au jiwe, *i.e.* wa kuweka mbele ya moto; (*curbstone*) jiwe la kando ya njia, jiwe la ukingo.
curd, *n.* maziwa yaliyoganda, magandi ya maziwa, maziwa mabivu. **curdle**, *v.t.* gandisha; — *v.t.* ganda, gandamana. *His blood curdled*, damu yake ilisisimka, aliogopa sana.
cure, *v.t.* ponya, ponyesha; (*meat &c.*) ng'onda, kausha, tia chumvi au dawa isioze; koleza. — *n.* dawa, mapozo; tendo la kupona au la kuponya. **curable**, *a.* -a kuponyeka. **curative**, *a.* -a kuponya, -a dawa.
curfew, *n.* kengele inayopigwa jioni kuonya watu kuzima taa na moto.
curio, *n.* tunu, azizi, kitu cho chote kilicho kigeni (cha kustaajabisha, cha sanaa). **curiosity**, *n.* kama *curio*; (*inquisitiveness*) utafiti, upekuzi, udadisi, uchunguzi. **curious**, *a.* -a tunu, -a mtindo, - a peke yake, geni, -a ajabu; (*inquisitive*) -tafiti, -chunguzi, -dadisi. **curiously**, *adv.* kwa jinsi lilivyo ajabu; ajabu.
curl, *v.t.* sokota, kunja, pinda, pota, suka, fanya viwimbiwimbi, jipindapinda; jinyonganyonga; — *v.t.* pindamana, kunjamana (kama viwimbi), zongamana. — *n.* msongo wa nywele, msokoto. **curly**, *a.* -a kusokotwa, -a msongo, -a kusokoteka. *Curly headed*, -enye nywele zilizoviringana (za kipilipili).
curlew, *n.* sululu, kipila. *Stone-curlew*, chekeamwezi.
curly, *a.* taz. *curl.*
curmudgeon, *n.* mchoyo, bahili, mnyimivu; mwenye chuki.
currant, *n.* zabibu kavu ndogo.
current, *a.* -a desturi, -a kutumika au kutendeka sasa au siku hizi, -a kukubaliwa na wengi. — *n.* (*of water*) mkondo; (*of air*) upepo mwepesi au hewa inayopita; (*course, succession*) njia, maendeleo, mfululizo, mafuatano (ya mambo).
currency, *n.* desturi, matumizi; (*money*) sarafu, fedha, senti, shilingi, noti *&c.*
curriculum, *n.* taratibu, kawaida (hasa ya mafundisho ya chuoni).
curry, (1) *n.* mchuzi; (*powder*) bizari. — *v.t.* pika kwa bizari.
curry, (2) *v.t.* chana nywele za farasi, punda *&c.*; (*hides*) tengeneza ngozi iwe laini, isioze. *Curry favour*, jipendekeza, bembejea.
curse, *v.t.* (*p.t. and pf.t.* **cursed**). laani, tukana, apiza, hizi, takia maovu; (*torment*) tesa, udhi sana; — *v.i.* apiza. — *n.* laana, apizo, hizaya, matukano, matusi; (*torment &c.*) mateso, malemezo, ukuba.
cursive, *a.* -a kwenda; -a mwandiko wa herufi zilizoungana wa michoro, si za chapa.
cursory, *a.* -a haraka, -zembe, -a juu juu tu.
curst, *p.t. and pf.t.* ya *curse.*
curt, *a.* -a haraka, -chache, -a kukatiza, -sio adabu. **curtail**, *v.t.* fupisha, punguza, kata, katiza.
curtain, *n.* pazia, msuto, chandalua; (*screen*) ukingo.
curtsy, **curtesy**, *n.* tendo la kujiinamia, la kukunja goti moja (ni tendo la heshima la wanawake na watoto). — *v.i.* jiinama, kunja goti moja kwa heshima.
curvature, *n.* taz. *curve.*
curve, *n.* kizingo, mviringo, tao.

pindi, kombo, kigosho, ukombo. — *v.t.* kunja, pinda, benua, peta; — *v.i.* kunjika, pindika, petamana, benuka, betabeta. **curved,** *a.* -a kuviringa, -a tao, -a kupetamana, -a kupindika. **curvature,** *n.* mpindo, kigosho, mpindiko; ukubwa au kiasi cha pindi (cha kombo *&c.*).

curvet, *v.t.* rukaruka, randa (hasa kwa farasi).

cushion, *n.* mto, takia.

cuspidor, *n.* kopo au chombo cha kutemea mate, tasa.

custard, *n.* mchanganyiko wa maziwa, mayai na sukari. **custard-apple,** *n.* (*tree*) mtopetope, mstafeli, mtomoko; (*fruit*) topetope, stafeli, tomoko.

custodian, *n.* taz. *custody.*

custody, *n.* (*guarding, care &c.*) ulinzi, usimamizi, utunzi, uangalizi; (*imprisonment*) kifungo. *Have in safe custody,* funga imara, tunza sana. **custodian,** *n.* mwangalizi, mtunza, mlinzi, msimamizi.

custom, *n.* desturi, kawaida, mazoea, ada, madhehebu, mila; (*regular trade*) biashara ya kawaida. **customs,** *n. pl.* (*custom duties*) ushuru (utozwao forodhani kwa vitu vinavyotoka na kuingia nchi). **customary,** *a.* -a desturi, -a kawaida, -a mazoea. **customer,** *n.* mnunuzi (hasa aliyezoea kununua kwa mchuuzi fulani ni *customer* wake). **custom house,** *n.* forodha.

cut, *v.t.* (*p.t. and pf.t.* **cut**) kata; (*planks*) pasua; (*logs*) chonga; (*chop, prune*) chenga; (*firewood*) tema, changa, chanja; (*carve*) chora, nakshi; (*slice*) lenga, chanyata, checha; (*affect deeply*) umiza, choma moyo, chukiza; (*break off acquaintance*) vunja urafiki; (*pass without notice*) ambaa; (*castrate*) hasi; (*cut down, expenses &c.*) punguza; (*shorten*) punguza, fupisha, kusuru; (*hair*) nyoa, chega. — *v.i.* kata, umiza, weza kukatwa. *Cut a caper,* ruka, randa. *Cut and dried,* tayari yote tangu hapo. *Cut dead,* -pa kisogo. *Cut a fine figure,* fanya fahari. *Cut hair,* kata nywele, nyoa, chega. *Cut in,* jiingiza. *Cut off,* katia mbali, katiza, zuia, komesha, nyima. *Cut open,* tumbua. *Cut out,* tengeneza; (*debar*) ondoa; (*supplant*) jitia mahali pa, (*a garment*) fasili. *Cut a pencil,* chonga kalamu. *Cut and run,* kimbia upesi. *Cut the teeth,* nunuza, ota meno. *Cut up,* kata vipande vipande; (*annoy*) sumbua, huzunisha. *Cut up rough,* gombana. — *n.* mkato, mpasuo; (*blow*) kipigo, dharuba, chapa; (*wound*) jeraha; (*style*) jinsi, mtindo, babu kuu (au dogo). *A short cut,* njia ya kukata. *Get a cut* (*be cut*) katwa; (*with a stick &c.*) pigwa, chapwa. **cutter,** *n.* akataye; (*vessel*) chombo chembamba (chenye mlingoti mmoja). **cut-throat,** *n.* mwuaji, mkatili. **cutting, cut,** *n.* (*act of*) mkato, mchongo; (*piece cut*) kato; (*with tool*) choro, mchoro, nakshi; (*of plant*) kitawi, kipandikizi. **cutting,** *a.* -a kukata; (*causing pain*) -a kuchoma, -kali, -a kuchukiza. **cut-water,** *n.* (*of vessel*) hanamu.

cute, *a.* -erevu, -enye hila, -enye akili.

cuticle, *n.* ngozi. **cutaneous,** *a.* -a ngozi.

cutlass, *n.* upanga mfupi, jisu, sime, buchari.

cutler, *n.* mjume, mfanyiza na mwuza visu, mkasi, nyembe *&c.* **cutlery,** *n.* vitu vikali kama visu, nyuma, mkasi, nyembe *&c.*

cutlet, *n.*, kipande cha nyama hasa cha mbavu za kondoo au ndama.

cutter, *n.*, **cut-throat,** *n.*, **cutting,** *a. and n.* taz. *cut.*

cuttle-fish, *n.* pweza.

cut-water, *n.* taz. *cut*

cwt. = *hundredweight,* ratli 112.

cycle, *n.* (*regular period*) muda, (muhula) mzima, kipindi; muda ambao mambo yatokeayo humo hufuata kawaida, tena, hutokea tena na tena kwa kawaida ile ile; duara, andamo, mafuatano; (*bicycle*) baisikeli.

cyclone, *n.* tufani, tufani ya chamchela, kimbunga, dhoruba.
cyclopaedia, *n.* kitabu chenye habari za kila namna ya maarifa, kamusi.
cyclopean, cyclopic, *a.* -kubwa mno (kama kazi ya majitu).
cyclostyle, *n.* chombo cha kunakilia hati, barua &c.
cygnet, *n.* kinda la (mtoto wa) *swan*.
cylinder, *n.* kitu cho chote kirefu cha mviringo kama mzinga au bomba. **cylindrical**, *a.* -a kama *cylinder*.
cymbal, *n.* toazi.
cynic, *n.* mdharau yaliyo mema (sanaa, utajiri, mazungumzo, maadili); mdharau kibinadamu; mgumu. **cynical**, *a.* -a kudharau au kutweza mambo ya kibinadamu. **cynicism**, *n.* ugumu wa moyo, dharau ya kibinadamu; tabia ya kutojali (kutopenda) watu.
cynosure, *n.* cho chote kivutacho macho au cha kutazamisha watu, au cha kushangaza kwa uzuri wake &c.
cypher, *n.* taz. *cipher*.
cypress, *n.* namna ya mti.
cyst, *n.* kifuko chenye maji mazito (mwilini).
Czar, Tzar, *n.* mfalme wa *Russia*.

D

D. herufi ya Kirumi, maana yake mia tano.
dab, *v.t.* chachaga, paka kidogo, donoa. — *n.* kipako cha ghafula, mdono; kibonge kidogo cha kitu chororo au cha maji maji.
dabble, *v.t.* chovyachovya; — *v.t.* chezacheza majini; (*trifle with*) shughulika (fanya) kwa juujuu tu, purukusha, cheza. **dabbler**, *n.* mfanyi (kazi, sanaa &c.) juujuu tu, mpurukushani.
dabchick, *n.* kibisi.
dacoit, *n.* mwizi (mmojawapo wa kundi la wezi).
dad, daddy, *n.* baba (usemi wa kitoto).
daffodil, *n.* namna ya ua, rangi ya manjano.
daft, *a.* -pumbavu, -puzi, -enye kichaa.
dagger, *n.* jisu, sime, hanjari; (*curved*) jambia. *At daggers drawn*, katika hali ya uadui. *Look daggers*, tazama kwa chuki (kwa uadui).
dahlia, *n.* namna ya ua.
daily, *a.* -a kila siku, -a kila kutwa. — *adv.* sikuzote, kutwa.
dainty, *a.* -a kupendeza, -tamu, -zuri, -enye ladha nzuri; (*fastidious*) -teuzi, chaguzi; (*about food*) -enye kidomo. — *n.* kitu (hasa chakula) kizuri (cha anasa). **daintiness**, *n.* uteuzi, uchaguzi; uzuri.
dairy, *n.* chumba au nyumba mnamowekwa maziwa (inamotengenezwa siagi, jibini &c.); duka viuzwapo vitu hivyo.
dais, *n.* jukwaa, dungu; kiti cha sherehe kilichowekwa juu ya jukwaa.
daisy, *n.* namna ya ua la kizungu; jina la kike.
dale, *n.* bonde.

dalliance, *n.* taz. *dally.*
dally, *v.i.* chezacheza, poteza wakati (kwa uvivu, uzembe); chelewa, kawia, limatia; (*amorously*) fanya ubembe, bembeleza. **dalliance,** *n.* mchezo, uchezaji; usiri, uzembe.
dam, (1) *n.* boma la kuzuia maji (mtoni, baharini &c.). — *v.t.* zuia maji (ya bahari au mto) kwa boma.
dam, (2) *n.* mama mzazi (hasa mnyama).
damage, *v.t.* haribu, hasiri, vunja. *Be damaged,* haribika, hasirika, vunjika, tetereka. — *n.* uharabu, hasara, madhara, maafa.
damask, *n.* namna ya kitambaa chenye urembo uliofumwa; namna ya chuma cha pua; namna ya waridi.
dame, *n.* bibi mkubwa, mwanamke mzee, bibi mzee.
damn, *v.t.* laani, apiza, tukana, tia au takia adhabu ya milele. **damnable,** *a.* -baya sana, -laanifu, -a kuchukiza mno. **damnation,** *n.* laana ya milele, adhabu ya kutengwa na Mungu. **damnatory,** *a.* -a kupasisha hukumu, -a kuleta laana, -a kuapiza. **damned,** *a.* -enye kulaaniwa milele, maleuni, -a kuchukiza; (mara nyingi maana yake ni sana, au mno tu).
damp, *n.* unyevu, uchepechepe, rutuba, umaji. — *a.* -nyevu, -a chepechepe, -a majimaji, -bichi, -enye rutuba. **damp, dampen,** *v.t.* lowesha kidogo, tia maji kidogo, rutubisha, fanya chepechepe; (*discourage*) shusha moyo; punguza, fupisha (tamaa, furaha, bidii &c.); zuia. **damper,** *n.* kitu kinachotia unyevu &c.; kitu kinachopunguza (kufupisha, kuzuia, kupoozesha). **dampness,** *n.* rutuba, uchepechepe, unyevu.
damsel, *n.* kijana mwanamke, msichana, mwanamwali.
damson, *n.* tunda kama zambarau.
dance, *v.i.* cheza ngoma, randa, rukaruka; — *v.t.* (*a child*) vinyavinya. — *n.* ngoma, mchezo, mandari. **dancing,** *n.* mchezo, tendo au jinsi ya kucheza ngoma. *Dancing place,* batobato.
dandle, *v.t.* vinyavinya, chezesha mikononi.
dandruff, *n.* mba.
dandy, *n.* mmalidadi, mlimbwende, mmbeja, mbuji, mshaufu, mtanashati, mfuauji.
Dane, *n.* mtu wa nchi ya *Denmark.*
danger, *n.* hatari, hofu, kicho, mashaka, janga, ogofyo. *Put in danger,* hatirisha, tia hatarini, ponza. **dangerous,** *a.* -a hatari &c.
dangle, *v.t.* ning'iniza, yumbisha; — *v.i.* ning'inia, yumbayumba, chezacheza, wayawaya.
dank, *a.* -nyevu, -chepechepe (hewa).
dapper, *a.* -epesi, -nadhifu. *A dapper man,* mtu (hasa mdogo kwa kimo) mwepesi, nadhifu, mmbeja.
dappled, *a.* -enye madoadoa, -enye mabaka.
dare, *v.i.* thubutu, jasiri, jaribia, toogopa kufanya; — *v.t.* (*defy, challenge*) shindanisha, taka shari. *I dare you to strike me,* huthubutu kunipiga. *I dare say,* naona, nadhani. **dare-devil,** *n.* mjasiri sana. **daring,** *a.* hodari, -jasiri, -sio na hofu. — *n.* uhodari, ujasiri.
dark, *a.* -a giza, -eusi, -a gizagiza, -a utusitusi; (*difficult to understand*) -a fumbo, -gumu; (*secret*) -a siri; (*wicked*) -ovu; (*unenlightened*) -jinga, -shenzi. — *n.* giza, weusi, mazimbwezimbwe, utusitusi; ujinga. **darken,** *v.t.* tia giza, ondoa mwangaza; (*perplex*) tia mashaka, fumba; (*sadden*) huzunisha; — *v.i.* (*of sky*) tanda (mawingu); ingia giza. **darkness,** *n.* taz. *dark, n.*
darling, *n.* mpenzi, kipenzi.
darn, *v.t.* tililia, shona (kufuata namna nguo ilivyofumwa). — *n.* mshono wa kutililia; kiraka.
dart, *n.* kishale, kiparara, mkuki mdogo; cho chote kichomacho; (*sudden rush*) ruko, tendo la kurukia (la kutokea ghafula). — *v.i.* ruka (toka, enda) upesi, au kwa ghafula;

— *v.t.* (*throw*) tupa (piga, vurumisha) upesi; (*emit*) toa ghafula.
dash, *v.t.* (*throw violently*) tupa kwa nguvu; (*destroy*) vunja, haribu; (*put hastily*) tia kwa haraka, fanya kwa haraka; — *v.i.* (*rush*) enda mbio, puruka; (*of waves &c.*) pigapiga, rukaruka. — *n.* mshindo wa ghafula; mruko (mwendo) wa mbio; (*vigour*) bidii, ujasiri, nguvu, wepesi; (*small quantity*) kidogo; (*line*) kistari, kama hiki (—). **dashing,** *a.* -a kwenda mbio sana, -epesi sana; -jasiri, hodari.
dastard, *n.* mwoga, mnyonge, mwovu. **dastardly,** *a.* -a woga, -nyonge, -ovu.
data, *n.* mambo ya hakika (au yaliyokubaliwa kuwa hakika).
date, (1) *n.* tarehe; mwaka na mwezi na siku ya jambo fulani; muda uliotajwa. — *v.t.* tia tarehe; andika mwaka, mwezi na siku ya jambo fulani. *It dates from,* mwanzo wake ulikuwa. *Out of date,* -a zamani, -a kale, si namna ya siku hizi. *Up to date,* -a siku hizi, -a sasa, -pya.
date, (2) *n.* (*tree*) mtende; (*fruit*) tende.
daub, *v.t.* kandika, paka, rashia, sirima, paka ovyo ovyo.
daughter, *n.* binti, mtoto (kijana, mwana) wa kike. **daughter-in-law,** *n.* mkwe (mke wa mwana). **daughterly,** *a.* -a binti, kama binti.
daunt, *v.t.* zuia kwa hofu, ogofya, tisha, tia hofu; (*subdue*) tiisha. **dauntless,** *a.* hodari, jasiri, sio na hofu, -shupavu. **dauntlessly,** *adv.* bila hofu, kwa uthabiti, kwa ujasiri.
davit, *n.* slingi, winchi (hasa ya melini ya kupandishia na kutelemshia mashua).
Davy Jones's locker, *n.* bahari. *Go to Davy Jones's locker,* tota baharini.
daw, *n.* ndege kama kunguru mdogo.
dawdle, *v.i.* poteza wakati, chelewa (kawia) kwa kuchezacheza (kwa uzembe), enda polepole, tangatanga.
dawn, *v.i.* pambazuka, pambauka, -cha; (*begin*) anza. *It dawned upon me,* nilianza kufahamu, inilielea, nia (maana) iliniingia moyoni. — *n* mapambazuko, alfajiri, kucha, macha ya jua, kichea, ucheo, uche, ucheachea; ukungu wa alfajiri, weupe wa alfajiri; (*beginning*) mwanzo, asili, chimbuko. **dawning,** *n.* kama *dawn.*
day, *n.* siku; (*time of daylight*) mchana, kuchwa; (*period of life*) wakati, muda, maisha, aushi. *All day,* mchana kutwa. *Day by day,* kila siku. *Day after day, From day to day,* siku kwa siku. *The day after to-morrow,* kesho kutwa. *The third day,* mtondo. *The fourth day,* mtondogoo. *One of these days,* baada ya siku kadha wa kadha, siku moja. *Yesterday,* jana. *The other day,* juzi juzi. *Good-day* (*greeting*) hujambo, jambo, (*morning*) sabalkheri, (*afternoon*) masalkheri. **day book,** *n.* kitabu cha kuandikia shughuli za kila siku; hutumiwa na wafanya biashara na wengineo. **daybreak,** *n.* taz. *dawn, n.* **daydream,** *n.* mawazo au matamani ya moyoni yamjiayo mtu angali yu macho. **day labour,** *n.* kazi ya kibarua ya kutwa. **day labourer,** *n.* kibarua. **daylight,** *n.* mchana, mwangaza wa mchana. **day-spring,** *n.* taz. *dawn, n.* **daytime** *n.* mchana.
daze, *v.t.* tunduwaza, pumbaza, fadhaisha, shangaza, rusha akili, tia bumbuazi, shtusha. — *n.* bumbuazi, mshangao, mzumbao, fadhaa. **dazzle,** *v.t.* fanya kiwi, tia kiwi machoni, fanya unyenyezi, shangaza, staajabisha (kwa mng'ao, uzuri, akili &c.). — *n.* kiwi, mng'ao, unyenyezi.
deacon, *n.* shemasi; (katika madhehebu nyingine za Wakristo, ni mtu aliyechaguliwa kuangalia mambo ya kanisa). **deaconess,** *n.* *deacon* wa kike.
dead, *a.* -fu, -liokufa, -siyo na maisha (uzima, uhai); kama kifu, -kavu, baridi, bila nguvu, bila faida, dhaifu; (*without sense of feeling*) -pooza. *Be dead,* fariki, -fa, isha. *Dead body,* (*of man*) maiti, mfu; (*of animals*)

pinda, mzoga. **dead-beat,** *a.* -a kuchoka kabisa. **dead-drunk,** *a.* -a kulewa kabisa, -a chakari. **deaden,** *v.t.* fisha, poozesha, fifisha, dhoofisha, legeza, ondoa nguvu; nyamazisha, tuliza. **dead heat,** *n.* usawa (suluhu) katika shindano. **dead-letter,** *n.* barua isiyoweza kuonekana mwenyewe; sheria (amri) isiyo na nguvu. **dead-level,** *a.* sawasawa kabisa. **dead-lock,** *n.* mgogoro, kizuizi; mambo yaliyotatizwa au kupingana hata yamesimama, hayaendelei. **dead-loss,** *n.* hasara kabisa, hasara tupu. **deadly,** *a.* -a kufisha, -a mauti, -a kudhuru sana. **deadness,** *n.* upoozo, uzito, baridi, ulegevu, utepetevu, ufu, udhaifu. **dead set,** *n.* jaribio (shambulio, mruko) la bidii nyingi. *Be dead set against,* pinga kabisa, tokubali kabisa, zuia iwezekanavyo. **dead-shot,** *n.* shabaha barabara; mtu mwenye shabaha barabara. **death,** *n.* mauti, kifo, kufa, ufu, ajali, faradhi; (*end, ruin*) mwisho, maangamizi, uangamizo. *Be at death's door,* -wa kufani, chungulia kuzimu (kaburi). *Die a natural death,* (*of animal*) -fa kipinda, -fa kibudu; (*of man*) -fa ajali, -fa kibudu. *Do or put to death,* ua, fisha. *Jaws of death,* kufani, kuchungulia kuzimu (kaburi). **death-agony,** *n.* shindano linalotangulia kufa pengine, gharighari ya kufa. **death-bed,** *n.* kitanda anachofia mtu; ugonjwa wa mauti (wa kufa). **death-duty,** *n.* ushuru unaotozwa na serikali katika mali ya marehemu. **deathless,** *a.* -a milele, -siyo na mwisho, -siyokufa. **deathly,** *a.* kama mauti. **death-rate,** *n.* hesabu ya watu wanaokufa mahali katika kila mia katika muda fulani.

deaf, *a.* -ziwi, -sioweza kusikia vizuri au kabisa; -a kuziba masikio, -a kutosikiliza. *A deaf person,* kiziwi. *A deaf mute,* mtu aliye kiziwi na bubu pia. **deafen,** *v.t.* tia uziwi, shinda masikio.

deal, (1) *n.* sunobari.

deal, (2) *v.t.* (*p.t. and pf.t.* **dealt**) (*distribute*) gawa, gawanya; — *v.i.* (*act*) tenda; (*trade*) fanya biashara. *Deal a blow,* piga. *Deal a blow at,* jaribu kupiga. *Deal with,* shughulika na, -wa na neno na; (*arrange*) tengeneza, kata shauri. *Deal in,* fanya biashara kwa, uza na kununua. — *n.* (*portion*) mgawo; (*quantity*) wingi. *A great deal,* wingi. *A good deal of,* -ingi kidogo. **dealer,** *n.* mchuuzi, mfanya biashara, mwenye duka. **dealing,** *n.* (*trade*) biashara, ubazazi; (*affairs, conduct*) mambo, matendo, mwenendo.

dealt, *p.t. and pf.t.* ya *deal.*

dean, *n.* mkuu wa makasisi wa *cathedral*; mkuu mmojawapo wa chuo kikubwa (*college*). **deanery,** *n.* kazi au makao ya *dean.*

dear, *a.* ghali, -a tunu, -a thamani nyingi; (*beloved*) -penzi, -a kupendeza; (*in letters after the Arab style*) muhebi. — *n.* mpenzi, kipenzi, muhebi. — *int. Oh dear! Dear me! Dear dear!* maneno ya kuonyesha mshangao, huruma, majonzi *&c.*, kadiri sauti ilivyo, *e.g.* loo! pole! masalale! mama wee! *&c.*

dearth, *n.* upungufu, ukosefu, haba, uchache, njaa, hali ya kuadimika (ya kuwa ghali).

death, *n.*, **death-agony,** *n.*, **death-bed,** *n.*, **death-duty,** *n.*, **deathless,** *a.*, **deathly,** *a.*, **death-rate,** *n.* taz. *dead.*

debar, *v.t.* pinga, zuia, kataza, harimisha.

debase, *v.t.* (*lower condition*) shusha, dhili, tweza, adhiri, haribu cheo (hali, sifa, jina); (*lower value*) rahisisha, vunja bei (thamani), ghoshi. **debased,** *a.* -nyonge, -baya, -potovu, -dhilifu, -fisadi, fasiki. **debasement,** *n.* unyonge, ubaya, utwezo, udhilifu, udhaifu, hali nyonge, upotovu, ufasiki, ufisadi; (*depreciation*) uharibifu, upungufu wa thamani (bei *&c.*).

debatable, *a.* taz. *debate.*

debate, *v.t. and i.* bishana, shindana kwa maneno, jadiliana; (*consider*) fikiri, fanya shauri. — *n.* mashindano, mashindano ya maneno, hoja, jadiliano, mdahili. **debatable**, *a.* -a mashaka, -a kushindaniwa (bishaniwa).

debauch, *v.t.* potosha, fisidi, haribu kwa zinaa (uasherati, ulevi *&c.*); (*corrupt*) pevusha, komaza, tongoza. — *n.* karamu au mfululizo wa (kipindi cha) uasherati (zinaa, ulevi ulafi, ufasiki, ufisadi *&c.*). **debauchee**, *n.* mwasherati, mlafi, mlevi, mfisadi, mfasiki, mtongozi. **debauchery**, *n.* zinaa, uasherati, ulevi, ufasiki, ufisadi, utongozi.

debenture, *n.* hati ya fedha, stakabadhi ya fedha iliyokopeshwa.

debilitate, *v.t.* dhoofisha, kondesha, punguza afya, ondolea nguvu, fanya dhaifu. **debility**, *n.* udhaifu, ulegevu, ugoigoi.

debit, *n.* hesabu iliyoandikwa upande wa mapato wa daftari. — *v.t.* andika fedha, karidhisha, andika mapato. **debt**, *n.* deni. *Be in debt*, wiwa, -wa na deni, daiwa. *Have in one's debts*, wia. **debtor**, *n.* mdeni.

debonair, *a.* -a madaha, -a adabu, -a jamala, -zuri sana, -kunjufu, -changamfu.

debouch, *v.i.* toka (*e.g.* mto katika mahali pembamba hata mahali papana; askari kutoka katika korongo au bonde jembamba hata katika uwanda *&c.*).

debris, *n.* takataka, kifusi, mabaki ya nyumba *&c.*

debt, debtor, *n.* taz. *debit.*

debut, *n.* utokezi *e.g.* jaribio la kwanza la mwimbaji kuimba mbele ya watu *&c.*

decade, *n.* mwongo (hesabu); muda wa miaka kumi.

decadence, *n.* upunguo, uharibifu, uchakavu, upoozi (wa uzuri, sanaa *&c.*). **decadent**, *a.* -a kupungua (kupooza, kuharibika, kuchakaa).

decalogue, *n.* amri kumi za Nabii Musa.

decamp, *v.i.* kimbia, toroka, ondoka (hasa kwa siri au hila); vunja kambi.

decant, *v.t.* chingirisha, gida, miminia divai katika chupa ili kuacha mashapo. **decanter**, *n.* chupa nzuri ya kumiminia mvinyo, divai *&c.*

decapitate, *v.t.* kata kichwa. **decapitation**, *n.* mkato wa kichwa.

decarbonize, *v.t.* ondoa *carbon*, *e.g.* kwangua masizi magumu katika mashine ya motakaa *&c.*

decay, *v.i.* oza, haribika, chakaa, fifia, pooza, pungukiwa na uzuri au nguvu. — *n.* upunguo, uharibifu, hali ya kuoza (kuchakaa, kuharibika, kupungukiwa).

decease, *v.i.* fa, fariki. — *n.* kifo, kufa mauti. **deceased**, *a.* -liokufa. *The deceased*, marehemu, hayati.

deceit, *n.* hila, udanganyifu, werevu, uwongo, ulaghai, leba, hadaa, ujanja, ughilibu, ubilisi. **deceitful**, *a.* -erevu, -a uwongo, -enye hila, -danganyifu, -janja. **deceitfulness**, *n.* hila *&c.* kama *deceit.* **deceive**, *v.t.* danganya, punja, hadaa, ghilibu, kopa, rubuni, laghai, kenga, haini, karamkia, shaua, tega, bilisi, ghuri. **deceiver**, *n.* mdanganyi, mlaghai, ayari, mwongo, mhaini *&c.* **deception**, *n.* kama *deceit.* **deceptive**, *a.* -a kudanganya, -a hila, -a kutia mashaka.

December, *n.* mwezi wa kumi na mbili wa mwaka wa kizungu, Desemba.

decency, *n.* taz. *decent.*

decent, *a.* -a adabu, -a heshima, -zuri, stahifu, -a kufaa. **decency**, *n.* adabu, heshima, ustahifu, haya, uzuri wa mazoea na mwenendo.

decennial, *a.* -a kila mwaka wa kumi.

deception, *n.*, **deceptive**, *a.* taz. **deceit.**

decide, *v.t.* (*determine*) kata (shauri, neno); (*a quarrel*) amua; — *v.i.* (*resolve*) azimu, nia, kusudia. **decided**, *a.* (*determined, resolute*) thabiti, imara, -a nguvu, -enye nia au kusudi thabiti, -gumu; (*clear*) dhahiri, wazi, bila shaka. **decision**, *n.* hukumu, maamuzi, neno mkataa; (*resolution*) nia thabiti, uthabiti, nguvu. **decisive,** *a.* (*clear*) dhahiri, thabiti, wazi, halisi, bila shaka; (*final*) mkataa, -a kukata (shauri, maneno), -a kushinda, -a nguvu, tama.

deciduous, *a.* -a kufifia, -a kupungua kwa wakati wake, -a kupukutika (kama majani ya miti mingine).

decimal, *a.* -a miongo, -a kumi, -a sehemu za kumi. *Decimal system,* njia ya kuandika hesabu kwa miongo, yaani makumi na hesabu zinazogawanyika sawasawa na kumi. — *n.* sehemu ya kumi. **decimate,** *v.t.* ua kila mtu wa kumi; punguza sana hesabu kwa kuua (kwa ugonjwa &c.).

decipher, *v.t.* fumbua (fasiri) maandiko ya siri au ya fumbo; fumbua (fasiri) yaliyo magumu kufahamika au kusomeka.

decision, *n.*, **decisive,** *a.* taz. *decide.*

deck, *v.t.* pamba, vika vizuri. — *n.* sitaha; (*of cards*) jozi ya karata.

declaim, *v.i.* sema kwa sauti kuu, paliza sauti; (*practise speaking*) jifunza usemaji, jizoeza kunena. *Declaim against,* leta udaku, dakuliza. **declamation,** *n.* maneno ya makelele, usemi wa kiburi, usemaji. **declamatory,** *a.* -a makelele, -a ufasaha lakini maana imepungua.

declaration, *n.*, **declaratory,** *a.* taz. *declare.*

declare, *v.t.* tangaza, julisha, vumisha; — *v.i.* nena kwa nguvu (kwa uthabiti). **declaration,** *n.* habari, taarifa, tangazo, ilani, maneno; hati ya kujulisha au kueleza habari. **declaratory,** *a.* -a kueleza, -a kuhubiri, -a kujulisha, -a kutangaza.

decline, *v.i.* (*refuse*) kataa; (*slope*) inama; (*go down*) shuka; (*fail*) (*decay*) pungua, punguka, haribika, chakaa; (*turn aside*) enda upande, potoka; — *v.t.* inamisha. — *n.* (*sloping*) mtelemko, mwinamo, mshuko, mainamizi; (*falling off*) mpunguo, uharibifu, uchakao; (*consumption*) kifua kikuu. **declension,** *n.* (*sloping*) mwinamo, mainamizi, telemko, mshuko; (*diminution*) upunguo, uchakavu, uharibifu; (*grammatical*) jinsi jina (*noun*) linavyobadilika. **declivity,** *n.* mtelemko, mwinamo.

declutch, *v.i.* tengua *clutch* (ya motakaa), taz. *clutch* (2).

decoct, *v.t.* fanya (dawa &c.) kwa kupika. **decoction,** *n.* mchemko (wa dawa &c.); dawa &c. iliyofanywa kwa kupika au kuchemsha.

decode, *v.t.* fasiri maandiko ya siri (fumbo). Taz. *code.*

decompose, *v.t.* (*analyse*) changanua, vunja, geuza hali ya asili, geuza; (*rot*) ozesha, haribu; — *v.i.* oza, nyekenya, haribika. **decomposition,** *n.* (*analysis*) mchanganuo, mvunjo; (*putrefaction*) ubovu, uozi, kioza.

decorate, *v.t.* pamba, remba, tia uzuri; (*with badge or medal*) visha nishani ya heshima (cheo &c.). **decoration,** *n.* pambo, urembo, uzuri, bombwe; (*medal*) nishani. **decorative,** *a.* -a kupamba, -a urembo, -a kutia uzuri, -a sherehe.

decorous, *a.* -a adabu, adibu, -a heshima, -stahifu, makini. **decorum,** *n.* adabu, heshima, ustahi, makini.

decorticate, *v.t.* ambua gamba.

decoy, *v.t.* tega, nasa, vuta, shawishi, bilisi, kamata kwa hila au werevu, — *n.* mtego, kitu cha kutegea; (*bait*) chambo, mtu (au kitu) aliyewekwa kuwavuta wengine kwa hila ili wategwe.

decrease, *v.t.* punguza, tuliza; — *v.i.* pungua, punguka, fifia, nyamaa, tulia. — *n.* upunguo, kipunguo.

decree, *n.* amri, agizo, hukumu. *v.t.* toa amri, amuru.

decrement, *n.* upunguo, kipunguo, upungufu.

decrepit, *a.* dhaifu (kwa uzee, kuchakaa &c.), -kuukuu, -kongwe, -chakavu. **decrepitude,** *n.* ukongwe, udhaifu, uchakavu.

decry, *v.t.* rahisisha, umbua, vunja bei (heshima, sifa, cheo, jina *&c.*); laumu, tia hatiani, singizia.

dedicate, *v.t.* weka wakf, tenga (weka) kwa matumizi ya dini au kwa utukufu wa Mungu, tabaruku, zindua; (*devote*) toa (weka), funga kabisa) kwa ajili ya kusudi fulani maalum; (*a book*) andikia ukumbusho au heshima ya mtu au kusudi maalum. **dedication**, *n.* (*speech, ceremony*) hotuba (hitima) ya kuzindulia, mazinduo, kutabaruku; (*offering*) kutoa, kuweka.

deduce, *v.t.* eleza, fasiri maana, pata maarifa au maono juu ya jambo kwa dalili au maonyo au mambo yaliyopo au yaliyotangulia. *I deduce*, kwa mambo yalivyo, nasema (au naona). **deduct**, *v.t.* toa, chukua, katia, twalia. **deduction**, *n.* mambo yalivyofasiriwa au kukisiwa kwa jinsi mengine yalivyo; mkato, matoleo. **deductive**, *a.* -a kuonya maana, -a kueleza, -a kudhihirisha.

deed, *n.* tendo, kitendo, kazi; (*great deed*) tendo kubwa (la ushujaa, la ujasiri); (*legal*) hati, mkataba. *Indeed*, kwa kweli.

deem, *v.t.* dhani, ona, hesabu, sadiki.

deep, *a.* -a kwenda chini; -a kwenda nyuma, -a ndani, -enye kina kirefu au kilindi; -ingi, -nene, -zito; (*cunning*) -erevu, -janja, -enye hila. *A deep river*, mto wa maji mengi. *Deep respect*, heshima (staha) nyingi. *Deep silence*, kimya kabisa. *Deep darkness*, giza nene (nzito). *Deep colour*, rangi nyingi (nyeusi, nzito). *Deep thought*, fikira nyingi. *Deep sound*, sauti nene. *Deep subject*, jambo la fumbo (la siri, gumu, lenye matata). *Deep secret*, siri kabisa. *Deep mourning*, huzuni nyingi, nguo za kuugulia. *Soldiers six deep*, askari safu sita. *He is deep in his book*, anasoma sana kitabu chake. — *n.* bahari kuu; (*deep water*) kilindi, lindi. *In the deep of the heart*, moyoni kwa ndani, kimoyomoyo. **deepen**, *v.t.* ongeza (urefu wa kwenda chini, nyuma au ndani); — *v.i.* ongezeka. **deeply**, *adv.* sana. **deep-seated**, *a.* imara, -enye msingi imara, -a nguvu. **depth**, *n.* hali ya kuwa *deep*; urefu wa kwenda chini, uketo, kina. *Depths of the sea*, vilindi. *Depth of winter*, kati ya wakati wa baridi. *Depths of ignorance*, upeo wa ujinga. *Depth of night*, usiku wa manane. *Be (get) out of one's depth*, jitatanya, tatizwa, fumbwa, potea.

deer, *n.* mnyama, mfano wa paa, kulungu *&c.* **deer-stalking** *n.* mwindo wa *deer*.

deface, *v.t.* umbua, haribu sura au uzuri, rembua. **defacement**, *n.* mwumbuo, uharibifu, mrembuo, tendo la kuumbua (kurembua, kuharibu) au hali iletwayo nalo.

defalcate, *v.i.* iba, tumia au poteza mali iliyowekwa amana. **defalcation**, *n.* wivi (upotevu) wa mali iliyowekwa amana; upunguo.

defamation, *n.*, **defamatory**, *a.* taz. *defame*.

defame, *v.t.* singizia, sengenya, umbua, rahisisha, vunja sifa (jina, heshima). **defamation**, *n.* masengenyo, masingizio. **defamatory**, *a.*-a kusingizia, -a kuumbua *&c.*

default, *n.* ukosefu, ukosekano, upungufu; ulegevu; kosa (la kutofanya ipasavyo), kutokufanya. *In default of*, ikiwa hapana, isipokuwa, mahali pa, badala ya. — *v.i.* kosa (kufanya, kuhudhuria). **defaulter**, *n.* mkosaji; asiyelipa deni; asiyeweza kutoa hesabu ya fedha impasayo; asiyehudhuria mbele ya baraza wakati unaompasa.

defeat, *v.t.* shinda, kimbiza, piga, vunja, angamiza. — *n.* ushinde, mtanguo, kimbizo, mapigo, mvunjo, maangamizi, mwangamio.

defecate, *v.t.* safisha, chuja na kuondoa taka; — *v.i.* -nya, enda choo, enda haja. **defecation**, *n.* mchujo, tendo la kusafisha; tendo la kunya (la kwenda choo).

defect, *n.* upungufu, ila, kombo, kipunguo, kosa, kasoro, waa, dosari, taksiri, walakini. **defection,** *n.* uasi, uhuni, usalata, kosa (la kutoroka, la kuacha kazi, dini *&c.*). **defective,** *a.* punguani, -enye upungufu (ila, waa, kombo, kasoro *&c.*).

defend, *v.t.* (*guard*) linda, hifadhi, simamia, kinga, shindania, hami; (*speak for*) tetea, shuhudia. **defence,** *n.* ulinzi, himaya, mlindo; (*plea, answer*) mateteo, udhuru, majibu, madai; (*anything which protects*) kinga, mkingo. **defenceless,** *a.* pasipo nguvu (rafiki, boma, askari, msaada, mlinzi, kinga *&c.*), -tupu, -dhaifu. **defendant,** *n.* mshtakiwa, mdaiwa. **defender,** *n.* mlinzi, mtetezi, msaidizi. **defensible,** *a.* -a kulindwa, -a kulindika, -a nguvu; (*capable of vindication*) -a maana, -a kuthibitika. **defensive,** *a.* -a kujilinda tu, -a kujitetea, -a kukingia. — *n.* kikao cha kujilinda (kujitetea, kukinga). *Be on the defensive,* jilinda, kita, -wa katika hali au kikao cha kujilinda.

defer, (1) *v.t.* ahirisha, weka (hata wakati mwingine), rajua, cheleza, kawisha. *Be deferred,* ahiri, wekwa.

defer, (2) *v.i.* jinyenyekea, ondokea, kubali mradi wa (nia ya, kusudi la, maneno ya) mwingine. **deference,** *n.* ukubali, heshima, utii, ustahifu, unyenyekeo. **deferential,** *a* stahifu, -a heshima, -nyenyekevu.

defiance, *n.*, **defiant,** *a.* taz. *defy.*

deficiency, *n.*, **deficient,** *a.*, taz. *deficit.*

deficit, *n.* hasara, kipunguo (hasa cha fedha au mali), nakisi. **deficiency,** *n,* upungufu, kipunguo, uchache, haba, kasoro. **deficient,** *a.* -pungufu, -kosefu, haba, -dogo. *He is deficient in sense,* yu punguani; hana akili hata kidogo, ana akili afkani.

defile, (1) *v.i.* pita mmoja mmoja (askari). — *n.* njia nyembamba ya milimani, bonde jembamba.

defile, (2) *v.t.* najisi, chafua, tia taka. **defilement,** *n.* unajisi, uchafu, ujusi, janaba.

define, *v.t.* weka mpaka; dhihirisha, eleza wazi kabisa, eleza maana yote, ainisha. **definite,** *a.* halisi, dhahiri, wazi, -enye maana dhahiri. **definition,** *n.* elezo, tafsiri, fafanusi. **definitive,** *a.* mkataa, -a kukata maneno, tama.

deflect, *v.t.* vuta upande, potosha, geuza upande, kengeusha, inamisha; — *v.i.* enda upande (au chini), potoka, geuka, kengeua. **deflection, deflexion,** *n.* upotoe, mwendo wa upande, mwinamo.

defloration, *n.* kubikiri, mtomo.

deflower, *v.t.* bikiri, tomoa.

deforest, *v.t.* kata miti ya mwituni, haribu mwitu.

deform, *v.t.* umbua, haribu, geuza vibaya, lemaza. **deformation,** *n.* mwumbuo, ugeuzi (kuwa-baya); mageuko mabaya; kilema, kombo. **deformed,** *a.* -a kilema, -enye kombo, -liyoumbuka, -lioatilika. **deformity,** *n.* kilema, kombo, kigosho.

defraud, *v.t.* danganya, punja, kopa, nyang'anya, laghai, rubuni, ghilibu.

defray, *v.t.* lipa gharama.

deft, *a.* stadi, bingwa, mahiri, -erevu, -epesi.

defunct, *a.* -fu, marehemu, hayati.

defy, *v.t.* taka vita, taka shari, ita kuja kupigana; (*set at nought*) toogopa, dharau, asi; (*provoke*) tolea ujuvi, kaidi, fanya kiburi kwa, piga masharti. *I defy you to do it,* huthubutu; huwezi; ukiweza, juu yangu kulipa, usipoweza, juu yako. **defiance,** *n.* tendo au maneno ya kusai (ya kutaka vita, ya kuita kuja kupigana, ya kutaka shari, ya kudharau adui). *In defiance of orders,* kuasi (kutojali) amri. **defiant,** *a.* -a kutaka vita, -a shari, -a kiburi, -asi, -dharaulifu.

degeneracy, *n.* taz. *degenerate.*

degenerate, *v.i.* haribika tabia, rudia ushenzi, geuka vibaya, zidi kuwa -baya, punguka, dhoofika. — *a.*

-lioharibika, -liogeuka vibaya. — *n.* mtu (mnyama) ambaye tabia yake imeharibika, *e.g.* mtu mwema kugeuka mwasherati *&c.* **degeneracy,** *n.* uharibifu wa tabia. **degeneration,** *n.* uharibifu wa tabia.

degradation, *n.* taz. *degrade.*

degrade, *v.t.* shusha, ondoa cheo (heshima, jina), dhili, tweza, aibisha; — *v.i.* dhilika, potea cheo (heshima *&c.*). **degradation,** *n.* udhilifu, aibu, uduni, hali mbaya *e.g.* ufisadi, ufasiki, uasherati *&c.*; upunguo wa cheo.

degree *n.* (*rank*) cheo, daraja, manzili; (*amount*) kadiri, kiasi; (*university*) cheo cha elimu fulani; (*in measurement*) kipimo cha kupimia duara (pembe, joto). *By degrees,* kidogo kidogo, nusu. *To a degree,* sana, mno.

deify, *v.t.* fanya Mungu, abudu (heshimu) kama Mungu.

deign, *v.t.* kubali, ridhia, penda. *Deign to listen,* tafadhali usikilize. *He did not deign to answer,* hakujibu.

deism, *n.* imani ya kukubali kwamba kuna Mungu, lakini kutokubali mambo yaliyofunuliwa na dini.

deist, *n.* mtu mwenye imani ya *deism.*

deity, *n.* Mungu; Uungu, Umungu.

deject, *v.t.* huzunisha, sikitisha, vunja moyo, tia majonzi. **dejected,** *a.* -a huzuni, -zito. **dejection,** *n.* huzuni, sikitiko, majonzi, moyo mzito.

delay, *v.t.* kawisha, chelewesha, ahirisha, usirisha, weka, faitisha; — *v.i.* kawia, chelewa, faitika, limatia, taahari, usiri. — *n.* ukawa, ukawio, usiri, zuio, taahira; (*interval*) muhula, muda, kitambo, kipindi.

delectable, *a.* -a kupendeza, -tamu, -a kufurahisha, -anisi. **delectation,** *n.* furaha, mapendezi, anasa.

delegate, *v.t.* tuma wakilisha, agiza. *Delegate to;* wekea, tolea, agizia. — *n.* mjumbe, wakili, kaimu, makamu. **delegation,** *n.* kutuma, kuwakilisha, kuagiza, ujumbe; mjumbe, wakili *&c.*, jamii ya wajumbe (mawakili *&c.*).

delete, *v.t.* futa, ondoa, tangua (herufi, neno, maandiko).

deleterious, *a.* -haribifu, -potevu, -a kudhuru.

deliberate, *v.i.* (*reflect*) fikiri, waza, angalia; (*take counsel*) fanya shauri, shauriana, hojiana, barizi; — *v.t.* pima, fikiri, zungumza (ongea) habari za. — *a.* -angalifu, -a hadhari, bila haraka, -a kusudi. **deliberately,** *adv.* kwa kuangalia, makusudi, kwa kusudi; (*slowly*) polepole, taratibu, kidogo kidogo. **deliberation.** *n.* (*discussion*) maneno, shauri; (*consideration*) fikira, uangalifu, taratibu, hadhari. **deliberative,** *a.* -a kufanya shauri. *A deliberative assembly,* baraza.

delicate, *a.* (*pleasing*) -a kupendeza, -tamu, -zuri; (*soft*) -ororo; (*fine*) -dogo; (*slender*) -embamba; (*smooth*) laini; (*slight*) -epesi; (*refined*) -enye malezi mema, -a adabu; (*careful*) -angalifu; (*of health*) dhaifu, si -enye nguvu. *A delicate business,* jambo gumu. *He is in delicate health,* hana afya nzuri; mara kwa mara huugua.

delicacy, *n.* (*refinement*) adabu, malezi mema; (*care*) uangalifu; (*nice dish*) chakula kitamu. **delicious,** *a.* -a kupendeza sana, -a kufurahisha sana, -tamu, -zuri.

delight, *v.t.* pendeza sana, furahisha sana, teremesha, anisi; — *v.i.* penda, furahi. — *n.* furaha, anasa, mapendezi, mteremo. **delightedly,** *adv.* kwa furaha, kwa moyo. **delightful,** *a.* -a kupendeza sana, -a kufurahisha sana, -zuri sana.

delimit,, **delimitate,** *v.t.* weka mpaka. **delimitation,** *n.* kuweka mpaka; mpaka.

delineate, *v.t.* (*draw, paint*) andika, piga picha (sanamu) ya; (*describe*) fafanua kwa maneno, eleza, onyesha barabara. **delineation,** *n.*. mwandiko (wa picha, wa sanamu, wa maelezo); maelezo, picha, sanamu.

delinquency, *n.* taz. *delinquent.*

delinquent, *n.* mkosaji, mwenye hatia. **delinquency,** *n.* kosa, hatia.

delirium, *n.* mapayo, weweseko, wazimu, mahoka. **delirious,** *a.* -enye kupayukapayuka au kuweweseka (kwa ugonjwa au ulevi), -a kupayuka.

deliver, *v.t.* (*save*) okoa, opoa, ponya, hifadhi, afu, afua, linda, fanya huru (katika hatari, utumwa, kifungo, maumivu, mauti, dhambi &c.); (*give up, hand over*) kabidhi, toa, weka, salimisha. *Deliver a speech,* hutubu, hubiri. *Be delivered of a child,* zaa, jifungua. *Deliver a blow,* piga. **deliverance,** *n.* wokovu, ulinzi, uhuru, ukombozi, afua; (*utterance*) kutoa (maneno wazi), mahubiri, hotuba; (*childbirth*) uzazi. **deliverer,** *n.* mwokozi, mkombozi. **delivery,** *n.* kama *deliverance;* (*mode of speaking &c.*) jinsi ya kusema (kupiga &c.); matamko.

dell, *n.* bonde, kibonde.

delta, *n.* mahali mto unapoingia baharini uliojigawanya sehemu mbili au zaidi.

delude, *v.t.* danganya, hadaa, shaua, ghilibu, laghai, tia mchanga wa macho. *Be self-deluded,* ghururika. **delusion,** *n.* maono ya uwongo (hasa yaletwayo na wazimu); madanganyo, madanganyiko. *He is a victim of delusion,* amedanganyika sana; amerukwa na akili. **delusive,** -a kudanganya, -a uwongo &c. *Make a delusive show,* jishaua.

deluge, *v.t.* gharikisha, funikiza. — *n.* gharika, mafuriko ya maji; mvua kubwa sana.

delusion, *n.*, **delusive,** *a.* taz. *delude.*

delve, *v.t.* chimba, chimba sana; chungua sana (kitabu, elimu, masomo).

demagogue, *n.* mfitini, msukumizi.

demand, *v.t.* taka (omba) kwa nguvu (kwa haki), dai, uliza; (*require*) hitaji; (*in marriage*) posa. — *n.* haja, matakwa, ulizo, swali, agizo, madahili; (*need*) hitaji, tamaa; (*in marriage*) posa. *On demand,* mara itakwapo. *There is a great demand for cloth, Cloth is in demand,* nguo inatakiwa sana, watu wananunua nguo nyingi, wanunuzi ni wengi.

demarcate, *v.t.* andika (weka) mpaka. **demarcation,** *n.* kuandika (kuweka) mpaka; mpaka.

demean, *v.t.* (*refl.*) (*debase*) jitweza, jitia aibu, jiumbua, jiharibia heshima (cheo &c.); (*behave*) enda, enenda, jitenda, jiweka, jichukua. **demeanour,** *n.* mwenendo, matendo, mazoea.

demented, *a.* -enye wazimu (kichaa, kurukwa na akili). **dementia,** *n.* kichaa.

demesne, *n.* taz. *domain.*

demerit, *n.* kosa, upunguo, upungufu.

demi-god, *n.* nusu Mungu, kama Mungu.

demise, *n.* mauti, kufa.

demobilize, *v.t.* changua (askari, manowari); ruhusu askari kwenda kwao baada ya vita.

democracy, *n.* (*people*) watu, akina yahe; (*Government*) utawalaji wa nchi kwa baadhi ya watu waliochaguliwa na watu wa nchi wenyewe; (*country*) nchi inayotawaliwa na baadhi ya watu waliochaguliwa na watu wenyewe. **democrat,** *n.* mfuasi wa *democracy.* **democratic,** *a.* -a *democracy.*

demolish, *v.t.* bomoa, vunja, haribu, angamiza, maliza; (*eat*) -la. **demolition,** *n.* uharibifu, maangamizi, kubomoa (hasa nyumba, majengo).

demon, *n.* pepo mbaya, jini mbaya, shetani, mtu katili (mwovu, mharibifu, mwangamizi). **demoniac,** *a.* -enye pepo mbaya, -a shetani, katili, -ovu sana. **demoniacal,** *a.* -a shetani, -a pepo mbaya. **demonology,** *n.* elimu ya pepo.

demonstrable, *a.* taz. *demonstrate.*

demonstrate, *v.t.* onya wazi, thibitisha, onyesha, fafanua. **demonstrable,** *a.* -a kuthibitika, -a kuweza kuthibitishwa. **demonstration,** *n.* (*proof*) mathubutu, ushahidi, mafafanusi; (*certainty*) hakika; (*show*) onyesho, onyeshano tamasha. **demonstrative,** *a.* -a kuthibitisha, -a kuonyesha, -a kuainisha, -a kuhakikisha, -a kuonyesha wazi maono (upendo, furaha *&c.*). demonstrator, *n.* mwalimu afundishaye kwa kuonyesha matendo (*e.g.* kuchanganya dawa, kuendesha mashine *&c.*), msaidizi (mshiriki) wa onyesho *&c.*

demoralization, *n.* taz. *demoralize.*

demoralize, *v.t.* potoa, potosha; (*of young*) pevusha; (*dispirit*) vunja moyo, chafua. **demoralization,** *n.* uharibifu wa moyo (tabia, hali), upotoe, uharibifu wa utii (ushujaa, nguvu *&c.*) hasa wa askari vitani.

demur, *v.i.* sita, kinza, kataa, onea shaka, bisha, kaidi. — *n.* kusita, mgogoro, mabishano, makinzano, makatao. **demurrage,** *n.* ushuru unaotozwa kama vitu (bidhaa *&c.*) vikiachwa stesheni (forodhani *&c.*) zaidi ya muda maalum. **demurrer,** *n.* kinzano, dakizo, udaku.

demure, *a.* -nyamavu, -pole, -a taratibu, -enye kiasi, -enye haya.

demurrage, *n.* **demurrer,** *n.* taz. *demur.*

den, *n.* tundu (la mnyama wa mwitu), kitundu, pango; (*hovel*) nyumba (au chumba) mbaya isiyofaa kukaa watu; (*of thieves*) pakutanapo wevi *&c.*; (*study*) chumba cha faragha cha kazi.

denationalize, *v.t.* ondoa cheo (au tabia) cha taifa lisiwe taifa tena; ondoa mtu katika taifa asiwe wa taifa lile au asifuate desturi (tabia) za taifa lile.

denaturalize, *v.t.* haribu tabia ya asili, geuza desturi za asili, ondoa haki ya mtu kuwa wa taifa (au nchi) fulani.

dengue, *n.* kidinga popo.

deniable, *a.*, **denial,** *n.* taz. *deny.*

denizen, *n.* mkaa mahali fulani, mkazi, mzalia.

denominate, *v.t.* taja, ita, -pa jina. **denomination,** *n.* (*name*) jina, (*class*) aina, namna, jinsi, jamii; (*sect*) madhehebu. **denominational,** *a.* -a madhehebu fulani, -enye mafundisho mbalimbali. **denominator,** *n.* kigawanyo.

denotation, *n.* taz. *denote.*

denote, *v.t.* onya, -wa ishara ya, -wa na maana fulani. **denotation,** *n.* maana, jina, alama.

denouement, *n.* mwisho wa hadithi (shauri, mfululizo wa mambo), mfumbuo wa fumbo (matatizo).

denounce, *v.t.* shtaki, suta, shutumu, laumu, nenea. **denunciation,** *n.* mashtaka, masuto, shutumu, lawama.

dense, *a.* -zito, -nene, -ingi, -liyosongamana; -gumu. **density,** *n.* uzito, unene.

dent, *v.t.* bonyeza. — *n.* kishimo, kibonyeo.

dental, *a.* -a meno. **dentate,** *a.* -a menomeno. **dentifrice,** *n.* dawa ya kusugulia meno. **dentist,** *n.* daktari wa meno. **dentition,** *n.* mpango wa meno; kuota meno. **denture,** *n.* meno, hasa yaliyofanyizwa ya kutumia badala ya meno ya asili.

denudation, *n.* taz. *denude.*

denude, *v.t.* funua, vulia nguo (mavazi) zote; komba mali, twalia, ondolea. *A country denuded of vegetation,* nchi iliyoondolewa mwitu na majani. **denudation,** *n.* kufanya wazi, hasa kukata mwitu wote na mvua kuchukua udongo mzuri wa juu na kuacha mawe mawe.

denunciation, *n.* taz. *denounce.*

deny, *v.t.* kana, kanisha, kaidi; (*refuse*) kataza; (*withhold*) nyima, hini. *Deny oneself,* jinyima, jihinisha, jikatalia; (*in order to achieve object*) kusuru. **deniable,** *a.* -a kukanika. **denial,** *n.* mkano, ukani; (*withholding*) mnyimo, kuhini, katazo.

deodorize, *v.t.* ondoa harufu. **deodorant,** *n.* dawa inayoondoa harufu mbaya.

depart, *v.i.* ondoka, toka, enda, fanya safari, shika njia, safiri; (*die*) fariki, -fa, shikwa na faradhi; (*alter*) badilika, geuka; (*forsake*) acha.

departed, *a.* (*dead*) marehemu, hayati. **departure**, *n.* kuondoka, kutoka, kuenda, safari. *A new departure*, jambo jipya, mwanzo.
department, *n.* sehemu, kazi, idara.
departure, *n.* taz. *depart.*
depend, *v.i.* (*on*) (*be connected with*) fungamana na, fuatana na, tungika na; (*rest on*) -wa mtoto wa (mfuasi wa, kazi ya, juu ya, chini ya), inamia, elekea; (*trust*) amini, tegemea, tumaini; (*be maintained by*) pata riziki kwa, kaa kwa, ponea. *Everything depends on you*, yote ni juu yako. *It depends*, labda, inategemea mambo yalivyo. **dependable**, *a.* -tumainifu, -a kutumainika. **dependence**, *n.* hali ya kutumainia au kufuatana na; hasa ni nchi iliyo chini ya himaya ya nchi nyingine. **dependent**, *n.* mfuasi, mtoto, mtumishi. — *a.* -a kufuatana na &c. taz. *depend*; -a kutegemea, -a kutumaini.
depict, *v.t.* andika (piga) picha au sanamu ya; eleza kwa maneno au maandiko, fafanua.
depilatory, *a.* -a kuondoa nywele, *n.* dawa ya kuondoa nywele.
deplete, *v.t.* ondolea vyote vilivyomo, fanya -tupu, punguza, maliza. **depletion**, *n.* kufanya (kufanyika) -tupu, upungufu, ukosekano.
deplorable, *a.* taz. *deplore.*
deplore, *v.t.* sikitikia, jutia, lilia. **deplorable**, *a.* -a kuhuzunisha, -a kusikitisha, -baya.
deploy, *v.t.* eneza, tanua (safu ya askari vitani); — *v.i.* enea.
deponent, *n.* shahidi.
depopulate, *v.t.* hamisha (punguza, angamiza) watu wa mahali. **depopulation**, *n.* upunguo (maangamizi) wa watu wa mahali.
deport, *v.t.* hamisha, fukuza, ondoa katika nchi; (*deport oneself*) jichukua, -wa na mwendo (wa kiburi, madaha &c.) **deportation**, *n.* uhamisho, ufukuzo, ondoleo la mtu katika nchi.
deportment, *n.* mwenendo, kikao, tabia.
depose, *v.t.* uzulu, ondosha, shusha; — *v.i.* (*give evidence*) shuhudia, toa ushuhuda. **deposition**, *n.* (*evidence*) ushuhuda, mathubuti; (*removal from office*) kuuzulu.
deposit, *v.t.* weka, toa, salimisha. — *n.* amana, arabuni, akiba, kitu kilichowekwa; rehani; (*sediment*) mashapo, takataka za chini (ya maji, mafuta &c.). **depository**, *n.* (*store*) ghala, bohari; (*guardian* &c.) mlinzi, mwenye kuwekewa kitu, mtunzi, mtunzaji.
deposition, *n.* taz. *depose.*
depository, *n.* taz. *deposit.*
depot, *n.* (*store*) ghala, bohari; (*military station*) kambi wanamofundishwa askari na kuwekewa zana na vyombo vya askari.
deprave, *v.t.* haribu tabia, geuza vibaya, potosha. **depraved**, *a* -baya, -ovu, -potovu, -potoe, fisadi fasiki. **depravity**, *n.* upotovu ufisadi, ufasiki, uovu.
deprecate, *v.t.* lalama, zuia, kwa maombi, ombea; (*disapprove*) kataza, kanya, tokubali; (*regret*) jutia. **deprecation**, *n.* lalamiko, uombezi; (*disapproval*) kanyo, katazo, mazuio. **deprecative**, *a.* -a kukanya, -a kukataza, -a kutokubali, -a kuzuia. **deprecatory**, *a.* taz. *deprecative.*
depreciate, *v.t.* rahisisha, punguza bei au thamani (kwa kutumia sana, kuchakaza &c.); (*disparage*) kashifu, singizia, umbua, vunja sifa (heshima, jina); — *v.i.* (*decline in value* &c.) punguka, rahisika, chakaa. **depreciation**, *n.* upunguzo (upunguo, upungufu) wa thamani (matumizi, manufaa); (*disparagement*) ukashifu; urahisi; (*allowance*) kipunguo (kwa ajili ya kutumika, kuchakaa). **depreciatory**, *a.* -a kupunguza (thamani, manufaa, matumizi), -a kurahisisha; -a kukashifu, -a kuvunja sifa (heshima, jina), -umbufu.
depredation, *n.* uharibifu, unyang'anyi, wivi, wizi. **depredator**, *n.* mharabu, mnyang'anyi, mwizi.
depress, *v.t.* (*lower*) inamisha,

shusha; (*weaken*) dhoofisha, punguza nguvu; (*make dejected*) huzunisha, sikitisha, legeza, kefyakefya. **depressing**, *a.* -a kuhuzunisha, -a kusikitisha, -a kutia majonzi, -a kuondoa furaha (uchangamshi *&c.*). **depression**, *n.* bonde, shimo, mvungu, mwinamo, kibonyeo; (*dejection*) huzuni, uzito, unyogovu, unyong'onyevu, majonzi; (*diminution*) upungufu, ulegevu.

deprivation, *n.* taz. *deprive*.

deprive, *v.t.* twalia, ondolea, nyima. **deprivation**, *n.* kutwaa, kutwaliwa; (*want, loss*) uhitaji, ukosekano, hasara.

dept, *n.* ufupisho wa *department*.

depth, *n.* taz. *deep*.

deputation, *n.* taz. *depute*.

depute, *v.t.* tuma, agiza, wakilisha, weka naibu (makamu). **deputation**, *n* agizo, ujumbe; (*person*) mjumbe, wajumbe. **deputize**, *v.i.* fanya badala ya mtu mwingine, -wa naibu (makamu). **deputy**, *n.* mjumbe, tume, wakili, naibu, makamu.

derail, *v.t.* ondosha (gari la moshi) katika reli zake.

derange, *v.t.* chafua, fuja, haribu, vunja; (*make mad*) tia kichaa (wazimu). **derangement**, *n.* machafuko, fujo, mavurugiko, uharibifu; (*madness*) wazimu, kichaa, upunguani wa akili.

derelict, *n.* mali (meli, chombo, mtu) iliyoachwa (iliyotupwa). — *a.* -liotupwa, -lioachwa. **dereliction**, *n.* kuacha (kuachwa), kutupa (kutupwa); kosa la kuacha au kutofanya kazi iliyopasa.

deride, *v.t.* cheka, dhihaki, fanyizia mzaha, dharau, bera, beua, beza. **derision**, *n.* mzaha, dhihaka, dharau, macheko. **derisive**, *a.* -a dhihaka, -a mzaha, -a kudharau, -a bure, -batili.

derivable, *a.*, **derivation**, *n.*, **derivative**, *n. and a.* taz. *derive*.

derive, *v.t.* pata, pokea. *Be derived from*, toka katika, tokana na, patikana kwa. *It is derived from . . .*, asili (mwanzo, chimbuko) yake ni . . . **derivable**, *a.* -a kupatikana, -a kujulikana, -a kutokana. **derivation**, *n.* (*origin*) asili, mwanzo, chimbuko; (*getting*) kupata. **derivative**, *n. and a.* kitu (neno, dawa) kisicho cha asili, kilichotokana na kingine.

derogate, *v.i.* punguza, toa sehemu katika, ondolea (uzuri, wema, tabia njema). **derogation**, *n.* punguzo (la cheo, heshima *&c.*), dhara. **derogatory**, *a.* -a kuaibisha, -enye aibu, -a kuvunja heshima (cheo *&c.*), -a kudharau, -a kuhasiri.

derrick, *n.* winchi, slingi, mashine ya kuinua vitu vizito, hasa katika meli.

dervish, *n.* derweshi, mtawa wa madhehebu fulani ya kiislamu.

descant, *v.i.* (*on*) toa maneno mengi juu ya, piga domo juu ya, semea sana.

descend, *v.i.* (*go or come down*) shuka, enda (-ja) chini, telemka; (*slope*) inama, telemka; (*of origin*) toka, tokana na, zaliwa, -wa katika ukoo wa . . .; (*of property, character &c.*) rithishwa (na); — *v.t.* (*descend upon*) angukia, shambulia, endea ghafula. *He is descended from a king*, yu mtoto wa mfalme, yu wa ukoo wa mfalme. **descendant**, *n.* mtoto, mzao. *Descendants*, watoto, wazao, dhuria. **descent**, *n.* mshuko, mtelemko, mwinamo; (*of origin*) nasaba, ukoo, jadi, kizazi, uzazi; (*raid*) shambulio, vita.

describe, *v.t.* eleza, toa habari, aridhia, simulia habari ya, hadithia, fafanua, wasifu. **description**, *n.* maelezo, habari, kisa, hadithi, maneno, sifa; (*kind*) jinsi, namna, aina, mfano. **descriptive**, *a.* -a kueleza, -a kusimulia habari, -a sifa, -a kuwasifu, -a kuainisha.

descry, *v.t.* ona, weza kuona (kwa mbali), chungulia, pata kuona, hisi, nabihi.

desecrate, *v.t.* kufuru, najisi, aibisha. **desecration**, *n.* ukufuru, makufuru, unajisi, kunajisi.

desert, (1) *n.* (*merit*) ustahili; (*reward*) thawabu; (*punishment*) adhabu, radà; (*what one deserves*) haki, stahili.

desert, (2) *v.t.* (*abandon*) acha, tupa; — *v.i.* (*run away*) toroka, kimbia; (*remove from*) hama. *A deserted* (*solitary*) *person*, mkiwa. *A deserted village*, mahame, ganjo, tongo.

desert, *n.* jangwa, nyika, ukiwa, pori, mahame. **deserter,** *n.* mtoro, mkimbizi, mhaini. **desertion,** *n.* utoro; (*abandonment*) kuacha, kutupa, mtupo; (*removal*) uhame; (*desolation*) ukiwa.

deserve, *v.t. and i.* stahili. *He deserves a beating*, ataka (amestahili) kupigwa. **deservedly,** *adv.* kama ilivyostahili, vyema, kwa haki. **deserving,** *a.* stahilifu, -enye sifa njema, -stahiki.

déshabille, *n.* taz. *dishabille.*

desiccate, *v.t.* kausha (na kufanya kama unga); — *v.i.* kauka kabisa.

desiderate, *v.t.* (*want*) taka sana, hitaji; (*regret*) jutia. **desideratum,** *n.* kitu kilichotakwa sana; hitaji, punguo, faradhi.

design, *v.t.* (*devise*) buni, vumbua, tunga, sanii, andika; (*trace out*) fanya (andika) shauri, tunga, rekabisha; (*intend*) kusudia, nia, azimia. *Design work*, toa kazi. — *n.* (*intention*) kusudi, mradi, shauri, nia, maarubu, madhumuni; (*sketch, pattern*) sanamu, kiolezo, kielelezo, namna, picha; (*plot*) hila, mtego.

designate, *v.t.* onyesha, taja, agiza; (*appoint*) chagua; (*denote*) -wa na maana fulani. — *a.* -liyechaguliwa. **designation,** *n.* jina, agizo, wonyesho; (*meaning*) maana. **designedly,** *adv.* makusudi. **designer,** *n.* mwandishi wa violezo vya kazi, mapambo &c.; mbuniji, mwongozi wa kazi; (*in bad sense*) mtunga mashauri yenye hila, mfitini. **designing,** *a.* -a hila, -erevu, -janja.

desirability, *n.*, **desirable,** *a.* taz. *desire.*

desire, *v.t.* taka, tamani, onea shauku; onea uchu; (*sexual*) ashiki, taka (*with obj. prefix*); (*request*) omba. — *n.* tamaa, uchu, shauku, hamu, hawa; (*need*) haja, matakwa, utashi, mapenzi, matilaba; (*sexual*) ashiki, shauku, ngoa. **desirability,** *n.* uzuri, ufao. **desirable,** *a.* -zuri, -a kupendeza, -a kutamanika, -a kutamanisha, -a kufaa. **desirous,** *a.* -enye kutaka (shauku, tamaa, uchu, ashiki &c.), -a kutamani.

desist, *v.i.* acha kufanya, koma, isha, tulia, nyamaza, hulu.

desk, *n.* meza (ya kuandikia), dawati, deski.

desolate, *v.t.* fanya ukiwa, haribu, vunja, kumba, teka; (*make sad &c.*) huzunisha, tia majonzi. — *a.* -a ukiwa, -a jangwa (nyika, pori); -liyoachwa, -liyotupwa; -enye huzuni (majonzi). **desolation,** *n.* kufanya (kufanyika) ukiwa, mkumbo, ukiwa; (*solitariness*) upweke, ukiwa.

despair, *v.i.* kata tamaa, -fa moyo, shindwa, tokuwa na tumaini. — *n.* ukosefu wa tumaini, kukata tamaa, kufa moyo. **desperado,** *n.* mjasiri aliye tayari kufanya lo lote (hasa mtu mwovu, katili, mshari). **desperate,** *a.* -enye kukata tamaa, bila tumaini, -a kufanya yo yote, -sioponyeka, -baya mno; (*dangerous*) -a hatari sana. *A desperate struggle*, shindano kali sana. **desperation,** *n.* taz. *despair.*

despatch, *v.t.* taz. *dispatch.*

desperado, *n.*, **desperate,** *a.*, **desperation,** *n.* taz. *despair.*

despicable, *a.* taz. *despise.*

despise, *v.t.* tweza, dharau, hizi, hakiri, nyarafu, kirihi, mena, turufu. **despicable,** *n.* -nyonge, hafifu, -baya.

despite, *n.* *In despite of his wishes* (*efforts, opposition &c.*), ijapokuwa hataki (hakubali, hapendi &c.).

despoil, *v.t.* nyang'anya, tekea, twalia, chukulia. **despoilation,** *n.* kunyang'anya, unyang'anyi.

despond, *v.i.* kata tamaa, -fa moyo, vunjikiwa, shindwa moyo, legea.

despondence, *n.* kukata tamaa, kufa moyo, majonzi, uzito. **despondent,** *a.* -a kukata tamaa, -a kushindwa moyo, bila tumaini (ushujaa, wepesi wa moyo), -zito.

despot, *n.* mtawala peke yake (pasipo baraza wala shauri la watu), sultani, bwana; (*tyrant*) mdhalimu. *Play the despot, act despotically,* piga ubwana, fanya jeuri, dhulumu. **despotic,** *a.* **despotical,** *a.* -enye nguvu peke yake; -dhalimu, -jeuri. **despotism,** *n.* hali au utawala wa *despot*; udhalimu, jeuri.

dessert, *n.* matunda, maandazi *&c.* mwisho wa kula kizungu (yaani chakula cha kumalizia).

destination, *n.* taz. *destine.*

destine, *v.t.* weka (chagua, agiza) kwa hali au kazi au mahali fulani. *This is destined for Zanzibar,* hii inakwenda Unguja. *He is destined for the army,* anakusudiwa kuwa askari. *You are destined to die,* ajali yako (mwisho wako) utakufa. **destination,** *n.* mahali mtu (au kitu) anapopelekwa, au anapokusudia kufika, mwisho wa (kikomo cha) safari. **destiny,** *n.* ajali, tua, Mungu; (*fortune, condition*) hali, maisha, mambo.

destitute, *a.* -kiwa, maskini, fukara, pasipo, *e.g. destitute of clothes* (*trees, water &c.*) pasipo nguo (miti, maji *&c.*). **destitution,** *n.* ufakiri, ufukara, umaskini, uhitaji, ukiwa.

destroy, *v.t.* haribu, vunja, angamiza, avya, teketeza, maliza, umbua, ua, batili. **destroyer,** *n.* mharabu, mwangamizi hasa namna ya manowari. **destruction,** *n.* kuharibu (kuvunja, kuangamiza *&c.*), uharibifu, upotevu, maangamizi, mauaji. **destructive,** *a.* -a kuharibu, -a kuua, -a shari, -harabu, -haribifu. **destructiveness,** *n.* uharibifu, upotevu.

desuetude, *n.* kutotumika, kubatilika. *To fall into desuetude,* kubatilika, kutotumika, kufa, kuisha.

desultory, *a.* -badilifu, -siyo na taratibu, -geugeu, -siyoendelea mfululizo, -siyo na maana sana, -a kuchezacheza.

detach, *v.t.* tenga, kata, toa, vunja, bandua. **detachment,** *n.* mtengo, mabanduko; (*of soldiers*) kikosi; (*impartiality*) uadilifu, hali (tabia) ya kutokuvutwa na maneno ya watu; (*aloofness*) ukinaifu.

detail, *v.t.* simulia habari yote; tuma (agiza, amuru) kufanya kazi maalum. — *n.* habari (ya mambo moja moja, hata yaliyo madogo), habari zote, kila kitu. *In detail,* moja moja, yote pia, kinaganaga.

detain, *v.t.* kawisha, chelewesha, shindisha, faitisha, zuia, funga. **detention,** *n.* kuzuia, kuzuiwa, uzuio, uzuizi, kukawilishwa, kufungwa, kifungo.

detect, *v.t.* vumbua, gundua, ona. **detection,** *n.* kugundua, kugundulìwa, upelelezi. **detective,** *n.* mpelelezi (polisi), askari kanzu, jasusi.

detention, *n.* taz. *detain.*

deter, *v.t.* kataza, ogofya, zuia (kwa kutia shaka, hofu). **deterrent,** *n.* shaka, ogofyo, linalozuia (kwa kutia shaka, hofu). — *a.* -zuifu, -a shaka, -a kutisha.

deteriorate, *v.t.* punguza thamani (manufaa, matumizi); — *v.i.* pungua thamani, haribika, chakaa, punguka, kwajuka. **deterioration,** *n.* uharibifu, upunguo wa thamani (manufaa, matumizi), uchakao.

determinate, *a.*, **determinately,** *adv.*, **determination,** *n.*, **determinative,** *a.* taz. *determine.*

determine, *v.t.* (*limit, define*) weka mpaka, kaza, onyesha, dhihirisha, ainisha, yakinisha; (*fix beforehand*) weka (miadi, tarehe); (*settle, decide*) amua, kata maneno, maliza; (*prescribe*) amuru, shurutisha, lazimisha, kusudisha; — *v.i.* (*resolve*) yakinia, azimu, kusudia, ukilia; (*end*) isha. **determinate,** *a.* thabiti, maalum, -dhahiri, mkataa. **determinately,** *adv.* imara, thabiti, barabara, -siyosita *&c.* **determination,** *n.* (*resolve*)

kusudi, nia, shauri; (*resoluteness*) uthabiti, bidii, ushupavu, ugumu. **determinative,** *a.* -a kudhihirisha, -a kushurutisha, -a kuyakinisha. **determined,** *a.* imara, thabiti, dhahiri, hodari, -shupavu, -gumu, -tendaji, -enye nia thabiti.
deterrent, *n. and a.* taz. *deter*.
detest, *v.t.* chukia sana, kirihi, zia. **detestable,** *a.* -a kuchukiza, makuruhi. **detestation,** *n.* machukio makuu, karaha, kirahi.
dethrone, *v.t.* uzulu, ondoa (mfalme). **dethronement,** *n.* kuuzulu.
detonate, *v.t.* pasua kwa mshindo (*e.g.* baruti, fataki *&c.*); — *v.i.* pasuka kwa mshindo. **detonation,** *n.* mshindo (wa baruti kupasuka, wa bunduki, wa mzinga, wa fataki *&c.*).
detour, *n.* kipengee, njia ya kuzunguka. *Make a detour,* zunguka.
detract, *v.t.* ondoa sehemu, toa; (*slander*) umbua, punguza sifa, chongea; (*lessen value*) rahisisha, **detraction,** *n.* mpunguo wa sifa (thamani) masingizio, uchongezi. **detractor,** *n.* msingizia, mchongezi.
detriment, *n.* hasara, madhara. **detrimental,** *a.* -a kutia hasara, -a kudhuru.
deuce, *n.* karata au upande wa dadu wenye ng'anda mbili; (*the devil*) shetani, ibilis..
Deuteronomy, *n.* kitabu cha tano cha Nabii Musa, Kumbukumbu ya Torati.
devastate, *v.t.* teka, kumba, haribu, teketeza. **devastation,** *n.* kuteka, kutekwa; teketeo, teketezo; kumbo, mkumbo, uharibifu.
develop, *v.t.* (*augment*) endeleza, endesha, sitawisha, kuza, fanikisha; (*a film &c.*) tia dawa ili kutokeza picha; (*explain*) funua, eleza; — *v.i.* (*grow*) kua, endelea, funuka, dhihirika; (*quickly*) vuvumka. **development,** *n.* maendeleo, kukua, usitawi; (*explanation*) ufunuo; (*addition*) mazidio.
deviate, *v.i.* enda upande, toka (acha) njia, potoka, kosa. **deviation,** *n.* kwenda upande, kipengee; (*error*) upotovu, kosa.
device, *n.* taz. *devise*.
devil, *n.* shetani, ibilisi. *A poor devil,* maskini, fukara. **devilish,** *a.* kama shetani, -baya mno, -ovu sana. **devilry,** *n.* ushetani, ubilisi, ukatili, uovu.
devious, *a.* -potovu, -enye vipengee, -a kuzunguka, -a vizingo vingi.
devise, *v.t.* fanya (tafuta, vumbua, tunga, zaa, waza, buni) shauri (hila, werevu, njia *&c.*). *Devise to,* wakifia, usia, rithisha. **device,** *n.* shauri, hila, njia (ya kufanya); (*contrivance*) chombo, ala, sanaa, kitu; (*emblem*) chapa, alama, sanamu, picha. *Full of devices,* -enye mashauri (hila, vipengee) mengi. *Follow your own devices,* fuata yako (shika lako).
devitalize, *v.t.* ondoa uzuri (uhai, nguvu), dhoofisha.
devoid, *a.* (*of*), -tovu, pasipo, bila, *&c. He is devoid of sense* (*fear, shame &c.*), hana akili (hofu, haya *&c.*), mtovu wa akili (hofu *&c.*). *A country devoid of inhabitants,* nchi isiyo na (pasipo na, pasina) watu.
devolve, *v.t.* (*on*) tolea, -pa, wakilisha (kazi, madaraka *&c.*); — *v.i.* (*upon*) jia, pata, pasa. *It devolved upon me to bury him,* ilikuwa juu yangu (ilinipasa) kumzika.
devote, *v.t.* toa, wakifu, funga. *Devote oneself,* jifunga, jitia, jiweka. **devoted,** *a.* -enye bidii, -a kushika kazi kwa moyo, -aminifu, -a kupenda sana; (*victim*) -liolaaniwa, -a kupotea, maskini. *Be devoted to* (*work &c.*) shiriki, shika sana (kazi *&c.*). *Devoted to good works,* tengwa kwa mambo mema. **devotee,** *n.* mtawa, sufii, walii. **devotion,** *n.* (*religious*) ibada, sala; moyo wa ibada (wa dini, wa kumwabudu Mungu); (*earnestness*) upendo, bidii, moyo; (*application*) kujifunga, kushiriki. **devotional,** *a.* -a ibada, -a dini, -a kuonyesha ibada, -a kuamsha fikara njema za ibada. **devout,** *a.* -a

kumcha Mungu, -chaji, -a ibada, -a bidii, -a kushika dini, -tawa. *A devout person,* mcha Mungu, mtu wa dini.

devour, *v.t.* -la, meza; (*as a wild beast*) tafuna, nyafua; (*greedily*) -la kwa pupa, lafua; (*destroy*) teketeza, angamiza; (*a book*) soma kwa bidii; (*gaze*) angazia macho, kazia macho.

devout, *a.* taz. *devote.*

dew, *n.* umande. **dewlap,** *n.* ngozi inayoning'inia chini ya shingo ya ng'ombe, refurefu, dehedehe. **dewy,** *a.* -enye umande.

dexterity, *n.* ustadi, ubingwa, umahiri, wepesi, welekevu. **dexterous, dextrous,** *a.* -stadi, mahiri, -epesi, -elekevu wa kazi, hodari, bingwa.

dhow, *n.* jahazi, chombo.

diabolic, diabolical, *a.* -a shetani, -a ibilisi, -ovu sana, -baya sana, -katili.

diadem, *n.* taji.

diagnose, *v.t.* pima, yakinisha ugonjwa &c. kwa hali na dalili zilizopo. **diagnosis,** *n.* uchunguzi na yakini ya ugonjwa (jambo) kwa hali na mambo yalivyo, ujuzi wa ugonjwa na dalili zake.

diagonal, *a.* -a kutoka pembe mpaka pembe iliyoielekea, -a kukata mraba pembe kwa pembe, -a mshazari, -a hanamu. — *n.* mstari wa kutoka pembe ya mraba (au mstatili) mpaka pembe inayoielekea.

diagram, *n.* picha (sanamu) ya kufundishia, kiolezo, kielelezo, mfano.

dial, *n.* uliao wa kuonyeshea saa ngapi kwa kivuli cha jua; bamba la uso wa saa.

dialect, *n.* lugha, maneno, namna ya kunena, matamko. *Dialect of Zanzibar,* Kiunguja. **dialectic,** *a.* -a lugha.

dialectic, *n.* elimu ya kuhoji mambo kwa majibizano au majadiliano (ya kupata ukweli kwa kusemezana kwa akili, ya kutoa hoja vyema au kujadiliana).

dialogue, *n.* mazungumzo, maneno, maandiko yaliyotungwa kama kwamba watu wanasemezana.

diameter, *n.* mstari ulionyoka unaopita kati hasa ya duara, kipenyo.

diametrically, *adv.* kabisa, halisi, sawasawa, *e.g. be diametrically opposite,* elekea sawasawa kabisa, -wa kinyume kabisa.

diamond, *n.* almasi. — *a.* kama almasi, -a almasi. *In playing cards,* uru.

diapason, *n.* sauti zote za wimbo zimelingana; sauti zote za mtu (kuimba), za kinanda, za zomari &c. toka chini hata juu; mshindo mzuri wa muziki.

diaphanous, *a.* -a kupenya nuru, -angavu, -a kuona.

diaphragm, *n.* kiwambo (cha moyo, ngoma, sikio &c.).

diarrhoea, *n.* tumbo la kuendesha (la kuhara).

diary, *n.* kitabu chenye habari za mambo ya kila siku taratibu, habari za kila siku, tarehe.

diatribe, *n.* maneno (hotuba) yaliyojaa lawama (makaripio, makemeo, matusi &c.).

dibber, dibble, *n.* mwuo, kijiti cha kufanyia makoongo ya kupandia mbegu. — *v.t.* panda mbegu kwa mwuo.

dice, *n. pl.* ya *die.* **dice-box,** *n.* kikombe cha (kopo la) kuchezea dadu.

dichotomy, *n.* mgawo wa sehemu mbili.

dicky, dickey, *n.* kiti cha tatu nyuma ya motakaa yenye viti viwili mbele.

dicky-bird, *n.* ndege (usemi wa kitoto).

dictate, *v.t.* (*read aloud*) soma wazi; (*cause to write*) andikisha; (*declare*) onyesha, tangaza, amuru; (*order*) nena (amuru) vikali. *Dictate to,* somea; (*direct*) amuru. — *n.* maneno, maonyo, amri. **dictation,** *n.* kuandikisha, imla; (*orders*) amri nzito, maonyo makali. *I will not submit to dictation,* sitaki kuamriwa, sikubali kutii amri, siambiliki mimi, **dictator,** *n.* mwenye amri peke yake, mtawala wa peke yake, sultani. **dictatorial,** *a.* -a kutoa amri na kushurutisha watu kuzitii, -a kutiisha, -gumu, -kali. **dictatorship,** *n.* utawalaji wa *dictator,* usultani. **diction,** *n.* usemi, jinsi ya kusema. **dictionary,** *n.* kamusi. **dictum,** *n.* neno kubwa, fumbo, neno la maana, neno la amri.

did, *p.t.* ya *do.*

didactic, *a.* -a kufundisha, -a kujulisha, -a kuadilisha.

die, (1) *n.* (*pl. dice*) dadu; (*pl. dies*) chapa ya chuma ya kupigia chapa sarafu, nishani, karatasi *&c. To play with dice,* kucheza dadu. *The die is cast,* shauri limekwisha, jambo limekatika.

die (2), *v.i.* -fa, fariki, kata roho, salimika, salimisha roho; (*fail, cease*) isha, fifia, legea, koma. *Die away, die out,* fifia, zimia, pungukapunguka, toweka. *Die outright* (*on the spot*), -fa fofofo. *Die natural death,* -fa kibudu, -fa upinda. **dying,** *n.* kufa, kifo. — *a.* -a kufa, -a kufani.

diet, (1) *n.* baraza, mkutano.

diet, (2) *n.* chakula, ulaji, maakuli. — *v.t.* gunga, zia, shika mwiko. **dietary,** *n.* ulaji, taratibu (kawaida) ya vyakula vya kila siku, posho; (*prescribed*) mwiko, mzio, ugunga. **dietetics,** *n.* elimu ya kupambanua vyakula na jinsi vinavyohusiana na afya ya mwili.

differ, *v.i.* (*be different*) hitilafiana, -wa mbalimbali (namna nyingine), achana, kosana, topatana; (*think differently*) tokubali, ona sivyo. **difference,** *n.* tofauti, hitilafu, hali ya kuwa mbalimbali; (*quarrel*) ugomvi, mateto, shindano. **different,** *a.* mbalimbali, si sawa, si mamoja, -ingine. **differential,** *n.* (*gear*) mtambo unaowezesha magurudumu ya nyuma ya motakaa yaachane kwa mwendo mahali inapopinda. **differentiate,** *v.t.* pambanua, ainisha, tofautisha; — *v.i.* achana, hitilafiana. **differently,** *adv.* kwa jinsi nyingine, kwa jinsi isiyo sawa.

difficult, *a.* -gumu, -zito, -a shida, -a mashaka, -a fumbo. **difficulty,** *n.* shida, matata, dhiki, uzito, ugumu, kizuio, udhia, kingo, mgogoro, janga, kayaya. *Be in difficulties,* -wa na shida *&c.,* dhikika, zidiwa. *Get oneself into difficulties,* jifunga.

diffidence, *n.* taz. *diffident.*

diffident, *a.* -oga, -enye haya, -a shaka. *He is diffident of his powers,* hajiegemei nafsi. **diffidence,** *n.* haya, woga, mashaka.

diffuse, *v.t.* toa, eneza, tawanya. — *a.* -a maneno mengi. **diffusely,** *adv.* kwa kueneza; kwa maneno mengi. **diffusion,** *n.* eneo, enezo. **diffusive,** *a.* -a kuenea, -a kueneza.

dig, *v.t.* (*p.t. and pf.t.* **dug, digged**) chimba (udongo, mfereji, handaki *&c*), chimbua (muhogo, viazi *&c.*), lima (shamba), checha, omoa (udongo). — *v.i.* chimba, chimbua, lima. *Dig up, out,* chimbua, fukua. *Dig in* (*cover by digging*) fukia; (*thrust in*) ingiza, choma, chomeka, tumbukiza. **digging,** *n.* chimbo, mahali pa kuchimba.

digest, *v.t.* badili (yeyusha) chakula kinywani na matumboni ili kifae kuchukuliwa na damu mwilini; (*consider*) fikiri, fahamu; (*bear with*) vumilia; *v.i.* yeyuka (badilika, pokewa, nywewa) tumboni. *I cannot digest this food, This food is indigestible,* chakula hiki hakitulii tumboni, tumbo halikiweki. — *n.* muhtasari, mafupisho, ufupisho, matengenezo. **digestible,** -a kutulia tumboni. **digestion,** *n.* uwezo wa kubadili chakula kifae mwilini, (kazi ya) tumbo. **digestive,** *a.* -a kutuliza (au kutulia) tumboni.

digging, *n.* taz. *dig.*

digit, *n.* kidole; tarakimu.

dignified, *a.* taz. *dignify.*

dignify, *v.t.* tukuza, heshimu, zidisha heshima, adhimisha. **dignified,** *a.* -a heshima, -a adabu, makini, -adhimu. **dignitary**, *n.* mkuu, mkubwa, mwenye cheo (daraja) kikuu. **dignity**, *n.* heshima, adabu, makini, jaha, adhama; (*greatness*) ukuu, ubora; (*rank*) daraja, cheo.

digress, *v.i.* potoka, potea; acha kwa kitambo habari inayosemwa (au kuandikwa) na kushika vingine, zunguka. **digression**, *n.* mzunguko, kupotea, kuacha kwa kitambo habari inayosemwa (au kuandikwa) na kushika vingine.

dike, *n.* handaki, mfereji; (*embankment*) boma (la kuzuia maji yasienee yakifurika.

dikkop, *n.* chekea mwezi.

dilapidate, *v.t.* haribu, chakaza; — *v.i.* haribika, chakaa. **dilapidated**, *a.* -bovu, -gofu, goigoi. **dilapidation**, *n.* uharibifu, uchakavu, ugofu, ugoigoi.

dilate, *v.t.* tanua, panua, vimbisha, kubaza; — *v.i.* tanuka, panuka, vimba. *Dilate upon a subject*, sema (andika) maneno mengi juu ya jambo. **dilatation**, *n.* mtanuo, mpanuo, uvimbe, kivimbe; mtanuko, upanuko.

dilatory, *a.* (*slow, idle*) -vivu, -zembe, si -epesi, si -tendaji; (*delaying*) -a kukawia, -a kuchelewa, -a kukawilisha, -a kuweka, -a kuchelewesha.

dilemma, *n.* mashaka (hasa ya kuchagua moja katika mawili na yote ni mabaya au ya shida). *You are on the horns of a dilemma*, huna budi kuchagua, ukipenda usipende.

dilettante, *n.* mpenda sanaa (asiyejua sana habari zake); kijoyojoyo.

diligence, *n.* taz. *diligent.*

diligent, *a.* -enye bidii, -tendaji, -a kazi, -angalifu, -enye juhudi, -a kushika kazi, -a kubiabia. **diligence**, *n.* bidii, utendaji, uangalifu, jitihada, juhudi, jadi. **diligently**, *adv.* kwa uangalifu, kwa bidii, kwa juhudi &c.

dilly-dally, *v.i.* sitasita, chezacheza, poteza wakati.

dilute, *v.t.* zimua; fifisha; (*adulterate*) ghoshi; (*weaken*) punguza nguvu. — *a.* -liyozimuliwa, -liyofifia &c.

dilution, *n.* mchanganyo au mchanganyiko (wa kuzimua au kuzimuliwa au kupunguza nguvu, ukali, maana &c.).

dim, *v.t.* tia giza, fifisha; — *v.i.* ingia giza, fifia. — *a.* (*of light*) -a giza kidogo, -a utusitusi, -siyo na mwangaza mwingi; (*indistinct*) si dhahiri, -sioonekana vizuri, -a unyenyezi; (*of sounds*) -siosikilikana vizuri; (*of ideas &c.*) si dhahiri; -liofifia. *I have a dim idea*, nafahamu kidogo tu. *His eyes are dim*, macho yake yameingia giza (tandabui). **dimness**, *n.* giza, utusitusi.

dimension, *n.* ukubwa, kadiri, cheo, kimo, urefu, upana, eneo, kivimbe.

diminish, *v.t.* punguza; — *v.i.* pungua, punguka. **diminution**, *n.* mpunguo, mpunguzo, kipunguo. **diminutive**, *a.* -dogo sana.

dimple, *n.* kifinyo au kishimo kidogo, hasa katika shavu la uso au kidevu. — *v.t. and i.* fanya vifinyo (vishimo, vikunjo); *e.g.* juu ya maji, usoni mtu achekapo &c.

din, *n.* makelele, mshindo, ghasia. — *v.i.* fanya kelele (mshindo, ghasia); — *v.t.* chagiza (kumwambia mtu yale yale tena na tena mpaka achoke).

dine, *v.i.* -la chakula kikubwa cha kutwa (ama mchana ama usiku); — *v.t.* karibisha kwenye chakula hicho; weka chakulani, *e.g. this table dines six people*, meza hii yatosha (yaweka) watu sita chakulani. **dining-room**, *n.* chumba cha kulia, mezani. **dinner**, *n.* chakula kikubwa cha kutwa.

ding-dong, *n.* mlio wa kengele au mlio uliofanana nao.

dinghy, *n.*, **dingey**, *n.* mashua ndogo.

dingle, *n.* kibonde, hasa chenye uvuli wa miti.

dingy, *a.* -chafu, -siong'aa, -liyofifia, -liokwajuka, -enye taka, si nadhifu, -eusi, -enye gizagiza.

dining-room, *n.*, **dinner**, *n.* taz. *dine.*

dint, *n.* kishimo, kibonyeo; nguvu, ajili, *e.g. by dint of good luck*, kwa nguvu (ajili, sababu) ya bahati.

diocese, *n.* jimbo la askofu. **diocesan**, *n.* askofu. — *a.* -a jimbo la askofu.

dip, *v.t.* chovya, zamisha; chovya kitambaa katika rangi; ogesha (kondoo, ng'ombe *&c.*) kwa dawa; telemsha na kupandisha tena upesi; *e.g. dip a flag* (bendera); — *v.i.* inama, nepa, enda chini, telemka kidogo. *Dip into*, onja (soma, chungua, tazama) kidogo. — *n.* mchovyo, mzamo; dawa ya kuogeshea kondoo *&c.*; mwinamo, mtelemko.

diphtheria, *n.* ugonjwa mbaya wa koo ndani wa kuambukiza.

diphthong, *n.* vokali (*vowels*) mbili zinazotamkwa kama kwamba ni moja tu, *e.g.* au.

diploma, *n.* hati ya sifa, hati ya cheo, shuhuda.

diplomacy, *n.* maarifa ya ujumbe (hasa kati ya taifa na mataifa mengine); upatanishi, usuluhishi; (*cunning*) werevu, ujanja. **diplomat**, *n.* mjumbe wa serikali (hasa kati ya taifa na mataifa mengine); mpatanishi, msuluhishi. **diplomatic**, *a.* -a ujumbe, -patanishi, -suluhivu; (*cunning*) -erevu, -janja.

dipper, *n.* kata, sila, ndau, upo, mdila, ndoo, chombo cha kuchotea maji.

dipsomania, *n.* shauku (tamaa, uchu, wazimu) ya ulevi. **dipsomaniac**, *n.* mtu mwenye wazimu (tamaa, uchu *&c.*) wa kutaka ulevi.

diptera, *n.* jamii ya wadudu wenye mabawa mawili tu, kama inzi. **dipterous**, *a.* -enye mabawa mawili.

dire, *a.* -a kutisha, -a kuogofya, -enye misiba, -baya. **direful**, *a.* kama *dire.*

direct, *v.t.* ongoza, elekeza, nyosha, rekebisha, simamia; (*order*) amuru, agiza; (*a letter*) andika (tia) anwani. *Direct attention to*, angalia, tazama; onyesha, angaliza, tazamisha. — *a.* -nyofu, barabara, sawasawa, halisi. *Direct road*, njia moja kwa moja.

direction, *n.* (*course*) majira, njia, uelekeo, mwendo; (*order*) agizo, amri, fundisho, usia; (*superintendence*) uongozi, usimamizi; (*address*) anwani (ya barua); (*information &c.*) maelezo. *In the direction of*, upande wa. **directly**, *adv.* (*at once*) mara, mara moja, sasa hivi; (*presently*) halafu, baadaye kidogo; (*plainly*) wazi, halisi, sawasawa, barabara.

director, *n.* mwongozi, msimamizi, mwelekezi, mkuu, mkurugenzi

directory, *n.* kitabu chenye majina, anwani, kazi na habari nyinginezo za watu wa mtaa (mji *&c.*).

direful, *a.* taz. *dire.*

dirge, *n.* maombolezo, wimbo wa huzuni, wimbo wa maziko; (*Moslem*) tahlili.

dirt, *n.* uchafu wa namna yo yote (kinyesi, matope, taka); udongo, kifusi; kitu cho chote kilicho duni, kisicho na thamani. *Cheap as dirt*, rahisi sana. *Treat a person like dirt*, dharau mtu. *Eat dirt*, jinyenyekea sana. **dirty**, *a.* -a taka, -chafu; (*of weather*) -a mvua na upepo mwingi. **dirty**, *v.t.* tia taka, fanya kuwa chafu.

dis- (hutiwa mwanzo wa maneno mengi, na maana yake ni 'si' au hugeuza maana kuwa kinyume kabisa).

disable, *v.t.* dhoofisha, vunja, ondolea nguvu, shinda, weza, lemaza. **disability**, *n.* udhaifu, upunguani, utovu wa nguvu. *Be under a disability*, -wa na punguani. **disablement**, *n.* kama *disability*, hasa udhaifu, kilema.

disabuse, *v.t.* ondolea kosa (ujinga), arifu ukweli (sahihi, hakika), erevusha.

disadvantage, *n.* zuio, matata, upungufu, madhara, hasara, udhaifu. **disadvantageous**, *a.* -zuifu, -a hasara, -a kutofaa.

disaffected, *a.* -a kuchukizwa, -a kutaka maasi, -a uadui. **disaffection,** *n.* chuki, uchungu, ununi, uadi, ukimwa.

disagree, *v.i.* gombana, tetana, bishana, kosana, topatana; (*of food*) totulia tumboni, chafua, dhuru, (*repeat or nauseate &c.*) puzia. *This food disagrees with me,* chakula hiki kinaninuka. **disagreeable,** *a.* (*of persons*) -chungu, -gumu, -enye chuki, -enye nongwa; (*annoying*) -a udhia, -sumbufu; (*unpleasant*), -a kuchukiza, -a kuudhi, -sumbufu. **disagreement,** *n.* ugomvi, hali mbali, kutopatana, tofauti.

disallow, *v.t.* kataza, tokutoa idhini, tokubali; (*reject*) kanusha.

disappear, *v.i.* toweka, tokomea, toka, enda zake, didimia, fifia; (*comes to an end*) isha, koma, potea. **disappearance,** *n.* kutoweka, kuondoka; (*conclusion*) mwisho.

disappoint, *v.t.* tofanya iliyotumainiwa; totekeleza ahadi; topendeza, tia uchungu, chukiza; (*thwart*) zuia, pinga, batilisha. **disappointed,** *a. Be disappointed,* topata (yaliyotumainiwa, yaliyotazamiwa, yaliyoahidiwa &c.), zuiwa, pingwa, udhika. **disappointment,** *n.* uchungu, udhiko, chukizo; (*failure*) hasara, kutofanikiwa.

disapprobation, *n.*, **disapproval,** *n.* taz. *disapprove.*

disapprove, *v.i.* tokubali, toridhia, topenda, kataa; — *v.t.* chukiwa na. **disapproval, disapprobation,** *n.* lawama, katazo.

disarm, *v.t.* ondolea (twalia, chukulia) silaha; (*subdue, quiet*) tiisha, tuliza, patanisha, suluhisha; — *v.i.* punguza silaha za vita &c. **disarmament,** *n.* mpunguo (mpunguzo) wa silaha za vita za taifa, nchi, manowari &c.

disarrange, *v.t.* chafua, fuja, tungua. **disarrangement,** *n.* uchafuko, machafuko, fujo.

disarray, *v.t.* chafua, fuja. — *n.* uchafuko, fujo.

disaster, *n.* msiba, hasara, teketezo, afa, maafa, baa, masaibu, maangamizo, taabu. **disastrous,** *a.* -a msiba, -a hasara, -a taabu, -a maafa.

disavow, *v.t.* kana, kania, kataa. **disavowal,** *n.* mkano, mkatao, kukania.

disband, *v.t.* vunja (jeshi), changua, tawanya, likiza; — *v.i.* fumukana, tawanyika, changukana. **disbandment,** *n.* mlikizo (wa jeshi), mtawanyo; mtawanyiko, fumukano.

disbelief, *a.* taz. *disbelieve.*

disbelieve, *v.t. and i.* tosadiki, toamini. **disbelief,** *n.* kutoamini, kutosadiki, ukosefu (ukosekano) wa imani. **disbeliever,** *n.* asiyeamini, mkosefu (mtovu) wa imani.

disburden, *v.t.* ondolea mzigo, tuliza.

disburse, *v.t. and i.* toa (fedha), lipa. **disbursement,** *n.* lipo, gharama.

disc, *n.* taz. *disk.*

discard, *v.t.* tupa, ondosha, kataa, beua.

discern, *v.t.* ona, fahamu, tambua, pambanua, hisi, nabihi, maizi. **discernible,** *a.* -a kuonekana (fahamikana, tambulikana, pambanulikana). **discerning,** *a.* -a akili, -juzi, -chaguzi. **discernment,** *n.* busara, akili, utambuzi, ufahamivu, uchaguzi.

discharge, *v.t.* (*dismiss*) ondosha, toa (katika kazi); (*put out*) toa, toka, foka, fuka; (*let off*) piga, fyatua (bunduki &c.), tupa (mshale &c.); (*release*) fungua, ruhusu, feleti; (*unload*) shusha, telemsha (shehena &c.); (*pay*) lipa (deni &c.); (*from an obligation*) feleti, tangua; (*execute, fulfil*) fanya, fanyiza, timiza, tekeleza. — *n.* kuondosha, kutoa &c. (*of firearm &c.*) mshindo, kishindo; (*from an abcess &c.*) usaha; (*liberation*) ruhusa.

disciple, *n.* mwanafunzi, mfuasi, mtoto. **disciplinarian,** *n.* mtiisha, mtoa amri nyingi, mshikisha utaratibu na utii, mgumu. **disciplinary,** *a.* -a kurudi, -a kuadilisha, -a kuongoza, -a kutiisha. **discipline,** *n.*

(*educational*) malezi, maongozi, marudi; (*of pupil*) utii, usikizi, usikivu; (*of teacher*) utawala; (*moral*) maadili; (*drill*) taratibu, amri moja; (*trial*) jaribu. — *v.t.* rudi, tiisha, ongoza, adilisha, tawala.

disclaim, *v.t.* kana, kania, kataa, kanusha.

disclose, *v.t.* funua, onyesha, dhihirisha, vumbua, fumua. **disclosure**, *n.* ufunuo, mafunuo, mambo yaliyofunuliwa, uvumbuzi, wonyesho.

discolour, *v.t.* geuza (haribu) rangi; — *v.i.* geuka (haribika) rangi, kwajuka.

discomfit, *v.t.* fadhaisha, pumbaza, bumbuaza, tahayarisha; (*baffle*) vunja, batilisha; (*rout*) piga, shinda. **discomfiture**, *n.* fadhaa, mashaka, haya, bumbuazi; (*defeat*) kupigwa, kushindwa, ushinde; (*prostration*) ubatilisho.

discomfort, *v.t.* sumbua, udhi, taabisha, kalifu, kera. — *n.* udhia, masumbuo, taabu, maumivu, kero, hali isiyo na raha, adha, utakalifu.

discommode, *v.t.* sumbua, udhi, taabisha.

discompose, *v.t.* (*vex*) chukiza, sumbua, udhi, harakisha, hamanisha, tia wasiwasi; (*disarrange*) chafua, fuja, vuruga. **discomposure**, *n.* wasiwasi, fadhaa, maudhiko, machafuko, haraka, hamaniko.

disconcert, *v.t.* taz. *discompose*. **disconcertment**, *n.* taz. *discomposure*.

disconnect, *v.t.* tenga, fungua, tungua, kata, achanisha, ungua. **disconnected**, *a.* -a kutengwa (funguliwa, katwa &c.); (*of thought &c.*) -siofungamana vizuri, -siofuatana barabara.

disconsolate, *a.* -enye huzuni (majonzi, sikitiko), -zito, -siofarijika, -sio na faraja.

discontent, discontentment, *n.* uchungu, (ukosefu) wa ridhaa, chuki, manung'uniko. *Show discontent*, guna, nuna, nung'unika. **discontented**, *a.* -enye chuki (uchungu), -a kutokuridhika.

discontinuance, *n.* taz. *discontinue*.

discontinue, *v.t.* acha, komesha, kataza; — *v.i.* isha, hulu. **discontinuance**, *n.* mwisho, ukomo, kikomo, kituo. **discontinuous**, *a.* -a kukatikakatika, -siyofuatana moja kwa moja, -enye nafasi katikati.

discord, discordance, *n.* -a kutopatana, -enye mashauri (nia, maono, sauti &c.) yasiyopatana (ya mbalimbali); (*quarrel*) ugomvi, fitina, fii, sabasi, mabishano; (*in music*) sauti zisizolingana. **discordant**, *a.* -a kutopatana, -a kutolingana, -siyopendeza, -a kuchukiza, -baya, -siyo barabara.

discount, *n.* mshusho wa bei (thamani), kipunguzi (cha bei kwa sababu ya kulipa fedha taslimu). *Be at a discount*, dharauliwa, rahisishwa. — *v.t.* kata faida, punguza bei; (*allow for*) sadiki nusu tu ya habari (kwa ajili ya kupigwa chuku, kubadilishwa &c.).

discountenance, *v.t.* nyima msaada (idhini, ruhusa, upendeleo), tokubali, zuia, kataa.

discourage, *v.t.* shusha moyo, tia mashaka, punguza tamaa (nia, kusudi), zuia shauri, pinga, kefyakefya. *Discourage a person from doing*, shauri (shawishi, vuta) mtu asifanye. **discouragement**, *n.* jambo la kuzuia au kukatisha tamaa; hali ya kutotumaini, kushusha moyo; mazuizi, mapinzo, mgogoro.

discourse, *n.* maongezi, maneno, mazungumzo, hotuba. — *v.i.* ongea, zungumza; hutubu, hubiri; toa habari (kwa kusema au kuandika).

discourteous, *a.* -siyo na heshima (adabu, ustahi), -baya, -a kudharau, -dharaulifu, -a kubeza. **discourtesy**, *n.* ukosefu (ukosekano, utovu) wa adabu (heshima, ustahi), dharau, bezo.

discover, *v.t.* vumbua, kuta, gundua, pata kujua habari ya; (*in the act of doing wrong*) feli, fumania; (*show*) onyesha, dhihirisha, toa, funua.

discovery, *n.* kuvumbua, kuvumbulika, mvumbuo, uvumbuzi; (*new fact*) jambo jipya (geni, lisilojulika kwanza, ajabu).

discredit, *v.t.* (*disbelieve*) tosadiki; (*bring into*) onyesha (dhihirisha) uwongo; (*dishonour*) aibisha, punguza sifa, vunja uso, tahayarisha, tia fedheha. — *n.* aibu, fedheha, tahayuri, sifa mbaya, mashaka. **discreditable,** *a.* -a aibu, -baya, -a kudhuru sifa (jina, cheo); -a kufanya watu wasisadiki (wasitumaini).

discreet, *a.* -a busara, -aminifu, -a akili, -a kutanadhari. **discretion,** *n.* busara, akili, uchunguzi, uteuzi. *Surrender at discretion,* jitoa bila masharti. *At your discretion,* upendavyo, hiari yako. *He has reached years of discretion,* amepata umri wa kuweza kuchagua apendavyo, ana busara, amefika miaka ya rushd.

discrepancy, *n.* tofauti, hitilafu. **discrepant,** *a.* -a mbalimbali, -a kinyume, -a kutopatana, -enye tofauti, -a kuhitilafiana.

discretion, *n.* taz. *discreet.*

discriminate, *v.i.* pambanua, chagua, ainisha, tofautisha, teua; (*make distinctions*) pendelea. *Discriminate between so and so and so and so,* ona (pambanua) tofauti baina ya fulani na fulani. *Discriminate a person of so and so against so and so,* pendelea fulani kuliko fulani. *Discriminate against,* onea. **discriminating,** *a.* -a kupambanua (kuchagua, kutofautisha), -enye uweza wa kupambanua (kuchagua, kuainisha, kutofautisha). **discrimination,** *n.* busara, utambuzi, akili ya kupambanua, kupambanua.

discursive, *a.* -a maneno mengi, -enye habari ya mambo mengi mbalimbali.

discuss, *v.t.* zungumza (ongea) juu ya, hoji; (*consume with enjoyment*) -la kwa furaha. **discussion,** *n.* mazungumzo, maongezi, hoja, huja, kisa, mabishano ya kutengeneza jambo, mdahili.

disdain, *v.t.* dharau, tweza, beza, beja, bekua, bera, beua, nyarafu, chukia, kataa (kwa kiburi, dharau). — *n.* dharau, kiburi, makuu, usodawi, unyarafu. **disdainful,** *a.* -a kiburi, -a kutakabari, kudharau, -dharaulifu, -sodawi.

disease, *n.* ugonjwa, maradhi, uele, ndwele.

disembark, *v.i.* shuka (telemka) pwani (chomboni, melini); — *v.t.* shusha (telemsha) pwani. **disembarkation,** *n.* kushuka (kushusha) pwani, mshuko.

disembody, *v.t.* toa katika mwili; (*of troops*) changua, likiza. *A disembodied spirit,* pepo, kivuli.

disembowel, *v.t.* tumbua, toa matumbo.

disenchant, *v.t.* ondoa uchawi, zindua, zingua, logoa, tegua, topoa, zingulia, punga pepo; (*disillusion*) fumbulia macho. **disenchantment,** *n.* uzinguo, mzinguo, zinguo, kupungwa, mtopoo.

disencumber, *v.t.* ondolea mzigo (kizuizi, mgogoro, mapinzo), fungulia.

disendow, *v.t.* twalia mali.

disengage, *v.t.* tenga, fungua, kongoa, namua, nasua, toa, fumua; — *v.i.* tenguka, funguka, fumuka, fumukana. **disengaged,** *a.* -liyotengwa au kutenguka, -liyofunguliwa au kufunguka, -sabili; (*persons*) pasipo na shughuli, faraghani, -enye nafasi (wasaa); (*of room &c.*) pasipo na watu (kazi). **disengagement,** *n.* kufunguliwa, kutengwa, faragha, nafasi, wasaa.

disentangle, *v.t.* tatanua, fundua, funua, kunjua; (*make clear*) eleza, fumbua; (*set in order*) tengeneza, panga; — *v.i.* tatanuka, funduka, funuka, kunjuka; (*become clear*) elea, dhihirika.

disestablish, *v.t.* chafua, ondoa, geuza hali. *Disestablish the Church,* tenga Kanisa na Serikali.

disfavour, *v.t.* chukia, topenda. — *n.* chukio, kutopenda, hali ya kutopendwa (ya kutwezwa).

disfigure, *v.t.* umbua, haribu sura (umbo, uzuri, thamani, babua), rembua. *Be disfigured,* umbuka, kwajuka, sawajika. **disfiguration,** *n.* taz. *disfigurement.* **disfigurement,** *n.* kuumbua (kuumbuka), kilema, kulemaa, waa, ila, hitilafu, kasoro.

disfranchise, *v.t.* ondolea haki ya uraia (ya kupeleka au kuchagua mtu wa kuwamo katika halmashauri (*Parliament*). **disfranchisement,** *n.* kuondoa (kuondolewa) *franchise.*

disgorge, *v.t.* toa, kokomoa, tapika; (*yield up*) rudisha kwa sharti (yaliyonyang'anywa); (*of a river*) mimina; — *v.i.* miminika; (*make restitution*) rudisha.

disgrace, *n.* ila, aibu, fedheha, ari, tahayuri, soni, tua, hizaya, izara, janaha. — *v.t.* tia aibu, aibisha, fedhehi, fedhehesha, kebehi, hizi, tahayarisha, tweza, aziri. **disgraceful,** *a.* -a aibu *&c.*

disgruntled, *a.* -sioridhika, -siopendezwa, -a kuudhika.

disguise, *v.t.* geuza, fanya -ingine, ficha, funika. — *n.* mavazi ya kujigeuza (ya uigaji), umbo la uwongo, hila.

disgust, *v.t.* chukiza, chafua moyo, kirihi. — *n.* machukio, karaha, kirahi, ikirahi, unyarafu, kinyaa.

dish, *n.* sahani, kombe, bunguu, kibunguu; (*food*) chakula. — *v.t.* (*dish up*) pakua, leta chakula.

dishabille, *n.* hali ya kuvaa nguo ovyo ovyo (ya kuvaa nguo chache, yaani nyingine zimevuliwa au hazijavaliwa bado); nguo za kuvaa faraghani.

dishearten, *v.t.* vunja (legeza) moyo, ogofya, tia hofu (huzuni).

dishevelled, *a.* -a kuchafuka, -a kuvurugika, -a kufujika. *Dishevelled hair,* nywele za matimutimu.

dishonest, *a.* (*person*) si amini, si -aminifu; (*of actions*) -danganyifu, -a uwongo. *Dishonest person,* mjanja, mkopi, mdanganyi, mdanganyifu, ayari, laghai; (*a thief*) mwivi, mwizi.

dishonesty, *n.* uwongo, udanganyifu, hila, ujanja, wizi, wivi.

dishonour, *v.t.* aibisha, fedhehesha, hizi, tahayarisha; (*refuse to redeem*) totekeleza (ahadi, deni); (*treat rudely*) dharau, beza. — *n.* aibu, ari, hizaya, fedheha; dharau. **dishonourable,** *a.* (*untrustworthy*) si -aminifu, si -nyofu; (*disgraceful*) -a aibu.

disillusion, *v.t.* onyesha ukweli (hakika), ondosha uwongo. **disillusionment,** *n.* onyo la ukweli (la hakika), kuonya ukweli (hakika), hali ya kuonyeshwa (ya kujua) ukweli (hakika).

disinclination, *n.* ukosefu (ukosekano) wa kupenda, machukio, moyo wa kutotaka. **disincline,** *v.t.* punguza tamaa (mapenzi, nia), geuza (zuia) moyo. *He is disinclined for food,* hataki chakula.

disinfect, *v.t.* safisha pachafu, ondoa (katika nyumba, mahali, nguo *&c.*) yale yanayoambukiza ugonjwa, fukiza, takasa. **disinfectant,** *n.* dawa ya kuondoa yanayoambukiza ugonjwa, fukizo.

disingenuous, *a.* -enye nia (sababu, maarubu, matilaba, madhumuni) isiyonyoka, -enye hila, danganyifu, -janja, si -nyofu.

disinherit, *v.t.* kata urithi, toa katika urithi.

disintegrate, *v.t.* vunja, changanua, tenga sehemu mbalimbali; — *v.i.* vunjika, changanuka, tengeka sehemu mbalimbali.

disinter, *v.t.* fukua, chimbua (kitu kilichozikwa; (*bring into view*) vumbua, gundua.

disinterested, *a.* si -enye kupendelea, si -enye kutaka faida. *A disinterested person,* mtu adili, asiyependelea, asiyejitakia.

disjoin, *v.t.* tenga, ungua, achanisha, kata, tungua. **disjoined,** *a.* -siyofungamana, -siyofuatana moja kwa moja, -liyokatikakatika. **disjointedly,** *adv.* bila kufuatana vizuri, bila kufungamana, kwa kukatikatika.

disk, *n.* kitu cha duara (kama sahani).

dislike, *v.t.* chukia, iza, wenga, kirihi, topenda. — *n.* machukio, kirahi.

dislocate, *v.t.* tegua, kutua, shtua, shtusha; (*disturb*) vuruga, fuja, tia fujo, chafua. **dislocation,** *n.* mteguo, mteguko, mkutuo, mshtuo, mshtuko; (*disturbance*) fujo, chafuko, vurugiko.

dislodge, *v.t.* ondoa, ondosha, fukuza, hamisha.

disloyal, *a.* si -amini, si -aminifu, -siyefanya yapasayo, si -aminifu kwa mfalme (mkubwa) amhusuye.

dismal, *a.* -a kufisha moyo (kwa sababu ya giza, weusi, ukiwa &c.), -a kuhuzunisha, -a kuchukiza, -a kuondoa furaha; (*of the spirits*) -enye huzuni (majonzi), -siye na furaha.

dismantle, *v.t.* pambua, rembua, ondoa mapambo; (*raze*) vunja, bomoa.

dismast, *v.t.* ondoa (vunja) milingoti ya chombo (*e.g.* kwa dhoruba, tufani, mzinga &c.).

dismay, *v.t.* ogofya, tisha, tia hofu, fadhaisha. — *n.* hofu, fadhaa, machugachuga, mang'amung'amu, mang'ang'amu.

dismember, *v.t.* changua, kongonyoa, rarua (vunja) vipande vipande.

dismiss, *v.t.* (*allow to go*) ruhusu, likiza, fungua; (*send away*) ondosha, achia mbali, uzulu, fukuza. **dismissal,** *n.* kuondoshwa, kutolewa, kufukuzwa; (*leave to go*) ruhusa, likizo, kuaga.

dismount, *v.t.* shusha, telemsha, tungua; — *v.i.* shuka juu ya farasi.

disobedience, *n.*, **disobedient,** *a.* taz. *disobey.*

disobey, *v.t. and i.* asi, kaidi, halifu, totii. **disobedience,** *n.* maasi, uasi, ukaidi, uhalifu, kutotii. **disobedient,** *a.* -asi, -kaidi.

disoblige, *v.t.* tojali mapenzi (matakwa, haja) ya (mwingine), tenda jambo asilotaka mwingine, totenda jambo analotaka mwingine. **disobliging,** *a.* -siyejali wengine, si -fadhili, si -hisani.

disorder, *v.t.* chafua, fuja, tia fujo, buruga, rabishi. — *n.* fujo, machafuko; (*illness*) ugonjwa, maradhi, uele; (*tumult*) udhia, fitina, ghasia, rabsha, zahama, msukosuko. **disorderly,** *a.* si -enye taratibu, -a fujo, -a machafuko, hobelahobela, shaghalabaghala; (*riotous*) -a jeuri, -fitini, -asi, maasi, -a ghasia. *Disorderly house,* danguro, nyumba ya malaya (kahaba).

disorganize, *v.t.* chafua, haribu, fuja, haribu uzuri wa, vunja taratibu ya. **disorganization,** *n.* machafuko, uharibifu, fujo.

disown, *v.t.* kana, kataa; (*renounce*) kanusha.

disparage, *v.t.* umbua, vunja heshima, kashifu, haribu sifa, singizia, rahisisha, tusha, aziri, jugumu. *Disparaging remarks,* matusi. **disparagement,** *n.* kuumbua, mwumbuo, uumbuaji, matusi, kashifa.

disparity, *n.* hitilafu, tofauti.

dispassionate, *a.* si -pendelevu, -siyependelea, adili, -adilifu, -a haki, -tulivu. **dispassionately,** *adv.* kwa haki, bila kupendelea, kwa uadilifu.

dispatch, despatch, *v.t.* (*send person*) tuma; (*send thing*) peleka; (*do*) fanya upesi, maliza. — *n.* kufanya upesi, wepesi, haraka; (*written*) barua, waraka; (*urgency*) bidii, himizo.

dispel, *v.t.* ondoa, fukuza, tawanya, towesha.

dispensable, *a.*, **dispensary,** *n.*, **dispensation,** *n.* taz. *dispense.*

dispense, *v.t.* gawanya, toa (dawa &c.). *Dispense with,* totumia, totaka, ondoa, weka mbali. **dispensable,** *a.* si -a lazima, si -a kanuni. **dispensary,** *n.* nyumba ya kutoa dawa, nyumba ya tabibu (daktari). **dispensation,** *n.* kutoa, mgawo; (*divine*) maongozi ya Mungu, madaraka; (*special leave*) ruhusa.

disperse, *v.t.* tawanya, eneza, ondoa, towesha; — *v.i.* tawanyika, enea, ondoka; (*vanish*) toweka, tokomea.

dispersion, *n.* eneo, tawanyiko, enezo, tawanyo.
dispirit, *v.t.* legeza (vunja) moyo; toa tamaa, tia majonzi (huzuni).
displace, *v.t.* hamisha, sogeza, toa katika mahali pake, weka vibaya; twaa mahali pa. **displacement,** *n.* kutoa (kutolewa, kutoka) katika mahali pake; uhamisho; nafasi iliyoachwa na kitu kilichohamishwa, hasa kadiri ya maji iliyohamishwa na kitu kinachoelea juu yake, *e.g.* meli yenye *displacement* kadiri ya tani 10,000 ya maji.
display, *v.t.* onyesha, tembeza, angaza; (*for sale*) zinza. — *n.* wonyesho, wonyeshano, tamasha, sherehe, urembo, mkogo. *Make a display,* fanya sherehe, fanya fahari; (*insincere*) jisingizia kama una (furaha, majonzi, masikitiko &c.); (*show off*) takabari, koga.
displease, *v.t.* chukiza, tia uchungu, kasirisha, udhi. **displeasure,** *n.* chuki, uchungu, kasirani, ghadhabu, hasira, maudhiko.
disport, *v.i.* chezacheza. *Disport oneself,* chezacheza, jifurahisha, koga, fanya mikogo.
dispose, *v.t.* (*arrange*) andaa, andika, weka taratibu, tengeneza, panga; (*use*) tumia; (*direct*) ongoza, elekeza, vuta, shawishi; — *v.i.* (*determine*) amuru, weka, kata shauri. *Dispose of* (*settle*) hukumia, kata mambo ya, amria; (*make away with*) komesha, uzia mbali, tumilia mbali, acha, toa, maliza. *Be disposed to,* taka, penda, elekea. **disposal,** *n.* (*arrangement*) matengenezo, madaraka, andao; (*rule, control*) amri, hukumu, idhini; (*use, distribution*) mgawo, maenezi, matumizi; (*sale*) kuuza. *At the disposal of,* chini ya, katika mikono (amri) ya, tayari kwa. **disposer,** *n.* mtengenezaji, mwenye amri. *Title of God,* Mwawadhi. **disposition,** *n.* (*character*) tabia, silika, moyo; (*inclination*) elekeo, nia, kutaka; (*arrangements*) madaraka, taratibu, mapango.
dispossess, *v.t.* toa, ondosha, fukuza; (*dispossess of*) twalia (mali, shamba &c.); (*evil spirit*) punga (chuchia) pepo.
disproof, *n.* taz. *disprove.*
disproportion, *n.* kutolingana, hali ya kutokuwa cheo au kadiri inayofaa (yaani -kubwa zaidi au -dogo zaidi). **disproportionate,** *a.* -a kadiri (cheo, kimo, ukubwa) isiyofaa (isiyolingana na kitu kingine).
disprove, *v.t.* kanusha, bainisha uwongo (au ya kuwa kinyume chake ni kweli), shuhudia (thibitisha) ya kuwa sivyo. **disproof,** *n.* kanusho, ushuhuda wa kuthibitisha au kubainisha uwongo wa fumbo.
disputable, *a.*, **disputant,** *n.*, **disputatious,** *a.* taz. *dispute.*
dispute, *v.i.* shindana (kwa maneno), tetana, bishana, hojiana; (*quarrel*) gombana; — *v.t.* (*call in question*) kaidi, kana, pinga. — *n.* shindano (la maneno), mateto, mabishano, maneno, ugomvi, manza. **disputable,** *a.* -enye mashaka, si hakika, si yakini. **disputant,** *n.* mshindani, mtetaji, mhoji. *I was one of the disputants,* mimi nilikuwamo katika maneno yale. **disputatious,** *a.* -kaidi, -gomvi, -bishi.
disqualification, *n.* taz. *disqualify.*
disqualify, *v.t.* (*debar*) ondolea haki, gombeza, harimisha; (*render unfit, incapacitate*) zuia, ondolea nguvu (uwezo &c.). *Be disqualified,* ondolewa haki &c.; (*be unfit*) tofaa, tostahili, toweza. *He is disqualified,* hawezi, hastahili, hafai; (*debarred*) amegombezwa &c. **disqualification,** *n.* (*deprivation*) kuondolewa (ondoleo la) haki &c.; (*incapacity*) kutoweza; (*stop, obstruction*) kizuio, kikomo.
disquiet, *v.t.* fadhaisha, hangaisha, tia wasiwasi, kera, shtusha, sumbua, hamanisha, pekecha, tia hofu, ogofya. — *n.* fadhaa, dukuduku, masumbuko, wasiwasi, hangaiko, hamaniko, kero, hangaisho, udhiko, mapinduko, hofu, maogofyo, machugachuga, mang'ang'amu, mang'a-

mung'amu. **disquietude,** *n.* taz. *disquiet.*

disquisition, *n.* hotuba ndefu (maneno mengi, maandiko marefu) yenye maelezo mengi juu ya jambo.

disregard, *v.t.* tojali, toangalia, tofikiri, dharau, acha. *We may disregard this item,* tunaweza, kuacha (kutoangalia, kutofikiri) jambo hili. — *n.* kutoangalia, kutojali, dharau, ukosefu (utovu) wa kujali &c.

disrepair, *n.* hali ya kuharibika (kuchakaa).

disreputable, *a.* taz. *disrepute.*

disrepute, *n.* tabia (sifa) mbaya, utovu wa heshima. *Bring into disrepute,* adhiri, tusha, aziri. **disreputable,** *a.* -enye tabia (sifa) mbaya, duni, -ovu.

disrespect, *n.* utovu wa heshima (ustahi, adabu), ufidhuli, usafihi, ukavu wa macho, ujuvi. **disrespectful,** *a.* -tovu wa heshima ustahi, adabu). *Be disrespectful,* dharau, vunja heshima (uso), kosa adabu.

disrobe, *v.t. and i.* vua (vulia) nguo.

disruption, *n.* kupasuka, mpasuko, mvunjiko, farakano.

dissatisfaction, *n.*, **dissatisfied,** *a.* taz. *dissatisfy.*

dissatisfy, *v.t.* topendeza, toridhisha, chukiza, tia uchungu. **dissatisfaction,** *n.* uchungu, kutopendezwa, kutoona radhi. **dissatisfied,** *a.* -enye uchungu, -a kuchukiwa, -a kutoridhika.

dissect, *v.t.* changua, kata vipande vipande, tenga sehemu mbalimbali (hasa ili kuchunguza viungo au sehemu mbalimbali). **dissection,** *n.* tendo la kukata kama *dissect;* sehemu iliyokatwa.

dissemble, *v.t.* ficha, geuza, fanya (kitu, nia, maono &c.) kuonekana kama kwamba ni vingine; — *v.i.* jificha, jigeuza (nia, maono &c.), danganya. **dissembler,** *n.* mdanganyi, mnafiki, mzandiki.

disseminate, *v.t.* eneza, tawanya, hasa mafundisho ya dini (ya fitina &c.).

dissent, *v.i.* tokubali, kaidi, topatana, toridhia. — *n.* ukaidi, kutokubali, makatao; (*in religion*) farakano (waliofarakana na, wasiokubali) Kanisa la Uingereza. **dissension,** *n.* kutopatana, fitina, faraka, ugomvi.

dissenter, *n.* asiyekubali mafundisho ya Kanisa la Uingereza.

dissentient, *a.* -a kuona vingine, -a kutokubali, -enye kukaidi, -enye shauri jingine (mbalimbali). — *n.* asiyekubali (shauri, maneno &c.).

dissertation, *n.* hotuba ndefu (maandiko mengi) yenye maelezo mengi juu ya jambo.

disservice, *n.* tendo linalodharau (linalopinga).

dissever, *v.t.* tenga, kata.

dissimilar, *a.* si sawa, mbalimbali, -enye tofauti, -siyofanana. **dissimilarity,** *n.* tofauti, hitilafu.

dissimulate, *v.t.* ficha, geuza (maono, nia &c.); — *v.i.* jificha, jigeuza (maono, nia), danganya. **dissimulation,** *n.* unafiki, udanganyifu (wa kuficha maono, nia, kusudi &c.).

dissipate, *v.t.* tawanya, fukuza, ondolea mbali, ondoa kabisa; (*waste by extravagance &c.*) tapanya, poteza, fuja; — *v.i.* (*pass away*) toweka, pita, ondoka; (*engage in frivolity &c.*) zungumza, cheza; (*in dissipation*) fanya uasherati (ufisadi, ufasiki, ulevi &c.). **dissipation,** *n.* uasherati, ulevi, ufisadi, ufasiki; (*dispersion, loss*) ondoleo, upotevu; (*frivolity*) mazungumzo matupu, kucheza, machezo.

dissociate, *v.t.* tenga, kata, weka mbali; (*repudiate connexion &c.*) kaidi, kanusha, jitenga na.

dissoluble, *a.* -a kuyeyushikana, -a kutangukana.

dissolute, *a.*, **dissolution,** *n.* taz. *dissolve.*

dissolve, *v.t.* (*melt*) yeyusha; (*destroy*) vunja, fungua, komesha, tangua; — *v.i.* vunjika, tanguka, isha; (*vanish*) toweka polepole, fifia, potea.

dissolute, *a.* -fisadi, -potovu, -potoe, -asherati, -levi, -ovu. **dissolution,** *n.* (*end*) mwisho; (*death*) mauti; (*destruction*) kuharibika. **dissolvent,** *n.* kitu kinachofanya kingine kuyeyuka.

dissonance, *n.* taz. *dissonant.*

dissonant, *a.* -a sauti mbalimbali (zisizolingana, zisizo nzuri), -a makelele; (*different*) -a mbalimbali. **dissonance,** *n.* sauti zisizolingana, makelele; (*difference*) tofauti.

dissuade, *v.t.* shawishi (shauri, vuta) vingine, jaribu kuzuia (kwa shauri, maneno); faulu katika kushawishi mtu, asifanye jambo. **dissuasion,** *n.* kushawishi &c.; hoja (inayoletwa kuzuia mtu asifanye jambo). **dissuasive,** *a.* -a kuelekea (-enye kusudi) kushawishi &c.

dissyllable, *n.* -enye silabi (matamko) mbili, *e.g.* paka, ni *dissyllable.*

distaff, *n.* kijiti cha kukunjia uzi, chenye bonge la uzi. *The distaff side,* kuukeni.

distance, *n.* urefu; (*in travelling*) mwendo; (*interval*) nafasi; (*in time*) wakati, muda; (*distant place*) palipo mbali, mbali. — *v.t.* fanya nafasi katikati, tenga; pita kabisa (katika mashindano, adui &c.). **distant,** *a.* -a mbali; (*indistinct*) -a kufanana kidogo sana; (*cold, reserved*) baridi, si -kunjufu. *A distant relative,* jamaa lakini si ndugu wa karibu.

distaste, *n.* kutopenda, machukio, chuki. **distasteful,** *a.* -a kuchukiza.

distemper, (1) *n.* ugonjwa (wa mbwa).

distemper, (2) *n.* (*thin glue*) rangi ya maji, sherizi, na vingine vya kupaka ukuta. — *v.t.* paka rangi ya *distemper.*

distend, *v.t.* vimbisha, tanua; — *v.i.* vimba, kubaza, tanuka. **distension,** *n.* kuvimba, kuvimbisha, uvimbe.

distich, *n.* wimbo (shairi) wa mistari miwili miwili.

distil, *v.i.* tiririka, tona; — *v.t.* tiririsha, tonesha; fanya maji kuwa mvuke na kuugeuza maji tena; pata kiini cha kitu kwa kuchemsha na kugeuza mvuke wake kuwa maji, *e.g.* dawa au mvinyo. **distillation,** *n.* kutona, kutonesha &c.; tendo la kukamata mvuke na kuugeuza maji tena. **distillery,** *n.* nyumba ya *distillation,* hasa mvinyo inapofanyizwa.

distinct, *a.*, **distinction,** *n.*, **distinctive,** *a.*, **distinctiveness,** *n.* taz. *distinguish.*

distinguish, *v.t.* pambanua, bainisha, ainisha, chagua, weka mbali; (*confer honour*) tukuza, pasha sifa; (*perceive*) ona, tambua. *He greatly distinguished himself,* alijipatia sifa bora. **distinct,** *a.* (*different*) -ingine, -a mbalimbali, -a -moja -moja; (*clear*) dhahiri, wazi, kiada. *Speak slowly and distinctly,* sema kiada, pambanua. *These matters are entirely distinct from each other,* mambo haya yameachana kabisa. **distinction,** *n.* (*difference*) tofauti; (*honour*) heshima, sifa. **distinctive,** *a.* -a kupambanua, -a kuonyesha, -a peke yake, -a mtindo. **distinctness,** *n.* udhahiri. **distinguishable,** *a.* -a kutambulikana, -a kuonekana dhahiri. **distinguished,** *a.* -teule, -a fahari, -tukufu, mashuhuri, bora.

distort, *v.t.* potoa, umbua, rembua; (*pervert*) geuza vibaya, haribu maana ya. **distortion,** *n.* (*by disease*) kilema, kuumbuka; (*perversion*) uharibifu, upotovu.

distract, *v.t.* (*draw attention*) vuta (mawazo, fikira) pengine, fikirisha vingine, achisha kazi, ondoa katika shughuli; (*occupy*) shughulisha; (*unsettle*) fadhaisha, tia wasiwasi, hangaisha, tia mashaka (wazimu); (*amuse*) pumzisha, tuliza. **distracted,** *a.* -enye wasiwasi (fadhaa, mashaka, hangaiko, wazimu). **distraction,** *n.* (*unsettlement*) fadhaa, mashaka, wasiwasi, hangaiko, haraka, wazimu; (*rest*) pumzisho, kitulizo, mchezo, tafrija, mazungumzo.

distrain, *v.t.* lipiza, toza kwa nguvu,

twaa kwa nguvu, filisi. **distraint,** *n.* lipizo, kufilisi.

distress, *v.t.* sumbua, udhi, dhiisha, dhikisha, lemea, chosha, taabisha. *Distress oneself,* hangaika, ona wasiwasi. — *n.* taabu, shida, dhiki, udhia, msiba, mashaka, huzuni, kibuhuti, wasiwasi, hangaiko; (*distraint*) kufilisi, kufilisika.

distributive, *v.t.* (*give out, divide*) toa, gawa, gawanya, eneza, tanda, tandaza; (*arrange*) ainisha, panga, andika. **distributer,** *n.* mgawanyi, mwenezi, mtoa, mtoaji. **distribution,** *n.* mgawanyo, mgawo, maenezi.

district, *n.* (*of country*) nchi, upande, jimbo, wilaya, tarafa; (*of town*) mtaa, buldani.

distrust, *v.t.* shuku, tuhumu, dhania, toamini, tosadiki, totumaini, fanyia hadhari. — *n.* tuhuma, shaka, hadhari, hofu. **distrustful,** *a.* -enye hadhari, -enye mashaka, -a kushuku, -sioamini.

disturb, *v.t.* (*disarrange*) pindua, chafua, fuja, vuruga, buruga, vunja utaratibu; (*annoy*) sumbua, amsha, udhi, shtua, shtusha, shughulisha, pekecha. *Do not disturb yourself,* starehe. **disturbance,** *n.* (*uproar*) ghasia, zahama, kishindo, msukosuko; (*disarrangement*) machafuko, fujo.

disunion, *n.* taz. *disunite.*

disunite, *v.t.* tenga, farakisha, kata; — *v.i.* tengana, farakana. **disunion,** *n.* farakano, kutengana; (*discord*) kutopatana, ugomvi.

disuse, *v.t.* acha kutumia, acha. — *n.* kutotumika. *This path has fallen into disuse,* njia hii imekufa, haitumiki.

ditch, *n.* handaki, shimo, mfereji. *Die in the last ditch,* linda mpaka mwisho, endelea mpaka mwisho. *Ditch water,* maji yanayosimama (kama yale yaliyobaki katika handaki). *Dull as ditch water,* -jinga (-gumu, baridi) kabisa.

ditto, *n.* ile ile, kama kwanza, sawasawa—ufupisho wake ni *do.*

ditty, *n.* wimbo mdogo mwepesi.

diuretic, *a.* -a kuongeza mkojo, -a kukojosha.

diurnal, *a.* (*daily*) -a kila siku, siku kwa siku; (*of daylight*) -a mchana.

divan, *n.* kiti (kikubwa chenye mito), matakia.

dive, *v.i.* zama majini, piga mbizi; (*hand into*) tia mkono (majini, chomboni, mfukoni &c.); (*go deeply into*) jitia kabisa. *He dived into the bush,* alijitoma chakani. — *n.* mzamo, mzamio. **diver,** *n.* mpiga mbizi, mzamia (lulu &c.). **diving-bell,** *n.* chombo cha mtu kuingia ili azame chini ya maji.

diverge, *v.i.* gawanyika njia mbalimbali, tawanyika, enda mbalimbali, acha njia (majira, tabia), achana (maono, mashauri), -wa mbalimbali. **divergence,** *n.* kugawanyika (kuenda) njia mbalimbali, kuenda upande; (*difference*) tofauti. **divergent,** *a.* -a kwenda upande, -a mbalimbali.

divers, *a.,* **diverse,** *a.,* **diversely,** *adv.,* **diversify,** *v.,* **diversion,** *n.,* **diversity,** *n.* taz. *divert.*

divert, *v.t.* geuza upande, bekua, potosha; (*relieve, amuse*) achisha kazi, furahisha, chekesha. **divers,** *a.* -ingi, -ingine -ingine, -inginezo. **diverse,** *a.* -a namna mbalimbali, -a namna nyingine nyingine. **diversely,** *adv.* kwa namna (jinsi) mbalimbali (nyingine nyingine). **diversify,** *v.t.* badili namna, fanya kuwa -a namna mbalimbali (nyingine nyingine). **diversion,** *n.* kugeuza, kupotoa, kupotosha; (*pastime*) mchezo, mazungumzo, tafrija; (*restful change*) jambo la kuachisha kazi, pumzisho; (*stratagem*) hila (kudanganya adui). **diversity,** *n.* tofauti, hitilafu. **diverting,** *a.* -a kugeuza (kugeuka) upande; -a kufurahisha; -a kuchekesha.

divest, *v.t.* vua, vulia, twalia.

divide, *v.t.* (*into parts*) kata, pasua, vunja, changua; (*separate*) tenga, bagua, pita kati ya; (*distribute*) gawa, gawanya; (*set at variance*) farikisha, fitini, gombanisha; (*make classification*) pambanua, ainisha, panga; (*in arithmetic*) gawanya; — *v.i.* (*cease to be one*) tengana, tengeka, gawanyika. **dividend,** *n.* sehemu ya faida, faida ya gawio; (*in arithmetic*) kigawanye, hesabu yenye kugawanyika. **divider,** *n.* mgawanyi, kitu kigawanyacho. *Dividers* (*compasses*), bikari. **divisible,** *a.* -a kugawanyikana. **division,** *n.* (*separation*) kutenga, mtengo; (*in arithmetic*) kugawanya, mkasama (*rare*); (*distribution*) mgawo, mgawanyo, mgawanyiko; (*partition*) kitengo, kitu cha kutengea; (*wall*) kiambaza, ukuta; (*part*) fungu, mkato, sehemu, nusu, kitu kilichotengeka; (*of army*) kikosi, tapo, sehemu ya jeshi. **divisor,** *n.* kigawanyo.

divine, *v.t.* (*foretell*) agua, bashiri, jua mbele; (*guess*) bahatisha, kisi. — *a.* -a Mungu, kama -a Mungu, -a dini, -takatifu; (*surpassing*) bora sana, -tukufu, -a fahari, -a ajabu. — *n.* mwenye elimu nyingi ya mambo ya Mungu (dini). *Divine service,* ibada ya Mungu, dini. **divination,** *n.* uaguzi, maaguzi, ubashiri, kupiga bao (ramli, falaki), uramali. *To find offender,* mburuga. **diviner,** *n.* mwaguzi. *Divining board,* bao, ramli, kisango, kibunzi. **divinity,** *n.* uungu, umungu, tabia ya Mungu, Mungu; (*theology*) elimu ya mambo ya Mungu.

diving-bell, *n.* taz. *dive.*

divinity, *n.* taz. *divine.*

divisible, *a.*, **division,** *n.*, **divisor,** *n.* taz. *divide.*

divorce, *n.* talaka. — *v.t.* taliki, tangua ndoa, acha; (*separate*) tenga.

divulge, *v.t.* funua, toa wazi, tangaza, fumbua (siri).

dizziness, *n.* taz. *dizzy.*

dizzy, *a.* -enye kizunguzungu (kisuli, kisulisuli, mbasua); -a kutia kizunguzungu &c.; (*perplexed*) -enye wasiwasi, -a kufumbwa; (*precipitate*) -a haraka, si -angalifu. — *v.t.* tia kizunguzungu, hangaisha, tia wasiwasi. **dizziness,** *n.* kizunguzungu, kisuli, kisulisuli, mbasua.

do, *v.t.* (*p.t.* **did,** *pf.t.* **done**) fanya, tenda; (*complete, finish*) maliza, timiliza, isha, (*cook*) pika; (*visit*) zuru, tembelea, tazama, angalia; (*cheat*) danganya, punja, laghai, kopa, rubuni, ghilibu, shinda; (*suit*) faa; (*travel*) safiri, enda; — *v.i.* shughulika; (*be concerned with*) husu; (*be fitting, suit*) faa; (*be, go on*) -wa na hali, endelea. *How do you do?* u hali gani? hujambo? jambo? *I am doing well,* sijambo, hali njema, nafanikiwa. *It will not do,* haifai, haiendi. *It is done* (*finished*), imekwisha, imemalizika, imetimizwa; (*cooked*) imeiva. *He is done,* amechoka, ameshindwa. *Do over,* funika, paka. *Be done for,* shindwa, potea. *Do for,* poteza, angamiza, ua; (*suffice*) faa, tosha; (*affect*) fanyia, tendea. *Do without,* totumia, totaka, tohitaji. *Do with* (*find use for*), tumia; (*have dealings with*) shughulika na. *Have to do with,* shughulika na; (*concern*) husu. *I have done with it,* simo tena, sifanyi tena, situmii tena, sina neno nayo tena. *Do away with,* ondoa kabisa. *Do do it,* tafadhali ufanye, nataka sana ufanye. *Do you want it? I do,* waitaka? naitaka. *Do* (*well, ill*) *by,* tendea (mazuri, mabaya). **do,** *n.* (*swindle*) hila, ujanja; (*party &c.*) tafrija, karamu. **doable,** *a.* -a kuwezekana, -a kufanyikana, -a kutendekana. **doer,** *n.* mtenda, aliyetenda (jambo fulani). **doings,** *n.* matendo, mwenendo. *Grand doings,* sherehe, tamasha, michezo, sikukuu.

docile, *a.* -tii, -tiifu, -sikivu, -sikizi, -sikilivu, makini, welekevu.

dock, (1) *v.t.* kata, katiza, fupisha, punguza.

dock, (2) *n.* (*in criminal court*) mahali (kitundu) pa kuwekwa mfungwa katika korti.

dock, (3) *n.* (*for ships*) gudi, majahaba. — *v.t.* tia gudini. **dockage,**

n. nafasi ya meli (merikebu, chombo) katika gudi; ada ya kutumia gudi. **dock-dues,** *n.* ada ya kutumia gudi. **dockyard,** *n.* gudi, majahaba, furutile, flotile.

docket, *n.* karata, cheti, orodha.

dockyard, *n.* taz. *dock* (3).

doctor, *n.* tabibu, mganga, daktari; (*learned man*) mtu aliyepata cheo kilicho bora cha elimu katika *University*; mwalimu. — *v.t.* ganga, tibu, uguza, tia dawa, agua; (*mend, repair*) tengeneza. **doctrinal,** *a.* -a elimu, -a mafundisho; -a madhehebu (ya dini &c.). **doctrine,** *n.* elimu, mafundisho ya dini, madhehebu, imani, kanuni; (*idea*) nia. *It is his doctrine,* ndivyo aonavyo yeye.

document, *n.* hati, maandiko, cheti, mkataba. **documentary,** *a.* -a hati, -enye kuandikwa.

dodder, *v.i.* enda mwendo wa kutetemeka (kwa udhaifu, uzee, ugonjwa); payuka, payapaya (kama mzee), tetereka.

dodge, *v.t.* epa, epuka, epukana, piga chenga, kwepa; — *v.i.* (*of moral activities*) tumia hila (werevu). — *n.* hila, mtego, werevu; (*in good sense*) njia, namna, akili, shauri. **dodger,** *n.* mwerevu, mwenye hila, mlaghai, ayari.

doe, *n.* jike la *deer.*

doer, *n.* taz. *do.*

doff, *v.t.* vua (kofia, nguo, mavazi); (*abandon*) acha.

dog, *n.* mbwa, (*pariah*) mbwa koko. *Go to the dogs,* haribika, potoka. *Throw to the dogs,* tapanya, poteza, toa kama si kitu. *Rain cats and dogs,* nyesha mvua kubwa. *Lead a dog's life,* sumbuliwa, sumbuka, ishi maisha ya kuhangaikahangaika. *To be a dog in the manger,* kuwa na inda. — *v.t.* fuata (kama mbwa wa kuwinda), fuata karibu, shikilia, andama (misiba, hasara &c.). **dog-days,** *n.* siku za jua kali. **dogged,** *a.* (*obstinate*) -kaidi, -shupavu, -gumu; (*firm*) thabiti, imara. **dog-tired,** *a.* -a kuchoka sana. **dog-watch,** *n.* (*nautical*) zamu tangu saa kumi za usiku mpaka saa kumi na mbili asubuhi, au tangu saa kumi na mbili jioni mpaka saa mbili za usiku.

doggerel, *a.* mashairi (hafifu ya upuzi).

dogma, *n.* fundisho la kanuni (la sharti), hasa la wakuu wa Kanisa. **dogmatic,** *a.* -a sharti, -a kanuni; (*arbitrary*) -a kukata maneno, enye maneno makavu; (*insistent*) -shupavu, -a kushikilia kauli. **dogmatism,** *n.* ushupavu wa maneno, kushikilia kauli, maneno makavu. **dogmatize,** *v.t.* kata maneno, toa kanuni; — *v.i.* shikilia kauli (shauri, maneno).

dog-star, *n.* shiraa (Ar.).

dog-tired, *a.* taz. *dog.*

dog-watch, *n.* taz. *dog.*

doings, *n.* taz. *do.*

doldrums, *n.* uzito wa moyo, huzuni; (*nautical*) baharini karibu na ikweta ambapo kwa kawaida kuna shwari.

dole, *n.* sadaka (ya posho, nguo, fedha—hasa kidogo tu). — *v.t.* (*out*) gawia kidogo kidogo (kwa unyimivu).

doleful, *a.* -a huzuni, -zito. **dolorous,** *a.* kama *doleful.*

doll, *n.* mtoto wa bandia, mwanasesere.

dollar, *n.* reale. *Black dollar,* reale ya Sham. *Spanish Pillar dollar,* reale mzinga. *American,* sarafu yenye thamani ya shilingi nne na senti ishirini hivi.

dolorous, *a.* taz. *doleful.*

dolphin, *n.* samaki kama nyangumi mdogo.

dolt, *n.* mjinga, baradhuli, mzuzu.

domain, *n.* milki, nchi, kitende, makao. *That is my domain,* kazi yangu hiyo.

dome, *n.* kuba, zege.

domestic, *a.* -a nyumbani, -a nchi yenyewe; (*of animals*) -liofugwa. *A domestic person, of domestic tasks,* mkaa nyumbani. *A domestic,* mtumishi. **domesticate,** *v.t.* fuga, fundisha (vuta, lea) kupenda nyumbani na mambo yake.

domicile, *n.* nyumba, makao, kitende, kaya.
dominant, *a.* taz. *dominate.*
dominate, *v.t.* (*rule*) tawala, -wa na amri juu ya, amuru; (*prevail*) shinda, -wa na nguvu, -wa -kubwa kuliko (*e.g.* mlima, nyumba, sauti *&c.*); — *v.i.* tawala. **dominant,** *a.* -kuu, -a nguvu, -a kutawala, -enye hukumu (amri). **domination,** *n.* utawala, hukumu, amri, nguvu. **domineer,** *v.t.* fanya jeuri, dhulumu, piga ubwana, onyesha nguvu, onea; (*assert opinion*) shikilia kauli. **domineering,** *a.* -dhalimu, -jeuri, -onevu, -a kupiga ubwana.
dominion, *n.* mamlaka, utawala, hukumu, amri; (*country*) milki, ufalme, nchi. *Be under the dominion of,* shindwa na, -wa chini ya.
dominoes, *n.* (*game of*) dhumna.
don, *v.t.* vaa, valia, jivika.
donate, *v.t.* -pa (zawadi, msaada wa fedha). **donation,** *n.* zawadi, kipaji, sadaka. **donor,** *n.* mpaji, mtoa (sadaka, zawadi).
done, *v. pf.t.* ya *do. Be done,* (*finished*) isha, malizika; (*overcome*) shindana; (*deceived*) danganyika; (*tired out*) choka sana.
donga, *n.* korongo.
donkey, *n.* (*riding*) punda; (*for loads*) punda kihongwe, kihongwe; (*stupid person*) mpumbavu, mpuzi.
donor, *n.* taz. *donate.*
don't = *do not.*
doom, *n.* (*fatal*) ajali; (*ruin*) maangamizi; (*death*) kifo, mauti; (*judgement*) hukumu. — *v.t.* (*destine*) weka; (*sentence*) pasisha hukumu. **doomsday,** *n.* siku ya mwisho (ya kuhukumiwa ulimwengu).
door, *n.* mlango; (*of two valves*) tarabe. *Indoors,* ndani, ndani ya nyumba, nyumbani. *Out of doors,* nje ya nyumba, nje. *Next door to,* karibu na. *To lay at his door,* kumshtaki, kumlaumu, kumtwisha, kumsukumia. **door-keeper,** *n.* bawabu, mngoje mlango. *Door-chain,* riza, tumbuu. *Door-post,* mhimili, mwimo. *Door-step,* (*sill*) kizingiti.
dope, *n.* dawa inayolevya (*e.g.* afyuni, kasumba, bangi *&c.*). — *v.t.* -pa dawa (hasa inayolevya); (*hoodwink*) ghilibu, rubuni, laghai (kwa maneno ya uwongo).
dormant, *a.* -a kulala; (*disused*) -siotumika, -liokufa. **dormitory,** *n.* chumba cha kulala; (*in native villages and school, where separate sleeping huts for unmarried boys and girls are customary*) gane, bweni.
dormouse, *n.* mnyama mdogo kidogo kama kipanya mwenye mkia kama komba.
dorsal, *a.* -a mgongo, -a nyuma.
dose, *n.* kiasi cha dawa, kadiri ya dawa ya siku moja au ya mara moja. — *v.t.* nywesha dawa.
dossier, *n.* hati (karatasi) zenye habari (tarehe) ya mtu.
dot, (1) *n.* nukta, alama ndogo, kitone. — *v.t.* tia nukta. *Dot about,* tia huko na huko. *Be dotted about,* tapakaa, tawanyika.
dot, (2) *n.* mahari.
dotage, *n.* ukongwe, udhaifu wa akili na mwili wa uzeeni, uzulu, upuzi wa kizee. **dotard,** *n.* mkongwe aliyepungua akili na nguvu, mzulu, mpumbavu. **dote,** *v.i.* pungukiwa akili, zulu, konga; (*dote upon*) penda sana, pendelea, tunuka, tia habani.
dotterel, *n.* chekehukwa.
double, *a.* maradufu, mara mbili; (*in pairs*) -wili -wili, kwa jozi; (*deceitful*) -a hila, -a nia mbili, -kauleni, si -aminifu. *Double dealing,* ujanja, urubuni, ughilibu, udanganyifu, hila, ukopi. — *n.* mara mbili; (*counterpart*) mwenzi, sawa, mfano. *At the double,* mbio. — *v.t.* rudufya, zidisha kwa mbili; (*fold*) kunja, pinda; (*of sleeves, trousers &c.*) sega, pania; (*a cape—nautical*) zunguka (pitia) rasi, faulu; (*the fists*) fumba; — *v.i.* zidi (ongezeka) mara mbili; (*go quickly*) kaza mwendo, enda mbio, piga mbio; (*be capable of being folded &c.*) kunjika, pindika

Double back, kunja, pinda; rudi mbio. *Double up*, pinda, kunja; (*a person with pain &c.*) fanya kujikunja kwa maumivu *&c.*; (*intrans.*) kunjika, pindika; (*of a person in pain &c.*) jikunja (kunjika, kunjamana) kwa maumivu. **double-barrelled**, *a.* -a midomo (mitutu) miwili, -a kasiba mbili. **double-minded**, *a*, -a nia mbili, si -nyofu, -enye hila, kauleni, mnafiki, mzandiki. **double-quick**, *a. and adv.* upesi sana, kwa mbio sana. **doublet**, *n.* vazi kama fulana.

doubt, *n.* shaka, wasiwasi, tashwishi, tuhuma. — *v.i.* -wa na shaka, ona shaka, fanya tashwishi; —*v.t.* shuku, tuhumu, onea shaka; (*disbelieve*) tosadiki. **doubtful**, *a.* (*irresolute*) -enye wasiwasi (mashaka); (*uncertain*) si hakika, si yakini, -siyojulika, si dhahiri. **doubtless**, *adv.* bila shaka, hakika, yakini.

douche, *v.t.* tia maji (ya kusafisha, ya kuogesha) mwilini nje (au ndani kwa bomba). — *n.* maji (au dawa) ya *douche*.

dough, *n.* kinyunga, unga uliotiwa maji na chachu tayari kuokwa.

doughty, *a.* hodari, -shujaa, -jasiri.

dour, *a.* -gumu, -shupavu, -kaidi.

douse, *v.t.* lowesha, mwagia maji, chovya majini; (*extinguish light*) zima.

dove, *n.* (*lesser red-eyed*) hua, njiwa; (*ring-necked*) tetere; (*tambourine*) pugi kikombe; (*wood*) pugi, pugi wanda; (*large*) mwigo. **dovetail**, *v.t.* (*mortise*) umanisha kwa ndimi; — *v.i.* umana kwa ndimi. — *n.* kiungo cha mbao cha kuumana kwa ndimi.

dowager, *n.* mwanamke mjane aliyerithishwa mali na mumewe, hasa ni jina la heshima la mjane wa mwana wa mfalme. **dower**, *n.* sehemu ya urithi apewayo mjane mwanamke; mahari.

dowdy, *a.* (*of woman*) -enye kuvaa nguo zisizopendeza (ovyo ovyo).

down, (1) *n.* (*fine hair*) ulaika, *usu. in plur.* malaika. **downy**, *a.* laini, -ororo, -a malaika.

down, (2) *n.* nchi ya vilima vilima vyenye majani.

down, (3) *adv.* (*below*) chini; (*low, depressed*) katika hali dhaifu, katika huzuni; (*of descent, duration, decrease*) toka juu, tokea zamani, (kwa jinsi ya kushuka au kupunguza). *Come down*, shuka; (*decrease*) punguka. *Down with it!* angusha! vunja! angamiza! — *n.* ukosefu wa usitawi, hali dhaifu. *Ups and downs*, mabadiliko, mapinduzi. **downcast**, *a.* -enye huzuni, -zito. *Be downcast*, vunjikiwa (moyo). **downfall**, *n.* maanguko, maangamizi. *A downfall of rain*, mvua nyingi. **downhearted**, *a.* kama *downcast*. **downhill**, *a. and adv.* -a kuja (kwenda) chini, kwa kutelemka, -a kutelemka; -a kugeuka hali mbaya. **downpour**, *n.* mvua nyingi. **downright**, *a. and adv.* -nyofu, wazi, halisi; kabisa, sana. **down-trodden**, *a.* -a kudhulumiwa, -a kuonewa, -a kulemewa. **downward**, *a. and adv.* kama *downhill*.

downy, *a.* taz. *down* (1).

dowry, *n.* mahari.

doxology, *n.* wimbo wa kumsifu Mungu.

doyen, *n.* mzee (wa chama, kazi fulani *&c.*).

doze, *v.i.* sinzia. — *n.* usingizi mwepesi.

dozen, *n.* kumi na mbili, dazan. *A baker's dozen*, kumi na tatu.

dr. = *doctor*.

drab, (1) *a.* -a rangi ya hudhurungi nyeusi, -siyo na rangi nzuri; -a kuondoa furaha, -a kudhikika.

drab, (2) *n.* mwanamke mchafu, mkoo; malaya, kahaba.

drachm, *n.* kipimo cha dawa, kadiri ya *grains* 60, sehemu ya nane ya *ounce*; (*avoird.*) grains 27⅓, sehemu ya kumi na sita ya *ounce*; kiasi (kadiri) kidogo sana.

draft, *n.* (*of soldiers &c.*) kundi dogo la askari (watu) lililotolewa katika kundi kubwa kwa kazi maalum; (*sketch, design*) kiolezo, kielelezo, rasimu, ramani, mfano (wa kazi *&c.*)

ulioandikwa; (*rough copy of document*) mwandiko wa upesi (wa kujaribia, wa kufikiria &c.) wa hati (barua &c.); (*cheque*) hundi, hawala, hati ya kulipa fedha; (taz. **draught**.) — *v.t.* (*select, separate*) tenga (chagua) kundi dogo katika kundi kubwa (la askari &c.); (*design*) andika (piga) sanamu ya, toa, rasimu. **draftsman, draughtsman**, *n.* mwandishi wa ramani (rasimu, violezo, vielelezo, hati &c.).

drag, *v.t.* kokota, kokoteza, vuta, burura, buruta, gugurusha, gurugusha, tambaza; (*search*) tafutia, tafuta katika; — *v.i.* (*go slowly*) enda kwa shida; (*of time*) chelewa, kawia; (*of pain*) vuta. — *n.* (*hindrance*) kizuio, mgogoro, mzigo; (*net*) wavu. **draggle**, *v.t.* tambaza, tambarisha; kokoteza; (*through mud &c.*) chafua (kwa kutambarisha katika matope, maji); — *v.i.* burutwa, burutika, bururika, kokoteka, kokotezwa. **drag-net**, *n.* juya, jarifa.

dragoman, *n.* mkalimani (wa Kiarabu, Kituruki, Kiajemi), kiongozi.

dragon, *n.* joka (la hadithi) lenye mabawa, magamba, miguu minne yenye kucha, litoalo moto na moshi kinywani; namna ya mjusi anayeweza kuruka; namna ya njiwa. **dragon-fly**, *n.* kereng'ende. **dragon's-blood**, *n.* maziwa ya watu wawili. **dragoon**, *n.* askari mpanda farasi. — *v.t.* onea vibaya, tiisha kwa nguvu, dhulumu.

drain, *n.* mfereji, mfumbi; (*removal, waste*) upotevu, mpunguo, ondoleo; (*heavy expense*) gharama kubwa; (*small drink*) funda, maji kidogo. — *v.t.* ondoa maji (kausha) kwa mifereji; (*drink*) nywa yote pia; (*exhaust*) kumba, tumia mbali; (*draw off*) tiririsha, pitisha; (*make drainage*) fanyia mifereji ya kuchukulia taka; (*of wound*) ondoa usaha kwa vibomba; (*carry off water of*) chukua maji yote ya; — *v.i.* (*trickle away*) tiririka, churuzika. **drainage**, *n.* kuchukua maji; kupita maji kwa vijito; (*sewers*) mifereji ya taka. **drain-pipe**, *n.* bomba la kuchukulia taka, maji machafu &c.

drake, *n.* bata dume.

dram, *n.* taz. *drachm*; kiasi kidogo sana cha ulevi.

drama, *n.* hadithi (mtungo) iliyotungwa makusudi ya kuigizwa kama mchezo mbele ya watu; mchezo wa kuigiza mambo ya hadithi hiyo; mfululizo wa mambo ya shani yaliyompata mtu (au watu) hata ni kama kwamba yametungwa kama *drama*. **dramatic**, *a.* -a *drama*. **dramatist**, *n.* mtunga hadithi &c. ya *drama*. **dramatization**, *n.* maigizo ya matendo na mambo ya hadithi, uigaji. **dramatize**, *v.t.* tunga hadithi ya kuigizwa mbele ya watu kama mchezo; tunga habari ili ziweze kuigizwa kama mchezo.

drank, *p.t.* ya *drink*.

drape, *v.t.* pamba kwa nguo. **draper**, *n.* mwuza nguo. **drapery**, *n.* nguo, kitambaa.

drastic, *a.* -a nguvu sana. *Make drastic alterations*, badili (pindua) sana.

draught, *n.* taz. *draft*; (*carrying, drawing*) uchukuzi, uvutaji; (*of fish*) mvuo wa samaki kwa wavu; (*act of drinking*) mnywo, funda; (*of medicine*) kiasi cha dawa iliyofanywa tayari kunywewa; (*nautical*) kadiri ya meli (chombo) kwenda chini katika maji, au kadiri ya maji inayohitajiwa ili meli ielee; (*current of air*) upepo, mvuto wa upepo, mwendo hewa kama inavyopita katikati ya mlango wa dirisha lililo wazi. *Draughts* (*game*), dama. — *v.t.* taz. draft. **draught-horse**, *n.* farasi mwenye nguvu nyingi mwenye kazi ya kuvuta gari &c. zito. **draughtsman**, *n.* taz. *draftsman*. **draughty**, *a.* -a upepo mwingi.

draw, *v.t.* (*p.t.* **drew**, *p.t.* **drawn**) (*drag*) kokota, vuta, buruta, burura; (*depict*) andika, piga (picha, sanamu, kiolezo &c.); (*of water*) teka, (*by small quantities*) chota; (*sword &c.*) futa, chomoa; (*money*) toza, pata; (*tears, blood &c.*) toa; toza. *Draw a battle, or a game*, fanya sawa, shinda na pasipo mmojwapo kushinda, shindana sawa-sawa. *Draw a bow*, piga upindi. *Draw breath*, paaza pumzi, vuta pumzi, tanafusi, (*rest*) pumzika. *Draw a conclusion*, ona, dhani (baada ya kutoa au kusikia sababu). *Draw to an end*, -wa karibu na mwisho. *Draw a game*, fanya suluhu (usare). *Draw a lesson*, jifunza. *Draw a line*, piga mstari. *Draw the long bow*, piga chuku, tia chumvi. *Draw lots*, piga kura. *Draw a nail*, kongoa, zidua, (*a tooth*) ng'oa, (*a cork*) zibua. *Draw near*, karibia, sogea karibu, jongea karibu. *Draw off* (*retire*) rudi, enda zake (zao &c.); (*take off*) vua, ondoa; (*drain off*) churuzisha. *Draw on* (*approach*), karibia; (*of money*) lipiza; tumia; (*of clothes*) vaa; (*bring*) leta; (*of resources*) twaa sehemu ya, gharimisha, twaa katika; (*entice*) vuta. *Draw out* (*write clearly*) andika vizuri; (*explain*) eleza, fafanua; (*enlarge*) ongeza; (*cause to talk*) toa, toza, futua. *Draw together*, kusanyika; (*oneself*) jikunyata. *Draw up* (*arrange*), panga, ratibu; (*stop*) simama; (*write*) andika. *Draw water*, teka maji. *It draws six feet of water*, merikebu (meli, chombo) yataka maji ya futi sita. — *n.* jambo (kitu) linalovuta (linalotamanisha); (*lottery*) bahati nasibu, kupiga kura; (*drawn game*) sare, suluhu, shindano lililokwisha bila mmojawapo kushinda. **drawback,** *n.* kizuio, kizuizi, ila; ushuru wa bidhaa uliotozwa ambao unarudishwa kama bidhaa hiyo ikipelekwa kutoka nchi. **drawbridge,** *n.* daraja (ulalo, mtatago) linaloweza kuinuliwa au kuvutwa kuzuia watu wasivuke. **drawer,** *n.* (*of a table*) mtoto wa meza; (*of chest of drawers*) saraka, mtoto; (*draughtsman*) mwandishi (wa ramani, violezo &c.). **drawers,** *n.* suruali. *Chest of drawers*, almari, sanduku (kabati) lenye watoto. **drawing,** *n.* kuandika sanamu (picha, ramani, violezo &c.); (*picture*) picha, sanamu, andiko, choro, taswira. **drawing-room,** *n.* sebule. **drawl,** *v.t.* kokota (tambaza, kokoteza) maneno (sauti), dodosa, ganzaganza — *n.* usemi wa kukokoteza maneno **drawn,** *v.pf.t.* ya *draw*; — *a. A d. wn battle, game &c.*, vita (shindano, mchezo) pasipo kushinda mtu, ushindani wa sawa-sawa.

dray, *n.* namna ya gari la kuchukulia mizigo mizito. **dray-horse,** *n.* farasi mwenye nguvu kwa kuvuta gari.

dread, *v.t.* ogopa, hofia. — *n.* woga, hofu. **dread, dreadful,** *a.* -a hofu, -a kutisha, -a kuogofya; (*disagreeable*) -a kuchukiza, -baya; (*as intensive*) sana. **dreadnought,** *n.* namna ya manowari kubwa sana.

dream, *n.* ndoto, njozi, ruya. — *v.i.* (*p.t. and pf.t.* **dreamt, dreamed**) ota (ndoto). **dreamer,** *n.* mwota ndoto; awazaye mambo kama ya ndoto. **dreamy,** *a.* -a kama ndoto, -enye kuota ndoto, -sinzia. *Dreamy eyes*, macho ya kusinzilia. *A dreamy person*, mtu afanyaye mambo kama kwamba anasinzia; awazaye sana mambo yasivyo.

drear, dreary, *a.* pasipo furaha, -a kama ukiwa, -a kutia huzuni, -a kufanya moyo mzito, -baya, -a kuchosha.

dredge, (1) *n.* wavu au chombo cha kuzolea taka chini ya maji. — *v.t.* zoa taka chini ya maji ili kufanya mfereji (kilindi) mkubwa zaidi. **dredger,** *n.* kama *dredge*.

dredge, (2) *v.t.* nyunyiza unga (sukari) juu ya nyama (maandazi &c.). **dredger,** *n.* chombo kama kopo lenye vitundu vidogo vidogo cha kunyunyizia unga, sukari &c.

dregs, *n.* takataka, kishinda, tama, machujo, mashapo, masimbi, mashudu, mashata.

drench, *v.t.* lowesha, mwagia maji, nywesha (wanyama) dawa.

dress, *v.t.* (*arrange*) panga; (*hair*) chana (suka) nywele; (*apply medicine*) tia dawa, funga dawa; (*put clothes upon*) vika; (*supply with clothes*) visha; (*adorn*) pamba; (*cook*) pika; (*set ready*) tengeneza, andaa; (*prepare raw material*) chambua, chamvua; (*soil*) simadi, tia mbolea; — *v.i.* (*get into line*) pangana; (*put on clothes*) vaa, valia; (*dress finely*) piga umalidadi. *Dress down* (*scold*) kemea, karipia. *Dress out*, pamba. *Dress up*, pamba, valisha nguo nzuri; (*intrans.*) vaa nguo za kuigiza. — *n.* nguo, mavazi, mvao; (*woman's*) kisutu, kanga. **dresser,** *n.* (*kitchen*) meza au kabati ya jikoni; (*surgeon's assistant*) msaidizi wa daktari. **dressing,** *n.* (*of calico*) dondo; (*medical*) dawa ya kubandika; (*on wound after circumcision*) alfafa; (*keeping time*) utaratibu (wa kupanga askari); (*love of dress*) umalidadi; (*sauce*) mchuzi, kitoweo; (*manure*) mbolea, samadi.

drew, *p.t.* ya *draw.*

dribble, *v.i.* tiririka, dondoka; — *v.t.* toa udelele (udende, mate) kama mtoto au mzee afanyavyo; (*football*) piga chenga (kumzungusha mtu katika kucheza mpira). **dribblet,** *n.* kidogo. *By dribblets*, kidogo kidogo.

drift, *v.i.* chukuliwa (*e.g.* kwa mkondo wa maji &c.), enda (*e.g.* juu ya maji yanayopita &c.); peperushwa na kufanya chungu (*e.g.* majani yaliyopukutika, mchanga laini &c.); ingia polepole bila kujua (*e.g.* nchi vitani, mtu katika umaskini au ulegevu &c.). — *n.* mkondo (*e.g.* wa maji), mvuto wa meli au chombo katika majira yake kwa mkondo; (*meaning*) maana; (*heap*) chungu (ya majani, mchanga, theluji &c.) iliyofanywa kwa upepo, bahari &c. **drift-ice,** *n.* barafu baharini inayochukuliwa na mikondo. **drift-wood,** *n.* mbao zilizoachwa pwani maji yarudipo.

drill, (1) *n.* namna ya kitambaa, katani au amerikani nzito.

drill, (2) *n.* (*military*) utaratibu wa askari, kwata, gwaride, taburu. — *v.t.* amrisha (chezesha, fundisha) askari; — *v.i.* cheza (askari), cheza gwaride (taburu).

drill, (3) *n.* (*boring tool*) kekee. — *v.t.* zua, toboa, pekecha.

drill, (4) *n.* mfuo (wa kupandia mbegu); namna ya mashine ya kufanyia mifuo na kupandia mbegu humo. — *v.t.* panda mbegu katika mifuo.

drink, *v.t.* *and* *i.* (*p.t.* **drank,** *pf.t.* **drunk**) -nywa. *Drink in*, (*receive gladly*) pokea (sikia, ona) kwa furaha. *Get drunk*, lewa. *Drink to*, *Drink the health of*, salimu (kwa kunwyea divai), pigia salamu. — *n.* kinwaji, kinyweo; (*alcoholic*) kileo, ulevi. **drinkable,** *a.* -a kunyweka. **drinker,** *n.* mnywaji; (*drunkard*) mlevi. **drinking,** *n.* kunywa, mnywo, unywaji. *Given to, fond of, drinking*, penda sana kunywa (ulevi). **drunk,** *a.* *Be drunk*, lewa. **drunkard,** *n.* mlevi. **drunken,** *a.* -a kulewa, -levi, -a ulevi. **drunkenness,** *n.* ulevi.

drip, *v.i.* tiririka, chururika, dondoka, tona; — *v.t.* tiririsha, dondosha, tonesha. — *n.* mtiririko, tone, sauti ya maji kutona. **dripping,** *n.* *of meat*) uto wa nyama; (*dropping*) kutona, manyunyu.

drive, *v.t.* (*p.t.* **drove,** *pf.t.* **driven**) endesha (ongoza) kwa nguvu; (*in carriage*) chukua kwa gari; (*force, urge*) sukuma, sukumiza, shurutisha; (*of a nail*) pigilia, kongomea; (*cattle*) swaga, shunga; (*a car, engine &c.*) endesha; (*tunnel, cavity &c.*) fukua, fanya shimo (tundu); — *v.i.* (*rush*) enda kwa nguvu; (*travel in vehicle*) enda (tembea) kwa gari. *Drive away*, fukuza, shunga, winga, furusha, kimbiza; (*birds from field*) amia. *Drive at*, taka, jaribia. *Let drive*, piga. *What are you driving at?* wataka nini? — *n.* mwendo katika gari, njia ya kuendea gari; (*of ball &c.*) mpigo, mrusho;

(*energy*) nguvu. **driver,** *n.* mwendeshi, mwendeshaji, msimamizi wa gari (farasi *&c.*), saisi. **driver-ant,** *n.* siafu. **driving,** *n.* kuendesha, kusukumiza, kufukuza *&c.* **drove,** *n.* kundi (la ng'ombe *&c.*) linaloongozwa. **drover,** *n.* mwongozaji wa kundi (la ng'ombe *&c.*).

drivel, *v.i.* toka ute (udende, udelele); (*talk foolishly*) payuka, payapaya, bwabwaja, puza. —*n.* upuzi, mapayo, mapiswa. **driveller,** *n.* mpayukaji.

driven, *pf.t.* ya *drive.*

driver, *n.,* **driver-ant,** *n.,* **driving,** *n.* taz. *drive.*

drizzle, *n.* manyunyu, wasa la mvua, mvua ya marasharasha. — *v.i.* nyunya, nyonyota.

droll, *a.* -a kuchekesha, -cheshi. **drollery,** *n.* ucheshi, uchekeshaji, ubishi, mzaha.

dromedary, *n.* ngamia.

drone, *n.* nyuki dume; (*lazy person*) mvivu, mkunguni, mtepetevu, mlegevu, goigoi; (*sound*) uvumi, mvumo. — *v.i.* vuma (kama nyuki *&c.*); sema au imba kwa sauti ya kivivu.

drongo, *n.* (*glossy backed*) mramba.

droop, *v.i.* fifia, zimia, dhoofika, shuka, inama; — *v.t.* (*let down*) inamisha, shusha. — *n.* mwinamo, mshuko.

drop, *v.i.* anguka, ponyoka, shuka, telemka, poromoka; (*stop*) koma, isha; (*utter*) toa (neno); (*of water*) tona; (*grain*) dondoka; (*leaves*) pukutika; (*wind*) legea; — *v.t.* (*let go*) acha, angusha, bwaga, poromosha. *Drop off,* pungua. *Drop into,* tumbukia. — *n.* tone, kitone; cho chote kinachoshuka au kushushwa; (*decrease*) kipunguo; (*distance*) urefu kati ya kitu kilicho juu na kingine kilicho chini. **droppings,** *n.* matone; mavi ya wanyama.

dropsy, *n.* tumbo la maji, istiska.

dross, *n.* (*of metals*) mavi (ya chuma, ya madini); (*scum*) povu; (*rubbish*) taka, takataka.

drought, *n.* kukosa (ukosefu wa) mvua siku nyingi, kiu.

drove, *n. and p.t.* ya *drive.*

drover, *n.* taz. *drive.*

drown, *v.t.* tosa majini, fisha kwa maji; (*submerge*) zamisha, tumbukiza; (*overwhelm, silence*) shinda, nyamazisha, hinikiza; — *v.i.* (*be drowned*) tota, fa majini.

drowse, *v.i.* sinzia. **drowsily,** *adv.* kivivu. **drowsiness,** *n.* lepe, lepe ya usingizi, ndezi. **drowsy,** *a.* -enye lepe, -enye usingizi, -zito kwa usingizi.

drub, *v.t.* piga.

drudge, *n.* mtu mwenye kazi ya kuchosha (inayokulia, inayolemea, isiyopendeza). — *v.i.* fanya kazi ya kuchosha (isiyopendeza, ya kitumwa). **drudgery,** *n.* kazi ngumu (isiyopendeza), kazi ya taabu (inayokulia, inayolemea).

drug, *n.* dawa; (*in sinister sense*) dawa inayotumika vibaya, hasa ya kulevya; bidhaa isiyouzikana kwa sababu ya wingi wake, *e.g. a drug in the market.* — *v.t.* nywesha dawa (hasa ya nguvu, sumu, kileo); tia (ghoshi kwa) dawa, hasa ya sumu au ya kudhuru; (*indulge in narcotics &c.*) zoea kunywa dawa zinazolevya *&c.* kwa kiasi cha kudhuru. **druggist,** *n.* mwuza dawa, mwenye duka la dawa.

drugget, *n.* namna ya zulia.

druggist, *n.* taz. *drug.*

Druid, *n.* kuhani wa Uingereza wa zamani.

drum, *n.* ngoma (ya kupiga), cho chote chenye mfano wa ngoma, *e.g.* pipa, kopo *&c.*; (*of ear*) ngozi katikati ya sikio, kiwambo cha sikio; (*sound of drum*) dundo. — *v.t. and i.* piga ngoma; pigapiga, gongagonga. **drumstick,** *n.* mkwiro.

drunk, *a.,* **drunkard,** *n.,* **drunken,** *a.,* **drunkenness,** *n.* taz. *drink.*

dry, *a.* -kavu, yabisi; (*waterless*) kame, pasipo mvua, pasipo maji; (*plain*) si -a kupendeza; (*severe*) -kali, -gumu; (*thirsty*) -enye kiu, -a kutia kiu; (*of wine*) -chungu, -siyo -tamu; (*of speech*) baridi; (*of facts*) dhahiri, waziwazi. — *v.t.* kausha; (*clothes*) anika; (*hands, tears, eyes*) futa; — *v.i.* (*become dry*) kauka, nyauka. **dryness,** *n.* ukavu, uyabisi; (*of teeth after eating fruit, e.g. unripe banana*) ukafu, ukakasi, ukamvu, ugege. **dry-nurse,** *n.* aya, mlezi (asiyenyonyesha). **dry-rot,** *n.* siridado, uozi wa mti na mbao.

dryad, *n.* kizimwi (zimwi) wa mwituni.

dry-nurse, *n.*, **dry-rot,** *n.* taz. *dry.*

dual, *a.* -a watu wawili, -a vitu viwili.

dub, *v.t.* pasha jina la heshima, taja, pasha jina.

dubious, *a.* -enye mashaka, si hakika, si -aminifu, -a kutia mashaka.

ducal, *a.* taz. *duke.*

ducat, *n.* fedha ya Ulaya zamani, thamani yake kadiri ya shilingi tisa.

duchess, *n.*, **duchy,** *n.* taz. *duke.*

duck, (1) *n.* namna ya kitambaa kizito cha pamba au katani.

duck, (2) *n.* (*white backed*) kotwe; (*applied to many sp.*) bata, salili; (*darling &c.*) mpenzi, muhibu, tiba. *Make ducks and drakes of,* tapanya, poteza, fuja, tupa. **duckling,** *n.* mtoto wa bata. — *v.i.* zama ghafula chini ya maji; (*bend down*) inama, jikunja; — *v.t.* chovya, tumbukiza majini.

duct, *n.* mchirizi, kichirizi, kifereji, nyweleo. **ductile,** *a.* -a kuvutikana (kama madini kufanyika uzi); -a kufinyangikana (kama udongo wa ufinyanzi); -a kunama, -a kinamo; (*of character*) -sikivu, -sikizi, -tiifu. **ductless,** *a.* -siyo na mchirizi *&c.*

dud, *n.* (*slang*) kitu (au mtu) kisichofaa, kisichositawi, kipooza.

dudgeon, *n.* chuki, mfundo, uchungu, hasira, kinyongo, undani, kasirani.

due, *n.* haki, halali, mali, stahili, desturi, ada; (*tax*) ushuru, kodi. — *a.* -a haki, -a halali *&c. Due to,* kwa sababu ya; (*befitting*) -a kupasa, -a wajibu. *It is due to the sun,* ni kwa sababu ya jua. *The ship is due to-day,* meli inatazamiwa kufika leo. — *adv.* barabara, sawasawa. *The ship will sail due south,* meli itasafiri kusini barabara.

duel, *n.* pigano (shindano, jadiliano) la watu wawili.

duet, *n.* wimbo wa watu (vinanda *&c.*) wawili.

duffer, *n.* mjinga, baradhuli, mzito wa akili.

dug, *n.* titi, chuchu (ya mnyama), kiwele.

dug, *v. p.t. and pf.t.* ya *dig.*

dugong, *n.* nguva.

dug-out, *n.* (*canoe*) mtumbwi; (*in a trench*) mfano wa chumba katika handaki ya vita.

duiker, *n.* (*Abbotts*) mindi; (*common*) funo.

duke, *n.* mtu mwenye cheo bora kuliko wote ila mfalme; katika nchi nyingine, mfalme mdogo. *The dukes* (*slang*) ngumi. **ducal,** *a.* -a *duke.* **duchess,** *n. duke* wa kike, mke wa *duke.* **duchy, dukedom,** *n.* milki au cheo cha *duke.*

dulcet, *a.* -tamu (kusikia). **dulcify,** *v.t.* fanya kuwa -tamu. **dulcimer,** *n.* namna ya kinanda.

dull, *a.* -zito, -pumbavu, punguani wa akili; (*slow*) -tepetevu, -vivu, goigoi, si -epesi, si -elekevu, si -a bidii, si -a furaha; (*dim*) -siong'aa, si -angavu; (*dark*) -a giza, -a mawingu, -eusi kidogo, -a utusitusi; (*tedious*) -a kuchukiza; (*blunt*) butu. *A dull discourse,* maneno baridi, maneno mazito (yasiyokolea). *Get dull* (*colour*), chujuka, fifia, chakaa, kwajuka. — *v.t.* pumbaza, chosha akili; (*reduce force of*) nyamazisha, tuliza, punguza; (*blunt*) fanya butu, tia ubutu, seneza; (*make cloudy &c.*) tia giza (ukungu, weusi), ondoa (punguza) uangavu. **dullard,** *n.* baradhuli, mpumbavu, mzito wa akili. **dullness,** *n.* mazimbwezimbwe, giza, weusi, utusitusi; (*of intellect*) uzito, upumbavu *&c.*

duly, *adv.* vizuri, ipasavyo, taratibu, kwa kawaida, kwa wakati wake, sawasawa, barabara.

dumb, *a.* bubu; (*silent*) -a kimya, -a

kunyamaa. *Dumb animal*, mnyama. **dumb-bells**, *n.* vyuma vya kuchezea vya kuzoeza viungo vya mwili (mchezo wa juhudi). **dumbfound**, *v.t.* duwaza, pumbaza, shangaza, fadhaisha. **dumbness**, *n.* ububu.

dummy, *n.* mfano, mwigo, sanamu. — *a.* -a uwongo, -a kuigiza. *Dummy cartridge*, kiasi kisicho na risasi.

dump, *v.t.* (*rubbish*) tupa (taka, takataka); (*commercial*) leta bidhaa ya kuuza rahisi sana (hasa katika nchi nyingine ili kuiuza rahisi kuliko bidhaa ya namna ile ile ya kwao); — *v.i.* (*drop down*) anguka ghafula (kwa kishindo). — *n.* jaa (ya taka); ghala (akiba) kubwa, hasa ya zana za vita.

dumpling, *n.* namna ya maandazi mazito, bumunda.

dumps, *n.* chuki, hasira, uchungu, mifundo, kasirani. *In the dumps*, udhika, kasirika, -wa na mfundo.

dumpy, *a.* -fupi na -nene.

dun, (1) *a.* -eusi kidogo, -enye rangi ya majivu meusi.

dun, (2) *v.t.* taka fedha kwa makelele, chagiza, kamia, kalia, shikilia, lipiza deni, toza fedha; (*harass*) udhi, sumbua.

dunce, *n.* mjinga kabisa, punguani wa akili, mzito wa akili, baradhuli, mzuzu.

dunderhead, *n.* mjinga, punguani wa akili, mzito wa akili, afkani.

dune, *n.* eneo la mchanga wa tifutifu pwani lenye miinuko.

dung, *n.* mavi, kinyesi, shonde, samadi; (*dried cake for fuel*) shonde. **dunghill**, *n.* jaa, chungu ya samadi.

dungaree(s), *n.* vazi linalovaliwa nje na wenye kazi ya kuangalia mashine *&c.*, kuhifadhi nguo za ndani.

dungeon, *n.* gereza, kifungo; gereza ya chini ya ngome.

dunghill, *n.* taz. *dung*.

dunnage, *n.* makwa, mbao (matawi *&c.*) zilizotiwa kati ya mizigo ya shehena kuizuia isijongee, au chini ngamani kuzuia shehena isipate maji.

duodenum, *n.* sehemu ya utumbo (inchi kumi na mbili) iliyo karibu na tumbo lenyewe.

dupe, *v.t.* danganya, punja, kopa, laghai, rubuni, ghilibu. — *n.* baradhuli, mjinga, mzuzu.

duplicate, *v.t.* nakili, fuatisha, andika (fanya) -ingine sawasawa; (*increase*) zidisha kwa mbili. — *n.* nakili, mwenzi, -ingine mfano mmoja, -ingine sawasawa. — *a.* -a mfano mmoja, -a sawasawa, -a nakili.

duplicator, *n.* mashine ya kupigia chapa nakili za hati, maandiko *&c.*

duplicity, *n.* hila, udanganyifu, unafiki, hitilafu, kauleni.

durable, *a.* -a kudumu sana, -a kukaa sana, -a daima, -a aushi, -sioharibika upesi. **durance**, *n.* kifungo, kufungwa (gerezani). **duration**, *n.* maisha, muda, wakati, uendeleo, kikao, aushi, udumifu. **during**, *prep.* wakati wa, pindi ya, kwa.

durbar, *n.* baraza. *Hold a durbar*, fanya baraza, barizi.

duress(e), *n.* kifungo, hali ya kufungwa (ya kuzuiwa, ya kushurutishwa).

durian, *n.* fenesi la kizungu.

during, *prep.* taz. *durable*.

durst, *p.t.* ya *dare*.

dusk, *n.* giza la jioni, magharibi. **dusky**, *a.* -a giza kidogo, -eusi kidogo.

dust, *n.* vumbi; (*on a road*) tifutifu; (*powder*) unga. *Throw dust in the eyes of*, kosesha, danganya, laghai. *Raise a dust*, tifua; (*make a disturbance*) fanya fitina (makelele, ghasia). *Bite the dust*, anguka chini; uawa; jeruhiwa. *Lick the dust*, jinyenyekea sana. — *v.t.* nyunyizia kitu kama unga (vumbi, sukari nyembamba, dawa ya unga *&c.*); (*wipe*) pangusa, futa; (*by beating*) kung'uta. **dust-bin**, *n.* pipa la kutia taka. **dust-cart**, *n.* gari la kuchukulia taka. **duster**, *n.* kitambaa (cha kupangusia). **dust-man**, *n.* topasi, mtu mwenye kazi ya kuondoa taka katika mapipa ya taka mijini;

dust-proof, *a.* -siopenyezeka (-sio-ingilikana) na mavumbi. **dusty**, *a.* -enye mavumbi, -a tifutifu.

Dutch, *a.* -a *Holland.* — *n.* lugha ya *Holland*; watu wa *Holland.* **Dutchman**, *n.* mzalia wa nchi ya *Holland.* **Dutch oven**, *n.* námna ya jiko la bati kuweka mbele ya moto.

duty, *n.* wajibu, ipasayo, mujibu, haki, kazi, kiwango; (*toll*) ushuru, kodi; (*compliments*) salaam, maamkio. *It is my duty*, imenipasa, ni wajibu wangu. *Duty bids me*, imenibidi. *Duties of social station*, daraja, cheo, madaraka. *Duty* (*customs*), ushuru wa forodhani. **duteous, dutiful**, *a.* -tii, -tiifu, -sikivu, -sikizi, -a kufanya wajibu (ipasayo), -a kuheshimu wazazi (wazee).

dwarf, *n.* mbilikimo, kibeti, kidurango. *Be dwarfed* (*dwarfish*), via, kundaa, dumaa. — *a.* -dogo (-fupi) kuliko -a kawaida; -a namna ndogo. — *v.t.* fanya kuonekana kama kwamba ni -dogo (kwa kupambanua, kwa kulinganisha); (*hinder growth*) kundaza, viza, dumaza, zuia mmea *&c.* usimee zaidi. **dwarfish**, *a.* -dogo, -liovia, -liokundaa, liodumaa, -a kibeti.

dwell, *v.i.* (*p.t. and pf. t.* **dwelt**) kaa, keti, shinda, fanya makao (kitende, mastakimu, maskani), sakini. *Dwell on, Dwell upon* (*a subject, point &c.*) toa maneno mengi juu ya, fikiri sana, eleza sana, sumbukia, fululiza, endeleza. **dweller**, *n.* mkaa, mkaaji, mkazi, mzalia. **dwelling**, *n.* makao, makazi, maskani, nyumba, kitende, mastakimu, chengo, kaya.

dwindle, *v.i.* pungua, punguka, chakaa, dhoofika, fifia, sinyaa.

dye, *n.* rangi. *Fast dye*, rangi isiyochujuka. — *v.t.* tia rangi; — *v.i.* (*take on colour*) tilika rangi. **dyer**, *n.* mwenye uchumi (kazi) wa kutia rangi.

dying, *n. and a.* taz. *die.*

dyke, *n.* taz. *dike.*

dynamics, *n.* elimu ya nguvu zinazoendesha.

dynamite, *n.* namna ya baruti yenye nguvu nyingi. — *v.t.* haribu (pasua, teketeza) kwa *dynamite.*

dynamo, *n.* mashine inayogeuza nguvu za kuendesha kuwa umeme.

dynasty, *n.* nasaba (jamaa, jadi, ukoo) ya mfalme.

dysentery, *n.* tumbo la (ugonjwa wa) kuhara damu.

dyspepsia, *n.* ugonjwa wa kutoweza kuyeyusha (kubadili, kupokea) chakula vizuri tumboni; (*heartburn, eructation*) kiungulia. **dyspeptic**, *a.* (-enye) ugonjwa wa *dyspepsia. I have dyspepsia, I am dyspeptic*, tumbo langu haliweki vizuri chakula; chakula hakikai vizuri tumboni mwangu; chakula hakinitulii tumboni.

E

each, *a.* kila -moja, -moja; (*with verbs*) -ana, *e.g. beat each other*, pigana; *go with each other*, fuatana; *help each other*, saidiana. *Each man, each of the men*, kila mtu, watu wote. *Each one*, kila mtu mbalimbali. *Each other*, wao kwa wao, kila mtu na mwenziwe.

eager, *a.* -enye bidii (moyo, shauku, tamaa, harara, pupa). **eagerly**, *adv.* kwa moyo, kwa bidii &c. **eagerness**, *n.* moyo, bidii, juhudi, shauku, tamaa; (*excessive*) pupa, harara.

eagle, *n.* (*Vulturine fish-*) koho; (*African sea-*) furukombe, fukombe; tai. **eagle-eyed**, *a.* -enye macho makali kama ya tai. **eaglet**, *n.* kinda la tai.

ear, (1) *n.* (*of corn &c.*) suke.

ear, (2) *n.* sikio. *Give ear*, sikia, sikiliza, tega sikio. *Bring about the ears*, letea matata (maangamizi, madhara). *Set by the ears*, fitini, gombanisha. *Ear ornaments*, kipuli, kipini, jasi. **ear-ache**, *n.* kuumwa sikioni; maumivu ya sikioni. **ear-drum**, *n.* kiwambo cha sikio. **ear-mark**, *v.t.* tia alama (ya kujulisha mwenyewe); (*set aside*) weka (kwa kusudi maalum). **ear-ring**, *n.* bali, kipuli, pete ya sikio. **earshot**, *n.* kadiri ya kusikia maneno. *He is not within earshot*, hawezi kusikia (kwa kuwa yu mbali).

earl, *n.* jina la heshima la mtu mwenye cheo kikubwa, wa chini yake ni *marquis*. **earldom**, *n.* daraja au milki ya *earl*.

early, *a. and adv.* mapema, -a alfajiri, -a asubuhi na mapema; (*premature*) mbele ya wakati wake, upesi, -tangulifu; (*ancient*) -a kale, -a zamani; (*near the beginning*) mwanzo; mwanzoni, -a karibu na kwanza (mwanzo).

earmark, *v.* taz. *ear* (2).

earn, *v.t.* pata (kwa kazi), chuma; (*deserve*) stahili. **earnings**, *n.* mshahara, chumo.

earnest, (1) *n.* arabuni, rehani, amana.

earnest, (2) *a.* -a juhudi, -a bidii, -a moyo, -a nguvu, -a kweli. — *n.* bidii juhudi &c. *In earnest*, kwa kweli, kwa moyo. *Be in earnest*, kaza moyo, taka (fanya) kwa moyo, jifunga, jitahidi. **earnestly**, *adv.* kwa moyo, kwa bidii &c.

earnings, *n.* taz. *earn*.

ear-ring, *n.*, **earshot**, *n.* taz. *ear* (2).

earth, *n.* (*land*) nchi, ardhi; (*soil*) udongo, ardhi; (*the planet*) dunia, ulimwengu; (*dry land as opposed to sea*) bara, nchi kavu; (*animals' hole or lair*) pango, shimo. — *v.t.* funika kwa udongo, fukia; tia uzi wa simu ya umeme ardhini. **earthen**, *a.* -a udongo. *Earthenware*, vitu (vyombo) vya udongo; (*china*) vyombo vya kauri. **earthly**, *a.* -a dunia hii; (*bad*) -nyonge, -baya. *No earthly use*, haifai hata kidogo. **earthquake**, *n.* tetemeko, (tetemo, tikisiko) la nchi. **earthwork**, *n.* boma la udongo. **earthy**, *a.* -a udongo.

ease, *n.* raha, utulivu, amani, buraha; (*after pain*) faraja, nafuu, ashekali, hueni. *Be ill at ease*, fadhaika, taharuki, sumbuka, hangaika, ona wasiwasi. *Be at ease, feel at ease*, starehe, kunjuka, changamka, ona raha. *Put at ease*, starehesha, teremesha, changamsha, ondoa shaka. *With ease*, rahisi, upesi, bila bidii, bila kuchoka (kuhangaika). — *v.t.* tuliza, fariji, starehesha, pumzisha; (*of pain*) nyamazisha, punguza, ondolea maumivu; (*make easy*) rahisisha; (*ease oneself*) enda chooni; (*make loose*) legeza; — *v.i.* (*ease down*) pumzika, legaza mbio; (*ease off*) jongea (sogea) mbali kidogo. **easily**, *adv.* kwa urahisi, kwa upesi, bila taabu, vizuri. **easiness**, *n.* urahisi, wepesi; (*comfort*) raha, ustarehe. **easy**, *a.* rahisi, -epesi, -a mara moja, sahala; (*quiet*) -a raha, -tulivu, -radhi, -siyo na udhia; (*lax*) -pole, si -gumu, si -zito, -epesi. **easy**, *adv.* *Go easy, take things easy*, enda polepole (bila kutumia nguvu). **easy-going,** *a.* -pole, si -gumu, si -kali; (*placable*) -radhi, -epesi, -kuridhika; (*careless*) -zembe, -vivu.

easel, *n.* chombo cha kuegemeza picha (sanamu), au cha kuwekea ubao wa kuandikia.

easily, *adv.*, **easiness,** *n.* taz. *ease.*

east, *n.* mashariki, matlai, maawao, maawio, macheo. *The Near East,* nchi ya *Turkey, Balkans* na jirani. *The Far East,* nchi za *China, Japan* na jirani. *The Middle East,* nchi za *Persia, Mesopotamia* na jirani. — *adv.* masharikini. **easterly, eastern,** *a.* -a mashariki. **eastward,** *adv.* masharikini. **east-wind,** *n.* matlai.

Easter, *n.* Pasaka, sikukuu ya kufufuka Yesu Kristo.

easterly, *a.*, **eastern,** *a.*, **eastward,** *adv.*, **east-wind,** *n.* taz. *east.*

easy, *a. and adv.*, **easy-going,** *a.* taz. *ease.*

eat, *v.t.* (*p.t.* **ate,** *pf.t.* **eaten**) -la, tafuna; (*take food with fingers*) mega; (*destroy*) -la, haribu, teketeza; — *v.i.* -la. *Eat enough,* shiba. *Eat too much,* jivimbisha, sakarika, sakara. *Eat* (*ye*) kuleni. *Eat one's words,* rudi (rudisha, geuza) maneno, omba radhi, kiria uwongo. **eatable,** *a.* -a kulika, -a kutafunika. **eatables,** *n.* vyakula. **eaten,** *pf.t. Eaten up with pride,* -enye kiburi kingi. **eating,** *n.* ulaji, malaji. **eating-house,** *n.* mkahawa, hoteli.

eaves, *n.* mchirizi, upenu. **eaves-dropper,** *n.* mdukizi, mduzi.

ebb, *v.i.* (*of tide*) -pwa, rudi; (*lessen*) pungua, punguka, fifia. — *n.* maji kupwa (mafu); (*decline*) kutoka, kuisha, mwisho.

ebon, *a.* -a mpingo; (*black*) -eusi kabisa. **ebonite,** *n.* kitu kigumu cheusi, kidogo kama mpingo, kifanyizwacho kwa kuyeyusha mpira pamoja na kiberiti. Pia huitwa *vulcanite.* **ebony,** *n.* mpingo; (*colour*) weusi. — *a.* -a mpingo.

ebriety, *n.* ulevi, kulewa.

ebullient, *a.* -a kuchemka, -a kufoka, -a kububujika, -a kujaa furaha. **ebullition,** *n.* mchemko, foko, bubujiko; (*outburst*) ukali, mkazo, kipindi.

eccentric, *a.* -geni, -a kinyongo, -a kasirani, si -a taratibu, si -a kawaida, punguani -a akili. *He is eccentric,* afuata roho yake, ashika yake. **eccentricity,** *n.* ajabu, ugeni; nia mbali, desturi mbali, kinyongo.

Ecclesiastes, *n.* kitabu kimoja cha Agano la Kale kiitwacho Mhubiri.

ecclesiastic, *n.* kasisi, padre, mtu mwenye daraja katika Kanisa la kikristo. **ecclesiastical,** *a.* -a Kanisa la kikristo, -a padre, -a dini.

echo, *n.* mwangwi; (*likeness*) mfano, kifani, kivuli; (*response*) jibu, itiko. — *v.i.* toa mwangwi; — *v.t.* (*repeat*) rudisha sauti, kariri, fuatisha maneno.

éclat, *n.* uzuri, urembo, fahari, sifa nyingi; (*applause*) vifijo.

eclectic, *n.* mteuzi, mchaguzi (katika mengi, asiyefuata madhehebu moja). — *a.* -chaguzi, -teuzi. **eclectism,** *n.* namna (taratibu, tabia) ya *eclectic;* uteuzi, uchaguzi.

eclipse, *n.* kupatwa mwezi (jua); (*obscuration*) kupitiliwa, kushindwa. — *v.t.* shinda, pita, acha nyuma. *Be eclipsed,* patwa, liwa; (*obscured*) shindwa, pitiliwa mbali. **ecliptic,** *n.* njia ya jua angani na mstari wa chini yake katika nchi.

economic, *a.* -a kuhusu kuendesha nyumba au mali; -a kuhusu kuendesha nchi na fedha zinazopatikana na kutumika; -a kuhusa kuwapatia wanadamu mahitaji yao. **economics,** *n.* elimu inayohusu upataji wa mahitaji ya wanadamu. **economical,** *a.* -wekevu, -enye kupunguza gharama, -enye kiasi katika kutumia fedha (vitu), -kabidhi, -gumu; (*cheap*) rahisi. **economize,** *v.i.* punguza gharama, shika kiasi katika kutumia fedha na vitu; weka akiba, tumia kwa kiasi, kabidhi. **economy,** *n.* uwekevu, iktisadi, ukabidhi, kiasi katika kutumia fedha na vitu, uangalifu kuzuia upotevu wa fedha (vitu, mali *&c.*); (*domestic*) kanuni za kuendesha nyumba vizuri; (*political economy*) taz. *economics*.

ecstasy, *n.* kipindi cha furaha (mshangao, huzuni *&c.*), upeo wa furaha *&c.*; (*frenzy*) hali ya kurukwa na akili. **ecstatic**, *a.* -a nguvu mno, -ingi mno, -a kurusha akili; -a kurukwa na akili.

ecumenical, *a.* -a ulimwengu wote, -a mambo ya walimwengu wote. *An ecumenical council*, mkutano mkuu wa maaskofu wote wa Kanisa la kikristo.

eczema, *n.* ugonjwa wa ngozi kama upele mbaya sana.

eddy, *n.* mzunguko (wa maji, hewa), kizingia, mzingo, mkondo wa maji unaozungukazunguka, chamchela (kinyamkela) ndogo. — *v.i.* zungukazunguka.

Eden, *n.* bustani ya Aden, makao ya Adamu na Hawa walipoumbwa.

edge, *n.* (*of river, rock &c.*) ukingo; (*of a cloth*) upindo; (*of a weapon, tool*) machinjioni, makali; (*of a place*) mpaka; (*keenness*) ukali. *Give an edge to*, tia makali, noa. *Set the teeth on edge*, tia ganzi la meno; (*give offence*) chukiza. *Take the edge off*, punguza nguvu (utamu, furaha, maana *&c.*). — *v.t.* tia makali, noa; (*of a cloth*) tia upindo. *Edge away*, jongea, sogea (hasa upande, mshazari). *Edge into*, ingiza kwa hadhari (shida, siri). *Edge out*, toka polepole, kwa hadhari. **edgeways, edgewise**, *adv.* kwa makali juu au mbele; kwa upande, ubavuni. *I could not get a word in edgeways*, sikuweza kusema hata neno moja (kwa kuwa mtu au watu) alikuwa na domo. **edging**, *n.* ukingo, (*of cloth*) upindo.

edible, *a.* -a kulika na wanadamu.

edict, *n.* amri, sheria.

edification, *n.*, **edifice**, *n.* taz. *edify*.

edify, *v.t.* fundisha mema, ongoza vizuri, adilisha. **edification**, *n.* wema, mafundisho (malezi) mema; maongozi mema, maongozo mema. **edifice**, *n.*, jumba. **edifying**, *a.* -a kuongeza wema (maarifa, malezi mema), -a kufundisha wema, -a kukuza roho.

edit, *v.t.* tengeneza kitabu tayari kupigwa chapa (hasa chenye maandiko ya mwingine au wengine), tengeneza tayari habari kupigwa chapa katika gazeti. **edition**, *n.* jumla ya nakala za kitabu fulani iliyopigwa chapa wakati mmoja. **editor**, *n.* mtengenezaji wa kitabu (chenye maandiko ya mwingine au wengine); msimamizi au mtengenezaji wa gazeti. **editorial**, *a.* -a *editor*. — *n.* habari zilizoandikwa na *editor* wa gazeti au chini ya uangalifu wake.

educate, *v.t.* zoeza, kuza na kuongoza akili, tabia na uwezo; funza, fundisha, elimisha, somesha; (*bring up*) lea; (*morally*) ongoza, adilisha, rudi; (*in manners*) adibisha; (*provide schooling for*) chukulia (lipia) gharama ya kuelimisha. *An educated person* (*a person of education*) mtaalamu, mwana chuoni; mtu wa adili; mtu wa adabu, mwenye kujua mambo, mjuzi. **education**, *n.* kuzoeza, kukuza na kuongoza akili, tabia na uwezo; mafundisho, mafunzo, malezi, ulezi, masomo; kusoma, kufundishwa; (*results of teaching*) maarifa, elimu. **educational**, *a.* -a kufundisha, -a kusomesha, -a kuelimisha, -enye mafundisho. **educationalist**, *n.* mtu anayehusiwa na elimu, kazi au utengenezaji wa *education*.

educe, *v.t.* toa, toza, dhihirisha; (*infer*) ona, fahamu (kwa sababu ya mambo mengine). *Educe all that is best in a man*, toa (dhihirisha) tabia (maarifa *&c.*) zilizo bora za mtu.

eel, *n.* mkunga, nyoka wa maji.

e'en, *n. and adv.* = *even*.

e'er, *adv.* = *ever*.

eerie, eery, *a.* -a kutia hofu, -a kioja, -a kutisha.

efface, *v.t.* futa, futia mbali, ondoa kabisa, haribu kabisa. *Efface oneself.*

jifanya kama ni mdogo, kama si mtu astahiliye kufikiriwa.

effect, *n.* (*result*) mwisho, matokeo, mambo ya baadaye, yafuatayo, kazi; (*practical outcome*) jambo, tendo; (*meaning*) maana; (*force*) nguvu. *In effect*, maana yake, kweli. *To this effect* (*to the following effect*) kama hivi, kwa maana hii. *Without effect*, bure. *For effect*, kwa kujitokeza (kujitanguliza, kujifaharisha). *Effects* (*property*), vyombo, mali. *Take effect*, tenda kazi yake, -wa na njia. *Give effect to*, tendesha kazi, tia nguvu. *Produce an effect*, tenda kazi (ya kushangaza, ya kushtusha, ya kuogofya, ya kufurahisha, ya kuhuzunisha &c.). *Carry into effect*, tumia, fikiliza, faulu, tekeleza, timiliza, jirisha. *Be the effect of*, mwisho wake ni, kazi yake ni. *The effects of the war*, mambo yaliyotukia kwa sababu ya vita, mambo ya baada ya vita. — *v.t.* fanya, fanyiza, amili, timiliza, tekeleza, jirisha, pata. **effective**, *a.* -a kufaa, -a nguvu, -enye njia, -a kuleta lililotakiwa (lililokusudiwa). **effectively**, *adv.* kwa kufaa (kwa kuleta lililotakiwa). **effectual**, *a.* kama *effective*. **effectually**, *adv.* kama *effectively*. **effectuate**, *v.t.* tekeleza, timiliza, fanya, fanyiza, faulu. **efficacious**, *a.* -a kufaa, taz. *effective*. **efficaciously**, *adv.* kama *effectively*. **efficacy**, *n.* nguvu, mafaa, kazi, manufaa.

effeminacy, *n.* tabia ya kike. **effeminate**, *a.* -a kike, dhaifu; -oga, -tepetevu, -a anasa (kama mwanamke).

effervesce, *v.i.* chemka, fura, fanya povu, umuka. **effervescence**, *n.* mchemko, povu. **effervescent**, *a.* -a kuchemka, -a kutoa povu, -a kuumuka.

effete, *a.* -chakavu, -liochakaa, -liyoishiwa nguvu, dhaifu, -siyofaa kitu.

efficacious, *a.*, **efficaciously**, *adv.*, **efficacy**, *n.* taz. *effect*.

efficiency, *n.* taz. *efficient*.

efficient, *a.* -a nguvu, -a kufaa, -enye njia, -a kazi; (*of persons*) -stadi, -bingwa, hodari. **efficiency**, *n.* utendaji, uhodari, uwezo, kazi. **efficiently**, *adv.* kwa ustadi, kwa uhodari, kwa kufaa.

effigy, *n.* sanamu, mfano, sura, kinyago.

effloresce, *v.i.* chanua (maua); (*chemical*) geuka unga kwa kufunuliwa hewani, fanya chunyu. **efflorescence**, *n.* kuchanua (maua); (*chemical*) kukauka maji hewani na kubakiza unga (namna ya chumvi), unga, mavumbi meupe, utando.

effluence, *n.* taz. *effluent*.

effluent, *a.* -a kutoka, -a kumiminika. — *n.* mto utokao katika mto mkubwa zaidi au ziwa. **effluence**, *n.* miminiko, kutoka (kwa mwangaza, umeme &c.). **effluvium**, *n.* uvundo, harufu mbaya. **efflux**, *n.* kutoka, miminiko, kitu kitokacho (kama maji).

effort, *n.* bidii, jaribio, juhudi, jitihada, idili, nguvu. *Make an effort*, jitahidi, fanya bidii, tumia nguvu; (*moral*) jibidiisha. **effortless**, *a.* -zembe, -tepetevu, -vivu, pasipo bidii (juhudi &c.).

effrontery, *n.* ujuvi, ukavu wa macho, usafihi, kiburi, ufidhuli.

effulgence, *n.* taz. *effulgent*.

effulgent, *a.* -a kuangaza, -enye kutoa nuru (mwangaza, mng'ao), -a kung'aa. **effulgence**, *n.* mwangaza, mwanga, uangavu, ung'ao, fahari.

effuse, *v.t.* toa (maji, hewa, nuru, mwangaza, harufu &c.); — *v.i.* toka (maji &c.). **effusion**, *n.* kutoka, kumwaga, kumwagika; maneno mengi. **effusive**, *a.* -kunjufu, -ingi wa maneno, -ingi wa upendo.

e.g. = kwa mfano.

egg, (1) *v.t.* (*on*) sukuma, sukumiza, chocha, himiza, harakisha.

egg, (2) *n.* yai; (*white*) ute; (*yolk*) kiini; (*shell*) kaka, ganda. **egg-plant**, *n.* mbilingani. **egg-shaped**, *a.* -enye umbo la yai. **egg-shell**, *n.* ganda la yai; (*empty*) kaka.

ego, *n.* nafsi. **egoism,** *n.* tabia ya kujifikiri (ya kutafuta raha, faida *&c.* ya mwenyewe). **egoist,** *n.* mtu mwenye tabia ya *egoism*. **egotism,** *n.* taz. *egoism*; tabia ya kujipendelea (ya kujisifu, ya kujikinai), majisifu. **egotist,** *n.* mjisifu, mtu mwenye tabia ya *egotism*.

egregious, *a.* -a kupita kiasi (upeo) kwa ubaya, -baya sana.

egress, *n.* njia (uwezo, ruhusa) ya kutoka, matokeo. **egression,** *n.* kutoka.

egret, *n.* (*little*) yangeyange, taz. *aigrette*.

Egypt, *n.* Misri. **Egyptian,** *n.* Mmisri mtu (mzalia) wa Misri. — *a.* -a Misri, -a kimisri.

eh, *int.* ati. — *interrog.* ulisema nini?

eider, *n.* namna ya bata. **eider-down,** *n.* manyoya laini ya *eider*; (*quilt*) furushi lililotiwa manyoya laini ya *eider*.

eight, *n. and a.* nane, themanya. **eighteen,** *n. and a.* kumi na nane, themantashara. **eighteenth,** *a.* -a kumi na nane. **eighth,** *a.* -a nane. *An eighth part,* themuni, thumuni. **eightieth,** *a.* -a themanini. **eighty,** *n. and a.* themanini.

eirenicon, *n.* neno (shauri) la kuleta amani (mapatano).

either, *a.* -moja -o -ote, -mojawapo; (*both*) -ote -wili. *A man stood at either side,* mtu alisimama upande huu na huu (pande zote mbili). — *n.* -mojawapo. — *adv. and conj.* ama . . . ama, au . . . au, *e.g. either this or that,* au hii au hii, ama hii ama hii; (*with negative*) wala, *e.g. nor did I do that either,* wala hilo sikulifanya.

ejaculate, *v.t.* toa neno ghafula, toa (maji *&c.*) ghafula. **ejaculation,** *n.* neno la ghafula, maji *&c.* yaliyotolewa ghafula.

eject, *v.t.* toa, ondosha, fukuza, foka, fuka; (*vomit*) tapika. **ejection,** *n.* kutoa, kutoka, ondoleo *&c.* **ejective,** *a.* -a kutoa, -a kuondosha *&c.* **ejector,** *n.* mtu (kitu) anayetoa *&c.*

eke, *v.t.* (*out*) ongeza, zidisha, dumisha, fuliza.

elaborate, *a.* -a kazi nyingi, -zuri, -enye matengenezo (maelezo, mambo, madoido) mengi. — *v.t.* fanyiza sana, timiliza, kamilisha; zidi kutia kazi (matengenezo, maelezo *&c.*), tia madoido. **elaboration,** *n.* kazi (matengenezo, maelezo, mambo) nyingi, uzuri, madoido.

eland, *n.* pofu.

elapse, *v.i.* pita, jiri.

elastic, *a.* -a kunyumbuka, -a kunapukia, kama mpira; (*capable of adaptation*) -a kubadilikana kufaa mambo yalivyo. *Be elastic,* kunyumbuka, kunapukia. — *n.* ugwe wa pamba au hariri wenye nyuzi za mpira. **elasticity,** *n.* hali ya kunyumbuka (ya kubadilikana kufaa mambo yalivyo).

elate, *v.t.* furahisha, tia moyo (matumaini, kiburi). **elation,** *n.* furaha, matumaini, moyo mwepesi.

elbow, *n.* kiko (cha mkono), kivi. — *v.t.* piga kikumbo. **elbow-room,** *n.* nafasi ya kufaa.

elder, (1) *n.* namna ya mti wa Ulaya.

elder, (2) *n.* mzee. — *a.* -kubwa (kwa umri). **elderly,** *a.* -zee kidogo.

eldest, *a.* -kubwa (kwa umri).

elect, *v.t.* chagua (kwa kazi au daraja bora, kuwa -kubwa), chagua, teua; — *v.i.* (*decide*) nia, azimu, azimia. — *a.* -teule, -liyochaguliwa. *Bishop elect,* kasisi aliyechaguliwa kuwa askofu, lakini bado hajawekwa. **election,** *n.* mchaguo (wa mkubwa au wakubwa, hasa mtu au watu wa baraza kuu ya nchi), kuchagua, kuteua. **electioneer,** *v.t.* shawishi (sukumiza, vuta) watu kuchagua mtu fulani kuwa mkubwa (hasa kuwa mtu wa baraza kuu ya nchi). **elective,** *a.* -enye kuchaguliwa, -enye ruhusa (haki *&c.*) ya kuchagua. **elector,** *n.* mwenye haki ya kuchagua katika *election*. **electoral,** *a.* -enye kuchagua, -a *election*. **electorate,** *n.* jumla ya watu wote wenye haki kuchagua katika *election* ya nchi.

electric, *a.* -a umeme, -a asili ya umeme, -a kuendeshwa (kufanyika) kwa umeme; (*rapid*) -a upesi mno ajabu (kama umeme). *Electric light*, taa ya umeme. (*In some places* stimu *is used for electricity*). **electrical,** *a.* -a umeme; (*fig.*) -a kushtusha sana, -a upesi mno ajabu. **electrician,** *n.* fundi wa umeme, mwenye maarifa ya umeme. **electricity,** *n.* umeme, asili ya umeme; elimu ya umeme na asili yake. **electrification,** *n.* kazi ya kutia nguvu ya umeme ili kuendesha (kuwasha taa &c.); hali ya kutiwa nguvu ya umeme. **electrify,** *v.t.* tia nguvu ya umeme (ili kuendesha mashine, kuwasha taa &c.); (*astonish*) shangaza mno, shtusha sana. **electro-,** *pref.* -a kuhusu (kufanyika kwa) nguvu ya umeme. **electrocute,** *v.t.* fisha (ua) kwa nguvu ya umeme. **electrocution,** *n.* tendo la kufisha (kuua) kwa nguvu ya umeme. **electrode,** *n.* ncha zitokapo nguvu ya umeme katika *battery* &c. **electro-magnet,** *n.* sumaku ya nguvu ya umeme.

electuary, *n.* dawa iliyochanganyika na kitu kitamu kama asali &c.

elegance, *n.* taz. *elegant.*

elegant, *a.* -zuri, -a jamala, -a madaha, -enye adabu, -enye malezi mazuri, -a anasa, -a sanaa, -sanifu. **elegance,** *n.* uzuri, jamala, madaha, madahiro, matuko, umbuji; (*of speech*) usemaji, ufasaha. **elegantly,** *adv.* kwa madaha, kwa adabu &c.

elegy, *n.* mashairi (ya kuomboleza).

element, *n.* (*environment*) ulimwengu; (*four elements*) ardhi (udongo), maji, hewa, moto; (*elementary substance or fact*) kitu cha asili, jambo la asili; (*chem. and phys.*) kitu cha asili kisichogawanyikana sehemu mbalimbali; (*part*) sehemu. *Elements* (*in teaching*) mwanzo, mlango. *He is in his element*, ajiona kuwa kwake, (kwao &c.). *Strife* (*fury*) *of the elements*, dhoruba, tufani, machafuko ya bahari, upepo mwingi. **elemental,** *a.* -a ardhi (maji, hewa, moto), -a asili, -a mwanzo. **elementary,** *a.* -a asili, -a mwanzo, -a kwanza.

elephant, *n.* tembo, ndovu. **elephantiasis,** *n.* ugonjwa wa matende, jethamu. **elephantine,** *a.* -kubwa mno, -a kama tembo.

elevate, *v.t.* inua, kweza, pandisha, panza, paliza, tweka; (*elate*) furahisha, changamsha, tumainisha; (*promote*) zidishia cheo, heshimu, kuza; (*improve*) ongoza vema, adilisha. **elevated,** *a.* -a juu, -a kuinuka; -kuu, bora, -a furaha, -a tumaini. **elevation,** *n.* mwinuo, mwinuko, mkweo &c ; cheo bora, utukufu, neshima; (*height*) urefu wa kwenda juu, kimo; (*hill*) kilima, mwinuko; (*drawing*) sanamu (picha, ramani) ya kuonyesha urefu wa jengo au kitu kingine. **elevator,** *n.* mtambo (mashine, mtu, kitu cho chote) unaoinua au kupandisha.

eleven, *n. and a.* kumi na moja, edashara. **eleventh,** *a.* -a edashara, -a kumi na moja.

elf, elfin, *n.* zimwi, kizimwi, jini; (*mischievous child*) mtoto mtundu; (*dwarf*) mbilikimo, kijitu. **elfin,** *a.* -a kizimwi &c. **elfish,** *a.* -a kama zimwi (jini, mtoto mtundu), -tundu.

elicit, *v.t.* toza, tokeza, dhihirisha. *Elicit a reply*, jibisha, vuta mtu ajibu. *Elicit the truth*, vuta mtu aseme kweli.

elide, *v.t.* fupisha tamko la neno kwa kutotamka vokali, *e.g.* Mungu badala ya Muungu. **elision,** *n.* ufupisho wa tamko la neno.

eligible, *a.* -a kuchagulikana; -a kufaa, -a kustahili, -stahilifu, -teule. **eligibility,** *n.* haki (ustahilifu, hali) ya kuchagulikana, uteule, hali (tabia) ya kufaa.

eliminate, *v.t.* toa, futa, ondosha, acha. **elimination,** *n.* tendo la kutoa (kufuta, kuondosha).

elision, *n.* taz. *elide.*

élite, *n.* kilicho (walio) bora kabisa.
elixir, *n.* dawa iliyodhaniwa kuwa na nguvu ya ajabu ya kuongeza urefu wa maisha; dawa inayotia nguvu ya mwili.
elk, *n.* mnyama kama kulungu mkubwa mwenye pembe za panda panda.
ell, *n.* kipimo cha urefu, yadi 1¼. *If you give him an inch, he will take an ell. Swahili versions of the Prov.* are: (1) Wakiisha tia chanda watatia na mkono: wakiisha tia mkono, watatia na guu, *When they have put in the finger, they will also put in the hand, when they have put in the hand, they will also put in the foot*; (2) Ukimpa shibiri atachukua pima, *If you give him a span (9 inches) he will take a fathom.*
ellipse, *n.* umbo la yai; (*in Gram.*) utovu (ukosekano) wa neno (au maneno) linalofahamikana kwa akili, *e.g.* yeye alikuwa mweusi na nduguye mweupe, *i.e.* alikuwa mweupe. **ellipsis**, *n.* kama *ellipse*. **elliptic**, *a.*, **elliptical**, *a.* -enye umbo la yai; -enye utovu (ukosekano) wa sehemu.
elm, *n.* namna ya mti wa Ulaya.
elocution, *n.* usemaji, usemi, utamko wa maneno: ustadi wa kusema kwa ufasaha. **elocutionist**, *n.* mstadi wa kusema kwa ufasaha, msemaji; mwalimu afundishaye ufasaha wa usemaji.
elongate, *v.t.* ongeza urefu, tawilisha, tanua, nyosha; — *v.i.* -wa -refu, tuili. — *a.* -refu, tuili. **elongation**, *n.* mwongezo wa urefu, mtanuo, mtawilio.
elope, *v.i.* toroka, hasa mtu na mchumba ili kuoana bila idhini ya wazee, au mwanamke kutoroka na hawara na kuacha mumewe. **elopement**, *n.* utoro, taz. *elope*.
eloquence, *n.* taz. *eloquent*.
eloquent, *a.* -enye ufasaha wa maneno, -enye uwezo wa kushawishi (wa kuamsha moyo, huzuni, furaha *&c.*) kwa maneno (au maandiko), -semaji. **eloquence**, *n.* usemaji unaokolea, ufasaha wa maneno (au kuandika); uwezo wa kuamsha moyo (maono, huzuni, furaha *&c.*) kwa maneno (au maandiko); maneno ya kushawishi au kuvuta. **eloquently**, *adv.* kwa ufasaha, kwa maneno yanayokolea (kushawishi, kuvuta *&c.*).
else, *adv.* (*besides*) tena, juu ya hayo, zaidi. *What else shall I say?* nitasema nini tena (zaidi, juu ya hayo)? *Did you see any one else?* ulimwona mtu mwingine (zaidi)?; (*otherwise*) kama sivyo, au. *Take care or else you will fall*, jihadhari, kama sivyo (au sivyo) utaanguka. **elsewhere**, *adv.* pengine, penginepo.
elucidate, *v.t.* eleza, dhihirisha, fafanua, angaza, fumbua. **elucidation**, *n.* maelezo, mafafanusi, ufumbuzi.
elude, *v.t.* epa, epuka, epukana na, epusha, okoka kwa werevu (hila), kimbilia; (*baffle*) fumba, tatiza.
elusion, *n.* hila, werevu (wa kuepusha, wa kujiokoa, wa kukimbia).
elusive, *a.* -a hila, -danganyifu, -gumu kufahamu au kukumbuka, -a fumbo. **elusory**, *a.* kama *elusive*.
Elysian, *a.* taz. *Elysium*.
Elysium, *n.* (*final bliss*) peponi, ahera; (*gate of Paradise*) mlango wa jaha; (*happiness*) raha mustarehe, hali ya heri halisi. **Elysian**, *a.* -a *Elysium*.
emaciate, *v.t.* dhoofisha, kondesha, gofusha. *Become emaciated*, nywea, konda, nyorora. *A very emaciated person*, gofu la mtu. **emaciated**, *a.* -embamba sana, -dhoofu, -liyekonda sana, -liyechuruzika, -a kusawajika.
emaciation, *n.* wembamba, udhaifu (kwa ajili ya njaa au ugonjwa).
emanate, *v.i.* (*from, in*) toka, anza.
emanation, *n.* kitokacho; (*smell*) harufu.
emancipate, *v.t.* weka huru, toa utumwani. **emancipated**, *a.* huru, -siyetawalwa, -enye kufuata moyo wake (wao *&c.*) wala si mambo ya desturi. **emancipation**, *n.* uhuru, kuweka huru, uondoleo wa udhalimu.

emasculate, *v.t.* hasi; (*weaken*) dhoofisha, ondolea nguvu, legeza. **emasculated,** *a.* hanithi, dhaifu, bila nguvu ya mwili (ya akili, ya roho).

embalm, *v.t.* (*a corpse*) tia dawa (maiti) isioze; (*preserve carefully*) linda, hifadhi, tunza; (*perfume*) tia harufu nzuri. **embalmment,** *n.* kutia dawa (maiti) isioze.

embank, *v.t.* jengea boma. **embankment,** *n.* boma (la kuzuia maji), njia ya juu juu, fungu la udongo lililojengwa kupitishia reli za gari la moshi au barabara.

embargo, *n.* makatazo, marufuku. *Lay an embargo on,* piga marufuku, funga, zuia.

embark, *v.t.* panda, ingia (melini); (*put on board*) pakia, ingiza; (*embark in, or upon*) anza, shika, ingia, maliki. **embarkation,** *n.* mapakizi, kupandisha chomboni; kupanda, kuingia melini (chomboni).

embarrass, *v.t.* zuia, hangaisha, tatiza, sumbua, udhi, tahayarisha, fadhaisha; (*financial*) dhikisha, fanyia shida ya fedha. **embarrassment,** *n.* fadhaa, mashaka, haya, soni, matata, hangaiko, wasiwasi; dhiki, zuizi.

embassy, *n.* ubalozi, jumba la balozi, ujumbe.

embed, *v.t.* tia ndani sana na kukaza imara.

embellish, *v.t.* pamba, tia uzuri, rembesha, tia madoido; (*a story*) piga chuku, tia chumvi. **embellishment,** *n.* mapambo, uzuri, madoido, urembo; (*of story*) chuku.

ember, *n.* kaa la moto, majivu ya moto.

Ember days, *n.* nyakati nne za kufunga Wakristo, siku tatu katika kila robo mwaka.

embezzle, *v.t.* iba (tumia) bila haki fedha zilizowekwa amana au katika kabidhi. **embezzlement,** *n.* wizi wa fedha zilizowekwa amana. **embezzler,** *n.* mwizi aibaye fedha zilizowekwa amana kwake.

embitter, *v.t.* chukiza, tia uchungu, ongezea chuki (uchungu), vunja moyo. **embitterment,** *n.* chuki, uchungu wa moyo.

emblazon, *v.t.* pamba kwa rangi nyingi, kama vile ngao kwa alama za ukoo, marika *&c.*; tangaza sifa za, tukuza. **emblazonment,** pambo la rangi nyingi, taz. *emblazon.*

emblem, *n.* mfano, kifani, alama, methali. **emblematic,** *a.* -enye mfano, -enye maana, -a methali.

embodiment, *n.* taz. *embody.*

embody, *v.t.* fanyia mwili (umbo); unganisha, -wa -moja na, tia pamoja, tia ndani, weka. **embodiment,** *n.* kupata mwili (umbo); mfano hasa, asili, umbo, onekano. *He is the embodiment of goodness,* yu mwema halisi, amejaa wema.

embolden, *v.t.* tia moyo, -pa moyo, tumainisha, thibitisha, fanya kuwa hodari, sukuma.

embonpoint, *n.* unene (wa tumbo).

embosom, *v.t.* kumbatia, tia moyoni, tia ndani (kati) ya, zungusha.

emboss, *v.t.* nakshi, kata (tia) nakshi. *Embossed work,* kazi yenye mapambo (urembo, nakshi) ya vinundunundu (yanayotokeza, yaliyoinuka). **embossment,** *n.* nakshi, mapambo (urembo) yanayotokeza (ya vinundunundu).

embower, *v.t.* zungushia (miti, maua *&c.*).

embrace, *v.t.* kumbatia, kumbatiana, pambaja, sogeza kifuani; (*accept*) kubali kwa moyo, tumia kwa bidii, fuasa; (*include*) shika, -wa na, weka; (*take in*) fahamu, ona, tambua. — *n.* kumbatio, pambajo.

embrasure, *n.* tundu ukutani (la kupenyeza mzinga au bunduki), dirisha, buruji.

embrocate, *v.t.* sugua kwa dawa, paka dawa. **embrocation,** *n.* dawa ya kusugulia (kupaka), *e.g.* kwa mguu ulioteguka *&c.*

embroider, *v.t.* tarizi, tia nakshi (almaria); (*a story &c.*) piga chuku, tia chumvi. **embroidery,** *n.* almaria, nakshi; (*stitched*) tarizi, tarazo, taraza; (*adornment*) mapambo, urembo, uzuri.

embroil, *v.t.* fitini, fitinisha, gombanisha, pekecha, chochea, tia shonga, tia chonjo; (*bring into confusion*) fuja, chafua, tia fujo, buruga. **embroilment,** *n.* fitina, ugomvi, matata, shonga, chonjo, machafuko, fujo, ghasia, upekecho.

embryo, *n.* mimba; (*germ*) mbegu, kiini, moyo; (*origin*) mwanzo, asili, chimbuko.

emend, *v.t.* sahihisha, safi, toa makosa, rekebisha, tengeneza maneno (maandiko &c.). **emendation,** *n.* tengenezo la maandiko, kusahihisha.

emerald, *n.* zumaradi.

emerge, *v.i.* zuka, tokea, ibuka or. '.ana; (*become known* &c.) julikana, dhihirika. **emergency,** *n,* kizushi, uzushi, jambo la ghafula (lisilotazamiwa), udhuru; (*danger*) hatari, mashaka. **emergent,** *a.* -a kutoka, -a kuzuka. **emersion,** *n.* utokezi.

emery, *n.* namna ya vumbi ambayo chembe zake ni ngumu mno, la kusugulia na kukatulia madini, msasa. *Emery-cloth* (*paper*) msasa.

emetic, *n.* tapisho, dawa ya kutapisha.

emigrant, *n.* taz. *emigrate.*

emigrate, *v.i.* hama, hamia ugenini, hajiri, hujuru. **emigrant,** *n.* mtu ahamiaye ugenini, mhajiri. — *a.* -enye kuhama, -hamaji. **emigration,** *n.* kuhama, kuhajiri, kuhujuru, uhamaji, uhame, uhajiri. **emigratory,** *a.* -enye tabia (desturi, kawaida) ya kuhama, kama vile ndege wahamao wakati wao na kurudi tena.

eminence, *n.* taz. *eminent.*

eminent, *a.* -kuu, -enye cheo (daraja) kikuu, mashuhuri, -enye sifa na kujulikana. **eminence,** *n.* ukuu, ubora, utukufu (wa daraja, cheo, tabia, sifa, uwezo); (*hill*) kilima, mwinuko. **eminently,** *adv.* sana, kabisa.

emir, *n.* amiri, shehe, sheik.

emissary, *n.* mjumbe, tume, mpelelezi.

emission, *n.* taz. *emit.*

emit, *v.t.* toa, tokeza. **emission,** *n.* kutoa, kutoka, utoko, utokezi.

emmet, *n.* mdudu wa jamii ya siafu, mchwa, chungu &c.

emollient, *n.* dawa ya kutuliza (punguza, nyamazisha) maumivu (uchungu). — *a.* -a kulainisha, -a kutuliza (kupunguza, kunyamazisha) maumivu (uchungu).

emolument, *n.* mshahara, ujira, pato, chumo, faida.

emotion, *n.* maono (furaha, huzuni, sikitiko, chuki, upendo &c.); hangaiko (shtuko, mchomo) la moyo. **emotional,** *a.* -enye tabia ya kuvutwa kwa urahisi kuona furaha (huzuni, sikitiko &c.) **emotionless,** *a.* baridi, bila kuona (kuonyesha, kuamsha) furaha (huzuni, sikitiko &c.).

empanel, *v.t.* andika jina katika orodha ya *jury.*

emperor, *n.* mfalme, hasa atawalaye falme mbili au zaidi. **empire,** *n.* ufalme, milki, mamlaka; (*sovereignty*) enzi kuu. **empress,** *n.* mke wa *emperor.*

emphasis, *n.* mkazo, nguvu. **emphasize,** *v.t.* kaza sauti (katika kunena), paaza sauti, tamka kwa nguvu; (*give force to*) tia nguvu, kaza, tokeza, dhihirisha. **emphatic,** *a.* -a nguvu, -a mkazo; (*distinct*) dhahiri, waziwazi. **emphatically,** *adv.* kwa nguvu; (*certainly*) sana, bila shaka.

empire, *n.* taz. *emperor.*

empirical, empiric, *a.* jarabati, -a kutegemea majaribio wala si elimu na maarifa, -a kubahatisha. **empiricism,** *n.* kazi (matendo &c.) inayotegemea majaribio wala si elimu na maarifa, ubahatisho.

emplacement, *n.* mahali, mahali hasa jengo lilipojengwa, mahali pa kuweka mzinga.

employ, *v.t.* tuma, -pa kazi, ajiri,

tumikisha, shughulisha; (*make use of*) tumia. *Employ oneself in*, jishughulisha na. — *n*. kazi. *I am in his employ*, nafanya kazi kwake. **employable**, *a*. -a kutumikana, -a kuajirika. **employé, employee**, *n*. mtu wa kazi, mtumishi, mtu wa mshahara, mtu aliyeajiriwa (aliyetumwa), kibarua. **employer**, *n*. bwana (tajiri) (mwenye mtu wa kazi) aajiriye watu kwa mshahara. **employment**, *n*. kazi, utumishi, uchumi, shughuli, amali; (*use*) utumizi, matumizi.

empoison, *v.t.* tia sumu, sumisha, haribu, ghoshi; (*fig.*) tia uchungu, fitini.

emporium, *n*. mji wenye biashara nyingi; (*market*) soko; (*shop*) duka kubwa.

empower, *v.t.* wezesha, -pa amri (nguvu, hukumu, mamlaka *&c.*).

empress, *n*. taz. *emperor*.

emptiness, *n*. taz. *empty*.

empty, *a*. -tupu, pasipo na kitu, wazi ndani. *An empty bottle*, chupa isiyo na kitu ndani yake. *To feel empty*, kuona njaa. *Empty words*, maneno yasiyo na maana, ubatili, upuzi, maneno baridi. *Empty promises*, ahadi za bure (zisizokusudiwa kutekelezwa). — *n*. kitu kisicho na kitu ndani, *e.g.* kasha, chupa, behewa. — *v.t.* mwaga, miminia mbali, toa yote yaliyomo, kumba, futa; — *v.i.* mwagika, fanyika tupu. *The river empties itself into the sea*, maji ya mto huingia baharini. **emptiness**, *n*. uwazi, nafasi wazi, hali ya kuwa -tupu (pasipo na kitu ndani); (*stupidity*) akili chache, upunguani; (*without sense*) ubatili, upuzi.

empty-handed, *a*. bila kitu. *He came (went) empty-handed*, alikuja (alikwenda) bila kupata kitu.

empty-headed, *a*. -enye akili chache, -jinga.

empyrean, *n*. anga ya juu, mbingu.

emu, *n*. ndege mkubwa wa nchi ya Australia anayefanana na mbuni.

emulate, *v.t.* jaribu kufanya (kuwa) sawa na mwingine; jaribu kushinda mwingine (kwa ustadi, tabia, akili, uwezo, ushujaa *&c.*); fuatisha, igiza, shindana na; (*rival*) -wa sawa na, fanana na, karibia. **emulation**, *n*. ushindani, moyo wa (bidii ya) kushindana, maigizo, mwigo; (*envy*) wivu, husuda. **emulous**, *a*. -enye moyo wa bidii ya *emulate*; -enye moyo au bidii ya kufaulu (kuendelea, kusitawi *&c.*).

emulsify, *v.t.* fanya kuwa kama maziwa mazito kidogo. **emulsion**, *n*. namna ya dawa nzito kidogo kama maziwa.

enable, *v.t.* wezesha, tia nguvu, jalia. **enabling**, *a*. -a kuwezesha.

enact, *v.t.* fanya sheria, toa (simamisha, thibitisha) amri. *Be enacted*, fanyika, tendeka, tokea. **enactment**, *n*. amri, sheria; (*making a law*) kufanya sheria.

enamel, *n*. namna ya rangi ngumu ya kung'aa kama kioo, tabaka ngumu ya nje kama juu ya jino *&c.* — *v.t.* paka *enamel*.

enamour, *v.t.* tamanisha, washia (amshia) tamaa, tia shauku (ashiki), chunusha, ashikisha. *Be enamoured of*, ashiki, tamani sana, chunuka, penda sana, vutwa sana na.

en bloc, *adv*. kwa jumla.

encage, *v.t.* tia (funga) tunduni, funga ndani kama katika kitundu.

encamp, *v.i.* tua, fanya kituo, piga kambi, panga. **encampment**, *n*. kituo, kambi.

encase, *v.t.* funika, funga, zungushia.

encaustic, *a*. -a kuokwa, -a kuchomeka (moto). *Encaustic tile*, tofali lenye pambo la rangi lililookwa.

enceinte, *a*. -enye mimba, -zito (kwa mimba).

enchain, *v.t.* funga katika minyororo; (*fig.*) shika, shikilia, shikiza, shinda.

enchant, *v.t.* loga, fanyia uchawi, nuizia uchawi, sihiri; (*delight*) pendeza mno, liwaza, shangaza, shinda moyo. **enchanter**, *n*. mganga, mchawi, mlozi; (*by beauty*) mtiisha moyo, aliwazaye, afurahishaye. **en-**

chanting, *a.* -enye mapendezi, -a kushinda moyo, -a kupendeza (kufurahisha, kuliwaza) sana, -zuri sana. **enchantment**, *n.* uchawi, ulozi, usihiri, uramali, uganga; (*beauty*) uzuri, uliwazo. **enchantress**, *n.* *enchanter* wa kike.

enchase, *v.t.* tia (kama kito katika pete &c.), tia nakshi, nakshi.

encircle, *v.t.* zunguka, zingira, zingia, zungusha.

enclasp, *v.t.* kumbatia, fumbatia.

enclave, *n.* nchi iliyozungukwa na nchi ya kigeni pande zote.

enclitic, *n.* neno linalojiunga nyuma ya neno jingine, *e.g.* mwanawe, we ni *enclitic*; wendapi? pi ni *enclitic*.

enclose, *v.t.* zunguka kabisa, zungusha kabisa, zingira kabisa; (*shut up*) tia (funga) ndani (ya kasha, bahasha, furushi &c.). **enclosure**, *n.* kiwanja (ua) kilichozungushiwa na ua (boma, kitalu &c.); (*thing enclosed*) kitu cha ndani (kama barua katika bahasha &c.); (*wall, fence*) kitalu, boma, ua; (*for cattle*) boma chaa.

encomium, *n.* sifa.

encompass, *v.t.* zunguka, zingia; zungusha (kwa ukuta, kitalu, askari &c.).

encore, *int.* (fanya, cheza, imba &c.) tena—ni mwito wa wasikiaji kuomba mwimbaji &c. kuimba tena. — *n.* mwito wa *encore*, wimbo (mchezo &c.) unaoimbwa kwa sababu ya mwito wa wasikiaji. —*v.t.* fanya vifijo na kuomba mwimbaji (mchezaji &c.) kuimba tena.

encounter, *v.t.* kutana na, pambana na, pigana na, kuta, pata, jipasha; — *v.i.* onana. — *n.* kukutana, mkutano, kupambana, mpambano; (*fight*) pigano.

encourage, *v.t.* tia moyo, tia nguvu, thibitisha, saidia, endeleza, bembeleza, fariji, shawishi, vuta, juburu. **encouragement**, *n.* kutia moyo &c., jambo la kutia moyo, msaada, faraja. **encouraging**, *a.* -a kutia moyo &c.

encroach, *v.i.* jiingiza, jiingiliza, jipenyeza, -la, twaa isiyo haki, iba mpaka. **encroachment**, *n.* kujiingiliza.

encrust, incrust, *v.t.* funika utando, funika kwa vito au madini yenye thamani; — *v.i.* fanya utando, tanda. **encrustment**, *n.* kufunika utando.

encumber, *v.t.* zuia, tatiza, sumbua, lemea, songa; (*put in debt*) pasha deni. **encumbrance**, *n.* zuizi, zuizo, mgogoro, mzigo; (*financial*) deni. *Without encumbrance*, bila mtoto.

encyclopaedia, *n.* kitabu cha maarifa yote.

end, *n.* (*limit*) mwisho, kikomo, mpaka, ncha, pembe, kilembwa; (*remnant*) kipande; (*conclusion*) mwisho, kikomo, aheri; (*destruction*) ajali, maangamizo, mwisho; (*death*) kufa, kifo, mauti, ajali; (*of a journey*) kifiko; (*purpose, object*) kusudi, nia, shauri, maarubu, madhumuni, matakwa, azimio, mradi. *He gains his end*, apata atakacho, apata mradi wake. *The ends of the earth*, pembe za dunia. *Bring to an end*, maliza, komesha, ishiliza. *No end*, wingi sana. *On end*, mfululizo. *In the end*, mwishowe, hatimaye. *Put an end to*, maliza, komesha. *Be at a loose end*, -wa bila kazi (shughuli). *He is at the end of his tether*, ameishiwa maarifa (nguvu, akili &c.). — *v.t.* komesha, kata; (*complete, finish*) maliza, ishiliza; — *v.i.* isha, koma. *He shall end by doing* (*marrying, killing* &c.), atakuja kufanya (kuoa, kuua &c.). **ending**, *n.* mwisho, hasa wa neno (hadithi, habari &c.). **endless**, *a.* -a daima, -a milele, -a kale na kale, pasipo mwisho; (*over long*) -ingi sana, -a bure. **endmost**, *a.* -a mwisho, -a mbali zaidi. **endways**, *adv.* **endwise**, *adv.* ncha kwa ncha, kiwimawima, kwa kusimama.

endamage, *v.t.* taz. *damage*.

endanger, *v.t.* hatirisha, tia hatarini, ponza.

endear, *v.t.* pendekeza. *His kindness endeared him to all,* ukarimu (wema, upaji) wake ulifanya watu wote wampende. **endearing,** *a.* -a kupendeza, -a kupendekeza. **endearment,** *n.* mapendezi, ubembelezi, maneno (matendo) ya kuonyesha upendo.

endeavour, *v.i.* jaribu, fanya bidii, jitahidi. — *n.* jaribio, juhudi, bidii, jitihada.

endemic, *n.* (*disease*) ugonjwa ulio wa kawaida au unaodumu katika watu fulani (mahali fulani, nchi fulani). — *a.* (*of plants &c.*) -a kienyeji, -a nchi (mahali) fulani.

ending, *n.*, **endless,** *a.*, **endmost,** *a.* taz. *end.*

endorse, *v.t.* andikia jina, tia mkono, tia sahihi, sahihisha (katika nyuma ya hati, hawala &c.); (*accept*) kubali, penda, sifu, ridhia. **endorsement,** *n.* mwandiko wa jina (sahihi, maneno) katika upande wa nyuma ya hati (hawala &c.); kibali, ridhaa.

endow, *v.t.* -pa, tolea, jalia; (*give property to*) sihia, kabidhisha mali, wekea mali wakf. *He is endowed with great gifts,* amejaliwa akili (maarifa, karama) nyingi. **endowment,** *n.* kuwekea (kuwekewa) wakf, matoleo, mali; karama, jambo zuri la kufaa kama akili, uzuri, nguvu &c. *Endowment policy,* hati ya bima ya kuahidi kulipa fedha fulani tarehe fulani, au mtu afapo ikiwa siku ya kufa kwake inatangulia ile tarehe.

endue, *v.t.* -pa, jalia, tolea, karimu.

endurable, *a.*, **endurance,** *n.* taz. *endure.*

endure, *v.i.* (*last*) ishi, dumu, endelea, sedeka; (*remain firm*) vumilia, stahimili; — *v.t.* vumilia, stahimili. **endurable,** *a.* -a kuvumilika, -a kustahimilika, -a kuchukulika. **enduring,** *a.* -a kudumu, -a kuendelea.

endways, *adv.*, **endwise,** *adv.* taz. *end.*

enema, *n.* bomba la kuingizia dawa mkunduni; dawa ya kuingizwa mkunduni.

enemy, *n.* adui, mtesi, hasimu mshindani, jeshi la maadui. — *a* -a adui. **enmity,** *n.* uadui, husuma uhasama, sabasi.

energetic, *a.* -enye nguvu (bidii, juhudi), -tendaji, -epesi. **energize,** *v.t.* tilia nguvu, bidiisha. **energy,** *n.* nguvu, bidii, kani, wepesi, utendaji, mkazo, uwezo wa kufanya kazi.

enervate, *v.t.* dhoofisha, legeza, ondolea nguvu, nyong'onyeza. — *a.* dhaifu, -tepetevu. **enervation,** *n.* udhaifu, ulegevu, unyong'onyevu, utepetevu, unyogovu.

enfeeble, *v.t.* dhoofisha, legeza, ondolea nguvu, nyong'onyeza.

enfilade, *v.t.* pigia bunduki (mizinga) mstari mzima wa adui; panga bunduki (mizinga) ili ziweze kupiga mstari mzima wa adui.

enforce, *v.t.* tilia nguvu, toza kwa nguvu; (*a law*) fikiliza, fanya kuwa, jirisha. **enforced,** *a.* -a lazima, -a sharti, -a nguvu. **enforcement,** *n.* kütumia nguvu, kutiwa nguvu, nguvu.

enfranchise, *v.t.* pasha haki ya kusaidia kuchagua mtu wa kupelekwa halmashauri kubwa ya nchi (*Parliament*); weka huru, toa katika utumwa; (*of a town*) pasha mji haki ya kuchagua mtu kupelekwa halmashauri kubwa ya nchi. **enfranchisement,** *n.* uhuru; (*citizenship*) uraia, uenyeji.

engage, *v.t.* (*promise*) ahidi, jipa sharti; (*agree*) afikana, patana, fanya sharti; (*bind*) funga, bidisha; (*hire*) tuma, ajirisha; (*fight*) piganisha; (*interlock with*) ingia, shika; (*occupy*) shughulisha; — *v.i.* (*in*) shughulika; (*undertake*) ahidi, diriki. *He is engaged,* ana kazi (shughuli); (*to marry*) ameposa. *Engage for digging,* limisha; (*for harvesting*) vunisha; (*for milking*) kamisha; (*for service generally*) tumisha. **engaged,** *a.* shughulika, -wa katika kazi; (*betrothed*) poswa; (*hired*) ajiriwa, tumwa. **engagement,** *n.* shughuli, kazi, utumishi; (*in war*) mapigano;

(*promise*) ahadi, sharti, mapatano, maagano, maafikano; (*betrothal*) uchumba, ahadi ya ndoa. **engaging,** *a.* -enye mapendezi (haiba, uzuri), -a kupendeza.

engender, *v.t.* zaa, fanya, fanyika, -wa asili ya, amsha, anzisha, leta.

engine, *n.* mtambo, mashine, chombo, zana; (*locomotive*) gari la moshi. **engine-driver,** *n.* msimamizi wa gari la moshi, dereva. **engineer,** *n.* fundi wa mtambo (mashine, gari la moshi &c.), mwenye maarifa ya kufanya (kuendesha, kurekebisha) mtambo na mashine &c. — *v.t.* buni (tunga, fanya, simamia) kazi ya *engineer*; buni (tunga, fanya) shauri linalotaka akili (fikira, werevu) nyingi. **engineering,** *n.* kazi (maarifa, elimu) ya kufanya (kubuni, kutengeneza, kusimamia) mtambo na mashine &c. pia, ya kazi kubwa kama ya kufanyiza barabara kubwa (daraja, maboma, minara, mito &c.).

engird, engirdle, *v.t.* zungusha, zunguka (*e.g.* kwa ukanda).

English, *a.* -a kiingereza, -a Uingereza, -a Ingereza. — *n.* Waingereza. *Speak English,* sema Kiingereza. *King's English,* Kiingereza safi. **Englishman,** *n.* Mwingereza mwanamume. **Englishwoman,** *n.* Mwingereza mwanamke.

engorge, *v.t.* -la kwa wingi na kwa pupa, jivimbisha.

engraft, *v.t.* pandikiza (mche katika shina la mmea mwingine); (*in the mind*) tia ndani, tilia moyoni, fundisha. Taz. *ingraft.*

engrain, *v.t.* ingiliza, penyeza, ndani. *It is engrained in him,* ni asili (ibada, tabia, kazi, sifa, mazoea, amali) yake.

engrave, *v.t.* chora, tia (kata nakshi), nakshi; (*upon the mind*) kaza katika fikira (moyo, fahamu). **engraver,** *n.* mchora, mkata nakshi; (*jeweller*) sonara. **engraving,** *n.* mchoro, nakshi; (*picture*) picha, sanamu, taswira.

engross, *v.t.* andika (nakili) hati mwandiko mkubwa, andika hati kwa kisheria; (*occupy, absorb*) vuta, shughulisha, weza, shinda. **engrossing,** *a.* -a kushughulisha sana, -a kushika moyo (usikivu).

engulf, *v.t.* meza, didimika, gharikisha.

enhance, *v.t.* ongeza, zidisha, kuza, endeleza. **enhancement,** *n.* maongezo, uongezo, ziada, mazidio, mkuzo.

enigma, *n.* kitendawili, fumbo la maneno; (*difficulty*) ajabu, matata, tatizo. **enigmatic,** *a.* -a fumbo, -gumu kufahamika, -a kutatiza.

enjoin, *v.t.* amuru, agiza, shurutisha, lazimisha, onya, usia.

enjoy, *v.t.* penda, pendezwa na, furahiwa na, furahia; (*have*) -wa na, hozi, miliki, -wa hali ya. *Enjoy oneself,* furahi. *Did you enjoy it?* kulikufurahisha? **enjoyable,** *a.* -a kufurahisha. **enjoyment,** *n.* furaha, raha, anasa, mustarehe, kuzuri, kicheko, hadhi; (*state, condition, possession*) kuwa hali ya, kuwa na, kumiliki.

enkindle, *v.t.* washa, chocha, amsha, chochea.

enlarge, *v.t.* kuza, ongeza, zidisha, tanua; — *v.i.* (*grow large*) kua, tanuka, ongezeka; (*be capable of enlargement*) kuzika. **enlargement,** *n.* maongezo, mazidio, kukuza; (*of photograph*) mkuzo wa picha (sanamu).

enlighten, *v.t.* nurisha, tia nuru, angaza, angazisha; (*instruct*) erevusha, elimisha, fundisha, ongoza; (*inform*) arifu, aridhia. **enlightened,** *a.* -angavu, -enye maarifa. *Be enlightened,* elimika, ongoka. **enlightenment,** *n.* kuerevuka, mwangaza, wongofu, elimu, hekima.

enlist, *v.t.* andika, changa; pata (msaada, huruma, ushirika &c.); (*employ*) tia (katika kazi), tumia; — *v.i.* jiandika (ingia, jitia) katika kazi (uaskari), saidia, jitia. **enlistment,** *n.* kuandika (kujiandika) uaskari, chango; (*employment*) kutuma, kutumika.

enliven, *v.t.* furahisha, changamsha, teremesha, kunjua uso wa, shtua, tilia nguvu, sitawisha.

en masse, *adv.* kwa jumla, kwa jamii, -ote pamoja.

enmesh, *v.t.* tatiza, tega.

enmity, *n.* taz. *enemy*.

ennoble, *v.t.* (*give rank*) zidisha cheo, kuza, tukuza; (*improve*) ongoza vema, ongezea uzuri, adilisha.

ennui, *n.* uchovu, utepetevu, ukinaifu, unyong'onyevu, unyogovu, ulegevu.

enormity, *n.* taz. *enormous*.

enormous, *a.* -kubwa mno kupita kiasi. **enormity**, *n.* ubaya (wa kupita kiasi, wa kuchukiza), jambo baya mno, kosa kuu.

enough, *a.* -a kutosha, -a kadiri ya kutosha, -a kadiri ya (kiasi cha) kufaa. — *n.* kadiri ya (kiasi cha) kutosha au kufaa (kusudi, haja &c.); (*too much*) kadiri ya (kiasi cha) kuzidi (kusudi, haja &c.). — *adv.* kwa kadiri ya (kiasi cha) kufaa, kwa kiasi. *He has been good enough to give me*, kwa hisani yake amenipa. *Be enough*, tosha, kifu, akidi. *Have enough*, kinai, shiba, -wa na -ingi. *You will have enough of him one day*, atakuchosha (atakukinaisha) siku moja. *It is enough*, basi. *Have enough food*, shiba. *Enough of that!* basi! nyamaza! kelele! *The meat is not cooked enough*, nyama haijaiva (ya kutosha). *Sure enough*, bila shaka, hakika, yakini.

enquire, *v.i.*, **enquiry**, *n.* taz. *inquire*, *inquiry*.

enrage, *v.t.* kasirisha, ghadhibisha.

enrapture, *v.t.* furahisha mno, pendeza mno, shangaza (pumbaza) kwa furaha.

enrich, *v.t.* tajirisha, sitawisha, ongeza mali, -pa utàjiri, nafisi; (*of land*) zalisha, simadi, tia mbolea, rutubisha; (*a subject*) pamba, tia uzuri (urembo), rembesha, tia madoido. **enrichment**, *n.* kuongezeka (mali, uzuri, urembo, manufaa, rutuba &c.), kunafisika; (*additional matter*) nyongeza, kiongezo.

enrobe, *v.t.* valisha, visha, vika.

enrol, *v.t.* (*soldiers &c.*) andika, changa. **enrolment**, *n.* kuandika, mwandiko, mchango.

en route, *adv.* njiani, katika safari, katika kuenda.

ensample, *n.* mfano, kifano, kiolezo.

ensconce, *v.t.* ficha, funika, weka, imarisha, starehesha.

ensemble, *n.* (*tout ensemble*) mambo yanavyoonekana (kufikiriwa, kusikika &c.) yote pamoja.

enshrine, *v.t.* tunza (hifadhi, kumbuka) sana, weka kama tunu.

enshroud, *v.t.* funika, setiri, ficha.

ensign, *n.* bendera, hasa ya kiingereza, nyekundu, nyeupe na buluu, yenye *Union Jack* pembeni; (*officer*) mchukuzi wa bendera.

ensilage, *n.* majani &c. chakula cha ng'ombe, farasi &c. yaliyofukiwa shimoni yangali mabichi kuwa akiba. — *v.t.* fukia majani mabichi &c. shimoni.

enslave, *v.t.* tia utumwani, chukua mateka, fanya watumwa; (*fig*), shinda, tawala kabisa (moyo, tamaa, akili &c.). *Be enslaved by one's passions*, tawaliwa (shindwa) kabisa na tamaa za mwili. **enslavement**, *n.* utumwa, utawalwa, kutia (kutiwa) utumwani.

ensnare, *v.t.* tega, kamata kwa hila (werevu).

ensue, *v.i.* fuata, -ja nyuma, fuatana, andama, tokea (tukia) kwa sababu ya. **ensuing**, *a.* -a kufuata.

ensure, *v.t.* salimisha, linda, hifadhi; (*make certain of*) hakikisha; taz. *insure*.

entail, *v.t.* leta nyuma yake, fanya; (*law*) rithisha mali isivyoweza kutoka katika ukoo fulani.

entangle, *v.t.* tatanisha, tatiza, tia matata, zongomeza, tega. **entanglement**, *n.* matata, matatizo, mtego. *Wire entanglements*, seng'enge ya kutega, mitego ya seng'enge.

entente, *n.* mapatano ya urafiki baina ya serikali za nchi.

enter, *v.t.* ingia, enda ndani, penya;

(*write down*) andika; — *v.i.* ingia, penya; (*form part of*) -wa sehemu ya, -wamo. *Enter into* (*share*), shiriki. *Enter upon* (*begin*), shika, anza, ingia. **entrance,** *n.* mwingilio, mlango, ukumbi, njia, kuingia; (*beginning*) mwanzo; (*right of entrance*) ruhusa ya kuingia. **entrant,** *n.* aingiaye; (*in contest*) mshindani, **entrée,** *n.* ruhusa ya (uwezo wa, haki ya) kuingia; (*course of meal*) chakula kinachoandaliwa kisha kula samaki. **entry,** *n.* taz. *entrance*: (*written record*) kuandika (habari), mwandiko, habari, tarehe.

enteric, *n.* ugonjwa mmojawapo wa matumbo.

enterprise, *n.* jambo kubwa (hasa la ujasiri, hatari, ajabu), jambo la bidii, jambo, kazi; (*spirit, energy*) moyo, bidii, ujasiri, utendaji, uhodari. **enterprising,** *a.* -jasiri, -tendaji, hodari, -epesi.

entertain, *v.t.* karibisha, pokea, kirimu; (*amuse*) pendeza, furahisha, teremesha (*consider*) fikiria, wazia, (*favourably*) kubali. **entertaining,** *a.* -a kupendeza, -a kuchekesha, -teremeshi, -a mazungumzo. **entertainment,** *n.* karamu; (*amusement, show*), mazungumzo, machezo, tamasha, tafrija.

enthral, *v.t.* fanya mtumwa, tia utumwani; weza, shinda moyo, tiisha, loga, shangaza (kwa uzuri, habari, mambo ya ajabu &c.). **enthralment,** *n.* mshangao, kutisha (kutishwa) moyo, hali kama ya kupagawa.

enthrone, *v.t.* tawaza, fanya (mfalme au askofu), kalisha katika kiti cha enzi; (*fig.*) wekea heshima nyingi. **enthronement,** *n.* kutawaza, kutawazwa, kukalisha katika kiti cha enzi.

enthusiasm, *n.* shauku, harara, idili; hali ya kujaa upendo (bidii, shauku, furaha, mshangao) kwa mtu au jambo; vifijo, sherehe (ya kuonyesha furaha, upendo, bidii, shauku &c.). **enthusiast,** *n.* mwenye *enthusiasm*. **enthusiastic,** *a.* -a bidii, -a shauku, -a sherehe, -a vifijo, -a moyo.

entice, *v.t.* vuta kwa werevu, shawishi, tongoza, bemba, bembeleza. **enticement,** *n.* ushawishi, mvuto, shonga, chambo; (*trials*) majaribu. **enticing,** *a.* -a kuvuta (kwa uzuri, utamu &c.), -bembe.

entire, *a.* -zima, pia, -ote, kamili, -timilifu. **entirely,** *adv.* kabisa, pia. **entirety,** *n.* ukamili, utimilifu, hali ya kuwa -zima, pasipo kuzidi wala kupungua. *In its entirety*, -zima, -ote pia.

entitle, *v.t.* (*give title*) taja; (*give right*) pasha haki, stahilisha, ruhusu. *I am entitled to it*, ni haki (stahili) yangu.

entity, *n.* kitu chenyewe hasa.

entomb, *v.t.* zika, tia kaburini.

entomology, *n.* elimu ya wadudu.

entourage, *n.* mahali, kitende, mazingira, hali; (*followers*) wafuasi, akina.

entrails, *n.* matumbo.

entrain, *v.t.* pakia, pakiza (katika gari la moshi); — *v.i.* ingia, jipakia (katika gari la moshi).

entrammel, *v.t.* zuia, pinga, tatanisha.

entrance, (1) *n.* taz. *enter*.

entrance, (2) *v.t.* furahisha mno, pendeza mno, shangaza (pumbaza &c.) kwa furaha. **entrancing,** *a.* -a kushangaza (kufurahisha, kupendeza) mno.

entrant, *n.* taz. *enter*.

entrap, *v.t.* tega, kamata kwa hila (werevu), laghai, danganya.

entreat, *v.t.* sihi, omba; (*for mercy*) lalamia. **entreaty,** *n.* maombi, haja, malalamiko.

entrée, *n.* taz. *enter*.

entrench, *v.t.* zungushia handaki, zungushia boma (la kulinda mji, kambi, jeshi &c.). *Entrench oneself*, jiweka salama mahali. **entrenchment,** *n.* handaki, boma (la kulinda mahali, &c.).

entrust, *v.t.* wekea amana, aminia, aminisha, kabidhi, salimia, akifia.

entry, *n.* taz. *enter.*
entwine, *v.t.* pota, suka, tatiza, tatanya, zongomeza, funganisha, kumbatia.
enumerate, *v.t.* hesabu, taja moja moja, nena. **enumeration,** *n.* kuhesabu, mtajo wa moja moja.
enunciate, *v.t.* nena wazi, tangaza, hubiri; (*pronounce*) tamka. **enunciation,** *n.* kunena wazi; (*of pronouncing*) matamko.
envelop, *v.t.* zunguka, zungusha, funika, gubika; (*fig.*) ficha, fumba, tatiza, tatanisha. **envelope,** *n.* bahasha; (*covering*) kifuniko; (*rind, husk*) ganda. **envelopment,** *n.* kufunika, kugubika, kifuniko.
envenom, *v.t.* tia sumu (uchungu, ukali), sumisha; (*exasperate*) kasirisha.
enviable, *a.*, **envious,** *a.* taz. *envy.*
environ, *v.t.* zunguka, zungusha, zingira. **environment,** *n.* mazingira, kitendc, ukazi, makao, makazi, mastakimu, ulimwengu, hali, mambo, manzili. **environs,** *n.* ujirani, kandokando, mahali panapozunguka karibu, kiunga, pembizo.
envisage, *v.t.* fikiria, wazia.
envoy, *n.* mjumbe, tume.
envy, *n.* husuda, wivu, kijicho. — *v.t.* onea husuda, husudu, hasidi, onea wivu, tamani (mali au hali ya mwingine). **enviable,** *a.* -a kutamanika, -zuri. **envious,** *a.* -enye husuda, -enye kijicho.
enwrap, *v.t.* kunja, peta, funga, tia ndani, funika, vika, gubika.
epaulet, *n.* purendi (la begani).
ephemeral, *a.* -a siku moja tu, -a kitambo, -a kupita upesi.
epic, *n.* utenzi.
epicure, *n.* mteuzi (wa chakula), apendaye sana vyakula vilivyoteuliwa, mwenye kidomo, mtu wa anasa (katika mambo ya kula na kunywa). **epicurean,** *a. and n.* -a jinsi ya *epicure*; (*Greek*) mfuasi wa mwalimu *Epicurus.*
epidemic, *a.* -a kushika (kuambukiza, kupata) watu wengi pamoja. — *n.* (*disease*) ugonjwa unaoshika wati wengi pamoja.
epidermis, *n.* ngozi ya nje.
epiglottis, *n.* kidakatonge, kimio.
epigram, *n.* shairi, mashairi; (*witticism*) neno jerevu la akili, fumbo la neno. **epigrammatic,** *a.* -a akili, -erevu.
epilepsy, *n.* kifafa. **epileptic,** *a.* -a kifafa.
epilogue, *n.* maneno ya mwisho wa hotuba (kitabu, mwandiko).
Epiphany, *n.* sikukuu ya kuonekana Yesu Kristo na Mamajusi.
episcopacy, *n.* uaskofu. **episcopal,** *a.* -a askofu, -enye maaskofu. **episcopalian,** *a.* -a kanisa lenye kuamriwa na maaskofu. **episcopate,** *n.* wakati (kazi) ya uaskofu; (*bishops*) jamii ya maaskofu.
episode, *n.* hadithi iliyoingizwa katika hadithi nyingine; jambo mojawapo katika mfululizo wa mambo, hasa jambo la maana sana.
epistle, *n.* barua, waraka. **epistolary,** *a.* -a jinsi ya barua, -a kwa barua.
epitaph, *n.* maneno yaliyoandikwa juu ya jiwe la kaburi, au sanamu ya ukumbusho wa marehemu; maneno (shairi) yaliyoandikwa kwa ukumbusho wa marehemu, hasa kumsifu.
epithet, *n.* neno la kuonyesha jinsi, sifa, tabia *&c.* taz. *adjective*; jina linaloeleza sifa (tabia, jinsi).
epitome, *n.* muhtasari, ufupisho wa habari. **epitomize,** *v.t.* fupisha habari, fanya muhtasari.
epoch, *n.* tarehe (muda, muhula, wakati wa jambo kubwa, wa kukumbukwa, mashuhuri); mwanzo wa muda maalum (wa elimu maalum *&c.*).
Epsom salts, *n.* chumvi ya haluli, dawa ya kuharisha.
equable, *a.* taz. *equal.*
equal, *a.* sawa, sawasawa, mamoja, si -geuzi, -a kulingana, linganifu, -a kulanda. *Be equal to the occasion,* weza, toshindwa, tofadhaika. *Are you equal to it?* waiweza?. — *n.* (*in*

age) hirimu, marika; (*in condition, quality*) mwenzi. — *v.t.* -wa sawa na, lingana na, landana na. **equable,** *a.* sawasawa, si -a kubadilika. *He has an equal temper*, habadiliki tabia, yu sawasawa siku zote. **equality,** *n.* hali ya kuwa sawa, usawa, umoja, hali moja, ulinganifu. **equalization,** *n.* kufanya sawasawa, usawa, mlinganyo, ulinganifu, ulingano. **equalize,** *v.t.* sawazisha, fanya sawasawa, linganisha. **equanimity,** *n.* utulivu wa moyo (tabia), utaratibu, upole, amani. **equation,** *n.* kusawazisha, kulinganisha, mlinganyo.

equator, *n.* ikweta (*Eng.*), istiwai (*Ar.*), duara ya kuizunguka dunia kati hasa ya ncha ya kaskazini na ncha ya kusini. **equatorial,** *a.* -a *equator*, -a karibu na *equator*.

equerry, *n.* bwana mwenye cheo kikuu amngojeaye mfalme (malkia, mwana wa mfalme); (zamani) mwangalizi mkuu wa farasi wa mfalme (mwana wa mfalme &c.). **equestrian,** *a.* -a kupanda farasi. — *n.* mpanda farasi. **equine,** *a.* -a farasi, -a kama farasi.

equi- *prefix.* ya kuanzia neno jingine, maana yake ni kama *equal*.

equiangular, *a.* -enye pembe zote sawa.

equidistant, *a.* -enye urefu (wa kuwa mbali) sawa, mbali sawa, mwendo sawa.

equilateral, *a.* -enye pande zote zilizo sawa.

equilibrium, *n.* sawa (kama vitanga vya mizani), uzito ulio sawa, usawa, uzani mmoja. *Be in equilibrium*, simama sawasawa, sawazikana.

equine, *a.* taz. *equerry*.

equinox, *n.* majira ya jua kupita juu ya ikweta, na urefu wa mchana na usiku ni sawasawa.

equip, *v.t.* fanya tayari, tengeneza, andaa. **equipage,** *n.* zana za safari, wafuasi; gari na wafuasi, saisi &c.; zana. **equipment,** *n.* mapambo, mavalio, vyombo, zana, vifaa, masurufu.

equipoise, *n.* taz. *equilibrium*.

equitable, *a.*, **equitably,** *adv.* taz. *equity*.

equity, *n.* haki, sawa, uadilifu, maadili. **equitable,** *a.* -a haki, adili, -adilifu, ipasayo, sawa, wajibu. **equitably,** *adv.* kwa haki, kwa adili.

equivalent, *n.* sawa, badala. — *a.* -enye maana (thamani) iliyo sawa, -a kulingana, -linganifu, mamoja.

equivocal, *a.* -enye maana isiyo dhahiri, -enye maana mbili au zaidi, -enye matata, si wazi, si amini, si -nyofu. **equivocate,** *v.i.* tatiza maneno, sema maneno yenye maana isiyo dhahiri (yenye maana mbili au zaidi), hasa kwa kusudi la kutatiza au kudanganya, sitasita, ogopa. **equivocation,** *n.* matata ya maneno, madanganya, upotovu (upotoe) wa maneno, uwongo, unafiki, uzandiki.

era, *n.* njia ya kuhesabu tarehe kuanzia jambo kubwa maalum, *e.g. Christian era* ni wakati unaofuata mwanzo wa dini ya kikristo.

eradicate, *v.t.* ng'oa kabisa, haribu kabisa, futia mbali. **eradication,** *n.* kung'oa, kuharibu, kufutia mbali.

erase, *v.t.* futa, futia mbali, batili. **eraser,** *n.* kitu (kipande cha mpira) cha kufutia maandiko &c. **erasure,** *n.* kufuta, mfuto, mtanguo.

ere, *conj.* kabla; (*rather than*) kuliko.

erect, *v.t.* simamisha, simikisha; (*construct*) jenga, unda, fanyiza. — *a.* -a kusimama, -a wima, -a kiwimawima. **erectile,** *a.* -a kusimikana, -a kuweza kusimama wima. **erection,** *n.* kusimika, kusimikisha, msimiko, kujenga; (*buildings &c.*) majengo; (*of wood*) kiunzi.

ermine, *n.* mnyama mdogo kama cheche; ngozi ya mnyama huyo.

erode, *v.t.* -la, bomoa, fukua, monyoa, mong'onyoa, mega (mawe na udongo, kazi ya maji, mvua &c.). **erosion,** *n.* kula, mmego, kumonyoa, kumonyoka, mmonyoko, kumong'onyoka, mmong'onyoko.

erotic, *a.* -a ngoa, -a ashiki, -a shauku

nyingi, -kware, -a uchu, -a tamaa (ya kiume na kike); (*person*) mkware, mtiriri.

err, *v.i.* kosa, potoka, fanya vibaya, fanya dhambi. **errant,** *a.* -a kutembeatembea kutafuta mambo ya ujasiri (uhodari *&c.*); -a kutembeatembea, -a kutangatanga; -a kupotoka, -potoe, -a kukosa. **erratic,** *a.* -a kupotea, -potoe, -a kupotoka, -potovu, -a kuzungukazunguka, -a kugeukageuka, -geni, -geugeu. **erratum,** *n.* (*plur.* **errata**) kosa (katika kuandika au kufuasa chapa au kunakili). **erring,** *a.* -enye hatia, -enye kufanya dhambi, -a dhambi, -a kufanya kosa, -kosaji, -a kupotoka. **erroneous,** *a.* -enye kosa, -a uwongo, -kosefu. **error,** *n.* kosa.

errand, *n.* utume, ujumbe, maagizo, amri; (*business*) kazi, neno, amali. *He has gone on an errand,* ametumwa. *What is his errand?* amejia nini? ameendea nini?

erratic, *a.,* **erratum,** *n.,* **erring,** *a.,* **erroneous,** *a.,* **error,** *n.* taz. *err.*

erst, *adv.,* **erstwhile,** *adv.* zamani, kale, kwanza, mwanzoni.

eructation, *n.* kiungulia, kokomoko, cheuo, mbweu.

erudite, *a.* -enye maarifa, -enye elimu, -juzi. **erudition,** *n.* maarifa, elimu, ujuzi.

erupt, *v.i.* foka, bubujika, toka ghafula. **eruption,** *n.* (*volcanic*) kutoka moshi (moto, mawe *&c.*); (*disease*) kutoka upele, vipele, upele, ukurutu; (*uproar*) fitina, udhia, msukosuko.

erysipelas, *n.* ugonjwa mmojawapo wa kutoka namna ya upele mbaya sana.

escalade, *n.* kupanda kwa ngazi. *To take by escalade,* kuteka mji kwa kushambulia boma (kwa ngazi).

escalator, *n.* namna ya ngazi (daraja) inayojiendea, yaani watu husimama tu na ngazi hiyo huwapandisha au kuwatelemsha.

escapade, *n.* taz. *escape.*

escape, *n.* wokovu, kuokoka, kupona; (*other way*) budi, njia ya wokovu (ya kuokoka); (*surprising*) kuokoka kwa ajabu; (*of prisoner &c.*) kutoroka; (*of gas &c.*) mvujo, kuvuja; (*mechan.*) bomba la kutoka moshi, mvuke *&c.* *He had a narrow escape,* aliokoka kwa shida. *Fire-escape,* ngazi ya kupandishia nyumba inayoungua ili watu waliomo watelemke na kuokoka. —*v.i.* okoka, pona, futahi; (*run away*) kimbia, toroka; (*avoid*) epa; (*get away*) (*be lost*) toka pasipo ruhusa, toka bure, potea; (*as a spring*) fyatuka; (*slip from*) chopoka, ponyoka, kurupuka; — *v.t.* (*avoid*) epuka, epusha. *Escape notice, observation,* toangaliwa, totambulika, fichikana. *Escape memory,* pitia, sahauliwa. *It escaped me,* nilipitiwa, sikusikia. **escapade,** *n.* tendo la ujinga (la kuasi, la ujasiri, la upuzi) hasa kwa ajili ya furaha moyoni.

escarpment, *n.* genge, mlima wa kiwimawima, mahali palipochongoka, palipoinuka kiwimawima.

eschew, *v.t.* epua, epusha, epukana na, kimbia, kataa.

escort, *n.* mlinzi, mfuasi (katika safari), askari, jamii ya walinzi. — *v.t.* fuatana na (ili kulinda, kwa heshima, kusindikiza).

esculent, *a.* -a kulika, -a kufaa kwa chakula. — *n.* chakula.

escutcheon, *n.* ngao yenye alama ya kuonyesha cheo au nasaba ya mtu. *Blot on his escutcheon,* aibu kwake.

esoteric, *a.* -a ndani, -a siri, -a watu wenye elimu tu.

esparto, *n.* namna ya nyasi inayotumika kufanya karatasi, nguo nzito *&c.*

especial, *a.* bora, -a peke yake, -a mtindo, -kuu, -a kwanza, mahsusi, maalum, hasa. **especially,** *adv.* zaidi, hasa, sana.

espionage, *n.* upelelezi, uchungulizi, kuchungulia, udadisi, kudoya.

esplanade, *n.* uwanja, barabara pana, hasa kwa watu kutembelea.

espousal, *n.* kuposa, poso; kuoa, ndoa, arusi, nikaha. *Espousal of a* *cause,* kushika (kusaidia) shauri.

espouse, *v.t.* oza, oa; (*support*) jitia katika, fuata mambo ya, saidia.

esprit de corps, *n.* moyo (juhudi) wa kupenda na kusitawisha jamii na heshima yake.

espy, *v.t.* ona, angalia, chungulia, gundua, fumania.

-esque, *suff.* ya kufuata neno, maana yake ni -a jinsi ya, -a namna ya, -a kufanana na, *e.g. Arabesque,* -a kiarabu.

esquire, *n.* jina la heshima la kuandika kufuata jina la mwungwana (kwa uzazi, malezi, maarifa *&c.*); mwungwana.

essay, *n.* (*effort*) bidii, juhudi, jaribio; (*written*) insha, habari, taarifa, mtungo (wa habari, maneno). *Make an essay,* jitahidi, jaribu. *Write an essay on,* andika habari ya, andika insha ya, tunga habari ya. — *v.t.* jaribu, fanya bidii ya, jitahidi; (*try, prove*) hakiki, pima. **essayist,** *n.* mwandishi (mtungaji) wa insha (habari, taarifa).

essence, *n.* asili, nafsi, kitu chenyewe hasa; (*real character*) hali, tabia, johari; (*extract, perfume*) mafuta, ute, uturi, marashi; (*inmost part, meaning*) moyo, kiini, maana halisi.

essential, *a.* -a asili, -a kitu chenyewe; (*indispensable*) -a kanuni, a kawaida, -a lazima; (*pure*) safi. — *n.* kanuni, asili, lazima.

establish, *v.t.* weka, fanyiza, anzisha, simamisha; (*make firm*) imarisha, weka imara, thibitisha; (*appoint*) amuru, tengeneza; (*prove*) kubalisha, shuhudia. **established,** *a.* imara, thabiti, madhubuti. **establishment,** *n.* kuweka imara *&c.*; (*government*) serikali; (*household*) nyumba, kikao, maskani, kitende; (*ecclesiastical*) kanisa (dini) la serikali, kanisa la Uingereza; (*of a department &c.*) jumla ya watu wa kazi.

estate, *n.* (*land*) shamba; (*property*) mali; (*state*) hali, cheo, manzili.

esteem, *v.t.* (*honour*) heshimu, stahi, jali, sharifu, thamini; (*consider*) ona, dhani, kadiri, hesabu. — *n.* heshima, ustahi, ustahiki, itibari, staha, upendo; (*judgement*) mawazo, maono; (*merit*) sifa, thamani. *High esteem,* sifa njema, thamani. **estimable,** *a.* -a kuheshimiwa, -a kusifiwa, -stahifu, -ema. **estimate,** *v.t.* kadiri, kiasi, atikali, pima; (*by comparison*) enenza; — *v.i.* (*make estimate*) fanya hesabu. — *n.* kisio (la hesabu, thamani, gharama *&c.*); hesabu ya kisio; upimaji (wa tabia, sifa *&c.*). **estimation,** *n.* heshima, sifa; (*judgement*) nia, moyo. *In my estimation,* nionavyo mimi.

estop, *v.t.* kataza, zuia. **estoppel,** *n.* katazo, zuio.

estrange, *v.t.* farikisha, tenga, vunja urafiki, chukiza, geuza. **estrangement,** *n.* mvunjo wa urafiki, kufarikisha.

estuary, *n.* hori, mahali papana mto unapoingia baharini, mlango mpana wa mto.

et cetera, etcetera, na vingine vivyo, kadha wa kadha. Ufupisho ni *etc.* au *&c.*

etch, *v.t.* chora (sanamu, picha) juu ya madini kwa dawa kali ili kufanya chapa ya kupigia picha; piga chapa picha (sanamu *&c.*) kwa chapa iliyochorwa kwa dawa kali. **etching,** *n.* picha (sanamu) iliyopigwa chapa kwa namna ya *etch;* mchoro wa picha (sanamu *&c.*) kwa namna ya *etch.*

eternal, *a.* -a milele, -a kale na kale, -a azali, pasipo mwanzo wala mwisho, -a abadi, -a daima, -a kuendelea bila kikomo. **eternity,** *n.* milele, wakati usio na mwanzo wala mwisho; (*the next world*) ahera.

ether, *n.* anga ya juu, hewa nyembamba (nyepesi) sana; (*in medicine*) namna ya dawa ikaukayo upesi inayotumika kuzimisha roho kwa muda au kunyamazisha maumivu. **ethereal,** *a.* -a mbinguni, -a peponi, -epesi sana (kama hewa), -a kufanana na -a mbinguni kuliko -a duniani.

ethical, *a.* -a mambo ya adili, -a wema na ubaya, -enye habari (ya kutupasa kwa) wema na ubaya. **ethics,** *n.* elimu ya wema na ubaya, elimu ya maadili.

ethnic, ethnical, *a.* -a kabila (taifa), -a kuhusu tabia za kabila (taifa). **ethnography,** *n.* maelezo ya taratibu ya tabia za kabila (taifa). **ethnology,** *n.* elimu ya tabia (makao, umbo, desturi *&c.*) za mataifa (wanadamu).

etiquette, *n.* adabu, mwenendo (desturi, matendo) wa kawaida ya kiungwana.

etymology, *n.* elimu ya asili (jinsi na maana) ya maneno moja moja; kuchunguza asili ya neno kadiri inavyowezekana kwa kulinganisha lugha na habari za lugha inayotumia lile neno.

eucalyptus, *n.* namna ya mti.

Eucharist, *n.* Ushirika Mtakatifu wa kikristo.

eugenics, *n.* elimu ya jinsi ya kusitawisha wanadamu (wanyama) kwa kuchagua wazazi kwa uangalifu sana.

eulogist, *n.* taz. *eulogium.*

eulogium, *n.* maneno ya kusifu, sifa. **eulogist,** *n.* msifu. **eulogize,** *v.t.* sifu. **eulogy,** *n.* kama *eulogium.*

eunuch, *n.* towashi, mhasi.

euphemism, *n.* neno zuri (safi, lisilochukiza, lisilo mwiko) litumikalo badala ya neno chafu (linalochukiza, lisilo la heshima, la mwiko *&c.*). **euphemistic,** *a.* -zuri, -a kutokuchukiza.

euphonic, *a.* taz. *euphony.*

euphony, *n.* sauti ya kupendeza, sauti zinazolingana, ulinganifu wa sauti, sauti tamu, tamko tamu. **euphonic,** *a.* -a *euphony.*

euphorbia, *n.* jamii ya miti kama mganga, mbono, mchongoma, mnyara *&c.*

Eurasian, *n.* mtu (hasa wa Uhindi) ambaye mzazi mmoja ni wa kihindi na mwingine wa Ulaya (*Europe*).

Europe, *n.* Ulaya, Uzunguni. **European,** *n.* Mzungu. — *a.* -a kizungu

europeanize, *v.t.* geuza kizungu, zoeza mambo na desturi za Wazungu.

euthanasia, *n.* kifo kisicho na maumivu; kufisha bila maumivu (hasa watu wenye ugonjwa usioponyeka wenye maumivu mengi mno).

evacuate, *v.t.* ondoka katika, toka, hama katika, acha; (*of bowels*) -nya; (*vomit*) tapika. **evacuation,** *n.* kuacha mahali, kuhama; (*excreta &c.*) mavi, kinyesi, choo; (*vomit*) matapishi.

evade, *v.t.* (*a blow*) epa; (*avoid*) piga chenga, epuka, epukana na, epa; (*escape by trickery*) kimbia (tolipa, tojibu, tofanya *&c.*) kwa kutumia hila (werevu). **evasion,** *n.* kuepa, kuepuka, kupiga chenga, hila, werevu, maneno ya werevu. **evasive,** *a.* -enye hila, -erevu; (*elusive*) -gumu kufahamu, -a kuendelea muda mfupi tu.

evanescent, *a.* -a kupita upesi, -a kuwapo muda mfupi tu, -a kutoweka, -a kufifia, -a kupotea..

evangelic, evangelical, *a.* -a Injili, -a jinsi ya Injili, -a imani ya Injili; (*of the evangelical school*) -a madhehebu ya Wakristo wanaoshikilia ya kuwa kiini cha imani ya Injili ni kuokoka kwa kufanya mambo mema wala si kutumainia mafumbo (*sacraments*) ya dini. **evangelist,** *n.* mwandika Injili, mweneza Injili. **evangelization,** *n.* eneo (enezo) la mafundisho ya Injili; kufundisha imani ya Injili. **evangelize,** *v.t.* fundisha imani ya Injili, eneza habari za Injili.

evaporate, *v.i.* geuka hewa; (*be absorbed*) nywewa, kauka, toweka, potea; — *v.t.* kausha, geuza kuwa hewa (mvuke). **evaporation,** *n.* kugeuka hewa, kukauka, kunywewa.

evasion, *n.*, **evasive,** *a.* taz. *evade.*

Eve, (1) *n.* (*Proper name of first woman*) Hawa.

eve, (2) *n.* (*evening*) jioni, magharibi; (*of festival*) siku kabla ya sikukuu; (*time before*) wakati unaotangulia jambo. **even, evening,** *n.* jioni, magharibi. **evensong,** *n.* sala za jioni za Kanisa la kiingereza **eventide,** *n.* jioni.

even, *a.* (*level*) sawasawa; (*smooth*) laini; (*quiet*) -tulivu; (*unchanging*) imara, -siyobadilika; (*fair*) -a haki, -adilifu, adili; (*of numbers*) kamili, shufwa, inayogawanyika kwa mbili bila kubaki. — *adv.* sawasawa; kama -vyo, *e.g. It has turned out even as I expected,* limetokea kama nilivyofikiri; (*at that moment*) sawia, *e.g. even as he was speaking a shot rang out,* katika kusema na bunduki kulia sawia; (*even if*) ijapo, ijapokuwa, angao, hata. *Even if you die,* ujapokufa, hata ukifa, hata kama ukifa. *Even if you go, it is all the same to me,* hata ukienda ni mamoja kwangu. — *v.t.* sawazisha. **even-handed,** *a.* -a haki, -adilifu.

evening, *n.* **evensong,** *n.* taz. *eve* (2).

event, *n.* jambo, tukio, mkasa; (*result*) mwisho, matokeo; (*sporting*) shindano moja (katika mashindano ya mbio &c.); (*startling*) shani, kizushi, jambo kubwa. *At all events,* kwa vyo vyote, viwavyo vyote, hakuna budi. *In the event of his death,* akifa. **eventful,** *a.* -enye mambo mengi, -a ajabu. **eventual,** *a.* -a mwisho, mwishoni. **eventuality,** *n.* jambo liwezalo kutokea, mwisho, tukio. **eventually,** *adv.* mwisho, hatimaye. **eventuate,** *v.i.* tukio, tokeo.

eventide, *n.* taz. *eve* (2).

eventual, *a.*, **eventuality,** *n.*, **eventually,** *adv.*, **eventuate,** *v.* taz. *event.*

ever, *adv.* (*always*) sikuzote, daima, kila mara, abadi; (*any time*) wakati wo wote. *Whoever,* ye yote. *Whenever, wherever,* po pote. *Wherever he goes,* kila aendapo. *Whatever,* iwayo yote. *Ever and anon,* mara kwa mara. *Ever so,* -a kadiri yo yote, sana sana. *For ever,* hata milele. *Now and for ever,* maisha na milele.

evergreen, *a.* (mti) -siokauka, -siofifia, -siokufa.

everlasting, *a.* -a milele, -a kudumu (kuendelea) bila kukoma. **everlastingly,** *adv.* kwa milele, kwa muda mrefu sana.

evermore, *adv.* milele.

every, *a.* kila. *Every now and then,* pengine pengine, mara kwa mara. **everybody,** *n.* kila mtu, watu wote. **everyday,** *a.* -a kila siku, -a mara kwa mara, -a kawaida, -a desturi. **everyone,** *n.* kila mtu, watu wote. **everything,** *n.* kila kitu (jambo, neno). **everywhere,** *adv.* pote pote, kote kote, kila mahali.

evict, *v.t.* toa katika (shamba, nyumba); toza (nyumba, mahali &c.) kwa nguvu ya haki. **eviction,** *n.* kutoa katika nyumba (shamba &c.); kutoza &c. kwa nguvu ya haki.

evidence, *n.* ushahidi, ushuhuda, mathubutu. *Be in evidence,* -wamo, -onekana. *Give evidence,* shuhudia, toa ushuhuda. **evident,** *a.* dhahiri, wazi. **evidential,** *a.* -a kuthibitisha, -a kushuhudia. **evidently,** *adv.* kwa dhahiri, kwa wazi.

evil, *a.* -ovu, -baya, -fasiki, fisadi, -potovu; (*unfortunate*) -a kisirani, -a ndege mbaya. *The Evil One,* Shetani, Ibilisi. — *n.* uovu, ubaya, baa, ufasiki, ufisadi, upotovu, uasherati. **evil-doer,** *n.* mwovu, mtenda mbaya, mfasiki, mfisadi, mpotovu. **evil-eyed,** *a.* -enye kijicho. **evilly,** *adv.* kwa uovu, viovu. **evil-minded,** *a.* -ovu, -baya.

evince, *v.t.* onyesha, toa wazi, dhihirisha.

eviscerate, *v.t.* tumbua; (*fig.*) haribu maana (tabia).

evoke, *v.t.* ita, tokeza, zusha, leta, toza, amsha.

evolution, *n.* (*growth*) kukua, kuendelea, kuota; (*progression*) maendeleo; (*change and progress*) mageuzi yenye kuendelea, mabadili na maendeleo; (*of soldiers*) kazi, miendo michezo, mazunguko. **evolve,** *v.t.* (*produce*) toa, toza, tokeza, fanyiza; (*disclose*) bainisha, onyesha; — *v.i.* funuka, kua na kuendelea, tokea (dhihirika, badilika) kwa taratibu.

ewe, *n.* kondoo jike.
ewer, *n.* kopo (kubwa la maji).
exacerbate, *v.t.* zidisha (maumivu, ugomvi, hasira, chuki, uchungu &c.); (*irritate* &c.) kasirisha, sumbua, udhi, chukiza. **exacerbation**, *n.* kuzidisha (maumivu &c.); uchungu, udhiko, hasira, chuki &c.
exact, *a.* halisi, barabara, sawasawa; (*true*) kweli; (*careful*) -angalifu, -a bidii, -aminifu. — *v.t.* (*payment*) toza, lipiza; (*of work, circumstances*) hitaji, taka; (*compel*) shurutisha, lazimisha. *Exact obedience*, tiisha, shurutisha (lazimisha) kutii. *This work exacts closest attention*, kazi hii inataka (inahitaji) uangalifu sana. **exacting**, *a.* -kali, -a kuonea, -a kutaka kazi (uangalifu) nyingi, -zito, -gumu, -dhalimu. **exaction**, *n.* kutoza, kulipiza; (*unjust tolls* &c.) kodi nyingi (isiyo ya haki), hongo, udhalimu; (*of life, profession* &c.) kazi, uangalifu, wajibu. **exactitude**, *n.* uhalisi, usahihi. **exactly**, *adv.* halisi, barabara, sawasawa, sahihi, sawia, mahsusi. **exactness**, *n.* uhalisi, usahihi, kweli, uaminifu.
exaggerate, *v.t.* ongeza sifa (habari) mno, zidisha, piga chuku, tia chumvi, tukuza mno, tokeza kupita kiasi; — *v.i.* piga chuku (domo). **exaggeration**, *n.* maongezo, sifa nyingi mno, kiungo, chuku, domo.
exalt, *v.t.* (*raise*) inua, kweza, paaza; (*promote*) kuza, pandisha (cheo, daraja); (*praise*) tukuza, adhimisha, adhimu; (*elate*) furahisha, faharisha. **exaltation**, *n.* kuinua &c.; utukufu, adhama; (*elation*) furaha, majivuno, kutukuka. **exalted**, *a.* -a cheo bora, -tukufu, bora, -a furaha, -adhimu.
examination, *n.* mtihani, mkaguo, ukaguzi, uchunguzi, kutazamia, kuhoji, kujaribu. kuchunguza. **examine**, *v.t.* (*test, try*) onja, jaribia; (*inspect*) angalia, tazamia, aua, kagua; (*inquire into*) hoji, hakiki, chungua, dadisi, nyenya. **examinee**, *n.* mtu anayejaribiwa katika mtihani. **examiner**, *n.* mkaguaji, mchunguzi, mpelelezi, mwulizi, mhoji.
example, *n.* mfano, namna, kiolezo, kielelezo, onyo. *I will make an example of him*, nitamwadhibisha ili wengine waonywe. *Set an example to*, fuasisha, tolea namna. *For example*, hivi, kama hivi, jinsi hii, kwa mfano, madhalani. **exemplar**, *n.* mfano, namna, kiolezo. **exemplary**, *a.* -a namna -a kuonya, -a kufuatishika, -ema sana, bora, -stahifu, -a kustahili kufuatwa. **exemplify**, *v.t.* onyesha kwa mfano, onyesha namna.
exasperate, *v.t.* kasirisha, ghadhibisha, tia ukali, chachisha, chochea (hasira, chuki &c.). **exasperation**, *n.* hasira kali, ghadhabu, uchungu mwingi.
excavate, *v.t.* chimba, chimbua, fukua, fukulia. **excavation**, *n.* shimo, tundu, ufuo. **excavator**, *n.* mchimbaji, mchimbuaji, mashine ya kuchimbulia.
exceed, *v.t.* pita, ruka mpaka, zidi, -wa zaidi ya; — *v.i.* zidi. **exceedingly**, *adv.* mno (ajabu), sana (sana). **excess**, *n.* kupita kiasi, kuzidi mno, mazidio, wingi; (*intemperance*) ulafi (ulevi, ufisadi), upotovu. *In excess*, mno, kwa mno. **excessive**, *a.* mno, zaidi, -a kupita kiasi.
excel, *v.t.* pita, shinda, zidi, kulula; — *v.i.* -wa bora, zidi. **excellence**, *n.* ubora, uzuri, wema. **excellency**, *n.* kama *excellence*; jina la heshima wapewalo mabwana wengine wenye cheo kikubwa. *His Excellency the Governor*, Bwana *Governor* mtukufu. **excellent**, *a.* bora, -zuri sana, -ema sana, aali, -adhimu.
except, *v.t.* toa, acha, tenga, weka mbali, tohesabu, tofikiri, totia. — *prep.* ila, isipokuwa, ghairi ya, minghairi, baghairi. — *conj.* isipokuwa. **excepting**, *prep.* kama *except, prep.* **exception**, *n.* jambo la peke yake, hitilafu, tofauti, jambo lisilo sawa (lisilo la kawaida); (*objection*) makatazo, kinzano. *Take exception to*, kataa, chukizwa na,

tokubali, dakiza, *With the exception of* = *except*. **exceptionable,** *a.* -baya, -kosefu, -a kubishikana, -a kushindanikana. **exceptional,** *a.* -a peke yake, mbali, si -a kawaida, -a tofauti, -a hitilafu. **exceptionally,** *adv.* kwa kadiri (kiasi) inavyozidi (inavyopungua, isiyo ya kawaida &c.).

excerpt, *n.* teuzi, dondoo, maneno kadha wa kadha ya kitabu, hotuba &c.

excess, *n.*, **excessive,** *a.* taz. *exceed.*

exchange, *v.t.* badili, badilisha; (*in comp.*) -ana. *Exchange presents,* pelekeana (peana) zawadi; (*compliments*) salimiana, amkiana; (*services*) fadhiliana, faliana; (*blows*) pigana. — *n.* badilisho, kubadilisha; (*conversion of coin &c.*) mvunjo wa fedha, faida ya fedha; (*current price*) bei; (*place of exchange*) nyumba ya kubadilisha fedha. *Rate of exchange,* sarafu. *In exchange for,* mahali pa, badala ya. **exchangeable,** *a.* -a kubadilikana, -a kubadilishikana.

exchequer, *n.* hazina ya serikali, fedha ya serikali.

excisable, *a.* taz. *excise* (1).

excise, (1) *n.* ushuru, kodi. **excisable,** *a.* -a kulipa kodi, -a kutozeka kodi. **exciseman,** *n.* mtoza ushuru, mlipiza kodi, mtu wa forodhani.

excise, (2) *v.t.* kata, ondoa, toa. **excision,** *n.* kukata, kutoa, kuondoa, mkato.

exciseman, *n.* taz. *excise* (1).

excision, *n.* taz. *excise* (2).

excite, *v.t.* amsha, shtua, chocheza, taharakisha, washa, sukasuka, chomesha; (*cause*) fanya, fanyiza, leta. *Exite attention,* tazamisha, vuta macho, shtusha. *Excite desire,* tamanisha, vuta, tia shauku (ashiki, tamaa), sisimua. *Be excited, in an excited state,* hangaika, tahamaki, hamanika, sisimka. **excitable,** *a.* -epesi (kwa hasira, furaha &c.), -a haraka. **excitement,** *n.* wasiwasi, msisimko, kichocho, haraka, juhudi, fadhaa, hangaiko, hamaniko; (*exciting object*) jambo la kuhamakisha (kushtua, kufurahisha, kuogofya, lenye hatari &c.). *Be in a state of excitement,* hangaika, taharuki, fadhaika, ona wasiwasi, sisimka. **exciting,** *a.* -a kushtusha, -a kuharakisha, -a kutia furaha (hofu, ajabu, wasiwasi &c.).

exclaim, *v.i.* sema ghafula (kwa sauti kuu, kwa haraka, kwa nguvu, kwa mkazo), lia, paliza sauti, piga kelele (kwa mshangao, hasira, maumivu, harara &c.). **exclamation,** *n.* mlio, kilio, msemo wa ghafula &c., ukelele wa mshangao &c. *Note of exclamation,* alama ya kushangaa, alama hii (!) iliyoandikwa kufuata maneno ya mshangao.

exclude, *v.t.* (*remove, shut out*) toa, ondoa, weka mbali, tenga, fungia mlango; (*refuse*) kataa, kataza, zuia. **exclusion,** *n.* kutoa, kutolewa &c. **exclusive,** *a.* -a peke yake (yao &c.), -a kuchaguachagua, pasipo wengine, -moja, -zuivu. *Exclusive of,* pasipo, ghairi ya, minghairi. *An exclusive person,* mkinaifu, pweke. **exclusively,** *adv.* peke yake, tu, basi. *Refer exclusively to,* husika na. *Almost exclusively,* karibu yote.

excogitate, *v.t.* tunga, buni, vumbua, zua, jua kwa kufikiri.

excommunicate, *v.t.* harimisha, ondolea haki ya kushirikiana katika ibada za kanisa la kikristo, tenga katika Ushirika Mtakatifu. **excommunication,** *n.* kuharimisha &c., taz. *excommunicate.*.

excoriate, *v.t.* chubua, ambua, chuna.

excrement, *n.* mavi, kinyesi.

excreta, *n.* taka za mwili hasa kinyesi na mkojo. **excrete,** *v.t.* toa (jasho, mkojo &c.), -nya. **excretion,** *n.* kitolewacho mwilini kama jasho, mkojo &c. **excretory,** *a.* -enye kazi ya kutoa katika mwili.

excrescence, *n.* kitu kinachojitokeza katika kitu kingine; nywele ni *excrescence* ya kichwa; kitu kisicho cha kawaida kinachojitokeza katika mwili au mmea; tezi, kinundu.

excreta, *n.*, **excrete**, *v.*, **excretion**, *n.*, **excretory**, *a.* taz. *excrement.*
excruciate, *v.t.* tesa, umiza sana. **excruciating**, *a.* -a kuumiza mno, -a kutesa sana.
exculpate, *v.t.* toa katika hatia (lawama), burai. **exculpation**, *n.* kutoa katika hatia (lawama).
excursion, *n.* matembezi, safari, kwenda kushinda mahali; (*hostile*) shambulio. **excursive**, *a.* -a maneno mengi, -a kuongeza maneno.
excusable, *a.* taz. *excuse.*
excuse, *v.t.* (*pardon*) achilia, samehe, udhuru; (*allow*) ruhusu, halalisha; (*obtain pardon or allowance*) patia masamaha, toa katika hatia, ridhisha. *Excuse me*, kunradhi, niwie radhi, naomba radhi, pole. — *n.* udhuru, matetesi; (*false excuse*) singizio, kisingizio, kiongopeo. *Make a false excuse*, zua, jisingizia, ongopa. **excusable**, *a.* -a kusameheka, -dogo, -a kustahili kusamehewa (kuachiliwa).
execrable, *a.* taz. *execrate.*
execrate, *v.t.* chukia mno, kirihi; — *v.i.* (*curse*) laani, apiza. **execrable**, *a.* -a kuchukiza mno, -a kirahi, makuruhi, baya sana. **execration**, *n.* maapizo, laana, matukano.
execute, *v.t.* maliza, fanyiza, tekeleza, timiliza; (*ratify*) tia sahihi, sahihisha; (*obey, carry out*) fikiliza, fuasa (amri, maneno); (*put to death*) fisha, ua; (*behead*) kata kichwa; (*hang*) nyonga (kwa amri ya hakimu au ya serikali). *Execute a dance, piece of music &c.*, cheza, piga ngoma &c. **execution**, *n.* (*performance*) utimizo, tendo, kufanyiza, kazi; (*putting to death*) kufisha, kuua, kuuawa; (*hanging*) kunyonga, kunyongwa. **executioner**, *n.* mfishaji, mwuaji, mnyongaji (kwa amri ya hakimu au ya serikali). **executive**, *a.* -enye amri, -a nguvu, -tendaji. — *n.* serikali. **executor**, *n.* mtenda, mfanyiza; (*trustee*) wakili (kwa mambo ya usia). **executrix**, *n.* *executor* wa kike.
exegesis, *n.* maelezo, ufasiri, mafafanusi (hasa ya maandiko matakatifu. **exegetic**, *a.* -a kueleza &c.
exemplar, *n.*, **exemplary**, *a.*, **exemplify**, *v.* taz. *example.*
exempt, *v.t.* samehe, achilia, ruhusu. **exemption**, *n.* ruhusa, kuachiliwa, achilio, ondoleo.
exequies, *n.* maziko.
exercise, *n.* utembezi, mchezo, kazi (hasa kwa ajili ya kunyosha viungo na kupata afya); (*lesson*) msomo, somo; (*practice*) matumizi, mazoezi; (*test*) majaribu, majaribio, mashindano; (*religious*) ibada, sala. *Take exercise*, tembea, punga hewa, cheza, nyosha miguu (viungo), jiendea. — *v.t.* tendeza, endesha, zoeza; (*use*) tumia, fanya; (*trouble*) sumbua, tesa, hangaisha, tia wasiwasi; (*test*) jaribia. *Exercise a horse*, endesha (tembeza) farasi. *Exercise authority, office &c.*, tumia, fanya. *Exercise patience*, subiri, saburi, vumilia, stahimili. *Exercise oneself*, jifundisha, jizoeza, jitahidi, fanya bidii (juhudi).
exert, *v.t.* toa, tumia; (*oneself*) fanya juhudi (bidii), jitahidi. **exertion**, *n.* bidii, juhudi, jadi; (*difficulty*) shida, kazi.
exhalation, *n.* taz. *exhale.*
exhale, *v.t.* toa (pandisha, paaza) pumzi, toa mvuke (harufu, uvundo); — *v.i.* toweka (kama mvuke &c.). **exhalation**, *n.* pumzi, kutoa pumzi, harufu, uvundo, ukungu, mvuke.
exhaust, *v.t.* (*finish*) isha, maliza kabisa; (*consume, use up*) ondoa (chukua, tumia) -ote; (*weary*) chosha, legeza, shinda, taabisha. — *n.* bomba &c. la mashine la kutolea mvuke uishapo kufanya kazi yake. **exhausting**, *a.* -chovu, -a kuchosha, -a kutaabisha, -a taabu, -a kumaliza nguvu &c. **exhaustion**, *n.* kuishiwa nguvu, kushindwa, kuisha tumiwa -ote; uchovu, taabu, ulegevu, unyong'onyevu, mavundevunde. **exhaustive**, *a.* -a kumaliza kabisa, -a uangalifu sana hata kumaliza kabisa.

exhibit, *v.t.* onyesha, toa wazi, tembeza, zinza. — *n.* kitu cha kuonyesha (kama hati, kisu *&c.*) cha ushuhuda katika mashtaka; kitu kinachoonyeshwa. **exhibition**, *n.* onyesho, onyeshano, wonyeshano, tamasha; (*prize*) fedha zinazotolewa na chuo kusaidia mwanafunzi kama tuzo kwa sababu ya ustahili wake. **exhibitioner**, *n.* mwanafunzi aliyepewa *exhibition*. **exhibitor**, *n.* mwonyeshi, hasa katika wonyeshano.

exhilarate, *v.t.* tia moyo (furaha, matumaini), changamsha, furahisha, teremesha, burudisha. **exhilarating**, *a.* -changamfu, -a kufurahisha, -a kuburudisha, -a kutia moyo (furaha, matumaini *&c.*). **exhilaration**, *n.* furaha, uchangamfu, uchangamshi, ukunjufu, moyo mkuu.

exhort, *v.t.* sihi, omba, usia, tia moyo; onya, fundisha, shauri. **exhortation**, *n.* mausia, shauri, maonyo, maombi, maowidha.

exhumation, *n.* taz. *exhume*.

exhume, *v.t.* (*dig up*) fukua, chimbua (hasa maiti kaburini); (*bring to light*) fufua, funua. **exhumation**, *n.* kuchimbua, mchimbuo.

exigency, *n.* (*need*) mahitaji, sharti, lazima; (*emergency*) jambo la ghafula (la hatari, la kuhitaji msaada). **exigent**, *a.* -a kuhitajiwa kufanyika bila kukawia, -a haraka, muhimu.

exiguity, *n.* taz. *exiguous*.

exiguous, *a.* -chache, -dogo, haba. **exiguity**, *n.* uchache, udogo, uhaba.

exile, *n.* kuhamisha (kufukuzwa, kukaa) mbali na kwao; (*a person*) mtu aliyefukuzwa *&c.* mbali na kwao, hasa kwa ajili ya kosa alilofanya; (*place, time*) mahali au muda wa kukaa *&c.* mbali na kwao. — *v.t.* fukuza, hamisha.

exist, *v.i.* -wa, -wako, -wa -zima, -wa hai, kaa, ishi. *He existed on grass*, aliponea majani. *Where does it exist?* makao yake wapi? *Do spirits exist? They do.* Kuna (ziko) pepo? Ziko. **existence**, *n.* kuwako, kukaa, kuishi, uzima, maisha, hakika; (*creature*) kiumbe. *There is no such thing in existence*, hakuna kabisa kitu cha namna hiyo. **existent**, *a.* -enye kuwa (kuwako, hakika), -zima, -hai.

exit, *n.* njia ya (mlango wa) kutokea, kutoka. **exodus**, *n.* kutoka, kuhama, kuondoka; kitabu cha pili cha Agano la Kale.

ex officio, *adv.* kwa sababu ya kuwa na kazi (cheo) fulani.

exogamic, exogamous, *a.* -enye desturi ya kuoa mke (kuolewa na mume) wa kabila jingine. **exogamy**, *n.* desturi ya mwanamume kuoa mke (mwanamke kuolewa na mume) wa kabila jingine.

exonerate, *v.t.* toa katika lawama (hatia), burai.

exorbitant, *a.* -a kupita kiasi, -kubwa mno, -ingi mno. *The price of this is exorbitant*, bei ya hiki ni kubwa mno, ni ghali sana.

exorcism, *n.* chuchio, kupunga pepo. **exorcist**, *n.* mpungaji pepo. **exorcize**, *v.t.* punga pepo, lema, chuchia.

exordium, *n.* dibaji, mwanzo (hasa wa hotuba, wa kuhubiri).

exoteric, *a.* -a nje, -wazi, -a watu wote, -a kufahamikana na watu wote.

exotic, *a.* -geni, -a nchi nyingine.

expand, *v.t.* tanua, panua, eneza, zidisha, kuza, vimbisha; — *v.i.* tanuka, panuka, enea, zidi, kua, vimba. **expanse**, *n.* eneo, mapana, nafasi. **expansion**, *n.* kutanua, kutanuka *&c.*; eneo, uvimbe, mpanuo, mtanuo. **expansive**, *a.* -enye kutanua (kuvimba *&c.*); (*frank &c.*) -kunjufu.

ex parte, *a.* -a kupendelea (kufadhili, kusaidia, kufaidi) upande mmoja. — *adv.* kwa kupendelea (kufadhili, kusaidia, kufaidi) upande mmoja.

expatiate, *v.i.* (*upon*) simulia kwa maneno mengi, piga domo, ongea-ongea.

expatriate *v.t.* hamisha (ondosha)

mbali na kwao, toa katika nchi, fukuza. **expatriation**, *n.* kufukuza (kufukuzwa) kutoka kwao.

expect, *v.t.* ngoja, ngojea, tumaini, tazamia; — *v.i.* ona, dhani. *I expect so*, naona, labda, haikosi. **expectant**, *a.* -enye kungojea, -a kutazamia, tayari. **expectation**, *n.*, **expectancy**, *n.* kungojea, matumaini, kutazamia; (*prospect*) mambo ya mbele (ya baadaye), yatakayokuwa; (*inheritance*) urithi.

expectorate, *v.t.* tema mate, toa kohozi (belghamu). **expectoration**, *n.* kutema mate, kutoa kohozi (belghamu); mate, kohozi, belghamu.

expediency, *n.* taz. *expedient.*

expedient, *a.* -a kufaa, -enye njia, -enye faida (manufaa). *It is expedient*, afadhali, yafaa, inafaa. — *n.* shauri, njia, hila. **expediency**, *n.* faida, njia, shauri la kufaa, manufaa, ufanidi. **expedite**, *v.t.* himiza, endeleza, saidia. **expedition**, *n.* safari; (*speed*) wepesi, hima, haraka. **expeditious**, *a.* -epesi, -a haraka. **expeditiously**, *adv.* kwa upesi, kwa haraka, muhimu.

expel, *v.t.* toa, ondosha, fukuza. **expulsion**, *n.* fukuzo, ondoleo, uhamisho. **expulsory**, *a.* -enye nguvu (tabia) ya kutoa (kuondosha &c.)

expend, *v.t.* tumia (fedha, nguvu, akili, fikira, uangalifu &c.), toa fedha &c., fanya (toa) gharama, hariji. **expenditure**, *n.* gharama, haraja, matumizi (ya fedha, nguvu, fikira, uangalifu &c.). **expense**, *n.* gharama, haraja. *Go to expense about*, *Be at expense*, toa (fanya) gharama nyingi. *At the expense of*, kwa hasara ya, kwa gharama ya, kwa aibu ya. **expensive**, *a.* ghali, -a thamani, -a bei kubwa.

experience, *n.* kupata (kujua, kuona, kuonja) mwenyewe, mambo ya maisha, mambo yenyewe, ulimwengu; (*knowledge*) maarifa, hakika ya mambo, ustadi kwa kuzoea (kusimamia watu, kuamrisha askari, kufanya kazi fulani &c.). — *v.t.* pata -enyewe, jua -enyewe, patwa na. **experienced**, *a.* -enye maarifa, -enye kujua (kazi, mambo), -juzi, -stadi. **experiment**, *n.* jaribu, jaribio, tendo (si maneno). — *v.i.* jaribia. **experimental**, *a.* -a kujaribia, -a mambo yenyewe, -a hakika.

expert, *a.* -zoevu, -stadi, fundi, bingwa, hodari, mahiri, -elekevu. — *n.* mzoevu, mstadi, fundi, mbingwa &c. **expertly**, *adv.* kwa ustadi (uhodari, ufundi &c.). **expertness**, *n.* ustadi, ufundi, ubingwa &c.

expiate, *v.t.* lipa, lipia, toa sadaka kwa, fidia. **expiation**, *n.* malipo, sadaka, fidio; (*for murder*) dia. **expiatory**, *a.* -a kulipia, -a kufidia.

expiration, *n.* taz. *expire.*

expire, *v.i.* (*exhale*) toa (pandisha, paaza) pumzi, pumua; (*die*) -fa, kata roho; (*end*) koma, isha, tekelea. **expiration**, *n.* kutoa (kupandisha, kupaaza) pumzi, kupumua; (*end*) mwisho.

explain, *v.t.* -eleza, pambanua, fasiri, fafanua, fumbua, funua, toa wazi, dhihirisha, aridhia, toa maelezo. *Explain away*, eleza vingine, geuza maana, vuta. **explanation**, *n.* maelezo, fafanusi, tafsiri; (*reason*) sababu, kisa, hoja; (*meaning*) maana; (*understanding*) mapatano. **explanatory**, *a.* -a kueleza &c. -a kutoa sababu (kisa, maana &c.).

expletive, *n.* neno lisilochukua maana hasa, sana ni neno la kutukana, laana, kiapo, matusi, *e.g.* Audhubilahi! Walahi! Nyoo!

explicable, *a.* taz. *explicate.*

explicate, *v.t.* funua, fumbua, tambulisha, eleza maana zaidi. **explicable**, *a.* -a kufasirikana, -a kuelezekana. **explicit**, *a.* (*things*) wazi, dhahiri, baini; (*persons*) -nyofu, amini. **explicitly**, *adv.* dhahiri, waziwazi.

explode, *v.t.* (*blow up*) washa, pasua, lipusha; (*bring to an end*) komesha, isha, maliza; (*let off*) tegua; — *v.i.* (*go off*) waka, lipuka, pasuka, lia;

(*with laughter*) angua kicheko; (*with rage, anger*) hamaki. **explosion,** *n.* shindo kubwa (la baruti kupasuka *&c.*), kipindi cha hasira *&c.* **explosive,** *a.* -enye mshindo, -enye kuvunja (kutoa mshindo, kupasuka kwa nguvu) kama baruti. — *n.* baruti (ya namna nyinginezo).

exploit, *n.* tendo hodari (la ujasiri, la ushujaa, la sifa, la hatari). — *v.t.* tumia kwa jinsi ya kupata faida yote iwezekanavyo.

exploration, *n.* taz. *explore.*

explore, *v.t.* peleleza nchi, jasisi, tafutia, chunguza, vumbua, safiri katika. **exploration,** *n.* safari, upelelezi, uvumbuzi, ujasusi. **explorer,** *n.* msafiri, mpelelezi, mvumbuaji wa nchi.

explosion, *n.*, **explosive,** *a. and n.* taz. *explode.*

exponent, *n.* mtoa habari, mtambulishi, mfasiri, mwenye kueleza.

export, *v.t.* peleka vitu (bidhaa) nchi nyingine kuuzwa. — *n.* kupeleka vitu (bidhaa) nchi nyingine kuuzwa; bidhaa, mali (inayopelekwa nchi nyingine). **exportation,** *n.* kupeleka bidhaa *&c.* nchi nyingine kuuzwa.

expose, *v.t.* (*put out*) toa nje, weka wazi, benua, futua; (*uncover*) funua; onyesha; (*faults*) chongea, fumua; (*a child*) tupa, acha; (*to danger*) hatirisha, tia hatarini; (*to punishment*) pasisha hukumu (adhabu). **exposed,** *a.* (*open*) wazi, -tupu; (*liable*) -a kupatikana, -a kupasishwa. **exposition,** *n.* habari, ufasiri, maelezo; taz. *exhibition.* **expositor,** *n.* mwenye kueleza (kufasiri). **exposure,** *n.* (*openness*) uwazi; (*being unprotected*) kukaa nje (penye hatari, baridi, mvua, jua kali, vita *&c.*); (*being outcast*) kutolewa nje, kutupwa; (*telling of faults*) machongezi.

expostulate (*with*), *v.i.* onya kosa, taradhia, shauri ili kuzuia, zuia kwa maneno, gombeza, dakiza. **expostulation,** *n.* maonyo, mausia, maneno (shauri) ya kuzuia, madakizo, magombezo, udaku. **expostulatory,** *a.* -a kuonya, -a kutaradhia.

exposure, *n.* taz. *expose.*

expound, *v.t.* eleza, fasiri.

express, *v.t.* kama, minya, binya; (*make clear*) eleza, dhihirisha, onyesha; (*state*) nena. — *a.* (*precise*) halisi; (*plain*) dhahiri, wazi; (*speedy*) -a kwenda mbio sana, -a haraka, muhimu. — *n.* tarishi, mjumbe wa haraka; (*train*) gari la moshi liendalo mbio sana. — *adv.* mbio, muhimu, kwa upesi sana, kwa tarishi aendaye mbio, kwa gari la moshi liendalo mbio. **expression,** *n.* (*words*) neno, maneno, usemi; (*face*) uso, sura; (*statement*) wonyesho, kutoa habari. **expressionless,** *a.* -a kipumbavu, pasipo akili, pasipo maana. **expressive,** *a.* -a maana sana, -a akili nyingi, -enye habari (kuonyesha akili, furaha, huzuni *&c.*). **expressly,** *adv.* halisi, makusudi.

expropriate, *v.t.* ondolea mali. **expropriation,** *n.* kuondolea mali.

expulsion, *n.*, **expulsory,** *a.* taz. *expel.*

expunge, *v.t.* futa, futia mbali, toa.

expurgate, *v.t.* takasa, safisha, sahihisha.

exquisite, *a.* bora sana, -zuri sana, -tamu sana; (*extreme*) -ingi sana, -kubwa mno. — *n.* mmalidadi, mlimbwende.

exscind, *v.t.* katia mbali, ng'oa.

ex-service, *a. Ex-service man,* mtu aliyekuwa askari (katika jeshi, manowari *&c.*) hasa wakati wa vita vikuu 1914–18, lakini sasa amekwisha toka uaskari.

extant, *a.* -enye kuwapo, -a kukaa hata leo, -liopo sasa.

extempore, *adv.* bila kujiweka tayari, palepale, papo hapo. — *a.* -a papo hapo bila kujiweka tayari. *An extempore sermon,* hotuba iliyotolewa papo hapo bila kufikiriwa au kutungwa kwanza. **extemporaneous,** *a.*, **extemporary,** *a.* kama *extempore.* **extemporize,** *v.t. and i.* tenda bila kuweka tayari kwanza (bila kufikiri kwanza, bila kulinga kwanza), tunga hotuba, wimbo, shairi *&c.*) papo hapo.

extend, *v.t.* laza kirefurefu, nyosha, panua, tanua, tandaza; (*stretch*) vuta, nyosha, eneza; (*prolong*) ongeza; (*give*) nyosha, tolea; — *v.i.* (*continue*) tandaa, tambaa; (*reach*) fika; (*spread*) enea. **extended**, *a.* -a kuenea, -a kuendelea muda mrefu, -lionyoshwa, -nayotambaa, -nayotandaa. *Lie with legs extended*, tandawaa. **extensive**, *a.* -enye eneo kubwa, -kubwa, -pana, -ingi, -a kutandaa (kutambaa) sana. **extent**, *n.* eneo, ukubwa; (*degree*) cheo, kadiri.

extenuate, *v.t.* punguza (hasa ukubwa wa hatia au kosa), toa udhuru wa (jambo baya). *Nothing can extenuate his baseness*, hakuna neno linaloweza kupunguza ukubwa wa uovu wake. **extenuating**, *a.* -a kupunguza (hasa ukubwa wa hatia au kosa). *Extenuating circumstances*, mambo yanayopunguza ukubwa (wa kosa, hatia *&c.*). **extenuation**, *n.* udhuru, sababu ya kupunguza ukubwa wa kosa *&c.*

exterior, *n.* umbo, sura, nje. — *a.* -a nje.

exterminate, *v.t.* (*root out*) ng'oa; (*destroy*) haribu kabisa, komesha, maliza, ulia mbali. **extermination**, *n.* kuharibu kabisa, kuharibika kabisa *&c.*

external, *a.* -a nje; (*foreign*) -a nchi nyingine, -a wageni; (*unessential*) si -a asili, -a kuonekana kwa macho tu. **externals**, *n.* umbo, sura, mambo ya nje, maonekano. **externally**, *adv.* kwa nje.

extinct, *a.* -fu, -liozimika -liokwisha, -siopo sasa. **extinction**, *n.* kufa, kuzimika, kwisha, kukomesha. **extinguish**, *v.t.* zima, zimisha, komesha. **extinguisher**, *n.* kitu cha kuzimishia taa (moto, mshumaa *&c.*).

extirpate, *v.t.* (*root out*) ng'oa; (*destroy*) haribu kabisa, komesha, maliza, ulia mbali. **extirpation**, *n.* kung'oa, kuharibu kabisa *&c.*

extol, *v.t.* sifu, himidi, tukuza.

extort, *v.t.* toza kwa nguvu, lipiza kwa jeuri, pokonya, nyang'anya, pata (fedha, ahadi *&c.*) kwa kutumia nguvu (jeuri, maogofya). **extortion**, *n.* kutoza (kupata *&c.*) kwa nguvu; kutaka bei kubwa sana kwa kitu. **extortionate**, *a.* -a jeuri, -dhalimu, -a kupokonya, -a kutaka -ingi kupita kadiri, -a kutaka bei kubwa sana. **extortioner**, *n.* mtoza fedha (ahadi *&c.*) kwa jeuri (kwa nguvu), mnyang'anyi, mdhalimu.

extra, *a.* -a zaidi, -a zaidi ya desturi (kawaida, iliyotazamiwa *&c.*), -a bure (yaani bila kulipiwa fedha). — *adv.* zaidi, juu, sana. *Extra good*, -ema sana. *Try extra hard*, jitahidi sana (kuliko kawaida). — *n.* ziada, hasa ni jambo (kazi, utumishi *&c.*) ambalo kwalo fedha zaidi kuliko ile iliyotajwa inatozwa.

extract, *v.t.* (*tooth, root &c.*) ng'oa; (*nails &c.*) kongoa, zidua; (*from bundle &c.*) chopoa, vura; (*select*) chagua; (*distil out, press out &c.*) toa sumu (nguvu, uzuri, maji, dawa, *&c.*) kwa kusindikiza (kukamua, kuchemsha na kupata mvuke *&c.*); (*obtain*) toza kwa nguvu, pata kwa kuhojihoji *&c.* — *n.* maji (dawa, mafuta, sumu *&c.*) matokeo ya kusindika (kuchemsha, kuloweka *&c.*); (*selected pieces*) mateuzi, madondoo. **extraction**, *n.* kutoa, kung'oa; (*crushing*) kusindika *&c.*; (*lineage*) kizazi, nasaba, jamaa, jadi.

extradite, *v.* taz. *extradition.*

extradition, *n.* kurudisha kwake ili ahukumiwe mkosaji wa nchi nyingine aliyekimbia. **extradite**, *v.t.* fanya *extradition.*

extraneous, *a.* -a nje, -a kigeni, -a zaidi, -siyofungamana na (jambo linalofikiriwa *&c.*).

extraordinarily, *adv.* taz. *extraordinary.*

extraordinary, *a.* ajabu, -geni, -a

peke yake, -a mtindo; (*irregular*) si -a kawaida, si -a desturi. *Extraordinary beauty*, uzuri wa ajabu sana, uzuri kama nini? **extraordinarily**, *adv*. ajabu mno, sana.

extravagance, *n*. taz. *extravagant*.

extravagant, *a*. -a kupita kiasi, -potevu wa mali (fedha), -a gharama nyingi (kupita kiasi), -badhirifu. **extravagance**, *n*. upotevu wa mali (fedha), budhara, ubadhirifu, gharama kubwa (kupita kiasi); (*folly*) ujinga, upotovu, wazimu.

extreme, *a*. -a mwisho, -a kipeo, -a mpakani, -a mbali kabisa, -a juu kabisa, -a chini kabisa, -a nguvu kabisa, -a kupita kadiri, -a mno, -kali kabisa; (*opinionated*) -shupavu, si taratibu, si kiasi. — *n*. mwisho, upeo, kipeo, mpaka, ncha, kupita kadiri. **extremely**, *adv*. sana, mno, kabisa, upeo. *Extremely barbarous people*, washenzi wa mwisho. **extremity**, *n*. mwisho, mpaka, pembe, kipeo, upeo, ncha; (*limb*) kiungo (cha mwili, mkono, mguu &c.); (*emergency*) hali mbaya mno, hatari kubwa.

extricate, *v.t.* toa, okoa, tatanua. **extrication**, *n*. kutoa, kutoka &c.

extrinsic, *a*. -a nje, si -a asili, -a zaidi.

extrude, *v.t.* toa nje, sukumia nje. **extrusion**, *n*. kutoa (kutolewa) nje.

exuberance, *n*. taz. *exuberant*.

exuberant, *a*. -a kusitawi, -ingi sana, tele, maridhawa; (*of persons*) -enye nguvu (afya, ukunjufu &c.). **exuberance**, *n*. usitwai, wingi.

exudation, *n*. taz. *exude*.

exude, *v.t.* toa (maji, jasho &c.), papa, rishai; — *v.i.* toka, vuja, dondoka. **exudation**, *n*. matokeo (ya jasho, maji &c.); kupapa maji, kuvuja, kurishai.

exult, *v.i.* (*at, over*) furahi, shangilia; (*against*) simanga. **exultant**, *a*. -a furaha nyingi, -a shangwe. **exultation**, *n*. furaha kuu, shangwe.

eye, *n*. jicho; (*of needle*) tundu, kitundu. *Up to the eyes*, sana, kabisa. *Have in one's eye*, kumbuka, taka, tamani. *Give a blow in the eye*, piga konde la jicho. *Keep an eye on*, angalia, tunza. *A sharp eye*, macho makali, hodari kuona. *Open the eye*, fumbua jicho. *Shut the eye*, fumba jicho. *In the twinkling of an eye*, kufumba na kufumbua. *As far as the eye can see*, upeo wa macho. *Dreamy eyes*, macho ya kusinzia. *Have one eye, Have lost an eye*, -wa na chongo. *Keep one's eye open*, -wa macho, angalia, jihadhari. *Open a person's eye to something*, fahamisha, arifu, onyesha. — *v.t.* angalia, kazia macho, chungua, kodolea; (*with envy, ill will*) tupia kijicho; (*with contempt*) tazama kitongotongo. **eyeball**, *n*. mboni ya jicho. **eyebrow**, *n*. nyushi. **eyeglass**, *n*. rodi, kioo cha jicho moja. *Eyeglasses*, miwani. **eyelash**, *n*. ukope. **eyelet**, *n*. tundu, kitundu; (*in decoration, button-hole*) kiua. **eyelid**, *n*. ukope. **eyeshot**, *n*. upeo wa macho. **eyesight**, *n*. macho, kuona kwa macho, uwezo wa kuona kwa macho. *My eyesight is bad*, macho yangu dhaifu, sioni vema. *Bad eyesight*, kiwaa. **eyesocket**, *n*. tundu la (kishimo cha) jicho. **eyesore**, *n*. chukizo. **eye-tooth**, *n*. jino kubwa chini ya jicho. **eyewitness**, *n*. shahidi (aliyeona mwenyewe kwa macho yake).

eyrie, *n*. tundu (la kozi, tai, kapungu au ndege wakubwa). taz. *aerie*.

F

fable, *n.* hadithi, kisa, ngano, hekaya; (*fiction*) uwongo. — *v.t. and i.* buni hadithi *&c.*, zua uwongo, eneza (simulia, hadithia) habari za uwongo. **fabled,** *a.* -a kubuniwa, -a uwongo. **fabulous,** *a.* -a uwongo, -a kubuniwa; (*marvellous*) -kubwa mno, -ingi mno, ajabu.

fabric, *n.* kitu kilichofanyizwa (nguo, kitambaa, nyumba *&c.*); namna ya kufanyiza, jinsi; (*system, construction*) kazi, matengenezo. **fabricate,** *v.t.* (*construct*) fanyiza, jenga; (*invent*) buni, tunga, zua. **fabrication,** *n.* (*manufacture*) kufanyiza, kifanyizwacho; (*structure*) jengo; (*falsehood*) uwongo, maneno ya kubuniwa.

fabulous, *a.* taz. *fable.*

façade, *n.* upande wa mbele wa nyumba.

face, *n.* uso, sura, wajihi; (*front, top, exterior*) upande (wa mbele, wa juu, wa nje); (*prepared side*) upande uliofanyiziwa kazi; (*side*) upande; (*smoothness*) usawa, ulaini; (*boldness*) ukavu wa macho, ufidhuli, usafihi, ushupavu, ujuvi; (*grimace*) uso uliofinywa (uliokunjamana). *A long face,* uso wa huzuni (wa kuonyesha chuki, kutopenda *&c.*). *Fall on the face,* anguka kifudifudi (fudifudi, uso chini). *Have the face to,* thubutu, toonelea haya, fanya kwa ukavu wa macho (pasipo haya, kwa ushupavu, kwa ufidhuli, kwa nguvu). *Lie on the face,* lala kitumbotumbo (tumboni), lala fudifudi. *Set the face against,* kataza, gombeza, zuia, kinza. *Face to face,* uso kwa uso, kwa kupambana, kwa kukabiliana, kwa kuelekeana, dafurao. *Meet (see, visit) face to face,* wajihi; (*recip.*) wajihiana. *In the face of,* mbele ya macho ya, machoni pa, kwa kudharau. *Make faces,* geuza (finya, kunja) uso. *Face value,* thamani iliyoandikwa juu ya sarafu (noti, hawala, hundi *&c.*) kuonyesha hesabu ya kima chake. *Put a bold face on,* fanya kama haidhuru (kama si kitu). — *v.t.* simamia, simama mbele ya, -wa na uso kwa; (*oppose*) zuia, shindana na; (*be opposite*) elekea, kabili; (*give surface to*) fanyiza nje, kandika, tomea, fanya sawa, lainisha; — *v.i.* (*turn*) geuka. *Face out,* jasiria, fanya kwa uthabiti. **facer,** *n.* pigo la uso; (*problem*) jambo la shida (la ghafula). **facet,** *n.* upande. **facial,** *a.* -a uso. **facing,** *n.* upande wa nje; (*in masonry*) kutomea, mtomo; (*in dress*) mapambo, tepe. *Put through facings,* tazamia, jaribia.

facetious, *a.* -bishi, -chekeshi, -a mzaha.

facial, *a.* taz. *face.*

facile, *a.* rahisi, -epesi, -a juu juu tu; (*of persons*) -kunjufu, -pole, -a adabu. **facilitate,** *v.t.* fanya rahisi, rahisisha, himiza, saidia, endesha. **facility,** *n.* (*ease*) urahisi, wepesi, welekevu; (*means*) njia, msaada; (*affability*) utu mwema, ukunjufu, upole.

facing, *n.* taz. *face.*

facsimile, *n.* nakili (nakala) halisi, mwigo sawasawa, mfano mmoja.

fact, *n.* jambo la hakika, kweli, hakika, jambo. *In fact,* kweli, hasa. *The fact is (that),* kweli, hakuna shaka, hakika. *It is a fact,* kweli hiyo, si uwongo, ndivyo ilivyo. *As a matter of fact,* kwa kweli.

faction, *n.* jamii ya wafitini wenye shauri moja, fitina, farakano, chamkano. **factious,** *a.* -fitini, -a kutia fitina.

factitious, *a.* -liofanyizwa, -a kutungwa, si -a asili, -a uwongo, si -a kawaida.

factor, *n.* (*agent*) wakili, karani; (*part*) schemu. *Highest Common Factor,* kigawanyo kilicho kikubwa. **factory,** *n.* kiwanda, nyumba ya kufanyizia vitu, karakana, banda la kazi. **factotum,** *n.* mtumishi wa kazi zote, mfanya kazi zote au za namna zote peke yake.

faculty, *n.* welekevu (ustadi, ufundi, uwezo) wa kufanya tendo lo lote; (*licence*) ruhusa; (*corporation*) jamii, chama (cha watu wenye kazi moja); (*natural function*) nguvu, akili, uwezo.

fad, *n.* mfundo, kinyongo, kombo. **faddist,** *n.* mwenye kinyongo (kombo, mfundo). **faddy,** *a.* -a kinyongo, -enye kombo.

fade, *v.i.* fifia, chujuka, kwajuka, kauka, dhoofika, pungua, chakaa, -fa; — *v.t.* fifisha, chujusha. **fadeless,** *a.* imara, -a kudumu (kuendelea, kuishi).

faeces, *n.* mavi, kinyesi.

fag, *v.i.* fanya kazi kwa taabu; — *v.t.* chosha, taabisha, legeza kwa kazi, nyong'onyeza; (*at schools*) tuma mtoto kwa kazi nyinginezo; — *v.t.* tumika kwa kazi nyinginezo. — *n.* taabu, kazi (ngumu) nzito, uchovu, unyogovu, unyong'onyevu; (*at school*) mtoto amtumikiaye mkubwa kwa kazi nyinginezo; (*slang*) sigareti. **fag-end,** *n.* kipande kilichosalia kisichofaa kitu.

faggot, *n.* tita (la kuni, la pao za chuma).

Fahrenheit, *n.* namna ya kipimo cha joto na baridi, kilichotiwa alama 32° kuonyesha baridi inayoganda, na 212° kuonyesha joto la kuchemsha.

fail, *v.i.* ((*be missing or insufficient*) kosekana, adimika, punguka; (*miss*) kosa; (*grow weak &c.*) legea, pungua; (*be unable to do*) shindwa, toweza, topata, tofaulu, tofuzu; (*come to an end*) isha, tindika; (*be bankrupt*) filisika. *He failed me,* hakunifaa, hakunisaidia, hakufanya kama alivyoahidi. *He tried but failed,* alijitahidi asipate, alijaribu asifaulu. *Come without fail,* usikose kuja. **failing,** *n.* kushindwa, upungufu, udhaifu, hitilafu; (*fault*) kosa. **failure,** *n.* upungufu, ukosefu, ulegevu; (*want of success*) kushindwa, kutofaulu, kutofuzu; (*person &c. who is unsuccessful*) mtu asiyeweza kazi vizuri aliyojaribu; kitu kisichofaa kazi yake; tendo lisilofaulu; (*bankrupt*) kufilisika.

fain, *a.* (*be*) kubali, -wa radhi, ridhika, taka. — *adv.* kwa kutaka, kwa furaha.

faint, *a.* (*weak*) dhaifu, hafifu, -legevu, -chovu, -nyong'onyevu; (*of character*) -oga, -baridi, -a hofu; (*deficient*) pasipo bidii (nguvu, maana wazi), -dogo, -nyonge; (*dim*) -sioonekana vema; (*dizzy*) -a kizunguzungu, -a kutaka kuzimia (kuzirai). — *v.i.* zimia roho, zirai, ghumia, ona kizunguzungu, legea, nyong'onyea. — *n.* kuzimia roho, kuzirai. **faint-hearted,** *a.* -oga, -enye roho (moyo) chache, udhaifu wa moyo. **faintly,** *adv.* kidogo kidogo. **faintness,** *n.* udhaifu, ulegevu, unyong'onyevu, upungufu; (*dimness*) giza; (*dizziness*) kizunguzungu; (*of things at a distance*) unyenyezi.

fair, (1) *n.* mkutano wa watu kuuza vitu na kujifurahisha kwa kutazama michezo &c.; ramsa, tamasha, sikukuu ya ramsa na kuuza vitu.

fair, (2) *a.* -zuri, -eupe, safi; (*just*) -a haki, adili, -adilifu, sawa; (*moderate*) -a kiasi, -a kadiri, kidogo. *The fair sex,* wanawake. *Fair weather,* kuzuri, kweupe, kumetakata. *Fair voyage,* safari ya heri, safari njema. *Fair play,* hali moja, kila mtu sawasawa, pasipo kupendelea. *Bid fair to be,* taka kuwa, elekea kuwa. **fairly,** *adv.* vizuri, kwa haki, kwa uadilifu, bila kupendelea; (*completely*) kabisa.

fairy, *n.* pepo, jini, zimwi, kizimwi. **fairy-tale,** *n.* hadithi (kisa, ngano, hekaya) ya kizimwi &c.

faith, *n.* imani, amini, uaminifu, itibari; (*promise*) ahadi, miadi; (*religion*) dini, itikadi. **faithful,** *a.* -amini, -aminifu, -nyofu. **faithfully,** *adv.* kwa uaminifu. **faithfulness,** *n.* uaminifu, amini, unyofu. **faithless,** *a.* -danganyifu, -erevu, -janja, -wongo, -sioaminika. **faithlessness,** *n.* udanganyifu, utovu wa uaminifu.

fake, *v.t.* fanyiza kitu hafifu kuigiza kitu cha thamani (hasa ili kudanganya); geuza maneno ya maandiko (hati), tengeneza ili kuigiza. — *n.* mwigo, kitu cha uwongo.

falchion, *n.* jambia, sime.

falcon, *n.* kipanga (ndege kama tai mdogo). **falconer,** *n.* mfugaji vipanga, mwindaji awindaye kwa msaada wa vipanga waliofugwa. **falconry,** *n.* ufugaji (uwindaji) wa vipanga.

faldstool, *n.* kiti cha (meza ya) kupigia magoti wakati wa kusali.

fall, *v.i.* (*p.t.* **fell,** *pf.t.* **fallen**) anguka, poromoka, -gwa; (*be ruined*) angamia, haribika; (*err*) kosa; (*like rain*) -nya, nyesha; (*in drops*) tona, dondoka; (*from hand, slip*) ponyoka, chopoka; (*flat*) lala; (*diminish*) punguka, pungua; (*mercury &c. in thermometer*) shuka; (*of temperature*) zidi kuwa baridi; (*fail to produce desired effect*) pooza, tokolea, topendeza, tofaa; (*slope*) inama, telemka, shuka; (*as leaves*) pukutika. *Fall among,* angukia, kutana na. *Fall asleep,* shikwa na usingizi, sinzia. *Fall away,* (*get thin*) konda, dhoofu, dhoofika; (*revolt*) asi, huni; (*be lost*) potea; (*lapse*) kufuru, kosa. *Fall back,* enda nyuma, rudi; (*decrease*) punguka. *Fall down,* (*worship*) sujudu. *Fall flat, i.e. of speech &c.,* pooza, tokolea, topendeza, tofaa. *Fall foul of,* pambana na. *Fall in,* tumbukia; (*of walls*) bomoka; (*soldiers*) jipanga. *Fall in love with,* ashiki, shikwa na mapenzi (haba, shauku) ya. *Fall into,* (*a river*) tokea; (*a custom*) zoea; (*a hole*) tumbukia. *Fall off,* punguka, zidi kuwa -baya. *Fall on,* endea, shambulia, rukia. *Fall out,* kosana, gombana; (*soldiers*) likizwa, tawanyika; (*result*) tokea, tukia. *Fall short,* kosa kufika, punguka. *Fall sick* (*ill*), ugua, patwa (shikwa) na ugonjwa. *Fall through,* isha, tanguka, -fa, vunjika, pooza, haribika. *Fall to,* shika kazi; (*be allotted to*) -wa mali ya (kazi ya). *Fall under,* -wa chini ya (katika). *Let fall,* angusha, bwaga. — *n.* kuanguka &c., maanguko; (*decrease*) upungufu; (*error*) kosa, dhambi; (*ruin*) maangamizi; (*death*) mauti; (*defeat*) kushindwa, kutekwa (mji); (*descent*) telemko, mwinamo, bonde; (*distance down*) kadiri ya mwanguko; (*of rain*) mvua, manyunyu; (*of water, cascade*) maporomoko ya maji, maanguko ya maji; (*of tone*) mshuko, mpunguo wa sauti; (*autumn*) mwisho wa mwaka. *The Fall of Man,* dhambi ya Adamu na Hawa.

fallacious, *a.* taz. *fallacy.*

fallacy, *n.* neno linalodanganya, hoja ya uwongo, kosa, uwongo. **fallacious,** *a.* -danganyifu, -a uwongo, -a kukosesha.

fallen, *pf.t.* ya *fall.*

fallibility, *n.* taz. *fallible.*

fallible, *a.* -a kuweza kukosa, -a kuweza kuwa kosa. **fallibility,** *n.* welekeo wa kukosa, welekeo wa kukosana na kweli.

fallow, *a.* -a kulimwa na kuachwa bila kupandwa mbegu; (*fig.*) -jinga, -siofundishwa. — *n.* shamba lililolimwa na kuachwa bila kupandwa mbegu.

false, *a.* -a uwongo, -nafiki, -danganyifu, -wongo, -mbea, si amini; (*incorrect*) si kweli, si halisi, si hakika; (*artificial*) -a kufanyizwa, si -a asili. **falsehood,** *n.* uwongo. **falsely,** *adv.* kwa uwongo, kwa udanganyifu, kwa kudanganya. **falseness,** *n.* uwongo, udanganyifu, hila, werevu. **falsification,** *n.* ugeuzi mbaya, ughoshi, mageuzi yenye kusudi la kudanganya. **falsify,** *v.t.* geuza maana (namna) kusudi la kudanganya, ghoshi. **falsity,** *n.* uwongo, udanganyifu, uhaini.

falsetto, *n.* sauti ya kiume inayofanana na ya kike, sauti ya kiume iliyogeuzwa kuiga sauti ya kike.

falsification, *n.*, **falsify,** *v.*, **falsity,** *n.* taz. *false.*

falter, *v.i.* sita, sesetuka, sesereka, sepetuka, kwaa; (*speak falteringly*) sema kwa kigugumizi, kokoteza maneno, babaika.

fame, *n.* sifa; (*good repute*) sifa njema, fahari, utukufu, umaarufu. *House of ill fame,* danguro, nyumba ya malaya. *Woman of ill fame,* malaya, kahaba. **famed, famous,** *a.* maarufu, mashuhuri, -a sifa, -a kusifiwa, -tukufu, -bayana. *Make famous,* tukuza, faharisha, adhimisha.

familiar, *a.* -zoevu, -juzi, -a kujuana sana, -a kusuhubiana sana; (*sociable, familiar*) -kunjufu; (*well known*) -a kujulika, -a siku zote, -a zamani. *A familiar friend,* msiri, rafiki sana. *Be familiar* (*on familiar terms*) *with,* jua sana, zoelea sana, fanya utani na, taniana. *Talk familiarly to,* zungumza na, ongea na. **familiarity,** *n.* (*friendliness*) mazoea, uzoevu, urafiki, utani; (*knowledge*) kujua sana, ujuzi. **familiarize,** *v.t.* zoeza.

family, *n.* (*relations*) jamaa, ndugu, ukoo, ahali, ufungu; (*household*) nyumba, watu wa nyumbani; (*class*) jinsi, aina, namna, jamii, kabila, kizazi; (*rank*) cheo bora. *A person of family,* mtoto wa watu. *Be in the family way,* -wa na mimba, -wa mzito.

famine, *n.* njaa, shida ya chakula. **famish,** *v.t.* shindisha na njaa, taabisha kwa njaa; — *v.i.* ona njaa sana, taabika kwa njaa; taabika kwa baridi.

famous, *a.* taz. *fame.*

fan, *n.* pepeo, kipepeo, upepeo. — *v.t. and i.* pepea, punga; (*grain*) pepeta. **fan-palm,** *n.* mlala, mwaa, mkoche.

fanatic, *n.* mshupavu (hasa wa dini), mtu ashikiliaye sana jambo (dini &c.), hasa bila akili. **fanatical,** *a.* -shupavu (-a dini, jambo), -a mno, -a kupita kiasi, -a kukithiri, kwa moyo, si kwa akili. **fanaticism,** *n.* ushupavu wa dini (jambo), bidii ya moyo katika dini (jambo) isiyo ya akili.

fancier, *n.*, **fanciful,** *a.* taz. *fancy.*

fancy, *v.t.* (*imagine*) waza, tunga moyoni, ota, dhani; (*like*) penda, pendelea, chagua. *I fancy so,* naona. — *n.* wazo, mawazo, kuwaza, nia, dhana; (*liking*) mapendezi, upendeleo. *Take a fancy to,* tia habani, penda. *Mere fancy,* wazo tu, ndoto tu. — *a.* -a kupendeza si -a kweli (si -a kufaa); (*of work, articles &c.*) -a kazi, -enye kutiwa kazi, -a urembo; (*extravagant*) -a mno, ghali. *Fancy articles,* vitakataka, vitu vya sanaa (vilivyotiwa kazi au urembo). **fancier,** *n.* mjuzi wa habari, hasa ya wanyama. *Dog-fancier,* mjuzi wa habari za mbwa, mfugaji mstadi wa mbwa. **fanciful,** *a.* -a kuwaza tu, -a kuwaziwa tu, -a kuota kama ndoto, -pumbavu, -a kuchekesha, -a kutunga (kutungwa) moyoni isivyo akili; (*persons*) -enye kuwaza moyoni isivyo akili, -enye kombo, -enye kinyongo, -puzi. **fancy-work,** *n.* darizi, almaria, kazi.

fane, *n.* hekalu, kanisa.

fanfare, *n.* mshindo wa matarumbeta.

fang, *n.* chonge, jino la mnyama (hasa la wanyama walao nyama), jino lenye sumu la nyoka; (*of tooth*) shina la jino; (*of hoe &c.*) msuka.

fantastic, *a.* taz. *fantasy.*

fantasy, *n.* mawazo, uwazo, ndoto, njozi, ruya, mazingaombwe. **fantastic,** *a.* -a kigeni, -a kuchekesha, si -a kawaida, -a kuwazika tu, -a kinyongo.

far, *a. and adv.* mbali, sana. *By far,* zaidi sana. *Far between,* mbali wao kwa wao. *As far as,* hata, mpaka, hadi, kadiri, -vyo. *Far and wide,* kote kote. *Far from* (*let alone, not *to mention, not only*), licha ya, sembuse. *Far from it*, hasha, sivyo. *Be it far from me*, iepukane nami, 'inipitie mbali, sithubutu. **far-away,** *a.* -a mbali sana. **far-famed,** *a.* maarufu sana, mashuhuri sana, -a kujulikana kote kote. **far-fetched,** *a.* si halisi, -siokolea, -sio na maana, -a kubahatisha tu. **far-seeing, far-sighted,** *a.* -a akili, juzi, -a busara, -a kufikiri mambo kwanza. **farther,** *a.* -a mbali zaidi; (*later*) mbele; (*additional*) -a zaidi. — *adv.* mbali zaidi; (*besides &c.*) tena, zaidi, juu ya hayo. **farthermost,** *a.* -a mbali zaidi; -a mbali kupita -ote. **farthest,** *adv. and a.* mbali sana, mbele kabisa, kupita yote. *At farthest*, ndio mwisho, hakuna zaidi.

farce, *n.* mchezo (jambo, hadithi) wa kuchekesha sana; (*joke*) ubishi, upuzi. **farcical,** *a.* -a kuchekesha sana, -a ubishi, -puzi.

fare, *v.i.* (*proceed*) enda, safiri, pata; (*happen &c.*) tukia, tokea; (*get on*) -wa na hali, patwa na mambo; (*be entertained*) tendewa, lishwa. — *n.* nauli, uchukuzi; (*passenger*) msafiri, abiria; (*food*) chakula. *Bill of fare*, orodha ya vyakula vya karamu (hoteli). **farewell,** *int.* kwa heri. — *n.* kuaga, maagano; (*final*) buriani. *Bid farewell*, aga; (*finally*) agana (takana, peana) buriani; (*leave*) acha, toka, ondokea. — *a.* -a kuaga, -a mwisho.

far-famed, *a.*, **far-fetched,** *a.* taz. *far.*

farina, *n.* unga; (*chem.*) wanga. **farinaceous,** *a.* -enye unga, -a unga.

farm, *n.* shamba, konde, mgunda, nyumba ya mwenyeji wa shamba. — *v.t.* lima, -wa na shamba; (*let out on hire*) pangisha, kodisha, ajirisha; (*take on hire*) kodi, panga. **farmer,** *n.* mwenyeji wa shamba, mlimaji, mkulima. **farming,** *n.* kilimo, ukulima, ulimaji. **farmstead,** *n.* nyumba ya mwenyeji wa shamba pamoja na mabanda yake ya shambani.

farrago, *n.* fujo, machanganyiko.

farrier, *n.* fundi wa kutia viatu vya chuma miguuni mwa farasi.

farrow, *v.t. and i.* zaa (nguruwe).

far-seeing, *a.*, **far-sighted,** *a.*, **farther,** *adv. and a.*, **farthermost,** *a.*, **farthest,** *adv. and a.* taz. *far.*

farthing, *n.* sarafu ya kiingereza, kadiri ya senti mbili.

fascinate, *v.t.* loga, fanyia uchawi, sihiri; (*captivate*) shinda, weza, vuta, tiisha (kwa uzuri, si kwa nguvu). **fascination,** *n.* kuloga, ulozi, kufanyia uchawi, uchawi; (*of beauty*) mvuto, mapendezi, uzuri.

Fascism, *n.* taz. *Fascist.*

Fascist, *n.* mfuasi wa jamii ya watu wasiotaka kutawaliwa na watu waliochaguliwa na watu wote, bali na mtu mmoja tu, *e.g.* serikali aliyosimamisha Mwitalia aitwaye Mussolini katika nchi ya Italia, kupigania ufitina uliozuka mwisho wa vita vikuu, mwaka 1919. **Fascism,** *n.* utaratibu wa *Fascists*; utawala unaofuatwa na *Fascists.*

fash, *v.t. and reflex. fash oneself*, jisumbua, jikalifu, jihangaisha, kasirika; (*cause annoyance to*) sumbua, hangaisha, kasirisha, tia wasiwasi, kalifu.

fashion, *n.* (*appearance*) umbo, namna, sura; (*habit*) desturi, nguo za desturi; (*mode of dressing*) desturi ya kuvaa nguo, mvao, mviko; (*rank*) uungwana, cheo; (*kind*) jinsi, njia, namna; (*way of the world*) ya malimwengu. *After a fashion*, kwa kadiri. *It is the fashion at present*, ndio mtindo wa siku hizi, ndiyo desturi ya kisasa. — *v.t.* fanya, fanyiza; (*create*) umba; (*construct*) unda, tengeneza. **fashionable,** *a.* -a desturi, -a siku hizi.

fast, *n.* mfungo, kujinyima chakula, kutokula, kufunga. — *v.i.* funga. — *a.* -epesi, -a mbio; (*sure, firm*) imara, mathubuti, -a kufungwa imara (kikiki), thabiti, -a kukaza; (*trusty*) amini, -aminifu; (*vicious*) -potovu, fasiki, fisadi; (*lasting*) -a kudumu, -a daima. (*He is*) *fast* *asleep*, (ana) usingizi mzito (amelala foo). *A fast friend*, rafiki kwa kweli. *Fast colour*, rangi ya nguo isiyofifia (isiyochujuka, isiyotoka kwa kufuliwa). *Make fast*, funga, kaza. *Hold fast*, shika sana, shikilia. *A fast man*, mpotovu, mfisadi, mfasiki. *A fast day*, siku ya kufunga. — *adv.* hima, upesi, kwa haraka, mbio; (*much*) sana, kwa kukaza; (*extravagantly*) kwa upotovu, kipotovu. ***fasten**, *v.t.* funga, kaza, fanya mathubuti, fungasha; (*loosely*) shaliki; (*door with bolt or bar*) komea; — *v.i.* fungika. *Fasten on*, kamata, shika sana; (*cause to be imputed to*) sukumiza; (*fasten one's eyes upon*) angazia (kazia, kodolea) macho. **fastener**, *n.* (*button, stud &c.*) kifungo, kizuizi; (*bar of door*) komeo, kiwi. **fastening**, *n.* (*act, way of*) mfungo; (*means of*) kifungo, kiungo. **fasting**, *n.* kufunga, mfungo. — *a.* -a kufunga. **fastish**, *a.* -a mbio kidogo, -a upesi kidogo. **fastness**, *n.* wepesi, mbio, haraka; (*fortress &c.*) boma, ngome, husuni.

fastidious, *a.* -a kuchaguachagua, -chaguzi, -teuzi; (*in matters of food*) -enye kidomo.

fasting, *n.*, **fastish**, *a.*, **fastness**, *n.* taz. *fast.*

fat, *n.* (*liquid*) mafuta, uto; (*animal*) mafuta, shahamu, unono; (*best part*) kilicho bora. *Live on the fat of the land*, ishi maisha ya anasa. — *a.* -enye mafuta, -nono; (*of person*) -nene. *Grow fat*, (*man*) nenepa, wanda, tonoka; (*beasts*) nona. **fathead**, *n.* mpumbavu, baradhuli. **fatless**, *a.* -sio na mafuta(shahamu). **fatling**, *n.* ndama (mwana kondoo &c.) aliye mnono. **fatness**, *n.* unene, unono. **fatten**, *v.t.* (*man*) nenepesha; (*animal*) nonesha; — *v.i.* (*get fat*) nenepa, nona. **fatty**, *a.* -a mafuta (shahamu), -a kama mafuta.

fatal, *a.* (*fated*) -a ajali; (*deadly*) -a mwisho, -a kufisha, -a mauti, -a maulisho, -haribifu, -potevu, -angamizi. **fatalism**, *n.* kuamini (imani) ya kuwa yote yameandikwa tokea hapo na binadamu hana hiari, hawezi kubadili mambo, yote ni ya ajali tu. **fatalist**, *n.* aaminiye *fatalism.* **fatality**, *n.* (*fate*) ajali, katiba; (*death*) kufa, mauti, maulisho; (*accident*) msiba. **fate**, *n.* (*doom*) ajali; (*fortune*) bahati; (*law of nature*) katiba, maumbile, amri ya Mungu. **fated**, *a.* -a ajali, -a katiba, -a amri ya Mungu.

fathead, *n.* taz. *fat.*

father, *n.* baba mzaa, mzazi; (*ancestor*) baba, babu, mzee. *Stepfather*, baba wa kambo. *Father-in-law*, mkwe. *Grandfather*, babu. **fatherhood**, *n.* ubaba. **fatherland**, *n.* nchi ya kuzaliwa, kwetu (kwenu, kwao). **fatherless**, *a.* -liofiwa na baba, -kiwa, yatima. **fatherly**, *a.* -a kama baba, -ema, -pole.

fathom, *n.* pima, futi sita (hasa kina cha maji), wari mbili. — *v.t.* pima (urefu wa kwenda chini; (*understand*) tambua, elewa. **fathomless**, *a.* siopimika (urefu wa kwenda chini) -siotambulikana.

fatigue, *n.* ulegevu, unyong'onyevu, uchovu, mavundevunde, mavune; (*trouble*) taabu, kazi. — *v.t.* chosha, legeza, taabisha. *Be fatigued*, choka, taabika.

fatless, *a.*, **fatling**, *n.*, **fatness**, *n.*, **fatten**, *v.*, **fatty**, *a.* taz. *fat.*

fatuity, *n.* upuzi, upumbavu, ujinga.

fatuous, *a.* -jinga, -a upuzi, -puzi, -pumbavu.

faucet, *n.* bilula.

fault, *n.* kosa, hatia, taksiri; (*defect*) hitilafu, upungufu, baa, waa, walakini, ila, kasoro, dosari. *Be at fault*, sitasita. *Be in fault*, kosa, -wa na hatia. *Find fault with*, onea makosa, karipia, ambilia, atibu, suta. **fault-finding**, *n.* masuto. **faultless**, *a.* -tovu wa makosa, si -kosefu wa neno lo lote, pasipo kosa, sahihi, kamili, -nyofu. **faultlessness**, *n.* ukamilifu, hali ya kuwa bila kosa (hatia, upungufu, hitilafu &c.). **faulty**, *a.* -enye makosa (hatia, hitilafu, upungufu, waa &c.); -kosefu, -pungufu, -baya, si sawa, si sahihi.

fauna, *n.* jamii ya wanyama wa namna zote wa nchi fulani (wakati fulani).

fauteuil, *n.* kiti cha mikono.

faux pas, *n.* tendo la kukosa adabu.

favour, *n.* upendeleo, majaliwa; (*acceptance*) kibali; (*a favour*) pendeleo, fadhili, hisani, wema, tajamala. *Do me a favour*, tafadhali. *It was in my favour*, ilikuwa njema (heri) kwangu. *The matter was decided in my favour*, nilishinda. *In favour of*, kwa ajili ya, kwa upendo wa, kwa kupendelea, kwa upande wa. *Be in favour of*, penda, taka, kubali, *Speak in favour of*, sifu, tetea, ombea. *Be in favour*, pendelewa. *Find favour*, kubalika, pendeza. *Curry favour with*, jipendekeza kwa. — *v.t.* pendelea, kubali; (*aid*) saidia, faa, tajamali; (*resemble*) fanana na, landa. *Favour with*, jalia, -pa. **favourable**, *a.* -ema, -a kufaa. **favourably**, *adv.* kwa kufaa, kwa kupendeza. **favourite**, *n.* kipenzi, mpenzi, kipendezi. — *a.* -a kupendeza, -penzi, -pendezi. **favouritism**, *n.* kupendelea, mapendeleo, upendeleo.

fawn, (1) *n.* mtoto wa *deer*, paa mdogo; (*colour*) rangi ya paa (kama hudhurungi nyeupe).

fawn, (2) *v.i.* onyesha upendo (kama mbwa anavyorukaruka na kusukasuka mkia &c.); (*upon*) jipendekeza, bemba, rairai, bembeleza, sifusifu mno.

fay, *n.* kizimwi, jini.

fealty, *n.* uapo au ahadi ya kumtumikia mtu; amini, kutumikia kwa moyo (kwa uaminifu).

fear, *n.* (*dread*) hofu, woga; (*reverence*) kicho, uchaji; (*object of fear*) kicho, kitisho. — *v.t.* ogopa, hofu; (*revere*) -cha; — *v.i.* ogopa, ona hofu, chelea. *Never fear*, usiogope. **fearful**, *a.* -a kutisha, -a hofu, -a kuogofya; (*timid*) -oga. **fearfully**, *adv.* kwa woga, kwa hofu, kwa kuchelea; (*as intens.*) mno, sana. **fearfulness**, *n.* woga, uchaji, hofu. **fearless**, *a.* -jasiri, hodari, -gumu, -kavu wa macho, -shupavu, -juba, pasipo hofu. **fearlessness**, *n.*, ujasiri, uhodari, ushupavu, ugumu, ukavu wa macho, ujuba. **fearsome**, *a.* -a kutisha, -a kuogofya &c.

feasible, *a.* -a kuwezekana, -a kutendekana, yamkini.

feast, *n.* karamu, chakula kingi; (*festival*) sikukuu, idi; (*abundance*) wingi wa vitu vya (mambo ya) kufurahisha; (*marriage, banquet*) wali wa lima. — *v.t.* (*entertain*) karimu, kirimu, karibisha; (*delight*) furahisha, shibisha; (*enjoy*) jifurahisha; — *v.i.* (*eat largely*) -la karamu, -la sana, -la shibe (kefu). **festal**, *a.* -a sikukuu, -a furaha, -a karamu. **festival**, *n.* sikukuu, karamu, idi. **festive**, *a.* -a sikukuu, -a furaha; (*playful*) -cheshi, kunjufu. **festivity**, *n.* furaha, shangwe, michezo, furaha ya sikukuu. **festoon**, *n.* msokoto wa (masongo ya) maua, karatasi za rangi rangi, vitambaa vya rangi rangi &c.

feat, *n.* tendo la ajabu (la ujasiri, la uhodari, la nguvu), tendo kubwa.

feather, *n.* unyoya, nyoya; (*wing*) ubawa; (*tail*) mleli, msusi. **feather-brained**, *a.* -puzi, -pumbavu. **feathery**, *a.* -enye manyoya, -a kama manyoya; laini, -epesi sana.

feature, *n.* sehemu ya uso (pua, midomo &c.); (*appearance*) sura, umbo; (*remarkable point*) jambo la kuangaliwa (la kuvuta macho, la kutazamisha). — *v.t.* onyesha. **featureless**, *a.* bila sura (umbo), bila kitu kinachovuta macho, bila jambo linalovuta akili.

febrifuge, *n.* dawa ya homa. **febrile**, *a.* -a homa.

February, *n.* mwezi wa pili wa mwaka wa kizungu, Februari.

feckless, *a.* -zembe, -potevu. **fecklessness**, *n.* uzembe, upotevu.

fecund, *a.* -zazi, -a kuzaa sana. **fecundate**, *v.t.* tia rutuba; tia mimba. **fecundity,** *n.* (*animals*) uzazi; (*land*) baraka, neema, kuzaa sana, rutuba.

fed, *p.t.* ya *feed.*

federal, *a.* -a kuunganika (kutangamana) katika mambo ya utawala. **federate,** *v.t.* unganisha katika mambo ya utawala; — *v.i.* ungana katika mambo ya utawala. **federation,** *n.* kuunganisha (kuungana, tangamano) katika mambo ya utawala; (*group*) jamii ya makabila (mataifa, vyama &c.) yaliyoungana katika mambo ya utawala.

fee, *n.* ada, karo, (*of doctor,* daktari; *native doctor,* mganga; *cook,* mpishi; *mason,* mwashi; *carpenter,* seremala &c.) udaktari, uganga, upishi, uashi, useremala &c.

feeble, *a.* dhaifu, hafifu, goigoi, duni, ajizi. *Feeble minded,* -enye kichaa. **feebleness,** *n.* udhaifu, uajizi.

feed, *v.t.* (*p.t. and pf. t.* **fed**) lisha, chunga; — *v.i.* (*eat*) -la, jilisha; — *v.t.* (*fire*) chochea; (*a machine &c.*) endesha, zidishia nguvu; (*gratify, increase*) zidisha, ridhisha, dumisha. — *n.* chakula, malisho, maakuli; (*fuel*) kuni, makaa; (*additional matter*) zaidi. **feeder,** *n.* mlishi, mchungaji; kitu kizidishacho au kutia nguvu kitu kingine.

feel, *v.i.* (*p.t. and pf.t.* **felt**) ona, jiona, ona moyoni; (*appear*) onekana, oneka kama; — *v.t.* (*with fingers*) tomasa, bonyeza; (*touch*) papasa, gusa; (*be affected by*) ingiwa na, patwa na, shtushwa na. *Feel, feel deeply,* tia moyoni, tia maanani, fanya msiba, -wa na msiba. *Feel (something) about (a person &c.),* onelea. *Feel for,* hurumia; (*with hand, feel about for*) papasa; (*in the dark*) tutusa (sunza). *Feel the pulse,* pima vipigo vya mshipa wa damu. *I feel ill,* naona vibaya, najiona siwezi. *How do you feel?* waonaje? *It feels soft,* kama nyororo. *He feels his loss,* msiba umemhuzunisha. *Feel sure, feel certain,* jua sana, ona hakika. — *n.* kuona, kugusa. *Be hard to the feel,* onelea -gumu. **feeler,** *n.* pembe, mkono, papasi; (*test*) jaribu. **feeling,** *n.* kuona, kujiona &c., (*internal*) kuona moyoni, nia, moyo, mawazo ya ndani. *Hurt feelings of,* chukiza, udhi, tia uchungu wa moyo, kosesha. *Without power of, feeling (dead),* pooza. *Loose feeling,* pooza. — *a.* -a huruma, -ema. **feelings,** *n.pl.* maono, *e.g.* hasira, upendo, uchungu &c.

feet, *pl.* ya *foot.*

feign, *v.t.* tunga, buni, fanya; (*pretend*) jifanya, jisingizia. *Feign an attack,* fanya kama kushambulia.

feint, (1) *n.* mwigo, madanganya, hila, uwongo.

feint, (2) *a.* -embamba, -epesi. *Feint lines,* mistari isiyoonekana sana kwa kuwa ni myembamba myepesi.

felicitate, *v.t.* takia heri (furaha), shangilia, -pa mkono, (taz. *congratulate*), pongeza, hongeza. **felicitation,** *n.* kutakia heri &c.; pongezi, hongera. **felicitous,** *a.* -a kufurahisha, -a kupendeza, -a heri, -zuri, -a kufaa, -a kukolea. **felicity,** *n.* heri, neema, usitawi, baraka, furaha kuu, sudi, nyota nzuri, maneno yanayokolea.

feline, *a.* -a paka, -a kipaka, -a kama paka, -a jamii ya paka.

fell, (1) *p.t.* ya *fall.*

fell, (2) *n.* mlima.

fell, (3) *a.* -kali, -korofi, -katili, -a jeuri, -harabu, -haribifu.

fell, (4) *v.t.* angusha; (*of tree*) kata. *Run and fell a seam (in sewing),* piga bandi, kisha piga jongo nene.

fellow, *n.* mwenzi, mshiriki (hasa katika mabaya); (*person*) mtu; (*in contempt*) mtu hafifu (duni, asiye na adabu); (*of college*) mwana chuoni aliyechaguliwa kuwa wa halmashauri wa chuo kikubwa na kuchunguza elimu fulani; (*of society*) mtu aliyechaguliwa kuwa mwana chama. *Poor fellow!* maskini! *You fellows!* jamani. **fellow countryman,** *n.* ndugu (yaani mtu wa kabila, taifa, au nchi moja). **fellow creature,** *n.*

kiumbe mwenzake (mwenzio *&c.*); kiumbe sawasawa. **fellow feeling,** *n.* upendano, huruma. **fellow servant,** *n.* mjoli, mtumishi mwenzi. **fellowship,** *n.* ushirika, urafiki, upatano; (*of a society &c.*) uanachama.

felo de se, *n.* mtu aliyejiua, kujiua.

felon, *n.* mtu aliyefanya kosa kubwa (*e.g.* kuua, kuunguza nyumba ya mtu mwingine *&c.*) **felonious,** *a.* -ovu, -a hatia. **felony,** *n.* kosa kubwa, *e.g.* kuua, kuunguza nyumba *&c.*

felt, (1) *n.* namna ya nguo iliyofanywa kwa kugandamiza manyoya ya wanyama pamoja na sherizi, *e.g.* ya tarbushi.

felt, (2) *p.t. and pf.t.* ya *feel.*

female, *n.* mwanamke; (*of animals*) jike. — *a.* -ke, -a kike; (*of animals*) jike. **feminine,** *a.* -ke, -a kike, -a namna ya kike, -a kufanana na kike (mwanamke).

femoral, *a.* -a paja. **femur,** *n.* paja, mfupa wa paja.

fen, *n.* mbuga yenye kinamasi, bwawa.

fence, *n.* ua; (*of stone*) kitalu; (*as defence*) boma; (*slang*) mpokeaji wa mali iliyoibwa. *Sit on the fence,* sitasita, kutojitia upande huu wala huu. — *v.i.* cheza wawili kwa panga, shindana; (*equivocate*) ongopa, sitasita; — *v.t.* (*enclose*) jenga ua, zungushia ua (kitalu). **fencing,** *n.* ua, kujenga ua; (*materials*) majengo ya ua (seng'enge, miti *&c.*); (*game*) mchezo wa kupigana kwa panga.

fend, *v.t.* (*off*) kinga, epusha; (*for*) tunza, kimu, ruzuku. **fender,** *n.* kinga, kingio, mkinga, ukingo.

fennel, *n.* shamari (*Ar.*).

fenugreek, *n.* uwatu.

feral, *a.* (*of animals*) -kali, -siofugwa, -a mwituni; (*of plants*) -a mwitu; (*of humans*) -kali, -shenzi, -katili.

ferment, *n.* uchachu, chachu, hamira; (*boiling*) chemko; (*disorder*) fujo, vurugiko, ghasia, zahama, msukosuko. *Be in a ferment,* chemka, toa povu, chachuka; (*be excited*) fujika, vurugika, chafuka, taharuki, kasirika, hangaika. — *v.t.* chachisha; (*stir up*) chochea fitina (fujo, ghasia *&c.*); —*v.i.* chacha, chachuka; (*with anger*) panda hamaki, hamaki. **fermentation,** *n.* kuchachuka, kazi ya uchachu; (*excitement*) fujo, ghasia, machafuko, msukosuko, zahama, hasira, haraka, hamaki.

fern, *n.* kangaga, dege la watoto, *Pteris longifolia*; madole matano.

ferocious, *a.* -kali, katili. **ferocity,** *n.* ukali, ukatili.

ferret, *n.* kinyama kama cheche. — *v.t.* (*out*) tafutatafuta, peleleza, chunguza, toa wazi.

ferro-, *pref.* -a chuma, -enye chuma. **ferruginous,** *a.* -enye chuma, -enye rangi kama ile ya kutu.

ferrule, *n.* (*ring*) pete manoleo; (*on end of stick*) kitu kama subana cha kuchomeka mwisho wa bakora, kijiti cha mwavuli *&c.*, kuzuia kisipasuke wala kulika upesi.

ferry, *n.* kivuko; (*boat*) chombo (mashua) cha kuvushia watu mtoni (kivukoni). — *v.t.* (*over*) vusha, vukisha. **ferryman,** *n.* mvushaji.

fertile, *a.* -a kuzaa sana, -zazi; (*of soil*) -enye rutuba; (*country*) -a neema, -a baraka. **fertility,** *n.* kuzaa sana, uzaaji, neema, baraka. **fertilization,** *n.* -a kuongeza uzuri (rutuba) wa udongo kwa kuulima au kuutia mbolea; (*impregnation*) kutia mimba. **fertilize,** *v.t.* (*earth*) tia rutuba (mbolea, samadi); simadi; (*impregnate*) tia mimba. **fertilizer,** *n.* mbolea, samadi, cho chote kinachotia udongo nguvu.

fervency, *n.* bidii, moyo wa bidii, juhudi. **fervent,** *a.* -enye moyo wa bidii, -a juhudi, -a nguvu. **fervently,** *adv.* kwa moyo, kwa nguvu, kwa bidii. **fervid,** *a.* -enye moyo wa bidii, -a juhudi, -a nguvu. **fervour,** *n.* bidii, moyo wa bidii, juhudi, nguvu.

festal, *a.* taz. *feast.*

fester, *v.i.* tunga usaha; (*rot*) oza;

(*rankle*) kasirika, ona uchungu; — *v.t.* (*cause to decay &c.*) ozesha, fanya kutunga usaha.

festival, *n.*, **festive**, *a.*, **festivity**, *n.*, **festoon**, *n.* taz. *feast.*

fetch, *v.t.* leta, toza; (*be sold for*) uzwa kwa, pata; (*strike*) piga.

fête, *n.* sikukuu, ramsa, tamasha, tafrija. — *v.t.* shangilia, karibisha kwa furaha.

fetich, *n.* taz. *fetish.*

fetid, *a.*, **foetid**, *a.* -a kunuka, -enye uvundo, -enye harufu mbaya.

fetish, *n.* hirizi, kago, tambiko, kitu kinachoabudiwa kwa sababu kinafikirwa kina pepo ndani yake; kitu (jambo) kinachopendwa na kuheshimiwa mno. **fetishism**, *n.* imani ya kusadiki vitu vinavyoweza kusaidia au kudhuru kwa sababu ya kuwa na pepo ndani yake.

fetlock, *n.* kishungi cha nywele mguuni pa farasi chini; mahali ziotapo nywele hizo.

fetter, *n.* pingu, mnyororo, silisili; (*fig.*) kizuizi, kifungo.

fetus, *n.* taz. *foetus.*

feud, (1) *n.* uadui baina ya makabila mawili (watu wa koo mbili *&c.*); uadui wa kurithiwa (wa kutaka kisasi), uadui wa kuendelea muda mrefu.

feud, (2) *n.* shamba alilopewa mtu na mkubwa kwa kumtumikia kazi *&c.* **feudal**, *a.* utumishi kwa ajili ya kupata shamba. **feudalism**, *n.* desturi ya watu kupata mashamba kwa mkubwa kwa kumtumikia kazi.

fever, *n.* homa; (*excitement*) hali ya fadhaa (wasiwasi, haraka, uchafuko), msukosuko, harara. *East Coast fever* (*cattle*) ndigano. *Spirillum* (*tick fever*), homa ya papasi. *Relapsing fever*, homa ya vipindi. *Malaria*, homa ya malaria. *Dengue fever*, kidinga popo. *Newcomer's* (*acclimatization*) *fever*, mkunguru, ukunguru. **feverish**, *a.* -a homa kidogo; (*excited*) -enye pupa, -enye wasiwasi, -a haraka.

few, *a.* -chache, haba. *A few of*, akali ya, kidogo, -ingine -chache. **fewness**, *n.* uchache, kuwa haba.

fez, *n.* tarbushi. *Different kinds*: kitunga, takshi.

fiancé, *n.* mchumba (mwanamume). **fiancée**, *n.* mchumba (mwanamke).

fiasco, *n.* jambo lililopooza (lisilofaulu, lisilotimilika).

fiat, *n.* amri, neno la nguvu, sharti.

fib, *n.* uwongo. — *v.i.* sema uwongo, ongopa. **fibber**, *n.* mwongo.

fibre, *n.* (*single*) uzi, kitembwe; (*of coco-nut*) ukumbi, usumba; (*of young coco-nut leaves*) kidifu, difu; (*of banana plant*) ugomba; (*of pine-apple plant*) unanasi; (*of sisal*) katani, ukonge; (*general*) utembwe, utembo, ufumwale, nyuzinyuzi; (*root*) mzizi. **fibrous**, *a.* -a nyuzinyuzi.

fibula, *n.* muundi (wa mguu), goko.

fickle, *a.* -geugeu, -a kugeukageuka, -geuzi.

fiction, *n.* (*untruth*) uwongo, habari za uwongo; (*story*) hadithi ya kubuniwa, hadithi tu, uzushi, uzuli, mabuniko. **fictitious**, *a.* -a uwongo, -a kubunika, -a kutungwa (si -a kweli).

fiddle, *n.* fidla, udi (zeze) ya kizungu (yenye nyuzi na upinde wa kupigia). — *v.t. and i.* piga zeze; — *v.i.* (*waste time*) chezacheza, poteza wakati. **fiddlededee**, *int. and n.* upuzi, mawe! **fiddle-faddle**, *n.* mambo madogomadogo, mapuzi. — *a.* -a upuzi, -dogodogo, hafifu. — *v.i.* chezacheza, poteza wakati. **fiddler**, *n.* (mpiga) fidla. **fiddlestick**, *n.* upinde wa kupigia fidla. **fiddlesticks**, *int.* upuzi! mawe! **fiddling**, *a.* -a upuzi, -dogodogo, hafifu.

fidelity, *n.* amini, uaminifu, uthabiti.

fidget, *n.* wasiwasi, hangaiko, utukutu; mtukutu, asiyetulia. — *v.i.* chezacheza, totulia; — *v.t.* (*disturb*) sumbua, harakisha, tia wasiwasi, hangaisha. **fidgety**, *a.* -tukutu, -sumbufu, -enye wasiwasi, -a kuchezacheza.

fidibus, *n.* kibahaluli, kimwenge.

fiduciary, *n.* mwenye amana. — *a.* -a amana.
fie, *int.* kefule! sefule!
field, *n.* konde, shamba, mgunda; (*of battle*) mahali pa mapigano; (*space*) nafasi; (*expanse*) eneo la nchi, uwanda; (*competitors*) washindani wote (jamii). *Take the field,* enda vitani (mashindanoni). **field-day,** *n.* siku ya askari kucheza vita; siku ya jambo kubwa, sikukuu. **field-glass,** *n.* namna ya darubini ndogo. **field-marshal,** *n.* cheo cha kiaskari kilicho kikubwa kushinda vyote. **field-officer,** *n.* afisa wa kiaskari mwenye cheo cha *major, lieutenant-colonel* au *colonel.* **field-piece,** *n.* mzinga unaoweza kukokotwa.
fiend, *n.* shetani, ibilisi, jini, zimwi, pepo mbaya; (*wicked man*) katili, mdhalimu, jeuri, mtu mwovu sana. **fiendish,** *a.* -a kishetani, katili, -ovu sana.
fierce, *a.* -kali, -a nguvu; (*of animals*) -kali, mbwai; (*of persons*) katili, -kali, nduli, -uaji. **fiercely,** *adv.* kwa ukali, kwa ukatili, kwa nguvu. **fierceness,** *n.* ukali, ukatili; (*of sun*) ukali, ukalifu; (*violence*) nguvu, jeuri.
fiery, *a.* -a moto, -a joto; (*fierce*) -kali; (*violent*) -a nguvu; (*hasty, angry*) -epesi, -enye hasira, -a harara. (Taz. *fire.*)
fife, *n.* filimbi.
fifteen, *n. and a.* kumi na tano, hamstashara. **fifteenth,** *a.* -a kumi na tano. **fifth,** *a.* -a tano. **fiftieth,** *a.* -a hamsini. **fifty,** *n. and a.* hamsini.
fig, *n.* (*tree*) mtini; (*fruit*) tini. *I don't care a fig,* haidhuru hata kidogo.
fight, *v.i.* (*p.t. and pf.t.* **fought**) pigana, fanya vita, shindana; (*with, against*) pigana na; (*for*) pigania, shindania. *Fight off,* rudisha (zuia) kwa nguvu (bidii, juhudi). *Fight shy of,* epuka, epukana na, epusha. — *n.* vita, mapigano, kondo, shindano; (*brawl*) fitina, ugomvi.
fighter, *n.* mpigani, mshindani. **fighting,** *n.* vita, mapigano, kama *fight.* — *a.* -a kupigana, -a kiaskari, -a kuweza kupigana. **fighting-men,** *n.* askari.
figment, *n.* uwongo, kitu kilichotungwa (kilichowazwa tu), ndoto, mawazo.
figurative, *a.,* **figuratively,** *adv.* taz. *figure.*
figure, *n.* (*appearance*) umbo, sura; (*representation*) mfano, sanamu, choro; (*number*) tarakimu; (*show*) fahari; (*price*) bei; (*in dance*) gungu. *Quick at figures,* -elekevu wa kuhesabu. *What is your figure?* kiasi gani? wauzaje? kem? *Have a fine figure,* umbika vizuri, onekana vizuri, piga umalidadi (fahari, urembo). — *v.t.* onyesha kwa picha (sanamu &c.); (*mentally*) waza (fikiri) moyoni (katika akili); (*make a show*) jifaharisha; (*represent*) -wa mfano wa, -wa kama; (*typify*) onyesha mbele; — *v.i.* (*reckon &c.*) hesabu. *Figure largely,* -wamo (tajwa) sana. *Figure out,* hesabu, fikiria, wazia. *Figure as,* jifanya, jifananisha na. **figurative,** *a.* -enye mfano (wa maneno), -a methali. **figuratively,** *adv.* kwa mfano. **figure-head,** *n.* nakshi ya gubetini katika jahazi au chombo; (*person*) mkubwa kwa jina tu.
filament, *n.* uzi, mzizi.
filbert, *n.* namna ya lozi ya kizungu.
filch, *v.t.* iba, kwepua.
file, (1) *n.* (*soldiers*) safu (askari wawili mmoja mbele na mmoja nyuma); (*Indian file*) sanjari, mwandamo mmoja mmoja. — *v.i.* fuatana, andamana, enda mwandamo.
file, (2) *n.* tupa; (*for wood*) tungu. — *v.t.* chua, piga tupa, kata kwa tupa; (*teeth*) chonga. **filings,** *n.* unga wa chuma, shaba &c. (uliotoka katika kupiga tupa).
file, (3) *n.* uzi wa chuma wenye ncha kali wa kuchomekea karatasi, barua &c. kwa taratibu; jalada ya (au kitu cho chote cha kuwekea barua

&c. kwa taratibu); fungu la barua &c. lililofungwa pamoja kwa taratibu. — *v.t.* tunga (weka, funga) barua &c. kwa taratibu.

filial, *a.* -a mtoto kwa baba yake (mama yake), -a kupenda baba yake (mama yake).

filibuster, *n.* haramia, mnyang'anyi, mjeuri.

filigree-work, *n.* temsi.

filings, *n.* taz. *file* (2).

fill, *v.t.* jaza; (*fill up*) jaliza; (*fill spaces*) chomelea (chomekea); (*fill in holes in the earth*) fukia; (*with food*) shibisha; (*office occupation*) tia katika (kazi), fanya (kazi); — *v.i.* (*get full*) jaa. *Have one's fill,* shiba. *Fill in,* tia, maliza. *Fill out* (*grow*), kua, pata maungo, nenepa; (*expand*) tanuka, vimba. *Fill up,* jaza; (*a form* &c.) tia (andika) habari zinazotakiwa katika nafasi zilizoachwa. — *n.* kiasi cha kujaza; shibe; wingi. **filling,** *n.* kitu cha kujaza au kutia.

fillet, *n.* utepe; (*of meat*) sarara; (*of fish*) nofu (ya samaki). — *v.t.* toa miiba ya samaki na kutenga nofu zake.

filling, *n.* taz. *fill.*

fillip, *v.t.* *Give a fillip to,* piga kwa kidole; (*rouse*) amsha, shtua. — *n.* kipigo cha kidole, kiamsha, mshtuo.

filly, *n.* mwana farasi jike.

film, *n.* utando; (*in eye*) chamba; (*photographic, cinema*) kitu kama karatasi cha gamba jembamba cha kupigia sanamu, cha kuonyeshea sanamu katika sinema. — *v.i.* tanda utando; — *v.t.* tandaza utando; (*photograph*) pigia sanamu (picha, sinema). **filmy,** *a.* -embamba, -epesi, -a utando.

filter, *n.* chujio, chombo cha kusafishia maji (cha kuchujia taka, cha kuchujia); (*of basket*) kung'uto, kiteo; (*bag*) kifumbu; (*netting*) kimia, kilifu. — *v.t.* safisha kwa *filter,* chuja; — *v.i.* (*pass through*) vuja, pita kidogokidogo, papa, rishai. **filtrate,** *v.t. and i.* taz. *filter.* **filtration,** *n.* kuchuja, uchujo, mchujo.

filth, filthiness, *n.* uchafu, taka, kinyaa, unajisi. **filthy,** *a.* -chafu, -najisi, -a taka, -a kinyaa, -nyarafu.

filtrate, *v.,* **filtration,** *n.* taz. *filter.*

fin, *n.* pezi. **finny,** *a.* -enye mapezi, -a samaki.

final, *a.* -a mwisho, -a kukata maneno, mkataa. *Final cause,* kusudi. *Final word,* neno tama. — *n.* mwisho. **finale,** *n.* sehemu ya mwisho (wa kuimba, wa kucheza ngoma, wa kazi, wa mfululizo wa mambo). **finality,** *n.* mkataa, mwisho. **finally,** *adv.* mwishoni, kwa kumaliza; (*completely*) kabisa.

finance, *n.* mambo ya fedha, mali, fedha ya serikali. — *v.t.* lipa gharama ya, toa fedha kwa. **financial,** *a.* -a fedha (na mambo yake), -a fedha ya serikali, -a mali. **financially,** *adv.* kwa habari za fedha. **financier,** *n.* mstadi katika mambo ya fedha na mali.

finch, *n.* (*Golden weaver*) mnana; (*Kersten's weaver*) binti chuma, kinanda; (*Brown's red-faced weaver*) tunguribi; (*diff. sp.*) chiriku; (*small black and white*) komakanga.

find, *v.t.* (*p.t. and pf.t.* **found**) ona, pata, kuta; (*look for*) tafuta; (*ascertain*) pata kujua, hakiki, baini, ng'amua; (*provide*) patia; (*judge*) hukumu; (*discover*) vumbua; (*unexpectedly*) gundua; (*detect*) chungulia. *Find fault with,* laumu, shtaki, chongea. — *n.* (*lucky discovery*) bahati. **finding,** *n.* kuona, kupata &c.; (*law*) hukumu. **foundling,** *n.* mtoto mkiwa, kiokote, mtoto wa kuokotwa.

fine, (1) *n.* faini, fedha inayotozwa kwa adhabu, fedha ya kulipia kosa, ukombozi; (*for murder*) dia, haki ya damu. *In fine,* mwisho, basi, kwa ufupi. — *v.t.* toza fedha, lipiza ukombozi, toza fedha ya adhabu, pasisha adhabu (ya kulipa fedha).

fine, (2) *a.* -zuri; (*slender*) -embamba; (*point*) -kali; (*soft*) laini, -ororo; (*well grown*) -kuza; (*pure*) safi; (*healthy*) -a afya; (*large*) -kubwa,

-pana; (*well trained &c.*) -stadi. *It is a fine day, fine weather,* jua leo, kuzuri leo, kumetakata leo. *To run it, cut it (rather fine),* kufanya kwa jinsi (wakati) ya kufaa tu bila kuzidi. **finely,** *adv.* vizuri sana. **fineness,** *n.* uzuri, ulaini, wembamba, wepesi. **finery,** *n.* umalidadi, urembo, mangwaji, ulimbwende, mavazi mazuri, mavalio. **finesse,** *n.* ustadi, utendaji wa kupata mradi bila kukasirisha au kuamsha uadui; (*artfulness*) ujanja, hila.

finger, *n.* kidole, kidole cha mkono, chanda. *Have a finger in,* shirki, -wamo katika. *Burn one's fingers,* jipatia hasara (matata) kwa kujitia katika shauri &c. *Have at one's finger tips,* jua sana. — *v.t.* tia vidole, papasa, tomasa, gusa, piga (cheza) kinanda &c. kwa vidole. **finger-alphabet,** *n.* jinsi ya kuweka vidole kujulisha herufi mbalimbali; hutumika na mabubu na viziwi. **fingering,** *n.* taratibu ya kutumia vidole katika kupiga kinanda &c. **finger-mark,** *n.* alama ya kidole. **finger-nail,** *n.* kucha. **finger-print,** *n.* alama ya kidole. **finger-tip,** *n.* ncha ya kidole.

finical, finicking, *a.* -teuzi, -chaguzi. **finicky,** *a.* (*having much detail*) -enye mambo madogo mengi, -a matata.

finis, *n.* mwisho, tamati. **finish,** *v.t.* maliza, timiza, timiliza, hitimisha, akidi; (*bring to an end*) maliza, fanya mwisho, ishiliza; (*put an end to*) zuia, komesha, nyamazisha; (*kill*) ua, fisha; (*consume*) -la -ote; — *v.i.* (*come to an end*) isha, koma. *Finish education,* hitimu. — *n.* uzuri; (*end*) mwisho, aheri. **finished.** *a.* kamili, -kamilifu, -zuri.

finite, *a.* -enye mpaka (kikomo), -enye kuisha, -a kuishika.

finny, *a.* taz. *fin.*

fir, *n.* msunobari, mti wa jamii ya msunobari, mvinje &c.

fire, *n.* moto (*blaze*) mwako; (*brightness*) wangavu; (*excitement*) juhudi, harara; (*energy*) nguvu; (*of fire-arms*) mshindo wa bunduki, kupiga bunduki. *Light a fire,* washa moto. *Set on fire,* washa moto, tia moto, unguza. — *v.t.* tia moto, washa, choma moto, unguza, teketeza, oka; (*a gun*) piga (bunduki); — *v.i.* waka, lipuka. *Fire off,* piga. *Fire up,* kasirika, panda hamaki. **fire-alarm,** *n.* kamsa, alama (mlio &c.) ya kujulisha watu nyumba imeshika moto. **fire-arm,** *n.* bunduki, bastola. **fireball,** *n.* kimwondo. **firebrand,** *n.* kinga cha moto, mwenge; (*agitator*) mfitini, mchochezi. **fire-brigade,** *n.* jamii ya askari wenye kazi ya kuzima moto mjini. **firedamp,** *n.* hewa mbaya inayolipuka pengine, hasa huwapo katika mashimo ya kuchimbua makaa ya mawe. **fire-engine,** *n.* chombo cha kuzimia moto, kinachotumiwa na *fire-brigade.* **fire-escape,** *n.* ngazi ndefu ya kutelemkia watu katika nyumba inayoungua. **fire-extinguisher,** *n.* chombo cha kuzimia moto. **firefly,** *n.* kimulimuli, kimerimeti. **fire-insurance,** *n.* kulipa bima (jukumu) ya moto. **fire-irons,** *n.* vichocheo, vyombo vya kuchochelea moto nyumbani. **fire-light,** *n.* mwangaza wa moto. **fire-place,** *n.* mahali nyumbani pa kukokea moto, meko; (*of stones*) mafya, mafiga. **fireproof,** *n.* -sioshika moto, -sioteketea, -sioharibika kwa moto. **fireside,** *n.* pa kuota moto; (*home*) kwake (kwao &c.). **firestick,** *n.* upekecho. (ulindi, wimbombo). **firewood,** *n.* kuni; (*one piece*) ukuni. **fireworks,** *n.* fataki au viberiti vya michezo. **fire-worship,** *n.* kuabudu moto kama kwamba ni Mungu. **firing,** *n.* kuchoma moto, kuwasha moto; (*firewood*) kuni; (*coal*) makaa ya mawe.

firkin, *n.* kipipa kinachoweka kadiri ya madebe mawili.

firm, (1) *n.* kumpuni, shirika la biashara, watu wa bia, bia.

firm, (2) *a.* imara, thabiti, mathubuti, -gumu, -a kukita, liokazwa, -a kusimama; (*resolute*) hodari, -gumu, -a nguvu, -shupavu, -siosita. *Make firm,* imarisha, thibitisha, kita, shupaza. *Be firm,* zinda, kita, dinda, -wa imara (thabiti &c.), kazana. **firmly,** *adv.* kwa uthabiti, kwa nia imara, kwa nguvu, kwa mkazo. **firmness,** *n.* uthabiti, usimeme, imara, ushupavu.

firmament, *n.* anga, mbingu.

firmly, *adv.,* **firmness,** *n.* taz. *firm* (2).

first, *a.* -a kwanza; (*earliest*) -a kwanza, -a kutangulia; (*chief*) -kuu, bora; (*new*) -pya. *Experience for the first time,* limbuka. *At first, In the first place,* kwanza. *From the first,* tangu mwanzo. — *adv.* kwanza, mbele. *Be first,* takadamu, kadimu. *Go first,* tangulia. — *n.* mwanzo, chanzo, awali, asili, chimbuko; (*best quality*) kilicho bora. **first aid,** *n.* msaada wa mgonjwa (mtu aliyeumia, &c.) wakati wa kungoja daktari afike. **first-begotten, first-born,** *n.* kifungua mimba. **first-class,** *a.* -a kwanza, -a jinsi iliyo nzuri (bora, halisi), namba ya kwanza. **first-fruits,** *n.* malimbuko. **first-hand,** *a.* -pya kabisa, -liopatika kwa shahidi (mahali -lipotokea, kwa mtu aliyehusiwa hasa). **firstly,** *adv.* kwanza, mwanzoni. **first-rate,** *a.* bora, kadiri, halisi, vizuri, aali.

firth, *n.* hori ya kuingia sana, mlango mrefu wa mto.

fiscal, *a.* -a hazina (-a mali) ya serikali.

fish, *n.* samaki, nswi. *To drink like a fish,* kunywa sana. *A pretty kettle of fish,* matata. — *v.i.* vua samaki; (*use craft*) tumia hila, jaribia kwa werevu. *Fish up,* opoa. **fishbone,** *n.* mwiba wa samaki. **fisher, fisherman,** *n.* mvuvi. **fishery,** *n.* mahali pa kazi ya kuvua samaki. **fish-hook,** *n.* ndoana. **fishing,** *n.* uvuvi. **fish-kettle,** *n.* chungu au sufuria, ya kupikia samaki. **fish-like,** *a.* -a kama samaki. **fish-monger,** *n.* mwuzaji samaki. **fish-plate,** *n.* taruma la kufungashia reli za gari la moshi. **fish-trap,** *n.* dema, lema, mgono; (*fence of sticks* &c.) uzio. **fishy,** *a.* -a samaki, -enye samaki tele, kama samaki.

fissible, *a.* -a kupasulika, -enye kupasuka upesi. **fissure,** *n.* ufa, mpasuko, mwanya.

fist, *n.* ngumi; (*knuckles*) konde, konzi. *Hit with fist,* piga ngumi (konde).

fistula, *n.* nasuri, jipu lenye tundu.

fit, (1) *n.* kifafa, kipindu, kushikwa; (*of passion*) hasira ya ghafula, kiruu, hamaki. *By fits and starts,* mara kushika mara kuacha; kwa vishindo, kwa vipindi. **fitful,** *a.* a-kugeukageuka, -a mara kushika mara kuacha, -a vipindi, -a vishindo. **fitfully,** *adv,* kwa vipindi, kwa vishindo.

fit, (2) *v.t.* faa, lingana (na), -wa sawasawa, -wa barabara, afiki; (*adapt, make* &c.) fanyiza, fanya sawasawa, tia barabara, tengeneza, linganisha, unga; — *v.i.* (*be suitable, seemly*) stahili, laiki, agia, juzu; (*of clothes*) kaa, enea, faa, shimiri, agia. *His clothes fit him,* nguo zake zimemkaa (zimemwenea, zimemfaa, zimemwagia). *Fit out,* -pa matumizi (mahitaji, masurufu, vifaa, zana &c.). *Fit tight,* saki. *Fit up* (*a house* &c.), pamba, tengeneza, tononosha. *It fits me,* ni kiasi (cheo) changu; (*of clothing*) zimenikaa, zimenienea, zimenifaa, zimeniagia. — *n.* kifaacho, matengenezo. — *a.* -a kufaa, -a kustahili, -enye hali (kimo, tabia &c.) ya kufaa, -a kuweza, wajibu. *Be fit,* faa, stahili, weza. *Feel fit, Fit as a fiddle,* -wa na afya. *Think fit,* taka, chagua. **fitly,** *a.* kwa jinsi ya kufaa, kwa haki, vizuri. **fitment,** *n.* pambo, tengenezo, zana. **fitness,** *n.* kufaa, usawa, uzuri, ulinganifu. **fitter,** *n.* fundi mshonaji apimishaye nguo; fundi wa kutengeneza mashine (mitambo). **fitting,** *a.* -a kufaa, -a adabu, -ema, -stahiki, -zuri, -a haki, wajibu, fani, -a kufuzu. — *n.* mapambo, zana, matengenezo.

fitful, *a.*, **fitfully,** *adv.* taz. *fit* (1).

fitly, *a.*, **fitment,** *n.*, **fitness,** *n.*, **fitter,** *n.*, **fitting,** *a. and n.* taz. *fit* (2).

five, *n. and a.* tano, -tano. **fivefold,** *a.* -a mara tano, -a kuzidi mara tano. — *adv.* mara tano. **fives,** *n.* mchezo wa kutupa mpira ukutani kwa mkono.

fix, *v.t.* kaza; (*establish*) fanya imara, imarisha, thibitisha; (*arrange*) tengeneza; (*as with a wedge*) kokomea; (*appoint*) weka, agizia, amuru; (*decide*) azimu, kata shauri; — *v.i.* (*become fixed*) kazana, kwama; (*congeal*) ganda, gandamana. *Fix attention,* angalia. *Fix eyes on,* kodolea, kazia macho. *Fix in the memory,* tia (weka) moyoni, fahamisha, kumbusha. *Fix upon,* chagua. — *n.* mashaka, matata, hatari. *Get into a fix,* tia mashakani, kwamisha. *Get out of a fix,* toa mashakani, kwamua; (*be saved &c.*) pona, okoka, kwamuka. **fixed,** *a.* imara, thabiti, -a kukazwa, -siogeuka, -sioondoka, mkataa. **fixity,** *n.* uthabiti, ugumu, usimeme, mkazo, imara. **fixture,** *n.* jambo la sharti, neno la mkataa, mapatano, kuwekeana; (*fittings*) mapambo, vyombo (visivyoondoka).

fizz, *v.i.* chemka, fanya sauti kama maji yanayochemka na kutoa povu.

fizzle, *v.i.* kama *fizz*; (*fizzle out*) pooza.

flabbergast, *v.t.* shangaza, pumbaza, duwaza.

flabby, *a.* teketeke, teke, -enye kulegea, dabwadabwa, debwedebwe; (*of character*) -tepetevu, -legevu, dhaifu, duni. **flabbiness,** *n.* hali ya kuwa teketeke, ulegevu, ulaini; (*of character*) udhaifu, utepetevu, ulegevu.

flaccid, *a.* taz. *flabby.* **flaccidity,** *n.* taz. *flabbiness.*

flag, (1) *n.* (*plants*) kangaga, nyasi, tete.

flag, (2) *n.* jiwe pana jembamba la kutengenezea njia wanapotembelea watu.

flag, (3) *n.* bendera, beramu. — *v.t.* pamba kwa bendera; peleka habari kwa kupunga bendera. **flagship,** *n.* manowari inayotweka bendera ya *admiral.* **flagstaff,** *n.* mlingoti.

flag, (4) *v.i.* legea, nyong'onyea, choka, shindwa, tepetea; (*diminish &c.*) fifia, pungua.

flagellate, *v.t.* piga mijeledi. **flagellation,** *n.* kupiga mijeledi, mpigo wa mijeledi.

flageolet, *n.* filimbi, zomari.

flagitious, *a.* -ovu sana, -a aibu.

flagon, *n.* gudulia, chupa ya ubapa, kopo la kunywea.

flagrant, *a.* -a uovu wazi, -baya sana, baini.

flagship, *n.*, **flagstaff,** *n.* taz. *flag* (3).

flail, *n.* kipande cha mti cha kufikichia (kuputia) mtama, mpunga *&c.*

flair, *n.* moyo wa kupenda (mashairi, kazi fulani, elimu fulani); wepesi, karama, wangavu (wa kufanya kazi fulani, kujua elimu fulani).

flake, *n.* gamba; (*of metal*) mavi, bamba, kibamba; (*flakes of snow*) theluji kama manyoya; (*piece*) kipande chembamba. — *v.t.* funika kwa (nyunyizia) vipande vyembamba; — *v.i.* (*scale*) pasuka vipande vipande vyembamba. **flaky,** *a.* -a kupasuka vipande vyembamba, -a vipande vyembamba.

flambeau, *n.* mwenge. **flamboyant,** *a.* -enye urembo (mapambo) kuzidi kiasi, -a rangi inayong'aa sana. — *n.* (*acacia*) mkakaya.

flame, *n.* mwako wa moto, mwali wa moto, ulimi wa moto; (*sweetheart*) mchumba; (*of emotion*) mwako (wa upendo, wa hasira, wa bidii *&c.*). — *v.i.* waka, lipuka, toa moto. **flaming,** *a.* -a moto, -a kuwaka. *Nandy flame tree,* kifabakazi.

flamingo, *n.* heroe, ndege kama korongo mwekundu sana.

flange, *n.* kipande (ulimi) kinachotokeza (katika gurudumu, boriti *&c.*)

flank, *n.* ubavu; (*side*) upande, kando, janibu. *A flank movement,* mwendo wa kupita upande, mzunguko. — *v.t.* kaa (pita, weka) ubavuni kwa (upande wa, kando ya), — *v.i.* -wa kandoni, pakana na.

flannel, *n.* kitambaa cha sufi au manyoya ya kondoo. *Flannels,* nguo (suruali, koti &c.) za kitambaa cha sufi. **flannelette,** *n.* kitambaa chororo cha pamba kilichofanana na kitambaa cha sufi.

flap, *v.t.* piga (mabawa), pigapiga, punga; — *v.i.* tapatapa, papatika, pigapiga, punga. — *n.* pigo; (*loose piece*) kipande; (*of garment*) upindo, lisani. **flap-valve,** *n.* kilango.

flare, *v.i.* waka, toa moto, ng'aa, lipuka, bimbiriza; (*fly into passion*) panda hamaki, bimbiriza, hamaki. — *n.* mwako, moto, lipuko. **flare-up,** *n.* lipuko. **flaring,** *a.* -a kuwaka sana, -enye rangi inayovuta macho.

flash, *v.i.* piga (kama umeme), metameta, mulika, tokea ghafula, pita upesi sana; — *v.t.* mulika, memetesha, lipusha. *It suddenly flashed upon him,* fikira (wazo) ilimpata ghafula. — *n.* nuru ya (mwanga wa) kumulika ghafula, kianga, kimulimuli; (*lightning*) umeme; (*space of time*) dakika, muda mfupi sana kama kupigwa kwa umeme. *In a flash,* kufumba na kufumbua tu. — *a.* -a kimalidadi, -shaufu, hafifu. **flashlight,** *n.* taa inayowaka na kuzimika ghafula, hasa katika mnara wa taa wa baharini; taa ya kupelekea habari kwa kuiwasha na kuizima ghafula. **flashy,** *a.* -shaufu, hafifu, -a kimalidadi.

flask, *n.* chupa ndogo ya ubapa; (*powder-flask*) pembe ya baruti.

flat, *n.* (*of sword*) ubapa; (*place*) mahali sawa na pana papana, wangwa; (*in a house*) orofa ya nyumba; (*symbol in music*) kitelemsho; (*dupe*) baradhuli. — *a.* sawa, sawasawa, panapana; (*smooth*) laini; (*insipid, dull*) baridi, dufu, si -tamu, chapwa; (*depressed*) -legevu, -enye moyo mzito; (*of liquor*) -liotulia, dufu. *The dance fell flat,* ngoma haikupendeza (ilipooza). *His speech fell flat,* maneno yake hayakukolea. *He gave a flat denial,* alikana kabisa. **flat-iron,** *n.* pasi. **flatness,** *n.* kuwa sawa, usawa, ubaridi, udufu, ulegevu, upoozo &c. **flatten,** *v.t.* fanya sawasawa, sawazisha, lainisha, tandaza; (*by hammering*) tambuza. — *v.i.* -wa (fanyika) sawasawa, lainika.

flatter, *v.t.* sifu mno, sifu (isivyostahili), rairai, bembeleza, jipendekeza kwa. **flatterer,** *n.* msifu mno, mbembelezi. **flattery,** *n.* ubembelezi, kusifu mno (bila kustahili).

flatulence, *n.* riahi. **flatulent,** *a.* -a riahi.

flaunt, *v.t.* angaza mno, tembeza mno, onyesha waziwazi, shaua, koga; — *v.i.* jishaua, tambatamba, fanya mikogo.

flautist, *n.* taz. *flute.*

flavour, *n.* utamu, mwonjo, ladha; (*style*) namna; (*sign*) alama. — *v.t.* koleza, tia utamu, unga, tia viungo, towea, towelea, chapukiza. **flavouring,** *n.* utamu, kiungo, kitu cha kukoleza au kutia utamu, *e.g.* mdalasini, karafuu, ndimu &c. **flavourless,** *a.* -chapwa, dufu, -isiokolea.

flaw, *n.* kombo, ufa, waa, ila, hitilafu, upungufu, kosa. **flawless,** *a.* kamili, -zima, bila waa (ila, hitilafu, upungufu &c.).

flax, *n.* kitani. **flaxen,** *a.* -a kitani, -enye rangi ya kitani, -a kama kitani. *Flaxen hair,* nywele za singa zenye rangi ya kitani.

flay, *v.t.* chuna, chunua.

flea, *n.* kiroboto. **fleabite,** *n.* alama ya kuumwa na kiroboto; jambo dogo sana (hafifu).

fleck, *n.* kiraka, paku, doa. — *v.t.* tia viraka (mapaku, madoa).

fled, *p.t. and pf. t.* ya *flee.*

fledge, *v.i.* pata manyoya ya kurukia, pata nguvu ya kuruka (ndege). **fledged,** *a.* (makinda ya ndege)

-enye mabawa ya kurukia, -enye nguvu ya kuruka. **fledgling**, *n.* kinda (kifaranga) la ndege; (*child &c.*) mtoto, kijana.

flee, *v.i.* (*p.t. and pf.t.* **fled**) kimbia.

fleece, *n.* manyoya ya kondoo; kitu kilichofanana na manyoya ya kondoo, *e.g.* mawingu. — *v.t.* kumba mali, twalia mali yote. **fleecy**, *a.* -a manyova ya kondoo, -kama manyoya ya kondoo.

fleet, (1) *n.* jamii (kundi) ya manowari, meli (merikebu, mashua, vyombo) nyingi pamoja.

fleet, (2) *a.* -epesi, -enye mbio. **fleeting**, *a.* -a kuisha (kupita) upesi, -a muda mfupi tu. **fleetness**, *n.* wepesi, mbio, mwendo wa mbio.

flesh, *n.* nyama; (*lean*) mnofu; (*body*) kiwiliwili, mwili; (*mankind*) wanadamu, binadamu; (*humanity*) utu; (*present life*) maisha ya duniani (ya sasa); (*original sin*) uovu wa asili. *Flesh and blood*, mwili (mwenye uhai); (*kindred*) jamaa, ndugu. *Put on flesh*, nenepa. *Lose flesh*, konda, churuzika. *In the flesh*, hai, -zima. — *v.t.* onjesha damu (mauaji). *Flesh the sword*, tumia upanga kwa mara ya kwanza (katika vita, kuua, kujeruhi). **fleshiness**, *n.* mnofu, unono. **fleshly**, *a.* -a mwili; (*carnal*) -a tamaa za mwili, -kware. **fleshy**, *a.* (*fat*) -nene, -nono; (*of flesh*) -a nyama, -enye nyama.

flew, *p.t.* ya *fly*.

flex, *v.t.* kunja (mkono, mguu); — *v.i.* kunjana, kunjikana (mguu, mkono). — *n.* uzi wa taa za umeme.

flexibility, *n.* hali ya kuwa *flexible*.

flexible, *a.* -a kupindikana, -a kunama, -a kunyumbuka, -a kunapukia, -a kukunjikana; (*adaptable*) -a kutengenezeka, -a kubadilikana; (*complaint*) -tiifu, -a kukubali mambo (hali) mapya. **flexion**, *n.* mkunjo (mkono, mguu), kukunja (mkono, (mguu). **flexor**, *n.* mkunja, kikunja.

flick, *v.t.* piga kidogo, shtua.

flicker, *v.i.* (*of light*) sinzia; (*of things*) wayawaya, yumbayumba, yungayunga, tapa, papatika, chezacheza.

flier, *n.* taz. *flyer*.

flight, (1) *n.* kukimbia, ukimbizi. *To take flight, to take to flight*, kimbia. *To put to flight*, kimbiza, fukuza, winga.

flight, (2) *n.* kuruka, kupuruka; mruko; (*sudden display of energy*) bidii; (*of birds*) kundi (la ndege); (*of arrow &c.*) mrusho wa wingi wa mishale *&c.*; (*of steps*) madaraja, ngazi. **flightiness**, *n.* ushaufu, ugeugeu, ubatilifu. **flighty**, *a.* -shaufu, -geugeu, hafifu, -a kukusa.

flimsy, *a.* -embamba laini, dhaifu, -a kuvunjikana (kutatuka) kwa urahisi, hafifu, goigoi.

flinch, *v.i.* nywea, epa, shtuka, jikunja, jikunyata; (*give way*) legea, shindwa, ogopa.

fling, *v.t.* (*p.t. and pf.t.* **flung**) tupa, rusha, vurumisha, angusha, toa kwa nguvu, peleka upesi (ghafula, kwa nguvu); — *v.i.* (*go angrily &c.*) enda (taka) kwa nguvu (kwa sababu ya hasira, hamaki *&c.*). *Fling up*, acha; (*an appointment*) jitoa, toka. *Fling open*, fungua (sindua) kwa nguvu. — *n.* kipindi (cha hasira, furaha, ufisadi, ufasiki, upotovu *&c.*) (*throw*) mrusho, pigo; (*dance*) namna ya ngoma.

flint, *n.* namna ya jiwe gumu sana, kipande cha jiwe gumu sana, jiwe la bunduki. **flint-gun**, *n.* bunduki ya gumegume. **flinty**, *a.* -a *flint*, -gumu sana, -shupavu.

flip, *v.t.* piga kwa ncha ya kidole, shtua. — *n.* kipigo. **flippancy**, *n.* upurukushani, upuzi, haraka. **flippant**, *a.* hafifu, -puzi, -a kupurukusha. **flipper**, *n.* kikono, mkono.

flirt, *v.t.* punga, chezesha, suka, tikisika; — *v.i.* shtukashtuka, yumbayumba, wayawaya; (*coquet*) cheza, bemba (mwanamke kwa mwanamume au mwanamume kwa mwanamke) kama kwamba ataka uchumba, lakini bila nia hasa.

flirt, *n.* mbembe, mwanamume

(mwanamke) apendaye kucheza au kusuhubiana na mwanamke (mwanamume) kama kwamba ni mchumba bila nia hasa; mwanamke (mwanamume) anayejirahisisha kwa wanaume (wanawake) kwa mazungumzo &c. **flirtation**, *n.* uchumba wa kucheza, ubembe, maongezi ya uchumba.

flit, *v.i.* ruka huko na huko kwa wepesi; pita kwa wepesi au kimya; (*move home*) hama.

flitch, *n.* pande la nyama ya nguruwe.

float, *v.i.* elea, ogelea; (*be carried along*) chukuliwa na maji (upepo &c.), pita polepole; — *v.t.* (*cause to float*) eleza; (*set going*) endesha, anzisha. — *n.* chelezo. **floating**, *a.* -a kuelea, -nayoelea, -nayoogelea, huru, -siyokazwa. **flotation**, *n.* kuelea, mweleo, kuanzisha kumpuni. **flotilla**, *n.* kundi la mashua (la jahazi, la vyombo, la manowari ndogo). **flotsam**, *n.* mbao (mabaki ya vyombo vilivyovunjika baharini) zinazoelea baharini.

flock, (1) *n.* kundi, umati, jeshi. — *v.i.* -ja wengi, jaa, kusanyika, songana, kutana.

flock, (2) *n.* kibonge cha sufu, sufu ya manyoya ya kondoo yaliyochambuliwa kujazia godoro, mto &c. **flock-bed**, *n.* godoro lililojazwa manyoya ya kondoo au sufu iliyochambuliwa.

floe, *n.* pande kubwa la barafu linaloelea baharini.

flog, *v.t.* piga sana, pigapiga, chapa, puta. **flogging**, *n.* adhabu ya kupigwa.

flood, *n.* gharika, furiko, maji mengi, maji ya kujaa; (*abundantly*) wingi. *Flood of tears*, machozi mengi. — *v.t.* gharikisha, funikiza (kwa maji), toa tele juu ya; — *v.i.* furika, jaa sana (mto). **floodgate**, *n.* mlango (wa kuzuia maji). **flood-tide**, *n.* maji (bahari) kujaa.

floor, *n.* chini; (*concrete*) sakafu; (*threshing*) uga; (*upper*) dari; (*story*) orofa. — *v.t.* sakifu, pigilia, tia mbao za chini; (*overcome*) angusha, shinda, fumba, pumbaza, shangaza. **flooring**, *n.* mbao (sakafu) za chini.

flop, *v.i.* jipweteka, jitupa, enda kwa vishindo; anguka kwa kishindo, tapatapa. — *n.* kishindo.

flora, *n.* jamii ya mimea yote ya nchi fulani, mimea. **floral**, *a.* -a maua. **florescence**, *n.* kutumbuka (kuchanua, kufumbua) maua; wakati mmea unapotoa maua. **floret**, *n.* ua dogo. **floriculture**, *n.* ulimaji wa maua. **florid**, *a.* (*red*) -ekundu; (*showy*) shaufu, -a kufanya fahari, -a uzuri, -a umalidadi, -a ulimbwende. **florist**, *n.* mwuzaji maua, mlimaji maua.

florin, *n.* sarafu ya kiingereza, thamani yake shilingi mbili.

florist, *n.* taz. *flora.*

floss, *n.* nyuzi laini za hariri, manyoya membamba. *Embroider with floss silk*, tia kazi, tarizi.

flotation, *n.* (*floatation*), **flotilla**, *n.*, **flotsam**, *n.* taz. *float.*

flounce, (1) *v.i.* jitapatapa, enda kwa vishindo (haraka, hamaki, harara), jitikisa, jisukasuka.

flounce, (2) *n.* marinda ya upindo wa nguo.

flounder, *v.i.* tapatapa, gaagaa; (*blunder*) sitasita, kosakosa, hangaika, -wa na wasiwasi, tatanika.

flour, *n.* unga; (*wheaten, maize &c.*) unga wa ngano (mahindi &c.). — *v.t.* nyunyizia unga. **flour-dredge, -dredger**, *n.* kopo la kunyunyizia unga. **flour-mill**, *n.* kinu cha kusagia unga. **floury**, *a.* -a unga, -lionyunyiziwa unga, -a kama unga.

flourish, *v.i.* sitawi, fanikiwa, kua, tonoka, vuvumika, endelea vizuri, -wa na afya; — *v.t.* (*brandish*) punga, tikisa; (*in writing &c.*) tia madoido, tia urembo. — *n.* (*show*) fahari; (*of style*) urembo, madoido; (*of trumpets*) mshindo, mdundo; (*of arms &c.*) tikiso, mpungo, kupunga. **flourishing**, *a.* -enye afya (nguvu, hali njema, neema), -a kusitawi, -a raha.

flour-mill, *n.*, **floury**, *a.* taz. *flour.*

flout, *v.t.* dhihaki, dharau, beza, fanyia mzaha, cheka. — *n.* dhihaka, dharau, mzaha, matusi, matukano.

flow, *v.i.* enda (kama maji) tiririka,, pita, jiri, toka; (*of tides*) jaa; (*hang loose*) ning'inia; (*gush out*) foka, bubujika. *Ebb and flow,* kupwa na kujaa. *Flowing language,* maneno mengi ya ufasaha. *He gave a flowing address,* maneno yalimtoka kama maji. — *n.* mkondo, mvuto (wa maji), mwendo; (*abundance*) wingi; (*outburst*) bubujiko, mtoko. **flowing,** *a.* -a kwenda (kupita, kutiririka, kububujika &c.); (*of language*) -enye ufasaha, -zuri, -tamu; (*hanging loosely*) -a kuning'inia, -a kupwaya.

flower, *n.* ua; (*of speech &c.*) uzuri, dibaji, madoido; (*choicest part &c.*) kipeo cha uzuri (uzima, maisha, nguvu, afya &c.). *Flower of an age,* ujana, uzima. *Flower (of an army &c.)* sehemu bora, -a kwanza. — *v.i.* toa maua, chanua. **flower-bud,** *n.* tumba la ua. **flowering,** *a.* -enye maua. **flower-stalk,** *n.* kikonyo. **flowery,** *a.* -enye maua mengi; (*of speech*) -zuri, -a ufasaha.

flowing, *a.* taz. *flow.*

flown, *pf.t.* ya *fly.*

fluctuate, *v.i.* panda na kushuka, enda na kurudi; sitasita, tangatanga, badilibadili, geukageuka, badilika-badilika. **fluctuation,** *n.* kupanda na kushuka &c., mageuzi.

flue, *n.* bomba la moshi, dohani.

fluency, *n.* taz. *fluent.*

fluent, *a.* -epesi wa kusema, -semaji, -enye usemaji, -a ufasaha; (*of words*) kama maji. **fluency,** *n.* usemaji, ufasaha, wepesi wa kusema (kunena), unenaji. **fluently,** *adv.* kwa ufasaha, kwa wepesi.

fluff, *n.* kibonge cha sufi (manyoya, malaika, pamba &c.); (*beard*) ndevu nyembamba laini za kwanza. — *v.t.* chambua (chamvua) (sufi, pamba &c.). **fluffy,** *a.* laini, -embamba (kama malaika, manyoya, sufi &c.).

fluid, *n.* (kitu kama) maji, hewa. — *a.* -a maji (au hewa), kama maji (au hewa). **fluidity,** *n.* hali ya (kuwa kama) maji (au hewa).

fluke, (1) *n.* (*of anchor*) kombe.

fluke, (2) *n.* bahati njema.

flume, *n.* mfereji wa kupitishia maji kwenye kinu (mtambo, mashini), korongo lenye mto.

flummery, *n.* upuzi, mapayupayu, maneno ya ovyo; (*sweet*) namna ya chakula kitamu.

flummox, *v.t.* fadhaisha, pumbaza, duwaza.

flung, *p.t. and pf.t.* ya *fling.*

flunkey, *n.* mtumishi mwanamume.

flurry, *v.t.* harakisha, hangaisha, tia wasiwasi, pumbaza (kwa haraka, ghasia &c.). *Be flurried,* hangaika, ona wasiwasi. — *n.* haraka, ghasia, wasiwasi, hangaiko, msukosuko.

flush, (1) *v.i.* ruka, bumburuka (ndege); — *v.t.* rusha, bumburusha. — *n.* kundi la ndege lililorushwa pamoja.

flush, (2) *v.i.* (*drain*) pitisha maji, safisha; (*cause to blush*) geuza uso; (*excite*) chomesha, washa, harakisha; (*level*) sawazisha; — *v.i.* (*spurt*) foka, bubujika toka; (*blush*) geuka uso (kwa haya, furaha, matumaini, tamaa &c.), iva usoni; (*turn red*) -wa (geuka) -ekundu. — *n.* wekundu usoni (kwa haya &c.), kuiva uso, kugeuka rangi usoni; (*redness*) wekundu; (*sudden motion*) hali ya ghafula (hasira, furahá &c.); (*body of water*) wingi (wa maji), mkondo wa ghafula. — *a.* -a kujaa mpaka juu, -enye wingi wa (fedha); (*level*) -a sawasawa (bila kutokeza).

fluster, *v.t.* hangaisha, harakisha, tia wasiwasi fadhaisha, buruga; — *v.i.* hangaika, ona wasiwasi, fadhaika. — *n.* hangaiko, wasiwasi, ghasia, msukosuko.

flute, *n.* filimbi, zomari; (*in a column &c.* nakshi ya mifuo. *v.t.* piga filimbi (zomari); (*in a column &c.*) tia nakshi ya mifuo. **fluted,** *a.* -enye nakshi ya mifuo. **fluting,** *n.* kupiga filimbi; nakshi ya mifuo. **flutist,** *n.* mpiga filimbi.

flutter, *v.i.* pigapiga mabawa (bila kuruka, au kurukaruka kidogo kidogo tu), papatika, tetemeka, tikisika, punga; suka; (*agitate &c.*) hangaisha, harakisha, ogofya, fadhaisha, tia wasiwasi; (*of loose material &c.*) yumbayumba, yongayonga, pepesuka, cheza, punga. — *n.* hangaiko, wasiwasi, fadhaa, msukosuko.

fluvial, *a.* -a mto, -a mtoni.

flux, *n.* mwendo wa maji; (*change*) mabadilibadili; (*fusion*) hali ya kuyeyuka; (*discharge*) kutoka kwa wingi (damu, choo *&c.*).

fly, *v.i.* (*p.t.* **flew,** *pf.t.* **flown**), ruka, puruka; (*be borne by the air &c.*) chukuliwa (peperushwa) na upepo; (*go quickly*) enda mbio, kimbia, pita upesi; (*of a flag &c.*) pepea; — *v.t.* rusha: (*of an aeroplane*) endesha hewani; (*a flag*) tweka (bendera). *Fly at,* rukia, shambulia. *Fly into a passion,* futuka, panda hamaki, hamaki. *Fly off,* toka (enda) ghafula. *Let fly* (*arrow, gun*), piga. *Fly a kite,* rusha kishada. *The door* (*window*) *flew open,* mlango (dirisha) ulifunguka ghafula. — *n.* inzi; (*flap*) lisani, kipande cha kitambaa (mlango wa hewa, kufunika vifungo vya suruali *&c.*); (*carriage*) gari (la kuchukulia watu). — *a.* -juzi, -erevu, -janja. **flycatcher,** *n.* (*Paradise*) shore kishungi, tiva. **fly-fish,** *v.i.* vua samaki kwa chambo cha mainzi. **flying,** *a.* -a kuruka, -a muda mfupi, -a haraka, -a mbio sana; (*loose*) -siyokazwa, sabili. **flying-ant,** *n.* kumbikumbi. **flying-column,** *n.* jeshi la askari wa kwenda mbio. **flying-fish,** *n.* panzi la bahari, samaki mwenye (mapezi kama) mabawa. **fly-leaf,** *n.* ukurasa wa kwanza na wa mwisho wa kitabu usiopigwa chapa. **fly-paper,** *n.* karatasi iliyopakwa gundi (limbolimbo) ya kunasa mainzi. **fly-wheel,** *n.* gurudumu la kusawazisha mwendo wa mashine.

foal, *n.* mwana farasi (punda). — *v.i.* zaa mwana farasi.

foam, *n.* povu, ukafu. — *v.i.* toa povu, chafuka, umuka.

fob, *n.* mfuko mdogo wa kutia saa wa ubindo wa suruali.

focus, *n.* mahali mishale ya nuru (au moto) inapokutana baada ya kupindika kwa kioo *&c.*; mahali kitu kinapoonekana vizuri zaidi kwa macho (au lenzi (kioo), darubini *&c.*); kuweka kitu (darubini, macho, miwani *&c.*) mahali kinapoonekana vizuri kuliko pengine; mahali penye jambo hasa. — *v.t.* kutanisha mishale ya nuru kwa lenzi (kioo); weka kitu (macho, darubini *&c.*) ili kuona vizuri iwezekanavyo; (*attention &c.*) kaza (fikira, uangalifu *&c.*).

fodder, *n.* chakula (isipokuwa majani yanayoota) cha farasi, ng'ombe, kondoo *&c.*; (*grass*) ukoka, majani (makavu).

foe, *n.* adui.

foetus, *n.* mimba, mtoto kabla ya kuzaliwa; (*of four months*) kijusu, kilenga.

fog, *n.* ukungu, kunge, kungugu, shemali, wingu la chini, umande; (*blurred condition*) unyenyezi; (*bewilderment*) wasiwasi, matata. **foggy,** *a.* -a ukungu, -enye ukungu *&c.* **foghorn,** *n.* paipu ya meli inayopigwa wakati wa ukungu kujulisha ilipo.

fogey, *n.* mtu mzima (au mzee) ashikiliaye ya zamani asijali ya siku hizi, mzito, mjinga.

foggy, *a.,* **foghorn,** *n.* taz. *fog.*

foible, *n.* kipunguo, kinyongo, kombo fikira (isiyo kweli). *One of his foibles is to think he can sing,* ajiona kwamba aweza kuimba (lakini hawezi).

foil, (1) *n.* jaribosi, bamba la madini (bati *&c.*); kitu kinachotokeza uzuri (ubora) wa kingine kikiwekwa karibu nacho.

foil, (2) *n.* upanga mwembamba wa kuchezea.

foil, (3) *v.t.* shinda, zuia, tatanisha, pinga.

foist, *v.t.* tia (leta) kwa hila (werevu),

ingiza kwa uwongo, toa (-pa, uza *&c.*) kama kwamba ni halisi, bali ni -a uwongo.

fold, (1) *n.* (*enclosure, pen*) zizi, boma.

fold, (2) *v.t.* kunja, pinda; (*the arms*) pakata, pachika (mikono); (*embrace*) kumbatia; — *v.i.* kunjikana, pindikana. — *n.* (*drapery*) kunjo, mkunjo, kikunjo, mkuto, pindo, tabaka, finyo; (*of man's loin cloth, used as a pocket*) kibindo; (*of rope, snake &c.*) songo, pindo, kunjo; (*times*) mara. *Tenfold*, mara kumi. **folder**, *n.* mkunja, kikunja, kitu kinachokunjikana. **folding**, *a.* -a kukunjikana, -a kupindikana.

foliage, *n.* majani (ya mti).

folio, *n.* ukurasa, sahifu; (*of ledger*) kurasa mbili za daftari zinazoelekeana, upande mmoja wa matumizi na wa pili wa mapato; (*page number*) hesabu ya ukurasa wa kitabu; (*size of paper*) ukurasa mkubwa wa karatasi uliokunjwa mara moja; (*volume*) kitabu kikubwa.

folk, *n.* watu, umati. **folk-lore**, *n.* hadithi, ngano (desturi, habari) za watu wa kale. **folk-song**, *n.* wimbo wa zamani unaojulikana na umati wa watu.

follicle, *n.* kinyeleo, kinyweleo.

follow, *v.t.* fuata, andama; (*attend*) ngojea; (*pursue, hunt*) winda, fukuzia, andamia; (*a road*) fuata, shika (njia); (*imitate*) iga, igiza, fuatisha; (*obey*) tii; — *v.i.* fuata. *It follows that*, kwa sababu hiyo, kwa hiyo, hivyo. *Follow a pattern*, fuatisha, oleza. *Follow after*, fuata, andamia, enda nyuma ya, -ja baadaye. *Follow up*, fuata, patia; (*carry on*) shika, endeleza, fuliza, fanya. *The following month*, mwezi mwandamo, mwezi wa pili. *The following day*, siku ya pili, asubuhi yake, kesho yake. *As follows*, hivi. **follower**, *n.* mfuasi, chokora; (*disciple, pupil*) mwanafunzi. **following**, *a.* -a kufuata, -a baadaye, -a pili. — *n.* wafuasi, wanafunzi, akina, umati.

folly, *n.* upuzi, upumbavu, ujinga.

foment, *v.t.* osha kwa dawa au maji ya moto, bandika dawa; (*excite*) chochea, fitini, tia shonga (chonjo), washa, saidia, ongeza. **fomentation**, *n.* josho la moto, dawa ya kubandikia; (*instigation*) fitina, machocheo, kichocheo, chonjo, shonga.

fond, *a.* -enye kupenda, -a mahaba; (*over-fond*) -enye kupenda mno, -a kupendelea, -pendelevu; (*foolish*) -jinga, -a kijinga. *Be very fond of*, penda sana, pendelea. **fondle**, *v.t.* bembeleza, kumbatia, fanya (fanyana)mahaba. **fondling**, *n.* mpenzi, kipenzi. **fondness**, *n.* mapenzi, mahaba, uchu, upenzi, ashiki.

fondant, *n.* chakula kitamu laini, kama halua.

fondle, *v.*, **fondling**, *n.*, **fondness**, *n.* taz. *fond.*

font, *n.* birika la maji ya ubatizo; kitungi cha taa; taz. *fountain.*

fontanel, **fontanelle**, *n.* utosi wa mtoto mchanga.

food, *n.* chakula, maakuli, kilaji, mlo, lukuma; (*necessary*) riziki; (*on a journey*) masurufu; (*ration of food*) posho. **foodstuffs**, *n.* vyakula.

fool, *n.* mpumbavu, mjinga, baghami, bozi, bunga, daba, juha, jura; (*dupe*) baradhuli; (*jester*) mchekeshaji, mcheshi. *Make a fool of oneself*, jipumbaza. *A stupid fool*, hayawani. *Fool!* mpumbavu! ng'ombe! ngamia! mbuzi! *Play the fool with*, danganya, laghai, zuzua, haribu. — *v.t.* zuzua, zulisha, pumbaza, kejeli, kenga, renga; (*hoax*) danganya, laghai, hadaa, ghilibu; — *v.i.* (*behave as a fool*) jipumbaza, fanya upuzi. *Fool about*, chezacheza. *Fool away*, poteza, tumia vibaya. *Fool with*, chezeachezea. **foolery**, *n.* ujinga, upumbavu, upuzi. **foolhardy**, *a.* -jasiri, -a kujihatirisha bure, pasipo akili, -enye wazimu. **foolish**, *a.* pumbavu, -jinga, -puzi, chege, jahili. *Foolish talk*, mapayo, vijineno, upuzi. *Become foolish*, pumbazika, pumbaa. *He is foolish*, hana akili. **foolishness**, *n.* upuzi, upumbavu, ujinga, ubozi. **foolproof,** *a.* -a salama kabisa, -sioharibika kwa urahisi, -a namna ya kuwa hata mjinga aweza kutumia bila kuharibu.

foolscap, *n.* karatasi, kipimo chake inchi 13 kwa inchi 8½.

foot, *n.* (*pl.* **feet**) mguu, guu; (*sole of foot*) wayo, unyayo; (*lower part*) upande wa (kipande cha) chini, tako, liwato; (*cloven*) ukwato; (*measure*) urefu wa mguu, inchi thenashara, inchi kumi na mbili, futi; (*soldier*) askari. *Deformed* (*club*) *foot,* kiguu, kibwiko. *At the foot of* (*the hill*), chini ya (mlima). *Fall on one's feet,* fanikiwa. *Go on foot,* enda kwa miguu, enda chini. *Set on foot,* anzisha, fanyiza. **football,** *n.* mpira wa teke, futboli, mchezo wa kupiga teke mpira; mchezo wa mpira. **footboard,** *n.* ubao wa kukanyagia mtu anapoingia motakaa, ubao kandoni pa behewa ya gari la moshi. **footbridge,** *n.* daraja dogo la kupisha watu, ulalo, mtatago. **footfall,** *n.* kishindo cha mguu. **footguards,** *n.* askari walinzi. **foothill,** *n.* kilima, chini ya mlima. **foothold,** *n.* pa kuwekea au kutegemezea mguu, tegemeo la mguu. **footing,** *n.* pa kusimama, msingi; (*position*) kikao; (*starting-point*) mwanzo, chimbuko; (*state*) hali, cheo; (*of figures*) jumla ya hesabu. *To make pay his footing,* kumshika hakali. **footman,** *n.* mtumishi. **footmark,** *n.* wayo, unyayo, alama ya mguu, mguu. **footnote,** *n.* maelezo yaliyoandikwa chini katika ukurasa. **footpad,** *n.* mwizi, mwivi, mkwepuzi, pakacha. **footpath,** *n.* kijia. **footprint,** *n.* wayo, unyayo, alama ya mguu, mguu. **foot-rule,** *n.* kipimo cha futi moja, futi, cheo. **foot-soldier,** *n.* askari mwenda miguu. **footstep,** *n.* hatua; kishindo cha mguu; wayo, unyayo, alama ya mguu, mguu. *Follow his footsteps,* mfuate, fanya kama alivyofanya yeye, mwige. **footstool,** *n.* kiti cha kuegemesha miguu. **footwear,** *n.* viatu.

footle, *v.i.* chezacheza, fanya upuzi. — *n.* upuzi, mapayapaya, mapayuko. **footling,** *a.* hafifu, -a upuzi, duni.

footman, *n.*, **footmark,** *n.*, **footnote,** *n.*, **footpad,** *n.*, **footpath,** *n.*, **footprint,** *n.*, **foot-rule,** *n.*, **foot-soldier,** *n.*, **footstep,** *n.*, **footstool,** *n.*, **footwear,** *n.* taz. *foot.*

foozle, *v.t.* haribu kazi, buruga jambo, purukusha, fanya kwa uzembe.

fop, *n.* mmalidadi, mlimbwende. **foppery,** *n.* umalidadi, mangwaji, ulimbwende. **foppish,** *a.* kimalidadi, -malidadi.

for, *prep.* kwa; — *also expressed by Prep. form of verb, e.g. bring for,* letea; *do for,* fanyia &c.; (*because of*) kwa sababu ya, kwa ajili ya; (*instead of*) mahali pa, badala ya; (*of direction*) kwenda kwa; (*of time*) muda wa, mwendo wa. *As for,* lakini, kwa habari ya. *For nothing,* bure, bilashi. *For all the world,* pia, halisi. *For all I know,* kadiri nijuavyo mimi. *Forasmuch as,* kwa sababu, kwa kuwa, kwa maana. *For all that,* yajapokuwa hayo, walakini. *For ever,* hata milele. *Oh for a gun!* ningekuwa na bunduki! Laiti ningekuwa na bunduki! — *conj.* kwa kuwa, kwa maana, maana.

forage, *n.* chakula cha farasi, punda, ng'ombe &c.; kutafuta chakula. — *v.t.* tafuta chakula; tafuta (kitu cho chote); nyang'anya.

forasmuch, *conj.* taz. *for.*

foray, *n.* vita, shambulio.

forbade, forbad, *p.t.* ya *forbid.*

forbear, *v.t.* (*p.t.* **forbore,** *pf.t.* **forborne**) jizuia, stahimili, vumilia, chukua; (*bear with*) chukuliana na; — *v.i.* (*refuse*) kataa; (*abstain from*) epuka, epusha, acha, tofanya. **forbearance,** *n.* saburi, uvumilivu, ustahimili, ustahimilivu. **forbearing,** *a.* -enye kuvumilia (kustahimili), -enye saburi, -enye kusamehe, -pole, -vumilivu, -stahimilivu.

forbearance, *n.*, **forbearing,** *a.* taz. *forbear.*

forbears, *n.* baba, babu.
forbid, *v.t.* (*p.t.* **forbade,** *pf.t.* **forbidden**) gombeza, kataza, kanya, katalia, piga marufuku, asa, checha; (*prevent*) zuia, katiza, fingiza. **forbidden,** *a.* haramu, marufuku, si halali, -liogombezwa, -liokatazwa. **forbidding,** *a.* -a kuchukiza, -a kuogofya, -a kutisha, -kali, -chungu. **forbiddingly,** *adv.* kwa kutisha, kwa kuogofya, kwa kuchukiza.
forbore, *p.t.,* **forborne,** *pf.t.* ya *forbear.*
force, *n.* nguvu, lazima, sharti; (*energy*) bidii, juhudi, jitihada, uwezo; (*violence*) jeuri, dhulumu; (*army*) jeshi (la askari, mapolisi, manowari &c.). — *v.t.* lazimisha, shurutisha, juburu, tia nguvu, tiisha, pata (twaa, sukuma, endesha, vunja) kwa nguvu; (*by moral means*) bidisha; (*ravish*) bikiri, twaa kwa lazima; (*hasten growth*) ivisha, pevusha, otesha upesi. *Come into force,* (amri) anza, -wa na nguvu. *He was forced to go,* alikwenda kwa shida (nguvu, lazima). *Force apart,* mamanua, nanua. **forced,** *a.* -a lazima, -a shida, -a kukaza. *Make a forced march,* kaza mwendo. *Forced labour,* shokoa, hidima. **forceful,** *a.* -a nguvu, hodari, -a bidii, -a maana sana. **forcefully,** *adv.* kwa nguvu, kwa bidii. **forceless,** *a.* bila nguvu, dhaifu, bila maana. **force-pump,** *n.* bomba la kusukumiza maji. **forcible,** *a.* -a nguvu, hodari, -a bidii, -a maana sana. **forcibly,** *adv.* kwa nguvu, kwa mkazo. **forcing,** *n.* kuotesha upesi (maua, matunda, miche).
forcemeat, *n.* nyama iliyokatwakatwa (au kusagwa) na kutiwa viungo. Hutumika kujazia kuku &c. kabla ya kumpika.
forceps, *n.* kikoleo, mentari, kibano.
force-pump, *n.,* **forcible,** *a.,* **forcibly,** *adv.,* **forcing,** *n.* taz. *force.*
ford, *n.* kivuko. — *v.t.* vuka kwa miguu. **fordable,** *a.* -a kuvukika.
fore, *n.* upande wa mbele, mbele. *To the fore,* mbele. — *pfx.* -a mbele, -a kutangulia.
forearm, (1) *n.* kigasha, mkono (tangu kiko mpaka kitanga).
forearm, (2) *v.t.* -pa silaha mbele, weka tayari (kwa vita).
forebode, *v.t.* agua, bashiri, onya, onyesha; ona mbele moyoni (mambo mabaya yanayokuja). **foreboding,** *n.* ndege mbaya, kisirani, kuona mbele (mabaya), kibuhuti.
forecast, *v.t.* kisi, bahatisha, agua, tabiri. — *n.* maaguzi, bahatisho, utabiri.
forecastle, *n.* sitaha ya gubeti au omo, sitaha ya mbele na chini yake.
foreclose, *v.t.* zuia, komesha. **foreclosure,** *n.* zuio, zuizo.
forefather, *n.* baba, babu, mzee.
forefinger, *n.* kidole cha shahada, cha pili cha kidole gumba.
forefoot, *n.* mguu wa mbele.
forego, *v.t.* tangulia, enda mbele. Taz. *forgo.* **foregoing,** *a.* -a kutangulia, -liotangulia, -liokwisha nenwa (andikwa). *A foregone conclusion,* neno lililokwisha katika, neno linaloweza kujulikana mbele kwa yakini.
foreground, *n.* mahali pa mbele, palipo karibu na mtu anayetazama; (*fig.*) mahali mtu anapoonekana vizuri zaidi.
forehead, *n.* paji la uso, kikomo cha uso. *A broad forehead,* bapa la uso. *A projecting forehead,* komo la uso.
foreign, *a.* -geni, -a kigeni, -a nchi -ingine; (*distinct, irrelevant*) mbali, -siopasa, -siohusu. *There is a foreign body in his throat,* kitu kimemkwama kooni. **foreigner,** *n.* mtu wa nchi nyingine.
forejudge, *v.t.* kata shauri (hukumu) kabla ya kujua mambo yake yote.
foreknow, *v.t.* (*p.t.* **foreknew,** *pf.t.* **foreknown**) jua mbele. **foreknowledge,** *n.* kujua mbele.
foreland, *n.* rasi, pwani.
forelock, *n.* panja.
foreman, *n.* msimamizi, mnyapara.
foremast, *n.* mlingoti wa mbele.

foremost, *a.* -a mbele, -a kwanza, -kuu.
forenoon, *n.* asubuhi, mchana kabla ya saa sita.
forensic, *a.* -a korti (na mambo yake, maneno yake), -a barazani.
foreordain, *v.t.* amuru mbele.
forepart, *n.* sehemu ya mbele, upande wa mbele; (*in a dhow*) gubeti, omo.
forerunner, *n.* mtangulizi, mtakadamu; (*sign*) dalili.
foresail, *n.* tanga la mbele.
foresee, *v.t.* (*p.t.* **foresaw,** *pf.t.* **foreseen**) ona mbele, jua mbele. **foresight,** *n.* kuona mbele yatakayokuja, busara, akili.
foreshadow, *v.t.* onyesha mbele (kwa fumbo, si wazi).
foreshew = **foreshow.**
foreshore, *n.* ufuoni, pwani.
foreshorten, *v.t.* andika (chora) vizuri zitokezazo katika picha (sanamu).
foreshow, *v.t.* (*pf.t.* **foreshown**) onyesha mbele, onya, tabiri.
foresight, *n.* taz. *foresee.*
foreskin, *n.* ngovi.
forest, *n.* mwitu, pori, pululu. **forester,** *n.* msimamizi wa mwitu, mkaa mwituni. **forestry,** *n.* elimu (kazi) ya kusitawisha mwitu.
forestall, *v.t.* (*anticipate*) tangulia, twaa kwanza; (*obstruct*) zuia, pinga njia.
forester, *n.*, **forestry,** *n.* taz. *forest.*
foretaste, *n.* kuonja mbele, kionjo cha (mwonjo wa) mbele, kupata mbele, malimbuko.
foretell, *v.t.* (*p.t. and pf.t.* **foretold**) tabiri, bashiri, agua.
forethought, *n.* busara, akili (ya kuwa tayari kwa, au kuandalia mambo ya baadaye).
foretoken, *v.t.* toa mbele mfano wa, toa dalili, ashiria mbele.
foretold, *p.t. and pf.t.* ya *foretell.*
forever, *adv. and n.* kwa milele, hata milele.
forewarn, *v.t.* onya (asa, kanya) mbele.
foreword, *n.* dibaji, utangulizi.
forfeit, *v.t.* potewa na, nyang' anywa twaliwa, tozwa (kwa adhabu ya kosa), stahili kutwaliwa *&c.* (kwa sababu ya kosa). — *n.* malipo (ya kosa), adhabu, haka, kulipa fedha, ukombozi, hasara, faini. **forfeiture,** *n.* kutwaliwa (kwa sababu ya kosa), ukombozi.
forfend, *v.t.* kinga, kinza, epusha, kinda.
forgather, *v.i.* kutana, onana (kwa urafiki, mazungumzo *&c.*).
forgave, *p.t.* ya **forgive.**
forge, (1) *v.i.* (*of a ship*) *forge ahead,* endelea mbele polepole; (*of a horse &c.*) endelea polepole mpaka kutangulia.
forge, (2) *n.* kiwanda cha mhunzi (mfua chuma), meko ya mfua chuma. — *v.t.* (*iron &c.*) fua; (*make*) fanyiza; (*make falsely*) fanyiza isivyo halali, iga kwa kudanganya, jiandikia uwongo, buni; — *v.i.* fua chuma *&c.* iga ili kudanganya. **forger,** *n.* mwandishi wa uwongo (wa kudanganya), mbini. **forgery,** *n.* ubini; (*document*) mwandiko wa (hati ya) uwongo wa kudanganya; (*false signature*) sahihi ya uwongo. *It is a forgery,* imebuniwa, si mkono wake, si sahihi yake.
forget, *v.t.* (*p.t.* **forgot,** *pf.t.* **forgotten**), sahau, pitiwa, kosa kukumbuka. *Forget oneself,* pitiwa. **forgetful,** *a.* -sahaulifu. **forgetfulness,** *n.* usahaulifu, tabia ya kusahau, usahau. **forgotten,** *a.* -liyosahauliwa.
forgive, *v.t.* (*p.t.* **forgave,** *pf.t.* **forgiven**) samehe, achilia; (*obligation*) burai, bihi. *Forgive me,* niwie radhi, kunradhi, pole. *Forgive each other,* radhiana. **forgiveness,** *n.* kusamehe, usamehe, usamehevu, buraa. **forgiving,** *a.* -samehevu, -enye huruma.
forgo, *v.t.* acha, toa, bihi, jinyima, kataa, epukana na, epusha, totwaa, totumia.
forgot, *p.t.* **forgotten,** *pf.t.* ya *forget.*
fork, *n.* kiuma; (*of a road, river,*

tree &c.) panda; (*of body*), msamba, kitako. — *v.i.* fanya (gawanyika) panda; — *v.t.* twaa kwa kiuma, toa kwa kiuma. *Fork out* (*slang*), lipa fedha (gharama). **forked,** *a.* kama kiuma; (*branched*) -enye panda.

forlorn, *a.* maskini, -tupu, -lioachwa, -liotupwa, -kiwa, -pweke. *Forlorn hope,* kundi la askari lililopelekwa mbele kushambulia boma vitani, shambulio la boma, kundi la mashujaa walio tayari kujasiria lo lote; (*fig.*) tendo la ujasiri lenye tumaini kidogo tu la kufaulu. **forlornness,** *n.* ukiwa, upweke, umaskini, hali ya kuachwa (ya kutupwa).

form, *n.* umbo, maumbile, namna, sura, wajihi, aina, jinsi; (*prescribed order*) taratibu, kawaida, desturi; (*pattern*) mfano, cheo, kiolezo; (*elegance*) uzuri, madaha, madahiro, utaratibu, matengeneo; (*outward show, unreality*) mifano mitupu, matendo matupu, ushaufu, upuzi, unafiki; (*condition*) hali; (*bench*) kiti; (*class*) darasa. — *v.t.* fanya, fanyiza; umba, tengeneza, tunga; (*train*) ongoza, fundisha, zoeza; (*articulate*) taja, sema; — *v.i.* (*take shape &c.*) fanyika, umbika, pata umbo (sura), tokea; (*be*) -wa, -wamo, -wa sehemu ya. **formal,** *a.* (*prescribed*) -a kawaida, -a desturi, -a taratibu; (*meaningless*) -tupu, pasipo maana, -puzi; (*dull, uninteresting*) baridi, -siokolea, si -zuri, si -a kupendeza, si -a moyo. **formalism,** *n.* kushika dini au desturi kwa sababu ni desturi (si kwa akili wala kwa moyo), unafiki, uzandiki. **formalist,** *n.* mwenye kufuata jambo kwa sababu ni desturi (si kwa moyo wala kwa akili). **formality,** *n.* kawaida, desturi, taratibu. **formally,** *adv.* kwa desturi, kwa jinsi yake; (*exactly*) halisi, sahihi. **formation,** *n.* kufanyiza, jinsi ya kufanyiza, umbo, maana, mapangano, mpango, matengenezo, majenzi, ujenzi, upangaji, mfanyo, mfanyizo. **formative,** *a.* -a kufanyiza, -a kujenga, -a kutunga. — *n.* sehemu (ya neno, sarufi). **formless,** *a.* bila sura maalum, -sio dhahiri. **formula,** *n.* (*set form, rule*) kanuni, kawaida, amri, utaratibu; (*written directions*) maelezo ya kufanya (kutunga, kuchanganya, kuunga). **formulary,** *n.* kitabu chenye kanuni (maelezo namna ya kufanya &c.). **formulate,** *v.t.* eleza kanuni (jinsi ya kufanya), eleza kwa taratibu.

former, *a.* -a kwanza, -a zamani, -liopita. **formerly,** *adv.* kwanza, zamani.

formidable, *a.* -a kutisha, -a kuogofya, -a kutia hofu, -kubwa, -kali, -enye hatari.

formless, *a.*, **formula,** *n.*, **formulary,** *n.*, **formulate,** *v.* taz. *form.*

fornicate, *v.i.* fanya uasherati, zini. **fornication,** *n.* uasherati, uzinzi, uhawara. **fornicator,** *n.* mwasherati, mzinzi, hawara. **fornicatress,** *n.*, mwanamke mzinzi, hawara.

forsake, *v.t.* (*p.t.* **forsook,** *pf.t.* **forsaken**) acha, tupa, kataa. **forsaken,** *a.* -lioachwa, -liotupwa.

forsooth, *adv.* kweli, labda, naona.

forswear, *v.t.* (*p.t.* **forswore,** *pf.t.* **forsworn**) kataa kabisa (kwa kiapo) acha, kana; — *v.i.* (*swear falsely*) apa uwongo, zuri.

fort, *n.* ngome, boma, gereza, husuni. **fortification,** *n.* kutia nguvu, kuongeza nguvu, ongezo la nguvu; kujenga boma, boma. **fortify,** *v.t.* tia (ongeza) nguvu, imarisha, jenga boma. **fortitude,** *n.* nguvu, uhodari, ushujaa, uvumilivu (wa maumivu, shida, taabu, hatari &c.). **fortress,** *n.* mji uliojengwa maboma, boma.

forte, *n.* nguvu, sifa. *His special forte is teaching,* yu hodari hasa katika kufundisha. — *adv.* kwa nguvu. **forte-piano,** *adv.* kwa nguvu, kisha kwa utulivu. **fortissimo,** *adv.* kwa nguvu nyingi.

forth, *adv.* (*onwards*) kwenda mbele, mbele, tena; (*outwards*) kwenda nje, kutoka nje, nje. *And so forth*, na vingine vivyo hivyo. *Back and forth*, kwenda na kurudi, huko na huko. **forthcoming**, *a.* tayari kutokea, -a pili, -naokuja. **forthwith**, *adv.* mara hivo, sasa hivi, mara, bila kukawia.

fortieth, *a.* taz. *forty*.

fortification, *n.*, **fortify**, *v.* taz. *fort*.

fortissimo, *adv.* taz. *forte*.

fortitude, *n.* taz. *fort*.

fortnight, *n.* majuma mawili, siku kumi na nne. **fortnightly**, *a.* -a kila siku ya kumi na nne.

fortress, *n.* taz. *fort*.

fortuitous, *a.* -a bahati, -a nasibu.

fortunate, *a.*, **fortunately**, *adv.* taz. *fortune*.

fortune, *n.* bahati, nasibu; (*destiny*) ajali; (*condition*) hali, cheo, mambo, manzili; (*success*) usitawi, kufanikiwa, heri, neema, baraka; (*wealth*) mali, utajiri, rasilmali. *A large fortune*, mali nyingi. *A man of fortune*, tajiri, mwenye mali nyingi. **fortunate**, *a.* heri, -a heri, -a bahati, -a baraka, -a neema. **fortunately**, *adv.* kwa bahati nzuri. **fortune-hunter**, *n.* mtu ajaribuye kujitajirisha upesi kwa werevu (hasa kwa kuoa au kuolewa na mtu mwenye mali nyingi). **fortune-teller**, *n.* mtu anayejidai uwezo wa kujulisha mambo yatakayompata mwingine, mtabiri, mpiga ramli.

forty, *n.* and *a.* kumi mara nne, arobaini. **fortieth**, *a.* -a arobaini.

forum, *n.* baraza.

forward, **forwards**, *adv.* mbele, kwenda mbele, kuzidi kuendelea. — *int.* haya! — *a.* -a mbele, -a kutangulia, -a kwenda mbele; (*progressive*) -a kuendeleza hali; (*hasty, officious*) -a haraka, si -enye haya, -juvi, -shupavu, -fidhuli, -enye macho makavu. — *n.* (katika michezo mingine) mcheza katika mstari wa (safu ya) mbele. — *v.t.* endesha, himiza, saidia, kuza; (*letters &c.*) peleka. **forwardness**, *n.* hali ya kuwa mbela &c.; (*pertness &c.*) ufidhuli, ujuvi, ukavu wa macho, ushupavu; (*readiness &c.*) wepesi.

fossil, *n.* and *a.* mabaki ya wanyama, mimea &c. ya zamani yaliyogeuka mawe, ambayo huonekana katika tabaka za miamba inapopasuliwa. — *a.* -liogeuka mawe; (*person or thing*) -a kikale. **fossiliferous**, *a.* -enye *fossils*. **fossilize**, *v.t.* geuza jiwe; — *v.i.* geuka jiwe.

foster, *v.t.* lea, lisha; (*promote*) ongeza, chochea, kuza, saidia; (*harbour feeling*) weka moyoni. **foster-brother**, *n.*, **foster-sister**, *n.* ndugu wa kunyonya. **foster-child**, *n.* mtoto wa kunyonya. **foster-parent**, *n.* (*father*) baba wa kulea; (*mother*) mama wa kunyonyesha.

fought, *p.t.* and *pf.t.* ya *fight*.

foul, *a.* -chafu, -a kirahi, -a taka, -najisi, -baya, -ovu. *Fall foul of*, pambana na, gombana na. — *adv.* (katika michezo, mashindano) kwa jinsi isivyo halali. — *n.* kucheza kwa jinsi isivyo halali, mvunjo wa sheria (ya machezo, mashindano), kosa. — *v.i.* zibwa (zuiwa) na taka, tatanika; (*come into collision*) pambana; — *v.t.* (*defile &c.*) tia taka, najisi, chafua; (*a person's name &c.*) haribu (ondoa, vunja) jina (sifa, hesima &c.) — *v.i.* (*in sport*) cheza isivyo halali, kosa. **foul-mouthed** *a.* -a kutukana, -tukanaji, -a kusema matusi. **foulness**, *n.* uchafu, taka, unajisi, uovu, ukuba.

found, (1) *p.t.* and *pf.t.* ya *find*.

found, (2) *v.t.* (*establish &c.*) weka msingi wa, imarisha, weka imara, kaza, thibitisha; (*institute*) anzisha, -wa mwanzo wa (asili ya, shina la). **foundation**, *n.* msingi, shina, asili; (*reason*) sababu, hoja, kisa; (*endowment*) mali wakf. *A religious foundation*, nyumba wakf. *To be on an educational foundation*, kupata malezi bure. **foundationless**, *a* -siyo na msingi (sababu, kisa &c.) **founder**, *n.* mwenye kuanzisha asili, mwanzo. — *v.i.* zama, tota didimia.

found, (3) *v.t.* subu, ita, yeyusha madini na kuimiminia katika kalibu. **founder,** *n.* fundi wa kusubu. **foundry,** *n.* kiwanda cha kusubia madini (cha mfua chuma, cha mhunzi).

founder, *n.* taz. *found* (1) & (3).

founder, *v.* taz. *found* (2).

foundling, *n.* taz. *find.*

foundry, *n.* taz. *found* (3).

fount, fountain, *n.* bomba la kurusha maji juu kwa nguvu; (*spring*) chemchemi, kisima; (*source*) asili, mwanzo, shina; (*of lamp, pen &c.*) cha kuwekea maji (wino &c.). **fountain-head,** *n.* jicho la maji; (*source*) mwanzo. **fountain-pen,** *n.* kalamu ya wino (yenye kuweka wino ndani).

four, *n.* and *a.* nne, -nne, aroba. *Four times,* mara nne. **fourfold,** *a.* mara nne. **fourteen,** *n.* and *a.* arobatashara, kumi na nne. **fourteenth,** *a.* -a kumi na nne, -a arobatashara. **fourth,** *a.* -a nne. **fourthly** *adv.* nne.

fowl, *n.* kuku; (*young*) faranga, kifaranga; (*cock*) jogoo, jimbi, (*young*) kipora; (*bird*) ndege, (*young*) kinda. **fowler,** *n.* mwindaji (mtegaji) ndege. **fowling-piece,** *n.* bunduki ya marisaa (ya kupigia ndege).

fox, *n.* mnyama kama mbweha; (*cheat*) ayari, mlaghai, mwerevu. — *v.t.* danganya, laghai; — *v.i.* fanya werevu, tumia hila. **foxhound,** *n.* mbwa wa kuwindia *fox.* **foxtrot,** *n.* namna ya ngoma ya kucheza. **foxy,** *a.* kama mbweha, -erevu, -danganyifu, -enye hila.

foyer, *n.* sebule, majilisi.

fracas, *n.* ghasia, zahama, ugomvi wenye kelele, msukosuko.

fraction, *n.*, **fractional,** *a.*, **fractious,** *a.* taz. *fracture.*

fracture, *n.*, mvunjo, mvunjiko, kuvunjika. *He has a fracture of the leg,* amevunjika mguu. — *v.t.* vunja; — *v.i.* vunjika. **fraction,** *n.* sehemu, kipande, mkato. *Decimal fraction,* sehemu ya kumi. **fractional,** *a.* -a sehemu, -a hesabu ya sehemu; (*minute &c.*) -dogo sana. **fractious,** *a.* -tukutu, -sumbufu, -gomvi, -enye chuki.

fragile, *a.* -a kuvunjika upesi, dhaifu, -a muda mfupi. **fragility,** *n.* hali (tabia) ya kuvunjika upesi. **fragment,** *n.* kipande, sehemu, kigeregenja, kigereng'enza. **fragmentary,** *a.* -a vipande vipande, -siokamilika, -a sehemu sehemu.

fragrance, fragrancy, *n.* taz. *fragrant.*

fragrant, *a.* -a kunukia, -enye harufu nzuri; (*fig.*) -tamu, -a kupendeza. **fragrance, fragrancy,** *n.* harufu nzuri, utamu (wa kunukia), manukato, kunukato.

frail, *a.* dhaifu, goigoi, hafifu, -a kupita au kuharibika upesi, -kosefu. **frailty,** *n.* udhaifu, ugoigoi, uhafifu, kosa.

framboesia, *n.* buba.

frame, *v.t.* fanya, fanyiza, tengeneza; (*invent*) tunga; buni; (*articulate*) sema, taja; — *v.i.* (*put in a frame*) zungushia mbao (chuma &c.); (*take shape &c.*) tengenea, endelea, tungamana. — *n.* (*body*) mwili, maungo; (*state*) hali, tabia; (*framework*) mbao, miti, kiunzi, boma; (*for mosquito net*) besera; (*of door or window*) mhimili, mwimo; (*iron*) chuma. **framework,** *n.* (*skeleton*) mifupa; (*in building*) mjengo; (*of native house*) boma, majengo; (*of wood*) kiunzi, miti; (*scaffold*) jukwaa.

franc, *n.* sarafu ya kifaransa, thamani yake zamani kadiri ya senti themanini, lakini sasa kadiri ya senti kumi na tisa.

France, *n.* Faransa, Ufaransa.

franchise, *n.* uhuru, uungwana, uenyeji, ruhusa ya serikali, ruhusa au haki ya kuchagua mtu wa baraza.

francolin, *n.* kwale.

frangipani, franjipani, *n.* namna ya mti uitwao mjinga, msanapichi, mwaka.

frank, (1) *v.t.* (*letter*) tia sahihi (barua) ipelekwe bure; (*person*) ruhusa kuingia (kusafiri) bila kulipa gharama (nauli).

frank, (2) *a.* -nyofu, -kunjufu, -a kusema (kuonyesha) kweli. **frankly,** *adv.* kwa kweli. **frankness,** *n.* unyofu, ukunjufu, tabia ya kusema kweli.

frankincense, *n.* ubani, uvumba, buhuri.

frankly, *adv.*, **frankness,** *n.* taz. *frank* (2).

frantic, *a.* -enye wazimu, -enye kiruu, kama -enye wazimu (kwa hasira, maumivu, majonzi *&c.*), -a kurusha akili.

fraternal, *a.* -a ndugu, -a kidugu. **fraternity,** *n.* udugu; (*society*) chama, shirika, jamii (ya watu wenye hali moja). **fraternize,** *v.i.* fanyia kama ni ndugu, fanya urafiki, suhubiana, andamana. **fratricide,** *n.* (*person*) mwua ndugu; (*act*) kuua ndugu.

fraud, *n.* hila, werevu, madanganyo, udanganyifu, hadaa, ukopi, ulaghai; (*person*) mdanganyi, mwerevu, mlaghai, mwongo. **fraudulently,** *adv.* kwa kudanganya, kwa hila (werevu).

fraught, *a.* (*with*) -enye (-liojaa, -enye kuleta) hatari, (maana, huzuni *&c.*).

fray, (1) *n.* ghasia, ugomvi wenye kelele; pigano, shindano.

fray, (2) *v.t.* chakaza, haribu kwa kusugua, chambua, chanua; — *v.i.* chakaa, chanika, chambuka.

freak, *n.* mchezo, mzaha, jambo la kigeni, kizushi. *Freak of nature,* kiumbe kigeni (kisicho cha kawaida), ajabu, kizushi, kioja, dubwana. **freakish,** *a.* -a mchezo, -a kizushi, -a kioja *&c.*

freckle, *n.* doa (katika ngozi).

free, *a.* huru, -ungwana; (*rude*) -juvi, fidhuli, -safihi, pasipo adabu; (*alone*) peke yake; (*unhampered*) -siofungwa, -siokazwa, -siozuiwa, sabili; (*unengaged*) pasipo kazi, -enye faragha; (*voluntary*) -a hiari, pasipo lazima, bila sharti; (*gratuitous*) bure, bilashi; (*liberal*) -karimu, -paji; (*open, unrestrained*) -kunjufu, kiasi; pasipo (*public*) wazi, -a watu wote. *Free from,* pasipo. *Free of cost or expense,* pasipo (pasina) gharama, bure. *Have a free hand,* -wa na nafasi, fanya upendavyo, tozuiwa na mtu. *A free agent,* mwenye hiari, mfanya apendavyo pasipo sharti. *A free port,* bandari ya kutumika na wote bila kutozwa kodi wala ushuru. *Make free with,* tumia pasipo ruhusa, tumilia mbali. *Make free to,* thubutu. — *v.t.* weka huru, tia huru, okoa, opoa, ponya; (*from prison*) toa, fungua; (*ransom*) komboa, fidi; (*from spell*) adua, zingua; (*relieve*) ondolea vizuizi (shida, matata); (*from spirit*) komoa. **free and easy,** *a.* -kunjufu, -a kuambilika. **freebooter,** *n.* mnyang'anyi, haramia. **freedman,** *n.* huru, huria, mtu aliyekuwa mtumwa akafanywa huru. **freedom,** *n.* uhuru, uungwana; (*permission*) ruhusa; (*choice*) hiari, uchaguo; (*frankness*) unyofu, ukunjufu. **free-hand,** *a.* (*drawing*) -a kuandikwa kwa wepesi na mkono. **free-handed,** *a.* -karimu, -paji. **freehold,** *n.* shamba (kiwanja *&c.*) lisilopasiwa kodi au ushuru, mali hasa ya mwenyewe. **free kick,** *n.* (*football*) teke la mpira bila kuzuiwa, adhabu ya kosa la adui. **free lance,** *n.* mtu afanyaye kazi apendavyo apendapo. **free-liver,** *n.* mfanya yo yote (mlafi, mlevi, mwasherati *&c.*). **free-love,** *n.* unyumba bila kuoana, uasherati, uzinzi. **freely,** *adv.* bila kuzuiwa, kwa unyofu; (*abundantly*) kwa wingi, tele; (*without reservation*) kabisa. **freeman,** *n.* mwungwana, mtu asiye mtumwa. **freemason,** *n.* mwana wa chama kimojawapo cha kusaidiana chenye utaratibu maalum wa siri. **freemasonry,** *n.* utaratibu wa mafundisho ya *freemason.* **freethinker,** *n.* mtu ashikiliaye nia (mawazo) yake mwenyewe katika mambo ya dini, asikubali mwongozo wa vitabu vya dini. **free-thought,** *n.* fikira juu ya dini zisizotegemea mapokeo wala vitabu vya dini. **free trade,** *n.* biashara baina ya nchi bila mazuizi ya serikali katika mambo ya ushuru wa forodhani &c. **free-wheel,** *n.* gurudumu lenye kuendesha baisikeli ambalo huendelea kuzunguka hali miguu inapumzika. **free-will,** *n.* hiari, kuchagua, uwezo wa kuchagua au mema au mabaya bila kulazimishwa wala kushurutishwa.

free-stone, *n.* mawe yanayoweza kukatwa bila kuvunjika hasa ya mchanga na chokaa.

free-thinker, *n.*, **free-thought,** *n.*, **free-wheel,** *n.*, **free-will,** *n.* taz. *free.*

freeze, *v.i.* (*p.t.* **froze,** *pf.t.* **frozen**) ganda (gandamana) kwa baridi; -wa baridi sana hata kugandisha maji kwa barafu; (*fig.*) ona baridi sana, sisimka (kwa hofu); — *v.t.* gandamiza (gandisha) kwa baridi; fanya mwili kusisimka (kwa hofu, hatari). **freezing-point,** *n.* kiasi cha baridi kinachogandisha maji kuwa barafu.

freight, *n.* shehena; (*cost of shipping*) nauli, mapakizi; (*load, burden*) uzito wa shehena (mizigo). — *v.t.* sheheneza. **freightage,** *n.* nauli, mapakizi.

French, *a.* kifaransa, -faransa. — *n.* lugha ya Wafaransa, Kifaransa; (*people*) Wafaransa. *Take French leave,* ondoka (fanya) bila kupata ruhusa. **French chalk,** *n.* jasi.

frenzy, *n.* wazimu, kiruu, kichaa, wasiwasi (kama ya mwenye wazimu).

frequency, *n.* taz. *frequent.*

frequent, *a.* -a mara nyingi, -a mara kwa mara, -a kufanyika mara nyingi katika muda mfupi; (*persons*) -zoevu, -a kwenda (kuja, kufanya) mara kwa mara. — *v.t.* enda (mahali) mara kwa mara, zoea kwenda (kukaa, kuzuru) kwa wingi. **frequency,** *n.* kufanyika mara kwa mara, kwa wingi, wingi. **frequenter,** *n.* mzoevu.

fresco, *n.* sanamu iliyoandikwa ukutani chokaa (lipu) ingali mbichi.

fresh, *a.* -bichi, -pya, -ingine; (*recent*) -a sasa, -a siku hizi, -pya; (*ready*) tayari; (*not salt*) -tamu, -siotiwa chumvi; (*of air*) safi, baridi; (*complexion*) safi, -zuri, -a kupendeza; (*brisk, healthy*) -a nguvu, -enye afya, enye hali nzuri. *Make a fresh start,* anza tena. *He is fresh from (school &c.)* ndiyo kwanza atoke (chuoni &c.); ametoka sasa hivi (chuoni &c.). **freshen,** *v.t.* burudisha, amsha, tia nguvu; — *v.i.* burudika, amka; (*wind*) zidi, kaza. **freshet,** *n.* mvo, mafuriko. **freshness,** *n.* ubaridi, upya &c.

fret, *v.t.* -la, chakaza; (*harass &c.*) sumbua, chokoza, huzunisha, hangaisha; (*chafe*) paruza, washa; — *v.i.* (*be worried &c.*) sumbuka, hangaika, huzunika, ona wasiwasi. **fretful,** *a.* -tukutu, -chungu, -sumbufu, -a kunung'unika.

fretwork, *n.* nakshi, machoro, matemo, bombwe.

friable, *a.* -a kufikichika, -a kumung'unyika, -a kusagika (kupondeka, kufikichika, kumung'unyika) kwa urahisi.

friar, *n.* mtu aliyejitenga na mambo ya dunia ili ashikilie dini, na kutii amri zihusuzo chama kimojawapo cha watawa.

fricasee, *n.* nyama (kuku &c.) iliyokatwa vipande na kupikwa pamoja na mchuzi na viungo.

fricative, *a.* taz. *friction.*

friction, *n.* kusugua, msuguo, mkwaruzo, kuchua, kuchuana, mchuo; (*quarrel*) ugomvi, mabishano, mazuio. **fricative,** *a.* -a mkwaruzo, -a kukwaruza.

Friday, *n.* Ijumaa. *Good Friday,* Ijumaa Kuu (siku aliyosulibiwa Yesu Kristo, na siku ya ukumbusho wake).

fried, *p.t.* ya *fry.*

friend, *n.* rafiki, mwenzi, sahibu, mwandani, ahi, muhebi; (*confidential*) msiri; (*supporter*) mpenda, mpendelea, msaidia; (*Quaker*) mfuasi wa madhehebu mojawapo ya Wakristo iitwayo *Society of Friends,* chama cha marafiki. *Make friends,* patana, fanyiana urafiki; (*blood fellowship*) chanjiana. **friendless,** *a.* pasipo rafiki. *A friendless man,* mtu asiye na rafiki. **friendliness,** *n.* urafiki, upole, wema. **friendly,** *a.* -pole, -ema, -zuri. **friendly society,** *n.* chama cha kusaidiana. **friendship,** *n.* urafiki, upendano, usuhuba, huba.

frieze, *n.* mapambo ya picha *&c.* kiambazani juu.

frigate, *n.* manowari ya zamani ya matanga.

fright, *n.* hofu, woga, tisho; (*shock*) kituko, kishindo, mshtuko. **frighten,** *v.t.* ogofya, ogofisha, tia hofu, hofisha, tisha, shtua, shtusha. *Be frightened,* ogopa, ingiwa na hofu, shtuka, shtushwa. **frightened,** *a.* -oga, -enye hofu. **frightful,** *a.* -a kutisha, -a kitisho, -a kuogofya; (*unpleasant*) -baya, -a kuchukiza. **frightfully,** *adv.* kwa hofu; (*very*) sana.

frigid, *a.* baridi; (*of temperament*) baridi, si -enye shauku (ashiki, hamu), -enye damu (tabia) iliyopooza, si -enye bidii (juhudi); (*of manner*) baridi, si -kunjufu, si -a kuambilika, -a kuchukiza. *Frigid zone,* sehemu ya nchi yenye baridi kali. **frigidity,** *n.* ubaridi, utovu wa shauku (ashiki, ukunjufu, bidii), upoozi.

frill, *n.* upindo (wa nguo) wenye marinda madogo (wenye virinda); (*useless adornment &c.*) marembo ya bure (ya kuzidi), madoido. — *v.t.* tia (fanya) virinda (vikunjo); — *v.i.* (*become crinkled*) kunjamana.

fringe, *n.* matamvua, taraza; (*edge*) ukingo, mpaka; (*of hair*) nywele kipajini, kishungi; (*beard*) ndevu kidogo kidevuni. — *v.t.* tia matamvua, tarizi, tia ukingo, -wa ukingoni.

frippery, *n.* nguo za umalidadi kupita kiasi, takataka, marembo hafifu.

frisk, *v.i.* rukaruka, randa, chachawa, chezacheza (kama watoto au wana mbuzi *&c.*); — *v.t.* sukasuka; (*flick &c.*) pungapunga. **frisky.** *a.* -a kuchezacheza, -a kurukaruka, -a kupenda machezo.

fritter, *n.* kikaimati, bumunda, andazi kama kitumbua. — *v.t.* (*away*) katakata, haribu, poteza, tapanya.

frivol, *v.i.* chezacheza, fanya upuzi, shughulika na mambo hafifu. **frivolity,** *n.* upuzi, soga, porojo, mazungumzo hafifu, michezo, uhafifu. **frivolous,** *a.* hafifu, pasipo maana, -puzi, -a kijoyo.

friz, frizz, *v.t.* sokota (nywele); (*cloth, hide &c.*) sugua, chua; — *v.i.* (*become*) *curled* sokoteka, sokotana. **frizzle,** *v.t.* sokota (nywele); — *v.i.* (*become curled*) sokoteka, sokotana; — *v.t.* (*fry &c.*) kaanga, unguza; — *v.i.* kaangwa mpaka karibu kuungua; (*be exposed to great heat*) pigwa na (ona) jua kali. **frizzy,** *a.* (*of hair*) -enye visokoto, -a kipilipili.

fro, *adv.* *Go to and fro,* kwenda na kurudi, huko na huko.

frock, *n.* vazi kama kanzu (la kike, la *monk,* la mtoto wa kike), teitei. **frock-coat,** *n.* namna ya koti ndefu, vazi la kiume.

frog, (1) *n.* chura. *Frog in the throat,* kupwewa sauti. *Frog march,* watu wanne kumchukua mfungwa kila mmoja amemshika mguu au mkono, hali mfungwa ameelekea uso chini.

frog, (2) *n.* (*of waistbelt*) kipande cha ukanda cha kuchomekea upanga au singe.

frolic, *n.* mchezo, mzaha. — *v.i.* cheza. **frolicsome,** *a.* -a kuchezacheza, -purupuru.

from, *prep.* kwa, katika, toka, tangu, kwa sababu ya; (*locative*) -ni. *He is from home,* hayuko kwake, ametoka. *What is it from?* sababu yake nini? *Where are you from?* umetoka wapi? *I am from the mainland,* natoka bara.

frond, *n.* kitawi.

front, *n.* mbele, upande wa mbele, pa mbele, uso; (*of a house*) ngao ya nyumba. *In front of,* mbele ya. *Put in front,* weka mbele, tanguliza, elekeza. *Go in front,* tangulia, takadamu.

— *a.* -a mbele, -a kwanza. — *v.t.* kabili, elekea. **frontage**, *n.* upande wa mbele wa (nyumba, shamba), upande unaoelekea barabarani (njiani &c.). **frontal**, *a.* -a mbele. **frontier**, *n.* mpaka. **frontispiece**, *n.* picha (sanamu, chapa) mwanzo wa kitabu. **frontlet**, *n.* upindo, utepe wa kuvaa pajini.

frost, *n.* baridi kali, vipande vidogo vya theluji, umande ulioganda kwa baridi; (*black*) jalidi; (*white*) sakitu. **frosty**, *a.* -a baridi kali &c.

froth, *n.* povu, ukafu; (*folly*) upuzi. *Froth over*, chemka, furika. — *v.i.* toa povu, umuka, chemka; — *v.t.* (*cause to froth*) fanya povu, umua. **frothy**, *a.* -a povu, -a kuumuka, -a kuchemka; (*silly*) -puzi, hafifu, -a juu juu tu.

froward, *a.* -kaidi, -tundu, -shupavu, -asi. **frowardness**, *n.* ukaidi, utundu, ushupavu, uasi.

frown, *v.i.* kunja (finya) uso; kunja (finya) kipaji; (*disapprove*) chukia. — *n.* uso wa kukunjamana, chuki. **frowning**, *a.* -a kukunjamana (uso); (*inspiring terror* &c.) -a kutisha -a kuogofya.

frowzy, *a.* -a kunuka, -chafu, -kuukuu, -koo.

froze, frozen, *p.t. and pf.t.* ya *freeze*.

fructify, *v.i.* zaa, toa faida; — *v.t.* tia mimba, fanya kutoa faida (mavuno).

frugal, *a.* -wekevu, -angalifu (hasa kwa habari za chakula), -a kiasi, -a kula kidogo. *A frugal meal*, chakula kidogo, uchache wa chakula. **frugality**, *n.* kiasi, uchache, uwekevu, uangalifu.

fruit, *n.* tunda, zao; (*profit*) faida, mapato, chumo; (*result*) mwisho. *First fruit*, malimbuko. **fruiterer**, *n.* mwuzaji matunda. **fruitful**, *a.* -zazi, -a kuzaa sana; (*profitable*) -a faida, -a kufaa. **fruition**, *n.* uchumi, matumizi, kufurahia. **fruitless**, *a.* bure, pasipo faida, -siofaa.

frustrate, *v.t.* pinga, shinda, zuia, batili, vunja. **frustration**, *n.* mazuio, uzuizi, ubatilisho, mvunjo.

fry, (1) *n.* samaki wachanga.

fry, (2) *v.t.* kaanga; — *v.i.* kaangwa, kaangika. — *n.* chakula kilichokaangwa. **frying-pan**, *n.* (*metal*) tawa; (*earthen*) kaango, kikaango.

fuddle, *v.t.* pumbaza, tia wasiwasi.

fudge, *int.* upuzi! mawe! — *n.* upuzi, mapayuko.

fuel, *n.* (*sticks*) kuni; (*coals*) makaa; (*oil*) mafuta. — *v.t.* tia kuni (makaa, mafuta).

fug, *n.* ufukuto, uvuguvugu wa hewa mbaya chumbani, hewa nzito. — *v.i.* kaa katika chumba chenye joto kisicho na hewa safi. **fuggy**, *a.* -a vuguvugu, -enye hewa mbaya.

fugitive, *n.* mtoro, mkimbia (hatari, kazi, adhabu &c.). — *a.* -a kupita, -a kufiha, -a kupotea.

fugue, *n.* wimbo wa kufuatana sauti taratibu kwa ulinganifu mzuri.

fulcrum, *n.* egemeo la wenzo.

fulfil, *v.t.* timiza, timiliza, fanya yapasayo, maliza, isha; (*a promise*) tekeleza, fikiliza. **fulfilment**, *n.* mwisho, utimilizo, kutekeleza.

fulgent, *a.* -a kung'aa, -a kuwaka.

full, *a.* -enye kujaa, -liojaa, -enye tele, nomi; (*abundant*) -ingi, tele, -a kutosha; (*complete, whole*) -zima, -ote, kamili, kabisa, halisi; (*content*) -enye uradhi, -a kushiba; (*devoted to*) -enye kujitia kabisa, -a kushughulika (na). *Full moon*, mwezi mkubwa (mpevu, duara). *Of full age*, -zima. *A full heart*, moyo wa huzuni (wa fikira). *A full meal*, kushiba, shibe. *Brimful*, furifuri, farafara. *Full of talk*, -ingi wa maneno. *A full account*, hadithi yote, habari zote. *A full stop*, kikomo, nukta. *In full*, kamili, kabisa, -ote. *Be in full swing*, sitawi. *Be quite full* (*brimful, full up*) jaa farafara, jaa pomoni. **full-blooded**, *a.* -enye nguvu, -a kiume. **full-blown**, *a.*, **full-grown**, *a.* -pevu, -kuza; (*of men*) -zima. *Become full-grown* pevuka, komaa, pata kimo. **fullness**, *n.* hali ya kuwa *full*, kujaa, shibe, ujalivu, ujazi;

(*satiety*) ukinaifu, kushiba, kefu; (*completion*) utimilifu. **fully**, *adv*. kabisa, sana, pia.

fulminate, *v.i.* metameta; lipuka, pasuka kwa kishindo; toa ngurumo, vuma; — *v.t.* (*threaten*) toa ukali (maneno ya makelele, ya ghadhabu), ogofya, kamia, kemea, karipia; pasua (lipusha) baruti *&c*. **fulmination**, *n*. makelele, ngurumo, kishindo, ghadhabu, amri kali, makamio, makaripio, ukeme.

fulsome, *a*. -a kusifu mno (kwa uwongo, kwa kujipendekeza), -a kurairai, -a kukinaisha, -ingi mno, -a kuchukiza (kwa wingi wake).

fumble, *v.t. and i.* papasa, shikashika kwa vidole vizito, sitasita, buruga-buruga.

fume, *n*. moshi, mvuke mzito, vukizo, uvuke; (*agitation*) hangaiko, wasi-wasi; (*anger*) hasira, ghadhabu. — *v.i.* toa mvuke, foka moshi; (*fret &c.*) hangaika, fanya kwa wasi-wasi; (*be irritable*) kasirika. *A fuming passion*, kiruu, ghadhabu kali. **fumigate**, *v.t.* fukiza, toa moshi, tia mafusho, takasa kwa fukizo (moshi). **fumigation**, *n*. ufukizo, mafusho, utakaso kwa moshi (marashi *&c*.). **fumigator**, *n*. mfukiza, chetezo. **fumy**, *a*. -a kujaa moshi (mvuke, uvuke *&c*.).

fun, *n*. mchezo, mzaha, macheko, masihara, furaha. *Make fun of*, cheka, fanyia mzaha, dhihaki. **funny**, *a*. -a kuchekesha, -a mzaha, -cheshi, -chekeshaji; (*strange*) -geni, -a kigeni, ajabu.

function, *n*. kazi, matumizi, manufaa; (*ceremony*) adhimisho, ibada, tamasha. — *v.i.* fanya kazi, faa. **functional**, *a*. -a kufanya kazi, katika kufanya kazi. **functionary**, *n*. mwenye kuamriwa kazi fulani, mtu wa serikali, mtumishi.

fund, *n*. akiba, wingi; (*for particular purpose*) fedha (mali) iliyowekwa kwa kusudi maalum; (*funds*) rasilmali; (*of government*) hazina ya serikali. *To invest in the funds*, kuweka fedha kwa serikali (ili kupata faida).

fundament, *n*. matako, kitako. **fundamental**, *a*. -a asili, -a kwanza, -kubwa. — *n*. msingi, asili, kanuni. **fundamentally**, *adv*. toka mwanzo wake, kabisa.

funeral, *n*. maziko. *Requisites for funeral*, mazishi. *Provide a funeral*, zisha, toa mazishi (yaani gharama). *Attend a funeral*, enda kuzika (mazikoni). *Perform funeral service* (*Muhammedans*) soma fatiha. *Make funeral arrangements*, tengeneza andao la maiti. — *a*. -a maziko, -a mazishi. **funereal**, *a*. -a jinsi ya maziko, -a huzuni, -a matanga; (*dark*) -eusi.

fungus, *n*. ukungu, kuvu; (*mushroom-like growth*) uyoga, kiyoga.

funicular, *a*. -a kamba, -a kuendeshwa (kuvutwa) kwa kamba.

funk, *n*. (*slang*) woga; mwoga.

funnel, *n*. (*chimney*) bomba, dohani; (*filler*) mrija, kikopo (cha kumiminia maji, mafuta *&c*. kama kawa lililopinduliwa).

funny, *a*. taz. *fun*.

fur, *n*. manyoya (ya mnyama), nywele ndogondogo, ngozi ya mnyama yenye manyoya; (*deposit*) masimbi; (*on tongue*) utando (ukoga, uchafu) wa ulimi. **furrier**, *n*. mwuzaji ngozi za manyoya. **furry**, *a*. -enye manyoya (ya mnyama), -a kama manyoya; (*of tongue*) -enye utando (ukoga, uchafu), -chafu.

furbelow, *n*. virinda, matamvua (ya mavazi ya kike).

furbish, *v.t.* sugua, katua, ng'arisha, safisha, tengeneza.

furious, *a*., taz. *fury*.

furl, *v.t.* kunja; — *v.i.* kunjika, kunjana, kunjamana. — *n*. kikunjo, kikuto.

furlong, *n*. yadi mia mbili na ishirini; sehemu ya nane kwa moja ($\frac{1}{8}$) ya maili.

furlough, *n*. ruhusa ya kupumzika (ya mtu wa serikali, askari), ruhusa ya kupumzika, likizo, livu.

furnace, *n.* (*for baking pottery &c.*) joko; (*for metal*) kalibu; (*for bricks, lime &c.*) tanuu.
furnish, *v.t.* toa, -pa, patia, pasha; (*a house*) pamba. *Furnished with*, -enye. *A furnished house*, nyumba na vyombo ndani, nyumba pamoja na mapambo. **furnisher**, *n.* mpambaji, mwuzaji mapambo na vyombo vya nyumbani &c. **furniture**, *n.* pambo la nyumba, vyombo, vifaa, zana.
furore, *n.* taz. *fury.*
furrier, *n.* taz. *fur.*
furrow, *n.* mfuo, ngungwe, mlizamu, mrizabu, mkondo, mfereji wa kupishia maji; (*wrinkle, cease*) kunjo, finyo, kunyato, kunyanzi.
further, *a.* -a mbele, -a zaidi, -a mbali zaidi. — *adv.* mbele, zaidi, tena, aidha, waama, juu ya hayo, mbali zaidi. — *v.t.* saidia, endesha, endeleza, himiza. **furtherance**, *n.* msaada, maendelezi, maongozi, kuendesha. **furthermore**, *adv.* zaidi, tena, juu ya hayo. **furthermost, furthest**, *a.* -a mbele sana, -a mbali kabisa, -a mwisho.
furtive, *a.* -a hila, -a siri, -a ujanja; (*of person*) -a siri, -fichaji. **furtively**, *adv.* kwa hila, kwa siri, kwa kufichaficha.
fury, *n.* ghadhabu kali, kiruu; (*of passions*) nguvu, harara; (*avenging spirit*) shetani. **furious**, *a.* -a ghadhabu, -kali mno, -a nguvu (mbio) sana; -enye kiruu; (*of passions*) -a nguvu mno, -siozuilika. **furore**, *n.* ukelele wa kushangilia, vifijo.
furze, furze-bush, *n.* mti wa kizungu kidogo kama mchongoma wenye maua ya rangi ya manjano.
fuse, (1) *n.* fataki.
fuse, (2) *v.t.* yeyusha; (*blend*) unganya, changanya; — *v.t.* (*melt*) yeyuka; (*blend*) ungana, changamana. — *n.* kipande cha uzi (madini kinachoyeyuka (au kukatika) nguvu ya elektrisiti (umeme) ikizidi kadiri. **fusibility**, *n.* uwezo wa kuyeyushika (kuchanganyika) na kadiri yake. **fusible**, *a.* -a kuyeyushika. **fusion**, *n.* kuyeyuka, kuyeyusha; myeyuko, myeyusho; (*mixture*) mchanganyiko.
fusee, *n.* kiberiti.
fuselage, *n.* kiunzi cha eropleni.
fusibility, *n.*, **fusible**, *a.* taz. *fuse* (2).
fusil, *n.* namna ya bunduki za zamani. **fusilier**, *n.* askari wa jeshi waliochukua *fusil* zamani. **fusilade**, *n.* mfululizo wa bunduki, bunduki nyingi kupigwa pamoja.
fusion, *n.* taz. *fuse* (2).
fuss, *n.* udhia, makelele, ghasia, zahama, fujo, wasiwasi, msukosuko, haraka. — *v.i.* hangaika, shughulikashughulika; — *v.t.* sumbua, hangaisha, tia wasiwasi. **fussy**, *a.* -sumbufu, -tukutu, -enye wasiwasi; -a kushughulikashughulika katika mambo madogo.
fustian, *n.* namna ya nguo nzito.
fusty, *a.* -a kuchakaa, -chakavu, bovu, -a kunuka (kama kitu kikuukuu).
futile, *a.* -a bure, -siofaa, hafifu, duni. **futility**, *n.* uhafifu, ubatili, utupu, kutofaa, upuzi.
future, *a.* and *n.* wakati ujao, -a baadaye, -a kuja halafu, -a pili, -ingine. *For the future*, baadaye, tangu leo, tokea hapo. **futurity**, *n.* wakati ujao, wakati wa (hali ya, mambo ya) baadaye, ahera, aheri.
fuzzy, *a.* -a nyuzinyuzi, -a kimbimbi. *Fuzzy hair*, nywele ndefu zilizotatanika (za nyuzinyuzi, za kimbimbi).

G

gabble, *v.i.* sema (soma) upesi bila kutamka vizuri maneno, tatarika, payuka, piga domo. — *n.* mapayo, mtatariko, domo, vijineno.

gaberdine, *n.* namna ya nguo nyepesi.

gable, *n.* sehemu ya kiambaza iliyo katikati ya mapaa ya nyumba ya kigongo.

gad, *v.i.* (*about*), tembeatembea, zurura, zururuka, zunguka, zinga, tangatanga. *She does not gad about,* hana kitango. **gadabout,** *n.* mtembezi, mwenye kitango.

gadfly, *n.* kipanga, pange.

gadget, *n.* zana, ala, chombo (cha kazi).

gaff, *n.* kingoe cha (mkuki wa) kuvulia samaki, chocho, chusa.

gaffer, *n.* msimamizi, mnyapara.

gag, *v.t.* ziba (funga) kinywa; (*silence*) tuliza, nyamazisha. — *n.* kuziba kinywa, kizibo cha kinywa.

gage, *n.* amana, arabuni, dhamana; (*as challenge*) alama ya kumwalika mtu kupigana (kushindana); mwaliko wa kupigana (kushindana).

gaiety, *n.*, **gaily,** *adv.* taz. *gay.*

gain, *n.* faida, chumo, pato, halasa, ongezo, ziada. — *v.t.* pata faida, faidi, chuma, nufaika, pata; (*a battle*) shinda; (*reach*) fika; — *v.i.* faidi, pata faida &c. *Gain ground,* endelea mbele. *Gain on* (*upon*), patia, shinda; (*encroach on*) jiingiza katika, -la. **gainings,** *n.* mapato, machumo, faida, halasa.

gainsay, *v.t.* (*p.t. and pf.t.* **gainsaid**) kaidi, kana.

gait, *n.* mwendo.

gaiter, *n.* ngozi au kitambaa cha kuvaa mguuni toka goti mpaka kifundo.

gala, *n.* fahari, tamasha, shangwe, sikukuu, ramsa.

galago, *n.* komba.

galaxy, *n.* jamii ya (kundi la) wanawake wazuri au wanaume mashuhuri.

galbanum, *n.* ubani.

gale, *n.* upepo mwingi, dhoruba.

gall, *n.* nyongo; (*bitterness*) uchungu, ukali, chuki; (*of horse*) lengelenge, kidonda, chubuko. — *v.t.* washa, sumbua, kasirisha, chukiza; (*injure by rubbing*) chubua, kwaruza. **gall-bladder,** *n.* nyongo. **galling,** *a.* kutia uchungu, -a kukasirisha, -a kuudhi, -sumbufu.

gallant, *a.* hodari, jahili, -shujaa; (*gay*) -zuri, -a urembo; (*chivalrous*) -a kujipendekeza kwa wanawake; (*amorous*) -a ashiki, -a mahaba. — *n.* kijana mmalidadi, mshaufu, ajipendekezaye kwa wanawake; astahiye wanawake; (*in bad sense*) hawara. **gallantry,** *n.* (*courage*) ushujaa, uhodari, ujahili; (*chivalry*) kujipendekeza kwa wanawake; mambo ya ashiki (ya mahaba, ya uhawara).

gall-bladder, *n.* taz. *gall.*

galleon, *n.* namna ya jahazi kubwa ya zamani.

gallery, *n.* chumba (kirefu); (*passage*) ujia (mrefu mwembamba); (*balcony*) roshani; (*for pictures &c.*) nyumba ya sanamu &c.; (*in theatre*) orofa ya juu.

galley, *n.* namna ya jahazi ya zamani ya matanga na makasia; (*ship's boat*) mashua ya manowari; (*ship's kitchen*) jiko la melini (merikebuni); (*printing*) kikasha cha kuwekea herufi. **galley-slave,** *n.* mtumwa mvuta kasia katika jahazi.

gallinaceous, *a.* -a jamii ya kuku, kanga &c.

galling, *a.* taz. *gall.*
gallivant, *v.i.* tangatanga, tembea tembea, zurura, zururuka.
gallon, *n.* kipimo cha kiingereza kadiri ya pishi mbili.
gallop, *v.i.* enda shoti, piga shoti, enda mbio, enda kwa kuruka ;(*hurry*) fanya (soma, enda &c.) kwa haraka sana; — *v.t.* endesha shoti. — *n.* mwendo wa shoti.
gallows, *n.* miti ya kunyongea watu waliohukumiwa kufa kwa sheria. **gallows-bird**, *n.* mtu mwovu astahiliye kunyongwa.
galore, *adv.* kwa wingi. — *n.* wingi.
galvanic, *a.* -a nguvu ya umeme, -a elektrisiti. **galvanism**, *n.* nguvu ya umeme (elektrisiti) iliyofanywa kwa kuchanganya dawa fulani. **galvanize**, *v.t.* paka madini (chuma, bati); (*startle* &c.) shtua, amsha. *Galvanized iron*, bati.
gambit, *n.* mwanzo wa mchezo wa sataranji, mwanzo wa jambo (shughuli).
gamble, *v.i.* cheza kamari, cheza karata kwa fedha, chezea fedha, shindana kwa masharti, pingana kwa fedha, bahatisha; (*dice*) cheza dadu. **gambler**, *n.* mchezaji kamari (karata, dadu &c.) kwa fedha. **gambling**, *n.* kuchezea fedha, mchezo wa kamari.
gamboge, *n.* rangi kama manjano.
gambol, *v.i.* randa, rukaruka, chachawa, cheza. — *n.* mruko, mchezo, kuranda, kuchachawa.
game, *n.* mchezo, chezo, shindano, zungumzo; (*animals* &c. *hunted*) mawindo, wanyama (ndege) wa kuwinda; (*plan*) shauri. *Make game of*, fanyia mzaha, zuzua, dhihaki, cheka. *The game is up*, shauri limeshindwa. — *a.* -jasiri, hodari. — *v.i.* cheza kamari (dadu), chezea fedha; (*away*) poteza, tapanya katika kucheza kamari &c. **game-cock**, *n.* jogoo kuchi. **gamekeeper**, *n.* mlinzi (wa wanyama wa kuwinda shambani (mwituni). **game-licence**, *n.* cheti cha ruhusa ya kupiga wanyama. **gamely**, *adv.* kwa ushujaa (uhodari, ujasiri). **gamester**, *n.* mchezaji kamari, dadu &c. taz. *gambler*. **gaming**, *n.* mchezo wa kamari, kuchezea fedha, taz. *gambling*.
gamin, *n.* mtoto wa kikopo, mtoto aliyetupwa.
gaming, *n.* taz. *game*.
gammon, *n.* paja (au sehemu ya paja) ya nyama ya nguruwe.
gamut, *n.* eneo la sauti ya mtu (kinanda &c.) yaani toka chini mpaka juu; ngazi ya sauti; (*whole extent* &c.) jumla ya (huzuni, ukali, taabu, furaha, maovu &c.).
gander, *n.* bata dume la Bukini.
gang, *n.* kundi, jamii (ya watu wafanyao kazi pamoja, ya wafungwa, ya watu washirikio katika maovu &c.). **ganger**, *n.* msimamizi, mnyapara. **gangway**, *n.* ujia, ulalo, ubao (wa kuingilia melini).
ganglion, *n.* kifundo cha neva (mishipa ya fahamu).
gangrene, *n.* kidonda kinachooza, kioza cha kidonda; (*fig.*) sababu ya kitu (jambo) kuoza (kupooza, kuharibika). **gangrenous**, *a.* -liooza, -nachoozesha, -lionyekenya.
gangway, *n.* taz. *gang*.
gantry, *n.* jukwaa.
gaol, *n.* **jail**, *n.* gereza, kifungo, mahabusi. **gaol-bird**, *n.* mfungwa (hasa aliyefungwa mara nyingi). **gaoler**, *n.* mlinzi wa gereza &c.
gap, *n.* nafasi (katika ukuta, kitalu &c.) tundu (ukutani &c.); (*crack*) ufa; (*in teeth* &c.) pengo; (*in knife* &c.) pelezi; (*pass*) mwanya, mlango, kipito; (*interval*) nafasi; (*break in continuity*) ukosefu; (*divergence in views*) hitilafu. **gape**, *v.i.* achama, fumbua kinywa, simama kinywa wazi, pumbaa; (*yawn*) piga miayo; (*of earth* &c.) atuka, pasuka, fanya ufa. **gappy**, *a.* -enye mapengo (mianya, nafasi katikati &c.).
garage, *n.* banda la kuwekea motakaa, kiwanda cha kutengenezea motakaa.

garb, *n.* vazi, vao, nguo. — *v.t.* visha, vika.
garbage, *n.* matumbo ya mnyama; (*filth*) taka.
garble, *v.t.* potoa, geuza vibaya makusudi.
garden, *n.* bustani, shamba la maua, kiunga (cha miti ya matunda, mboga, maua). *Kitchen garden*, shamba la mboga. — *v.i.* lima bustani. **gardener**, *n.* (mlimaji) bustani. **gardening**, *n.* kilimo (ulimaji) cha bustani.
gargantuan, *a.* -kubwa sana.
gargle, *n.* dawa ya kusukutua. — *v.t.* sukutua (kooni).
gargoyle, *n.* mlizamu ambao kinywa chake ni sanamu ya mtu au mnyama.
garish, *a.* -shaufu, -a rangi nyingi sana, -enye marembo kupita kiasi.
garland, *n.* shada la maua, msongo wa maua. — *v.t.* visha shada la maua.
garlic, *n.* kitunguu saumu.
garment, *n.* vazi, vao, nguo.
garner, *n.* ghala, kilindo. — *v.t.* weka ghalani, weka akiba.
garnet, *n.* namna ya kito chekundu.
garnish, *v.t.* pamba. — *n.* pambo, urembo. **garniture**, *n.* pambo, urembo.
garret, *n.* kijumba (kipenu) cha orofani.
garrison, *n.* askari (walinzi wa mji, ngome, boma). — *v.t.* tia askari walinzi (bomani, mjini, ngomeni).
garrotte, *v.t.* nyonga, songa (mtu).
garrulity, *n.* usemi mwingi, domo, maneno mengi, mapayo. **garrulous**, *a.* -enye domo, -enye maneno mengi, -payapaya, -a kuchagiza.
garter, *n.* ukanda wa kuzuia soksi; (*as decoration*) alama ya cheo cha heshima kubwa sana Uingereza.
garth, *n.* ua, bustani.
gas, *n.* hewa, kitu kama hewa au mvuke mwembamba; (*fig.*) mapayo, maneno yasiyo na maana. — *v.t.* sumisha kwa namna ya hewa mbaya; — *v.i.* (*colloq.*) payapaya, payuka, bwabwaja, piga domo kaya. **gas-bag**, *n.* mfuko wa kupulizia hewa; (*person*) mpayapaya, mpiga domo. **gas-coal**, *n.* namna ya makaa ya mawe yanayotoa namna ya hewa inayoweza kuwaka. **gaseous**, *a.* -a kama *gas*. **gasometer**, *n.* chombo cha kupimia au cha kuwekea *gas*. **gas-helmet**, *n.* kofia yenye mfuko wa kufunika uso kumlinda mtu asidhurike kwa sumu ya hewa mbaya. **gas-mask**, *n.* namna ya *gas-helmet*. **gas-meter**, *n.* chombo cha kupimia *gas*.
gasconade, *n.* majivuno, majisifu. — *v.i.* jivuna, jisifu.
gaseous, *a.* taz. *gas*.
gash, *v.t.* kata, keketa, tema, chanja, toja, — *n.* (*for ornament*) tojo, chale, nembo, taruma.
gas-helmet, *n.* taz. *gas*.
gasket, *n.* kamba ya kufungia foromali tanga lililokunjwa; (*of engine &c.*) kipande (tabaka) cha pamba (karatasi &c.) cha kuzibia mahali sehemu mbili za mashine zinapoungana.
gas-mask, *n.*, **gas-meter**, *n.*, **gasometer**, *n.* taz. *gas*.
gasp, *v.i.* tweta, hema, vuta pumzi kwa shida, kokota pumzi, kata pumzi (kwa mshangao, hofu &c.); — *v.t.* (*gasp out words*) sema kwa shida (kwa ajili ya kutweta &c.) *At the, one's, last gasp*, gharighari ya kufa, kufani.
gastric, *a.* -a tumbo. **gastritis**, *n.* ugonjwa mmojawapo wa tumbo.
gastronomy, *n.* elimu ya upishi.
gate, *n.* mlango, lango; (*spectators*) hesabu ya watu walipao fedha kutazama mchezo kiwandani (*e.g.* mchezo wa mpira &c.); jumla ya fedha ilipwayo na watu hao. **gatekeeper**, *n.* bawabu, mngoja mlango **gate-post**, *n.* mhimili, (mwimo) wa mlango. *Between you and me and the gate-post*, kwa siri, baina sisi wawili tu. **gateway**, *n.* taz. *gate*.
gather, *v.t.* kusanya, changa, kutanisha, (*fruit*) chuma, tunda; (*maize*

&c. by breaking off heads) goboa, konyoa; (into folds, pleats &c.) kunja; (conclude) fahamu; — v.i. kusanyika, kutanika, hudhuria; (of a boil &c.) tunga (fanya) usaha. *Gather up*, okota, zoa. **gathering**, *n.* mkutano, kusanyiko; (*harvest*) kuchuma (matunda), mavuno; (*boil*) jipu.

gauche, *a.* -siyejua desturi za kufanya mbele za watu.

gaudy, *a.* -shaufu, -a umalidadi, -a urembo mwingi, -a fahari.

gauge, *n.* (*carpenter's*) mahati; (*size*) kipimo (unene, upana); (*measure*) kipande cha kupimia, kipimio. — *v.t.* pima, kadirisha, hesabu, linganisha, kisi.

gaunt, *a.* -embamba sana, -a kimbaombao, -a kukonda.

gauntlet, *n.* mfuko wa kulindia mikono (wa kuvaa vitani au wakati wa kuendesha gari &c.). *Run the gauntlet*, jitia katika hatari ya maisha, vumilia mapigo, matukano &c. au adhabu kali.

gauze, *n.* shashi, nguo nyembamba sana ya kupenya nuru (jicho). **gauzy**, *a.* -embamba laini sana.

gave, *p.t.* ya *give*.

gavotte, *n.* namna ya ngoma ya kucheza (na muziki yake).

gawk, *n.* mjinga, mtu mzito, msungo. **gawky**, *a.* -jinga, -zito.

gay, *a.* -a furaha, -changamshi, -changamfu, -kunjufu, -enye moyo mwepesi; (*in bad sense*) fisadi, fasiki, -a uasherati. **gaiety**, *n.* furaha, ukunjufu, michezo, shangwe, tafrija, ramsa. **gaily**, *adv.* kwa furaha, kwa shangwe, kwa moyo mwepesi.

gaze, *v.i.* (*at, upon, on*) tazama, kodolea macho, kazia, macho, angazia macho. — *n.* tazama, nadhari. **gazing-stock**, *n.* kitu cha kuchekwa, mzaha, twezo.

gazelle, *n.* paa, kinokera; (*grants*) swala.

gazette, *n.* gazeti, karatasi yenye habari, karatasi yenye matangazo ya serikali &c. — *v.t.* tangaza katika gazeti. **gazetteer**, *n.* kamusi ya jiografia (habari za nchi na watu wake).

gazing-stock, *n.* taz. *gaze*.

gear, *n.* vyombo, samani, ala, zana, vifaa, matandiko; (*of machine &c.*) matengenezo yanayoanzisha, kuzidisha au kupunguza mwendo wa mashine (motakaa &c.). *High gear*, matengenezo yanayoanzisha mwendo wa mbio. *Low gear*, matengenezo yanayopunguza mwendo (mwendo wa polepole). *Out of gear*, matengenezo yanayoendesha yametengana. *In gear*, matengenezo yanayoendesha yameingiana. *Change gear*, badili mwendo.

geese, *pl.* ya *goose*.

gelatin(e), *n.* kitu kama sherizi safi iliyoganda kuwa nyembamba kama karatasi.

geld, *v.t.* hasi. **gelding**, *n.* farasi mhasi, maksai.

gem, *n.* kito cha thamani, johari; (*treasure*) kitu kizuri sana, kilicho bora.

gendarme, *n.* polisi (wa Ufaransa).

gender, *n.* jinsi (kwa kuwa kiume au kike). *Feminine gender*, -a kike. *Masculine gender*, -a kiume. *Neuter gender*, si -a kike wala -a kiume.

genealogical, *a.* -a nasaba, -a kizazi. **genealogy**, *n.* nasaba, kizazi, ukoo, -jadi; hati ya nasaba.

general, *a.* -a vitu vyote, -a mambo yote, -a watu wote, -a vitu (mambo, watu) vingi; (*common*) -a desturi, -a kawaida, -a siku zote; (*chief, principal*) -kuu, kubwa. *A general dealer*, mfanya biashara ya namna nyingi. *General idea, outline*, dokezo, namna, maelezo ya juujuu tu. *A general statement*, maelezo ya juujuu tu (bila kuarifu habari zote). *In general*, kwa kawaida (desturi), mara nyingi, mahali pengi, kote kote. — *n.* jemadari mkuu wa jeshi la askari. **generality**, *n.* jambo (neno &c.) lihusulo jamii (aina, jinsi &c.), maelezo (maarifa) ya juujuu tu; (*greater number*) wengi. **generaliza-**

tion, *n.* jambo (shauri, neno, maono, maarifa *&c.*) la kijuujuu tu (bila kuhoji au kufikiri mambo yote), kijuujuu. **generalize,** *v.i.* hukumu (kata shauri, fikiri, ainisha) kwa kuangalia kijuujuu tu mambo yote; (*speak vaguely*) sema (eleza, arifu, tolea habari) kijuujuu; — *v.t.* (*bring into general use*) eneza, tumikisha pote. **generally,** *adv.* kwa kawaida (desturi), taz. *general, a. Generally speaking, to speak generally,* mara nyingi, kwa kawaida. **generalship,** *n.* ujemadari, maarifa ya vita; usimamizi, utengenezaji, ustadi wa kutengeneza mashauri.

generate, *v.t.* zaa, fanyiza, tokeza, leta. **generation,** *n.* uzazi, kizazi, kufanyiza; (*time, era*) zamani, wakati, siku; (*people of one age*) watu wa wakati fulani, kizazi; (*period of time*) kadiri ya miaka thelathini. *Three generations,* baba na mwanawe na mjukuu. **generative,** *a.* -a kuzaa, -zazi. *Generative organs,* viungo vya uzazi; (*male*) mboo, uume, dhakari; (*female*) kuma, uke. **generator,** *n.* mfanyiza, kifanyiza. **generic,** *a.* -a kuhusu jamii (jinsi, namna, aina) nzima; (*comprehensive*) -a vitu maana, mambo, jinsi, namna) vingi.

generous, *a.* (*liberal*) karimu, -paji; (*noble, good*) -ema, -zuri; (*abundant*) -ingi, -enye kutoa nyingi; (*wine*) -a nguvu, -zuri. **generosity,** *n.* ukarimu, upaji, wema, utu mwema.

genesis, *n.* asili, mwanzo, chimbuko, uzazi; (*first book of Old Testament*) kitabu cha kwanza cha Agano la Kale, Mwanzo.

genet, *n.* fungo, ngawa.

genetic, *a.* -a uzazi, -a kizazi, -a kuzaa. **genetics,** *n.* elimu ya tabia zinazorithishwa.

genial, *a.* -kunjufu, -changamfu, -a kufurahisha, -a kuambilika; (*of climate*) -a kupendeza, -a kufurahisha. **geniality,** *n.* ukunjufu, uchangamfu, wema, upole.

genie, *n.* jini, zimwi, pepo; (*evil*) afriti, shetani.

genitals, *n. pl.* viungo vya uzazi; (*male*) mboo, uume, dhakari, mapumbu; (*female*) kuma, uke.

genitive, *a. and n.* jinsi ya (*noun, pronoun, adjective*) kujulisha -enyewe.

genius, *n.* pepo mwema au mbaya anayetawala (anayelinda) mahali au watu; (*evil*) afriti; (*great talent*) akili halisi; (*disposition*) akili, tabia; (*special capacity*) welekevu, ustadi; (*person*) mwenye akili (ustadi, welekevu) ya namna fulani maalum.

genre, *n.* namna, aina, jinsi.

genteel, *a.* -a kiungwana, -a adabu, -pole, makini. **gentility,** *n.* uungwana, adabu, upole, malezi mazuri, jamala.

gentile, *a.* si Myahudi. — *n.* mtu asiye Myahudi.

gentility, *n.* taz. *genteel.*

gentle, *a.* -pole, -tulivu, -a makini, raufu, -si -enye makelele (ukali, (nguvu); (*of wind, water*), -anana; (*of birth*) -ungwana. **gentlefolk**(s), *n.* waungwana, watoto wa watu. **gentleman,** *n.* mwungwana, mtoto wa watu; (*independent*) mwenye mali asiye na hoja kufanya kazi; (*any male person*) mwanamume. **gentlemanly,** *a.* -a adabu, -a kiungwana, -pole. **gentleness,** *n.* upole, utulivu, makini, latifu. **gently,** *adv.* kwa upole, kwa utaratibu, siasa, kwa utulivu (makini) kinyerenyere. **gentry,** *n.* waungwana, watoto wa watu, wakubwa.

genuflect, *v.i.* piga goti (katika kusujudu au kuheshimu). **genuflection,** *n.* kupiga goti, mpigo wa goti.

genuine, *a.* halisi, -a kweli, safi, -ema, -zuri, -sioghoshiwa.

genus, *n.* (*pl.* **genera**) jinsi, namna, aina, mbegu, jamii.

geographical, *a.* taz. *geography.*

geography, *n.* elimu ya habari za dunia, tabia zake, mazao yake, nchi zake na watu wake; (*book*) kitabu chenye habari za dunia *&c.* **geographical,** *a.* -a *geography.*

geological, *a.*, **geologist**, *n.* taz. *geology.*

geology, *n.* elimu ya habari za mawe, udongo na uso wa dunia kujua jinsi zilivyofanyika. **geological**, *a.* -a *geology.* **geologist**, *n.* mtu atafutaye habari za mawe *&c.*

geometrical, *a.* taz. *geometry.*

geometry, *n.* elimu ya mistari na maumbo. **geometrical**, *a.* -a *geometry.*

gerenuk, *n.* twiga, mdogo.

germ, *n.* mimba, mbegu, yai; (*source*) asili, mwanzo; (*microbe &c.*) kijidudu. **germicide**, *n.* (dawa) kinachoweza kuua *germ.* **germinal**, *a.* -a *germ.* **germinate**, *v.i.* kua, chipuka, anza; — *v.t.* kuza, chipuza, anzisha.

German, *n. and a.* -dachi; Mdachi; (*language*) Kidachi.

germane, *a.* -a kuhusu, -a kupasa.

germicide, *n.*, **germinal**, *a.*, **germinate**, *v.* taz. *germ.*

gestation, *n.* kuchukua mimba; muda wa kuchukua mimba (kutoka kutunga mpaka kuzaa).

gesticulate, *v.i.* onyesha maana (maono) kwa kupunga (kutumia) mikono, ashiria (onya) kwa mkono. **gesticulation**, *n.* ishara (ya kupunga mkono, kukonyeza), konyezo.

gesture, *n.* kama *gesticulation.* — *v.* kama *gesticulate.*

get, *v.t.* (*p.t. and pf.t.* **got**) pata, hozi; (*become*) pata kuwa, ingia; (*induce*) shawishi, ongoza, shurutisha; (*cause to be*) fanyiza, amuru (kufanyika); (*arrive*) fika; (*go*) enda, toka. *Get across*, vuka, fika ng'ambo. *Get ahead*, tangulia, pita, shinda. *Get along!* nenda zako! *Get angry*, futuka, kasirika, fanya ukali, panda hamaki, hamaki. *Get better*, pona, -wa hajambo, pata ashekali (nafuu). *Get the better of*, shinda, pita, ghilibu. *Get beyond*, pita. *Get my heart*, jifunza sana. *Get drunk*, lewa. *Get into*, ingia. *Get into a rage*, futuka, kasirika. *Get off*, toka, okoka, achiliwa. *Get on*, endelea mbele, fanikiwa. *How are you getting on?* U hali gani? Habari ya siku nyingi? Hujambo? *Get out*, toka. *Get out of the way*, jitenga, epuka; (*as exclamation*) simile! jihadhari! habedari! *Get over* (*recover*) pona katika; (*by flattery*) bembeleza, rairai. *Get through* (*money*) tumia; (*work*) maliza, isha. *Get together*, kusanya, kutanisha; (*come together*) kusanyika. *Get under*, ingia chini ya; (*subdue*) shinda, weza, zuia. *Get up*, ondoka; (*climb*) panda, kwea; (*learn*) jifunza; (*arrange*) tengeneza, pamba. *Get well*, pona. **get-at-able**, *a.* -a kufikika; (*persons*) -pole, -a kuambilika.

get-up, *n.* mwao, mavazi, matengenezo.

gewgaw, *n.* kishaufu, kitakataka, kipuzi.

geyser, *n.* chemchemi (bubujiko) ya maji ya moto yanayoruka juu sana; (*for heating water*) chombo cha kupasha moto maji ya kuoga *&c.*

ghastly, *a.* -a kutisha, -a kuchukiza, -baya; (*deathly*) -eupe sana, kama kifu.

ghee, *n.* samli.

gherkin, *n.* namna ya tango dogo.

ghetto, *n.* mtaa mjini wanamokaa Wayahudi.

ghost, *n.* pepo, kivuli, kizuka. *Give up the ghost*, kata roho, -fa, fariki dunia. *A ghost of a smile*, mcheko mdogo (kama kwamba ni kivuli cha mcheko). *The Holy Ghost*, Roho Mtakatifu. **ghostly**, *a.* kama kivuli cha mtu; (*spiritual*) -a roho, -a kiroho.

ghoul, *n.* zimwi, jini, pepo (alaye maiti); mtu katili apendaye kufanya maovu.

giant, *n.* jitu, pandikizi (pande) la mtu; (*outstanding person*) mwenye akili (ushujaa, uhodari, ustadi *&c.*) kupita ile ya kawaida. — *a.* -refu (-kubwa) mno.

gibber, talk gibberish, *v.i.* tatarika, payapaya, payuka, babaika, bwabwaja, bwata.

gibbet, *n.* miti ya kunyongea watu waliohukumiwa kufa kwa sheria.

gibbon, *n.* namna ya nyani wa *Malay* aliyefanana sana na bin adamu.
gibe, *v.i.* (*at*) dharau, fanyia mzaha, dhihaki, cheka. —*n.* dharau, mzaha.
giblets, *n.* maini, moyo na firigisi ya kuku, bata *&c.*
giddy, *a.* -a kizunguzungu, -a kisulisuli; (*causing giddiness*) -a kutia kizunguzungu; (*flighty &c.*) -puzi, -a kujitia katika mazungumzo (michezo *&c.*) kuliko kazi. *Be giddy,* -wa na kizunguzungu, sulika; levyalevya; (*be foolish*) pumbazika. **giddiness,** *n.* kizunguzungu, kisulisuli, masua, mbasua, gumbizi; (*folly*) upumbavu.
gift, *n.* (*in general*) zawadi, majazi, karamu, adia, kipaji; (*for merit*) tuzo; (*from God*) thawabu, upaji, baraka, karama; (*customary fee*) ada, kinyosha mgongo, kilemba, ufito *&c.* (*casual*) bakshishi; (*charitable*) sadaka; (*congratulatory*) mapukusa, pukuso, hongera, pongezi; (*for rescue*) maokozi; (*for ransom*) makombozi; (*for services*) malipo; (*talents*) akili, nguvu; (*keepsake*) hiba. **gifted,** *a.* hodari, -a akili.
gig, *n.* gari jepesi lenye magurudumu mawili; (*boat*) mashua ya meli (manowari *&c.*).
gigantic, *a.* -kubwa mno, -refu mno, -a kupita kiasi.
giggle, *v.i.* cheka kipumbavu, chekelea.
gild, *v.t.* (paka) dhahabu, chovya katika maji ya dhahabu; (*brighten &c.*) pamba. **gilded,** *a.* -liopakwa (-liotiwa) dhahabu; -liopambwa sana. **gilding,** *n.* mpako wa dhahabu, rangi ya dhahabu. **gilt,** *n.* kama *gilding*; uzuri wa kijujuu tu. — *a.* kama *gilded.*
gill, (1) *n.* shavu la samaki.
gill, (2) *n.* kipimo kidogo cha kiingereza, kadiri ya robo *pint.*
gilt, *a.* taz. *gild.*
gimcrack, *n.* kitakataka, kitu hafifu, kipuzi.
gimlet, *n.* chombo kidogo cha kutobolea.
gin, (1) *n.* mtego; (*crane*) winchi, silingi; (*cotton ginnery*) kinu cha (mtambo wa) kuchambulia pamba.
gin, (2) *n.* namna ya kileo cheupe kama maji.
ginger, *n.* tangawizi; (*colour*) rangi ya hudhurungi nyekundu; (*energy &c.*) bidii, nguvu, juhudi. **gingerly,** *adv.* kwa hadhari sana, kwa uangalifu mno.
gipsy, gypsy, *n.* mtu wa taifa la kigeni la Uhindi lililotawanyika Ulaya ambalo hutembeatembea tu pasipo kikao.
giraffe, *n.* twiga.
gird, *v.t.* (*p.t. and pf.t.* **girt, girded**) zungushia, vika (kiunoni). *Gird up the loins,* jifanya tayari kwa kazi (safari, kitendo). **girder,** *n.* boriti, mhimili (ubao au chuma). **girdle,** *n.* mshipi, ukanda, mahazamu, masombo, ukumbuu; (*of beads*) kondavi, utunda. **girth,** *n.* kivimbe, uvimbe, mzingo, kizingo; (*in harness*) ukanda wa kufungia matandiko ya farasi, wa tumbo.
girl, *n.* kijana mwanamke, mtoto wa kike, msichana, kigori, mwanamwali; (*servant*) mtumishi kijana wa kike. **girlhood,** *n.* ujana (wa mwanamke). **girlish,** *a.* -a kitoto (cha kike).
girt = *girded,* taz. *gird.*
girth, *n.* taz. *gird.*
gist, *n.* maana, kiini cha habari, maana hasa.
give, *v.t.* (*p.t.* **gave,** *pf.t.* **given**) toa, -pa, lipa, jazi, kidhi, jalia, gawia; (*furnish*) fanyia; (*infect with*) ambukiza, eneza, (*hand over*) kabidhi, salimisha, wekea, tolea; (*concede*) achia; —*v.i.* (*slacken*) legea, bonyea; (*be elastic &c.*) nyumbuka. *Give a congratulatory present to,* pukusa. *Give oneself,* jitoa, jifunga, jiweka. *Be given to* (*drink &c.*) -wa mtu wa, elekea (kulewa *&c.*). *Be given to understand,* fahamishwa. *Give away,* toa zawadi, -pa sadaka; (*in marriage*) oza. *Give back,* rudisha, rejesha, rejeza, lipa. *Give birth to,* zaa. *Give*

chase to, fuata, winda. *Give ear to*, sikiliza. *Give forth* (*out*), toa, tangaza. *Give ground*, rudi, enda nyuma, shindwa. *Give the hand in marriage*, taz. *marry*. *Give in*, legea, shindwa. *Give the lie to*, kana, kanusha. *Give out*, isha, koma, -fa, legea; (*announce*) toa, tangaza; (*distribute*) gawanya, eneza. *Give over*, koma, isha. *Give place to*, ondokea. *Give trouble to*, sumbua, udhi. *Give up* (*surrender*), acha, toa; (*be beaten*) shindwa, kata tamaa, ruzu. *Give oneself up*, jitoa, kubali kushindwa, legea; (*surrender*) salimisha, toa. *Give way*, vunjika, katika, legea; shindwa; (*under pressure*) bonyea, nepa. *I will give it you* (*punish*), nitakuadhibu, nitakupiga, nitakurudi. **given**, *a. and conj.* -liotolewa &c. taz. *give*; (*granted, assuming*), ikiwa, iwapo, tukikubali ya kwamba, tukisema, tukipatana kwa; (*such and such*) fulani, -mojawapo maalum. **giver**, *n.* mpaji, mwenye kutoa, mtoaji. **giving**, *n.* upaji, kutoa &c.

gizzard, *n.* firigisi.

glacier, *n.* mto wa maji yaliyoganda kwa baridi, mto wa barafu. **glacial**, *a.* -a barafu.

glad, *a.* -a furaha, -kunjufu, -changamfu. **gladden**, *v.t.* furahisha, changamsha, teremesha;—*v.i.* furahi, changamka. **gladly**, *adv.* kwa furaha, kwa moyo. **gladness**, *n.* furaha, ukunjufu, uchangamfu, shangwe, nderemo. **gladsome**, *a.* furaha, -a kufurahisha, -a kuchangamsha.

glade, *n.* mahali peupe mwituni.

gladiator, *n.* mpiganaji aliyepigana na watu au wanyama katika michezo ya zamani ya Warumi.

gladly, *adv.*, **gladness**, *n.*, **gladsome**, *a.* taz. *glad.*

glamour, *n.* uzuri wa kudanganya (unaofanya mambo kuonekana yasivyo); (*sorcery*) uchawi, kiinimacho.

glance, *n.* tazamo, nadhari, konyezo, mtupo wa jicho (macho). — *v.t.* (*at*) tupia jicho, angalia kidogo, chungulia upesi; — *v.i.* (*glitter*) metameta, ng'aa; (*off*) piga na kugeuka upande. *Glance at* (*mention*), taja tu, nenea kidogo.

gland, *n.* sehemu ya mwili kama kifuko mnamofanyizwa maji yenye dawa yaingiayo damuni na kufanya kazi nyinginezo mwilini. *Swollen gland*, tezi; (*in groin*) mtoki, (*in throat*) makororo. **glanders**, *n.* ugonjwa wa wanyama wa kutoka kamasi nyingi. **glandular**, *a.* -a *gland.*

glare, *v.i.* ng'aa, ng'ariza; (*stare*) kodolea, kazia (macho). — *n.* mng'aro; tazamo la hasira (la ukali). **glaring**, *a.* -a kung'ara; (*evident*) wazi, dhahiri, -a kujulika na wote.

glass, *n.* kioo; (*for drinking*) bilauri; (*telescope*) darubini; (*spectacles*) miwani; (*as a measure*) kadiri ya bilauri; (*hour-glass*) shisha. **glass-paper**, *n.* msasa. **glassy**, *a.* -a kama kioo, -eupe, laini (kama kioo); (*lifeless*) baridi. **glaze**, *v.t.* tia kioo, paka rangi nyeupe inayong'aa (kama sahani na vikombe); — *v.i.* geuka kama kioo, yaani bila dalili ya uhai (kama macho ya mgonjwa au mtu kufani). **glazier**, *n.* fundi wa kutia kioo (madirishani &c.). **glazing**, *n.* kazi ya *glazier.*

gleam, *v.i.* ng'aa, mulika; (*reveal itself*) jionyesha; onekana. — *n.* kianga, kimeta, kimulimuli; (*sign*) dalili.

glean, *v.t. and i.* buga, bugabuga, okota masazo ya wavunaji, okota, kusanya (pata) kwa shida.

glebe, *n.* shamba lililowekwa wakf (kwa matumizi ya dini au maskini).

glee, *n.* furaha, shangwe, uchangamfu; (*in music*) wimbo ulioimbwa na watu kwa sauti zinazolingana.

gleet, *n.* ute utokao katika kidonda au uume.

glen, *n.* bonde dogo.

glib, *a.* -enye maneno mengi, -epesi wa kusema. *Glib speech*, maneno kama maji.

glide, *v.i.* pita (ingia, toka, enda) kwa mwendo laini (kama kwamba miguu haiendi), tiririka, nyinyirika, teleza, pita mbio kwa mwendo laini, enda kinyerenyere. **glider,** *n.* ya cropleni isiyo na mashine.

glimmer, *v.i.* mulika kidogo kidogo; (*flicker*) sinzia. — *n.* mwangaza (wa taa, mshumaa &c.) mdogo, kianga, kimeta, kimulimuli; (*of hope &c.*) kidogo, alama.

glimpse, *n.* tazamo la mara moja, kuona kwa mara moja kuona kidogo tu katika kupita.

glint, *v.i.* metameta, ng'aa. — *n.* kianga, kimulimuli.

glisten, *v.i.* zagaa, ng'aa, metameta.

glitter, *v.i.* metameta, ng'aa. — *n.* kimeta, wangavu, mng'arizo, mng'aro.

gloaming, *n.* jioni, karibu na wakati wa giza, utusitusi wa jioni.

gloat, *v.i.* (*over*) tazama (fikiri) kwa furaha; (*over another's misfortunes*) simanga, simbulia.

globe, *n.* kitu kilichoviringana pande zote kama chungwa, mpira, tufe; (*terrestrial*) mfano wa dunia; (*the earth*) dunia. **globe-fish,** *n.* bunju. **globe-trotter,** *n.* msafiri ugenini asiyeweza kutulia mahali. **globular,** *a.* -a kuviringana kama mpira. **globule,** *n.* mpira mdogo, gololi, tone.

gloom, *n.* giza, weusi, utusitusi; (*sorrow*) huzuni, majonzi, ghamu, uzito. **gloomy,** *a.* -a giza, -zito, -a huzuni &c.

glorify, *v.t.* tukuza, sifu, adhimisha, fahirisha, adhimu. **glorious,** *a.* -tukufu, -a fahari, -zuri mno, adhimu. **glory,** *n.* hali anayokaa Mungu na malaika; fahari, utukufu, sifa, adhama, uzuri, upeo wa usitawi (neema). *To go to glory,* kufa. *To be in one's glory,* kuwa katika kufanya unayopenda hasa. **glory-hole,** *n.* ghala.

glossary, *n.* orodha ya maneno na maelezo yake, kamusi.

gloss, *v.t.* ng'arisha; (*over a mistake &c.*) setiri, rahisisha. — *n.* mng'ao, kung'aa. **glossy,** *a.* -a kung'aa.

glove, *n.* mfuko wa mkono. *To be hand in glove,* kuwa rafiki sana na kusaidiana katika jambo.

glow, *v.i.* meka, -wa -ekundu (au -eupe) kwa joto bila kutoa ndimi za moto; metameta; (*feel warm &c.*) ona joto; (*with anger*) kasirika; (*pride*) jiona, takabari, ona kiburi; (*joy*) furahi. — *n.* mwangaza wa moto; kuona joto mwilini (kwa ajili ya afya, ya kuoga &c.); mng'ao. **glow-worm,** *n.* kimulimuli, kimetameta.

glower, *v.i.* tazama (kunja uso, kodolea macho) kwa hasira (chuki).

glow-worm, *n.* taz. *glow.*

glucose, *n.* sukari iliyo katika matunda na mimea.

glue, *n.* sherizi, gundi, embwe. — *v.t.* unga (ambatisha, kaza) kwa *glue.* **glutinous,** *a.* -a kunata.

glum, *a.* kimya kwa uzito wa moyo (kuudhika), -chungu.

glut, *v.t.* shibisha, kinaisha; peleka (fanyiza, toa) wingi kuliko inayohitajiwa. — *n.* wingi mno, shibe. **glutton,** *n.* mlafi. **gluttonous,** *a.* -lafi. *To eat gluttonously,* kula kwa pupa. **gluttony,** *n.* ulafi.

glutinous, *a.* taz. *glue.*

glutton, *n.,* **gluttonous,** *a.,* **gluttony,** *n.* taz. *glut.*

glycerine, *n.* ute mtamu mweupe kama maji, unaopatikana katika mafuta ya namna nyinginezo. Hutumika katika kufanyiza dawa &c.

gnarled, *a.* -a vinundunundu, -enye vifundo vingi (kama mti wa zamani), (*of character*) -chungu, -enye chuki.

gnash, *v.t.* (*teeth*) kereza (meno), saga (meno).

gnat, *n.* mdudu mdogo kama mbu.

gnaw, *v.t. and i.* tafuna, guguna, ng'ong'ona, ng'ota; (*torment &c.*) sumbua, udhi. **gnawing,** *n.* kutafuna, kuguguna; maumivu. — *a.* -a kuguguna, -a kuumiza, -a kusumbua.

gnome, *n.* zimwi, kizimwi.

gnu, *n.* nyumbu.

go, *v.i.* (*p.t.* **went,** *pf.t.* **gone**) enda; (*away*) enda zangu (zako, zake *&c.*), toka, ondoka; (*on or back*) endelea; (*tend*) elekea; (*intend*) taka, nuia, kusudia; (*perish, pass away*) pita, isha, potea, angamia; (*reach*) fika, fikia. *Go about,* zunguka; zurura, zururuka; (*attend to*) shika (kazi). *Go about it in the right way,* anza vizuri. *Go abroad,* tembea ugenini, safiri. *Go after,* fuata nyuma, fuatia, andamia; (*search for*) enda kutafuta. *Go against,* endea, enda kupiga, endea kwa shari; (*thwart*) zuia, kinga, pinga, topendeza. *Go along with you!* usifanye upuzi. *Go at,* jaribia. *Go back on a person,* tomsaidia mtu hali uliahidi. *Go bad,* oza, haribika. *Go bail for,* dhamini, -wa dhamini ya. *Go before,* tangulia, takadamu, sabiki. *Go by,* pita; (*copy*) fuata. *Go down,* zama, telemka, shuka, tua; (*decrease*) punguka, pungua; (*be acceptable*) pendeza, kubalika. *Go for* (*nothing*), uzwa rahisi, tokuwa na maana (thamani). *Go halves,* shiriki sawasawa (wawili); gawana nusu bi nusu. *Go hard* (*well, ill*); -wa shida (heri, shari). *Go in for,* tafuta sana, jitia katika, fanya bidii ya. *Go mad,* shikwa na wazimu, ingia wazimu. *Go off,* (*trap*) fyatuka, teguka, (*gun*) lia, piga; (*pass away*) pita, isha; (*happen*) -wa, jiri, fanyika. *Go off with,* toroka na, iba. *Go on,* endelea, enda mbele, tangulia, pita; (*continue*) fululiza, fuliza, ishi, dumu, shinda. *Go out,* toka; (*as lamp*) zimika. *Go over,* pita juu, vuka; (*examine*) angalia taratibu. *Go round* (*suffice for all*) enea, tosha. *Go shares,* shiriki. *Go through with,* maliza, timiliza, fikiliza. *Go to meet,* laki. *Go together* (*in company*), andamana, fuatana. *Go with* (*agree with*), patana na, agia, laiki. *Go without,* topata, kosa kupata. *Let go,* acha, fungua. *It is no go,* haifai neno. *He has no go,* hana moyo (bidii, juhudi). *He has gone out for the day,* amekwenda shinda mahali leo. *The matter is going off well,* jambo linasitawi. *Let's have a go at it,* ebu tujaribu. **go-ahead,** *a.* -enye bidii (nguvu), -enye nia ya kuendelea. **go-as-you-please,** *a.* bila taratibu, bila matengenezo ya mbele, bila kanuni. **go-by,** *n.* *Give you the go-by to,* ambaa, epukana na, piga chenga.

Goa, *n.* Goa.

goad, *n.* fimbo ya kuongozea ng'ombe, mchokoro; (*stimulus*) mchomo, mchocheo, kichocheo. — *v.t.* sukuma, ongoza kwa uchungu na nguvu, chochea, chomesha.

go-ahead, *a.* taz. *go.*

goal, *n.* kikomo, kifiko, mede, mwisho (wa mahali pa kushindania mbio); (*end, object*) mwisho, kusudi, nia, mradi, maarubu, madhumuni; (*in football*) mlango; (*score*) bao. **goal-keeper,** *n.* mlinda (mngoja) mlango. **goal-post,** *n.* mhimili (mwimo) wa mlango.

go-as-you-please, *a.* taz. *go.*

goat, *n.* mbuzi; (*he goat*) beberu, denge wa mbuzi. *Act* (*play*) *the* (*giddy*) *goat,* fanya upuzi. *Separate the sheep from the goats,* tenga watu wema na wabaya. *Get one's goat,* udhi, sumbua, kasirisha. **goat-biter,** *n.* (*a kind of black lizard*) kiumambuzi. **goatee,** *n.* ndevu kama za mbuzi. **goat-pepper,** *n.* pilipili.

gobble, *v.t. and i.* meza kwa pupa, -la kwa pupa; — *v.i.* gugumiza. **gobbler,** *n.* bata mzinga dume.

go-between, *n.* kijumbe; (*pander*) kawadi.

goblet, *n.* kopo la kunywea.

goblin, *n.* zimwi, kizimwi, jini, afriti, shetani.

go-by, *n.* taz. *go.*

God, *n.* Mungu, Mola; (*by Muhammadans only*) Allah. *God willing,* inshallah. *God be with you,* Mungu akuweke. *God forbid! God preserve us!* audhu bilahi! **godfather,** *n.* mdhamini (wa kiume) wa ubatizo. **God-fearing,** *a.* -chaji Mungu. **God-**

head, *n.* Uungu, Umungu. **godless,** *a. A godless person,* asiyejali (asiyeamini) Mungu, kafiri. **godlike,** *n.* kama Mungu, -a Kimungu, -ema mno. **godliness,** *n.* wema, utawa. **godly,** *a.* -tawa, -ema, -enye kushika dini. *A godly person,* mchaji Mungu. **godmother,** *n.* mdhamini (wa kike) wa ubatizo. **God-speed,** *n.* kwa heri, salamu, Allah bilheri.

go-down, *n.* ghala, bohari.

God-speed, *n.* taz. *god.*

goggle, *v.i.* kodolea macho (kwa mshangao, hofu &c.); (*of the eyes*) tokeza. **goggles,** *n.* miwani ya kuzuia mavumbi, miwani. **goggling,** *a.* (*of the eyes*) -a nje, -a kutokeza.

goitre, *n.* tezi.

gold, *n.* dhahabu; (*money*) fedha, mali, utajiri. — *a.* -a dhahabu. **gold-digger,** *n.* mchimbaji dhahabu. **gold-diggings,** *n.* mahali pa (shimo la) kuchimbua dhahabu. **golden,** *a.* -a dhahabu, kama dhahabu, -enye rangi ya dhahabu; (*precious*) -a thamani sana, -a tunu; (*surpassing*) -zuri mno, bora. *A golden opportunity,* nafasi ya kufaa sana, bahati kubwa. *Golden opinions,* sifa njema. *The golden age,* zamani za heri wanadamu walipokaa kwa amani na kufanikiwa. *The golden rule,* usia: Wafanyie wengine kama unavyotaka wakufanyie wewe. *Golden syrup,* asali ya miwa. **golden oriole,** *n.* mramba mweupe, kurumbizi. **gold-field,** *n.* mahali dhahabu inapochimbuliwa. **gold-finch,** *n.* namna ya ndege. **gold-fish,** *n.* namna ya samaki mdogo mwenye rangi ya dhahabu. **gold-smith,** *n.* mfua dhahabu, sonara.

golf, *n.* mchezo wa mipira midogo kupiga kwa fimbo za vingoe.

goloshes, *n.* viatu vya mpira vya kuvaa nje ya viatu vya kawaida kuzuia maji.

gondola, *n.* namna ya mashua ndefu.

gone, *pf.t.* ya *go.*

gong, *n.* upatu

gonorrhoea, *n.* kisonono.

good, *n.* wema, uzuri, hali njema, heri, faida. — *a.* -ema, bora, salihi, nakawa, -zuri; (*useful*) -a kufaa, -a maana, -enye manufaa, hodari; (*considerable*) -kubwa kidogo, -ingi kidogo; (*fine*) -zuri; (*true*) -a kweli; (*accurate*) halisi; (*sound*) -zima, -kamili, -zuri. *A good deal,* wingi, tele. *A good deal of work,* kazi nyingi kidogo. *A good many,* -ingi. *As good as,* kama, sawa na. *Be good for,* faa. *Be so good as to (go),* tafadhali sana (uende). *For good,* ndio mwisho, basi. *Good-bye,* kwa heri, alamsiki. *Hold good,* -wa na nguvu, -wako. *In good time,* mapema. *Make good,* thibitisha; (*repair*) tengeneza; (*repay*) lipa. *Think good,* ona radhi kwa, ridhia, kubali; (*resolve*) penda, kusudia, azimu. *To the good,* faida. *Good!* vyema! vema! haya! basi! inshallah! **good-breeding,** *n.* adabu, uungwana, jamala. **good-bye,** *int.* kwa heri, nakwenda (*I am going*). *Say good-bye to,* aga, agana na. **good-day,** *int.* jambo, salamu, sabalkheri. **good-for-nothing,** *a.* hafifu, dhaifu, ovyo, -nyangarika. **Good Friday,** *n.* taz. *Friday.* **good-humour,** *n.* wema, utu mwema, upole, ukunjufu, uchangamfu; (*patience*) saburi, uvumilivu; (*calmness*) utulivu, makini, utaratibu **good-luck,** *n.* bahati, sudi, heri, ndege njema. **goodly,** *a.* -ema, -kubwa, -zuri. **good-nature,** *n.* wema, utu wema, upole, makini, ukunjufu &c.; taz. *good-humour.* **goodness,** *n.* wema, uzuri, upaji, ufadhili, hisani, adili, maadili, latifu; (*strength, quality*) nguvu, utamu. **good-night,** *int.* kwa heri. *Go to bid good-night to,* tuesha. **goods,** *n.* mali; (*household*) vyombo (vya nyumbani), vikorokoro, vifaa; (*commercial*) bidhaa. **good-temper,** *n.* taz. *good-humour.* **goodwill,** *n.* hisani, ukarimu, uradhi, ridhaa, mapendezi, upendeleo; (*in trade*) sifa iliyopatikana kwa ustadi (bidii &c.).

goose, *n.* (*pl.* **geese**) bata Bukini;

(*Pigmy goose*) salili, bata; (*fool*) mjinga, baradhuli. *A wild goose chase*, kutafuta bure, kazi bure. **goose-flesh**, *n.* kimbimbi, msisimko, hali ya mwili kusisimka kwa baridi (hofu &c.). **goose-step**, *n.* namna ya kwenda kiaskari bila kukunja magoti. **gosling**, *n.* mtoto wa bata Bukini.

gooseberry, *n.* namna ya tunda dogo la kizungu.

goose-flesh, *n.*, **goose-step**, *n.* taz. *goose*.

Gordian, *a.* *To cut the Gordian knot*, kukata shauri kwa nguvu bila kujaribu taratibu.

gore, (1) *v.t.* guta, piga pembe (ng'ombe).

gore, (2) *n.* damu, mavilio ya damu. **gory**, *a.* -a damu, -enye kutiwa damu.

gore, (3) *n.* (*in garment*) kijambia, kiraka; (*under arm*) kikwapa.

gorge, *n.* koo, shingo, umio; (*pass*) bonde jembamba, genge, kipito kati ya milima mirefu. — *v.i.* -la kwa pupa, lafua, akia, jivimbisha; — *v.t.* shibisha, vimbisha kwa chakula kingi.

gorgeous, *a.* -zuri sana, -enye marembo (mapambo) mengi, -a kutazamisha (kwa uzuri wake).

gorilla, *n.* nyani mkubwa anayefanana na mtu.

gormand, *n.* mlafi. **gormandize**, *v.i.* lafua, -la sana, jivimbisha. **gormandizer**, *n.* mlafi.

gorse, *n.* mti wa kizungu wenye miiba na maua yenye rangi ya manjano.

gory, *a.* taz. *gore*, *n.* (1).

goshawk, *n.* (*East African*) kozi, kikozi.

gosling, *n.* taz. *goose*.

gospel, *n.* Injili, imani ya kikristo, msahafu wenye habari za Maisha ya Yesu Kristo; (*doctrine, tenets*) mafundisho, madhehebu; (*truth*) maneno ya hakika, kweli.

gossamer, *n.* nyuzi laini nyembamba; matando ya buibui wadogo; nguo kama shashi nyembamba sana.

gossip, *n.* maneno, maongezi, mazungumzo, dakizo, soga, porojo; (*foolish talk*) upuzi, maneno matupu, vijineno, maongezi hafifu, udaku; (*of persons*) mzungumzi, mpiga domo, mdaku. *Talk gossip, to detain with gossip*, puzisha. — *v.i.* ongea, piga domo, puzika, dakua.

got, *p.t. and pf.t.* ya *get*.

Goth, *n.* (*barbarian*) mshenzi, mjeuri. **Gothic**, *a.* (*architecture*) ujenzi wenye matao yenye pembe juu.

gouge, *n.* patasi, bobari, ukombo. — *v.t.* piga mfuo; (*out*) toa, ng'oa.

gourd, *n.* (*fruit*) boga, mumunya; (*vessel*) kitoma, buyu.

gourmand, *n.* mlafi, mpenda chakula kizuri. **gourmet**, *n.* mpenda chakula kizuri, mchaguzi, mteuzi wa chakula.

gout, *n.* jongo; (*drop*) tone (hasa la damu iliyoganda).

govern, *v.t.* tawala, miliki, hukumu; (*direct, control*) ongoza, zuia. **governess**, *n.* mwanamke mlezi wa watoto. **governing**, *a.* -enye kutawala (hukumu, amri, nguvu); (*supreme*) -kuu, -enye enzi. **government**, *n.* serikali, dola; (*control, power*) utawala, hukumu, amri; (*direction*) kuongoza, mwongozo, kuzuia; (*sphere of power*) nchi, ufalme, utawala, milki. **governor**, *n.* (*English word generally used*); (*Arabic*) liwali; (*director*) msimamizi, (*tutor*) mlezi; (*of machine*) mtambo unaorekebisha mwendo wa mashine; (*father*) baba (mzazi).

gown, *n.* vazi la kike la kizungu, teitei; vazi kama joho la walimu, wana sheria, jaji &c.

grab, *v.* nyakua, pokonya, shika ghafula (kwa pupa), nyang'anya.

grace, *n.* (*elegance*) uzuri, madaha, madahiro, matuko, umbuji, adabu; (*kindness*) hisani, mapenzi, upendeleo, huruma, rehema; (*of God*) neema, rehema, majaliwa, huruma; (*sanction, permission*) ruhusa, achilio; (*prayer at meals*) sala (ya kushukuru chakulani); (*as form of address*) jina la heshima la kiingereza la kumtaja *Duke* au *Archbishop*. *Means of grace*, njia za kupata neema ya Mungu. *To say grace*, kushukuru chakulani. *With a good grace*, vizuri, kwa moyo. *With a bad grace*, vibaya, kwa chuki (uchungu). *Good graces*, upendeleo, upenzi. — *v.t.* sitawisha, stahilisha, pendekeza. **graceful**, *a.* -zuri, -enye madaha. **gracefully**, *adv.* kwa madaha, dalji. **graceless**, *a.* -baya, -bovu. **gracious**, *a.* -enye neema, -a rehema; (*beneficient*) -enye hisani, -fadhili, -enye mapendezi. **graciously**, *adv.* kwa hisani (huruma, neema, rehema &c.).

gradate, *v.t.* panga kwa taratibu hata tofauti baina vitu vilivyopangwa haionekani sana. **gradation**, *n.* daraja, utaratibu. **grade**, *n.* cheo, daraja, jinsi; (*slope*) mshuko, mtelemko, kadiri ya kushuka au kupanda (kusitawi au kupooza). — *v.t.* panga jamii (kundi, chungu &c.) kwa kadiri ya ujuzi (ukubwa, udogo, cheo, kipimo &c.); kuza (zidisha uzuri &c.) ng'ombe na mifugo kwa mbegu nzuri zaidi; (*a road*) sawazisha, punguza vilima. **gradient**, *n.* mtelemko, mshuko, kadiri ya kushuka au kupanda. **gradual**, *a.* kidogo kidogo, -a taratibu, -a polepole, punde kwa punde. **gradually**, *adv.* kwa taratibu, polepole, kidogo kidogo. **graduate**, *v.t.* gawanya (panga) kwa cheo (uzuri &c.), tia alama ya kuonyesha cheo &c.; — *v.i.* (*get a degree*) pata daraja katika cheo kikubwa (*University*). — *n.* mwenye daraja katika chuo kikubwa (*University*).

graft, (1) *n.* chipukizi ya mti (iliyotiwa shinani mwa mti mwingine, iliyopandikizwa kwa mti usio wake). — *v.t.* pandikiza ((chipukizi katika mti usio wake).

graft, (2) *n.* fedha za rushwa, rushwa, udanganyifu.

grain, *n.* nafaka, mbegu; (*unripe*) tete; (*single grain*) punje; (*of sand &c.*) chembe, uvumbi; (*small quantity*) kidogo, kipimo kidogo sana; (*of wood &c.*) nyuzi; (*of marble*) marembo. *In the grain*, asili, maumbile. *Against the grain*, vigumu, haipendezi. *Go against the grain*, chukiza, tia uchungu, kasirisha. *Take it with a grain of salt*, sadiki kidogo tu. **granivorous**, *a.* -laji nafaka.

graminivorous, *a.* -laji majani.

grammar, *n.* sarufi, nahau, elimu ya kazi na matumizi ya maneno. **grammatical**, *a.* -a kufuata sheria (kanuni) za sarufi, sahihi.

gramme, *n.* kipimo cha uzito, gramme 353 = *ounce*.

gramophone, *n.* (*usu.* gramofoni), semakweli, santuri.

grampus, *n.* mnyama mkubwa wa bahari kama pomboo. *Snore like a grampus*, koroma kwa sauti kubwa.

granary, *n.* ghala ya nafaka.

grand, *a.* -kubwa, -kuu, -a fahari, -tukufu, -zuri, bora, -enye cheo, -a heshima, -sharifu. **grandchild**, *n.* mjukuu. *Great-grandchild*, kitukuu, kilembwe. *Great-great-grandchild*, kining'ina. **grand duke**, *n.* mfalme wa nchi ndogo fulani. **grandee**, *n.* mtu wa cheo, mkuu, mtu wa fahari. **grandeur**, *n.* fahari, ukuu, utukufu, usherehe, adhama. **grandfather**, *n.* babu; (*ancestor*) mzee. **grandiloquent**, *a.* -a kujivuna (maneno), -a kupiga domo. **grandiose**, *a.* -a sherehe, -tukufu; (*in bad sense*) -a kujivuna. **grandmother**, *n.* bibi, mzee. **great-grandmother**, *n.* mzaa bibi. **grandsire**, *n.* babu, mzee.

granite, *n.* namna ya jiwe gumu sana.

granny, *n.* kizee, bibi (mzaa baba au mama).

granivorous, *a.* taz. *grain*.

grant, *v.t.* -pa, jalia, ruzuku, toa, kidhi, lipa; (*allow, acquiesce in*) kubali, ridhia, achia. *Granted that they differ*, hata na waachane. *Granted that &c.* ikiwa, ijapokuwa, hata tukisema ya kwamba, iwapo. *Grant request*, fanya haja, kidhi (timiza) haja. — *n.* ruhusa, mlipo, kıpaji, zawadi, karama; (*bestowal*) kutoa, kulipa; (*of money*) fedha iliyotolewa kwa makusudi maalum. **grantee**, *n.* mwenye kupewa. **grantor**, *n.* mwenye kupa, mtoa.

granular, *a.* -a chembe (punje), -a kama chembe (punje), -a kinundu-nundu. **granulate**, *v.t. and i.* fanya kama chembe (punje, mchanga mnene). **granulated**, *a.* -a chembe-chembe. **granule**, *n.* chembe, punje.

grape, *n.* zabibu; (*vine*) mzabibu. *Sour grapes*, kusema kitu hakina thamani (si kizuri) kwa sababu hakipatikani. **grape-fruit**, *n.* balungi; (*tree*) mbalungi. **grape-shot**, *n.* marisaa makubwa.

graph, *n.* mwandiko wa mistari na matao kuonyesha mabadiliko (ulinganifu &c.) ya mambo, *e.g.* joto la jua linavyozidi au kupungua kutwa &c. **-graph**, *suffix*, -a kuhusu kuandika (mwandiko).

graphic, *a.* -a kueleza (kukolea, kusimulia, kufahamisha, kuonyesha) vizuri.

graphite, *n.* kinywe, namna ya jiwe jororo jeusi linalotumika kufanyizia kalamu za kuandikia (si za wino).

grapnel, *n.* nanga ndogo ya makombe manne, nanga toto au ya parua; (*hook*) kulabu.

grapple, *v.t.* kamatana, shikana; shika sana, jitia kwa, jifunga kwa; (*hook*) pemba, bemba.

grasp, *v.t.* shika, fumbata; (*understand*) fahamu -ote, sikia sana. — *n.* kushika kwa mkono, mkono; (*power*) nguvu, uwezo; (*comprehension*) ufahamu, akili. **grasping**, *a.* -choyo, -kabidhi, -bahili.

grass, *n.* majani; (*coarse, rushy*) nyasi, unyasi; (*soft creeping*) ukoka. *Go to grass*, pumzika kwa muda. **grasshopper**, *n.* panzi, funutu. **grass-plot**, *n.* uwanja wa majani mafupi. **grass widow**, *n.* mwanamke ambaye mume wake amesafiri kwa muda. **grassy**, *a.* -enye majani mengi.

grate, (1) *v.i* paruza, kwaruza, lia kwa kuparuza; — *v.t.* (*rub small*) saga, chua, sugua; (*of coco-nut*) kuna. *Grate on*, chukiza. **grater**, *n.* (*for coco-nuts*) mbuzi. **grating**, *a.* -enye mparuzo, -a kuparuza; (*unpleasing*) -a kuchukiza. — *n.* mparuzo, kwaruzo, sauti (mlio) wa kuparuza.

grate, (2) *n.* fito za chuma za kuwekea moto jikoni. **grating**, *n.* kiunzi cha fito (za chuma) zinazokingamana.

grateful, *a.* -a kushukuru, -enye shukrani; (*pleasant*) -tamu, -a kupendeza. **gratefully**, *adv.* kwa furaha. **gratification**, *n.* furaha; (*giving pleasure*) mapendezi; (*contentment*) uradhi, ridhaa; (*accomplishment*) kupata, kutimiza, timizo. *It gave him much gratification*, ilimpendeza sana. **gratify**, *v.t.* pendeza, furahisha, anisi, ridhisha, tosheleza. **gratifying**, *a.* -a kupendeza (kufurahisha, kuridhisha) sana. **gratitude**, *n.* shukrani.

grater, *n.* taz. *grate* (1).

gratification, *n.*, **gratify**, *v.*, **gratifying**, *a.* taz. *grateful.*

grating, *a.* and *n.* taz. *grate* (1).

gratis, *adv.* bure, bilashi, pasipo faida, pasipo malipo, bila gharama.

gratuitous, *a.* -a bure, bilashi, pasipo faida, bila malipo, bila kisa (sababu). **gratuity**, *n.* zawadi, bakshishi; (*customary*) ada, kilemba, ufito &c.

gratitude, *n.* taz. *grateful.*

gratuitous, *a.*, **gratuity**, *n.* taz. *gratis.*

grave, (1) *a.* -zito, -a taratibu; (*important, critical*) -kubwa, -a mashaka, -a hatari. *A grave offence*, kosa kubwa. **gravitate**, *v.i.* elekea, taka kwenda, vutwa. **gravitation**, *n.* uzito; (*attraction*) uvutano. **gravity**, *n.* uzito; (*sobriety*) utaratibu; (*importance*) ukubwa, habari kubwa, maana, nyingi; (*critical state*) hatari, mashaka. *Specific gravity*, uzito wa kitu kulingana na ule wa maji. *Centre of gravity*, palipo uzito hasa.

grave, (2) *n.* kaburi, ziara; (*place of*

dead) ahera, kuzimu. *Have one foot in the grave*, chungulia kuzimu. **grave-digger**, *n*. mchimba kaburi. **graveyard**, *n*. makaburini, mava.
gravel, *n*. changarawe, mawe madogo, vijiwe.
graven, *a*. -liochorwa, -lionakishiwa.
graveyard, *n*. taz. *grave* (2).
graving-dock, *n*. gadi, jahabu, mahali meli zinapotolewa katika maji ili zisafishwe chini.
gravitate, *v*., **gravitation**, *n*., **gravity**, *n*. taz. *grave* (1).
gravy, *n*. mchuzi, rojorojo.
gray, *a*. taz. *grey*.
graze, (1) *v.t.* (*rub*) paruza, chubua kidogo. — *n*. paruza, chubuko dogo.
graze, (2) *v.t.* (*feed cattle*) lisha, chunga (ng'ombe, mbuzi *&c.*); — *v.i.* (*eat grass*) -la majani. **grazier**, *n*. mchungaji. **grazing**, *n*. malisho.
grease, *n*. mafuta, shahamu (*for caulking*) bereu, deheni; (*adhering to pan &c.*) uge, ugea. — *v.t.* paka (tia) mafuta. **greasy**, *a*. -enye mafuta; (*slippery*) -a matelezi, -a kuteleza.
great, *a*. -kubwa, -kuu, bora, -ingi, -a nguvu, adhimu. *Become great*, (*of persons*) tukuka; (*of things*) kua. *A great deal*, wingi. *A great deal of rain*, mvua nyingi. *It is too great for me*, imenikulia. *Great-grandfather*, baba mzazi wa babu. *Great-grandmother*, mama mzazi wa bibi. **greater**, *a*. -kubwa (zaidi, kuliko). **greatest**, *a*. -a kubwa (kupita -ote). **greatly**, *adv*. sana. **greatness**, *n*. ukuu, ukubwa, utukufu, nguvu, adhama.
greaves, *n*. vyuma vya kuvaa kulinda miundi ya miguu.
grebe, *n*. (*little*) kibisi.
Grecian, *a*. taz. *Greek*.
greed, *n*. choyo, tamaa, ulafi, pupa, roho, tutuo. **greedily**, *adv*. kwa choyo (ulafi, pupa *&c.*). **greediness**, *n*. choyo, ulafi, tamaa *&c.* **greedy**, *a*. -lafi, -enye choyo, -enye tamaa. *Be greedy*, -la kwa pupa, -wa na roho, -wa na choyo, fanya tamaa.

Greek, *n*. *and a*. Mgiriki, Giriki; (*ancient*) Myunani. **Grecian**, *a*. -a kigiriki; (*ancient*) -a kiyunani.
green, *a*. -a rangi ya majani, kijani kibichi, chanikiwiti; (*unripe*) -bichi; (*simple*) -zuzu, -jinga. — *n*. rangi ya majani (kijani kibichi). **greengage**, *n*. tunda la kizungu kidogo kama embe dogo. **greengrocer**, *n*. mwuza mboga na matunda. **greenhorn**, *n*. mzuzu, mjinga. **greenhouse**, *n*. nyumba ya kuotesha maua na matunda. **greenness**, *n*. kuwa *green*. **greens**, *n*. mboga.
greet, *v.t.* salimu, salimia, amkia, pokea (kwa furaha, vifijo, huzuni *&c.*); (*with excessive humility*) kongowea. **greeting**, *n*.salamu, maamkizi. **greeting**! salaam! jambo!
gregarious, *a*. -enye kukaa (au kupenda kukaa) makundi makundi (wengi pamoja).
grenade, *n*. kombora dogo. **grenadier**, *n*. askari (wa kikosi au jeshi fulani).
grew, *p.t.* ya *grow*.
grey, *a*. -a kijivu, rangi ya majivu, -eupe, -eupe kidogo; (*of weather*) -a mawingu; (*dreary*) bila furaha, -zito, -a huzuni. **greybeard**, *n*. mwenye mvi, mzee. **grey-haired**, *a*. -enye nywele za mvi.
greyhound, *n*. namna ya mbwa mrefu mwembamba mwenye mbio sana.
grid, *n*. chombo cha fito za chuma kukaangia nyama; kiunzi cha fito (za chuma) zinazokingamana; (*electric*) kiunzi kidogo cha nyuzi za chuma *&c.* zinazokingamana kinachotumika katika simu za upepo.
griddle, *n*. kama *grid*; kikaango.
gridiron, *n*. namna ya kikaango.
grief, *n*. sikitiko, huzuni, ghamu, majonzi, kibuhuti, kihoro. *Come to grief*, umia, potea, angamia, pata hasara (maumivu *&c.*). **grievance**, *n*. jambo zito, dhulumu; (*complaint*) kisa, nung'uniko. **grieve**, *v.t.* sikitisha, huzunisha, udhi, tia huzuni (majonzi); — *v.i.* sikitika, -wa na

huzuni (majonzi), fanya msiba (majonzi). **grievous**, *a.* -zito, -gumu, -a kutia kuzua, -a kulemea.

griffin, *n.* mnyama (wa hadithi) mwenye mwili wa simba na kichwa na mabawa ya tai.

grill, *n.* chombo cha fito za chuma cha kuchomea nyama, samaki *&c.*; nyama, samaki *&c.* iliyochomwa. — *v.t.* choma (nyama, samaki *&c.*); — *v.i.* pigwa na joto (jua) kali.

grille, *n.* dirisha dogo lenye fito zilizokingamana.

grim, *a.* -kali, -katili, -korofi; (*ghastly*) -a kutia hofu, -a kuogofya; (*sullen*) -shupavu, -gumu.

grimace, *v.i.* finya (kunja) uso. — *n.* finyo (kunjo) la uso, kicheko.

grime, *n.* masizi, taka, uchafu.

grimy, *a.* -enye taka, -chafu, -enye masizi.

grin, *v.i.* toa meno (kwa kucheka), cheka kipumbavu, finya (kunja) uso. — *n.* kicheko (cha kipumbavu), kufinya uso, finyo la uso.

grind, *v.t.* (*pt. and pf.t.* **ground**) (*grain*) saga, chua; (*coarsely*) paaza; (*to fine powder*) tikita; *tools &c. by rubbing, filing &c.*) chua, noa; (*oppress*) onea; dhulumu; (*the teeth*) kereza (gwaraza), saga (meno); (*cram, coach &c.*) fundisha kwa bidii; — *v.i.* (*work hard*) shikilia kazi, soma kwa bidii; (*be capable of being ground*) sagika. *Grind down*, saga tikita; (*a knife &c.*) noa; (*oppress &c.*) onea, dhulumu, taabisha. — *n.* kazi ngumu, kazi ya taabu. **grinder**, *n.* msaga, kisaga; (*tooth*) chego, gego.

grindstone, *n.* jiwe la kunolea, kinoo, cherehe; (*for grinding grain*) kijaa. *Keep one's nose to the grindstone*), jishurutisha kufanya kazi.

grip, *v.t.* shika (kamata) sana, pelekea kucha. — *n.* kushika (kukamata) sana (kwa mkono, makucha); mikono, makucha. **gripe**, *v.t.* kama *grip*; tia maumivu tumboni, umiza tumbo. **gripes**, *n.* maumivu ya tumboni, kushikwa tumbo, sokoto la tumboni.

grisly, *a.* -a kutisha, -a kuogofya.

grist, *n.* nafaka ya kusagwa.

gristle, *n.* ufupa mwororo.

grit, *n.* mchanga, changarawe; (*courage*) moyo mgumu, uthabiti, ushupavu, bidii. *He has no grit*, hana moyo, yu mkulifu, yu mwepesi kushindwa. — *v.i.* fanya sauti ya kukwaruza; (*teeth*) kereza (meno).

gritty, *a.* -a kukwaruza, -enye mchanga (changarawe).

grizzle, *v.i.* (hasa huhusu watoto) lialia, nung'unika bila kuacha.

grizzled, *a.* -enye mvi, -a kijivu.

groan, *v.i.* ugua, piga kite. *Groan at* (*down*), zomea, zuma. — *n.* mauguzi, kuugua, kite, mlio wa huzuni (maumivu, taabu), zomeo, kuzomea.

grocer, *n.* mwuza vyakula. **groceries**, *n.* vyakula na vitu kama sabuni *&c.*

grog, *n.* kileo, ulevi. **groggy**, *a.* -dhaifu, hafifu, goigoi.

groin, *n.* manena, kinena.

groom, *n.* mchunga farasi, saisi; (*bridegroom*) bwana arusi. — *v.t.* (*horse*) sugua, safisha, chana; (*persons*) fanya nadhifu, katua. *A well-groomed man*, mtu nadhifu.

groove, *n.* mfuo; (*routine*) desturi. — *v.t.* tia (kata) mfuo.

grope, *v.i.* tafuta kwa kupapasa (kama kipofu, au mtu gizani), papasa, sitasita; (*in the dark*) tutusa.

gross, *a.* -baya sana, -chafu; (*thick*) -nene (*dull*) -zito. *Gross amount*, jumla bila kupunguzwa. *Gross weight*, ghafi. — *n.* jumla ya mia moja arobaini na nne (144).

grotesque, *a.* -a kigeni hata kuchekesha.

grotto, *n.* kipango, pango.

ground, (1) *v. p.t. and pf.t.* ya *grind*.

ground, (2) *n.* nchi; (*soil*) ardhi, udongo; (*bottom*) chini; (*land*) shamba, konde, kiwanja, uwanja; (*foundation*) chimbuko, msingi; (*source*) asili, mwanzo; (*sediment*) takataka za chini, tama; (*reason, principle*) sababu, hoja, kisa, tegemeo. *Gain ground,* endelea, enea zaidi. *Loss or give ground,* rudi, shindwa, punguka. *Stand one's ground,* simama, kita, jiweka imara, tokubali kushindwa. — *v.t.* weka imara; (*give reason for*) toa sababu (kisa, hoja) ya; (*teach rudiments*) fundisha mianzo ya elimu, fundisha vyema; (*arms*) weka chini, shusha, telemsha; — *v.i.* (*run ashore*) pwelewa, kwama, panda mwambani. **ground-floor,** *n.* vyumba vya chini. **groundless,** *a.* pasipo sababu, -a bure, -a upuzi, -tupu. **ground-nuts,** *n.* (*hard*) njugu mawe; (*pea-nuts*) njugu nyasa. **ground-rent,** *n.* kodi ya kiwanja. **grounds,** *n.* mashapo, mashata, taka. **ground-swell,** *n.* mawimbi ya mkoba, kwelea ya mawimbi. **groundwork,** *n.* msingi, asili, chimbuko, mwanzo, mlango.

group, *n.* jamii, kundi, mkutano, fungu; (*cultivating together*) chaa. *So and so's group,* umati wa fulani, akina fulani. — *v.t.* panga jamii jamii *&c.*, ainisha, gawanya mafungu mafungu; — *v.i.* kusanyika jamii (kundi) pamoja.

grouse, (1) *n.* namna ya ndege anayewindwa Ulaya.

grouse, (2) *v.i.* nung'unika.

grove, *n.* kichaka, miti mingi kidogo mahali pamoja.

grovel, *v.i.* tambaa, lala kifudifudi; (*abase oneself*) nyenyekea, jifanya, -nyonge, jidhili.

grow, *v.i.* (*p.t.* **grew,** *pf.t.* **grown**) kua; (*of plants*) ota, mea; (*become*) pata kuwa, -wa; (*increase*) zidi, ongezeka; (*become more and more*) zidi kuwa; (*spread, advance*) endelea, enea, fanikiwa; — *v.t.* (*cultivate*) otesha, panda, lima. *Be grown over,* melewa. *Grow old,* konga, chakaa. *Grow small* (*less*), pungua. *Grow up,* komaa, pevuka, -wa zima. *Grow out of,* toka kwa, -wa sababu ya. *Let the hair grow,* kalia nywele. *Cause to grow,* otesha, meesha, kuza. **grown up,** *a.* -zima. *Grown ups,* watu wazima. **growth,** *n.* kuzidi, maendeleo, eneo, kukua, ukuzi kutoa; (*vegetation*) woto, mmea; (*outcome*) mwisho, matokeo.

growl, *v.i.* nguruma, vuma, koroma; (*complain*) nuna, guna, janga, nung'unika. — *n.* ngurumo, uvumi, mvumo, maguno, manung'uniko.

grown, *v.*, **growth,** *n.* taz. *grow.*

grub, *n.* mdudu, funza, buu, jana; (*slang*) chakula. — *v.t.* pekua, (*grub about*) chimbachimba; (*grub up*) ng'oa, fukua; — *v.i.* (*drudge*) fanya kazi ya taabu; (*about*) tafutatafuta; (*dig*) chimbachimba. **grubby,** *a.* wadudu (mafunza, mabuu); -chafu, -enye taka.

grudge, *v.t.* husudu, hasidi, onea kijicho kwa unyimivu (kwa sababu ya husuda, kijicho, chuki), sunza. — *n.* chukio la siri, inadi, ugomvi wa kale, fundo (mfundo wa, kifundo cha) la roho, kinyongo, undani, nongwa. *Bear a grudge against,* kamia, onea chuki. **grudgingly,** *adv.* kwa unyimivu, kinyiminyimi, kwa husuda (chuki).

gruel, *n.* uji; (*of rice*) mashendea, uji wa mapande; (*of milk and maize flour*) faluda; (*spiced*) fuka (*of wheat flour*) kikaimati; (*thin*) ubwabwa. *Have* (*get, take*) *one's gruel,* adhibishwa sana. *Give a man his gruel,* mwadhibisha. — *v.t.* adhibisha vikali, taabisha, tendea vikali. **gruelling,** *a.* -kali, gumu, -a taabu.

gruesome, *a.* -a kutisha, -a kuogofya, -a kuchukiza.

gruff, *a.* (*voice, manner*) -kali.

grumble, *v.i.* nuna, nung'unika, guna, janga; (*rumble*) nguruma, vuma. **grumbler,** *n.* mnuni, mnung'unikaji. **grumbling,** *n.* kununa *&c.*; mnuno, nung'uniko; ngurumo, mvumo.

grumpy, *a.* -a kasirani, -enye hasira, -a harara, -chuki.

grunt, *v.i.* guna, koroma.

guano, *n.* taka za ndege wa bahari zinazotumika kama mbolea au samadi.

guarantee, *v.t.* (*a debt*) hawili; (*a*

work) diriki, tadariki, dhamini, jukumu; (*assure*) hakikisha, thibitisha; (*give pledge or assurance*) toa hakika (dhamana, rehani, daraka), ahidi. — *n.* dhamana, stakabadhi, masharti, amana, rehani, daraka, ahadi.

guard, *n.* mlinzi; (*conductor*) msimamizi; (*caution*) hadhari; (*protecting thing*) kinga, kitu cha kukingia au kulindia. *Be on one's guard,* jihadhari, -wa na hadhari, kaa macho. *Be off one's guard,* toangalia, sinzia. *Be on guard,* shika kingojo, fanya zamu, ngoja. *Mount guard,* shika zamu (kingojo). — *v.t.* linda, tunza, hifadhi, ngojea; zuia, kinga. *Guard against,* kinga, epuka kwa hadhari. **guarded,** *a.* -a hadhari, -angalifu. **guard-house,** *n.* korokoni, mahabusi. **guardian,** *n.* mlinzi, mlezi. **guardianship,** *n.* ulinzi, ulezi, ukabidhi. **guard-room,** *n.* korokoni.

guava, *n.* (*tree*) mpera; (*fruit*) pera.

gubernatorial, *a.* -a *governor,* -a kuhusu *governor.*

gudgeon, *n.* namna ya samaki za mitoni.

guerdon, *n.* zawadi, tuzo, malipo.

guerilla, *n.* mapigano (vita) ya watu wasio askari hasa.

guess, *v.t.* kisi, bahatisha; (*think*) ona, dhani; — *v.i.* bahatisha. — *n.* kisio, dhana, bahatisho, neno la kukisi. **guesswork,** *n.* kisio tu, dhana tu.

guest, *n.* mgeni, mtu aliyekaribishwa.

guffaw, *n.* cheko kubwa. — *v.i.* cheka kwa sauti kubwa.

guide, *n.* kiongozi, rubani, mkurugenzi, mwongozi; (*directing object*) alama, kitu cha kuelekezea &c.; (*book, instruction*) maelezo, maongezi, mwongozo. — *v.t.* ongoza, elekeza, onyesha njia.

guild, *n.* chama, ushirika wa watu (kwa biashara, kusaidiana &c.).

guile, *n.* ujanja, werevu, hila. **guileful,** *a.* -enye hila, -erevu, -janja. **guileless,** *a.* -nyofu.

guillotine, *n.* mashine yenye kisu cha kukata watu vichwa (cha kukata kurasa za vitabu). — *v.t.* kata kichwa.

guilt, *n.* hatia, uovu, dhambi, kosa, janaha, jinaya. *He is guilty,* amekosa, amevunja sheria. **guilty,** *a.* -enye hatia, -kosefu, -a dhambi.

guinea, *n.* sarafu ya dhahabu yenye thamani ya shilingi ishirini na moja, shilingi ishirini na moja. **guinea-corn,** *n.* mtama. **guinea-fowl,** *n.* (*crested*) kororo; (*helmeted*) kanga.

guise, *n.* sura, umbo, vao, mwendo.

guitar, *n.* gambusi, udi, zeze (yenye nyuzi sita).

gulf, *n.* hori, ghuba; (*cavity*) shimo kubwa.

gull, (1) *n.* shakwe, membe.

gull, (2) *n.* (*simpleton*) mjinga, mzuzu, baradhuli. — *v.t.* danganya, ghilibu, kopa, laghai, punja. **gullible,** *a.* -jinga, -zuzu, -a kudanganywa kwa urahisi.

gullet, *n.* umio, koo.

gully, *n.* mvo, mvo mkavu, korongo, mfereji.

gulp, *v.t.* gugumiza; (*gulp down*) meza upesi, akia. — *n.* mkupuo.

gum, (1) *n.* (*of teeth*) ufizi, sine. *Rub child's gums to aid teething,* nunuza. **gumboil,** *n.* kijipu cha ufizi.

gum, (2) *n.* (*gum Arabic*) sumughu; (*copal*) sandarusi; (*paste &c.*) gundi; (*sticky stuff, birdlime &c.*) ulimbo, ulimbolimbo, ambo. **gummy,** *a.* -a gundi &c.; -enye gundi &c., -a kunata.

gumption, *n.* akili, busara.

gun, *n.* bunduki; (*cannon*) mzinga. *Double barrelled,* bunduki ya midomo (kasiba, mitutu) miwili. *Matchlock,* bunduki ya mrao. *Muzzle-loader,* bunduki ya fataki (ya kushindiliwa). *Breech-loader,* bunduki ya korofindo, ya viasi (ya kuvunja). *Flint gun,* bunduki ya jiwe (y gumegume). **gun-barrel,** *n.* mtutu, kasiba, mwanzi. **gunboat,** *n.* manowari ndogo. **gun-cap,** *n.* fataki. **gun-carriage,** *n.* magurudumu ya mzinga. **gun-cotton,** *n.* baruti ya pamba. **gun-lock,** *n.* mtambo, kitasa cha bunduki. **gunner,** *n.* mkuu wa mzinga, mtu wa mzinga. **gunpowder,** *n.* baruti. **gun-running,** *n.* kuingiza bunduki katika nchi bila ruhusa (inapokatazwa, inapopigwa marufuku). **gunshot,** *n.* mpigo wa bunduki. **gunsmith,** *n.* fundi wa kufua bunduki.

gunny, *n.* gunia.

gunpowder, *n.*, **gun-running,** *n.*, **gunshot,** *n.*, **gunsmith,** *n.* taz. *gun.*

gunwale, *n.* ubao wa mbavuni mwa chombo juu.

gurgle, *v.i.* lia kama maji kooni, lia guruguru, gugumia. — *n.* mlio wa maji kooni, guruguru.

gush, *v.i.* (*of water*) bubujika, foka, toka kwa nguvu, churuzika; (*talk too much*) toa maneno mengi. — *n.* mkondo; (*outburst*) bubujiko, shindo, (*abundance*) wingi. **gushing,** *a.* -a kutokota, -a kububujika, -a kufoka, -a kujiajia; (*talkative*) -a maneno mengi.

gusset, *n.* upapi wa nguo, kijambia, kiraka; (*under arm*) kikwapa.

gust, *n.* (*of wind*) mkondo wa upepo, upepo wa ghafula, dhoruba. *A gust of passion,* hamaki, harara, hasira ya ghafula, kishindo.

gusto, *n.* furaha, pupa.

gut, *n.* tumbo, uzi wa utumbo. *He has no guts,* hana moyo, yu mwoga. — *v.t.* (*remove guts*) tumbua; (*destroy &c.*) teka, komba, haribu, angamiza.

gutta-percha, *n.* mpira.

gutter, *n.* mchirizi, mlizamu, mrizabu, kopo; (*lowest environment &c.*) unyonge, kinyonge, umaskini. — *v.i.* chururika, churuzika, tiririka. **guttersnipe,** *n.* mtoto mnyonge achezaye barabarani asiye na adabu, mtoto wa kikopo, mhuni.

guttural, *a.* (sauti) -a kooni (kama sauti ya *gh* katika ghafula &c.).

guy rope, *n.* kamba ya kukazia (kuimarishia &c.).

guzzle, *v.t. and i.* gugumiza, -la (kunywa) kwa pupa; — *v.i.* lafua.

gymkhana, *n.* kiwanja cha kuchezea michezo kama mpira &c.

gymnasium, *n.* chumba au kiwanja cha michezo ya kuzoeza viungo vya mwili. **gymnast,** *n.* fundi wa michezo ya (juhudi) kuzoeza viungo vya mwili. **gymnastics,** *n.* mazoezi ya viungo vya mwili, juhudi.

gynaecology, *n.* elimu ya magonjwa ya wanawake.

gypsum, *n.* jasi, jiwe kama chaki.

gypsy, *n.* taz. *gipsy.*

gyrate, *v.i.* zunguka. **gyration,** *n.* mzunguko. **gyratory,** *a.* -a kuzungukazunguka. **gyroscope,** *n.* gurudumu zito ambalo linapozunguka upesi hukaa mahali pale pale na kwa hiyo huweza kuzuia eropleni, meli &c. zisisukesuke sana.

gyves, *n. pl.* pingu.

H

ha! *int.* (kuonyesha furaha, mshangao, huzuni, mshtuko), lo! ehe! ama! salale! masalale! *&c.*

haberdasher, *n.* mwuza nguo, uzi, sindano *&c.*

habiliments, *n.* mavazi, nguo.

habit, *n.* mazoea, desturi, kazi, ibada, tabia, ada, hali; (*dress*) vazi, nguo. **habitual**, *a.* -a mazoea, -zoevu, -a desturi, -a ibada, -a kawaida. **habitually**, *adv.* kwa desturi (kawaida). **habituate**, *v.t.* zoeza.

habitable, *a.* -a kukaa watu, -a kukalika na watu. *Be habitable*, kalika, kalikana. **habitation**, *n.*, **habitat**, *n.* kikao, makao, makazi, masikani, kitende, chengo, mastakimu, kaya.

habitual, *a.*, **habitually**, *adv.*, **habituate**, *v.* taz. *habit.*

hack, (1) *v.t.* katakata, tema, chonga, keketa; (*kick*) piga teke. — *n.* pigo. *Hacking cough*, kukohoa kwa nguvu.

hack, (2) *n.* (*horse*) farasi wa kazi; (*drudge*) mtu aliyeajiriwa kufanya kazi ya taabu (ya kutaabisha). **hackneyed**, *a.* -liotumika sana (hata kuchakaa au kuchosha).

had, *p.t. and pf.t.* ya **have**. *Be had*, *Be to be had*, patikana. *Had rather*, *Had better*, afadhali, heri, zaidi.

haddock, *n.* namna ya samaki wa bahari.

Hades, *n.* jehanum.

haemoglobin, *n.* kitu chekundu katika damu kinachotwaa *oxygen* katika hewa na kuipeleka kila mahali mwilini.

haemoptysis, *n.* kutoa ukohozi wenye damu.

haemorrhage, *n.* kutoa damu, mtoko wa damu.

haemorrhoids, *n.* bawasiri, futuri, kikundu, mjiko.

haft, *n.* mpini, kipini, pini, kipande cha mti au chuma cha kushikia (cha kisu, jembe, chombo *&c.*).

hag, *n.* kizee (kibaya kikongwe), kichawi.

haggard, *a.* -a kukonda, -a kuumbuka (kwa ugonjwa, njaa, taabu *&c.*), -a kusawajika sura, -a kudhoofu.

haggle, *v.i.* pigania bei, piga ubazazi.

hail, (1) *v.i.* nya mvua ya mawe. **hailstones**, **hailstorm**, *n.* mvua za mawe.

hail, (2) *v.t.* salimu, toa salamu, pongeza, pokea kwa shangwe; — *v.i.* (*a ship &c.*) ita, pigia ukelele. *Hail from*, toka. — *n.* salamu.

hair, *n.* unywele (nywele), usinga (singa); (*of beard*) udevu (ndevu); (*of lower lip*) kinywa mchuzi; (*of animal*) singa, unyoya; (*of hand and arm*) laika (malaika); (*of pubes and under armpit*) vuzi (mavuzi); (*straight*) nywele za singa; (*woolly*) nywele za kipilipili; (*soft, wavy*) nywele za ukoka; (*frizzy*) nywele za kimbimbi. *Split hairs*, shindania madogo bure. *He did not turn a hair*, hakuogopa hata kidogo. **hairbreadth**, *a.* -embamba sana. *A hairbreadth escape*, kuokoka kwa shida sana, kunusurika. **hairdresser**, *n.* kinyozi. **hair-splitting**, *n.* kuleta maneno (kisa, sababu) mengi ya bure, mabishano ya bure. **hairy**, *a.* -enye nywele nyingi, kama unywele.

halcyon days, *n.* siku za heri (shwari, raha, amani, faraja, neema, starehe, fanaka, baraka, mapato).

hale, *a.* -zima, -enye afya (rai, siha, nguvu), -shupavu, kakawana.

half, *n.* (*pl.* **halves**) nusu. *Half-orange*, *half-coco-nut &c.* (*i.e. of anything round*) kizio. *Cut in half*, kata nusu bi nusu. **half-breed**, *n.* chotara (mtu) -nusu mweupe nusu mweusi, yaani baba na mama yake ni wa mataifa mbalimbali. **half-brother**, **half-sister**, *n.* ndugu upande wa kuumeni au wa kukeni, ndugu baba mmoja (mama mmoja), ndugu. **half-caste**, *n.* taz. *half-breed.* **half-crown**, *n.* shilingi mbili na nusu, sarafu yenye thamani ya shilingi mbili na nusu. **half-hearted**, *a.* zembe, -sio na bidii, tepetevu. **halfpenny**, *n.* sarafu ya kiingereza yenye thamani ya senti 4½. **half-seas-over,** *a.* nusu kulewa. **half-tone,** *n.* namna ya kunakili picha kuzipiga chapa katika vitabu. **half-witted,** *a.* -enye akili chache, -pungufu wa akili, -enye akili afkani, -enye kichaa (mafuu, wazimu), -punguani. **half-yearly,** *a.* -a kila mwezi wa sita, -a mara mbili kila mwaka. **halve,** *v.t.* kata nusu bi nusu, kata vipande viwili vilivyo sawa, gawanya sawasawa. **halves,** *n.* (*pl.* ya *half*). *Go halves,* gawanya sawasawa, shirikiana.

halibut, *n.* namna ya samaki.

halitosis, *n.* pumzi inayonuka vibaya.

hall, *n.* chumba kikubwa (cha kulia, cha kubarizia, cha kukutanikia), (*entrance hall*) sebule. *Public hall,* kilinge. **hall-mark,** *n.* chapa inayopigiwa fedha au dhahabu kuonyesha kama ni safi.

hallelujah, *int.* neno la kumsifu Mungu.

hallo, halloa, *int.* ukelele wa kuita au kushtuka. **halloo,** *v.t.* piga ukelele (wa kuita, wa kutomeshea mbwa kuwinda &c.).

hallow, *v.t.* toa (weka) kwa matumizi ya ibada ya Mungu tu, fanya wakf; (*reverence*) tukuza, adhimisha.

hallucination, *n.* kupotewa akili, chechele, ndoto, kosa.

halo, *n.* duara ya mwangaza (nuru) hasa kuzunguka kichwa cha mtakatifu; (*of moon or sun*) uzunguko, uzingo.

halt, *v.t.* simamisha; — *v.i.* simama; (*on a journey*) tua; (*limp*) chechemea; (*hesitate*) sita. **halting,** *a.* -a kusita, -a kutanga. **halting-place,** *n.* kituo, kikomo; (*camp*) kambi, kigono, rago.

halter, *n.* kamba yenye tanzi (ya kuongozea farasi, ya kunyonga mtu).

halting, *a.,* **halting-place,** *n.* taz. *halt.*

halve, *v.,* **halves,** *n.* taz. *half.*

halyards, *n.* henza, jarari, kamba ya kupandishia na kutelemshia tanga, foromali au bendera.

ham, *n.* mvungu wa paja, kiga, kiweo, paja la nguruwe lililokolea chumvi au kukaushwa katika moshi.

hamadryad, *n.* kizimwi wa mitini.

hamlet, *n.* mji mdogo, kijiji, kitongoji.

hammer, *v.t.* gonga, piga nyundo; (*metal*) fua; (*metal in thin sheets*) babata; (*nails &c.*) gongomea; (*defeat*) shinda. *Hammer away,* fululiza. *Go at it hammer and tongs,* shikilia kwa bidii nyingi. — *n.* nyundo; (*auction*) mnada. *Bring to the hammer,* nadi.

hammock, *n.* wavu wa kulalia (au kuchukulia) mtu kama machela, susu.

hamper, (1) *n.* tunga (kapu) lenye kifuniko, jamanda.

hamper, (2) *v.t.* zuia, tatanisha.

hamstring, *v.t.* kata mshipa wa mguu nyuma (uvunguni mwa goti).

hand, *n.* mkono (toka kitanga mpaka ncha za vidole), kitu cho chote kama mkono; (*labourer*) mtu wa kazi, kibarua; (*sailor*) baharia; (*skill*) nguvu, uwezo, ustadi, ufundi; (*writing*) mwandiko, hati; (*of watch*) mkono, mshale, akarabu; (*side*) upande; (*left hand*) upande wa kushoto; (*right hand*) mkono wa kuume (wa kulia, wa mlio); (*handbreadth*) upana wa mkono (ndio wa vidole au vyanda vinne). *All hands,* kila mtu, watu wote. *At hand,* karibu, tayari. *Hand in hand* pamoja, hali moja, shauri moja. *Hand over hand,* upesi, rahisi. *On the one hand,* kwanza. *Hand-to-hand fight,* vita vikali, vita vya kushikiliana sana. *Pass from hand to hand,* pokezanya. *In the hand, The money is in hand,* mkononi, fedha iko tayari, iko kwangu (kwake &c.). *Cash in hand,* fedha taslimu (mkononi), nakidi. *The matter is in hand,* jambo linatendeka, linaendelea, limeanzishwa. *At first hand,* -pya, kwa fundi mwenyewe, kwa mwenyeji, -siotumika bado. *At second hand,* si -pya, -liotumika, -kuukuu. *Hands* *off!* acha! usiguse! *Hands up!* jitoe! *Off-hand,* ghafula, mara moja, pasipo fikira, kwa kupurukusha. *Do in an off-hand way,* ghafilisha, purukusha. *It is off my hands,* simo, si juu yangu. *Change hands,* badilishwa. *Come to hand,* wasili, fika. *Get one's hand in,* jifunza, zoelea. *Have a hand in,* -wamo, shiriki. *Have in hand,* tendea kazi; (*control*) weza, shinda. *Have one's hand full,* shughulika sana, -wa na shughuli, ona mashaka. *Get the upper hand,* shinda, weza. *Lay hands on,* pelekea mkono, funga, tendea jeuri. *Lend a hand,* tia mkono, saidia. *Live from hand to mouth,* kaa maskini, -wa fukara, fukarika, hali ya kijungu meko. *Wash the hands of,* jitoa katika, jitenga na, tupia mbali. *Under the hand of,* kwa usahihi wa, wakatabahu. — *v.t.* -pa, toa, tia mkononi; (*convey*) leta, peleka kwa mkono; (*escort*) sindikiza. *Hand down,* pokeleza, rithisha. *Hand over,* toa, salimisha, weka, kabidhi, lipa. — *a.* -a mkono, -a kadiri ya mkono, -a kutumika kwa mkono, kama mkono. **hand-barrow,** *n.* gari dogo (la kukokotwa na mtu). **handbill,** *n.* hati ndogo ya kueneza habari. **handbook,** *n.* kitabu cha maelezo. **hand-cart,** *n.* gari dogo la kukokotwa na mtu. **handcuff,** *n.* pingu ya mikono. **handful,** *n.* ukofi, chopi, konzi; (*on palm of hand*) gao; (*small quantity*) kidogo; (*troublesome person*) mtukutu, mkaidi, mwenye matata (udhia), mkorofi. **handicap,** *n.* shindano (walimosaidiwa washindani, wengine mbele, wengine nyuma, kwa kadiri ya kuwasawazisha nguvu); (*disability*) kizuizi, upungufu. — *v.t.* weka nyuma (zuia) ili kusawazisha nguvu katika shindano; (*place at disadvantage*) zuia, tatanisha. **handicraft,** *n.* sanaa, uchumi, kazi ya mikono (kama kufuma, kusuka vikapu, kufinyanga &c.). **handiwork,** *n.* kazi ya mikono, kitu kilichofanyizwa kwa mikono. **handkerchief,** *n.* leso, kitambaa. *Pocket-handkerchief,* leso (kitambaa) cha kufutia kamasi. **handle,** *n.* (*of tool &c.*) mpini, kipini; (*of saucepan &c.*) kono, mkono; (*of pail &c.*) utambo. — *v.t.* gusa, papasa, tomasa; (*use*) tumia; (*treat*) tendea kazi; (*control*) ongoza. zuia. **handle-bar,** *n.* usukani. **hand-loom,** *n.* kitanda cha mfumi (cha mikono). **handmaid,** *n.* mtumishi wa kike. **hand-mill,** *n.* kinu (cha kuendeshwa kwa mikono). **handsome,** *a.* -zuri (uso, umbo, sura); (*large*) -ingi, -kubwa. **handspike,** *n.* mtaimbo, wenzo, mti, kipande. **hand-to-mouth,** *a.* -a shida, -a kijungu meko. **handwork,** *n.* kazi ya mikono. **handwriting,** *n.* mwandiko, hati. **handy,** *a.* -elekevu wa kazi, -epesi; (*useful*) -a kufaa; (*ready*) -a tayari.

hang, *v.t.* (*p.t.* **hung,** *pf.t.* **hung, hanged**) (*on wall*) angika; (*up*) tundika, tungika; (*so as to swing*) pembeza, yongesha; (*strangle*) nyonga, songa; (*decorate*) funika, pamba; — *v.i.* (*delay*) sitasita, tanga; (*swing*) ning'inia. *Hang back,* kataa, totaka, sita. *Hang down,* shusha; (*intrans.*) shuka. *Hang over,* tokeza, fanya domo; (*impend*) -wa karibu, taka kuja, karibia, -wa tayari. *Hang on,* (*persevere*) dumu, endelea; (*depend on*) -wa juu ya, tungika na, rejea, fungamana na. *They hung on his words,* walimsikiliza sana. *Hang together,* -wa hali moja; fungamana. *It all hangs together,* yote barabara, yote sawasawa. *Go and be hanged!* potelea mbali. — *n.* jinsi kitu (nguo &c.) kinavyokaa, kikao; (*meaning*) maana. **hang-dog,** *a.* -a aibu, -nyonge, -enye haya. **hanger,** *n.* upanga mfupi. **hanger-on,** *n.* chokora, mfuasi, mdoya, mwenye kurondea (kudusia). **hanging,** *n.* kusongwa; (*curtains &c.*) nguo za kupamba (mapazia, bendera &c.). — *a.* -a kutokeza, -a kufanya domo, -a mbavuni pa kilima. **hangman,** *n.* mwenye kazi ya kutundika

(kunyonga) watu waliohukumiwa kufa na serikali.
hangar, *n.* banda la eropleni.
hanger, *n.*, **hanger-on,** *n.*, **hanging,** *n.*, **hangman,** *n.* taz. *hang.*
hank, *n.* shada, kibonge, kidonge (cha uzi, hariri &c.).
hanker, *v.i.* (*after, for*) taka sana, tamani, -wa na shauku (ya). *Have a hankering,* wa na uchu (shauku), tamani. **hankering,** *n.* uchu, shauku, tamaa.
hansom-cab, *n.* gari lenye magurudumu mawili la kuchukulia watu.
hap, *n.* bahati, nasibu, tukio, kikuti. — *v.t.* tukia, jiri. **haphazard,** *n.* bahati. — *a.* ovyo. *He did it at haphazard,* alifanya ovyo ovyo (shaghala baghala, kwa bahati, kwa kubahatisha, ghafula). **hapless,** *a.* -siye na bahati, maskini. **haply,** *adv.* kwa bahati, kwa nasibu; huenda, labda. **happen,** *v.i.* tukia, jiri, -wa. *Happen to,* pata. *It happened,* kwa nasibu, kwa bahati. **happily,** *adv.* kwa furaha; (*well*) vema, vizuri, kwa bahati. **happiness,** *n.* raha, furaha, kicheko, heri, sudi, nderemo, hadhi, raha mustarehe, baraka. **happy,** *a.* -a furaha, -a heri, -a bahati; (*in disposition*) -chekevu, -changamfu, -kunjufu, -chekeshi, -cheshi, -a furaha; (*skilful*) hodari, -elekevu, -ema. **happy-go-lucky,** *a.* -enye kubahatisha, -zembe, ovyo.
harangue, *v.t.* hutubu, toa hotuba (hasa ya maneno makali au ya ukelele). — *n.* hotuba, maneno mengi (makali ya ukelele).
harass, *v.t.* udhi, sumbua, chokoza, hangaisha, sai, tia wasiwasi, chosha, chusha, taabisha.
harbinger, *n.* mjumbe, mtangulizi, mleta habari, kijumbe.
harbour, *n.* bandari, kimbilio, kituo. — *v.t.* weka, pakea, karibisha, ficha, linda; (*keep in mind*) shika, weka moyoni.
hard, *a.* -gumu, -kavu, yabisi, -zito, kali, -shupavu. *Go hard with,* kulia, dhiki, lemea. *Get hard,* shupaa, shupana, pindamana, kazana, ganda, kauka. *Be hard up,* zidiwa, dhii, taiti, wamba. *Hard times,* siku za dhiki (taabu, shida), utaiti, wambo. *Be hard of hearing,* tosikia vyema. — *adv.* sana, kwa nguvu, shida. *Hard by,* karibu, pale pale. **hard-earned,** *a.* -liopatika (-liopatwa) kwa shida (taabu &c.) -liyochumwa kwa taabu. -a shida. **harden,** *v.t.* fanya gumu, tia ugumu, fanya madhubuti, kaza, gandamiza, shupaza; — *v.i.* imarika, -wa madhubuti shupaa, ganda, kazana. **hardened,** *a.* -gumu, -shupavu, -zoevu (hasa wa mabaya). **hard-featured,** *a.* -enye uso mkali (mchungu). **hard-fisted,** *a.* bahili, -nyimivu, kabidhi, -gumu. **hard-headed,** *a.* -a busara, -a akili barabara. **hard-hearted,** *a.* -enye moyo mgumu, -kali, bila huruma, katili. **hardihood,** *n.* uhodari, uthabiti, ugumu, ujasiri. **hardly,** *adv.* vikali, vigumu; (*with difficulty*) kwa shida; (*scarcely &c.*) tu. **hardiness,** *n.* ugumu, uyabisi, ukavu, ushupavu, ukali &c. **hard-set,** *a.* -gumu, -kavu, -shupavu; (*of an egg*) -viza. **hardship,** *n.* taabu, shida, mkasa, matata, mgogoro, msiba; (*grievance*) jambo zito, udhalimu. **hardware,** *n.* vyombo vya chuma, pua &c., kama sufuria, birika &c. **hardy,** *a.* hodari, -tendaji, -zoevu wa kazi na taabu; (*shameless*) bila haya, -enye macho makavu, -juvi, -jasiri, -kalamzi.
hare, *n.* sungura, katiti. **hare-brained,** *a.* -zembe, -a harara, si -angalifu, -jasiri. **hare-lip,** *n.* mdomo wa pande.
harem, *n.* nyumba ya wake na masuria wa mtu; wake na masuria wa mtu.
haricot, *n.* namna ya haragwe; nyama na mboga zilizopikwa pamoja.
hark, *int.* sikiliza! *Hark back,* rudia. **harken,** *v.i.* sikia, sikiliza.
harlequin, *n.* mchekeshaji, mcheshi, mtu wa kuchezacheza.

harlot, *n.* kahaba, malaya, mtembezi.
harm, *n.* madhara, udhalimu, hasara, maumivu. — *v.t.* dhuru, dhulumu, haribu, hasiri, umiza, wenga. **harmful,** *a.* -enye madhara, -a kuumiza, -baya. **harmless,** *a.* si -a kudhuru, si -a shari, -pole; (*feeble*) dhaifu, -nyonge.
harmonic, *a.*, **harmonics,** *n.*, **harmonious,** *a.*, **harmonium,** *n.*, **harmonize,** *v.* taz. *harmony.*
harmony, *n.* amani, mapatano, upatano, umoja, moyo mmoja; (*in music*) ulinganifu wa sauti. **harmonic,** *a.* -a kufanya sauti zinazopendeza (zinazolingana). **harmonics,** *n.* maarifa ya sauti zinazolingana. **harmonious,** *a.* -a kupatana, -a amani; (*in music*) -a kulingana, -enye ulinganifu (wa sauti). **harmonium,** *n.* kinanda, santuri. **harmonize,** *v.t.* patanisha, linganisha; — *v.i.* lingana, patana, chukuana.
harness, *n.* lijamu na kigwe cha kuongozea farasi (punda *&c.*). *He died in harness,* alikufa angali akifanya kazi yake. *Double harness,* vigwe vya kuongozea farasi wawili. *To work* (*run*) *in double harness,* kushirikiana katika kazi (mambo ya maisha *&c.*)
harp, *n.* kinubi. — *v.i.* piga kinubi. *Harp upon,* nena mara nyingi, rudia mara nyingi, kimu, chagiza. *Harp upon the same thing,* rudiarudia yale yale. **harper, harpist,** *n.* mpiga kinubi. **harpsichord,** *n.* namna ya kinanda.
harpoon, *n.* chusa, mundu. — *v.t.* piga chusa (mundu).
harpsichord, *n.* taz. *harp.*
harpy, *n.* (katika hadithi za kiyunani) mnyama mwenye mwili kama mwanamke, na miguu, makucha, mkia na mbawa za ndege; (*rapacious person*) mdhalimu, mkorofi, ajaribuye kupata yote kwa mwenyewe.
harridan, *n.* kizee mwovu.
harrier, *n.* mbwa wa kuwindia sungura.
harrow, *n.* chombo cha kulimia chenye meno mengi ya kuvunjavunja udongo. — *v.t.* tumia *harrow;* (*vex &c.*) huzunisha, chokoza, sumbua, udhi. **harrowing,** *a.* -a kuhuzunisha, -a kutesa, -a kuchoma moyo, -baya, -a kutia uchungu wa moyo, -a kuudhi sana.
harry, *v.t.* teka, teka nyara, onea, sumbua, haribu, tesa, dhulumu.
harsh, *a.* (*of texture*) -a kukwaruza, -a kuwasha; (*of sound*) -a kuchukiza, -kali: (*of disposition &c.*) -kali, -gumu, -katili, -onevu, -zito. **harshness,** *n.* ugumu, ukali, jeuri, uzito, uonevu, udhalimu, ukatili.
hart, *n.* ayala, mnyama kama paa dume.
hartebeest, *n.* kongoni.
harum-scarum, *n.* mzembe, mjasiri, mtu asiyejali mambo. — *a.* -jasiri, -a harara, hafifu, -zembe.
harvest, *n.* mavuno, mazao; (*profit*) faida, chumo, pato; (*season*) majira ya kuvuna; (*consequence*) matokeo. **harvester,** *n.* mvunaji, mvuni; (*machine*) chombo cha kuvunia. **harvest home,** *n.* sikukuu mwisho wa kuvuna.
has, taz. *have.*
hash, *n.* vipande vidogo vya nyama iliyokwisha pikwa ikapashwa moto tena; (*muddle &c.*) machafuko, vurugiko, fujo. *Make a hash of,* buruga, chafua, fuja, haribu, purukusha. *I'll settle his hash,* nitamshinda, nitakomesha matata yake.
hashish, *n.* bangi.
hasp, *n.* peto (ya kufungia).
hassock, *n.* takia la kupigia magoti.
haste, *n.* haraka, wepesi, hima, kikaka, pupa, harara, tutuo, hamaniko. **hasten,** *v.t.* himiza, harakisha, kimbiliza; — *v.i.* fanya hima, fanya haraka, enda upesi, enda mbio. **hastily,** *adv.* kwa haraka (harara, pupa *&c.*). **hastiness,** *n.* haraka, wepesi, uharara, kikaka, kakara, uhamaniko. **hasty,** *a.* -a haraka, -a ghafula, -a harara, -a pupa, *Speak hasty words,* kimbiliza maneno.

hat, *n.* kofia, chapeo; (*turban*) kilemba. *Pass (send round, go round with) the hat,* changa fedha. *Talk through one's hat,* payapaya, bwabwaja, sema upuzi, piga chuku. **hatter,** *n.* mwuza kofia.

hatch, (1) *n.* **hatchway,** *n.* mlango wa kushukia ndani ya meli.

hatch, (2) *v.t.* (*sit on*) atamia, kalia; (*bring out*) angua, toa; (*a plot &c.*) buni, tunga, fanyiza.

hatchet, *n.* shoka, kishoka. *Bury the hatchet,* fanya amani, patana, acha ugomvi *&c.*

hatchway, *n.* taz. *hatch* (1).

hate, *v.t.* chukia, onea chuki sana, onea kinyongo, kirihi, mena, zia. — *n.* uchuki, machukio, karaha, kirahi, kinyongo, kasirani. **hateful,** *a.* -a kuchukiza, -a kukirihi, makuruhi, -a kinyongo, -a kasirani, -a kuchukia. **hatred,** *n.* machukio, chuki, kinyongo, kasirani.

hath. *He hath = he has.*

hatter, *n.* taz. *hat.*

haughty, *a.* -a kiburi, -a kudharau, -a kupiga makuu, -a kubeza, -a kujivuna, -a kujideka, -a kutakabari.

haul, *v.t.* kokota, vuta kwa nguvu, burura, buruta, buruza, gugurusha. *Haul over the coals,* karipia, kemea. — *n.* (*of fish*) vuo, numbi; (*acquisition &c.*) pato.

haunch, *n.* paja, tako.

haunt, *v.t.* enda mara kwa mara, rudia mara nyingi, penda kukaa, zoelea (mahali), fanya makao, dumia. — *n.* makao, makazi, maskani, faradhi.

have, *v.i.* (*p.t. and pf.t.* **had**) -wa na; (*possess*) miliki, hozi; (*take, get*) twaa, pata; (*be under obligation*) paswa, shurutishwa, lazimishwa; (*cause*) amuru, fanyiza, diriki; (*effect*) pata, shinda; (*in comp.*) -eza, -esha, -isha *&c.* (*In verbs*) -me-, *e.g. I have gone,* nimekwenda. *I have to go,* sina budi kwenda, imenibidi kwenda. *I will have it done,* nitaifanyiza, itafanyika, juu yangu hii, nitaamuru ifanyike. *Have a house built,* jengesha nyumba. *I will have it divided among you,* nitawagawanyizia. *She had a child,* alizaa mtoto. *Have in mind,* kumbuka, fahamu, nia, nuia. *Have in honour,* heshimu, jali. *Have a care,* jihadhari; (*take care of*) tunza. *Have it out,* sema wazi, kata neno, isha. *Have on,* vaa. *What has he on?* amevaa nini? *I won't have it,* sikubali, sitaki. *I would have you know,* nataka ufahamu (ujue). *Had I known I would not have gone,* ningalijua nisingalikwenda. *You have been had,* umedanganyika. **having,** *a.* -enye.

haven, *n.* bandari, kituo, mahali pa raha, kimbilio.

haversack, *n.* mkoba, bahasha, mfuko, shanta.

having, *a.* taz. *have.*

havoc, *n.* maangamizi makuu, uharibifu mwingi, shari, hasara, upotevu mwingi.

hawk, (1) *n.* (*African Harrier*) hajivale, kengewa, shakevale; (*black sparrow*) kozi, kikozi. **hawk-eyed,** *a.* -enye macho makali (yawezayo kuona upesi na mbali).

hawk, (2) *v.t.* chuuza, tembeza biashara ndogo ndogo, fanya kazi ya ubazazi. **hawker,** *n.* mchuuzi, mtembeza bidhaa, bazazi.

hawk-eyed, *a.* taz. *hawk* (1).

hawser, *n.* kamba kubwa nene.

hawthorn, *n.* namna ya mti mdogo wa kiingereza wenye miiba.

hay, *n.* majani yaliyokatwa na kukaushwa kulisha ng'ombe, farasi *&c.*; ukoka mkavu. *Make hay while the sun shines,* chumia juani uje ule uvulini; tumie udongo ungali na maji. *Make hay of,* fuja, buruga. **haycock,** *n.* tita la *hay.* **hay fever,** *n.* makamasi yaletwayo na mavumbi ya maua *&c.* yakiingia puani na kooni. **hayrick, haystack,** *n.* chungu kubwa ya *hay.*

hazard, *n.* mchezo wa kubahatisha, kamari; (*danger*) hatari; (*chance*) bahati. *At haphazard,* kwa bahati. — *v.t.* hatirisha, jasiri, ponza, fanya kwa bahati, bahatisha. **hazardous,** *a.* -enye hatari.

haze, *n.* umande, ukungu, mvuke, giza, kunge, kungugu, utusitusi; (*of vision*) unyenyezi; (*perplexity*) mashaka. **haziness,** *n.* unyenyezi, utusitusi. **hazy,** *a.* -enye haze; (*indistinct*) si dhahiri si baini.

he, *pron.* yeye (mwanamume); (*emphat.*) yule; (*in comp.*) -a yu- *It is he, He is the man,* ndiye. *There he is! That is he!* huyo!

head, *n.* kichwa; (*of a ship*) omo; (*intellect*) akili; (*chief*) mkuu, jumbe; (*front*) mahali pa mbele; (*single individual*) watu (au wanyama) mmoja mmoja; (*source*) mwanzo, asili, chimbuko; (*cape*) rasi; (*top*) mahali pa juu; (*force*) nguvu; (*perfection*) usitawi, upeo, kipeo, kuiva (jipu); (*division, section*) sehemu, fungu (la maneno); (*of spear &c.*) chuma, chembe; (*of a bed*) mchago. *Come to a head,* iva, sitawi. *From head to foot, Over head and ears,* pia, kabisa, -ote. *Out of his head,* kwa peke yake, kwa akili zake. *Off one's head,* -enye wazimu (kichaa). *Over his head,* kijuujuu, kupita akili zake. *Turn one's head* (*delude*), pumbaza. *Lay heads together,* fanya shauri pamoja. *Take one's head,* nuia, kusudia, nia, azimu. *Put out of one's head,* sahaulisha. *Lose one's head,* potewa akili, fadhaika, hangaika. *Make head,* pata, nguvu, endelea, fanya nguvu, anza kushinda. *I can't make head or tail of it,* siwezi kuifahamu, imenishinda. *Show one's head,* toa kichwa, onekana wazi. — *v.t.* -wa mkuu wa, ongoza, tangulia; (*head off*) zuia mbele, pingia njia; — *v.i.* (*make for*) elekea, kabili, endea. **headache,** *n.* kichwa. *My head aches, I have a headache,* kichwa chaniuma. **headband, head-dress,** *n.* (*of women*) ukaya, dusumali; (*turban*) kilemba. **header,** *n.* kuanguka kichwani, kupiga mbizi kutanguliza kichwa. **heading,** *n.* anwani, dibaji. **headland,** *n.* rasi. **headlight,** *n.* taa ya mbele (ya motakaa, gari meli &c.). **headlong,** *a.* -a kishindo, -a nguvu, -a kasi. — *adv.* kichwa mbele, kwa harara, kwa ujasiri. **headman,** *n.* mzee, mkuu, jumbe, msimamizi. **headmaster,** *n.* mwalimu mkubwa wa chuo. **headmistress,** *n.* bibi mwalimu mkubwa wa chuo. **head-on,** *adv.* dafurao. **headpiece,** *n.* kichwa, akili, mtu mwenye akili. **head-quarters,** *n.* makao ya wakuu (wa kazi, serikali, jeshi la askari &c.). **headrest,** *n.* (*wooden*) msamilo. **headship,** *n.* ujumbe, ukuu. **headstrong,** *a.* -kaidi, -gumu, -a harara, -shupavu, -siyesikia shauri la mtu. *He is headstrong,* afuata nafsi yake. **headway,** *n.* maendeleo; nafasi juu ya kichwa katika mlango &c. **head-wind,** *n.* upepo wa mbisho. **heady,** *a.* kama *headstrong*; (*intoxicating*) -a kulevya, -a kileo.

heal, *v.t.* ponya; — *v.i.* pona. (*Note:* poza *and* poa *are often used, but their true meaning appears to be improve rather than heal absolutely*). **healing,** *a.* -a kuponya; (*things*) -a kupoza. — *n.* kuponya. **health,** *n.* uzima, afya, siha, rai, nguvu, hali. **healthful, healthy,** *a.* -a afya, -zima, -a kutia afya (siha, rai, nguvu).

heap, *n.* fungu, chungu, lundo; (*of stone collected for building*) boma; (*of refuse from plantation, for burning*) biwi; (*ant-hill*) kichuguu, chuguu; (*raised bed in garden*) tuta. *Lie in heaps* (*one on top of another*) elekana, pandana, lundikana. *Heaps of times,* mara nyingi. — *v.t.* kusanya fungu, fanya chungu, tia -ingi, lundika; (*one on top of another*) andikanya, lundikanya, omekeza; (*earth &c.*) fusia, palia. **heaped,** *a.* -a fara.

hear, *v.i.* (*p.t. and pf.t.* **heard**) sikia; (*listen to*) sikiliza; (*grant*) kubali; (*judge*) hukumu, amua; (*be told*) ambiwa, arifiwa. *Hear from,* pata barua ya. *Hear of,* pata habari ya; (*agree to*) kubali, ridhia. **hear! hear!** *int.* ndivyo hasa (*often expressed by* *repeated* Ehe! ehe!). **hearer,** *n.* msikizi, (*listener*) msikilizi. **hearing,** *n.* kusikia, kuona kwa masikio; (*audience*) ruhusa (nafasi) ya kusema maneno; (*legal*) baraza, hukumu. **hearsay,** *n.* tetesi, uvumi, wasemayo watu, maneno ya watu (yasiyo thibitishwa).

hearken, *v.i.* taz. *hark.*

hearsay, *n.* taz. *hear.*

hearse, *n.* gari la kuchukulia maiti mazikoni.

heart, *n.* moyo; (*poetic*) mtima, fuadi; (*disposition*) tabia, silika, roho, nia, dhati; (*energy*) bidii, nguvu; (*feeling*) huruma, haba; (*inmost part*) asili, kiini; (*meaning*) maana ya ndani, maana ya siri, asili; (*beloved*) kipenzi, muhebi; (*suit in cards*) kopa. *A soft heart,* huruma nyingi. *After one's own heart,* -a kupendeza halisi. *At heart,* kwa kweli. *Have at heart,* penda moyoni, kusudia kwa moyo, taka kwa bidii. *Be out of heart, Lose heart,* kata tamaa, legea. *Lose one's heart* (*fall in love*) ingia uchumba, pata mchumba, shikwa na upendo, ashiki, chunuka. *Take heart,* jipa moyo, piga moyo konde. *Take to heart,* onea sikitiko (uchungu) rohoni, sikitikia, fikiri sana. *Open the heart to,* funulia haba. *Set the heart on,* kazia moyo, tamani sana, onea shauku, taka kwa moyo, jifunga kwa, tia habani. *With all one's heart,* sana, kwa moyo wa bidii, kwa juhudi. *Heart and soul,* pia, kabisa, hasa, halisi. *Have the heart to,* thubutu. *Have one's heart in one's mouth,* shtushwa, tishwa. *His heart was in his throat,* moyo ulimpalia rohoni, alikuwa na tanzi la roho. *In the heart of Africa,* katikati ya Afrika. **heart-beat,** *n.* pigo la moyo. **heartbreaking,** *a.* -a kuhuzunisha sana, -a kuvunja moyo, -zito sana, -a taabu nyingi, -a kutaabisha mno, -a kukatisha tamaa kabisa, -a kulegeza moyo, -a kuondoa jitihadi. **heartbroken,** *a.* -a kushindwa na taabu, -enye huzuni (sikitiko, majonzi) nyingi, -a kuvunjika moyo (jitihadi, bidii &c.). **heartburn,** *n.* kiungulia. **heartburning,** *n.* ugomvi, uchungu, chuki, mfundo, dukuduku, kinyongo. **hearten,** *v.t.* tia moyo, fariji, pa moyo, changamsha; — *v.i.* pata moyo, jipa moyo. **heartfelt,** *a.* -a moyoni, -a kweli. **heartless,** *a.* pasipo huruma, -kali, -korofi, -katili. **heart-rending,** *a.* taz. *heart-breaking.* **heartstricken,** *a.* -enye huzuni (majonzi, sikitiko) nyingi. **heart-string,** *n.* moyo ndani. *Pull at one's heart-strings,* huzunisha sana, sikitisha sana, chochea huruma (huzuni, sikitiko &c.). **hearty,** *a.* -enye afya njema, -a nguvu; (*genial, frank*) -kunjufu, -changamfu, -nyofu, -enye utu mwema; (*energetic*) -a bidii, -a moyo. *A hearty meal,* chakula tele, shibe.

hearth, *n.* meko, moto; (*home*) nyumba, kwake (kwao &c.), makao, mastakimu, kitende. **hearthstone,** *n.* jiwe pana chini ya meko; (*home*) nyumba ya mtu &c. taz. *hearth.*

heartless, *a.*, **heart-rending,** *a.*, **heartstricken,** *a.*, **heart-string,** *n.*, **hearty,** *a.* taz. *heart.*

heat, *n.* moto, joto, hari, jasho; (*anger*) hasira, harara, ghadhabu, ukali, moyo juu, hamaki; (*vehemence*) bidii; (*in racing &c.*) mara, zamu, sehemu, shindo, safari; (*sexual*) nyege. *Prickly heat,* harara. — *v.t.* pasha moto, tia moto; (*enrage, excite*) kasirisha, tia bidii, sukumu, washa, chochea; — *v.i.* pata joto. **heated,** *a.* -a moto, -enye joto, -liopashwa moto; (*excited &c.*) -a harara, -a hamaki, -a nguvu, -a hasira.

heath, *n.* pori, nyika, mbuga; (*plant*) namna ya mimea iotayo nyikani &c.

heather, *n.* namna ya mimea iotayo nyikani &c.

heathen, *n. and a.* mtu asiye na habari za kweli za Mungu; kwa kawaida ni mtu asiye na dini ya kikristo, kiyahudi wala kiislamu, ila afuataye dini ya mapokeo ya wazee wake ya kutambikia mizimu &c. mshenzi.

heather, *n.* taz. *heath.*

heave, *v.t.* (*p.t.* pengine **hove**) inua (nyanyua) kwa juhudi, sukuma kwa nguvu, jitahidi; (*throw*) tupa, vurumisha; — *v.i.* (*palpitate*) pigapiga, puma; (*undulate*) panda na kushuka kama mawimbi, kwelea; (*haul*) vuta. *Heave anchor,* ng'oa nanga. *Heave a sigh,* ugua, kokota roho. *Heave to* (*ship*), simama, tua. *Heave in sight,* onekana baharini. — *n.* (*effort*) kusukuma kwa juhudi, shindo; (*undulation*) mwendo wa mawimbi juu na chini, kwelco; (*of the heart*) pigo.

heaven, *n.* peponi; (*sky*) uwingu, samawati; (*air*) anga, hewa; (*beautiful place*) mahali pa raha, pazuri sana; (*providence*) Mungu; (*bliss*) heri, hali ya raha mustarehe. **heavenly,** *a.* (*celestial*) -a mbinguni, -a juu; (*saintly*) -a kumpendeza Mungu, -ema sana, -takatifu; (*beautiful, blissful*) -zuri mno. **heavenward,** *a.* -a kwenda mbinguni, -a kumpendeza Mungu.

heaviness, *n.* taz. *heavy.*

heavy, *a.* -zito, -a kulemea, -kulivu; (*abundant*) -ingi, -kubwa. *A heavy loss,* hasara kubwa. *A heavy storm,* mvua nyingi, tufani, dhoruba. *A heavy sea,* mawimbi makubwa. *A heavy heart,* moyo wa huzuni. *Heavy fire,* bunduki (mizinga) nyingi zikipigwa. **heaviness,** *n.* uzito, uzani, ukulivu; (*grief*) ghamu, huzuni, majonzi.

Hebrew, *a.* -ebrania, -yahudi, -israeli. — *n.* Ebrania, *pl.* Maebrania, *or* Mwebrania *pl.* Waebrania; Myahudi, *plur.* Wayahudi; (*language*) Kiyahudi, Kiebrania.

hecatomb, *n.* kafara (dhabibu, sadaka) ya kuchinjwa ng'ombe 100, mauaji makubwa.

heckle, *v.t.* udhi (sumbua) kwa maswali magumu.

hectic, *a.* -a ugonjwa unaoendelea siku nyingi, -a homa. *A hectic time,* kipindi cha shughuli (furaha) nyingi sana.

hecto- = 100, *e.g. hectogram* = *gram* 100.

hector, *v.t.* chokoza, sumbua, udhi, fanyia fidhuli, jeuri &c.

hedge, *n.* ua, boma la miti (miba, michongoma), kitalu. — *v.t.* zungushia ua, jengea boma; — *v.i.* (*secure oneself*) jilinda, jihadhari; (*hesitate &c.*) sita. **hedgehog,** *n.* mnyama kama nungunungu mdogo. **hedge-sparrow,** *n.* namna ya ndege mdogo.

hedonic, *a.* -a anasa, -a raha. **hedonist,** *n.* mtu atafutaye anasa (raha).

heed, *v.t.* sikia, angalia, jali, kubali, tii. — *n.* usikizi, usikivu, utii, hadhari. **heedful,** *a.* -angalifu, -sikivu, -tii. **heedless,** *a.* -zembe, -jinga. **heedlessness,** *n.* uzembe, ujinga.

heel, *n.* kifundo (kisigino) cha mguu, kisigino; (*lower part*) upande wa chini, tako, liwato, mwisho. *At heel,* karibu kwa nyuma, -kifuata. *Take to one's heels, Show the heels,* kimbia. *Come to heel,* tii (kama mbwa). — *v.i.* (*over*) inama upande, jiinika; — *v.t.* inamisha, pindua. *Heel over,* pinduka.

hefty, *a.* -enye nguvu, -kubwa.

heifer, *n.* mtamba wa ng'ombe, mfarika (wa ng'ombe), mori.

heigh, *int.* sauti ya kuonyesha mshangao (ya kuuliza, ya furaha, ya kutia moyo &c.).

heigh-ho, *int.* sauti ya kuonyesha uchovu, majonzi &c.

height, *n.* urefu wa kwenda juu, kimo, utambo, urefu, kwenda juu; (*high place*) mahali pa juu, mlima, kilima, kilele, mwinuko; (*rank*) cheo kikubwa; (*highest, best state*) wingi, upeo, kipeo, nguvu, usitawi. *At the height of,* -lipositawi, -lipokuwa -ingi. *The height of folly,* ujinga mtupu.

heighten, *v.t.* ongeza kwa juu, ongeza urefu, fanya kuwa -refu zaidi, refusha kwa juu; — *v.i.* ongezeka urefu wa kwenda juu; — *v.t.* (*intensify &c.*) zidisha, — *v.i.* zidi, ongezeka. Taz. *high.*

heinous, *a.* -a kuchukiza, -baya sana, -ovu sana.

heir, *n.* mrithi. **heir-apparent**, *n.* mtu atakayekuwa mrithi. **heiress**, *n.* mwanamke mrithi, bibi tajiri. **heirloom**, *n.* mali ya urithi isiyoweza kutolewa wala kuuzwa. **heir presumptive**, *n.* mrithi (kama mwingine hazaliwi karibu zaidi).

held, *p.t. and pf.t.* ya *hold.*

helicopter, *n.* namna ya eropleni inayoweza kupaa na kushuka moja kwa moja kiwima.

helio-, *pref.* -a kuhusu jua, *e.g.* **heliograph**, *n.* chombo cha kuashiria kwa kioo na mwanga wa jua.

heliotrope, *n.* namna ya ua linalopenda kuelekea jua; rangi yake, ndiyo kama zambarau nyeupe kidogo.

hell, *n.* jehanum; makao ya mashetani na wafu wasiotubu dhambi zao; (*place of departed spirits*) ahèra, peponi, kuzimu; (*place of punishment*) mahali zinapoadhibiwa roho za watu waliokufa; (*bad place*) mahali pabaya, nyumba ya watu wabaya. *Gambling hell*, nyumba watu wanamocheza kamari na michezo mingine ya kubahatisha kwa fedha. **hellish**, *a.* -a kishetani, -baya mno.

Hellenic, *a.* -a kiyunani. **Hellenist**, *n.* Myahudi msema Kiyunani; (*scholar*) ajuaye Kiyunani.

hellish, *a.* taz. *hell.*

hello, *int.* neno la kusalimu rafiki au mtani (la mshangao, la kuita mtu).

helm, *n.* usukani. **helmsman**, *n.* rubani, mshika usukani.

helmet, *n.* kofia ya chuma.

helmsman, *n.* taz. *helm.*

help, *v.t.* saidia, auni, leta shime, nusuru; (*in building, cultivating &c. in return for similar help*) fanya ujima; (*be of use, encourage*) tia nguvu, faa, nafidhi; (*stop, check*) zuia; (*give food to*) gawia chakula. *He helped me to some meat*, alinigawia nyama (katika sahani yangu). *Help yourself*, twaa kadiri unayotaka; (*food*) mega. *I cannot help doing this*, sharti (sina budi) kufanya. *It cannot be helped*, sharti iwe, haina budi kuwa; (*never mind*) haidhuru. — *n.* msaada, auni, muawana, shime; *mutual help of neighbours*) ujima, kusaidiana; (*of food*) mego, sehemu. **helper**, *n.* msaidia, msaidizi, mtu wa kufaa. **helpful**, *a.* -a kufaa, -a kusaidia. **helpless**, *a.* hoi, bila msaada, dhaifu, -jinga, -siye na shauri. **helpmate, helpmeet**, *n.* mwenzi, rafiki; (*wife*) mke.

helter-skelter, *adv.* mbio mbio, kwa fujo, kwa haraka, ovyo ovyo, kwa vuruguvurugu.

hem, *v.t.* kunga, pinda, minika. *Hem in*, zunguka, funga, zingia. — *n.* upindo.

hemi-, *pref.* nusu, *e.g.* **hemisphere**, *n.* nusu ya mviringo kama mpira; (*of the earth*) kizio cha dunia.

hemlock, *n.* namna ya mmea wenye sumu.

hemorrhage, *n.* taz. *haemorrhage.*

hemp, *n.* katani. *Indian hemp*, bangi. **hempen**, *a.* -a katani. *Hempen rope*, kamba ya katani.

hen, *n.* kuku; (*not laying*) kiweto; (*ready to lay*) tembe; (*laying*) koo; (*female bird*) ndege jike, koo la ndege. **hen-coop**, *n.* tundu la kuku. **henpecked**, *a.* -enye kutawalwa na mkewe.

hence, *adv.* (*of place*) huku, hapa, toka hapa; (*of time*) tangu leo; (*by reason of*) kwa hiyo, kwa sababu hiyo. *Hence!* toka! ondoka! **henceforth**, *adv.* tangu leo, toka sasa.

hen-coop, *n.* taz. *hen.*

henna, *n.* hina; (*plant*) mhina.

henpecked, *a.* taz. *hen.*

hepatic, *a.* -a maini.

hepta-, *pref.* saba, *e.g.* **heptagon**, *n.* umbo lenye pande saba.

her, *pron.* yeye (mwanamke), yule; (*in verbs*) -m-. *She gives her*, (mwanamke) ampa (mwanamke). — *a.*

-ake (mwanamke). **hers,** *a.* -ake (mwanamke). **herself,** *pron.* yeye mwenyewe, yule yule (mwanamke); *reflex.* -ji-.

herald, *n.* mjumbe, mtangulizi, mleta habari, mpiga mbiu. — *v.t.* tangaza mbele, onya, piga mbiu. **heraldic,** *a.* -a *heraldry.* **heraldry,** *n.* maarifa ya nasaba na ya alama zake.

herb, *n.* mmea. *Herbs (eatable),* mboga, majani. **herbaceous,** *a.* -a mimea. **herbage,** *n.* majani. **herbalist,** *n.* mwenye maarifa ya mimea (hasa ifaayo kwa dawa).

herculean, *a.* (*strong*) -a nguvu nyingi mno; (*difficult*) -a hatari, -a shida, -kubwa sana, -a kazi.

herd, *n.* kundi (la wanyama wakubwa); (*common people*) jamii ya watu wa vivi hivi, akina yahe. — *v.t.* kusanya katika makundi, chunga (ng'ombe, mbuzi *&c.*); — *v.i.* kutanika makundi; kaa katika kundi. **herdsman,** *n.* mchunga, mchungaji.

here, *adv.* huku, humu, hapa; (*of time*) sasa. *Here!* Njoo! (*pl.*) njoni! *Here* (*i.e. present*) saa! nipo! *That's neither here nor there,* haimo. *Hereabouts,* kama hapa, karibu. *Hereafter,* baadaye, halafu. *Here and there,* huko na huko. *Hereby, Herein, Herewith, Hereupon,* hivi, kwa hiyo, hapa, humo. *Heretofore,* mbele, hata sasa, zamani. *Hereof,* juu ya hii, juu yake, habari zake.

hereditary, *a.* -a kurithiwa (kurithika), -a urithi. **heredity,** *n.* maelekeo ya tabia (udhaifu, nguvu, ugonjwa *&c.*) kurithiwa na mtoto. **heritage,** *n.* urithi.

heresy, *n.* mafundisho ya imani yasiyopatana na yale yaliyotangazwa na Kanisa kuwa kweli; mafundisho yasiyopatana na yale yaliyokubaliwa na wingi wa watu; uzushi. **heretic,** *n.* mzushi, afundishaye *heresy.* **heretical,** *a.* -a *heresy.*

heritage, *n.* taz. *hereditary.*

hermaphrodite, *n.* huntha (mtu au mnyama aliye na dalili ya uume na uke pia).

hermetic, *a.* -liozibwa kabisa hata hewa haiwezi kuingia.

hermit, *n.* mkaa pekee (wa peke yake), mtawa, walii, mpweke. **hermitage,** *n.* makao ya *hermit.*

hernia, *n.* mshipa (wa utumbo kutokeza), mshipa.

hero, *n.* mwanamume shujaa, jabari, jasiri; (*metaphor.*) simba, fahali; mtu mkuu (katika habari za kale, hadithi, utenzi *&c.*). **heroic,** *a.* -shujaa, hodari, jasiri. **heroics,** *n.* majivuno, makuu, majisifu. **heroine,** *n.* *hero* wa kike. **heroism,** *n.* ushujaa, uhodari, ujasiri, utu uume.

heron, *n.* (*certain species, esp. Black*) kulasitara. (*African green-backed, and other smaller species*) ngojamaliko; (*larger species*) korongo. (*White form of Red Sea Reef-*) yangeyange.

herpes, *n.* ugonjwa wa ngozi wa vilengelenge.

herring, *n.* namna ya samaki mdogo wa baharini.

hers, *a.*, **herself,** *pron.* taz. *her.*

hesitate, *v.i.* sita, shangaa, ingiwa na shaka, kwaa, fanya wasiwasi; (*in speaking*) sema kwa kisita, dodosa, ganzaganza, kokoteza maneno, sita. **hesitation,** *n.* kusita, mshangao, wasiwasi, kukawia, kuchelewa; (*in speaking*) kisita, kitata, kigugumizi.

Hessian, *n.* nguo nzito ya katani kama gunia; (*boot*) namna ya kiatu kirefu kifikacho karibu na goti.

hetero-, *pref.* -a namna nyingine, *e.g.* **heterodox,** *a.* -a kushika (desturi, imani *&c.*) mbalimbali na wingi wa watu. **heterogeneous,** *a.* -a namna nyingi mbalimbali.

hew, *v.t.* (*pf.t.* pengine **hewn**) kata, tema, chanja, chonga.

hexa-, *pref.* -a sita, *e.g.* **hexagonal,** *a.* -enye pande sita.

hey! *int.* neno la kuonyesha mshangao, kuuliza, kuita! ala! wewe! we!

heyday, *n.* siku za (wakati wa)

nguvu nyingi, afya bora, usitawi, upeo wa kusitawi (afya, furaha *&c.*).

hiatus, *a.* ufa, pengo, nafasi wazi, pungufu.

hibernate, *v.i.* pisha majira ya baridi kwa usingizi. **hibernation**, *n.* usingizi wa kupisha majira ya baridi.

Hibernian, *a.* -a *Ireland.*

hiccup, hiccough, *n.* kwikwi, kitefutefu, kekevu, kikwifukwifu.

hid, hidden, taz. *hide* (2).

hide, (1) *n.* ngozi (ya mnyama). *Give him a hiding*, mpige sana. **hide-bound**, *a.* -a kufuata mambo ya kawaida (desturi) tu.

hide, (2) *v.t.* (*p.t.* **hid**, *pf.t.* **hidden, hid**) ficha, funika setiri; — *v.i.* jificha, jisetiri. *Hide and seek*, bui, kizuizui, kibemasa. **hiding**, *n.* maficho, kuficha.

hide-bound, *a.* taz. *hide* (1).

hideous, *a.* -enye sura (umbo) ya kuchukiza sana, -a kukirihi, -a kirahi, -a kioja.

hiding, *n.* taz. *hide* (2).

hie, *v.i.* enda kwa haraka.

hierarchy, *n.* serikali ya Kanisa; jamii ya mapadre; (*gradation of ranks*) madaraja.

hieroglyphics, *n.* mwandiko wa kutumia picha (sanamu) badala ya herufi; (*secret writing*) mwandiko wa siri; fumbo la herufi.

higgledy-piggledy, *a.* -a fujo, -a machafuko, hobelahobela. — *adv.* kwa fujo, kwa machafuko, shelabela, ovyo ovyo, shaghalabaghala. — *n.* fujo, machafuko, mavurugiko.

high, *a.* -a juu, -refu (kwa kwenda juu); (*excellent, glorious*) bora, -tukufu, -a heshima, aali, adhimu; (*presumptuous*) -enye kiburi (makuu); (*powerful*) -a nguvu, -kubwa, jabari, -enye enzi; (*difficult*) -gumu; (*dear*) ghali; (*of sound*) -embamba, -a juu; (*of meat &c.*) -nayovunda, -nayonuka, -liyooza. *High and low*, (*of place*) kila mahali, kote kote; (*of persons*) wakubwa kwa wadogo. *High art*, sanaa halisi. *High church*, Wakristo wa Kanisa la kiingereza walitukuzao Kanisa na siri zake, na desturi zake na uzuri wa ibada. *High day*, sikukuu; (*noon*) mchana mkuu, adhuhuri, jua kichwani. *High spirits*, moyo mwepesi, wepesi wa moyo. *High tide, High water*, maji ya kujaa, maji makuu. *High treason*, kumwasi mfalme au serikali. *High words*, maneno ya hasira. *On high*, juu. *With a high hand*, kwa nguvu, kwa jeuri. *The Most High*, Mungu, Mwenyezi Mungu, Mola, Allah. *Speak in high terms of*, sifu. *The highest pitch* (*point, degree*) kipeo, kikomo, usitawi. *It is high time*, wakati umewadia. **high-born**, *a.* -a cheo kikubwa, -a jamaa (ukoo, jadi) bora, -toto wa watu. **high-bred**, *a.* -a mbegu njema; (*polite*), -a adabu, -a heshima, makini, -a malezi mazuri. **highbrow**, *n.* mtu ajidaiye akili na busara nyingi. — *a.* -a kupita akili za wingi wa watu. **high-coloured**, *a.* -a rangi za kung'aa; (*exaggerated*) -a kupiga chuku, -enye habari za kustaajabisha. **high court**, *n.* baraza (korti) ya hukumu kuu ya nchi. **high-falutin**, *a.* -a kuonekana kama ni ufasaha lakini ni mapayo tu. **high-flown**, *a.* -a juujuu, -a kupiga makuu, -a maneno ya ufasaha bila maana. **high-handed**, *a.* -a jeuri, -a nguvu, jahili, -dhalimu. **highland**, *n.* nchi ya juu, milima, palipoinuka. **highlander**, *n.* mkaa milimani, hasa watu wa *Scotland.* **highly**, *adv.* sana, vema. *Speak highly of*, sifu. **high-minded**, *a.* -nyofu, -enye moyo mzuri (safi), -enye nia njema, -a utu bora. **highness**, *n.* utukufu, fahari. *Your Highness*, -namna ya kumwitikia (kumtaja) mtoto mwanamume wa mfalme. **high-pressure**, *a.* -a nguvu nyingi; (*busy*) -a shughuli nyingi, -a juhudi. **high-priest**, *n.* kuhani mkuu. **high-principled**, *a.* -nyofu, -a haki, -enye tabia bora, -a utu mwema. **highroad**, *n.* barabara, njia kuu, njia. **high-seasoned,** -a kutiwa viungo vingi. **high-spirited,** *a.* -jasiri, hodari; (*of horse*) -tukutu, -a kurukaruka. **high-strung,** *a.* -epesi wa kuchochewa (wa kuhangaika, wa kuona wasiwasi), -a hamaki, -a harara. **highway,** *n.* barabara, njia kuu, njia. **highwayman,** *n.* haramia, mnyang'anyi wa wasafiri (hasa mwenye bunduki au bastola), pakacha.

hike, *v.i.* safiri kwa miguu kutazama nchi.

hilarious, *a.* -a furaha, -changamfu, -a moyo mwepesi (pamoja na ukelele). **hilarity,** *n.* furaha, uchangamshi, kicheko, ukunjufu.

hill, *n.* kilima, kiduta. **hillock,** *n.* kilima kidogo; (*ant-hill*) kichuguu, chuguu. **hilly,** *a.* -enye vilima, -a vilima vilima.

hilt, *n.* mpini, kipini. *Up to the hilt,* kabisa.

him, *pron.* yeye (mume), yule; (*in verbs*) -m-. *He gives him,* (mwanamume) ampa (mwanamume). **himself,** *pron.* yeye mwenyewe, yule yule (mwanamume); (*reflex.*) -ji-. *The injured man came to himself,* mtu aliyeumia alipata fahamu tena, alijirudia.

hind, (1) *n.* paa jike.

hind, (2) *a.* -a nyuma. *Hind legs,* miguu ya nyuma (ya mnyama). **hinder,** *a.* -a nyuma. — *v.t.* zuia, pinga, kinza, tatanisha; (*delay*) kawilisha, chelewesha, faitisha. **hindermost,** *a.* -a nyuma kabisa, -a mwisho. **hind-quarters,** *n.* matako; (*of animals*) mgongo wa nyuma. **hindrance,** *n.* kizuizo, kizuio, mgogoro, pingamizi.

Hindu, *n.* Banyani. **Hinduism,** *n.* dini ya kibanyani. **Hindustani,** *n.* lugha mojawapo ya kihindi.

hinge, *n.* pata, bawaba. *Hinge on* (*upon*), tegemea, husiana na, fungamana na. *His mind is off its hinges* (*or unhinged*), ana wazimu.

hint, *v.t.* dokeza, nong'oneza, konyeza onya kidogo (kwa siri), fumbia. — *n.* dokezo, mnong'ono, onyo dogo, neno la fumbo, habari kidogo. *Give a hint, Throw out hints* = *hint, v.*

hinterland, *n.* bara, yaani sehemu ya nchi iliyo mbali na pwani.

hip, *n.* nyonga, kiweo.

hip! hip! hurrah! *int.* mlio wa kushangilia.

hippopotamus, *n.* kiboko, tomondo.

hire, *n.* ujira, ijara, mshahara, upangaji, kodi. — *v.t.* panga, ajiri, kodi, tuma; (*hire out, let on hire*) pangisha, ajirisha, kodisha. **hireling,** *n.* mtumishi, mtu wa mshahara, kibarua, mtu wa kazi ya kipande.

hirsute, *a.* -enye nywele (malaika, manyoya, ndevu).

his, *a.* -ake (mwanamume).

hiss, *v.i.* lia kama nyoka (kama sauti ya s); — *v.t.* (*show disapproval, contempt*) fyonya, fyoza, cheka, fanyia mzaha, pigia kelele, fukuza. — *n.* mlio kama wa nyoka (kama sauti ya s).

hist! *int.* nyamaza! kimya! sikiliza!

historian, *n.,* **historic, historical,** *a.* taz. *history.*

history, *n.* historia, habari za kweli za mambo yaliyopita, tarehe, habari, masimulizi. **historian,** *n.* mwandishi wa historia, mtungaji wa tarehe, msimulizi. **historic, historical,** *a.* -a historia. *An historical event,* jambo la maana sana.

histrionic, *a.* -a uigaji wa mambo (hadithi, habari), -a si nyofu, -a uwongo.

hit, *v.t.* (*p.t. and pf.t.* **hit**) piga, gonga; (*attain*) pata. *Hit against each other,* gongana. *Hit on,* kuta, pata. *Hit off,* eleza, fafanisha vizuri. *You have hit it,* ndivyo hasa usemavyo. *They hit it off well,* ni rafiki sana, wanapatana sana.

hitch, *v.t.* (*hitch up*) vuta; jongeza; (*hitch on to*) fungia; (*be joined with*) fungamana; (*stick, go by jerks*) kwama, kokota mwendo, tatanika. — *n.* fundo, kifungo, kizuio, kizuizi, mgogoro, kikwazo.

hither, *adv.* huku, hapa. *Hither and*

thither, huko na huko. **hitherto,** *adv.* hata sasa (leo), mpaka sasa (leo).
hive, *n.* mzinga (wa nyuki), tundu la nyuki, kundi la nyuki; (*crowded place*) penye watu wengi, penye ghasia, penye shughuli nyingi.
ho! *int.* sauti ya kuonyesha mshangao, taabu, shauku &c.: loo! ala! ama!
hoar, *a.* -eupe, -enye mvi. **hoar-frost,** *n.* sakitu, theluji, umande wa theluji. **hoary,** *a* (*white*) -eupe (kwa maisha marefu); (*grey-haired*) -enye mvi; (*old*) -a kale sana.
hoard, *n.* akiba, kande. — *v.t.* weka akiba, dunduliza, weka kwa choyo (ubahili), kabidhi. **hoarding** (1), *n.* ukabidhi, ubahili, choyo.
hoarding, (2) *n.* ua wa mbao.
hoar-frost, *n.* taz. *hoar.*
hoarse, *a.* (*voice*) -liyopwea, -liyokauka, -kavu. **hoarseness,** *n.* kupwewa sauti, kukaukiwa sauti.
hoary, *a.* taz. *hoar.*
hoax, *n.* ubishi, mchezo, mzaha, shere. — *v.t.* danganya, dhihaki, chezea shere, fanyia mzaha.
hob, *n.* bamba la chuma juu ya moto jikoni.
hobble, *v.i.* chechemea, enda chopi, enda pecha, chegea; — *v.t.* (*fetter*) fungia miguu (ya farasi asiweze kwenda ila kidogo).
hobbledehoy, *n.* kijana mzembe (asiye na desturi wala adabu nzuri), mtwana.
hobby, *n.* jambo (kazi, elimu &c.) analoshughulikia mtu kupisha wakati, yaani kujifurahisha tu wala si kwa uchumi.
hobgoblin, *n.* zimwi, kizimwi, jini mbaya.
hobnail, *n.* msumari wa viatu wenye kichwa kikubwa.
honob, *v.i.* (*with*) suhubiana (na), fanya urafiki (na).
Hobson's choice, *n.* hapana hiari, hapana uchaguo.
hock, (1) *n.* namna ya divai nyeupe ya kidachi.
hock, (2) *n.* goti la farasi nyuma.
hockey, *n.* mchezo wa mpira mdogo unaochezwa kwa kupigwa na fimbo yenye kingoe.
hocus-pocus, *n.* maneno ya kilinge, kiinimacho, madanganyo ya maneno na matendo.
hod, *n.* chano, karai.
hodge-podge, *n.* taz. *hotch-potch.*
hoe, *n.* jembe. — *v.t.* lima, palilia.
hog, *n.* nguruwe dume; (*wild*) nguruwe wa mwitu; (*dirty person*) mtu mchafu, mpujufu. *Eat like a hog,* -la kwa pupa, lafua. *Go the whole hog,* fanya jambo mpaka kulimaliza (kufaulu, mpaka mwisho).
hogshead, *n.* pipa kubwa, hasa la kutilia mvinyo.
hoist, *v.t.* inua, pandisha, kweza; (*sail, load &c.*) tweka, twika. *Hoist with his own petard,* tegwa na tendo lake mwenyewe.
hold, (1) *n.* (*of a ship*) ngama, tumbo, falka, feuli, banduru.
hold, (2) *v.t.* (*p.t. and pf.t.* **held**) shika, kamata, bamba, nasa; (*think*) dhani, dhania; (*contain*) weka, chukua; — *v.i.* (*be in force*) kaa, -wa na nguvu; (*continue*) dumu. *Hold!* simama! basi! *It holds water,* haivuji; (*of statement, plan*) yafaa, ni nzuri. *Hold the breath,* zuia (paaza) pumzi. *Hold out* (*endure*), vumilia, tosha, stahimili, toshindwa; (*extend*) nyosha, toa. *Hold forth* (*of speech*), toa maneno wazi, toa hotuba ndefu. *Hold in,* zuia. *Hold good,* wa na nguvu, faa. *Hold a meeting,* fanya mkutano; (*a court, council*) barizi. *Hold off,* jitenga, kaa mbali; (*prevent*) zuia, pinga. *Hold on,* fuliza, fuluiza, dumu, endelea; (*keep hold*) shikilia. *Hold on!* ngoja kwanza! *Hold up,* inua; (*take courage*) jipa moyo, piga moyo konde; (*of weather*) anuka; (*a traveller &c.*) tisha (msafiri &c.) na kuiba mali kwa nguvu. *Hold by, to, or with,* wa hali moja na, -wa upande wa, pendelea, taka. *Hold together,* shikamana; (*appear true*) thibitika. *Hold in the hollow of one's hand,* -wa na amri zote juu ya. *Hold a man to his promised word*), shurutisha (pasi-

sha) mtu kutukeleza (kufikisha) ahadi yake. *Hold one's tongue*, nyamaza, nyamaa kimya, kaa kimya. — *n.* mshiko; (*stronghold*) ngome, boma, husuni; (*authority*) uwezo, amri. *Get hold of*, kamata, shikilia, weza, pata. *Keep a hold on him*, usimwache. *Lay hold of*, shikilia. *I have a hold on him*, namwia. **holdback**, *n.* kizuio, kizuizi, mgogoro. **holder**, *n.* kitu cha kuwekea (kutilia) kitu au vitu vingine; (*person*) mwenyewe, mpangaji. **holding**, *n.* kiwanja (shamba).

hole, *n.* tundu, kitundu, shimo, pango, kipango, kuo; (*through a thing*) kipenyo, tobo, kitobo; (*for seed*) koongo; (*for light, air*) mwangaza; (*in ear for ornament*) ndewe. *Be in a hole* (*difficulty*), -wa na mashaka, kwama. *Make a hole*, zua, toboa; (*with drill*) pekecha; (*with spade &c.*) fukua, chimbua. *Pick holes in*, pekua. *Hole and corner methods*, uayari, ulaghai, ujanja, werevu, udanganyifu.

holiday, *n.* (*festival*) sikukuu, idi; (*free from work*) ruhusa, likizo, livu. *Be given a holiday*, achiwa siku, likizwa, ruhusiwa kupumzika.

holiness, *n.* taz. *holy*.

hollow, *a.* wazi ndani, -vungu, -tupu, -enye uvungu; (*false*) si kweli, si halisi, -enye hila. — *n.* bonde, shimo, mvungu, uvungu. — *v.t.* (*out*) komba, fukua. **hollow-eyed**, *a.* -enye macho ndani. **hollow-hearted**, *a.* -erevu, -danganyifu, si amini. **hollowness**, *n.* uwazi, uvungu; (*falsity*) hila, udanganyifu, matupu.

holly. *n.* namna ya mti wenye majani yaliyo na ncha kali.

holocaust, *n.* maangamizi (hasa ya watu kwa kuchomwa moto).

holster, *n.* mfuko wa bastola.

holy, *a.* -takatifu, safi; (*consecrated*) wakf, -a kutengwa (kuwekwa) kwa kazi ya Mungu (dini). *Holy Ghost*, Roho Mtakatifu. **holiness**, *n.* utakatifu, usafi, utawa, usufii, uwalii.

homage, *n.* heshima kuu, ustahi, ibada. *Do homage*, -pa heshima, sujudia, shika miguu.

home, *n.* (*of house*) kwangu (kwako, kwake &c.), nyumba, kiambo, chengo, mastakimu, maskani; (*of place, country &c.*) kwetu (kwenu, kwao &c.), nchi, makao; (*locality*) mahali; *refuge*) makimbilio. *He is at home*, yuko (kwake). *I feel myself at home*, najiona niko kwetu. *Make yourself at home*, usifanye haya, hapa kama kwako. *Be at home in*, jua sana, zoelea sana. *Drive a nail home*, pigilia (kongomea) msumari kabisa. *His words went home*, maneno yake yalichoma moyo. *Go home*, enda kwake; (*have effect*) -wa na nguvu, shinda. — *a.* -a kwetu, -a karibu; (*telling*) -a kupenya moyoni, -enye njia. *Home-thrust*, pigo la nguvu, neno la kuchoma (kupenya) moyo. — *adv.* kwake (kwao &c.), hata kwake, hata ndani, hata mwisho, sana. **home-bred**, *a.* -zalia, -a kwetu. **homeless**, *a.* -a kutupwa, -a kupotea. *He is homeless*, hana kwake. **homely**, *a.* -a kama kwetu, -a kukumbusha mtu kwake (kwao); -a kawaida, -a mazoea; -siyo na mapambo (fahari, urembo, uzuri, nahau &c.) mengi. **home-sick**, *a.* (*be*) tamani sana nchi yetu (yao &c.) kumbuka kwetu (kwao &c.); waza kwao. **home-sickness**, *n.* hamu ya kukumbuka kwao; (*sickness on leaving home and settling in a strange place*) mkunguru, ukunguru. **homestead**, *n.* nyumba na shamba lake.

homeward, *adv.* -a kwenda kwetu, -a kurudi. *Homeward-bound* (*ship*), njiani kurudi kwao, -a kwenda kwao, -nayorudi.

homicide, *n.* (*person*) mwuaji; (*act*) kuua mtu.

homily, *n.* hotuba.

hominy, *n.* unga wa mahindi.

homo-, *pref.* -a kufanana, -a jinsi moja, *e.g.* **homoeopathy**, *n.* mauguzi ya kulisha dawa kidogo kidogo, ambayo inaleta dalili kama zile zile za ugonjwa wenyewe. **homogeneous,** *a.* -a jinsi moja, -a namna moja tu, -ote sawa pia, -ote namna moja. **homologous,** *a.* sawa, -a namna moja, -a kufanana. **homonym,** *n.* neno lililotamkwa kama neno jingine ila maana yake si sawa, *e.g.* paa (mnyama), paa (la nyumba); kaa (la moto), kaa (mnyama wa bahari).

hone, *n.* kinoo, jiwe la kunolea. — *v.t.* noa.

honest, *a.* amini, -aminifu, -nyofu, -a haki, adili, -adilifu, madhubuti. **honestly,** *a.* kwa haki (uadilifu, unyofu, uaminifu). **honesty,** *n.* amini, uaminifu, unyofu, uadilifu, moyo safi.

honey, *n.* asali ya nyuki, uki. **honey-bee,** *n.* nyuki. **honeycomb,** *n.* masega, mkate wa nyuki (nta yenye asali), majana, mazana, kamba ya nyuki. **honeycombed,** *a.* -enye vitundu vingi, -a kupenyezwa vipenyo vingi. **honeymoon,** *n.* muda wa kukaa faraghani pamoja bwana na bibi arusi baada ya kuoana, fungate.

honorarium, *n.*, **honorary,** *a.*, **honorific,** *a.* taz. *honour.*

honour, *n.* heshima, utukufu, staha, ustahi, adhama, taadhima, ustahiki, jaha; (*trustworthiness, justice*) uaminifu, amini, kweli, haki, uadilifu, maadili; (*rank*) daraja bora, sifa njema. *Debt of honour,* deni ya ahadi, si ya sharti. *Word of honour,* ahadi. *It is a point of honour with me,* nimeahidi, imenibidi. *On my honour,* natoa ahadi. *Honour bright,* kweli, ndiyo ahadi. *Be held in honour,* heshimiwa, stahiwa &c. *He did honour to the meal,* chakula kilikuwa kizuri akala shibe yake. *Your Honour* (namna ya kusema na jaji). — *v.t.* heshimu, jali, tukuza, stahi, sifu, adhimu, adhimisha, sharifu. *Honour a promise,* fikiliza ahadi *Honour a debt,* lipa deni. **honorarium,** *n.* malipo ya hiari kwa kazi yasiyodaiwa, bakshishi, ada, karo. **honorary,** *a.* -a heshima tu, si -a mshahara. *An honorary office,* kazi bila mshahara. **honorific,** *a.* -a heshima. **honourable,** *a.* -a heshima, amini, -stahiki, -aminifu, adili, adilifu, mahashumu. *Honourable, Right Honourable,* jina la heshima la kutaja watu wenye cheo fulani.

hood, *n.* kifuniko cha kichwa na mabega; (*woman's*) shela; (*of a car*) chandalua. — *v.t.* funika, setiri.

hoodwink, *v.t.* danganya, pofusha macho, hadaa.

hoodoo, *n.* kisirani, ndege mbaya.

hoof, *n.* ukwato, kwata. *Cattle on the hoof,* ng'ombe wazima (wahai).

hook, *n.* kulabu; (*fishing*) ndoana; (*hooked stick &c.*) upembo, kiopoo, mti uliopetemana; (*for gathering fruit*) ngoe, kingoe; (*to hang things on*) chango. *By hook or by crook,* kwa vyo vyote, kwa njia zote, viwavyo vyote. *Bill-hook,* mundu. — *v.t.* (*fish*) vua, tega, pata; (*branch of tree, fruit &c.*) ngoeka, koeka; — *v.i.* (*form a hook*) petamana. **hooked,** *a.* kama ndoana, -a kupindika, -liopindamana, -enye kombo, -liopetamana. **hookworm,** *n.* kichango kinacholeta ugonjwa wa safura kikiingia na kukaa tumboni.

hookah, *n.* buruma, kikororo.

hookworm, *n.* taz. *hook.*

hooligan, *n.* mtu azoeaye kupigana na kufanya ghasia na makelele katika njia za mji.

hoop, *n.* pete kubwa, duara, gurudumu. *Hoop-iron,* bambo ya chuma ya kuzungushia pipa.

hooping-cough, *n.* taz. *whooping-cough.*

hoot, *v.i.* lia kama bundi, lia kama paipu ya meli au honi ya motakaa; — *v.t.* zomea, pigia makelele, fukuza kwa makelele, lia 'Huyo! huyo!' — *n.* mlio wa bundi (wa paipu, wa honi), makelele ya mzaha, zomeo.

hooter, *n.* honi, paipu.

hop, (1) *v.i.* ruka kwa mguu mmoja, rukaruka kama ndege warukavyo chini na kama chura afanyavyo;

— *v.t.* (*over*) kiuka. *Hop it* (*slang*) nenda, toka, ondoka. — *n.* mruko wa mguu mmoja.

hop, (2) *n.* mti wenye maua yanayotumiwa kufanyizia pombe ya kizungu; maua ya mti huo.

hope, *v.i.* tumaini, taraji; (*desire*) taka, tamani; (*fancy*) dhani, ona. — *n.* matumaini, taraja, rajua. **hopeful,** *a.* -enye kutumaini, tumainifu, -a taraja; (*giving hope*) -a kutia taraja, -a tumaini, -a kupendeza, -a kufaa. **hopeless,** *a.* -a bure, -a kukata tamaa, -baya kabisa, -sioponyeka, -sio na matumaini.

hoopoe, *n.* hudhud, golegole.

horde, *n.* kundi (la watu wanaofanya ghasia, la maharamia, la watu wenye jeuri).

horizon, *n.* mstari wa upeo wa macho kama kwamba mbingu na nchi zimeungana hapo, upeo wa macho; (*of a person*) ulimwengu, fikira. **horizontal,** *a.* kama *horizon,* yaani -a sawa na nchi (kulala), inayolala sawasawa (si wima).

hormone, *n.* kitu kilichomo damuni kinachochukuliwa mpaka viungo vingine vya mwili na kuvichochea.

horn, *n.* pembe; (*for blowing*) baragumu, mbiu, siwa, gunda, kigunda; (*of motor-car &c.*) honi, paipu. *To be in the horns of a dilemma,* kuwa na budi kuchagua moja katika mawili, ukipenda usipende. *Butt with the horns,* piga pembe, guta. *Draw in one's horns,* tulia. *Take the bull by the horns,* fanya jambo gumu kwa uthabiti (kwa ujasiri *&c.*). **hornbill,** *n.* (*crowned*) kwembe. **horned,** *a.* -enye pembe. **hornpipe,** *n.* namna ya ngoma (ya kucheza), hasa ya kibaharia. **horny,** *a.* -a kama pembe, -a pembe, -gumu.

hornet, *n.* nyigu, mavu, bungu.

hornpipe, *n.*, **horny,** *a.* taz. *horn.*

horoscope, *n.* falaki, maaguzi kwa nyota (hasa kwa kutazama nyota zilizvyo mtoto azaliwapo). *Cast a horoscope,* piga falaki, agua kwa nyota.

horrible, *a.*, **horrid,** *a.*, **horrify,** *v.* taz. *horror.*

horror, *n.* hofu kuu, tisho, machukio, kirahi, karaha; (*horrible object*) kitisho, kioja, maafa, kitu cha hofu. *Strike with horror* = *horrify.* **horrible,** *a.* -a kuogofya, -a kutisha, -a kuchukiza, -a kukirihi. **horrid,** *a.* -a kuchukiza, -baya sana. **horrify,** *v.t.* ogofya, hofisha, tia hofu, tisha, chukiza mno, kirihi.

hors de combat, *a.* -enye kuzuiwa -sipigane (hasa kwa sababu ya kujeruhiwa).

hors d'œuvre, *n.* namna ya vyakula vilivyokolezwa sana vinavyoletwa mezani mwanzo wa kula.

horse, *n.* farasi; (*cavalry*) askari wapanda farasi; (*frame, support*) tegemeo. *On horseback,* juu ya farasi. *Mount* (*get on*) *a horse,* panda farasi. *Get off a horse,* shuka juu ya farasi. *To ride the high horse,* takabari. *Work like a horse,* fanya kazi kwa bidii nyingi. *Put the cart before the horse,* fanya mambo kinyume cha taratibu yake. *To look a gift horse in the mouth,* nung'unikia zawadi (kitu kilichopewa bure). *Horse sense,* busara. **horseman,** *n.* mpanda farasi. **horsemanship,** *n.* uhodari (ustadi) wa kupanda farasi. **horseplay,** *n.* mchezo wenye ghasia. **horse-power,** *n.* kipimo cha kupimia nguvu ya mashine (mtambo) ndiyo nguvu iwezayo kuinua ratli 550 futi moja kwa nukta moja. **horse-radish,** *n.* (*tree*) mronge. **horseshoe,** *n.* chuma cha kupigilia kwato za farasi. **horsewhip,** *v.t.* piga sana kwa mjeledi.

hortatory, *a.* -a kuonya, -enye shauri.

horticulture, *n.* kilimo cha bustani, ukulima wa bustani. **horticulturist,** *n.* mkulima wa bustani.

hosanna, *int. and n.* neno la kumsifu Mungu au kumwabudu.

hose, *n.* (*stockings*) soksi (ndefu), vifuniko vya miguu; (*pipe*) bomba la mpira la kutupia maji (bustanini, kuzimia moto *&c.*). **hose-pipe,** *n.*

bomba la mpira la kutupia maji. **hosier,** *n.* mwuza soksi, shati, nguo za kuvaa ndani (ya nguo nyingine) kama fulana *&c.* **hosiery,** *n.* bidhaa za *hosier* ndiyo soksi, fulana, kala *&c.*

hospice, *n.* nyumba ya kupumzikia wasafiri. **hospitable,** *a.* -karimu, -a kupokea wageni, -a kukaribisha watu, -enye mlango mzuri. **hospital,** *n.* hospitali (nyumba ya kuuguzia wagonjwa). **hospitality,** *n.* ukarimu, upaji, kukaribisha wageni, utu mwema.

host, (1) *n.* (*sacramental*) mkate unaotumika katika Ushirika Mtakatifu.

host, (2) *n.* mwenyeji, mwenye kukaribisha wageni. **hostel,** *n.* nyumba ya kukaa wanafunzi wa chuoni; nyumba ya kupumzikia wasafiri. **hostelry,** *n.* nyumba ya kupumzikia wasafiri. **hostess,** *n.* *host* wa kike.

host, (3) *n.* jeshi, wingi. **hostage,** *n.* mdhamini, kole, mtu aliyeshikwa au kuwekwa rehani; (*pledge*) dhamana. **hostile,** *a.* -a adui, -a kukinza, -a uhasama, -a kushindana (kupigana, kupinzana). **hostility,** *n.* uadui, uhasimu, chuki, ukinzani.

hostel, *n.*, **hostelry,** *n.*, **hostess,** *n.* taz. *host* (2).

hostile, *a.*, **hostility,** *n.*, taz. *host* (3).

hostler, *n.* taz. *ostler.*

hot, *a.* -a moto, -enye joto; (*angry, vehement*) -kali, -a hasira, -a harara, -a hamaki, -epesi kukasirika, -a kasirani; (*appetent*) -enye ashiki (nyege) nyingi. *Hot work,* kazi ya hari, kazi moto. *Hot water,* maji ya moto; (*trouble*) mashaka, matata. *Hot sun,* jua kali. *The sun is hot,* jua linachomoza. *This room is hot,* chumba hiki kina joto. *I am hot,* nina jasho (hari). *Get hot* (*excited*), sisimka, taharuki. *Hot air* (*slang*), upuzi, mapayo. *Give it to him hot,* mpige (mwadhibu) sana. **hotbed,** *n.* tuta (lenye mbolea au samadi la kuotesha sana mboga); (*of evil &c.*) mahali penye maovu (mabaya, fitina *&c.*) mengi. **hot-blooded,** *a.* -enye harara ya moyo, -a harara, -kali, -a hamaki, -epesi wa hasira, habali (*appetent*) -enye ashiki nyingi, -a harara. **hotfoot,** *adv.* mbio, kwa haraka, upesi. **hot-headed,** *a.* -a harara, -kali, taz. *hot-blooded.* **hot-house,** *n.* kibanda cha kuoteshea maua na matunda. **hotly,** *adv.* kwa ukali, kwa hasira, kwa hamaki *&c.*

hotchpotch, *n.* changanyiko.

hotel, *n.* hoteli, nyumba ya wageni.

hotfoot, *adv.* **hot-headed,** *a.*, **hot-house,** *n.*, **hotly,** *adv.* taz. *hot.*

Hottentot, *n.* mtu mweusi wa kabila moja la Afrika ya Kusini.

hough, *v.t.* taz. *hamstring.*

hound, *n.* mbwa mkubwa wa kuwindia; (*person*) mtu mbaya (mjuvi, mfidhuli, duni, hafifu). — *v.t.* fukuza, winda, toa; (*incite*) sukuma, sukumiza (kwa mabaya), chomesha, tomesha.

hour, *n.* saa; (*time, opportunity*) wakati, siku, nafasi, wasaa. *What is the hour?* saa ngapi? *After hours,* kwa kuchelewa. *Keep good hours,* enda kulala mapema. *Small hours,* (tangu usiku wa manane mpaka alfajiri). *The eleventh hour,* saa (wakati, nafasi) ya mwisho kufanya jambo. *His hour has come,* saa ya kufa kwake (*or,* nafasi yake ya kufanya jambo) imewadia. *In an evil hour,* kwa bahati mbaya. **hour-glass,** *n.* shisha, chupa yenye mchanga ya kuhesabia saa. **hour-hand,** *n.* mkono (mshale) wa saa unaoonyesha saa, ndio ule mdogo. **hourly,** *a.* -a kila saa, -a kutokea (kufanyika *&c.*) katika muda wa saa. — *adv.* baada ya kila saa, saa yo yote, wakati wo wote.

houri, *n.* hurulaini, mwanamwali mzuri; Waislamu husadiki *houri* hukaa peponi kuwafurahisha watu wafao na kwenda huko.

hourly, *a.* taz. *hour.*

house, *n.* nyumba, makao; chengo; (*household*) madaraka ya nyumba, mambo ya nyumbani, watu wa nyumbani; (*family*) jamaa; (*in trade*) kumpuni, shirika la wafanyi biashara; (*parliament*) baraza. —*v.t.* pokea nyumbani, karibisha; (*shelter*) peleka ndani, linda. *Keep house*, -wa na nyumba, pata nyumba. *Keep open house*, karibisha wote. **house-breaker**, *n.* mwizi, mwivi aingiaye nyumba ya mtu mwingine mchana kusudi aibe; mwenye uchumi wa kubomoa nyumba au majengo. **household**, *n.* watu wa nyumbani. **householder**, *n.* mwenyeji, mwenye nyumba. **housekeeper**, *n.* (mwanamke msimamizi wa nyumba mwenye madaraka ya nyumba). **housekeeping**, *n.* madaraka ya nyumba, maangalizi (matunzaji) ya nyumba. **houseless**, *a. He is houseless*, hana kituo, hana kwake, yu mhuni, mwenda ovyo. **housemaid**, *n.* mwanamke mtumishi wa nyumbani kwa mshahara. **house-warming**, *n.* karamu ya kuzindua (kuzindikia) nyumba. **housewife**, *n.* bibi mkubwa wa nyumba, bibi mwenye nyumba; (*for needles &c.*) kibumba (mfuko) chenye sindano, uzi, vifungo &c. **housing**, *n.* kupatia watu nyumba za kukaa; (*cavity &c.*) tundu (uvungu &c.) katika mti (boriti &c.) la kukaa mti mwingine; (*of plane &c.*) chumba.

hove, *p.t.* ya *heave*.

hovel, *n.* kibanda kibovu, nyumba mbovu (ya kimaskini, chafu).

hover (*about*), *v.i.* rukaruka juu, zungukazunguka kwa mabawa; (*hesitate, waver*) kaa kwa mashaka, sitasita, tanga; (*of a bird in the air*) sinzia hewani.

how, *adv.* je? jinsi gani? hali gani? kwa sababu gani? *How to (do)* jinsi ya, njia ya (kufanya;) (*in comp.*) -vyo, -je. *How are you? How do you do?* Hujambo? Jambo? U hali gani? Waonaje? Habari ya siku nyingi? *How much?* kiasi gani? Kem? Wauzaje? *How beautiful!* nzuri kama nini! nzuri mno! nzuri ajabu! *Howbeit, however, howsoever*, lakini, walakini, iwayo yote, kwa vyo vyote. *He will buy it, however dear it is*, atanunua ijapo ni ghali sana.

howdah, *n.* kiti juu ya tembo aliyefugwa.

however, *conj.* walakini. Taz. *how.*

howitzer, *n.* namna ya mzinga mfupi wa kutupia risasi katika handaki.

howl, *v.i.* lia (kama mbwa, kama upepo wa nguvu), zoma, lia kwa ukelele (kwa sababu ya maumivu, hasira, mzaha &c.); vuma. — *n.* lio, mlio, mvumo, uvumi. *Howl of laughter*, ukelele wa kicheko, kucheka kwa makelele. **howler**, *n.* kosa (hasa katika mtihani) la kuchekesha. **howling**, *a.* -a kulia (kuvuma &c.). *It was a howling success*, ilisitawi sana.

hub, *n.* kitovu (kikombe) cha gurudumu; mahali penye shughuli (kazi, biashara &c.) nyingi.

hubbub, *n.* makelele, ghasia, udhia, zahama, msukosuko.

huckster, *n.* mchuuzi, mfanya biashara ya kutembeza vitu vidogo vidogo.

huddle, *v.t.* weka (tupa, tia, songa) pamoja ovyo ovyo; songasonga; (*oneself up*) jikunyata, jikunja; (*of wearing clothes*) vaa ovyo ovyo; —*v.i.* (*together*) songana, songamana.

hue, (1) *n.* rangi.

hue, (2) *n. Raise a hue and cry*, lia Huyo! Huyo! piga makelele.

huff, *n.* chuki, uchungu, moyo juu, kinyongo, shonde, undani, kununa. *Take the huff*, chukizwa, udhika. **huffy**, *a.* -a chukichuki, -epesi wa hasira, -a kinyongo, -enye undani, -a shonde, -nunaji.

hug, *v.t.* kumbatia, ambatana na; (*the shore*) sogea pwani, ambaa, sairi. — *n.* kikumbatio.

huge, *a.* -kubwa mno.

hulk, *n.* (*old ship*) meli (jahazi, chombo) mbovu; (*person*) mtu mkubwa mzito. **hulking**, *a.* -kubwa -zito.

hull, (1) *n.* jahazi (meli, chombo) tupu (pasipo milingoti, matanga, kamba *&c.*).

hull, (2) *n.* ganda, kumvi, kumbi. — *v.t.* toa ganda, menya, pura, puna, papatua, ambua, goboa.

hullabaloo, *n.* ghasia, makelele, zahama, msukosuko.

hullo, *int.* neno la kumfanya mtu atazame (la mshangao, la kumwamkia mtu, hasa rafiki au mtani).

hum, *v.i.* vuma, imba (hali midomo imefumbwa), vuma kama nyuki. *To hum and haw,* sitasita katika kusema. *Make things hum,* tia nguvu. — *n.* uvumi, mavumi, mvumo, vumo.

human, *a.* -a mwanadamu, -a mtu, -a kibinadamu. **humane,** *a.* -ema, -enye huruma, -pole, -a fadhili. **humanitarian,** *a.* -a huruma, -a kujaribu kupunguza maumivu na taabu. **humanity,** *n.* huruma, wema utu mwema; (*the human race*) jamii ya wanadamu wote, walimwengu, watu wote; (*human nature*) utu, asili ya kibinadamu, ubinadamu, uanadamu. **humanize,** *v.t.* sitawisha utu, staarabisha, ongoza kwa mafundisho na desturi njema, zoeza mema, toa ushenzini, ondoa ukali na ukatili.

humble, *a.* -nyenyekevu, -enye haya, -enye soni, -siyetaka makuu, -siyetakabari, -siyetaka fahari, -adilifu; (*mean, poor*) -nyonge, maskini, duni. *Eat humble pie,* kiri makosa, upungufu *&c.* na kuomba radhi. — *v.t.* shusha, tweza, dhilisha, aibisha. *To be humbled,* twezwa, shushwa *&c.* **humbly,** *adv.* kwa unyenyekevu, kwa haya. **humiliate,** *v.t.* shusha, tweza, dhilisha; (*mortify, abash*) tahayarisha, fedhehesha, tia haya, ingiza uchungu, kashifu, vunjia heshima (daraja, cheo, jina *&c.*). **humiliation,** *n.* aibu, udhilifu, uchungu, tahayuri, haya. **humility,** *n.* unyenyekevu, uvumilivu, haya.

humbug, *n.* upuzi, mapayo; (*imposter*) mjanja, ayari, laghai; (*act*) ujanja, uayari, ulaghai, werevu. — *v.t.* danganya, laghai, ghilibu.

humdrum, *a.* (*monotonous*) -a siku zote (bila mabadiliko), -a vivi hivi, -a kuchosha.

humerus, *n.* mfupa wa mkono katikati ya kiko na bega.

humid, *a.* majimaji, chepechepe, -nyevu, chege, -a rutuba; (*of climate*) -a jasho. **humidity,** *n.* unyevu, uchepechepe, rutuba; kiasi cha maji yaliyo hewani.

humiliate, *v.,* **humiliation,** *n.,* **humility,** *n.* taz. *humble.*

humming, *n.* uvumi. **humming-bird,** *n.* ndege mzuri mdogo afanyaye uvumi kwa mabawa yake.

hummock, *n.* kilima kidogo; mwinuko mdogo, kiduta.

humorist, *n.,* **humorous,** *n.* taz. *humour.*

humour, *n.* (*disposition*) tabia, moyo; (*whim, idea*) nia, wazo, shauri; (*wit, playfulness*) ucheshi, uchekeshaji, ubishi; (*fluid*) maji (ya mwilini). *He has a sense of humour,* yu mwepesi kuona na kufahamu mambo ya ubishi. *He is good humoured,* yu mkunjufu (mchangamfu). — *v.t.* bembeleza (tuliza, furahisha) kwa kukubali mashauri (matakwa). **humorist,** *n.* mcheshi, mchekeshaji, -a kuchekesha, -enye ubishi.

hump, *n.* kigongo; (*of a cow &c.*) nundu. **humpbacked,** *a.* -enye kigongo (kinundu).

humph, *int.* sauti ya kuonyesha chukizo au kutokusadiki.

humus, *n.* udongo uliofanyika kwa majani kuoza, rutuba.

hunch, *n.* kinundu, kigongo; bumba, kipande kikubwa. **hunchback,** *n.* kigongo, kibiongo. — *v.t.* kunja mgongo kufanya kinundu au kigongo.

hundred, *n.* mia. *Two hundred,* miteen. *Hundreds,* -ingi, mia mia. **hundredfold,** *a.* -a mara mia. — *adv.* mara mia. **hundredth,** *a.* -a mia, -a sehemu mia kwa moja.

hundredweight, *n.* ratli mia na kumi na mbili.
hung, *p.t. and pf.t.* ya *hang*.
hunger, *n.* njaa, ukosefu wa chakula, uhitaji wa chakula; (*craving*) tamaa, shauku, uchu, kwiu. — *v.i.* (*hunger for, after*) tamani sana, taka sana. **hungry**, *a.* -enye njaa, -a kutaka kula; (*of soil, land*) -siotoa chakula, -bava.
hunk, *n.* kipande kikubwa kinene (hasa cha mkate).
hunkers, *n.* mapaja. *On one's hunkers*, kuchutuma.
hunt, *v.t.* winda, saka; (*drive away*) fukuza, winga. *Hunt for*, tafuta kwa bidii. — *n.* mwindo, msako, kuwinda, kusaka. **hunter**, *n.* mwinda, mwindaji, msaka, msakaji, msasi; (*horse*) farasi wa kuwindia. **hunting**, *n.* kuwinda, uwindaji, usakaji, usasi. **huntsman**, *n.* taz. *hunter*.
hurdle, *n.* kiunzi kama cha kufanyizia ua au kitalu (cha miti au fito zilizosokotwa). Pia hutumika kurukia katika mashindano ya kwenda mbio na ya farasi.
hurdy-gurdy, *n.* santuri, kinanda.
hurl, *v.t.* tupa kwa nguvu, vurumisha.
hurly-burly, *n.* makelele, udhia, ghasia, zahama, msukosuko.
hurrah, *n.* mlio wa shangwe (wa furaha, wa kushangilia).
hurricane, *n.* tufani, kimbunga.
hurry, *n.* haraka, harara, ghasia, hima, kikaka, kakara. — *v.t.* himiza, harakisha, kimbiza; — *v.i.* enda kwa haraka, kimbia, ghafilika, enda hima. **hurry-scurry**, *n.* ghasia, zahama, kikaka, kakara.
hurt, *v.t.* (*p.t. and pf.t.* **hurt**) dhuru, umiza, uma, vuaza, changa, wanga, sononesha; (*damage*) haribu, vunja, hasiri, athiri; (*annoy*) sumbua, udhi, huzunisha, kasiri; — *v.i.* uma, umiza. *Hurt the feeling of*, hizi, chukiza, tia uchungu. *Where are you hurt?* Waumwa wapi? *Be hurt*, umwa, umia, umizwa; (*in feelings*) chukizwa, udhika, tiwa uchungu.
hurtful, *a.* -a kudhuru, -a kuumiza, -enye madhara, -enye hasara.
hurtle, *v.i.* enda mbio sana, pita mbio sana.
husband, *n.* mume. — *v.t.* tumia kwa uangalifu (kwa kiasi), weka akiba, punguza gharama, kabidhi. **husbandman**, *n.* mkulima, mlimaji. **husbandry**, *n.* mlimo, maarifa ya kilimo, ulimaji, ukulima.
hush, *int.* kimya! nyamaza! kelele! — *v.t.* tuliza, nyamazisha; — *v.i.* nyamaa kimya, tulia. *Hush up*, setiri, ficha. *Hush money*, rushwa ya kumvuta mtu asetiri kosa (maovu &c.).
husk, *n.* ganda; (*of rice*) kumvi; (*of coco-nut &c.*) makumbi. — *v.t.* ambua; (*coco-nut*), fua.
husky, *a.* -a nguvu na afya; (*of voice*) -liyopwewa.
hussar, *n.* askari mpanda farasi.
hussy, *n.* mwanamke mtundu (asiye na adabu, mjuvi, mkavu wa macho).
hustings, *n.* (mahali pa kufanyia *election*).
hustle, *v.t.* songa, sukuma, kumba, fanya haraka, sukumiza. — *n.* mkumbo, msukumo, haraka, hangaiko, msukosuko. **hustler**, *n.* mwenye bidii, atiaye bidii ili kazi ifanyike, msukumizi.
hut, *n.* kibanda, nyumba. **hut-tax**, *n.* kodi ya nyumba.
hutch, *n.* tundu, kitundu, kirimba, kizimba.
huzza, *n.* = *hurrah*.
hyaena, *n.* taz. *hyena*.
hybrid, *a.* -a wazazi wa namna (mataifa) mbalimbali, -a mbegu mbili mbalimbali, -a kuchanganyika mbegu.
hydrant, *n.* bomba la maji.
hydraulic, *a.* -a maji, -nayoendeshwa kwa maji. **hydraulics**, *n.* maarifa ya mwendo wa maji. **hydrocele**, *n.* mshipa wa maji, toma. **hydrodynamics**, *n.* maarifa ya mwendo na nguvu za maji. **hydrogen**, *n.* namna ya hewa nyepesi sana, iliyochanganyika na *oxygen* hufanya

maji. **hydrography,** *n.* elimu ya kufanya ramani ya bahari na mito. **hydrometer,** *n.* chombo cha kupimia uzito wa maji na vilivyo kama maji, tena cha kupimia nguvu ya vileo. **hydrophobia,** *n.* kalab (*Ar.*), ugonjwa wa kuumwa na mbwa mwenye wazimu. **hydroplane,** *n.* eropleni inayoweza kwenda majini. **hydrostatics,** *n.* maarifa ya hali ya uzito wa maji yakiwa yamesimama.

hyena, *n.* fisi, kingugwa.

hygiene, *n.* maarifa ya kufanyiza na kuhifadhi afya mwilini, elimu ya afya. **hygienic,** *a.* -a afya, -a kuleta afya.

hygrometer, *n.*, **hygroscope,** *n.* chombo cha kupimia maji ya hewani, na umande na mvua.

hymen, *n.* kizinda, ubikira. **hymeneal,** *a.* -a ndoa, -a nikahi.

hymn, *n.* wimbo wa dini, mashairi, utenzi. — *v.t.* pigia (imbia) wimbo, imba. **hymnal,** *n.* kitabu cha nyimbo za dini.

hyperbolic, *a.* -a kupiga chuku, -a kuongeza, -kuu.

hypertrophy, *n.* kukua (kunenepa) mno sehemu ya mwili.

hyphaene palm, *n.* mwaa, mkoma, mkoche, mlala.

hyphen, *n.* kistari, alama hii (-) inayotumika kuunganisha maneno mawili, *e.g. self-praise.*

hypnotism, *n.* nguvu (uwezo) wa kumtia mtu hali kama ya usingizi na kumfanya atende mambo yanayoamriwa katika usingizi huo. **hypnotize,** *v.t.* tia mtu hali kama ya usingizi kwa nguvu ya kunuiza; shinda akili (kwa uzuri wa maneno, kwa ukali wa macho &c.).

hypochondria, *n.* ulegevu wa moyo, hasa kwa kuona mashaka juu ya afya. **hypochondriac,** *n.* mtu mwenye *hypochondria.*

hypocrisy, *n.* unafiki, uzandiki, kujisingizia wema (tabia njema, dini &c.), udanganyifu wa moyo. **hypocrite,** *n.* mnafiki, mzandiki, kauleni, mdanganyifu, mjisingizia wema (tabia njema &c.). **hypocritical,** *a.* -nafiki, -erevu, -danganyifu.

hypodermic, *a.* -a chini ya ngozi. — *n.* dawa ya kuingiza chini ya ngozi.

hypotenuse, *n.* upande mrefu wa pembetatu yenye pembe mraba.

hypothecate, *v.t.* weka rehani.

hypothesis, *n.* neno linalokubaliwa ingawa halikuthibitika, kusudi kueleza jambo; neno la kubahatisha, udhani. **hypothetical,** *a.* -a kubahatisha, -a kukisi, -a kutafuta hakika.

hyrax, *n.* wibari, kwanga, pelele.

hysteria, *n.* hali ya kushikwa na shetani (pepo) wa kulia au kucheka bila sababu. **hysterical,** *a.* -enye kushikwa na shetani (pepo). **hysterics,** *n.* hali ya kutoweza kuzuia kucheka au kulia, shetani, pepo.

I

I. herufi ya kirumi, maana yake moja.
I, *pron.* mimi, mwenyewe, nafsi yangu; (*in comp.*) ni-, na-.
ib. taz. *ibid.*
ibex, *n.* mbuzi mwitu.
ibid., ib., ibidem, *adv.* katika kitabu (mstari, kifungo, ukurasa) kile kile kilichotajwa.
ibis, *n.* kwarara, namna ya korongo wa maji.
ice, *n.* barafu. *Break the ice,* anzisha maneno, jasiria maneno. *On thin ice,* katika hatari au mashaka. — *v.t.* gandisha kwa baridi, funika kwa barafu; (*a cake*) ikiza sukari. **iceberg,** *n.* kilima cha barafu kinachoelea baharini. **icebound,** *a.* (*a ship*) iliyozungukwa kwa barafu (isiweze kutoka). **ice-cream,** *n.* chakula kitamu kilichofanyizwa kwa maziwa na vitu vingine na kugandishwa kwa baridi. **ice-pack,** *n.* mapande makubwa ya barafu baharini.
icicle, *n.* barafu iliyojitunga kama kishada au kishungi. **icing,** *n.* sukari ya kuikiza keki. **icy,** *a.* -liofunikwa kwa barafu, -a kama barafu, baridi sana.
ichneumon, *n.* nguchiro, mnyama kidogo kama paka auaye nyoka; (*fly*) namna ya inzi atagaye mayai yake mwilini mwa wadudu wengine.
ichthyology, *n.* elimu ya samaki zote.
ichthyosaurus, *n.* mnyama wa zamani sana mwenye mwili kama samaki na kinywa kirefu sana.
icicle, *n.*, **icing,** *n.* taz. *ice.*
icon, *n.* kitu kitakatifu (kilichowekwa wakf), *e.g.* picha au sanamu ya mtakatifu. **iconoclast,** *n.* mvunja sanamu takatifu; mvunja sanamu za kuabudika; mtu ajaribuye kuvunja desturi na imani za kale.
icy, *a.* taz. *ice.*
idea, *n.* wazo, nia, shauri, fikira; dhana; (*sketch, outline*) mwanzo, dokezo, kionyesho. *I have no idea,* sijui mwenyewe. *Only an idea,* wazo tu. **ideal,** *a.* (*mental*) -a akili, -a moyoni; (*unreal, fanciful*) -a kuwazika tu, si -a kweli, si -a amali; (*perfect, absolute*) kamili, pasipo upungufu, bila kombo lo lote, bora halisi na kupita yote. — *n.* wazo (fikira) la ukamilifu (utimilifu, upeo wa uzuri), kipeo, kilicho (lililo, aliye &c.) bora kabisa, mfano wa (kiolezo cha) ukamilifu. **idealism,** *n.* elimu ya watu wasemao: Hakuna hakika ya kitu ulimwenguni, ila ya nia tu na mawazo ya akili, ndiyo hakika hasa; tabia ya kuwaza mambo na mashauri kama yanayopaswa kuwa (yaani kamili kabisa); kutaka ukamili. **idealist,** *n.* mtu ashikaye au mwenye tabia ya *idealism*; mtaka ukamili. **idealize,** *v.t.* fanya kamili, tia ukamilifu; dhania kuwa kamili, kamilisha, fikiria mtu (au kitu) kuwa kamili na kutoangalia upungufu wake.
idem, *n. and adv.* neno (kitabu, mwandishi) lile lile.
identify, *v.t.* fanya mamoja, dhania (tendea) sawasawa, shirikisha, fungamanisha; (*recognize*) tambua, fahamu. **identical,** *a.* (*man*) yule mwenyewe, yule yule; (*thing*) kile kile &c., mfano mmoja. **identically,** *adv.* halisi, kabisa, barabara, hasa, vivyo hivyo. **identity,** *n.* umoja, kuwa yule yule (kile kile &c.), hali moja, usawa. *Prove one's identity,* thibitisha nafsi (ya kuwa ndiye hasa anayefikiriwa). **identification,** *n.* kuthibitisha (kuthibitishwa) nafsi.
id est, ndiyo, yaani, maana yake, kwa kawaida hufupishwa na kuandikwa *i.e.*
idiom, *n.* lugha, maneno; (*good style*) usemi mzuri safi, ufasaha wa maneno, nahau; (*special use*) fungu la maneno ambayo yanapoungwa pamoja huleta maana isiyo ya kawaida ya maneno yale mbalimbali, *e.g.* maji yamekwenda kuletwa, lakini kweli maji hayakuenda mahali. **idiomatic,** *a.* safi, -enye nahau, fasihi.

Idiomatic Swahili, Kiswahili cha kienyeji.

idiosyncrasy, *n.* tabia (nia, desturi, mwenendo, mazoea *&c.*) ya mtu peke yake; (*fad*) fundo, kinyongo.

idiot, *n.* mwenye kichaa, mjinga, mpumbavu, baradhuli, hayawani, juha, jura. *You are an idiot!* mpumbavu! umepumbaa! ng'ombe! ngamia! hayawani! **idiocy,** *n.* (*madness*) wazimu, kichaa; (*folly*) upumbavu mkuu, upuzi kabisa. **idiotic,** *a.* -pumbavu, -a upuzi *&c.*

idle, *a.* -vivu, -zembe, -legevu, -a bure, -siofaa, batili. *Idle words,* maneno ya bure, upuzi, maneno matupu. **idleness,** *n.* uvivu, uzembe, ulegevu, ukunguni.

idol, *n.* sanamu ya kuabudika; (*great favourite*) mpenzi, kipenzi, mtu (au kitu) anayependwa (kustahiwa, kuheshimiwa) mno. **idolater,** *n.* mwabudu sanamu, kafiri, mwabudu mungu wa uwongo. **idolatrous,** *a.* -a kuabudu sanamu. **idolatry,** *n.* ibada ya sanamu, ibada ya miungu ya uwongo, kupenda (kuheshimu) mno. **idolize,** *v.t.* abudu kama Mungu, penda mno, heshimu mno.

idyl(l), *n.* mashairi mafupi, hasa yanayosimulia habari za maisha ya shambani. **idyllic,** *a.* -a *idyl*; -zuri sana, -a kupendeza sana.

i.e. taz. *id est.*

if, *conj.* kama, ikiwa, iwapo, asaa; (*in comp.*) -ki-. *If I die,* nikifa. *If you please,* tafadhali. *If so,* hivi, kwa hiyo. *If it happens that,* endapo kwamba. *If* (*when*) *they come to hear,* waendapo wakasikia, wakipata habari.

ignite, *v.t.* washa, tia moto; — *v.i.* waka, shikwa na moto. **igneous,** *a.* -a moto, (mawe) yaliyofanyika kwa moto. **ignition,** *n.* mwako, kuwasha; (*of motor-car &c.*) vyombo vinavyotia moto vepa (mvuke) kuanzisha mashine.

ignoble, *a.* -nyonge, -duni, -dhaifu, -a kuchukiza, -baya, -a aibu, -a kutahayarisha. **ignominious,** *a.* -a aibu, -a kufedhehesha, -a kutahayarisha. **ignominy,** *n.* aibu, fedheha.

ignoramus, *n.*, **ignorance,** *n.*, **ignorant,** *a.* taz. *ignore.*

ignore, *v.t.* pitia makusudi, toangalia, tojali, achia mbali, puza. **ignoramus,** *n.* mjinga, mpumbavu, juha, jura. **ignorance,** *n.* ujinga, ukosefu wa maarifa, kutokujua. **ignorant,** *a.* -jinga, -a kijinga, -kosefu wa maarifa, -siojua, jahili.

iguana, *n.* mnyama kama kenge.

ikon, *n.* taz. *icon.*

ilk, *a.* *Of that ilk,* -a namna (jinsi, jina) ile.

ill, *a.* -gonjwa; (*bad*) -baya, -ovu; (*harmful*) -a madhara. *Be ill,* ugua. *He is ill,* hawezi. *Ill at ease,* -enye mashaka. *Ill done,* -liofanyika vibaya. *Ill fame,* sifa mbaya. *House of ill fame = brothel,* danguro, nyumba ya makahaba (malaya). *Ill will,* chuki, machukio. *Ill usage,* kutumia (kufanyia) vibaya. *A bird of ill omen,* ndege mbaya, kisirani. — *adv.* vibaya. — *n.* ubaya, uovu; (*harm, loss*) hasara, msiba, shari, mashaka, madhara, shida. **ill-advised,** *a.* -siyo na akili (busara), -jinga, -pumbavu. **ill-affected,** *a.* -a kutopenda, -a kutokubali, -a kuchukia. **ill-bred,** *a.* -siyo na adabu, -siyo na malezi mazuri. **ill-disposed,** *a.* -enye nia ya kudhuru, -ovu, -enye chuki, -a kutopenda (kutokubali). **ill-favoured,** *a.* -a kuchukiza, -baya, -enye sura (maungo) inayochukiza. **ill-looking,** *a.* -enye sura mbaya. **ill-mannered,** *a.* -sio adabu, -sio na malezi mazuri. **ill-natured,** *a.* -kali, -baya, -korofi. **illness,** *n.* ugonjwa, uele. **ill-omened,** *a.* **ill-starred,** *a.* ndege mbaya, -a kisirani, -a shari, -enye bahati mbaya, -a baa, -churo, -chimvi. **ill-tempered,** *a.* -gomvi, -tundu, -korofi, -chungu, -kali. **ill-timed,** *a.* si wakati wake, -sipofaa. **ill-treat,** *v.t.* tendea mabaya, tumia vibaya, dhuru, onea, dhulumu, chokoza. **ill-will,** *n.* uadui, husuda, kijicho, machukio.

illegal, *a.* -sio haki, -sio halali, -sioruhusiwa na sheria ya dini au serikali, haramu. **illegality,** *n.* jambo lisiloruhusiwa na sheria, jambo lililo haramu.

illegible, *a.* -siosomeka, -sioandikwa vizuri, -bayabaya.

illegitimate, *a.* -a haramu; (*irregular, incorrect*) si haki, si kanuni, si halisi, si halali.

ill-favoured, *a.* taz. *ill.*

illiberal, *a.* -enye choyo, -a moyo dhaifu, bahili, si karimu, si -ema, si -a kupenda wote sawa; (*narrow-minded*) -chache wa majuzi, -siojua mengi. **illiberality,** *n.* choyo, ubahili; (*meanness*) unyonge, udhaifu.

illicit, *a.* haramu, marufuku, -liogombezwa, -liyokatazwa, -sioruhusiwa.

illimitable, *a.* -kubwa sana, -ingi sana, -siopimikana, -a kukithiri.

illiterate, *a.* (*person*) asiyefundishwa, mjinga, asiyeweza kusoma wala kuandika; (*thing*) -jinga, -a kijinga.

ill-looking, *a.*, **ill-mannered,** *a.*, **ill-natured,** *a.*, **illness,** *n.* taz. *ill.*

illogical, *a.*, -siyo na maana, -sio kwa akili, -sipatana na akili.

ill-omened, *a.*, **ill-starred,** *a.*, **ill-tempered,** *a.*, **ill-timed,** *a.*, **ill-treat,** *v.* taz. *ill.*

illuminate, illumine, *v.t.* tia nuru, angaza, mulika; (*paint*) pamba kwa rangi; (*explain*) eleza, onyesha, fafanisha, dhihirisha. **illumination,** *n.* mwanga, nuru, mwangazu; (*coloured illustration*) herufi na sanamu za rangi; (*decoration with lights*) kupamba mji kwa taa.

illusion, *n.* (*deception*) madanganyo, uwongo, mangazimbwe, mauzauza; (*fancy*) wazo, kivuli, njozi; ndoto, ruya. **illusive, illusory,** *a.* -a kudanganya akili.

illustrate, *v.t.* fafanisha, eleza kwa mifano; (*furnish with pictures*) tia picha za kueleza (jambo, kitabu). **illustration,** *n.* (*picture*) picha, sanamu; (*explanation*) mafafanusi, maelezo, mfano, kielelezo. **illustrious,** *a.* maarufu, mashuhuri, -tukufu, bora, -enye sifa, -adhimu.

ill-will, *n.* taz. *ill.*

im- taz. **in-**; (*in comp.*) si, pasipo, bila.

image, *n.* sanamu, sura, mfano. *He is the image of his father,* amefanana kabisa na baba yake, analanda baba yake. **imagery,** *n.* sanamu, mifano, machoro; (*imitation*) mfano mtupu, mwigo; (*in writing, speech*) maneno yanayoleta mifano (picha) katika akili. **imaginary,** *a.* -a kuwazika tu, -a mawazo tu, -a uwongo, si -a kweli. **imagination,** *n.* akili, mawazo, kuwaza, dhana; (*fanciful idea*) wazo la upuzi, wazo la jambo lisiloelekea kuwa kweli; (*creative faculty*) uwezo wa mtu kuwazia mambo asiyoona ila amesikia yanatajwa. **imaginative,** *a.* -enye mawazo mengi, -enye mawazo ya mambo yasiyofaa kitu. **imagine,** *v.t.* (*form a mental picture of*) wazia, dhania; (*suppose*) waza, ona, dhani, fikiri; (*guess*) kisi.

imbecile, *a.* -punguani, -pungufu wa akili, -enye akili afkani. — *n.* punguani, bozi, zebe, mtu mwenye akili chache; (*fool*) mpumbavu. **imbecility,** *n.* upungufu wa akili, kichaa; upuzi.

imbibe, *v.t.* nywa; (*learn*) jifunza, weka, hifadhi moyoni.

imbroglio, *n.* ghasia, machafuko.

imbrue, *v.t.* chafua, tia taka (rangi, damu &c.).

imbue, *v.t.* lowesha; chovya (katika maji, rangi &c.); (*instil into*) tia moyoni, jaza.

imitate, *v.t.* iga, fuatisha, fuasa, fanya sawasawa, nakili. **imitation,** *n.* mwigo, ufuasi, uigaji; (*likeness*) mfano, nakili; (*meant to deceive*) madanganyo, si halisi. **imitative,** *a.* -a kuiga, -a kufuatisha.

immaculate, *a.* safi kabisa, pasipo mawaa, pasipo kosa, pasipo dhambi. *Immaculate conception,* imani ya

kuwa Bikira Mariamu alizaliwa pasipo dhambi ya asili.
immanent, *a.* -a kudumu ndani, -a kuwapo pote.
immaterial, *a.* pasipo umbo la kiwiliwili, -sio na mwili, -a pepo, -a roho; (*unimportant*) -sio na maana sana, si kitu. *It is quite immaterial*, haidhuru, mamoja.
immature, *a.* -changa, -siopevuka, -bichi; (*of fallen fruit*) -pooza. **immaturity**, *n.* uchanga, ubichi, hali ya kuwa bado kukomaa (kupevuka).
immeasurable, *a.* -sioweza kupimika, -a kupita kiasi, -sio na mwisho (mpaka, kadiri).
immediate, *a.* (*instant*) -a mara moja, -a ghafula, -a sasa hivi; (*close*) -a pili -a karibu, -a jirani; (*direct, personal*) -a -enyewe tu, bila msaada, -a kutenda (kutendeka) na mwenyewe pasipo kitu kingine. **immediately**, *adv.* sasa hivi, papo hapo, mara moja, bila kukawia, halahala, karibu.
immemorial, *a.* tangu zamani za kale, -a kale sana, -a zama zisizokumbukwa.
immense, *a.* -kubwa sana, -ingi mno. **immensity**, *n.* ukubwa (wa kupita kadiri), wingi.
immerse, *v.t.* chovya, tosa, zamisha, didimisha, tumbukiza; (*occupy fully*) shughulisha, tia katika shughuli (taabu, shida &c.). **immersion**, *n.* chovyo, mchovyo, kuchovyeka, kutumbukia, tumbukio; (*occupation*) kushughulika.
immigrant, *n.* mtu aingiaye nchi isiyo kwake na kukaa, mgeni, mjaji, mhamiaji. **immigrate**, *v.i.* ingia nchi kusudi kukaa, hamia nchi, hajiri, gura. **immigration**, *n.* kuja kukaa, majilio, kuhamia, hijira.
imminent, *a.* -a karibu sana, -a kuelekea kutokea upesi.
immobile, *a.* -sioweza kuendeshwa (kuhamishwa, kujongezwa), -sioweza kwenda (kuhama, kujongea).
immoderate, *a.* pasipo kadiri, bila kiasi, -ingi mno, -a kukithiri.
immodest, *a.* pasipo haya, -chafu, -pujufu. **immodesty**, *n.* upujufu, ukosefu wa haya (wa adabu), uhayawani.
immolate, *v.t.* chinja kwa kafara, dhabihu. **immolation**, *n.* kuchinja (kuchinjwa) kwa kafara.
immoral, *a.* -baya, -ovu, -enye tabia mbaya, si adili; (*licentious*) -fisadi, fasiki, asherati, -tongozi. **immorality**, *n.* ubaya, uovu; (*sexual*) uasherati, ufisadi, uzinzi.
immortal, *a.* -a kuishi milele, -a kudumu milele, -siokufa, -sio na mwisho, -a kale na kale, -sioharibika. **immortality**, *n.* maisha ya milele, uzima (uhai) usio na mwisho, kutokufa, ukale, kutoharibika. **immortalize**, *v.t.* fanyia ukumbusho wa daima, fanya kukaa (kuishi) milele, pasha sifa za daima.
immovable, *a.* -sioondoka, -siojongezeka, -siogeuka, -siotikisika, imara, madhubuti. **immovability**, *n.* kuwa *immovable*.
immune, *a.* (*from taxation*) huru; (*from disease*) -sioweza kupatwa na ugonjwa; (*from harm by poison &c.*) -sioweza kudhurika kwa sumu &c. **immunity**, *n.* (*exemption*) uhuru, ruhusa, kuachiwa; (*privilege*) haki, mapendeleo, faida; (*being without*) kutokuwa na, kuwa pasipo, kutopasiwa.
immure, *v.t.* funga, tia ndani, weka, tia.
immutable, *a.* -siobadilika, -siogeuka.
imp, *n.* shetani mdogo, kishetani, pepo mbaya; (*of a child*) mtoto mtundu. **impish**, *a.* -a kishetani, -tundu.
impact, *n.* mgongano, mpambano, pigo, kishindo.
impair, *v.t.* punguza nguvu (thamani, manufaa &c.), haribu, punguza, dhoofisha, kasiri.
impale, *v.t.* choma (penyeza) kwa kitu chenye ncha kali (mti, mkuki, upanga &c.).
impalpable, *a.* -sioonekana, -embamba sana, -dogo mno, laini.

impanel, *v.* taz. *empanel.*

impart, *v.t.* gawa, gawanya, shirikisha; (*by words*) toa, sema, funua, simulia, arifu, aridhia.

impartial, *a.* -adilifu, -adili, -a haki, -nyofu, -siopendelea, sawa. **impartiality,** *n.* uadilifu, maadili, unyofu, haki, kutopendelea.

impassable, *a.* -siopitika, -sioendeka. *The rivers are impassable,* mito haipishi (haivushi).

impasse, *n.* mahali pasipo na njia ya kutoka, shida kubwa, pingamizi, mgogoro.

impassioned, *a.* (*speech*) -a moyo (harara, hasira &c.).

impassive, *a.* baridi, -tepetevu, -kavu.

impatience, *n.* haraka, wepesi, kutosubiri, pupa, tutuo. **impatient,** *a.* -a harara, -a haraka, -enye pupa (tutuo).

impeach, *v.t.* shtaki, laumu, vunja heshima (jina, sifa), punguza sifa. **impeachment,** *n.* mashtaka.

impeccable, *a.* -sioweza kutenda dhambi, -siokosa, bila kosa (hatia, waa). **impeccability,** *n.* hali ya kuwa *impeccable.*

impecunious, *a.* maskini; (*person*) maskini, fukara, kibapara, mkata, suta, fakiri.

impede, *v.t.* zuia, pinga, tatanisha, kawilisha, chelewesha, kinza. **impediment,** *n.* kizuio, kizuizi, matata mgogoro, pingamizi; (*in speech*) kigugumizi, kitata. **impedimenta,** *n.* mizigo ya msafiri, vikorokoro.

impel, *v.t.* sukuma, sukumiza, endesha, himiza, tia chonjo, chochea, tomesha.

impend, *v.i.* karibia, -wa karibu. **impending,** *a.* -a karibu sana.

impenetrable, *a.* -siopenyeka, -siopenyezeka; (*unintelligible*) -siotambulikana, -a fumbo, -sioelea.

impenitent, *a.* -siotubu, -gumu -a moyo. **impenitence,** *n.* hali ya kuwa *impenitent,* ugumu wa moyo.

imperative, *a.* -a kuamuru; (*necessary*) -a lazima, -a sharti.

imperceptible, *a.* -sioonekana, -dogo mno.

imperfect, *a.* si kamili, si barabara; (*deficient*) -kosefu, -pungufu, dhaifu; (*in growth, development*) -viza, -liovia, -liodumaa, -liokundaa. **imperfection,** *n.* ukosefu, upungufu, kasoro, kombo, udhaifu, hitilafu, kipunguo, waa, ila.

imperial, *a.* -a ufalme wote (hasa wa kiingereza). -a kifalme; (*grand, magnificent*) bora, -kubwa; (*measure*) -a kiingereza. — *n.* kinywa mchuzi. **imperialism,** *n.* kutaka kueneza na kuhifadhi ufalme. **imperious,** *a.* -enye kupenda kuamuru na kutumia nguvu, -a kutawala, -a amri nyingi, -kali, -a sharti. *He is very imperious,* hupiga ubwana, hutoa amri nyingi.

imperil, *v.t.* hatirisha, tia hatarini, ponza.

imperious, *a.* taz. *imperial.*

imperishable, *a.* -sioharibika, siooza, -siochakaa, -a kuishi milele, -a aushi, -a daima, -a kale na kale.

impersonal, *a.* (*of verbs*) -a kutumika nafsi ya tatu ya umoja bila kutaja mtu au kitu maalum, *e.g. it is raining,* yaani inanyesha mvua; bila kutaja mwenyewe wala mtu ye yote maalum; -siyo na nafsi hai wala akili wala hiari, kama kitu si kama mtu. **impersonate,** *v.t.* iga, jifanya, geuka.

impertinence, *n.* ufidhuli, ujuvi, usafihi, ukavu wa macho. **impertinent,** *a.* -fidhuli, -safihi, -kavu wa macho, -juvi. *He was impertinent to me,* alinitolea ujuvi, alinifidhulikia.

imperturbable, *a.* (*quiet, unmoved*) -tulivu, -gumu; (*fearless*) pasipo hofu, -kavu wa macho, -shupavu. **imperturbability,** *n.* utulivu, ukavu wa macho, ushupavu.

impervious, *a.* -siopisha kitu, -siopenyeka. *He is an impervious person,* hasikii (hakubali, hafahamu) shauri.

impetuous, *a.* -a harara, -a haraka, -a nguvu, -a bidii bila kufikiri, -a kishindo. **impetus,** *n.* nguvu, mwendo, mvuto, mkazo; (*sudden*) shindo.

impiety, *n.* ukosefu wa heshima kwa Mungu, kutojali Mungu; ukosefu wa heshima (ustahi) wa mtu kwa wazazi wake, (mtu) kutojali wazazi wake. **impious**, *a.* -a kutomheshimu Mungu, -a kumdharau Mungu, -baya, -ovu, -potovu, -kufuru.

impinge, *v.i.* piga, angukia; pambana na, ingiana na.

impious, *a.* taz. *impiety*.

impish, *a.* taz. *imp*.

implacable, *a.* -enye hasira (chuki, uchungu) isiyotulizika, -siyosamehe, -gumu -a moyo, -korofi, -kali.

implant, *v.t.* tia (ingiza) moyoni, fundisha; tia (kaza) ndani imara.

implement, *n.* chombo cha kazi, samani, kipande, ala.

implicate, *v.t.* tia hatiani (katika makosa), pasisha hatia, shirikisha (jambo baya), tatanisha. **implication**, *n.* (*inference*) maana halisi, maana hasa; (*suggestion*) maana (isiyo wazi), kidokezi.

implicit, *a.* -a kufungamana na, -a ndani, -a siri; (*unquestioning*) kabisa, kamili.

implore, *v.t.* omba sana, sihi, lalama, nasihi, ronga.

imply, *v.t.* (*indicate*) onya, dokeza, -wa na maana, onyesha bila kutaja; (*involve*) husika na, leta, fanya.

impolite, *a.* -sio adabu, pasipo heshima, -tovu -a makini.

impolitic, *a.* -sio busara, -siofaa, -a bure, -a ujinga.

imponderable, *a.* -siopimikana (kwa kuwa -epesi), -dogo sana.

import, (1) *v.t.* leta (ingiza) bidhaa katika nchi (kutoka nchi nyingine). — *n.* bidhaa zinazoingia (zinazoletwa) katika nchi. *Imports and exports*, bidhaa zinazoingia na zinazotoka. **importer**, *n.* mleta (mwingiza) bidhaa katika nchi.

import, (2) *n.* maana. — *v.t.* onyesha, -wa na maana. **importance**, *n.* ukubwa, maana, amali, heshima, fahari. **important**, *a.* -kubwa, -kuu, -enye amri (nguvu), -a maana, -a amali, muhimu, bora, -a kupasa watu wengi.

importune, *v.t.* ombaomba, udhi (chosha, sumbua) kwa maombi, chagiza. **importunity**, *n.* usumbufu (udhia) wa kuomba. **importunate**, *a.* -a kuombaomba, -a kuchosha kwa maombi, -enye udhia, -sumbufu, -a kushurutisha.

impose, *v.t.* amuru, pasha, lazimisha, twisha; (*exact*) toza, lipiza; — *v.i.* (*on, upon*) danganya, hadaa, laghai, ghilibu, rubuni, punja. *Impose a difficult task on*, kalifu. **imposing**, *a.* -a kushangaza, -a ajabu, -a fahari, -kubwa, -zuri. **imposition**, *n.* kutoza, kutwisha; (*tax*) kodi, ushuru; (*swindle*) madanganya, hadaa, ulaghai &c. *Imposition of hands*, kuweka (kutia) mikono. **impost**, *n.* ushuru, kodi. **impostor**, *n.* ayari, laghai, jambazi, mjanja, mdanganyi, mpunjaji. **imposture**, *n.* ujanja, hila, hadaa, ulaghai.

impossible, *a.* -siowezekana, -siofanyika, -sioweza kuwa, -siomudikana, muhali. **impossibility**, *n.* jambo lisilowezekana, lisiloweza kuwa, lisilomudikana, muhali.

impost, *n.*, **impostor**, *n.*, **imposture**, *n.* taz. *impose*.

impotence, *n.* udhaifu; (*sexual*) uhanithi. **impotent**, *a.* dhaifu, pasipo nguvu, -siofaa neno; (*of males*) hanithi, -siofaa.

impound, *v.t.* funga, weka kifungoni.

impoverish, *v.t.* fukarisha, fanya kuwa maskini, dhiisha, dhikisha; (*weaken &c.*) punguzia nguvu, dhoofisha, chakaza. **impoverished**, *a.* maskini, -liochakaa, dhai **impoverishment**, *n.* umaskini, ufukara, kudhoofika, &c.

impracticable, *a.* -siofanyika, -siowezekana, muhali; (*person or character*) -gumu, -kaidi, -shupavu; (*of roads, &c.*) -siotumika, -siopitika. **impracticability**, *n.* jambo lisilofanyika (lisilowezekana), muhali; kutowezekana, kutofanyika.

imprecate, *v.t.* apiza, toa laana, laani. **imprecation**, *n.* apizo, laana. **imprecatory**, *a.* -a kuapiza, laanifu, -a kulaani.

impregnable, *a.* -siotwalika (vitani), -sioshindika (kwa maneno), -siovunjikana; (*in moral sense*) -sioshawishika, -siovutika, -siopotoka.

impregnate, *v.t.* tia (pa) mimba (himila), zalisha; (*mix*) changanya, tia ndani.

impress, *v.t.* (*imprint*) piga chapa; (*urge upon*) tia moyoni, ingiza sana; (*force to work*) tumikisha, tia kazini kwa nguvu, shokoa; (*affect*) choma moyoni; ingia, vuta, shinda, fanya kuona huzuni (mapendezi, furaha *&c.*). — *n.* chapa, alama, mfano. **impressible**, *a.* -epesi kuona (huruma, huzuni, furaha, upendo *&c.*). **impression**, *n.* chapa, alama; (*notion*) dhana, wazo, maono; (*of books*) jumla ya manakala ya vitabu yaliyopigwa chapa pamoja. *It is my impression*, naona, ndiyo nionayo. *Make an impression*, penya (ingia) moyoni, shinda (vuta) moyo, shawishi, vuta; (*stir up*) chomesha, chocha; (*weigh down, sink into*) topea. **impressionable**, *a.* taz. *impressible*. **impressive**, *a.* -a kufanya kuona (ajabu, upendo, uzito *&c.*), -a kushinda (kuvuta) moyo, -enye ushawishi, -enye nguvu.

imprest, *n.* fedha anayopewa mtu wa serikali kutumia kwa kazi ya serikali.

imprimatur, *n.* idhini ya kupiga chapa kitabu. *The book has received the imprimatur of the Government*, serikali imeruhusu kitabu.

imprint, *v.t.* piga chapa; (*in mind*) tia moyoni.

imprison, *v.t.* funga, tia kifungoni (gerezani). **imprisonment**, *n.* kifungo, kufungwa.

improbable, *a.* si yamkini, -sioelekea kutokea (kuwa kweli, kuwa, kufanyika *&c.*), -sio hakika, -enye shaka, -gumu. *I think it improbable*, naona sivyo. *Not improbable*, labda, huenda.

impromptu, *a.* bila kutengenezwa kwanza; bila kufikiriwa kwanza.

improper, *a.* -siofaa, si adabu, si -zuri; (*indecent*) -chafu, -pujufu. **impropriety**, *n.* jambo lisilofaa (lisilo adabu, lisilo heshima).

improve, *v.t.* kuza hali (thamani, manufaa *&c.*), sitawisha, endeleza, ongoza vizuri, tengeneza, tumia vizuri; *v.i.* endelea, sitawi, tengenea, pata nafuu, ongoka. *Improve the occasion*, tumia vizuri wakati, chuma, faidi. *Improve in health*, pata nafuu (ashekali), poa. **improvement**, *n.* (*progress*) maendeleo; (*growth*) kukua, mazidi; (*making better*) matengenezo, mafundisho; (*profitable use*) matumizi mema, usitawi. **improver**, *n.* mtu (au kitu) anayekuza hali *&c.* taz. *improve*; (*apprentice*) mwanafunzi afanyaye kazi kwa mshahara mdogo tu ili azidi kupata maarifa (ufundi).

improvident, *a.* si -enye kufikiri siku za mbele, si -enye kuweka akiba ya mbele, -potevu. **improvidence**, *n.* kutofikiri siku za mbele, kutoweka akiba ya mbele, upotevu.

improvise, *v.t.* tunga (fanyiza, vumbua) papo hapo bila matengenezo, fanya kwa haraka bila vifaa (vyombo *&c.*) vyake hasa.

imprudent, *a.* bila fikira ya baadaye, bila hadhari, -a harara, si -enye busara. **imprudence**, *n.* utovu wa busara (akili, fikira za mbele), tendo lisilo la busara.

impudent, *a.* -fidhuli, -juvi, -safihi, -kavu wa macho, -shupavu, -tundu, -siye na haya. **impudence**, *n.* ufidhuli, ujuvi, usafihi, ukavu wa macho, ushupavu, utundu.

impugn, *v.t.* gomba, shindana na, nenea, teta, kana.

impulse, *n.* nguvu (ya kusukuma, kuendesha, kujongeza), msukumo, mvuto, shindo; (*desire*) nia (tamaa, kutaka) ya ghafula, kutaka kwa ghafula (kama kwamba kwa sharti). *Give an impulse to*, endesha, sukumiza. **impulsive**, *a.* -a kufanya bila kutunga shauri kwanza, -a harara, -a ghafula, -epesi.

impunity, *n.* *Do with impunity*, fanya bila hofu ya kupata adhabu.

impure, *a.* -chafu, -najisi, -a taka, -koo; (*adulterated*) -lioghoshiwa, -liochanganyika na kitu (au vitu) cha namna nyingine, si safi. **impurity**, *n.* uchafu, taka, takataka, unajisi.

impute, *v.t.* dhania, hesabia, tolea, wekea; (*charge with*) shtaki, singizia, zulia. **imputation**, *n.* (*charge*) mashtaka, mashutumu, masuto, masingizio; (*ascription*) kuhesabia, kudhania *&c.*

in, *prep.* kwa, katika, -ni, — *adv.* ndani, -mo. *Indoors*, ndani ya nyumba, ndani, nyumbani. *In front of*, mbele ya, hadhara ya. *He is in*, yumo. *I am in for*, sina budi kupata. *In that*, kwa sababu, kwa kuwa.

in-, *pref.* si, pasipo, bila, *e.g.* *inability*, *n.* = pasipo *ability*.

inability, *n.* utovu wa uwezo (nguvu, nafasi, manufaa *&c.*), hali ya kutoweza, kutoweza.

inaccessible, *a.* -siojilika, -siopandika, -siofikika, -sioendeka.

inaccurate, *a.* -enye kosa, -kosefu, si sahihi, -a uwongo. **inaccuracy**, *n.* kosa, kukosa, kutokuwa sahihi.

inactive, *a.* -fu, kama kifu, -a kimya, pasipo nguvu; (*dull, slow*) -vivu, -zembe, -zito, pasipo bidii, -tepetevu, -legevu. **inaction**, *n.* kimya, kukaakaa, kutotenda neno, uvivu, uzembe. **inactivity**, *n.* uvivu, uzito, ulegevu, utepetevu, ukosefu wa nguvu, hali ya kutotumika (ya kutofanya kazi, ya kukaa bure).

inadequate, *a.* -siotosha, -siofaa, -dogo, -pungufu, -chache, haba. **inadequacy**, *n.* udogo, upungufu, uchache, kuwa haba.

inadmissible, *a.* -sioruhusiwa, si halali, marufuku, -siokubalika, haramu.

inadvertent, *a.* -zembe, si -angalifu, -kosefu; (*unnoticed*) -a kupitiwa, -a kughafilika, si -a kusudi. **inadvertency**, *n.* uzembe, kutoangalia, ghafula; (*mistake*) kosa.

inalienable, *a.* -sioondoleka, -siotengeka, -a daima.

inane, *a.* -sio na maana, -puzi, -pumbavu, chege, baridi.

inanimate, *a.* -fu, si -enye uzima (uhai), kitu tu; (*spiritless, dull*) baridi, -tepetevu, pasipo nguvu.

inanition, *n.* njaa.

inapplicable, *a.* -siofaa, -siopasa, si -zuri, si wajibu.

inappreciable, *a.* -dogo sana, -dogo mno, kama si kitu, katiti.

inappropriate, *a.* -siofaa, -siopasa, si -zuri, si wajibu.

inapt, *a.* -siofaa, -siopasa; (*unskilled*) si -epesi, si -stadi.

inarticulate, *a.* (*words*) -siyotamkwa vizuri, si dhahiri, -siyoweza kusikika vizuri; (*of persons*) -siyeweza kusema dhahiri, -siyeweza kueleza maono (shauri, maana); -a kimya.

inasmuch (*as*), *conj.* kwa sababu, kwa kuwa.

inattention, *n.* kutoangalia, uzembe, ulegevu, purukushani, macho nje. **inattentive**, *a.* si -angalifu, -zembe. *Be inattentive*, jipurukusha, toangalia, sinzia, kukusa.

inaudible, *a.* -siosikika, (sauti) dogo sana.

inaugurate, *v.t.* (*public institution*) fungua, zindika, zingua, ingia; (*begin*) anzisha. **inaugural**, *a.* -a kuzindulia. *Inaugural ceremony, address &c.* mzinduo, mzindiko; (*address*) halbadili. **inauguration**, *n.* kuzindua, kuzindika, mzinduo, mzindiko.

inauspicious, *a.* -a ndege mbaya, -a kisirani, -a bahati mbaya.

inborn, *a.* -a asili, -a maumbile.

inbred, *a.* -a asili; -liozaliwa na wazazi wa ujamaa mmoja.

incalculable, *a.* -siopimika (au kuhesabika) kwa kuwa -kubwa au -ingi, -kubwa mno, -ingi mno.

incandescent, *a.* -enye kung'aa kwa moto mwingi, -enye moto mweupe,

-inayotoa nuru kwa sababu ya joto lake (kama uzi wa taa ya umeme).

incantation, *n.* wimbo (au maneno) wa kunuizia uchawi (uganga).

incapable, *a.* -sioweza, sio na nguvu, -siofaa neno, dhaifu. **incapability**, *n.* hali ya kutoweza. **incapacitate**, *v.t.* ondolea nguvu (uwezo, haki &c.). **incapacity**, *n.* kutoweza, ukosefu wa nguvu (akili).

incarcerate, *v.t.* funga, tia kifungoni.

incarnadine, *a.* -ekundu. — *v.t.* fanya kuwa nyekundu.

incarnate, *a.* -enye mwili (kiwiliwili), -enye asili na umbo la binadamu. **incarnation**, *n.* kutwaa utu, kugeuka mtu, kuwa mtu, kufanyika mtu; (*embodiment*) namna, mfano, halisi. *The Incarnation*, kufanyika mtu halisi Yesu Kristo.

incautious, *a.* pasipo hadhari, si -angalifu, -zembe, -jasiri, -a harara.

incendiary, *n.* and *a.* achomaye moto na kuteketeza nyumba au shamba makusudi; mfitini achocheaye watu kuasi na kupigana na serikali. **incendiarism**, *n.* kuchoma moto nyumba au shamba makusudi; maasi, fitina juu ya serikali.

incense, (1) *n.* ubani, udi, uvumba. *Burn incense*, fukiza.

incense, (2) *v.t.* tia uchungu, kasirisha ghadhibisha.

incentive, *n.* kichocheo, kishawishi, kinachovuta (kinachotia) moyo, kinachosukuma; (*motive*) sababu, madhumuni, maarubu, kisa.

inception, *n.* mwanzo.

incessant, *a.* -siokwisha, bila kukoma, -a daima, -a kufululiza.

incest, *n.* zinaa ya maharimu (kama vile baba na binti yake &c.). **incestuous**, *a.* -a uzini wa maharimu.

inch, *n.* inchi (kipimo cha urefu mara thenashara kwa futi). *By inches*, kidogo kidogo, punde kwa punde.

inchoate, *a.* -a kuanza, -a katika kuanza, -a kujaribia, -a kuonja, kama mbegu.

incidence, *n.* taz. *incident.*

incident, *n.* jambo, neno, tukio, kadhia. — *a.* -enye kupata (kuja, kutokea). **incidence**, *n.* kuja, majilio, namna ya kuangukia (ya kutukia, ya kupata). *The incidence of disease*, hesabu, au namna ya watu wapatwao na ugonjwa (fulani). **incidental**, *a.* (*casual*) -a bahati, -a nasibu; (*resulting*) -a kutokea, -a kufuata.

incinerator, *n.* jiko la kuchomea taka.

incipient, *a.* -a kwanza, -a katika kuanza.

incise, *v.t.* kata, chanja, tema, chora, toja. **incision**, *n.* kato, chanjo; (*small*) mtai; (*ornamental*) chale, tojo. **incisive**, *a.* -kali, -a nguvu, -enye njia. **incisor**, *n.* jino la mbele (la kuuma), chonge.

incite, *v.t.* chochea, sukuma, shawishi, vuta, ongoza, amsha, chonjomoa, tasliti, bimbiriza; (*a dog*) tomesha. **incitement**, *n.* kichocheo, kishawishi, mvuto, chonjo, shonga; (*motive*) sababu, kisa.

incivility, *n.* ufidhuli, utovu wa adabu, ujuvi, usodawi, usafihi.

inclement, *a.* (*weather*) baridi, mawingu, mvua, dhoruba.

inclination, *n.* taz. *incline.*

incline, *v.i.* elekea, kabili; (*deviate*) enda mshazari (upande), potoka; (*down*) inamia, shuka; (*up*) panda, inuka; — *v.t.* elekeza, kabilisha; (*down*) inamisha; (*up*) pandisha. *Be inclined to*, taka, penda; (*have a tendency to*) elekea. — *n.* kilima, mpando, mshuko, telemko, mtelemko, mwinamo, mainamizi. **inclination**, *n.* (*slope*) mainamizi, mwinamo; (*propensity*) maelekeo, mapenzi, tamaa.

inclose, *v.* taz. *enclose.*

include, *v.t.* (*put, have inside*) tia, weka ndani, -wa na . . . ndani; (*cover, admit*) ona sawa, -wa na maana moja, chukua; (*in meaning*) husika na. **including**, *prep.* pamoja na. **inclusion**, *n.* kutia, kutiwa, kuweka ndani &c. **inclusive**, *a.* -a kushika

(kuweka, kutia) -ote ndani, -enye ndani yake, -ote pamoja, -ote pia.
incognito, *adv.* kwa jina jingine (lisilo lako, lake &c. la kawaida).
incoherent, *a.* -a kupayuka, -a kulopoka, -a kubwata, -a mapayo; (*inconsistent*) -sioshikamana, -siofungamana, -sio na taratibu. **incoherence, incoherency**, *n.* (*of speech*) msemo usio na maana (usiofungamana, uliochafuka), upayukaji, mapayo, kugotagota.
incombustible, *a.* -siowaka moto, -sioharibika kwa moto.
income, *n.* mapato, mshahara, chumo, faida, maduhuli.
incommensurate, *a.* -siolinganikana, si sawa, si -a kutosha. **incommensurable**, *a.* -siolinganikana.
incommode, *v.t.* sumbua, udhi. **incommodious**, *a.* -sumbufu, si -zuri, -siopendeza, -sio na nafasi.
incommunicable, *a.* -sioshirikika, -sioneneka, -siotoleka wazi, -a mtu mmoja, -a kitu kimoja, -a peke yake.
incomparable, *a.* -siolinganikana, -sioweza kufananishwa, pasipo kifani, -siofanana na kitu, -a kupita yote, bora sana.
incompatible, *a.* -siopatana, -enye tabia mbalimbali, si -linganifu, si sawa, -a kinyume.
incompetent, *a.* -sio na nguvu (akili, ustadi, uwezo, maarifa &c.) kwa kazi fulani, -siofaa, -sioweza.
incompetence, *n.* hali (tabia) ya kuwa *incompetent*, kutoweza, kutofaa, utovu wa nguvu (akili, ustadi, maarifa &c.) kwa kazi fulani.
incomplete, *a.* si kamili, si -zima, sehemu, -pungufu.
incomprehensible, *a.* -siotambulikana, -siofahamika, -a fumbo, -a siri; (*illimitable*) -sio na mipaka.
incompressible, *a.* -sioweza kupunguzwa kwa nguvu, -siosongeka, -siosindikika, siobonyezeka, -gumu sana.
inconceivable, *a.* -siowazikana, -siofahamika, -a kushinda akili, -a ajabu sana, -a kushangaza.
inconclusive, *a.* -enye mashaka, -siokata maneno (shauri), si -enye njia.
incongruous, *a.* -siofaa, -siopatana, mbalimbali, -a upuzi. **incongruity**, *n.* hitilafu, tofauti, jambo (kitu) lisilofaa, lisilopatana, upuzi.
inconsequent, inconsequential, *a.* -siofuata sawasawa, -siofungamana, -sio na akili (njia), -a ovyo.
inconsiderable, *a.* -dogo, hafifu, kidogo.
inconsiderate, *a.* -a kujifikiri -enyewe tu, -siojali wengine; (*rash*) -a haraka, -a harara, -pumbavu.
inconsistent, *a.* si -linganifu, -siopatana vema, si sawa, -sio -enye akili, -a kigeugeu, -badilifu. **inconsistency**, *n.* kutopatana, kuwa mbalimbali; (*absurdity*) upumbavu; (*unsteadiness*) ugeuzi, mageuzi.
inconsolable, *a.* -siofarijika, -siotulizika, -siotulia.
inconspicuous, *a.* -a sioonekana kwa wepesi, -dogo sana.
inconstant, *a.* -geugeu, -geuzi, -badilifu, -a kubadilika; (*not reliable*) si amini, si thabiti.
incontestable, *a.* -siokanika, -siokanushika, -a kukubalika na wote, pasipo shaka.
incontinent, *a.* -siojizuia, -kware, -siojizuia ashiki, -asherati, -fisadi. **incontinence**, *n.* ukware, ashiki nyingi, uasherati.
incontrovertible, *a.* = *incontestable*.
inconvenient, *a.* -sumbufu, -siofaa, -siotengenea, -sio na raha. **inconvenience**, *n.* sumbuo, taabu. — *v.t.* sumbua, udhi, taabisha.
inconvertible, *a.* -siobadilikana.
incorporate, *v.t.* fanya moja, unga, unganisha, changa; (*include*) tia ndani, changanya. **incorporation**, *n.* kuchanga, mchanganyo, kuungana, mwungano, kutia ndani.
incorporeal, *a.* si -enye mwili (umbo la wazi), kama kivuli, -a pepo, -a kiroho.
incorrect, *a.* -enye makosa, -kosefu, -si sahihi, si kweli, si halisi.

incorrigible, *a.* -siorudika, -enye moyo mbaya, -kaidi, -tundu, baa.
incorruptible, *a.* -sioharibika, -siochakaa, -siooza; (*honest*) amini, siotwaa rushwa, -nyofu. **incorruption,** *n.* kutoharibika.
increase, *v.t.* ongeza, zidisha, kuza, kithiri; — *v.i.* ongezeka, zidi, kua, kithiri, endelea, enea. — *n.* mazidi, mazidio, mwongezo, nyongeza, jazi, jazo, maendeleo, eneo; (*profit*) chumo, faida.
incredible, *a.* -siosadikika, -a kupita kiasi, ajabu mno, -a kushangaza. **incredibility,** *n.* hali ya kuwa *incredible.* **incredulity,** *n.* hali ya kuwa *incredulous.* **incredulous,** *a.* -siosadiki, -gumu.
increment, *n.* nyongeza, ongezo, kiongezo, mazidi, mazidio; chumo, faida, mapato.
incriminate, *v.t.* pasisha hatia, tia hatiani; shtaki, chongea.
incrust, *v.t.* funika, kandika, tomea. **incrustation,** *n.* utando; (*in cooking*) ukoko; (*on teeth*) ukoga; (*mould*) ukungu, kuvu; (*rust*) kutu; (*of salt*) chunyu; (*of masonry*) mtomo.
incubate, *v.i.* atamia (kalia) mayai. **incubation,** *n.* kuatamia.
incubus, *n.* taabu, udhia, jambo zito; (*nightmare*) jinamizi.
inculcate, *v.t.* fundisha, onyaonya, sisitiza. **inculcation,** *n.* kufundisha, kuonya.
inculpate, *v.t.* shtaki, chongea, tia hatiani, laumu.
incumbent, *a.* -a kupasa, -a kubidi. *It is incumbent upon me,* imenipasa, imenibidi, ni wajibu wangu, ni juu yangu. — *n.* padre wa mji, kasisi. **incumbency,** *n.* kuwa na kazi ya kasisi, mahali pa kasisi.
incur, *v.t.* pata, patwa na, pasiwa, pasishwa. **incursion,** *n.* shambulio, mjio wa ghafula (wa askari za adui, wa wageni &c.), ingilio la ghafula (katika nchi ya adui).
incurable, *a.* -sioponyeka. *It is incurable,* hakuna dawa yake.
incursion, *n.* taz. *incur.*
indebted, *a.* -enye kuwiwa, -enye deni, -a kupasiwa kushukuru. *Be indebted,* wiwa, -wa na deni, pasiwa, fadhiliwa.
indecent, *a.* si -a adabu (heshima, ustahi), -siofaa; (*immodest, obscene*) -chafu, -pujufu. **indecency,** *n.* utovu wa adabu (heshima, ustahi), jambo lisilofaa, uchafu, upujufu.
indecipherable, *a.* -siosomeka, -siotambulikana.
indecision, *n.* kusita moyoni, wasiwasi, kutanga, mashaka, kutoweza kuchagua. **indecisive,** *a.* -a mashaka, si dhahiri, si -a kukata maneno (shauri), -a wasiwasi, -a kusitasita.
indeclinable, *a.* -siobadilika (kisarufi).
indecorous, *a.* si -a adabu (heshima, ustahi), -siofaa. **indecorum,** *n.* utovu wa adabu (heshima, ustahi), jambo lisilofaa.
indeed, *adv.* kweli, halisi, ndiyo, naam; (*emphasis*) sana. — *int.* ala! kweli!
indefatigable, *a.* -siochoka, -siolegea, -a kudumu, -a kuendelea (kufululiza, kuchagiza, kushikilia) mpaka kupata mradi.
indefeasible, *a.* -siotanguka, -siotwalika, -sioondoleka.
indefensible, *a.* (*place*) -sioweza kulindwa; (*affair*) -sio na neno la kutetea, -baya kabisa.
indefinable, *a.* -sioelezeka, -siofanulika. **indefinite,** *a.* -sio wazi, -sio dhahiri, -siotajwa dhahiri. *Indefinite article,* taz. *a, an.* **indefiniteness,** *n.* mashaka, kutodhihirika, hali ya kuwa *indefinite.*
indelible, *a.* -siofutika, -sioondoleka.
indelicate, *a.* si -a adabu (heshima, ustahi), -siofaa, -chafu, -pujufu. **indelicacy,** *n.* utovu wa adabu (malezi mema, heshima), uchafu, upujufu.
indemnify, *v.t.* lipa, komboa, ondoa hasara. **indemnity,** *n.* malipo, ukombozi.
indemonstrable, *a.* -siothibitika, -sioonyesheka, -siodhihirika.

indent, *v.t.* tia pengo, bonyeza; (*in printing*) jongeza mstari ndani; — *v.i.* (*for goods*) pelekea maagizo (ya zana, vyakula &c.). — *n.* hati (barua, cheti) ya kuagizia vitu; (*notch*) pengo, bonyezo (bonyeo). **indentation,** *n.* pengo; (*of coast &c.*) kizingo, kighuba; (*groove*) mfuo. **indenture,** *n.* sharti, maagano, hati, mkataba.

independent, *a.* -a kujitawala (kujitegemea, kujiwezea, kujitoshelea, kujisimamia, kujiruzuku) -enyewe; (*having means*) -enye mali, tajiri. *An independent air* (*manner*), ukinaifu, ushupavu, ujuvi. **independence,** *n.* upweke, upekee, ukinaifu, hali au tabia ya kuwa *independent*; (*insubordination*) ushupavu, ugumu, kutokurudika, kutoambilika; (*private property*) mali, nafuu, riziki.

indescribable, *a.* -sioelezeka, -sionekana, -siotajika, -a kupita maneno, -a ajabu, -a kushangaza.

indestructible, *a.* -sioharibika, -a daima, -a aushi.

indeterminate, *a.* -sio wazi, -sio dhahiri, si yakini.

index, *n.* fahirisi, orodha ya mambo yaliyo kitabuni na hesabu ya ukurasa wake; (*indication, mark*) onyo, elezo. *Index finger,* kidole cha shahada. — *v.t.* tunga katika taratibu ya Alfabeti, a, b, ch &c.; tengeneza fahirisi (faharasa).

Indian, *n.* Mhindi; (*Hindu*) Banyani; (*N. American*) mwenyeji (mtu mwekundu) wa Amerika. **Indian corn,** *n.* (*plant*) muhindi; (*cob of grains*) hindi, ma-; (*grains*) mahindi; (*cob without grains*) gunzi, bunzi. **Indian file,** *n.* mwandamo, ufuatano, sanjari, mpororo. **india-rubber,** *n.* mpira.

indicate, *v.t.* onya, onyesha. **indication,** *n.* alama, dalili, ishara, madhubutu, onyo; (*hint*) kidokezo. *Give an indication* (*by signs*), ashiria, pungia, konyezea. **indicative,** *a.* -a kuonya, -a kuarifu. *Ind. mood.,* kiarifa (*verb*) chenye hali ya kuonyesha habari hasa, si amri, si kusudi.

indict, *v.t.* shtaki. **indictable,** *a.* -a kushtakiwa, -a kushtakika mbele ya korti. **indictment,** *n.* mashtaka, hati ya mashtaka.

indifference, *n.* ubaridi, kutojali, ukavu wa macho, upurukushani, uzembe. *It is a matter of indifference,* mamoja, sawasawa, haidhuru. **indifferent,** *a.* baridi, -a kutojali, -kavu wa macho, -zembe; (*of medium quality &c.*) -a vivi hivi, -a kadiri; (*inferior*) hafifu, duni. **indifferently,** *adv.* sawasawa, bila kupendelea; (*slightly*) kidogo, kadiri.

indigence, *n.* umaskini, ufukara, uhitaji. **indigent,** *a.* maskini, -a kimaskini, fukara.

indigenous, *a.* -zalia, -a nchi yenyewe, -a kuko huko, -a asili, si -a kigeni, -a mumo humo.

indigent, *a.* taz. *indigence.*

indigestible, *a.* -siotulia tumboni (kwa kuwa -gumu, -zito &c.), -bichi. **indigestion,** *n.* tumbo* (kuuma), ugonjwa (maumivu) tumbo kutoweza chakula.

indignant, *a.* -enye uchungu (hasira, hamaki), -a kuudhika. **indignation,** *n.* uchungu, hasira. **indignity,** *n.* ufidhuli, aibu, jeuri, utwezo.

indigo, *n.* nili; (*plant*) mnili.

indirect, *a.* si -a kunyoka, -a vipengee, si -nyofu, si wazi (dhahiri), -a kuzunguka; (*secondary &c.*) si -a kukusudiwa, -a kufuata. **indirectly,** *adv.* kwa vipengee, kwa kuzunguka, kwa fumbo (siri, mfano, hila), si sawasawa.

indiscreet, *a.* si -a busara (akili, hadhari), -pumbavu, -jinga. **indiscretion,** *n.* tendo lisilo la akili (busara, hadhari), ujinga, ukosefu wa busara.

indiscriminate, *a.* kwa -ote sawasawa, pasipo tofauti, iwezavyo, vyo vyote; (*disorderly*) -siochaguliwa kwa busara, -a kifujo; (*wholesale*) jumla, shelabela.

indispensable, *a.* -a lazima (sharti, kanuni).
indisposed, *a.* si -zima, -gonjwa; (*unwilling*) -a kutopenda (kutotaka, kutoridhika). *He is indisposed,* hawezi, yu mgonjwa. *He is indisposed to go,* hapendi (hataki) kuenda. **indisposition,** *n.* ugonjwa; (*dislike*) chuki, hasira, kutoridhika.
indisputable, *a.* -siokanikana, -a kukubalika na wote, pasipo shaka.
indissoluble, *a.* -siotanguka, -siochangukana, -siovunjikana, -a daima.
indistinct, *a.* si wazi (dhahiri, baini), -siotambulikana vizuri. *Become* (*grow*) *indistinct,* fifia. **indistinctness,** *n.* unyenyezi, kiwi.
indistinguishable, *a.* -siotambulikana, -siobainikana, -sioonekana vizuri, si dhahiri.
indite, *v.t.* andika; (*compose*) tunga, buni.
individual, *a.* -moja, -moja peke yake, kila -mojawapo, -ake mtu mmoja, -a kila mtu. — *n.* mtu mmoja, kitu kimoja. **individualism,** *n.* mafundisho ya kuwa haki ya kila mtu mmoja mmoja ni ya maana sana kuliko haki ya watu wote pamoja. **individuality,** *n.* nafsi, roho; (*character*) tabia, maumbile, sifa, chapa; (*singleness*) umoja, upweke. **individualize,** *v.t.* tofautisha, pambanua, ainisha. **individually,** *adv.* kila -moja peke yake, -moja -moja.
indivisible, *a.* -siogawanyikana, -sioweza kuvunjika (kukatika, kuchangukana, kupunguzwa &c.).
indocile, *a.* -kaidi, -siorudika, -sioambilika.
indoctrinate, *v.t.* funza, fundisha.
indolence, *n.* uvivu, utepetevu, ulegevu, uzembe, ukunguni. **indolent,** *a.* -vivu, -tepetevu &c.
indomitable, *a.* -sioshindika, -siokubali kushindwa, -siotiishika, -siokata tamaa, hodari, imara, madhubuti.
indoors, *adv.* ndani ya nyumba, ndani.
indorse, *v.* taz. *endorse.*
indubitable, *a.* pasipo shaka, bayana, wazi, hakika, yakini.
induce, *v.t.* vuta, shawishi, shurutisha, bidi; (*cause*) fanya, leta. **inducement,** *n.* mvuto, kishawishi, kitu cha kutamanisha, kitamanisho.
induct, *v.t.* ingiza, ingiliza, tia katika kazi. **induction,** *n.* *inductive reasoning;* kuingiza kasisi katika kazi yake; (*electricity*) kufanya nguvu ya umeme (elektrisiti) ipite katika uzi wa ndani kwa kupitisha nguvu ya umeme katika uzi ulionyongwa na kuuzungusha bila kuugusa.
inductive, *a.* *inductive reasoning,* maneno au hoja ya kuongeza maarifa, kuyatumia yaliyojulika ili yasiyojulika yajulikane.
indulge, *v.t.* pendelea, achia, endekeza; (*desires*) timiza, jitoa kwa. *To indulge in,* kujifurahisha kwa. **indulgence,** *n.* huruma, upendeleo, kuachiwa, ruhusa; (*of desires*) anasa, kujitoa, uzoefu wa kujifurahisha. **indulgent,** *a.* -pole, -ema, -taratibu, -a kupendelea.
indurate, *v.t.* fanya -gumu, gandamiza, shupaza.
industry, *n.* utendaji, bidii, ujitahidi; (*employment*) kazi, uchumi. **industrial,** *a.* -a kazi. **industrious,** *a.* -a kushika kazi, -enye bidii ya kazi, -tendaji, hodari.
indwelling, *n.* and *a.* kukaa ndani (moyoni, rohoni).
inebriate, *v.t.* levya. — *n.* mlevi. **inebriation,** *n.* ulevi, kulewa.
ineffable, *a.* -sioelezeka kwa kuwa -zuri, -ema, -ajabu sana, -tukufu.
ineffaceable, *a.* -siofutika, -sioondoleka.
ineffective, ineffectual, *a.* -siofaa, -sio na nguvu, si -enye njia, hafifu, dhaifu, -dogo, -a bure.
inefficiency, *n.* taz. *inefficient.*
inefficient, *a.* -sioweza, si -stadi, -siofaa, -siofanya kazi vizuri, hafifu. **inefficiency,** *n.* utovu wa kuweza (wa ustadi, wa maarifa &c.), uhafifu.
inelegance, *n.* taz. *inelegant.*

inelegant, *a.* si -zuri, si -enye madaha, -zito. **inelegance,** *n.* utovu wa uzuri (wa madaha), uzito, jambo (neno, tendo) lisilopendeza (lisilo la adabu).

ineligible, *a.* -siochagulika, -siostahili, -siofaa.

inept, *a.* -pumbavu, -siofaa, -a upuzi. **ineptitude,** *n.* upumbavu, upuzi.

inequality, *n.* kutokuwa sawa, tofauti, ubadilifu.

ineradicable, *a.* -sioondoleka, -siong'oleka, imara, madhubuti.

inert, *a.* -fu, kama kifu, -vivu, -zembe, -tepetevu, -zito. **inertia,** *n.* hali ya kutokuwa na nguvu, ulegevu, uzito, uvivu; (*scientific*) nguvu inayofanya kitu kisijongee kinapokaa mahali, na kufanya kiendelee kinapokwenda.

inestimable, *a.* -siokadirika (kwa kuwa -kubwa, -ingi, -a thamani nyingi), -kubwa mno, -ingi mno, -a thamani nyingi sana.

inevitable, *a.* -sioepukika, pasipo budi, -a sharti, -a lazima kutukia (kufuata).

inexact, *a.* si sahihi, -enye kosa, -enye hitilafu.

inexcusable, *a.* -sioachilika (kwa kuwa -baya sana), -baya mno.

inexhaustible, *a.* -sioisha, -sioishika, -siomalizika (kwa kuwa -ingi), -ingi mno; (*unwearied*) -siochoka.

inexorable, *a.* -gumu, -sio na huruma, -siosamehe, -siobadilika wala kuzuilika.

inexpedient, *a.* -siofaa.

inexperience, *n.* ujinga, utovu wa maarifa (ujuzi), kutojua. **inexperienced,** *a.* -jinga, -siojua.

inexpert, *a.* si -stadi, si -bingwa, si -elekevu.

inexpiable, *a.* -sioondoleka kwa malipo au sadaka, -siokomboleka, -siosameheka.

inexplicable, *a.* -sioelezeka, -siofumbulikana, -a fumbo (ajabu, matata).

inexpressible, *a.* -sioelezeka, -sionekana, -a kupita maneno, -a ajabu, -a kushangaza.

inextinguishable, *a.* -siozimika, -siotulizika, -siotulia.

inextricable, *a.* -sionyosheka, -siotengenezeka, -siofungulika, -enye matata mengi (asiweze mtu kutoka).

infallibility, *n.* kutoweza kukosa, hakika, kuwa na hakika, kujua pasipo kosa. *Papal infallibility* mafundisho ya Kanisa la Rumi ya kuwa askofu wa Rumi (*Pope*) hawezi kukosa anapotoa amri juu ya mambo ya imani ya kikristo au ya kupambanua mema na mabaya. **infallible,** *a.* -enye hakika, -sioweza kukosa, pasipo kosa.

infamous, *a.* -enye sifa mbaya, -ovu sana, -a aibu. **infamy,** *n.* sifa mbaya, fedheha, aibu.

infancy, *n.* taz. *infant.*

infant, *n.* mtoto mchanga; (*legal minor*) mtu asiyepata miaka 21. **infancy,** *n.* utoto, uchanga, mwanzo. **infanticide,** *n.* kuua watoto wachanga; mtu aliyeua mtoto mchanga. **infantile,** *a.* -a kitoto, -a mwanzoni. **infantine,** *a.* -a kitoto, -jinga

infantry, *n.* askari (wa kwenda kwa miguu).

infatuate, *v.t.* rusha akili, pumbazisha, pumbaza, tia ashiki (hamu, upendo) hata kurusha akili. *Be infatuated* (*with a person*), pumbazika, (*with worldly goods &c.*) ghururika. **infatuation,** *n.* ghururi, kupumbazika, kupotewa akili, kuchukuliwa, kushikwa.

infect, *v.t.* ambukiza, tia wito, eneza. **infection,** *n.* ambukizo, uambukizo, kuambukiza, wito, nguvu ya kujieneza, (*moral*) ushawishi mbaya. **infectious,** *a.* -a kuambukiza, -enye wito, -enye nguvu ya kujieneza.

infelicity, *n.* bahati mbaya, shari, uchungu, uzito wa moyo, kosa.

infer, *v.t.* ona, fahamu (kwa kujua sababu yake). *I infer,* kwa sababu hivo nadhani, basi naona. **inference,** *n.* (*inferring*) kujua jambo kwa kujua sababu yake; (*conclusion*) mwisho wa maneno. *The inference is*, basi kwa sababu hii, mwisho wa maneno ndio huu.

inferior, *a.* -a chini, -dogo, -baya, hafifu, ghafi. **inferiority**, *n.* kuwa chini &c.

infernal, *a.* -a jehanamu, -a shetani; (*utterly bad*) -baya sana, -liolaaniwa. **inferno**, *n.* jehanamu, mahali pa joto sana.

infest, *v.t.* jaa tele, tapakaa (adui, wadudu &c.). *A house infested with rats*, nyumba iliyojaa (iliyotapakaa) panya (yenye panya wengi sana).

infidel, *n.* kafiri, mtu asiye na dini yo yote; mtu asiye Mkristo, mtu asiye Mwislamu. **infidelity**, *n.* ukafiri, kumkana Mungu, kukataa imani ya kikristo; (*conjugal*) uzini.

infiltrate, *v.i.* nywewa, penya, ingia, chuja; — *v.t.* penyeza (ingiza) maji &c. kwa kuyachuja. **infiltration**, *n.* kuchuja, machujo, mchujo.

infinite, *a.* pasipo mwisho (kikomo, mpaka, kiasi), -sio na mwisho. *The Infinite*, Mungu. **infinitely**, *adv.* sana. **infinitesimal**, *a.* -dogo mno kabisa. **infinitive mood**, *n.* namna ya kiarifa (*verb*) chenye kutumika kama jina (*noun*). **infinitude**, *n.* wingi, pasipo mwisho. **infinity**, *n.* nafasi (wakati, wingi) usio na mwisho kwa kuwa mkubwa, pasipo kiasi, bila mwisho, wingi.

infirm, *a.* dhaifu, -gonjwa, goigoi, si thabiti, -a kusita. **infirmary**, *n.* hospitali, nyumba ya wagonjwa, nyumba ya dawa. **infirmity**, *n.* udhaifu, ugonjwa, upungufu.

inflame, *v.t.* washa, kasirisha, chochea, amsha; (*of sore &c.*) tia wekundu, vimbisha; — *v.i.* waka, kasirika, panda hamaki. **inflammable**, *a.* -a kuwaka moto, -a kuwashika, -epesi kushika moto; (*of temperament*) -a harara, -epesi kukasirika. **inflammation**, *n.* mwako, moto; (*swollen place*) uvimbe unaoumiza (unaowasha, unaochoma). **inflammatory**, *a.* -a kuwasha, -a kuchochea, -a kuamsha (fitina ugomvi, chuki, ashiki, tamaa &c.), -a kufitinisha, -a kukasirisha, -a kusukasuka.

inflate, *v.t.* pulizia; (*expand*) vimbisha, panua; (*elate*) tia moyo (kiburi, tumaini), kweza; (*enlarge*) ongeza, kuza. **inflated**, *a.* -a kiburi, -kuu. **inflation**, *n.* kuvimba; (*pride*) majivuno, makuu.

inflect, *v.t.* badili, geuza. **inflection**, *n.* taz. *inflexion*. **inflexibility**, *n.* kutopindika, kutonyumbuka; (*determination*) ugumu, ushupavu, uthabiti. **inflexible**, *a.* -siopindika, -sionyumbuka; (*determined*) -gumu, -siobadili, -shupavu, thabiti, mathubuti. **inflexion**, *n.* mabadili, kubadilika.

inflict, *v.t.* piga, tia, pasha, pasisha, pelekea. **infliction**, *n.* kutia, kupasha; (*punishment*) adhabu; (*calamity &c.*) msiba, taabu, baa.

inflorescence, *n.* hali ya kuwa na maua.

inflow, *n.* kuja ndani, mjio, mwingio, kuletwa, majilio.

influence, *v.t.* vuta, ongoza, rudi, shawishi, geuza, athari. — *n.* mvuto, maongozi, nguvu, ushawishi, athari. **influential**, *a.* -enye nguvu (kuvuta, kuongoza, kurudi, kushawishi, kugeuza, kuathari &c.), -kubwa, -kuu.

influenza, *n.* makamasi, mafua, kamata.

influx, *n.* kuja ndani, mjio, majilio, mwingio, kuingia, kuletwa.

inform, *v.t.* juvya, julisha, arifu, -pa (pasha) habari, hubiri, aridhia, simulia, hadithia bashiri; — *v.i.* (*against*) shtaki. *A well-informed person*, mjuzi, mwenye maarifa, ajuaye mambo. *I am informed*, nimeambiwa, nimesikia habari. **informant**, *n.* mleta habari, mjumbe. **information**, *n.* habari, taarifa, maarifa, bayana, msimulizi. **informer**, *n.* mshtaki, mchongezi, mdukizi, mleta habari.

informal, *a.* (*irregular*) si -a kawaida, si -a taratibu; (*without ceremony*) bila sherehe, vivi hivi, -a haraka.

informant, *n.*, **information**, *n.*, **informer**, *n.* taz. *inform*.

infraction, *n.* kuvunja, kuasi, uhalifu, kukosea, kutoshika.

infrequent, *a.* si mara nyingi, -a mara chache, shida, si -zoevu.

infringe, *v.t.* vunja, asi, halifu, kosea. **infringement,** *n.* kuvunja, kuasi, uhalifu, kukosea, kutoshika.

infuriate, *v.t.* ghadhibisha, fanya kuwa -kali, kasirisha.

infuse, *v.t.* mwagia, miminia, tia katika maji yanayochemka, nywesha; (*in the mind*) tia ndani, tilia moyoni, ingiza, nywesha. **infusible,** *a.* -a kutilika, -a kunywesha; (*not fusible*) -sioyeyuka. **infusion,** *n.* kumwagia *&c.*, taz. *infuse*; maji yenye nguvu ya mboga (dawa *&c.*) zilizochemshwa ndani yake. **infusoria,** *n.* vidudu vidogodogo vya maji yenye maozo.

ingathering, *n.* mkusanyo, mchango, (*harvest*) mavuno, mapato.

ingenious, *a.* -enye akili, -stadi, -erevu, hodari, -juzi, -bingwa, waria, arifu. **ingenuity,** *n.* ustadi, ubingwa, ufundi, ujuzi, umahiri, akili, busara.

ingenuous, *a.* -nyofu, -kunjufu, -adilifu, adili, -sio na hila.

inglorious, *a.* -nyonge, -a aibu, pasipo heshima.

ingot, *n.* kipande, kidonge, kinoo (cha madini).

ingrained, *a.* -a ndani, -a kujaza, imara. *Ingrained dirt,* taka iliyoingia sana (ya ndani). *Ingrained habits,* mazoea yaliyokwisha thibitika.

ingratiate, *v.t.* pendekeza, rairai.

ingratitude, *n.* utovu wa shukrani, kutokuwa na shukrani, kutoshukuru.

ingredient, *n.* sehemu, kitu kilichomo, ndani yake, kichanganyiko.

ingress, *n.* kuingia, mwingilio, mlango, ruhusa ya kuingia, njia.

inguinal, *a.* -a manena.

inhabit, *v.t.* kaa katika, kaa penye, kalia, kaa. **inhabitable,** *a.* -a kukaa watu, -a kukalika na watu. **inhabitant,** *n.* mkazi, mkaa, mtu (wa mji au nchi fulani), mwenyeji.

inhale, *v.t.* vuta (shusha) pumzi, vuta hewa, pisha puani (kooni).

inhalation, *n.* kuvuta pumzi (hewa), pumzi.

inharmonious, *a.* si -linganifu, si -enye kupatana vema, -baya.

inhere, *v.i.* shikamana na, fungamana na, kaa ndani ya, -wamo. **inherent,** *a.* -a ndani, -a asili.

inherit, *v.t.* rithi. **inheritance,** *n.* urithi. **inheritor,** *n.* mrithi.

inhibit, *v.t.* zuia, kataza, gombeza, harimisha, pinza, chelewesha. **inhibition,** *n.* makatazo, mazuio; (*psychol.*) moyo wa mtu kumzuia asifanye jambo kwa sababu amezoezwa au kufundishwa kufikiri ni marufuku (haramu, baya, mwiko *&c.*).

inhospitable, *a.* -siopokea wageni, si -karibishaji, -tovu wa ukarimu, -enye mlango mbaya; (*of place, country &c.*) pasipofaa watu kukaa, pasipo mahali pa kukaa, baridi, -baya. **inhospitality,** *a.* utovu wa ukarimu, kutopokea wageni, ubaya (wa kutofaa watu).

inhuman, *a.* -kali sana, -katili, kama mnyama, jahili, -sio na huruma, -korofi. **inhumanity,** *n.* ukatili, ujahili, ukorofi, ukali mbaya.

inimical, *a.* -a uadui, si -enye urafiki, -a kuzuia, -a kudhuru, -a kupinga, -a kushindana.

inimitable, *a.* -sioigika, -sio na kifani, -ema sana, bora, -sioshindika, -a ajabu.

iniquitous, *a.* -ovu sana, -baya sana. **iniquity,** *n.* uovu, ubaya, udhalimu.

initial, *a.* -a mwanzo, -a kwanza. — *n.* herufi ya kwanza ya jina la mtu.

initiate, *v.t.* anza, anzisha, anzilisha, maliki, amiri; (*teach elements*) anza kufundisha; (*admit*) ingiza, ingiliza; (*into tribal customs*) tia jandoni (unyagoni, ukumbi). — *n.* mtu aliyeingizwa (aliyepokewa) katika chama *&c.*; (*in tribal rites*) mwali. **initiation,** *n.* mwanzo, kuingiza, mwingizo, kuingia, mwingio. *Tribal initiation rites,* jando, unyago, ukumbi. **initiative,** *a.* -a kuanza, -a kuingiza. — *n.* akili (tabia, uwezo nguvu *&c.*) ya kuanzishia mambo (ya kuvumbua njia &c.). *He has no initiative*, hana akili (uwezo, nguvu, bidii &c.) kuanza mambo mwenyewe.

inject, *v.t.* ingiza kwa nguvu, penyeza ndani; (*of medicine*) piga sindano. **injection**, *n.* kuingiza, mwingizo; (*medicine*) dawa ya sindano (ya kuingiza ndani). *Give an injection*, piga sindano.

injudicious, *a.* si -a busara (akili), -jinga, -siofaa.

injunction, *n.* amri, agizo, usio; (*law*) hati ya kuamuru jambo lifanyike (au lisifanyike).

injure, *v.t.* dhuru, umiza, haribu, kasiri, vunja, hasiri, dhulumu, onea. **injurious**, *a.* -a kudhuru, -enye madhara, -a kutia hasara, -a kuhasiri, -dhulumu, -onevu, -a shari. **injury**, *n.* madhara, hasara, maumivu, jeraha, uharibifu, maafa.

injustice, *n.* udhalimu, jeuri, jambo lisilo la haki.

ink, *n.* wino. — *v.t.* paka (tia) wino. **inkstand**, **inkwell**, *n.* kidau cha wino. **inky**, *a.* -enye wino, -eusi kama wino, -a giza sana.

inkling, *n.* kidokezo, dalili. *Get an inkling of*, sikia (onja) kidogo.

inkstand, *n.*, **inkwell**, *n.*, **inky**, *a.* taz. *ink*.

inlaid-work, *n.* taz. *inlay*.

inland, *a.* -a bara, -a ndani, -a nyuma.

inlay, *v.t.* (*p.t.* and *pf.t.* **inlaid**) fanya kazi ya njumu. **inlaid-work**, *n.* njumu.

inlet, *n.*, njia, mlango; (*creek*) hori, ghuba ndogo.

inmate, *n.* mkaa (wa nyumba fulani), mkazi, mkaaji.

inmost, *a.* -a ndani kabisa.

inn, *n.* hoteli, mkahawa, nyumba ya kupokea wageni. **innkeeper**, *n.* mwenye hoteli (mkahawa &c.).

innate, *a.* -a asili, -a maumbile, -a tabia, -siyoepukika.

inner, *a.* -a ndani, -a ndani zaidi.

innings, *n.* zamu (katika mchezo).

innkeeper, *n.* taz. *inn*.

innocent, *a.* safi, bila hatia (kosa) -siokosa, -eupe, -siyefanya dhambi (kosa, jambo aliloshtakiwa); (*simple*) -jinga, -a kitoto; (*morally harmless*) -sioleta maovu (mabaya, dhambi); (*innocuous*) -siodhuru. *Declare innocent*, ondoa hatiani, achilia. *He is innocent*, hakukosa, hana hatia. **innocence**, *n.* hali ya kuwa innocent.

innocuous, *a.* -siodhuru, -sio na madhara, -sioumiza, -ema, -zuri.

innovate, *v.i.* zua, anzisha jambo jipya, geuza mambo. **innovation**, *n.* (*novelty*) uzuzi, uzushi, uzuli; (*change*) mageuzi, mabadili, mambo mapya, mageni. **innovator**, *n.* mzushi, mwanza jambo jipya.

innuendo, *n.* kilinge, masingizio, kusengenya, masengenyo, machongezi, maneno yenye maana mbaya iliyofichwa.

innumerable, *a.* -siohesabika (kwa kuwa -ingi sana), -ingi mno.

innutritious, *a.* (*food*) -siotia nguvu, -siofaa.

inoculate, *v.t.* ambukiza (mtu au mnyama) ugonjwa usio mkali kumlinda asipatwe nao kwa ukali, chanja, piga sindano makusudi kuzuia uambukizo wa ugonjwa; (*teach, insinuate*) fundisha (mabaya), julisha (kwa werevu), tia moyoni. **inoculation**, *n.* kuchanjwa (kuambukizwa, kupigwa sindano) makusudi kuzuia uambukizo wa ugonjwa.

inodorous, *a.* -sionuka, pasipo harufu.

inoffensive, *a.* -siodhuru, si -kali, -pole, si -enye shari.

inoperative, *a.* -sio na nguvu, -siofanya kazi, -liotanguka, -fu, -liokufa.

inopportune, *a.* -sumbufu, -siofaa. *It is inopportune*, si wakati wake.

inordinate, *a.* -sio na kiasi, -a kupita kiasi, bila taratibu, -ingi mno.

inorganic, *a.* -a kitu kisicho sehemu ya mwili wala kitu cho chote chenye uhai, si -enye uhai, -a kifu, -a kama jiwe.

inquest, *n.* baraza ya kuhoji sababu ya kifo.

inquietude, *n.* kutotulia, wasiwasi, fadhaa, hangaiko.

inquire, *v.t.* uliza, tafuta habari, saili, hoji, tafiti; — *v.i.* uliza. *Inquire after,* ulizia hali. *Inquire for,* taka, omba. *Inquire into,* chungua, chunguza, peleleza, dadisi, pekua, fatiisha. **inquirer,** *n.* mwenye kuuliza *&c.* **inquiring,** *a.* -a kutafuta, -tafiti, -dadisi. **inquiry,** *n.* ulizo, swali, hoja; (*legal, formal*) hukumu, baraza, maneno; (*general*) kutafuta habari, uchungulizi. *Hold an inquiry into,* barizi kwa.

inquisition, *n.* kuhoji sana. *The Inquisition,* baraza kuu ya kuhukumia wazushi wa dini. **inquisitive,** *a.* -pekuzi, -pelelezi, -tafiti, -jasusi, -a kufatiisha, -chunguzi, -dadisi. *An inquisitive person,* mdadisi, duzi, mchunguzi, mpelelezi, mtafiti. **inquisitiveness,** *n.* utafiti, udadisi, ujasusi. **inquisitor,** *n.* mhoji, hakimu, mtu wa *Inquisition.*

inroad, *n.* vita, shambulio; (*encroachment*) kutwaa sehemu. *Make inroads on,* -la, vunja, haribu, kasiri, katia.

ins and outs, *n.* vipengee, mapindi, mizingo. *To know all the ins and outs,* kujua habari zote.

insalubrious, *a.* si -enye afya.

insane, *a.* -enye wazimu, -enye kichaa. **insanity,** *n.* wazimu, kichaa.

insatiable, *a.* -siotosheleka, -sioridhika, -sioisha; (*voracious*) -lafi, -sioshiba.

inscribe, *v.t.* andika, andikia, chora. **inscription,** *n.* mwandiko, andiko, maneno (yaliyoandikwa); (*on tomb &c.*) tarehe, machoro.

inscrutable, *a.* -siofahamika, -siotambulikana, -a fumbo, -a siri.

insect, *n.* mdudu. **insecticide,** *n.* dawa ya kuua wadudu. **insectivorous,** *a.* -enye kula wadudu.

insecure, *a.* -sio salama (imara, thabiti, mathubuti), -enye hatari, -a mashaka. **insecurity,** *n.* hatari, mashaka, udhaifu, ubovu.

insensate, *a.* pasipo akili, -pumbavu, -a hayawani, kama mnyama.

insensible, *a.* -sioona, -siohisi; (*imperceptible*) -sioonekana, -dogo. *Be insensible,* zimia, zirai. *He is insensible to pity,* hana huruma. *He is insensible to praise,* sifa hazimpendezi. **insensibility,** *n.* hali ya kuwa *insensible.* **insensibly,** *adv.* kidogo kidogo.

inseparable, *a.* -siotengeka, -siochangukana, siku zote pamoja, mamoja. *Inseparable companions,* rafiki wanaoandamana siku zote.

insert, *v.t.* tia ndani, tia, penyeza, ingiza. **insertion,** *n.* mwingizo, kuingiza, kitu kilichoingizwa.

inset, *n.* kitu kilichotiwa, *e.g.* picha ndogo iliyopigwa chapa katika picha kubwa.

inside, *a. and n.* upande wa ndani, ndani, ndani ya, -a ndani.

insidious, *a.* -erevu, -a hila, -danganyifu, -a kudhuru kwa siri.

insight, *n.* busara, ufahamu, akili, utambuzi, ujuzi, maarifa.

insignia, *n.* alama za cheo (kama nishani, tepe, taji *&c.*).

insignificance, *n.* taz. *insignificant.*

insignificant, *a.* (*person*) -dogo, -nyonge, dhaifu; (*thing*) hafifu, duni, ghafi. **insignificance,** *n.* udogo, uhafifu, unyonge, utovu wa maana.

insincere, *a.* -si amini, si -aminifu, si -nyofu, -danganyifu, -nafiki. **insincerity,** *n.* udanganyifu, hila, unafiki.

insinuate, *v.t.* penyeza kidogo kidogo (kwa hila), ingiliza, nena kwa fumbo; (*ingratiate*) pendekeza; (*suggest darkly*) dokeza, singizia. **insinuating,** *a.* -a kupendekeza, -a kudokeza. **insinuation,** *n.* kupenyeza *&c.*; neno la kusingizia (la kuchongea kwa siri), uchongezi, dokezo, kidokezo.

insipid, *a.* (*dull*) -dufu, -zito, baridi; (*tasteless*) chapwa, -sio na kiungo, -siokolewa, pasipo utamu. **insipidity,** *n.* udufu, uzito, ubaridi, uchapwa.

insist, *v.t. and i.* (*on*) nena kwa nguvu (kwa bidii, kwa uthabiti), chagiza, shurutisha, amuru kwa nguvu, zidi kuomba, shikilia, taka kwa nguvu, sisitiza.

insobriety, *n.* utovu wa kiasi, hasa katika kunywa, ulevi.

insolence, *n.* taz. *insolent.*

insolent, *a.* -fidhuli, -a jeuri, -juvi, -kavu wa macho, -shupavu, -safihi, -enye kiburi, -a kutakabari. **insolence**, *n.* ufidhuli, jeuri, ujuvi, ukavu wa macho, ushupavu, usafihi, kiburi.

insoluble, *a.* -sioyeyuka; (*inexplicable*) -siofumbulikana, -a fumbo, -gumu sana. **insolubility**, *n.* hali (tabia) ya kuwa *insoluble.*

insolvent, *a.* -sioweza kulipa deni, -liofilisika. **insolvency**, *n.* kufilisika, hali ya kutoweza kulipa deni (ya kufilisika).

insomuch, *adv.* hata, kwa jinsi.

insomnia, *n.* hali ya kutoweza kupata usingizi.

insouciant, *a.* -zembe, -kavu wa macho, upurukushani.

inspan, *v.t.* fungia (farasi, ng'ombe &c.) garini.

inspect, *v.t.* kagua, tazama, tazamia, aua, chungua, chunguza, simamia, angalia. **inspection**, *n.* kuangalia &c.; mkaguo, ukaguzi. **inspector**, *n.* msimamizi, mwangalizi, mkaguzi.

inspire, *v.t.* vuta pumzi, puzia; (*suggest*) tia moyoni (shauri, hofu, tumaini &c.); (*direct*) ongoza, endesha, sukuma, sukumiza. *He is inspired,* amefunguliwa heri, anaongozwa na Mungu. **inspiration**, *n.* kuvuta pumzi, upuzio; (*guidance, direction*) maongozi, shauri, onyo; (*divine guidance*) maongozi ya Mungu, upuzio wa Roho Mtakatifu, Mungu.

inspirit, *v.t.* pa moyo, tia moyo, amsha, teremesha, changamsha, ondoa huzuni.

inst. taz. *instant.*

instability, *n.* utovu wa imara (uthabiti), udhaifu, ulegevu, ugoigoi, kutikisika, kutosimama, kugeuka, kigeugeu, mleoleo.

install, *v.t.* tia katika kazi, weka, tia. **installation**, *n.* kuweka, kiweko. **instalment**, *n.* taz. *installation*; (*portion*) sehemu, fungu (la deni, malipo, mali, maandiko, hadithi &c.).

instance, *n.* mfano, namna; (*request*) shauri, uombezi, maongozi. *In the first instance,* mwanzoni, kwanza. *At the instance of so and so,* kwa shauri la fulani, *i.e.* fulani aliomba au alishauri. *For instance,* kwa mfano, mathalan. — *v.t.* taja, nena.

instant, *a.* -a mara moja, -a ghafula, -a pale pale; (*close*) -a karibu; (*with specified date*) -a mwezi huu. *The 2nd inst.*, siku ya pili ya mwezi huu. — *n.* dakika, mara hii, papo hapo, sasa hivi. *Do it this instant,* fanya sasa hivi (mara hii, papo hapo). *Wait an instant,* ngoja kidogo, ngoja kwanza. *In an instant, Instantaneously,* ghafula hiyo, mara hiyo, sasa hivi. **instantaneous**, *a.* -a dakika moja, -a mara hiyo, pale pale. **instanter**, *adv.* mara, bila kukawia, papo hapo.

instead (*of*), adv. mahali pa, badala ya.

instep, *n.* kiganja cha mguu (juu ya wayo).

instigate, *v.t.* anzisha, anza, chochea, sukumiza, vuta, chomesha, tomesha, amsha, vuruga, ongoza, tia shonga (chonjo). **instigation**, *n.* kichocheo, kichomo, sukumizo, usukumizi, shauri, maongozi, ushawishi, mvuto, shonga, chonjo. **instigator**, *n.* mchochea, msukumizi, mshauri, mwongozi &c.

instil(l), *v.t.* tia kwa taraibu (polepole, kidogo kidogo), fundisha kidogo kidogo.

instinct, *n.* silika, akili (ya asili inayofunza watu na wanyama watende mambo bila kufundishwa); (*propensity*) tabia, tamaa, moyo, kutaka; (*unreasoned impulse*) nia ya ghafula. **instinctive**, *a.* -a tabia,

-a silika, -a moyo (bila shauri au ufahamu) -a ghafula, -a mara moja.

institute, *v.t.* anzisha, fanyiza, simamisha, amuru, maliki, weka, — *n.* chama, shirika, jamii ya watu (iliyofanyika kwa kusudi la kazi maalum), nyumba ya chama (jamii *&c.*). **institution,** *n.* kuanzisha *&c.*, taz: *institute, v.*; (*rule, established practice*) kawaida, desturi, sheria; chama *&c.*, kama *institute, n.*

instruct, *v.t.* funza, fundisha, elimisha, adilisha, hekimisha; (*of household and tribal affairs*) funda; (*give orders*) agiza, amuru; (*young children*) lea. **instruction,** *n.* mafunzo, mafundisho, malezi; (*tribal rites*) (*girls*) unyago; (*boys*) jando, kumbi, ukumbi; (*tribal teachings*) mizungu, malango; (*commission*) maagizo; (*advice &c.*) shauri, usia. **instructive,** *a.* -a kufundisha, -a kufaa kwa maarifa na adili, -a maana. **instructor,** *n.* mwalimu, mkufunzi; (*in arts and crafts*) fundi; (*in initiation rites*) kungwi, kungu.

instrument, *n.* chombo, ala, kipande, samani, kitu cha kufanyizia kazi; (*in law*) hati; (*agent*) mtumishi, mjumbe, wakili, mtu afanyaye jambo; (*musical*) ala ya ngoma (muziki), *e.g.* ngoma, kinanda, fidla, gambusi, zeze *&c.* **instrumental,** *a.* -a kutendea kazi, -a kutumika, -a kufaa, -a kusaidia; (*music*) -a ngoma namna namna (mbalimbali). *He was instrumental,* alitumika, alitenda kazi, alikuwamo. **instrumentality,** *n.* matumizi, utume, utumi, nguvu, njia.

insubordinate, *a.* -asi, -kaidi, -halifu.

insubordination, *n.* maasi, kuasi, ukaidi, uhalifu.

insufferable, *a.* -a kuchukiza, -siovumilika, -siostahimilika, -siochukulika, -baya sana.

insufficient, *a.* haba, -chache, kidogo, -siotosha, -siofaa, shida. **insufficiency,** *n.* kutotosha, kuwa haba, uchache, upungufu.

insular, *a.* -a kisiwa, -a kukaa kisiwani; (*narrow, selfish*) -enye ulimwengu mdogo, -enye mawazo (maarifa *&c.*) ya mumo humo tu, -a peke yake, -a kujiona, -kinaifu. **insularity,** *n.* kuwa kisiwa; ukinaifu, tabia ya kufikiri ya mumo humo tu.

insulate, *v.t.* tenga, weka peke yake; (*electricity &c.*) funika kwa mpira *&c.* ili nguvu ya umeme (joto *&c.*) isitoke. **insulation,** *n.* kutengwa, kukaa pekee.

insult, *n.* matukano, ufidhuli, usafihi, jeuri, jefule, ujuvi. — *v.t.* tukana, fidhulika, kebehi, tenda jeuri. **insulting,** *a.* -a kutukana, -fidhuli, -a jeuri, -kavu wa macho, -safihi.

insuperable, *a.* -sioshindika, -siopitika, -sioondoleka, -kubwa sana.

insupportable, *a.* -siovumilika, -siostahimilika, siochukulika, -baya sana.

insure, *v.t.* fanya bima ya, lipa jukumu, (lipa fedha kila mwaka kwa masharti ya kuwa ukifa, jamaa watalipwa fedha fulani, au, ya kuwa hasara ikitokea fedha kiasi fulani italipwa). **insurance,** *n.* bima, masharti ya bima, jukumu.

insurgent, *n. and a.* mwasi, mfitini (wa serikali); -asi, -halifu, -fitini. **insurrection,** *n.* maasi, fitina (juu ya serikali).

insurmountable, *a.* -sioshindika, -siopitika, -sioondoleka, -kubwa sana.

insurrection, *n.* taz. *insurgent.*

insusceptible, *a.* -siopatika, -sioona, -sioamshika, -siovutika.

intact, *a.* -zima, kamili, -ote, salamu (salama), pasipo hasara (upungufu).

intake, *n.* mlango (kilango, tundu) wa kuingia maji au hewa.

intangible, *a.* -siooneka kwa kugusa, -sioonekana, -siotambulikana, kama kivuli tu, kama si kitu.

integer, *n.* kitu kizima (kamili), hesabu kamili, -zima (bila upungufu), -a kanuni, -a asili. **integrate,** *v.t.* unganisha sehemu zote kufanya -zima, kamilisha. **integrity,** *n.* uzima, ukamilifu; (*of character*) amini, uaminifu, haki, unyofu, wema, tabia bora, maadili, uadilifu.

integument, *n.* kifuniko, ngozi, ganda.

intellect, *n.* akili. **intellectual,** *a.* -enye akili, -a akili. **intelligence,** *n.* akili, ufahamu, busara, ujuzi, welekevu, utambuzi, wangavu; (*news &c.*) habari, maarifa. **intelligent,** *a.* -enye akili, -tambuzi, -fahamivu, -juzi, -angavu. **intelligentsia,** *n.* watu wenye akili (maarufu) wa nchi.

intemperate, *a.* -sio na kiasi, hasa katika kunywa ulevi. **intemperance,** *n.* utovu wa kiasi, kutojizuia, ulevi.

intend, *v.t.* kusudia, nia, nuia, azimu, taka, dhamiri, ukilia. **intended,** *n.* mchumba. **intent,** *n.* nia, kusudi, shauri, moyo, maana, mradi, azimio, dhamiri, garadhi, maarubu, madhumuni. *To all intents and purposes,* kweli, barabara, sawa kama. — *a.* (*on*) -enye bidii (ya), -a kujikaza (kwa). **intention,** *n.* taz. *intent, n.* *Well intentioned,* -enye nia njema, -enye moyo mwema. **intentional,** *a.* -a kusudi, -a moyo. **intentionally,** *adv.* makusudi, kwa moyo, kwa kutaka. **intently,** *adv.* kwa kukaza, kwa nguvu. **intentness,** *n.* mkazo, bidii, uangalifu.

intense, *a.* -a mkazo, -a nguvu, -ingi sana, -kubwa sana, -kali sana, -a bidii nyingi, -a juhudi. *Intense heat,* joto kali sana. **intensely,** *adv.* kwa nguvu, kabisa, sana. **intensify,** *v.t.* kaza, ongeza, zidisha, kithiri; — *v.i.* pata nguvu, zidi, ongezeka, kithiri. **intensity,** *n.* mkazo, bidii, nguvu, ukali, ukalifu. **intensive,** *a.* -a bidii, -a juhudi, -a uangalifu, -a kutia mkazo, -a kuzidisha nguvu.

intent, *n. and a.*, **intention,** *n.*, **intentional,** *a.*, **intentionally,** *adv.*, **intently,** *adv.*, **intentness,** *n.*, taz. *intend.*

inter, (1) *v.t.* zika. **interment,** *n.* maziko, kuzika.

inter-, (2) *pref.* baina, kati ya, miongoni mwa, katika, *e.g. international,* baina (miongoni mwa) mataifa. *In comp.* -ana, *e.g. interact,* tendana; *interchange,* badiliana, badilishana.

inter alia, katika (pamoja na, miongoni mwa) mambo mengine.

interact, *v.i.* tendana, vutana, amshana, chocheana. **interaction,** *n.* kutendana, utendano (kazi ya -enyewe kwa -enyewe), uvutano, uamshano, uchocheano.

intercalate, *v.t.* tia kati, penyeza.

intercede, *v.i.* (*for*) ombea, tetea, sihi (toa maneno) kwa ajili ya, nenea. **intercession,** *n.* kuombea, maombezi, mateteo. **intercessor,** *n.* mwombezi, mnenezi, mtetezi. **intercessory,** *a.* -a kuombea, -a kutetea.

intercept, *v.t.* kamata (zuia, pinza) njiani, zuia, kinga.

intercession, *n.*, **intercessor,** *n.*, **intercessory,** *a.* taz. *intercede.*

interchange, *v.t. and i.* badiliana, badilishana. **interchangeable,** *a.* -a kubadilikana, sawasawa kabisa, mfano mmoja.

intercolonial, *a.* (-a *Colonies* zenyewe kwa zenyewe).

intercommunion, *n.* ushirika, kushirikiana.

intercourse, *n.* (*social*) mazungumzo, maongezi, urafiki, kujiliana, ushirika; (*commercial*) biashara, kubadilishana vitu; (*sexual*) mambo ya mume na mke, unyumba, ngono, ugoni, kujamii, (*vulgar*) kutomba.

interdict, *v.t.* gombeza; kataza, rufuku, piga marufuku, harimisha, zuia, pinza &c., (kwa amri ya serikali, kanisa &c.). — *n.* makatazo, kuharimisha; amri ya Kanisa ya kutenga watu na ibada zake.

interest, *n.* moyo wa kupenda (kutaka, kutunza, kuangalia, kuogopa, kusikitikia, kuhurumia &c.), usikizi, usikivu; (*profit*) faida; (*share*) sehemu, shirika; (*earnestness*) bidii; (*influence*) nguvu, kupendelewa. *He takes no interest in me,* hanipendi, haniangalii, hanijali. *He listened with great interest,* alisikiliza sana. *He got on by interest,* alipata cheo kwa kupendelewa. *It involves many interests,* yapasa watu wengi (mambo mengi). *He charges 5 per cent. interest,* mia kwa tano ndiyo faida yake. *In the interests of,* kwa ajili ya, kwa faida ya. — *v.t.* tia moyo wa kupenda &c. (taz. *interest, n.*); vuta, angaliza, pendeza, pasa, tamanisha, tazamisha, chomesha, chochea amsha. **interested,** *a.* -enye *interest, n. From interested motive,* kwa ajili ya faida. **interesting,** *a.* -enye kutia *interest, n.* -a kuvuta, -a kupendeza, -a kusikiza, &c.

interfere, *v.i.* jipenyeza, jiingiliza, jitia kati, jidukiza, taradhia; (*check*) katiza, zuia, pinza. **interference,** *n.* kujitia kati, kuzuia, kizuizi, pingamizi, mgogoro.

interfuse, *v.t.* changanya; — *v.i.* changanyika.

interim, *n.* muda wa kati.

interior, *n. and a.* upande wa ndani, ndani, -a ndani; (*of country*) bara.

interject, *v.t.* tia kati, dakiza (kwa), katiza (kwa). **interjection,** *n.* neno la kuonyesha mshangao &c. *e.g.* ee! loo! ati! kumbe! haya! hebu! weye! &c.

interlace, *v.t.* tatanisha, changanya; — *v.i.* tatana, ingiana, pitanapitana.

interlard, *v.t.* changanya, tia kati.

interleave, *v.t.* changanya kurasa tupu kitabuni, pangilia karatasi kati ya kurasa.

interline, *v.t.* andika kati ya mistari ya kitabu (mwandiko).

interlinear, *a.* -a kati ya mistari.

interlock, *v.t.* unganisha, fungamanisha; — *v.i.* fungamana, ungamana.

interlocutor, *n.* mwenye kuuliza au kusema na.

interloper, *n.* mdukizi, mpelelezi.

interlude, *n.* kipumziko, nafasi kati ya sehemu za mchezo.

intermarry, *v.i.* oana.

intermeddle, *v.i.* jitia kati, jishughulisha (hasa na mambo ya watu wengine).

intermediate, *a.* -a kati, -a baina. **intermediary,** *n.* mjumbe, mwamuzi. — *a.* -a kati, -a baina.

interment, taz. *inter.*

interminable, *a.* pasipo mwisho, -a kufululiza; (*wearisome*) -a kuchosha.

intermingle, *v.t.* changanya, changamanisha; — *v.i.* changamana.

intermit, *v.t.* simamisha, katiza, komesha (kwa muda); — *v.i.* simama, tulia, koma. **intermission,** *n.* kituo, kutulia; (*interval*) muda wa kati, kikomo. **intermittent,** *a.* -a vipindi, -a kwenda na kurudi, -a kukoma na kurudi mara, si -a kufululiza.

intermix, *v.t.* changanya; — *v.i.* changamana.

intern, *v.t.* funga, zuia (kataza) mtu asitoke mahali fulani (*e.g.* kambi la waliotekwa vitani &c.). **internal,** *a.* -a ndani, -a moyoni, -a jambo lenyewe, -a nchi yenyewe.

international, *a.* -a kuhusu mataifa, -a kati ya mataifa.

internecine, *a.* -a kuuana, -kali sana.

interpellate, *v.t.* katiza kuuliza swali (kutaka maelezo). **interpellation,** *n.* (*question*) swali, ulizo; (*interruption*) kukatiza maneno.

interpolate, *v.t.* tia (maneno yasiyokuwamo) katika kitabu (hati), maandiko). *The book has been interpolated,* kitabu kimetiwa maneno yasiyokuwamo kilipoandikwa. **interpolation,** *n.* kutia kitabuni (katika hati, maandiko) maneno yasiyokuwamo kilipoandikwa; maneno yaliyotiwa ambayo yasiyokuwamo.

interpose, *v.t.* tia kati, ingiza, penyeza; — *v.i.* ingia kati, jitia kati. **interposition,** *n.* kutia kati, kujiingiza.

interpret, *v.t.* fasiri, tafsiri, eleza maana, fafanisha, fafanua, dhihirisha, fumbua; (*dreams*) agua. **interpretation,** *n.* tafsiri, maana, mafafanusi, maelezo; (*of dreams*) uaguzi, maaguzi. **interpreter,** *n.* mfasiri, mfafanusi; (*of foreign language*) mkalimani; (*of dreams*) mwaguzi.

interregnum, *n.* muda kati, *e.g.* kati ya kufariki mfalme na kutawazwa mrithi wake.

interrogate, *v.t.* uliza, hoji, saili, tafutia habari, dadisi. **interrogation,** *n.* ulizo, swali. *Note (mark, point) of interrogation,* alama hii (?), yaani alama ya kuuliza. **interrogative,** *a.* -a kuuliza. **interrogatory,** *n.* ulizo, swali, maulizo. — *a.*, -a kuuliza.

interrupt, *v.t.* dakiza, katiza, jitia kati, pinga, jidukiza, kingamisha, viza, komesha, chachawiza. **interruption,** *n.* madakizo, kizuizo, zuio, kukatiza, katizo, kukingamisha.

intersect, *v.t.* kata, katakata; — *v.i.* katana, kingamana, pambana, kutana. **intersection,** *n.* kukatana, mkutano, mkingamo.

intersperse, *v.t.* changanya, tia huko na huko kati ya vitu vingine.

interstice, *n.* ufa, mwanya, kipenyo, kitundu, nafasi ndogo.

intertwine, *v.t.* pota, sokota, suka, tatiza; — *v.i.* tatana, kingamana.

interval, *n.* hatua, nafasi, wakati (katikati ya mahali pawili, mambo mawili, nyakati mbili). *At intervals,* huko na huko, pengine pengine, kwa vipindi.

intervene, *v.i.* -ja (tokea) kati, jitia (ingia) kati. **intervention,** *n.* kujitia kati, ujumbe, uamuzi.

interview, *n.* mkutano (wa watu wawili au baadhi mbili za watu), mkutano wa kupata shauri au kufanya shughuli.

interweave, *v.t.* tatanisha, changanya, sokota.

intestate, *a.* pasipo usia, pasipo kurithisha mali.

intestine, *a.* -a nchi yenyewe, -a taifa lenyewe, -a wenyewe kwa wenyewe, -a ndani. **intestines,** *n.* matumbo; (*small*) chango, uchengelele.

intimate, *a.* -a ndani, -a moyo, -a moyoni; (*thorough, complete*) kamili, -a -ote. *An intimate friend,* msiri. *Intimate knowledge,* kujua sana. — *v.t.* arifu, tangaza, hubiri, onya. **intimacy,** *n.* urafiki, ushirika; (*sexual*) ngono, tendo la kulalana (kujamii). **intimation,** *n.* habari, taarifu, neno, onyo, ishara.

intimidate, *v.t.* tisha, ogofya, kamia. **intimidation,** *n.* kitisho, ogofya, makamio.

into, *prep.* (kuingia, kuja, kuenda) katika, kwa, ndani ya, -ni.

intolerable, *a.* -siovumilika, -sistahimilika, -siochukulika, -zito mno, -a kulemea.

intolerance, *n.* taz. *intolerant.*

intolerant, *a.* -sioweza kuvumilia (kustahimili, kukubali) maneno (mashauri *&c.*) ya wengine, -shupavu. **intolerance,** *n.* kutovumilia, kutosikia maneno, ushupavu.

intone, *v.t.* sema kwa sauti ya kuimba. **intonation,** *n.* kusema kwa sauti ya kuimba, sauti, kuimba, tamko.

intoxicate, *v.t.* rusha akili, shinda, chukua; (*make drunk*) levya. **intoxicant,** *n.* kileo, ulevi; (*excitement*) kupotewa akili, kuchukuliwa na furaha (kiburi, tumaini *&c.*).

intractable, *a.* -tundu, -kaidi, -gumu, -baya.

intramural, *a.* -a ndani (ya kanisa, mji, chuo *&c.*).

intransigent, *a.* -siotaka kupatana, -siokubali kupatana.

intrepid, *a.* -siotishika, -sioona hofu, -jasiri, -kavu -a macho, -enye moyo mkuu, hodari. **intrepidity,** *n.* ujasiri, uhodari, ukavu wa macho, hali ya kuwa *intrepid.*

intricacy, *n.* taz. *intricate.*

intricate, *a.* -enye sehemu nyingi, -enye matatizo, -liotatanika, -a kazi nyingi, -a fumbo, -gumu. **intricacy,** *n.* matatizo, mambo mengi, sehemu nyingi, ugumu.

intrigue, *v.i.* fanya shauri kwa hila (kwa werevu, kwa siri); — *v.t.* (*rouse interest*) amsha, vuta, chochea, kanganya. — *n.* hila, werevu, shauri la siri, fitina.

intrinsic, *a.* -a kitu chenyewe peke yake, -a ndani, -a asili, halisi.

introduce, *v.t.* leta, ingiza, penyeza; (*bring into notice*) anza, tangaza, tembeza; (*make acquainted*) julisha, julishana. **introduction,** *n.* kuleta, kuingiza &c. (taz. *introduce*); (*primer*) mlango, mwanzo; (*preface*) dibaji, maneno ya mbele (kitabuni), utangulizi. **introductory,** *a.* -a mwanzo, -a kuanzisha.

introspection, *n.* kujiangalia nafsi, kutafakari mawazo na maono ya nafsi, kujifikiri, kujiwazia.

introvert, *v.t.* geuza ndani, elekeza ndani, peleka ndani. — *n.* mtu mwenye tabia ya kufikiri mawazo na maono ya nafsi yake.

intrude, *v.i.* ingia bila kukaribishwa wala kutakiwa; — *v.t.* leta au ingiza pasipo adabu (kwa jeuri au ufidhuli), jipenyeza, jidukiza. **intruder,** *n.* mdukizi, mpelelezi, mzushi. **intrusion,** *n.* kujipenyeza &c. taz. *intrude.* **intrusive,** *a.* -a kuingia bila kutakwa, -dukizi.

intuition, *n.* ujuzi (maono) unaoingia akili ghafula bila kufikiri (kwa kutupia jicho tu). *Intuition as to the character of a person,* ujuzi (maono) juu ya tabia ya mtu, bila kuwa na sababu thabiti. **intuitive,** *a.* -a mara moja, ghafula bila kufikiri.

inundate, *v.t.* gharikisha, funikiza, maji, furika katika; (*fill up*) jaza, eneza, songa. **inundation,** *n.* furiko, gharika; (*abundance*) wingi.

inure, enure, *v.t.* zoeza. *Inured to,* -zoevu wa.

invade, *v.t.* leta vita, ingia kwa vita, shambulia, ruka mpaka, ingia ghafula, ingia -ingi. **invader,** *n.* mleta vita, adui (aingiaye nchi kwa vita). **invasion,** *n.* mwingilio kwa vita, mruko wa mpaka kwa vita, shambulio; (*encroachment*) mwingilio.

invalid, *n.* mgonjwa, mwele, — *a.* -sio na nguvu, -liotanguka, -siofaa, -a bure, batili. **invalidate,** *v.t.* tangua, batili, batilisha. **invalidity,** *n.* utovu wa nguvu, kutofaa, kutanguka.

invaluable, *a.* -a thamani sana, -a tunu, -siokadirika kwa kuwa na thamani sana (kwa kuwa na manufaa &c.)

invariable, *a.* -siobadili, -siogeuka, sawasawa siku zote.

invasion, *n.* taz. *invade.*

invective, *n.* maneno makali ya kushtaki (kulaumu, kushutumu), mashutumu, mashtaka makali. **inveigh,** *v.i.* (*against*) sema, nenea, amba, shtaki, shutumu.

inveigle, *v.t.* vuta kwa werevu (hila &c.) laghai, shawishi, ghilibu.

invent, *v.t.* zua, buni, tunga, vumbua, fanyiza. **invention,** *n.* uvumbuzi, ubuni; (*something invented*) kitu (chombo, mashine &c.) kipya, njia (namna) mpya; (*untruth*) uwongo, hila; (*inventiveness*) akili ya kuvumbua (kubuni &c.), werevu. **inventive,** *a.* -elekevu, hodari wa kubuni &c. -zushi, -vumbuzi. **inventor,** *n.* mwenye kubuni, mzushi, mvumbuaji, mfanyi, mtungaji.

inventory, *n.* orodha, hesabu, daftari, jedwali.

invert, *v.t.* pindua, geuza, weka kinyume. **inverse,** *a.* -a kinyume, mbalimbali, -a kupinduka. **inversion,** *n.* kugeuza, mgeuzo, kupindua, mapinduzi, hali ya kuwa kinyume (ya kupinduka).

invertebrate, *a.* -sio na uti wa mgongo; (*of person*) -geugeu, dhaifu, si -aminifu.

invest, *v.t.* (*money*) tuma fedha ili kupata faida, *e.g.* shirikisha katika kumpuni (duka, shamba &c.); (*clothe*) -pa, vika, pamba; (*besiege*) zunguka, zingia, fanya mazingiwa. *Invest in* (*a car* &c.) nunua. **investiture,** *n.* weka katika (kabidhisha, ingiza) kazi (cheo, daraja &c.). **investment,** *n.* kutuma fedha &c. taz. *invest*; fedha iliyotumika kupata faida; (*siege*) mazingiwa.

investigate, *v.t.* chungua, chunguza, peleleza, tafuta habari ya, hoji, hakiki. **investigation,** *n.* kuchungua &c.; hoja, mchunguo, uchunguzi.

investiture, *n.*, **investment,** *n.* taz. *invest.*

inveterate, *a.*, -a zamani, -a nguvu, -a siku nyingi, -a kuzoea, -zoevu. *An inveterate thief (drunkard &c.)* mwizi (mlevi) wa kupindukia.

invidious, *a.* -a kuchukiza, -a kutia chuki, -a kuchochea uchungu, -a kupendelea (na kwa hiyo kutia uchungu).

invigilate, *v.i.* simamia mtihani.

invigorate, *v.t.* tia nguvu (uzima), imarisha, thibitisha, burudisha.

invincible, *a.* -sioshindika.

inviolate, *a.* -zima, safi, -sioharibika. **inviolable,** *a.* -sioharibika, -siodhurika, wakf, -a heshima.

invisible, *a.* -sioonekana. *Become invisible (vanish),* toweka, tokomea.

invite, *v.t.* ita, taka, omba; *(attract)* vuta, shawishi; *(guests)* karibisha, alika. **invitation,** *n.* barua ya kukaribisha (ya kualika), mwaliko, jaliko, aliko, kuita, mwito. *I have received an invitation,* nimekaribishwa, nimealikwa, nimeitwa. **inviting,** *a.* -a kutamanisha, -a kuvuta.

invocation, *n.* taz. *invoke.*

invoice, *n.* orodha, hesabu.

invoke, *v.t.* *(ask for)* omba, sihi, taka; *(pray to)* tolea sala, omba kwa; *(summons up)* ita, leta. **invocation,** *n.* maombo, sala, kuomba.

involuntary, *a.* -siokusudiwa, pasipo kutaka, bila kujua, si kwa akili.

involve, *v.t.* funika, tatanisha; *(bring)* leta, fanya, -wa sababu ya, pasha; *(place)* tia, weka. **involved,** *a.* *(in debt)* -enye deni; *(embarrassed, difficult)* -enye matata, -gumu, -sioelea.

invulnerable, *a.* -siotilika jeraha, -siodhurika, -siovunjika, -siotwalika (boma &c.).

inward, *a.* -a ndani, -a moyoni, rohoni. **inwardly,** *adv.* kwa ndani, ndani, moyoni. **inwards,** *adv.* ndani. — *n.* matumbo.

iodine, *n.* *Tincture of iodine,* namna ya dawa ya kupaka vijeraha, &c. dawa ya joto.

iota, *n.* kipande kidogo, kidogo. *There is not an iota of truth in the statement,* maneno si kweli hata kidogo.

I.O.U. = *I owe you,* yaani naahidi kulipa deni.

ipecacuanha, *n.* dawa ya kutapisha iliyofanyika kwa mizizi ya mzikoziko.

irascible, *a.* -epesi wa hasira, -a harara, -kali, -enye chukichuki, habali.

ire, *n.* hasira, ukali, harara, ghadhabu.

irate, *a.* -a hasira, -kali.

iridescent, *a.* -a kung'aa kwa rangi zote za upindi wa mvua. **iridescence,** *n.* mng'ao wa kitu chenye rangi zote zilizo katika upindi wa mvua.

iridium, *n.* namna ya madini nyeupe ngumu sana.

iris, *n.* namna ya ua; *(of eye)* duara ya rangi inayozunguka mboni ya jicho.

irk, *v.t.* chosha, taabisha, udhi, sumbua, lemeza. **irksome,** *a.* -a kuchosha, -a kutaabisha, -a taabu, -a kuudhi, -a kusumbua, -sumbufu, -a kulemea, -a kuchukiza.

iron, *n.* chuma; *(for laundry)* pasi. *Cast iron,* chuma cha kusubu. *Wrought iron,* chuma cha kufua. *Pieces of iron,* vyuma. *Put in irons,* tia pingu, funga minyororo, funga. *Strike while the iron is hot,* fanya hapo mambo yangalipo ya kufaa. *A man of iron,* mtu mgumu. *Have too many irons in the fire,* shughulika na mambo mengi zaidi pamoja. — *a.* -a chuma; *(hard)* -gumu mno. — *v.t.* piga pasi. **iron-bar,** *n.* ufito wa chuma, upao; *(thick)* mtaimbo. **ironclad,** *n.* manowari. **ironmonger,** *n.* mfanya biashara ya vyombo vya chuma. **ironmongery,** *n.*, biashara ya vyombo vya chuma. **iron-mould,** *n.* doa lililofanyika nguoni kwa kutu au wino.

ironical, *a.* taz. *irony.*

ironmonger, *n.*, **iron-mould,** *n.* taz. *iron.*

irony, *n.* ubishi, dhihaka, matumizi ya maneno ya kinyume, *e.g.* hapa pazuri (lakini kwa kweli ni pabaya sana); mambo yaliyotokea kinyume cha yaliyotazamiwa, *e.g. the irony of fate*, kinyume kilicholetwa na ajali kama kwamba inafanya mzaha. **ironical,** *a.* -a *irony.*

irradiate, *v.i.* toa mwanga pande zote; — *v.t.* angaza, mulika, tia nuru; (*rejoice*) furahisha; (*give lustre to*) fahirisha; (*enlighten*) pasha elimu (maarifa). **irradiation,** *n.* kutoka mwanga, mwanga; (*brilliancy*) fahari, wangavu.

irrational, *a.* -sio na akili si kwa akili, -pumbavu.

irreclaimable, *a.* -siorudika, -siotengenezeka.

irreconcilable, *a.* -siopatana kabisa, -sioweza kupatanishwa, mbalimbali.

irrecoverable, *a.* -siopatikana tena, -siorudi, -siokomboleka.

irredeemable, *a.* -siokomboleka, -siorudika.

irreducible, *a.* -siopunguka, -sioweza kupunguzwa.

irrefragable, *a.* -siokanikana, -siokanushika, -siobatilika.

irrefutable, *a.* -siokanikana, -siokanushika, madhubuti.

irregular, *a.* si sawa, -liopotoka, -liochafuka, -sio -a kawaida, si -a desturi, si -a taratibu, -baya. **irregularity,** *n.* kukosa taratibu, si kawaida, ubaya, lisilo la kawaida.

irrelevant, *a.* -siopasa, -siohusu, -siofaa, -siofungamana. **irrelevancy,** *n.* kutofaa, kutohusu, kutopasa; neno lisilofungamana, lisilohusu.

irreligious, *a.* -sioshika dini, -siopenda Mungu, -a kuchukia dini (Mungu), -siopatana na dini. *He is irreligious,* hajali Mungu, hana dini, hashiki dini. **irreligion,** *n.* utovu wa dini, kutompenda Mungu.

irremediable, *a.* -sioponyeka, -siorudika, -siotengenezeka.

irremovable, *a.* -sioondoleka, imara, madhubuti, thabiti.

irreparable, *a.* -siotengenezeka, -sioponyeka, -siorekabika.

irrepressible, *a.* -siozuilika, -siotulizika, -siozimika, -a nguvu.

irreproachable, *a.* -siolaumika, -sio na hatia, -sio na kosa, -ema, -adilifu, -a mwenendo mzuri kabisa.

irresistible, *a.* -a kushinda yote, -a nguvu nyingi sana, -sioweza kuzuiwa na mtu, -kubwa.

irresolute, *a.* -a kusitasita, -sio thabiti, -a waisiwasi, dhaifu. **irresolution,** *n.* wasiwasi, kusita moyoni, shaka, kutanga, udhaifu, hangaiko.

irresolvable, *a.* -siochangukana, -siogawanyikana; -siotambulikana.

irrespective (*of*), *a.* pasipo kujali (kuangalia, kufikiri, kuhesabu), pasipo, isipokuwa, ila, mbali (ya).

irresponsible, *a.* -siokuwamo, -siopasiwa; (*unreliable*) si -aminifu, -siotumainika, habali, -zembe. *He is irresponsible,* si chini ya mtu (amri), hana mtu (kitu) juu yake; hajali mtu (neno), hadiriki neno, yote juu yake mwenyewe.

irretrievable, *a.* -siopatikana tena, -siorudika, -siotengenezeka, -sioponyeka.

irreverent, *a.* -sio na heshima, -siostahi, -siojali, -sio na adabu, -dharau, -fidhuli, -safihi. **irreverence,** *n.* utovu wa heshima (ustahi), usafihi, kutomhesimu Mungu (watu), dharau, ufidhuli.

irreversible, *a.* -siogeuka, -siorudika, -siotanguka, -siobadilika.

irrevocable, *a.* -siorudika, -siotenguka, -siobadilika.

irrigate, *v.t.* tilia maji (hasa kwa njia ya mifereji au handaki); (*medical*) osha kidonda (jeraha &c.) kwa maji yanayopita. **irrigation,** *n.* kutia maji (hasa shamba kwa mifereji au handaki), kuleta maji, mito, mafuriko.

irritate, *v.t.* washa, choma, chomesha, chokoza, kasirisha, sumbua, udhi. **irritability,** *n.* wepesi wa hasira, unyeti, harara, chukichuki, uchuki. **irritable,** *a.* -epesi wa hasira, -a kuudhika upesi, -a harara, -a hamaki, -a chuki, -a kuchacha. **irritant,** *a. and n.* -a kuwasha, -a kutia uchungu, -a kuchoma, -a kuchukiza, -a kukasirisha. — *n.* kitu kiwashacho &c. **irritation,** *n.* moto, kuwasha, kichomi, mchomo, kiwasho, chuki, uchungu.

irruption *n.* (*of enemies*) shambulio; (*water*) mafuriko; (*sudden coming*) majilio ya ghafula, kuingia kwa tadi (kwa nguvu).

is, *v.* (taz. *am, be*), ni; (*in comp.*) -na, *He is good,* ni (yu) mwema. *He is eating,* anakula.

isinglass, *n.* kitu kama gundi kinachotumika kuweka mayai yasioze.

Islam, *n.* Islamu, dini ya Muhammadi, dini ya kiislamu.

island, *n.* kisiwa. **islander,** *n.* mkaa kisiwani. **isle,** *n.* kisiwa. **islet,** *n.* kisiwa kidogo.

isolate, *v.t.* tenga, weka peke yake (yao &c.). **isolation,** *n.* kukaa upweke, kutenga, upekee.

isosceles, *a. Isosceles triangle,* pembetatu yenye pande mbili zilizo sawa kwa urefu.

isotherm, *n.* mstari wa ramani unaounganisha mahali penye kadiri ile ile ya joto.

issue, *v.t.* (*send out &c.*) toa; — *v.i.* (*come out*) toka, tokea; (*end*) isha. *Issue in,* leta. — *n.* kutoa, kutoka, kitokacho, matokeo; (*children*) watoto; (*end*) mwisho; (*point*) jambo lenyewe, kisa, hoja; (*test, trial*) jaribu, shindano; (*thing or amount issued*) toleo, kitu kitokacho, jamii ya vitu vilivyotolewa pamoja. *Be at an issue,* shindaniwa, topatana. *Join issue with,* shindana na, gombana na.

isthmus, *n.* shingo (ya nchi inayounganisha mafungu mawili ya nchi).

it, *pron.* hii (huu, hiki &c.), ile (ule, kile &c.); (*in comp.*) i- (u-, ki- &c.). *It is good,* njema hiyo, ni njema. *I love it,* naipenda.

italics, *n.* herufi za namna hii *italic.*

itch, *n.* upele, pele, ukurutu. — *v.i.* waka, washa, nyea, chochota, cheneta, chonyota, (*long for*) taka sana, tamani. **itching,** *n.* mnyeo; kiwasho; (*yearning*) uchu, shauku. *Have an itching for,* tamani, taka sana.

item, *n.* kitu kimoja, kitu kimoja katika orodha, dondoo la habari. — *adv.* tena.

iterate, *v.t.* kariri, sema mara ya pili au mara nyingi, sisitiza. **iteration,** *n.* kukariri, kusema mara nyingi (yale yale).

itinerant, *a.* -a kuzungukazunguka, -a kutembeatembea, -a kwenda huko na huko. **itinerary,** *n.* utaratibu wa safari, njia ya safari, habari ya mambo ya safari, tarihi.

its, *a.* -ake. **itself,** *pron.* -enyewe; (*in comp.*) -ji-. *By itself,* peke yake, nafsi yake, -tupu tu. *Go by itself,* jienda. *He hid himself,* alijificha.

ivory, *n.* pembe.

ivy, *n.* namna ya mmea wenye majani unaotambaa juu ya kuta, miamba, nyumba &c.

J

jab, *v.t.* dukua, piga mdukuo. — *n.* mdukuo.

jabber, *v.i.* tatarika, sema upesi bila kutamka vizuri maneno, payuka. — *n.* mapayo.

jacana, *n.* Sile maua.

Jack, (1) *n.* (jina = *John*); (*fellow, man*) mtu, *e.g. every man jack*, kila mtu; (*sailor*) baharia; (*in cards*) mzungu wa tatu, ghulamu; (*for lifting*) mtambo wa kuinulia vitu vizito; (*flag*) bendera. *Before you could say Jack Robinson*, mara hiyo, kufumba na kufumbua, upesi sana. *Jack of all trades*, mtu awezaye kila kazi. *Union Jack*, bendera ya Waingereza wote na serikali yao, bendera ya ufalme wa Uingereza. **jackass**, *n.* punda dume; (*fool*) mpumbavu. **jack-boot**, *n.* kiatu kinachofika juu ya goti. **jackdaw**, *n.* ndege mweusi kama kunguru; ni mwizi sana. **Jack-in-office**, *n.* mwenye cheo kidogo afanyaye makuu, mtu ajikuzaye kwa sababu ya cheo chake (ambacho ni kidogo tu). **Jack-in-the-box**, *n.* mchezo wa kitoto ambao ni kikasha chenye sanamu ndogo ndani inayoruka juu kikasha kifunguliwapo. **jack-knife**, *n.* kisu kikubwa cha kukunja. **jack-plane**, *n.* randa kubwa. **jack-tar**, *n.* baharia.

jack, (2) *n.* kikombe (kopo) cha kunywea cha ngozi.

jackal, *n.* mbwa wa mwitu, mbweha, bweha.

jackanapes, *n.* mtu mtundu, mtoto mtukutu, mkavu wa macho, mjuvi, mfidhuli, mmalidadi.

jackass, *n.*, **jack-boot**, *n.*, **jackdaw**, *n.* taz. *jack* (1).

jacket, *n.* koti; (*cover*) kifuniko. *To dust a person's jacket*, kumpiga mtu.

jack-fruit, *n.* fenesi; (*tree*) mfenesi.

Jack-in-office, *n.*, **Jack-in-the-box**, *n.*, **jack-knife**, *n.*, **jack-plane**, *n.*, **jack-tar**, *n.* taz. *jack*, *n.* (1).

jade, (1) *n.* jiwe zuri gumu la thamani lenye rangi ya kijani kibichi.

jade, (2) *n.* farasi aliyechakaa; (*woman*) mwanamke mbaya, pia jina la kumtaja mwanamke kwa mchezo (ubishi). — *v.t.* chosha, legeza, taabisha, nyong'onyeza, chakaza. **jaded**, *a.* -liotaabika, -liochoka kwa kazi au taabu, -liochakaa.

jag, *n.* chonge, ncha, jino; (*notch*) pengo (kama la msumeno). — *v.t.* keketa, kata (pasua) na kufanya mapengo. **jagged**, *a.* -enye vichonge, -liochongoka, -enye pelezi, -enye menomeno na mapengo.

jaguar, *n.* chui (wa Amerika).

jail, *n.* (*gaol*) gereza, kifungo. **jailer**, *n.* bawabu wa gereza, msimamizi (mlinzi) wa gereza na wafungwa. Taz. *gaol*).

jam, (1) *n.* (*preserve*) mraba (matunda yaliyochemshwa pamoja na sukari).

jam, (2) *v.t.* bana, kwamisha, shindilia; — *v.i.* kwama, songamana, sakama. — *n.* msongano, msongamano, mbano.

jamb, *n.* (*of door*) mwimo, mhimili.

jamboree, *n.* mkutano wa furaha (shangwe), *e.g.* wa *Boy Scouts*.

jangle, *v.i.* lia (kama kengele zisizopigwa vizuri); (*quarrel*) gombana, zozana. — *n.* ukelele wa *jangle*.

janitor, *n.* bawabu, mngojaji mlango.

janissary, *n.* askari wa Sultani Rumi zamani.

January, *n.* mwezi wa kwanza wa mwaka wa kizungu, Januari.

japan, *n.* namna ya rangi ngumu. — *v.t.* paka rangi.

jape, *v.i.* fanya ubishi, dhihaki, fanya mzaha. — *n.* ubishi, dhihaka, mzaha.

jar, *n.* (*water*) mtungi, gudulia, kasiki, (*large stone*) balasi; (*for jam &c.*) chupa.

jar, *v.i.* fanya sauti ya kuchukiza, fanya (piga) kishindo; — *v.t.* paruza, kwaruza, tikisa; (*not agree*) gombana, tia uchungu, sumbua, udhi; (*shock*) shtusha, shtua, gutusha, shangaza, kasirisha, chukiza. — *n.* kishindo, kwaruzo, paruzo; (*discord*) ugomvi, fitina, mateto. *The news gave me a nasty jar*, habari ilinishtusha sana.

jargon, *n.* changanyiko la maneno (ya kishenzi, yaliyogoteka).

jasmine, *n.* yasmini; (*wild, flower*) afu, (*tree*) mwafu.

jasper, *n.* jiwe zuri la rangi (nyekundu, ya manjano au ya hudhurungi).

jaundice, *n.* ugonjwa wa ngozi na macho kugeuka rangi ya manjano unaofanywa na nyongo.

jaunt, *n.* mandari, matembezi, kwenda kutembea. **jaunty**, *a.* -a kucheza, -a kupiga fahari, kimalidadi, -a madaha.

javelin, *n.* sagai, mkuki mfupi.

jaw, *n.* taya, utaya. **jaws**, *n. plur.* kinywa; (*of machine &c.*) kitu kama kinywa; (*talk*) domo, maneno mengi ya kukaripia (kukemea, kuonya *&c.*). **jaw-bone**, *n.* taya, utaya. **jaw-breaker**, *n.* neno lililo gumu kutamka.

jay, *n.* ndege kama kunguru mdogo mwenye rangi nzuri na milio mingi.

jazz, *n.* namna ya muziki ya ngoma.

jealous, *a.* -wivu, -a husuda. *Be jealous*, ona wivu, fanya kijicho, husuda. **jealousy**, *n.* wivu, husuda, ghera.

jeer, *v.i.* cheka, dhihaki, fanya mzaha, fanya ubishi. — *n.* cheko, dhihaka, mzaha, ubishi.

Jehovah, *n.* Mungu (Kiyahudi).

jejune, *a.* hafifu, duni, -chache, -tupu, -a bure, baridi.

jelly, *n.* ute mzito, kitu chororo, yaani si maji wala kigumu, kitu kitamu kilichofanana na halua. **jelly-fish**, *n.* mnyama wa bahari wa yavuyavu.

jemmy, *n.* mtaimbo mfupi unaotumika na wevi kufungulia milango.

jenny, *n.* mashine ya kusokota nyuzi.

jeopardy, *n.* hatari, mashaka. **jeopardize**, *v.t.* hatirisha, tia hatarini, ponza.

jeremiad, *n.* malalamiko, manung'uniko.

jerk, *v.t.* tupa, (rusha, piga, vuta, sogeza, endesha, jongeza) ghafula, shtua, shtusha, kutua; — *v.i.* shtuka, enda (mudu, jongea *&c.*) ghafula, shtuka shtuka. — *n.* mshtuo, mshtusho, mkutuo, mshtuko.

jerkin, *n.* koti fupi la kusaki (hasa la ngozi).

jerry-built, *a.* -liojengwa vibaya, (nyumba) hafifu.

jersey, *n.* namna ya fulana nzito.

jest, *n.* ubishi, mzaha, neno la kuchekesha, masihara, upuzi. — *v.i.* bisha, toa mzaha. **jester**, *n.* mcheshi, mtu wa kuchekesha, majununi.

Jesuit, *n.* mwana wa chama kimojawapo cha dini ya kikristo; (*intriguer &c.*) mwerevu, mwenye hila. **Jesuitical**, *a.* -a kama *Jesuit*; (*intriguing, &c.*) -erevu, -enye hila.

Jesus, *n.* Yesu Kristo, Masiya, bin Mariamu, (*Muhammedan name*) Isa.

jet, (1) *n.* tokeo la ghafula (la maji, la moto), bubujiko, foko, mruko, mshindo; (*pipe*) bomba la kuletea maji (hewa *&c.*); (*hole*) kitundu cha kutokea maji (hewa *&c.*).

jet, (2) *n.* namna ya jiwe jeusi sana linalotumika kufanyizia mapambo ya mavazi. **jet-black**, *a.* -eusi sana.

jetsam, *n.* shehena *&c.* iliyotupwa baharini kupunguza uzito wa jahazi (chombo, meli *&c.*); shehena iliyotupwa baharini na kukokotwa pwani, *e.g. Flotsam and jetsam.* **jettison**, *v.t.* tupa shehena baharini kupunguza uzito wa jahazi *&c.*

jetty, *n.* boma pwani litokezalo baharini; (*landing-stage*), gati.

Jew, *n.* Myahudi; (*fig.*) mkabidhi, bahili. **Jewish**, *a.* -a kiyahudi.

jewel, *n.* kito, johari, jiwe la thamani; (*beloved*) kipenzi. **jeweller**, *n.* mwuza *jewel.* **jewellery**, *n.*, **jewelry**, *n.* vitu vilivyofanyizwa kwa vito na dhahabu (fedha, madini ya thamani).

Jewish, *a.* taz. *Jew.*

jib, *n.* tanga la mbele (la mlingoti wa maji).

jib, *v.i.* (*of horse*) simama ghafula, chezacheza, enda upande; (*fig.*) simama (koma) ghafula, kataa kuendelea; sitasita.

jibe, *n.* taz. *gibe.*

jiffy, *n.* muda mfupi. *I shall come in a jiffy*, nitakuja sasa hivi (nitakuja punde).

jig, *n.* namna ya mchezo wa ngoma;

muziki ya mchezo huo. — *v.i.* cheza ngoma ya namna fulani, rukaruka.

jigger, *n.* (*flea*) tekenya, funza.

jilt, *v.t.* vunja uchumba bure. — *n.* mvunja uchumba bure.

jingle, *v.i.* lia; — *v.t.* liza (kama njuga au senti *&c.*). — *n.* mlio wa vitu kama njuga au senti *&c.* kugongana.

jinks, *n. High jinks*, michezo (furaha) ya makelele.

job, *n.* kazi, kazi moja fulani, kazi ya mkato, kazi ya makataa; (*stroke of business*) chumo, jambo la biashara; (*unjust dealing*) jambo baya (lisilo nyofu, la ujanja) linaloleta faida; (*habitual work*) kazi, uchumi. *That's a good job*, vizuri, heri. *Give him a job*, mpe kazi. *Job lot*, vitu vya bidhaa shelabela. **jobber**, *n.* anunuaye na kuuza tena apate faida; (*cheat*) mjanja, mkopi, ajipatiaye faida kwa njia mbaya (werevu, hila, ujanja). **jobbery**, *n.* kazi ya kujipatia faida kwa njia mbaya (werevu, hila, ujanja).

jockey, *n.* mpanda farasi katika mashindano. — *v.t.* hadaa, laghai, danganya, ghilibu.

jocose, *a.* -cheshi, -a mzaha, -a ubishi. **jocular**, *a.* -cheshi, -a mzaha, -a ubishi. **jocularity**, *n.* ucheshi, ubishi. **jocund**, *a.* -cheshi, -changamfu, -kunjufu.

jog, *v.t.* shtua, shtusha, amsha, dukua, piga mdukuo, gusa, piga kikumbo, gongana na; — *v.i.* (*go slowly*) enda polepole vizito lakini kwa taratibu, fululiza taratibu. — *n.* mdukuo, kikumbo, mwendo wa polepole.

Johanna (*Island*), *n.* Anzwani.

John Bull, *n.* Mwingereza (ye yote), taifa la kiingereza; tabia ya kiingereza.

join, *v.t.* unga, unganisha, fanya -moja; — *v.i.* ungana, ungana na, unganika, kutana, kutanika, pakana, changanyika, jitia katika, changamana na. *Join battle*, pigana. *Join issue*, shindana, tetana. **joiner**, *n.* seremala. **joinery**, *n.* useremala, kazi ya seremala. **joint**, *n.* kiungo, mwungo, fundo, kifundo; (*piece of meat*) kipande kizima cha nyama—*called by various appropriate names*—*leg*, mguu; *ham*, paja; *neck*, shingo *&c.* *Be out of joint*, teguka, shtuka. — *a.* -a wengi pamoja, -a chango, -a shirika. **jointly**, *adv.* pamoja, kwa umoja, kwa shirika. **joint stock**, *n.* mali ya chango, mali ya shirika (bia). *Joint stock company*, kumpuni ya (ushirika wa) watu waliochanga fedha zao kufanya biashara *&c.*

joist, *n.* boriti; (*for carrying deck of vessel*) darumeti.

joke, *n.* ubishi, mzaha, masihara. — *v.i.* fanya ubishi, fanya mzaha, dhihaki. **joker**, *n.* mcheshi, mfanya mzaha (masihara).

jolly, *a.* -a furaha, -changamfu, -kunjufu, -a kupendeza, -zuri, -a kufurahisha, -a kuchangamsha. — *v.t.* bembeleza. — *adv.* sana. **jollity**, *n.* furaha, ukunjufu, michezo, uchangamfu.

jolly-boat, *n.* mashua (ya meli).

jolt, *v.t.* shtua, shtusha, tikisa, sukasuka, gutusha; — *v.i.* shtuka, shtukashtuka, tikisika, enda kwa vishindo. — *n.* mshtuo, mshtusho mshtuko, msukosuko, kishindo, mdukuo, kikumbo.

jostle, *v.t.* songa, sukumia, kumba, piga kikumbo, sukuma kwa nguvu.

jot, *n.* kipande kidogo, nukta. *Not a jot*, (hapana) hata kidogo. — *v.t.* (*down*) andika ukumbusho. **jotting**, *n.* ukumbusho wa maneno machache.

journal, *n.* tarehe, kitabu cha mambo ya kila siku, habari za kila siku; (*newspaper*) gazeti; (*in account*) daftari. **journalese**, *n.* maandiko kama yale ya magazeti. **journalism**, *n.* mtungo wa habari kwa magazeti. **journalist**, *n.* mwandishi wa habari kwa magazeti.

journey, *n.* safari, mwendo. *Money* (*provisions*) *for journey*, masurufu. — *v.i.* safiri. *Prepare for a journey*, fanya safari. **journeyman**, *n.* fundi.

joust, *n.* mchezo wa kushindana wapanda farasi kama vitani.

Jove, *n.* mungu wa kirumi (katika habari na hadithi za zamani). *By Jove!* (neno la kuonyesha mshangao, furaha *&c.*); Loo! **jovial,** *a.* -a furaha, -kunjufu, -changamfu, -a kucheka, -a kucheza.

jowl, *n.* taya, mashavu ya uso na kidevu. *Cheek by jowl,* karibu karibu sana.

joy, *n.* furaha, shangwe, nderemo. **joyful, joyous,** *a.* -a furaha, -a shangwe. **joyfulness,** *n.* furaha, shangwe.

jubilant, *a.* -a shangwe. **jubilation,** *n.* shangwe, furaha. **jubilee,** *n.* sikukuu ya ukumbusho wa mwaka wa hamsini (wa kutawala, kuolewa *&c.*). *Silver Jubilee,* sikukuu ya ukumbusho wa mwaka wa ishirini na tano. *Diamond Jubilee,* sikukuu ya ukumbusho wa mwaka wa sitini.

Judaism, *n.* dini na desturi za kiyahudi.

Judas, *n.* mhaini, msaliti.

judge, *n.* (*European*) jaji; (*Muhammedan law*) kadhi; (*general*) hakimu; (*arbitrator*) mwamuzi; (*critic*) mwenye maarifa, mjuzi, apambanuaye na kuchagua kwa akili. — *v.t.* hukumu, hukumia; (*arbitration*) amua; (*pass sentence*) toa hukumu, kata maneno; (*estimate, distinguish*) pambanua, chagua kwa akili, fahamu, tabia; (*be of opinion*) dhani, ona; (*criticize, examine*) chungua, chunguza, pima, tazamia, peleleza enenza. **judgement,** *n.,* **judgment,** *n.* hukumu, maamuzi, neno la mwisho; (*opinion*) shauri, nia, maono; (*wisdom*) akili, busara, ujuzi; (*providential punishment*) adhabu, Mungu; (*taste*) akili ya kutambua au kuchagua mazuri. **judicature,** *n.* jamii ya wanasheria wa nchi. **judicial,** *a.* -a *judge*; (*fair*) -adilifu, adili, -a haki, sawa, -nyofu. **judicious,** *a.* -enye akili, -a busara, -juzi.

jug, *n.* kopo, mdumu. — *v.t.* pika katika chungu kilichofunikwa.

juggle, *v.i.* fanya kiinimacho, fanya mizungu au michezo ya kushangaza; (*distort &c.*) fanya ujanja, danganya, potoa. **juggler,** *n.* mfanya kiinimacho, mfanya miujiza *&c.*; (*impostor*) mwerevu, ayari, mlaghai, jambazi. **jugglery,** *n.* kiinimacho, mauzauza, miujiza; (*imposture*) werevu, ujanja, ulaghai.

jugular, *a.* -a shingoni. — *n.* (*jugular vein*) halkumu, mshipa mkubwa (vena) wa shingoni unaorudisha damu moyoni.

juice, *n.* maji ya mti (tunda *&c.*), utomvu; (*of grated coco-nut*) kasimele, (*same with water*) tui. **juicy,** *a.* -enye *juice.*

July, *n.* Julai, mwezi wa saba wa mwaka wa kizungu.

jumble, *v.t.* changanya, chafua, boruga, fuja. — *n.* fujo, machafuko, changanyiko.

jump, *v.i.* ruka, chupa; (*start, twitch*) shtuka; (*for joy*) randa, jitapa, chachawa; — *v.t.* (*pass over*) kiuka, dakia, ruka juu ya; (*leave out*) pitia, acha; (*hoodwink &c.*) danganya, laghai, chukua (twaa) kwa hila au werevu. *Jump at* (*an offer &c.*) kubali (pokea, twaa) kwa furaha. *Jump in,* ingia upesi. *Jump out,* toka upesi. *Jump on,* panda upesi. *Jump down,* shuka upesi. — *n.* mruko, ruko, chupo (mchupo); (*start*) mstuko, mshtuo. *The price* (*temperature*) *has jumped,* bei (joto) imezidi ghafula.

jumper, *n.* gwanda fupi, namna ya fulana.

junction, *n.* mkutano, mwungano, kiungo; (*of roads*) njia panda.

juncture, *n.* taz. *junction*; hali ya jambo, jambo (kuu, la hatari, la hofu *&c.*), wakati. *At this juncture,* hapo, ndipo, mara hiyo.

June, *n.* Juni, mwezi wa sita wa mwaka wa kizungu.

jungle, *n.* kichaka, msitu, mwitu, magugu.

junior, *a.* -dogo (kwa umri, kwa cheo), -a chini. — *n.* mdogo (wa umri au wa cheo).

juniper, *n.* mreteni.

junk, (1) *n.* jahazi la Kichina.
junk, (2) *n.* (*rubbish*) takataka; (*old rope*) kamba kuukuu; (*salt meat*) nyama iliyotiwa chumvi; (*nonsense*) upuzi.
junket, *n.* maziwa yaliyogandishwa na kutiwa sukari.
Jupiter, *n.* mungu mkuu wa Warumi (wa zamani); (*planet*) sayari iliyo kubwa, mshtarii.
juridical, *a.* -a sheria.
jurisdiction, *n.* hukumu, mamlaka, amri. **jurisprudence,** *n.* maarifa ya sheria. **jurist,** *n.* mwanasheria. **juror,** *n.* mtu wa *jury*. **jury,** *n.* baraza la watu (kumi na wawili) waliochaguliwa kusikiliza maneno ya shauri la kumwambia hakimu (jaji) wanayofikiri juu yake bila kupendelea. **juryman,** *n.* mtu wa *jury*.
just, *a.* -a haki, -nyofu, -adili, -adilifu; salihi; (*well-deserved*) -a haki, -liostahili. —*adv.* (*exactly*) barabara, sawasawa, halisi, vivi hivi; (*only*) tu, shida. *Just now,* sasa hivi. *He has just come,* ndiyo kwanza aje. *He has just gone,* ndiyo kwanza aende. *He just succeeded,* alifaulu, (aliweza, alifanya) kwa shida (alikuwa karibu kushindwa). *That is just right,* ndivyo hasa. *Just what I said,* ndiyo hasa niliyosema. **justice,** *n.* haki, moyo sawa, usawa, unyofu, uadilifu, maadili; (*vengeance*) kisasi; (*judge*) jaji. *Justice of the Peace,* jaji mdogo (wa mji, au mtaa fulani). **justifiable,** *a.* -a haki, -a kuthibitika kuwa -a haki. **justification,** *n.* sababu, hoja, kisa, sababu (njema, ya kufaa, ya haki). **justify,** *v.t.* thibithisha kuwa -a haki (-a kweli); (*acquit, declare guiltless*) hesabia haki, achilia, weka (mtu) haki. *He was justified in doing it,* alifanya kwa haki. *Justify oneself* (*one's conduct*), jiweka wema (haki).
jut (*out*), *v.i.* tokeza, fanya mdomo, benuka.
jute, *n.* katani ya kihindi, katani ya gunia.
juvenile, *a.* -a watoto, -a kitoto, -a kijana. — *n.* kijana, mtoto.
juxtaposition, *n.* hali ya kuwa karibu (jirani, ya kupakana), ujirani, ulinganifu, mpambano.

K

Kaffir, *n.* mtu mweusi mwenyeji wa Afrika ya Kusini. **Kaffir-corn,** *n.* mtama.
kaiser, *n.* mfalme.
kakelaar, *n.* (*Tanganyika*) goligoli.
kaleidoscopic, *a.* -a kubadilibadili, -a kubadilikabadilika, -geugeu.
kangaroo, *n.* mnyama wa *Australia* aendaye kwa miguu yake ya nyuma kwa mwendo wa kurukaruka.
kapok, *n.* sufi; (*tree*) msufi.
kedge, *n.* nanga ndogo.
kedgeree, *n.* wali kwa samaki &c.
keel, *n.* mkuku. — *v.t.* (*over*) inamisha; — *v.i.* inama.
keen, *a.* hodari, -epesi, -a bidii; (*sharp*) -kali, -enye makali, -a kupenya ndani. *Be keen on,* penda taka, pendelea. **keenness,** *n.* bidi, juhudi, ukalifu, ukali.

keep, *v.t.* (*p.t. and pf.t.* **kept**) linda, hifadhi, tunza, weka, kalisha, shindisha, shika, hozi; (*of live stock*) fuga, chunga, lisha; (*maintain*) ruzuku, lisha, kimu; (*adhere to*) shika, fuata; (*suppress*) zuia, tuliza, nyamazisha; (*continue*) fuliza, endelea, fululiza, kaa, shinda, dumu; (*not spoil*) tooza, toharibika. *It will keep*, haiharibiki, haiozi, itakaa vema. *Keep a holiday* (*festival*), fanya (adhimisha) sikukuu (idi). *Keep at home*, tawa, kaa ndani. *Keep back*, zuia, nyima, ficha. *Keep company*, zungumza, fanyana uchumba. *Keep counsel*, ficha shauri, nyamaa. *Keep down*, zuia, tuliza, punguza. *Keep house*, -wa na nyumba, pata nyumba, oa, angalia madaraka ya nyumba. *Keep in view*, angalia, kumbuka. *Keep in with*, patana na. *Keep off*, kinga, epua, bekua, zuia. *Keep on*, fuliza, fululiza, endelea, dumu, shika, shinda. *Keep one's bed*, ugua, lala. *Keep order*, simamia, tengeneza. *Keep school*, fanya darasa ya watoto, fundisha. *Keep shop*, -wa na duka, weka duka, fanya uchuuzi. *Keep to*, shika, linda. *Keep under*, tiisha, zuia; (*oppress*) onea, dhulumu. *Keep up*, dumisha, endeleza, fuliza, fululiza; (*maintain*) weka. *He keeps up*, hajambo, yu mzima, hashindwi. *Keep watch*, ngoja zamu, shika zamu, kesha. *Keep watch over* (*protect*) linda, hifadhi; (*spy upon*) chungulia, peleleza. — *n.* riziki, chakula, posho, malisho; (*stronghold*) ngome, gereza, boma. **keeper**, *n.* mlinzi, mlinda, mchunga, mchungaji, mtunza, msimamizi. **keeping**, *n.* utunzo, lindo, ulinzi, hifadhi. *In keeping*, sawa, -linganifu, -a kupatana. **keepsake**, *n.* kikumbusho, tunu, zawadi, hiba.

keg, *n.* kipipa.

kelp, *n.* majani ya bahari, mwani.

ken, *v.t.* jua, tambua, fahamu. — *n.* ujuzi, kutambua, ulimwengu. *It is beyond my ken*, sina habari nayo, siifahamu.

kennel, *n.* tundu la mbwa, mahali pa kuweka mbwa wa kuwinda; (*hovel*) nyumba hafifu, kibanda kibovu.

kept, *p.t. and pf.t.* ya *keep*.

kerb(stone), *n.* jiwe la ukingo wa barabara (kutenga mahali pa magari na pa watu kutembea).

kerchief, *n.* kitambaa, leso, ankachifi.

kernel, *n.* (*of stone*) kiini; (*stone*) kokwa, koko; (*essential part*) kisa, kiini.

kerosene, *n.* mafuta ya taa.

ketch, *n.* chombo kidogo cha matanga.

ketchup, *n.* mchuzi wa achali.

kettle, *n.* birika, kanderinya. *This is a pretty kettle of fish*, mambo yametatanika sana. **kettledrum**, *n.* mdundo, namna ya ngoma ndogo ya madini.

key, *n.* ufunguo; (*explanation*) ufunuo, ufumbuo, ufumbuzi, tafsiri, mafafanusi, jibu, jawabu; (*in music*) msingi, jamii ya sauti nane zinazolingana zenyewe kwa zenyewe; (*of keyboard*) kipande cha kinanda cha kupigwa kwa vidole; (*important post*) mlango; (*decisive point*) neno la nguvu, jambo kubwa, kitu cha kushindia; (*in machinery*) kipande cha kukaza, kifungo. — *v.t.* funga, kaza kwa kabari; (*tune up*) pandisha sauti ya kinanda, fidla &c. *Key up*, amsha, chochea. **keyboard**, *n.* sehemu ya kinanda &c. yenye vipande vya kupigwa kwa vidole. **keyhole**, *n.* tundu la ufunguo. **keynote**, *n.* sauti inayoonyesha (inayojulisha) msingi (*key*) katika kuimba. **keystone**, *n.* jiwe la katikati ya tao.

khaki, *n.* kaki (namna ya nguo yenye rangi kahawia, inayotumika sana kushonea suruali na koti kama zile za askari), rangi ya kahawia.

kick, *v.t.* piga teke; — *v.i.* (*of gun*) &c. piga katika kurudi, rudi ghafula kwa kishindo; (*resist*) kaidi, halifu. — *n.* teke, ukwato. *Kick one's heels*, kaa bure, ngoja bure. *Kick up a dust*, fanya matata, fanya ghasia. *Kick* *the bucket*, kufa, fariki. *Be kicked out*, tolewa (nyumbani, kazini *&c.*). *Kick off*, anza, anzisha.

kid, *n.* mwana mbuzi; (*leather*) ngozi ya mwana mbuzi; (*slang*) mtoto. — *v.t.* danganya, laghai. **kidnap**, *v.t.* iba mtoto, chukua na kuweka. mtu kwa nguvu bila hiari yake.

kidney, *n.* nso, figo, buki; (*fig.*) namna, aina, jinsi. *A man of that kidney*, mtu wa namna hiyo.

kill, *v.t.* ua, fisha; (*by cutting throat*) chinja; (*destroy, bring to an end*) haribu, vunja, komesha, angamiza, teketeza. — *n.* kuua; (*of hunt*) windo. **killer**, *n.* mwuaji. **killing**, *a.* -a kuua, -a kufisha, -a kuharibu *&c.*; (*laughable*) -a kuchekesha sana; (*ravishing*) -a kupendeza sana, -a kutazamisha, -a kuvuta macho.

kill-joy, *n.* mtu aondoaye furaha (aharibuye michezo).

kiln, *n.* (*for lime*) tanuu, tanuru; (*for pottery*) joko, chocho, chomeo.

kilo = **kilogram**, *n.* ratli 2½. **kilo** = **kilometre**, *n.* yadi 1093 au ⅝ maili **kilowatt**, *n.* kipimo cha elektrisiti; ni *watt* 1000.

kilt, *n.* vazi la watu wa *Scotland* kama shuka ya kufika gotini, nzito, yenye vikunjo.

kin, *n.* ukoo, jamaa, mlango, ndugu; (*kind*) namna, jinsi, aina. — *a.* -a jamaa moja, -a namna moja, -a kufanana. **kindred**, *n.* ndugu, jamaa, ufungu, ukoo, ahali. — *a.* sawa, kama sawa, -a namna moja, -a namna ile ile, ndugu. **kinsfolk**, *n.* taz. *kindred*. **kinship**, *n.* udugu, ukoo, ujamaa. **kinsman**, *n.* ndugu, jamaa, ahali, akraba.

kind, (1) *n.* namna, jinsi, aina, hali, tabia, babu, launi. *Pay in kind*, lipa vitu (si fedha). *A kind of dog*, namna ya mbwa. *Of a (given) kind*, ki-. *Of the European kind*, Kizungu. *All kinds of*, jamii ya, namna zote za, kila aina ya. *Of what kind?* -a namna gani?

kind, (2) **kind-hearted**, **kindly**, *a.* -ema, -pole, -enye huruma: -fadhili, -karimu, -paji. **kindly**, *adv.* kwa upole. *Would you kindly*, tafadhali... **kindness**, *n.* wema, upole, huruma, latifu; (*service*) fadhili; hisani; (*generosity*) upaji, ukarimu; (*sympathy*) huruma, moyo, kite.

kindergarten, *n.* chuo cha watoto wadogo.

kindle, *v.t.* washa, tia moto; (*excite*) amsha, chochea, tamanisha; — *v.i.* (*take fire*) waka, shika moto; (*be roused*) amka, panda hamaki, kasirika. **kindling**, *n.* vidondo.

kindly, *a. and adv.*, **kindness**, *n.* taz. *kind* (2).

kindred, taz. *kin*.

kine, *n.* ng'ombe (wengi).

king, *n.* mfalme. **kingdom**, *n.* ufalme, milki, dola, nchi (ya mfalme mmoja). **kingfish**, *n.* nguru. **kingfisher**, *n.* mdiria, (*pied*) dete, detepwani; (*Natal Pigmy*) kisharifu, msharifu; (*mangrove*) kijimbimsitu.

kingly, *a.* -a kifalme, -a fahari, -kuu, bora sana.

kink, *v.t.* nyonga. — *n.* kinyongo, kombo, dosari.

kinsfolk, *n.*, **kinship**, *n.*, **kinsman**, *n.* taz. *kin*.

kipper, *n.* namna ya samaki aliyekaushwa kwa moshi na kutiwa chumvi.

kirk, *n.* kanisa.

kismet, *n.* ajali.

kiss, *v.t.* busu, nonea. — *n.* busu.

kit, *n.* vyombo (vifaa, zana) vya askari au msafiri, vikorokoro.

kitchen, *n.* jikoni, mekoni, chumba cha kupikia chakula. **kitchen-garden**, *n.* shamba la mboga. **kitchen-range**, *n.* jiko la chuma, jiko la kizungu.

kite, *n.* (*African*) mwewe, kengewa, kipanga; (*toy*) tiara, shada, portangi.

kith, *n.* *Kith and kin*, jamaa, ndugu, watani.

kitten, *n.* paka mtoto, mwana paka, kipaka.

kleptomania, *n.* wazimu wa kuiba vitu. **kleptomaniac**, *n.* mwenye wazimu wa kuiba vitu.

kloof, *n.* bonde jembamba la kuenda chini sana (*South Africa*).

knack, *n.* wepesi, welekevu, ubingwa, ustadi.

knapsack, *n.* mkoba (wa kuchukulia masurufu safarini), shanta, bahasha, mfuko.

knave, *n.* mjanja, ayari, mlaghai, jambazi; (*in cards*) mzungu wa tatu, ghulamu. **knavery,** *n.* ujanja, uayari, ulaghai, ujambazi. **knavish,** *a.* -a ujanja, -danganyifu, -laghai.

knead, *v.t.* kanda (unga, mwili &c.).

knee, *n.* goti, futi. **knee-cap,** *n.* pia ya goti, kilegesambwa. **knee-deep,** *a.* -a mpaka gotini. **kneel,** *v.i.* piga magoti.

knell, *n.* shindo la kengele (ikigongwa moja moja kama kwa maziko. *Death-knell*, onyo la mauti.

knelt, *p.t. and pf.t.* ya *kneel.*

knew, *p.t.* ya *know.*

knickerbockers, *n.* suruali fupi, suruali kipande, kapatula.

knick-knack, *n.* takataka, vitu vidogovidogo vya pambo.

knife, *n.* (*pl. knives*) kisu; (*large*) jisu, sime, buchari, geli; (*large, curved*) jambia, shembea; (*for tapping palm-trees*) kotama. *Pocket-knife*, kisu cha kukunja, kijembe. *War to the knife*, kupigana na (kukinzana na, kushindana na) bila huruma; vita vya kufa au kupona. *Before you could say knife*, mara hiyo, upesi sana, ghafula, kufumba na kufumbua. — *v.t.* jeruhi kwa kisu, choma kisu. **knife-edge,** *n.* makali ya kisu (*the back is* mafutuni).

knight, *n.* mwenye cheo cha kuitwa *Sir* kutangulia jina lake. **knight-bachelor,** *n.* mwenye cheo cha chini cha *knight.* **knight-errant,** *n.* (katika habari na hadithi za zamani) *knight* azungukaye huko na huko akifanya kazi njema ya ujasiri na huruma. **knighthood,** *n.* cheo cha *knight.* **knightly,** *a.* -a kumstahili *knight*, -a *knight*, -a heshima, -a cheo bora.

knit, *v.t.* (*p.t. and pf.t.* **knit, knitted**) suka, sokota, fuma; (*join closely*) unga, unganisha; — *v.i.* (*become joined*) ungana, fungamana. *Knit the brows*, kunja uso, kunja vipaji. *Well-knit*, -shupavu, -a kushupana, -kakawana. **knitting,** *n.* kazi ya kusokota (ya kufuma, ya kusuka) msokoto.

knives, *n.* (*pl.* ya *knife*).

knob, *n.* nundu, kinundu, fundo; (*on the end of a stick*) rungu, kirungu. **knobby,** *a.* -a kinundu, -a vinundunundu, -enye mafundo. **knobkerrie,** *n.* rungu.

knock, *v.t. and i.* gonga, bisha, piga, gota, dunda, ng'ota. *Knock about*, pigapiga, piga sana, tangatanga. *Knock at a door*, bisha mlango, piga hodi. *Knock up*, amsha, chosha, taabisha, shinda. *Knock down*, angusha, bomoa; (*and hurt*). (*Knock into a cocked hat*, shinda kabisa. *Knock on the head*, gonga kichwa, haribu, komesha, zuia. *Knock off*, ondosha; (*reduce price*) punguza bei; (*stop work*) acha kazi. *Knock together*, gonganisha; (*make quickly*) fanyiza upesi. — *n.* pigo, kipigo, shindo, kishindo, bisho. **knocker,** *n.* kipande cha kubishia mlango. **knock-kneed,** *a.* *Be knock-kneed*, -wa na vigosho. **knock-out,** *n.* pigo la mwisho (katika shindano la ngumi).

knoll, *n.* kilima, mwinuko, kiduta.

knot, *n.* fundo, kifundo; (*in stalks &c.*) pingili, kipingili; (*difficulty*) fumbo, matata; (*group*) kundi, jamii; (*tie*) kifungo; (*measure*) futi 6080; (*of speed*) mwendo wa futi 6080 katika muda wa saa. **knotty,** *a.* -enye mafundo, -enye vipingili; (*difficult*) -a matata, -a fumbo, -gumu kufahamu (kutambua, kuwa na hakika).

knout, *n.* mjeledi (wa ngozi na uzi wa (chuma).

know, *v.t. and i.* (*p.t.* **knew,** *pf.t.* **known**) jua, fahamu, tambua, komanya, ng'amua, atikali, pata hakika ya. *He knows what's what*, mjuzi huyo, hadanganyiki. *Know of*,

-wa na habari ya. **knowing,** *a.* -juzi, -a busara; (*sly*) -erevu, -janja. **knowledge,** *n.* (*learning*) elimu, hekima; (*information, notice*) maarifa, habari, taarifa, bayana. *To the best of my knowledge,* kadiri nijuavyo. **known,** *a.* -liojulikana. *Make known,* julisha, tangaza, toa habari ya.

knuckle, *n.* konde, konzi, kiungo cha kidole. *Rap with the knuckles,* piga konzi, piga konde. — *v.i.* (*down, or under*) jitoa, shindwa.

kodak, *n.* namna ya *camera* ya kupigia picha.

kopje, *n.* (katika Afrika ya Kusini) mlima, mwinuko, kiduta.

Koran, *n.* Alkorani, kurani, msahafu wa Waislamu.

kraal, *n.* (katika nchi ya Afrika ya Kusini) mji wa kienyeji.

kudos, *n.* heshima (kwa sababu ya tendo).

kudu, *n.* (*greater*) tandala.

L

L. herufi ya Kirumi, maana yake 50.

laager, *n.* kambi (iliyopangwa kati ya duara ya magari).

label, *n.* kipande (cha karatasi) cha kubandikia mzigo, kasha &c., kipande (cha karatasi) chenye anwani (namba, jina, maelezo &c.). — *v.t.* bandika (tia, fungia) *label.*

labial, *a.* -a midomo, -a kufanyika kwa midomo. **labio-dental,** *a.* -a kufanyika kati ya mdomo wa chini na meno.

laboratory, *n.*, **laborious,** *a.* taz. *labour.*

labour, *n.* kazi, utumishi, uchumi; (*wearisome toil*) taabu; (*exertion*) juhudi, bidii, jitihada; (*workers*) watu wa kazi, jamii ya wafanya kazi; (*childbirth*) utungu (uchungu) wa kuzaa. *Labour and capital,* wafanyi kazi na wanaowaajiri. — *v.t.* fanya kazi, tumika, toa bidii, jitahidi; (*of a ship*) fuawa na mawimbi, fanya mrama; (*in childbirth*) -wa na utungu wa kuzaa; — *v.t.* (*elaborate unduly*) eleza sana (kuliko haja). *The labouring classes,* watu wa kazi. **laboratory,** *n.* nyumba ya kufanyia kazi wavumbuzi wa dawa, mashine &c. **laborious,** *a.* -a kazi, -a taabu, -a kuchosha, -a juhudi, -a bidii, -kulifu. **laboured,** *a.* -a juhudi, -a kufanyiwa kazi, -a shida. **labourer,** *n.* mfanya kazi, mtu wa kazi, mtumishi; (*casual, daily*) kibarua; (*monthly, by card*) mfanya kazi wa kipande; (*agricultural*) mkulima mlimaji.

laburnum, *n.* namna ya mti wenye maua ya rangi ya manjano.

labyrinth, *n.* mahali penye vipengee vingi (pa kupotelea njia, penye matata), mazingile mwanambije; vichochoro vinavyokatana; (*puzzle*) matata mengi, matatanisho.

lac, (1) *n.* utomvu mwekundu, kama gundi ya mti fulani, unaotumika kufanyizia rangi.

lac, (2) *n.* laki, 100,000.

lace, *n.* (*of shoe*) kitani, kigwe, ukanda; (*fabric*) nguo nyembamba ya nyuzi zilizosukwa vizuri, nguo ya kimia. — *v.t.* funga kwa *lace.*

lacerate, *v.t.* papura, papua, rarua, jeruhi; (*fig.*) choma moyo, hangaisha, tia uchungu. **laceration,** *n.* kupapura, upapuro, jeraha.

lachrymal, *a.* -a machozi. **lachrymose,** *a.* -a machozi, -a huzuni.

lack, *n.* utovu, ukosefu, upungufu, uhitaji, shida. — *v.t.* kosa, pungukiwa, hitaji, taka, tokuwa na, -wa si -enye. *Proverb: The borrower lacks not; he who lacks is the owner of the vessel,* mwenye kuazima hatoi: mtovu ni mwenye chombo. *He lacks good manners,* hana adabu, yu mtovu wa adabu. **lacking,** *a.* -tovu. *Lacking in sense,* -tovu wa akili.

lackadaisical, *a.* -zembe, -tepetevu, baridi, dhaifu, hafifu, -a kujipurukusha.

lackey, *n.* mtumishi mwanamume; (*fig.*) mnyonge, ajifanyaye kama mtumishi.

laconic, *a.* -a maneno machache, -a kusema kwa maneno machache.

lacquer, *n.* rangi ya kupaka ngumu inayong'aa. — *v.t.* paka *lacquer.*

lactate, *v.t.* tunga maziwa; nyonyesha maziwa. **lactation,** *n.* kunyonyesha maziwa. **lacteal, lactic,** *a.* -a maziwa.

lacuna, *n.* sehemu (kipande) iliyokosekana, nafasi wazi.

lad, *n.* kijana (mwanamume), kivulana, mvulana.

ladder, *n.* ngazi, madaraja ya kupandia.

lade, *v.t.* (*pf.t.* **laden**) pakia, sheheni, sheheneza, tia shehena, chukuza mizigo; (*water out of a boat*) kumba, vua maji. **laden,** *a.* -enye shehena, -enye mizigo, -liohna, -enye -ingi; (*overburdened by load, grief &c.*) -a kulemewa. **lading,** *n.* shehena, mizigo, mapakizi. *Bill of lading,* cheti, hesabu, orodha.

ladle, *n.* upawa, kata, mkamshi. — *v.t.* (*out*) toa kwa upawa (kata), pakua; (*of liquid in small quantities*) chota, danga.

lady, *n.* bibi, mwanamke wa kiungwana; jina la heshima kwa mabibi wa cheo fulani, *e.g.* mke wa *knight. Our Lady,* Bikira Mariamu Mbarikiwa, mama wa Yesu Kristo (Isa Masiya). *Lady of the home* (*addressed as*) mwana, bibi mkubwa, bi mkubwa. *The ladies* (*generally*) akina bibi. **Lady Day,** *n.* tarehe ishirini na tano Machi. **ladylike,** *a.* kama bibi, -a kiungwana, -a adabu, -a malezi mazuri. **lady-love,** *n.* mchumba (mwanamke). **ladyship,** *n.* (jina la kumtaja bibi wa cheo fulani, *e.g. Your Ladyship.*

lag, (1) *n. an old lag,* mtu aliyefungwa mara nyingi. — *v.t.* funga gerezani (kifungoni), kamata, bamba.

lag, (2) *v.i.* kawia, chelewa, vunja mwendo, kaa nyuma, usiri. **laggard,** *n.* mvivu, mzembe, mlegevu, mkunguni.

lager, *n.* (*beer*) namna ya pombe ya kizungu.

lagoon, *n.* wangwa.

laid, *p.t. and pf.t.* ya *lay.*

lain, *pf.t.* ya *lie.*

lair, *n.* tundu, pango, malalo (ya mnyama wa mwitu).

laity, *n.* watu wote wasio mapadre (wasio na maarifa fulani, wasio wa kazi fulani).

lake, *n.* ziwa la maji.

lake, *n.* (*crimson lake*) namna ya rangi nyekundu (taz. *lac* (1)).

lamb, *n.* mwana kondoo, kikondoo; (*flesh*) nyama ya mwana kondoo; (*term of affection*) mpenzi.

lambent, *a.* -a kumetameta.

lame, *a.* -enye kilema, kiwete, -liolemaa, -a kuchechemea, chopi, kiguu; (*unsatisfactory*) -siofaa, si -zuri. *Be* (*walk*) *lame,* chechea, chechemea, -enda chopi. **lameness,** *n.* kilema, mwendo wa chopi &c.

lament, *v.i.* lia, omboleza, piga maombolezo, kaa matanga; — *v.t.* lilia. — *n.* kilio, maombolezo. **lamentable,** *a.* -a huzuni, -a kusikitisha, -a msiba. **lamentation,** *n.* kilio, maombolezo.

laminated, *a.* -a magamba, -a tabaka nyembamba.

lamp, *n.* taa; (*lantern*) kandili, fanusi; (*small, without chimney*) kibatari. **lamp-black,** *n.* masizi ya taa. **lamp-post,** *n.* nguzo ya (kuchukua) taa. **lamp-stand,** *n.* mwango, kinara.

lampoon, *n.* mashairi ya maneno makali (hasa ya kuchekesha) ya kusingizia mtu au ya kukashifu.

lamp-post, *n.* taz. *lamp.*

lamprey, *n.* namna ya samaki kama mkunga.

lamp-stand, *n.* taz. *lamp.*

lance, *n.* mkuki, mfumo. — *v.t.* choma kwa mkuki; (*with lancet*) kata, pasua, chanja, tumbua (jipu &c.). **lancer,** *n.* askari mpanda farasi mwenye mkuki. **lancet,** *n.* kisu kidogo kinachotumiwa na madaktari.

land, *n.* nchi, ardhi, bara; (*estate*) shamba, konde, mgunda, kiunga; (*garden*) bustani; (*shore*) bara, nchi kavu, pwani; (*soil*) udongo, ardhi; (*ready for planting*) ucheu, uchoo. *By land, By overland route,* kwa njia ya nchi kavu, kwa njia ya bara. — *a.* -a nchi kavu. — *v.t.* shusha, telemsha; (*cause to reach*) fikisha, leta; — *v.i.* (*come to land*) shuka pwani, telemka. **land breeze,** *n.* upepo utokao nchi kavu. **landed,** *a.* -enye shamba. *Landed property,* shamba, mashamba. **landholder,** *n.* mwenye shamba. **landing,** *n.* kushuka (kutelemka) pwani (nchi kavu); (*of stairs*) kituo kati ya sehemu mbili za madaraja ya kupandia; (*landing-stage*) gati, mahali pa kutelemkia, diko. **landlady,** *n.* mwenyeji wa nyumba (mwanamke). **landlocked,** *a.* -liozungukwa na nchi. **landlord,** *n.* mwenyeji, mwenye kupangisha shamba au nyumba (mwanamume). **landmark,** *n.* alama ya mpaka, mpaka, kitu (*e.g.* mlima, mnara, nyumba kubwa &c.) cha kuonya mahali au kuongoza njiani; (*in life &c.*) jambo kubwa la maisha (la habari za watu, nchi &c.). **landowner,** *n.* mwenye shamba (kiwanja &c.). **landscape,** *n.* sanamu (picha) ya nchi, kipande cha nchi, kipande cha nchi yenye tabia au sura ya kupendeza macho, mandhari. **landslip, landslide,** *n.* poromoko la kipande cha nchi, *e.g.* cha magenge, mtelemko wa mlima &c. **landward,** *adv.* kuelekea pwani, kwenda pwani, upande wa pwani, pwani.

landau, *n.* gari la magurudumu manne lenye kifuniko kinachoweza kukunjwa.

land breeze, *n.* **landed,** *a.,* **landholder,** *n.,* **landing,** *n.,* **landlady,** *n.,* **landlocked,** *a.,* **landlord,** *n.,* **landmark,** *n.,* **landowner,** *n.,* **landscape,** *n.,* **landslip,** *n.,* **landslide,** *n.,* **landward,** *adv.* taz. *land.*

lane, *n.* njia nyembamba, kijia, ujia. *It is a long lane that has no turning,* hakuna marefu yasiyo na ncha, *lit. there is no length without an end.*

language, *n.* lugha, maneno, msemo, usemi, ki-, *e.g. The language of Zanzibar,* Kiunguja, *of the Swahili,* Kiswahili, *of the Nyamwezi,* Kinyamwezi. *Bad language,* matukano, matusi.

languid, *a.* (*of disposition*) -tepetevu, -legevu, baridi; (*from fatigue, weary*) -chovu, -nyong'onyevu. *Be* (*become*) *languid,* nyong'onyea, choka. **languish,** *v.i.* nyong'onyea, dhoofika, fifia, punguka, sinzia. **languishing,** *a* -a kunyong'onyea &c. *A languishing look,* macho ya kusinzilia. **languor,** *n.* utepetevu, unyong'onyevu, udhaifu, ulegevu, uchovu; (*sentimental, dreaminess*) kusinzilia.

lank, lanky, *a.* -refu, -embamba, -a kimbaombao; (*of hair*) -lionyoka.

lanolin, *n.* mafuta ya manyoya ya kondoo yaliyosafika; hutumika kupakaa kama dawa ya ngozi.

lantern, *n.* fanusi, kandili, taa ya mkono.

lanyard, *n.* kitani kilichofungiwa kisu au filimbi cha kuvaa shingoni au begani.

lap, *n.* paja, pajani. *Live in the lap of luxury*, kaa maisha ya anasa. *Take in the lap*, pakata, tia pajani.

lap, (1) *v.t.* songa, zungusha, funga, kunja, funika. *Lap over*, pita, pitana. — *n.* (*in racing*) mzunguko (katika shindano la kuzunguka mara mbili tatu), fungu, sehemu. **lapel**, *n.* kunjo la koti kifuani. **lappet**, *n.* mkunjo, kishungi.

lap, (2) *v.t.* -nywa (kwa ulimi kama paka); (*of human beings*) -nywa kwa pupa, -nywa bila kiasi; (*of flattery, tales &c.*) sikiliza sana, sadiki upesi, pendezwa sana na; — *v.i.* -nywa (kwa ulimi); (*of sound*) fanya sauti kama mnyama anayekunywa kwa ulimi, *e.g.* mawimbi madogo pwani.

lapel, *n.* taz. *lap* (1).

lapidary, *n.* fundi wa kukata na kukatua vito na kuchora mazuri (urembo), fundi wa vito.

lappet, *n.* taz. *lap* (1).

lapse, *v.i.* potoka, rudia dhambi; (*fail, pass away*) tanguka, pita, potea, -fa, punguka. — *n.* kosa, kurudia dhambi; (*of time &c.*) kupita.

lapwing, *n.* namna ya ndege.

larboard, *n.* upande wa kushoto wa merikebu (meli).

larceny, *n.* wizi, wivi.

larch, *n.* namna ya mti kama mvinje.

lard, *n.* mafuta ya nguruwe, shahamu. — *v.t.* tia (chakulani) vipande vya mafuta au nyama ya nguruwe kuongeza utamu; (*writing, speech*) tia nahau (ufasaha, mifano, maneno ya lugha nyingine &c.). **larder**, *n.* chumba (ghala) cha kuwekea vyakula, nyama &c.

large, *a.* (*in size, importance*) -kubwa, -kuu; (*in quantity*) -ingi; (*thick*) -nene; (*long*) -refu; (*broad*) -pana; (*well-grown*) -kuza; (*liberal, comprehensive*) -ema, -a huruma, -a kukumbuka mengi, -a kushirikisha watu, -karimu. *Of large heart*, -ema, -enye huruma, -karimu. *Of large views*, -enye akili njema, hodari, -juzi. *At large*, kwa maneno mengi vikubwa. *Set at large*, fungua, fungulia, acha. *Be at large*, funguliwa, tembea po pote, -wa huru, -enye nafasi. *Be a gentleman at large*, jikalia, -wa mwungwana. *People at large*, watu wengi. **large-hearted**, *a.* -enye moyo mwema (wa upole, ukarimu &c.). **largely**, *adv.* hasa, zaidi, aghalabu. **largeness**, *n.* ukubwa, ukuu &c. taz. *large.* **larger**, *a.* -kubwa (zaidi), -kuu (zaidi). **largess**, *n.* bakshishi, zawadi, takarimu.

lariat, *n.* kamba ya kufungia farasi, kamba yenye tanzi ya kukamatia farasi, ng'ombe &c.

lark, (1) *n.* namna ya ndege mdogo arukaye juu sana mwenye sauti tamu sana; (*clapper lark*) kipozamataza.

lark, (2) *v.i.* cheza kwa furaha. — *n.* mchezo.

larva, *n.* (*pl.* **larvae**) mtoto wa mdudu kama funza, buu, kiluwiluwi; (*of bee*) jana.

larynx, *n.* kikoromeo, zoloto, kongomeo, sehemu ya koo inayotoa sauti. **laryngitis**, *n.* ugonjwa wa kuumia kikoromeo.

Lascar, *n.* baharia wa kihindi.

lascivious, *a.* -shaufu, -a tamaa, -zinifu, -enye ngoa, -kware, -a asherati, -fisadi, -potovu, -talaleshi, tongozi. **lasciviousness**, *n.* ukware, uzinifu, utongozi, matongozi, uasherati, utalaleshi.

lash, *v.t.* piga mjeledi, chapa kwa mjeledi au mchapo, pigapiga; (*excite violently*) amsha, chochea, tia hamaki; (*move rapidly backwards and forwards*) sukasuka; (*bind*) funga, fungasha; — *v.i.* (*attack suddenly, lash out at*), piga ghafula, shambulia ghafula. — *n.* pigo; (*part of whip*) kamba ya mjeledi (mchapo). **lashing**, *n.* pigo, kupiga; (*cord*) kamba ya kufungia.

lass, *n.* kijana mwanamke, msichana, kisichana, mwamwali, mwali.

lassitude, *n.* uchovu, ulegevu, u-nyong'onyevu, kuchoka.
lasso, *n.* kamba yenye tanzi ya kukamatia wanyama.
last, (1) *n.* chuma kama fuawe cha kufanyizia viatu; (*of fez cap*) foroma.
last, (2) *a.* -a mwisho, -a kwisha (kwa kwenda juu, chini, mbali *&c.*); (*nearest*) -a karibu huyu (hii, hiki *&c.*). *A last farewell,* kuaga buriani. *At last,* mwisho, kwa shida, kwa kuchelewa; (*of surprise*) kwa ajabu, kumbe. *Last night,* usiku wa leo, usiku huu uliopita. *Last time,* mara hiyo. *At the last,* mwisho, hatima. *To the last,* hata mwisho. *Breathe his last,* kata roho, fariki, -fa. *The last man to steal,* si mtu wa kuiba hata kidogo, wizi mbali, haibi kamwe. *Last week,* juma hili lililopita. *Last year,* mwaka wa jana. *Of the last importance,* -a maana sana, -a thamani nyingi, -kubwa mno. — *adv.* mwishoni. — *n.* mwisho. **lastly,** *adv.* mwisho, hatima.
last, (3) *v.i.* endelea, ishi, dumu, kaa; (*be suffice*) tosha. *It lasts,* yakaa, haiozi, haichakai, ina aushi. **lasting,** *a.* -a aushi, -enye kudumu.
lastly, *adv.* taz. *last* (1).
latch, *n.* kia, komeo, kikomeo. — *v.t.* funga kwa komeo (kwa kia).
latchet, *n.* kigwe cha kufungia kiatu.
late, *a.* (*near the end, last*) -a nyuma, -a mwisho; (*just past, recent,* -a mbele, -a karibu na mwisho, -pya, -a kisasa; (*in past time*) -liopita, -liokwisha, -liotaka kuwa; (*deceased*) marehemu, hayati; (*in the day*) -a jioni, -a usiku. *Be late,* kawia, chelewa, limatia, taahari, ajazi, -ja nyuma, -ja kinyume, kosa saa (wakati). *Of late* (*lately*) siku hizi, karibu, juzi, juzijuzi, si zamani, sasa hivi. **lately,** *adv.* hivi karibu, juzi-juzi. **lateness,** *n.* usiri, kuchelewa, taahira, uajizi, kuja nyuma, kukosa saa. **latest,** *a.* -a mwisho, -a karibu, -a sasa hivi, -a kisasa. *The latest fashion,* mtindo wa kisasa. **latter,** *a.* -a pili, -a nyuma, -liofuata. **latterly,** *adv.* baadaye, siku hizi.
lateen (*sail*), *n.* tanga la pembetatu.
lately, *adv.*, **lateness,** *n.* taz. *late.*
latent, *a.* -liofichwa, -a siri, -a ndani, -sioonekana, -liostirika, -siokomaa bado, -siopevuka bado.
lateral, *a.* -a upande, -a kwenda upande, -a mbavuni, -a kando.
latest, *a.* taz. *late.*
latex, *n.* utomvu mweupe wa baadhi ya miti, *e.g.* wa mpira.
lath, *n.* uwasa, wasa, ufito, upao, papi.
lathe, *n.* kerezo.
lather, *n.* povu la sabuni; (*sweat*) jasho.
Latin, *a.* -a kirumi, Kirumi.
latitude, *n.* (*space, liberty, choice*) nafasi, ruhusa, kuachiliwa, hiari; (*in geography*) urefu wa kwenda toka *equator* mpaka mahali fulani kaskazini au kusini, latitudo. **latitudinarian,** *n.* asiyefuata kabisa kanuni na taratibu (za watu wengine, za dini *&c.*) ila hufuata azipendazo yeye.
latrine, *n.* choo. *Go to the latrine,* enda chooni (msalani, haja).
latter, *a.*, **latterly,** *adv.* taz. *late.*
lattice, *n.* kiunzi cha fito au vibao vinavyokingamana, kimia, kiunzi kama wavu wa mti au chuma, kazi ya kimia.
laud, *v.t.* sifu, himidi. **laudable,** *a.* -a kusifiwa, -a kustahili sifa. **laudatory,** *a.* -a kusifu, -a kuhimidi, -a kutolea sifa.
laudanum, *n.* dawa ya kutia usingizi inayofanyizwa kwa afyuni.
laudatory, *a.* taz. *laud.*
laugh, *v.i.* cheka; (*be mirthful*) chekelea, cheza, furahi. *Laugh at,* cheka, fanyia mzaha, dhihaki, dharau, tweza. *Laugh in a person's face,* dharau mtu. *Laugh in one's sleeve,* cheka kwa siri, furahi kwa siri. — *n.* cheko, kicheko. **laughable,** *a.* -a kuchekwa, -a kuchekesha, -cheshi.
laughing-stock, *n.* mtu wa kuchekwa (wa kudhihakiwa), mpumbavu, dhihaka, mzaha, twezo; (*dupe*) bara-

dhuli. **laughter,** *n.* cheko, kicheko, macheko, masihara.

launch, *v.t.* (*throw*) piga, tupa, vurumisha; (*set afloat*) cheleza, shusha, shua baharini; (*make begin*) toa, anzisha; — *v.i.* (*make a beginning*) jitoa, ingia, anza. — *n.* kushua (merikebu au meli mpya); mashua kubwa ya melini, motaboti.

launder, *v.t.* fua nguo. **laundress,** *n.* dobi (mwanamke). **laundry,** *n.* kiwanda cha dobi, pa kufulia nguo, josho.

laureate, *a. Poet Laureate,* jina la heshima la mtunga mashairi wa mfalme.

laurel, *n.* mti fulani wa Ulaya na majani yake. **laurels,** *n.* heshima, fahari.

lava, *n.* mawe yaliyoyeyuka yatokayo mlima wa moto (volkeno).

lave, *v.t.* osha. **laver,** *n.* birika. **lavatory,** *n.* josho, chumba cha kunawa, choo. *Go to the lavatory,* enda chooni (msalani, haja).

lavender, *n.* mmea wenye maua madogo yenye rangi ya urujuani nyeupe yanayonukia sana; (*colour*) rangi ya urujuani nyeupe.

laver, *n.* taz. *lave.*

lavish, *v.t.* toa -ingi mno, toa kwa ukarimu; (*waste*) poteza, tapanya, fuja. — *a.* -ingi mno, maridhawa, tele, -paji mno; (*extravagant*) -potevu, -badhirifu.

law, *n.* sheria, hukumu, amri; (*custom, rule*) desturi, kawaida, kanuni; (*Jewish*) Torati; (*natural*) utaratibu wa ulimwengu, tabia, katibu, maumbile; (*necessary process*) lazima, sharti. *Go to law,* teta, shtaki, enda sheriani, enda kwa kadhi, enda korti. *Reign of law,* yote kwa desturi na taratibu. **law-abiding,** *a.* -tii sheria, -sikivu wa sheria. **law court,** *n.* mahakma, korti, baraza ya jaji (kadhi). **lawful,** *a.* -a haki, halali, -ema, -a sheria. **lawgiver,** *n.* mtoa sheria. **lawless,** *a.* -asi, -siotii sheria, -potovu, -dhalimu, -a jeuri, -baya. **law-suit,** *n.* daawa, madai, maneno (mbele ya jaji, kadhi &c.), mashtaka. **lawyer,** *n.* mwana sheria, mwalimu wa sheria, mdai, mwombezi, mnenezi, wakili.

lawn, (1) *n.* bustani (ya majani mazuri mororo). **lawn-tennis,** *n.* mchezo wa tufe na vibao.

lawn, (2) *n.* bafta nzuri nyembamba.

lawsuit, *n.*, **lawyer,** *n.* taz. *law.*

lax, *a.* (*negligent, careless*) -zembe, -legevu, -tepetevu, si -angalifu; (*morally*) -potovu, -baya, si -nyofu; (*loose*) -legevu. **laxative,** *n.* dawa ya kuharisha. **laxity, laxness,** *n.* ulegevu, utepetevu, uzembe, udhaifu, upotovu.

lay, (1) *v.t.* (*p.t.* & *pf.t.* **laid**) weka, tia, laza; (*spread*) tanda, tandaa, tandaza, tandika; (*cause to be still*) tuliza; (*eggs*) taga, kuta; (*a wager*) pinga, weka (sharti); (*a table, food*) andika. *Lay about,* piga pande zote. *Lay by* (*up, in*), weka akiba, weka. *Lay by the heels,* kamata na kufunga. *Lay down,* toa, acha; (*assert with authority*) fundisha, amuru, toa. *Lay hands on, Lay hold of,* kamata, shika, bamba, pelekea mikono. *Lay heads together,* fanya shauri pamoja. *Lay on,* pigapiga; (*apply*) paka, bandika. *Lay* (*a charge*) *against, Lay to* (*one's charge*) pakiza, pakilia, sukumia, wekea, tilia. *Lay open,* funua, eleza; (*by cutting*) tumbua. *Lay out,* tengeneza; (*spend*) toa gharama, tumia. *Lay siege to,* zungushia mji jeshi vitani, zingia, fungia mazingiwa, husuru. *Lay wait for,* otea. *Lay waste,* haribu, teka, kumba, angamiza. **lay,** *n. Lay* (*lie*) *of the land,* sura ya nchi, hali ya mambo. **layer,** *n.* safu, kunjo, tabaka, rusu; (*hen*) kuku anayetaga mayai, koo la kuku. *In layers,* kwa kupangana juu kwa juu, kwa kupangilika, tabaka tabaka, safu safu, rusu rusu. **lay-out,** *n.* taratibu, matengenezo.

lay, (2) *n.* wimbo, utenzi.

lay, (3) *a.* -a mtu (asiye wa kazi

fulani, *e.g.* asiye padre, daktari, mwana sheria *&c.*). **layman,** *n.* mtu asiye padre (daktari, mwana sheria *&c.*).

lay, (4) *v. p.t.* ya *lie.*

layer, *n.* taz. *lay* (1).

layman, *n.* taz. *lay* (2).

lay-out, *n.* taz. *lay* (1).

lazaretto, *n.* nyumba ya kuuguza maskini wenye ukoma na magonjwa ya kuambukiza.

laze, *v.i.* jikalia, kaa kwa uvivu, -wa -vivu. **laziness,** *n.* uvivu, uzembe, utepetevu, ulegevu, ukunguni. **lazy,** *a.* -vivu, -zembe, -tepetevu, -legevu.

lea, *n.* shamba la majani, konde.

lead, (1) *n.* risasi; (*for sounding*) bildi, timazi. *Lead pencil,* kalamu (isiyo ya wino), pensili. **leaden,** *a.* -a risasi; (*colour*) -a kijivu, -eusi; (*heavy, dull*) -zito, -gumu.

lead, (2) *v.t.* (*p.t. and pf.t.* **led**) ongoza, peleka, fikisha; (*by bridle*) akania; (*induce*) ongoza, vuta, shawishi; (*direct, superintend*) tawala, simamia, -wa na ukuu; — *v.i.* (*precede*) tangulia, sabiki; (*proceed*) enda (katika); (*begin*) anza (mchezo); (*in music*) toa kongwe, imbisha; (*be superior*) pita, shinda, -wa -a kwanza (bora); (*result in*) leta. *Lead a life,* enenda, ishi, fanya. *It leads to,* inaelekea, inaleta, mwisho wake ni; (*of a road*) yaenda (mahali). *Lead aright,* hidi. *Lead astray,* poteza, kosesha. — *n.* kuongoza, mwongozo, welekezo *&c.*; (*direction*) ukuu, uwezo, amri, usimamizi; (*precedence*) kutangulia, utangulizi, kuanza (katika mchezo *&c.*); (*amount of lead*) kadiri ya kutangulia; (*in singing*) kongwe; (*for dog*) kamba (kigwe) ya kuongoza mbwa. *Take the lead,* tangulia. *Give a lead* (*in singing*), toa kongwe. **leader,** *n.* kiongozi, kurugenzi, mkuu, wa kwanza, mtangulizi, msimamizi. **leading,** *n.* uongozi, usimamizi. — *a.* -kubwa -kuu, -a kwanza, -tangulizi. **leading article,** *n.* masimulizi ya gazeti yatoayo mawazo (fikira mashauri) ya mtengenezaji. **leading-strings,** *n.* kamba (kigwe) ya kumwongoza mtoto anayefundishwa kuenda. *Be in leading-strings,* -wa mjinga, -wa kama mtoto.

leaf, *n.* (*pl.* **leaves**) jani; (*of a book*) ukurasa, gombo; (*of coco-nut tree*) kuti; (*of banana*) gomba; (*thin piece*) bamba, kipande chembamba; (*a table*) ubao unaoweza kutolewa kufanya meza iwe ndogo zaidi. *To take a leaf out of somebody's book,* kuiga mtu, kutumia akili yake. *Turn over new leaf,* ongoka, rekabisha mambo ya maisha, rekabisha mwenendo. **leafless,** *a.* bila majani, -tupu. **leaflet,** *n.* ukurasa. **leafy,** *a.* -enye (-a) majani mengi.

league, (1) *n.* (*measure*) kipimo cha urefu, kadiri ya maili 3, mwendo wa maili 3.

league, (2) *n.* mapatano baina ya watu (au mataifa) ya kusaidiana, sharti, ushirika, chama. *Be in league with,* -wa na shauri moja na, shirikiana na. — *v.i.* shiriki.

leak, *v.i.* vuja. *Leak out,* toka, fumbulika (siri), julikana. *Spring a leak,* anza kuvuja, funuka. — *n.* kuvuja, mvujo; (*hole*) ufa, tundu; (*escape of water*) maji yakivuja. **leakage,** *n.* kuvuja, mvujo. **leaky,** *a.* -enye kuvuja; (*of boat*) -bovu.

lean, (1) *a.* -embamba, -liokonda, -a kimbaombao, -gofu, -sio na shahamu (mafuta); (*of meat*) -nofu; (*scanty*) -chache, haba. *Become lean,* konda, dhoofika. — *n.* (*of meat*) mnofu.

lean, (2) *v.i.* inama, enda upande, lala upande; — *v.t.* (*cause to rest*) tegemeza. *Lean on, against,* egemea, tegemea, jiegama na (katika), gandamia. *Lean to, towards,* elekea, taka zaidi, pendelea, inamia. **leaning,** *n.* kuinamia, mainamizi *&c.*; (*inclination*) kuelekea, maelekeo, kutaka, kukabili, upendeleo. **lean-to,** *n.* kipenu, upenu.

leap, *v.i.* (*p.t. and pf.t.* **leapt, leaped**) ruka, chupa; (*for joy*) rukaruka, randa, chachawa; — *v.t.* (*over*) kiuka.

Leap at, pokea, (kubali, twaa) kwa furaha nyingi. *Look before you leap*, usifanye jambo mpaka kulifikiri kwanza. — *n*. mruko, ruko. *By leaps and bounds*, upesi sana. **leap-frog**, *n*. mchezo wa kurukana. **leap year**, *n*. mwaka wa kuzidi siku moja (kila mwaka wa nne).

learn, *v.t.* (*p.t. and pf.t.* **learnt, learned**) jifunza, fundishwa, zoea; (*be informed*) arifiwa, pata habari, ambiwa. **learned**, *a*. -enye elimu, -juzi. *A learned man*, mwenye maarifa, mwalimu, hakimu, mtaalamu. **learner**, *n*. mwanafunzi. **learning**, *n*. elimu, hekima, maarifa. *A man of learning*, mtu mwenye maarifa, mwana vyuoni, mwalimu, mtaalamu.

lease, *v.t.* panga, kodi; (*let*) pangisha, kodisha. — *n*. masharti ya kupangisha (kukodisha) nyumba (duka, shamba), mkataba wa kukodisha, hati ya kukodisha. *Let on lease*, pangisha, kodisha. *Take on lease*, panga, kodi. **leasehold**, *n*. nyumba (duka, shamba) iliyopangishwa (iliyokodishwa). — *a*. -a kupanga, -a kukodi. **lessee**, *n*. mwenye kupanga (kukodi). **lessor**, *n*. mwenye kupangisha (kukodisha).

leash, *n*. kamba (kigwe) ya kuzuia mbwa. — *v.t.* zuia (funga) kwa kamba.

least, *a. and adv.* -dogo kuliko -ote, -lio -dogo, -dogo sana. *Least, in the least*, kidogo tu, hata kidogo. *At least*, lakini, basi, iwayo yote, kwa vyo vyote; (*quite, certainly*) pasipo shaka, haikosi.

leather, *n*. ngozi (iliyotengenezwa -isioze). — *v.t.* (*slang*) piga sana. **leatherette**, *n*. namna ya nguo iliyofanana na ngozi. **leathern**, *a*. -a ngozi. **leathery**, *a*. -a ngozi, -a kama ngozi.

leave, *n*. (*permission, consent*) ruhusa, idhini; (*holiday*) ruhusa, kipumziko, livu, likizo. *By your leave*, kunradhi, simile, jihadhari, habedari. *Take leave of*, aga, agana na; (*presume*) thubutu. — *v.t.* (*p.t. and pf.t.* **left**) acha, achia; (*depart from*) toka katika, ondoka katika; (*bequeath*) rithisha; (*as a remainder*) saza, bakiza, cheleza; — *v.i.* ondoka, toka. *Leave off*, acha, isha, koma, hulu. *Leave out*, pitia, ruka, totia. *Be left*, achwa, baki, salia. *There is some left*, shinda liko bado. *Leave off!* acha! koma! basi! **leavings**, *n*. mabaki, masalio, masazo, makombo. **leave-taking**, *n*. maagano.

leaven, *n*. chachu, hamira; (*principles*) mafundisho, madhehebu, elimu. — *v.t.* chacha, chachua, tia hamira; (*affect*) geuza, changanya na; (*spoil*) haribu, ghoshi.

leaves, *pl*. ya *leaf*.

leave-taking, *n*., **leavings**, taz. *leave*.

lecherous, *a*. -zinifu, -kware, -talaleshi, -asherati. **lechery** *n*. ukware, uzinzi, uasherati, utalaleshi.

lectern, *n*. meza ya kusomea kanisani, marufaa. **lectionary**, *n*. utaratibu au kawaida ya kusoma Maandiko Matakatifu kanisani.

lecture, *n*. mafundisho, hotuba. — *v.t.* hutubu; (*reprove*) karipia, kemea. **lecturer**, *n*. mwalimu, mtoa hotuba.

led, *p.t. and pf.t.* ya *lead*.

ledge, *n*. ushi, mdomo, ukingo; (*shelf*) ubao, kibao, kidaka, kishubaka, shubaka. *A ledge of rock*, mwamba.

ledger, *n*. daftari kubwa (ya hesabu).

lee, leeward, lee-shore, lee-side, *n*. upande wa chini (usioelekea upepo), upande wa demani. **leeward**, *adv*. kwa demani. **leeway**, *n*. mwendo wa chombo kikichukuliwa upande wa demani.

leech, *n*. mruba, ruba (mdudu mfyonza damu akaaye majini); (*doctor*) daktari, mganga, tabibu.

leek, *n*. namna ya kitunguu kidogo.

leer, *v.i.* tazama kitongotongo. — *n*. jicho upande, kijicho.

lees, *n*. (*of wine*) sira, masira, kishinda; (*of oil &c.*) mashapo, masimbi, mashata, mashudu.

leeward, *adv.*, **leeway,** *n.* taz. *lee.*
left, (1) *p.f. and pf.t.* ya *leave.*
left, (2) *a.* -a kushoto, -a kuukeni, -a kikeni. **left-hand,** *a.* -a kushoto, -a kuukeni. — *n.* upande wa kushoto. **left-handedness,** *n.* shoto.
leg, *n.* mguu; (*of a bed*) tendegu; *of garment*) mguu. *Be on his legs,* simama ili kutoa maneno; (*recover oneself*) okoka, -wa -zima. *Have no leg to stand on,* shindwa. *To pull a person's leg,* kumfanyia mtu mzaha, kumdhihaki mtu. *On its last legs,* -wa karibu kuisha. *To give a person a leg up,* kumsaidia mtu. **leggings,** *n.* mavazi ya ngozi ya miguu toka visigino mpaka magoti.
legacy, *n.* urithi, hiba; (*religious*) wakf. *Leave a legacy to,* rithisha, achia, usia; (*for religious purposes*) wakifia. **legatee,** *n.* mrithi.
legal, *a.* halali, -a haki, -a sheria, sahihi. **legality,** *n.* uhalali, haki, usahihi. **legalize,** *v.t.* halalisha, sahihisha.
legate, *n.* mjumbe, balozi. **legation,** *n.* ujumbe, ubalozi; (*residence*) nyumba ya balozi.
legatee, *n.* taz. *legacy.*
legation, *n.* taz. *legate.*
legend, *n.* hadithi, ngano, kisa, hekaya (hasa ya mambo ya ajabu au isiyo kweli); (*passed down by word of mouth*) mapokeo; (*inscription*) mwandiko, tarehe. **legendary,** *a.* -a hadithi, -a hekaya, -si -enye hakika.
legerdemain, *n.* kiinimacho, mizungu, miujiza, mauzauza.
leggings, *n.* taz. *leg.*
leghorn, *n.* namna ya kuku.
legible, *a.* -a kusomeka, dhahiri, -zuri. **legibility,** *n.* kusomeka, uzuri (wa kuandika), ufasihi.
legion, *n.* jeshi la askari (kirumi); (*abundance*) wingi. **legionary,** *n.* mtu wa *legion,* askari wa kirumi.
legislate, *v.i.* fanya sheria, toa sheria. **legislation,** *n.* kufanya sheria; sheria. **legislative,** *a.* -a kufanya sheria. **legislator,** *n.* mfanya sheria.
legislature, *n.* jamii ya wafanya sheria; serikali.
legitimate, *a.* halali, -a haki, -a sheria. **legitimacy,** *n.* uhalali, haki. **legitimize,** *v.t.* fanya kuwa halali, halalisha.
leguminous, *a.* -a jamii ya kunde, maharagwe *&c.*
leisure, *n.* faragha, nafasi, wakati, wasaa. **leisurely,** *adv.* taratibu, polepole.
lemon, *n.* limau; (*tree*) mlimau. **lemonade** *n.*, **lemon squash,** *n.* maji ya limau.
lemur, *n.* komba wa Bukini.
lend, *v.t.* (*p.t. and pf.t.* **lent**) azima, kopesha, karidhi; (*supply*) toa, -pa. *Lend a hand,* saidia, auni. *Lend an ear,* sikiliza. *It lends itself to,* inafaa kwa. **lender,** *n.* mkopeshi; (*of money on interest*) mla riba.
length, *n.* urefu, kadiri ya urefu. *At length,* mwisho, baadaye; (*fully*) kwa wingi, kwa maneno mengi. *Measure one's length on the ground,* anguka fudifudi. *At full length,* -ote pia, kamili. *Go to great lengths,* jasiria, jaribia yote; (*use efforts*) fanya vingi, jitahidi. *Keep at arm's length,* sukumia mbali, kataa urafiki, tenga. **lengthen,** *v.t.* nyosha, ongeza urefu, fanya -refu, eneza; — *v.i.* (*grow longer*) zidi urefu, enea. **lengthwise,** *adv.* kwa urefu, kirefu. **lengthy,** *a.* -refu, -refu mno, -a kuchosha.
lenient, *a.* -pole, -a huruma, si -kali. **leniency,** *n.* upole, huruma. **lenity,** *n.* upole, huruma.
lens, *n.* kioo (cha miwani, darubini *&c.*).
lent, (1) *p.t. and pf.t.* ya *lend.*
Lent, (2) *n.* kwaresima, siku arobaini za kufunga kikristo. **lenten,** *a.* -a *Lent.*
lentil, *n.* dengu, adesi.
leonine, *a.* -a kama simba.
leopard, *n.* chui.
leper, *n.* mwenye ukoma. **leprosy,** *n.* ukoma, matana, balasi, jethamu. **leprous,** *a* -enye ukoma, -a ukoma.

lesion, *n.* donda, jeraha.

-less, *suff.* pasipo, bila, si -enye.

less, *a. and adv.* -dogo zaidi, -dogo, -dogo sana, duni. *Less than,* -dogo kuliko, duni ya. *Less by,* kasa, kasoro, kupungua. **lessen,** *v.t.* punguza, fanya -dogo; — *v.i.* (*become less*) punguka. **lesser,** *a.* -dogo zaidi, -lio -dogo.

lessee, *n.* taz. *lease.*

lessen, *v.,* **lesser,** *a.* taz. *less.*

lesson, *n.* somo, fundisho; (*reproof*) maonyo; (*portion of Bible*) sehemu ya Maandiko Matakatifu ya kusoma kanisani, sura. *Let that be a lesson to you,* hayo yakuonye (yakuonye-she). *Teach him a lesson,* mrudi (mwadhibu) asifanye tena.

lessor, *n.* taz. *lease.*

lest, *conj.* isiwe, (*by use of neg. subj.*) *e.g.* kwa hofu -si-, kwa maana -si-, ili -si-. *Lest he die,* asife. *Take heed lest ye fall,* angalia usije ukaanguka.

let, (1) *v.t.* (*p.t. and pf.t.* **let**) acha, ruhusu, toa ruhusa; (*for hire*) pangisha, kodisha. *Let me die,* nife. *Let him be beaten,* apigwe. *Let be, Let alone,* acha. *Let blood,* toza damu. *Let down,* inamisha, shusha, tua. *Let drive, Let fly,* piga kwa nguvu. *Let fall,* angusha, (*a remark*) nena. *He let it fall,* ilimponyoka. *Let in,* fungulia mlango, karibisha, ingiza, pisha. *Let go* (*loose*), fungulia, acha, puliza. *Let off* (*trap &c.*) tegua, fyatua, piga. *Let out,* fungulia, funua, feleti, toa nje; (*expand*) panua, eneza, kunjua, legeza; (*on hire*) pangisha, kodisha. (*House*) *to let,* (nyumba) -a kupanga. *Let alone* (*not to mention, not only*) licha ya, sembuse.

let, (2) *n.* kizuio, mgogoro, pingamizi.

lethal, *a.* -a kufisha, -a kuua.

lethargy, *n.* usingizi, kusinzia, uzito, ulegevu, unyong'onyevu, utepetevu, uzembe. **lethargic,** *a.* -zito, -legevu, -zembe, -tepetevu, -nyong'onyevu.

letter, *n.* barua, waraka, hati; (*of alphabet*) herufi; (*written words*) maneno yenyewe, maneno halisi. *I acted according to the spirit rather than the letter of his instructions,* nilifanya kama alivyotaka si kama alivyoandika, nilifikiliza shauri lake kuliko maneno yake. *To the letter,* kabisa, halisi, pia. *Letters,* maarifa, vitabu, vyuo. *A man of letters,* mwana vyuoni, mtaalamu, mtu mwenye maarifa. **lettered,** *a.* -enye elimu, -enye malezi mazuri, -taalamu. **letter-press,** *n.* maneno yaliyopigwa chapa, maandiko, maneno.

lettuce, *n.* saladi, mboga ya majani ya kizungu.

levee, *n.* baraza. *Hold a levee,* barizi.

level, *a.* sawa (bila kuinuka), sawasawa. *He did his level best,* alifanya vizuri awezavyo. — *n.* (*position*) hali (ya juu, ya chini), cheo, daraja; (*flat area*) mahali pa sawa; (*spirit level &c.*) pimamaji, kipande cha kupimia usawa. *On a level,* sawa. *On different levels,* moja chini moja juu, mbalimbali. — *v.t.* sawazisha fanya sawa; (*knock down*) angusha, bomoa; (*aim*) elekeza, linga. **leveller,** *n.* msawazishi, mtu atakaye watu wote wawe na cheo (hali) kile kile.

lever, *n.* wenzo; (*of iron*) mtaimbo, msaha; (*of wood*) mti. **leverage,** *n.* nguvu au matumizi ya wenzo au mtaimbo.

leveret, *n.* kisungura, mtoto wa sungura.

leviathan, *n.* mnyama mkubwa wa majini, mamba, kitu cho chote kikubwa mno.

levitate, *v.t.* angaza; — *v.i.* anga, angama. **levitation,** *n.* kuanga, kuangama, kuangaza.

Levite, *n.* Mlawi. **Levitical,** *a.* -a Walawi, -a kilawi. **Leviticus,** *n.* kitabu cha tatu cha Musa katika *Bible.*

levity, *n.* purukushani, utovu wa staha (kicho, heshima).

levy, *n.* mchango, chango (la askari, kodi &c.); (*muster*) kundi la askari. — *v.t.* changa, toza.

lewd, *a.* -chafu, -pujufu, -fisadi, -asherati, -zinifu. **lewdness,** *n.* uchafu, upujufu, ufisadi (wa maneno, matendo *&c.*).

lexicographer, *n.* mbuni kamusi.

lexicon, *n.* kamusi.

liability, *n.* taz. *liable.*

liable, *a.* -enye madaraka, -enye kupasiwa, -a kupaswa, -enye kustahili (kupatwa, kushikwa, kuelekea); (*of debts*) -enye kuwiwa. **liability,** *n.* madaraka, kupasiwa, kuwiwa; (*tendency*) kuelekea, mwelekeo, maelekeo. *Unlimited liability,* madaraka bila kiasi. *Limited liability,* madaraka ya kiasi.

liaison officer, *n.* afisa aliyewekwa kuwa mjumbe baina ya sehemu za jeshi, au baina ya majeshi mawili (moja la adui).

liar, *n.* mwongo, mmbea, mzandiki, mnafiki, mdhabidhabina.

libation, *n.* sadaka ya kumimina (divai *&c.*).

libel, *n.* maandiko (hati, tangazo) yenye masingizio, masengenyo, chongelezo, uchongezi, machongezi, masingizio, kashifa, mashtaka ya bure (ya uwongo). — *v.t.* singizia vibaya (bure), sengenya, chongea, kashifu. **libeller,** *n.* mchongezi, mtoa *libel.* **libellous,** *a.* -a kusingizia, -a kuchongea.

liberal, *a.* (*generous*) -karimu, -paji, -ema; (*abundant*) -ingi, tele, maridhawa, -kubwa; (*of ideas*) -enye utu mwema, -fadhili, -a nia bora, bora. *A liberal education,* malezi ya kiungwana, malezi bora. *Liberal ideas,* moyo wa kukumbuka vingi na kufalia wengi; (*in politics*) moyo wa kufuata *Liberal Party. Liberal Party,* jina la jamii mojawapo ya watu wa Uingereza inayojitia katika mambo ya utawala wa nchi. **liberalism,** *n.* nia na mashauri ya *Liberal Party.* **liberality,** *n.* ukarimu, upaji, wema, ufadhili, nia bora za kufalia wengi. **liberalize,** *v.t.* angaza, ongoza, tengeneza. **liberate,** *v.t.* fungua, achilia, toa utumwani, fanya huru, toa nje. **liberator,** *n.* mwenye kuweka huru, mwokozi, mkombozi.

libertine, *n.* mfisadi, mwasherati, mzinzi. **liberty,** *n.* uhuru, uungwana; (*permission, choice*) ruhusa, nafasi, hitiari, kuachiwa, kutozuiwa, kufunguliwa. *To take liberties with,* kufanya yasiyo haki (yasiyofaa).

libidinous, *a.* -enye shauku (ashiki, tamaa za mwili, ukware) nyingi, -chafu, -zinifu, -asherati, -fisadi, -talaleshi, -a kuchochea nyege.

library, *n.* (*books*) jamii ya vitabu; (*room*) chumba (nyumba) cha kuwekea vitabu, maktaba, chumba cha kusomea. **librarian,** *n.* mlinzi wa vitabu, msimamizi wa *library.*

libretto, *n.* maneno ya nyimbo za *opera.*

lice, *n.* (*pl.* ya *louse*) chawa; (*chicken lice*) utitiri.

licence, *n.* (*permission*) ruhusa; (*written*) cheti, hati; (*outrage*) jeuri, upotovu. *Poetic licence,* haki ya watungaji mashairi kutumia maneno na sarufi isiyo sahihi, kwa ajili ya ushairi. **licensee,** *n.* mwenye cheti (hati) cha ruhusa. **licentiate,** *n.* mwenye ruhusa (kufundisha, kufanya kazi ya udakatari *&c.*). **licentious,** *a.* -asherati, -fisadi, -kware, -zinifu, -talaleshi. **licentiousness,** *n.* uasherati, ufisadi, uzinifu, upotovu, ukware, utalaleshi.

lichen, *n.* ukoga, ukungu, kuvu (wa miti na miamba).

lick, *v.t.* lamba; (*one's lips*) lambitia; (*slang*) piga sana; (*excel*) shinda. *Lick a person's boots,* jinyenyekea mbele ya mtu. *Lick into shape,* fundisha mwanafunzi mgumu; maliza kazi ya kufanya kitu. — *n.* kulamba, kipande kidogo, kilicholambwa. **licking,** *n.* kulamba. *We gave them a beating,* tuliwashinda, tuliwapiga.

lid, *n.* kifuniko, kipande cha juu; (*of box*) ubao wa juu; (*of earthenware pot &c.*) mkungu (wa kufunikia), kibia.

lie, (1) *v.i.* sema (toa) uwongo, ongopa. — *n.* uwongo. *Give the lie* *to,* kanya, kanisha, onya uwongo, shtakia uwongo. *Tell a lie about,* singizia. **lying,** *a.* -a uwongo, -a kuongopa.

lie, (2) *v.i.* (*p.t.* **lay,** *pf.t.* **lain**) lala, gona, jinyosha; (*be placed, rest*) kaa, -wako, wekwa. *Lie on, with, at the door of,* -wa juu ya. *As far as in me lies,* kadiri niwezavyo. *Lie doggo,* kaa kimya. *Lie over,* kaa, baki, salia, wekwa. *Lie hard, heavy on,* lemea. *Lie in wait for,* otea, vizia. *Lie across each other,* pandana, kingamana. *Lie at the mercy of, Lie under,* -wa chini ya. *Lie up,* lala nyumbani kwa ugonjwa. *Lie with,* lala na, lala. — *n.* hali. *The lie of the land,* hali ya nchi ilivyo. **lying-in,** *n.* hali ya mwanamke anayezaa mtoto.

liege, *a.* na *n.* -enye amri, bwana.

lieu, *n.* *In lieu of,* mahali pa, badala ya.

lieutenant, *n.* afisa mwenye cheo kilicho chini ya *Captain*; (*deputy &c.*) wakili, naibu.

life, *n.* (*pl.* **lives**) uzima, uhai, maisha; (*existence*) kuwa na uzima, kuishi, kuwa, kuwako; (*vital force*) roho, damu; (*person*) mtu mzima; (*living creatures*) viumbe; (*vigour*) nguvu, bidii, wepesi; (*way of living*) maisha, mwendo, mwenendo; (*human affairs*) ulimwengu, mambo; (*history*) habari ya maisha, hadithi, kisa; (*darling*) kipenzi. *To the life, as large as life,* sawasawa, kama -livyo halisi. *Seek the life of,* taka kuua. *Have the life of,* ua. *Life-blood,* roho, damu. *Life-interest, Life annuity,* faida ya kitambo, ya muda wa maisha. **life-belt,** *n.* mshipi wa kuvaa mtu asiweze kuzama majini. **life-boat,** *n.* mashua iliyoundwa makusudi kuopolea watu katika hatari ya majini; mashua inayochukuliwa melini kusudi watu watoke katika meli iwapo katika hatari ya kuzama. **life-buoy,** *n.* taz. *life-belt*; chelezo cha kuopolea watu katika hatari ya majini. **life-guard,** *n.* askari (wa kumngojea mfalme mwenyewe). **lifeless,** *a.* -fu, -liozimia; (*feeble, dull*) pasipo nguvu, -legevu, nyong'onyevu, -tepetevu, baridi. **lifelike,** *a.* kama kitu chenyewe, sawasawa, kama -livyo halisi. **lifelong,** *a.* -a maisha pia, mpaka kufa. **lifetime,** *n.* maisha, muda au wakati wa kuwa hai.

lift, *v.t.* inua, pandisha, paza, paliza, tweka, nyanyua, kweza; (*improve*) ongoza, tengeneza, tukuza; — *v.i.* (*rise*) panda, inuka. — *n.* msaada; (*hoisting machine*) mtambo wa kupandishia vitu na watu mpaka orofa za juu nyumbani.

ligament, *n.* mshipa, kamba. **ligature,** *n.* uzi, kamba, kitambaa.

light, (1) *n.* nuru, *weupe, mwanga, mwangaza, anga; (*daylight*) mchana; (*brightness*) wangavu, mng'ao; (*window*) dirisha, mwangaza; (*enlightenment*) maarifa, akili; (*publicity*) ubayani, kuwa wazi; (*famous person*) mtu wa sifa, mashuhuri; (*point of view*) jinsi ya kufahamu; (*lamp*) taa; (*match*) kiberiti. *Show light on,* mulikia; (*explain*) eleza, *fafanisha. *Bring to light,* funua, vumbua, onyesha, bainisha. *According to my lights,* nionavyo mimi. *By the light of grammar,* kwa kukumbuka sarufi. *Light of nature,* akili. *In this light, in that light,* hivi, vile. — *a.* -enye nuru, -enye mwangaza, -eupe. — *v.t.* (*p.t. and pf.t.* **lighted, lit**) (*kindle*) washa; (*make light*) nawiri, angaza, mulikia; (*help with light*) peleka kwa taa, mulikia njiani; — *v.i.* waka. **lighten,** *v.t.* (*give light*) angaza, ng'ariza, mulikia; — *v.i.* (*emit lightning*) toa umeme. **lighter,** *n.* mwenye kuwasha (taa). **lighthouse,** *n.* mnara wenye taa (ya kuonya hatari ya mwamba, ya kuashiria njia &c.). **lightning,** *n.* umeme. **lightning-conductor,** *n.* uzi (chuma, shaba) wa kukingia umeme. **lights,** *n.* (*knowledge*) maarifa, akili. *He lives up to his lights,* afanya vyema kadiri ajuavyo, mwema kwa kadiri yake.

light, (2) *a.* (*in weight*) -epesi, rahisi, sahala; (*gay, pleasing*) -a furaha, -a kupendeza, -changamfu; (*worthless*) -nyonge, -baya, hafifu, ghafi; (*slight*) -dogo, kidogo, -chache; (*gentle*) -a polepole, -anana, laini; (*loose, crumbling*) tifutifu; (*troops*) -enye silaha nyepesi. *Light coin*, sarafu mbaya hafifu. *Make light of*, dharau, tweza, toangalia. **light-armed**, *a.* -enye silaha chache si nzito. **lighten**, *v.t.* rahisisha, punguza, fanya -epesi; — *v.i.* (*become lighter*) pungua, punguka (uzito); — *v.t.* (*enliven*) changamsha; (*relieve*) fariji, burudisha; — *v.i.* (*become more cheerful &c.*) changamka, kunjuka. **light-fingered**, *a.* -a kuiba, kijivi. **light-headed**, *a.* -a kurukwa na akili, -enye kichaa, -a akili chache. **light-hearted**, *a.* -kunjufu, -changamfu, -a furaha, -a kucheza. **light-heartedness**, *n.* wepesi wa moyo, ukunjufu, uchangamfu. **light-infantry**, *n.* askari wa kwenda mbio wenye silaha nyepesi. **lightly**, *adv.* (*easily*) upesi, rahisi; (*hastily*) pasipo kufikiri, kwa haraka; (*slightly*) kidogo, upesi, bure; (*gracefully*) kwa madaha (mangwaji). **lightness**, *n.* wepesi, urahisi; (*worthlessness*) uhafifu.

light, (3) *v.i.* shuka, tua; (*as birds*) tua, tenga; (*light on, upon*) tulia, jia; (*meet with*) pata, kuta, angukia; (*discover*) vumbua.

lighten, *v.* taz. *light* (1) & (2).

lighter, *n.* tishari; taz. *light* (1).

light-fingered, *a.*, **light-headed**, *a.*, **light-hearted**, *a.*, **light-heartedness**, *n.* taz. *light* (2).

lighthouse, *n.* taz. *light* (1).

light-infantry, *n.*, **lightly**, *adv.*, **lightness**, *n.* taz. *light* (2).

lightning, *n.*, **lightning-conductor**, *n.* taz. *light* (1).

lights, *n.* mapafu, yavuyavu; taz. *light* (1).

like, *v.t.* penda, taka, chagua, ona -tamu, hebu, stahabu. *As you like*, upendavyo, hiari yako. *Do as one likes*, tumia roho, fanya -pendavyo. — *n.* mfano, kifani, mwenzi; (*desire*) mapenzi. — *a.* sawa, -a kufanana, -a mfano mmoja, mamoja. *As like as not*, naona, labda. (*In comp.*) *-like*, kama, *e.g. childlike*, kama mtoto. *Be like*, fanana na, landa, -wa mfano mmoja, shabihi, twazana, twaana, lingana, -wa sawa. — *conj.* sawa na, mfano wa, kama, mithili ya. **likelihood**, *n.* *There is a likelihood*, yamkini, huenda, labda. **likely**, *a.* *It is likely, There is a likelihood of it, Most likely*, naona itakuwa, nadhani, inakabili kuwa, yaelekea, yataka kuwa, labda, huenda, haikosi. *A likely man*, mzuri, wa kupendeza.

liken, *v.t.* fananisha, linganisha.

likeness, *n.* mfano, kifani, mshabaha, sanamu, picha, sura, taswira, mithili, mlingano, ufanani. *Have a likeness*, -wa mfano mmoja, fanana, landa. *They have a great likeness*, wamefanana sana. **likewise**, *adv.* na tena, kadhalika, vivyo. **liking**, *n.* mapenzi, kutaka, matakwa, upendeleo, tamaa, shauku. *Take a liking to*, penda, tia habani, elekea.

lilt, *n.* mwendo (mpigo) wa wimbo, ngoma.

lily, *n.* ua zuri, jamii ya yungiyungi. *Water-lily*, yungiyungi. **lily-white**, *a.* -eupe kabisa.

limb, *n.* sehemu ya mwili, kiungo, mkono, mguu; (*of a tree*) tawi, tanzu. *There is pain in all my limbs*, maungo yote yaniuma.

limber, (1) *n.* sehemu ya mbele ya gari la mzinga. — *v.t.* fungia *limber*.

limber, (2) *a.* -a kupindika kwa urahisi, -epesi.

limbo, *n.* ahera.

lime, (1) *n.* (*fruit*) ndimu; (*tree*) mdimu. *Lime-juice*, maji ya ndimu.

lime, (2) *n.* chokaa. *Bird-lime*, ulimbo. **lime-kiln**, *n.* tanuu (chomeo) la chokaa. **limelight**, *n.* nuru nyeupe kali ya namna ya taa ya kuangazia michezo. *He is fond of the limelight*, apenda kujitokeza (kujionyesha) mbele ya watu.

limestone, *n.* gange, mawe ya chokaa.

limit, *n.* mpaka; (*restriction*) kizuio; (*extent*) kadiri, kiasi, eneo; (*utmost extent*) upeo, kipeo, mwisho. — *v.t.* zuia, katiza, funga, wekea mpaka, kata ruhusa. *Limit to*, gombeza yote ila. *Be limited to* (*in scope, meaning*), husika na. **limitation**, *n.* kuzuia, kizuio, kizuizi, mpaka, sheria, sharti. **limited**, *a.* -a kadiri -pungufu; (*small*) -dogo, -embamba, -chache. **limitless**, *a.* pasipo kiasi, bila kadiri, kupita kadiri yote, -siyo na mpaka.

limn, *v.t.* andika picha (sanamu).

limp, (1) *a.* teketeke, laini; (*relaxed*) -legevu, -nyong'onyevu.

limp, (2) *v.i.* chechema, sita, enda chopi.

limpet, *n.* namna ya koa wa bahari anayeambatana sana na miamba.

limpid, *a.* safi, -eupe, -angavu. **limpidity**, *n.* wangavu.

line, *n.* mstari, mfuo, safu; (*cord*) kamba, kitani, uzi; (*for fishing*) mshipi, ugwe; (*of verse*) mstari; (*of book*) aya; (*course*) njia, mwendo; (*kind*) jinsi, namna, aina; (*direction*) maelekeo, upande; (*of shooting*) shabaha; (*occupation, conduct*) kazi, mwenendo, shughuli; (*succession, procession, file*) mwandamo, mafuatano, msago, mtawalio, mpororo; (*line of descent*) ukoo, ufungu, jamaa, nasibu, nasaba, jadi; (*military*) jeshi la askari; (*fortification*) boma, kituo cha askari; (*camp*) kituo, kambi; (*of battle*) mpango wa vita; (*railway*) reli, njia ya magari ya moshi; (*of ships &c.*) meli (merikebu) za kumpuni, jamii ya meli nyingi; (*mathemat.*) mstari (wenye urefu, si upana wala unene); (*as a measure*) sehemu ya thenashara ya inchi; (*equator*) ikweta, isitiwai; (*telegraph*) simu; (*contour*) sura, uso; (*border*) mpaka. *Draw a line*, piga (andika) mstari; (*make a limit*) piga (weka) mpaka, fanya mwisho (kikomo). *Hard lines*, jambo zito, udhalimu. *Out of line*, si sawa, si taratibu, mshazari. *Fall into line*, jipanga. *Place in line*, panga, ratibisha. *Line-of-battleship*, manowari kubwa. *There is no hard and fast line in these matters*, mambo haya yanapitana. — *v.t.* andika (piga) mistari; (*of clothes*) tabiki, tia tabaka; (*fill inside*) jaza ndani; — *v.i.* pangana, jipanga safu (mstari). *Line with*, panga ndani ya. **lineage**, *n.* ufungu, jamaa; (*pedigree*) nasaba, ukoo, jadi. **lineal**, *a.* -a nasaba (ukoo, jadi) fulani. **lineament**, *n.* sura, uso, wajihi, umbo. **linear**, *a.* -a mstari, -a mistari. **lineate**, *a.* -enye mistari. **lined**, *a.* -enye mistari; (*with material*) -enye bitana, -enye tabaka ya nguo ndani. **liner**, *n.* (*ship*) meli. **lining**, *n.* tabaka, nguo ya kutia ndani ya nguo nyingine, bitana.

linen, *n.* kitani, nguo ya kitani; nguo za kuvaa ndani, nguo za meza na kitanda &c. — *a.* -a kitani. **linen-draper**, *n.* mwuza nguo.

liner, *n.* taz. *line.*

linger, *v.i.* kawia, limatia, kaa, sita, tanga, usiri. **lingering**, *a.* -a kudumu siku nyingi, -a kuendelea sana.

lingerie, *n.* nguo za ndani za kike.

lingering, *a.* taz. *linger.*

lingual, *a.* -a ulimi, -a lugha. **lingo**, *n.* lugha (neno la kudharau lugha yenyewe). **lingua franca**, *n.* lugha yenye maneno yaliyotoka katika lugha nyingi, inayotumika na watu wa makabila au mataifa mengi.

linguist, *n.* mtu ajuaye lugha nyingi, mtu mwenye elimu ya lugha. **linguistic**, *a.* -a lugha, -a kuhusu elimu ya lugha.

liniment, *n.* dawa ya mafuta ya kusugua.

lining, *n.* taz. *line.*

link, *n.* pete; (*joining*) kiungo; (*torch*) mwenge. — *v.t.* unga, fungasha, fungamanisha; — *v.i.* (*link up with*) ungana na, jiunga na.

links, *n.* kiwanja cha kucheza *golf.*

linnet, *n.* namna ya ndege wa Ulaya.

linoleum, *n.* namna ya nguo ngumu ya kutandika chini nyumbani.
linotype, *n.* mashine inayopanga herufi za kupiga chapa na kuziunganisha mistari mistari.
linseed, *n.* mbegu za kitani.
lint, *n.* nguo ya pamba nyororo ya kubandikia dawa.
lintel, *n.* kizingiti, kizimba.
lion, *n.* simba dume; (*important person*) mtu mashuhuri. *The lion's share*, fungu kubwa. **lioness**, *n.* simba jike. **lionize**, *v.t.* tukuza, tendea kama ni mtu mashuhuri. **lion-like**, *a.* kama simba, hodari.
lip, *n.* mdomo, kitu kama mdomo; (*edge*) ukingo; (*impudence &c.*) maneno ya ujuvi (ya ufidhuli). *Hang on a person's lips*, sikiliza sana maneno ya mtu. *Smack* (*lick*) *the lips*, lambitia. — *v.t.* gusa kwa midomo, busu; (*utter*) nena, sema, tamka. **lip-ring**, *n.* ndonya. **lip-service**, *n.* kusifu bure, ahadi za bure, kilemba cha ukoka. **lip-stick**, *n.* namna ya rangi inayotumiwa na wanawake wengine ya kupaka midomo.
liquefaction, *n.*, **liquefy**, *v.*, **liqueur**, *n.* tax. *liquid.*
liquid, *a.* -a maji, kama maji, -nayoweza kumiminika; (*smooth*) laini, -ororo; (*clear*) -eupe; -angavu. — *n.* maji, kitu kiwezacho kumiminika. **liquefaction**, *n.* kuyeyuka, kugeuka maji. **liquefy**, *v.t.* yeyusha; — *v.i.* yeyuka; — *v.t.* geuza maji; — *v.i.* geuka maji. **liqueur**, *n.* divai ya nguvu iliyokolea utamu, namna ya mvinyo bora. **liquidate**, *v.t.* lipa deni, funga hesabu na kulipa deni kwa urari; — *v.i.* (*become bankrupt*) filisika. **liquidation**, *n.* kufanya hesabu na kulipa deni kwa urari, kufungwa hesabu. *Go into liquidation*, filisika. **liquidator**, *n.* mfunga hesabu (wa kumpuni, duka &c.). **liquor**, *n.* maji; (*beverage*) kinywaji; (*intoxicating*) kileo, ulevi, pombe, tembo, akari, gimbi &c. *Be in liquor*, lewa.
liquorice, *n.* susu. *Cough medicine made from liquorice*, urukususu.
lisp, *v.i.* sema kitembe. — *n.* **lisping**, *n.* kitembe. — *a.* -a kitembe.
lissom, *a.* -epesi, -a madaha.
list, (1) *n.* hesabu, fahirisi, orodha, jedwali. *Enter the lists*, ingia kiwanjani kushindana, shindana. — *v.t.* fanya (andika) orodha (hesabu, jedwali &c.); — *v.i* (*enlist as soldier*) ingia uaskari, andika kiaskari.
list, (2) *v.i.* (meli, merikebu) inamia upande.
list, (3) *v.i.* taka, penda. *He does as he lists*, afanya apendavyo.
list, (4) *v.i.* taz. *listen.*
listen, *v.i.* sikiliza, sikia. **listener**, *n.* msikilizaji.
listless, *a.* -tepetevu, -legevu, -nyong'onyevu, -zito.
lit, *p.t.* na *pf.t.* ya *light.*
litany, *n.* sala za kuomba za padre na watu wakiitikiana, litania.
litchi, *n.* (*tree*) mgulabi; (*fruit*) gulabi.
literal, *a.* -a herufi; (*exact*) hasa, halisi, -a maneno yenyewe, -a maana iliyo wazi. *Literal translation*, ufasiri wa maneno yote moja moja. **literally**, *adv.* kwa jinsi ya maana hasa ya maneno, halisi, kweli. *He did literally nothing*, hakutenda hata neno. **literary**, *a.* -a vitabu, -a mambo ya elimu, -enye kujua vitabu na maarifa yaliyomo, -enye habari ya vitabu na kusoma. **literate**, *a.* -enye elimu, -taalamu, -enye kuweza kuandika na kusoma. — *n.* mtu awezaye kuandika na kusoma; mwenye elimu ya kadiri au ya kutosha. **literature**, *n.* vitabu, jamii ya vitabu na maandiko; (*profession*) kazi ya kusoma na kuandika vitabu; (*classical*) vitabu vya maandiko mazuri na vyenye ufasaha.
lithe, *a.*, **lithesome**, *a.* -liopindikana kwa urahisi, -epesi -a kupindikana, -epesi, -a madaha.
lithograph, *n.* maandiko (picha &c.) yaliyochorwa juu ya namna ya jiwe la kupigia chapa. — *v.t.* piga chapa kwa *lithograph.*

litigate, *v.i.* dai mbele ya sheria, enda sheriani. **litigant,** *n.* mdai, mdaawa. **litigation,** *n.* daawa, shauri mbele ya sheria. **litigious,** *a.* -a kupenda daawa, -a mashauri mengi, -gomvi.

litre, *n.* kipimo kadiri ya *pints* 1¾ (kadiri ya vibaba viwili kasa robo).

litter, *n.* machela, susu, kitanda cha kumchukulia mtu; (*for cattle*) majani ya kulalia; (*mess*) takataka, fujo, machafuko; (*of animals*) watoto wote wa uzazi mmoja (mkumbo mmoja). — *v.t.* chafua, fuja, tia takataka; — *v.t. and i.* (*produce young*) zaa (wanyama).

little, *a.* -dogo, -chache, kidogo, haba; (*insignificant*) -nyonge, hafifu, duni, dhaifu, ki-. *A little,* kidogo, punde. *A little more,* bado kidogo, punde zaidi. *Little by little,* kidogo kidogo, punde kwa punde. *Take up little by little,* chota. *Little one,* mtoto. *A little boy,* kitoto. *A little thing,* kidude. *Make little of,* dharau, tweza, punguza, beza. **littleness,** *n.* udogo; (*meanness*) unyonge, udhaifu, uhafifu, uduni.

littoral, *a.* -a pwani. — *n.* pwani.

liturgy, *n.* kawaida ya ibada na sala ya dini, kawaida ya Ushirika Mtakatifu.

live, *v.i.* -wa na uzima, -wa hai; (*exist, remain*) -wa, ishi, kaa, dumu; (*get maintenance*) pata riziki, pata nafuu. *Live on,* -la, ponea, lishwa. *What does he live on?* hula nini? *What does he live by?* kazi yake nini? *Live down,* sahaulisha mwendo mbaya (tendo baya) kwa kuishi mwendo mzuri. — *a.* -zima, -hai; (*burning*) -a moto. *Live coals,* makaa ya moto. **livelihood,** *n.* uchumi, kazi, nafuu, riziki, maishilio. **livelong,** *a.* *Livelong day,* mchana kutwa. *Livelong night,* usiku kucha. **lively,** *a.* -epesi, -changamfu, -cheshi, -kunjufu, -a kuenda mbio. **live stock,** *n.* wanyama wa kufuga, *e.g.* ng'ombe, farasi, kondoo, mbuzi &c. **living,** *n.* nafuu, riziki, uchumi, kazi, maishilio; (*of priest*) kazi yenye uchumi wa padre mahali fulani, pa kukaa padre. — *a.* hai, -zima; (*working, energetic, moving*) -enye nguvu, -a bidii, -a moto, -tendaji, -enye mwendo. **living-room,** *n.* sebule, ukumbi, chumba cha kukaa na kuzungumza, majilisi.

liver, *n.* ini, nso.

livery, *n.* nguo za urembo, nguo za rasmi, mavalio, mavalio ya mtumishi. **livery-stable,** *n.* banda la farasi wa kuajiri.

lives, *pl.* ya *life.*

live stock, *n.* taz. *live.*

livid, *a.* -a maji ya risasi. *Become livid with fear* (*rage, illness &c.*) geuka rangi, (sisimka) kwa hofu (hasira, ugonjwa &c.).

living, *n., a.,* **living-room,** *n.* taz. *live.*

lizard, *n.* (*common climbing*) mjusi, kijusi; (*burrowing*) guruguru, nguruguru; (*large, water*) kenge.

llama, *n.* mnyama kama kondoo mwenye shingo ndefu na manyoya marefu, wa *South America.*

lo, *int.* tazama! loo! kumbe! *Lo and behold!* fahamu! tahamaki!

load, *v.t.* (*a ship*) pakia, sheheni, tia shehena; (*a man*) twisha, chukuza; (*a gun*) shindilia, shamiri; (*heap up*) tia -ingi, lemeza. *He loaded him with favours,* alimtendea fadhili nyingi, alimtendea hisani nyingi. *Load with reproaches,* shutumu, kemea. — *n.* mzigo, mtumba; (*abundance*) wingi. *A load of sorrow,* huzuni nyingi. **loadstone,** *n.* sumaku, chuma cha magnetisi.

loaf, *n.* (*pl.* **loaves**) mkate.

loaf, *v.i.* pitisha wakati bila kufanya kazi, jikalia, kaakaa, jizungumza, susurika, zurura, zururika. **loafer,** *n.* mhuni, mtu awezaye kazi asitake kuifanya, mvivu, mtembezi.

loan, *n.* udongo mzito na mchanga pamoja.

loan, *n.* maazimo, mwazimo, karadha, ukopi, mkopo. *Give on loan,* karidhi, kopesha. *Get on loan,* kopa.

loathe, *v.t.* chukia kabisa, kirihi, zia. **loath**, *a.* *Be loath*, totaka, tokubali, toridhia, kataa. *He was loath to go*, hakutaka kwenda. **loathing**, *n.* machukio makuu, karaha. **loathsome**, *a.* -a kuchukiza mno, makuruhi.

loaves, *pl.* ya *loaf*.

lobby, *n.* sebule, ukumbi.

lobe, *n.* (*of ear*) ndewe; (*of other organ &c.*) kipande, sehemu.

lobster, *n.* kamba (wa bahari).

local, *a.* -a mahali maalum, -a mahali pale pale, -a mahali pamoja. **locality**, *n.* mahali, nchi, upande, janibu, mtaa; (*neighbourhood*) ujirani. **localize**, *v.t.* weka (zuilia) mahali maalum, tumia kwa mahali maalum. **locally**, *adv.* katika mahali (mtaa, upande &c.) maalum. **locate**, *v.t.* weka mahali, vumbua mahali pa.

loch, *n.* ziwa la maji (*Scotland*).

lock, *n.* (*of hair*) shungi, kishungi. **locks**, *n. plur.* nywele.

lock, *n.* (*of box*) kitasa; (*padlock*) kufuli; (*wooden*) komeo; (*of gun*) mtambo; (*of canal*) milango. *A deadlock*, mwisho, kikomo, pasipopitika, kusimama; (*great difficulty*) matata makuu, mgogoro. *Lock, stock and barrel*, -ote pia. — *v.t.* funga kwa *lock*; (*close up*) kaza, weka ndani; (*fasten together*) shikamanisha. **locker**, *n.* kasha lenye kufungwa na *lock*, kabati. **locket**, *n.* kibweta kidogo cha tunu. **lockjaw**, *n.* pepo punda. **locksmith**, *n.* fundi wa kufanyiza *lock*. **lock-up**, *n.* kifungo, gereza, korokoni, mahabusi.

locomotion, *n.* mwendo, nguvu ya kwenda. **locomotive**, *n.* gari la moshi, mashine. — *a.* -enye nguvu ya kwenda.

locum tenens, *n.* padre (daktari) afanyaye kazi kwa muda badala ya mwingine.

locust, *n.* nzige, maige; (*young*) funutu, tunutu, kimatu.

lode, *n.* mstari (uzi) wa madini ndani ya mawe. **lodestone**, *n.* = *loadstone* sumaku.

lodge, *v.i.* (*rest, remain*) tua, lala, kaa, shinda; (*stick*) kazwa, kwama, sakama; (*have hired lodgings*) kaa katika nyumba ya kupanga; — *v.t.* (*place*) weka, tia. *Lodge a complaint* (*against*), shtaki. — *n.* kibanda, nyumba ndogo; (*club-house*) nyumba ya chama. **lodgement, lodgment**, *n.* mahali pa kukaa; (*military*) mahali pa nguvu, boma, kituo; (*accumulation*) vipande vya kitu vilivyozuiwa vikakaa mahali, *e.g.* mferejini &c. **lodger**, *n.* mkaa katika nyumba ya kupanga, mpanga chumba. **lodging**, *n.* nyumba (chumba) ya kupanga; (*place to sleep*) mahali pa kulala, malalo. **lodging-house**, *n.* nyumba yenye vyumba vya kupanga. *Lodging-house keeper*, mwenyeji wa *lodging-house*.

loft, *n.* orofa ya juu kabisa. **lofty**, *a.* -a juu sana, -refu; (*noble*) bora, -ema sana, -a fahari; (*arrogant*) -a kiburi.

log, *n.* gogo, kishiku, kisiki, (*of ship*) batli. **log-book**, *n.* kitabu cha batli (chenye habari zote za safari ya merikebu, (meli) mwendo, majira &c.), tarehe. **log-cabin**, *n.* kibanda cha magogo. **loggerheads** (*Be at*) gombana, tetana.

logic, *n.* elimu ya kuwaza kwa akili halisi, elimu ya kujua elimu yenyewe ni nini, njia gani ya kuipata halisi. **logical**, *a.* -enye hoja au maneno ya akili, -enye kuonya hakika, -a *logic*. **logician**, *n.* mtu hodari kwa *logic*, mtu mwenye akili safi, mwenye kuthibitisha maneno yake.

loin, *n.* kiuno. *Gird up one's loins*, jifunga tayari. **loin-cloth**, *n.* shuka, nguo, doti.

loiter, *v.i.* sita, tanga, jikalia, fanya uzembe, fanya usiri, usirika, chezacheza, susurika, zurura, zururika. **loiterer**, *n.* mzembe, mvivu, mchezaji, mtangatanga.

loll, *v.i.* lala (kaa) kivivu, jikalia, tandawaa, gaagaa, jizungumza; — *v.t.* (*let hang*) tokeza kinywani (ulimi).

lone, lonely, lonesome, *a.* -a kukaa peke yake (yao &c.), -a pekee, -a ukiwa, pasipo watu. **loneliness,** *n.* kuwa peke yake (yao *&c.*), ukiwa, kujiona -kiwa, kitwea.

long, *a.* (*in space*) -refu, -enye urefu, -a kunyosha; (*in time*) -a wakati mwingi, -a siku (saa) nyingi; (*slow*) si -epesi, -a polepole, -a kuchosha; (*enduring*) -a kukaa, -a kudumu, -a aushi. *In the long run,* mwisho. *The long and short of it,* jambo lenyewe, asili ya maneno, maana halisi. *Long ago,* zamani sana. *Long* (*before, after &c.*) siku nyingi, muda mrefu (mbele ya, baada ya *&c.*). *Long measure,* kupima urefu. *A long time,* siku nyingi. *Be* (*stay*) *a long time,* kaa sana, kawia. — *v.i.* (*for*) -wa na tamaa (uchu, shauku), tamani sana, taka sana, ashiki, chunuka. — *adv.* wakati mwingi tangu zamani. *I have long known it,* nimeijua tangu zamani. *Long forgotten,* -liosahauliwa siku nyingi. **longbow,** *n.* upindi. *To draw the longbow,* piga chuku. **longcloth,** *n.* namna ya amerikani nzito. **longer,** *a.* -refu zaidi. *No longer, not any longer,* si zaidi, si tena, si tangu sasa. *He no longer loves me,* hanipendi tena, ameacha kunipenda. **longevity,** *n.* maisha mengi, uzee. **longheaded,** *a.* -enye busara. **longing,** *n.* tamaa, uchu, shauku, hawa, hamu, jadi, kwiu. **longitude,** *n.* urefu wa kuenda mahali fulani kwa mashariki au kwa magharibi tokea *meridian* ya *London,* longitudo. **long-lived,** *a.* -enye maisha mengi, -a aushi. **longshoreman,** *n.* mtu afanyaye kazi pwani. **long-sighted,** *a.* -enye kuona vyema mbali, si karibu. **long-standing,** *a.* -a siku nyingi, -a tangu siku nyingi. **long-suffering,** *a.* -vumilivu, -stahimilivu, -pole. — *n.* uvumilivu, ustahimilivu, saburi. **long-winded,** *a.* -a maneno mengi, -enye domo.

loofah, *n.* dodoki; (*tree*) mdodoki.

look, *v.i.* tazama, elekeza (tupa) jicho, angalia, ona; (*appear*) onekana -wa kama, fanana na; (*face*) elekea, elekeana na, kabili; (*show by the face*) -wa na uso wa, onyesha kwa uso. *Look as if,* -wa kama, elekea, kabili. *It looks as if it would rain,* yataka kunya mvua. *Look alive,* amka, fanya hima. *Look at,* tazama, angalia; (*consider*) fikiri, fahamu. *Look after,* angalia, tunza; (*investigate*) tafuta habari ya. *He has much to look after,* ana maangalizi mengi. *Look for,* tafuta, peleleza, duhushi, londea, chungua; (*expect*) tazamia, tumainia. *Look down on,* dharau, tweza, nyarafu. *Look forward to,* tazamia kwa furaha. *Look like,* fanana na, landa, -wa mfano wa, -wa kama, kabili. *It looks like rain,* inakabili mvua. *Look out,* tafuta; (*attend*) -wa macho, jihadhari, angalia. *Look out!* simile! jihadhari! habedari! jiponye! *Look on,* dhani, dhania, hesabu; (*be spectator*) simama karibu, hudhuria. *Look to,* angalia, tunza; (*hope in*) tarajia, tumainia. *Look through,* penyeza jicho; (*examine*) chungulia, tafutia. *Look up,* tazama juu, inua macho; (*learn*) jifunza, tafuta habari ya; (*visit*) zuru, amkia. *His affairs are looking up,* hayajambo mambo yake, anaondokea. *Look up to,* heshimu, ondokea, stahi. *Look about, or round,* tupa jicho huko na huko, tazama pote, -wa macho, fanya bidii. — *n.* nadhari tazamo; (*appearance*) sura, umbo, hali, uso. *Things have a bad look,* mambo yanaonekana kama si mazuri. *Good looks,* uso mzuri, sura ya kupendeza. *Look of envy,* kijicho. **looker-on,** *n.* mwenye kuona (kutazama) jambo, ila asiingie. **looking-glass,** *n.* kioo (cha kujitazamia). **look-out,** *n.* mlinzi, mpelelezi; (*prospect*) mambo ya mbele, yatakayokuwa; (*view*) mandhari. *It is your look-out,* juu yako, kazi yako. *Keep a good look-out,* kaa macho, angalia sana, jihadhari sana.

loom, (1) *n.* kitanda cha mfumi, mtandi.

loom, (2) *v.i.* onekana kama -kubwa (kama -a kutisha), onekana kama kivuli kwa taratibu.

loop, *n.* kitanzi; (*of rope used like rowlock or handle of box &c.*) kishwara, duara. — *v.t.* piga kitanzi; — *v.i.* fanya duara, pinda na kufanya duara.

loophole, *n.* kitundu cha kupenyezea bunduki; (*way of escape*) mlango, pa kukimbia, njia ya kuokoka, budi.

loose, *a.* (*unfastened*) -liofunguka, -liofunuka, -a kulegalega, sabili, -legevu, -lioachwa, -lioachiwa; (*not tight*) -siokazwa, -a kupwaya; (*of abrics*) -embamba, si -nene; (*friable*) tifutifu; (*irregular, inexact*) si halisi, si -ema, si -a kawaida, si -a taratibu; (*profligate*) -potovu, -baya; (*of bowels*) -a kuenenda, -a kuendesha, -a kuhara. **loose, loosen,** *v.t.* fungua, fungulia, feleti, fumua, bandua, legeza, acha, sabili, achia, fyatua. *Loose off a gun* (*arrow*) piga bunduki (upindi). *Let loose* = *loose. Break loose,* jifungua, jitoa, jipoteza. *Play fast and loose,* fanya upuzi, danganya, fanya werevu. **looseness,** *n.* ulegevu, upotovu *&c.*

loot, *v.t.* teka, teka nyara. — *n.* mateka, nyara.

lop, *v.t.* pogoa, punguza (kata, fyeka) matawi, chenga. **lop-eared,** *a.* -enye masikio yanayoning'inia. **lop-sided,** *a.* -a kwenda upande, si sawa, mshazari, chopi.

loquacious, *a.* -enye domo, -piga domo, -enye maneno mengi, -semaji, -limi. **loquacity,** *n.* mapayo, usemaji, domo.

lord, *n.* (jina la heshima la mtu mwenye cheo kikuu fulani cha kiingereza), mtawala, mkuu, hababi, maulana, bwana, seyidi (*—but note that these last two words are often equivalent to the English mister*); (*God*) Mungu, Mwenyezi Mungu, Mola, Allah (*many Christian bodies use* bwana *for God and Jesus Christ also, but see note above*). *Lord's day,* Jumapili, siku iliyowekwa wakf kwa ibada ya Mungu. *Lord's Supper,* Ushirika Mtakatifu. *Lord Bishop,* askofu. *House of Lords,* baraza ya wakuu wa cheo na maaskofu Uingereza; (*place*) chumba cha kubarizia wakuu. **lordly,** *a.* -a heshima, -a fahari; (*arrogant*) -a kupiga ubwana, -a kiburi. **lordship,** *n.* hali, milki ya *Lord. Your Lordship,* bwana wangu, seyidi yangu.

lore, *n.* elimu, maarifa.

lose, *v.t.* (*p.t.* na *pf.t.* **lost**) potewa na, twaliwa, poteza, angamiza, kosa kupata, kosa kusikia; — *v.i.* (*suffer loss*) pata hasara, punguka; (*be defeated*) shindwa. *I have lost a knife,* kisu kimenipotea. *Lose ground,* anza kushindwa (kurudishwa, kupitiwa). *Lose heart,* legea, kata tamaa. *Lose one's heart to,* shikwa na upendo wa (shauku ya), penda sana, ashiki. *Lose one's senses,* rukwa na akili, zimia roho, zirai, ghumia. *Lose one's head,* shikwa na fadhaa, (na bumbuazi, na wasiwasi). *Lose strength,* via, legea, haribika, fifia, dhoofika. *Lose a battle,* shindwa vitani. *I shall lose no time in doing it,* nitaifanya sasa hivi. **losing,** *a.* -a hasara, -a kushindwa. **losings,** *n.* hasara. **loss,** *n.* hasara, msiba, maangamizi, kupotea, kipunguo. *We retired without loss of life,* tulirudi bila mtu kuuawa (kupotea). **lost,** *a.* (*p.t.* ya *lose*). *Be lost,* potea, angamia, isha, hiliki, ghibu. *I am lost,* nimepotea, nimeangamia. *All is lost,* imekwisha, nimeshindwa. *Be lost in astonishment* (*surprise, amazement*), shangaa, maka, staajabu, shikwa na mshangao, tunduwaa, pumbaa. *Be lost in thought* (*meditation &c.*), -wa na mawazo mengi, -wa katika fikira. *Lost in shame,* -pujufu, pasipo haya.

lot, *n.* kura; (*portion*) sehemu, katiba, ajali; (*collection heap*) fungu, jamii; (*quantity*) wingi. *In a lot,* shelabela, jamii, jumla. *Cast lots,* piga kura. *A lot of people* (*lots of*), watu wengi, umati wa watu. **lottery,** *n.* mchezo wa bahati, bahati nasibu; (*risk*) bahati, hatari.

loth, *a.* taz. *loath.*

lotion, *n.* dawa ya kuoshea, ya kutia vidonda (ngozi *&c.*).

lottery, *n.* taz. *lot.*

lotus, *n.* yungiyungi (la kimisri, la kihindi).

loud, *a.* -enye sauti kuu, -a makelele, -a kishindo, -a nguvu; (*of colour &c.*) -a kutazamisha, -a rangi nyingi. *A loud report,* shindo kubwa. *Speak loud,* sema sana, nena kikelele. **loudly,** *adv.* kwa makelele, kwa kishindo.

lounge, *v.i.* kaa (lala) kivivu, jikalia, tandawaa, jiegemeza; (*stroll about*) tembea (zunguka) kivivu, susurika, zurura, zururika. — *n.* chumba cha kukaa na kuzungumza, kiti cha kukalia na kupumzika, kitanda. *Lounge suit,* nguo za kizungu za kuvaa mchana.

louse, *n.* (*pl.* **lice**) (*head louse, chicken louse*) utitiri; (*body louse*) chawa.

lout, *n.* mtu asiye na adabu, mjinga, baradhuli.

love, *n.* upendo, pendo, upendano, mapenzi, shauku, huba; (*desire*) tamaa, uchu, ashiki, hawa, hamu; (*courtship*) uchumba; (*sympathy*) huruma, wema; (*beloved*) kipenzi, halili, muhebi, tiba. *Be in love,* penda mwanamke (mwanamume), -wa na mchumba, taka kuoa mwanamke. *Fall in love,* shikwa na. upendo (huba), ashiki, pata mchumba. *Make love to,* pendeleza, bembeleza. *A labour of love,* kazi bure (pasipo faida, kwa ajili ya kupenda tu). — *v.t.* penda, taka, tamani, pendana, -wa na mahaba, hebu, -wa na ashiki, chunuka na. **lovable,** *a.* -a kupendwa, -a kupendeza. **loveliness,** *n.* uzuri. **lovely,** *a.* -zuri sana, -a kupendeza. **lover,** *n.* mchumba (mwanamume). **loving,** *a.* -a kupenda, -enye moyo wa kupenda sana. **loving-kindness,** *n.* wema, huruma, upendo, fadhili, mapenzi.

low, (1) *v.i.* lia (kama ng'ombe). **lowing,** *n.* mlio (wa ng'ombe).

low, (2) *a.* -a chini; (*short*) fupi; (*of price, number &c.*) -dogo; (*of sound*) -nene; (*of condition &c.*) -nyonge, -baya, -a kadiri; (*deficient*) -dogo; (*cheap*) rahisi. *Low life,* maisha manyonge, watu wabaya. *Low principles,* tabia mbaya. *Lie low,* kaa kimya (bila kufanya neno). *Be laid low,* uawa. *Low Church,* madhehebu mojawapo ya Kanisa la kiingereza. *Of the lowest kind,* duni kabisa, hafifu kabisa, -a kwisha. — *adv.* chini; (*cheaply*) rahisi; (*of sound*) kwa sauti ndogo, -pole. **lower,** *a.* -a chini zaidi, -a chini *&c.* taz. *low. The lower classes,* watu wadogo, walio watu tu. — *v.t.* shusha, telemsha, inamisha; (*bucket &c.*) tumbukiza, puliza; (*sail*) tua; (*lessen*) punguza; (*abase*) dhili, adhiri, tusha; (*cheapen*) rahisisha; (*sky*) tanda, fanya mawingu; (*face*) kunjamana, toa ukali. **lowland,** *n.* nchi ya chini (pana na sawa), bonde. **lowliness,** *n.* unyenyekevu. **lowly,** *a.* -nyenyekevu, si -enye kiburi, -dogo. **low-spirited,** *a.* -a huzuni, -a kukata tamaa, -a roho nzito. **low-tide,** *n.*, **low-water,** *n.* maji ya kupwa, maji mafu.

lowing, *n.* taz. *low* (1).

lowland, *n.*, **lowliness,** *n.*, **lowly,** *a.*, **low-spirited,** *a.*, **low-tide,** *n.*, **low-water,** *n.* taz. *low* (2).

loyal, *a.* -aminifu, -tiifu, amini, -a kudumia, -a kushika kwa moyo. **loyalist,** *n.* mwaminifu kwa mfalme. **loyalty,** *n.* uaminifu, utii.

lozenge, *n.* kidonge cha sukari na dawa cha kufyonza, peremendi; umbo lenye pembe nne, mfano wa ng'anda ya uru ya karata za kuchezea.

L. s. d. = *pounds, shillings, pence.*

Ltd. = *limited.*

lubber, *n.* mjinga, mtu asiye ustadi wa kazi.

lubricate, *v.t.* tia mafuta, tia utelezi, lainisha (legeza) kwa mafuta. **lubricant,** *n.* mafuta.

lucerne, *n.* mmea wenye majani matatu matatu kila kikonyo, majani yake yafaa sana kwa chakula cha ng'ombe.

lucid, *a.* -a kufahamika kwa urahisi, wazi, dhahiri, -a kuelea rahisi, -a akili; (*transparent*) -angavu, -eupe. **lucidity,** *n.* wangavu, weupe; (*in style*) udhahiri, urahisi wa kufahamika, nahau.

Lucifer, *n.* Shetani, ibilisi; (*star*) nyota ya asubuhi; (*match*) kiberiti.

luck, *n.* bahati, nasibu, sudi; (*fate*) Mungu; (*good luck*) heri, neema, jaha, ndege njema, futahi, ghanima, sudi njema. *Good luck to you,* kwa heri, bashiri heri. *He is in good luck,* ana bahati nzuri, amependelewa, ameneemeka. *Bad luck,* shari, ndege mbaya, nuhusi. **luckless,** *a.* -a bahati mbaya, -a shari. **lucky,** *a.* -a bahati, -a bahati njema, -a heri. *A lucky find,* dafina.

lucre, *n.* faida, fedha, mali. *Filthy lucre,* faida iliyopatikana kwa njia mbaya. **lucrative,** *a.* -a faida nyingi, -a kuleta faida, -enye faida.

lucubration, *n.* kazi ya kusoma kwa bidii usiku.

ludicrous, *a.* -a kuchekesha, -puzi, -pumbavu, -a mzaha.

luff, *v.i.* bisha.

lug, *v.t.* kokota, vuta, burura, buruta.

luggage, *n.* vyombo, mizigo, vikorokoro, takataka.

lugger, *n.* chombo cha kizungu cha matanga.

lugubrious, *a.* -a huzuni, -zito.

lukewarm, *a.* -a uvuguvugu, fufutende, -a moto kidogo, si baridi, si -enye baridi. *Be lukewarm,* vuvuwaa. **lukewarmness,** *n.* uvuguvugu, utepetevu.

lull, *v.t.* tuliza, tia usingizi, tumbuiza. — *n.* kikomo cha kitambo, muda wa kutulia. **lullaby,** *n.* utumbuizo, kitumbuizo.

lumbago, *n.* maumivu ya viunoni, baridi viunoni. **lumbar,** *a.* -a viuno.

lumber, (1) *n.* takataka; (*timber*) mti, mbao, magogo. — *v.t.* jaza na vyombo, takataka &c.

lumber, (2) *v.i.* enda kwa shida (kwa sababu -zito), enda kwa kishindo. **lumbering,** *a.* -a mwendo mzito, -a kwenda kwa shida na kishindo (kwa sababu -zito), -a kujikokota.

luminary, *n.* mwezi, jua, nyota; (*person*) mtu mashuhuri. **luminous,** *a.* -a kung'aa; (*clear*) dhahiri, wazi, -a kufahamika kwa urahisi, -a kuelea vizuri.

lump, *n.* kitumba, bonge, fungu, fumba; (*small*) kibonge, kidonge, kitonge; (*of meat*) chinyango, kinofu; (*mass*) jamii, jumla. *Lumps caused by a sting &c.,* marugurugu. *In a lump,* shelabela, kwa jumla, jamii, kititi. *A lump sum,* fedha (ya kulipia vitu vingi pamoja, badala ya kila kitu peke yake). —*v.t.* (*together*) tia pamoja, changanya, jumlisha; — *v.i.* changamana, changanyika. **lumpy,** *a.* -a vibumba, -a vidonge, kinundunundu, -liobudaa.

lunacy, *n.* wazimu, kichaa. **lunatic,** *n.* mwenye wazimu (kichaa), mwenda wazimu, mkichaa.

lunar, *a.* -a mwezi.

lunatic, *n.* taz. *lunacy.*

lunch, luncheon, *n.* chakula cha adhuhuri.

lung, *n.* pafu, buhumu, pumu; (*of animal*) yavuyavu.

lunge, *n.* pigo la ghafula (la upanga, la kuchoma). — *v.t.* (*at*) piga ghafula ili kuchoma.

lurch, (1) *n.* (*of a ship*) mrama, mwendo wa kulala upande ghafula; (*stagger*) kupepesuka, kupeperuka. — *v.i.* lala upande ghafula, fanya mrama, enda mrama, peperuka, pepesuka.

lurch, (2) *n. Leave in the lurch,* acha pasipo msaada, acha katika shida.

lurcher, *n.* namna ya mbwa wa kuwinda.

lure, *v.t.* vuta, shawishi, tega. — *n.*

(*bait*) chambo; (*trap*) mtego; (*attraction*) mvuto, kishawishi.

lurid, *a.* -a kung'aa, -a rangi nyingi, -a kutia hofu, -a kuogofya, -a kutisha.

lurk, *v.i.* jificha, jibanza, otea.

luscious, *a.* -tamu sana.

lush, *a.* (majani) -bichi sana, -enye maji maji, -a kusitawi sana.

lust, *n.* tamaa mbaya, ngoa, ashiki, hawa, uzinifu, ukware. **lustful,** *a.* -a tamaa nyingi, -enye ashiki nyingi, -kware. **lustily,** *adv.* kwa nguvu. **lusty,** *a.* -a nguvu, -a bidii, hodari, -kuza.

lustration, *n.* utakaso.

lustre, *n.* mng'aro, mwanga, nuru, weupe, wangavu; (*glory, honour*) sifa, heshima, fahari. **lustrous,** *a.* -a kung'aa.

lusty, *a.* taz. *lust.*

lute, *n.* zeze, udi, kinubi.

Lutheran, *a.* -a *Luther,* -a kufuata mafundisho ya *Luther.* — *n.* mfuasi wa mafundisho ya *Luther.*

luxuriant, *a.* -a kuota sana, -a kusitawi sana, -a kuzaa sana, tele, -zuri. **luxuriance,** *n.* usitawi, wingi wa uzazi, wingi. **luxurious,** *a.* -a kupenda anasa, -a kujipendeza, -zuri sana, -a anasa. **luxury,** *n.* anasa, vitu vingi, hali ya ukwasi, utajiri, wingi wa mali; (*rarity*) tunu.

lying, *a.* taz. *lie* (1).

lying-in, *n.* taz. *lie* (2).

lymph, *n.* maji ya mwilini kama damu nyeupe. **lymphatic,** *a.* -a *lymph.*

lynch, *v.t.* ua bila hukumu ya sheria, *e.g. The crowd lynched him,* kundi la watu walimwua (kwa ghadhabu, kulipiza kisasi &c.).

lynx, *n.* mnyama kama paka mwitu mwenye macho makali sana. **lynx-eyed,** *a.* -enye macho makali sana, -a kuona sana, -chungulizi.

lyre, *n.* kinubi, udi, zeze. **lyric,** *n.* mashairi ya kinubi, ya furaha au huzuni.

M

M. herufi ya kirumi, maana yake, elfu moja.

ma'am, *n.* = **madam,** bibi. *Yes ma'am,* (kuitika) lebeka bibi.

macadamize, *v.t.* fanya njia (barabara) ya kokoto laini na sawa. *Macadamized road,* njia ya baraste, njia ya kokoto zilizogandamizwa mpaka kuwa laini na sawa.

macaroni, *n.* tambi, unga wa ngano uliofanyizwa kama mfano wa chango.

mace, (1) *n.* (*spice*) basibasi.

mace, (2) *n.* (*club*) rungu; alama ya cheo cha mtu.

macerate, *v.t.* fanya laini (kwa kulowesha majini), dhoofisha.

machete, *n.* panga, mundu.

Machiavellian, *a.* -erevu, -danganyifu.

machine, *n.* (*instrument*) chombo, samani, ala; (*mill*) kinu; (*sewing*) cherehani; (*in general*) mashine, mtambo. **machination,** *n.* shauri ovu, hila. **machine-gun,** *n.* bombom. **machinery,** *n.* vyombo, vinu, mashine; mtambo; (*arrangements*) matengenezo, madaraka. **machinist**, *n.* fundi wa *machine*.

mackerel, *n.* namna ya samaki.

mackintosh, *n.* koti la mvua.

mad, *a.* -enye wazimu; (*angry*) -a kukasirika sana, -enye kiruu. *Go mad*, shikwa na wazimu, rukwa na akili. **madcap**, *n.* mjasiri. **madden** *v.t.* tia wazimu, rusha akili, kasirisha sana. **mad-house**, *n.* nyumba ya kufungia wenye wazimu. **madman**, *n.* mwenye wazimu, majununi. **madness**, *n.* wazimu, kupotewa na akili, ujinga mkuu, pepo, shetani, mahoka.

Madagascar, *n.* Buki, Bukini.

madam, *n.* bibi, bibi mkubwa, bi mkubwa.

madcap, *n.*, **madden**, *v.* taz. *mad*.

madder, *n.* mmea fulani unaotumika kufanyia rangi nyekundu.

made, *p.t.* na *pf.t.* ya *make*.

mad-house, *n.*, **madness**, taz. *mad*.

Madeira, *n.* namna ya divai tamu.

Madonna, *n.* Bikira Mariamu mama wa Yesu Kristo au sanamu au picha yake.

madrigal, *n.* wimbo mdogo mzuri, wimbo wa sauti tatu au zaidi.

maelstrom, *n.* machafuko, fujo, msukosuko; (*eddy*) kizingia cha maji.

Magadoxa, *n.* Mogadishu, Mkuchyo.

magazine, *n.* nyumba ya kuwekea bidhaa, bohari, ghala, nyumba ya kuwekea baruti; (*book*) kitabu chenye habari au hadithi kitolewacho mara kwa mara, kama gazeti; (*of rifle*) kitasa cha bunduki.

magenta, *n.* rangi kama zambarau nyekundu.

maggot, *n.* funza, buu.

magic, *n.* (*white*) uganga; (*black*) uchawi, ulozi, usihiri, uramali; (*for finding offender*) mburuga; (*conjuring*) mwujiza, mzungu, kiinimacho. **magic, magical**, *a.* -a *magic*, ajabu, -a mwujiza. *Magic lantern*, taa ya kuangazia picha katika ukuta au nguo iliyotandwa. **magician**, *n.* mchawi, mlozi.

magistrate, *n.* jaji, hakimu, mwamuzi; (*Moslem*) kadhi. **magisterial**, *a.* -a jaji *&c.*, (*weighty*) -a nguvu, -kali. **magistracy**, *n.* jamii au kazi ya majaji *&c.*

magnanimous, *a.* -ema, -adilifu, -enye moyo mkuu, -enye huruma (haki) -nyofu. **magnanimity**, *n.* utu mwema, moyo mkuu, maadili, unyofu, huruma, haki.

magnate, *n.* tajiri mkuu.

magnesia(*sulphate of*), *n.* chumvi ya haluli.

magnet, *n.* magnetisi, sumaku, sindano ya dira, chuma chenye nguvu ya kujivutia vipande vingine vya chuma. **magnetic**, *a.* -a magnetisi, -enye nguvu ya kuvuta. **magnetism**, *n.* nguvu ya magnetisi (ya sumaku); (*power*) nguvu ya kuvuta.

magnetize, *v.t.* tia nguvu ya magnetisi. **magneto**, *n.* mashine ya umeme (elektrisiti) iwashayo mvuke wa petroli katika motakaa *&c.*

magnify, *v.t.* tukuza, adhimisha, adhimu, ongeza, sifu, kuza. **Magnificat**, *n.* wimbo wa Bikira Mariamu Mtakatifu unaoanza kwa maneno '*My soul doth magnify the Lord*'. **magnificence**, *n.* utukufu, uzuri, fahari, adhama. **magnificent**, *a.* -zuri (-kubwa, -kirimu) kabisa, -tukufu, -adhimu. **magniloquent**, *a.* -a maneno makuu, -a maneno ya fahari, -piga domo. **magnitude**, *n.* (*size*) ukubwa, cheo; (*greatness*) ukubwa, ubora, ukuu. **magnum**, *n.* chupa kubwa yenye kuweka *quart* mbili.

magpie, *n.* ndege kama kunguru.

mahogany, *n.* mkangazi, mbambakofi, namna ya mti mwekundu.

Mahometan, *a.* taz. *Muhammedan*.

maid, maiden, *n.* mwanamwali, mwali, bikira; (*young women*) kijana mwanamke; (*house servant*) mtumishi wa kike; (*spinster*) mwanamke asiyeolewa bado. **maiden**, *a.* -a kike (asiyeolewa bado); (*first, new*) -a kwanza, -pya, -bichi. **maidenhood**, *n.* ujana (wa mwanamke); (*vir-*

ginity) ubikira, kizinda. **maiden-name**, *n.* jina la mwanamke kabla hajaolewa. **maidservant**, *n.* mtumishi wa kike.

mail, (1) *n.* (*armour*) deraya, nguo ya pete za chuma, kisibau cha chuma cha kuvaa vitani.

mail, (2) *n.* barua za posta; (*system*) posta; (*boat*) meli; (*runner*) tarishi. — *v.t.* peleka kwa posta. **mail-bag**, *n.* mfuko wa barua za posta.

maim, *v.t.* haribu kiungo (mguu, mkono, jicho *&c.*) cha mtu; vunja, umbua, kasiri. **maimed**, *a.* -a kilema, kiwete.

main, *n.* (katika mashairi) bahari. *Water (sewage) main*, bomba (mfereji) kubwa. *Electric main*, uzi mkubwa unaoleta umeme (elektrisiti) nyumbani. *With might and main*, kwa bidii (nguvu) nyingi. *In the main*, zaidi, aghalabu, hasa, kwa vingi, ila kidogo tu. — *a.* -kubwa, -kuu, -a kwanza, -a maana. *Main road*, njia kuu, barabara. *By main force*, kwa nguvu tupu, kwa nguvu, kwa jeuri. **mainland**, *n.* bara, nchi kuu; (*opposite Zanzibar*) mrima. **mainspring**, *n.* kamani, mtambo wa kuendesha saa (wa kupigisha bunduki *&c.*); (*chief cause*) mwanzo, sababu halisi. **mainstay**, *n.* (*support*) msaada, nguzo, tegemeo.

maintain, *v.t.* (*keep, hold*) shika, kaa katika; (*preserve*) dumisha, hifadhi, shindisha, kaza; (*support*) lisha, kimu, -pa riziki, chukua, tegemeza, gharimia; (*assert*) sema, thibitisha, shikilia. **maintenance**, *n.* tegemezo, uthabiti, msaada, teteo; (*means of living*) posho, cha kuponea, nafuu, riziki, chakula, masurufu.

maize, *n.* (*plant and fruit*) muhindi; (*grain*) mahindi; (*cob*) gunzi, kigunzi, kibunzi; (*parched*) bisi; (*flour*) unga wa mahindi.

majesty, *n.* enzi, ezi, utukufu, adhama, fahari. *Your Majesty*, (namna ya kusema na mfalme). **majestic**, *a.* -enye enzi, -adhimu, -tukufu.

major, *a.* -kubwa, -ingi, zaidi ya nusu. — *n.* afisa wa kiaskari kati ya *captain* na *lieutenant-colonel*. **major-domo**, *n.* mtumishi mkuu wa nyumba kubwa. **majority**, wingi, zaidi ya nusu; (*full age*) umri wa miaka ishirini na mmoja.

make, *v.t.* (*p.t. and pf.t.* **made**) fanya, fanyiza; (*create*) umba, huluku; (*earn &c.*) pata, chuma; (*compel*) lazimisha, shurutisha; (*become*) -wa, pata kuwa; (*construct*) fanyiza, buni; (*a ship*) unda; (*a house*) jenga; (*a drawing*) andika, chora, piga; (*a story*) tunga, buni; (*be, form*) -wa, -wamo; (*understand*) fahamu, ona; (*reach*) fika; (*cause to be*) *by terminations in* -eza, -iza, -esha, -isha, -sha, -za, -ya, *e.g. make thin*, kondesha; *make great*, kuza; *make sick*, tapisha; *make well*, ponya, *&c.* *Make a bed*, tandika kitanda. *Make account of*, heshimu, tukuza. *Make away with*, tupa, poteza, ua, haribu. *Make believe*, *Make as if*, jifanya, jisingizia. *Make at*, endea. *Make bold*, thubutu, jasiria. *Make choice of*, chagua, hiari. *Make fast*, kaza, funga. *Make for*, shika njia kuenda, endea, elekea. *Make free with*, tumia upendavyo pasipo ruhusa, poteza, tapanya, fuja. *Make good*, rudisha, lipa, tengeneza, thibitisha. *Make light of (little of)*, dharau. *Make headway*, pata nguvu, endelea. *Make money*, pata fedha, chuma mali, jitajirisha. *Make merry*, furahi. *Make much of (honour)*, heshimu, dhani -kubwa; (*understand*) fahamu vema. *Make off*, ondoka, kimbia, puruka. *Make out*, fahamu; (*prove*) thubutisha. *Make over*, toa, pa, pisha, lipa; (*transfer property &c.*) sihia. *Make sail*, tweka, ondoka. *Make sure*, pata hakika, hakikisha, yakinisha. *Make up*, fanya, fanyiza, tengeneza, buni, tunga; (*complete*) timiza, maliza; (*compensate*) lipa. *Make up one's mind*, kaza shauri, nia, kusudia, azimu. *Make up a quarrel*, patana, tulia. *Make up for*, lipa sawa, -wa sawa, komboa. *Make up to*, jipendekeza kwa, rairai. **make**, *n*. umbo, sura, namna, aina. **maker**, *n*. muumba, mfanya, fundi. **makeshift**, *n*. badala, kitu kinachotumika kwa sababu kitu chenyewe (hasa) hakipo (hakipatikani). **make-up**, *n*. rangi na unga wa kupakaa uso unaotumika na wanawake wengine na *actors*. **make-weight**, *n*. kitu kisicho na maana, cha bure, kidogo tu (cha kutimiza hesabu, uzito &c.).

malachite, *n*. namna ya jiwe lenye rangi ya majani.

maladministration, *n*. uongozi mbaya, kutawala vibaya.

malady, *n*. ugonjwa, uele, maradhi.

malaria, *n*. homa iletwayo na namna ya mbu.

malapert, *a*. -juvi, -fidhuli, -safihi, -enye macho makavu.

malcontent, *a*. -sioridhika, -a chuki; (*rebellious*) -asi, -kaidi.

male, *a*. -ume, dume, -a kiume. — *n*. mume, dume; (*man*) mwanamume.

malediction, *n*. laana, matukano, maapizo.

malefactor, *n*. mfanya maovu, mwovu (*e.g.* mwizi, mwuaji &c.).

malevolence, *n*. nia ovu, ukorofi, chuki. **malevolent**, *a*. -enye nia ovu, -baya, -korofi, habithi.

malformation, *n*. kombo, kipunguo, kilema, kiwete.

malice, *n*. uovu, ukorofi, kijicho, nia ya kudhuru wengine. **malicious**, *a*. -ovu, -korofi, -enye nia ya kudhuru wengine, habithi.

malign, *a*. -ovu, -a nia mbaya, -a kudhuru; (*unpropitious*) -a kisirani, -a ndege mbaya, -a shari. — *v.t.* singizia, sengenya, shtaki uwongo, tweza, vunja, heshima (jina). **malignant**, *a*. -ovu, -enye nia mbaya, -a kudhuru, -enye chuki nyingi, -a shari. *Malignant disease*, ugonjwa unaoelekea kuleta kufa. **malignity**, *n*. uovu, ubaya, chuki.

malinger, *v.i.* jisingizia ugonjwa. **malingerer**, *n*. ajisingiziaye ugonjwa.

mallard, *n*. bata wa mwitu.

malleable, *a*. -a kufulika, -a kufulikana, -a kufanyika -embamba au -enye umbo jingine kwa kupigwa na nyundo, *e.g.* dhahabu; (*of character*) -epesi kuongozwa, -tiifu, -sikivu. **malleability**, *n*. hali au tabia ya kuwa *malleable*.

mallet, *n*. nyundo (ya mti).

malnutrition, *n*. kutopata chakula cha kutosha au chakula cha kufaa.

malodorous, *a*. -a kunuka vibaya, -a kuvunda, -enye harufu mbaya.

malpractice, *n*. tendo baya, mwenendo mbaya.

malt, *n*. kimea (cha pombe &c.).

maltreat, *v.t.* tendea mabaya (jeuri, udhalimu &c.), dhulumu, onea. **maltreatment**, *n*. udhalimu, kutenda (kutendewa) mabaya &c.

malversation, *n*. matumizi mabaya, kupoteza mali (amana).

mamma, *n*. mama.

mammal, *n*. mnyama anyonyeshaye watoto wake. **mammalia**, *n*. jamii ya wanyama wanyonyeshao watoto wao.

mammon, *n*. mali utajiri.

mammoth, *n*. tembo wa kikale. — *a*. -kubwa mno.

man, *n*. (*pl.* **men**), (*male*) mwanamume; (*human being*) mwanadamu, binadamu; (*individual, person*) mtu; (*hero*) mtu wa kiume, dume, simba, fahali; (*old*) mzee; (*white*) Mzungu; (*young*) kijana, mvulana; (*servant*) mtumishi, boi; (*husband*) mume. *To a man*, wote pia. *Play the man*, tenda kiume. *The inner man*, tumbo. — *v.t.* tia watu, pakia baharia, wekea askari. **man-at-arms**, *n*. askari. **man-eater**, *n*. mlaji watu, mnyama (simba) alaye watu. **manful**, *a*. hodari, -a kiume. **manfully**, *adv*. kwa kiume, hodari. **manhood**, *n*. utu uzima (wa mwanamume); (*manliness*) moyo mkuu, uhodari, moyo wa kiume. **mankind**, *n*. watu, wanadamu, jamii ya wanadamu, walimwengu. **manliness**, *n*. tabia ya kiume, uhodari, ushujaa, utu mume. **manly,** *a.* -a kiume, hodari, bora. **man-of-war,** *n.* manowari. **manslaughter,** *n.* kuua mtu, mauaji.

manacle, *n.* pingu ya mikono.

manage, *v.t.* (*direct, arrange*) amuru, simamia, tengeneza, ongoza; (*control*) tawala, tiisha; (*influence*) vuta; (*transact*) fanya shughuli; (*be in charge of*) tunza; — *v.i.* (*effect*) fanya, amili, pata, faulu. *I can manage* (*do by myself*) najiweza. **manageable,** *a.* -liowezekana, -a kadiri; (*tractable*) -a kutii, -tiifu, -sikivu, -a kuonyeka, -a kuongoka, -a kutumika. **management,** *n.* usimamizi, uongozi, maongozi, matengenezo, madaraka, matumizi; (*skill*) werevu, shauri la akili. *The management,* wakuu. **manager,** *n.* msimamizi, mwongozi, mkubwa.

man-at-arms, *n.* taz. *man.*

manatee, *n.* nguva.

mandarin, *n.* mtu wa serikali wa *China*; (*orange*) chenza; (*smaller kind*) kangaja.

mandate, *n.* amri, agizo, hukumu; (*to act for another*) uwakili; (*by the League of Nations*) amri (mamlaka, nguvu) iliyopewa nchi kwa *League of Nations* (Ushirika wa Mataifa) kutawala nchi fulani. **mandatary, mandatory,** *n.* mtu (nchi) aliyepewa amri (agizo, mamlaka, uwakili).

mandible, *n.* utaya; (*of birds &c.*) mdomo.

mandolin(e), *n.* namna ya zeze (udi, gambusi, kinubi).

mandrake, *n.* mmea unaofanyizwa dawa kama afyuni au bangi.

mandrill, *n.* namna ya nyani mkubwa wa *West Africa.*

mane, *n.* manyoya ya shingoni (mwa mnyama kama farasi na simba), nywele za singa.

man-eater, *n.*, **manful,** *a.*, **manfully,** *adv.* taz. *man.*

manganese, *n.* namna ya madini nyeusi inayotumika katika kufanyiza kioo.

mange, *n.*, ugonjwa kama upele wa wanyama. **mangy,** *a.* -enye ugonjwa wa *mange*; (*bad &c.*) -baya, hafifu, -nyonge.

mangel-wurzel, *n.* mboga kidogo kama kiazi kikuu; chakula cha ng'ombe.

manger, *n.* hori, chombo (sanduku) cha kuwekea chakula cha ng'ombe, farasi *&c.*

mangle, (1) *n.* chombo chenye magogo ya mviringo cha kukamulia na kulainishia nguo, guruto. — *v.t.* guruta, kamua kwa *mangle.*

mangle, (2) *v.t.* rarua, tatua, pasua; (*spoil*) haribu, potoa.

mango, *n.* (*tree*) mwembe; (*fruit*) embe; (*large*) embe dodo, dodo.

mangrove, *n.* mkandaa, mkoko, msindi, mchu.

mangy, *a.* taz. *mange.*

manhood, *n.* taz. *man.*

mania, *n.* wazimu shetani; (*great interest*) moyo wa kupenda sana. *He has a mania for dancing,* apenda sana kucheza. **maniac,** *n.* mwenye (mwenda) wazimu. **maniacal,** *a.* -a wazimu, kama wazimu, -a shetani.

manifest, *a.* dhahiri, wazi, baini, -bayana. — *v.t.* onyesha, toa, toa wazi, dhihirisha; — *v.i.* (*appear &c.*) onekana, jitokeza, tokea. **manifestation,** *n.* onyesho, ufunuo, kutoa wazi. **manifesto,** *n.* hati ya kutangaza habari.

manifold, *a.* -ingi, -a namna nyingi, -a mara nyingi. — *v.t.* fanya nakili nyingi.

manikin, *n.* kibeti, kijitu, mbilikimo, kipande cha mtu; (*figure*) sanamu ya umbo la mtu; (*bird, brown-backed*) tongo kanga; (*bronze*) tongo pofu; (*magpie and other manikin finches*) tongo simba.

manil(l)a, *n.* namna ya katani (ukonge).

manioc, *n.* muhogo.

manipulate, *v.t.* fanya (fanyiza, tengeneza, umba) kwa mikono; (*influence*) vuta kwa hila (werevu, akili). **manipulation,** *n.* kufanya, kufanyiza *&c.*

mankind, *n.*, **manliness,** *n.*, **manly,** *a.* taz. *man.*
manna, *n.* chakula Waisraeli walichopewa jangwani na Mungu kwa namna ya mwujiza.
manner, *n.* jinsi, namna, njia. *What manner of?* gani? *In a manner,* nusu, kama, kidogo; (*badly*) vibaya. *After this manner,* kwa namna hii, hivyo.
mannerism, *n.* jinsi ya peke yake, jinsi ya mtu fulani tu, desturi, ada, mtindo. **manners,** *n.* tabia, mambo, mwenendo, hali, kikao. *Good manners,* adabu, tasfida, madaha, jamala, heshima, makini, upole. *Well-mannered,* -a adabu, -a heshima. *Ill-mannered,* si adabu, kimashamba, kishenzi, -a kuchukiza, -safihi, -fidhuli.
manœuvre, *n.* (*clever management*) madaraka ya akili, maongozi merevu; (*device*) werevu, hila; (*warlike*) matengenezo au madaraka ya vita, mchezo wa vita, kuenda askari au manowari huko na huko vitani, luteka. — *v.t.* peleka askari au manowari huko na huko vitani; tengeneza vita; — *v.i.* (*scheme*) fanya hila (werevu), enda (askari, manowari) huko na huko vitani. *Manœuvre* (*person*) *into,* shawishi (mtu) kufanya.
man-of-war, *n.* taz. *man.*
manor, *n.* shamba la mtu mkubwa. **manor-house,** *n.* jumba la *manor.*
manse, *n.* nyumba ya padre (*Scotland*). **mansion,** *n.* jumba. **Mansion House,** *n.* jumba la *Lord Mayor of London* (jumbe mkuu wa *London*).
manslaughter, *n.* taz. *man.*
mantel, mantelpiece, mantel-shelf, *n.* ubao wa ukutani juu ya meko.
mantis, *n.* vunjajungu.
mantle, *n.* vazi la kike la kujitanda, tandio, kitandio, mtandio, tandiko. — *v.t.* funika, tanda; — *v.i.* (*of colour*) enea, tokea.
manual, *a.* -a mikono, -liofanyika kwa mikono. — *n.* kitabu kidogo cha mafundisho au maelezo; (*of organ*) vipande vinavyopigwa na vidole.
manufacture, *v.t.* fanya, fanyiza, tunga, buni. — *n.* kazi (ya kufanyiza kitu), kitu kilichofanyizwa.
manufactory, *n.* kiwanda, nyumba inamofanyizwa vitu, nyumba ya kazi, banda la kazi, kinu, karakana.
manufacturer, *n.* mwenye *manufactory,* mfanyiza vitu.
manumit, *v.t.* weka huru, toa utumwani. **manumission,** *n.* kuweka huru, kutoa (kutoka) utumwani.
manure, *n.* mbolea, samadi. — *v.t.* tia mbolea, simadi.
manuscript, *n.* mwandiko, maandiko, karatasi yenye maandiko (wa mkono si wa chapa).
many, *a.* -ingi, maridhawa, tele, kadha wa kadha.
map, *n.* ramani. — *v.t.* andika (fanya) ramani. *Map out,* tengeza, onyesha vizuri, andika wazi, tunga shauri (namna, njia).
maple, *n.* namna ya mti (mingine hutumika kutengezea vyombo, mingine kutengezea sukari).
mar, *v.t.* haribu, hasiri, vunja, umbua, athiri. *Be marred,* sawajika, umbuka, haribika.
marauder, *n.* mnyang'anyi, mtekaji, mwizi.
marble, *n.* marmar (namna ya mawe mazuri yanayong'aa, ya rangi); (*playing*) gololi, tufe ndogo ya jiwe.
March, (1) *n.* (*month*) Machi, mwezi wa tatu wa mwaka wa kizungu.
march, (2) *v.i.* enda taratibu (mwendo wa askari); (*start*) ondoka, safiri; — *v.t.* (*conduct*) peleka, endesha. — *n.* mwendo wa askari, mwendo, safari; (*musical*) wimbo wa kusawazisha mwendo wa askari.
marches, *n.* mipaka ya nchi.
marchioness, *n.* mke wa *marquis.*
marconigram, *n.* simu ya hewani (bila uzi).
mare, *n.* farasi jike. *Mare's nest,* jambo lililodhaniwa limevumbuliwa, kumbe ni wazo tu.

margarine, *n.* namna ya siagi iliyofanyizwa kwa mafuta au ute wa njugu &c.

margin, *n.* ukingo, kando, ubavu, upande; (*of a book*) pambizo, nafasi (ya kandoni); (*extra amount*) ziada. **marginal**, *a.* -a upande (ukingo, kando &c.), -a pambizoni.

marine, *a.* -a bahari, -a baharini, -a pwani, -a mambo ya bahari. — *n.* askari ya manowari; (*shipping*) jamii ya merikebu (meli) zote za taifa fulani. **mariner**, *n.* baharia, mwana maji. **maritime**, *a.* -a bahari, -a pwani, -enye shughuli kwa bahari.

marital, *a.* -a mume, -a ndoa.

maritime, *a.* taz. *marine.*

mark, *v.t.* tia alama, pigia chapa, athiri; (*be a mark*) -wa alama ya; (*put a mark*) fanya alama, andika hesabu; (*observe*) angalia, tazama; (*body with a stick &c.*) alia. *Mark out*, pambanua, ainisha, chagua, teua. *Mark time*, kanyagisha (chapa) miguu bila kuendelea; kaa na kungojea amri (au nafasi). — *n.* alama, dalili, ishara, athari; (*stamp*) chapa; (*evidence*) mathubutu; (*target*) shabaha; (*position, rank*) cheo; (*number*) hesabu; (*coin*) sarafu mojawapo ya kidachi; (*tribal mark*) nembo, chale; (*of skin, animals &c.*) doa, batobato, baka, waa; (*weal*) walio; (*scar*) kovu. *It is beside the mark*, haina maana, haihusu, haimo. *Up to the mark*, -zima, tayari, hali njema. *A man of mark*, mtu wa cheo, mashuhuri. *A trade mark*, chapa (ya bidhaa). **marking-ink**, *n.* wino usiochujuka wa kuandikia nguo. **marksman**, *n.* mtu hodari wa kupiga shabaha.

market, *n.* soko, gulio, mahali pa biashara, biashara; (*demand for goods*) tamaa, kutakwa. *There is no market for these goods*, watu hawataki kununua bidhaa hizi. *Ready market*, tamaa tele. — *v.t.* peleka kuuza. **marketable**, *a.* -a kuuzikana. **market-garden**, *n.* bustani (shamba) ya mboga za kuuza.

marking-ink, *n.*, **marksman**, *n.* taz. *mark.*

marl, *n.*, udongo mzuri wenye chokaa.

marlinespike, *n.* kipande cha chuma cha kutengea nyuzi za kamba.

marmalade, *n.* machungwa yaliyokatwakatwa na kupikwa pamoja na sukari, mraba wa machungwa.

marmoset, *n.* namna ya kima mdogo wa Amerika.

marmot, *n.* namna ya komba au kindi.

maroon, *v.t.* acha (mtu au watu) katika kisiwa au nchi isiyo na watu.

maroon, *n.* namna ya fataki inayofanya mshindo mkubwa.

marquee, *n.* hema kubwa.

marquis, *n.* jina la cheo kikubwa kiingereza, kati ya *duke* na *earl* mtu mwenye cheo hicho.

marriage, *n.*, **marriageable**, *a.* taz. *marry.*

marrow, *n.* ubongo, mafuta yaliyo ndani ya uwazi wa mifupa; (*vegetable*) boga.

marry, *v.t.* (*perform the ceremony*) oza, funga ndoa (nikahi); (*of male*) oa; (*female*) olewa; (*of parents*) oza; (*of the parties*) fanya arusi, oana. *The married state*, hali ya kuwa mke (mume). **marriage**, *n.* ndoa, nikahi; (*ceremony*) arusi, uozi. *Ask in marriage*, posa. *Give in marriage*, oza. **marriageable**, *a.* -zima, -pevu. *Become marriageable*, balehe.

Mars, *n.* mungu wa vita kiyunani (zamani); jina la sayari mojawapo.

marsh, *n.* bwawa, ziwa lenye matope, kinamasi. **marshy**, *a.* -enye mabwawa, -a maji maji, -a matope, -a kinamasi.

marshal, *v.t.* panga kwa taratibu, ongoza, simamia. — *n.* msimamizi, mwandikaji. *Field-Marshal*, jemadari mkuu.

marshy, *a.* taz. *marsh.*

mart, *n.* soko, gulio, duka la dalali (mnadi).

marten, *n.* karu.

martial, *a.* -a vita, -a kupenda vita, -a kiaskari, -a kiume.

martin, *n.* ndege kama mbayuwayu.
martinet, *n.* mtoa amri nyingi, mtu mkali, atakaye wengine kumtii kabisa, mpiga ubwana.
martyr, *n.* mfia dini, mtu aliyeuawa (au kuteswa) kwa sababu ya kukataa kuikana dini yake, shahidi (wa dini); (*victim*) mteswa bure. *A martyr to toothache,* mtu aumwaye jino kila mara. **martyrdom,** *n.* mauti au mateso ya *martyr.*
marvel, *n.* ajabu, kitu (jambo) cha kushangaza, mwujiza, kioja, shani, mzungu. — *v.i.* shangaa, staajabu, toshewa, roja, ona ajabu, maka. **marvellous,** *a.* -a ajabu, -a kushangaza.
masculine, *a.* -ume, -a kiume, dume.
mash, *v.t.* ponda, seta. — *n.* mseto.
mask, *n.* kifuniko cha uso; (*women's*) barakoa; (*disguise*) mwigo, hila, maficho; (*of head, face &c.*) kinyago. — *v.t.* ficha, geuza setiri. **masquerade,** *n.* mchezo wa watu wanaovaa vinyago. — *v.i.* iga mtu mwingine. **masquerader,** *n.* mwiga mtu mwingine.
mason, *n.* mwashi; (*freemason*) mwana chama cha *Freemasons.* **masonic,** *a.* -a chama cha *Freemasons.* **masonry,** *n.* uashi, kazi ya mawe na chokaa.
masquerade, *n. and v.,* **masquerader,** *n.* taz. *mask.*
Mass, (1) *n.* (*Eucharist*) kawaida ya Ushirika Mtakatifu, misa.
mass, (2) *n.* (*quantity*) wingi, jamii; (*lump, aggregate*) fungu, chungu; (*mixture*) changanyiko, tungamo; (*volume*) ukubwa, uzito, cheo; (*total quantity*) jumla, yote pamoja. *The masses,* watu wengi, akina yahe. *In a mass,* pamoja, jumla, kikundi, mshindo mmoja, dharuba moja; (*promiscuously*) vivi hivi, shelabela. *A mass of iron,* chuma kitupu. *The mass of, The great mass of,* schemu kubwa ya, wingi wa. *A mass-meeting,* mkutano mkubwa. — *v.t.* kusanya pamoja, unga pamoja, songanisha; — *v.i.* kusanyika, ungamana, songamana. **massive, massy,** *a.* -kubwa, -nene, -zito.
massacre, *v.t.* chinja ovyo wanaume na wanawake na watoto. — *n.* mchinjo wa ovyo ovyo, machinjo, mauaji ya bure.
massage, *v.t.* kanda, singa, sia.
massive, massy, *a.* taz. *mass* (2).
mast, *n.* mlingoti. *Mizzen-mast,* mlingoti wa galme.
master, *n.* bwana, bwana mkubwa, hababi; (*of house*) bwana, mwenyeji; (*of school*) mwalimu; (*of a trade, art &c.*) fundi, msimamizi, waria, mstadi, mjuzi; (*of dhow*) nahodha; (*of ship*) kapiteni. *Master of Arts, M.A.,* mtu aliyepewa daraja iliyoitwa hivyo ya *University.* —*v.t.* shinda, weza; (*learn*) jifunza, jua sana. **masterful,** *a.* hodari; (*domineering*) -gumu, -shupavu, -a kupiga ubwana. **master-key,** *n.* kifunguo (cha kufungulia namna nyingi za kufuli). **masterly,** *a.* -a akili, hodari. **masterpiece,** *n.* kazi bora. kazi nzuri halisi, kipeo. **master-stroke,** *n.* tendo la akili sana. **mastery,** *n.* uwezo, nguvu, amri; (*complete knowledge*) maarifa mengi, ustadi, ujuzi.
mastic, *n.* kitu kama sandarusi.
masticate, *v.t.* tafuna; tikita.
mastiff, *n.* namna ya mbwa mkubwa.
mastodon, *n.* mnyama mkubwa wa kikale kama tembo.
mastoid, *n.* sehemu ya mfupa nyuma ya sikio.
masturbate, *v.i.* jichua, jipura, fanya (piga) punyeto. **masturbation,** *n.* kujichua &c., punyeto.
mat, (1) *n.* (*sleeping, oblong*) mkeka, kirago; (*praying, oval*) msala (*floor*) jamvi, busati; (*round*) kitanga, tuguu, utanga. — *v.t.* tatanisha, tatiza; — *v.i.* tatana, tatanika. **matted,** *a.* -liosukwa, -liosokoteka, -liotatanika. **matting,** *n.* jamvi, busati.
mat, (2) *a.* -enye uso usio lain. (usiong'aa).

matador, *n.* mchinjaji fahali katika mchezo wa kupigana na fahali.

match, (1) *n.* (*lucifer*) kiberiti; (*of matchlock gun*) mrao. *Match box,* gamba (ganda) la kiberiti.

match, (2) *n.* (*equal*) mwenzi, sawa, mshindani; (*contest*) shindano, pigano, mchezo; (*marriage*) maozi. *Be a match for,* -wa sawa na, weza. — *v.t.* (*make equal*) pata sawa, fanya sawa, linganisha; (*set to fight*) shindanisha, piganisha; — *v.i.* (*be like*) -wa mfano mmoja, -wa mwenzi, lingana, landana. *This matches well,* linganifu hiyo, ndiyo sawa, inalinga, inalanda. **match-board,** *n.* ubao mwembamba wenye kingo zinazoweza kuunganishwa na mwenzake kwa urahisi, ukingo mmoja una ulimi, mwingine una mfuo. **matchless,** *a.* -sio na kifani, -a kupita -ote. **matchmaker,** *n.* mtu apendaye sana kufanya mashauri ya watu kuoana.

mate, *n.* mwenzi (mke au mume), rafiki; (*of ship*) nahodha mdogo. — *v.t.* oza; — *v.i.* oa.

material, *a.* (*physical*) -enye asili ya kitu (cha kuoneka, cha kugusika &c., si kama roho au pepo), -lio kitu, -a kuoneka, -a kugusika; (*corporeal*) -a mwili, -a kiwiliwili; (*important*) -a maana, -kubwa, kanuni. *It is not material,* haidhuru, mamoja. — *n.* (*substance*) kitu, nyama. **materialism,** *n.* kusadiki ya kuwa hakuna roho, wala ulimwengu usiooneka na akili zetu, ila huu tu. **materialist,** *n.* asadikiye *materialism.* **materialize,** *v.t.* fanya kuwa kitu, tokeza -enye umbo; (*lower*) geuza, haribu, umbua; — *v.i.* (*appear*) onekana, tokea -enye umbo (mwili, kiwiliwili); (*be realized &c.*) -wa, tokea, timizwa, kamilika, tekelezwa. **materials,** *n. plur.* vitu vya kufanyizia kitu, vitu, vyombo, vifaa, zana (*for building*) majengo; (*for carpentry*) miti, mbao, misumari &c.; (*for clothes*) nguo, kitambaa &c.; (*for ship*) maunzi.

maternal, *a.* -a mama, -a kuukeni.

maternity, *n.* umama, kuwa mama. *Maternity nurse,* mzalishi.

mathematics, *n.* elimu ya hesabu. **mathematical,** *a.* -a hesabu, -a jinsi ya hesabu; (*exact &c.*) sawasawa kabisa, halisi, hakika. **mathematician,** *n.* mwenye maarifa ya hesabu.

matins, *n.* sala ya asubuhi. **matinee,** *n.* mchezo wa *theatre* wa alasiri.

matricide, *n.* kumwua mama; (*person*) aliyemwua mama yake.

matriculate, *v.t.* ingiza (pokea) katika *University*; — *v.i.* pokewa katika *University,* shinda katika mtihani ya kuingia *University.* **matriculation,** *n.* kuingia au kuingizwa katika *University*; (*examination*) mtihani ya kuingia *University.*

matrimony, *n.* ndoa, kuoa. **matrimonial,** *a.* -a kuoa, -a ndoa.

matrix, *n.* tumbo (la kuzaa); (*mould*) kalibu; (*stone*) mawe ya asili (yenye madini, vito &c.).

matron, *n.* mwanamke aliyeolewa; (*of hospital &c.*) bibi mkubwa. **matronly,** *a.* -a kumpasa *matron*; (*of women*) -a kama mwanamke aliyeolewa, -zima, -enye maungo makubwa.

matted, *a.* taz. *mat* (1).

matter, *n.* kitu cho chote (cha kinyama, cha kimti, cha kijiwe); (*pus*) usaha, udusi; (*subject &c.*) jambo, kigambo, neno, jawabu, kisa, hoja, habari; (*business*) shughuli, kazi; (*amount, quantity*) kadiri; (*stuff, object &c.*) vitu. *As a matter of fact,* jambo la hakika, hakika, kweli. *A matter of course,* jambo la kawaida, desturi. *No laughing matter,* jambo zito, si mchezo (masihara). *No matter,* haidhuru, mamoja. *What is the matter?* Kuna nini? *A matter of ten miles,* kadiri ya maili kumi. *Printed matter,* vitabu, magazeti &c. — *v.i.* pasa, faa, -wa na maana. *It does not matter,* haidhuru, mamoja. **matter-of-fact,** *a.* (*practical*) -a busara, -a amali, -enye kujua mambo; (*dull, uninteresting*) -a vivi hivi, -a ovyo, baridi, -kavu.

matting, *n.* taz. *mat* (1).
mattock, *n.* jembe.
mattress, *n.* godoro.
mature, *a.* -zima, -pevu, -bivu; (*ready*) tayari, kamili, -liotengenezwa. — *v.t.* ivisha, pevusha; — *v.i.* (*come to maturity*) iva, pevuka, komaa; — *v.t.* (*get ready*) maliza, kamilisha, andaa; — *v.i.* (*be ready*) kamilika, -wa tayari. **maturity,** *n.* uzima, upevu, ubivu; (*perfection*) ukamilifu. *Come to maturity,* pevuka, komaa, iva.
matutinal, *a.* -a asubuhi.
maudlin, *a.* -epesi kuona huzuni (ashiki *&c.*) ya kipumbavu, -pumbavu, dhaifu.
maul, *v.t.* piga, umiza vibaya, paruza, chubua, ponda.
maunder, *v.i.* enda (sema) kivivu.
Maundy Thursday, *n.* Alhamisi kabla ya Ijumaa Kuu.
mausoleum, *n.* kaburi (kubwa zuri).
mauve, *n.* (rangi ya) urujuani.
maw, *n.* tumbo, tumbo la nne la mnyama acheuaye (ng'ombe, mbuzi *&c.*).
mawkish, *a.* -a kuchukiza, -a kukinaisha; (*of books &c.*) -a huzuni (ashiki *&c.*) ya kipumbavu, hafifu.
maxillary, *a.* -a taya.
maxim, *n.* neno la hekima, kanuni; (*proverb*) mithali, mfano, fumbo la maneno.
maxim (*gun*), *n.* bombom.
maximum, *n.* upeo, kipeo, cheo (hesabu, kadiri *&c.*) kilicho kikubwa. — *a.* -kubwa kabisa, -ingi kabisa, -a mwisho, -a upeo.
may, (1) *v.i.* (*p.t.* **might**) weza, -wa na ruhusa, wezekana. *I may go,* naweza (halali yangu, hiari yangu) kwenda, labda nitakwenda. (*That*) *I may go,* niende. *May I go?* Niende? *May you be happy,* uwe heri. *May be,* labda, huenda, sijui. **maybe,** *adv.* labda, huenda.
May, (2) *n.* Mei, mwezi wa tano wa mwaka wa kizingu; (*tree*) namna ya mti wenye maua meupe. **May Day,** *n.* siku ya kwanza ya *May.* **maypole,** *n.* mti mrefu (kama mlingoti) uliopambwa kwa maua *&c.*, pengine watu hucheza kuuzunguka *May Day.*
mayonnaise, *n.* namna ya mchuzi uliofanyizwa kwa mayai, mafuta na siki.
mayor, *n.* mkubwa (jumbe) wa mji. **mayoralty,** *n.* kazi (muda) ya *mayor.* **mayoress,** *n.* mke wa *mayor.*
maypole, *n.* taz. *may* (2).
maze, *n.* (*labyrinth*) mzingile mwanambije, mazunguko, mizingo; (*perplexity*) matata, mashaka, fadhaa.
me, *pron.* mimi (*in comp.*) -ni-.
mead, (1) *n.* kileo cha asali ya nyuki na maji.
mead, (2) **meadow,** *n.* shamba (konde) la majani.
meagre, *a.* (*of persons*) -embamba, -a kimbaombao; (*of things*) haba, -chache, kidogo.
meal, (1) *n.* chakula, mlo.
meal, (2) *n.* (*flour*) unga. **mealy,** *a.* kama unga, -a kufikichika. **mealy-mouthed,** *a.* -enye kutumia maneno yasiyo na nguvu (yasiyo dhahiri), si -nyofu, -janja, -sifu mno, -a kujipendekeza.
mealie, *n.* hindi. *Mealie meal,* unga wa mahindi.
mealy, *a.,* **mealy-mouthed,** *a.* taz. *meal* (2).
mean, (1) *a.* -nyonge, -baya, hafifu, duni; (*stingy*) -bahili, -enye choyo. **meanness,** *n.* unyonge, udhaifu, uhafifu; (*avarice*) ubahili, choyo.
mean, (2) *a.* (*middle*) -a kati, -a kadiri; (*average*) wastani; (*of time*) -a katikati. *In the meantime,* wakati wa kati, huku, katika ku-. — *n.* kati, cheo cha kati; (*average*) kadiri, wastani. *Means,* njia, jinsi, namna, vyombo; (*wealth*) fedha, mali, utajiri, wasaa. *By all means!* hakika, vyema. *By no means,* hasha, sivyo kabisa. *By any means,* kwa vyo vyote. *A man of means,* tajiri. *Ways and means,* gharama, fedha.
meanwhile, *adv.* huko nyuma, wakati ule ule, pale pale, sasa hivi.

mean, (3) *v.t.* (*p.t. and pf.t.* **meant**) -wa na maana; taka kuonyesha (kuarifu); (*purpose*) azimu, nia, taka, kusudia. *It means,* yaani, maana yake. **meaning,** *n.* maana, nguvu. *The meaning is,* yaani, maana yake. **meaningless,** *a.* bila maana, hafifu, duni, bila kusudi.

meander, *v.i.* zungukazunguka, fanya mapindi (mizingo).

meaning, *n.*, **meaningless,** *a.* taz. *mean* (3).

meanness, *n.* taz. *mean* (1).

means, *n.* taz. *mean* (2).

meant, *p.t.* na *pf.t.* ya *mean* (3).

meanwhile, *adv.* taz. *mean* (2).

measles, *n.* surua. **measly,** *a.* hafifu, duni, -chache, kidogo.

measure, *n.* kipimo, kadiri, kiasi, cheo; (*rod or line*) chenezo, kigezo; (*operations*) kazi, matendo, mashauri, madaraka; (*foot rule*) futi; (*of poetry &c.*) mwendo. *Take measures,* anza, shika kazi, fanya mashauri. *Take a man's measure,* angalia (pima, tazama) akili (uwezo, nguvu &c.) ya mtu. — *v.t.* (*take measure*) pima, kadiri, hesabu, linga, enenza, angalia cheo (tabia &c.); (*be by measure*) -wa na kadiri (kipimo); (*measure by comparison*) enenza, linganisha. *It measures six feet,* urefu wake ni futi sita. *Measure one's length on the ground,* anguka fudifudi (chalichali). *Measure oneself with,* shindana na, jaribia nguvu ya. **measured,** *a.* -a taratibu, -a sawasawa, -a kadiri. **measureless,** *a.* -a kupita kiasi, -sio na mwisho. **measurement,** *n.* kipimo, mpimo, kupima &c.

meat, *n.* nyama; (*scrap of*) kinofu, chinyango; (*toasted on a stick*) mshakiki, subana; (*with rice &c.*) kitoweo; (*food*) chakula. *Lean of meat (not fat),* mnofu. *A book full of meat,* kitabu chenye mambo mengi ya akili.

mechanic, *n.* fundi wa mashine. **mechanical,** *a.* -a mashine, -a kufanyika (kuendeshwa) kwa mashine; (*machine-like*) -a kufanya (kufanyika) kama kwamba kwa mashine, yaani tena na tena, bila fikira, bila akili. **mechanician,** *n.* fundi wa kutengeneza (kufanyiza, kuendesha) mashine. **mechanics,** *n.* maarifa ya kutumia nguvu za mashine, vyombo na vitu visivyo na akili, kama za kabari, mtaimbo, gurudumu, roda &c. **mechanism,** *n.* mashine, mtambo; nguvu ya vyombo na vitu vya kutumika kwa kazi, mitambo, magurudumu &c.

medal, *n.* nishani, kipande cha madini kama sarafu. **medallion,** *n.* kipande cha duara cha madini au jiwe kilichochorwa sanamu.

meddle, *v.i.* jitia, jidukiza, jiingiliza (bure katika mambo ya watu), udhi; (*touch*) gusa, chezea. **meddler,** *n.* mdukizi, mdakuzi, mfidhuli. **meddlesome,** *a.*, **meddling,** *a.* -sumbufu, -fidhuli, -juvi.

mediaeval, medieval, *a.* -a zamani za kati ya A.D. 500 na 1500, -a kikale.

medial, *a.* -a kati.

mediate, *v.i.* (*intervene*) jitia kati, -wa jumbe, amua; (*intercede*) ombea, tetea, nenea; — *v.t.* patanisha, suluhisha, pata (fanya) kwa *mediation.* **mediation,** *n.* upatanisho, uombezi. **mediator,** *n.* (*of enemies, rivals &c.*) msuluhishi, mpatanishi, mwamuzi; (*go between*) kijumbe.

medical, *a.* -a tabibu, -a uganga, -a dawa. *To be under medical orders (treatment),* alikwa. *Medical man,* daktari, mganga, tabibu. **medicament,** *n.* dawa, uganga. **medicated,** *a.* -enye dawa, -liotiwa dawa, -liofanyizwa kwa dawa. **medicinal,** *a.* -a dawa, -a kuponya. **medicine,** *n.* dawa; (*art*) uganga, udaktari, utabibu. *Give medicine to,* -pa dawa, nywesha dawa.

mediocre, *a.* -a kadiri (si -ema wala si -baya), hafifu, duni, -baya kidogo. **mediocrity,** *n.* hali ya kuwa si -ema wala si -baya; (*person*) mtu asiye akili nyingi lakini si mjinga.

meditate, *v.i.* fikiri, tafakari, waza; — *v.t.* (*intend*) azimu, kusudia, nia, taka. **meditation,** *n.* fikira, mawazo, taamuli. **meditative,** *a.* -a kufikiri, -a fikira nyingi.

medium, *n.* hali (kadiri) ya kati, wastani; (*means*) njia, chombo; (*go-between*) kijumbe. — *a.* -a kati, -a kadiri, wastani.

medley, *n.* machanganyiko, machafuko, kifujofujo.

medular, *n.* sehemu ya nyuma ya ubongo.

meed, *n.* (*reward*) tuzo, zawadi; (*merit*) stahili.

meek, *a.* -pole, -ema, -tii, -tiifu, -vumilivu, -sikivu. **meekness,** *n.* upole, uvumilivu, usikivu.

meerschaum, *n.* udongo laini mweupe unaotumika kufanyizia viko vya tumbako; kiko cha *meerschaum.*

meet, (1) *a.* -zuri, -a kufaa, -a kustahili, wajibu, -a haki.

meet, (2) *n.* mkutano (wa wawindaji) wa watu wanaosaka. — *v.t.* (*p.t. and pf.t.* **met**) kuta, kutana na; (*for hostilities*) jiana kwa vita, pigana; (*confront*) kabili; (*come to terms*) patana, fanya suluhu, afikana; (*meet with*) pata, patwa na, patikana na; (*a person*) onana na, kutana na; — *v.i.* (*come in contact*) gusa; (*come together*) kutanika, kutana, onana, kusanyika. *Go to meet,* laki. *Meet the eye* (*ear &c.*), fikiliwa na jicho, tazamwa, onekana (sikiwa &c.). *Meet a person's wishes,* fanya atakayo mtu. *Meet the requirements,* faa. *Meet a bill,* lipa hesabu. **meeting,** *n.* mkutano, kusanyiko, jamii ya watu. **meeting-house,** *n.* nyumba ya kufanyia ibada ya Mungu.

megalith, *n.* jiwe kubwa sana (katika majengo ya watu wa kale).

megalomania, *n.* tamaa nyingi (kama wazimu) ya ukuu, dhana ya wazimu ya kuwa ni mkuu.

megaphone, *n.* kitu kama pembe pana cha kuzidishia sauti au kuipeleka mbali.

megrim, *n.* kichwa (cha kuuma), maumivu ya kichwa. *Have the megrims,* huzunika, kata tamaa.

melancholy, *n.* huzuni, ghamu, uzito, uchungu. **melancholia,** *n.* ugonjwa (kama wazimu) wa huzuni (uzito, uchungu, kukata tamaa) nyingi.

mélange, *n.* changanyiko.

mêlée, *n.* mapigano yenye ghasia nyingi.

melliferous, *a.* -tamu kama asali.

mellifluous, *a.* (sauti) -tamu, laini, -zuri.

mellow, *a.* -bivu, -ororo, laini, -zuri, -liofanyika -pole (tamu, -zuri &c.) kwa umri (maisha, siku) mwingi.

melodious, *a.* taz. *melody.*

melodrama, *n.* mchezo wa kuiga mambo ya hadithi, wenye mambo mengi ya kuchoma moyo (ya kusikitikisha, ya kuhuzunisha &c.)

melody, *n.* sauti tamu zinazofuatana; (*music*) ngoma, ghani, wimbo, mafuatano ya sauti, muziki. **melodeon, melodion,** *n.* kinanda. **meldious,** *a.* -a sauti tamu, -a sauti zinazolingana vizuri.

melon, *n.* tikiti (maji).

melt, *v.t.* yeyusha; (*move to pity*) tia huruma, sikitisha; (*smooth*) lainisha; — *v.i.* yeyuka; (*be absorbed, fade*) nywewa, fifia; (*disappear*) toweka taratibu, tokomea; (*become smooth*) lainika. **melting,** *a.* (*of looks, glances*) -a kusikitikisha, -a kugeuza moyo, -a kusinzilia; (*of sounds*) -tamu sana, -a kulainisha moyo. **molten,** *a.* -liyoyeyuka, -a kuyeyusha.

member, *n.* (*of body*) sehemu, kiungo, mkono, mguu &c.; (*of a whole*) sehemu, kipande, nusu; (*of company, society &c.*) mtu, mwana, mshiriki; (*of a group*) -mojawapo, -moja. *Member of Parliament, M.P.,* mtu wa baraza kuu ya Waingereza. **membership,** *n.* hali ya kuwa *member,* ushirika, kuwa mtu wa chama, hesabu ya wanachama wote wa chama &c.

membrane, *n.* ngozi nyembamba ya ndani ya mwili, utando.

memento, *n.* ukumbusho, kumbukumbu.

memoir, *n.*, **memoirs,** *n.*, **memo,** *n.*, **memorable,** *a.*, **memorandum,** *n.*, **memorial,** *n.*, **memorialize,** *v.* taz. *memory.*

memory, *n.* uwezo wa kukumbuka, ufahamu, ukumbuko, kukumbuka, akili, ufahamivu; (*past events*) mambo yaliyokwisha pita. *Repeat from memory,* soma kwa ghaibu, sema kwa moyo, kariri. *Keep in memory,* tia moyoni, kumbuka. *Not in the memory of man,* tangu zamani sana, zamani sana hata mtu hawezi kukumbuka. *Within living memory,* siku hizi, siku zetu. **memoir,** *n.* kitabu chenye habari za maisha ya mtu kilichoandikwa na mtu mwingine, tarehe, habari. **memoirs,** *n.* habari ya mambo yaliyotokea katika maisha ya mtu, zilizoandikwa na yeye mwenyewe. **memo,** *n.* taz. *memorandum.* **memorable,** *a.* -kubwa, -a sifa, -a kukumbukwa, mashuhuri. **memorandum,** *n.* maandiko ya kukumbusha habari, hati, taarifu, ukumbusho, cheti. **memorial,** *n.* kumbukumbu, ukumbusho; (*written*) hati yenye maombi, haja. **memorialize,** *v.t.* peleka hati ya maombi serikalini; wekea ukumbusho. **memorize,** *v.t.* jifunza kwa moyo, tia katika akili, andika.

men, *n. pl.* ya *man.*

menace, *v.t.* ogofya, kamia, tia hofu, tiisha, taka kuja, taka kuumiza (kudhuru, kuhatirisha &c.). — *n.* ogofya, tisho, kamio, hatari.

menagerie, *n.* jamii ya wanyama wa mwitu wanaotembezwa katika vitundu ili watu wawaone.

mend, *v.t.* tengeneza, fanyiza; — *v.i.* (*get better*) poa, pona, pata hajambo, pata ashekali; (*in character*) tulia, ongoka.

mendacious, *a.* -wongo, -mbea. **mendacity,** *n.* uwongo, udanganyifu, umbea.

mendicant, *n.* maskini aombaye riziki. **mendicity,** *n.* hali ya mwombaji, umaskini.

menial, *n.* mtumishi. — *a.* -a mtumishi, -nyonge.

meningitis, *n.* ugonjwa wa ngozi inayofunika ubongo.

menopause, *n.* wakati wa mwanamke kuingia ugumba (wa kuacha kupata hedhi).

menses, *n.* ugonjwa wa mwezi, hedhi.

menstruate, *v.i.* -wa na hedhi, ingia mwezini, ingia damuni. **menstruation,** *n.* hedhi, mwezi, damu.

mensuration, *n.* mpimo (wa marefu na maeneo), elimu ya kupima marefu na maeneo.

mental, *a.* -a akili, -a moyoni. *A mental case,* mtu mwenye kichaa (wazimu). *Mental arithmetic,* hesabu za kichwani. **mentality,** *n.* akili, tabia. **mentor,** *n.* mshauri, mwongozi, nasiha.

mention, *v.t.* taja, nena, semea, dhikiri. *Not to mention,* licha ya, sembuse. — *n.* mtajo, kutaja, kunena, kumbukumbu, habari taarifa.

mentor, *n.* taz. *mental.*

menu, *n.* orodha ya vyakula.

mephitic, *a.* -enye uvundo, -a kunuka.

mercantile, *a.* taz. *merchant.*

mercenary, *a.* -a mshahara, -a kutaka faida (mapato), -a tamaa, -a biashara. *For mercenary ends,* kwa ajili ya faida. — *n.* askari mgeni wa mshahara.

mercer, *n.* mwuza nguo (za hariri, za pamba, za usufu).

merchandise, *n.* taz. *merchant.*

merchant, *n.* mfanyi biashara, tajiri. **mercantile,** *a.* -a biashara, -a mambo ya biashara, -a kufanya biashara. *The mercantile marine,* meli zinazopakia abiria na bidhaa (si manowari). **merchandise,** *n.* bidhaa, biashara, mali. **merchantman,** *n.* meli (merikebu) ya kupakia bidhaa.

merciful, *a.*, **merciless,** *a.* taz. *mercy.*

mercury, *n.* zebaki; (*planet*) sayari moja karibu na jua. **mercurial,** *a.* -geuzi, -a kigeugeu, -epesi (kuona furaha, huzuni *&c.*).

mercy, *n.* rehema, huruma, upole, wema; (*pardon*) msamaha, masamaha, achilio. *Beg for mercy,* lalama, lalamika. *Be at the mercy of,* tiishwa na, -wa chini ya. *Sisters of mercy,* wanawake watawa wa chama kitakatifu. *That's a mercy,* ni jambo la kutia shukrani, alhamdulilahi, (*praise be to God*). **merciful,** *a.* -a rehema, -a huruma, -pole, -ema, rahimu. **merciless,** *a.* -kali, -korofi, pasipo rehema, bila huruma, -katili, dhalimu, jahili.

mere, (1) *n.* ziwa la maji.

mere, (2) *a.* tupu, tu, halisi. **merely,** *adv.* tu.

meretricious, *a.* -a uzuri (wema) wa nje tu, -a kutazamisha (kwa uzuri au wema wa uwongo), -danganyifu.

merge, *v.t.* unganisha, changanya, tia; — *v.i.* ungana, ungamana, unganika, changanyika, **merger,** *n.* mwungano wa makumpuni mengineyo ya biashara *&c.*

meridian, *n.* (*noon*) adhuhuri, jua kichwani; (*highest point, best state*), upeo, kipeo, usitawi; (*geograph.*) mstari kutoka kaskazini mpaka kusini.

meringue, *n.* namna ya andazi la yai na sukari.

merino, *n.* namna ya kondoo mwenye manyoya marefu laini sana; (*cloth*) nguo ya manyoya ya *merino* (ya usufu).

merit, *n.* ustahili, ustahiki, tabia nzuri, sifa njema, uzuri, ujira, ijara; (*good service*) fadhili, matendo mema, kazi njema. — *v.t.* stahili, stahiki. *He merits it,* ni haki yake, yamemstahili, amestahili. **meritorious,** *a.* -a kustahili, -a sifa njema.

mermaid, *n.* zimwi la bahari, nusu mwanamke na nusu samaki (la hadithi tu). **merman,** *n.* zimwi la bahari nusu mwanamume, na nusu samaki (la hadidhi tu).

merry, *a.* -a furaha nyingi, -a kufurahisha, -changamfu, -a moyo mwepesi, -kunjufu. **merriment,** *n.* furaha, uchangamfu, ukunjufu, macheko. **merry thought,** *n.* mfupa wa kuku shingoni mwisho wa kidari.

mesh, *n.* jicho la wavu (kimia), wavu, kimia; (*snare*) mtego. — *v.t.* tega, nasa; — *v.i.* (*of wheels*) ingiana.

mesmerize, *v.t.* tia mtu usingizi au hali kama usingizi au kumtiisha kwa kushinda akili yake (kupunga mikono mbele ya macho yake na kwa njia nyingine kadhalika). **mesmeric,** *a.* -a *mesmerism.* **mesmerism,** *n.* kutia usingizi *&c.* taz. *mesmerize.*

mess, *n.* (*complication, difficulty*) matata, fujo, machafuko, udhia; (*mixture*) changanyiko, vurugiko; (*dirt &c.*) taka, takataka; (*meal*) chakula, mlo, posho; (*meal in common*) jamii ya watu wanaokula pamoja, chakula cha bia, kikoa. *Here's a pretty mess,* matata hayo barabara. *Make a mess of things,* fuja, buruga, tatanisha, — *v.t.* (*make a mess of*) chafua, buruga, fuja, boronga, gurugusha; — *v.i.* (*eat at common table*) -la bia, -la kikoa; (*mess about*) chezacheza, purukusha. **messmate,** *n.* mwenzi wa kula pamoja, mwenzi wa bia (wa kikoa).

message, *n.* maneno, habari, taarifa, agizo; (*written*) barua, cheti, waraka.

messenger, *n.* mjumbe, tume, tarishi.

Messiah, *n.* Masiya, Masiha, Kristo.

messmate, *n.* taz. *mess.*

met, *p.t. and pf.t.* ya *meet.*

messrs. mabwana.

metabolism, *n.* mabadiliko, *e.g.* chakula kilicholiwa kubadilika kuwa nyama ya mwili *&c.*

metacarpus, *n.* kiganja cha mkono, hasa katikati ya kiwiko na vidole.

metal, *n.* madini (chuma, fedha, dhahabu *&c.*); (*for road making*) kokoto. *The metals,* reli za gari la moshi. **metallic,** *a.* -a madini, kama madini. **metalliferous,** *a.* (*rock &c.*) -enye madini ndani yake. **metallurgy,** *n.* kazi na maarifa ya kutengeneza madini tayari kufuliwa.

metamorphosis, *n.* badiliko la tabia (umbo, namna), ubadili, kugeuka. **metamorphic,** *a.* (*rocks &c.*) -liogeuzwa namna (hasa kwa moto na kushindiliwa). **metamorphose,** *v.t.* geuza badili (tabia umbo, namna).

metaphor, *n.* mfano wa maneno, mithali. **metaphorical,** *a.* -enye *metaphor,* -enye fumbo, -a mfano. **metaphorically,** *adv.* kwa mfano.

metaphysics, *n.* elimu ya kuchunguza asili ya kila kitu, ya asili na mwanzo wa uhai, tabia ya Mungu &c.

metatarsus, *n.* kiganja cha mguu, hasa katikati ya kiwiko na vidole.

mete, *v.t.* pima, hesabu; (*allot*) gawia, tolea. **meter,** *n.* chombo cha kupimia.

meteor, *n.* kimwondo, nyota ipitayo upesi mbinguni. **meteoric,** *a.* -a *meteor,* kama kimwondo, yaani -a kupita upesi sana. **meteorite, meteorolite,** *n.* mavi ya nyota, jiwe lililotoka katika nyota. **meteorology,** *n.* maarifa ya hewa na anga na mambo yake.

meter, *n.* taz. *mete.*

methinks, *v.* nadhani, naona.

method, *n.* (*system, order*) taratibu, madaraka, kawaida, desturi; (*way, plan*) shauri, njia, jinsi (namna) ya kufanya. **methodical,** *a.* -a taratibu.

Methodist, *n.* mfuasi wa mafundisho (ya dini) ya *John Wesley,* Mwingereza.

methought, *v.* nilidhani, niliona.

methylated spirits, *n.* *alcohol* iliyotiwa dawa kuifanya isifae kunywewa.

meticulous, *a.* -angalifu sana katika mambo madogodogo.

metier, *n.* kazi inayomfaa hasa mtu.

metre, *n.* kawaida ya ulinganifu wa sauti za maneno katika mashairi na nyimbo; jinsi ya wimbo au utenzi; (*as a measure*) kipimo cha urefu, kadiri ya inchi 39½. **metric, metrical,** *a.* -a *metre.*

metropolis, *n.* mji mkuu wa nchi. **metropolitan,** *a.* -a *metropolis.* — *n.* askofu mkuu wa sehemu ya nchi yenye maaskofu wengine.

mettle, *n.* (*disposition*) moyo, tabia; (*energy, spirit*) wepesi, bidii, moyo mkuu, juhudi, uhodari. *Put on his mettle,* amsha, tia bidii. **mettlesome,** *a.* -enye nguvu na mikogo mingi.

mew, (1) *v.i.* lia (kama paka).

mew, (2) *v.t.* (*fasten up*) funga, fungia ndani. **mews,** *n.* mabanda (mazizi) ya farasi.

miasma, *n.* ukungu mbaya (wa kuleta ugonjwa).

mica, *n.* ulanga, namna ya jiwe kama tabaka za kioo, mavi ya nyota.

mice, *pl.* ya *mouse.*

Michaelmas, *n.* sikukuu ya Mikael malaika mkuu, 29 *September.*

micro-, *pref.* -dogo sana.

microbe, *n.* kijidudu.

microcosm, *n.* ulimwengu mdogo, mfano wa ulimwengu, mtu.

micrometer, *n.* chombo cha kupimia vidogo sana.

microphone, *n.* chombo cha kugeuza mawimbi ya sauti kuwa mawimbi ya umeme (*electricity*).

microscope, *n.* darubini ya kutazamia vitu vidogo sana. **microscopic,** *a.* -a *microscope,* -dogo mno.

micturition, *n.* kukojoa, kutabawali.

mid, *a.* -a kati. *Midday,* adhuhuri, jua kichwani, saa sita ya mchana. *Midnight,* usiku wa manane, kati ya usiku, saa sita ya usiku. **middy,** *n.* taz. *midshipman.* **mid-rib,** *n.* ujukuti; (*of raffia palm*) mwali, (*of coco-nut tree*) upongoo. **midriff,** *n.* kiwambamoyo, pazia la tumboni. **midship,** *n.* katikati ya meli (merikebu). **midshipman,** *n.* mwanafunzi anayefundishwa kuwa afisa manowarini. **midst,** *n.* *In the* *midst,* kati, baina. **midsummer,** *n.* siku za jua kali, kiangazi. **midway,** *a.* -a katikati. **midwinter,** *n.* siku za baridi kali.

midden, *n.* jaa, jalala.

middle, *n.* *and* *a.* kati, -a kati, wastani; (*of the body*) mwili wa kati, tumbo. *Middle finger,* kidole cha kati. *Middle Ages,* wakati baina ya A.D. 500—A.D. 1500. **middle-aged,** *a.* -enye umri wa kati ya miaka 40–60, -zima. **middleman,** *n.* mchuuzi, dalali. **middlemost,** *a.* -a kati kabisa, -a katikati. **middle watch,** *n.* zamu (ya baharia) baina ya saa sita na saa kumi za usiku. **middling,** *a.* -a katikati; (*moderate*) -a kadiri, kadiri, wastani.

middy, *n.* taz. *mid.*

midge, *n.* usubi, inzi kama mbu mdogo aumaye. **midget,** *n.* kibeti, mbilikimo, mtu mdogo sana.

midnight, *n.*, **mid-rib,** *n.*, **midriff,** *n.*, **midship,** *n.*, **midshipman,** *n.*, **midst,** *n.*, **midsummer,** *n.*, **midway,** *a.*, taz. *mid.*

midwife, *n.* mzalishi, mkunga. **midwifery,** *n.* uzalishi, ukunga.

midwinter, *n.* taz. *mid.*

mien, *n.* sura, umbo, uso, mwendo, mwenendo, silika.

might, (1) *v. p.t.* ya *may.*

might, (2) *n.* uwezo, nguvu, ukuu.

mighty, *a.* -enye nguvu (uwezo, amri, ukuu) nyingi.

mignonette, *n.* ua dogo linalonukia vizuri sana.

migrate, *v.i.* hama, hajiri, enda kukaa mahali pengine. **migration,** *n.* kuhama; (*of birds &c.*) uhamaji. **migratory,** *a.* -a kuhama na kurudi kila mwaka, -a kuhamahama, -a kupotea.

milch, *a.* -enye kutoa maziwa, -a kukama (kwa maziwa).

mild, *a.* -pole, laini, -tamu, -siye -kali. *A mild attack of fever,* homa kidogo. *A mild medicine,* dawa isiyo kali. **mildness,** *n.* upole, ulaini.

mildew, *n.* kawa, kuvu.

mildness, *n.* taz. *mild.*

mile, *n.* maili, mwendo wa robo saa kwa miguu, kipimo cha urefu, yadi 1,760. **mileage,** *n.* hesabu ya maili zilizoendwa. **milestone,** *n.* jiwe lililowekwa kando ya barabara kila mwendo wa maili.

militant, *a.* -a kupigana, -a vitani, -a kutaka vita. *The Church militant,* Wakristo waliopo hapa duniani ndio vitani, hawajapata raha ndio peponi (*Church triumphant*). **militarism,** *n.* moyo wa (tabia) kutaka vita. **military,** *a.* -a askari, kiaskari, -a vita, -a kupigana. — *n.* jeshi la askari, jamii ya askari. **militate,** *v.i.* (*against*) -wa mbali, -wa upande mwingine, kingamana (na), zuia, pinza. **militia,** *n.* jamii ya watu wanaofundishwa mambo ya kiaskari na vita kuilinda nchi yao.

milk, *n.* maziwa; (*curdled*) maziwa mabichi, robu. *Buttermilk,* mtindi. *Condensed milk,* maziwa ya kopo. *A land of milk and honey,* nchi yenye neema (mavuno na vyakula vingi). *It's no good crying over spilt milk,* maji yaliyomwagika hayazoleki. — *v.t.* kama; (*get profit from*) toza faida, teka. **milkman,** *n.* mkamishi, mkamuzi, mtembeza maziwa ya kuuza. **milksop,** *n.* mwoga, mwanamume dhaifu. **milk-tooth,** *n.* jino la kitoto. **milky,** *a.* kama maziwa. *The Milky Way,* zile nyota ndogo nyingi sana pamoja, kama wingu jeupe mbinguni usiku.

mill, *n.* kinu, kiwanda cha vinu, taz. *manufactory.* *Flour mill,* kinu cha kusagia unga. *Sugar mill,* kinu cha kusindikia miwa. *Steam mill,* kinu cha moshi. *Oil mill,* kinu cha kusindikia mafuta, shindikizo. — *v.t.* tia (sindikiza) kinuni, saga, ponda. **millboard,** *n.* namna ya karatasi nene. **mill-dam,** *n.* boma la kuzuia maji ili kufanya mkondo wa kuendesha *mill.* **miller,** *n.* msimamizi (mwenyeji) wa kinu. **milling,** *n.* kazi (tendo, namna) ya kusindika (kusaga, kuponda) katika kinu; (*of a coin*) michoro ya ukingoni mwa sarafu. **mill-pond**, *n.* ziwa lililofanywa kwa kuziba maji ili kufanya mkondo wa kuendesha kazi ya *mill. Calm as (like a mill-pond)*, maji matulivu sana. **mill-race**, *n.* mto au mkondo wa maji uendeshao kazi ya *mill.* **millstone**, *n.* jiwe la kusagia, (*top stone*) kijaa. **mill-wheel**, *n.* gurudumu kubwa linalozunguka na kuendesha kazi ya *mill.* **millwright**, *n.* fundi wa kutengeneza *mill.*

millennium, *n.* muda wa miaka elfu; siku Yesu Kristo atakazomiliki duniani atakapokuja mara ya pili; siku za raha na neema kabisa.

millepede, *n.* jongoo.

miller, *n.* taz. *mill.*

millet, *n.* mtama. *Bulrush millet*, wimbi, mawele. *Millet stalks*, mabua. *Stalks of sweet millet*, vikota. *Millet flour*, unga wa mtama.

milliner, *n.* mshona nguo na kofia za kike, mwuza nguo na kofia za kike. **millinery**, *n.* vitu vinavyouzwa na *milliner.*

milling, *n.* taz. *mill.*

million, *n.* 1,000,000; elfu mara elfu, milioni. **millionaire**, *n.* mtu mwenye (*pounds, dollars, francs &c.*) milioni moja, tajiri mkuu.

mill-race, *n.*, **millstone**, *n.*, **mill-wheel**, *n.*, **millwright**, *n.* taz. *mill.*

milt, *n.* (*spleen*) wengu; (*male roe of fish*) mbegu za samaki dume.

mime, *n.* mchezo kama unyago; mchezi; mwigaji. — *v.i.* iga. **mimeograph**, *n.* chombo cha kunakilia barua, hati *&c.* **mimetic**, *a.* -a kuiga. **mimic**, *v.t.* iga, iga kwa dhihaka. — *n.* mwigaji. **mimicry**, *n.* mwigo, kuiga, dhihaka.

mimosa, *n.* namna ya mti, jamii ya mganga, mgunguti, mguruka, mguruti, *&c.*

minaret, *n.* mnara wa msikiti.

mince, *v.t.* kata vipande vidogo; — *v.i.* (*of speech*) toa kidogo kidogo, sema kitembe (si wazi); (*of gait*) enda kwa hatua ndogo, piga madaha. *Do not mince matters*, sema waziwazi, sema kweli ilivyo. — *n.* kima, nyama iliyokatwa vipande vidogodogo. **mincemeat**, *n.* mchanganyiko wa zabibu, matunda, mafuta, sukari, unga *&c.* wa kufanyia maandazi. **mince-pie**, *n.* andazi lenye *mincemeat*, ndani yake. **mincing-machine**, *n.* kinu kidogo cha kukatia nyama *&c.*, vipande vidogodogo.

mind, *n.* moyo, akili, nia, roho, dhati, dhamira. *Keep (bear) in mind*, kumbuka. *Have a mind, Have a great mind*, taka, nia, elekea. *Make up one's mind*, azimu, kusudia, jifunga, kaza shauri. *Call to mind*, fahamu, kumbuka. *Bring to mind, Put to mind*, kumbusha, fahamisha. *It is to my mind*, inanipendeza, ndiyo nitakayo. *Be of one mind*, patana. *Be of two minds*, sita. *Be absent-minded*, chukuliwa na chechele. — *v.t.* (*observe, watch*) angalia, kumbuka, tunza; (*attend to*) shika, jitia katika angalia; (*obey*) sikia, tii; — *v.i.* (*take to heart*) weka moyoni, onea uchungu (huzuni); (*be careful*) hadhari, angalia. *Never mind!* haidhuru! mamoja! *Mind you do it*, usikose kufanya; (*in letters*) halahala (alaala). *Mind! Mind yourself!* jihadhari! habedari! *I do not mind*, mamoja kwangu. *Mind your own business*, shika lako, wewe humo. **mindful**, *a.* -angalifu, -fahamivu, -enye hadhari.

mine, (1) *a.* -angu, -angu mimi.

mine, (2) *n.* (*pit*) shimo, chimbo (la kuchimbulia mawe, madini, makaa *&c.*); (*explosive*) shimo la kupenyezea baruti chini ya kitu, kusudi kukivunja; (*submarine*) pipa la baruti baharini chini, la kuvunja meli (merikebu, manowari) zikipita; (*great store*) akiba kubwa, wingi. — *v.t. and i.* fanya *mine*, fukua chini. **minefield**, *n.* mahali penye mashimo ya kuchimbulia makaa, madini *&c.*; mahali palipowekwa baruti ya kuvunjia vitu (meli *&c.*). **miner**, *n.* afanyaye kazi katika *mine*, mchimbuzi. **mineral**, *n.* jiwe, mawe (cho chote kisicho cha kimea wala kinyama; hasa huchimbuliwa chini ya nchi.) — *a.* -a mawe, -a vitu vitokavyo katika mawe. *Mineral waters*, soda (maji yaliyotiwa namna ya hewa). **mineralogy**, *n.* elimu ya *minerals*. **mining**, *n.* kazi ya *mine*. — *a.* -a kuhusu *mine*.

mingle, *v.t.* changanya, unga, unganisha, tia pamoja; — *v.i.* changanyika, ungamana, changamana. **mingling**, *n.* mchanganyo.

miniature, *n.* sanamu (picha) ndogo ya rangi, mfano ndogo. *In miniature*, sawasawa lakini -ndogo, kwa vidogo.

minim, *n.* kipimo kidogo cha dawa, tone moja. **minimize**, *v.t.* punguza, punguzia sifa, rahisisha, tweza, ona si kitu, dharau. **minimum**, *n.* kadiri iliyo ndogo iwezekanavyo. — *a.* -a mwisho (kwa kuwa -dogo), -dogo sana.

mining, *n.* taz. *mine*.

minion, *n.* kipenzi; (*flatterer*) msifu, mjipendekeza vibaya; (*slave*) mtumwa.

minister, *n.* (*of state*) waziri, balozi, mjumbe wa serikali, mtu mkubwa wa serikali; (*of religion*) padre, kasisi; (*preacher*) hatibu, mhubiri; (*of a mosque*) mwalimu, imamu; (*servant*) mtumishi, mjumbe, mhudumu, mngoje. — *v.i.* (*to*) ngojea, tumikia, saidia, -wa -tumishi; (*supply*) toa, tolea. **ministerial**, *a.* -a *minister*; (*helping*) -a kufaa, -a kusaidia. **ministration**, *n.* utumishi, msaada. **ministry**, *n.* kazi ya *minister*; jamii ya mawaziri wa mfalme, serikali; jamii ya mapadre wa Kanisa, kazi ya mapadre, ukasisi, upadre.

mink, *n.* mnyama mdogo kama cheche akaaye majini na nchi kavu mwenye ngozi inayouzwa kwa bei kubwa; ngozi ya mnyama huyo.

minnow, *n.* samaki mdogo wa mtoni.

minor, *a.* -dogo, -a chini, hafifu. — *n.* mtu asiyepata bado umri wa miaka ishirini na mmoja, mtoto. **minority**, *n.* hali ya *minor*; (*smaller number*) wachache, walio wachache. *In a minority*, -chache, -enye wafuasi wachache.

minster, *n.* kanisa kubwa.

minstrel, *n.* mwimbaji, mutribu, mtunga mashairi, mpiga kinubi (zeze, kinanda &c.). **minstrelsy**, *n.* kazi ya *minstrel*, nyimbo, ghani, mashairi.

mint, (1) *n.* nanaa; (*plant*) mnanaa.

mint, (2) *n.* kiwanda cha kufanyiza sarafu (cha kupiga chapa sarafu); (*abundance*) wingi, neema.

minuet, *n.* ngoma moja ya kizungu.

minus, *prep.* (*without*) kasa, kasoro, pasipo, bila, kupungua. *Minus sign*, alama ya kutoa au kuondoa, ndiyo hii —.

minute, *a.* -dogo sana, -dogodogo; (*trifling*) hafifu; (*exact*) halisi, barabara; (*exacting, precise*) -a kutaka usahihi, (uhalisi, usawa, utaratibu &c.). — *n.* dakika, sehemu ya sitini ya saa moja; (*short time*) kitambo kidogo, kipindi, muda mdogo; (*note*) ukumbusho wa mambo, tarehe, taarifa, cheti. *Minutes* (*of a meeting*) muhtasari ya maneno yaliyosemwa na kukatwa katika mkutano. *Minute-gun*, mzinga unaopigwa mmoja mmoja (kila dakika) kujulisha msiba au kutaka msaada. *Minute-hand*, mshale (mkono) mrefu wa saa. *In a minute*, karibu, sasa hivi, mara. *Wait a minute*, ngoja kwanza, ngoja kidogo. **minutely**, *adv.* kwa uangalifu sana. **minutiae**, *n.* mambo madogo.

minx, *n.* mtoto wa kike mtundu (mjuvi, mfidhuli, mtukutu, asiye na adabu).

miracle, *n.* mwujiza, shani, ajabu, jambo geni lisilo na kifani (wala kwa kawaida ya viumbe vyote, lisilo la ulimwengu huu). **miraculous**, *a.* -a mwujiza, -a ajabu sana.

mirage, *n.* mazigazi, mangazimbwe, sarabi, madanganyo ya macho (ya vitu kuonekana jinsi visivyo).

mire, *n.* tope, matope, kinamasi. **miry**, *a.* -a matope mengi.
mirror, *n.* kioo (cha kujitazamia).
mirth, *n.* furaha na macheko. **mirthful**, *a.* -a macheko, -a furaha.
miry, *a.* taz. *mire.*
misadventure, *n.* jambo baya, hasara, msiba, shari. *By misadventure,* kwa bahati mbaya, kwa nasibu, bila kukusudiwa.
misanthrope, *n.* mchukia wanadamu wenziwe, mkaa pweke. **misanthropic**, *a.* -a kuchukia watu, -a kudharau na kuepukana na watu. **misanthropy**, *n.* kuchukia watu.
misapply, *v.t.* tumia vibaya, poteza, tupa. **misapplication**, *n.* utumizi mbaya (wa fedha, akili, wakati &c.).
misapprehend, *v.t.* kosa kufahamu vema, kosea maana. **misapprehension**, *n.* kukosa kufahamu maana.
misappropriate, *v.t.* twaa bila haki, tumia vibaya, iba. **misappropriation**, *n.* kutwaa bila haki, utumizi usio wa haki.
misbehave, *v.i.* kosa adabu, fanya yasiyofaa, kosa. **misbehaviour**, *n.* matendo mabaya, makosa, ubaya.
miscalculate, *v.t.* hesabu vibaya, kosea hesabu, fikiri (ona, dhani) yasivyo. **miscalculation**, *n.* kukosa katika kuhesabu (katika kufikiri, katika kupima &c.).
miscarry, *v.i.* tokea vibaya, haribika, pooza, enda upande, koseka, kosa kupata, potea, kosa kufika; (*of birth*) haribu mimba. *The letter miscarried,* barua haikufika. *The plan miscarried,* shauri halikufaulu. **miscarriage**, *n.* kuharibika mimba; (*failure*) kosa, ukosefu, upotovu.
miscellaneous, *a.* -a namna nyingi pamoja. **miscellany**, *n.* mchanganyiko wa vitu vya namna mbalimbali.
mischance, *n.* bahati mbaya, tukio la ajali, msiba.
mischief, *n.* madhara, hasara, uharibifu, fujo, fitina, utundu. *To do him a mischief,* kumdhuru. *Make mischief between,* tia fitina, gombanisha. *The fire did great mischief,* moto ulifanya hasara kubwa. *The child did it out of mischief,* mtoto alifanya kwa utundu. **mischief-maker**, *n.* mfitini. **mischievous**, *a.* -harabu, -tundu, -potevu, -baya, -tiriri, -a chachari.
misconceive, *v.t.* kosa kufahamu vema. **misconception**, *n.* kosa (la akili), kutofahamu vema.
misconduct, *n.* kutenda mabaya, makosa, ubaya; (*adultery*) uzinzi, uzini, kuzini.
misconstrue, *v.t.* kosa kuelewa vema. kosea maana, fahamu (fikiri) yasivyo. **misconstruction**, *n.* kukosa maana.
miscreant, *n.* mtu mbaya kabisa, baa, mtu mwovu.
misdeal, *v.t. and i.* gawia (karata za kuchezea) vibaya. — *n.* mgawanyo mbaya. **misdealings**, *n.* matendo mabaya, makosa.
misdeed, *n.* tendo baya, kosa.
misdemeanour, *n.* kosa.
misdirect, *v.t.* ongoza (peleka, onyesha, fundisha, onya) vibaya.
miser, *n.* bahili, mtu mwenye choyo (awekaye mali asiitumie). **miserly**, *a.* -a choyo, bahili.
misery, *n.* taabu, shida, mashaka, umaskini, udhilifu, huzuni kuu, hali mbaya sana. **miserable**, *a.* -enye taabu (huzuni, mashaka), maskini; (*in bad condition*) -enye hali mbaya, -nyonge, hafifu, duni.
misfit, *n.* vazi lisilokaa (lisilo sawa na kimo).
misfortune, *n.* msiba, taabu; (*loss*) hasara, ukuba.
misgiving, *n.* mashaka, wasiwasi, hangaiko, tashwishwi, kusita.
misgovern, *v.t.* tawala vibaya. **misgovernment**, *n.* kutawala vibaya.
misguided, *a.* -lioongozwa vibaya.
mishap, *n.* bahati mbaya, tendo baya lisilokusudiwa, msiba.
misinform, *v.t.* arifu vibaya (yasivyo kweli), simulia uwongo. *I was misinformed,* sikuambiwa vema, niliambiwa uwongo.

misjudge, *v.t.* kosa kusikia (kudhania, kuhukumu) vema, kosea, dhania mtu mpumbavu (mwoga, mbaya *&c.*) hali yu mwenye akili (hodari, mwema *&c.*).

mislay, *v.t.* (*p.t. and pf.t.* **mislaid**) weka (kitu) pasipo pake na kutoweza kukiona, potewa na kwa muda.

mislead, *v.* (*p.t. and pf.t.* **misled**) ongoza (arifu, onyesha ambia) vibaya, kosesha, poteza, danganya.

mismanage, *v.t.* chafua, fuja, buruga, ongoza vibaya, haribu madaraka au taratibu.

misname, *v.t.* taja kwa jina lisilo lake. **misnomer,** *n.* jina lisilofaa (lisilo lake, -kosefu, -baya).

misogynist, *n.* mchukia wanawake wote.

misplace, *v.t.* weka mahali pasipo pake (pasipofaa, pasipostahili).

misprint, *n.* kosa (katika chapa ya kitabu).

mispronounce, *v.t. and i.* tamka vibaya. **mispronunciation,** *n.* tamko baya.

misquote, *v.t. and i.* geuza maneno ya. **misquotation,** *n.* kugeuza maneno ya.

misrepresent, *v.t.* eleza vibaya, geuza habari za, singizia. **misrepresentation,** *n.* maarifa (habari) ya uwongo, masingizio.

misrule, *n.* kutawala vibaya; (*disorder*) ghasia, fujo, fitina.

miss, (1) *n.* jina la kutaja mwanamke asiyeolewa, bibi.

miss, (2) *v.t.* kosa shabaha, kosa kupiga (kupata), epea; (*pass over*) ruka, pitia; (*feel loss of*) jutia, onea majuto, kumbuka kwa uchungu, sikitikia, lilia; (*want*) taka, hitaji; — *v.i.* kosa. *He missed the train,* alichelewa, gari lilikwisha kuondoka. *We shall miss you if you go,* ukienda tutahuzunika. — *n.* kosa la shabaha, kukosa kupata, kuepea. **missing,** *a.* -siopo. *It is missing* (inayotakiwa) haipo, imepotea.

missal, *n.* kitabu cha sala za Ushirika Mtakatifu.

misshapen, *a.* -enye makombo, -lioumbuka, -liopotoka.

missile, *n.* kitu cha kutupia kama mshale, mkuki, mawe *&c.*

missing, *a.* taz. *miss* (2).

mission, *n.* kutuma (kutumwa) kwa kazi fulani, ujumbe, utume, upelekwa; (*errand*) kazi, maagizo; (*religious*) jamii ya watu wanaofundisha habari za Injili katika nchi ya kigeni, na mahali wakaapo, nyumba yao. **missionary,** *n.* mtu mwenye kazi ya kueneza habari za Injili kwao wasioijua au wasioiangalia vema, mpelekwa, mjumbe.

missis, *n.* jina la kumtaja mwanamke aliyeolewa, pamoja na jina lake, huandikwa *Mrs* (fulani).

missive, *n.* barua, waraka, taarifa.

mis-spell, *v.t.* (*p.t. and pf.t.* **misspelt**) kosa katika kuendeleza neno.

mis-spend, *v.t.* (*p.t. and pf.t.* **misspent**) tumia vibaya, poteza, fuja.

mis-state, *v.t.* kosa katika kunena (kueleza, kusimulia). **mis-statement,** *n.* habari za uwongo, uwongo.

mist, *n.* ukungu, shemali, umande, kunge, kungugu. **misty,** *a.* -a ukungu, -a umande; (*obscure*) si wazi, si dhahiri.

mistake, *v.t.* (*p.t.* **mistook,** *pf.t.* **mistaken**) kosea, dhania (ona fahamu, fikiri) lisilo la kweli, si fahamu vema. *I mistook him for a thief,* nilimdhania mwizi (kumbe sivyo). *I mistook your meaning,* sikufahamu vema maneno yako. — *n.* kosa, tendo (neno, dhana *&c.*) lisilokusudiwa. *You are a fool and no mistake,* wewe mpumbavu bila shaka.

mister, *n.* bwana, jina la kumtaja mwanamume pamoja na jina lake, huandikwa *Mr* (fulani).

mistress, *n.* (*of house*) bibi, mwana, mwenyeji; (*sweetheart*) mchumba; (*paramour*) hawara, kinyumba; (*ruler*) mkuu, mtawala. *Schoolmistress,* bibi mwalimu.

mistrust, *v.t.* shuku, tuhumu, toamini, totegemea, dhania mabaya, onea mashaka. — *n.* shaka, tuhuma. **mistrustful,** *a.* -enye kushuku, -enye shaka *&c.*

misty, *a.* taz. *mist.*

misunderstand, *v.t.* kosa kufahamu, kosa kuelewa maana. **misunderstanding,** *n.* kosa, kukosea maana, kutosikia vema.

misuse, *v.t.* tumia vibaya (si kama ipasavyo). — *n.* matumizi mabaya, utumizi mbaya.

mite, *n.* kidudu kidogo sana; (*coin*) senti moja, msaada kidogo.

mitigate, *v.t.* punguza, tuliza, nyamazisha. **mitigation,** *n.* kipunguo, kipunguzo, kupunguza, kitulizo.

mitre, *n.* kofia ya kiaskofu; (*carpentry*) namna ya kuunga vipande viwili vya ubao, na chombo cha kuviunganisha.

mitten, *n.* mfuko wa kufunika mkono wenye vitundu vya kupenyeza vidole.

mix, *v.t.* changa, changanya; (*food*) unga; (*stir*) vuruga, buruga; — *v.i.* changanyika, changamana. **mixture,** *n.* mchanganyo, mchanganyiko; (*medical*) dawa (ya kunywa).

mix-up, *n.* ghasia, fujo, machafuko.

mizzen-mast, *n.* mlingoti wa galme (wa nyuma).

mnemonics, *n.* elimu ya kusaidia akili ya kukumbuka.

moan, *v.i.* ugua, lia, piga kite. — *n.* kilio, kite.

moat, *n.* shimo refu lenye maji nje ya boma, handaki ya maji, mto.

mob, *n.* watu, watu wengi, watu wenye makelele, ghasia ya watu. — *v.t.* songa, kumba, zunguka (kwa jeuri au vifijo), fanyia jeuri.

mobile, *a.* -a kuenda (kuendeshwa) kwa wepesi, -epesi kugeuka (kujongea huko na huko), -enye mwendo. **mobility,** *n.* wepesi wa kugeuka, mwendo. **mobilize,** *v.t.* kusanya (askari, baharia, zana za vita) tayari kwenda vitani.

mock, *v.t.* iga, dhihaki, cheka, fanyia mzaha; (*triumph over*) simanga. — *n.* mwigo, mzaha, dhihaka. — *a.* -a kuiga, -a mzaha. **mockery.** *n.* mwigo, dhihaka, mzaha, usimango,

mode, *n.* jinsi, namna, njia, desturi, kawaida, kanuni. **model,** *n.* mfano mdogo wa kitu kikubwa, mfano, kifani, kielezo, kielelezo; (*perfect example*) kipeo, kitu kikamilifu, kitu kizuri sana, namna ya uzuri, kitu (mtu, mwendo *&c.*) kilichostahili kufuatwa; (*of artist &c.*) kitu (mtu) ambacho umbo lake (sura yake) laandikwa (lafuatishwa) na mwandishi wa picha (mchora wa sanamu) — *v.t.* finyanga kwa udongo *&c.*, fanyiza (umba) kwa kufuata namna (umbo, sura) au kwa kuiga mtu (au kitu), fanya mfano.

moderate, *v.t.* punguza (joto, ukali, harara, nguvu *&c.*), tuliza, zimua, zuia; — *v.i.* pungua, tulia, nyamaza. — *a.* -a kiasi, -a kadiri, wastani, -pole. **moderately,** *adv.* kwa kiasi, si sana. **moderation,** *n.* kiasi, kadiri, utaratibu, upole. **moderator,** *n.* mwamuzi, msuluhishi, mpatanishi.

modern, *a.* -a siku hizi, -a kisasa, -a zamani zetu, -pya, -geni. **modernism,** *n.* namna ya sasa, kipya si kikale, kizushi, kisasa. **modernize,** *v.t.* fanyiza kwa desturi za siku hizi, geuza vipya.

modest, *a.* -enye haya, -enye adabu, -enye kiasi, si -enye majivuno (kiburi, kichwa kikubwa), si -a kujitanguliza, -dogo. **modesty,** *n.* haya, adabu, utulivu, makini, stara.

modicum, *n.* kidogo.

modify, *v.t.* punguza (ukali, nguvu *&c.*), geuza (badilisha, badili) kidogo. **modification,** *n.* ugeuzi, ubadili, kugeuza (kubadili) kidogo.

modulate, *v.t.* badili sauti. **modulation,** *n.* ubadili wa sauti. **modulator,** *n.* ramani yenye kanuni ya kubadili sauti.

modus operandi, jinsi (namna) ya kufanya.

mohair, *n.* manyoya mazuri laini ya namna ya mbuzi; nguo iliyofumwa kwa manyoya hayo.

Mohammedan, *n.* Mwislamu. — *a.*

-a islamu, -a kiislamu. **Mohammedanism**, *n.* dini ya Waislamu, Islamu.

moiety, *n.* nusu.

moil, *v.i. toil and moil*, fanya kazi ya kuchosha (ya taabu).

moist, *a.* -a maji, chepechepe, chege, -bichi, -a unyevu, -a kulowa, -enye rutuba, chelema. *A moist atmosphere*, umande mwingi. **moisten**, *v.t.* tia maji kidogo, lowesha, rutubisha, fanya kuwa chepechepe. **moisture**, *n.* maji, unyevu, uchepe, rutuba, ubichi, umande, maji ya mvuke.

molar, *n.* chego, gego, jino la nyuma la kutafunia.

molasses, *n.* machujo ya asali ya miwa.

mole, (1) *n.* (*spot*) kiwaa cheusi, baka jeusi.

mole, (2) *n.* (*animal*) fuko, mnyama mdogo anayefukua chini. **molehill**, *n.* chungu ya udongo inayofanywa na *mole* anapofukua chini. *Make mountains out of molehills*, hangaika sana kwa ajili ya shida (matata) kidogo tu. **moleskin**, *n.* ngozi ya *mole*; namna ya nguo nzito inayotumika kufanyizia suruali za kazi ngumu.

mole, (3) *n.* (*breakwater*) boma la mawe majini la kuzuia mawimbi.

molecule, *n.* kipande kilicho kidogo sana cha kitu.

molehill, *n.*, **moleskin**, *n.* taz. *mole* (2).

molest, *v.t.* sumbua, udhi, chokoza, nyanyasa, kera, endea kwa jeuri (ili kudhuru, kuzuia *&c.*) **molestation**, *n.* kusumbua, usumbuo, udhia, dhara, kero.

mollify, *v.t.* tuliza, punguza, ridhisha, bembeleza.

mollusc, *n.* (*pl.* **mollusca**) (*univalve*) konokono, koa; (*bivalve*) kombe.

mollycoddle, *n.* mtu ajipendaye (ajidekezaye). — *v.t.* engaenga, dekeza.

molten, *a.* taz. *melt.*

moment, *n.* kitambo kidogo, muda mfupi sana, kope la juu na chini, kufumba na kufumbua; (*velocity*) mwendo, nguvu ya kwenda; (*importance*) maana, ukuu, thamani. *At that moment*, wakati ule ule. *Go this moment*, nenda sasa hivi. **momentary**, *a.* -a mara moja, -a kupita upesi sana. **momentous**, *a.* -a maana sana, -kubwa, -kuu, -enye habari kubwa. **momentum**, *n.* nguvu ya kwenda, mwendo.

monarch, *n.* mfalme. **monarchial**, *a.* -a mfalme. **monarchy**, *n.*, ufalme.

monastery, *n.* nyumba ya *monks*. **monastic**, *a.* -a *monks*. **monasticism**, *n.* maisha na desturi za *monks*.

Monday, *n.* Jumatatu.

monetary, *a.* taz. *money*.

money, *n.* fedha (sarafu, noti) inayotumika katika kuuza na kununua; (*wealth*) utajiri, mali. *Make money*, pata (chuma) fedha. **monetary**, *a.* -a mambo ya fedha. **money-broker**, **money-changer**, *n.* mbadili (mvunja) fedha. **moneyed**, *a.* -enye mali, -tajiri. **money-grubber**, *n.* ajishughulishaye sana kuchuma fedha. **money-lender**, *n.* mkopeshaji fedha; (*at a usurious rate*) mla riba. **money-order**, *n.* hawala ya fedha inayonunulika posta (*post office*) ya kupeleka mahali pengine na yule apelekewaye aweza kuivunja katika posta ya huko.

monger, *n.* mfanyi biashara, *e.g. ironmonger*, mwuzaji wa vitu vya chuma; *fishmonger*, mwuzaji wa samaki.

mongoose, *n.* nguchiro.

mongrel, *a.* mbwa (mnyama, mtu) wa mbegu mbili; (*person*) chotara, suriama.

monitor, *n.* mshauri; (*in schools*) msimamizi; (*warship*) manowari ndogo yenye mizinga mikubwa; (*lizard*) mnyama kama kenge. **monition**, *n.* onyo, shauri. **monitorial**, *a.* -a *monitor*.

monk, *n.* mtu ajitengaye na mambo ya dunia ili azidi kujifunga kwa mambo ya dini, akikaa katika *monastery* pamoja na wengine chini ya *abbot*, mtawa, sufii. **monkery**, *n.* jamii ya *monks*, hali na desturi ya *monks*, nyumba ya *monks*. **monkish**, *a.* -a *monk*, -a kama *monk*.

monkey, *n.* (*small lightish coloured*) tumbili, ngedere; (*small dark coloured*) kima; (*colobus*) mbega; (*large*) nyani; (*mischievous child*) mtundu. —*v.i.* chezacheza; (*monkey with*) chezea, sumbua, hasiri. **monkey-puzzle**, *n.* namna ya mti usiopandika kwa sababu una miiba mingi. **monkey-wrench**, *n.* namna ya koleo yenye meno ya kushikia vitu imara.

monkish, *a.* taz. *monk*.

mono-, *pref.* -a -moja tu, -a mara moja tu, -enye -moja tu.

monocle, *n.* rodi, kioo cha miwani cha jicho moja.

monogamy, *n.* hali au desturi ya kuwa na mke mmoja tu.

monogram, *n.* chapa ya herufi mbili zilizochanganyika pamoja, moja juu ya nyingine.

monograph, *n.* kitabu kidogo chenye habari ya jambo (kitu, elimu) moja tu.

monolith, *n.* nguzo ya jiwe moja tu.

monologue, *n.* maneno ya mtu mmoja akisema peke yake.

monomania, *n.* namna ya wazimu ambao humfanya mtu ashikilie neno (jambo, habari) moja tu.

monoplane, *n.* eropleni yenye bawa moja tu upande huu na upande huu.

monopolize, *v.t.* pata (shika, miliki) -ote, jipatia -ote, jitumilia -ote (pasipo kushiriki na wengine). *Monopolize the conversation*, sema maneno mengi (zungumza sana) hata mwingine asipate nafasi kusema. **monopoly**, *n.* (*in general*) kumiliki -ote *&c.*, taz. *monopolize*; (*commercial*) ruhusa (nguvu, haki) ya kuuza na kununua bidhaa fulani au kufanya uchumi fulani, bila kushirikisha wengine, peke yake (yao *&c.*) kufaidi, faida ya mtu peke yake (ya kumpuni moja peke yake). *Get a monopoly of ivory*, kumba biashara yote ya pembe.

monosyllable, *n.* neno lenye sauti moja tu, *e.g.* la, tu. **monosyllabic**, *a.* -enye sauti moja tu.

monotheism, *n.* kumwamini Mungu mmoja tu.

monotone, *n.* sauti moja isiyobadilika (kama kusema maneno mengi bila kubadili sauti). **monotonous**, *a.* -siobadilika, -a sawasawa, -a kuchosha (kwa sababu hapana mabadiliko). **monotony**, *n.* uchovu (ubaridi, uchoshi *&c.*) kwa ajili ya kutobadilika mambo.

monsieur, *n.* bwana (Kifaransa).

monsoon, *n.* (*north*) msimu, kaskazi; (*south*) kusi, demani.

monster, *n.* mnyama mkubwa mno ajabu, kitu kikubwa ajabu; (*portent*) kitisho, kioja, dubwana; (*unnatural object*) kitu (mtu) kisicho cha kawaida (*e.g.* mtu mkubwa sana, mdogo sana, mwenye vichwa viwili *&c.*); (*brutal person*) mkali, mkatili, mkorofi, (*giant*) pande (pandikizi) la mtu. **monstrosity**, *n.* kioja, dubwana, kitu kinachotia hofu (ajabu, machukio *&c.*) kwa kuwa kibaya na kigeni. **monstrous**, *a.* -kubwa mno, ajabu; (*terrifying &c.*) -a kuogofya, -a kuchukiza, -a baya mno.

month, *n.* (muda wa) mwezi. *What is the day of the month?* mwezi ngapi? *It is the fifth day of the month*, leo mwezi tano. **monthly**, *a.* -a kila mwezi, -a mwezi. *Monthly pay*, mshahara. **monthly**, *n.* kitabu kinachopigwa chapa na kutolewa kila mwezi, gazeti la mwezi. *Monthlies*, hedhi, damu, mwezi.

monument, *n.* kaburi; (*memorial*) nguzo (mnara, sanamu *&c.*) ya ukumbusho, kumbukumbu. **monumental**, *a.* -kubwa sana, -a sifa za daima, -a ukumbusho.

mooch, mouch, *v.i.* tembea huko na huko kivivu, tangatanga kivivuvivu, susurika, zurura, zururika.

mood, *n*. namna, jinsi; (*temper*) moyo, nia, tabia. **moody**, *a*. -enye moyo mzito (wa huzuni, wa uchungu, wa chuki), -epesi kuona hasira, -a kukata tamaa, -enye undani.

moon, *n*. mwezi. *Full moon*, mwezi mkubwa (mduara, mpevu). *New moon*, mwezi mwandamo. *Young moon*, mwezi mchanga. *Moonbeam*, kianga cha mwezi. **moon-blindness**, *n*. kiwi. **moonlight**, *n*. mbalamwezi. **moonshine**, *n*. mbalamwezi; (*nonsense*) upuzi. **moonstone**, *n*. namna ya kito, rangi yake buluu yenye kijani kibichi. **moonstruck**, *a*. -enye wazimu.

moor, (1) *n*. jangwa, wangwa, nyika. **moorhen**, *n*. kuku ziwa. **moorland**, *n*. *moor*.

moor, (2) *v.t.* funganisha, tia (puliza) nanga. **mooring**, *n*. kutia nanga, kufunga, kufunganisha; (*place*) maelezi, mahali pa kutia nanga *&c.*, bandari; (*anchor*) nanga; (*cable*) amari, kamba.

moorhen, *n*. taz. *moor* (1).

mooring, *n*. taz. *moor* (2).

moorland, *n*. taz. *moor* (1).

moose, *n*. mnyama kama kongoni wa Amerika.

moot, *v.t.* leta kisa cha kuhoji (cha kubishania, cha kushindania, cha kugombania). — *a*. -a kubishania, -siyoyakinika bado.

mop, *n*. ufagio uliofanyizwa kwa vipande vyembamba vya kitambaa au nyuzi nene. — *v.t.* sugua (futa, pangusa) kwa *mop*; (*wipe face*) pua uso; (*tears*) futa machozi.

mope, *v.i.* nyamaa kimya kwa huzuni, -wa na moyo mzito, jitenga, kaa pekee.

moraine, *n*. fungu la mawe patokeapo *glacier*.

moral, *a*. -enye adili, -adilifu, -ema, -zuri, -nyofu; (*pure, chaste*) safi, -takatifu; (*having moral sense, free will*) -enye hiari (akili) ya kuchagua mema au mabaya; (*teaching morality*) -enye mafundisho mazuri, -a kuongoa vizuri. *A moral certainty*, jambo linaloelekea kuwa kweli, yamkini. *Moral law*, kanuni ya mema na mabaya. *A matter of moral obligation*, wajibu, lipasalo, linalobidi. *He gained a moral victory*, alishindwa, lakini kwa jinsi alivyofanya bidii ikawa kama alishinda. — *n*. fundisho, maana. **morale**, *n*. tabia, moyo. **morality**, *n*. wema adili, adilifu, uzuri; (*chastity*) kuwa safi, usafi; (*moral science*) maarifa ya wema na ubaya; (*character*) tabia, sifa. **moralist**, *n*. mfundishi wa *morality*, mtu adilifu. **moralize**, *v.i.* ongea juu ya wema na ubaya; — *v.t.* (*make moral*) ongoza, adilisha, fundisha mema. **morally**, *adv*. kwa adili, vema; (*sufficiently, nearly*) jinsi ya kutosha, kama, karibu, yamkini. **morals**, *n*. maarifa ya wema na ubaya, taz. *morality*. *A person's morals*, maono ya mtu juu ya wema na ubaya, mwendo wake katika mambo ya mwili wake, hasa ya kiume na kike. *He has no morals*, mtu mbaya huyu, mzinifu, mwasherati.

morass, *n*. bwawa, ziwa la tope, kinamasi; (*perplexity*) matata, tataniko.

moratorium, *n*. sheria ya serikali ya kuruhusu kukawilisha au kuahiri malipo ya deni.

morbid, *a*. -enye hali mbaya, si -zima, -gonjwa (-a mwili, -a roho); (*of the mind*) -enye kuwazia huzuni (mambo ya kutisha, mambo mabaya, mambo ya kuchukiza).

mordant, *a*. -kali; (*of disease*) -a kuoza.

more, *a*. zaidi, tena, bado, kupita, kuzidi, juu. *A little more*, punde. *More than*, kuliko, zaidi ya, licha ya, fauka ya. *Be no more*, -fa, -isha. *Do more and more*, zidi kufanya. *More or less*, kwa kadiri. *Grow (get, be) more*, zidi kuwa. **moreover**, *adv*. tena, na, aidha, waama.

morganatic marriage, *n*. mwana wa mfalme kuoa mke asiye wa cheo chake (mke hawezi kurithi cheo wala mali isipokuwa mali isiyo ya kifalme).

morgue, *n.* nyumba ya kuwekea maiti mpaka wajulikane ni nani.

moribund, *a.* -a kufani, karibu kufa; (*ceasing*) -a karibu kwisha, -lioisha, -liofifia.

Mormon, *n.* mfuasi wa *Joseph Smith*, na kitabu chake.

morn, morning, *n.* asubuhi; (*early*) alfajiri, mapambazuko, kucha.

morocco, *n.* namna ya ngozi laini, sana hutumika kufanyizia majalada ya vitabu.

moron, *n.* mpunguani, mwenye kuvia akili, mwenye akili afkani.

morose, *a.* -a huzuni, -a kasirani, -a chuki, -chungu. **moroseness**, *n.* uchungu, chuki.

morphia, morphine, *n.* dawa mojawapo ya usingizi yenye asili ya afyuni.

morphology, *n.* elimu ya (uchunguzi katika) umbo na ujenzi wa wanyama, mimea na lugha.

morris-dance, *n.* namna ya ngoma ya kiingereza ya zamani.

morrow, *n.* kesho, asubuhi.

morse, *a. morse signalling*, namna ya kupeleka habari kwa mapigo marefu na mafupi ya sauti au ya vimulimuli vya taa.

morsel, *n.* kidogo, chembe, kipande kidogo, mmego.

mortal, *a.* (*causing death*) -a maulisho, -a mauti, -a kufisha; (*liable to death*) -enye kufa, -a kibinadamu. *Mortal conflict*, pigano la kufa au kupona. *A mortal foe*, adui hata mwisho. — *n.* mwanadamu, binadamu. **mortality**, *n.* (*death*) mauti, kifo, kufa wengi; (*mortal state*) utu, hali (maisha) ya binadamu; (*death rate*) hesabu ya watu wanaokufa mahali katika muda maalum. *There was great mortality*, wengi walikufa.

mortar, *n.* (*for building*) chokaa; (*for pounding*) kinu; (*gun*) kombora.

mortar-board, *n.* chano, ubao wa kuwekea chokaa (mwashi anapojenga &c.); (*cap*) namna ya kofia inayovaliwa na wanafunzi wa vyuo vingine.

mortgage, *n.* rehani, amana, poni; (*document*) hati ya kuweka rehani, wasili. — *v.t.* weka rehani.

mortification, *n.* taz. *mortify*.

mortify, *v.i.* oza; — *v.t.* (*vex, shame*) tia uchungu (haya, huzuni, aibu); (*restrain, subdue*) tiisha, zuia, fungisha. *Mortify oneself*, jirudi, jitesa, jitiisha. **mortification**, *n.* kuoza; (*vexation &c.*) uchungu, haya, hasira; (*restraint*) kutiisha. **mortifying**, *a.* -a kutia uchungu (haya, huzuni, aibu).

mortise, *n.* tundu katika ubao la kutia ulimi (*tenon*) wa ubao mwingine ili kuziunga. — *v.t.* unga kwa *mortise*.

mortuary, *n.* chumba cha kuwekea maiti.

mosaic, *n.* sanamu iliyofanyizwa kwa kupanga vijiwe au vigae vyenye rangi mbalimbali.

moselle, *n.* namna ya divai.

Moslem, *n.* na *a.* Mwislamu, -islamu, -a kiislamu.

mosque, *n.* msikiti.

mosquito, *n.* mbu. **mosquito-net**, chandalua; (*frame*) besera. **mosquito proof**, *a.* -siopisha mbu, -nayozuia mbu wasiingie.

moss, *n.* majani madogodogo laini yaotayo penye maji. **mossy**, *a.* -enye *moss*.

most, *a.* -ingi kupita -ote, -ingi sana, -ingi. *For the most part*, zaidi, kwa kawaida, aghalabu. — *adv.* sana, kupita yote, kuliko yote. **mostly**, *adv.* mara nyingi, desturi, kwa wingi, aghalabu, kwa kawaida, hasa.

mote, *n.* chembe, *e.g.* ya vumbi.

moth, *n.* nondo, kipopo. **moth-eaten**, *a.* -liliwa na nondo; (*worn-out*) -liochakaa, -bovu.

mother, *n.* mama mzazi; (*term of respectful reference*) mwana. *Mother country*, nchi ya kuzaliwa, kwao (kwetu, kwenu). *Mother tongue*, lugha ya kwao (kwetu, kwenu). *Stepmother*, mama wa kambo.

— *v.t.* tunza (*lea*) kama mama. **motherhood,** *n.* umama, hali ya kuwa mama. **mother-in-law,** *n.* mkwe. **motherless,** *a.* pasipo mama, -siye na mama. **motherly,** *a.* kama mama, -pole, -ema. **mother-of-pearl,** *n.* lulumizi, ubamba wa ndani ya kombe la chaza.

motif, *n.* taz. *motive.*

motion, *n.* mwendo, kwenda, nguvu ya kwenda; (*mental*) nia, wazo, tamaa, madhumuni, azimio; (*proposal*) shauri, onyo, haja; (*in medicine*) kwenda chooni, kinyesi. *Set in motion,* anzisha. *Move a motion,* uliza watu wa mkutano kama wanakubali shauri fulani. *Have a motion,* enda chooni, -nya. — *v.t. and i.* ashiria, pungia mkono, onya kwa mkono. **motionless,** *a.* bila kujongea (kusita, kwenda), kimya, tuli.

motive, *n.* (*purpose*) nia, kusudi, azimio, maarubu, matilaba, madhumuni; (*reason*) hoja, kisa, sababu, mwanzo; (*object*) mwisho, maana. **motif,** *n.* wazo (sehemu ya wimbo, habari) linalorudiwa mara kwa mara katika maandiko (wimbo &c.), kiini.

motley, mottled, *a.* -a rangi nyingi mbalimbali, -enye madoadoa, -a marakaraka. **mottle,** *v.t.* tia madoadoa ya rangi mbalimbali.

motor, *n.* mashine inayogeuza nguvu kuwa mwendo, mashine (mtambo) inayoendesha. *Motor-cycle,* baisikeli inayoendeshwa na *motor. Motor-boat,* mashua inayoendeshwa na *motor. Motor-car* gari linaloendeshwa na *motor,* motakaa. — *v.t.* chukua katika motakaa; — *v.i.* safiri (enda) katika motakaa. **motorist,** *n.* mwendhi motokaa, msafiri katika motakaa.

mottle, *v.,* **mottled,** *a.* taz. *motley.*

motto, *n.* maneno (usemi, mithali) yanayoshikilia mtu kuongoza maisha yake, mithali, fumbo la maneno.

mould, (1) *n.* (*earth*) udongo wenye rutuba, udongo mweusi mzuri, udongo.

mould, (2) *n.* ukungu, kawa, koga, kuvu. **moulder,** *v.i.* oza, chakaa, haribika kwa kutu (kuvu, kawa, koga). **mouldy,** *a.* -enye ukungu (kawa, kuvu, koga), -liochakaa, -a zamani.

mould, (3) *n.* (*for casting*) kalibu; (*pattern*) kielezo, na nna; (*character*) tabia, moyo, chapa. — *v.t.* (*in clay &c.*) finyanga, fanyiza kwa udongo; (*in metal*) subu kwa kalibu, fanya kwa madini iliyoyeyuka; (*form, give shape to*) tengeneza, fanyiza kwa akili. **moulder,** *n.* mwumbaji, mfanyi vitu kwa kalibu &c. **moulding,** *n.* (*in masonry*) ushi; (*of wood*) nakshi, mchoro.

moulder, *v.* taz. *mould* (2).

moulder, *n.,* **moulding,** *n.* taz. *mould* (3).

mouldy, *a.* taz. *mould* (2).

moult, *v.i.* jigeua manyoya, pukutika (futuka) manyoya, monyoka manyoya.

mound, *n.* (*earth*) chungu, kilima, mwinuko; (*of white ant*) kichuguu; (*of stone*) boma. — *v.t.* lundika (udongo mawe), fanya chungu.

mount, *v.t.* panda, kwea, rekebu; (*put in position, complete*) weka vema, tengeneza, maliza; — *v.i.* inuka, fika juu, kwea; (*increase*) zidi, ongezeka. *Mount a horse,* panda farasi. *Mount guard,* weka mlinzi, weka zamu (askari); -wa mlinzi, linda, shika zamu. — *n.* mlima, kilima; (*horse*) farasi; (*card*) karata. **mountain,** *n.* mlima, jabali. **mountaineer,** *n.* mkaa mlimani, mpanda mlima. **mountainous,** *a.* -enye milima mingi. **mounted,** *a.* (*on back*) juu ya mnyama (farasi); (*on card &c.*) katika karata, katika ubao &c. *Mounted troops,* askari wapanda farasi. **mounting,** *n.* kupamba, mapambo, uzuri; (*going up*) kupanda, kukwea, mpando.

mountebank, *n.* ayari, jambazi, mjanja.

mounted, *a.* **mounting,** *n.* taz. *mount.*
mourn, *v.i.* lia, huzunika, sikitika; (*formal*) kaa matanga, omboleza, kaa msiba; — *v.t.* (*for*) lilia, huzunikia, sikitikia. *Mourn with* (*join in mourning*), hani. **mournful,** *a.* -a huzuni, -enye majonzi, -zito, -a kuhuzunisha, -a kusikitisha. **mourning,** *a.* kulia, huzuni, majonzi; (*formal*) matanga, kilio, maombolezo, msiba, (*dress*) nguo za kuugulia. *Be in mourning,* kaa matanga, vaa nguo za mfiwa. *Go out of mourning,* ondoa matanga.
mouse, *n.* (*pl.* **mice**) panya mdogo.
moustache, *n.* sharubu, ndevu za mdomo.
mouth, *n.* kinywa; (*entrance*) mlango, pa kuingia, pa kutokea. *Down in the mouth,* -enye huzuni. — *v.t. and i.* sema kwa sauti kubwa mno; (*chew*) tafunatafuna. **mouthful,** *n.* (*of liquid*) funda; (*of food*) mego. **mouth-organ,** *n.* kinanda (cha kupuliza kwa mdomo). **mouthpiece,** *n.* mdomo, tundu la kupulizia; (*of tobacco pipe*) mdakale; (*spokesman*) msemaji, mnenaji, mkuu.
move, *v.t.* endesha, sogeza, jongeza, tikisa, sukuma, sukumiza; badilisha mahali, hamisha, ondoa, peleka, chukua; (*influence*) ongoza, shawishi, vuta; (*excite*) kasirisha, huzunisha, amsha moyo, chocha, choma moyo; (*advise*) shauri, nena shauri; — *v.i.* (*go*) enda, sogea, jongea, tikisika, cheza, jimudu, jichukua; (*change residence*) hama, gura, hajiri, hujuru, jitanibu. *He cannot move himself,* hawezi kujimudu. *Appliances for moving,* nyenzo. — *n.* mwendo; (*turn*) zamu (katika mchezo); (*action*) tendo jambo (katika vita, shughuli, kazi). *He is always on the move,* hana kituo, mhamishaji huyu. **movable,** *a.* -enye mwendo, -a kwenda (kuendeshwa, kuchukulika, kujongezeka, kuondoleka, kutikisika); (*varying*) -a kubadilika, -a kucheza. **movables,** *n.* mali, vifaa, mapambo (ya nyumba), vikorokoro.
movement, *n.* mwendo, mazunguko, mabadili, tetemo, mshindo; (*working*) kazi; (*agitation*) fitina, udhia, msukosuko; (*progress*) maendeleo; (*opinion*) shauri; (*of musical composition*) sehemu yenye mwendo mbalimbali na nyingine. **mover,** *n.* mwendeshi, mchochezi, aletaye shauri (hoja, kisa). **moving,** *a.* -a kuendesha, -a kusukuma, -enye mwendo, -a kwenda; (*affecting*) -a kutia huzuni (huruma, hasira, nguvu *&c.*) moyoni.
mow, *v.* (*pf. t.* **mown**) kata majani.
mower, *n.* mkata majani.
Mozambique, *n.* Msumbiji.
Mr. taz. *mister.*
Mrs. taz. *missis.*
much, *a. and n.* -ingi, tele, sana, neema, maridhawa, wingi. *Be too much for,* kulia, shinda, lemea. *Make much of,* pendelea; (*exaggerate*) ongeza mno, zidisha. *How much is it?* (*of price*) kem? wauzaje? kiasi gani? *It is too much* (*costly*) ghali. *Much too dear,* ghali sana mno. *Much more,* zaidi sana.
mucilage, *n.* ute, maji yañayonata, utomvu, gundi.
muck, *n.* taka, takataka, uchafu, kinyaa, kifusi. *To make a muck of,* buruga, haribu, fuja, chafua.
mucous membrane, *n.* ngozi yenye ute ya ndani (ya kinywa, pua, pafu, tumbo *&c.*). **mucus,** *n.* ute wa ngozi *mucus membrane*; (*from nose*) kamasi, gole.
mud, *n.* tope, matope, kinamasi.
muddle, *v.t.* chafua, fuja, tatiza, tatanisha, buruga, changanya, haribu. *Muddle* (*make a mess of*) *work,* burugaburuga, boronga. — *n.* fujo, machafuko, matata, udhia. **muddle-headed,** *a.* -enye wasiwasi. **muddy,** *a.* -a matope, -a topetope, -enye matope mengi. — *v.t.* chafua, buruga, tifua. **mudfish,** *n.* kambare.
mudguard, *n.* bango.
muezzin, *n.* mwadhini.
muff, (1) *n.* namna ya mfuko wa kutia mikono isipate baridi.

muff, (2) *n.* mwoga, baradhuli, mjinga.

muffin, *n.* namna ya mkate unaochomwa na kuliwa ungali na moto pamoja na siagi.

muffle, *v.t.* funika kwa nguo (hasa shingo na kichwa); funika ili kupunguza mlio (ngoma, kengele). **muffler,** *n.* kitambaa au nguo ya kufunika.

mufti, *n.* nguo zinazovaliwa na askari wakati usio wa kazi (zisizo za kiaskari).

mug, (1) *n.* kopo, kikombe, mdumu; (*face = slang*) uso.

mug, (2) *n.* baradhuli, mzuzu, mjinga, mpumbavu.

muggy, *a.* -a joto na unyevu, -a jasho, -a mvua na mawingu pasipo baridi.

Muhammedan, *n.* taz. *Mohammedan.*

mulatto, *n.* mtu wa mbegu mbili, nusu mweupe nusu mweusi, -chotara, sariama.

mulberry, *n.* (*tree*) mforsadi; (*fruit*) forsadi.

mulch, *n.* samadi, mbolea, majani yanayooza (yanayotiwa shinani mwa miche michanga kuihifadhi na joto). — *v.t.* tilia *mulch.*

mulct, *v.t.* toza fedha (ya kulipia kosa), toza faini (ukombozi), lipiza hongo, ibia.

mule, *n.* nyumbu, baghala; (*stubborn person*) mkaidi, mshupavu. **muleteer,** *n.* mchunga nyumbu. **mulish,** *a.* -kaidi, -tundu, -shupavu.

mull, *v.t.* pasha moto mvinyo (divai) na kutia sukari *&c.*

mullet, *n.* namna ya samaki.

mulligatawny, *n.* namna ya mchuzi wenye bizari, pilipili *&c.*

mullion, *n.* nguzo ya kati ya dirisha.

multi-, *pref.* -enye -ingi, *e.g. multicoloured,* -enye rangi ya namna nyingi.

multifarious, *a.* -a namna nyingi, -ingi mbalimbali.

multiform, *a.* -enye mambo mengi, -a namna nyingi.

multiple, *n.*, **multiplex,** *a.*, **multiplicand,** *n.*, **multiplication,** *n.*, **multiplicity,** *n.* taz. *multiply.*

multiply, *v.t.* zidisha; — *v.i.* zidi, ongezeka. **multiple,** *n.* hesabu iliyo mara fulani ya hesabu nyingine. — *a.* (*manifold*) -a vitu vingi. **multiplex,** *a.* -a sehemu nyingi, -a mara nyingi. **multiplicand,** *n.* kizidishe, hesabu ya kuzidishwa. **multiplication,** *n.* kuzidisha. **multiplicity,** *n.* wingi. **multiplier,** *n.* kizidisho, hesabu ya kuzidisha.

multitude, *n.* wingi, kundi, jeshi, makutano, umati, kaumu. **multitudinous,** *a.* -ingi, tele.

multum in parvo, *n.* mambo (vitu, maarifa *&c.*) mengi katika nafasi ndogo.

mum, *a.* kimya. *Keep mum,* kaa kimya. **mummer,** *n.* mchezo wa kuigiza mambo (hasa bila kusema).

mumble, *v.t. and i.* sema bila kutamka vizuri (kama kwa kufumba midomo; (*chew*) mumunya.

mummer, *n.* taz. *mum.*

mummy, *n.* mumiani; maiti iliyotengenezwa kwa dawa na kuzungushiwa vitambaa isioze.

mumps, *n.* matubwitubwi, machubwichubwi, ugonjwa wa kuvimba tezi shingoni.

munch, *v.t.* tafunatafuna, guguna, mumunya.

mundane, *a.* -a ulimwengu huu, -a mambo yapitayo, -a kidunia.

mungoose, *n.* taz. *mongoose.*

municipal, *a.* -a kuhusu utawala wa mji. **municipality,** *n.* mji wenye baraza yake inayoutawala, baraza ya mji.

munificent, *a.* -karimu, -paji. **munificence,** *n.* ukarimu, upaji.

munition, *n.* zana za vita, vifaa vya vita.

mural, *a.* -a ukutani.

murder, *v.t.* ua kwa kusudi; (*spoil*) haribu, vunja. — *n.* uuaji wa mtu kwa kusudi, kuua mtu kwa kusudi. **murderer,** *n.* mwuaji (kwa kusudi). **murderous,** *a.* -a kuua, -a kuua wengi, -a kiuaji, -kali, -katili, -baya sana.

murky, *a.* -a giza, -eusi, -a utusitusi.

murmur, *v.i.* vuma (lia kama maji, kama watu wengi wakiongea pamoja); (*complain, grumble*) guna, nung'unika, zomea; — *v.t.* (*utter in subdued voice*) nong'ona, sema kwa sauti ndogo. — *n.* mlio mvumo, uvumi, kivumi, nung'unika, mnong'ono.

murrain, *n.* ugonjwa wa ng'ombe, mbuzi na kondoo.

muscatel, *n.* namna ya zabibu; namna ya divai.

muscle, *n.* musuli, mnofu, chavu, tafu, mshipa; (*sinew*) ukano. **muscular**, *a.* -enye nguvu ya mwili, -enye maungo, -shupavu, -a kakawana.

muse, (1) *v.i.* fikiri, tafakari, kumbuka moyoni, waza, taamuli.

muse, (2) *n.* Mungu wa kike katika hadithi za zamani za kiyunani. Tisa walitajwa, wa mashairi, wa nyimbo na ngoma *&c.*

museum, *n.* nyumba ya kuhifadhi na kuweka ili watu watazame, jamii ya vitu vya tunu, vya sanaa *&c.* vionyeshavyo maendeleo ya wanadamu, wanyama, kazi *&c.*; jamii ya vitu hivyo.

mushroom, *n.* kiyoga, uyoga.

mushy, *a.* teketeke.

music, *n.* muziki, ngoma, tarabu, sauti (ya kinanda, kinubi, zeze *&c.*) sauti tamu, mlio mzuri. **musical**, *a.* -a *music*. *Musical* box, santuri. **music-hall**, *n.* jumba wanamoimba na kucheza wachezaji mbele ya watu. **musician**, *n.* fundi wa *music*, mwimbaji, mpigaji ngoma, mutribu.

musk, *n.* meski.

musket, *n.* bunduki ya mrao. **musketeer**, *n.* askari wa *musket*. **musketry**, *n.* maarifa ya kupiga bunduki.

muslin, *n.* shashi, melimeli, doria, bushashi.

mussel, *n.* (*shell-fish*) kome, kijogoo.

Mussulman, *n.* Mwislamu.

must, (1) *aux. v.* hakuna budi, sharti, lazima, yapasa. *You must go*, sharti uende. *I must*, sina budi. *He must be honest*, yampasa kuwa aminifu.

must, (2) *n.* maji ya zabibu.

mustard, *n.* haradali.

muster, *v.t.* kusanya, changa, kutanisha; — *v.i.* (*come together*) kusanyika, kutana. *Muster courage*, jipa moyo, thubutu. — *n.* mchango, mkutano. *Pass muster*, faa, tosha, kubalika.

musty, *a.* -enye koga (kuvu), -baya, -lioharibika.

mutable, *a.* -a kubadilibadili, -geugeu, -geuzi, -a kuelekea kubadilika. **mutability**, *n.* tabia (hali) ya kubadilibadili (ya kubadilika), ugeuzi.

mutation, *n.* mabadili. **mutatis mutandis**, pamoja na mabadili yanayohusu.

mute, *a.* kimya, pasipo kusema, pasipo sauti; (*dumb*) bubu; (*not sounded*) -siyotamkwa (herufi) ingawa imeandikwa katika neno. — *n.* bubu; (*of violin &c.*) kitu cha kupunguzia sauti (ya fidla *&c.*). **mutely**, *adv.* kimya, bila sauti.

mutilate, *v.t.* kata, vunja, haribu, hasiri; (*cripple*) lemaza; (*remove essential part*) ondoa (toa, haribu) sehemu yenye maana sana. **mutilation**, *n.* mkato, mvunjo, hasara, kilema.

mutiny, *n.* maasi, uasi, fitina. — *v.i.* asi, halifu. **mutineer**, *n.* mwasi (hasa askari au baharia). **mutinous**, *a.* -a kuasi, -a kuhalifu, -fitini.

mutter, *v.i.* sema mashavuni, bubujika, nung'unika; (*speak indistinctly*) sema maneno yasiyosikika. **muttering**, *n.* msemo wa mashavuni, bubujiko, nung'uniko; (*of thunder*) ngurumo.

mutton, *n.* nyama ya kondoo.

mutual, *a.* -a wao kwa wao, -a wote wawili, -a wenyewe; (*in verbs*) -ana. *Mutual affection*, upendano. *Mutual agreement*, maafikano, mapatano. *Mutual help*, kusaidiana; (*in culti-*

vating, building &c.) ujima. *Mutual friend*, rafiki wa wote wawili.

muzzle, *n.* pua na mdomo wa mnyama (uliochongoka kama wa mbwa, paka mbweha *&c.*); (*to prevent biting &c.*) kitu cha kumfungisha mnyama mdomoni; kifungo cha mdomo; (*rifle &c.*) kitundu (cha kasiba, mtutu *&c.*) — *v.t.* tia *muzzle*; (*silence*) nyamazisha, fungisha, dakiza, katiza.

muzzy, *a.* -enye wasiwasi, -a kupumbazika (kama kwa kunywa sana).

my, *a.* -angu, -angu mimi. **myself**, *pron.* mimi mwenyewe, nafsi yangu; (*in comp.*) -ji-, *e.g. I hurt myself*, nilijiumiza.

myopia, *n.* hali ya kutoweza kuona vitu vya mbali (ila vya karibu tu).

myriad, *n.* kikwi, elfu kumi; wingi sana.

myrmidon, *n.* mtu (mtumishi, mtumwa) afikishaye amri bila huruma (kwa ukali).

myrrh, *n.* manemane.

myrtle, *n.* namna ya mti mdogo.

myself, *pron.* taz. *my.*

mystery, *n.* siri, fumbo, jambo asiloweza kufahamu mwanadamu. **mysterious**, *a.* -a siri, -a fumbo, -sioelezwa, -sioelezeka. **mystic**, *a.* -a siri *&c.* kama *mysterious.* — *n.* mtu ajaribuye kumshiriki Mungu kwa kujitoa na kutafakari sana habari za Mungu. **mystical**, *a.* taz. *mysterious.* **mysticism**, *n.* mafundisho (elimu, imani) ya *mystic.* **mystify**, *v.t.* fumba, tatanisha, tatiza, chafua akili, zulisha, zuzua, kikisa.

myth, *n.* hadithi, ngano, hasa za miungu, zimwi *&c.*; (*fiction*) uwongo. **mythical**, *a.* -a hadithi; -a uwongo, -a kubuniwa, -a kuzuliwa. **mythology**. *n.* maarifa ya *myth.*

N

nab, *v.t.* kamata, shika, bamba, dara.

nabob, *n.* tajiri wa kihindi, tajiri.

nacre, *n.* lulumizi, taz. *mother-of-pearl.*

nadir, *n.* palipo chini ya miguu hasa, taz. (*zenith*); cheo (kadiri *&c.*) cha chini.

nag, (1) *n.* farasi, hasa aliye mdogo.

nag, (2) *v.t. and i.* karipia, kemea; — *v.i.* nung'unika, kefyakefya, zoza. **nagger**, *n.* mzozi. **nagging**, *n.* mzozo, kuzozana. — *a.* -enye gubu.

naiad, *n.* zimwi wa majini.

nail, *n.* (*finger*) ukucha, nyaa; (*iron*) msumari. *Fight tooth and nail*, pigana sana (kwa ukali). *Hard as nails*, -enye afya na nguvu kabisa, -gumu sana, -shupavu. — *v.t.* kongomea, pigilia misumari.

naïve, *a.* -nyofu, -sio na hila, -jinga. **naïveté**, *n.* unyofu, kweli, ujinga wa mambo.

naked, *a.* -tupu, -a utupu, -a uchi; (*bare, plain*) -tupu, wazi, halisi. *See with the naked eye*, ona kwa macho, ona dhahiri. *Stark naked*, uchi wa nyama. **nakedness**, *n.* utupu, uchi.

namby-pamby, *a.* dufu, hafifu,

baridi. — *n.* mwanamume hafifu, mpuzi.

name, *n.* jina, neno ambalo kwalo kitu (au mtu) kinatajwa; (*fame*) sifa. *What is your name?* jina lako nani? *What is the name of this town?* mji huu unaitwaje? *What is the name of the book?* kitabu kinaitwaje? *In the name of God,* kwa jina la Mungu, bismillahi (*Arabic*). *Call names,* tukana. *In name,* kwa jina tu (si kweli). *In the name of,* kwa ajili ya, mahali pa, kwa amri ya. *Give a dog a bad name and hang him,* laumu mtu kwa ajili ya sifa anazopewa kwa watu. — *v.t.* -pa jina, taja jina. **nameless,** *a.* bila jina, -siofaa kutajwa (kwa kuwa -baya mno). **namely,** *adv.* ndiyo, hivi, yaani. **namesake,** *n.* mwenye jina lilo hilo, mwenye jina sawa, somo.

nandy flame tree, *n.* (*Spathodea nilotica*) kifabakazi.

nanny-goat, *n.* mbuzi wa kike, mbuzi jike.

nap, (1) *n.* manyoya (nywele) mafupi ya nguo, zulia *&c.*

nap, (2) *n.* usingizi kidogo. *Be caught napping,* ghafilika, shtushwa.

nap, (3) *n.* mchezo fulani wa karata. *To go nap on,* kuwa na hakika ya kuwa jambo ni kweli, au ya kuwa lilitukia.

nape, *n.* ukosi, kikosi.

napery, *n.* vitambaa vya (nguo za) nyumbani, *e.g.* vya mezani *&c.*

naphtha, *n.* namna ya mafuta mepesi. **naphthalene,** *n.* namna ya dawa yenye harufu kali inayotumika kufukuza wadudu.

napkin, *n.* kitambaa cha mikono mezani; (*baby's*) kitambaa cha uwinda cha kumfungia mtoto.

narcissus, *n.* nargisi.

narcotic, *n.* dawa inayotia usingizi. — *a.* -a kutia usingizi.

narrate, *v.t.* hadithia, simulia, toa habari, nena; (*tell to*) ambia. **narration,** *n.* kuhadithia, kusimulia *&c.*; maneno, masimulizi. **narrative,** *n.* maneno, hadithi, kisa, habari, masimulizi; (*anecdote*) hekaya.

narrow, *a.* (*not broad*) -embamba, -a kufinya, -a finyo, -liofinyana, -dogo, kabibu; (*of circumstances*) -embamba, -a shida, -a dhiki; (*niggardly*) -a choyo, bahili, -nyimivu; (*in mind*) -a akili chache, -shupavu, -gumu, -a kushika lake. — *v.t.* fanya kuwa -embamba; — *v.i.* -wa -embamba, punguka upana. **narrowly,** *adv.* (*with difficulty*) kwa shida; (*with care*) kwa bidii (uangalifu). **narrow-minded,** *a.* -shupavu, -gumu, -a kushika lake.

narwhal, *n.* namna ya nyangumi mdogo.

nasal, *a.* -a pua, -a puani.

nascent, *a.* -a kuanza kuwa, -a kuanza kuota (kuchimbuka, kuchanuka).

nasty, *a.* -a kuchukiza, makuruhi, -chafu, -a taka; (*malicious &c.*) -a chuki, -enye nia mbaya; (*painful, dangerous*) -a kuumiza, -enye hatari; (*awkward*) -a shida, -a matata.

natal, *a.* -a kuzaliwa. — *n.* nchi ya Kepi.

nation, *n.* taifa. **national,** *a.* -a taifa lote, -a watu wote (wa taifa fulani. — *n.* mtu wa taifa fulani au mwenye haki zote za mtu wa taifa fulani. **nationalism,** *n.* fahari anayoona mtu kwa ajili ya taifa lake; shauri la kuhifadhi au kusitawisha taifa. **nationality,** *n.* hali ya mtu aliyezaliwa au kukubaliwa katika taifa fulani, kuwa taifa, taifa.

nationalize, *v.t.* ingiza katika taifa, fanya taifa, fanya kuwa mali ya taifa (ya serikali).

native, *n.* mzalia; (*non-European*) mtu asiye Mzungu, mwenyeji; (*uncivilized*) mtu wa taifa lisilostaarabika; (*product*) kizao. — *a.* (*inborn, natural, original*) -a asili; (*of native country*) -a kwetu (kwenu, kwao). *Native country,* nchi ya asili, kwetu (kwenu, kwao). **nativity,** *n.* uzaliwa, siku ya kuzaliwa.

natron, *n.* magadi.

natty, *a.* nadhifu, -safi, -malidadi; (*quick &c.*) -epesi, -stadi.

natural, *a.* taz. *nature.*
nature, *n.* asili, hali, maumbile, katiba, tabia, johari; (*natural appearance, shape*) umbo, hali, sura; (*kind*) jinsi, namna, aina; (*world*) ulimwengu, viumbe vyote, jamii ya vitu; (*habit*) desturi, kawaida, mazoea, silika; (*mortal*) moyo, tabia. *Calls of nature,* haja. *Laws of nature,* utaratibu wa ulimwengu, jambo la asili, kawaida ya vitu vyote, kanuni. *In the nature of,* kama, mfano wa. *Nature study,* elimu ya viumbe. *Nature worship,* kuabudu viumbe (kitu kilichoumbwa). *Ill-nature,* ukali, ubaya, utu mbaya, chuki. **natural,** *a.* -a asili *&c.* taz. *nature*; ake (-ao *&c.*) halisi; (*inevitable*) pasipo budi, sharti, -a kanuni; (*customary*) -a kawaida, -a desturi, kama siku zote; (*proper, fitting*) wajibu, ipasavyo, -zuri, -a kufaa. *Natural child,* mwana haramu. *Natural shape, form, constitution &c.* asili. hali ya asili, umbo, maumbile. *Natural history,* habari za vitu vyote, hasa ya vitu vyenye uhai. *Natural law,* kawaida, kanuni, kawaida za vitu vya ulimwengu, katiba. *Natural philosophy,* elimu ya vitu vya ulimwengu. *Natural science,* maarifa ya vitu vyote. *Natural selection,* maendeleo ya vitu vyenye uhai (dhaifu huisha, na -enye afya huishi na kuzaana). *Natural result* (*consequence, effect*) lisilo na budi kutokea, tokeo la faradhi. *Die a natural death,* -fa kibudu. **naturalist,** *n.* achunguzaye habari za mimea, wanyama, wadudu *&c.* **naturalize,** *v.t.* ingiza mgeni katika taifa; (*of animals, plants &c.*) zoeza (tabia za nchi nyingine). *Naturalized Frenchman,* Mfaransa kwa sheria lakini si kwa kuzaliwa. **naturally,** *adv.* kwa *nature*; (*easily*) kwa urahisi, sikuzote, kwa desturi; (*necessarily*) sharti, hakuna budi.
naught, *n.* hapana kitu. *All for naught,* bure, kazi bure. *Set at naught,* dharau, beza. *Bring to naught,* haribu, shinda. **naughtiness,** *n.* utundu, utukutu, ukaidi. **naughty,** *a.* -baya, -tundu, -tukutu, -kaidi.
nausea, *n.* ugagazi, uchefuchefu, kigagazi, kutaka kutapika, kutapika, kuchafuka moyo, kinyaa, unyarafu. **nauseate,** *v.t.* chukiza sana, chefuka, chafua moyo, tapisha; (*of food repeating*) puzia. **nauseous, nauseating,** *a.* -a kuchafua moyo, -a kunyarafu, -a kutapisha, -a kupuzia, -a kuchukiza sana, -a kutia kinyaa.
nautical, *a.* -a baharia, -a mambo ya meli (merikebu *&c.*), -a kusafiri baharini. *Nautical mile,* yadi 6080.
naval, *a.* -a manowari, -a mambo ya manowari. **navy,** *n.* jamii ya manowari zote za taifa fulani, manowari.
nave, *n.* sehemu kubwa ya kanisa katikati wasalipo watu.
navel, *n.* kitovu; (*protruding*) tungu (tovu).
navigate, *v.t.* ongoza (elekeza) meli (merikebu, eropleni *&c.*), safiri baharini (hewani). **navigable,** *a.* -a kuendeka kwa meli (merikebu *&c.*). **navigation,** *n.* safiri baharini, safari ya baharini; (*as a science*) maarifa ya kuongoza vyombo baharini, ya mambo ya meli (merikebu *&c.*). **navigator,** *n.* mwenye kujua *navigation,* kiongozi wa meli (merikebu, eropleni *&c.*), nahodha; (*pilot*) rubani.
navvy, *n.* kibarua, mtu wa kazi (hasa wa kazi ya kuchimba na kufanyiza barabara).
navy, *n.* taz. *naval.*
nay, *adv.* siyo, la, a-a.
naze, *n.* rasi.
neap, *n.* maji mafu (ya mbande), maji ya kupwa sana.
near, *a.* karibu; (*like*) kama sawa; (*miserly*) -a choyo, bahili, -nyimivu; (*critical*) -a shida. *He lives near* (*is a near neighbour*), anakaa karibu, yu jirani. *A near friend,* rafiki sana, msiri. *A near road,* njia ya kukata. *A near escape,* shida kuokoka. — *v.t.* karibia, sogea (jongea) karibu.

nearly, *adv.* karibu, kama. **nearness,** *n.* kuwa *near.* **near-sighted,** *a.* -sioona vema ila vitu vilivyo karibu.

neat, (1) *n.* ng'ombe. *Neat's-foot oil,* mafuta ya miguu ya ng'ombe.

neat, (2) *a.* -a taratibu, -zuri, nadhifu; (*person*) -nadhifu, -mbeja, -malidadi; (*of liquor*) bila kutia maji. *Make neat,* safidi, tengeneza, katua, kwatua. **neatly,** *adv.* vizuri; kwa akili. **neatness,** *n.* unadhifu, uzuri, usafi, utaratibu.

nebula, *n.* jamii ya nyota nyingi ndogo kama wingu. **nebulous,** *a.* (*indistinct*) kama wingu, -a unyenyezi, si wazi, si dhahiri.

necessary, *a.* -a lazima, -a faradhi, -a kanuni, -a sharti, -a juzu. **necessaries,** *n.* riziki, vifaa, manufaa; (*for a journey*) masurufu, posho. **necessarily,** *adv.* kwa lazima, sharti, kanuni. **necessitate,** *v.t.* fanya lazima ya, lazimisha, juzu. *It necessitates war,* haina budi italeta vita. **necessitous,** *a.* -a maskini, -a fukara.

neck, *n.* shingo, kitu kirefu chembamba kama shingo, rasi. *Neck and crop,* pia, kabisa. *Neck and neck,* sawasawa. *Neck or nothing,* kwa vyo vyote, kufa au kupona. *Stiff necked,* -shupavu, -kaidi, -gumu. **neckcloth,** *n.* kitambaa cha shingoni. **necklace,** *n.* mkufu. **necktie,** *n.* utepe wa shingoni.

necro-, *pfx.* -a kuhusu mauti. **necromancer,** *n.* mchawi (mlozi), hasa anayejidai uwezo wa kusema na wafu. **necromancy,** *n.* uchawi, ulozi, usihiri, uramali (hasa wa kusema na wafu). **necropolis,** *n.* makaburini, maziara. **necrosis,** *n.* kuoza kwa sehemu ya mwili (hasa mfupa).

nectar, *n.* (katika hadithi za kiyunani za zamani) kinywaji cha miungu; (*sweet drink*) kinywaji kitamu sana; (*of plants*) maji matamu yaliyo katika maua, asali. **nectarine,** *n.* namna ya tunda.

née, *a.* (-a kuzaliwa) *e.g. Mrs. Brown née Robinson,* yaani jina lake kabla hajaolewa lilikuwa *Robinson.*

need, *n.* uhitaji, hitaji, haja, matakwa udhuru; (*poverty*) umaskini, ufukara, ukata; (*lack*) ukosefu, upungufu, utovu; (*danger*) hatari, mashaka. — *v.t.* hitaji, taka, pungukiwa na; (*deserve*) stahili; — *v.i.* dhikika. *He need not come,* si lazima aje. **needful,** *a.* -liotakwa, -liohitajika, -a kufaa sana; (*indispensable*) kanuni, sharti. **needless,** *a.* -siotakwa, -a bure. **needs,** *adv.* sharti, hakuna budi. *He needs must do,* sharti afanye. **needy,** *a.* maskini, -a fukara, -kosefu, -hitaji.

needle, *n.* sindano; (*packing*) shazia, shasira; (*magnetic*) dira. *Thread a needle,* tunga sindano. **needlewoman,** *n.* mshoni (mwanamke). **needlework,** *n.* ushoni, kazi ya kushona.

needless, *a.* taz. *need.*

needlewoman, *n.*, **needlework,** *n.* taz. *needle.*

needs, *adv.*, **needy,** *a.* taz. *need.*

ne'er = **never.** *Ne'er-do-well,* mpotovu, mpotevu.

nefarious, *a.* -baya sana, -ovu.

negate, *v.t.* kana, kanusha, tangua. **negation,** *n.* kukana, kikano; (*opposite*) mbalimbali kabisa, kinyume. **negative,** *n.* kukana, kikano, kusema 'siyo, la'. *He replied in the negative,* alijibu, La. *A negative* (*photograph*), picha ya kufanyia nakala (sehemu nyeusi hutokea kuwa nyeupe katika nakala). — *a.* -a kukana, -a kukanusha, -a kutoa, -sio kitu, -a kinyume kabisa. *It had a negative result,* haikufaa neno. — *v.t.* kana, kanusha; sema, la; (*render useless*) tangua, zuia, pinza.

neglect, *v.t.* (*not attend to*) totunza, toangalia, tojali, tofanya, acha; (*slight*) tupa, dharau, hizi; (*do carelessly*) fanya kwa uzembe (kwa uvivu), purukusha, ghafilisha, kukusa. — *n.* kuacha, kutofanya kwa bidii, uzembe, udharau, ukosefu, utovu, upurukushani, kukosea; (*state of being neglected*) hali ya kuachwa (ya kutupwa, ya kudharauliwa). **neglectful**, *a.* -vivu, -zembe, -si -angalifu, si -ene kutunza, -sahaulifu, -a kukukusa. **negligence**, *n.* kutoangalia, kutojali, upukurushani, ukosefu, ulegevu, uvivu, usahaulifu, uzembe. **negligent**, *a.* taz. *neglectful.*

negotiate, *v.t.* fanya (fanyana) shauri, tengeneza; (*get over &c.*) pata, pita, fanyiza, weza; (*get money for*) badili kwa fedha; — *v.i.* fanya (fanyana) shauri. **negotiable**, *a.* -a kufaa kwa biashara, -a kupatikana, -a kutumikana; (*of roads &c.*) -a kupitika. **negotiation**, *n.* shauri, shughuli, maneno, biashara, mapatano.

negro, *n.* mtu mweusi (mwanamume). **negress**, *n.* mtu mweusi (mwanamke). **negroid**, *a.* -a watu weusi, kama watu weusi, -enye baadhi ya tabia za *negro.*

negus, *n.* divai ya moto iliyochanganyika na maji, sukari na limau.

neigh, *v.i.* lia (farasi). — *n.* mlio wa farasi.

neighbour, *n.* jirani, mtu akaaye karibu; (*in wider sense*) ndugu. **neighbourhood**, *n.* ujirani, nchi ya kandokando. *In the neighbourhood of*, upande wa, karibu ya, katika mtaa wa. *Neighbouring estates*, mashamba yanayopakana. **neighbourly**, *a.* -ema, -fadhili.

neither, *adv.* wala. *Neither . . nor*, wala . . . wala. — *a.* si . . . ote, wala hii wala hii, si . . . hata -moja.

nemesis, *n.* kisasi, hasara (maumivu, madhara &c.) iletwayo na mambo mabaya aliyofanya mtu mwenyewe.

neo-, *pfx.* -a siku hizi, -pya. **neolithic**, *a.* -a mawe mapya. *Neolithic age*, zamani za miaka 10,000 watu walipofanyiza vyombo vya mawe vilivyoshinda vile vya kabla ya wakati huo. **neology**, *n.* uzushi wa kubuni maneno mapya au maana mpya kwa maneno ya zamani, elimu mpya ya kigeni. **neophyte**, *n.* mtu mpya, yaani aliyeingia kazi (dini, cheo &c.) siku hizi, mwanafunzi.

nephew, *n.* mtoto (mwanamume) wa ndugu, mpwa, *e.g. my nephew*, mpwangu. *Their nephew*, mpwao.

nephritis, *n.* ugonjwa wa mafigo.

nepotism, *n.* kuwapendelea jamaa (kuwapa daraja kuu zenye mshahara mkubwa).

nerve, *n.* neva, mshipa wa fahamu; (*courage*) moyo mgumu, uthabiti, nguvu; (*impudence*) ujuvi, ukavu wa macho, ufidhuli, usafihi. *Strain every nerve*, jitahidi sana. *Have the nerve to*, thubutu, jasiria. *Suffer from nerves*, shikwa na majonzi (wasiwasi, harara, hasira ya ghafula &c.). — *v.t. e.g. nerve oneself*, jipa moyo mkuu. **nerveless**, *a.* -legevu, dhaifu, -nyogovu, -nyong'onyevu. **nervous**, *a.* -epesi kushtuka, -a harakaharaka; (*excitable, timid*) dhaifu, -oga; (*courageous*) thabiti, -a nguvu. *A nervous breakdown*, ugonjwa wa akili uletwao na mashaka au kazi nyingi. **nervousness**, *n.* woga, wasiwasi, haya, fadhaa, chachari, machachari.

nest, *n.* kiota, kioto, tundu. *Feather one's nest*, jipatia mali (pengine kwa njia mbaya). *A nest of vice*, makao ya watu wafanyao maovu. *Nest-egg*, akiba. — *v.i.* jenga kiota, taga mayai katika kiota na kuyaatamia.

nestle, *v.i.* vamia, songelea kitu kama ndege afanyavyo katika kiota chake, au mtoto anaposogelea mama yake, tulia; — *v.t.* sogeza, weka. **nestling**, *n.* kinda, kidege; (*chicken*) kifaranga.

net, (1) *n.* wavu; (*casting*) kimia; (*seine*) jarifa, juya. *Mosquito net*, chandalua. — *v.t.* vua, nasa, tega; (*gain*) pata, faidi; — *v.i.* (*make net*) fanyiza wavu &c. **netting**, **network**, *n.* wavu, kimia &c. taz. *net.*

net, (2) *a.* bila kupunguzika. *Net price*, bei halisi (haipunguziki). *Net gain* (*profit*), faida halisi, faida tupu.

nether, *a.* -a chini. **nethermost**, *a.* -a chini kabisa.

netting, *n*. taz. *net* (1).
nettle, *n*. kiwawi. — *v.t.* kasirisha, chokoza, udhi, sumbua.
network, *n*. taz. *net* (1).
neuralgia, *n*. hijabu, maumivu ya neva (mishipa ya fahamu), hasa kichwani. **neurasthenia**, *n*. udhaifu (ugonjwa) usio wa mwili ila uletwao na uchovu wa *nerves*. **neuritis**, *n*. kama *neuralgia*. **neurotic**, *a*. -sioweza kutulia (kujizuia, kujiweza).
neuter, *a*. wala -a kiume wala -a kike.
neutral, *a*. wala -a upande huu wala -a upande huu, katikati, wala hivi wala hivi, -siopendelea, peke yake (yao &c.). *I am neutral*, mimi simo. *A neutral person*, mtu baki. **neutrality**, *n*. kuwa *neutral*, hali ya *neutral*, kutopendelea, kutokuwamo.
neutralize, *v.t.* tangua, batilisha, komesha.
never, *adv*. si . . . kamwe, si . . . wakati wo wote (wa sasa, uliopita, utakaokuja), si . . . aushi, si . . . abadan. *With neg., e.g. it is never used now*, haitumiki siku hizi; *it never has been used*, haijatumika; *it never was used*, haikutumika; *it never shall be used*, haitatumika kamwe; *never refuse work*, usikatae kazi hata siku moja; *never despair*, usikate tamaa wakati wo wote. *He answered never a word*, hakujibu hata neno. *I will do it, never fear*, bila shaka nitafanya. **nevermore**, *adv*. si tena kabisa. **nevertheless**, *conj*. walakini, lakini, hata hivyo.
new, *a*. -pya; (*strange, novel*) -geni; (*different*) -ingine; (*fresh*) -bichi; (*unaccustomed*) -jinga, si -zoevu, -zuzu; (*late, modern*) -a karibu, -a siku hizi, -a kisasa. *New moon*, mwezi mwandamo, mwezi mchanga. *New Testament*, Agano Jipya, maandiko matakatifu ya Wakristo. *New World*, Amerika. *A new fashion* (*new of its kind*), mtindo. *Newfangled*, -a kizushi, -a kigeni. *A newcomer*, mgeni; (*lacking experience*) mjinga, mzuzu. **newness**, *n*. kuwa *new*, upya, ugeni, ubichi. **news**, *n*. habari za mambo yaliyotokea karibuni; habari; (*written*) taarifa; (*fresh information*) habari mpya. *Break the news*, ambia habari (hasa ya msiba). *News of a death*, tanzia. **newsagent**, *n*. mwuza magazeti. **newsmonger**, *n*. mdakuzi, mpayukaji. **newspaper**, *n*. gazeti, karatasi yenye habari. **newsvendor**, *n*. mwuza magazeti.
Newfoundland (*dog*), *n*. namna ya mbwa mkubwa mwenye manyoya marefu.
newness, *n*., **news**, *n*., **newsagent**, *n*., **newsmonger**, *n*., **newspaper**, *n*., **newsvendor**, *n*. taz. *new*.
newt, *n*. mnyama mdogo wa ziwani kama mjusi.
next, *a*. -a pili, -a karibu, -a kufuata, -nayokuja. — *adv*. tena, baadaye, aidha, halafu. — *prep*. karibu ya, -a pili ya.
nib, *n*. ncha ya kalamu ya wino.
nibble, *v.i.* tafuna (mega) kidogo kidogo, guguna.
nice, *a*. -ema, -zuri, -a kupendeza, -a furaha; (*to taste*) -tamu, -zuri; (*exact*) halisi; (*precise, dainty*) -a kuchagua, -chaguzi, -teuzi; (*minute*) -dogo sana. *A nice argument*, neno linalotatiza sana, lililo gumu kukata, linalohitajiwa kufikiriwa sana. **nicely**, *adv*. vizuri. **nicety**, *n*. uzuri, uhalisi, usahihi, bidii ya kuchagua, kupambanua kwa akili. *To a nicety*, hasa, halisi. **niceties**, *n*. mambo madogo madogo; (*of style* ufasaha.
niche, *n*. kidaka, kishubaka, pembe.
nick, *n*. pengo, kipengo, pelezi. *The nick of time*, wakati ufaao hasa, papo kwa papo.
nickel, *n*. namna ya madini nyeupe ngumu kama fedha; (*coin*) sarafu ya Amerika kadiri ya senti 30.
nicknacks, *n*. taz. *knick-knack*.
nickname, *n*. jina la kupanga, jina la fumbo (msimbo, simo).
nicotine, *n*. sumu iliyo katika tumbako.

nidification, *n.* (ndege) kufanya tundu (kiota).
niece, *n.* mtoto (mwanamke) wa ndugu, mpwa wa kike.
niggard, *n.* mtu wa choyo, bahili, mnyimivu. **niggardly,** *a.* -choyo, bahili, -nyimivu, -nyiminyimi.
nigger, *n.* mtu mweusi (hasa ni neno la dharau).
niggle, *v.i.* shughulikia mambo madogodogo.
nigh, *adv.* karibu. *Draw nigh,* karibia.
night, *n.* usiku; (*darkness*) giza. *All night,* usiku kucha. *Last night,* usiku wa leo. *To-night,* usiku huu (ujao). *A night and a day,* kuchwa kucha. **nightcap,** *n.* kofia ya kuvaa wakati wa kulala; (*drink*) kinywaji (hasa kileo) cha kunywa kabla ya kulala. **nightfall,** *n.* magharibi, mshuko wa esha, kuchwa, jioni. **nightingale,** *n.* ndege mdogo wa Ulaya aimbaye usiku vizuri sana. **nightjar,** *n.* pwaju, mraruasanda, mpasuasanda, kirukanjia. **nightly,** *a.* -a usiku, -a kila usiku. **nightmare,** *n.* jinamizi. **nightshade,** *n.* mtua, mtunguja. **night-watch,** *n.* zamu za usiku; mlinzi wa usiku, mngoja zamu usiku.
nihilist, *n.* mchukia serikali.
nil, *n.* hapana kitu.
Nilotic, *a.* -a mto *Nile* na kandokando zake.
nimble, *a.* -epesi, hodari (-a kazi), -elekevu.
nimbus, *n.* wingu la mvua; (*halo*) uzingo duara ya rangi ya dhahabu au nuru.
nincompoop, *n.* mjinga, baradhuli, mzuzu, mpumbavu.
nine, *n. and a.* kenda, tisa. **nineteen,** *n. and a.* kumi na kenda, tisatashara. **nineteenth,** *a.* -a kumi na kenda. **ninetieth,** *a.* -a tisini. **ninety,** *n. and a.* tisini. **ninth,** *a.* -a tisa, -a kenda.
ninny, *n.* mjinga, baradhuli, mzuzu, mpumbavu.
ninth, *a.* taz. *nine.*
nip, *v.t. and i.* minya, finya, binya, nyakua, uma ghafula; (*destroy*) songa, kata, haribu. *Nip in the bud,* komesha mwanzoni. *Nip along,* enda upesi. — *n.* mminyo, mfinyo mbinyo, msongo, mkato, pigo. **nipper,** *n.* (*of crab &c.*) gando, gondi; (*forceps*) kibano; (*for depilation*) mentari; (*pincers, pliers*) koleo; (*boy*) mtoto mwanamume, kivulana. **nippy,** *a.* -epesi.
nipple, *n.* (*of breast*) chuchu, titi; (*of gun*) kifa; (*generally*) kinundu.
nippy, *a.* taz. *nip.*
nirvana, *n.* raha baada ya kufa (kwa dini ya Buddha).
nit, *n.* yai la chawa (la utitiri).
nitre, *n.* shura.
nitrogen, *n.* *gas* iliyomo hewani, sehemu ya tano kwa nne ya jumla ya hewa. Imo katika kila kitu chenye uhai *e.g.* wanyama na miti. **nitrogenous,** *a.* -enye *nitrogen.*
nix, *n.* (*slang*) hapana kitu.
no, *adv.* siyo, la, hakuna, hapana. — *a.* hapana, si. *There is no food,* hapana chakula. *He is no fool,* yeye si mpumbavu (ni mtu mwenye akili). *No doubt,* hapana shaka. *He had no luck (food &c.),* hakuwa na bahati (chakula &c.). *He will come no more,* haji tena.
noble, *a.* bora, -kuu, -enye cheo kikubwa, -enye tabia nzuri, -sharifu. — *n.* mtu mwenye cheo fulani kama *peer.* **nobility,** *n.* daraja bora, cheo kikubwa, *e.g.* cha *peer*; (*character*) wema, ubora; (*class*) watu wakubwa, watu wa cheo. **nobleman,** *n.* mtu mwenye cheo (daraja) kikubwa, *e.g. peer.* **nobly,** *adv.* vema, vizuri, kwa uhodari.
nobody, *n.* si mtu. *Nobody is there,* hapana mtu. *Nobody knows,* hajui hata mtu, hakuna ajuaye. *A mere nobody,* mtu tu (asiye na cheo).
nocturnal, *a.* -a usiku.
nod, *v.t.* inamisha kichwa (ishara ya kukubali, kuamkia au kusinzia); — *v.i.* (*doze*) sinzia, kupia; (*bend*) inama, yumbayumba. — *n.* mwi-

namo wa kichwa. *The land of Nod,* usingizi, ndoto.
noddle, *n.* kichwa.
node, *n.* kivimbe, kinundu, kifundo. **nodular,** *a.* -enye vifundo (vivimbe, vinundu). **nodule,** *n.* kinundu, kifundo, kivimbe, kijiwe, kipumba.
Noel, *n.* sikukuu ya Kuzaliwa kwake Kristo.
noggin, *n.* kikombe, kopo dogo.
noise, *n.* sauti, mlio, kishindo, uvumi; (*uproar*) makelele, ghasia, hoihoi, zahama. **noiseless,** *a.* pasipo *noise,* -a kimya. **noisily,** *adv.* kwa kelele (kishindo). **noisy,** *a.* -a makelele, -a kishindo kikubwa, -a ghasia.
noisome, *a.* -a kuchukiza, -a kinyaa, -a kudhuru, -baya sana.
noisy, *a.* taz. *noise.*
nomad, *a.* -siokaa mahali ila huhamahama, -sio na makao. — *n.* mtu asiye na makao maalum ila huhamahama. **nomadic,** *a.* taz. *nomad, a.*
nom de plume, *n.* jina la kujipa (analotumia mwandishi wa vitabu).
nomenclature, *n.* majina, utaratibu wa majina au kutia majina.
nominal, *n.* -a jina -a jina, tu, -a maneno tu, si kweli, si halisi, -a uwongo. **nominally,** *adv.* kwa jina, kwa maneno tu, si kweli. **nominate,** *v.t.* (*name*) ita, taja, andika; (*appoint*) amuru, chagua, weka. **nomination,** *n.* kuita, kutaja, mtajo, kuandika, kuchagua, mchaguo. **nominee,** *n.* mtu aliyechaguliwa (aliyeandikwa, aliyewekwa).
non- (mwanzoni pa neno, maana yake kama **not, un-, in-**) si.
nonage, *n.* utoto, kama utoto.
nonagenarian, *n.* mtu mwenye umri wa miaka tisini.
nonce, *n.* *For the nonce,* kwa sasa.
nonchalance, *n.* uzembe, utepetevu, ubaridi, ukavu wa macho, ujuvi.
non-combatant, *n.* mtu asiye askari, raia.
non-commissioned officer, *n.* afisa mdogo (*sergeant, corporal*).
non-committal, *a.* -a kutosema kusudi lake (lao *&c.*), -a kutokana wala kukubali, -a kutosema ndiyo wala siyo.
non-conductor, *n.* kitu kisichopitisha kitu kingine (yaani kisichopitisha nguvu ya kitu kama umeme, joto *&c.*), kizuio.
nonconformist, *n.* mtu asiyekubali kutenda (au kuamini) wanayotenda (au kuamini) wengine, hasa ni Mkristo asiyekubali kawaida nyingine nezo za Kanisa.
non-content, *n.* asiyekubali shauri kwa jambo fulani.
nondescript, *a.* -sioelezeka vizuri, -sio -a namna (aina, jinsi) maalum, -sio na tabia maalum.
none, *a.* si hata moja, hapana mtu, hapana kitu. *There were none present,* hapana aliyekuwapo.
nonentity, *n.* mtu tu (asiye wa maana); (*thing*) si kitu; (*insignificant object*) kinyonge, hafifu.
nonesuch, *n.* taz. *nonsuch.*
non-existence, *n.* kutokuwa kabisa. **non-existent,** *a.* *It is simply non-existent,* hapana kitu hicho kabisa, si kitu.
nonpareil, *a.* bila mfano (kwa kuwa -zuri, bora *&c.*), -zuri kabisa, bora kabisa.
nonplus, *n.* mashaka, fadhaa. — *v.t.* pumbaza, tunduwaza, fadhaisha, duwaza, bumbuaza, rabishi. *Be nonplussed,* pumbaa, duwaa, shangaa, fadhaika, bahashika.
nonsense, *n.* upuzi, puo, mapiswa, maneno tu. *Talk nonsense,* puzika, payuka, piga domo, sema, upuzi, bwata, babaika, bwabwaja. *Nonsense!* upuzi! mawe! **nonsensical,** *a.* -a upuzi, -a kuchekesha.
nonsuch, *n.* mtu (kitu) asiye na mfano, aliye (kilicho) bora kabisa.
nonsuit, *n.* kutolewa sheriani (kwa sababu ya kutokuwa na ushuhuda).
noodle, *n.* mjinga, baradhuli, mpumbavu, mzuzu.
nook, *n.* pembe, kipembe, kificho.
noon, noonday, noontide, *n.* adhuhuri, jua kichwani; (*prime &c.*)

kipeo cha usitawi, wakati (siku) wa kusitawi.

noose, *n.* tanzi, kitanzi, shalaka, kishwara.

nor, *conj.* wala. *Neither ... nor*, si ... wala, wala ... wala.

norm, *n.* kawaida, kanuni, cheo (namna) cha kawaida. **normal**, *a.* -a kawaida, -a sikuzote, -a desturi, kadiri. *A normal school*, chuo wanamofundishwa walimu. **normally**, *adv.* kwa kawaida, kwa desturi.

north, *n.* kaskazini, kibla. *North winds*, kaskazi, shemali. *The north*, upande wa kaskazini, nchi za kaskazini. *Steer to the north* (*northwards*), shika majira ya jaa. — *a.* -a kaskazini. **north-east**, *n.* *and a.* kati ya kaskazi na matlai, mashariki ya kaskazini. **northerly, northern**, *a.* -a kaskazini. **northernmost**, *a.* -a kaskazini kabisa. **northward**, *adv.* upande wa kaskazi. **north-west**, *n.* *and a.* kati ya kaskazi na magharibi, magharibi ya kaskazini. **north-western, north-westerly**, *a.* -a *north-west.*

Norwegian, *a.* -a *Norway* (nchi moja ya Ulaya).

nose, *n.* pua; (*projecting part*) mdomo, mkono. *Nose-ring*, hazama. *Speak through the nose*, semea puani, sema kwa puani, sema king'ong'o. *Cut off one's nose to spite one's face*, jifanyia mwenyewe hasara katika hasira. *Follow one's nose*, enda mbele moja kwa moja. *Keep one's nose to the grindstone*, shikilia kazi, jikalifu. *Turn up the nose at*, dharau. — *v.t.* (*out*) vumbua, gundua; (*nuzzle*) gusagusa kwa pua; — *v.i.* (*sniff, smell*) nusa; (*interfere. meddle*) jitia, jidukiza. **nosegay**, *n.* fungu (shada) la maua. **nosey, nosy**, *a.* -enye tabia ya kujitia (ya kujidukiza). **nostril**, *n.* tundu la pua, mwanzi wa pua.

nostalgia, *n.* majonzi (huzuni, moyo mzito) ya mtu anapokumbuka kwake.

nostril, *n.* taz. *nose.*

nostrum, *n.* dawa ya siri, dawa ya uwongo, dawa ya hila.

not, *adv.* si; (*in verbs*) si-, ha- &c. *Not so*, sivyo, hakuna, la, *Not at all, Not a bit*, si hata kidogo, hasha. *Not to say, Not only not*, licha ya, sembuse. *Not a man spoke*, hakusema hata mtu. *He is not going*, haendi. *I am not going*, siendi.

notability, *n.*, **notable**, *a.*, **notary**, *n.*, **notation**, *n.* taz. *note.*

notch, *n.* pengo; (*of arrow*) koleo; (*in upright poles for building*) makwa. — *v.t.* tia pengo, katia.

note, *n.* (*letter*) barua, hati, waraka, cheti; (*mark*) ishara, alama; (*fame*) sifa, jina; (*memorandum*) ukumbusho, maneno ya kukumbusha, muhtasari, fahamu; (*musical*) sauti (moja moja); (*written*) nukta, chapa. *Note of hand*, hati, hawala. *A man of note*, mtu mkubwa (mashuhuri). *Take note!* fahamu! **note** *v.t.* (*observe*) angalia, fahamu; (*make a note of*) kumbuka, andika. **notability**, *n.* kujulikana sana; (*person*) mtu mkubwa (mashuhuri). **notable**, *a.* -a kujulika sana, -enye jina, -kubwa ajabu, -zuri, mashuhuri, -enye sifa. **notary**, *n.* karani, mwandishi (wa hati za sheria. **notation**, *n.* mwandiko. **noted**, *a.* -enye sifa, mashuhuri, maarufu, -a kujulikana, -kubwa, -zuri. **noteworthy**, *a.* -a kustahili kukumbukwa, (kuangaliwa).

nothing, *n.* si kitu. *A mere nothing*, jambo (kitu) dogo sana. *For nothing*, bure, bilashi, pasipo faida, bila hesabu. *Good for nothing*, -siofaa neno, -ovu kabisa. *Make nothing of*, toweza kufahamu (kutumia), toelewa, shindwa na. *To say nothing of*, sembuse, licha.

notice, *n.* habari, maarifa, taarifa, tangazo, ilani; (*warning*) onyo, ishara; (*document*) hati; (*attention*) heshima, upendeleo. *Give notice*, (*advertise*), tangaza. — *v.t.* (*observe*) angalia, sikia, ona, tanabahi; (*mention*) taja, nena; (*favour*) heshimu, pendelea, tendea mazuri. **notice-**

able, *a.* -a maana, -zuri, -a kutazamisha, -a kukumbukwa.

notify, *v.t.* julisha, arifu, toa habari, tangaza. **notification,** *n.* taarifa, habari; (*written*) tangazo, ilani, hati, cheti.

notion, *n.* wazo, nia, fikira, dhana. *I have not a notion,* sifahamu hata kidogo, sijui mwenyewe. **notional,** *a.* -a mawazo, -a akili; (*fanciful*) -a kuwaza tu (si halisi).

notorious, *a.* -bayana, -enye sifa mbaya, -liojulika kuwa -baya. **notoriety,** *n.* ubayana, ubaini, sifa mbaya; (*person*) mtu maarufu.

notwithstanding, *adv. prep. and conj.* walakini, lakini, ijapo, ijapokuwa, ingawa. *Notwithstanding advice, he went,* ijapokuwa alionywa, alikwenda.

nought, *n.* si kitu, si neno; (*arith.*) sifuri. *Come to nought,* batilika, tanguka, angamia. *Bring to nought,* batilisha, tangua, angamiza.

noun, *n.* (katika elimu ya sarufi) jina la kitu.

nourish, *v.t.* lisha, chunga, lea, otesha; (*increase*) ongeza, zidisha; (*a design &c.*) shika moyoni, azimu, kusudia. **nourishment,** *n.* kulisha, kuotesha; (*food*) chakula, maakuli.

nous, *n.* akili, busara.

novel, *a.* -pya, -geni, -zushi. *A novel occurrence,* kizushi, shani, kioja, ajabu. — *n.* kitabu chenye hadithi (iliyobunika). **novelette,** *n.* *novel* fupi. **novelist,** *n.* mwandishi wa *novel.* **novelty,** *n.* upya, ugeni; (*new thing*) kitu kipya, kizushi, shani.

November, *n.* mwezi wa edashara wa mwaka wa kizungu, Novemba.

novice, *n.* mwanafunzi, mtu mpya wa kazi *&c.*; (*religious*) mwanafunzi wa dini (wa chama cha dini). **noviciate,** *n.* hali ya kuwa *novice,* uanafunzi.

now, *adv.* sasa, sasa hivi, mara hiyo, mara moja. *Now and then,* pana siku, pengine. *Now then, come along!* haya, twende zetu. — *n.* sasa. *Up to now,* mpaka sasa. — *conj.* ikawa, lakini, basi, sikiliza *&c.* **nowadays,** *n.* siku hizi, siku zetu.

noways, *adv.* si . . . kwa njia yo yote, sivyo kabisa.

nowhere, *adv.* si . . . mahali po pote.

nowise, *adv.* si . . . kwa jinsi yo yote, si vyo vyote.

noxious, *a.* -a kudhuru, -enye madhara, -a kuchukiza, -baya.

nozzle, *n.* mdomo, pua.

nuance, *n.* hitilafu ndogo, tofauti ndogo (katika maana ya neno, ya rangi, ya jinsi ya kuonyesha maono *&c.*).

nubile, *a.* -a kuoleka (mwanamke).

nucleus, *n.* kiini, chanzo, asili, sehemu ya kati.

nude, *n.* -tupu, uchi, bila kuvaa nguo. **nudity,** *n.* utupu, uchi.

nudge, *v.t.* kumba, piga kikumbo, dukua, tia mdukuo. —*n.* mdukuo, kikumbo.

nudity, *n.* taz. *nude.*

nugatory, *a.* hafifu, -siofaa kitu, -sio na thamani, -a bure, batili.

nugget, *n.* kipande, kibumba (cha dhahabu au madini).

nuisance, *n.* udhia, usumbuo, machukizo, jambo (kitu, mtu, tendo) linaloudhi (linalodhuru, linalochukiza), kero.

null, *a.* batili, -liotanguka. *Be null and void,* tanguka, -fa. **nullify,** *v.t.* batili, batilisha, tangua, vunja, futa, ondoa. **nullity,** *a.* si kitu, si neno.

numb, *a.* -enye ganzi, -zito, -legevu. — *v.t.* tia (fanya) ganzi. **numbness,** *n.* ganzi, uzito, ufu.

number, *n.* hesabu, kiwango, idadi, namba; (*many*) wingi, watu wengi, kundi; (*poetic*) mashairi; (*arith.*) hesabu (*written*) tarakimu. *A number of books,* vitabu vingi. *A number of people,* watu wengi. *A book in numbers,* kitabu kwa sehemu (kwa mafungu). *In great numbers,* -ingi, tele. *They are without number* (*numberless*), hayana idadi. — *v.t.* tia hesabu (namba); (*amount to*) pata, *e.g. the people numbered fifty,* watu walipata hamsini; (*count,* *reckon*) hesabia. **numberless,** *a.* -ingi, -ingi sana, kupita hesabu, pasipo idadi.

numbness, *n.* taz. *numb.*

numeral, *a.* -a hesabu, -a tarakimu. — *n.* tarakimu, herufi ya hesabu. **numeration,** *n.* hesabu, kuhesabu. **numerator,** *n.* kadiri ya sehemu. **numeric, numerical,** *a.* -a hesabu. **numerous,** *a.* -ingi.

numismatics, *n.* elimu ya sarafu na nishani.

numskull, *n.* mpumbavu, baradhuli.

nun, *n.* *monk* wa kike. **nunnery,** *n.* nyumba ya *nuns.*

nuncio, *n.* mjumbe wa *Pope.*

nunnery, *n.* taz. *nun.*

nuptial, *a.* -a arusi. **nuptials,** *n.* arusi.

nurse, *n.* (*children*) mlezi, aya; (*of sick*) mwuguzi (hasa wa kike). — *v.t.* (*sick*) uguza, tunza (mgonjwa); (*feed child*) nyonyesha; (*look after*) lea; (*use with care &c.*) tunza, angalia (*entertain in mind*) weka, fikiri. **nursery,** *n.* chumba cha watoto wadogo. **nursling,** *n.* mtoto mchanga.

nurture, *n.* malezi; (*food*) chakula. — *v.t.* lea.

nut, *n.* kokwa; (*ground-nut, peanut*) njugu nyasa, karanga, (*hard*) njugu mawe; (*coco-nut*) nazi; (*almond*) lozi; (*African almond*) kungu. **nutcrackers,** *n.* kitu cha kubanjia kokwa. **nutshell,** *n.* gamba (ganda) la kokwa; (*of coco-nut*) kifuu. *In a nutshell,* kwa maneno machache sana, kwa vichache, rahisi kufahamu.

nutmeg, *n.* kungumanga; (*spice*) basibasi.

nutriment, *n.* chakula, maakuli. **nutrition,** *n.* kulisha, kuotesha; (*food*) chakula. **nutritious, nutritive,** *a.* -a kulisha, -a kuotesha, -a kukuza, -enye chakula.

nutshell, *n.* taz. *nut.*

nuzzle, *v.t. and i.* gusagusa (kumba) kwa pua (kama mbwa afanyavyo).

nymph, *n.* mwanamwali mzuri; (*fairy*) zimwi.

O

O, *int.* taz. *oh*; (*as invocation &c.*) ee, (*pl.*) enyi.

oaf, *n.* mpumbavu, mjinga, mzuzu.

oak, *n.* mti wa Ulaya unaoishi miaka mingi sana; mbao zake ni ngumu mno.

oakum, *n.* nyuzinyuzi za kamba iliyochakaa na kufumuliwa; hutumika kwa kukalfati.

oar, *n.* kasia. **oarsman,** *n.* mpiga kasia, baharia.

oasis, *n.* mahali penye miti na chemchemi katika jangwa.

oaten, *a.* taz. *oats.*

oath, *n.* uapo, kiapo, halafa; (*Mohammedan*) yamini; (*curse*) laana, apizo. *To take an oath on the Koran,* kuapa Kurani, kula yamini. *Put on oath,* apisha. *Upon your oath!* utaapa! *Exchange oaths,* apiana. *Administer an oath,* apisha.

oats, *n.* nafaka kama shayiri. *Sow one's wild oats* (kijana) jifurahisha katika maisha ya ufasiki kabla ya kutungamana na kukaa vizuri. **oaten,** *a.* -a *oats.* **oatmeal,** *n.* unga wa *oats.*

obdurate, *a.* -shupavu, -gumu, -kaidi. **obduracy,** *n.* ushupavu, ugumu, ukaidi.

obedient, *a.*, **obedience,** *n.* taz. *obey.*

obeisance, *n.* *Make an obeisance,* inama kichwa (ishara ya kuheshimu, kustahi &c.), sujudu, shika miguu.

obelisk, *n.* nguzo (mnara) ndefu yenye pande za mraba iliyochongoka juu.

obese, *a.* -nene sana, -enye tumbo kubwa, -a kitumbo. **obesity,** *n.* unene, tumbo.

obey, *v.t. and i.* tii, sikia, tumikia, fanya jinsi ilivyoagizwa au kuamriwa. **obedient,** *a.* -tii, -tiifu, -sikivu, -sikizi. **obedience,** *n.* utii, usikivu, usikizi.

obfuscate, *v.t.* fumba, tatiza, pumbaza, shangaza.

obituary, *n.* tanzia, orodha ya majina ya watu waliofariki.

object, (1) *n.* kitu, neno, jambo; (*aim, purpose*) nia, wazo, kusudi, gharadhi; (*matter for pity, ridicule &c.*) maskini, kitu (mtu, jambo) cha kuchukiza (cha kuhurumisha, cha kuhuzunisha &c.); (*grammat.*) neno linaloonyesha 'nini' au 'nani' aliyetendewa tendo la *verb. My object is,* kusudi langu ni, nataka, ndiyo nitakayo. *An object lesson,* mafundisho juu ya kitu kwa kukionyesha kitu chenyewe. **objective,** *a.* -a kitu (jambo &c.) kilichopo wala si cha kuwaziwa tu. — *n.* shabaha, kusudi; (*military*) mahali panaposhambuliwa (panapoendewa). **objectless,** *a.* pasipo kusudi (shauri, maana); -a bure, -pumbavu.

object, (2) *v.t.* kataa, bisha, teta, dakuliza, tokubali, toridhia; (*resist*) shindana, zuia. **objection,** *n.* katazo, kinzano, dakizo, teto, udaku; (*obstacle &c.*) kizuizi, zuio; (*feeling of dislike &c.*) uchungu, machukio, kutopenda. **objectionable,** *a.* -a kuchukiza, -a kutia uchungu, -baya, -siopendeza.

objective, *a. and n.*, **objectless,** *a.* taz *object* (1).

objurgate, *v.t.* kemea, karipia, shutumu, tukana. **objurgation,** *n.* kemeo, karipio, mashutumu, matukano.

oblate, *a.* -a kubenuka au kutokeza kidogo mbavuni.

oblation, *n.* kutoa, toleo, sadaka, dhabihu, kafara.

oblige, *v.t.* lazimisha, shurutisha, juzu, bidi; (*do service to*) fadhili, tendea mema, fanyia hisani. **obligation,** *n.* sharti, lazima, kanuni; (*contract*) mapatano; (*debt*) deni; (*duty*) jambo lipasalo (linalobidi), wajibu. *Moral obligation,* amri ya Mungu, kawaida, wema wa asili. *Positive obligation,* amri ya mtu, neno la binadamu, jambo la sharti. *Put under an obligation,* bidi, pasisha, fadhili, funga. *Be under an obligation,* paswa, fungwa, wiwa. **obligatory,** *a.* faradhi, -a lazima, -a sharti, -a kujuzu. **obliging,** *a.* -a fadhili, -ema, -karimu, tayari kusaidia.

oblique, *a.* -a kwenda upande, mshazari, -a kukingama -enye matemo; (*indirect, bad*) -potovu, -baya, -a kukosa. **obliquity,** *n.* kuwa *oblique.*

obliterate, *v.t.* futa, futia mbali, ondoa kabisa, haribu.

oblivion, *n.* usahaulifu, kutokumbuka, kusahauliwa. *Be buried in oblivion,* sahauliwa kabisa. **oblivious,** *a.* -sahaulifu, -a kupotea katika fikira.

oblong, *a.* -refu kuliko -pana. — *n.* mstatili, umbo kama mraba lakini pande mbili zinazoelekeana ni ndefu kuliko zile nyingine.

obloquy, *n.* matukano, mashutumu, masingizio; kemeo, karipio, lawama; (*shame*) aibu, fedheha.

obnoxious, *a.* -a kuchukiza, makuruhi.

oboe, *n.* namna ya zomari.

obscene, *a.* -chafu, -a kinyaa, -pujufu. **obscenity**, *n.* uchafu, kinyaa, upujufu.

obscure, *a.* (*dark*) -a giza; (*hidden, indistinct*) -a siri, -a mbali, -a kujificha, -a unyenyezi; (*puzzling*) -a fumbo, -a kutatiza, -gumu, -a mashaka, -si dhahiri; (*base, insignificant*) -nyonge, hafifu, duni. — *v.t.* tia giza, fumba, tatiza, ficha, setiri; (*disguise*) geuza. **obscuration**, *n.* kutia (kutiwa) giza, hali ya kufumba (ya kutiwa giza &c.). **obscurity**, *n.* giza; (*indistinctness*) fumbo, matata; (*baseness*) unyonge.

obsequies, *n.* maziko.

obsequious, *a.* -enye kutii kwa unyenyekevu sana, -a kujipendekeza, -a kujifanya kama mtumwa, -a kurairai.

observe, *v.t.* angalia, ona, chungua, chunguza, tanabahi; (*say*) nena, sema; (*obey*) tii, sikia; (*keep*) fuata, shika, shikilia; (*keep solemnly*) adhimisha, tukuza. **observable**, *a.* -a kukumbukwa, -a kuangalika, -a maana. **observance**, *n.* kuangalia, kukumbuka, kushika; (*practice*) desturi, kawaida. **observant**, *a.* -angalifu, -epesi, -elekevu. **observation**, *n.* kuangalia, kuangalika, uangalizi; (*remark*) neno, maneno; (*things observed*) mambo yaliyoangaliwa (yaliyoonwa). *Make an observation*, toa neno, nena, sema; (*with telescope &c.*) angalia (tazama, chunguza) kwa darubini &c. *By personal observation*, kwa kutazama (kuchungua) mwenyewe, kwa macho. **observatory**, *n.* mahali pa kuangalia jua, mwezi, nyota &c. **observer**, *n.* mwangalizi, mwangazi, mchunguzi, mpelelezi.

obsess, *v.t.* shika, shikilia, jaza (akili, moyo). **obsession**, *n.* kushikwa na shetani (pepo); (*desire &c.*) tamaa, shauku (inayojaa moyoni) isiyotulizika.

obsolete, *a.* -siotumika siku hizi, -a kikale, -liokufa, -siofaa.

obstacle, *n.* kizuizi, zuio, mgogoro.

obstetrics, *n.* maarifa ya uzalishi, ukunga.

obstinate, *a.* -kaidi, -shupavu, -gumu, -shindani, -bishi, -enye inadi, -sugu. **obstinacy**, *n.* ukaidi, ushupavu, inadi, usugu.

obstreperous, *a.* -kaidi, -tundu, -tukutu, -potovu, -a makelele.

obstruct, *v.t.* zuia, pinga, pingamiza, kinza, kataza, shindana, simamia. **obstruction**, *n.* kuzuia; (*obstacle*) kizuizi, zuio, katazo, pingamizi, mgogoro, kinga. **obstructive**, *a.* -a kuzuia, -zuivu, -pingamizi. **obstructiveness**, *n.* upingamizi, ukaidi, ubishi, ushindani, uzuivu.

obtain, *v.t.* pata, pewa; — *v.i.* (*hold place, be accepted*) -wako, kubalika, enea, tumika, -wa desturi. **obtainable**, *a.* -a kupatikana, -liopatikana.

obtrude, *v.i.* jiingiliza, jitia kati, jidukiza, fumania. **obtrusion**, *n.* kujiingiliza &c. **obtrusive**, *a.* -fidhuli, -safihi; (*open, glaring*) wazi, baini, -a kutokeza.

obtuse, *a.* -zito wa akili, -pumbavu; (*of angles*) pembe kubwa kuliko ya mraba, pembebutu.

obviate, *v.t.* ondoa, katiza, toa.

obvious, *a.* wazi, dhahiri, -a kuonekana, pasipo shaka.

occasion, *n.* (*particular time*) wakati, siku, defa; (*circumstance*) jambo, tukio, hali; (*opportunity*) wakati, nafasi, faragha; (*reason*) sababu, haja, uhitaji, udhuru, kisa. *Take occasion to*, pata (tumia) nafasi ya. — *v.t.* fanya, leta, toa. *Be occasioned by*, tokana na, -wa kazi ya. **occasional**, *a.* mara kwa mara, pengine, si sikuzote, -a wakati wake, -a bahati, -a nasibu; -a kufaa wakati (siku, kazi) fulani. **occasionally**, *adv.* pana siku, pengine, mara kwa mara.

occident, *n.* magharibi, pande za magharibi. **occidental**, *a.* -a magharibi.

occiput, *n.* kogo (la kichwa).

occult, *a.* -a siri, fumbo. **occultation**, *n.* kustirika (nyota).

occupancy, *n.*, **occupant**, *n.*, **occupation**, *n.*, **occupier**, *n.*, taz. *occupy*.

occupy, *v.t.* twaa, shika, miliki, hozi; (*require*) taka; (*use, give work to*) shughulisha, tumia. **occupancy**, *n.* kutwaa, kushika, kumiliki, kukalia; (*term*) wakati wa kukaa (katika nyumba au shamba *&c.*). **occupant**, *n.* mwenye kukaa, kukalia, kushika *&c.*, mkazi, mwenyeji. **occupation**, *n.* shughuli, kazi, uchumi, maishilio; (*taking possession*) kutwaa, kumiliki *&c.* **occupier**, *n.* mwenyeji *&c.* taz. *occupant*.

occur, *v.i.* -wa, tukia, tokea; (*enter the mind*) ingia moyoni. **occurrence**, *n.* tukio, jambo, kadhia.

ocean, *n.* bahari kuu; (*large number*) wingi. **oceanic**, *a.* -a bahari kuu, -a kupita baharini.

ochre, *n.* (*red*) ngeu, udongo mwekundu.

o'clock, *What o'clock is it?* saa ngapi?

octagon, *n.* kitu chenye pande nane. **octagonal**, *a.* -enye pembe nane na pande nane.

octave, *n.* sauti nane za *scale*, sauti ya nane; (*of festival*) sikukuu na siku saba zinazofuata, siku ya nane baada ya sikukuu. **octavo**, *n.* karatasi iliyokunjwa mara tatu ili kufanya kurasa nane (za kitabu).

October, *n.* mwezi wa kumi wa mwaka wa kizungu, Oktoba.

octogenarian, *n.* mtu mwenye umri wa miaka themanini.

octopus, *n.* pweza mkubwa.

ocular, *a.* -a macho, kwa macho, kwa kuona. **oculist**, *n.* daktari wa macho.

odd, *a.* -moja pasipo mwenzi wake, -moja peke yake; (*number*) witiri, kitangulizi, si kamili; (*remnant*) -liobaki; (*worthless*) -a ovyo, hafifu; (*strange*) -geni, si desturi, -a mtindo, ajabu; (*ridiculous*) -a mzaha, -a kuchekesha. *Odds and ends*, takataka, ovyo. *Odds*, tofauti, ziada, maziada. *It makes no odds, What the odds?* haidhuru, mamoja. *Give odds to*, tanguliza, fadhili, pendelea. *Be at odds*, gombana, bishana, zozana.

Oddfellows, *n.* chama fulani cha kusaidiana. **oddity**, *n.* kigeni, ajabu, shani, mzaha, ubishi, kioja.

ode, *n.* mashairi, utenzi.

odious, *a.* -a kuchukiza, makuruhi, -a kirahi (karaha). **odium**, *n.* machukio, chuki, machukizo, kuchukiza. *I shall get the odium of it*, watu watanilaumu na kunichukia kwa sababu yake.

odour, *n.* harufu (nzuri au mbaya); (*pleasant*) manukato; (*unpleasant*) uvundo; (*of body*) gugumu, (*of perspiration under armpits*) kikwapa, kutuzi. **odoriferous, odorous**, *a.* -a kunukia, -a manukato, -tamu. **odourless**, *a.* -siyo na harufu.

o'er = *over*.

oesophagus, *n.* umio wa chakula.

of, *prep.* -a, kwa, katika; (*about*) juu ya, habari ya. *The city of London*, mji *London*. *Of himself* (*itself &c.*) peke yake, kwa akili zake, kwa nguvu zake. *Of old*, zamani. *Of late*, siku hizi. *What of?* Je, habari gani ya? *Of consequence*, -kubwa -a maana.

off, *prep.* katika, kwa, -ni, mbali na, juu ya. *Off duty*, pasipo kazi. *Off side*, si upande wake. *Off hand*, mara moja, kwa upurukushani, kwa haraka. *Off his head*, -enye wazimu, -enye kichaa. *Off the coast*, karibu na pwani, kuelekea pwani. — *adv.* mbali, si juu. *Be well off*, -wa na mali, -wa tajiri. *Be badly off*, -wa maskini, taiti, wamba. *Be worse* (*better*) *off*, -wa na hali mbaya (njema), zaidi. *Off and on*, pengine, mara kwa mara, si siku zote, wakati wake. *Be off*, ondoka, safiri; (*come to an end*) isha, achwa. *Go off*, enda zangu (zako, zake *&c.*), toka, ondoka; (*of a gun, trap &c.*) fyatuka. *Get off*, funga safari, enda; (*escape*) okoka, kimbia; (*a horse*) shuka juu (ya). *Take off* (*remove*) chukua; (*of clothes*) vua; (*imitate*) iga. *Ward off*, kinga. *Off with you!* ondoka, toka. — *a.* -a upande wa kuume.

offal, *n.* matumbo ya mnyama, takataka.
offence, *n.* taz. *offend.*
offend, *v.t.* chukiza, tia uchungu, kirihi, kasirisha; (*hurt, annoy*) umiza, chokoza, sumbua, udhi; — *v.i.* (*do wrong*) kosa, fanya dhambi, fanya mabaya. **offence**, *n.* uchungu, chuki, hasira; (*fault, crime*) kosa, dhambi, manza, taksiri, jambo baya. *Give offence,* chukiza. *Take offence,* chukizwa, udhika, futuka. *Weapons of offence,* silaha za kudhuru, silaha. **offender**, *n.* mtenda mabaya, mwenye hatia, mkosaji, mwenye dhambi. **offensive**, *a.* -baya sana, -a kuchukiza, makuruhi, -a kinyaa; (*causing anger*) -a kukasirisha; (*of attacking*) -a kutaka vita, -a kushambulia, -a shari. *Take the offensive,* anzisha (leta) vita. *Offensive and defensive alliance,* mapatano ya kusaidiana vitani au katika kushambuliwa.
offer, *v.t.* toa, tolea; (*make proposal*) toa (tolea) maneno; (*express willingness*) taka, jitoa, jitolea, -wa tayari; (*in sacrifice*) dhabihu, toa sadaka; (*to spirits* - mizimu) tambikia; (*propose as price*) tia bei, nunua; (*present*) elekeza, kabilisha; (*at an auction*) zabuni; (*final bid*) shtiri. — *v.i.* (*occur, present itself &c.*) -wa, tokea, tukia, onekana. *Offer marriage,* posa. — *n.* neno, maneno, shauri, ahadi, kutaka; (*bid*) bei, kuzabuni. *Make an offer,* tia bei, nunua; (*at an auction*) zabuni. **offering**, *n.* kutoa, toleo; (*gift*) sadaka; (*sacrifice*) dhabihu, kafara; (*to spirits*) tambiko; (*give up*) kutoa. **offertory**, *n.* sadaka zinazotolewa kanisani.
office, *n.* kazi, utume; (*form of prayers*) chuo cha sala; hitima; (*for the sick—Mohammedan*) buruda; (*room for work*) chumba cha kazi, afisi; (*services*) fadhili, msaada. *Office of,* u-, *e.g. office of sultan,* usultani. **officer**, *n.* mkuu, afisa, mtu wa serikali, msimamizi. **official**, *n.* mtu wa serikali, afisa, mkuu. — *a.* -a serikali, -a nguvu, -a mwenye amri; (*formal, regular*) -a kawaida, -a taratibu. **officiate**, *v.i.* fanya kazi, fanya. **officious**, *a.* -a kujidukiza, -a kujitia, -fidhuli, -safihi, -sumbufu. **officiousness**, *n.* udukizi, ufidhuli, usafihi, usumbufu.
offing, *n.* taz. *off.*
offscourings, *n.* takataka.
offset, *n.* kitu cha kusawazisha (kulipa hasara).
offshoot, *n.* kitawi, kichipuko, chipukizi, mtoto, kitu kitokacho.
offspring, *n.* mzao, mtoto.
oft, often, *adv.* mara kwa mara, mara nyingi. *More often* (*usually*) aghalabu, kwa kawaida, kwa desturi.
ogle, *v.t. and i.* tazama upande (kitongo), tazama kwa macho ya kusinzilia, tongoza.
ogre, *n.* jini (zimwi) baya (la hadithi) alaye watu; (*cruel man*) mtu mkatili, habithi.
oh, *int.* ee! loo! mama wee!
oil, *n.* mafuta; (*rock*) mafuta ya taa; (*castor*) mafuta ya mbarika (mbono); (*semsem*) mafuta ya uto; (*olive*) halzeti, mafuta ya zeituni; (*palm oil*) mawese; (*ground-nut*) mafuta ya karanga. — *v.t.* tia (paka) mafuta **oilcake**, *n.* shudu. **oil-can**, *n.* kopo la kutilia mafuta. **oilcloth**, *n.* nguo nzito iliyopakwa rangi ya mafuta. **oiliness**, *n.* kuwa na *oil* au kama *oil*; ulaini, utelezi, mafuta. **oil-painting**, *n.* picha iliyoandikwa kwa rangi ya mafuta. **oilskin**, *n.* nguo iliyotiwa mafuta isipenyezeke kwa maji. **oily**, *a.* -a mafuta, laini.
ointment, *n.* dawa (yenye mafuta) ya kupaka, marhamu.
okra, *n.* (*plant*) mbamia, mbinda; (*pods*) bamia, binda.
old, *a.* (*person*) -zee, -kongwe; (*thing*) -a kwanza, -a zamani, -a kale; (*antique*) -a kikale; (*worn out*) -kuukuu, -liochakaa. *How old is he?* umri wake apataje? *Be old* (*worn out*), chakaa. *Grow old,* konga, zeeka. **old age**, *n.* uzee, ukongwe. **olden**, *a.* -a zamani, -a kale. **old-fashioned**,

a. -a zamani, -a kama zamani, -a kupenda ya zamani. **old person,** *n.* mzee; (*very old*) kikongwe; (*woman*) kizee, ajuza, (*man*) shaibu.

oleaginous, *a.* -enye mafuta, -a kuteleza, laini kama mafuta.

olfactory, *a.* -a kunusa.

oligarchy, *n.* wengi kutawaliwa na wachache, wachache wenye utawala. **oligarchical,** *a.* -a *oligarchy.*

olive, *n.* (*tree*) mzeituni; (*fruit*) zeituni; (*oil*) halzeti; (*wild olive tree*) mchekele. *Olive branch,* tawi la mzeituni, ishara ya kutaka amani.

omega, *n.* herufi ya mwisho wa alfabeti ya Kiyunani; (*end*) mwisho. *Alpha and omega,* mwanzo na mwisho.

omelette, *n.* kimanda, andazi la mayai.

omen, *n.* ndege, fali; (*sign*) ishara, dalili, onyo. *Good omen,* ndege njema. *Bad omen,* ndege mbaya, kisirani, ukuba. **ominous,** *a.* -a ndege mbaya, -a kisirani, -a kuonya -a kuogofya.

omissible, *a.*, **omission,** *n.* taz. *omit.*

omit, *v.t.* acha, ruka, pitia, kosea. **omissible,** *a.* -a kuachika, -a kutolekana, -siotakwa kwa kuwa si ya lazima. **omission,** *n.* kuacha, kupitia, kukosa kufanya; (*error*) kosa.

omnibus, *n.* gari kubwa la abiria.

omnipotent, *a.* -enye enzi zote, -enyezi. **omnipotence,** *n.* kuweza, enzi kuu, uenyezi.

omnipresent, *a.* -a kuenea pote. **omnipresence,** *n.* kuenea pote, eneo, kuwako kote kote.

omniscient, *a.* -a kujua yote. **omniscience,** *n.* kujua yote, hekima kuu.

omnivorous, *a.* -a kula vyo vyote, -la vyote.

on, *prep. and adv.* (*upon, in addition to*) juu; (*forward*) mbele; (*at, in, by &c.*) kwa, katika, -ni. *Be on,* fanyika, -wako. *Go on* (*forward*), endelea mbele; (*continue at work*) fululiza, fuliza; (*continue at rest*) shinda, kaa. *On and on,* moja kwa moja, kwa kufuliza, mfululizo, mfulizo. *On board,* chomboni. *Be on sale,* tembezwa, uzanya. *On shore,* pwani. *Be on fire,* teketea moto, waka. *On the road,* njiani. *On and off,* pengine. *On your oath,* utaapa.

onanism, *n.* taz. *masturbation.*

once, *adv.* mara moja tu; (*one day*) siku moja, hapo kale, zamani. *Once and again,* mara kwa mara. *Once on a time,* hapo kale. *Once in a way,* pengine, si mara nyingi. *At once* (*immediately*) upesi, mara, mara moja, papo hapo, halahala; (*all together*) pamoja, jamii.

one, *a. and n.* -moja, mosi, kitu kimoja, mtu mmoja. *It is a good one,* ni kizuri, kizuri hicho. *Be at one,* patana. *On the one hand, on the other,* kwanza, ya pili (tena). *One . . . another,* huyu . . . huyu, hii . . . hii. *One eats what one gets,* watu hula wapatavyo. *One another,* wao kwa wao, -enyewe kwa -enyewe; (*in comp.*) -ana, *e.g. beat one another,* pigana; *love one another,* pendana. *Many a one,* wengi. *One by one,* -moja -moja. *It is all one to me,* haidhuru, mamoja kwangu. **one-eyed,** *a.* -enye chongo. **oneness,** *n.* umoja. **oneself,** *n.* mwenyewe; (*in comp.*) -ji-, *e.g. please oneself,* jipendeza. **one-sided,** *a.* -a pogo, -a kwenda upande, mshazari, kwa kujiinika; (*unfair*) si -a haki, si sawa, si vizuri, -a kupendelea.

onerous, *a.* -zito, -a kulemea, -a kukulia, -enye taabu, -a kutaabisha.

oneself, *n.*, **one-sided,** *a.* taz. *one.*

onion, *n.* kitunguu.

onlooker, *n.* mtu anayetazama, mwenye kuhudhuria.

only, *a.* -tupu, tu; (*alone*) peke yake, -a pekee. — *adv.* tu, hivi tu, basi. *If only he would come,* laiti angekuja. — *conj.* ila, lakini, isipokuwa. *I would do it with pleasure only I have not time,* ningefanya kwa furaha lakini sina nafasi.

onset, *n.* shambulio, kuendea, kurukia, mwendo wa ghafula, vita vya ghafula; (*beginning*) mwanzo.
onslaught, *n.* shambulio, mrukio, kuendea kwa ghafula.
onus, *n.* kazi, daraka, wajibu. *The onus (of proof) lies with you,* juu yako (kuthibitisha).
onward, onwards, *a. and adv.* mbele, kwenda mbele, kwa kuendelea.
onyx, *n.* kito cha rangi.
ooze, *v.i.* vuja, tona, tiririka, churuzika, nyinyirika, toka taratibu. — *n.* mvujo, tonesho; (*mud*) matope, kinamasi.
opacity, *n.* taz. *opaque.*
opal, *n.* kito chenye rangi ya maziwa na maji.
opaque, *a.* -siyopenyezeka kwa nuru, -siyoona. **opacity**, *n.* kuwa *opaque*; giza.
open, *a.* wazi; (*place*) wazi, -eupe; (*free*) -a watu wote, wazi; (*flower*) -liochanuka; (*loose*) -a kulegea, -a kufunguliwa, -a kufunuka; (*unreserved*) -kunjufu, -nyofu; (*uncovered*) -siofunikwa, bila kifuniko; (*generous*) -paji, -karimu; (*of a score*) -siopona bado; (*free of taxes &c.*) bila ushuru; (*of argument, verdict &c.*) -siyothibitika, -sio -a mkataa, -a kushindanika, -a kubishanika; (*of town &c.*) -siolindwa, -sio na boma (wala askari); (*not secret*) wazi, dhahiri, -siyo ya siri, -siofichwa. *An open question,* jambo lisilokwisha, neno lisilokatwa bado (la mashaka, la kubishaniwa). *An open secret,* jambo la siri lakini limejuliwa na watu wengi. *Open air,* hewa ya nje, nje. *Open place,* kiwanja, uwanda; (*waste*) uga. *Open weather,* jua, siku za jua. *Keep open house,* karibisha (kirimu) wageni wengi. *Be open with a person,* mwambia habari zote bila kuficha neno. — *v.t.* fungua, fumbua, funua; (*begin*) anza, maliki; (*spread out*) eneza, tandaza; (*flowers*) chanua; (*make known*) bainisha, julisha; (*inaugurate*) zindua; (*a door*) shindua; (*a bundle*) futua; (*fire of guns*) *&c.*) anza kupiga; (*the mouth*) funua; (*the eyes or hands*) fumbua; — *v.i.* (*become open &c.*) funguka, funuka, fumbuka, tandaa, chanuka *&c. Open into,* -wa na mlango (njia, kichochoro *&c.*) wa kuingilia.
opener, *n.* mfungua, kifunguo.
open-eyed, *a.* -enye macho, -enye macho wazi kwa mshangao (kustaajabika, kwa hadhari). **open-handed**, *a.* -kunjufu, -nyofu. **opening**, *n.* mwanzo, mlango, kipenyo, pa kutokea, pa kupenyea, tundu, ufa; (*opportunity*) chimbuko, nafasi. — *a.* -a kwanza. **openly**, *adv.* kwa wazi, mbele ya (hadhara ya) watu.
open-minded, *a.* -nyofu, -adilifu, -siyependelea.
opera, *n.* mchezo wa kuigiza hadithi (habari *&c.*) wa waimbaji. **opera-glasses**, *n.* darubini ya kutazamia mchezo wa *opera.* **operatic**, *a.* -a *opera.*
operate, *v.t.* endesha (mashine *&c.*); — *v.i.* tenda kazi, toa nguvu; (*medical*) pasua, kata, tumbua. **operation**, *n.* kazi, kutenda, nguvu; (*medical*) udaktari (wa kupasua, wa kukata). **operative**, *a.* -a nguvu, -a kutenda kazi. — *n.* mfanya kazi, mtu wa kazi. **operator**, *n.* mfanyi kazi; (*medical*) daktari.
operatic, *a.* taz. *opera.*
operation, *n.*, **operative**, *a. and n.*, **operator**, *n.* taz. *operate.*
ophthalmia, *n.* ugonjwa wa macho.
opiate, *n.* taz. *opium.*
opine, *v.t.* dhani, ona, shuku.
opinion, *n.* shauri, nia, hukumu, usia, kauli, rai; (*estimation*) sifa. *Be of the opinion,* dhani, ona. *A matter of opinion,* jambo lisilo hakika, si yakini, jambo lenye mashaka. *Golden opinion,* sifa bora. *I have no opinion of,* sioni ya kuwa ni -zuri, naona ni hafifu (-baya).
opinionated, *a.* (mtu) ashikaye shauri lake, asiyesikia maneno ya watu, -shupavu, -gumu, -bishi.

opium, *n.* afyuni; (*mixture*) kasumba. **opiate,** *n.* dawa ya kutia usingizi (ya kutuliza).

opossum, *n.* mnyama wa Amerika kama komba.

opponent, *n.* mshindani, adui, mtesi, mzuia, mkinzani; (*in litigation*) mdaawa.

opportune, *a.* -a bahati njema, -a kuja sawasawa, -a kufaa, tayari. **opportunely,** *adv.* -a wakati wa kufaa, barabara. **opportunity,** *n.* nafasi, wakati, chimbuko, faragha, wasaa, saa (siku) ya kufaa.

oppose, *v.t.* zuia, kinga, pinga, kinza, pinza, shindana, kataa, simamia mbele, dinda, zinda; (*place before*) weka mbele, elekeza, kabili, elekeana; (*match*) pambanisha. *Be opposed* (*opposite, different*), -wa mbalimbali, achana, hitilafiana, elekeana, kabiliana. **opposable,** *a.* -a kuzuilikana. **opposer,** *n.* mshindani, adui, mtesi, mzuia, mkinzani. **opposite,** *a.* (*facing*) -a kuelekea, -a kuelekeana, mbele, -a kukabili; (*wholly different*) mbalimbali kabisa. **opposition,** *n.* kuelekeana, kukabiliana; (*resistance*) ushindani, kuzuia, kupinga njia; mgogoro, uzuio, uzuizi; (*entire difference*) hali mbalimbali, tofauti. *The opposition,* watu wasio wa jamii yenye nguvu katika halmashauri (*Parliament*) ya Uingereza.

oppress, *v.t.* onea, dhulumu, tendea mazito, songa, lemea. **oppression,** *n.* (*injustice*) udhalimu, jeuri, mazito, dhulumu; (*trouble*) hali ya taabu, mateso; (*languor, depression*) uchovu, unyogovu, unyong'onyevu, majonzi; (*in breathing*) kisongo cha roho, uzito. **oppressive,** *a.* -a kulemea, -zito, -a kusonga, -a taabu, -kali, -dhalimu, -kalifu. **oppressor,** *n.* mdhalimu, jeuri, bwana mkali na mkorofi, mtesi.

opprobrious, *a.* -a kuaibisha, -a aibu, -a matukano, -a kufedhehesha. **opprobrium,** *n.* aibu, fedheha, haya; (*reproach*) shutumu, matukano.

optic, *a.* -a macho, -a jicho. — *n.* jicho. **optical,** *a.* -a macho. *Optical illusion,* madanganyo ya macho, mauzauza. *Optical instrument,* darubini, miwani *&c.* **optician,** *n.* mfanyi (mwuza) miwani. **optics,** *n.* elimu ya nuru (ya kuona kwa macho).

optimism, *n.* kusadiki (matumaini) ya kuwa mambo yote yatatokea vizuri (barabara, ya kufaa *&c.*). **optimist,** *n.* mtu asadikiye (mwenye tumaini thabiti) ya kuwa yote yatatokea vizuri.

option, *n.* kuchagua, uchaguzi, hiari; (*in commerce*) haki ya kununua au kuacha kwa kuwekeana miadi (pamoja na kulipa arabuni). *There is no option,* hakuna budi, sharti, lazima. **optional,** *a.* -a hiari, si -a lazima.

opulent, *a.* tajiri, -enye mali nyingi, -kwasi. **opulence,** *n.* utajiri, mali, ukwasi.

or, *conj.* au, ama; (*otherwise*) kama sivyo.

oracle, *n.* (katika habari za zamani za kiyunani) mahali mungu aliposema na watu; mtu aliyesikia maneno ya mungu; maneno aliyosema mungu; (siku hizi) mtu wa hekima, hakimu, mwaguzi; (*wise saying*) maneno ya hekima; (*prophetic utterance*) maaguzi, usia. **oracular,** *a.* -a *oracle*; -a hekima; (*mysterious*) -a fumbo, si dhahiri, -a mashaka.

oral, *a.* -a mdomo, -a kinywa, -a kunena, -a maneno, -sioandikwa. **orally,** *adv.* kwa kinywa (mdomo), kwa maneno, kwa kunena.

orange, *n.* chungwa; (*bitter*) danzi; (*mandarin*) chenza; (*smaller*) kangaja. *Orange tree,* mchungwa. — *a.* -a rangi ya dhahabu nyekundu. **orangeade,** *n.* maji ya machungwa. **orangery,** *n.* shamba la (kiungacha) michungwa.

orang-outang, *n.* namna ya nyani mkubwa kama mtu.

oration, *n.* maneno, hotuba. **orator,** *n.* msemi, mneni, msemaji, mwenye ufasaha wa kusema. **oratorical,** *a.* -a maneno, -a mneni, -a ufasaha wa maneno. **oratorio,** *n.* utenzi wa dini wa kuimba. **oratory,** *n.* ufasaha wa kusema, usemaji; (*chapel*) kanisa dogo la (kijumba cha) kusalia.

orb, *n.* tufe, kitu chenye umbo la tufe (cha kuviringana), mviringo, duara; (*star*) nyota; (*eye*) jicho. **orbit,** *n.* mzunguko, mwendo wa (njia ya) kuzunguka.

orchard, *n.* shamba la (kiunga cha) miti izaayo matunda.

orchestra, *n.* tarabu, jamii ya watu wapigao muziki (ngoma, zeze, vinanda, filimbi, zomari &c.). **orchestral,** *a.* -a *orchestra.*

orchid, *n.* namna ya mmea wenye maua mazuri.

orchilla, *n.* (*plant*) malele.

orchitis, *n.* mshipa, kipumbu.

ordain, *v.t.* amuru, agiza; (*of clergy*) fanya kasisi, tia mikono. **ordinance,** *n.* amri, agizo, sheria. **ordination,** *n.* kufanya kasisi kwa kutiwa mikono na askofu. **ordinal,** *n.* sala na kawaida za kufanya kasisi. — *a.* *Ordinal numbers,* hesabu za kuonyesha utaratibu wa kufuatana, ndiyo *first, second, third &c.* Kiingereza, *i.e.* -a kwanza, -a pili, -a tatu &c.

ordeal, *n.* kiapo; (*severe trial*) majaribu, hatari, mateso.

order, *n.* amri, agizo; (*custom, rule*) kanuni, kawaida, desturi; (*regularity*) taratibu, uzuri; (*cheque*) hawala, hundi, hati; (*rank*) cheo, daraja; (*society*) chama; (*class, kind*) aina, jinsi, namna, kabila; (*decoration*) nishani. *The lower orders,* watu wadogo, watu tu, maskini. *Orders, Holy orders,* ukasisi, upadre, (madaraja, huduma takatifu). *Be in orders,* -wa padre. *Take orders,* fanyika padre. *My watch is out of order,* saa yangu haiendi (imeharibika). *Be in good order,* -wa na afya, -wa -zima; tengenezwa vizuri. *I made it to his order,* aliagiza nikaifanya. *In order to* (*that*), makusudi, ili. *Keep order,* simamia, -wa mlinzi. *Put in order,* panga, tunga, tengeneza, safidi, rekabisha, ratibisha. — *v.t.* (*appoint*) amuru, agiza; (*arrange*) tengeneza, andika taratibu, ratibisha. **orderliness,** *n.* utaratibu, utii, amani, utangamano, siasa. **orderly,** *a.* -a taratibu, -zuri; (*quiet*) makini, -a amani. — *n.* askari mtumishi.

ordinance, *n.* taz. *ordain.*

ordinary, *a.* (*usual*) -a siku zote, desturi; (*common*) -a vivi hivi, ovyo, hafifu, -nyonge. *An ordinary person,* mtu tu. — *n.* mwenye hukumu, askofu. *In ordinary,* mara nyingi kwa desturi. **ordinarily,** *adv.* mara nyingi, kwa desturi, aghalabu.

ordination, *n.* taz. *ordain.*

ordnance, *n.* mizinga, zana za vita.

ordure, *n.* mavi, kinyesi, taka, samadi.

ore, *n.* mawe yenye madini.

organ, *n.* sehemu ya (kiungo cha) mwili wa mtu au mmea inayofanya kazi maalum, *e.g.* mapafu, moyo, mizizi &c. (*means &c.*) njia ya (jinsi ya, kitu cha) kufanyia kazi, *e.g.* gazeti; (*musical*) kinanda chenye mabomba yanayotoa sauti kwa nguvu ya mivukuto; kinanda. **organic,** *a.* -a sehemu ya (kiungo cha) mwili wa mtu au mmea; -enye sehemu (viungo) zinazofanya kazi maalum; -a kitu chenye uhai. **organism,** *n.* kitu chenye uhai, jamii ya sehemu ambayo kila moja inafanya kazi yake maalum. **organist,** *n.* mpiga kinanda. **organization,** *n.* matengenezo, utaratibu, madaraka; (*association &c.*) chama, shirika. **organize,** *v.t.* tunga, tengeneza, amuru, simamia. **organizer,** *n.* mtengenezaji, mtungaji, msimamizi.

orgasm, *n.* mshindo; (*sexual*) mshindo, mshushio.

orgy, *n.* karamu ya ulafi na ulevi na uasherati, ngoma mbaya.

oribi, *n.* kasia.

oriel, *n.* dirisha la kutokeza nje, roshani.

orient, *n.* mashariki. **oriental,** *a.*

-a mashariki, -a pande za *Asia*. **orientalist,** *n.* mwenye elimu (maarifa) ya nchi za mashariki. **orientate,** *v.t.* jenga ili mbele yake, nyuma yake na pande zake zikabili mashariki, magharibi, kaskazini na kusini (kama ni kanisa — ili upande wa madhabahu ukabili mashariki); jipanga kulingana na kitu au mahali; — *v.i.* geuka kukabili mashariki. *Orientate oneself,* hakikisha mahali ulipo. **orientation,** *n.* kukabilisha vema, kuelekeza, kuweka sawa.

orifice, *n.* tundu, kitundu, mlango, kipenyo, ufa, kishimo.

origin, *n.* asili, mwanzo, chimbuko; (*ancestry*) wazazi, ukoo, jadi, nasaba; (*cause*) sababu, maana. **original,** *a.* -a asili, -a kwanza; (*peculiar*) -a peke yake, -a mtindo, -enyewe, halisi; (*inventive*) -enye akili ya kubuni (ya kutunga, ya kuvumbua); (*extraordinary*) ajabu, -geni, -pya. — *n.* namna ya (kiolezo cha) kwanza. **originality,** *n.* kuwa na akili za kubuni (za kutunga, za kuvumbua); (*singularity*) ajabu, upya. **originally,** *adv.* kwanza, kwa asili. **originate,** *v.t.* anzisha, zaa, umba. fanya, buni, tunga; — *v.i.* (*start*) anza, tokana. **origination,** *n.* mwanzo, kuanza, kuanzisha.

oriole, *n.* (*golden*) kirumbizi, mramba mweusi.

orion, *n.* fungu la nyota lenye 'mpini wa kata'.

orison, *n.* sala.

ormolu, *n.* shaba iliyopakwa rangi kufanana na dhahabu.

ornament, *n.* pambo, kipambo, urembo, madoido. — *v.t.* pamba, tia uzuri, remba, tia madoido. **ornamental,** *a.* -a kupamba, -a urembo, -zuri. **ornate,** *a.* -a mapambo, -a urembo, -zuri, -enye madoido.

ornithology, *n.* maarifa ya ndege.

orphan, *n.* yatima, mwana mkiwa. **orphanage,** *n.* nyumba ya kutunza na kulea yatima. **orphanhood,** *n.* kuwa yatima.

orthodox, *a.* -enye imani (dini, maono, desturi) sahihi (halisi), sahihi, halisi, barabara. **orthodoxy,** *n.* kuwa *orthodox,* imani halisi.

orthography, *n.* kuendeleza maneno vema, kuandika sahihi, maendelezo sahihi ya maneno.

oryx, *n.* (*fringe eared*) choroa.

oscillate, *v.t.* ning'iniza, pembeza; — *v.i.* ning'inia, yumbayumba, wayawaya, pembea; (*shift*) geuka, enda huko na huko; (*waver*) sita, ona mashaka. **oscillation,** *n.* kuning'inia &c.

oscular, *a.* -a kinywa, -a midomo. **osculate,** *v.t.* busu. **osculation,** *n.* kubusu, busu.

osier, *n.* ufito wa kusukia viti, meza &c.

osprey, *n.* koho, furukombe, fukombe; (*egret's plume*) kishungi cha yangeyange.

osseous, *a.* -a mifupa, kama mfupa, kifupa. **ossification,** *n.* kufanyika mfupa. **ossify,** *v.t. and i.* fanya (fanyika) mfupa.

ostensible, *a.* (*avowed*) dhahiri, wazi, -a kubainika, -a nje; (*unreal*) si -a kweli, si halisi. **ostentation,** *n.* majivuno, makuu, fahari, urembo, ushaufu. **ostentatious,** *a.* -shaufu, -a mikogo, -a *ostentation.* **ostentatiously,** *adv.* kwa majivuno, kwa kujionyesha, kwa kutazamisha.

osteology, *n.* elimu ya mifupa ya watu na wanyama.

ostler, *n.* saisi, mchunga farasi.

ostracize, *v.t.* toa (ondosha) katika jamii, fukuza. **ostracism,** *n.* kutolewa (kuondolewa) katika jamii.

ostrich, *n.* mbuni.

other, *a.* -ingine, -a pili, mbalimbali, zaidi. *Bring others,* leta -ingine, ongeza. *The others,* wale wengine, vile vingine, mabaki, yaliyosalia. *Some people do . . . others do . . .,* watu wengine hu . . ., wengine hu . . ., baadhi ya watu hu . . . , wengine hu . . . . **otherwise,** *adv.* vingine, kwa vingine, kwa sababu nyingine; (*if not, or else*) kama sivyo, au.

otter, *n.* mnyama akaaye mtoni, hula samaki.
otto of roses, *n.* halwaridi, marashi.
ottoman, *n.* kitanda chenye matakia; (*Turk*). Turuki, Mturuki.
ought, *v. aux.* paswa. *I ought*, napaswa, imenipasa, imenibidi, ni juu yangu, ni kazi yangu, ni stahili yangu, vizuri, njema, ni wajibu wangu.
ounce, *n.* wakia.
our, ours, *a.* -etu. **ourselves**, *pron.* sisi wenyewe.
oust, *v.t.* ondosha, toa nje, fukuza.
out, *adv.* nje (kama kutoka, kupita, kuwa wazi, kuisha, kukamilika). *Out-and-out*, kabisa, pia. *An out-and-out fool*, mpumbavu wa mwisho. *An out-and-out thief*, mwizi wa kupindukia. *Be out*, -wa nje, tembéa; (*be mistaken*) kosa; (*finished*) isha. *Go out*, toka, enda nje; (*as a candle*) zimika. *Have it out with*, pigana na, shindana na, kosana na. *Out of*, pasipo. *He is out of cash*, hana fedha. *I am out of it*, simo; (*have none of it*) imenitindikia, nimeishiwa. *Out of character*, -siopatana, -siolingana, si sawa. *Out of date*, -a kikale kabisa, -siotumika siku hizi. *Out of doors*, nje, njiani, -a kutembelea. *Out of hand*, ghafula, mara, dharuba moja; (*ungovernable*) -siozuilika. *Out of joint*, -lioteguka, -lioshtushwa. *Out of kindness*, kwa hisani, kufadhili. *Out of mind*, -siokumbukwa, -a kupita akili, pasipo kiasi. *Be out of one's mind*, -wa wazimu, rukwa na akili. *Be out of one's time*, ishiwa majira ya kazi. *Out of order* (*course*), si taratibu. *Out of place*, -siofaa, si mahali pake. *Be out of pocket*, pata hasara, gharama nyingi. *Out of print* (*book*), -sichopatikana. *Out of the question*, -siowezekana. *Out of reach*, -siopatikana. *Out of season*, si -a wakati wake. *Out of sorts*, -gonjwa, si radhi, kali, -enye uchungu. *Out of temper*, -kali, -enye hasira. *Out of use*, -siotumika. *Out of the way*, -geni, ajabu; (*remote*) mbali. *Out of the way!* simile! jihadhari! habedari! *Out with it!* sema! toa! **outer**, *a.* -a nje. **outermost**, *a.* -a nje kabisa. **outing**, *n.* kwenda kutembea, kupunga hewa, kushinda mahali, mandari.
outbalance, *v.t.* pita, shinda, zidi.
outbid, *v.t.* shinda (kwa bei, kwa kununua).
outbreak, *n.* fitina, maasi, vita; (*of temper &c.*) mshindo, kipindi, hasira ya ghafula.
outbuilding, *n.* kibanda (zizi, jiko &c.) cha nje ya nyumba yenyewe.
outcast, *n.* maskini, fukara, fakiri, -liotupwa; (*vagabond*) mhuni.
outclass, *v.t.* shinda, -wa bora kuliko.
outcome, *n.* mwisho, tokeo.
outcrop, *n.* sehemu ya mwamba inayotokeza juu.
outcry, *n.* makelele (ya hofu, ghadhabu, hasira), yowe.
outdistance, *v.t.* shinda kwa mbio, pita, enda upesi zaidi.
outdo, *v.t.* (*p.t.* **outdid**, *pf.t.* **outdone**) pita, shinda; (*deceive*) kalamkia, punja, ghilibu, rubuni, laghai, hadaa.
outer, *a.*, **outermost**, *a.* taz. *out*.
outfit, *n.* zana, vyombo, vifaa, nguo.
outfitter, *n.* mwuza *outfit*.
outflank, *v.t.* zunguka upande; (*outwit*) shinda kwa akili, punja, danganya, ghilibu, rubuni.
outgoings, *n.* gharama, haraja, matumizi ya fedha.
outgrow, *v.t.* (*p.t.* **outgrew**, *pf.t.* **outgrown**) -wa -kubwa kuliko, pita, kulia.
outhouse, *n.* kipenu, (kibanda, zizi, jiko &c.) nje ya nyumba yenyewe.
outing, *n.* taz. *out*.
outlandish, *a.* -a kigeni, ajabu.
outlast, *v.t.* pita kwa aushi, ishi zaidi, dumu.
outlaw, *n.* haramia, mtoro. — *v.t.* harimisha, torosha, fukuza, fanya haramu.
outlay, *n.* gharama, haraja, matumizi ya fedha.
outlet, *n.* pa kutokea, mlango, tundu.
outline, *n.* mstari wa kuonyesha

umbo la kitu; (*sketch*) habari kidogo, maneno machache, kidogo, ishara, dokezo. — *v.t.* andika umbo la kitu; (*sketch*) eleza kwa maneno machache (kwa ufupi).

outlive, *v.t.* ishi (dumu) kuliko.

outlook, *n.* kutazama mbele, mambo ya mbele; (*view*) mandhari, sura ya ulimwengu.

outlying, *a.* -a mbali, -a nje, peke yake.

outmarch, *v.t.* tangulia mbele ya, enda upesi kuliko.

outmatch, *v.t.* shinda, pita.

outmost, *a.* -a nje kabisa.

outnumber, *v.t.* -wa -ingi kuliko, pita, zidi.

out-patient, *n.* mgonjwa apewaye dawa hospitali lakini halali humo.

outpost, *n.* doria, askari mpelelezi, mlinzi wa mbele.

output, *n.* mapato (ya makaa, madini &c.), vitu vilivyofanyizwa katika kiwanda &c.

outrage, *n.* jambo ovu (la ukatili, la jeuri, la uhalifu, la kudhuru, la kuharibu) kabisa, kosa kubwa taksiri, manza. — *v.t.* tendea maovu kabisa, halifu; (*of woman*) bikiri (zinisha) kwa jeuri. **outrageous,** *a.* -a *outrage*, -baya kabisa, -a jeuri.

outrider, *n.* mfuasi (mtumishi) mpanda farasi.

outrigger, *n.* (*of canoe*) tengo, ndubi, rengu.

outright, *adv.* pia, kabisa; (*at once*) mara, papo hapo; (*openly*) kwa wazi, dhahiri. *He killed him outright,* alimwulia mbali (papo hapo).

outrun, *v.t.* (*p.t.* **outran,** *pf.t.* **outrun**) shinda kwa mbio, tangulia mbele ya.

outset, *n.* mwanzo.

outshine, *v.t.* (*p.t. and pf.t.* **outshone**) shinda, pita (kwa uzuri, kwa wangavu).

outside, *adv.* nje. — *n.* upande wa nje, sura; (*limit*) upeo, mpaka. *At the outside,* wala si zaidi, ndio mwisho. **outsider,** *n.* mtu asiye wa jamii (iliyotajwa); (*ill-bred person*) mtu asiye na adabu, mfidhuli, msafihi.

outskirt, *n.* (*of town*) kiunga, pembizo, mpakani; kando.

outspan, *v.t.* fungulia farasi (ng'ombe, punda) katika gari.

outspoken, *a.* -enye kusema yalivyo, -nyofu.

outspread, *a.* (*be*) tawanyika, tapakaa, enea, nyoka, tandikwa.

outstanding, *a.* (*remaining*) -liobaki, -liosalia, -liopo; (*debt*) -siolipwa; (*prominent*) -a kutokeza, -a kuonekana dhahiri, -a kuvuta macho, -a kutazamisha.

outstrip, *v.t.* shinda, pita, zidi.

out-talk, *v.t.* hinikiza, pambanya, shinda kwa maneno.

outward, *a.* -a nje; (*apparent, visible*) -a kuonekana, -a sura; (*unreal*) si -a kweli, si -a moyo, -a unafiki (uwongo). **outwardly,** *adv.* kwa nje; (*not truly*) si kwa kweli. **outwards,** *adv.* (kwenda) nje.

outweigh, *v.t.* pita kwa uzito (kwa nguvu), -wa -kubwa (-zito).

outwit, *v.t.* shinda kwa akili, punja, danganya, rubuni, ghilibu, laghai, kalamkia, hadaa.

outwork, *n.* boma la mbele.

oval, *a.* -enye umbo la yai, mviringo wa yai.

ovary, *n.* kifuko cha mayai (au mbegu) tumboni (mwa wanawake, mwa wanyama); (*in flowers*) sehemu ya ua inayogeuka kuwa tunda.

ovation, *n.* vifijo, shangwe, makelele ya salamu, vigelele vya kupokea.

oven, *n.* tanuu, kalibu; (*cooking*) jiko.

over, *adv.* juu, zaidi, kupita, nje. *All over,* kote kote, pote pia. *It is all over,* imekwisha. *Over again,* tena, mara ya pili. *Over and over,* mara kwa mara, mara nyingi. *Over and above,* zaidi, juu, baki, sazo, kuzidi. *Be over,* salia, baki; (*be ended*) isha. *Give over,* isha, koma, tulia, nyamaa. — *prep.* juu ya, kukingama, toka upande huu mpaka upande huu; zaidi ya.

overabundance, *n.* wingi wa kuzidi.

overalls, *n.* vazi la kupwaya la kuvaa nje ya nguo za kawaida kuzilinda wakati wa kufanya kazi.
overawe, *v.t.* tisha, ogofya, fadhaisha.
overbalance, *v.t.* angusha, pita (kwa uzito, kwa thamani). *Overbalance oneself*, taka kuanguka.
overbear, *v.t.* shinda, tiisha, fanya nguvu; (*by talking*) hinikiza, pambanya, pambanisha. **overbearing**, *a.* -a jeuri, -dhalimu, -kali, -gumu, -a kuonea, -fidhuli, -safihi.
overboard, *adv.* (*fall, throw*) anguka (tupa) baharini.
overburden, *v.t.* lemeza, twisha mazito mno.
overcast, *a.* (*be*) tanda. *The sky is overcast.* kumetanda mawingu.
overcharge, *v.t.* taka bei kubwa kuliko haki, uza ghali; (*overload*) tia -ingi mno, lemeza.
overcloud, *v.t.* tanda (mawingu); tia majonzi (huzuni, uzito).
overcoat, *n.* koti kubwa (la kuvaa juu ya nguo nyingine).
overcome, *v.t. and i.* (*p.t.* **overcame**, *pf.t.* **overcome**) shinda, pita, tiisha, piga, weza, zuia.
overcrowd, *v.t.* weka (tia, ingiza, ruhusu) watu wengi kuliko nafasi iliyopo, songamanisha.
verdo, *v.t.* (*p.t.* **overdid**, *pf.t.* **overdone**) fanya mno; (*in cooking*) pika mno; (*weary*) choka sana, sumbua, udhi. **overdone**, *a.* -liopikwa mno; (*worn out*) -enye kushindwa na kazi, -enye kuchoka.
overdose, *n.* mnywesho wa dawa zaidi kuliko kufaa (hata kudhuru).
overdraw, *v.t.* (*an account*) jipasha deni, ingia deni. **overdraft**, *n.* deni (kwa *bank*).
overdue, *a.* -a kuchelewa, -a kuja kinyume, -siowadia.
overeat, *v.i. and refl.* -la kuliko kadiri, sakara, sakarika, -la mpaka kuvimbiwa, jivimbisha (kwa kula), lafua.
over-estimate, *v.t* sifu mno, dhania -kubwa (ingi, -a thamani mno).
overflow, *v.t.* furika, toka nje, enea, tawanyika, gharikisha; (*overwhelm*) tiisha; — *v.i.* (*be over-abundant*) -wa -ingi; (*be filled superabundantly*) -wa na -ingi mno. — *n.* mafuriko, gharika; (*superfluity*) masazo, wingi; (*outlet*) pa kutokea maji. **overflowing**, *a.* -a kufurika; (*abundant*) -ingi sana, -enye wingi. — *n.* mafuriko; wingi, masazo.
overgrown, *v.t.* (*grow over*) funika kwa majani (miti); (*outgrow*) kua mno, pita kiasi cha. **overgrown**, *a.* -liofunikwa kwa majani au miti; (*size*) -kuza mno.
overhang, *v.t.* (*p.t. and pf.t.* **overhung**) (*project*) tokeza, fanya mdomo; (*cover*) -wa juu ya, funika, tanda; (*threaten*) taka kuja, karibia.
overhaul, *v.t.* chungua na kutengeneza vizuri; (*pass*) pita.
overhead, *adv.* juu, kichwani. — *a.* -a juujuu, -a kichwani; (*of a business*) -siobadilika, -a sikuzote. *Overhead charges*, kodi, ushuru, mishahara ya watu.
overhear, *v.t.* (*p.t. and pf.t.* **overheard**) (*by accident*) sikia bila kukusudia; (*deliberately*) sikia kwa siri, dukiza.
overjoyed, *a.* (*be*) furahi mno.
overland, *adv.* kwa nchi kavu. — *a.* -a nchi kavu (si -a baharini). *Overland route*, njia ya nchi kavu.
overlap, *v.i.* pitana, pishana; (*be partly identical*) fanana, -wa na habari (maarifa, maelezo &c.) zilizo sawasawa (na).
overlay, *v.t.* (*p.t. and pf.t.* **overlaid**) tia juu, funika, tanda; (*lie on*) lala juu ya.
overlook, *v* (*superintend*) angalia, simamia, tazamia; (*let pass*) pitia, achilia, samehe, sahau; (*of a window &c.*) -wa juu ya, chungulia; (*with the evil eye*) tazama kwa jicho ovu, loga. **overlooker**, *n.* msimamizi, mwangalizi.
overmatch, *v.t.* -wa na nguvu za kupita, shinda, weza. **overmatched**, *a.* -lioshindwa (kwa sababu ya kuwa -dogo au -chache).

overmuch, *a.* -ingi mno.
overnight, *adv.* usiku (uliopita, wa leo), usiku mpaka asubuhi.
overplus, *n.* baki, masazo.
overpower, *v.t.* shinda, tiisha, piga.
overrate, *v.t.* tia thamani (sifa) zaidi kuliko stahili.
overreach, *v.t.* tokeza; (*outwit*) danganya, punja, kalamkia, ghilibu, rubuni.
override, *v.t.* tangua, vunja; (*a horse*) endesha mno.
overrule, *v.t.* amuru vingine, geuza, tangua.
overrun, *v.t.* pita, pita mbele, pitia; (*invade, attack*) leta vita (hasara) katika, ingia kwa shari (nguvu, jeuri); (*cover*) funika, enea katika, funikiza.
oversee, *v.t.* simamia, angalia. **overseer**, *n.* msimamizi.
overset, *v.t.* pindua, pindukiza, angusha; — *v.i.* pinduka, anguka.
overshadow, *v.t.* tia kivuli juu; (*lessen importance*) rahisisha; (*cast gloom over*) tia majonzi (huzuni).
overshoot, *v.t.* (*p.t. and pf. t.* **overshot**) pita, pitia, kosa kupiga (kupata).
oversight, *n.* (*supervision*) usimamizi, uangalizi; (*error, neglect*) kosa, kupitiwa, usahaulifu.
oversleep, *v.i. and reflex.* chelewa (usingizini), sinzia sana, pita saa ya kuamka asubuhi. *I overslept myself*, jua lilinichea, nilichewa na jua (usingizini).
overspread, *v.t.* (*p.t. and pf.t.* **overspread**) enea (tawanyika) katika, funika, funikiza, tapakaa.
overstate, *v.t.* ongeza mno, piga chuku.
overstep, *v.t.* pitia, kosea, ruka mpaka.
overt, *a.* wazi, dhahiri, mbele ya macho, hadhara ya watu, hadharani, kadamnasi.
overtake, *v.t.* (*p.t.* **overtook**, *pf.t.* **overtaken**) patia, fikia; (*catch*) pata, kamata.
overtax, *v.t.* toza ushuru (kodi) kuliko haki; (*overstrain*) lemea, chosha.
overthrow, *v.t.* pindua, pindukiza, angusha; (*ruin, destroy*) angamiza, shinda, vunja. — *n.* maangamizi, uharibifu.
overtime, *adv. Work overtime*, fanya kazi ya kuzidi saa yake.
overtook, *p.t.* ya *overtake*.
overtop, *v.t.* (*rise above*) inuka juu ya, nyanyuka; (*excel*) shinda, pita.
overture, *n.* maneno ya kutaka urafiki (amani, mapatano, suluhu), haja, shauri; (*musical*) mwanzo (wa ngoma na kuimba).
overturn, *v.t.* pindua, pindukiza, angusha, angamiza; — *v.i.* pinduka.
overweening, *a.* -a kujivuna, -enye makuu, -a kutakabari, -kinaifu, -a kinaya, -ingi mno.
overwhelm, *v.t.* fanyia nguvu nyingi, shinda, vunja, angamiza, haribu pia; (*overrun*) ingia kwa shari (nguvu), funika, gharikisha; (*cover*) funikiza pia. **overwhelming**, *a.* -a kuelemeza, -a kushinda, -a kufunikiza kabisa.
overwork, *v.t.* tumia mno, amria kazi kubwa mno (ya kupita kadiri), lemea, lemeza, chosha; — *v.i.* fanya kazi nyingi kupita kadiri. — *n.* kazi kubwa (nyingi) mno, kazi ya kupita kadiri. **overworked**, *a.* -liochoka mno, -lioshindwa na kazi, -liokuliwa.
overwrought, *a.* taz. *overworked*; -lioshindwa na huzuni (wasiwasi, hangaiko &c.).
oviparous, *a.* -a kutaga mayai.
owe, *v.t.* wiwa, -wa na deni; (*owe to*) -pashwa na, -wa na (kitu) kwa sababu ya, -wa haki ya. *I owe him ten shillings*) nawiwa naye shilingi kumi. *He owes me ten shillings*, namwia shilingi kumi. *I owe my wealth to my father*, mali zangu nilipashwa (nilipatiwa) na baba. *I owe respect to my father*, imenipasa kumheshimu baba. **owing**, *a.* -a deni, -a haki. *Money is owing by me*, nawiwa fedha na mtu. *Owing to* (*caused by*), kwa sababu ya. *It is*

all owing to you, yote ni juu yako, kwa sababu yako, kosa lako.

owl, *n*. (*wood*) bundi, babe watoto, babewana.

own, *v.t.* miliki, hozi, -wa na (mali); (*confess*) kiri, ungama; — *v.i.* kiri, ungama. — *a*. enyewe, halisi. *My own*, -angu mimi. *Your own*, -ako wewe *&c*. **owner**, *n*. mwenyewe, mwenyeji. **ownership**, *n*. uenyeji, kumiliki, kuhozi.

ox, *n*. (*pl*. **oxen**) ng'ombe dume, maksai. *Strong as an ox*, -enye nguvu nyingi sana.

oxygen, *n*. kitu kama hewa kilichomo kwa wingi (⅕) katika hewa yenyewe na maji na mawe pia. **oxidation**, *n*. kuchanganyika na *oxygen*, kuliwa na hewa (kutu). **oxide**, *n*. mchanganyiko wa *oxygen* na *element*, *e.g*. kutu ni *oxide* (*oxygen* na chuma). **oxidize**, *v.t. and i*. changanya (changanyika) na *oxygen*.

oyster, *n*. chaza, shaza, kombe ya pwani.

ozone, *n*. hewa (upepo) ya kuburudisha ya pwani.

P

pabulum, *n*. chakula.

pace, *n*. (*foot*) hatua, wayo; (*movement*) mwendo; (*speed*) wepesi. *Keep pace with*, enda sawasawa na. — *v.i.* enda (taratibu kwa miguu); — *v.t.* (*measure*) pima kwa hatua; (*traverse*) pitapita katika (kwa miguu), tembelea.

pachyderm, *n*. mnyama mwenye ngozi nene sana, *e.g*. tembo, kiboko, kifaru *&c*.

pacific, *a*., **pacification**, *n*., **pacifier**, *n*. taz. *pacify*.

pacify, *v.t.* fanya amani, tuliza, patanisha, suluhisha, ridhisha, afikinisha; (*spirits*) tambikia, gonya. **pacific**, *a*. -a amani -tulivu, -pole, -a kutaka amani. *The Pacific*, *Pacific Ocean*, bahari iliyo kati ya *America* na *Asia* na *Australia*. **pacification**, *n*. kufanya amani, suluhu, amani, mapatano. **pacifier**, *n*. mpatanishi, msuluhishi.

pack, *v.t.* funga pamoja, funga, fanya mzigo, tengeneza mzigo, funga safari, (*fill in*) jaza, tia -ingi, songameza, songamanya; (*of animals*) pakia mizigo; (*arrange artfully*) tengeneza kwa hila (werevu, ujanja); — *v.i.* (*crowd together*) songamana. *Pack off*, *Send packing*, safirisha kwa haraka, fukuza, ondosha. — *n*. mzigo, mtumba, robota, furushi, bahasha; (*of cards*) jozi, fungu zima la karata; (*of dogs*) kundi. **package**, *n*. peto, kipeto, kirobota, furushi, bahasha, kasha, sanduku. **packer**, *n*. mfunga mizigo. **packet**, *n*. kifurushi, bahasha, chopa, kichopa, bumba, bunda; (*steamship*) meli. **pack-horse**, *n*. farasi wa kuchukulia mizigo. **packing**, *n*. kufunga mizigo; (*stuffing*) kitambaa (majani makavu *&c*.) cha kujazia, kizibo, kisongo. **packing-case**, *n*. kasha kubwa la mbao. **packing-needle**, *n*. shazia, shasira. **packman**, *n*. mtembeza bidhaa, mchukuzi. **pack-saddle**, *n*. shogi, tandiko la farasi (saruji) la mizigo. **packthread,** *n.* kitani, uzi mnene.

pact, *n.* maafikano, mapatano, sharti, mwafaka, mkataba.

pad, *n.* (*of grass*) kata; (*small cushion*) mto mdogo, kitakia; (*of animal*) fumba; (*as protection*) kipande cha nguo *&c.*, cha kubandikia. *Writing-pad,* karatasi za kuandikia zilizofungwa pamoja. — *v.t.* tia *pad,* bandika. **padding,** *n.* kitu cha kujazia tu, si cha maana sana; (*in a speech &c.*), maneno nafifu, upuzi.

paddle, (1) *v.i.* tembea majini.

paddle, (2) *n.* kafi. — *v.t. and i.* endesha majini kwa kafi, piga kafi. *Paddle one's own canoe,* fanya kazi bila msaada. **paddle-wheel,** *n.* gurudumu (la upande au nyuma) la kuendesha merikebu ya moshi (meli).

paddock, *n.* shamba dogo la kuchungia wanyama, kiwanda, uwanda.

paddy, *n.* mpunga.

padlock, *n.* kufuli.

padre, *n.* kasisi.

paean, *n.* wimbo wa kusifu (wa shangwe kwa sababu ya kushinda vitani).

paederasty, pederasty, *n.* kufira, kulawiti.

pagan, *n. and a.* mtu asiye Mkristo; mtu asiye Mkristo (wala Myahudi, wala Mwislamu), mtu asiyemwamini Mungu; -shenzi, -a kishenzi. **paganism,** *n.* ushenzi, hali (desturi) ya *pagan.*

page, (1) *n.* mtoto mtumishi, boi.

page, (2) *n.* ukurasa, upande mmoja wa ukurasa.

pageant, *n.* tamasha, mchezo wa kuigiza mambo (habari, matokeo) ya zamani ya mji; (*vain show*) tamasha (sherehe) ya bure. **pageantry,** *n.* kama *pageant.*

pagoda, *n.* hekalu (la kihindi au kichina).

paid, *p.t. and pf.t.* ya *pay.*

pail, *n.* ndoo. **pailful,** *n.* kadiri ya ndoo moja, ndoo.

pain, *n.* maumivu, uchungu, kuuma; (*stabbing pain*) kichomi; (*mental*) huzuni, ghamu, sikitiko. *Take pains, Be at pains,* jitahidi, jikalifu, fanya juhudi, toa bidii, angalia. — *v.t.* umiza, wanga; (*grieve*) huzunisha, sumbua; — *v.i.* (*ache &c.*) uma, umia. **painful,** *a.* -a kuumiza *&c.* *It is painful,* inauma. **painless,** *a.* -sioumiza, bila maumivu. **painstaking,** *a.* -enye kujitahidi, -a bidii ya kazi, -angalifu, hodari, -a juhudi.

paint, *n.* rangi (ya kupaka). — *v.t.* paka (tia) rangi, andika picha ya rangi; (*describe*) eleza habari, fafanisha. **painter,** (1) *n.* mpaka rangi, fundi wa kupaka rangi; mwandishi wa picha za rangi. **painting,** *n.* kupaka rangi; (*picture*) picha (taswira, sanamu).

painter, (2) *n.* kamba ya kufungia (ya kufungashia) mashua.

painting, *n.* taz. *paint.*

pair, *n.* (*two of a kind*) jozi, vitu viwili vilivyo sawa (vinavyolingana), (*married*) mume na mke. *A pair of scissors,* mkasi. *A pair of trousers,* suruali. *A pair of stairs,* madaraja, ngazi. *A pair of spectacles,* miwani. *A pair of shoes,* jozi ya viatu. — *v.i.* -wa (lingana) wawili wawili (mbili mbili *&c.*); (*of animals*) tafuta mwenzi; — *v.t.* panga (weka, fanya, linganisha) viwili.

palace, *n.* jumba la mfalme (mtawala), jumba kubwa. **palatial,** *a.* -a *palace,* -kubwa, -zuri, -a anasa.

paladin, *n.* shujaa, mtu hodari mwema.

palaeolithic, *a.* -a zamani za kale watu walipotumia vyombo (shoka *&c.*) vilivyofanyizwa kwa mawe.

palaeontology, *n.* elimu ya viumbe vya kale sana na mabaki yao.

palaeozoic, *a.* zamani za kale sana.

palanquin, *n.* machela.

palate, *n.* kaakaa, kaa la kinywa; (*taste*) ulimi. **palatable,** *a.* -tamu, -a kupendeza. **palatal,** *a.* -a *palate.*

palatial, *a.* taz. *palace.*

palaver, *n.* maneno, mashauri, maongezi, baraza. *Hold a palaver*, barizi. — *v.i.* payapaya, payuka, bwata bwabwaja.

pale, (1) *n.* (*stake*) kiguzo, mti, ufito; (*boundary*) mpaka; (*enclosure*) ua, kiwanja. **paling,** *n.* nguzo, kiguzo. **palisade,** *n.* ua (wa nguzo), boma (la miti iliyosimikishwa na kuchongoka).

pale, (2) *a.* -eupe, -enye rangi kidogo. — *v.i.* geuka rangi -eupe, fifia.

palette, *n.* kibao cha kufanyizia rangi (cha mwandishi wa picha).

palfrey, *n.* farasi mdogo.

palimpsest, *n.* mwandiko wa zamani uliofutwa kidogo, ukaandikiwa mara ya pili juu.

paling, *n.*, **palisade,** *n.* taz. *pale* (1).

pall, (1) *v.i.* chosha, kinaisha, chukiza, pooza, punguka, haribika.

pall, (2) *n.* subaya, subahiya, deuli, kitambaa cha kufunikia jeneza mazikoni.

pallet, *n.* godoro (hasa lililojazwa majani makavu).

palliate, *v.t.* tuliza, punguza (maumivu, ugonjwa); (*extenuate &c.*) rahisisha hatia (kosa), setiri, toa udhuru kwa. **palliation,** *n.* kurahisisha, kisetiri, kitulizo. **palliative,** *a.* -a kusetiri &c., -a kutuliza. — *n.* kitulizo.

pallid, *a.* -eupe (-a uso). **pallor,** *n.* weupe wa uso (kwa ugonjwa &c.).

palm, *n.* (*of hand*) kitanga (kiganja) cha mkono, gao; (*tree*) mti wa jamii ya mnazi, mvumo &c.; (*date tree*) mtende; (*palm-oil tree*) mchikichi; (*trophy*) alama ya kushinda, tuzo; (*sailmaker's*) dopa. — *v.t.* ficha katika kitanga cha mkono. *Palm off* (*something*), pokeza (kitu) kwa hila. **palmate,** *a.* -enye umbo kama kitanga cha mkono; (*leaves*) -a kutokeza huko na huko katika sehemu ya kati. **palmer,** *n.* haji aliyekwenda *Jerusalem* kwa ibada. **palmist,** *n.* mtu anayejidai kuwa anaweza kujua tabia na mambo yatakayompata mtu kwa kuangalia kitanga cha mkono wake. **palm-oil,** *n.* mawese; (*bribe*) rushwa, hongo, kipenyezo. **Palm Sunday,** *n.* Jumapili ya mitende, Jumapili kabla ya *Easter*. **palm-wine,** *n.* tembo, zarambo. **palmy,** *a.* -enye minazi (mitende &c.); (*flourishing*) -a kusitawi, -a neema, -zuri, -a baraka.

palpable, *a.* -a kugusika, -a kuonekana; (*clear*) baini, dhahiri. **palpably,** *adv.* dhahiri. **palpate,** *v.t.* gusa, papasa. **palpitate,** *v.i.* pigapiga, puma, papa, pwita, tutuma. **palpitation,** *n.* (*of heart*) kiherehere cha moyo; (*fear*) tetemeko, kipapo, hofu, kupapa rohoni.

palsy, *n.* upooza, kitetemo cha viungo vya mwili.

palter, *v.i.* fanya ujanja, piga domo, toa maneno ya hila, sitasita, ganzaganza. **paltry,** *n.* hafifu, -nyonge, dhaifu, -dogo.

pampas, *n.* manyika za *America* ya kusini.

pamper, *v.t.* shibisha, lisha vyakula vitamu; (*coddle*) pendelea, dekeza, endekeza, engaenga, (*indulge*) lisha, ongeza vibaya, kinaisha.

pamphlet, *n.* juzuu, kitabu kidogo. **pamphleteer,** *n.* mwandishi wa *pamphlets*.

pan, *n.* chungu, sufuria; (*frying pan*) kikaango, tawa. **pancake,** *n.* andazi kama kitumbua.

panacea, *n.* dawa ya kuponya maradhi yote (maumivu yote).

pancake, *n.* taz. *pan*.

pancreas, *n.* kongosho.

pandemonium, *n.* makelele mengi, ghasia nyingi, machafuko, mafujo, msukosuko.

pander, *v.i.* (*to*) saidia katika mambo ya ngoa (ya kutongoza wanawake), dekeza, endekeza, ongeza vibaya. — *n.* kawadi.

pane, *n.* (*of glass*) kioo, kipande cha (ubamba wa) kioo.

panegyric, *n.* maneno ya kusifu, hotuba ya sifa, sifa.

panel, *n.* kibao kilichotiwa katika mlango au kupigiliwa ukutani; (*list* *of names*) orodha ya majina, hasa ya watu walioitwa kufanya hukumu.

pang, *n.* umivu kali la ghafula, kichomi, mchomo; (*mental*) kipindi cha hamu, juhudi. *Pangs of hunger*, umivu kali la njaa. *Birth pangs*, uchungu ((utungu) wa kuzaa.

panic, *n.* hofu ya ghafula (ieneayo katika kundi la watu), woga mkuu. **panic-stricken**, *a.* -lioshikwa na woga mkuu (wa ghafula).

pannier, *n.* shogi.

pannikin, *n.* kikombe cha bati, kopo.

panoply, *n.* deraya, mavalio yote ya vita, deraya na silaha.

panorama, *n.* picha ndefu ya kupitishwa taratibu mbele ya macho; (*view*) sura ya ulimwengu, sura ya nchi yote.

pansy, *n.* ua la kizungu.

pant, *v.i.* tweta, hema, kokota roho, shusha pumzi, kukuta. *Pant after*, taka sana, tamani, onea shauku.

pantaloon, *n.* mcheshi, mfanya ubishi mwingi; (*trousers*) suruali. **pants**, *n.* suruali.

pantechnicon, *n.* gari kubwa kama chumba, la kuchukulia vyombo vya nyumba (meza, viti, vitanda, kabati &c.).

pantheism, *n.* kusadiki ya kuwa ulimwengu wote ni Mungu; kusadiki kuna miungu mingi. **pantheon**, *n.* jamii ya miungu yote ya taifa.

panther, *n.* mnyama kama chui.

pantomime, *n.* mchezo wa kuigiza mambo ya hadithi, mwigo wa mambo kwa ishara bila kusema. — *v.t.* igiza kwa ishara bila kusema.

pantry, *n.* chumba cha kuwekea vyombo vya kulia (sahani, vikombe, visu &c.).

pants, *n.* taz. *pantaloon*.

pap, (1) *n.* ubwabwa.

pap, (2) *n.* titi, chuchu la ziwa.

papa, *n.* (neno la kitoto) baba.

papacy, *n.* cheo (kazi, utawala) cha *Pope*; Kanisa la kirumi na madhehebu zake. **papal**, *a.* -a *Pope*. **papist**, *n.* mfuasi wa Kanisa la kirumi.

papaw, *n.* (*tree*) mpapai; (*fruit*) papai.

paper, *n.* karatasi; (*document*) hati, cheti; (*newspaper*) gazeti; (*cheques*) hawala, hati za fedha; (*money, notes*) noti. — *v.t.* bandika karatasi, *e.g.* ukutani, pamba kwa karatasi nzuri. **paper-hanger**, *n.* fundi wa kubandika karatasi ukutani.

paprika, *n.* pilipili hoho.

papyrus, *n.* mafunjo, njaanjaa, namna ya nyasi za mabwawani; namna ya karatasi iliyofanyizwa zamani na Wamisri kwa mabua ya mafunjo yaliyolengwa.

parity, *n.* usawa, urari. *On a par with*, sawa na, -a kulingana na.

parable, *n.* mfano wa maneno, mithali, hadithi yenye mafundisho, fumbo. **parabolic**, *a.* -a *parable*.

parabola, *n.* mwendo wa mviringo kama wa mpira utupwapo.

parabolic, *a.* taz. *parable*.

parachute, *n.* kitu kama mwavuli mkubwa cha kumwezesha mtu ashuke taratibu kutoka juu (katika eropleni &c.).

paraclete, *n.* = *Holy Ghost*.

parade, *n.* njia kuu ya kutembelea; (*military*) mchezo wa askari, gwaride; (*show, pomp*) fahari, majivuno, mangwaji. *Make a parade of*, jivunia, onyesha kwa kiburi &c. — *v.t.* tembeza, jivunia: (*military*) panga (askari); — *v.i.* (*assemble*) pangana; (*march*) andamana.

paradigm, *n.* kiolezo (cha kuonyesha jinsi *verb* inavyobadilika kwa kisarufi.)

paradise, *n.* peponi, ferdausi, barazahi; (*bliss*) furaha kuu, jaha. *Gate of Paradise*, kilango cha jaha.

paradox, *n.* kweli iliyo kama uwongo, neno linaloonekana kama kwamba ni la kinyume kumbe ni sahihi, fumbo la maneno, kitendawili. **paradoxical**, *a.* -a *paradox*

paraffin, *n.* mafuta ya taa.

paragon, *n.* mfano uliostahili kufuatwa (kuigwa), kiolezo kikamilifu, kipeo.

paragraph, *n.* fungu la maneno, kipande (cha mwandiko), aya.

parakeet, *n.* ndege, namna ya kasuku mdogo.

parallax, *n.* tofauti ya kitu kionekanavyo mahali pawili, kama hapa na pengine.

parallel, *a.* -a kuambaana, sambamba, -a kupambana sawasawa, -a kwenda sawasawa pasipo kukutana; (*similar, corresponding*) -a kulingana, sawa, mwenzi. — *n.* mfano, kifani. — *v.t.* leta mfano (kifani). **parallelism,** *n.* hali ya kuwa *parallel*, mfano. **parallelogram,** *n.* mstatili (kama mraba ila pande mbili zinazoelekeana ni ndefu kuliko zile nyingine).

paralyse, *v.t.* poozesha; (*with fear &c.*) shangaza, pumbaza, fadhaisha, duwaza; (*disable*) legeza, fisha, komesha, zuia. **paralysis,** *n.* kipooza. **paralytic,** *a.* -enye kupooza. — *n.* mtu aliyepooza (mguu, mkono &c.).

paramount, *a.* -kuu, -a kupita yote, -kubwa sana, -a maana kuu, -a nguvu.

paramour, *n.* hawara, kinyumba, mbuya.

parapet, *n.* ukingo (wa ukuta au boma), kikuta, ombwe.

paraphernalia, *n.* vyombo, vifaa, zana, mapambo, mavalio, urembo, fahari.

paraphrase, *n.* fafanusi, fasiri, elezo. — *v.t.* eleza, fafanua.

parasite, *n.* (*plant*) kimelea, kirukia; (*animal*) kimelea, kijidudu kimelea; (*person*) mdusia, kimelea. **parasitic,** *a.* -enye kujilisha (kujipendekeza, kushikamana) na mwingine, -enye kudusa (kudusia).

parasol, *n.* mwavuli (wa kukinga jua).

parboil, *v.t.* tokosa (chemsha) kidogo.

parcel, *n.* kifurushi, kibumba, bumba bahasa, kipeto. *Parcel of land*, kiwanja, sehemu ya shamba &c. *Part and parcel*, sehemu yenye maana sana. — *v.t.* (*out*) gawanya, gawa.

parch, *v.t.* kausha, unguza, shindisha kwa kiu; (*roast lightly*) kaanga; — *v.i.* (*become dry*) kauka, nyauka, ungua. *Parched maize*, bisi.

parchment, *n.* ngozi ya mnyama iliyotengenezwa kama karatasi ya kuandikia; hati iliyoandikwa katika karatasi hiyo; cho chote kama karatasi hiyo.

pardon, *n.* samaha, masamaha, samahani, usamehe, uradhi, ghofira, hisa. *Beg for, ask for pardon*, omba (taka) radhi (masamaha &c.). — *v.t.* samehe, achilia, ridhia, ghofiri. *Pardon me*, niwie radhi, uwe radhi, kunradhi, toba, pole. **pardonable,** *a.* -a kusameheka.

pare, *v.t.* (*fruit*) ambua, menya, toa maganda; (*nails &c.*) kata; (*lessen*) punguza. **paring,** *n.* (*of nails*) kikuchia; (*small bits*) maganda (yaliyoambuliwa) vipande vidogo, takataka.

paregoric, *n.* dawa ya kutulizia maumivu.

parent, *n.* baba (mama) mzaa; (*ancestor*) mzee, baba, mama; (*origin*) asili, chanzo. **parentage,** *n.* ubaba, umama; (*descent*) nasaba, ukoo, jadi. **parental,** *a.* -a baba (mama), kama baba (mama).

parenthesis, *n.* maneno yaliyoingizwa katikati (yaliyotengwa na maneno mengine kwa vistari au vifungo; (alama ya kutia maneno hayo, hivi (. . .).

pariah, *n.* Banyani wa cheo kilicho kinyonge kabisa; (*outcast*) maskini, fakiri, mtu aliyetupwa; (*dog*) mbwa koko.

paring, *n.* taz. *pare*.

parish, *n.* mtaa (wenye padre wake), **parishioner,** *n.* mkaa katika *parish*, fulani. **parochial,** *a.* -a *parish*, -a mtaa, -a mambo ya mtaa; (*narrow &c.*) -dogo, hafifu, -nyonge.

parity, *n.* taz. *par*.

park, *n.* shamba (zuri la kutembelea), bustani kubwa; (*military*) kiwanja cha kuwekea mizinga, vyombo na zana; (*for cars*) kiwanda (mahali) kilichowekwa kwa ajili ya motakaa.

— *v.t.* weka katika kiwanja (motakaa, mizinga).

parlance, *n.* usemi, maneno, msemo.

parley, *n.* shauri la (maneno ya) kufanya amani na adui. — *v.i.* fanya maneno (shauri), semana, semezana. **parliament,** *n.* halmashauri kuu ya serikali ya kiingereza, mkutano mkuu wa serikali ya kiingereza. **parliamentary,** *a.* -a *parliament,* -a kustahili *parliament.*

parlour, *n.* sebule, ukumbi, baraza.

parlous, *a.* -a hatari.

parochial, *a.* taz. *parish.*

parody, *n.* mwigo wa kuchekesha (wa kufanya mzaha, wa maneno au mashairi). — *v.t.* iga kwa jinsi ya kuchekesha (ya kufanya mzaha).

parole, *n.* ahadi ya mfungwa kutojaribu kutoroka.

paroquet, *n.* taz. *parakeet.*

paroxysm, *n.* shindo, kishindo, kipindi, ukali, hali ya ghafula. **paroxysmal,** *a.* -a *paroxysm,* -a ghafula, -a kishindo.

parquet, *n.* vipande vya mbao kama vigae vilivyoungwa kufanya kama sakafu.

parricide, *n.* mwua baba, mauaji ya baba.

parrot, *n.* kasuku, dura; (*brown-headed*) kwao. — *v.t.* sema maneno bila kufahamu maana yake.

parry, *v.t.* kinga, bekua, zuia; (*avoid*) epuka, epa.

parse, *v.t.* ainisha maneno kisarufi. **parsing,** *n.* kuainisha maneno kisarufi.

Parsee, *n.* Parisi.

parsimony, *n.* ukabidhi, ukavu, choyo cha fedha, ubahili, ugumu, kukata gharama. **parsimonious,** *a.* -kabidhi, bahili, -nyimivu.

parsing, *n.* taz. *parse.*

parsley, *n.* mboga ya kizungu ya majani yaliyofinyana.

parsnip, *n.* mboga ya kizungu kidogo kama kiazi.

parson, *n.* kasisi mwenye kuchunga watu wa mtaa fulani, padre. **parsonage,** *n.* nyumba ya *parson.*

part, *n.* sehemu, kipande, nusu fungu, mkato, hisa; (*work*) kazi; (*district, side*) upande; (*certain number*) -ingine, baadhi; (*duty*) wajibu. *He took your part,* alikuwa upande wako. *For my own part I think it good,* mimi nafsi yangu naiona njema. *For the most part,* zaidi, hasa, aghalabu. *A man parts,* mtu mwenye kulelewa vema (wa akili, hodari). *In good part,* kwa upole. *In bad part,* kwa ukali. *Part of speech,* aina ya neno kisarufi. *Act a part,* jifanya mtu mwingine, jigeua, fanya hila, cheza. *Take part in,* -wamo, shiriki, saidia. — *v.t.* tenga, tengua, gawa, achisha, kata, farakisha, bagua, baidisha; — *v.i.* (*of road*) fanya panda; (*separate*) tengana, tengwa, farikiana, achana. *Part company,* achana na, tokana na. *Part with,* acha, toa, tupa. **partial,** *a.* (*incomplete*) -a sehemu, -a nusu, -a upande; (*biased*) -a kupendelea; (*having a liking for*) -a kuona tamu, -a kutaka, -a kuelekea, -a kupenda. **partiality,** *n.* kutaka, kupenda, shauku; (*special*) upendeleo. **partially,** *adv.* kwa sehemu, nusu; (*with bias*) kwa kupendelea, si sawa. **particle,** *n.* kipande kilicho kidogo mno, kitu kidogo, chembe, kivumbi, kitakataka. **parting,** *n.* kuachana, kuondokana, magawanyiko, mtengano, kutengwa; (*of roads*) njia pacha, njia panda; (*farewell*) kuagana, agano. *A final parting,* kutakana buriani, — *a.* -a kutenga, -a kuagana, -a mwisho. **partly,** *adv.* nusu, kwa sehemu, kidogo.

partake, *v.i.* (*p.t.* **partook,** *pf.t.* **partaken**) (*of*) shiriki, onja, gawiwa, twaa, twaa sehemu; (*resemble*) -wa kama, -wamo. **partaker,** *n.* mshiriki. **partaking,** *n.* ushirika.

partial, *a.*, **partiality,** *n.*, **partially,** *adv.* taz. *part.*

participate, *v.i.* shiriki, onja, gawiwa, twaa, twaa sehemu, -wamo. **participant,** *n.* mshiriki. **participation,** *n.* ushirika.

participle, *n.* namna ya *verb* iliyotumika kama *adjective.*

particle, *n.* taz. *part.*

parti-coloured, *a.* -enye rangi mbalimbali sehemu mbalimbali.

particular, *a.* (*individual*) -moja, -a mtu mmoja, -a kitu kimoja, peke yake; (*important*) -a maana, -kubwa, ingi, -a peke yake; (*special*) mahsusi, maalum; (*precise*) halisi, -a mambo yote pia; (*careful*) -angalifu, *chaguzi. *In particular,* zaidi, hasa. *A particular point,* jambo moja, jambo fulani, — *n.* jambo moja. *Particulars,* mambo moja moja, habari zote (hata za mambo madogo sana). **particularity,** *n.* udhahiri, uhalisi, kupambanua. **particularize,** *v.i.* nena (taja) -moja -moja, eleza halisi, pambanua. **particularly,** *adv.* zaidi, hasa, halisi, juu yote, sana.

parting, *n. and a.* taz. *part.*

partisan, *n.* mfuasi (hasa mshupavu afuataye kwa bidii bila kupima kwa akili), mtu wa kupendelea.

partition, *n.* kugawanyika, mgawo; (*wall*) ukuta, kiambaza cha kati; (*of wood*) mbao za kati, kisetiri. — *v.t.* gawa, tenga, kata. **partitive,** *a.* -a kugawa, -a kutenga.

partly, *adv.* taz. *part.*

partner, *n.* mshiriki, mwenzi, rafiki, mtu afanyaye kazi au kucheza pamoja na mwingine. **partnership,** *n.* ushirika, bia; (*firm*) kampani.

partook, *p.t.* ya *partake.*

partridge, *n.* kwale.

parturient, *a.* -a karibu kuzaa, -a katika kuzaa. **parturition,** *n.* uzazi, kuzaa.

party, *n.* (*company*) jeshi, kundi, umati, watu wengi; (*faction*) jamii ya watu wenye shauri moja, upande, baadhi, madhehebu, shauri, wafuasi; (*entertainment*) kikoa, karamu, tafrija; (*partner*) mshiriki; (*person*) mtu. *He was a party to their proceedings,* alishirikiana nao, alikuwa hali moja nao. *His party,* wafuasi wake, wenzi wake, umati wake. *Give a party,* fanya karamu, alika wageni.

parvenu, *n.* mtu aliyetajirika au kupata ukuu ghafula, mzushi.

paschal, *a.* -a Pasaka, -a *Easter.*

pasha, *n.* jina la cheo cha kiaskari au kiserikali cha Kituruki.

pass, *v.i.* (*go*) pita, jiri, enda, endelea; (*near, without touching*) ambaa; (*change*) geuka, badilika; (*end*) isha, koma, toweka; (*die*) -fa, fariki; (*be approved*) kubalika, pata ruhusa (idhini), pewa daraja; (*be known*) julikana; (*of money*) tumika; — *v.t.* pita; (*exceed*) pita, pita kadiri; (*of money*) tumisha; (*neglect*) ambaa, toangalia; (*cause to go, hand, give*) leta, pitisha, peleka, pisha; (*approve*) kubali, sahihisha, amuru, toa idhini; (*evacuate*) -nya. *Pass a law (resolution, motion &c.)* fanya sheria (amri, agizo, onyo &c.), sahihisha, idhinisha. *The law passed,* sheria ikafanyika. *Bring to pass,* fanya, fanyiza, timiliza. *Come to pass,* -wa, fanyika, tukia. *Pass an examination,* shinda katika mtihani. *Pass off* (*end*) isha, tulia; (*rid oneself of*) toa kwa hila. *Pass for,* dhaniwa kuwa, jitendekeza. *Pass on to,* sukumiza; (*go to*) pitia, enda kwa, -ja katika. *Pass into,* geuka, geuka kuwa. *Pass sentence,* hukumu, toa hukumu, amua, kata hukumu. *Pass master,* kubalika, tosha, faa. *Pass over,* pita acha; (*cross water*) vuka, abiri. *Pass time,* shinda, ongea. *Pass by, let pass,* pita, pisha, pishia mbali; (*without touching, avoid*) ambaa. — *n.* njia, mlango, kipito (*gap*) mwanya; (*passport &c.*) cheti; (*difficulty*) matata, mashaka; (*leave*) ruhusa. **passable,** *a.* -a kuendeka, -a kupitika; (*moderately good*) -a kadiri, wastani, hivi.

passage, *n.* kupita, mpito; (*way*) njia, pito, kipito; (*journey*) safari; (*crossing*) kuabiri, uvuko, kivuko; (*in house*) chochoro, ujia; (*narrow*) kipenyo; (*alley*) kichochoro; (*ford*) kivuko; (*in a book*) mahali, maneno, fungu la maneno; (*transition*) kugeuka, mgeuko. *Bird of passage,* ndege wa kuhama, mhamishi. *Pas-*

sage of arms, pigano, bishano. **pass-book,** *n.* daftari ya hesabu ya fedha inayowekwa au kutolewa katika *bank*. **passer-by,** *n.* mpitaji, mpita njia, mgeni, msafiri. **passing,** *a.* -a kupita, -a siokaa, -a mara moja. *Passing bell*, kengele inayopigwa kujulisha watu ya kuwa mtu anakufa. — *n.* kupita, kupitana; (*death*) kufariki, kufa. *In passing*, kwa kupitia, kwa haraka, kwa vichache.

passe, *a.* -a kuchakaa.

passenger, *n.* abiria, mpitaji, mjaja msafiri, mgeni.

passer-by, *n.*, **passing,** *a. and n.* taz. *pass*.

passion, *n.* bidii ya moyo, juhudi ya roho, harara; (*anger*) hasira, kiruu, hamaki; (*desire*) ngoa, tamaa, shauku, ashiki, uchu, hawa; (*suffering*) mateso, maumivu. *The Passion*, maumivu makali ya Yesu Kristo msalabani aliposulibiwa. **passionate,** *a.* -a *passion*, -epesi wa hasira, -kali, harara, -a ashiki (shauku, tamaa, uchu, ngoa) nyingi.

passive, *a.* -a kutendewa (si kutenda); (*submissive*) -tulivu, -vumilivu, -stahimilivu; (*inactive*) -siotenda neno, -a kukaa tu. *Passive voice*, aina ya *verb* yenye habari ya kutendwa (si kutenda). **passivity,** *n.* kuwa *passive*, uvumilivu, utulivu &c.

pass-key, *n.* ufunguo unaofungulia vingi.

Passover, *n.* Pasaka.

passport, *n.* cheti (hati) cha njia, ruhusa.

pass-word, *n.* neno la siri (la kupatia ruhusa ya kuingia kambi, kupita askari wa zamu &c.).

past, *p.t.* ya *pass*. — *a.* -a kwanza, -a zamani, -liopita. *Past Tense*, aina ya *verb* yenye habari ya wakati uliopita. — *adv.* kupita mbele. — *prep.* kupita, zaidi ya, mbele ya. *He is past cure*, hawezi kupona. — *n.* zamani, mambo ya zamani, mambo yaliyopita.

paste, *n.* mchanganyiko wa unga na maji &c. (wa kufanya mkate, maandazi &c.); mchanganyiko laini wa unga na maji (wa kuambatisha, karatasi &c.), wambiso, embwe, cho chote kinamo kama udongo wa kufinyanga, *e.g.* mseto wa nyama au samaki &c.; (*for artificial gems*) kitu kama kioo kinachong'aa sana; hutumika kufanya vito vya pete &c. — *v.t.* ambatisha kwa *paste*, bandika kwa *paste*. **pasteboard,** *n.* karatasi nene (kama ubao mwembamba). **pastry,** *n.* maandazi; (*cake of*) kinyunya; (*mixture*) unga uliochanganyika na maji na siagi &c. wa kufanyiza maandazi &c. **pasty,** *n.* sambusa (kama kitumbua chenye nyama). — *a.* -a *paste*, -a kama *paste*; (*of face*) -eupe (usio wa afya).

pastel, *n.* kalamu kama ya udongo wa rangi.

pastern, *n.* mguu wa farasi chini (juu ya kwata).

pasteurize, *v.t.* pika kitu (*e.g.* maziwa) bila kukichemsha ili kuua vijidudu vyote vya ugonjwa vilivyomo.

pastille, *n.* kibonge kidogo kitamu chenye dawa ya koo; (*aromatic*) kibonge cha ubani &c., cha kufukizia.

pastime, *n.* mchezo, maongezi, mazungumzo, maburudisho.

pastor, *n.* padre, kasisi, mchungaji wa roho. **pastoral,** *a.* -a *pastor*; (*of a shepherd*) -a kuchunga kondoo; (*rural*) -a mashamba. *Pastoral theology*, elimu ya kazi ya padre, maarifa ya uchungaji wa roho. — *n.* waraka wa askofu kwa mapadre. **pastorate,** *n.* upadre, ukasisi, kazi ya padre, jamii ya mapadre. **pasture, pasturage,** *n.* machunga, malisho.

pastry, *n.* taz. *paste*.

pasture, pasturage, *n.* taz. *pastor*.

pasty, *n.* taz. *paste*.

pat, *v.t.* pigapiga polepole (kwa kofi); (*pat gently, stroke, caress*) papasa. *Pat on the back*, pongeza, shangilia. — *n.* kipigo cha kofi (cha kuonyesha upendo, kushangilia, furaha &c.);

(*sound*) kishindo kidogo (kama cha mguu kupiga chini); (*small lump*) kibonge. — *adv.* sawia, papo hapo, mara. **patter,** *v.i.* fanya vishindo vidogodogo (kama mvua). — *n.* vishindo vidogodogo vya mfulizo.

patch, *n.* kiraka, gango, kipande; (*of wood, e.g. in a boat*) hasho; (*of ground*) kiwanja, kiwanda, mahali padogo, shamba dogo, kiunga konde; (*for eye*) kidoto, kinga ya jicho. — *v.t.* tia kiraka (gango, hasho &c.), tengeneza, chomelea. *Patch up,* fanyiza, tengeneza; (*a quarrel*) patana. **patchwork,** *n.* vipande vingi vya nguo vilivyoshonwa ili kufanya nguo kubwa, nguo ya vipande vingi; (*inferior make*) kazi mbovu. **patchy,** *a.* -a kama virakaraka, -a namna (rangi) mbalimbali.

patchouli, *n.* namna ya manukato.

patchwork, *n.,* **patchy,** *a.* taz. *patch.*

pate, *n.* kichwa.

patella, *n.* pia ya goti.

paten, *n.* kisahani kinachotumika katika *Eucharist.*

patent, *a.* (*open*) wazi, dhahiri, bayana; (*patented*) -liohifadhiwa na amri ya serikali -siigwe; (*new, ingenious &c.*) -pya, -a akili, -a kufaa. *Patent leather,* ngozi (*leather*) iliyopakwa rangi ngumu inayong'aa sana. — *n.* hati ya kugombeza kitu kisiigwe, kitu walichogombezwa kuiga watu wengine. — *v.t.* pata hati ya *patent.* **patentee,** *n.* -enye kupewa *patent.* **patently**. *adv.* kwa wazi, dhahiri.

pater, *n.* baba. **paterfamilias,** *n.* baba mwenye watoto. **paternal,** *a.* -a kuumeni; (*fatherly*) -a baba, -a kama baba, -pole. **paternity,** *n.* kuwa baba, ubaba, uzazi. **paternoster,** *n.* sala ya Yesu Kristo! 'Baba yetu', &c.

path, *n.* njia, kijia. **pathless,** *a.* -sioendeka, -siopitika. **pathway,** *n.* njia.

pathetic, *a.* taz. *pathos.*

pathless, *a.* taz. *path.*

pathology, *n.* utabibu, elimu ya dalili, asili na dawa za ugonjwa.

pathos, *n.* huruma, huzuni, uwezo wa kutia huruma (wa kuhuzunisha). **pathetic,** *a.* -a kutia huruma (huzuni, majonzi, sikitiko &c.).

pathway, *n.* taz. *path.*

patience, *n.* taz. *patient.*

patient, *a.* -stahimilivu, -vumilivu, -enye saburi. *Be patient with,* vumilia, stahimili, chukuana na. — *n.* mgonjwa, mwele. **patience,** *n.* saburi, uvumilivu, utulivu, ustahimilivu. **patiently,** *adv.* kwa saburi, kwa utulivu.

patois, *n.* usemi wa mahali fulani (padogo), usemi wa watu wa mahali (si wa maandiko).

patriarch, *n.* mzee mkuu mwenye heshima; (*ancestor*) baba; (*chief bishop*) askofu mkuu. **patriarchal,** *a.* -a *patriarch.*

patrician, *a.* -kuu. — *n.* mtu mkuu (wa Rumi zamani).

patrimony, *n.* urithi.

patriot, *n.* mtu mpenda nchi yake (kabila lake, taifa lake); ajitiaye katika kukuza hali ya nchi yake &c., asijali masumbuko, taabu &c. **patriotic,** *a.* -a *patriot.* **patriotism,** *n.* tabia au matendo ya *patriot.*

patristic, *a.* -a wazee na walimu wa kale wa kikristo.

patrol, *n.* doria, askari mwenye zamu, kundi la askari (mapolisi) wenye kazi ya kuzunguka njia za mji (mahali). — *v.t.* tembelea njia ya mji (mahali) kulinda &c.

patron, *a.* baba, bwana, mfadhili, msaidizi, mlinzi. *Patron saint,* mtakatifu marehemu, adhaniwaye kuwa hasa mtunza mtu (mji, nchi, kazi) fulani. **patronage,** *n.* fadhili, upendeleo, msaada, ulinzi. **patronize,** *v.t.* saidia, linda, fadhili, pendelea; (*buy of*) nunulia, nunua kwa; (*depreciate*) rahisisha, jiona (jifanya) mkuu kuliko.

patten, *n.* kiatu (cha mti), mtalawanda.

patter, (1) *n.* and *v.* taz. *pat.*

patter, (2) *v.t.* sema (kariri) upesi upesi (bila kufikiri maana ya maneno); — *v.i.* sema upesi upesi, payuka, tatarika. — *n.* usemi wa jamii ya watu fulani (*e.g.* wa wizi); mapayo, matatariko.

pattern, *n.* (*model &c.*) kiolezo, kielelezo, mtindo, mfano, kipeo, kitu bora, namna ya wema; (*design*) sanamu, picha, kazi, urembo, bombwe; (*sample*) namna; (*of work*) kielezo, kielelezo, cheo.

patty, *n.* sambusa (andazi lenye nyama ndani).

paucity, *n.* uchache, shida, uhaba.

paunch, *n.* tumbo (hasa kubwa).

pauper, *n.* maskini, fakiri, fukara, hohe hahe, mkata; (*as an insult*) kibapara. **pauperism,** *n.* umaskini, ufukara, ufakiri, ukata. **pauperize,** *v.t.* fanya maskini, vutia umaskini.

pause, *v.i.* simama kidogo, pumzika kidogo, koma kwa muda mfupi, sita, ngoja kidogo; (*be silent*) nyamaa, kaa kimya. — *n.* kikomo, kituo, pindi; (*interval*) kituo; (*from work*) kipumziko; (*silence*) kimya.

pave, *v.t.* tia mawe chini, sakifu. *Pave the way for,* fanya tayari kwa, andalia. **pavement,** *n.* mawe makubwa sawa ya kutembelea, sakafu ya mawe.

pavilion, *n.* hema kubwa, banda zuri.

paw, *n.* nguu wa mnyama (mafumba na makucha). — *v.t.* parapara, kanyaga, kwakura; (*touch*) gusa, shika (bila uangalifu); (*stroke &c.*) papasa, gusa; — *v.i.* parapara.

pawn, (1) *n.* (*chess*) kitunda; (*person*) baradhuli, mzuzu.

pawn, (2) *v.t.* weka (tia) rehani. *Put in pawn,* weke rehani. **pawnbroker,** *n.* akopeshaye fedha kwa rehani, atwaaye rehani. **pawnshop,** *n.* rehani, duka la rehani.

pawpaw, *n.* (*fruit*) papai; (*tree*) mpapai.

pay, *v.t.* (*p.t. and pf.t.* **paid**) lipa, toa fedha, kabidhi, ridhisha; (*reward*) jazi, tuza, lipa; (*punish*) tia adhabu, adhibisha, patiliza; — *v.i.* lipa; (*be of profit*) faa, -wa na faida, leta faida. *Pay attention* (*regard, respect &c.*) *to,* angalia, heshimu, stahi, jali. *Pay out,* lipiza kisasi. *Pay one's way,* lipa gharama ihusuyo. *Pay court to,* jipendekeza kwa. *Pay a visit,* enda kutazama (kusalimu, kuamkia, kuzuru). *Pay one's respects,* enda kuamkia. *Pay away,* tumia; (*of a rope*) legeza polepole, puliza. — *n.* ijara, ujira, mshahara, haki. **payable,** *a.* -a kulipwa. **paymaster,** *n.* karani (wa kulipa mshahara askari au mabaharia), bwana fedha. **payment,** *n.* malipo. **pay-roll, pay-sheet,** *n.* orodha ya majina ya watu wa kazi na mshahara wao.

pea, *n.* njegere, dengu, adesi, mbaazi (ya kizungu). **Peanut,** *n.* njugu, karanga.

peace, *n.* amani, salama, raha, utulivu. *Keep the peace,* tofanya udhia, tosumbua watu, tulia. **peaceable,** *a.* -tulivu, -enye amani, -a kutaka amani, taratibu, -pole. **peaceful,** *a.* -tulivu, bila ghasia wala fujo. **peacemaker,** *n.* mpatanishi, msuluhishi. **peace-offering,** *n.* dhabihu, uradhi, kitulizo.

peach, *n.* tunda la kizungu, kidogo kama embe.

peacock, *n.* tausi, kibibi. **pea-hen,** *n.* tausi jike.

peak, *n.* kilele, kileleta, ncha ya juu; (*highest degree &c.*) hesabu (kadiri, kiasi *&c.*) iliyozidi. **peaked,** *a.* -a kuchungoka, -enye kilele.

peal, *v.t.* piga kengele, liza, vumisha; — *v.i.* lia, vuma nguruma. — *n.* mlio (wa kengele), jamii ya kengele nyingi; (*of thunder*) ngurumo, radi.

peanut, *n.* taz. *pea.*

pear, *n.* tunda la kizungu kama pera.

pearl, *n.* lulu.

peasant, *n.* mkulima. **peasantry,** *n.* wakulima.

peat, *n.* majani na mimea iliyooza na kugandamizwa chini ya ardhi; hutumika pengine badala ya kuni.

pebble, *n.* mbwe, kijiwe cha mviringo, changarawe. **pebbly,** *a.* -enye changarawe.

peccadillo, *n.* kosa dogo.

peck, (1) *n.* kipimo cha kizungu kadiri ya pishi nne.

peck, (2) *v.t.* donoa, piga kwa mdomo. **pecker,** *n.* (*slang*) pua, mdomo (wa ndege). *Keep one's pecker up,* tokata tamaa changamka. *Feel peckish,* ona njaa.

pectoral, *a.* -a kifua, -a kidari.

peculate, *v.i.* iba, tumia fedha (mali) iliyowekwa amana. **peculation,** *n.* wizi.

peculiar, *a..* -e peke yake, -sio na kifani, maalum; (*particular*) -a bidii, halisi, zaidi; (*strange*) -geni, ajabu. *My own peculiar property,* mali yangu mimi mwenyewe. *It is a custom peculiar to the Jews,* ni desturi ya Wayahudi peke yao, si ya wengine. *An animal peculiar to Africa,* mnyama wa Afrika tu. **peculiarity,** *n.* (*difference*) tofauti, hali (mtindo, tabia) ya peke yake; (*strangeness*) upya, ugeni. **peculiarly,** *adv.* (*especially*) zaidi, hasa, halisi; (*strangely*) vigeni, ajabu.

pecuniary, *a.* -a fedha (ya kutumika).

pedagogue, *n.* mwalimu, mfunzi.

pedal, *n.* kipande cha mashine (kinanda, cherehani, baisikeli &c.) cha kukanyaga kwa mguu. — *v.t.* endesha kwa kukanyagia *pedal.*

pedant, *n.* ajivunaye kwa elimu yake, ashikiliaye sana kanuni kuliko kutumia elimu yake kwa akili. **pedantic,** *a.* -a *pedant.* **pedantry,** *n.* tabia ya *pedant.*

peddle, *v.t.* chuuza, tembeza bidhaa. **pedlar,** *n.* mchuuzi, mtembeza bidhaa.

pedestal, *n.* kiweko, kipande cha chini ya kitu kama kinara, nguzo.

pedestrian, *n.* mwenda kwa miguu. **pedestrianism,** *n.* kwenda kwa (mwendo wa) miguu.

pedigree, *n.* ukoo, nasaba, jadi, majina ya wazee tangu zamani, hesabu ya vizazi.

pedler, pedlar, *n.* taz. *peddle.*

peduncle, *n.* kikonyo (cha ua).

peel, *n.* ganda, gamba. — *v.t.* ambua, papatua, menya, kemba; (*skin*) chuna, bandua, ambua, bambua; — *v.i.* ambuka, chunuka, banduka, bambuka.

peep, (1) *v.i.* chungulia; (*appear*) chomoza, chimbuka, onekana. — *n.* kuchungulia, mtazamo wa upesi (wa siri); (*of light*) mapambazuko, mwanzo. *Peep-hole,* ufa wa (kitundu cha) kuchungulia.

peep, (2) *v.i.* lia (kama kinda la ndege au panya). — *n.* mlio wa kinda la ndege.

peer, (1) *v.i.* chungua, angazia macho kazia macho tazama sana; (*come in sight*) onekana (*of sun*) chomoza, chimbuza.

peer, (2) *n.* mwenzi, sawa, mfano; (*titled person*) mtu mwenye cheo fulani cha kiingereza. (*duke, marquis, earl, viscount* au *baron*). **peerage,** *n.* cheo cha *peer.* **peerless,** *a.* -sio na kifani.

peevish, *a.* -epesi wa kukasirika, -chungu, -a chuki, -a kasirani, -tukutu.

peg, *n.* kijiti, kigingi; (*to hang things on*) chango; (*plug*) nguruzi, kizibo; (*of musical instrument*) hesi. *Tent pegs,* mambo. *Wooden pegs,* misumari ya mti, vijiti. *A peg* (*whisky and soda &c.*) bilauri (ya *whisky* na *soda &c.*). — *v.t.* funga kwa *peg.* pigilia kwa *peg. Peg away,* fanya kazi kwa bidii (mfulizo). *Peg out,* pigilia vijiti &c. kuonyesha mpaka &c.; (*become exhausted*) isha; (*die*) -fa.

pelf, *n.* mali, fedha, mapato.

pelican, *n.* mwari, ndege mwenye mdomo mkubwa sana.

pellet, *n.* kidonge.

pell-mell, *adv.* kifujofujo, kwa harakaharaka, ghafula. — *a.* -a fujo, -liofujika.

pellucid, *a.* -angavu, -eupe.

pelt, (1) *n.* ngozi (ya mnyama).

pelt, (2) *v.t.* tupia, vurumishia, pigia (*stone*) rujumu; — *v.i.* (*of rain*) nya sana, nyesha kwa nguvu.

pelvis, *n.* fupa la nyonga.

pemmican, *n.* nyama kavu iliyopondwa na kuchanganywa na mafuta (kwa wasafiri).

pen, (1) *n*. kalamu (ya wino); (*nib*) ncha ya kalamu, kijembe, nibu. — *v.t.* andika (kwa kalamu). **penholder**, *n*. kijiti cha kalamu. **penknife**, *n*. kisu kidogo (cha kukunja). **penmanship**, *n*. mwandiko.

pen, (2) *n*. (*enclosure*) zizi, ua, kizimba, tundu. — *v.t.* funga. **pent**, *a*. -liofungwa.

penal, *a*. -a adhabu, -enye adhabu, -a watu waliopasiwa adhabu. *Penal servitude*, kazi ya adhabu kifungoni. **penalize**, *v.t.* adhibisha, tia adhabu; (*inflict hardship &c.*) taabisha, onea, dhulumu. **penalty**, *n*. adhabu, malipo, kisasi.

penance, *n*. taz. *penitent*.

pence, *pl*. ya *penny*.

penchant, *n*. *Have a penchant for*, penda, pendelea.

pencil, *n*. kalamu.

pendant, pendent, *n*. (*for ear*) kipuli, pete ya sikio, jasi; (*for neck*) jebu. **pendent**, *a*. -a kuning'inia, -a kuangika. **pending**, *a*. -siokwisha bado, -naokuja. —*prep*. wakati wa, mpaka. **pendulous**, *a*. kuning'inia, -a kuwayawaya, -a kuyumbayumba. **pendulum**, *n*. kitu cha kuning'inia sawasawa, *e.g.* mizani ya saa.

penetrate, *v.t.* ingia, penya, choma, pita kati ya, bokoa, gagamiza; (*to further side*) tumbuza; (*affect deeply*) ingia moyoni, shtusha roho; (*comprehend*) fahamu kwa akili, elewa maana. **penetrable**, *a*. -a kuingilika, -a kupenyezeka; (*intelligible*) -a kutambulikana. **penetrating, penetrative**, *a*. -a kupenya ndani; (*severe*) -kali; (*clever*) -elekevu, -a akili nyingi. **penetration**, *n*. kupenya, kuingilia; (*power of piercing*) nguvu ya kupenya, ukali; (*understanding*) akili, busara, welekevu.

penguin, *n*. namna ya ndege mnene wa maji mwenye miguu mifupi asiyeweza kuruka juu.

penholder, *n*. taz. *pen* (1).

peninsula, *n*. mkono wa nchi, nchi iliyozungukwa na bahari pande zote isipokuwa sehemu ndogo. **peninsular**, *a*. -a *peninsula*.

penis, *n*. uume, dhakari, firari; (*vulgar*) mboo.

penitent, *a*. -enye kutubu, -a toba. **penance**, *n*. adhabu ya kutubisha, kitubio. **penitence**, *n*. toba, majuto. **penitential**, *a*. -a *penitence*. **penitentiary**, *a*. -a *penitence*. — *n*. gereza, kifungo; (*refuge*) nyumba ya kukimbilia (watu watubiao dhambi zao), pa kutubia.

penknife, *n*., **penmanship**, *n*. taz. *pen* (1).

pennant, pennon, *n*. bendera ndefu nyembamba.

penniless, *a*. taz. *penny*.

pennon, *n*. taz. *pennant*.

penny, *n*. (*pl*. **pence, pennies**) sarafu ya kiingereza, thamani yake senti 8½. **penniless**, *a*. -siye na senti hata moja, fukara, hohe hahe. **pennyweight**, *n*. kipimo cha uzani *24 grains*. **pennyworth**, *n*. kitu cha *penny*.

pension, *n*. ujira anaopewa mtu tangu kuacha kazi yake mpaka kufa. — *v.t.* lipa *pension*. *Pension off*, ruhusu kuacha kazi, na kulipa *pension*. **pensioner**, *n*. mwenye kulipwa *pension*.

pensive, *a*. -enye mawazo, -a kuwazawaza, -a huzuni, -zito.

pent, *a. and v.p.t. and pf.t.* za *pen* (2).

pentagon, *n*. kitu chenye pande tano.

pentateuch, *n*. vitabu vitano vya kwanza vya *Bible*, vitabu vya Musa.

Pentecost, *n*. sikukuu ya kikristo, siku ya hamsini baada ya Pasaka, sikukuu ya Roho Mtakatifu.

penthouse, *n*. upenu, kipenu.

penult, *n*. mwisho ila -moja. **penultimate**, *a*. -a mwisho ila -moja.

penury, *n*. umaskini, ufukara, ukata. **penurious**, -a maskini.

people, *n*. watu; (*nation*) jamii ya watu, taifa; (*populace*) watu wa vivi hivi, akina yahe, makutano. *People say*, husema, huvuma. *Other people's*,

-a watu. *People like us,* wakina (akina) sisi. *Abdallah's people,* wakina (akina) Abdallah. — *v.t.* jaza watu.

pepper, *n.* pilipili manga; (*red*) pilipili hoho. — *v.t.* tia pilipili; (*sprinkle*) nyunyizia; (*pelt*) tupia, pigapiga. **peppermint,** *n.* peremende. **peppercorn,** *n.* punje ya pilipili. **peppery,** *a.* -kali, -a harara, -epesi kukasirika.

pepsin, *n.* dawa inayofanyizwa tumboni ya kusaidia chakula kuyeyushwa humo.

per, *prep.* kwa.

peradventure, *adv.* labda, huenda, kwa nasibu.

perambulate, *v.t.* tembea katika, tembelea, pita kati ya. **perambulator,** *n.* gari dogo la kutembeleza watoto.

per annum, *adv.* kwa mwaka, kila mwaka.

perceivable, *a.* taz. *perceive.*

perceive, *v.t.* ona, fahamu, tambua, sikia, hisi, nabihi. **perceivable,** *a.* -a kuoneka, -a kuonekana, -a kujulika, -a kutambulikana. **perceptible,** *a.* -a kuoneka, -a kuonekana, -a kusikika, -a kujulika, -a kutambulikana. **perception,** *a.* kuona, akili za kuona, ufahamivu. **perceptive,** *a.* -enye *perception.*

per cent, *adv.* kwa (kila) mia moja. (Alama yake ni %). **percentage,** *n.* kadiri kwa kila mia moja; (*interest*) faida; (*part*) sehemu.

perceptible, *a.,* **perception,** *n.,* **perceptive,** *a.* taz. *perceive.*

perch, (1) *n.* samaki wa maji matamu mwenye kigongo na mapezi yenye miiba.

perch, (2) *n.* kituo, kitulio, kiota; (*measure*) kipimo cha urefu, yadi 5½. — *v.i.* tua, tulia, tenga, kaa.

perchance, *adv.* labda, huenda kwa nasibu.

percolate, *v.i.* vuja, penya tone tone; — *v.t.* chuja, pitisha tone tone. **percolation,** *n.* kuchuja, mchujo, kuvuja, mvujo. **percolator,** *n.* (*strainer*) kung'uto, kumunto, kifumbu, kichujio.

percussion, *n.* kugonga, mgongo, mshindo, kishindo, mgongano, mpambano. **percussion cap,** *n.* fataki.

perdition, *n.* kupotea milele (bila tumaini la wokovu), jehanamu.

peregrinate, *v.i.* tembea, tembelea, tembea katika nchi ngeni, safiri, hamahama. **peregrination,** *n.* safari, matembezi.

peremptory, *a.* mkataa, -a tama; (*precluding opposition*) -a sharti, -a lazima; (*imperious*) -kali, -a ubwana. **peremptorily,** *adv.* vikali, kwa nguvu.

perennial, *a.* -a sikuzote, -a daima.

perfect, *a.* kamili, -kamilifu, -timilifu, -zima, halisi, sahihi; (*thorough, complete*) kabisa. — *v.t.* kamilisha, timiza; (*by practice &c.*) zoeza mpaka kuwa stadi &c. **perfection,** *n.* ukamilifu, utimilivu, usitawi, upeo. **perfectly,** *adv.* pia, kabisa, halisi, kamili. **perfectness,** *n.* ukamilifu &c. taz. *perfection.*

perfervid, *a.* -a bidii nyingi, -a juhudi nyingi.

perfidy, *n.* kuvunja ahadi, ujanja, ubaya, uwongo, uhaini. **perfidious,** *a.* si -aminifu, -janja, -baya, -wongo, -haini.

perforate, *v.t.* toboa, tumbua, zua, pekecha, dudumia. **perforation,** *n.* tundu, kitundu, kitobo. **perforator,** *n.* kipande cha kutobolea.

perforce, *adv.* sharti, lazima, hakuna budi.

perform, *v.t.* fanya, fanyiza, tenda, maliza, tekeleza, timiliza; (*represent, act*) cheza; — *v.i.* cheza. **performance,** *n.* kufanya &c.; (*deed*) kitendo, tendo, kazi; (*acting*) mchezo; (*achievement*) tendo bora, tendo kuu (la ujasiri, akili, ustadi &c.). *Give a performance,* cheza, toa mchezo, charaza. **performer,** *n.* mtu wa kutenda, mtenda; (*actor*) mcheza, mchezaji (mbele ya watu).

perfume, *n.* manukato, marashi, uturi, ituri. (*smell*) utamu, manuka.

perfumer, *n.* mwuza marashi (uturi). **pefumery,** *n.* jamii ya marashi; kiwanda marashi yanapofanyizwa.

perfunctory, *a.* -a uzembe, pasipo bidii, -a purukushani, -a haraka.

pergola, *n.* matao kando ya njia ya kutambalia mimea.

perhaps, *adv.* labda, huenda, kwa nasibu.

peril, *n.* hatari, mashaka. *You will go at your peril,* ukienda hasara itakayotokea ni juu yako mwenyewe. *Put in peril,* ponza, hatirisha, tia hatarini. **perilous,** *a.* -enye hatari.

perimeter, *n.* kizingo, mzingo, mstari wa kuzunguka.

perineum, *n.* msamba, kitako, winda.

period, *n.* muda maalum; (*time*) kipindi, wakati, muhula, majira; (*in rhetoric*) = *sentence.* fungu la maneno mengi pamoja. *Flowing periods,* usemi mwingi wa ufasaha, usemi kama maji. *Of the period,* -a zamani hizi. *Periods* (*woman's*), hedhi, mwezi, damuni. **periodic, periodical,** *a.* -a -enye muhula zake, -enye vipindi vyake, -a kurudiarudia, -enye kuja wakati wake sawasawa. **periodical,** *n.* kitabu cha habari au hadithi kitolewacho kipya mara kwa mara kwa siku zake, kama gazeti.

peripatetic, *a.* -a kwenda huko na huko, mji mpaka mji.

periphery, *n.* kizingo, mzingo.

periphrasis, *n.* maneno ya kuzunguka, fumbo la maneno, maneno mengi.

periscope, *n.* kitu kama darubini yenye vioo ndani inayowezesha mtu kuona vitu upande wa pili wa ukuta (boma *&c.*) au ikiwa ni katika manowari ya kuzama, vitu vilivyo juu ya maji, *e.g.* meli, manowari *&c.*

perish, *v.i.* -fa, potea, haribika, tilifika, angamia, hiliki; (*decay*) chakaa, fifia, oza; (*disappear*) toweka tokomea, enda zake (zao *&c.*), isha. **perishable,** *a.* -a kupotea, -a kuharibika, si -enye aushi. **perishing,** *a.* (baridi *&c.*) -a kutaabisha, -a kusumbua sana.

peritoneum, *n.* kitambi cha tumbo.

periwinkle, *n.* konokono dogo la pwani; (*flower*) namna ya ua dogo.

perjure (*oneself*), *v. reflex.* apa uwongo, zuri; shuhudia uwongo. **perjurer,** *n.* mwapa uwongo, mfanya zuri. **perjury,** *n.* ushuhuda wa uwongo, azur, zuri, kuapa uwongo.

perk, *v.t.* simikisha, inua; — *v.i.* (*up*) changamka. **perky,** *a.* -epesi, -changamfu.

permanent, *a.* -enye kuishi, -a daima, -a kuendelea bila kubadilika, -a siku zote. **permanence,** *n.* aushi, udumu, uthabiti, **permanency** *n.* aushi, uthabiti; (*employment &c.*) kazi *&c.* ya miaka mingi (si ya muda mfupi tu). **permanently,** *adv.* bila kubadilika, kwa muda mrefu, thabiti, madhubuti.

permanganate, *n.* (*of potassium*) dawa kidogo kama baruti; huchanganywa na maji kufanya dawa ya vidonda na *disinfectant &c.*

permeate, *v.i.* enea (jaza) sehemu zote za, chuja, lowesha, nywewa na, pita kati ya. **permeable,** *a.* -a kupitika kwa maji.

permit, *v.t.* acha, ruhusu, -pa ruhusa, jalia, halalisha. — *n.* ruhusa, cheti cha ruhusa. **permissible,** *a.* halali, -a kufaa, -a kukubalika, -a kujuzu. **permission,** *n.* ruhusa, idhini. **permissive,** *a.* -a kutoa ruhusa, -a kuruhusu.

permute, *v.t.* badili, geuza taratibu. **permutation,** *n.* kubadilika, mabadili.

pernicious, *a.* -enye madhara, -a kudhuru, -baya, -potevu.

pernickety, *a.* -tukutu, -tundu, -teuzi, -chaguzi, -enye tabia ya kuvumbua makosa madogo.

perforation, *n.* mwisho wa hotuba ndefu au maneno mengi.

perpendicular, *a.* -a wima, -a kiwima.

perpetrate, *v.t.* tenda, fanya (hasa tendo baya). **perpetration,** *n.*

kutenda, kufanya. **perpetrator,** *n.* mtenda, mfanya.

perpetual, *a.* -a daima, -a siku zote, -a mara kwa mara, -a kuendelea muda mrefu. **perpetually,** *adv.* sikuzote, bila kikomo, daima, mara nyingi. **perpetuate,** *v.t.* dumisha, endeleza.

perpetuity, *n.* umilele, aushi, ufulizo. *In perpetuity,* pasipo mwisho.

perplex, *v.t.* tatiza, tatanisha, fumba, fadhaisha, kanganya, bumbuaza, hangaisha. *Be perplexed,* fadhaika, hangaika, hamanika, ona wasiwasi. **perplexity,** *n.* matata, mashaka, fadhaa, bumbuazi, dukuduku.

perquisite, *n.* ada.

per se, *adv.* peke yake (yao *&c.*).

persecute, *v.t.* dhulumu, onea, tesa, sumbua, chokoza, fukuza. **persecution,** *n.* udhalimu, fukuzo, mateso. **persecutor,** *n.* mdhalimu, mchokozi, mtesi.

persevere, *v.i.* endelea kwa bidii, dumu, chagiza, shikilia, toshindwa. **perseverance,** *n.* udumu, uthabiti, uvumilivu, idili, uendelezi, ulabibu. **persevering,** *a.* -enye bidii, -enye moyo wa kuendelea.

Persia, *n.* Uajemi.

persiflage, *n.* ubishi.

persist, *v.i.* dumu, fuliza, endelea. shinda, kakamia, shikilia, chagiza; (*in begging*) ng'ang'ania, ronga, **persistence,** *n.* kudumu, bidii, ujitahidi. **persistency,** *n.* ushupavu, ukaidi. **persistent,** *a.* -a kukaa, -a kuendelea bila kubadilika, thabiti, -shupavu, -kaidi.

person, *n.* mtu; (*appearance*) sura, umbo; (*individuality*) nafsi; (*body*) mwili, kiwiliwili. *In person,* nafsi yake, -enyewe. **personable,** *a.* -enye sura nzuri, -zuri. **personage,** *n.* mtu mwenye cheo, mtu mashuhuri. **personal,** *a.* -a mtu, -a mwenyewe, -angu (ako, ake *&c.*) mwenyewe; (*individual*) -a peke yake; (*of a person*) -a sura, -a umbo; (*critical, offensive*) -a kuchukiza, -a kusuta, -a kushtaki. *Make personal remarks on,* sengenya, suta, singizia. **personality,** *n.* nafsi (ya mtu); (*offensive criticism*) masuto, masingizio. **personally,** *adv.* -enyewe, nafsi yake (yao *&c.*), peke yangu (yako *&c.*). **personality,** *n.* vyombo, fedha, vikorokoro, vifaa, mapambo. **personate,** *v.t.* jifanya, jigeuza, iga. **personify,** *v.t.* fanya kama kwamba ni mtu; (*embody*) -wa nafsi yake. **personnel,** *n.* jamii ya watu wa kazi wa meli (kiwanda fulani, jeshi *&c.*).

perspective, *n.* kuandika picha kwa jinsi ya kulinganisha ukubwa, kimo, urefu, upana *&c.*, kama vitu vionekanavyo kwa macho. **perspicacious,** *a.* -enye akili za kufahamu, -enye busara. **perspicacity,** *n.* ufahamivu, akili, busara. **perspicuity,** *n.* udhihirifu, uwazi. **perspicuous,** *a.* dhahiri, bayana, wazi, rahisi; (*of persons &c.*) -enye uwezo wa kueleza dhahiri.

perspire, *v.i.* toka jasho (hari). **perspiration,** *n.* jasho, hari, nongo. *Evil smell of perspiration,* gugumu; (*of under the armpits*), kikwapa, kutuzi.

persuade, *v.t.* shawishi, vuta, ongoza, sadikisha, bembeleza, shurutisha; (*to do evil*) bilisi. **persuasion,** *n.* ushawishi, mvuto; (*opinion*) nia, moyo; (*form of religion*) madhehebu, dini. **persuasive,** *a.* -a kushawishi, -shawishi, -a kubembeleza.

pert, *a.* -juvi, -fidhuli, -safihi, -kavu wa macho, -shupavu, -tundu. **pertness,** *n.* ujuvi, ufidhuli, ukavu wa macho, ushupavu, utundu.

pertain, *v.i.* -wa mali (ya), -wa katika pasa, husiana (na), fungamana (na), fuatana (na), faa, laiki, agia.

pertinacious, *a.* (*resolute*) thabiti, -gumu, -shupavu, -enye kushikilia kusudi (nia *&c.*); (*obstinate*) -kaidi, -tundu. **pertinacity,** *n.* uthabiti, ugumu, ushupavu, ukaidi *&c.*

pertinent, *a.* -a kufaa, -a kupasa, -a kuhusu, -a kufungamana na. **pertinence,** *n.* kufaa, kuwa na maana, ulinganifu.

pertness, *n*. taz. *pert*.

perturb, *v.t.* fadhaisha, hangaisha, harakisha, tia mashaka, ogofya, hofisha, tia wasiwasi. **perturbation**, *n*. fadhaa, wasiwasi, mashaka, hangaiko.

peruke, *n*. kofia ya nywele.

peruse, *v.t.* soma kwa uangalifu, chungua, tazamia. **perusal**, *n*. kusoma, msomo.

pervade, *v.t.* enea kote katika, penya pote pa. **pervasive**, *a*. -a kuenea kote, -a kupenya pote.

perverse, *a*. -kaidi, -tundu, -potoe, -enye inadi. **perversion**, *n*. kupotosha, kugeuka vibaya. **perversity**, *n*. upotoe, ukaidi, utundu, inadi. **pervert**, *v.t.* ongoza vibaya, potosha, geuza vibaya, haribu tabia (dini) ya. — *n*. mtu abadiliye dini yake, kafiri; (*degenerate*) mpotoe, mpotovu, ageukaye kufuata tabia mbaya (mwendo mbaya, mazoea mabaya), hanithi.

pervious, *a*. -a kupitika, -a kupenyezeka, -a kuendeka.

pessimism, *n*. tabia ya kuona ya kuwa mambo yote ni mabaya (ya kutazamia misiba, taabu &c.). **pessimist**, *n*. mtu aonaye ya kuwa mambo yote ni mabaya, atazamiaye misiba (taabu).

pest, *n*. maradhi, baa; (*nuisance*) mtu mbaya, mwudhi, mkorofi, kitu kibaya kisumbuacho, baa, balaa. **pestiferous**, *a*. -baya, -a kinyaa, -a kuleta maradhi, -a kunuka vibaya. **pestilence**, *n*. maradhi ya kuambukiza, tauni. **pestilent, pestilential**, *a*. -a kudhuru, -enye madhara, -a kuharibu afya, -baya, -haribifu.

pester, *v.t.* sumbua, udhi, chokoza, chagiza.

pestiferous, *a*., **pestilence**, *n*., **pestilent**, *a*., **pestilential**, *a*. taz. *pest*.

pestle, *n*. mchi (wa kutwangia), mtwango.

pet, (1) *n*. (*favourite*) kipenzi; (*animal*) mnyama aliyefugwa na kufanywa rafiki, mnyama rafiki. *It is his pet aversion*, ndiyo anayoichukia hasa. — *v.t.* pendelea, bembeleza, dekeza, endekeza, engaenga.

pet, (2) *n*. chuki ya ghafula, mfundo wa moyo, moyo juu. *He is in a pet*, amekasirika. **pettish**, *a*. -a chukichuki.

petal, *n*. jani la ua lenye rangi.

petard, *n*. namna ya kombora ya zamani. *Hoist with his own petard*, (mtu) kupata hasara (madhara) kwa hila zake mwenyewe.

peter, *v.i.* (*out*) toweka taratibu, isha taratibu, isha.

petite, *a*. -dogo, nadhifu, -zuri.

petition, *n*. haja, maombi, dua. — *v.t.* tolea haja, omba, sihi, lalama. **petitioner**, *n*. mwenye haja, mwombi, mhitaji.

petrel, *n*. namna ya ndege wa bahari.

petrify, *v.t.* geuza kuwa jiwe, fanya jiwe; (*astonish*) shangaza, duwaza, tia bumbuazi; — *v.i.* geuka jiwe. **petrifaction**, *n*. kugeuka jiwe, kufanyika jiwe.

petroleum, *n*. mafuta ya taa. **petrol**, *n*. mafuta ya motakaa &c. (mepesi yawakayo).

petticoat, *n*. nguo ya kike toka kiunoni mpaka miguuni (ya ndani).

pettifogger, *n*. kijoyojoyo, ajishughulishaye katika mambo manyonge ili kupata mradi wake; ajishughulishaye katika mambo madogodogo (visa vidogo, hoja hafifu &c.).

pettish, *a*. taz. *pet* (2).

petty, *a*. -dogo, hafifu, dhaifu.

petulant, *a*. -tukutu, -a chuki, -epesi kukasirika, -enye kinyongo. **petulance**, *n*. utukutu, chuki, kinyongo.

pew, *n*. kiti kirefu (kwa urefu si kimo) cha kukaa watu kanisani; kiti.

pewter, *n*. madini (mchanganyiko wa risasi na bati).

phaeton, *n*. gari la farasi la kuchukulia watu lenye magurudumu manne.

phalanx, *n*. kikosi cha askari waliosongamana; (*of finger or toe*) mfupa wa kidole.

phallus, *n.* sanamu ya uume jinsi unavyoheshimiwa katika dini nyingine kuwa mfano wa nguvu ya uzazi wa viumbe. **phallic,** *n.* -a *phallus.*

phantasm, *n.* njozi, maono yaliyowazika tu (si ya kweli), madanganyo ya macho; (*ghost*) kizuka. **phantasmagoria,** *n.* sanamu za kuchezacheza; njozi ya watu (vitu &c.) wanaokwenda. **phantasmal,** *a.* -a njozi, -a kuwazika tu. **phantom,** *n.* mtu &c. aliyeonekana katika njozi, kizuka; (*vision*) njozi; (*delusion*) maono yaliyowazika tu (si ya kweli).

Pharisee, *n.* Farisayo; mtu afuataye (ashikiliaye) mambo ya nje tu ya dini; (*hypocrite*) mnafiki, mzandiki. **pharisaic,** *a.* -a Mafarisayo, -nafiki, -zandiki. **pharisaism,** *n.* unafiki, uzandiki.

pharmacy, *n.* maarifa ya kufanyiza dawa; (*shop*) duka la mwuza dawa. **pharmaceutic,** *a.* -a *pharmacy.* **pharmacopoeia,** *a.* *n.* kitabu chenye habari ya jinsi zifanyizwavyo dawa zote.

pharynx, *n.* kishimo kilicho nyuma ya pua, kinywa na kikoromeo.

phase, *n.* sura (ya kitu), mabadili ya sura, namna, hali.

pheasant, *n.* ndege kama kuku mwitu mwenye manyoya marefu mkiani.

phenomenon, *n.* (*fact*) kitu, jambo, neno; (*curiosity*) tukio, tokeo, shani, ajabu, kizushi, kioja. **phenomenal,** *a.* -a ajabu sana, si -a kawaida.

phial, *n.* chupa ndogo, kichupa.

philander, *v.i.* fanya kama uchumba kwa uzungumzi tu (bila nia ya kuoa).

philanthropic, *a.*, **philanthropist,** *n.* taz. *philanthropy.*

philanthropy, *n.* kupendana na watu wote, upendano, huruma, ufadhili. **philanthropic,** *a.* -a kupenda watu wote, -enye huruma, karimu, -enye fadhili. **philanthropist,** *n.* mpenda watu wote, mfadhili, mtu afanyaye bidii kusitawisha hali ya watu.

philatelist, *n.* taz. *philately.*

philately, *n.* kuweka, *postage stamp* (tikiti za posta) na kuzipanga aina mbalimbali. **philatelist,** *n.* mtu mwenye maarifa ya *postage stamp* aziwekaye na kuzipanga aina mbalimbali.

philharmonic, *a.* -a kupenda *music.*

philological, *a.*, **philologist,** *n.* taz. *philology.*

philology, *n.* elimu ya lugha, asili na maendeleo yake. **philological,** *a.* -a elimu ya lugha. **philologist,** *n.* mtu achunguaye habari za lugha, asili na maendeleo yake.

philosopher, *n.*, **philosophical,** *a.*, **philosophize,** *v.* taz. *philosophy.*

philosophy, *n.* elimu ya elimu zote, ya asili ya mambo yote na vitu vyote, ya kujua sababu na maana; (*wisdom*) hekima, busara; (*calmness*) uthabiti, utulivu. **philosopher,** *n.* mtu achunguaye *philosophy*; mtu asiyeharakishwa (asiyetiwa wasiwasi) na mambo, mtu thabiti. **philosophical,** *a.* -a *philosophy*; (*calm*) -tulivu, -siyehangaika, -siyeshtuka, -thabiti. **philosophize,** *v.i.* jifunza *philosophy*; jifanya *philosopher.*

philtre, philter, dawa inyodhaniwa kumtia mtu ashiki (kwa mtu mwingine maalum), ndere.

phlegm, *n.* belghamu, kohozi, kamasi; gole; (*dullness*) utepetevu, baridi, uzito, unyogovu. **phlegmatic,** *a.* -tulivu, -thabiti, -sioshtuka, baridi, -tepetevu, -zito.

phoenix, *n.* ndege (wa hadithi) ambaye baada ya kila miaka 500 au 600 alijichoma moto na kufufuka pale pale katika majivu.

phonetic, *a.* -a mambo ya sauti (ya usemi) -a sauti (ya usemi) -a jinsi ya kutamka. **phonetics,** *n.* elimu ya sauti za usemi.

phonograph, *n.* chombo cha kuandika yatamkwayo na kuyatamka yale yale.

phonology, *n.* elimu ya sauti za usemi (lugha); elimu ya sauti za usemi (lugha) na jinsi zinavyobadilika katika muda fulani; jamii ya sauti za usemi (lugha) fulani wakati fulani (na jinsi zilivyokuwa zamani na jinsi zilivyobadilika).

phosphorescent, *a.* taz. *phosphorus.*

phosphorus, *n.* kitu kama nta kinachong'aa gizani; huwaka kwa urahisi. **phosphorescent**, *a.* -a kung'aa gizani, -a kumetameta.

photo, photograph, *n.* picha iliyopigwa kwa nuru kupita *lens* mpaka kioo (karatasi *&c.*) kilichopakwa dawa ya namna fulani. — *v.t.* piga *photograph.* **photographer**, *n.* mpiga *photograph.* **photographic**, *a.* -a *photograph.* **photography**, *n.* kupiga *photograph*; maarifa ya kupiga *photograph.*

phrase, *n.* fungu la maneno machache (lililo sehemu ya *sentence*), maneno, neno. **phraseology**, *n.* jinsi ya kutumia maneno, jinsi ya usemi.

phrenologist, *n.* taz. *phrenology.*

phrenology, *n.* maarifa ya kujua tabia (moyo, akili *&c.*) ya mtu kwa umbo la kichwa chake. **phrenologist**, *n.* mtu mwenye maarifa ya *phrenology.*

phthisis, *n.* kifua kikuu.

physic, *n.* dawa. — *v.t.* nywesha dawa. **physician**, *n.* tabibu, mtabibu, daktari, mganga.

physical, *a.* taz. *physics.*

physician, *n.* taz. *physic.*

physics, *n.* elimu ya hali na tabia za vitu vyote, na ya nguvu zote zilizomo duniani; *e.g.* ya joto, ya sauti, ya umeme, ya magnetisi *&c.* na mabadiliko yanayofanyika kwa nguvu hizo. **physical**, *a.* (*natural*) -a asili, -a vitu vyote, -a viumbe; (*visible*) -a vyote vionekanavyo; (*material*) -a kuonekana kwa macho; (*corporeal*) -a mwili; (*of objects*) -a vitu; (*external*) -a nje. *A physical necessity*, lazima, halisi, hakuna budi kabisa. *It is a physical impossibility*, haiwezekani kwa vyo vyote. *He is physically unfit*, hawezi mwili wake. **physicist**, *n.* mchunguaji wa *physics.* **physiognomy**, *n.* sura, uso. **physiography**, *n.* elimu ya hali na tabia ya uso wa dunia. **physiology**, *n.* elimu ya mambo ya vitu vyenye uhai, *e.g.* ya mwili wa mtu. **physique**, *n.* umbo, sura, umbo na hali ya mwili. *Fine physique*, umbo zuri, maungo.

piano, pianoforte, *n.* kinanda (kikubwa chenye nyuzi ndani). **pianist**, *n.* mpiga kinanda.

piazza, *n.* uwanja (wa kutembelea mjini); (*veranda*) baraza.

piccalilli, *n.* achali.

piccaninny, *n.* mtoto mdogo (hasa mweusi).

piccolo, *n.* filimbi.

pick, *v.t.* donoa, pekua; (*break up*) wekua; (*a hole*) chokoa; (*choose*) chagua, pembua, teua; (*pull apart*) chambua, chamvua; (*flowers, fruit*) chuma, tunda; (*remove*) ondoa, chomoa; (*take hold of*) twaa. *Pick off*, piga (mtu) bunduki. *Pick out*, chagua; (*recognize*) tambua. *Pick up*, okota, zoa; (*bit by bit*) chota, donoa, danga, kumba; (*get by chance*) kuta, kusanya, tafuta; (*recover health*) pata nguvu (afya), -wa hajambo (hujambo *&c.*), jipa nguvu, pata ashekali (ahueni, nafuu). *Pick the teeth*, chokoa meno. *Pick a fowl*, nyonyoa, futua. *Pick a quarrel*, vumbulia vita (ugomvi), taka vita. *Pick a lock*, fungua bila ufunguo (kwa msumari, kulabu, kingoe *&c.*). *Pick holes in, Pick to pieces* (*accuse*), singizia, chongea. *Pick a pocket*, ibia (mfukoni mwa mtu njiani kwa siri). — *n.* sululu, mchokoo; (*best part*) uteule, kilicho bora, kipeo. **pickaxe**, *n.* sululu. **picked**, *a.* -teule, bora, -liochaguliwa. **pickpocket**, *n.* mwizi (wa kuibia mfukoni mwa watu kwa siri) sinzia. **pick-me-up**, *n.* kinywaji cha kutia nguvu, kiburudisho.

pickaback, *adv.* *Carry pickaback*, yongoja. *Be carried pickaback*, yongoa.

pickaxe, *n.*, **picked,** *a.* taz. *pick.*

picket, *n.* kingojo cha askari, askari (watu) walinzi; (*peg*) kigingi, kijiti. — *v.t.* pigilia funga kwa kigingi; wekea walinzi, weka walinzi.

pickle, *n.* achali; (*plight*) matata, hali mbaya. — *v.t.* weka (lowesha) katika maji ya chumvi au siki.

pick-me-up, *n.*, **pickpocket,** *n.* taz. *pick.*

picnic, *n.* kwenda kula shambani, mandari, matembezi.

picture, *n.* picha, sanamu, taswira, sura; (*likeness*) mfano, mithali. — *v.t.* waza moyoni, eleza kwa maneno. **pictorial,** *a.* -a picha (sanamu &c.). — *n.* gazeti lenye picha nyingi. **picturesque,** *a.* kama picha nzuri, -enye sura nzuri, -a kupendeza macho.

pidgin, *a. Pidgin English* kiingereza cha kuvunjia.

pie, *n.* andazi; (*of meat*) sambusa. *Have a finger in the pie,* -wamo.

piebald, *a.* -a rangi mbili, -enye madoa ya rangi mbili. **pied,** *a.* -a rangirangi, -a madoadoa.

piece, *n.* kipande, fungu, mkato, sehemu; (*of cloth*) kiraka, kitambaa; (*whole length*) jora, taka; (*gun*) bunduki; (*coin*) sarafu; (*in music*) wimbo; (*in art generally*) kazi. *In pieces,* vipande vipande. *Take to pieces,* vunja, kongoa. *A piece of news* (*of work, of impudence &c.*) habari (kazi, ufidhuli &c.). *All of a piece,* yote sawasawa. — *v.t.* tengeneza, unganisha. **piecemeal,** *adv.* kidogo kidogo, kipande kipande. **piecework,** *n.* kazi ya kupata fedha kwa kadiri ya kazi yenyewe (si ya wakati wake, si kwa fedha ya kutwa).

pied, *a.* taz. *piebald.*

pier, *n.* boma litokezalo baharini; gati itokezayo baharini; (*pillar*) msingi, nguzo. **pier-glass,** *n.* kioo kikubwa cha kutundika ukutani.

pierce, *v.t.* toboa, zua, choma, penya, penyeza, tumbua, ingiza; (*of ears*) toga, dunga; (*affect deeply*) penya, ingia moyoni, umiza, choma; — *v.i.* penya, ingia, choma. **piercing,** *a.* -a kupenya, -kali, -a nguvu, -a kuchoma.

pier-glass, *n.* taz. *pier.*

pierrot, *n.* mmoja wa jamii ya waimbaji waimbao kwa uchumi wao. Huvaa nguo nyeupe za kupwaya na kupaka nyuso zao rangi nyeupe.

pierrette, *n. pierrot* wa kike.

piety, *n.* taz. *pious.*

piffle, *n.* upuzi, mapayo.

pig, *n.* nguruwe; (*piece of unwrought metal*) mkuo. **piggery,** *n.* zizi la nguruwe. **piggish,** *a.* kama nguruwe -chafu. **pigheaded,** *a.* -kaidi, -tundu, -gumu, -shupavu. **pigsty,** *n.* zizi la nguruwe. **pigtail,** *n.* nywele ndefu za singa zilizosokotwa kisogoni, shungi la kichina.

pigeon, *n.* njiwa; (*Delands' green*) ninga. **pigeon-hole,** *n.* tundu la njiwa; (*recess*) tundu la kashani la kuwekea barua; hati, karatasi &c., kishubaka.

piggery, *n.*, **piggish,** *a.*, **pigheaded,** *a.* taz. *pig.*

pigment, *n.* rangi.

pigmy, *n.* kibeti, mtu mfupi sana, mbilikimo.

pigtail, *n.* taz. *pig.*

pike, *n.* mkuki mfupi; mkuki mrefu mwembamba; (*fish*) namna ya samaki wa maji baridi. **pikestaff,** *n.* uti mrefu mwembamba wa *pike.* *Plain as a pikestaff,* dhahiri kabisa.

pilchard, *n.* namna ya samaki wa baharini.

pile, (1) *n.* (*post*) nguzo, mhimili, mwimo. **pile-driver,** *n.* mashine ya kushindilia nguzo.

pile, (2) *n.* (*heap*) fungu, chungu; (*building*) jumba kubwa; (*funeral*) chungu ya kuni za kuchomea maiti; (*of garden rubbish, weeds &c.*) biwi. *Make one's pile,* chuma fedha za kuridhisha, jitajirisha. — *v.t.* fanya chungu, lundika, tuta, pandikiza, kusanya, andikanya, panganya, omekeza; (*of earth, concrete &c.*) palia, fusia.

pile, (3) *n.* manyoya laini (ya nguo, zulia &c.)
pile-driver, *n.* taz. *pile* (1).
piles, *n.* bawasiri, kikundu, futuri.
pilfer, *v.t.* iba vidogo.
pilgrim, *n.* mhaji, mwenda haji, msafiri. **pilgrimage,** *n.* kwenda kuzuru patakatifu; (*tedious journey*) safari ya taabu; (*to Mecca*) haji. *Make a pilgrimage,* zuru, hiji.
pill, *n,* kidonge cha dawa.
pillage, *n.* kuteka, mateka, nyara. — *v.t.* teka.
pillar, *n.* nguzo, mhimili, mwimo.
pillion, *n.* kiti cha mtu wa pili nyuma ya farasi, baisikeli &c.
pillory, *n.* mkatale wa kumfungia mtu kichwa na mikono. — *v.t.* tia (funga) katika mkatale; (*ridicule*) fanyia mzaha.
pillow, *n.* mto; (*large*) takia; (*of wood*) msamilo. **pillow-case, pillow-slip,** *n.* foronya, mfuko wa mto.
pilot, *n.* rubani, kiongozi, mshika usukani. — *v.t.* ongoza, peleka, elekeza.
pimp, *n.* kawadi. — *v.t.* tongoza.
pimple, *n.* kiwe, kipele, chinusi, kidudusi, dutu, ukurutu.
pin, *n.* kisumari, sindano, pini, kipingo; (*peg*) kiwi, kisumari; (*peg of metal*) kipingo; (*of wood*) kiwi. *Pins and needles,* ganzi, kiharusi. *I don't care a pin,* si kitu kwangu kabisa. —*v.t.* funga, kaza. *Pin one's faith on,* amini, tegemea, jetea. **pin-cushion,** *n.* mto mdogo sana wa (kibumba cha) kuchomekea *pins.* **pin-money,** *n.* fedha anayopewa mke kununulia vitakataka anavyotaka, *e.g.* mapambo.
pinafore, *n.* nguo ya mtoto ya kuvaa nje ya nguo zake zisipate taka.
pince-nez, *n.* miwani ya kupachika puani.
pinch, *v.t.* finya, binya, minya, nyakua, bana; (*distress*) dhiki, dhili, dhiisha, kondesha, onea, tia mazito, sumbua, dhulumu; (*steal = slang*) iba, nyang'anya; (*arrest*) kamata, bamba, dara; — *v.i.* finya, bana, minya. — *n.* (*squeeze*) finyo, binyo, nyakuo; (*small quantity*) kidokoo, kidogo; (*difficulty*) shida, mashaka, hatari. *At a pinch,* katika mashaka, katika shida. *Take a pinch,* dokoa. **pincers,** *n.* koleo, mbano, kibano; (*of crustaceans &c.*) gando, gondi.
pin-cushion, *n.* taz. *pin.*
pine, (1) *v.i.* fifia, chakaa, legea, taka kufa, dhoofika, konda, sinyaa, nywea, churuzika, kwajuka, nyorora (kwa sababu ya ugonjwa, huzuni, majonzi &c.). *Pine for,* tamani sana, -wa na shauku ya, chunuka, kondea.
pine, (2) *n.* msunobari. **pineapple,** *n.* (*plant*) mnanasi; (*fruit*) nanasi.
pinion, (1) *n.* ubawa, bawa. — *v.t.* funga mikono.
pinion, (2) *n.* gurudumu dogo lenye meno na mapengo.
pink, (1) *a.* -ekundu -eupe; (*flower*) namna ya ua; (*perfection*) upeo.
pink, (2) *v.t.* choma, penyeza (risasi ya bunduki, upanga &c.).
pin-money, *n.* taz. *pin.*
pinnace, *n.* mashua kubwa ya melini (inayoendeshwa kwa makasia au *petrol*).
pinnacle, *n.* mnara mrefu mwembamba; (*summit*) kilele, kileleta; (*culminating point*) upeo, kipeo, usitawi.
pint, *n.* kipimo cha kizungu kadiri ya kibaba.
pioneer, *n.* mtangulizi, mpenyezi, mpelelezi, mkurugenzi, mvumbuzi, mtu wa kwanza. — *v.t.* tangulia, vumbua, ongoza.
pious, *a.* -cha Mungu, -tawa, -a dini. **piety,** *n.* uchaji wa Mungu, utawa, usufii, dini uwalii.
pip, (1) *n.* kokwa dogo (kama ya chungwa).
pip, (2) *n.* ng'anda (alama katika karata za kuchezea); (*of fowls*) ugonjwa wa makamasi wa kuku. *Give one the pip* (*slang*), kasirisha, chukiza.
pipe *n.* mwanzi, mrija, bomba, neli; (*musical*) zomari, filimbi; (*tobacco*)

kiko, mtemba; (*hookah*) buruma, kikororo, kiko cha pipa; (*for water*) mfereji, mlizabu, mlizamu, mchirizi; (*spout*) kopo. *Pipe bowl*, bori. *Pipe stem*, mwanzi; (*of hookah*) mdakale, digali. — *v.t.* piga filimbi (zomari). **pipe-clay**, *n.* chaki. **piper**, *n.* mpiga filimbi (zomari). **piping**, *a.* -enye sauti nyembamba (kama makinda ya ndege). — *n.* mwanzi, bomba &c. taz. *pipe*, *n.*; sauti ya filimbi (zomari). **pipkin**, *n.* kijungu kidogo.

pippin, *n.* taz. *pip* (1).

piquant, *a.* -kali, -chungu; (*attractive*) -a kutamanisha; (*amusing*) -a kukolea, -a kuchekesha.

pique, *n.* chuki, uchungu, kiburi, mfundo. — *v.t.* chukiza, tia uchungu, choma (moyo). *Pique oneself on*, jivunia, jisifu kwa.

pirate, *n.* haramia (wa bahari); (*of books &c.*) apigaye chapa vitabu &c. vya mtu mwingine na kuviuza bila idhini ya mwandishi. — *v.t.* piga chapa vitabu &c. vya mwingine na kuviuza bila idhini ya mwandishi. **piracy**, *n.* uharamia (baharini), kazi ya *pirate*. **piratical**, *a.* -a *pirate*.

pirouette, *v.i.* zunguka hali ya kuchuchumia katika kucheza ngoma.

pistil, *n.* kijiti chembamba kilicho kati ya ua, ndiyo sehemu ya ua inayoweka mbegu.

pistol, *n.* bastola.

piston, *n.* mchi wa mashine.

pit, *n.* shimo, tundu, chimbo; (*mine*) shimo la kuchimbulia makaa; (*for trapping game*) rima; (*hell*) ahera, jehanamu; (*in a theatre*) uwanja wa kati ya *theatre*; (*of stomach &c., depression*) uvungu, mvungu. *Coal-pit*, shimo la makaa. *Armpit*, kwapa. *Scar*, kovu. — *v.t.* fanya kovu. *His face is pitted with smallpox*, uso wake umeduduka. *Pit against*, shindanisha. **pitfall**, *n.* rima (shimo la kutegea wanyama); mtego, shida ya ghafula. **pitman**, *n.* mfanya kazi katika *pit*.

pitch, (1) *n.* (*tar*) lami; (*for ships*) bereu. *As dark as pitch*, -eusi kabisa, giza kabisa. — *v.t.* paka lami (bereu). **pitch-black**, *a.* -eusi sana. **pitch-dark**, *n.* giza sana. — *a.* -enye giza sana. **pitchy**, *a.* -eusi, -a giza.

pitch, (2) *v.t.* (*throw*) tupa, vurumisha; (*fix*) kaza, tengeneza, simikisha, simamisha; (*music*) kadirisha sauti (kuwa nene au nyembamba); (*a yarn*) simulia, hadithia; — *v.i.* (*settle*) tua, tulia; (*of a ship*) tupwa huko na huko, fanya mrama, sukasuka; (*fall*) anguka. *Pitch a tent*, simikisha (piga) hema. *Pitch camp*, tua, fanya kituo (kambi). *Pitch on*, kuta, angukia, patia, pata. *Pitch into*, piga, endea kwa nguvu. — *n.* (*customary place &c.*) mahali pake (pako, pao &c.) pa kawaida (pa kazi): (*throw*) mtupo, mvurumisho; (*in cricket*) uwanja wa kuchezea; (*degree*) kadiri (ya kuwa juu au chini); (*musical*) kadiri ya sauti (nene au nyembamba); (*slope*) mshuko mwinamo, anguko, mtelemko; (*of a ship*) mrama, msukosuko. *Come to a pitch*, iva, endelea sana. **pitch-and-toss**, *n.* mchezo wa kurusha sarafu. **pitched**, *a.* *a pitched battle*, vita vilivyoandaliwa tayari, vita vikubwa vilivyotengenezwa kwa ustadi. **pitchfork**, *n.* fimbo ya panda ya kupanga majani yaliyokatwa. *Pitchfork into*, tia ghafula (mtu katika kazi bila kufikiri kama atafaa &c.). **pitching**, *n.* msukosuko, mrama. **pitch-pipe**, *n.* kama filimbi ndogo ya kukadirisha sauti.

pitch-black, *a.*, **pitch-dark**, *n. and a.* taz. *pitch* (1).

pitcher, *n.* mtungi, gudulia, kuzi.

pitchfork, *n.*, **pitching**, *n.*, **pitch-pipe**, *n.* taz. *pitch* (2).

pitchy, *a.* taz. *pitch* (1).

piteous, *a.* taz. *pity*.

pitfall, *n.* taz. *pit*.

pith, *n.* moyo mwororo (laini) wa bua &c., kitu chororo upande wa ndani wa ganda la chungwa; (*of* *coco-nut)* joya, (*of shoot of coco-nut tree*) kilele, shaha; (*essence*) asili, maana, nguvu, kiini. **pithy,** *a.* -enye maana, -a nguvu, -a akili, -a kukolea; (*soft*) -ororo, kama kiini chororo cha bua *&c.*

pitiable, *a.*, **pitiful,** *a.*, **pitiless,** *a.* taz. *pity.*

pitman, *n.* taz. *pit.*

pittance, *n.* posho kidogo, sehemu ndogo, chakula (fedha) kidogo.

pitted, *a.* taz. *pit.*

pity, *n.* huruma; (*sad event*) jambo la kutia huruma (la kuleta majuto, la kusikitisha), msiba. *What a pity, It is a great pity,* msiba kweli huo, jambo la kujutika. *For pity's sake,* kwa huruma yako. **piteous,** *a.* -a huzuni, -a kuhuzunisha, -a kutia huruma. **pitiable,** *a.* -a kusikitikisha, -a kutia huruma, -a kuhuzunisha; (*wretched*) -baya, -nyonge, hafifu. **pitiful,** *a.* -enye huruma; (*exciting pity*) taz. *pitiable.* **pitiless,** *a.* -korofi, -gumu, -katili.

pivot, *n.* msumari wa kati (ya mviringo, au ya kitu kizungukacho, kama ya pia); (*turning-point, base, essence*), asili, chimbuko, moyo, kiini. — *v.i.* geuka (zunguka) katika *point.*

pixy, pixie, *n.* kizimwi.

placability, *n.*, **placable,** *a.* taz. *placate.*

placard, *n.* tangazo la (ilani ya) kubandika ukutani. — *v.t.* tangaza habari kwa *placard.*

placate, *v.t.* tuliza, ridhisha. **placability,** *n.* upole, usamehevu, utulivu, makini. **placable,** *a.* -pole, -tulivu, -a amani, -samehevu, -a kusamehe.

place, *n.* mahali, janibu; (*open area*) uwanja, uwanda; (*town*) mji; (*country*) nchi; (*position, rank*) cheo, daraja, hali, kiwango; (*space*) nafasi; (*in book*) maneno, panenwapo, mahali; (*employment*) kazi. *Take place,* -wa, tukia, fanyika, jiri. *Take the place of,* -wa mahali pa, -wa badala ya, shika makamu ya. *Give place to,* ondokea, fanyia nafasi, kubali. *In place,* pafaapo, mahali pake. *Out of place,* pasipofaa. — *v.t.* weka, ika, tia; (*recognize*) tambua.

placenta, *n.* kondo la nyuma.

placid, *a.* -tulivu, -pole, -anana. **placidity,** *n.* utulivu, upole, makini.

plagiarism, *n.* taz. *plagiarize.*

plagiarize, *v.t.* tumia kazi (mawazo, matengenezo, akili, maandiko *&c.*) ya mtu mwingine bila kukiri ya kuwa ni yake. **plagiarism,** *n.* kazi (maandiko *&c.*) ya mtu iliyotumiwa na mwingine kama kwamba ni yake mwenyewe.

plague, *n.* tauni; (*affliction, calamity*) msiba, mateso, baa, balaa, taabu; (*nuisance*) kitu kibaya kinachosumbua, kisumbuo; (*person*) baa. — *v.t.* sumbua, udhi, chokoza, tesa, taabisha, chagiza.

plaice, *n.* namna ya samaki wa bahari mpana na sawa.

plaid, *n.* nguo pana nene, kama blanketi.

plain, *a.* (*clear*) dhahiri, wazi; (*flat*) sawa (*unadorned*) pasina urembo, -a mfuto, bila mapambo (uzuri, madaha, fahari, elimu, adabu); (*straightforward*) -nyofu, -a kweli; (*common*) vivi hivi, ovyo, -a mfuto, -dufu; (*simple*) -tupu, peke yake. — *n.* uwanda, tambarare, nchi pana na sawa. — *adv.* dhahiri, wazi. **plainly,** *adv.* dhahiri, wazi, kwa jinsi ilivyo *plain.* **plain-dealing,** *n.* unyofu, uaminifu. **plainness,** *n.* kuwa *plain,* udhahiri, unyofu, udufu *&c.* **plain-spoken,** *a.* -nyofu, bila hitilafu.

plaint, *n.* maombelezo, kilio; (*grievance*) mashtaka; (*document*) hati ya mashtaka. **plaintiff,** *n.* kudai. **plaintive,** *a.* -a huzuni, -a majonzi.

plait, *v.t.* suka, sokota. — *n.* kunjo, kikunjo, kikoto, upindo; (*braid*) kigwe, ugwe. *Plaits of hair,* masongomano (masongo) ya nywele.

plan, *n.* shauri, mradi nia, kusudi, azimio; (*method*) njia; (*sketch, outline*) ramani, picha, kiolezo, tarakibu. *Make* (*draw*) *a plan of a house,* andika ramani ya nyumba; (*mark out on the ground*) toa nyumba. — *v.t.* fanya shauri ya, azimu, nia, nuia; (*design*) andika rekebisha; (*on the ground*) toa.

plane, (1) *n.* randa; (*figure*) picha iliyo sawa kwa upana; (*surface*) uso (wa kitu) ulio sawasawa (usioinuka wala kushuka); (*stage*) kiasi (cha uzuri, ustaarabu); (*aeroplane*) eropleni. — *a.* -enye uso ulio sawasawa (usioinuka wala kushuka). — *v.t.* piga randa; (*of an aeroplane*) enda (shuka) hewani bila kutumia mashine.

plane, (2) *n.* namna ya mti.

planet, *n.* nyota kubwa yenye mwendo wa kuzunguka jua; sayari. **planetary,** *a.* -a sayari.

plank, *n.* ubao.

plant, *v.t.* panda, panda mbegu katika; (*fix*) weka, kaza, simamisha; (*instil, teach*) fundisha, funza. *Plant out* (*seedlings*) atika, pandikiza. — *n.* mbegu, mche, chipukizi, mmea; (*equipment*) jamii ya vyombo (samani, zana, mashine &c.) vya kufanyia kazi fulani. **plantation,** *n.* shamba, mgunda, konde; (*garden, orchard*) bustani, kiunga. **planting,** *n.* mpando.

plantain, *n.* (*fruit*) ndizi; (*plant*) mgomba.

plantation, *n.*, **planting,** *n.* taz. *plant.*

plaque, *n.* kipande chembamba cha madini, pembe &c. cha kupamba.

plash, *n.* kidimbwi.

plasma, *n.* maji ya damu, maziwa &c. yanayoweka chembechembe, mafuta &c.

plaster, *n.* lipu, mchanganyiko wa chokaa, mchanga, maji na nyuzinyuzi (wa kupaka kuta za nyumba); (*for mud houses*) udongo, kandiko; (*medical*) dawa ya kubandika, kibandiko, mpakato. — *v.t.* paka, tia, lipu; (*mud house*) kandika; (*in medicine*) bandika, pakaza. **plasterer,** *n.* mwashi; (*of mud houses*) mkandiki.

plastic, *a.* -a kufinyanga, kinamo, -nama, -a kunama, -a kunyumbuka; (*soft*) -ororo, -a kugeuka vyo vyote; (*docile*) -sikivu, -sikizi, -elekevu. **plasticity,** *n.* kuwa *plastic.*

plate, *n.* (*for food*) sahani, kisahani, kombe; (*sheet of metal*) bamba; (*silver &c. vessels*) vyombo vya fedha &c.; (*picture*) picha ya kitabuni. — *v.t.* chovya vitu vya madini katika fedha, dhahabu &c.; (*with tin*) rasisi. **plate-glass,** *n.* kipande kikubwa cha kioo kinene cha kutia katika dirisha kubwa. **plated,** *a.* -a kutiwa fedha au dhahabu nje, si fedha tupu. **platter,** *n.* sahani, kombe, hero, chano, ulio.

plateau, *n.* nchi iliyoinuka sawa na pana, uwanda wa juu.

plated, *a.* taz. *plate.*

platform, *n.* jukwaa, mbao; (*for sentry, watchman, open*) ulingo; (*covered*) dungu; (*for grain &c.*) uchala, uchaga, utaa; (*design, programme*) nia, mawazo, mashauri, maazimio.

platinum, *n.* madini nzito nyeupe ya thamani.

platitude, *n.* maneno baridi, msemo unaojulikana sana kwa hiyo haustahili kusemwa tena.

platonic, *a.* *Platonic affection* (*love*), upendo kwa akili (si kwa ngoa, ashiki, tamaa).

platoon, *n.* kikosi cha askari wapatao sitini.

platter, *n.* taz. *plate.*

plaudit, *n.* makelele ya kusalimu (ya kusifu, ya kufurahia), masifu, vifijo.

plausible, *a.* -a kujipendekeza, -a kuvuta, -enye kishawishi, kama kweli, kama -ema, -a kuonekana kama kwamba ni kweli (-ema &c.) lakini labda sivyo. **plausibility,** *n.* mapendezi, kuwa *plausible.*

play, *v.i.* cheza; (*music*) piga; (*be active*) enda, tenda, kazi; (*move freely*) peperuka, yumbayumba, wayawaya, legalega, chezacheza, rukaruka &c; — *v.t.* (*direct, as a stream of water, searchlight &c.*) peleka, tupa, elekeza; (*a game*) cheza; (*act*) jifanya; (*execute*) fanya; (*instrument of music*) piga. *Play into the hands of*, -wa shauri moja na, saidia, patia faida. *Play (one) false*, danganya. *Play truant*, toroka. *Play upon*, geuza, fanyia werevu. *Play the fool with*, puzika na. *Play with*, chezea, laabu. — *n.* mchezo; (*free movement*) mwendo mwepesi, uhuru wa mwendo; (*jest*) mzaha, ubishi, masihara; (*drama*) mchezo wa kuigiza mambo; (*of words*) mageuzi, fumbo; (*room*) nafasi, ruhusa. *Keep in play*, shughulisha, shindisha, kawilisha. *Bring into play*, tendeza kazi yake, tumisha. *Come into play*, tenda kazi, tumika. **played-out**, *a.* (*be*) choka, legea, shindwa. **player**, *n.* mchezaji, mshindanaji (katika machezo). **playful**, *a.* -cheshi, -a kucheza, -a mzaha, purupuru. **playfulness**, *n.* ubishi, uchezaji. **playground**, *n.* kiwanja, uwanja (wa machezo). **playing-cards**, *n.* karata. **playmate**, *n.* rafiki mshiriki katika michezo. **plaything**, *n.* kitu cha kuchezea, kipuzi.

plea, *n.* maombi, majiteteo, maneno, sababu, hoja, udhuru, kisa, udaku.

plead, *v.t.* tetea, leta hoja (kisa, udhuru); — *v.i.* (*ask*) omba, sihi, omboleza. *Plead guilty*, kiri kosa, ungama. *Plead for*, ombea, tetea. **pleader**, *n.* mdai, mwana sheria, mwombezi. **pleading**, *n.* kuomba, kutetea, maombi, maombezi, mateto; (*in law*) maneno (ya mbele ya baraza, katika korti, hukumuni).

please, *v.t. and i.* pendeza, ridhisha, furahisha, pata ukubali, anisi, kora, tulilia; — *v.i.* (*like, choose*) penda, taka, chagua. *Be pleased*, pendezwa; (*think right*) penda, ona njema, taka. *Please oneself* (*do as one likes*) tumia roho, fanya -pendavyo. *Just as you please*, upendavyo, hiari yako. *It pleased him*, aliona njema, ilimkalia tamu. *Please, If you please*, tafadhali, uwe radhi, kunradhi.

pleasant, *a.* -a kupendeza, -zuri, -tamu, -a kukolea, -a kukora. *A pleasant person to talk to*, mtu wa kuambilika. **pleasantry**, *n.* ubishi, mzaha, ucheshi, mazungumzo matamu, upendezi. **pleasing**, *a.* -a kupendeza, -zuri, -tamu, -a anasa, anisi, -a kukora, -a kukolea, marini. **pleasurable**, *a.* -a kupendeza, -a kuridhisha. **pleasure**, *n.* furaha, anasa, mchezo, raha, ridhaa; (*pleasing thing*) upendezi.

pleat, *n.* kunjo, finyo; (*in a dress*) marinda. — *v.t.* kunja, fanya marinda.

plebeian, *a.* -a watu (wa vivi hivi).

plebiscite, *n.* mwonyesho wa nia (maono) ya watu wote wa nchi juu ya jambo fulani.

pledge, *n.* (*token*) rehani, arabuni, amana, kabidhi; (*promise*) ahadi, dhamana, sharti, daraka. — *v.t.* weka rehani, funga kwa ahadi, ahidi. *Pledge word, honour &c.* jifunga kwa uapo, weka sharti, diriki, ahidi.

Pleiades, *n.* kilimia.

plenary, *a.* kamili, -ote, zima, -ingi.

plenipotentiary, *n.* mjumbe wa serikali (mwenye nguvu kama serikali yenyewe katika mambo fulani), mjumbe mkuu. — *a.* -enye nguvu (amri) zote. **plenitude**, *n.* ukamilifu, wingi.

plenty, *n.* wingi, maridhawa, neema, usitawi. *Plenty of food*, chakula tele. **plenteous, plentiful**, *a.* -ingi, maridhawa, tele, furifuri, farafara.

pleonasm, *n.* maneno mengi, maneno ya bure. **pleonastic**, *a.* -a maneno mengi, -a bure.

plethora, *n.* wingi kupita kiasi; (*medical*) ugonjwa wa kuwa na damu nyingi kupita kiasi.

pleurisy, *n.* ugonjwa wa ngozi ya nje ya mapafu. **pleuro-pneumonia**, *n.* ugonjwa wa ngozi ya nje ya mapafu na mapafu pia.

pliable, *a.* -a kugeuka, -a kupindika, -namo, -a kunama; (*docile*) -sikivu, -sikizi, -elekevu; (*yielding*) laini, -ororo. **pliability**, *n.* kuwa *pliable*;

kupindikana, kugeuka; usikivu, usikizi, welekevu. **pliant,** *a.* taz. *pliable.*

pliers, *n.* koleo; (*used by jewellers &c.*) chamburo.

plight, (1) *n.* hali (hasa mbaya), mambo (hasa mabaya).

plight, (2) *v.t.* ahidi, ahidi kuoa. — *n.* ahadi.

plimsoll, *n.* alama ubavuni mwa meli kuonya ya kuwa maji yaifikiapo ni marafuku kutia shehena zaidi.

plinth, *n.* msingi (nguzo) ulioinuka wa nyumba au sanamu.

plod, *v.i.* enda (fanya kazi) polepole na kwa shida, shikilia (fululizia) kazi (kusoma &c.) hasa kama ni ya taabu. **plodder,** *n.* mwenye bidii ya kazi (hasa afanyaye kazi polepole kwa taabu lakini kwa moyo).

plop, *n.* kishindo (kama kitu kikitumbukia majini au kizibo kikizibuka ghafula). — *adv.* (*of cork &c.*) po; (*of thing falling into water*) chubwi.

plot, *n.* shauri, shauri baya, hila, mtego; (*of ground*) shamba, mgunda, konde, kiunga, kiwanja; (*of story*) mambo ya hadithi, kiini cha (asili ya) hadithi. — *v.* fanya shauri (baya, la hila, la siri). **plotter,** *n.* mfanya hila (shauri la siri).

plough, *n.* jembe la kukokotwa na ng'ombe (farasi au motakaa). — *v.t.* lima kwa *plough*, plau. **ploughman,** *n.* mlimaji. **ploughshare,** *n.* chuma cha *plough.*

plover, *n.* namna ya ndege wa jamii ya kitwitwi.

pluck, *v.t.* finya, minya, nyaka, nyakua; (*fruit, flowers &c.*) chuma; (*maize &c.*) goboa, konyoa, kongonyoa; (*rob*) komba; (*hair, feathers &c.*) nyonyoa, futua; (*in examination*) kataa. *Pluck up*, ng'oa. *Pluck up courage*, piga moyo konde. — *n.* finyo, mnyakuo; (*courage, spirit*) uhodari, ushujaa, uthabiti, ushupavu, moyo, ugumu, moyo wa kiume. **plucky,** *a.* hodari, -enye moyo wa kiume, -shujaa, -a kiume.

plug, *n.* zibo, nguruzi, kizibo, kihasho; (*of tobacco &c.*) bumba. — *v.t.* ziba, funga.

plum, *n.* tunda kama zambarau; (*good thing*) kitu bora, tunu, tuzo.

plumage, *n.* taz. *plume.*

plumb, *n.* timazi, chubwi. *Out of plumb*, si sawasawa (kwa wima). — *a.* sawasawa (kwa wima), kiwima, wima kabisa, sawasawa; (*absolute*) kabisa. — *adv.* kwa wima; (*exactly*) hasa, sawasawa. — *v.t.* pima kwa timazi (usawa wa ukuta, urefu wa maji &c.); (*of the eye*) ona mpaka chini; (*of the intelligence*) fahamu kabisa. **plumbago,** *n.* kitu kama risasi au chaki nyeusi. **plumber,** *n.* fundi wa mabomba ya risasi (ya chuma, ya udongo) ya kuleta maji nyumbani, &c. **plumbing,** *n.* kazi ya *plumber.* **plumb-line, plummet,** *n.* timazi, chubwi, bildi.

plume, *n.* nyoya (la ndege, jogoo); (*tuft*) pambo la nywele au manyoya kichwani, shungi, shada ya manyoya (ya ndege). — *v.t.* *plume oneself*, jivuna. **plumage,** *n.* manyoya (ya ndege).

plummet, *n.* taz. *plumb.*

plump, (1) *a.* -enye maungo, -nene, -a kuviringana, -a kubenuka; (*of animals*) -nono. **plumpness,** *n.* mafuta, unene, unono, maungo mazuri, kuviringana, mbenuko.

plump, (2) *v.i.* anguka kwa kishindo; — *v.t.* bwaga, angusha kwa kishindo, jitupa, jitumbukiza. *Plump for*, chagua (fulani) peke yake (kwa vote). — *adv.* kwa kishindo. **plumper,** *n.* *vote* ya kuchagua mtu mmoja peke yake.

plumpness, *n.* taz. *plump* (1).

plunder, *v.t.* (*in war*) teka, teka nyara; (*steal*) nyang'anya, iba; (*by fraud*) punja, ghilibu. — *n.* (*war*) mateka, nyara; (*by theft &c.*) mapato (kwa wizi, uyang'anyi &c.). **plunderer,** *n.* mtekaji, mnyang'anyi mwizi.

plunge, *v.t.* tumbukiza, chovya ghafula, tosa; (*force into*) ingiza, tia, chomeka, penyeza; — *v.i.* (*hurl* *oneself into*) jitupa, jiingiza ghafula (kwa nguvu), enda kwa nguvu (kwa haraka, ghafula); (*dive*) piga mbizi. — *n.* mtupo (mwendo) wa ghafula, mruko, mshindo; (*dive*) mbizi, kupiga mbizi. **plunging**, *a.*, -a kujitupa, -a kuruka, -a kusukasuka.

pluperfect, *a. and n. The pluperfect tense*, namna ya *verb* kuonyesha ya kuwa tendo lilikuwa limekwisha tendeka (tendwa), *e.g.* (kabla hajafa) alikuwa ameweka (yote tayari)

plural, *a.* zaidi ya -moja,- ingi, -a wingi. — *n.* wingi. **plurality**, *n.* wingi, hesabu (namba) zaidi ya moja.

plus, *prep.* pamoja na, zaidi ya. *Plus sign*, alama ya kujumlisha, ndiyo +. **plus fours**, *n.* namna ya suruali pana ya kufika kidogo chini ya magoti.

plush, *n.* nguo yenye malaika au manyoya kama mahameli.

plutocrat, *n.* mtu mwenye nguvu (amri) kwa sababu ya utajiri wake (mali yake). **plutocracy**, *n.* utawala wa *plutocrat*, utawala kwa watu kwa nguvu ya utajiri wao (mali yao).

plutonic, *a.* -a ahera, -a chini sana, -a moto.

pluvial, *a.* a mvua, -a kufanyika kwa mvua.

ply, (1) *v.t. and i.* tumia (chombo, jembe, sindano *&c.*) kwa bidii; (*follow diligently*) fanya kazi (biashara *&c.*) kwa bidii; (*offer, supply, repeatedly*) -pa (letea, fanyia) mara kwa mara; (*go regularly*) enda na kurudi siku fulani (saa fulani, njia fulani) kwa kawaida.

ply, (2) *n.* (*layer*) tabaka; (*thickness*) maki; (*strand*) uzi. *Three-ply wood*, tabaka tatu za mbao zilizogandamizwa pamoja kufanya ubao mmoja wenye nguvu.

pneumatic, *a.* -enye hewa ndani, -a kuendeshwa kwa nguvu ya hewa.

pneumatics, *n.* elimu ya hewa na mambo yake. **pneumonia**, *n.* ugonjwa wa pafu kuwa zito hata mgonjwa hawezi kuvuta pumzi vizuri.

poach, (1) *v.t.* (*egg*) tokosa ute na kiini katika maji yanayochemka.

poach, (2) *v.t.* winda (saka) katika mashamba ya watu isivyo haki, vua samaki katika mito iliyo mali ya watu bila ruhusa; twaa isiyo haki.

poacher, *n.* mwizi wa mawindo.

pock, *n.* kovu ya ndui. *Be pockmarked*, duduka.

pocket, *n.* mfuko; (*hole, cavity*) kishimo; (*air-pocket*) kama wimbi hewani linalofanya eropleni kupanda au kutelemka ghafula. *Be out of pocket*, pata hasara, toa gharama. — *v.t.* tia mfukoni, futika; (*steal*) iba; (*endure*) vumilia; (*make profit*) faidi, chuma. **pocket-book**, *n.* kitabu kidogo cha kuchukulia mfukoni. **pocket-handkerchief**, *n.* leso, kitambaa, ankachifu. **pocket-knife**, *n.* kisu kidogo cha kukunja. kijembe. **pocket-money**, *n.* fedha kidogo ya kununulia vitu vidogo kama sigareti *&c.*

pod, *n.* ganda, mfuko, tumba; (*of a bean*) kunde, ukunde.

podgy, *a.* -nene, -fupi.

poem, *n.* mashairi; (*religious*) utenzi. **poesy**, *n.* mashairi. **poet**, *n.* mtunga mashairi, mshairi. **poetic, poetical**, *a.* -a mashairi. **poetry**, *n.* mashairi; utungaji wa mashairi. *Write poetry*, tunga (buni) mashairi. *A line of poetry*, shairi.

poignant, *a.* -kali, -enye kutia -uchungu. **poignancy**, *n.* uchungu, ukali.

point, *n.* ncha, kilembwa; (*of instrument*) ncha, chembe, chuma; (*of rocks*) kilele, mchonge; (*dot*) nukta; (*place*) mahali padogo, mahali halisi, mahali hasa; (*time*) nukta (dakika, wakati) halisi; (*matter*) jambo moja, jambo, neno, kitu; (*meaning*) maana, kusudi, asili, kiini; (*degree*) daraja cheo. *At all points*, pande zote, kabisa, halisi. *To the point, In point*, -enye maana, -a akili, -a kufaa, -a kupasa. *At the point of death*, kufani, gharighari ya mauti. *On the point of*, katika, karibu na. *I was on the point of saying*, nilitaka kusema pale pale. *On the point of departure,* katika kuondoka. *Point of view,* jinsi ya kuangalia, shauri. *From my point of view,* nionavyo mimi. *Make a point of,* shika sana, shikilia, kaza, bidi, zoea sana, fanya sikuzote. *Make a point,* endelea, jipatia sifa (daraja, faida, kushinda *&c.*). *Carry a point,* shinda, pata. *Bring to a point,* kata maneno, jumlisha. *Come to the point,* isha, maliza, kata neno. *Strain (stretch) a point,* kubali kwa shida; ruka mpaka, fanya isiyo haki hasa, vuta hukumu. *A point, A strong point,* jambo kubwa, sababu njema, sifa nzuri. *Points of the compass, Cardinal points,* njia za pepo, majira ya dira. *Points (in a railway)* reli zenye njia panda, zinazoweza kujongezwa ili kupeleka gari njia hii au hii. *Good (bad) points,* tabia nzuri (mbaya). — *v.t.* (*make pointed*) chonga; (*iron*) tambuza; (*direct*) elekeza, kabilisha, nyosha, onyesha; (*punctuate*) tia nukta; (*finish off masonry*) tomea; — *v.i.* (*direct finger to*) onyesha kwa kidole, elekeza (soza) kidole; (*of a dog*) onyesha ndege. *Point out,* onyesha, ainisha. *Point to,* onyesha; (*suggest*) elekea, kabili. **point-blank,** *adv.* sawasawa kabisa, pale pale, wazi wazi. **pointed,** *a.* -liochongoka, -embamba mwishoni, -enye ncha kali, -kali, (*forcible*) -enye maana, -a akili, -a kukolea; (*sarcastic*) -a kutia uchungu, -kali. **pointer,** *n.* (*of watch &c.*) mkono, mshale, akarabu; (*rod &c.*) fimbo (fito) ya kuelekezea (ya kuonyeshea); (*dog*) namna ya mbwa wa kuwinda, mwepesi kuonya habari ya ndege au mnyama. **pointing,** *n.* kuchonga *&c.* taz. *point, v.*; kuonya; (*punctuation*) kutia nukta, nukta; (*in masonry*) kutomea, mtomo. **pointless,** *a.* pasipo *point*; (*blunt*) -butu; (*stupid*) hafifu, -pumbavu, -a ovyo, -siohusu. *It is pointless (dull speech),* haikolei, haina kiungo; baridi. **pointsman,** *n.* mlinzi wa njia panda ya reli.

poise, *v.t.* weka sawasawa (kama mtungi *&c.* kichwani), tuliza sawasawa; (*place so as to swing*) pembeza, yongesha; (*weigh*) pima; — *v.i.* (*hover*) sinzia angani; (*be balanced*) tulia sawasawa, simama; (*be in suspense*) -wa na shaka, sitasita. — *n.* mwendo (*e.g.* kuinua kichwa, kutanguliza kichwa, kusimama wima *&c.*); (*calmness &c.*) utulivu, makini.

poison, *n.* sumu, liga; (*for fish*) utupa. — *v.t.* tia (lisha) sumu, liga, sumisha; (*pervert &c.*) potosha. **poisonous,** *a.* -a sumu, -a kufisha. -haribifu, -baya sana, -a kuchukiza.

poke, *v.t.* sukuma, kumba, piga kikumbo; (*with the finger in contempt*) tia mdukuo; (*the fire*) chochea; (*grope about*) papasa; (*in the dark*) tutusa; (*thrust oneself where one is not wanted*) jidukiza. *Poke fun at,* fanyia mzaha. — *n.* msukumo, kikumbo, mdukuo, msubukuo.

poker, (1) *n.* kichocheo. **poky,** *a.* -dogo.

poker, (2) *n.* mchezo fulani wa karata.

poky, *a.* taz. *poke.*

pole, (1) *n.* ncha ya kaskazini au kusini ya dunia, pembe za dunia; (*magnetism*) mwisho wa sumaku (magnetisi). *Pole-star,* nyota ya kaskazini. *Be poles apart,* -wa mbali-mbali kabisa, hitilafiana kabisa. **polar,** *a.* -a kaskazini au kusini, -a nchi za baridi sana, -a *pole.*

pole, (2) *n.* mti, ufito; (*long thin*) kombamoyo; (*for fastening thatch on roof*) fito; (*on to which thatch is fastened*) pao; (*for carrying load*) mpiko; (*for punting*) upondo; (*rafter*) boriti; (*post*) nguzo, mhimili, mwimo; (*hooked*) kiopoo, konzo, kingoe, ngoe; (*measure*) kipimo cha urefu yadi tano na nusu. — *v.t.* sukuma (endesha) kwa upondo. **pole-axe,** *n.* shoka la vita.

polecat, *n.* mnyama kama fungo.

polemic, polemical, *a.* -a kubishana, -a kushindana, -a majadiliano.

police, *n.* polisi, jamii ya mapolisi. **policeman,** *n.* polisi. **police-**

station, *n.* nyumba ya mashauri ya mapolisi; wanapopelekwa watu wakamatwao na mapolisi ili washtakiwe.

policy, (1) *n. Insurance policy,* hati ya *insurance.*

policy, (2) *n.* mashauri, maongozi (ya mambo ya serikali, ya wakubwa, ya pasayo wote); (*prudence*) busara; (*cunning*) ujanja, hila. **politic,** *a.* -a kufaa, -a busara; (*of the state*) -a serikali. **political,** *a.* -a kuhusu utawala wa (serikali ya) nchi; -a *politics. Political party,* jamii ya watu wenye shauri moja kwa mambo ya serikali. *Political affairs,* mambo ya utawala wa nchi. **political economy,** *n.* elimu inayohusu upataji wa mahitaji ya wanadamu. **politician,** *n.* mtu wa *politics,* mwenye kujishughulisha na *politics.* **politics,** *n.* mambo ya serikali (ya utawala); maono ya mtu juu ya utawala (serikali). **polity,** *n.* utawala, kumiliki, matengenezo ya serikali (ya utawala).

polish, *v.t.* ng'arisha, katua, kwatua; (*educate*) adibisha, ongoza; — *v.i.* lainika, katuka, kwatuka, ng'arika. *Polish off,* maliza upesi; (*kill*) ua. — *n.* ulaini, mng'aro, mwanga; (*substance used*) dawa ya kung'arisha (ya kukatulia, ya kukwatulia); (*manners*) malezi mazuri, adabu. **polished,** *a.* -liokatuka, -liokwatuka, -nayong'aa, -angavu; (*well-mannered*) -a adabu, -a madaha, -enye malezi mazuri.

polite, *a.* -a adabu, -a heshima, adibu.

politeness, *n.* adabu, heshima.

politic, *a.,* **political,** *a.,* **political economy,** *n.,* **politician,** *n.,* **politics,** *n.,* **polity,** *n.,* taz. *policy* (2).

polka, *n.* namna ya ngoma ya kizungu.

poll, *n.* kichwa (hasa kisogo); (*counting of votes*) kuhesabu watu waliotoa *vote* katika *election;* (*register of voters*) orodha ya watu wenye haki ya kutoa *vote;* (*place of voting*) mahali watu wanapokwenda kutoa *vote;* (*total of voters*) hesabu ya watu waliotoa *vote.* — *v.t.* toa *vote,* pokea *votes;* (*prune*) pogoa, kata ncha za matawi. **poll-tax,** *n.* kodi ya kichwa.

pollen, *n.* mbelewele, uvumbi (unga) ulio ndani ya maua chavua.

poll-tax, *n.* taz. *poll.*

pollute, *v.t.* tia taka, najisi, chafua. **pollution,** *n.* taka, janaba, uchafu, unajisi, kinyaa.

polo, *n.* mchezo wa wapanda farasi kupiga tufe kwa fimbo; mchezo wa watu wanaogelea majini kutupiana mpira.

poltroon, *n.* mwoga.

poly-, *pref.* -ingi. **polyandry,** *n.* desturi (katika makabila mengine) ya mwanamke kuwa na waume wawili au zaidi. **polygamist,** *n.* mwenye wake wawili au zaidi. **polygamy,** *n.* desturi ya mwanamume kuwa na wake wawili au zaidi. **polyglot,** *a.* -a lugha nyingi. **polygon,** *n.* kitu chenye pembe nyingi. **polyp,** *n.* mdudu wa majini mwenye mikono mingi. **polysyllabic,** *a.* -enye silabi zaidi ya tatu. **polysyllable,** *n.* neno lenye silabi nyingi (hasa zaidi ya tatu) *e.g.* ta-ka-ta-ka. **polytechnic,** *a.* -a elimu (sanaa) nyingi. — *n.* chuo mnamofundishwa elimu (sanaa) nyingi. **polytheism,** *n.* dini ya kuabudu (kuamini) miungu mingi. **polytheist,** *n.* mtu aaminiye miungu mingi.

pomade, *n.* mafuta ya kupaka nywele; (*used by native women*) behedani, bedani.

pomegranate, *n.* (*tree*) mkomamanga, mkudhumani; (*fruit*) komamanga, kudhumani.

pomelo, *n.* furungu, balungi.

pommel, *n.* pembe ya saruji (matandiko ya farasi au punda); mwisho wa mpini wa upanga. — *v.t.* pigapiga, piga ngumi nyingi.

pomp, *n.* fahari, sherehe, uzuri, kushaua, mashaufu, urembo, makuu. **pomposity,** *n.* mangwaji, ushaufu, majivuno, makuu. **pompous,** *a.* -a fahari, -shaufu, -a majivuno, -a kiburi.

pond, *n.* ziwa, kiziwa, shimo lenye maji; (*on beach*) kidimbwi.

ponder, *v.t.* fikiri, tafakari, waza.

ponderous, *a.* -zito sana, kubwa -zito, -zito; (*dull*) baridi, -zito.

poniard, *n.* kisu; (*curved*) jambia.

pontiff, *n.* kuhani mkuu; (*bishop*) askofu; (*Pope*) askofu wa Rumi. **pontifical,** *a.* -a *pontiff*. **pontificate,** *n.* kazi na utawala wa *pontiff*, hasa wa *Pope*.

pontoon, *n.* chelezo cha kuegemesha daraja ya kuvuka mto; mashua ya kuvusha watu &c.

pony, *n.* farasi mdogo (wa mbegu ndogo).

poodle, *n.* namna ya mbwa mwenye manyoya mengi.

pooh, *int.* chut! kefule! sefule! **pooh-pooh,** *v.t.* dharau, beza, pisha, cheka.

pool, (1) *n.* kiziwa, kidimbwi; (*deep place in river*) kilindi mtoni.

pool, (2) *n.* (*in games*) fedha jamii ya kushindaniwa; (*receptacle*) kidau; (*in business*) jamii ya watu wakichanga fedha zao. —*v.t.* changa fedha.

poop, *n.* shetri, sitaha.

poor, *a.* maskini, fukara, -kata, -kosefu; (*destitute*) hohe hahe; (*feeble, worthless*) hafifu, dhaifu, -baya, -chache, goigoi, -nyonge, -siopendeza. *Be* (*become poor*) fukarika, kombeka (pangusika) mali. **poor house,** *n.* nyumba wanamotunzwa maskini. **poor-laws,** *n.* sheria zinazohusu kulisha maskini. **poorly,** *adv.* vibaya, kwa jinsi isiyo nzuri. — *a.* -gonjwa. *Be* (*feel*) *poorly*, -wa hawezi, ugua, ona vibaya. **poor-rate,** *n.* kodi ya kulisha maskini. **poor-spirited,** *a.* -oga, dhaifu.

pop, *n.* kishindo. — *v.i.* fanya kishindo, pasuka (vunjika, katika, funguka, zibuka) kwa kishindo; (*as of corn &c. being parched*) tatarika; — *v.t.* tia (weka, fanya, toka, ruka) ghafula. *Pop upon*, gundulia, zukia. *Pop the question*, posa. *Pop up*, zuka, ibuka. *Pop off*, ondoka ghafula (kwa mbio; (*die*) fariki, -fa.

pope, *n.* askofu mkuu wa Rumi na wa Kanisa la kirumi. **popedom,** *n.* kazi na utawala wa *Pope*. **popery,** *n.* mafundisho, desturi &c. za Kanisa la kirumi (hasa ni neno la kudharau). **popish,** *a.* -a *popery*.

popinjay, *n.* mmalidadi, mfuauji, mshaufu.

popish, *a.* taz. *pope*.

poplar, *n.* namna ya mti mwembamba mrefu wa Ulaya.

poplin, *n.* namna ya kitambaa cha hariri na sufu cha nyuzinyuzi.

poppy, *n.* namna ya ua jekundu; namna ya mmea wenye utomvu unaotumika kufanyiza dawa ya kutia usingizi.

populace, *n.* watu (wa vivi hivi, wa mji jamii). **popular,** *a.* -a kupendwa na watu wote, -a kupendeza watu wote; (*of the populace*) -a watu wengi; -a kufaa watu walio wengi. *Be popular*, pendwa na wengi. **popularity,** *n.* kuwa *popular*, hali ya kupendwa (ya kupendeza) watu wengi; (*good will of all*) sifa za watu.

popularize, *v.t.* (*spread*) eneza katika watu wengi; (*simplify*) fanya jinsi ya kufaa kwa watu wengi; (*cheapen*) fanya rahisi, rahisisha.

popularly, *adv.* na watu wengi, mahali pengi, wapendavyo watu.

populate, *v.t.* jaza (weka, tia, kalisha) watu. **population,** *n.* watu (wa nchi fulani, wa mji fulani), wenyeji, wakazi. **populous,** *a.* -enye watu wengi, -a kujaa watu.

porcelain, *n.* udongo mzuri mweupe wa kufinyanga, — *a.* -a kauri.

porch, *n.* ukumbi, sebule.

porcine, *a.* taz. *pork*.

porcupine, *n.* nungu.

pore, (1) *v.i.* *Pore over*, kazia macho, soma kwa bidii.

pore, (2) *n.* kitundu kidogo; (*of skin*) kinyweleo. **porosity,** *n.* tabia (hali) ya kuwa na *pores* nyingi, kupapa maji. **porous**, *a.* -enye vinyeleo (vinyweleo) vingi, -a kupapa maji.

pork, *n.* nyama ya nguruwe. **porcine**, *a.* -a nguruwe, kama nguruwe. **porker**, *n.* nguruwe mdogo mnono.

porosity, *n.*, **porous**, *a.* taz. *pore* (2).

porphyry, *n.* namna ya jiwe gumu la rangi.

porpoise, *n.* pomboo.

porridge, *n.* namna ya uji mzito. **porringer**, *n.* sahani, kombe, bakuli.

port, (1) *n.* divai nyekundu tamu ya kireno.

port, (2) *n.* (*harbour*) bandari; (*port-hole*) kishubaka; (*of ship*) upande wa kushoto. — *v.t.* elekeza (chombo) kuume. **portal**, *n.* mlango mkubwa, lango. **porter**, *n.* mngoji mlango, bawabu. **portcullis**, *n.* mlango wa kuinuka na kushuka.

port, (3) (*demeanour*) mwendo, mwenendo, sura, umbo. **portable**, *a.* -a kuchukulika, -epesi. **portage**, *n.* kuchukua, uchukuzi, upagazi. **porter**, *n.* hamali, mchukuzi; (*caravan*) mpagazi, (*black beer*) pombe nyeusi ya kizungu. **porterage**, *n.* uchukuzi, upagazi.

portable, *a.*, **portage**, *n.* taz. *port* (3).

portal, *n.*, **portcullis**, *n.* taz. *port* (2).

portend, *v.t.* onya mbele, bashiri, kabili. **portent**, *n.* ndege (njema au mbaya), ishara ya mambo mabaya yatakayokuwa, kisirani, kitisho, kioja. **portentous**, *a.* -a kutisha, -a kuogofya, -kubwa mno, -baya sana.

porter, (1) *n.* taz. *port* (2).

porter, (2) *n.*, **porterage**, *n.* taz. *port* (3).

portfolio, *n.* jalada ya kutia hati, barua, *&c.*; (*state office*) uwaziri.

portico, *n.* baraza ya kutembelea yenye matao na nguzo.

portière, *n.* pazia la mlangoni.

portion, *n.* sehemu, fungu, mkato, mgawo, hisa; (*dowry*) mahari; (*inheritance*) urithi.

portly, *a.* -nene -kubwa. **portliness**, *n.* unene (wa mtu).

portmanteau, *n.* kasha la ngozi la kuchukulia nguo.

portray, *v.t.* andika picha (sanamu) ya; (*describe*) eleza, simulia, fafanua. **portrait**, *n.* picha (sanamu) ya mtu; (*type*) mfano, kiolezo. **portraiture**, *n.* kuandika picha (sanamu), mwandiko wa picha; (*description*) kueleza, kufafanua, maelezo, nafafanusi, uelezo, ufafanusi.

Portuguese, *a.* -a kireno; (*native of Portugal*) Mreno; (*language*) Kireno.

pose, (1) *v.t.* (*embarrass &c.*) tia matata, fadhaisha; tatiza, shinda. **poser**, *n.* fumbo, tatizo, matata.

pose, (2) *n.* kikao, sura, hali; (*pretence*) kisingizio, tabia (hali, sifa *&c.*) ya kujipa. — *v.t.* weka (katika kikao); — *v.i.* jiweka (katika kikao); (*pretend to be*) jifanya, jivuna kuwa, jidai. **poseur**, *n.* mpiga makuu, mjifanya mrembo.

position, *n.* (*place*) mahali; (*condition*) hali, kikao; (*opinion*) nia, neno; (*rank*) cheo, daraja, kiwango. *Be in a position to*, weza.

positive, *a.* (*real, actual*) -a hakika; (*absolute*) -a asili, -siobadilika; (*definite*) waziwazi, bayana, dhahiri; (*certain*) pasipo shaka, yakini; (*specially enacted*) kwa amri ya watu, si kwa asili au amri ya Mungu; (*implying exact knowledge*) -a ujuzi, -a kujua hakika; (*dogmatic*) -shupavu, -a kukatiza maneno. *Be positive*, jua sana pasipo shaka. **positively**, *adv.* kwa kweli, pasipo shaka, pasipo tofauti. **positivism**, *n.* ukubali wa mambo tu yanayoonekana na kujulikana vema na wanadamu.

posse, *n.* kikundi cha mapolisi.

possess, *v.* -wa na, miliki, shika, hozi; (*bewitch*) pagaa. *Possess oneself* (*of*), pata, jipatia. *Be possessed*, pagawa, -wa na wazimu (pepo), -wa na shetani; (*of property*) -wa na. **possession**, *n.* kumiliki; (*property*) mali, milki; (*by spirit*) kupagawa, shetani, pepo. *Give* (*put in*) *possession*, milikisha, tawaza; (*inform*) arifu, julisha, pasha habari. *Take possession*, kamata, twaa, shika. **possessor,** *n.* mwenyewe, mwenye, mwenyeji, bwana.

posset, *n.* maziwa ya moto na divai.

possible, *a.* -liowezekana, yamkini. *It is possible*, yawezekana, labda, huenda. *As soon as possible*, upesi iwezavyo, muhimu, kwa haraka sana. **possibility,** *n.* kuwa *possible*; (*power*) uwezo, nguvu, nafasi; (*chance*) bahati, hatari. *There is a possibility*, yawezekana, labda. **possibly,** *adv.* labda, kwa kadiri iwezekanavyo. *I cannot possibly do it*, siwezi kabisa kuifanya (haiwezekani). *As soon as you possibly can*, upesi uwezavyo (iwezekanavyo).

post, (1) *n.* (*of wood*) mti; (*prop*) mhimili, tuka, nguzo, kiguzo; (*door post*) mhimili, mwimo. (*place*) mahali kituo; (*station*) kilindo, palipoamriwa. — *v.t.* ((*fix up notice*) weka (bandika) mahali wazi, tangaza; (*assign place to*) weka, amria mahali. **poster,** *n.* karatasi kubwa ya kutangaza habari ya kubandikia ukutani.

post, (2) *n.* (*messenger*) mjumbe, tarishi, tume; (*postal services*) posta, kazi ya posta, barua za posta. — *v.t.* (*go quickly*) enda mbio; (*enter in accounts*) andika katika daftari. **postage,** *n.* ada ya posta. *Postage stamp*, tikiti ya posta. **postal,** *a.* -a posta. **postal order,** *n.* hati (cheti) ya fedha inayonunulika posta na fedha kupatikana ikipelekwa posta mahali pengine. **postcard,** *n.* karata ya kupelekea katika posta badala ya barua. **post-free,** *a.* bila kulipa ada ya posta. **post-haste,** *adv.* kwa haraka. — *n.* haraka nyingi. **postman,** *n.* tarishi, mpelekaji barua (mtu wa posta). **postmark,** *n.* chapa ya posta. **postmaster,** *n.* mkuu wa nyumba ya posta. **post office,** *n.* nyumba ya posta.

post-date, *v.t.* andikia tarehe ya baadaye (siyo iliyo kweli).

poster, *n.* taz. *post* (1).

posterior, *a.* -a nyuma, -a baadaye. — *n.* tako. **posterity,** *n.* watu wa baadaye, watakaozaliwa baadaye, wazao, watoto. **postern,** *n.* mlango mdogo wa nyuma.

post-free, *a.*, **post-haste,** *n.* *and adv.* taz. *post* (2).

posthumous, *a.* -liozaliwa baada ya kufa baba; -a baada ya kufa mwenyewe.

postilion, *n.* mpanda farasi wa gari.

postman, *n.*, **postmark,** *n.*, **postmaster,** *n.* taz. *post* (2).

post mortem, *n.* baada ya kufa. *Post-mortem examination*, kutazamia maiti kuona sababu ya kufa kwake.

post office, *n.* taz. *post* (2).

postpone, *v.t.* weka, ahirisha, (*place after*) weka nyuma (chini); (*delay*) chelewesha, kawilisha. **postponement,** *n.* kuweka *&c.*

post-prandial, *a.* -a baada ya kula *dinner*.

postscript, *n.* maneno yaliyotiwa baadaye (mwisho wa barua), nyongeza.

postulate, *v.t.* kubali neno (jambo) lisilothibitika (hasa kwa kusudi la kuhojiana); (*request &c.*) taka, hitaji; (*assume*) jitwalia. — *n.* neno lisilothibitika ambalo limekubaliwa kwa mapatano (hasa kwa kusudi la majadiliano).

posture, *n.* kikao, mkao; (*condition*) hali.

posy, *n.* shada (fungu) la maua.

pot, *n.* (*metal*) kopo, kikopo, mkebe; (*for cooking metal*) sufuria; (*earthen*) chungu, ungu, mkungu, bia, kibia; (*large*) jungu; (*small*) kijungu (*for tea*) buli; (*for coffee*) mdila, dele; (*jug*) mdumu; (*small brass, for milk*) kalasia. — *v.t.* tia katika *pot* (hasa miche katika vyungu au nyama, matunda, chakula *&c.*, katika makopo, bilauri *&c.*, ili kuvihifadhi visioze); (*hit*) piga. **potable,** *a.* -a kunyweka. **potage,** *n.* mchuzi wa nyama, mboga *&c.* **pot-bellied,** *a.* -enye kitumbo, -enye tumbo kubwa. **pot-herb,** *n.* mboga. **pot-hole,** *n.*

shimo refu; kishimo barabarani. **pot-hook,** *n.* kulabu, choro kama S. **pot-luck,** *n. Take pot luck,* -la fikia, -la fumanizi. **pot-pourri,** *n.*, **pot-sherd,** *n.* kigae, gae, kigeregenja, kigereng'enza. **pottage,** *n.* mchuzi wa nyama na mboga. **potter,** *n.* mfinyanzi. *Potter's kiln,* joko. **pottery,** *n.* (*articles*) vyombo vya udongo; (*place*) mahali pa kufinyanga.

potash, *n.* (*nitrate*) shura; (*carbonate*) magadi.

potassium permanganate, *n.* namna ya dawa nyekundu kidogo kama baruti; hutumika sana kwa *disinfectant.*

potation, *n.* kunywa; (*drink*) kinywaji.

potato, *n.* kiazi cha kizungu; (*sweet, native*) kiazi. *Potato bed,* tuta.

pot-bellied, *a.* taz. *pot.*

potent, *a.* -a nguvu. **potency,** *n.* nguvu. **potentate,** *n.* mtu mwenye nguvu, mkuu, mfalme, mtawala. **potential,** *a.* -liowezekana, -lioweza kuwa, -lioko lakini si wazi. **potentiality,** *n.* nguvu zisizodhihirika; (*possibility*) maelekeo, mambo yawezayo kutokea. **potentially,** *adv.* kwa kuwezekana, si kwa kuwa, kwa siri. **potently,** *adv.* kwa nguvu.

pother, *n.* udhia, machafuko, fujo, ghasia.

pot-herb, *n.*, **pot-hole,** *n.*, **pot-hook,** *n.* taz. *pot.*

potion, *n.* kinywaji, dawa ya kunywa.

pot-luck, *n.*, **pot-pourri,** *n.*, **pot-sherd,** *n.*, **pottage,** *n.*, **potter,** *n.*, **pottery,** *n.* taz. *pot.*

pouch, *n.* mfuko, kifuko; (*for cartridges*) beti. — *v.t.* tia mfukoni, futika; — *v.i.* tokeza kama mfuko.

poulterer, *n.* taz. *poultry.*

poultice, *n.* dawa ya kubandika (kama ugali laini wa moto), kibandiko cha dawa. — *v.t.* bandika *poultice.*

poultry, *n.* jamii ya kuku, mabata &c. **poulterer,** *n.* mwuza kuku, mabata &c.

pounce, *v.i.* ruka kwa ghafula. *Pounce upon,* rukia ghafula, vamia, ona ghafula na kushika. — *n.* mruko wa ghafula.

pound, (1) *n.* (*weight*) ratli; (*money*) pauni, thamani ya shilingi ishirini. **pounder,** *n.* kitu chenye uzani wa ratli fulani, *e.g. a six-pounder,* mzinga wenye risasi za ratli sita uzani wake.

pound, (2) *n.* (*enclosure*) zizi la kuwekea wanyama (ng'ombe, mbuzi, farasi &c.) waliopotea.

pound, (3) *v.t.* twanga, ponda, funda, pigapiga, chakacha. **pounder,** *n.* mchi.

pounder, *n.* taz. *pound* (1) *and* (3).

pour, *v.t.* mimina, mwaga, kupua; (*leaving dregs in vessel*) chingirisha, gida; (*emit freely*) toa -ingi (kwa nguvu); — *v.i.* (*flow freely*) toka -ingi (kwa nguvu), miminika. *The rain is pouring down,* mvua inanyesha sana. *Pour into,* miminia, tia.

pout, *v.i.* tokeza midomo (kwa chuki au uchungu).

poverty, *n.* umaskini, ufukara, ufakiri, ukata, utaiti, dhiki, udhikifu, urumo; (*lack, deficiency*) uchache, ukosefu, upungufu, uhitaji, utovu. **poverty-stricken,** *a.* maskini, -a kudhikika.

powder, *n.* unga, uvumbi; (*gun-powder*) baruti. — *v.t.* (*pulverize*) ponda, saga, chua; (*put powder on*) tia (nyunyizia) *powder.* **powder-flask, -horn,** *n.* pembe, talakaki. **powdery,** *a.* kama *powder.*

power, *n.* uwezo, nguvu, mamlaka, enzi, ezi, amri; (*an authority*) mwenye nguvu, mkubwa; (*great nation*) taifa kubwa. *The powers,* mataifa makubwa, wakubwa. *Mental* (*intellectual*) *power,* akili. *Have power,* -wa na nguvu (uwezo, mamlaka, enzi, amri). *Power of attorney,* uwakili, hati ya kuwakilisha (ya uwakili). *Have power over,* miliki, tawala, -wa na amri juu ya. **powerful,** *a.* -enye *power,* hodari, -a nguvu &c. **powerless,** *a.* pasipo *power*, dhaifu, bila nguvu *&c*. *Be (become) powerless*, pooza, potewa na nguvu *&c*.

pow-wow, *n*. mkutano wa (baraza ya) kufanya shauri, shauri, maneno.

pox, *n*. ugonjwa wa upele; (*syphilis*) sekeneko, kaswende. *Chicken-pox*, tete kuwanga, tetewanga, tete maji. *Small-pox*, ndui.

practicable, *a*. -a kufanyika, -liowezekana, -a kutendeka; (*usable*) -a kutumika (kuendeka *&c*.), -a kufaa. **practicability**, *n*. kuwezekana, kufanyika.

practical, *a*. (*useful*) -a kufaa, -a kutumika; (*sensible*) -a busara, -a akili, -a amali; (*for work*) -a kutenda kazi, kwa kazi. **practically**, *adv*. kwa kufaa, kwa busara, kwa kweli.

practice, *n*. (*habit*) mazoea, desturi, ibada; (*occupation*) kazi, uchumi; (*repeated exercise &c*.) mazoezo, mazoezi. *Learn by practice*, zoea, zoelea; jizoeza. *He might learn by practice*, anazoezeka. **practise**, *v*. (*doing*) kutenda, kufanya mara kwa mara; — *v.t*. tenda (fanya) mara kwa mara; (*engage in, exercise*) shika, fuata, fuliza, fanya kazi. — *v.i*. (*exercise oneself in*) jizoeza, jifunza, jiendekeza. **practised**, *a*. -zoevu, -elekevu, -stadi. **practitioner**, *n*. (*doctor*) daktari, tabibu; (*lawyer*) mwana sheria.

practically, *adv*. taz. *practical*.

pragmatic, pragmatical, *a*. -sumbufu, -a kujidukiza, -a kujitia (kujiingiliza) katika mambo ya watu, -tendaji mno, -fidhuli.

prairie, *n*. uwanda mpana wa majani (usio na miti), mbuga pana.

praise, *n*. sifa, hamdu, himdu, himidi, masifio. — *v.t*. sifu, himidi; (*glorify &c*.) adhimisha, tukuza. **praiseworthiness**, *n*. kustahili sifa, ustahili, wema. **praiseworthy**, *a*. -a kustahili sifa, -a kusifiwa (kusifika), -ema.

prance, *v.i*. chezacheza (kama farasi) randa, ruka, chachawa.

prank, *n*. mchezo, mzaha, kiila, kitimvi, kitimbi. **prankish**, *a*. -a michezo, -chezaji, -chimvi, -chimbi.

prate, *v.i*. sema upuzi, toa maneno mengi, piga domo, payuka, bwata, bwabwaja. **prater**, *n*. mpuzi, mpayukaji, mpiga domo. **prating**, *a*. -payukaji, -payu wa maneno.

prattle, *v.i*. toa maneno mengi, kama mtoto. — *n*. maneno ya kitoto, vijineno, mapayo.

pratique, *n*. ruhusa (ya meli kutelemsha abiria na shehena).

prattle, *n*. taz. *prate*.

prawn, *n*. kamba mdogo, uduvi (duvi, nduvi).

pray, *v.t*. omba; (*request*) sihi, taka; — *v.i*. omba, sali. *Pray to*, omba, tolea dua, omba dua, lalamia. *Pray for*, ombea; (*beg*) omba, taka, sihi. *Pray, why?* Kwa nini ati? Kwa nini basi? *Pray do!* haya! *Pray what is the news?* niambie, nakusihi, habari gani? **prayer** *n*. (*formal*) ibada, sala; (*special petition*) dua; (*request*) haja, maombi. **prayer book**, *n*. kitabu cha sala. **prayerful**, *a*. -enye kuomba, -a kusali, -zoevu wa kuomba (kusali). **prayer-mat, prayer-rug**, *n*. msala.

preach, *v.t*. hutubu, toa hotuba, hubiri, tangaza, eneza habari za; (*advocate*) shawishi, shauri. *Practise what you preach*, fanya mwenyewe unayowashauri wengine kuyafanya. **preacher**, *n*. mwenye kuhutubu, hatiba, mhubiri, mweneza habari za. **preaching**, *n*. hotuba, mahabiri.

preamble, *n*. mwanzo wa maneno, maneno ya kwanza, dibaji, matangulizi.

prebendary, *n*. kasisi mshiriki kazi katika kanisa kubwa (*cathedral*) Uingereza.

precarious, *a*. -a shida, -a hatari, -a mashaka, si salama, si thabiti.

precaution, *n*. hadhari, kujilinda mbele, uangalifu. *Take precautions*, jihadhari. **precautionary**, *a* -a hadhari, -a kulinda.

precede, *v.t*. tangulia, tangulia mbele ya, enda mbele, sabiki. **precedence**, *n.* utangulizi, heshima za ziada, kuzidi cheo, kukaa mbele, haki ya kikao fulani katika utaratibu wa vyeo (heshima *&c.*). **precedent,** *n.* jambo la zamani lililofanana na jambo la siku hizi, mfano, kiolezo, mithali. *There is no precedent,* jambo jipya, halina mfano zamani, halijawa hivi, bado kabisa. **preceding,** *a.* -a kwanza, -a mbele, -liotangulia.

precentor, *n.* mwenye kuimbisha kanisani, mtoa kongwe.

precept, *n.* fundisho, agizo, usia, onyo, amri. **preceptive,** *a.* -a kuonya, -a kuusia *&c.* **preceptor,** *n.* mwalimu, mfunzi, mkufunzi.

precinct, *n.* (*bound*) mpaka; (*enclosed space*) ua, kitalu; (*neighbourhood &c.*) mahali jirani.

precious, *a.* (*valuable*) -a thamani, -a tunu, ghali; (*beloved*) -penzi, -a kupendwa sana. *Precious metals,* (*gold*) dhahabu; (*silver*) fedha. *Precious stone,* kito.

precipice, *n.* genge, jabali, mtelemko (mwinuko) wa ghafula (wa kiwima, uliochongoka). **precipitous,** *a.* -a *precipice.*

precipitate, *v.t.* (*hasten*) himiza, tia haraka, leta upesi (kabla ya wakati upasao); (*throw down*) angusha ghafula, tumbukiza, vurumisha (hasa kutoka juu); (*let fall*) telemsha, shusha chini, tuamisha. — *n.* vumbi (taka) liangukalo katika maji yakituama. — *a.* -a haraka, -epesi, -a harara. **precipitancy,** *n.* haraka, mbio, wepesi; (*rashness &c.*) harara, haraka. **precipitant,** *n.* kitu ambacho kitiwapo majini hufanya vumbi (taka) lililomo kuanguka. **precipitately,** *adv.* kwa haraka, kwa harara. **precipitation,** *n.* haraka nyingi, harara; (*settlement*) kutuama, kuanguka chini (*e.g.* vumbi katika maji).

precipitous, *a.* taz. *precipice.*

précis, *n.* muhtasari, ufupisho wa maneno (ya hati, barua *&c.*).

precise, *a.* (*accurate*) sawasawa, halisi; (*definite, clear*) wazi, dhahiri; (*careful*) -a taratibu, -angalifu; (*of conduct &c.*) -a kushika desturi (kawaida) barabara. **precision, preciseness,** *n.* usawa, uwazi, utaratibu. **precisely,** *adv.* sawasawa, halisi, dhahiri; (*expressing agreement*) kabisa, ndivyo, naam.

preclude, *v.t.* zuia, pinga, komesha. **preclusion,** *n.* kuzuia *&c.* **preclusive,** *a.* -a kuzuia *&c.*, -zuivu.

precocious, *a.* -enye kupevuka upesi akili, -tundu, -enye akili za mtu mzima. **precociousness, precocity,** *n.* kuwa *precocious,* utundu.

preconceive, *v.t.* waza mbele. **preconception,** *n.* wazo la mbele.

preconcerted, *a.* -liotengenezwa mbele, -liofanyiwa shauri mbele.

precursor, *n.* mtangulizi, mjumbe. **precursory,** *a.* -a kutangulia.

predatory, *a.* -a kuteka, -a kunyang'anya; (*fierce*) -kali, katili; (*of animals*) -a mwitu, -a kuua na kula wengine.

predecease, *v.t.* -fa mbele, tangulia kufa. **predecessor,** *n.* mtangulizi, wa mbele, wa kwanza.

predestine, predestinate, *v.t.* azimu hali mbele, wekea (amuria) hali ya baadaye (peponi au jehanamu). **predestinarian,** *n.* asadikiye kwamba kila mtu tangu milele ameamriwa hali yake ya baadaye, peponi au jehanamu pasipo hiari. **predestination,** *n.* amri ya Mungu juu ya kila mtu na hali yake ya baadaye.

predetermine, *v.t.* azimu mbele, amuru mbele.

predial, *a.* -a mashamba.

predicament, *n.* mashaka, shida, hatari.

predicate, *v.t.* sema, nena; toa habari fulani juu ya kitu fulani. *To predicate whiteness of snow,* kusema theluji ni nyeupe. — *n.* (*in grammar*) neno lenye (maneno yenye) habari ya kitu fulani.

predict, *v.t.* toa habari mbele, tabiri, bashiri, agua, onya. **prediction,** *n.* ubashiri, uaguzi, maaguzi, maonyo.

predictive, *a.* -a kubashiri, -a kuagua, -a kuonya.

predilection, *n.* kupenda sana, upendeleo, shauku.

predispose, *v.t.* elekeza, kabilisha, ongoza, vuta. **predisposition,** *n.* kuelekea, maelekeo.

predominant, *a.* -enye kuzidi, -kubwa, -kuu, -ingi, -enye nguvu. **predominance,** *n.* kuwa na nguvu, kuzidi, kushinda, ukuu, wingi. **predominate,** *v.i.* pita, -wa na nguvu, -wa -ingi, zidi, shinda.

pre-eminent, *a.* -a kutangulia, -enye sifa (fahari, cheo, uzuri, manufaa *&c.*) zaidi, -a kuzidi, -a kupita. **pre-eminence,** *n.* kutangulia, kuwa na sifa (fahari, cheo, uzuri, manufaa *&c.*) zaidi, cheo kikubwa.

pre-emption, *n.* *Right of pre-emption,* haki ya kununua mbele au kwanza (kabla ya wengine).

preen, *v.t.* nyosha manyoya kwa mdomo (ndege); (*of person*) kinai, jitoshelea nafsi, takabari, jifahirisha.

pre-exist, *v.i.* -wako (mbele, kwanza, awali). **pre-existence,** *n.* kuwako mbele *&c.* **pre-existent,** *a.* -enye kuwako mbele *&c.*

preface, *n.* utangulizi, matangulizi, dibaji, maelezo ya mbele katika kitabu. **prefatory,** *a.* -a *preface.*

prefect, *n.* msimamizi.

prefer, *v.t.* penda zaidi, chagua mbele, stahabu, hitari, hiari; (*a charge*) leta; (*promote*) ongeza cheo. **preferable,** *a.* afadhali, zaidi, heri, -ema zaidi, bora. **preference,** *n.* upendeleo, kuchagua mbele, hiari, kutangulia, kutanguliza. **preferential,** *a.* -a kupendelea. **preferment,** *n.* kuzidishiwa cheo, nyongeza ya cheo, kupata kazi (daraja) bora.

prefigure, *v.t.* onya mbele kwa mfano, oleza; (*imagine beforehand*) wazia mbele.

prefix, *v.t.* weka (tia) mbele, tanguliza. — *n.* neno au jina *&c.* lililotiwa kutangulia neno au jina jingine; (*in grammar*) sehemu ya neno inayotiwa mwanzoni.

pregnant, *a.* -enye mimba, -enye himila, -zito; (*important*) -kubwa, -a maana, -a nguvu. *Pregnant with,* -enye, -a kujaa, -a kuleta. *Be pregnant,* -wa na mimba (himila), himili, -wa -zito. *This is a very pregnant word,* neno hili lachukua maana nyingi (mambo kadha wa kadha). **pregnancy,** *n.* mimba, uzito, himila. *During pregnancy,* wakati wa kuwa mja mzito, wakati wa kuwa na mimba.

prehensible, *a.* -enye nguvu ya kushika, -enye nguvu ya kukamata na kushikilia, -a kukamatia.

prehistoric, *a.* -a zamani za kale sana (zisizo na habari za hakika).

prejudge, *v.t.* kata maneno kabla ya kusikia kisa chake, hukumu bila kusikiliza. **prejudice,** *n.* kuchukia au kupendelea bila sababu yenye akili, kuonea mabaya au mema pasipo haki; (*injury*) hasara, madhara, dhuluma, udhalimu. — *v.t.* chukiza (pendeleza) kwa vibaya; vuta mtu kupenda au kuchukia; (*damage*) dhuru, hasiri, punguza. **prejudicial,** *a.* -a kudhuru, -a kuzuia, -a kuhasiri.

prelate, *n.* askofu. **prelacy,** *n.* uaskofu, jamii ya maaskofu.

preliminary, *a.* -a mwanzo, -a kutangulia, -a kufanya tayari. *Preliminary remarks,* matangulizi.

prelude, *n.* mwanzo (wa matendo, habari, muziki *&c.*) unaotangulia matendo *&c.* yenyewe hasa; dibaji, matangulizi. — *v.t.* ingiza, anzisha, tangulia, onya.

premature, *a.* -a kabla ya wakati wake, -a haraka, -epesi. **prematurely,** *adv.* upesi, kabla ya wakati wake.

premeditate, *v.t.* waza (azimu, kusudia, tengeneza, andaa) mbele.

premier, *n.* waziri mkuu wa serikali ya kiingereza. — *a.* -a kwanza, -kuu, -a cheo kilicho bora.

premiss, *n.* asili au chanzo cha

maneno katika kujadiliana, hoja. — *v.i.* sema kwanza, patana mbele (kwa neno fulani). **premisses,** *n.* nyumba na kiwanja chake; (*in argument*) matangulizi, matengeneo, hoja.

premium, *n.* (*fee*) malipo ya mbele, ada; (*bonus*) zawadi, ziada; (*advance in price*) faida. *Be at a premium,* zidi kuwa na thamani, zidi bei, ghalika. *Sell at a premium,* uza na kupata faida.

premonition, *n.* maonyo; hofu (ya kuwa jambo litatukia).

preoccupy, *v.t.* tangulia kushika (kukamata); (*engage before*) shughulisha. **preoccupation,** *n.* kutangulia kutwaa (kutwaliwa); (*being busy*) kushughulika.

prepaid, *a.* taz. *prepay.*

prepare, *v.t.* fanya (weka) tayari, andaa, zatiti; (*accustom, train, instruct*) zoeza, fundisha; (*construct*) fanya, fanyiza; (*cook*) pika; (*raw material, e.g. cotton, cloves &c.*) chambua, chamvua; (*prepare oneself*) jiweka tayari, jiandaa, jizoeza. *Prepare for,* andalia. **preparation,** *n.* kufanya (kuweka, kutengeneza) tayari, matengenezo, kuandaa; (*mixture*) changanyiko; (*medicine*) dawa. *Make preparations for,* andalia. **preparative, preparatory,** *a.* -a küweka (kufanya) tayari, -a kwanza, -a kutangulia.

prepay, *v.t.* (*p.t. and pf.t.* **prepaid**) lipa mbele, lipia ada mbele. **prepaid,** *a.* -liokwisha lipiwa ada.

prepense, *a.* -liokusudiwa mbele.

preponderate, *v.i.* zidi, -wa na nguvu (wingi) zaidi. **preponderance,** *n.* kuwa *preponderant.* **preponderant,** *a.* -a kuzidi, -kubwa, -ingi.

preposition, *n.* (*in grammar*) neno la kutiwa kutangulia *noun* lionyeshalo uhusiano uliopo kati ya kiumbe kimoja (tendo moja) na kiumbe kingine (tendo jingine) *e.g.* chini ya, katika, kwa, kabla ya *&c.*

prepossess *v.t.* pendeza, pendeleza, vuta, tamanisha. **prepossessing,** *a.* -zuri, -a kuvuta, -a kutamanisha.

prepossession, *n,* shauku, upendeleo.

preposterous, *a.* si -enye akili, -a upuzi, -siosadikika.

prepuce, *n.* ngovi (govi) ya uume, zunga.

prerequisite, *n.* kanuni, sharti. *It is a prerequisite,* sharti hii kwanza.

prerogative, *n.* haki, mamlaka au milki ya mtu mmoja peke yake, au ya watu wenye daraja au kazi moja; haki ya desturi, haki ya asili, sharti. *Be the prerogative of,* -wa haki ya, husu.

presage, *v.t.* onya mbele, agua, bashiri mambo yatakayokuja. — *n.* dalili, onyo (la mambo yatakayokuja), maaguzi, uaguzi, ndege (mbaya au njema).

presbyter, *n.* mzee wa Kanisa, kasisi, padre. **presbyterian,** -enye kusadiki ya kuwa makasisi watosha katika Kanisa wala hakuna haja ya maaskofu. — *n.* mtu asadikiye makasisi tu watosha katika Kanisa.

presbytery, *n.* jamii ya wazee wa Kanisa, jamii ya makasisi.

prescience, *n.* kuona mbele (mambo yatakayokuja) busara. **prescient,** *a.* -enye *prescience.*

prescribe, *v. t.* amuru, agiza.

prescription, *n.* amri za daktari; dawa iliyoamriwa; (*if forbidding something*) mwiko, mzio; (*usage*) desturi, mazoea, matumizi ya zamani.

prescriptive, *a.* -a desturi tangu zamani.

present, (1) *a.* (*place*) karibu, mbele, -liopo, hapa, pale; (*time*) -a sasa, siku hizi, -a wakati huu; (*at hand*) -a mara moja, tayari. *Be present,* -wapo. *He is present,* yupo hapa, yupo. *At present, for the present,* sasa, wakati huu. — *n.* wakati uliopo, wakati wa sasa, siku hizi.

presence, *n.* kuwapo, kuwa karibu, eneo, pa mbele, machoni; (*appearance*) sura, umbo. *In the presence of,* mbele ya, hadhara ya, machoni pa, panapo. *Presence of mind,* welekevu wa akili, busara, macho. **presence-chamber,** *n.* baraza, sebule. **presently,** *adv.* halafu, baadaye, bado.

present, (2) *a. and n.* (taz. *gift*) zawadi, bakshishi, adia, tuzo, tunu, majazo, kipaji, karama, wapo, hiba; (*customary*) ada, ufito, kilemba; (*reward*) tuzo; (*gratuity*) bakshishi; (*from God*) thawabu, upaji, baraka; (*of congratulation*) pukuso. *Give away as a present, Make a present of* toa bure, tunukia.—*v.t.* (*give*) -pa, toa, karimia, tunukia, jalia, tuza; (*put forward*) toa mbele, weka mbele (wazi), onyesha; (*arms*) elekeza, shika mbele. *Present by way of congratulation,* pukusa. **presentable,** *a.* (*pleasing*) -a kupendeza, -zuri, -a kufaa; (*of persons*) -enye malezi mazuri, -a adabu; (*fit to be presented*) -a kufaa kwa zawadi (tuzo &c.), -a kuweza kutolewa (kutoleka). **presentation,** *n.*, **presentment,** kupa, kutoa, kuweka mbele; (*gift*) zawadi &c. taz. *present.*

presentiment, *n.* moyo wa kuona mbele; (*of fear*) hofu, woga; (*of hope*) taraja.

presently, *adv.* taz. *present* (1).

presentment, *n.* taz. *present* (2).

preserve, *v.t.* linda, hifadhi, okoa, ponya, afu, afua, nusuru; (*keep*) weka, shika; (*season*) koleza, unga (tia sukari, chumvi &c. kitu kisioze). — *n.* mraba, maandazi ya matunda; (*for game &c.*) mahali pa kuweka na kulinda salama wanyama, ndege, samaki, vyo vyote vya kufuga na kuwinda. **preservation,** *n.* kulinda, ulinzi, kuhifadhi, wokovu, kupona, afua, uzima, salama. **preservative,** *a.* -a kulinda, -a kuponya. — *n.* dawa ya kuzuia kitu kisioze (*e.g.* ngozi ya mnyama, chakula &c.). **preserver,** *n.* mlinzi, mhifadhi, mwokozi.

preside, *v.i.* -wa mkuu, tawala, ongoza. **presidency,** *n.* kazi, nyumba, cheo, mamlaka ya *president.* **president,** *n.* mkuu, msimamizi (wa kumpuni, wa chama, wa serikali isiyo na mfalme &c.). **presidential,** *a.* -a *president.*

press, *v.t.* gandamiza, shindika, shindilia, kaza, lemeza; (*with hand, fingers*) kamua, finya, minya, bonyeza; (*as in massage*) kanda; (*follow up closely, hurry*) songa, songanisha; (*as in a vice, of a shoe &c.*) bana; (*urge*) omba sana, sihi, bidi, bidisha, shurutisha, shawishi, harakisha, sukumiza, nyenya; (*squeeze juice, oil &c. out of*) shindika; (*push, a knob &c.*) bonyeza, sukuma; (*embrace*) kumbatia, sogeza; (*with an iron, iron*) piga pasi; (*remove creases*) nyosha; (*impend*) -wa karibu, lemea; (*force*) tumisha kwa nguvu; (*with argument*) hoji, shurutisha, chagiza; (*dun*) chagiza; (*oppress, weigh upon*) lemea; — *v.i.* gandamiza, shindilia. — *n.* shinikizo, kinu; (*throng*) masongano, ghasia ya watu, msukosuko, zahama, watu wakisongana; (*hurry*) haraka, shida, taabu; (*clothes press*) kabati ya kuwekea nguo; (*machine*) mtambo wa kubania (wa kugandamizia, wa kushindikia, wa kushindilia); (*for printing*) mtambo wa kupigia chapa; (*printing*) kazi ya kupiga chapa na kutoa vitabu; (*printing establishment*) kiwanda cha kupigia chapa; (*news-writers, newspapers*) jamii ya watu wenye kazi ya kutangaza habari za mambo ya kila siku katika magazeti, jamii ya magazeti. **press-gang,** *n.* askari waliokamata watu kwa amri na kazi ya serikali.

pressing, *n.* kusonga, kuomba &c. taz. *press, v.* — *a.* -a haraka, -a kulemea, -a nguvu, -a sharti, muhimu. **pressure,** *n.* shinikizo, msongo, uzito, mkazo, mbano, mshurutisho; (*trouble*) shida, taabu, shughuli nyingi. *Use moral pressure,* bidisha, vuta, shawishi. *He did it under pressure,* alifanya kwa kushurutishwa.

prestige, *n.* sifa (kwa ajili ya matendo, maarifa, tabia njema &c. inayojulikana), heshima, fahari, jina.

presume, *v.i.* (*dare*) thubutu, fanya pasipo ruhusa (pasipo haki), fidhulika; — *v.t.* (*suppose*) dhania mbele, dhania pasipo kujua hakika, ona, waza. **presumable,** *a.* -lio yamkini, -liowezekana. **presuming,** *a.* -juvi, -fidhuli, -safihi, -a kiburi, -a kujitanguliza, -shupavu. **presumption,** *n.* kiburi, ufidhuli, usafihi, majivuno, ujuvi, ukavu wa macho; (*likelihood*) sababu, hoja; (*probability*) neno lililo yamkini au kuwezekana, lisilo hakika. **presumptive,** *a.* -a kutazamiwa, -a kusadikiwa, -a kutarajiwa. **presumptuous,** *a.* -a kiburi, -fidhuli, -shupavu, -juvi, -a kujasiri mno, -kavu wa macho.

presuppose, *v.t.* dhania kabla ya kujua, kubali pasipo uthibitisho; (*imply*) -wa kwa sababu ya (neno fulani lililotangulia). **presupposition,** *n.* jambo au neno lisilothibitika, ladhaniwa tu kuwa ndivyo, la ruhusa tu si la hakika; (*reason*) sababu, mwanzo, asili.

pretence, *n.* taz. *pretend.*

pretend, *v.i.* jifanya, sema kwa uwongo, fanya hila, jisingizia, fanya kwa jinsi ya kusadikisha watu yasivyo. *Pretend to,* taka, tamani, jidaia. **pretence,** *n.* (*falsehood*) uwongo, hila, ujanja; (*pretext*) maneno, udhuru, sababu, kisingizio. **pretender,** *n.* mdai, mwenye kudai. **pretension,** *n.* kutaka makuu, kujidai, kiburi; (*pretext*) maneno ya hila, udhuru, kisingizio; (*fiction*) uwongo; (*claim*) madai. **pretentious,** *a.* -a fahari, -a kujidai makuu, -a kujivuna, -kuu.

preterite, *n.* namna ya *verb* yenye habari za wakati uliopita. — *a.* -enye habari za wakati uliopita.

preternatural, *a.* -sio kawaida ya vitu vyote, -sio desturi, -a mwujiza, -geni, -a ajabu, -a kutisha.

pretext, *n.* sababu (udhuru, maneno, hoja), hasa isiyo ya kweli ya kuficha ya kweli.

pretty, *a.* -zuri (kwa kutazama), nakawa, -enye sura nzuri, -a kupendeza; (*large &c.*) -kubwa, -ingi. — *adv.* kadiri, sana kidogo. *Pretty hot,* moto mwingi kidogo, jua kali. *I am pretty well,* sijambo kidogo. **prettily,** *adv.* vizuri. **prettiness,** *n.* sura nzuri, uzuri.

prevail, *v.i.* shinda, weza, -wa na nguvu; (*be prevalent &c.*) chaga, enea, -wa -ingi, -wa pote, -wa -kubwa, -wa sikuzote, -wa mazoea (desturi, kawaida). *Prevail upon,* shawishi, vuta, shinda, shurutisha. **prevailing,** *a.* -a kushinda *&c.* -a kawaida, -a desturi, -a sikuzote, -a watu wengi. *The prevailing wind,* upepo wa kawaida. *The prevailing sentiment,* maono ya watu wengi, watu wengi waonavyo. *The prevailing fashions,* mtindo wa sasa. **prevalence,** *n.* maeneo, mazoea; (*predominance*) kushinda *&c.*, kuchaga. **prevalent,** *a.* -a kuenea, -wa pote (-ingi, -kubwa, wakati wote), -a kuchaga. *Fever is prevalent,* homa imechaga *&c.*

prevaricate, *v.i.* sema uwongo, ongopa, toa maneno ya ujanja, diradira, ganzaganza, babaika. **prevarication,** *n.* uwongo, ujanja. **prevaricator,** *n.* mwongo, mjanja, kauleni, kauli mbili.

prevent, *v.t.* zuia, pinga, pinza, kinza, kinga, komesha, fingiza. **preventative,** *a.* -a kuzuia, -a kukinga. — *n.* kitu kinachozuia, kinga. **prevention,** *n.* kuzuia, zuio, pinzani. **preventive,** *a.* -a kuzuia, -a kulinda, -a kukinga, -a hadhari. — *n.* kinga, zuio, kizuizi, kitu kinachozuia (ugonjwa, uovu *&c.*).

previous, *a.* -a kwanza, -liotangulia, -a zamani. *Previous to,* kabla ya, kutangulia. — *adv.* kabla.

prevision, *n.* kuona mbele, busara.

prey, *n.* mawindo, mateka, nyara. *Beast of prey,* nyama mbuai, mnyama mkali. *Be the prey of,* shikwa na, patikana na, shindwa na. — *v.i.* *Prey on,* -la, teka, haribu; (*harass*) lemea, huzunisha.

price, *n.* bei, thamani, kima, saari;

(*reward*) ujira, ijara, tuzo; (*return*) faida, uchumi. *At the price of,* kwa ajili ya, kwa kutoa. *At any price,* kwa vyo vyote. — *v.t.* tia bei, kadirisha. *Priceless, a.* -a thamani nyingi, bora sana, -sionunulika kwa fedha. **price-list,** *n.* orodha ya vitu (bidhaa) na bei zake.

prick, *v.t.* choma, washa; (*make holes for seeds*) piga makoongo; (*plant out young plants*) atika, pandikiza; (*the ears*) toga masikio; — *v.i.* choma; (*of ears*) simama. — *n.* mwiba; (*wound*) mchomo. **pricker,** *n.* chombo cha kutobolea. **prickle,** *n.* mwiba. — *v.i.* choma-choma, washa. **prickly,** *a.* -enye miiba. **prickly-heat,** *n.* vipele vya harara. **prickly-pear,** *n.* (*plant*) mpungate.

pride, *n.* kiburi, majivuno, kinaya, kimene, usodawi; (*display*) fahari, makuu; (*subject of boast*) kitu cha kujivunia, kitu cha kusifiwa sana, tunu, moyo, kipenzi; (*best sort*) kipeo. *Feel pride at* (*in*) ona fahari kwa ajili ya. *Pride of youth,* kuji-jetea ujana. *Pride of lions* (*peacocks*), kundi la simba (tausi). *Pride oneself on,* dai, jivunia.

priest, *n.* (*heathen*) kahini; (*Jewish*) kuhani; (*Christian*) kasisi, padre. **priestcraft,** *n.* ujanja wa makahini au makasisi. **priesthood,** *n.* ukuhani, ukasisi, upadre; jamii ya makuhani (ya makasisi). **priestly,** *a.* -a *priest.* **priest-ridden,** *a.* -a kuonewa (kutawaliwa) na *priest.*

prig, *n.* ajivunaye kwa elimu au wema, mjuvi, mkinaifu. *Be a prig, Be priggish,* jijuvisha, jikinai, jivunia elimu au wema. **priggish,** *a.* -juvi, -enye kujivunia elimu au wema.

prim, *a.* taratibu, -zuri, kiasi, baridi, -a makini. *She is prim,* hataki upuzi, yu baridi, ana makini. **primness,** *n.* makini, uzuri, utaratibu; (*affectedness*) haya, kiburi, ubaridi.

prime, *n.* mwanzo, uzuri, usitawi, uzima, ukamilifu, upeo; (*morning prayers*) sala za alfajiri. — *a.* -a kwanza, -zuri sana, bora; (*first in order*) -kuu. — *v.t.* tia baruti (kifani mwa bunduki); (*teach*) somesha mafundisho ya kwanza, erevusha, julisha mambo; (*machinery*) tia maji (mafuta, *petrol*) kidogo. **primacy,** *n.* kazi na heshima ya askofu mkuu. **primal,** *a.* -a kwanza, -a asili (*important*) -kuu. **primary,** *a.* -a asili, -a kwanza; (*important*) -kubwa, -kuu, -a maana, -a nguvu; (*preparatory*) -a kwanza. **primate,** *n.* askofu mkuu. **prime minister,** *n.* waziri mkuu. **primer,** *n.* kitabu cha masomo ya kwanza. **primeval,** *a.* -a zamani za kwanza, -a zamani sana, -a kale. **priming,** *n.* baruti ya kifani; (*of engine*) maji yakichanganyika na mvuke ndani ya *steam-engine*; (*of paint*) mpako wa kwanza wa rangi. **primitive,** *a.* -a zamani za kwanza, -a kale. **primogenitor,** *n.* baba. **primogeniture,** *n.* kuzaliwa wa kwanza, kurithi mtoto aliyezaliwa kwanza. **primordial,** *a.* -a kwanza.

primness, *n.* taz. *prim.*

primogenitor, *n.*, **primogeniture,** *n.*, **primordial,** *a.* taz. *prime.*

primrose, *n.* ua dogo la kondeni Ulaya; (*colour*) rangi ya manjano.

prince, *n.* mfalme au mtawala (asiye na haki ya kuitwa *king*); (*king's son*) mwana (wa kiume) wa mfalme. **princedom,** *n.* hali au heshima ya *prince.* **princely,** *a.* -a *prince,* -a kustahili *prince,* -zuri, -a anasa, -a fahari, -karimu, -paji &c. **princess,** *n.* binti mfalme, mwana (wa kike) wa mfalme. **principal,** *n.* mkuu, msimamizi, bwana mkubwa; (*money*) rasilmali, akiba, asili ya mali. — *a.* -kubwa, -kuu, -a maana, -a kwanza, -a nguvu. **principality,** *n.* mamlaka ya *prince.* **principalities,** *n. pl.* daraja mojawapo ya malaika. **principally,** *adv.* zaidi, hasa, aghalabu, kwa kawaida (desturi). **principle,** *n.* jambo la asili, neno la awali, chanzo, chimbuko; (*rational rule*) mafundisho, madhehebu, kawaida, kanuni; (*character*) tabia, moyo, nia, dhati; (*good character*) tabia nzuri, utu mwema; (*reason*) sababu, hoja, kisa. *High principle,* moyo mzuri, tabia nzuri, mwenendo mzuri. *He acts on principle,* ashika kawaida, afuasa mafundisho, hatendi ovyo, hana haraka. *These are his principles,* hayo ndiyo mashauri (mawazo, kanuni &c.) ambayo kwayo huongoza maisha yake (mwenendo wake).

print, *v.t.* piga chapa; (*mark*) tia kama alama; (*impress*) ingiza moyoni, tia moyoni. — *n.* (*mark*) chapa; (*picture*) picha, sanamu, taswira; (*calico*) nguo kama amerikani ya rangirangi; (*printed works*) maneno yaliyopigwa chapa; (*of foot*) wayo; (*of finger, hand &c.*) alama ya kidole, mkono &c. **printed,** *a.* -a chapa, -liopigwa chapa. **printer,** *n.* mpiga chapa (vitabu &c.). **printing,** *n.* kupiga chapa (vitabu &c.); ufundi wa kupiga chapa.

prior, *a.* -a kwanza, -liotangulia. — *n.* mkuu wa nyumba ya *monks.* **priority,** *n.* kuwa kabla, ukuu, hali (tabia) ya kuwa kwanza (kubwa, kuu). **priory,** *n.* nyumba ya *prior.*

prism, *n.* kipande cha kioo chenye pande tatu cha kuonyesha rangi za nuru mbalimbali (cha kugeuzia nuru nyeupe iwe rangi nyingi mbalimbali). **prismatic,** *a.* (*colours*) rangi za nuru zilizooneka kwa *prism,* -a rangi mbalimbali, -enye *prism.*

prison, *n.* kifungo, gereza, mahabusi. **prisoner,** *n.* mfungwa, mahabusi.

pristine, *a.* -a zamani za kale, -a asili.

private, *a.* -a mwenyewe peke yake; (*retired, secluded*) -a faragha, -a upweke; (*unemployed*) pasipo kazi, pasipo nguvu, peke yake; (*unofficial*) si wa serikali; (*confidential*) -a siri. *Private life,* nyumbani. *Private property,* mali ya mwenyewe, mali ya watu. *Private means,* utajiri, mali. *This is my private opinion,* naona mimi. *A private person,* mtu tu (si mkubwa, si wa serikali). *Private prayer,* sala ya siri, sala ya mtu peke yake. *In private,* faraghani, peke yake, kwa siri. *A private road,* njia (barabara) ya mwenyewe. — *n.* (*soldier*) askari. *Privates,* mbeleni. **privacy,** *n.* faragha, pasipo watu, kujitenga, mahali pa siri, upweke, siri, kuficha, maficho. **privateer,** *n.* merikebu yenye ruhusa kufanya vita peke yake. **privily,** *adv.* kwa siri, kwa maficho. **privity,** *n.* siri, maarifa ya siri, kuwa shauri moja kwa siri. **privy,** *a.* -a mtu mmoja peke yake; (*secret*) -a siri; (*retired*) -a faragha. *Be privy to,* jua kwa siri, shiriki siri. *Privy council,* baraza ya mfalme mwenyewe. *Privy councillor,* mtu wa *privy council. Privy purse,* mali ya mfalme. *Privy seal,* muhuri ya mfalme. — *n.* choo.

privation, *n.* upungufu, ukosefu kutwaliwa; (*poverty, want*) ukosefu, uhitaji, utaiti, shida, taabu, dhiki.

privative, *a.* -a kunyima, -a kutwalia, -a kukana.

privilege, *n.* (*special*) haki, mapendeleo, nafuu, ruhusa, faida, heshima, uwezo (wa mtu mmoja peke yake); (*general*) sharti. *Be the privilege of,* husu. **privileged,** *a.* -enye haki (mapendeleo, nafuu, ruhusa &c.) ya mtu peke yake; (*confidential*) -a siri.

privily, *adv.*, **privity,** *n.*, **privy,** *a.* *and n.* taz. *private.*

prize, (1) *n.* (*spoil*) mateka, nyara. — *v.t.* fungua kwa mtaimbo (msaha).

prize, (2) *n.* tuzo, tuza, zawadi; (*precious thing*) tunu, kitu cha thamani, azizi, dafina; — *v.t.* penda sana, pendelea, tunza sana, dhani kuwa ya thamani nyingi, tunuka, thamini. **prize-fight,** *n.* shindano la ngumi kwa tuzo. **prize-fighter,** *n.* mshindaji kwa ngumi. **prize-money,** *n.* fedha ya *prize,* fedha ya kushindaniwa, tuzo.

probable, *a.* -lioelekea (kutokea, kuwa, kuwa kweli), yamkini. *It is probable,* labda, huenda, naona, inaelekea. *The probable result will be . . .*, huelekea ya kuwa mwisho utakuwa . . . **probability**, *n.* hali ya kuwa *probable*. *In all probability*, huelekea, naona haina budi, yamkini. **probably**, *adv.* huelekea, huenda, labda, yamkini, inshallah.

probate, *n.* mathibitisho ya wosia au kurithi; nakili ya wosia uliothibitishwa. **probation**, *n.* majaribu; (*period*) wakati mtu anapojaribiwa kazi. **probationer**, *n.* mtu anayejaribiwa kama atafaa kwa kazi fulani, mwanafunzi.

probe, *n.* sindano kubwa butu ya kupima kishimo cha kidonda *&c.* ya kutafutia risasi (aliyopigwa mtu). — *v.t.* pima (tafuta) kwa *probe;* (*examine*) hoji, chungua, tazamia.

probity, *n.* uaminifu, unyofu, adili, wema.

problem, *n.* swali, ulizo, hoja; (*difficult matter*) mashaka, fumbo, neno gumu, matatizo; (*riddle*) kitendawili. **problematic**, *a.* -a shaka, si hakika, ajabu.

proboscis, *n.* (*of insects*) mdomo; (*of elephant*) mkonga, mkono, mwiro.

proceed, *v.i.* (*advance*) endelea mbele, enda, shika njia; (*come out*) toka; (*act*) fanya tena (zaidi). *He proceeded to say*, tena akasema. *Proceed against*, shtaki, dai, peleka sheriani. **procedure**, *n.* (*formal*) utaratibu, kawaida; (*action*) jinsi ya kutenda, kazi; (*progress*) maendeleo, mwenendo. **proceeding**, *n.* jambo, mambo, tendo. *Take proceedings against*, shtaki, dai sheriani. **proceeds**, *n.* pato, faida, uchumi, halasa. **process**, *n.* (*method*) njia, jinsi, maana; (*series*) mafuatano ya mambo; (*operation*) kutenda, tendo, kufanya, kufanyika, kazi yenyewe. *In process of time*, baada ya siku, hatima. *Legal process*, daawa, mashtaka, hukumu. **procession**, *n.* mafuatano, mwendo wa taratibu, andamo, mwandamano, watu wakiandamana. **processional**, *a.* -a *procession*, -a mwandamano.

proclaim, *v.t.* tangaza, piga mbiu ya, eneza, toa wazi, bainisha. **proclamation**, *n.* tangazo, ilani, mbiu, amri wazi, kunena wazi, taarifa.

proclivity, *n.* maelekeo; (*aptitude*) welekevu. *He has a proclivity to steal*, tabia yake ni kuiba.

proconsul, *n.* balozi.

procrastinate, *v.i.* ahiri, weka, kawia, legea, chelewa, sitasita. **procrastination**, *n.* usiri, kukawia, mazoea ya kuahirisha mpaka kesho.

procreate, *v.t.* zaa. **procreation**, *n.* kuzaa, uzazi. **procreative**, *a.* -a kuzaa,- zazi.

proctor, *n.* wakili.

procumbent, *a.* -a kulala kifudifudi (kitumbo); -a kutambaa chini.

procure, *v.t.* pata, patia, fanya, fanyiza, tengeneza, -wa sababu ya, leta, nunua. **procurable**, *a.* -a kupatikana. **procurator**, *n.* wakili. **procurer**, *n.* wakili; (*pander*) kawadi. **procuress**, *n.* kawadi wa kike.

prod, *v.t.* choma, chokoa, piga kikumbo, dukua, tia mdukuo; (*rouse &c.*) amsha, chochea. — *n.* kikumbo, mdukuo, mchomo.

prodigal, *a.* -potevu wa mali, -ponda mali, -fujaji, -a kutapanya mali, -badhiri, -badhirifu. **prodigality**, *n.* upotevu wa mali, ufujaji, ubadhirifu, kutapanya mali, budhara.

prodigy, *n.* mwujiza, ajabu, kioja. **prodigious**, *a.* -kubwa, -ingi mno, ajabu, ajabu mno.

produce, *v.t.* toa, zaa; (*make*) fanya, fanyiza (*cause*) -wa sababu ya, leta; (*compose*) tunga, buni; (*lengthen*) ongeza urefu. — *n.* zao, mazao, mavuno, matunda; (*profit*) mapato, faida, chumo. **producer**, *n.* mfanyizaji, mtenda kazi. **producible**, *a.* -a kuweza kuletwa, -a kufanyika, -a kufanyiziwa, -liopatikana. **product**, *n. produce, n.*; mazao, mavuno *&c.*; (*in arithm.*) jumla (katika kuzidisha); (*result, outcome*) matokeo. **production**, *n.* kutoa, kufanyiza; (*lenghthening*) kuongeza urefu; (*product*) kazi, mazao. **productive,** *a.* -a kuzaa, -zazi, -a kutoa, -enye kutoa, -ingi, hodari kwa kutoa (kufanyiza, kuzaa).

proem, *n.* mwanzo wa maneno, dibaji, utangulizi.

profanation, *n.* taz. *profane.*

profane, *a.* -a ulimwengu (si -a dini) -a ukafiri; (*polluted*) -najisi, -baya. **profanation,** *n.* kuharibu (kutweza, kutumia vibaya) kitu kitakatifu, unajisi, ukufuru. **profaneness, profanity,** *n.* ukufuru, unajisi, ubaya (wa kumchukiza Mungu).

profess, *v.t.* (*declare*) toa habari wazi ya, tangaza; (*own, acknowledge*) shuhudia, ungama, kiri; (*claim for oneself*) jifanya, jipa sifa ya, jisifu (jidai) kuwa na, jitaja fundi wa; (*practice*) fanya kazi ya (udaktari, uwakili, uanasheria &c.). **professed,** *a.* wazi, bayana, -a kujulika. **profession,** *n.* kunena wazi, ungamo, kukiri, ushuhuda; (*promise*) ahadi; (*occupation*) kazi, uchumi, shughuli; (*class*) jamii ya watu wenye kazi moja, ufundi. **professional,** *a.* -a fundi wa kazi, -a kazi ya fundi, -a mwalimu; (*in sport*) -a kucheza kwa mshahara. — *n.* afanyaye kazi fulani kwa mshahara (si kwa kujizungumza tu). **professor,** *n.* mwalimu (hasa mwalimu mkuu katika *University*), fundi, ajifanyaye fundi. **professorial,** *a.* -a *professor.*

proffer, *v.t.* toa, -pa, taka kutoa.

proficiency, *n.* taz. *proficient.*

proficient, *a.* hodari, -enye maarifa, -stadi, -elekevu, -bingwa. **proficiency,** *n.* ustadi, welekevu, uhodari, ubingwa; (*progress*) maendeleo.

profile, *n.* sura ya (umbo la) mtu au kitu kwa upande (si kwa mbele yake).

profit, *n.* faida, uchumi, halasa, chumo, mapato, kufaliwa, mafaa, msaada. — *v.t.* toa faida, saidia, faa, falia; (*derive advantage &c.*) faidi, pata faida, saidiwa, nufaika. **profitable,** *a.* -a kufaa, -a kuleta faida, -a kusaidia, -enye msaada. **profitless,** *a.* -sioleta faida, -a bure, -siofaa, -tupu.

profligacy, *n.* taz. *profligate.*

profligate, *a.* -potovu, -fisadi, -fasiki, -asherati, -zinifu. — *n.* mpotovu, mfisadi, mfasiki, mwasherati, mzinzi. **profligacy,** *n.* upotovu, ufisadi, ufasiki, uasherati, uzinzi, uzinifu.

profound, *a.* (*deep*) -a kwenda chini sana; (*significant*) -a maana sana; (*clever*) -a akili nyingi; (*great, much*) -kubwa, -ingi; (*enigmatic*) -a siri, -a fumbo. **profoundly,** *adv.* sana, kwa ndani, kwa bidii, kwa akili. **profoundness, profundity,** *n.* kwenda chini, kwenda ndani; (*of feeling*) uzito.

profuse, *a.* -ingi sana, tele; (*liberal*) -karimu, -paji, -enye kutoa tele. **profusely,** *adv.* kwa wingi, chapa. **profuseness, profusion,** *n.* wingi, neema; (*liberality*) ukarimu, upaji.

progenitor, *n.* mzazi, baba. **progeny,** *n.* mzao, mtoto, mwana, wazao, watoto, wana.

prognathous, *a.* -enye taya zinazotokeza mbele.

prognosis, *n.* ubashiri, utabiri, onyo la mbele, uaguzi; (*medical*) kisio la maendeleo ya ugonjwa.

prognostic, *n.* ishara, dalili (ya mambo yatakuwaje baadaye), onyo.

prognosticate, *v.t.* tabiri, bashiri, onya mbele, agua. **prognostication,** *n.* kuonya mbele, maaguzi.

prognosticator, *n.* mwenye kuonya mbele, mwaguzi, piga bao (falaki, ramli).

programme, *n.* orodha ya mambo yaliyokusudiwa kutendwa (ya michezo iliyokusudiwa kuchezwa, ya nyimbo zilizokusudiwa kuimbwa &c.), utaratibu, azimio.

progress, *n.* maendeleo, mwendo, kuendelea mbele, ubele; (*journey*) safari ya mfalme au mtu mkubwa. — *v.i.* endelea mbele, shika njia, fanikiwa. **progression,** *n.* kuendelea mbele, maendeleo. **progressive,** *a.* -a kuendelea mbele, -a moja kwa moja, -a kidogo kidogo. **progressively,** *adv.* kwa kuendelea, kidogo kidogo, moja kwa moja.

prohibit, *v.t.* kataza, gombeza, zuia, piga marufuku, rufuku. **prohibition,** *n.* makatazo, amri ya kugombeza, rufuka. **prohibitive,** *a.* -a kukataza &c.; (*of price, changes &c.*) ghali (ingi, -kubwa) hata kuzuia -sinunuliwe (-situmiwe). **prohibitory,** *a.* -a kukataza, -a kuzuia, -zuifu.

project, *n.* shauri, nia, kusudi, azimio, mradi. — *v.t.* tupa mbele, vurumisha; (*design*) azimu, kusudia, fanya shauri la, toa; (*sketch*) andika picha (sanamu) ya; — *v.i.* tokeza, fanya mdomo. **projectile,** *n.* kitu kilichotupwa, *e.g.* risasi ya bunduki au mzinga, mshale &c. — *a.* -a kutupa mbele -a kuvurumisha, -a kurusha. **projection,** *n.* kutupa, kuvurumisha; (*thing projecting*) kitu kitokezacho, mdomo, nundu, ushi; (*design*) kufanya shauri; (*drawing*) sanamu, picha, ramani. **projector,** *n.* mtoa shauri, mtu wa mashauri mengi; (*of light*) kitu ndani ya taa kinachotupa nuru mbele; (*of picture*) chombo kinachotupa picha (sanamu) mbele katika nguo, *e.g.* katika *cinema.*

proletariat, *n.* watu (wa vivi hivi, wafanyi kazi).

prolific, *a.* -a kuzaa sana, -zazi sana; (*active*) -a kufanya mengi.

prolix, *a.* -a maneno mengi, -a kuchosha, baridi.

prologue, *n.* maneno ya mbele, mwanzo wa maneno, matangulizi.

prolong, *v.t.* ongeza urefu, zidisha, dumisha, fuliza. **prolongation,** *n.* kuzidisha urefu, urefu wa kuzidi, mazidio, nyongeza.

promenade, *n.* matembezi, mahali pa kutembelea. — *v.i.* tembeatembea.

prominence, *n.* taz. *prominent.*

prominent, *a.* -a kutokeza, -a kuonekana wazi; (*of person*) -a kujulikana, bayana, mashuhuri, maarufu. **prominence,** *n.* kitu kitokezacho kama mdomo, pua, nundu &c.; (*renown*) kujulikana, umashuhuri, umaarufu, ukubwa, sifa. **prominently,** *adv* wazi, dhahiri, mbele ya wote.

promiscuous, *a.* liochangamana, -sio na taratibu, vivi hivi, -a fujofujo, -a shelabela, -ovyo, -a namna nyingi. **promiscuously,** *adv.* ovyo, kifujo, -ote pamoja, shelabela.

promise, *n.* ahadi, kiaga; (*with reference to a particular time or date*) miadi; (*mutual*) agano, maagano; (*good prospect*) (jambo litialo) tumaini, taraja, jambo la kutumainiwa. *Keep a promise,* fikiliza (timiza, tekeleza) ahadi. *Break a promise,* vunja ahadi. *Make a mutual promise,* agana. *Make a promise,* ahidi, toa ahadi; (*with reference to a particular time or date*) weka miadi. —*v.t. and i.* ahidi, toa ahadi; (*give prospect of*) tia tumaini, elekea mema. **promising,** *a.* -a kutumainiwa, -a kutaka mema, -a tabia njema, -a kuelekea mema. **promissory,** *a.* -a ahadi, -enye ahadi. *Promissory note,* hawala.

promontory, *n.* rasi.

promote, *v.t.* anzisha, endeleza, fanyiza, saidia, ongeza; (*arouse*) amsha, chochea; (*raise in rank*) -pa daraja, ongeza cheo, fanya -kubwa. **promoter,** *n.* mfanyizaji, mchocheaji. **promotion,** *n.* kupata daraja (cheo) kuzidishiwa heshima, nyongeza ya daraja (cheo); (*setting forward &c.*) kuanzisha &c.

prompt, *a.* -epesi, -tendaji, tayari, hodari, -a wakati ule ule unaopasa. — *v.t.* ongoza, sukuma, -pa moyo, tia bidii; (*in reading &c.*) somesha. **prompting,** *n.* maongozi, shauri. **promptitude, promptness,** *n.* wepesi, utendaji &c. **promptly,** *adv.* mara, papo hapo, kwa wakati hasa unaopasa, bila kusita, bila kukawia.

promulgate, *v.t.* toa wazi, tangaza, hubiri, eneza, bainisha. **promulgation,** *n.* kutoa wazi &c.

prone, *a.* fudifudi, kitumbo, tumboni, (*prone to*) -a kutaka, -a kuelekea, -a kuzoelea, -zoevu wa. **proneness,** *n.*

kuelekea, maelekeo, kupenda, kuzoea.

prong, *n.* (*fork*) uma, kiuma; (*point*) chembe, ncha; (*of a fork, pitch-fork*) jino. **pronged,** *a.* -enye meno (ncha, panda).

pronoun, *n.* neno linalotumika mahali pa *noun*. **pronominal,** *a.* -a *pronoun*.

pronounce, *v.t.* tamka; (*declare*) nena wazi, tangaza. **pronounced,** *a.* wazi, thabiti, sana. **pronouncement,** *n.* kutamka, tangazo, maelezo. **pronunciation,** *n.* matamko, usemi, lafudhi.

proof, *n.* (*evidence*) ushahidi, ushuhuda, mathibitisho, neno la kuthibitisha, sababu, hakika, yakini; (*trial*) jaribu; (*print*) nakala ya kitabu *&c.* ya kujaribia, yaani kusahihishwa makosa. — *a.* hodari, thabiti, -sioshindika, imara; (*impenetrable*) -siopenyeka; (*of spirits*) -enye kiasi fulani cha *alcohol*, *e.g.* *Spirits 10 per cent. under proof*, ulevi wenye *alcohol* inayopungua mia kwa kumi kiasi chote kinachoruhusiwa na serikali. *Put to the proof*, jaribia, hakikisha.

prop, *n.* mhimili, mwimo, nguzo, tegemeo, egemeo, mwega, makwa; (*of ship &c.*) gadi, shiku. — *v.t.* tegemeza, egemeza, gadimu, shikiza, letea msaada.

propagate, *v.t.* zaa, zalisha; (*spread*) eneza, tangaza. **propaganda,** *n.* maenezi (ya dini, madhehebu, maarifa *&c.*). **propagandist,** *n.* mwenezi (wa dini *&c.*). **propagation,** *n.* kuzaa, kuzaliana; (*spreading*) kueneza, maenezi.

propel, *v.t.* sogeza mbele, sukumia mbele, endesha, jongeza, peleka mbele. **propeller,** *n.* (*of ship or aeroplane*) majembe, rafardha.

propensity, *n.* maelekeo, tamani, shauku, kutaka.

proper, *a.* -a (hiyo fulani) peke yake, maalum; (*right*) -a adabu, -ema, salihi, -zuri, wajibu; (*suitable*) -a kufaa, -a kustahili, -stahiki; (*in strict sense*) halisi. **properly,** *adv.* kwa kufaa, uzuri. **property,** *n.* mali, milki; (*nature, quality*) asili, hali, tabia, nguvu. *A man of property*, tajiri.

prophecy, *n.*, **prophesy,** *v.* taz. *prophet*.

prophet, *n.* nabii, mtume; (*foreteller*) mwaguzi, mbashiri, mwonya mbele. **prophecy,** *n.* uaguzi, unabii, ubashiri. **prophesy,** *v.t.* toa unabii; (*predict*) agua, bashiri, tabiri. **prophetic,** *a.* -a nabii, -a kubashiri.

prophylactic, *a.* -a kukinga (kuzuia) ugonjwa. — *n.* dawa ya kukingia (kuzuilia) ugonjwa.

propinquity, *n.* kuwa karibu, kupakana, ujirani.

propitiate, *v.t.* tuliza, ridhisha, patanisha, suluhisha. **propitiation,** *n.* kutuliza, kuridhisha, kitulizo, kipatanisho. **propitiatory,** *a.* -a kutuliza *&c.* **propitious,** *a.* -a ndege njema, -a neema, -a heri, -a kupendelea.

proportion, *n.* kadiri, ukadiri, kuwiana, ulinganifu, uzuri (wa sehemu kulingana barabara). — *v.t.* fanya kadiri, linganisha; (*share out*) gawanya, gawa. **proportional,** *a.* -a kadiri -liolingana barabara. **proportionate,** *a.* -a kadiri, -liolingana barabara, -linganifu, -a kufaa.

proposal, *n.* taz. *propose*.

propose, *v.t.* toa, toa shauri, leta maneno; — *v.i.* (*intend*) kusudia, azimu, taka, nuia, nia; (*advise*) shauri, onya, usia; (*offer marriage*) posa. **proposal,** *n.* neno, maneno, jambo, kisa, shauri, nia, kusudi, madhumuni, azimio; (*of marriage*) kuposa, maposo. **proposition,** *n.* taz. *proposal*.

propound, *v.t.* toa, leta, nena.

proprietor, *n.* mwenyeji, mwenyewe, bwana. **proprietary,** *a.* -a mtu fulani peke yake, -a mwenyewe. **proprietorship,** *n.* kumiliki, uenyeji. **proprietress,** *n.* *proprietor* wa kike. **propriety,** *n.* adabu, utaratibu, uzuri, makini; (*suitability*) ulinganifu.

propulsion, *n.* kusukuma, kupeleka mbele, msukumo. **propulsive**, *a.* -a kupeleka (kusukuma) mbele.

pro rata, *adv.* kwa kadiri (ya kulingana).

prorogue, *v.t.* katiza (maneno ya baraza kuu), ahirisha, weka. **prorogation**, *n.* kukatiza, kuweka &c.

prosaic, *a.* taz. *prose.*

proscribe, *v.t.* gombeza, kataza, harimisha. **proscription**, *n.* makatazo, kuharimisha.

prose, *n.* usemi wa kawaida (usio mashairi wala utenzi); (*dull discourse*) maneno baridi (yasiyokolea); (*tediousness*) ubaridi, uchovu. **prosaic, prosy**, *a.* -a baridi, -a vivi hivi, -a kuchosha, -siokolea. *It is prosy* (*dull*), haikolei, haina kiungo.

prosecute, *v.t.* shtaki sheriani, dai, peleka korti (sheriani); (*carry on*) fululiza, fuliza, endesha, shika kazi ya, dumia. **prosecution**, *n.* kudai, daawa, mashtaka; (*carrying on*) fululizo, fulizo, kuendesha, kudumia. **prosecutor**, *n.* mshtaki, mdai; (*prosecuting counsel*) wakili wa mshtaka.

proselyte, *n.* mwongofu wa dini. **proselytism**, *n.* kuongoa; kuongoka. **proselytize**, *v.t.* ongoa, jaribu kuongoa.

prosody, *n.* kanuni za kutunga mashairi.

prospect, *n.* kutazamia mbele, mambo ya mbele, mambo yajayo, matazamio, maelekeo; (*view*) yaliyo mbele ya macho, sura ya ulimwengu, mandhari; (*ground of hope*) sababu ya kutumaini; matumaini; (*probable future*) mambo yanayoelekea kuwapo siku zijazo, hali inayoelekea kuwa, maelekeo. *There is a prospect of war*, inakabili vita, inaelekea vita. — *v.t.* peleleza, chungua, tafuta. **prospective**, *a.* -a mbele, -a baadaye; (*looking forward*) -a kutazamia mbele. **prospector**, *n.* mchunguzi (wa dhahabu, mafuta, ardhini &c.). **prospectus**, *n.* muhtasari, maelezo mafupi (ya shauri, chuo, kumpuni &c.).

prosper, *v.t.* fanikisha, sitawisha, endesha, kuza; — *v.i.* sitawi, fanikiwa, fana, endelea vizuri, nufaika, kunjuka, -wa na heri. *God prosper you*, Allah bilkheri, Mungu akubariki, Mwenyezi Mungu akuweke. *My affairs have prospered*, mambo yamenifanikia. **prosperity**, *n.* mali, usitawi, heri, neema, baraka, kufanikiwa, fanaka, ufanisi, ghanima, jaha. **prosperous**, *a.* -enye *prosperity*, fani.

prostitute, *n.* kahaba, malaya, mbuya. — *v.t.* fanya ukahaba; (*abuse*) aibisha, tumia vibaya (kwa aibu). **prostitution**, *n.* ukahaba, umalaya; (*abuse*) matumizi mabaya (ya aibu).

prostrate, *a.* kifudifudi, chini, -liolala chini; (*overcome, exhausted*) -legevu, -chovu, -a kuzimia roho. — *v.t.* angusha chini; (*exhaust*) shinda kabisa, legeza nguvu za. *Prostrate oneself before*, sujudu, sujudia, jinyenyekea mbele. **prostration**, *n.* kusujudia; (*exhaustion*) ulegevu wa nguvu, kuvunjika nguvu, unyogovu, unyong'onyevu, * mavundevunde, uvunde.

prosy, *a.* taz. *prose.*

protagonist, *n.* mkuu (katika mchezo wa *theatre*), mwongozi.

protean, *a.* -a mageuzi mengi, -geugeu, -a kugeukageuka.

protect, *v.t.* linda, hifadhi, tunza, hami, ponya, funika; (*by charm*) finga; (*crops from birds &c.*) amia, linda. **protection**, *n.* himaya, tunza, ulinzi; (*something that protects*) kinga, ngao, kifuniko; (*charm*) fingo, hirizi, kago. **protectionist**, *n.* ashikaye shauri la kukuza biashara ya nchi kwa kutoza ushuru bidhaa zinazoingizwa. **protective**, *a.* -a kuhifadhi, -a kukinga. **protector**, *n.* mhifadhi, mlinzi, baba. **protectorate**, *n.* nchi iliyo chini ya himaya ya nchi nyingine. **protégé**, *n.* mtu anayehifadhiwa na mwingine, mtoto, mtu (anayelindwa).

protein, *n.* chakula cha namna

kilichomo katika nyama, ute wa yai na samaki (hakimo katika mafuta wala sukari).

protest, *v.t.* (*affirm &c.*) shuhudia, sema kwa uthabiti (*e.g.* kana, kubali, kataa &c.); — *v.i.* (*raise objection*) kataa, tokubali, dakuliza, teta, leta udaku (tetesi). *He protested*, alisema hapendi (hataki, hapendelei, hakubali), alileta tetesi (udaku). — *n.* ushuhuda, kushuhudia; (*objection*) makatazo, dakizo, udaku, teto, tetesi. **protestant**, *n.* Mkristo asiyekubali baadhi ya mafundisho ya Kanisa la kirumi. **protestantanism**, *n.* hali (mafundisho, madhehebu) ya *protestant*. **protestation**, *n.* maneno ya kushuhudia (ya kukataa, kukubali, ya kuteta &c.).

protocol, *n.* hali ya mapatano (ya muda tu mpaka hati halisi iwe tayari).

protomartyr, *n. martyr* wa kwanza.

protoplasm, *n.* kama ute ulio chanzo cha uhai wa miti na wanyama.

prototype, *n.* chanzo, cheo, kiolezo, namna ya asili (ya awali).

protract, *v.t.* ongeza wakati wa, fululiza, fuliza, zidisha, kawisha, tawilisha, tuiliza; (*plot out*) andika ramani. **protracted**, *a.* -refu, tuili, -a muda mrefu. **protraction**, *n.* kukawilisha &c.; (*drawing*) ramani. **protractor**, *n.* chombo cha kupimia pembe (za mraba &c.).

protrude, *v.t. and i.* tokeza, toa nje, benua, nyanya; (*stick out*) tokeza, toka nje, benuka, fanya mdomo (nundu). **protrusion**, *n.* mbenuko, kutoa, kutoka &c.

protuberance, *n.* kubenuka, kutokeza, kivimbe, uvimbe, nundu, mgongo, mbenuko.

proud, *a.* -a kiburi, -a kujisifu, -a kujivuna, -a majivuno, sodawi, -a kutakabari; (*exulting in, taking a natural and worthy pride in*) -a kuona fahari. *I am proud of my son* (*country*) &c. naona fahari kwa ajili ya mtoto wangu (nchi yangu &c.).

provable, *a.* taz. *prove.*

prove, *v.t.* thibitisha, shuhudia, bainisha, hakikisha, hakiki; (*try*) jaribu, jaribia, onja; — *v.i.* (*turn out*) tokea, tekelea, onekana, bainika. **provable**, *a.* -a kuweza kuthibitika &c. **proven**, *a.* -liothibitika, jarabati.

provender, *n.* chakula (cha ng'ombe au farasi &c., majani, nyasi, malisho).

proverb, *n.* methali, mfano wa maneno. **proverbial**, *a.* -a *proverb*; (*generally known*) -a kujulika na wote, -a kutumika kote.

provide, *v.t.* toa, andaa, weka tayari, auni; — *v.i.* (*prepare for*) amuru mbele, tazamia mbele, -wa tayari kwa, wekea akiba, andalia; (*support*) -wa riziki ya, -wa akiba ya, -wa mali ya. *Provide for* (*feed* &c.) lisha, -pa riziki, ruzuku, kimu, chukua. **provided**, *conj.* (*that*) kwa sharti ya, iwapo, kama, ikiwa. **providence**, *n.* Mungu, maongozi ya Mungu, amri ya Mungu, majaliwa; (*foresight*) busara, mawazo ya mbele, kutazamia mbele; (*thrift*) kuweka akiba, uwekevu, kukata gharama. **provident**, *a.* -enye busara, -a kutazamia mbele, -a kuweka akiba, -wekevu. **providential**, *a.* -a *providence*, -a bahati njema, -a kufaa. **provision**, *n.* madaraka, kufanya tayari; (*clause, agreement*) sharti, maafikano. — *v.t.* wekea chakula. **provisional**, *a.* -a wakati, kitambo, -a mara moja, si -a daima. **provisionally**, *adv.* kwa sharti. **provisions**, *n.plur.* vyakula, maakuli, riziki; (*for journey* &c.) masurufu. **proviso**, *n.* sharti, maafikano.

province, *n.* (*function*) kazi, shughuli, sehemu; (*territory*) nchi, wilaya, jimbo; (*class*) sehemu ya mambo, aina, jamii. **provincial**, *a.* -a mashamba, -a miji midogo; (*countrified*) -a kihenzi, -a mashamba, -geni. **provincialism**, *n.* ushenzi, ugeni; (*in speech*) usemi wa kimashamba.

provision, *n. and v.*, **provisional**, *a.*, **provisionally**, *adv.*, **provisions**, *n.*, **proviso**, *n.* taz. *provide.*

provoke, *v.t.* (*cause*) fanya, -wa sababu ya, toza, leta; (*rouse, stir up &c.*) kasirisha, ghadhibisha, chochea, amsha, tia uchungu, tashtiti, chachisha, futulia, sunza. *Be provoked* (*take offence*) futuka. **provocation**, *n.* kukasirisha, tashtiti, jambo la kukasirisha (la kuchochea), kichocheo. **provocative, provocatory**, *a.* -a kukasirisha, -a kuchochea (-a kuamsha) hasira; (*causal*) -a kutoza, -a kufanya, -a kuleta. **provoking**, *a.* -a kukasirisha, -tiriri, -a kusumbua, -a kuudhi.

provost, *n.* mkuu (wa chuo kikubwa); (*in Scotland*) jumbe mkuu.

prow, *n.* gubeti, omo; (*of small vessel*) 'kikomo.

prowess, *n.* ushujaa, ujasiri, uthabiti, ugumu, uhodari, ustadi.

prowl, *v.i.* zungukazunguka (kama simba usiku).

proximate, *a.* -a karibu, -a pili yake, -a pale pale. **proximity**, *n.* kuwa karibu, kupakana, ujirani. **proximo**, *a.* -a mwezi ujao.

proxy, *n.* badala, wakili.

prude, *n.* mtu (hasa mwanamke) mwenye haya (au makini) kupita kiasi, hasa ya kujipa au kujivunia, mwanamke baridi. **prudery**, *n.* kuwa na haya mno, kujivunia haya au makini, ubaridi. **prudish**, *a.* -enye *prudery*.

prudence, *n.* taz. *prudent*.

prudent, *a.* -enye busara, -enye kufikiri mbele, -a taratibu, -enye akili, -wekevu. **prudence**, *n.* busara, fikira, hadhari, uwekevu, utaratibu, akili.

prudery, *n.*, **prudish**, *a.* taz. *prude*.

prune, (1) *n.* tunda kama zambarau lililokaushwa.

prune, (2) *v.t.* kata (punguzia) matawi, chenga, pogoa, fyeka.

prurient, *a.* -enye udadisi wa mambo kama nyege (ng'oa, uzinzi, uasherati *&c.*), -enye ashiki (nyege) nyingi. **prurience**, *n.* ashiki (nyege) nyingi, udadisi wa mambo kama nyege (ashiki, uasherati *&c.*).

pry, *v.i.* chungulia, peleleza, dadisi, dukiza, bemba, tafiti, doea.

psalm, *n.* zaburi. **psalmist**, *n.* mtunga zaburi. **psalmody**, *n.* jamii ya zaburi, kuimba zaburi. **psalter**, *n.* kitabu cha zaburi za Daudi. **psaltery**, *n.* zeze la kiyahudi.

pseudo, *pref.* -a uwongo. **pseudonym**, *n.* jina la uwongo, jina la kubunika.

pshaw! *int.* (neno la kuonyesha dharau, kutosadiki *&c.*). upuzi! mawe!

psychic, psychical, *a.* -a roho ya binadamu.

psychological, *a.*, **psychologist**, *n.* taz. *psychology*.

psychology, *n.* elimu ya mambo ya roho (ya moyo, ya akili, ya ufahamu) ya binadamu. **psychological**, *a.* -a *psychology*, -a mambo ya roho ya binadamu. *The psychological moment*, wakati ufaao hasa. **psychologist**, *n.* mtu achunguaye habari za *psychology*.

ptomaine, *n.* sumu inayotoka katika nyama au mboga zikioza.

puberty, *n.* ubalehe, kuanza kuwa mtu mzima, mwanzo wa kuweza kuzaa, upevu. **pubes**, *n.* mavuzi; mbeleni. **pubescence**, *n.* ubalehe; (*of plants &c.*) malaika (manyoya) laini ya miti, majani na wadudu. **pubescent**, *a.* -nayebalehe; -enye malaika laini, *e.g.* majani, wadudu *&c.* **pubic**, *a.* -a mbeleni.

public, *a.* -a waziwazi, bayana, -a watu wote, hadharani ya watu; (*official*) -a serikali. *Public affairs*, mambo ya taifa (yahusuyo watu wote), mambo ya serikali. —*n.* *The public*, watu (wa taifa au nchi fulani). **publican**, *n.* (Kirumi zamani) mtoza ushuru; (*owner of public-house*) mwenye hoteli pauzwapo mvinyo, pombe *&c.* **publication**, *n.* kubainisha, kueneza habari, kutoa wazi; (*book*) kitabu, kutoa kitabu. **public-house**, *n.* hoteli (pauzwapo mvinyo, pombe *&c.*). **publicist**, *n.* mwalimu wa sheria. **publicity**, *n.* uwazi, ubayana, kujulikana, kuta ngaza, kueneza habari. **publicly,** *adv.* kwa wazi, hadharani ya watu, mbele ya watu. **public-spirited,** *a.* -enye moyo wa kufadhili (kusaidia) watu kuliko nafsi yake. **publish,** *v.t.* bainisha, tangaza, toa wazi, eneza habari; (*of books &c.*) toa, piga chapa. **publisher,** *n.* mweneza habari; (*of books*) mtoa vitabu.

pucker, *v.t.* kunja, finya; — *v.i.* kunjamana, finyana. — *n.* kikunjo, finyo, kunyanzi.

pudding, *n.* chakula kitamu (maandazi *&c.*) kinacholiwa mwisho wa kula; utumbo wa mnyama uliojazwa nyama iliyokatwakatwa na kutiwa viungo na kupikwa; unga uliochanganywa na mafuta, mayai *&c.* na kutiwa matunda au nyama *&c.* na kupikwa.

puddle, *n.* kiziwa cha maji, kidimbwi. — *v.t.* kanyaga (kanda) udongo, paka (kandika) udongo kuzuia maji yasipenye.

pudgy, *a.* -fupi, -nene.

puerile, *a.* hafifu, -a kitoto, -a upuzi. **puerility,** *n.* upuzi, uhafifu.

puerperal, *a.* -a uzazi.

puff, *v.t.* puliza kwa kishindo, toa (tia) pumzi kwa kishindo; (*pant*) tweta, hema, kokota roho; (*inflate*) jaza (vimbisha kwa) hewa; (*praise unduly*) sifu mno, tembeza, angaza, rairai; (*make swell*) furisha. — *n.* kishindo (cha pumzi au upepo); (*overpraise*) maneno ya kusifu mno; (*powder-puff*) kibonge cha manyoya laini au kitu chororo, cha kupakalia *powder*; (*pastry*) maandazi mepesi sana. **puff-adder,** *n.* pili, kifutu, bafe, moma. **puff-back,** *n.* (*Zanzibar*) tiva. **puffy,** *a.* -liovimbavimba, -liofurafura; (*panting*) -a kutweta; (*of wind*) -a vishindo.

pug, *v.t.* kanda udongo wa kufanyia matofali au kufinyanga. — *n.* udongo uliokandwa.

pugilist, *n.* mtu apiganaye kwa ngumi. **pugilism,** *n.* maarifa ya kupigana ngumi. **pugilistic,** *a.* -a kupigana ngumi.

pugnacious, *a.* -gomvi, -a kutaka vita, -piganaji, -kali, -a shari. **pugnacity,** *n.* kutaka vita, ushindani, shari.

puissant, *a.* -a enzi, -a nguvu kuu. **puissance,** *n.* nguvu kuu, enzi, uwezo mwingi.

pull, *v.t.* vuta, kokota, buruta, burura; (*gather fruit &c.*) chuma; (*extract*) ng'oa; (*pluck sharply*) nyakua; (*jerk*) shtua, kutua; — *v.i.* vuta; (*be capable of being pulled*) vutika. *Pull apart,* rarua, tatua, pasua, chambua, chamvua. *Pull down,* angusha, bomoa; (*weaken*) dhoofisha. *Pull a face,* kunja (finya) uso. *Pull off,* (*profit*) ambulia, chuma, pata; (*clothes*) vua. *Pull one's leg,* kejeli. *Pull on* (*clothes*), vaa. *Pull out,* ng'oa; (*of a bundle &c.*) chopoa, vura. *Pull through,* pona, okoka. *Pull together,* vuta pamoja, saidiana. *Pull up,* simamisha; (*come to a halt*) simama; (*root up*) ng'oa. — *n.* mvuto, nguvu ya kuvuta, uwezo; (*carrying on*) mfululizo, mfulizo. **pull-through,** *n.* kamba ya kusafishia bunduki.

pullet, *n.* mtoto wa kuku, faranga.

pulley, *n.* kapi, ayari, gofia, roda, korodani, abedari.

pull-through, *n.* taz. *pull.*

pulmonary, *a.* -a kifua, -a pafu, -a pumu.

pulp, *n.* kitu chororo kama nyama ya tunda bivu, kama ubongo, mseto. — *v.t.* fanya kuwa *pulp*, seta, ponda. **pulpy,** *a.* teketeke, laini.

pulpit, *n.* mimbara.

pulpy, *a.* taz. *pulp.*

pulse, (1) *n.* kupigapiga moyo, kipigo cha mshipa wa damu. *Feel the pulse,* pima vipigo vya mshipa wa damu. **pulsate,** *v.i.* pigapiga, puma, tutuma. **pulsation,** *n.* kupigapiga, kupuma.

pulse, (2) *n.* (*grain*) nafaka, kunde, choroko, dengu *&c.*

pulverize, *v.t.* fanya kuwa unga, ponda, twanga, funda, chua, saga.

puma, *n.* mnyama wa *America* kama simba.

pumice, *n.* jiwe jepesi, litokalo katika *volcano*, kidogo kama matumbawe ya kusingia (msio).
pummel, *v. and n.* = *pommel.*
pump, *n.* bomba (ya kuvutia maji au mafuta, ya kupulizia). — *v.t.* vuta kwa bomba, puliza kwa bomba; (*question*) hoji hoji, dadisi, nyenga, nyenya, susuika.
pumpkin, *n.* (*plant*) mboga; (*fruit*) boga.
pun, *n.* neno la ubishi lenye maana mbili. — *v.i.* chezea maneno, sema maneno yenye maana mbili kwa ubishi. **punster,** *n.* mfanya *pun.*
punch, (1) *n.* mvinyo na maji ya

rada. **punitive,** *a.* -a kuadhibu, -a adhabu.
punkah, *n.* pepeo kubwa.
punster, *n.* taz. *pun.*
punt, *n.* mashua iliyo sawasawa chini, isiyo na mkuku. — *v.t.* endesha mashua kwa pondo, piga pondo.
puny, *a.* -dogo, dhaifu sana, -liovia.
pup, *n.* mtoto wa mbwa; kijana mjuvi (mfidhuli, mkavu wa macho). — *v.i.* zaa (mbwa). **puppy,** *n.* taz. *pup,* *n.*
pupa, *n.* buu, hali ya mdudu kati ya kuwa kiluwiluwi na mdudu mzima; (*of bees*) jana.
pupil, *n.* mwanafunzi; (*of eye*) mboni

in order, panga, tunga, ratibisha, sabidi, zatiti. *Put in mind of,* kumbusha, fahamisha. *Put off* (*clothes &c.*) vua, ondoa; (*defer*) weka, ahirisha, cheleza, kawilisha, rajua; (*mislead*) danganya; (*leave shore*) toka pwani, tweka. *Put off on,* sukumiza, kumbishia. *Put on,* (*clothes &c.*) vaa, valia, vika; (*arrow on string, knife in belt, spectacles on nose*) pachika; (*on lap, knees, shoulder*) pakata; (*assign*) amria; (*employ*) tumia; (*attribute*) sukumia; (*deceive*) punja, danganya, ghilibu, laghai; (*set to*) tia katika; (*on the fire*) teleka; (*on a spit*) tunga kijitini. *Put on guard,* tahadharisha, onya. *Put on trial,* peleka hukumini; (*prove*) jaribu. *Put out,* toa, ondosha; (*extinguish*) zima, zimisha; (*dislocate*) shtusha, tegua; (*extend*) nyosha, toa nje; (*perplex*) fadhaisha; (*offend*) tia uchungu, kasirisha. *Be put out,* ona chuki, futuka, udhika, kasirika. *Put over,* vusha, abirisha; (*defer*) weka, ahirisha; (*make master of*) weka juu ya, fanya msimamizi wa. *Put through,* penyeza; (*carry out*) maliza, fikiliza. *Put to bed,* laza kitandani, laza, tuesha. *Put to death,* fisha, ua. *Put to,* (*door*) shindika. *Be put to,* zidiwa, sumbuka, fadhaika. *Put to flight,* kimbiza. *Put to rights,* tengeneza. *Put to sea,* tweka. *Put to the sword,* chinja. *Put up,* (*lodge*)

puttees, *n.* vitambaa virefu vya kuzungushia miguu kati ya kisigino na goti.
putty, *n.* mchanganyiko wa chaki na mafuta.
puzzle, *v.t.* zuzua, tatiza, fadhaisha, fumba, shinda, kanganya, kikisa, zonga, koroweza, tatanisha; (*use puzzling language*) fumba maneno. *Puzzle over,* fikiria sana. — *n.* matata, fumbo, kitendawili. **puzzling,** *a.* -a matata, -a kutatiza, -a fumbo.
pygmy, *n.* kibeti, mbilikimo. — *a.* -a *pygmy,* -dogo sana.
pyjamas, *n.* suruali na koti, nguo za kulalia.
pylon, *n.* mlango, hasa wa hekalu la kimisri; nguzo ndefu (ya kuegemeza, ya mipaka, ya pambo).
pyorrhoea, *n.* kimenomeno, ugonjwa wa ufizi kutoka usaha kwenye meno.
pyramid, *n.* jengo la mawe, kama mapaa manne ya nyumba yaliyo sawa yote, (*Ar.*) ihramu, haram; (*pile*) chungu ya mawe, chungu. **pyramidal,** *a.* -a *pyramid.*
pyre, *n.* chungu ya kuni ya kuchomea maiti. **pyrotechnics,** *n.* wonyesho wa kazi ya fataki na baruti &c.; kazi ya kufanya fataki na vitu vya baruti &c.
python, *n.* chatu.

Q

quack, (1) *v.i.* lia (kama bata). — *n.* mlio (wa bata).
quack, (2) *n.* (*doctor*) mtu ajifanyaye mganga asijue dawa; (*imposter*) jambazi, ayari, mwongo. **quackery,** *n.* dawa ya uwongo uwongo, madanganya, ujambazi, uayari.
quadrangle, *n.* umbo lenye pande nne na pembe nne, *e.g.* mraba &c., mstatili; (*court*) behewa kati ya nyumba, uwanja wenye nyumba pande zote. **quadrangular,** *a.* kama *quadrangle.*
quadrant, *n.* robo ya duara; (*instrument*) chombo cha kupimia pembe.
quadrilateral, *a.* -enye pembe nne.
quadrille, *n.* ngoma ya Ulaya ya kucheza watu wanane, wawili wawili.
quadroon, *n.* mtu ambaye mzazi wake mmoja ni mweupe, na mwingine ni suriama (chotara).
quadruped, *n.* mnyama mwenye miguu minne.
quadruple, *a.* -a kuzidi mara nne. — *v.t.* zidisha kwa nne. **quadruplet,** *n.* jamii ya vitu vinne, hasa watoto wanne waliozaliwa pamoja. **quadruplicate,** *v.t.* zidisha kwa nne, fanya nakili nne.
quaff, *v.t.* -nywa kwa kishindo, gugumiza.
quagga, *n.* namna ya pundamilia.
quagmire, *n.* bwawa, mahali penye matope mengi, kinamasi.
quail, (1) *n.* tombo, tomboro, tomboroko.
quail, (2) *v.t.* tetema kwa hofu, shindwa na hofu, jikunyata kwa hofu, nywea, chunga.
quaint, *a.* -a kupendeza kwa kuwa -a kigeni (-a zamani); -a mtindo.
quake, *v.i.* tetemeka, tapatapa, chunga. — *n.* tetemo, kitapo. **quaker,** *n.* mmoja wa madhehebu mojawapo ya kikristo, pengine huitwa *Friends* (marafiki).
qualification, *n.*, **qualify,** *v.*, **qualitative,** *a.* taz. *quality.*
quality, *n.* tabia, jinsi, aina, sifa, cheo, cheo bora. *A person of quality,* mtu bora, mtoto wa watu. **qualification,** *n.* sifa, tabia, hali, akili, ruhusa, uwezo; (*change*) mageuzi, tofauti; (*disparagement*) upunguo, kupungua sifa, kusahihisha. **qualify,** *v.t.* wezesha, stahilisha, tolea ruhusa (haki, sifa, uwezo); (*alter*) geuza, punguza; — *v.i.* (*by study &c.*) pata kufaa (kuweza, uwezo, kustahili). *Be qualified for,* faa, weza, stahili, -wa na akili. tumikana. *In qualified terms,* si sana, kidogo. **qualitative,** *a.* -a kuhusu *quality,* -a kuonyesha *quality.*
qualm, *n.* kigagazi, kuchafuka tumbo, kichefuchefu; (*scruple*) mashaka, uchungu.
quandary, *n.* matata, mashaka.
quantity, *n.* kiasi, kadiri, cheo, wingi, ukubwa. *He's an unknown quantity,* hatujui tabia (sifa, uwezo) yake.
quarantine, *n.* kuzuiwa (kutengwa) mahali kwa sababu ya ugonjwa, watu wasiambukizwe; karantini.
quarrel, *n.* ugomvi, mateto, mzozo. — *v.i.* gombana, pambana, zozana. *Quarrel with* (*complain of &c.*), nung'nunikia, kasirikia. **quarrelsome,** *a.* -gomvi. **quarrelsomeness,** *n.* ugomvi, ukaidi, ubishi.
quarry, (1) *n.* (*prey*) windo.
quarry, (2) *n.* mahali pa kuvunja au kuchimbua mawe, chimbo. — *v.t.* chimbua mawe. **quarryman,** *n.* mvunja (mchimbaji) mawe.
quart, *n.* kipimo cha kiingereza kadiri ya vibaba viwili, kisaga.
quarter, *n.* robo, sehemu ya nne; (*clemency*) huruma, hasa ya kuachia (kuachiwa) maisha; (*direction*) upande, majira; (*district, area*) upande, mtaa; (*weight*) ratli ishirini na nne.

Three-quarters, kasa robo. *Give quarter,* achia adui aishi, -pa amani, acha, hurumia. — *v.t.* kata vipande vinne; (*lodge*) kalisha, -pa kituo na chakula. **quarter-day,** *n.* siku ya robo mwaka. **quarter-deck,** *n.* shetri, sitaha ya nyuma. **quarterly,** *a.* -a kila mwezi wa tatu, -a mara nne kila mwaka. **quartermaster,** *n.* afisa wa kiaskari aangaliaye habari za chakula, nguo, vifaa, hesabu *&c.*; (*in ships*) serehangi, baharia msimamizi. **quartern,** *n.* mkate, kadiri ya ratli nne. **quarters** *n.*, (*lodgings*) makao, makazi, kituo; (*of soldiers &c.*) nyumba za kukaa askari *&c.* *Fore-quarters,* pande za mbele (za mnyama). *Hind-quarters,* pande za nyuma. *Head-quarters,* makao ya wakuu. *At close quarters,* karibu karibu. **quarter sessions,** *n.* baraza ya kuhukumu kila mwezi wa tatu. **quarter-staff,** *n.* gongo, rungu. **quartette,** *n.* jamii ya watu wanne (vitu vinne); watu wanne wakiimba pamoja, au wimbo wao. **quarto,** *n.* upande wa karatasi iliyokunjwa kufanya kurasa nne kadiri ya urefu wa inchi 12 na upana wa inchi 9; kitabu chenye kurasa kadiri ya urefu wa inchi 12 na upana wa inchi 9.

quartz, *n.* namna ya jiwe gumu jeupe la kung'aa.

quash, *v.t.* tangua, batili, futa; (*suppress*) komesha, nyamazisha.

quasi, *adv.* kama, kuonekana kama kwamba.

quaver, *v.i.* tetemeka, tikisika. — *n.* mtikiso; (*in singing*) madoido, jinsi moja ya sauti fupi katika *music.*

quay, *n.* gati, diko; boma la mawe pwani, au la kutokeza baharini, pa kutelemshia shehena.

queen, *n.* malkia, mkewe mfalme. **queenly,** *a.* kama *queen,* -a kifalme.

queer, *a.* -geni, -a kigeni, -a ubishi, -a kuchekesha; (*ill*) -gonjwa kidogo; (*slightly mad*) -enye kichaa; (*doubtful*) -a mashaka, -a matata. — *v.t.* haribu, potosha.

quell, *v.t.* komesha, zuia, tuliza, nyamazisha.

quench, *v.t.* (*fire, light*) zima, zimisha; (*anger, hatred, desire*) tuliza; (*hope*) fisha, komesha; (*thirst*) zima, tuliza.

querulous, *a.*, -a kuguna, -a kunung'unika, -a kutokuwa radhi, -epesi kugombana.

query, *n.* ulizo, swali; (*mark*) alama ya kuuliza, hii (?). — *v.t.* onea shaka, taka maelezo zaidi juu ya jambo.

quest, *n.* kutafuta, upelelezi, safari ya kwenda kuvumbua habari.

question, *n.* swali, ulizo; (*subject of discussion*) neno, kisa, hoja; (*matter, affair*) neno, jambo, kadhia. *Ask questions,* uliza, toa maswali, saili. *Press with questions,* hoji, dadisi. *Call in question,* fanyia maneno. *It is out of the question,* haiwezekani. *Be in question,* fanyiwa maneno. *A burning question,* neno lenye haraka au kubishaniwa, jambo lihitajilo kukatwa upesi. *Beyond question,* hakika, yakini, bila shaka. — *v.t.* uliza, dadisi, hoji, saili, lumba; (*doubt*) onea mashaka, tosadiki sana. *I question whether,* sijui kama, sidhani. **questionable,** *a.* (*doubtful*) -enye mashaka, si hakika; (*not right*) si -ema, si halisi, si barabara. **questionnaire,** *n.* orodha ya maswali yenye nafasi ya kuandikia majibu.

queue, *n.* mstari wa watu waliojipanga wakingoja kuingia mahali.

quibble, *n.* maneno ya kudanganya (ya kulaghai, ya kuficha kweli, kipengee). — *v.i.* danganya kwa maneno, laghai. **quibbling,** *n.* udanganyifu wa maneno, ulaghai.

quick, *a.* -epesi, -a upesi; (*clever*) hodari, -elekevu, -enye akili; (*in sly sense*) -erevu; (*living*) hai, -zima, -enye uhai. *Be quick,* fanya haraka, chapuka. — *n.* nyama ya ndani, mshipa; (*in most part*) moyo, kiini. *It touched him to the quick,* ilimchoma moyoni. **quicken,** *v.t. and i.* himiza; (*encourage*) chochea, amsha, tia moyo, tia nguvu; (*give life to*) huisha, fufua; — *v.i.* amka, fufuka; (*of child in womb*) shtuka; (*move rapidly*) zidi mwendo, enda upesi zaidi. **quicklime**, *n.* chokaa mbichi isiyotiwa maji. **quickly**, *adv.* upesi, hima, kwa haraka, mbio. **quickness**, *n.* wepesi, mbio. **quicksand**, *n.* mchanga uliochangamana na maji usioendeka kwa kuwa unavuta chini, mchanga wa kutopeza (wa kudidimiza). **quickest**, *n.* -a michongoma, -a miiba. **quick-sighted**, *a.* -epesi kuona, -enye macho, -enye macho makali. **quicksilver**, *n.* zebaki. **quick-tempered**, *a.* -epesi wa hasira, -a harara, -a hamaki.

quid, (1) *n.* tumbako ya kutafuna, mshuku; (*chewed betel &c.*) utembe.

quid, (2) *n.* pauni, shilingi ishirini. *A quid pro quo*, kitu cha kulipia kitu.

quiescent, *a.* -liotulia, kimya, -tulivu, -siojongea. **quiescence**, *n.* utulivu, kimya, amani.

quiet, *a.* -liotulia, -siojongea, kimya, -tulivu, -nyamavu, -a amani, makini. — *n.* utulivu, amani, kimya. — *v.t.* nyamazisha, tuliza, fariji, liwaza; — *v.i.* (*quiet down*) tulia, nyamaa, farijika. **quietism**, *n.* utulivu wa rohoni, amani rohoni. **quietly**, *adv.* polepole, taratibu, kwa saburi, kimya. **quietness, quietude**, *n.* utulivu, amani, kimya. **quietus**, *n.* malipo; (*death*) kifo, mauti.

quill, *n.* ubawa, ubawa wa kuandikia.

quilt, *n.* firashi, farishi, tandiko la juu ya kitanda, tabaka mbili za nguo zenye pamba (sufi, manyoya) katikati.

quince, *n.* tunda la Ulaya kama pera.

quinine, *n.* kwinini, dawa ya homa.

quinquennial, *a.* -a kila mwaka wa tano.

quinsy, *n.* ugonjwa wa kooni, jipu la kooni, kimio, halula.

quintessence, *n.* asili (tabia, nguvu) halisi ya kitu, kipee, kiolezo cha ukamilifu.

quintet, quintette, *n.* watu watano wakiimba pamoja, au wimbo wao.

quintuplet, *n.* jamii ya watu watano (ya vitu vitano). **quintuplicate**, *a.* -a kuzidi mara tano.

quip, *n.* neno lenye akili (la ubishi, la kuchekesha).

quire, *n.* fungu la karatasi (kurasa ishirini na nne).

quirk, *n.* hila, madanganya; (*in writing &c.*) madoido.

quit, *v.t.* (*leave*) acha, toka katika, hama, ondoka katika; (*acquit*) achilia; (*pay*) lipa. *Quit you like men*, fanya kinaume. — *a.* -lioachiliwa, -liookoka. *Be quit of*, ondolewa, okoka katika. *Be quits*, ridhiana, patana, peana sawa. **quittance**, *n.* malipo, kisasi; (*receipt*) stakabadhi, risiti. **quitter**, *n.* (*slang*) mwoga, aachaye kazi (jambo) kabla hajaimaliza.

quite, *adv.* kabisa, kamwe, halisi, pia. *Quite as bad*, -baya sawasawa. *Quite so*, ndivyo hivyo.

quittance, *n.*, **quitter**, *n.* taz. *quit*.

quiver, (1) *v.i.* tetemeka, tikisika, tapatapa, chunga. — *n.* tetemo.

quiver, (2) *n.* (*for arrows*) podo, zaka.

qui vive, *n.* *On the qui vive*, -wa macho, -wa tayari, -wa na hadhari.

quixotic, *a.* -enye kukirimu (kupa, kuheshimu) wengine hata kujisahau mwenyewe.

quiz, *n.* ubishi. — *v.t.* fanyia ubishi; kodolea macho, angazia macho.

quoit, *n.* pete (duara) ya chuma (ya mchezo).

quondam, *n.* -a zamani, -a siku zilizopita, lakini si sasa.

quorum, *n.* jamii (hesabu) ya kanuni.

quota, *n.* sehemu ya haki (iliyopasa).

quote, *v.t.* toa (ingiza, chagua, tumia) maneno ya mtu mwingine (ya kitabuni), dondoa, tumia maneno ya. **quotation**, *n.* maneno fulani ya kitabuni au yaliyosemwa na mtu mwingine zamani, mateuzi, madondoo; (*price*) kima, bei. **quotation mark(s)**, *n.* alama za kutaja. hivi (' ') au (" ").

quoth (*he, she, I*), *v.i.* asema, alisema (nasema &c.).

quotidian, *a.* -a kila siku.

quotient, *n.* (*in arithmetic*) hisa (jawabu la hesabu ya kugawanya).

R

rabbi, *n.* mwalimu au padre wa kiyahudi.

rabbit, *n.* sungura, kisungura, kitungule, kititi.

rabble, *n.* watu wengi wakifanya makelele (jeuri, udhia), ghasia ya watu wengi, msukosuko wa watu. *The rabble,* watu wa ovyo, watu wanyonge.

rabid, *a.* -enye wazimu. **rabies,** *n.* kalab (Ar.), ugonjwa wa wazimu wa mbwa; ugonjwa unaoletwa kwa kuumwa na mbwa mwenye wazimu.

race, (1) *v.i.* shindana mbio, enda mbio; — *v.t.* (*run horses &c.*) shindanisha. — *n.* shindano la mbio; (*swift movement*) mwendo wa mbio; (*swift current*) mkondo wa mto. **racecourse,** *n.* uwanja wa kushindana mbio. **racehorse,** *n.* farasi wa kushindania mbio. **racing,** *n.* mashindano ya mbio.

race, (2) *n.* (*division of mankind*) taifa; (*lineage*) ujamaa, udugu, mbegu, jadi. **racial,** *a.* -a taifa, -a ujamaa *&c.* **racy,** *a.* -enye tabia (utamu, moyo *&c.*) halisi ya namna (taifa *&c.*) yake. *A racy story,* hadithi ya mambo machafu.

racecourse, *n.,* **racehorse,** *n.* taz. *race* (1).

racial, *a.* taz. *race* (2).

racing, *n.* taz. *race* (1).

rack, *n.* mbao zenye vyango (vipande) vya kutundikia (kuwekea, kuandikia, kupangia) vitu ukutani; (*in railway carriage*) kama susu ya juu ya kuwekea mizigo midogo (*for torture*) kitanda cha kushtusha viungo vya watu kuwatesa. — *v.t.* nyosha kwa nguvu; (*torment*) shtusha viungo, adhibisha, tesa, umiza mno; (*vex greatly*) udhi, onea, sumbua, hangaisha. *Rack one's brains,* fikiri sana, tafuta shauri.

racket, (1) **racquet,** *n.* ubao wa kuchezea tufe.

racket, (2) *n.* (*disturbance*) ghasia, makelele, zahama, msukosuko, haraka. **racketeer,** *n.* mtu aogofyaye wengine ili kupata fedha kwao. **racketeering,** *n.* kuogofya watu ili kupata fedha kwao.

racy, *a.* taz. *race* (2).

radiant, *a.* -angavu, -a kung'aa, -a furaha, -enye kianga cha uso. **radiance,** *n.* mwanga, mwangaza, wangavu, weupe, uzuri, nuru. **radiate,** *v.t. and i.* toa (tapanya, eneza, toka, tokeza) nuru (moto, joto) pande zote. **radiation,** *n.* kutoa nuru *&c.* taz. *radiate.* **radiator,** *n.* chombo cha kuenezea joto nyumbani; (*of engine*) chombo cha kupoza joto la mashine.

radical, *a.* -a awali, -a asili, -a katiba. — *n.* asili, sehemu ya asili; (*politics*) mtu wa jamii ya watu watakao kugeuza mambo mengi ya serikali. **radically,** *adv.* sana, kabisa.

radio, *n.* kupeleka simu (habari),

maneno, muziki hewani kwa nguvu za umeme; simu ya hewani. **radiogram,** *n.* simu ya hewani.

radish, *n.* mboga kama figili.

radium, *n.* madini ya thamani kubwa inayotoa nuru na nguvu za umeme.

radius, *n.* mstari wa kutoka katikati hasa ya duara (*circle*) mpaka kizingo chake.

raffia, *n.* chane kama za ukindu; (*palm*) mwale.

raffle, *v.t.* piga (pigia) kura kwa fedha. — *n.* bahati nasibu.

raft, *n.* chelezo (cha mbao zilizofunganishwa pamoja).

rafter, *n.* (*for thatch*) kombamoyo; (*thin*) pao.

rag, (1) *n.* kitambaa; (*torn clothes*) nguo mbovumbovu (zilizotatuka), matambaa. — *v.t.* kasirisha kwa ubishi (kwa mchezo, kwa mzaha), chezea. **ragged,** *a.* -liopasuka, liotatuka, -lioraruka, -baya, -bovu. **ragamuffin,** *n.* mtoto aliyevaa nguo mbovumbovu (zilizotatukatatuka), mtoto wa kikopo; (*ruffian*) mtu mnyonge (hafifu, maskini). **ragtag,** *n.* *ragtag and bobtail,* watu ovyo wa kila namna. **ragtime,** *n.* namna ya ngoma ya kucheza.

rag, (2) *n.* (*coral rag*) matumbawe.

rage, *n.* hasira kali, ghadhabu, kiruu, ghaidi. — *v.i.* kasirika, ghadhibika; (*act violently*) fanya ukali, fanya mshindo; (*be in violent motion*) chafuka, sukasuka; (*be very prevalent &c.*) endelea vikali, chaga; (*be intensely violent, of fever &c.*) -wa -kali sana. **raging,** *a.* -liokasirika, -liochafuka, -kali sana, -a mshindo mkubwa.

ragged, *a.* taz. *rag* (1).

raging, *a.* taz. *rage.*

ragout, *n.* nyama, mboga na viungo vilivyopikwa pamoja.

ragtag, *n.,* **ragtime,** *n.,* taz. *rag* (1).

raid, *n.* vita vya ghafula, shambulio, kuleta vita, mwingilio wa ghafula. — *v.t.* shambulia, endea kwa vita ghafula, ingilia ghafula. **raider,** *n* afanyaye *raid.*

rail, (1) *v.i.* (*at, against*) kemea, karipia, laumu, shutumu. **railing,** *a.* -a kukemea, -a kukaripia *&c.* — *n.* kemeo, karipio, mzaha, dhihaka, kucheka. **raillery,** *n.* mzaha, dhihaka, kucheka.

rail, (2) *n.* mti au ubao (wa juu ya nguzo za kitalu, ngazi *&c.*), papi, kipande, fito; (*iron*) chuma cha njia ya gari la moshi; (*railway train*) gari la moshi. — *v.t.* zungushia kitalu; (*send by rail*) peleka katika gari la moshi. **railing,** *n.* kitalu, miti ya (nguzo za) kuzungushia. **railroad, railway,** *n.* njia ya gari la moshi, reli.

railing, *n.* taz. *rail* (2); *a. and n.* taz. *rail* (1).

raillery, *n.* taz. *rail* (1).

railroad, railway, *n.* taz. *rail* (2).

raiment, *n.* nguo, mavazi.

rain, *n.* mvua; (*drizzle*) manyunyu; (*wet season*) masika; (*lesser rains*) vuli, mvua za mwaka. — *v.i.* -nya, nyesha; toka kwa wingi, -ja (fika) kwa wingi; — *v.t.* toa kwa wingi. **rainbow,** *n.* upindi wa mvua. **raincloud,** *n.* ghubari, wingu la mvua. **raincoat,** *n.* koti la mvua. **raindrop,** *n.* tone la mvua. **rainfall,** *n.* mvua; (*amount*) kadiri ya mvua inayonyesha mahali katika muda fulani. **rain-gauge,** *n.* chombo cha kupimia mvua. **rainstorm,** *n.* mvua kubwa, tufani ya mvua. **rainwater,** *n.* maji ya mvua. **rainy,** *a.* -a mvua nyingi.

raise, *v.t.* inua, panza, paaza, tweka, nyanyua, pandisha, kweza (*collect*) kusanya, changa; (*grow*) otesha, zalisha; (*produce, make*) fanya, fanyiza; (*increase*) ongeza, kuza; (*strengthen*) thibitisha; (*excite*) amsha, harakisha, chochea; (*bring to life*) huisha, fufua, baathi; (*of money*) pata; (*price*) kweza, pandisha; (*make stand*) simamisha; (*dignify*) tukuza, adhimisha; (*of voice*) paaza, paliza; (*remove*) ondoa, ondokesha; (*hat, cap*) vua kofia; (*dust*) tifua; (*bread with yeast*) umua (kwa chachu, hamira).

raisin, *n.* zabibu kavu.

raison d'être, *n.* sababu ya kuwa (ya kuwapo).

rajah, *n.* jumbe (mtawala, sultani) wa kihindi.

rake, (1) *n.* jembe lenye meno la kukokotea taka; (*debauchee*) mfisadi, mwasherati. — *v.t.* tumia *rake* (jembe la meno); (*collect*) kusanya; (*fire on*) pigia mizinga (merikebu mbele na nyuma, si mbavuni). *Rake up*, chocheleza, vumbulia, paliliza. **rakish**, *a.* -penda uasherati, -zinifu.

rake, (2) *n.* (*slope*) uinamizi, mainamizi. — *v.i.* inama, enda mshazari, enda hanamu. **rakish**, *a.* -zuri, -malidadi.

rakish, *a.* taz. *rake* (1) *and* (2).

rally, *v.* (1) *v.t.* (*restore order &c.*) kusanya tena, rudisha, tengenezesha, ondolea hofu, tia moyo; — *v.i.* kusanyika tena, jirudia, pata moyo, pata nguvu tena. — *n.* kujirudisha, kurudisha *&c.*; (*assembly &c.*) kukusanyika, mkusanyiko.

rally, (2) *v.t.* fanyia ubishi (mzaha).

ram, *n.* kondoo dume; (*of war-ship*) mdomo wa manowari; (*battering-ram*) mtambo wa kubomolea; (*hydraulic*) mtambo wa kushindilia (wa kusukumia mazito). — *v.t.* (*a charge*) shindilia, shindika; (*a ship*) ponda mbavu, piga kwa nguvu. **rammer**, *n.* mti wa kushindilia, mchi.

ramble, *v.i.* tembea, zunguka, susurika, zurura, zururika, tanga; (*be crazy*) potewa na akili, payuka; (*of plants*) tambaa. — *n.* matembezi, mazunguko. **rambler**, *n.* mtambaa. **rambling**, *a.* (*crazy*) -a kupayuka, -a kichaa; (*irrelevant*) -sio na maana, -puzi, -siohusiana.

ramify, *v.i.* (*spread*) enea; (*branch out*) gawanyika. **ramification**, *n.* maeneo; (*part, branch*) sehemu.

rammer, *n.* taz. *ram.*

ramp, *v.i.* fanya ukali, ruka (enda) huko na huko kwa ukali (ghadhabu). — *n.* mahali penye hanamu; (*swindle*) madanganyo, ulaghai.

rampage, *n.* ghasia, ukali. — *v.i.* fanya ukali, enda huko na huko kwa ukali (ghadhabu). **rampant**, *a.* kupita kiasi, -a kuenea pote; (*raging*) -kali mno, -a ghadhabu nyingi.

rampart, *n.* boma.

ramrod, *n.* mdeki.

ramshackle, *a.* -liochakaa, -bovubovu.

ran, *p.t.* ya *run.*

ranch, *n.* uwanda wa kufugia ng'ombe, kondoo *&c.*

rancid, *a.* (mafuta, siagi *&c.*) -liochachuka, -kali. **rancidity**, *n.* ukali, kuchachuka.

rancour, *n.* ukali, uchungu, machukio, chuki. **rancorous**, *a.* -kali, -a chuki, -enye uchungu mwingi.

random, *a.* bila taratibu, bila shauri (fikira, kusudi), ovyo, -a bahati, -a nasibu, shelabela, iwezavyo, vyo vyote. *At random*, ovyo, bila kutengeneza tayari.

rang, *p.t.* ya *ring.*

range, *v.t.* (*level, train*) elekeza, linga (bunduki, darubini); (*rove, roam*) zunguka, tembea; (*arrange*) panga, andika, tengeneza, weka kwa taratibu; (*pass over*) pitia; — *v.i.* (*extend*) enea, -wa na eneo (cheo, kadiri, hesabu). — *n.* (*line*) safu, msafa; (*series*) jamii; (*fireplace*) jiko la chuma; (*reach, extent*) eneo, kadiri; (*walk*) matembezi; (*space*) nafasi; (*compass*) mfiko, mtupo (wa risasi ya mzinga, bunduki *&c.*); (*distance*) mfiko, urefu (wa kufikia kitu au mahali); (*shooting range*) mahali pa kupigia shabaha. *Range of mountains*, milima milima mingi, safu ya milima. **ranger**, *n.* msimamizi wa shamba la (mwitu wa) serikali.

rank, (1) *n.* daraja, cheo, usheha, manzili; (*row*) safu; (*high rank*) cheo kikubwa, daraja bora. *The ranks, Rank and file*, askari. *He has risen from the ranks*, alikuwa na cheo kidogo, sasa, ni mkubwa. — *v.t.* weka; (*arrange*) tengeneza, panga; — *v.i.* (*be placed*) wekwa, hesabiwa, -wa na sifa (cheo, hesabu).

rank, (2) *a.* -kuza, -kubwa mno, -ingi mno, -a kupita kiasi; (*strong smelling*) -a kunuka, -a kuvunda, -enye uvundo, -a harufu mbaya, -liochachuka, -kali. *A rank idler,* mvivu kabisa. *A rank liar,* mwongo sana.

rankle, *v.i.* choma moyo, tia uchungu, waka, pekecha, kereketa.

ransack, *v.t.* tafuta kila mahali; (*plunder*) teka, nyang'anya.

ransom, *n.* ukombozi, fidia. — *v.t.* komboa, fidi.

rant, *v.i.* piga domo, toa maneno mengi, toa makelele ya upuzi, bwabwaja, bwata. — *n.* makelele, domo, maneno, upuzi. **ranter,** *n.* mpiga domo &c.

rap, (1) *v.t.* bisha, gonga, piga, gota, ng'ota. — *n.* pigo, shindo. **rapper,** *n.* chuma cha kubishia mlango.

rap, (2) *n.* *I don't care a rap,* mamoja kwangu. *Not worth a rap,* haifai neno, haina thamani.

rapacious, *a.* -a kuteka, -a kula, -a kutamani, -a pupa, -a choyo, -a tamaa, -a jeuri, -kali. **rapacity,** *n.* pupa, choyo, tutuo, tamaa ya mali, jeuri.

rape, (1) *v.t.* teka, chukua (nyang'anya, iba) kwa jeuri; (*woman*) twaa (lala na, bikiri) kwa sharti (nguvu, jeuri, bila idhini yake). — *n.* jeuri, kufanyia mwanamke jeuri (kwa kumlala, kumbikiri). **rapine,** *n.* kuteka, jeuri.

rape, (2) *n.* namna ya mbegu zenye mafuta.

rapid, *a.* -epesi, -a kwenda upesi, -a kasi, -a haraka, -a mbio, -a ghafula. — *n.* maji yaendayo kwa kasi, matelemko (maporomoko) ya maji, mkondo wa nguvu. **rapidity,** *n.* upesi, hima, haraka, mbio. **rapidly,** *adv.* ghafula, mbio, hima, kwa haraka.

rapier, *n.* upanga mwembamba.

rapine, *n.* taz. *rape* (1).

rapscallion, *n.* mtu mwenye tabia mbaya, mlaghai, mhuni, mtundu, mtukutu.

rapper, *n.* taz. *rap* (1).

rapport, *n.* *Be in rapport,* sikilizana, arifiana.

rapt, *a.* -liochukuliwa na furaha, -a furaha nyingi, -a fikira nyingi, -a kushindwa moyo. **rapture,** *n.* furaha nyingi (kupita kiasi), kipeo cha furaha, hali ya heri. **rapturous,** *a.* -a *rapture.*

rare, (1) *a.* (*air*) -embamba, haba; (*precious*) -a tunu, ajabu; (*scarce*) adimu, -siopatikana ila -chache, -a shida, -chache; (*very excellent*) bora, -sio na kifani. *Be* (*become*) *rare* (*e.g. of a visitant*), ghalika; (*of food, money &c.*) adimika, ghalika. *It is a rare specimen,* -ko -chache, -a namna hii, shida kupatikana namna hii, tunu. **rarefaction,** *n.* (hewa) kuwa haba, kuwa nyembamba. **rarify,** *v.t.* fanya haba, punguzia uzito au wingi wa hewa &c. **rarity,** *n.* tunu, hedaya, azizi, ajabu; (*scarceness*) kuwa haba, uchache. *It is a great rarity,* shida sana kupatikana namna yake, imeghalika sana. **rarely,** *adv.* mara chache, shida.

rare, (2) *a.* (nyama) isiyopikwa sana, iliyopikwa kidogo tu.

rascal, *n.* mtu mwenye tabia mbaya kabisa, mlaghai, mshari, mtundu, mtukutu, mchimvi. **rascality,** *n.* ubaya, ulaghai. **rascally,** *a.* -baya, -ovu.

rash, (1) *n.* vipele, ukurutu. *Come out in a rash, as the result of eating anything taboo,* wenga.

rash, (2) *a.* -jasiri, -a kujihatirisha bure, -enye moyo mgumu, -shupavu; (*precipitate*) -a harara, -epesi; (*dangerous*) -a hatari sana; (*foolish*) -jinga, -a ujinga. **rashly,** *adv.* kwa kutofikiri hatari, kwa ujasiri, kwa ujinga, bila kufikiri. **rashness,** *n.* ujasiri, kuingia hatarini bure, harara.

rasher, *n.* kipande chembamba cha nyama ya nguruwe.

rashly, *adv.,* **rashness,** *n.* taz. *rash.*

rasp, *v.t.* (*file*) chua, piga tupa; (*grate*) kwaruza, paruza; (*irritate*) tia uchungu, kasirisha, udhi. — *n.* tupa, kwaruzo.

raspberry, *n.* tunda dogo la Ulaya.

rat, *n.* panya; (*large*) buku; (*person*) mhaini, mhuni, msaliti. *Smell a rat*, shuku hila. — *v.i.* winda (saka) panya kwa mbwa; (*desert*) haini, asi.

ratable, *a.* taz. *rate* (2).

ratchet, *n.* gurudumu lenye meno yanayoelekea upande mmoja ili lizunguke namna moja lisiweze kurudi.

rate, (1) *v.t.* karipia, kemea.

rate, (2) *n.* mwendo; (*tax*) kodi, ushuru; (*price*) bei, kima, thamani; (*degree*) kadiri, kiasi, kanuni; (*of ships*) namna, aina. *At any rate*, hakuna budi, iwayo yote, hakika, kwa kila hali, sharti. — *v.t.* kadirisha, amria kiasi cha (kadiri ya) kodi. **ratable**, *a.* -a kutoa kodi, -a kulingana na kiasi maalum. **ratepayer**, *n.* mtoa kodi. **rating**, *n.* kadiri ya kodi (ya ujira, ya cheo &c); (*on warship*) watu wa vyeo mbalimbali chini ya *captain*. **ratio**, *n.* kadiri, jinsi ya kuwiana (ya kuhusiana), uhusiano. **ration**, *n.* posho ya kila siku. — *v.t.* posha, -pa posha.

rather, *adv.* (*moderately*) kidogo, si sana; (*preferably*) zaidi, afadhali. *I should rather go*, napenda kwenda, afadhali niende. *I had rather not*, sipendi mwenyewe. *Rather!* ndiyo! sana!

ratify, *v.t.* tia idhini, sahihisha, tia hakika thibitisha. **ratification**, *n.* (*approval*) ukubali, idhini, usahihi; (*confirmation*) hakika, kuthibitisha, thibitisho.

rating, *n.*, **ratio**, *n.*, **ration**, *n.* taz. *rate* (2).

rational, *a.* -a akili, -a busara. **rationale**, *n.* maelezo, sababu, hoja, shauri. **rationalism**, *n.* kufuata akili za binadamu. **rationalist**, *n.* afuataye akili za binadamu katika kueleza mambo ya dini (ya ujuzi). **rationality**, *n.* kuwa na akili, kulingana na akili, akili. **rationalize**, *v.t.* eleza kwa jinsi ya akili za binadamu.

ratlins, ratlines, ratlings, *n.* kamba ndogo za ngazi ya kupandia mlingoti merikebuni.

rattan, *n.* namna ya henzerani.

ratten, *v.t.* nyang'anya (haribu, vyombo vya kazi (kuzuia kazi isifanyike).

rattle, *v.i.* tatarika, alikaalika, lia kama kayamba (kama kokoto katika buyu &c.); (*of talk*) sema upesi upesi, kimbiliza maneno; (*of motion*) enda mbiombio; — *v.t.* tatarisha, liza (kayamba &c.); (*disconcert*) fadhaisha, hangaisha. — *n.* vipande vya kualika, kayamba, mchezo wa kutatarika, mlio wa vitu vikigongana (kama wa kayamba &c.); (*in throat*) kikoroma. **rattling**, *a.* -a kutatarika, -a kulialia kama kayamba &c. **rattlesnake**, *n.* namna ya nyoka wa *America* mwenye sumu afanyaye mlio wa kutatarika kwa mkia akikasirishwa.

raucous, *a.* -a kukwaruza.

ravage, *v.t.* teka, haribu, kumba; (*destroy*) haribu, umbua, angamiza. **ravager**, *n.* mharabu, mwenye kuteka. **ravages**, *n.* madhara, kuumbuka, uharibifu, hatari, hasara, maangamizi.

rave, *v.i.* fanya (nena) kama mwenye wazimu, fanya kishetani, paya, payukapayuka, -wa na pepo. *Rave about*, sifu sana. **raving**, *a.* -enye wazimu. *Raving madness*, shetani, mahoka, pepo.

ravel, *v.t.* (*undo*) fumua, tatanua, chamvua; (*entangle*) tatanisha; — *v.i.* (*become frayed &c.*) fumuka, chamvuka, tatanika, tatana.

raven, (1) *n.* ndege kama kunguru mkubwa.

raven, (2) *v.i.* fanya kama mnyama anayetafuta chakula chake, toa ukali, -wa na uchu (shauku, njaa).

ravenous, *a.* -enye njaa kuu, -a kulafua, -lafi, -enye pupa.

ravine, *n.* bonde, shimo, genge.

raving, *n.* taz. *rave.*
ravish, *v.t.* chukua (mwanamke) kwa nguvu, tendea jeuri, twaa mwanamke (bikiri) kwa jeuri (bila ruhusa yake); (*charm*) shinda moyo (akili) kwa furaha kuu, shangaza mno. **ravishing**, *a.* -zuri sana, -a kufurahisha mno. **ravishment**, *n.* kuchukua kwa nguvu, furaha kuu ya kushinda moyo.
raw, *a.* -bichi; (*bare*) -tupu, wazi; (*weather*) baridi; (*inexperienced*) -jinga, -zuzu. *Raw material*, vitu vya kufanyizia vitu vingine, *e.g.* pamba, katani, manyoya, mbata *&c.* *Raw recruit*, askari mpya (mchanga) asiyefundishwa bado). **raw-boned**, *a.* (*animal*) gofu la mnyama, mafupa wazi. **rawness**, *n.* kuwa *raw*, ubichi, ujinga, uzuzu.
ray, *n.* mwanga, mwangaza, kianga, mshale wa nuru, miale; (*point*) ncha, pembe.
raze, *v.t.* angusha, bomoa, haribu kabisa.
razor, *n.* wembe, **razor-strop**, *n.* kinoo cha wembe, ukanda wa kunolea wembe.
re, in re, *prep.* kwa habari za, kwa, juu ya.
re-, *pref.* tena, *e.g. re-tell*, simulia tena.
reach, *v.t.* fika, fikia, pata, patia, soza, enea hata; (*extend*) nyosha mkono, toa mkono; (*hand, pass to*) toa (leta) kwa kunyosha mkono; (*attain*) pata; — *v.i.* (*make effort*) jitahidi; (*extend*) enea, tandaa, tambaa, fika. *As far as the eye can reach*, upeo wa macho. *Reach up*, nyanyua mkono, inua, chuchumia. — *n.* kunyosha mkono; (*extent*) eneo, mfiko; (*capacity*) uwezo, nguvu, akili; (*open space*) mahali pawazi, peupe.
react, *v.i.* tenda jambo (geuka hali, shtuka *&c.*) kwa sababu ya kutendewa jambo, tendewa na kutendea nguvu, rudisha hali, geuzana, rejeana. *React against*, geuka kinyume. **reaction**, *n.* kutenda kwa sababu ya kutendewa, hali iletwayo kwa kutendewa, urejeo, kurudia hali ya kwanza; (*mutual*) kugeuzana; (*physical exhaustion*) unyong'onyevu (udhaifu, uzito, uvunde, mavundevunde) unaofuata juhudi kubwa. **reactionary**, *a.* -a *reaction*, -a kutaka kurudia hali ya kwanza; (*revolutionary*) -a kutaka maasi, -a kupinga maendeleo.
read, *v.t.* (*p.t. and pf.t.* **read**) soma, soma wazi, soma kitabu; (*understand*) fahamu, tambua;—*v.i.* soma, weza kusoma, jifunza kusoma. *Read into*, tia maana. *It will read well*, (yakiandikwa) yatapendeza kusoma. — *a.* -enye elimu, -enye kusoma. *Well read, Widely read, Deeply read*, -liosoma sana, mwana vyuoni, -enye maarifa ya vitabu. **readable**, *a.* -tamu kwa kusoma, -a kupendeza, -a kukolea, -a kusomeka. **reader**, *n.* mwenye kusoma vitabu, msomaji; mtu asiye padre mwenye ruhusa kusoma kanisani; (*lesson-book*) kitabu cha kujifunza kusoma. **reading**, *n.* kusoma vitabu; (*style of*) jinsi ya kusoma; (*in public*) kusoma wazi mbele ya watu; (*text*) maneno yenyewe ya kitabu. **reading**, *a.* -a kusoma sana, -a kutaali. **reading-book**, *n.* kitabu cha kujifunzia kusoma. **reading-room**, *n.* chumba cha kusomea, chumba cha vitabu.
readily, *adv.*, **readiness**, *n.* taz. *ready.*
reading, *n. and a.*, **reading-book**, *n.*, **reading-room**, *n.* taz. *read.*
readjust, *v.t.* tengeneza tena, linganisha mara ya pili.
ready, *a.* tayari; (*quick*) -a upesi, -epesi, elekevu; (*easy*) rahisi; (*at hand*) karibu, -a kuwapo tayari. *Ready money*, fedha mkononi, fedha taslimu, nakidi. *Ready market*, tamaa tele. *Make ready*, andaa, zatiti, weka tayari. **readily**, *adv.* mara hiyo, upesi, rahisi. **readiness**, *n.* wepesi, welekevu; (*preparedness*) kuwa tayari. *Be in readiness*, -wa tayari. **ready-made**, *a.* -liokwisha fanyizwa tayari, tayari.

reagent, *n.* kitu kinachogeuza au kujaribia kitu mwenzake.

real, *a.* -a hakika, -a kweli, halisi, sahihi, -a asili, -liopo. *Real property,* mali zisizochukulika (zisizoondoleka), *e.g.* shamba, kiwanja, nyumba *&c.* **realism,** *n.* kufikiri vilivyopo, vilivyoonekana kuliko vinavyowazika tu. **realist,** *n.* aelezaye mambo yalivyo, si yanavyowazika kuwa. **reality,** *n.* hali ya kuwa kweli (hakika, halisi *&c.*); jambo la (kitu cha) hakika (si la kuwazika tu). **realizable,** *a.* -a kumalizikana, -a kupatikana, -a kufanyikana, -a kusadikiwa *&c.* **realization,** *n.* kujulisha hakika ya jambo, ujuzi halisi wa jambo, kufanya jambo kuwa hakika, utokezi wa jambo lililotumainiwa (lililotazamiwa, lililotamaniwa *&c.*) kupata. **realize,** *v.t.* (*execute*) maliza, timiliza, fikiliza; (*get*) pata; (*produce*) fanya, fanyiza; (*grasp*) ona kuwa kweli, ng'amua, sadiki, amini, fahamu moyoni; (*property*) uza kwa fedha. **really,** *adv.* kweli, hakika, hasa, kabisa.

realm, *n.* milki, ufalme, nchi; (*matters*) mambo; (*class*) aina.

ream, *n.* fungu la karatasi, kurasa 480.

reanimate, *v.t.* huisha, fufua; (*rally*) amsha, tia moyo na nguvu.

reap, *v.t.* vuna, chuma; (*obtain*) pata, pewa. **reaper,** *n.* mvunaji, mvuni.

reappear, *v.i.* onekana tena, tokea mara ya pili; (*on farther side*) tumbuza. **reappearance,** *n.* matokeo ya pili, kurudi, kuonekana tena.

reappoint, *v.t.* agiza (amuru, weka) mara ya pili.

rear, (1) *v.t.* simamisha, simikisha, inua, pandisha; (*build, construct*) jenga, fanyiza; (*bring up a child*) lea; (*animals*) fuga, lisha, chunga; (*plants*) panda, otesha; — *v.i.* (*of horse*) simama (kwa miguu miwili ya nyuma). **rearing,** *n.* kusimama, kusimamisha *&c.*; (*training*) malezi; (*of animals*) kufuga, ufugaji, kuchunga, kulisha.

rear (2), *n.* upande wa nyuma, kinyume. *Bring up the rear,* fuatana wa mwisho. — *a.* -a nyuma, -a mwisho. *Rear-guard,* askari wa nyuma, walinzi wa nyuma. **rearward,** *adv.* kwa nyuma, kinyume.

rearrange, *v.t.* geuza taratibu, tungua, pangilia. **rearrangement,** *n.* mageuzi, madaraka mapya.

rearward, *adv.* taz. *rear* (2).

reason, *n.* (*intellect*) akili; (*ground, motive*) sababu, kisa, sabiki, maarubu, madhumuni; (*sense*) maana; (*truth*) kweli; (*fairness*) haki; (*right*) adili; (*reasoning*) kutumia akili, hoja. *By reason of,* kwa sababu ya, kwa ajili ya, minajili ya, kwa maana ya. — *v.i.* tumia akili, fikiri, waza; (*argue*) hojiana, jadiliana, toa sababu (hoja). *Reason with,* hoji. *Reason out of,* fanya kuacha (kwa kueleza hoja). *Reason into,* fanya kukubali (kwa kueleza hoja). **reasonable,** *a.* -a akili, -zuri, -pole, -a haki, -a kweli, -a maana. **reasoner,** *n.* mtoa hoja, mleta sababu. **reasoning,** *n.* (*argument*) hoja, kuhojiana, majadiliano; (*intellectual process*) kutumia akili, kufikiri, fikira, mawazo.

reassemble, *v.t.* kusanya (kutanisha, unga, unganisha) mara ya pili (tena); — *v.i.* kutanika (kusanyika, ungana, ungamana) mara ya pili (tena).

reassert, *v.t.* sema mara ya pili.

reassure, *v.t.* rudishia moyo, ondolea mashaka, tumainisha, -pa moyo, tuliza, hozahoza.

rebate, *n.* upunguo, kipunguo, kukata, mkato.

rebel, *n.* mwasi, mhuni. — *v.i.* asi, halifu, huni; (*feel repugnance against*) chukia sana. **rebellion,** *n.* maasi, uhalifu. **rebellious,** *a.* -asi, -kaidi, -halifu.

rebind, *v.t.* (*p.t. and pf.t.* **rebound**) tia jalada mara ya pili, jalidi tena.

rebound, *v.i.* duta, rudi nyuma, rudishwa nyuma, ruka tena.

rebuff, *v.t.* jibia vikali, vunjia maneno, zuilia maneno, kanya, kataa.

— *n.* jibu kali, kanyo, kikanyo. *Give a rebuff to*, vunja uso.
rebuild, *v.t.* (*p.t. and pf.t.* **rebuilt**) jenga tena (upya), fanyiza mara ya pili (upya).
rebuke, *v.t.* karipia, kemea, onya, laumu; (*check*) zuia, nyamazisha. — *n.* karipio, kemeo, onyo, lawama, neno kali, magombezi.
rebut, *v.t.* kana, kanya, kanusha, kataa, onyesha uwongo, rudi neno, dakuliza. **rebutment,** *n.* kanyo, dakizo, udaku.
recalcitrant, *a.* -kaidi, -pinzani.
recall, *v.t.* ita tena, rudisha, amuru kurudi; (*an order*) tangua (amri ya kwanza); (*retract, unsay*) geuza, rudisha; (*recollect*) fahamu, kumbuka; (*revive*) fufua; (*remind*) kumbusha.
recant, *v.t.* jikania maneno ya kwanza, geuza (rudisha) maneno, tubu, ritadi.
recapitulate, *v.t.* simulia mara ya pili, eleza kwa maneno machache, jumlisha. **recapitulation,** *n,* kujumlisha habari, muhtasari, mafupisho.
recapture, *v.t.* twaa mara ya pili, kamata tena. — *n.* kutwaa (kutwaliwa) mara ya pili.
recast, *v.t.* (*p.t. and pf.t.* **recast**) (*metal &c.*) mimina katika kalibu mara ya pili, subu tena; (*alter*) fanyiza vingine, fanyiza upya; (*an account*) hesabu tena.
recede, *v.i.* enda nyuma, rudi; (*of water*) pwa; (*from view*) tokomea. *Recede from*, acha, ondoka.
receipt, *n.* kupokea, kuletewa, kukabidhi, kustakabadhi; (*for money*) hati, stakabadhi, risiti, wasili; (*income*) mapato, uchumi, maduhuli; (*prescription*) karatasi (hati, maelezo) ya dawa; (*for cookery*) habari, maelezo. — *v.t.* sahihisha (hati ya fedha).
receive, *v.t.* pokea, letewa, kubali, karibisha; (*get*) pata, pewa, tiwa; (*feel*) ona; (*contain*) weka. **receiver,** *n.* mwenye kupokea *&c.*; chombo cha kuwekea kitu, chombo cha kupokelea **receptacle,** *n.* chombo cha (chumba cha, mahali pa) kuwekea vitu, *e.g.* mfuko, kikapu kasha, chombo, chumba, ghala *&c.*
reception, *n.* kupokea, kukaribisha, kukubali, kuletewa; (*of guests &c.*) baraza, tafrija, karamu, mkutano, kukaribisha, kuamkia; (*acceptance*) ukubali. *Hold a reception*, barizi. *He had a warm reception*, alipokewa kwa furaha, alishangiliwa. **receptive,** *a.* -a kupokea, -a kuweka, -a kufahamu; (*of the mind*) -sikizi, sikivu, -elekevu, -fahamivu, -a kutaka maarifa. **receptivity,** *n.* kuwa *receptive,* sikizi, usikivu, wepesi, welekevu, ufahamivu.
recension, *n.* kusahihisha kitabu; kitabu kilichosahihishwa.
recent, *a.* -pya, -a siku hizi, -a karibu. **recently,** *adv.* siku hizi, karibu, si zamani, juzi, juzijuzi.
receptacle, *n.*, **reception,** *n.*, **receptive,** *a.*, **receptivity,** *n.*, taz. *receive.*
recess, *n.* mahali pa ndani, pembetundu; (*in a wall*) shubaka, kidaka; (*holiday*) siku za (muda wa) kupumzika, wakati wa kulikizwa, livu; (*withdrawal*) kurudi nyuma, kujitenga, kupunguka; (*of tides*) kupwa.
recherché, *a.* -zuri, sana, -a mtindo, -teule, haba.
recipe, *n.* maelezo ya kufanyiza (kuunga, kuchanganya) kitu cha kula (cha kunywa, au dawa). **recipient,** *n.* mwenye kupokea (kupewa, kuletewa).
reciprocal, *a.* -a kubadili, -a kulipa, -a kupana, -a kurudisha, -a wao kwa wao, -a -enyewe kwa -enyewe; (*in comp.*) -ana. *Reciprocal affection,* upendano. *Reciprocal action,* kutendeana sawasawa. **reciprocally,** *adv.* kwa jinsi ya kutendana. **reciprocate,** *v.t.* tendana, pana, oneana, badili; (*return*) lipa, rudisha. **reciprocation,** *n.* kubadili, kulipa *&c.*
reciprocity, *n.* kutendana sawasawa ushirika, maagano.
recite, *v.t.* sema, nena, soma; (*repeat by heart*) kumbuka, sema kim.yo-

moyo (kwa moyo), soma kwa ghaibu, (*narrate*) simulia, nena, toa habari ya; (*publicly*) soma mbele ya watu. **recital**, *n*. kunena, kusoma, kusimulia; (*narrative*) habari, kisa, masimulizi; mtu kusoma (kuimba, au kupiga ngoma *&c*.) ili kufurahisha wenzake. **recitation**, *n*. kusema, kusoma *&c*., masimulizi.

reck, *v.t.* angalia, jihadhari, ogopa, jali. **reckless**, *a*. jahili, -jasiri, -a kujihatirisha bure, -kavu wa macho, -shupavu, bila hadhari, -zembe, -potovu. *A reckless fellow*, mtu wa kujiendea, asiyejali mtu. **recklessly**, *adv*. bila hadhari, kwa ujinga, bure, ovyo. **recklessness**, *n*. kuwa *reckless*, upotovu, upumbavu, ujahili, kutojali, uzembe.

reckon, *v.t.* hesabu, dhani; (*class*) tia, weka. *Reckon on*, amini, sadiki, tumaini, tegemea; (*except*) tazamia. **reckoning**, *n*. hesabu, idadi, malipo; (*of ship*) hesabu ya mwendo, majira. *Be out of reckoning*, potea.

reclaim, *v.t.* rudisha; (*tame*) fuga; (*reform*) ongoa, hidi; (*civilize*) ongoza, adilisha, geuza kuwa -ema (-ungwana), staarabisha, tamaduni; (*cultivate*) fanya mashamba, fyeka. **reclaimable**, *a*. -a kurudika, -a kuonyesha. **reclamation**, *n*. kurudisha *&c*.

recline, *v.i.* inama, lala; (*lean on*) egemea, vamia; (*lie at ease*) tandawaa, jinyosha.

recluse, *n*. mtawa, mtu wa pekee, ajitengaye na ulimwengu.

recognize, *v.t.* tambua, fahamu, jua, baini, ng'amua, maizi, hisi; (*acknowledge*) ungama, kiri, kubali; (*show gratitude for*) shukuria, lipa. **recognition**, *n*. kutambua, utambuzi, ufahamu; (*acknowledgement*) mwungamo; (*gratitude*) shukrani, ushukuru. **recognizable**, *a*. -a kutambulika, -a kufahamika. **recognizance**, *n*. kama *recognition*; (*engagement*) sharti, ahadi, dhamana.

recoil, *v.i.* rudi nyuma, duta, shtuka; (*shrink from*) nywea, ngwea, epuka, kimbia. — *n*. kurudi nyuma, mshtuko, mshindo.

recollect, *v.t.* kumbuka, fahamu; (*oneself*) jirudia; (*re-collect*) kusanya tena (mara ya pili). **recollected**, *a*. -a fikira, -tulivu, -a kiasi. **recollection**, *n*. ukumbuko, ufahamu; (*thing recollected*) jambo lililokumbukwa, jambo lililopita, mawazo ya mambo yaliyopita. *Within my recollection*, katika zamani zangu (maisha yangu).

recommence, *v.i.* anza tena, chaga, chachawa, chamka; — *v.t.* anzisha mara ya pili. **recommencement**, *n*. mwanzo wa pili, kuanza tena, kuchaga *&c*.

recommend, *v.t.* sifu, pendekeza; (*advise*) usia, shauri, nasihi; (*commit*) weka, kabidhi; (*give favourable impression*) pendeza. **recommendable**, *a*. -a sifa (tabia) njema, -ema, -amini, -stahivu, -stahiki. **recommendation**, *n*. sifa (tabia) njema, ustahivu, ustahiki; kupendekeza; (*letter*) barua ya kupendekeza. **recommendatory**, *a*. -a kusifu, -a kupendekeza.

recompence, *v.t.* lipa, jazi, tuza, -pa zawadi. — *n*. malipo, ujira, ijara, tuzo, jazo, thawabu, zawadi, haki, wokozi, ukombozi; (*punishment*) adhabu, rada; (*revenge*) kisasi.

reconcile, *v.t.* patanisha, suluhisha, afikanisha, ridhisha, tuliza, tengeneza, ondoa tofauti, fanya sawa, sawazisha, linganisha. *Be reconciled*, tulia, ridhika, patana, afikana. **reconcilable**, *a*. -a kupatana, sawa. **reconciliation**, *n*. kusuluhisha, kufanya amani, kufanya sawa, kulinganisha; (*harmony, concord*) mapatano, uradhi, suluhu, urafiki, amani. **reconciliatory**, *a*. -suluhifu, -suluhishi, -a kupatanisha, -a kutuliza, -a amani.

recondite, *a*. -a siri, -a fumbo, -gumu, -siotambulikana kwa urahisi.

reconnoitre, *v.t.* peleleza, chungulia, doea, doya, enda kutazama nchi ya adui. **reconnaissance**, *n*. upelelezi, uchungulizi.

reconsider, *v.t.* fikiri tena, rudia, rejea. **reconsideration,** *n.* kufikiri (kufikirika, kufikiriwa) mara ya pili, kurudia, marudio, marejeo.

reconstruct, *v.t.* jenga tena, fanyiza mara ya pili, geuza. **reconstruction,** *n.* kujenga tena *&c.*; jengo lililojengwa upya; shauri lililotungwa upya (lililogeuzwa).

record, *v.t.* andika habari ya, andika. — *n.* habari (zilizoandikwa), tarehe; (*memorial*) kumbukumbu, ukumbusho; (*best of its kind*) kipeo; (*of gramophone*) sahani ya gramafoni. *Break* (*beat*) *the record*), shinda -ote pia, pitilia mbali. **recorder,** *n.* mwandishi, katiba, karani.

recount, *v.t.* simulia, eleza, hadithia, hubiri; (*re-count*) hesabu mara ya pili.

recoup, *v.t.* lipa, chuma faida (kulipa hasara).

recourse, *n.* *Have recourse to,* taka msaada wa, kimbilia, tumia, jaribia, rejea.

re-cover, *v.t.* funika tena (upya).

recover, *v.t.* jipatia tena, jirudishia, pata tena (kilichopotea); (*get well*) pata afya tena; (*get one's due*) pata (iliyo haki, *e.g.* deni); — *v.i.* pona, pata nafuu (ashekali, ahueni). **recoverable,** *a.* -a kurudika, -a kupona, patikana tena. **recovery,** *n.* kujipatia tena; (*cure*) kupona.

recreant, *a.* -wongo, -oga, -nyonge, kafiri. — *n.* mtu mwoga (mnyonge) asiyetekeleza ahadi.

recreate, *v.t.* umba tena, fanyiza mara ya pili (upya). **recreation,** *n.* mchezo, maburudisho, mazungumzo, maongezi, furaha, tafrija. **recreative,** *a.* -a mchezo, -a kutia afya, -a kuburudisha.

recriminate, *v.i.* gomba, gombana, lipa, rudisha maneno makali, rudisha mashtaka, shtakiana, laumiana. **recrimination,** *n.* kugomba *&c.*; mashtaka juu ya mashtaka yanayoletwa na mshtakiwa. **recriminative,** *a.* -a kugomba *&c.*, -a kurudisha mashtaka (maneno makali).

recrudescence, *n.* kuanza tena (vita, matata, ugonjwa *&c.*), kurudi, kuchaga, kucharuka. **recrudescent,** *a.* -a kurudia, -a kuchaga.

recruit, *v.t.* andika (changa) askari wapya; (*repair*) tia (rudisha) nguvu; — *v.i.* (*rest*) pumzika, pata afya, pata nguvu, punga hewa. — *n.* askari mpya (mchanga). **recruiting,** *n.* kutafuta watu kuwa askari, kuandika (kuchanga) askari.

rectangle, *n.* umbo lenye pande nne na pembe zote za mraba. **rectangular,** *a.* -a *rectangle,* -enye pembe zote za mraba.

rectification, *n.*, **rectified,** *a.* taz. *rectify.*

rectify, *v.t.* sahihisha, tengeneza, rekabisha, toa makosa, safisha. **rectification,** *n.* kusahihisha *&c.* **rectified,** *a.* -liosafika sana, -liorekabishwa. **rectitude,** *n.* adili, maadili, wema, utu mwema, haki, unyofu, amini, uaminifu.

rectilineal, *a.* -a mistari iliyonyoka.

rectitude, *n.* taz. *rectify.*

rector, *n.* kasisi wa mtaa; (*of school*) mkuu wa chuo kikubwa. **rectory,** *n.* nyumba ya *rector* (kasisi).

rectum, *n.* mkundu.

recumbent, *a.* -liolala, -a kulala.

recuperate, *v.i.* pona (katika ugonjwa au hasara). **recuperative,** *a.* -a kutia afya, -a kuponya.

recur, *v.i.* -wa (-ja, fanyika, tokea, rudi) mara ya pili (mara kwa mara), rudia, chamka; (*have recourse to*) rejea kwa, kimbilia; (*come to mind*) rudia moyoni. **recurrence,** *n.* kuwa (kutokea) mara ya pili (mara kwa mara). **recurrent,** *a.* -a kurudi mara ya pili (mara kwa mara), -a vipindi, -a kurudirudi.

recusant, *a.* -asi, -kaidi.

red, *a.* -ekundu; (*dull*) *red dye,* hina. *Red Sea,* Bahari ya Sham. *Red tape,* mazuio ya bure. *Red cross,* msalaba mwekundu katika bendera nyeupe, ni alama ya madaktari na wasaidizi wao vitani. — *n.* rangi nyekundu, wekundu. **redden,** *v.t.* tia wekundu;

— *v.i.* (*blush*) geuka (uso) kwa haya, iva usoni. **reddish,** *a.* -ekundu kidogo. **red-handed,** *a.* katika jambo lenyewe, katika kutenda, pale pale. **red-hot,** *a.* -enye moto sana (hata kuwa nyekundu). **red-letter day,** *n.* sikukuu. **redness,** *n.* wekundu.

redact, *v.t.* tengeneza, sahihisha (panga, tunga) tayari kupigwa chapa.

redan, *n.* ngome.

redden, *v.,* **reddish,** *a.* taz. *red.*

redeem, *v.t.* komboa, fidi, lipa; (*perform*) fikiliza, tekeleza (ahadi); (*recover*) jipatia tena, fanyiza. **redeemer,** *n.* mkombozi, fidia. **redemption,** *n.* ukombozi, fidia. **redemptive,** *a.* -a kuokoa, -a kufidi.

red-handed, *a.* **red-hot,** *a.* taz. *red.*

redintegration, *n.* kufanyizwa kamili, kupona, kupata uzima.

redirect, *v.t.* andika anwani nyingine katika bahasha ya barua.

rediscover, *v.t.* vumbua mara ya pili. **rediscovery,** *n.* kuvumbua (kuvumbuliwa) mara ya pili.

redistribute, *v.t.* toa (gawa, gawanya, eneza) mara ya pili (vingine); (*rearrange*) ainisha (panga, andika) mara ya pili (vingine).

red-letter day, *n.,* **redness,** *n.* taz. *red.*

redolent, *a.* -a kunukia. **redolence,** *n.* kunukia, harufu nzuri.

redouble, *v.t.* ongeza, zidisha; — *v.i.* (*become greater*) zidi.

redoubt, *n.* ngome ndogo, boma dogo.

redoubtable, *a.* hodari, mashuhuri, -kuu.

redound, *v.i.* rudi; (*issue, result*) -ja, toka, tokea. *It redounds to his credit,* inamletea heshima.

redress, *v.t.* tengeneza, rekabisha, lipia haki, okoa. — *n.* msaada, malipo ya haki, wokovu, kisasi.

reduce, *v.t.* (*lessen*) punguza, shusha, kata, nakisi; (*subdue*) piga, tiisha, vunja; (*change*) geuza hali (kwa kuponda, kusaga, kushindika &c.); (*in arith.*) geuza hesabu; (*arrange*) andika, panga, gawanya. **reduced,** *a.* -liopunguzwa &c.; (*circumstances*) -nyonge, -a dhiki, maskini. **reducible,** *a.* -a kupunguzwa, -a kuweza kupunguzwa, -a kupunguzika &c. **reduction,** *n.* kupunguza (kupunguka) &c., nakisi.

redundant, *a.* -a kuzidi, -ingi mno, -a kuzidi kadiri inayotakiwa (iliyo ya hoja). **redundance,** *n.* kuwa -ingi mno, wingi, kuzidi.

reduplicate, *v.t.* tia mara mbili, fanya maradufu. **reduplication,** *n.* kutia (kutiwa) mara mbili (maradufu).

re-echo, *v.t.* rudisha sauti; — *v.i.* lialia, toa mwangwi.

reed, *n.* unyasi, tete, kangaga, mafunjo, njaanjaa, mrija; (*pipe*) filimbi *A broken reed,* msaidizi asiyeweza kutumainiwa. **reedy,** *a.* -a nyasi &c. nyingi, -a matete mengi; (*of voice*) -embamba.

reef, (1) *n.* (*in the sea*) miamba, fungu, vipwa, kizingiti; (*of gold-bearing quartz*) miamba yenye dhahabu ndani yake.

reef, (2) *n.* (*in sail*) sehemu ya tanga (inayoweza kukunjwa). — *v.t.* punguza, kunja, tua kidogo.

reek, *n.* mvuke, uvundo, moshi. — *v.i.* nuka, toa mvuke (moshi).

reel, *n.* kijiti cha kukunjia uzi; (*dance*) namna ya ngoma ya kucheza. — *v.t.* (*thread &c.*) kunja (uzi &c.), tatiza kijitini; — *v.i.* (*stagger*) lewalewa, levyalevya, pepesuka, sitasita, sesetuka, sepetuka, yugayuga.

re-elect, *v.t.* chagua mara ya pili. **re-election,** *n.* kuchagua (kuchaguliwa) mara ya pili, mchaguo wa pili.

re-embark, *v.i.* panda chomboni (melini) mara ya pili; — *v.t.* pakia mara ya pili.

re-enact, *v.t.* amuru mara ya pili. **re-enactment,** *n.* kuamuru (kuamriwa) mara ya pili.

re-enter, *v.t.* ingia mara ya pili.

re-entry, *n.* kuingia mara ya pili, mwingilio wa pili.

re-establish, *v.t.* imarisha (thibitisha, weka, amuru, tengencza &c.) mara ya pili. **re-establishment,** *n.* kuweka (kuwekwa, kuimarisha, kuimarika &c.) mara ya pili.

re-examine, *v.t.* *examine* mara ya pili. **re-examination,** *n.* kuangalia mara ya pili, mkaguo wa pili &c.

refection, *n.* chakula. **refectory,** *n.* chumba cha kulia, pa kulia, mezani.

refer, *v.t.* (*to*), (*send back*) pelekea, rejezea, rudishia; (*assign*) hesabia, wekea; — *v.i.* (*have recourse to*) rejea kwa, kimbilia, tumia; (*mention*) nena, taja; (*have reference*) husika na (kwa), husu. *This word refers only to persons,* neno hili lahusu (lahusika na) watu tu. **referee,** *n.* mwamuzi. **reference,** *n.* kumbukumbu, marejeo; (*mention*) habari, mtajo; (*meaning*) maana, kiini; (*witness*) shahidi; (*quotation*) maneno fulani ya kitabu. *In reference to,* kwa habari ya, kwa mambo ya, juu ya. *What is the reference?* neno hili limetoka wapi? kumbukumbu la nini? larejea wapi? **referendum,** *n.* kuuliza watu wote (si wale waliochaguliwa tu).

refill, *v.t.* jaza tena, tia tena; — *v.i.* jaa tena.

refine, *v.t.* takasa, safisha, fanya safi; (*civilize*) adilisha, fanya -ungwana, ondolea ushenzi, staarabisha, tamaduni. **refined,** *a.* -liosafika, safi, -liotakata, -a kiungwana, -a adabu, -a malezi mazuri, makini. **refinement,** *n.* ustaarabu, utamaduni, uungwana, adabu, madaha, makini, malezi mazuri; (*purification*) kuwa safi, usafi, utakaso, uhalisi. **refinery,** *n.* (*sugar*) kinu cha kufanyizia sukari. **refining,** *n.* (kufanya, kufanyika) safi &c.

refit, *v.t.* tengeneza tena, pamba mara ya pili, tia zana (vifaa, mafaa, vyakula &c.) tena. — *n.* matengenezo (zana, mafao, mapambo, vyakula) mapya.

reflect, *v.t. and i.* rudisha (nuru, moto, mfano &c.); (*consider*) fikiri, waza. *Reflect upon* (*disparage*) shutumu, umbua, singizia, sengenya. *His action reflected great credit upon him,* tendo lake lilimpatia sifa bora. **reflecting,** *a.* -a kurudisha (nuru, moto, mfano &c.); (*thoughtful*) -a fikira nyingi. **reflection,** *n.* (*of light* &c.) kurudi, kurudisha; (*thoughts*) fikira, mawazo; (*censure*) masingizio, mashutumu; (*likeness*) mfano, methali; (*visual image*) picha (sanamu, sura, mfano) katika kioo (maji &c.). **reflective,** *a.* -a *reflection.* **reflector,** *n.* kioo &c. cha kurudishia nuru &c.

reflex, *a.* -liopindika nyuma; (*introspective*) -a kujiangalia nafsi; (*involuntary*) -liotendeka na mwili bila kukusudiwa (bila kuweza kuzuiwa), -a kujiendea. — *n.* mfano, methali; (*reflexion*) nuru iliyorudika. **reflexive,** *a.* kupindika nyuma, -a kukumbuka mambo ya zamani. *Reflexive verb* (*in Swahili Grammar*), *verb* yenye -ji- ndani yake, *e.g.* alijipiga.

refluent, *a.* -a kupwa, -a kurudi.

reflux, *n.* kupwa, kurudi.

reform, *v.t.* tengeneza, fanyiza, ongoza, ongoa, hidi, geuza kuwa -ema, rudi, ondolea makosa, adilisha; — *v.i.* ongoka, tengemana, tengenea, tulia. — *n.* matengeneo &c. **reformation,** *n.* kutengeneza &c., matengenezo. *The Reformation,* matengenezo ya Kanisa la kiingereza A.D. 1530–1680. **reformatory,** *n.* nyumba ya kuadibisha na kuongoza watoto wabaya. **reformed,** *a.* -liotengenezwa, -lioongoka, -liogeuka kuwa -ema, -liotengemana. **reformer,** *n.* mtengenezaji, mwongozi, mkufunzi.

refract, *v.t.* geuzia njia, pinda, vunja. **refraction,** *n.* kugeuzwa njia, kupinda, kupindika, upinduzi. **refractive,** *a.* -a *refraction,* -a kugeuzia (kupinda) njia. **refractoriness,** *n.* ukaidi, ushupavu, ugumu. **refrac-**

tory, *a.* -kaidi, -shupavu, -potoe, -bishi; (*hard*) -gumu.
refrain, (1) *v.t.* zuia; — *v.i.* (*abstain from*) jizuia, epuka, acha.
refrain, (2) *n.* sehemu ya wimbo unaorudiwa mara kwa mara, kiitikio, kipokeo.
refrangible, *a.* -liopindikana, -liogeukana. **refrangibility**, *n.* kupindikana, upindikano.
refresh, *v.t.* burudisha, fariji, amsha, tia moyo, -pa nguvu. **refresher**, *n.* kitu, mtu au jambo linaloburudisha (linaloamsha akili), kiburudisho. **refreshing**, *a.* -a baridi, -a kuburudisha *&c.* **refreshment**, *n.* kuburudika, kitu kinachoburudisha, kiburudisho, chakula *&c.*
refrigerate, *v.t.* tia baridi, gandisha kwa baridi. **refrigerator**, *n.* chombo cha kufanyia baridi, chombo cha kugandishia kwa baridi.
refuge, *n.* kimbilio, mahali pa salama (pa kukimbilia). **refugee**, *n.* mkimbizi, mtoro.
refulgent, *a.* -a kung'aa, -nayong'aa. **refulgence**, *n.* kung'aa, mng'aro, mng'ao, mwangaza.
refund, *v.t.* rudisha, lipa. —*n.* malipo.
refuse, (1) *n.* taka, takataka. — *a.* -baya, -siofaa neno, hafifu.
refuse, (2) *v.t.* kataa, iza; (*food, because of pique*) susia, zilia; (*withhold*) katalia, nyima, kania, hini. **refusal**, *n.* makatazo, kanyo; (*right to purchase*) ruhusa ya kununua au kuacha (kabla ya wengine kupata nafasi).
refute, *v.t.* kanusha, onyesha uwongo wa, thibitisha ya kuwa neno (jambo) si kweli, vunja, pindua, jibia. **refutation**, kukanusha, mkanusho, kuonyesha uwongo, jibu.
regain, *v.t.* pata tena, fikiri mara ya pili.
regal, *a.* -a kifalme, -a kustahili mfalme, -a sherehe nyingi, -a madaha. **regalia**, *n.* mapambo ya mfalme, taji, fimbo *&c.*
regale, *v.t.* karibisha vizuri, lisha, furahisha, pendeza.
regalia, *n.* taz. *regal.*
regard, *v.t.* (*look at*) angalia, tazama; (*consider*) fikiri, tafakari, dhani, ona, kumbuka; (*esteem*) heshimu, stahi, jali; (*concern*) pasa, husu. *As regards, Regarding,* kwa habari za, mintarafu ya. *Regard as,* tia katika, ona sawa na. — *n.* (*notice*) kuangalia sifa; (*esteem*) heshima, staha, itibari; (*affection*) upendo, mahaba. *Kind regards,* salamu sana. *Give my regards to,* unisalimie. *In* (*with*) *regard to,* kwa habari ya, kwa mambo ya, juu ya, mintarafu ya. **regardful**, *a.* -a kuheshimu, -a kustahi, -angalifu, -a kufikiria. **regardless**, *a.* bila kufikiri (kustahi, kujali, kuangalia, kukumbuka, hadhari), -zembe.
regatta, *n.* mashindano ya mashua (ya kuendeshwa kwa makasia au matanga).
regency, *n.* taz. *regent.*
regenerate, *v.t.* (*recreate*) zaa mara ya pili (kwa jinsi ya roho), tia uzima mpya, huisha upya; (*reform*) ongoza, rudi; (*cause to grow again*) kuza mara ya pili. **regeneration**, *n.* uzazi wa pili; (*reform*) wongofu, kuongoza. **regenerative**, *a.* -a *regeneration.*
regent, *n.* mtawala wa muda kidogo badala ya mfalme, naibu. **regency**, *n.* utawala wa *regent.*
regicide, *n.* (*person*) mwuaji wa mfalme; (*act*) kuua mfalme.
régime, *n.* utawala, serikali; (*method &c.*) utaratibu, desturi, kawaida, kanuni, sheria. **regimen**, *n.* taratibu, hasa ya chakula *&c.* iliyoshauriwa na daktari.
regiment, *n.* jeshi la askari, yaani kumpuni nne, kadiri ya askari elfu moja; (*general*) kundi. **regimental**, *a.* -a *regiment. Regimentals,* mavazi, ya askari.
region, *n.* nchi, upande, mahali jirani, ujirani; (*sphere, subject*) mambo, habari. **regional**, *a.* -a nchi, -a mahali penyewe, -a mahali maalum.
register, *n.* kitabu, daftari, orodha,

tarihi, hesabu; (*of voice*) kadiri ya sauti ya mtu, yaani toka ya chini mpaka ya juu. — *v.t.* andika katika kitabu (orodha, daftari); (*express, show*) onyesha; **registrar**, *n.* mwandishi wa tarihi (mambo, orodha &c.). **registration**, *n.* kuandika (kuandikisha) katika kitabu (orodha &c.). **registry**, *n.* afisi ya *registrar*.

regress, regression, *n.* kurudi, kusogea nyuma. **regressive**, *a.* -a kurudi nyuma.

regret, *v.t.* juta, jutia, sikitika, sikitikia, ona (ingiwa, shikwa na) majuto ya, ona majonzi (uchungu) kwa sababu ya kutenda (au kutotenda); (*repent*) tubu. — *n.* majuto, masikitiko, majonzi; (*repentance*) toba. **regretful**, *a.* -a kujuta, -a kusikitika. **regrettable**, *a.* -a kujutika, -a kusikitisha.

regular, *a.* -a kawaida, taratibu, sawasawa; (*moral*) -a kiasi, -a adili, -adilifu; (*symmetrical*) -linganifu, -a kulingana. *A regular thief*, mwivi wa kupindukia. — *n.* askari wa jeshi. **regularity**, *n.* kawaida, kiasi, utaratibu, ulinganifu. **regularize**, *v.t.* tengeneza, ratibisha, patanisha na sheria (kanuni, kawaida &c.). **regularly**, *adv.* kwa kawaida (desturi, taratibu). **regulate**, *v.t.* tengeneza, ratibisha, rekabisha, simamia, amuru, tawala. **regulation**, *n.* kusimamia &c.; (*order*) amri, madaraka, sharti, maagizo. **regulative**, *a.* -a kusimamia (kuamuru, kurekabisha, kutawala, kuongoza). **regulator**, *n.* (mtu, kitu) -enye kuweza, -enye nguvu ya kuzuia (ya kutawala &c.).

regurgitate, *v.t.* rudisha kinywani kutoka tumboni, cheua, tapika.

rehabilitate, *v.t.* rudishia cheo, rudishia heshima (sifa njema &c.).

rehearse, *v.t.* (*repeat*) nena mara ya pili, kariri; (*recount*) simulia, nena, soma; (*practice*) jifanya tayari, jisomesha, jizoeza. **rehearsal**, *n.* ukariri &c., jaribio la mchezo (hotuba &c.).

reign, *n.* utawala, mamlaka, enzi, ezi; (*period of rule*) utawala, wakati wa kumiliki; (*dominance*) uwezo, nguvu. — *v.i.* tawala, milki; (*prevail*) shinda, enea pote.

reimburse, *v.t.* lipa, rudisha gharama. **reimbursement**, *n.* malipo, kulipa.

rein, *n.* hatamu, ugwe, kigwe. *Give the reins to*, jitoa kwa, tozuia. — *v.t.* zuia kwa hatamu, zuia.

reindeer, *n.* mnyama kama kulungu wa nchi za baridi sana.

reinforce, *v.t.* leta msaada, peleka shime; (*strengthen*) tia nguvu, -ja kusaidia. *Reinforced concrete*, sakafu yenye mapao ya chuma ndani, zege. **reinforcement**, *n.* msaada, shime; (*military*) askari wa kuzidishia nguvu ya jeshi.

reins, *n. plur.* mafigo, kiuno.

reinstate, *v.t.* rudishia hali ya kwanza. **reinstatement**, *n.* kurudishia (kurudishiwa) hali ya kwanza.

reinvest, *v.t.* *invest* mara ya pili.

reinvigorate, *v.t.* tia nguvu tena, rudisha afya, -pa moyo tena, burudisha.

reissue, *v.t.* toa mara ya pili.

reiterate, *v.t.* sema mara ya pili; sema mara kwa mara (mara nyingi), kariri. **reiteration**, *n.* kusema mara ya pili &c., msemo (mtajo) wa pili.

reject, *v.t.* kataa, kana, tupia mbali, iza. **rejection**, *n.* kukataa, kanyo, kukatalika, katao, mardudi.

rejoice, *v.t.* furahisha, changamsha, teremesha; — *v.i.* furahi, shangilia, terema; (*after trouble, difficulty &c.*) koya. **rejoicing**, *n.* furaha, shangwe, shangilio, nderemo.

re-join, *v.t.* unganisha tena (mara ya pili), unga tena; — *v.i.* ungana (ungamana) tena.

rejoin, *v.t.* jiunga na . . . tena, rudia, ungana na . . . tena; — *v.i.* (*reply*) jibu, itika. **rejoinder**, *n.* jibu, itiko.

rejuvenate, *v.t.* rudishia ujana, rudishia nguvu za ujana. **rejuvenation**, *n.* kurudishia (kurudi) nguvu za ujana.

rekindle, *v.t.* washa (chochea, amsha) mara ya pili; — *v.i.* waka (chocheka, amka) mara ya pili.

relapse, *v.t.* rudia hali mbaya (uovu, mwendo mbaya, udhaifu, ugonjwa). — *n.* kurudia hali mbaya, kuugua tena, kurudiwa na ugonjwa. **relapsing fever,** *n.* homa ya kurudia (ya vipindi) kama iletwayo na papasi.

relate, *v.t.* (*narrate &c.*) simulia, hadithia, toa habari, hubiri; (*bring into relation*) fungamanisha, linganisha, unganisha; — *v.i.* (*refer to*) -wa na habari, rejea, fungamana na, husu, husiana na; (*have bearing on*) wia, wiana na. **related,** *a.* (*be*) wia, wiana; (*connected*) -wa mamoja (hali moja, jinsi moja), lingana, fungamana, husu, husiana na; (*by birth*) -wa ndugu (jamaa) ya; (*narrated*) hubiriwa, hadithiwa, simuliwa. **relation,** *n.* (*of kinship*) ndugu, jamaa, ufungu, ahali, akraba; (*general*) jinsi ya kuwia (kuwiana, kuhusu, kuhusiana na), uhusiano, hali ya watu au vitu, vyenyewe kwa vyenyewe, kuwia, kuwiana; (*reference*) urejeo; (*condition, position*) hali. *In relation to,* kuliko. **relationship,** *n.* (*kinship*) udugu, ufungu, ukoo; (*general*) = *relation.* **relative,** *n.* ndugu, jamaa, ufungu. *Relative pronoun,* neno lenye kurejea *noun* kama -o-, -vyo-, -lo-, -zo- *&c.* — *a.* (*having reference to*) -enye habari (ya kitu kingine), -a kuwiana au kuhusiana (na kitu kingine); (*not absolutely*) -a kadiri si halisi), -enye masharti. **relativity,** *n.* kuwiana, kuhusiana; kuwa kadiri, kuwa kadiri ya binadamu, si kamili.

relax, *v.t.* (*weaken*) legeza, dhoofisha, punguza, sabili; (*relieve*) pumzisha, burudisha; (*of bowels*) endesha choo, fungua; — *v.i.* (*become lax*) legea. *Relax* (*rest*) *the limbs,* achanisha viungo, jinyosha. **relaxation,** *n.* kulegea, ulegevu *&c.*; (*diversion*) pumziko, mchezo, burudisho, mazungumuzo, tafrija.

relay, *n.* (watu, farasi, vyombo *&c.* vilivyowekwa tayari kupokezana kazi kwa zamu). *Do by relays,* pokezana kazi. *Arrange relays,* amuru zamu kwa zamu, weka akiba. — *v.t.* weka mara ya pili; (*a message*) pokea na kupeleka mbele.

release, *v.t.* fungua, acha, weka huru, ondoa, feleti; (*of a spring &c.*) fyatua. — *n.* kufungua, kufungu-liwa *&c.* mafungulio.

relegate, *v.t.* peleka, weka, ondoa. **relegation,** *n.* kupeleka *&c.*

relent, *v.i.* poa (hasira, ukali, ukatili, ushupavu, ugumu), tulia na kupunguka hasira (ukali *&c.*), ona huruma, sikitika, acha ukali (ukatili, ugumu). **relentless,** *a.* pasipo huruma, -kali, -gumu, -katili, -kakamizi.

relevant, *a.* -a kuhusu, -a kuhusiana na, -a kupasa, -a kufaa, -a kufungamana na. **relevancy,** *n.* kuhusu, kupasa, kufaa, uhusiano.

reliable, *a.*, **reliance,** *n.* taz. *rely.*

relic, *n.* mabaki, masazo, masalio, kumbukumbu, ukumbusho (wa mambo ya zamani au ya watakatifu wa kale). **reliquary,** *n.* sanduku ya kuwekea *relic.*

relict, *n.* mjane (mwanamke aliyefiwa na mume wake).

relief, *n.* taz. *relieve.*

relieve, *v.t.* pumzisha, fariji, ondolea huzuni (maumivu, taabu *&c.*), punguza, tuliza; (*assist*) saidia, auni, achia, nafisi, nafisisha, pokea kazi; (*enhance, add effect to*) pendekeza, pamba, onyesha vizuri. **relief,** *n.* msaada, shime, ondoleo la huzuni (taabu, maumivu, shida mbaya, dhiki *&c.*), faraja, kitulizo; (*taking turns*) kubadili zamu, kupokezanya kazi, badala; (*projection*) kutokeza. *Relief map,* ramani yenye milima inayotokeza.

religion, *n.* dini, ibada, imani, mambo ya Mungu, utawa. **religious,** *a.* -a dini, -a ibada, -a mambo ya Mungu, -tawa. **religiously,** *adv.* kwa jinsi ipasavyo mtu wa dini, kwa heshima (ustahi, kicho); (*strictly*) barabara, sawasawa.

relinquish, *v.t.* acha, fungua, toa, tupa, weka; (*go from*) toka katika, ondokana na. **relinquishment,** *n.* kuacha &c., achilio.

reliquary, *n.* taz. *relic.*

relish, *n.* (*taste*) ladha, utamu, harufu; (*seasoning*) kiungo; (*meat &c. eaten with food*) kitoweo; (*pleasure*) furaha, kupendezwa sana, kupenda sana; (*inclination*) moyo. *Give a relish to,* pendekeza; (*food*) koleza, tia viungo. — *v.t.* penda sana, pendezwa na.

reluctant, *a.* (*be*) topenda, totaka, tokubali, chukia. *He was reluctant to go,* hakutaka kwenda. **reluctance,** *n.* kutotaka, kutokubali, chuki. *With reluctance,* kwa moyo usiotaka, kwa kujikalifu.

rely, *v.i.* (*on*) amini, sadiki, tumainia, tegemea, jetea, tawakali. **reliable,** *a.* amini, -aminifu, -a kutumainiwa, -a kusadikiwa, -a kutegemea, thabiti, madhubuti. **reliance,** *n.* wimani, tumaini, tegemeo, kujetea. *Place reliance on* (*in*), tumaini, amini, tegemea.

remain, *v.i.* (*be left*) baki, salia; (*continue*) shinda, ishi, dumu, kaa, chelewa, sakini; (*unsold, unused*) china, doda, selelea, **remainder, remains,** *n.* baki, sazo, masazo, salio; (*in vessel &c.*) shinda, kishinda. *Remains* (*corpse*) maiti.

remand, *v.t.* rudisha kifungoni mpaka siku ya shauri.

remark, *v.t.* (*notice*) angalia, ona; (*say*) sema, nena. — *n.* neno, maneno. **remarkable,** *a.* -a sifa, -a maana, -a ajabu, -geni, -kubwa, mashuhuri, -a kuangaliwa, -a kutazamisha. **remarkably,** *adv.* sana.

remarriage, *n.* kuoa (kuolewa) mara ya pili (tena).

remedy, *n.* (*medical*) dawa, mapoza, uganga; (*practical*) shauri la kutuliza, kitulizo, matengenezo, kuponya. *Remedies for hunger,* maponea njaa. — *v.t.* tengeneza, rekabisha, ponya, ponyesha. **remedial,** *a.* -a kuponya, -a kutuliza.

remember, *v.t.* kumbuka, fahamu, dhukuru, nabihi, zingatia; (*salute*) -pa salamu. *Please remember me to him,* tafadhali mpe salamu zangu, unisalimie. **remembrance,** *n.* ukumbuko, ufahamu; (*memento*) ukumbusho, kumbukumbu. **remembrancer,** *n.* ukumbusho, kumbukumbu.

remind, *v.t.* kumbusha, fahamisha. **reminder,** *n.* ukumbusho.

reminiscent, *a.* -a kukumbusha, -a kukumbuka mambo yaliyopita. **reminiscence,** *n.* kukumbuka, kufahamu; (*thing remembered*) jambo lililokumbukwa. *Personal reminiscences* kisa, tarehe.

remiss, *a.* -legevu, -zembe, -vivu, -sioangalia, ajizi. **remissness,** *n.* uzembe, ukosefu, uvivu, ulegevu, ajizi, uajizi.

remit, *v.t.* samehe, achilia; (*dowry*) burai; (*send payment*) peleka, lipa; (*lessen*) punguza, legeza; (*pay*) rudisha, salimisha, toa. **remittal,** *n.* kusamehe &c. **remittance,** *n.* fedha, malipo, kupeleka fedha. **remittent,** *a.* -a kuzidi au kupungua, -a vipindi.

remnant, *n.* baki, sazo, masazo &c. taz. *remainder;* kipande kidogo kilichobaki.

remodel, *v.t.* geuza umbo, geuza, fanyiza upya, tengeneza.

remonstrate, *v.i.* onya, zuia kwa maneno, gombeza, shauri vingine, taradhia. **remonstrance,** *n.* onyo, hoja, maneno ya kuzuia, magombezi, udaku. **remonstrative,** *a.* -a kuonya, -a kugombeza &c.

remorse, *n.* majuto, toba. **remorseful,** *a.* -a kujuta, -a kutubu, -enye majuto (toba). **remorseless,** *a.* pasipo kujuta, pasipo huruma, -katili, -kali, -korofi. **remorselessness,** *n.* ukatili, ukali mwingi, ukorofi.

remote, *a.* -a mbali, -a zamani; (*original*) -a asili; (*insignificant*) kidogo.

remould, *v.t.* geuza umbo, geuza, fanyiza upya, umba upya.
remount, *v.t.* panda mara ya pili (tena), *mount* mara ya pili.
remove, *v.t.* ondoa, ondosha, tenga, weka mbali, hamisha. farakisha; (*clothes*) vua; (*from office*) uzulu; (*erase*) futa; (*a spell, witchcraft*) agua, eua, adua, tegua, zindua; (*bark &c.*) ambua; — *v.i.* (*migrate &c.*) hama, hajiri, hujuru, jitanibu, ondoka. **removable,** *a.* -a kuondoka, -a kuchukulia, -a kuondoleka. **removal,** *n.* kuondoa, kuchukua, kutoa; (*migration*) kuhama, kuondoka.
remunerate, *v.t.* lipa, -pa ujira, jazi, tuza, -pa zawadi. **remuneration,** *n.* ujira, jazo, jaza, tuzo, zawadi, mshahara. **remunerative,** *a.* -a kuleta faida (uchumi, mapato), -enye uchumi.
renaissance, renascence, *n.* siku za kufufuka elimu na maarifa Ulaya, A.D. 1300 mpaka 1500. **renascent,** *a.* -a kutokea mara ya pili, -a kuchipuka tena, -a kupata nguvu tena.
renal, *a.* -a mafigo, -a kiuno.
rename, *v.t.* tia jina jipya, geuza jina.
renascence, *n.*, **renascent,** *a.* taz. *renaissance.*
recontre, rencounter, *n.* mkutano; (*fight*) mapigano, mpambano.
rend, *v.t.* (*p.t. and pf.t.* **rent**) tatua, pasua, rarua, vunja. **rent,** *a.* -liotatuka, -liopasuka *&c.* — *n.* mpasuko, mtatuko, mvunjo, ufa, shimo; (*division, schism &c.*) mtengano, farakano.
render, *v.t.* toa, lipa, rudisha; (*make*) fanya, geuza kuwa; (*translate, explain*) fasiri, onyesha, eleza; (*clarify fat &c.*) safisha siagi (samli *&c.*) kwa kuiyeyusha. **rendering,** *n.* (*translation*) ufasiri, tafsiri; (*representation*) mafafanusi, maelezo, onyesho.
rendezvous, *n.* mahali pa kukutanika; mahali palipoamriwa.
renegade, *n.* mtoro, mkimbizi, haini; (*in religion*) kafiri, abadiliye dini yake.
renew, *v.t.* fanya -pya, tengeneza, fanyiza, fanya mara ya pili, tia nguvu, -pa moyo. **renewal,** *n.* kufanya (kufanyika) tena (upya), kufanyiza mara ya pili (upya).
rennet, *n.* dawa ya kugandisha maziwa.
renounce, *v.t.* (*refuse*) kataa, kana, kanusha; (*give up*) acha, jinyima, jihini, ondokea; (*claim*) burai. **renouncement,** *n.* kukataa *&c.* **renunciation,** *n.* makatao, kanyo; (*relinquishment*) kuacha, kujinyima, kujihini.
renovate, *v.t.* fanyiza kama kwanza, fanyiza upya, tengeneza, burudisha, tia afya. **renovation,** *n.* kufanyika tena, kuburudika. **renovator,** *n.* mtu au kitu cha kufanya -pya (cha kuburudisha).
renown, *n.* sifa, utukufu, jina, fahari, adhama. **renowned,** *a.* -enye sifa, -adhimu, -tukufu, mashuhuri.
rent, (1) *p.t. and pf.t.* ya *rend*; — *a. and n.* taz. *rend.*
rent, (2) *n.* kodi ya nyumba, upangaji. — *v.t.* (*hold on rent*) kodi, panga (nyumba *&c.*); (*grant on rent*) pangisha, kodisha. **rental,** *n.* kadiri ya kodi ya nyumba *&c.*; orodha ya wapangaji na kodi zinazowahusu, jumla ya fedha mtu anayopata kwa kukodisha nyumba zake.
renunciation, *n.* taz. *renounce.*
reorganize, *v.t.* tengeneza upya, geuza taratibu.
repaid, *v. p.t. and pf.t.* ya *repay.*
repair, (1) *v.i.* (*go*) enda.
repair, (2) *v.t.* (*mend*) fanyiza tena, tengeneza; (*of clothes*) shona, tia kiraka; (*of hose, i.e. darn*) tililia; (*make amends*) lipa, rudisha. — *n.* matengenezo; (*state*) hali. *In good repair,* -zima. *In bad repair,* -bovu. **repairer,** *n.* mtengenezaji. **repairable,** *a.* -a kutengenezeka, -lioweza kutengenezwa. **reparation,** *n.* malipo, matengenezo.
repartee, *n.* jibu jerevu (la akili). — *v.i.* daka, dakuliza.

repast, *n.* chakula, karamu, kula.
repatriate, *v.t.* rudisha (peleka) kwake (kwao &c.).
repay, *v.t.* (*p.t. and pf.t.* **repaid**) lipa, rudisha, rejeza; (*reward*) jazi, tuza; — *v.i.* lipa, rudisha; (*make requital*) twaa kisasi. **repayment,** *n.* malipo, kulipa.
repeal, *v.t.* tangua, batilisha, futa, ondoa.
repeat, *v.t.* (*do again*) fanya tena, tenda mara ya pili; (*say again*) sema tena, kariri; (*speak*) sema, soma, kariri; (*say by heart*) sema kwa akili (moyo), soma kwa ghaibu; — *v.i.* (*of food*) puzia; (*recur*) rudiarudia, tokea tena (mara nyingi). **repeatedly,** *adv.* mara kwa mara, mara nyingi, papo kwa papo. **repeater,** *n.* (*watch*) saa ndogo inayogonga; (*gun*) bunduki ya kupigia mishindo mfululizo. **repetition,** *n.* kufanya (kufanyika, kusema, kusoma &c.) mara ya pili (mara kwa mara, mara nyingi), mardudi; (*saying by heart*) kusema kwa akili, kusoma kwa ghaibu, kusema yaliyosomwa kwanza, ukariri.
repel, *v.t.* rudisha nyuma, fukuza, zuia, sukuma mbali; (*displease*) chukiza. **repellent,** *a.* -a kukataza, -a kuchukiza.
repent, *v.t.* tubu, juta, sikitika; (*reform*) tulia, ongoka, tengemana. **repentance,** *n.* toba, majuto, sikitiko; (*reform*) kutulia, kuongoka, utengemano. **repentant,** *a.* -a toba, -a kutubu.
repercussion, *n.* kurudi, kurudisha, kupigapiga; matokeo (yasiyokusudiwa).
repertoire, repertory, *n.* kusanyiko, jamii; jumla ya michezo (nyimbo, ngoma &c.) ya jamii ya wachezaji fulani.
repetition, *n.* taz. *repeat.*
repine, *v.i.* -wa na uchungu (mfundo) rohoni, nung'unika, nuna, sikitika, guna, -wa na majonzi.
replace, *v.t.* rudishia hali (mahali), weka (rudisha) kitu badala ya kingine (kilichoharibika &c.); (*take place of*) ingia mahali pa, -wa badala ya. **replacement,** *n.* kurudisha hali &c., kuingia mahali pa -ingine.
replenish, *v.t.* jaza tena. **replenishment,** *n.* kujaa (kujaza) tena.
replete, *a.* -liojaa, -enye . . . tele.
repletion, *n.* kujaa tele, kushiba, shibe. *To eat to repletion,* kujivimbisha.
replica, *n.* nakili, nakala.
reply, *v.t.* jibu, itika, peleka jibu; — *v.i.* jibu. — *n.* jibu, jawabu, itiko.
report, *v.t.* toa habari, simulia; (*in writing*) arifu, andika habari; (*of police &c. to superior*) toa (leta) timamu; (*accuse*) shtaki, chongea. *Report oneself,* jionyesha. — *n.* (*orderly, account*) maneno ya taratibu, habari halisi, (*of police &c.*) timamu; (*by letter*) taarifa, ripoti; (*loud sound*) mlio, shindo, kishindo; (*rumour*) maneno, kivumo, uvumi. **reporter,** *n.* mwandikaji wa habari, msimulizi.
repose, *v.i.* pumzika, jinyosha, lala, sinzia, kaa raha, starehe; — *v.t.* (*cause to lie*) laza, egemeza; (*place*) weka. — *n.* kupumzika, utulivu, raha, kimya. *Deep (profound) repose,* raha mustarehe. **repository,** *n.* bohari, ghala, duka.
repossess, *v.t.* miliki (milikisha) mara ya pili, pata mara ya pili.
reprehend, *v.t.* laumu, karipia, kemea, shutumu, sema, nenea. **reprehensible,** *a.* -a kulaumika, -enye lawama, -a kustahili kukaripiwa (kukemewa, kulaumiwa). **reprehension,** *n.* lawama, shutumu, kemeo, karipio.
represent, *v.t.* (*make likeness of*) toa mfano wa, fanya sanamu (picha) ya; (*be in place of*) -wa mjumbe wa (wakili wa, upande wa, alama ya, badala ya, naibu ya, mahali pa); (*be like*) fanana na, iga sura ya; (*declare, explain*) onyesha, bainisha, hubiri, toa maneno, eleza. **representation,** *n.* picha, sanamu, mfano; (*statement*) maneno, maelezo.

representative, *n.* (*agent*) wakili, mjumbe; (*substitute*) badala, naibu; (*likeness*) namna, mfano. — *a.* -enye mfano wa (nguvu ya, namna ya, tabia ya &c.) kitu kingine; (*government*) -a wakuu waliochaguliwa na watu wote.

repress, *v.t.* tiisha, funga, zuia, tuliza, nyamazisha, komesha. **repression,** *n.* kuzuia (kuzuiwa) kwa nguvu, kunyamazisha, kutiisha. **repressive,** *a.* -a kutiisha, -a kuzuia, -zuivu, -a kukomesha.

reprieve, *v.t.* achilia (kwa muda au kabisa), achia nafasi, zuia hukumu. — *n.* kuachiliwa kwa kitambo, achilio la muda.

reprimand, *v.t.* laumu, karipia, kemea, nenea. — *n.* lawama, magombezi.

reprint, *v.t.* piga chapa mara ya pili, toa kitabu mara ya pili. — *n.* kitabu (maandiko) kilichopigwa chapa mara ya pili.

reprisal, *n.* kisasi. *Take reprisals,* lipiza kisasi.

reproach, *v.t.* karipia, kemea, laumu, suta, shutumu, kamia, kengemeka, atibu. *Reproach oneself,* jikamia, jilaumu. — *n.* laumu, karipio, kemeo, suto, shutumu, jambo la aibu. **reproachful,** *a.* -a kushutumu, -a kusuta, -a kulaumu, -a kuaibisha.

reprobate, *v.t.* laumu, tokubali, chukia, kataza. — *n.* baa, mwovu kabisa, mfisadi, mfasiki, mpotovu. — *a.* -ovu, -potoe. **reprobation,** *n.* kulaumu &c., laana, machukio.

reproduce, *v.t.* toa tena, leta mara ya pili; (*restore*) rudisha; (*propagate*) zaa; (*make likeness of*) fanya sura ya (mfano, wa, namna ya). **reproduction,** *n.* kuzaa, uzazi; (*likeness, copy*) namna, mfano, sanamu, mwigo; (*fresh growth*) kutoa mara ya pili.

reprove, *v.t.* laumu, nenea, karipia, kemea. **reproof,** *n.* lawama, karipio, kemeo magombezi.

reptile, *n.* mnyama mtambaazi, mnyama wa jamii ya wanyama wenye damu baridi watagao mayai, *e.g.* nyoka, mjusi, mamba, kasa, kobe &c.; (*person*) mtu mwovu mwenye hila.

republic, *n.* jamhuri, nchi inayotawaliwa na mtu aliyechaguliwa na watu wake, si mfalme. **republican,** *a.* -a *republic.*

republication, *n.* kutoa habari mara ya pili; (*book*) kitabu kilichopigwa chapa mara ya pili.

republish, *v.t.* toa (habari, kitabu &c.) mara ya pili, tangaza mara ya pili, bainisha tena.

repudiate, *v.t.* kataa, kania; (*put away*) tupa, jitenga na, achana na; (*a debt*) kataa kulipa. **repudiation,** *n.* kukataa, mardudi, kukania, kuachana.

repugnant, *a.* -a kuchukiza, -a kukirihi, makuruhi; (*contrary*) mbalimbali, -a kinyume. **repugnance,** *n.* (*dislike*) machukio, kirahi; (*antagonism*) ushindani; (*contrariety*) tofauti, hali mbali.

repulse, *v.t.* (*force back*) sukuma nyuma, shinda, fukuza, kimbiza; (*keep back, repel*) kataa, ondoa, komesha. — *n.* kufukuza, kufukuzwa, kushindwa, kanyo, makatazo. **repulsion,** *n.* machukio. **repulsive,** *a.* -a kuchukiza, -baya.

repurchase, *v.t.* nunua mara ya pili, nunua tena. — *n.* kununua tena.

repute, *v.t.* dhani, ona. *He is reputed to be,* anadhaniwa kuwa. —*n.* sifa, tabia, jina, heshima. *Of good repute,* -enye sifa njema. *Of bad repute,* -enye sifa mbaya. **reputable,** *a.* -a sifa njema, -zuri. **reputation,** *n.* sifa, heshima. *Good* (*bad*) *reputation,* sifa nzuri (mbaya). **reputed,** *a.* -a sifa njema, -zuri; (*not guaranteed*) -a kadiri ya. **reputedly,** *adv.* kama inavyodhaniwa, watu wasemavyo.

request, *n.* haja, maombi, matakwa. *Be in request,* takwa, tafutwa. — *v.t.* taka, sihi, omba, tolea haja. *May I request you,* tafadhali.

requiem, *n.* wimbo wa maziko kuombea waliofariki.

require, *v.t.* (*order*) taka kwa nguvu, amrisha, toza, shurutisha, lipiza; (*need*) taka, hitaji, -wa na sharti ya, -wa na faradhi ya. **requirement,** *n.* itakiwayo, matakwa, kanuni, mahitaji, masharti; (*request*) haja, maombi. **requisite,** *a.* -liotakiwa, -a sharti, -a kanuni. — *n.* hitaji, kifaa. **requisition,** *n.* haja, amri, sharti, hali ya kutakiwa. — *v.t.* toza (kwa matumizi ya askari &c.).

requite, *v.t.* (*reward*) lipa, -pa haki, jazi; (*punish*) twaa kisasi, lipiza, adhibu. **requital,** *n.* malipo, haki, tuzo, rada, thawabu; (*revenge*) kisasi, malipizi.

reredos, *n.* pambo juu ya madhabahu kwa nyuma.

rescind, *v.t.* tangua, ondoa, futa, vunja, batili.

rescript, *n.* amri ya mkuu.

rescue, *v.t.* okoa, ponya, fungua, toa, gandua, gangua, opoa. — *n.* wokovu, msaada, kufungua. *Go to the rescue of,* enda kusaidia (kuokoa). **rescuer,** *n.* mwokozi, msaidizi.

research, *n.* kuchungua (kupeleleza, kusoma, kutafuta) ili kuvumbua habari mpya, uchunguzi wa mambo (elimu &c.) kuvumbua habari mpya.

resemble, *v.t.* fanana na, lingana na, landa, shabihi, -wa mfano mmoja na, -wa sawa na, -wa kama. **resemblance,** *n.* mfano, methali, sura moja, usawa, mshabaha.

resent, *v.t.* chukizwa na, onea uchungu (chuki), udhika kwa. **resentment,** *n.* uchungu, chuki, machukio, hasira, mfundo.

reserve, *v.t.* weka akiba, weka, limbika, shika, setiri, bakiza, saza; (*a seat* &c.) andikisha. — *n.* akiba, limbiko; (*soldiers*) askari wa nyuma (wa akiba, wa msaada); (*silence, caution*) unyamavu, utaratibu, hadhari; (*concealment*) usetiri, stara, maficho. **reservation,** *n.* usetiri, kuficha moyoni; (*keep in store*) kujiwekea, kuweka makusudi; (*conditions*) sharti. *With this reservation,* ila (isipokuwa, bila) hii tu. **reserved,** *a.* -nyamavu, -a maneno machache, baridi, -a siri; (*kept for use*) -liowekwa &c. **reservoir,** *n.* birika, hodhi, ziwa, tangi, mahali panapowekwa maji.

reset, *v.t.* (*razor* &c.) noa, tia ukali; (*plant*) atika, pandikiza; (*refix*) weka tena.

reship, *v.t.* pakia mara ya pili, pakua katika meli moja na kupakia katika nyingine.

reshuffle, *v.t.* changanya tena, geuza (mambo).

reside, *v.i.* kaa, -wa na nyumba (makao, makazi), -wamo. **residence,** *n.* kukaa, nyumba, makao, makazi. **residency,** *n.* nyumba ya balozi. **resident,** *n.* (*inhabitant*) mwenyeji, mkaa mahali, mkazi; (*consul*) balozi. — *a.* -a kukaa mahali. **residential,** *a.* -a kukaa watu.

residue, *n.* baki, sazo, salio; (*in a vessel*) shinda, kishinda. **residuary,** *a.* -liobaki, -a mabaki, -a shinda.

resign, *v.t.* toa, acha, weka, jiuzulu. *Resign oneself,* tii, jitoa, shukuru. **resignation,** *n.* kujiuzulu, kutoa, kuacha; (*document*) hati ya kujiuzulu (ya kuomba ruhusa kuacha kazi); (*submission, acquiescence*) kushukuru Mungu, uvumilivu, utulivu, kukata tamaa. **resigned,** *a.* -tulivu, -a kushukuru, -a kukata tamaa, -vumilivu. *He is quite resigned,* amekubali, ameshukuru, ameridhika.

resilent, *a.* -a kunepa, -a kunapukia, -a kurudi (kama mpira ukivutwa).

resin, *n.* utomvu mzito wa baadhi ya miti kama sandarusi. **resinous,** *a.* kama *resin.*

resist, *v.t.* shindana na, simamia, pingia njia, zuia, pinga, kinza, kaidi, asi. **resistance,** *n.* ushindani, ukinzani, upingamizi, upinzani, ukaidi, nguvu ya kuzuia, uzuizi, ugumu, ubishi. **resistless,** *a.* -siozuilika &c.

resolute, *a.,* **resolutely,** *adv.,* **resolution,** *n.* taz. *resolve.*

resolve, *v.t.* azimu, kusudia, nuia,

waza, nia, kaza shauri, yakinia. — *n.* azimu, azimio, nia, kusudi, mradi, shauri; (*determination*) uthabiti, ushupavu, moyo mgumu. **resolute,** *a.* thabiti, -shupavu, -gumu, hodari, -a nguvu. **resolutely,** *adv.* kwa uthabiti. **resolution,** *n.* kusudi, shauri, nia, mradi, azimio; (*firmness*) uthabiti, ushupavu, moyo mgumu; (*decree*) hukumu, amri; (*breaking up*) mvunjo, mchanganuo, mgawo. *Make resolution,* nuia. *Cause (urge, teach) to form resolution,* nuiza.

resonant, *a.* (*of voice*) -nene; (*of room &c.*) -a kurudisha sauti. **resonance,** *n.* mlio, kulialia.

resort, *v.i.* enda mara kwa mara; (*to*) kimbilia, tumia, rudia, rejea kwa. — *n.* (*haunt*) matembezi, mahali pa kutembelea; (*help, resource*) msaada, tegemeo, kimbilio, faradhi.

resound, *v.i.* lialia, lia tena, vuma; (*of fame &c.*) enea pote, julikana pote.

resource, *n.* njia, nguvu, shauri, mali. *Resources,* vifaa, zana, makimbilio, msaada, machumo, mali, njia ya kupata mali. *A man of resources (of many resources),* mwelekevu, mtu wa mashauri mengi. *What resources have we?* tufanyeje? **resourceful,** *a.* -a busara, -elekevu, -erevu, -a mashauri mengi.

respect, *n.* heshima, staha, ustahi, kujali, ustahifu, itibari, taadhima, kicho, uchaji; (*reference, regard*) mambo, habari, kuangalia. *Respects,* salamu. *Send (pay) respects,* salimu. *In respect of,* kwa mambo ya, kwa habari ya, juu ya. *In this respect,* kwa haya, hivi, hivyo. *In all respects,* kwa yote. *In whatever respects,* kwa vyo vyote. *With all respect to him,* awe radhi sana, anisamehe. *Have respect to,* angalia, pendelea, hurumia. — *v.t.* heshimu, stahi, jali, pendelea, sharifu, adhimu, adhimisha, cha; (*take into consideration*) angalia, kumbuka. *Treat with respect,* heshimu, stahi. **respectability,** *n.* hali ya kukaa vizuri (kwa heshima), unyofu. **respectable,** *a.* -a heshima, -zuri, -nyofu, -stahiki, -a kufaa; (*moderate*) -a kiasi, -a kadiri, -a kutosha, si -nyonge. **respected,** *a.* mahashumu, -stahifu. **respecter,** *n.* mwenye kujali (kuheshimu, kuangalia). **respectful,** *a.* -stahifu, -a heshima, -a adabu. *Treat respectfully, Treat with respect,* wekea heshima, heshimu, stahi. **respecting,** *prep.* juu ya, kwa habari ya, kwa mambo ya, kwa. **respective,** *a.* -a (kitu au mtu fulani) peke yake, -moja -moja; (*relative*) -a kadiri, si halisi. *They returned to their respective homes,* walirudi kila mtu nyumbani kwake. *Their respective merits,* sifa zao moja moja.

respiration, *n.* taz. *respire.*

respire, *v.i.* vuta pumzi, pumua, pumzika, tanafusi. **respiration,** *n.* kupumua, kutanafusi.

respite, *n.* kuachiwa kwa muda, kuahirika; (*rest*) nafasi, pumziko, raha, amani. — *v.t.* achia kitambo, pumzisha, -pa nafasi.

resplendence, *n.* taz. *resplendent.*

resplendent, *a.* -a kung'aa, -zuri sana, -a sherehe, -a fahari. **resplendence,** *n.* mng'ao, uzuri, fahari.

respond, *v.i.* jibu, itika, itikia; (*act in answer to*) itikia; (*react to*) shawishika, vutika, ongozeka *&c.* **respondent,** *n.* (*in a law suit*) mshtakiwa, aletwaye hukumuni. — *a.* -a kulingana, -a kujibia. **response,** *n.* jibu, itiko, kulingana. **responsibility,** *n.* kazi, shughuli, usimamizi, daraka, jukumu. *Undertake responsibility of, Make onself responsible for,* chukua madaraka, diriki, tadiriki. **responsible,** *a.* -enye madaraka, -enye kutiwa kazi, -enye kuagizwa (kuaminishwa) shughuli, -enye kusimamia, -enye kutadiriki; (*trustworthy*) amini, -aminifu, -ema; (*onerous*) -kubwa. *Be responsible for,* pasiwa, husiwa, agizwa. *He is responsible,* ni juu yake, ni daraka lake. *A responsible office,* kazi kubwa, kazi yenye madaraka mengi.

You are responsible, juu yako, kazi yako. *Make oneself reponsible*, chukua madaraka, diriki, tadiriki. **respon-sive,** *a.* -a kujibu, -a kuitika, -a kuitikia, -a kushawishika *&c.* taz. *respond.*

rest, (1) *n.* (*remainder*) baki, sazo, salio, shinda, kishinda, mwisho. *The rest, All the rest, The rest of them*, wengine wote (nyingine zote, vingine vyote *&c.*). *For the rest*, mwisho. — *v.i.* kaa, dumu. *Rest assured that I will do what I can*, kaa ukijua ya kuwa nitafanya kadiri niwezavyo. *It rests with him*, ni juu yake, hiari yake.

rest, (2) *n.* raha, pumziko, buraha; (*sleep*) usingizi; (*resting-place, pause*) kikomo, kituo; (*in music*) kimya; (*prop*) kitegemeo, mhimili, nguzo. — *v.i.* pumzika, lala, starehe, tulia, kaa, burahi; (*settle*) tua; (*acquiesce*) -wa radhi, ridhika; (*stop*) isha; (*be supported*) tegemea; — *v.t.* pumzisha, starehesha, tegemeza. **resting-place,** *n.* pumziko, kituo, kupumzika. **restive,** *a.* -siotulia, a-kuchezacheza, -tukutu, -a chachari. **restless,** *a.* -tukutu, -siotulia. *Be restless* (*toss about*), gaagaa, furukuta. *Pass a restless night*, gaagaa usiku kucha. **restlessness,** *n.* utukutu, haraka, fadhaa, chachari.

restaurant, *n.* hoteli, mkahawa.

resting-place, *n.* taz. *rest* (2).

restitution, *n.* kulipa, malipo, ukombozi.

restive, *a.*, **restless,** *a.*, **restlessness,** *n.* taz. *rest* (2).

restoration, *n.*, **restorative,** *a.* taz. *restore.*

restore, *v.t.* (*return*) rudisha; (*repay*) lipa; (*repair*) tengeneza; (*cure*) ponya. **restoration,** *n.* matengenezo, kutengeneza, kurudisha, kuponya, kulipa. **restorative,** *a.* -a *restoration*, -a kutia nguvu (afya, uzima), -a kuburudisha.

restrain, *v.t.* zuia, shika, funga. **restraining,** *a.* -a kuzuia, -zuivu. **restraint,** *n.* kuzuia, kizuio, zuio, amri; (*self control*) kujizuia, kiasi; (*confinement*) kufungwa, kuzuiwa.

restrict, *v.t.* zuia, weka mipaka, husuru, tia amri (sharti). **restriction,** *n.* kizuio, amri, sharti, mipaka. **restrictive,** *a.* -a kuzuia, -zuivu.

result, *v.i.* tokea, tukia, -wa. *Result from*, -wa sababu ya, fuata, andama. *Result in*, tokea. — *n.* mwisho, tokeo, jambo, mambo ya baadaye, yafuatayo. *Be the result of*, -wa kwa sababu ya. *The result was*, kwa sababu hii, basi, mwisho. *Results of war*, mambo yatukiayo kwa sababu ya vita, matokeo ya vita. **resultant,** *a.* -a mwisho, -liotukia. **resultless,** *a.* -a bure, -siofaa.

resume, *v.t.* twaa tena, anza tena, chaga, charuka, shika tena, endelea. **résumé,** *n.* muhtasari, ufupisho, habari chache. **resumption,** *n.* kutwaa tena *&c.*

resurrection, *n.* ufufuo, ufufuko; (*general*) kiyama. *The day of resurrection*, siku ya kiyama, siku ya kubaathiwa.

resuscitate, *v.t.* huisha, fufua, amsha, chochea, rudisha, toa tena, rejeza uzima. **resuscitation,** *n.* kuhuisha *&c.*

retail, *n.* (*sale*) rejareja. — *a.* -a rejareja, -a kadiri (kiasi) ndogo ndogo. — *v.t.* uza rejareja, chuuza, toa kidogo kidogo; (*circulate*) eneza. **retailer, retail-dealer,** *n.* mchuuzi, mwuza dukani, mbazazi.

retain, *v.t.* shika, weka; (*hire*) ajiri. **retainer,** *n.* mfuasi, mtumishi; (*lawyer's fee*) ada ya wakili. **retention,** *n.* kuzuia, kufunga, kuweka. **retentive,** *a.* -a kushika; (*able to remember*) -a kufahamu. *He has a retentive memory*, anakumbuka sana, anafahamu mengi.

retaliate, *v.i.* lipa maovu kwa maovu, rudisha ukali kwa ukali, lipiza (twaa) kisasi. **retaliation,** *n.* kisasi, malipo. **retaliative,** *a.* -a kisasi, -a kurudisha maovu (ukali) kwa maovu (ukali).

retard, *v.t.* kawilisha, cheleza, ahirisha, weka, zuia, vunja mwendo wa, punguza mwendo, usirisha.

retch, *v.i.* kokomoka.

retention, *n.*, **retentive,** *a.* taz. *retain.*

reticence, *n.* taz. *reticent.*

reticent, *a.* -nyamavu, -a kimya, -fichifichi, -a siri, -a maneno machache. **reticence,** *n.* unyamavu, ustirifu.

reticular, reticulated, *a.* kama wavu, kama kimia. **reticule,** *n.* kibahasha, kifuko.

retina, *n.* kama kioo kilicho ndani ya jicho.

retinue, *n.* wafuasi, watumishi, jamii ya watu wanaoandamana na mkubwa.

retire, *v.i.* rudi, endelea nyuma, jitenga, ondoka, kaa faraghani; (*from office*) ondoka, acha kazi, jiuzulu; (*to rest*) enda kulala. **retired,** *a.* -a faragha; (*from business*) -liotoka kazini. **retirement,** *n.* kurudi nyuma; (*quiet, privacy*) faragha, raha, pasipo na ghasia (kazi, shughuli). **retiring,** *a.* -nyamavu, -a kimya, makini, -tulivu, -enye haya, -nyenyekevu, -siye na makuu, -pole.

retort, *v.t. and i.* jibu vikali, itika kwa nguvu, rudisha maneno. — *n.* jibu kali, jibu la nguvu; (*vessel*) chombo cha kioo au madini chenye shingo iliyopindika, cha kupikia dawa &c.

retouch, *v.t.* tengeneza, sahihisha.

retrace, *v.t.* fuasa nyuma, rudia; (*with pen &c.*) andika mara ya pili. *He retraced his steps,* alirudi nyuma.

retract, *v.t.* kana, kanya (geuza) maneno ya kwanza, rudisha, tangua. **retractile,** *a.* -a kurudika ndani, -a kufumbata, -a kuweza kurudishwa nyuma. **retraction,** *n.* kuvuta nyuma, kurudika ndani; kukanya, utanguo.

retreat, *v.i.* rudi nyuma, kimbia. — *n.* kurudi nyuma, kukimbia, marejeo; (*refuge*) kimbilio, mahali pa raha (pa salama, pa faragha).

retrench, *v.t.* punguza (katia) gharama, chekecha, punguza. **retrenchment,** *n.* kupunguza, upunguo, kukatia gharama, mchekecho.

retribution, *n.* malipo, kisasi, upatilizo, adhabu; (*of evil, recoiling on one*) mashumushumu, rada. **retributive,** *a.* -a kulipa, -a kulipiza kisasi, -a kupatiliza, -a kuadhibu, -a kurudi.

retrieve, *v.t.* pata tena, rudisha, komboa, geuza, ongoa, hidi. **retrievable,** *a.* -a kupatika tena, -a kutengeneka. **retriever,** *n.* namna ya mbwa hodari wa kuwindia.

retrocede, *v.i.* rudi nyuma, geuka; (*strike inwards*) ingia ndani.

retroflex, *a.* -liopindika nyuma.

retrograde, *a.* -a kurudi nyuma, -a kuwa -baya zaidi, -a kuharibika. **retrogression,** *n.* kurudi nyuma, kuharibika. **retrogressive,** *a.* -a kurudi nyuma, -a kuharibu, -a kuharibika.

retrospect, retrospection, *n.* kutazamia yaliyopita, kukumbuka mambo ya zamani. **retrospective,** *a.* -a kutazamia nyuma, -a kuhusu (-a kupasa) wakati uliopita.

return, *v.i.* rudi, rejea, endelea nyuma, rudia, rudia hali ya kwanza; — *v.t.* (*reply*) jibu, itika; (*repay*) rudisha, lipa; (*give account of*) toa hesabu ya. — *n.* marejeo, kurudi; (*payment*) kulipa, malipo, kisasi; (*account*) hesabu, daftari, habari; (*profit*) chumo, faida, mapato. *In return,* kwa kulipa, mahali pake, badala yake.

reunion, *n.* mkutano, kuunganika tena, kupatana.

reunite, *v.t.* kutanisha, unganisha, patanisha, suluhisha; — *v.i.* (*come together &c.*) kutana, kutanika, ungana, ungamana, unganika, patana.

reveal, *v.t.* funua, fumbua, fichua, dhihirisha, eleza siri, onyesha, vumbua. **revelation,** *n.* kufunua &c., ufunuo, ufumbulio.

réveillé, *n.* ngoma ya kuamsha askari asubuhi.

revel, *v.i.* fanya karamu ya furaha

nyingi; (*carouse*) fanya karamu (ya ulevi na ulafi); (*delight*) furahia, jifurahisha. — *n.* karamu ya furaha nyingi, mandari, karamu ya ulevi na ulafi. **revelry,** *n.* furaha kubwa karamuni, ulevi na ulafi.

revelation, *n.* taz. *reveal.*

revelry, *n.* taz. *revel.*

revenge, *v.t.* twaa (lipiza) kisasi cha. *Revenge oneself on,* jilipiza kisasi. — *n.* majilipo, kisasi. **revengeful,** *a.* -a kutaka kisasi, -a kisasi, -kali mno.

revenue, *n.* mapato, chumo, uchumi, maduhuli; (*public*) mapato ya serikali kwa kodi, ushuru &c.

reverberate, *v.t.* (*reflect*) rudisha sauti (joto, nuru); — *v.i.* (*of sound*) lialia, vumavuma, nguruma, duta, endelea, rindima. **reverberation,** *n.* mlio, uvumi, ngurumo, kurudisha sauti rindimo &c.

revere, *v.t.* heshimu, stahi, -cha, jali. **reverence,** *n.* heshima, kicho, staha, uchaji, unyenyekevu. — *v.t.* taz. *revere.* **reverend,** *a.* -a kupewa heshima, -a kustahili heshima, -stahiki, -stahifu; (*as title*) padre. **reverent, reverential,** *a.* -a kuheshimu, -a kutoa heshima, -a kustahi, -nyenyekevu. **reverently,** *adv.* kwa heshima, kwa staha (unyenyekevu, kicho).

reverie, *n.* kama ndoto, fikira, mawazo. *In a reverie,* katika fikira, kwa ndoto.

reversal, *n.* taz. *reverse.*

reverse, *v.t.* pindua, geuza, tangua, rejeza, rudi, rudisha nyuma. — *n.* (*other side*) upande wa nyuma (wa chini, wa pili); (*opposite, contrary*) kinyume, iliyo mbalimbali, mbalimbali; (*defeat*) kupigwa, kushindwa, ushinde; (*disaster*) mapinduzi, maangamizi, msiba. — *a.* -a pili, -a nyuma; (*quite different*) -liyo mbalimbali, -a kinyume, mbalimbali kabisa. **reversal,** *n.* kupindua, upinduzi, ugeuzi, tanguo, kushindwa, ushinde. **reversible,** *a.* -a kupindukana, -a kutumika kuwili. **reversion,** *n.* kurudia hali, kurudia (kurudishia) mwenyewe. **reversionary,** *a.* -a *reversion.* **revert,** *v.i.* rudi, rejea, rudia hali ya kwanza.

revet, *v.t.* funika (imarisha, zuia) kwa mawe &c. **revetment,** *n.* safu (tabaka, utando) ya mawe &c., ya kuzuia (kuimarisha).

review, *v.t.* angalia (fikiri, tafakari) mara ya pili, tazamia, kagua, chungua; (*criticize in writing*) andika maono juu ya (kazi, maandiko, ya mtu mwingine); (*inspect troops*) kagua. — *n.* kuangalia &c.; (*of troops*) kutazamia jeshi la askari, mkaguo; (*periodical*) kitabu chenye habari ya vitabu vingine na mambo pia, gazeti; (*of a book*) maandiko yenye maono (ya mtu) juu ya kitabu fulani; (*revise*) sahihisha. **reviewal,** *n.* kuangalia, kukagua, kuchungua &c. **reviewer,** *n.* mwandikaji wa *review,* msahihishi, mkaguzi.

revile, *v.t.* tukana, suta, shutumu, taya, kebehi. **reviling,** *n.* matayo, masuto, mashutumu, matukano.

revise, *v.t.* sahihisha, tengeneza, toa makosa, fanya safi, safisha; (*alter*) geuza, badili, tengeneza. **revisal,** *n.* kusahihisha &c. **revision,** *n.* kusahihisha &c., kitabu (maandiko &c.) kilichosahihishwa. **revisional,** *a.* -a kusahihisha.

revisit, *v.t.* amkia tena, zuru mara ya pili, rejea, rudia.

revival, *n.* taz. *revive.*

revive, *v.t.* fufua, huisha, amsha (anzisha, rudisha, eneza, chochea) mara ya pili; — *v.i.* (*recover*) fufuka, huika, amka; (*return*) rudi, anza tena. **revival,** *n.* ufufuo, kuhuisha, kuamsha, kuamka, kurudi &c.

revivify, *v.t.* rudishia nguvu (uzima), huisha, amsha.

revocable, *a.,* **revocation,** *n.* taz. *revoke.*

revoke, *v.t.* geuza (maneno ya kwanza), tangua, futa, ondoa; (*in cards*) kosa kucheza namna ya karata iliyochezwa hali unayo moja mkononi. **revocable,** *a.* -a kugeuka- -a kutanguka, -a kutangulia. **re-**

vocation, *n.* kugeuza maneno, utanguo.

revolt, *v.i.* (*rebel*) asi, halifu; (*be disgusted*) chukizwa, tiwa machukio, nyarafu; — *v.t.* (*disgust*) chukiza mno, kirihi. — *n.* maasi, uhalifu; machukio, unyarafu. **revolting,** *a.* -a kuchukiza mno, -baya kabisa, makeruhi.

revolution, *n.*, **revolutionary,** *a.*, **revolutionist,** *n.*, **revolutionize,** *v.* taz. *revolve.*

revolve, *v.i.* zunguka, pinduka, geuka; (*consider*) waza moyoni, tafakari, fikirifikiri. **revolution,** *n.* (*rebellion*) maasi; (*radical change*) mageuzi makuu, mapinduzi; (*circular motion*) mzunguko. **revolutionary,** *a.* -a kuasi serikali, -a fitina, -a kufanya *revolution,* -a kuzunguka. **revolutionist,** *n.* mwasi, atakaye maasi. **revolutionize,** *v.t.* geuza sana, pinduapindua, badili kabisa. **revolver,** *n.* bastola (yenye kitasa cha kuweka risasi sita au zaidi kinachozunguka baada ya kupigwa).

revue, *n.* mchezo wa ngoma, nyimbo na maigizo ya mambo.

revulsion, *n.* mageuzi ya moyo (*e.g.* kupenda kugeuka kuchukia *&c.*); (*disgust*) machukio.

reward, *n.* zawadi, thawabu, jaza, jazi; (*for thing lost*) kiokozi, kiangaza macho, utotole; (*for work*) ijara, ujira, mshahara; (*in competition*) tuzo; (*present*) zawadi, bakshishi. *May God reward you,* Mungu akujazi, heri, Mungu akuweke. — *v.t.* -pa zawadi, tuza, toa bakshishi, jazi, lipa.

rhapsodical, *a.*, **rhapsodist,** *n.* taz. *rhapsody.*

rhapsody, *n.* maneno (utenzi, ngoma) yaliyotungwa na mtu alipotaharuki kwa (aliposhikwa sana na) furaha (ashiki *&c.*), kama mapayo; (*poetical*) fungu la utenzi. **rhapsodical,** *a.* kama *rhapsody.* **rhapsodist,** *n.* mwandishi wa *rhapsody.*

rhetoric, *n.* elimu ya usemaji, usemaji; (*eloquence*) ufasaha wa kusema; (*bombast*) usemaji wenye maneno mazuri bali maana kidogo, ufasaha usio na maana sana; (*inaccurate statement*) chuku. **rhetorical,** *a.* -a usemaji, -a ufasaha; (*not serious*) -a kutia fahari tu, -a madoido. **rhetorician,** *n.* msemaji, mwalimu wa kufundisha usemaji.

rheumatism, *n.* baridi yabisi, uele wa viungo; (*when joints swell*) jongo. **rheumatic,** *a.* -a *rheumatism.*

rhino, *n.* (*slang*) fedha (ya kutumia).

rhinoceros, *n.* kifaru.

rhomboid, *n.* taz. *rhombus.*

rhombus, *n.* umbo lenye pande nne sawa na pembe zisizo za mraba (kama mraba uliopotoka). **rhomboid,** *n.* umbo kama *rhombus* ila pande mbili zinazoelekeana tu ni sawa (kama mstatili uliopotoka).

rhyme, *n.* mashairi ambayo sauti zake za mwisho ni sawa (zinalingana), sauti za mwisho sawa, kina; (*poetry*) mashairi. *Write rhyming verses,* fanya kina cha mashairi, tia vina. — *v.i.* -wa na sauti sawa mwishoni, -wa na sauti za mwisho zinazolingana, -wa na vina. **rhymer,** *n.* mwandishi wa *rhyme.* **rhyming,** *a.* -enye *rhyme,* -enye vina.

rhythm, *n.* mwendo, ulinganifu wa mwendo (wa ngoma, muziki), mfuatano mzuri wa mwendo.

rib, *n.* ubavu; (*of ship*) taruma; (*of coco-nut leaf*) uchukuti; (*of leaf*) uchukuti, mshipa, chelewa. **ribbed,** *a.* -a nyuzinyuzi (kama mishipa).

ribald, *a.* -siyo -a adabu, -pujufu, -chafu, -a matusi. **ribaldry,** *n.* maneno yasiyo ya adabu (machafu, ya upujufu), matusi.

ribbon, riband, *n.* utepe, ugwe, kigwe, jamdani.

rice, *n.* (*growing*) mpunga; (*grain*) mchele; (*cooked*) wali; (*ground*) unga; (*burnt in cooking*) ukoko; (*gruel*) uji, mashendea. *A dish of rice and fish* (*meat*), wali kwa samaki (nyama). *There are many sorts, e.g.* korowai, meli, melikora, sena, bungala *&c., &c.*

rich, *a.* (*man*) tajiri, -enye mali, -kwasi; (*country*) -enye mali, -a neema; (*soil*) -a kuzaa sana, -enye rutuba nyingi, -zuri; (*abundant*) -ingi, -tele; (*colour &c.*) -ingi, -zuri; (*taste &c.*) -tamu sana, -enye ladha nzuri. *Rich in metals,* -enye madini tele. *Get rich,* tajirika, nafisika. *That's rich!* yachekesha sana! **riches,** *n.* mali, utajiri, ukwasi; (*abundance*) wingi, neema. **richly,** *adv.* sana, kabisa. *He richly deserves punishment,* astahili sana kuadhibiwa. **richness,** *n.* wingi, neema, baraka; (*value*) thamani; (*productiveness*) uzaaji, neema; (*colour, dress*) uzuri, urembo; (*taste*) utamu, ladha.

rick, *n.* chungu ya majani makavu.

rickets, *n.* nyongea, chirwa; ugonjwa, wa watoto, mifupa yao huwa myororo. **rickety,** *a.* -enye *rickets*; -goigoi, -bovu, dhaifu, -sio imara.

ricochet, *n.* mruko wa kitu (risasi *&c.*) kikipiga kitu. — *v.i.* duta, ruka baada ya kupiga kitu.

rid, *v.t.* (*p.t. & pf.t.* **rid**) okoa, pona, toa. *Rid of anxiety,* toa mashakani. *He is rid of his trouble,* ametoka katika taabu. *Rid of,* ondolea, twalia, fungulia. *Be rid of,* okoka katika, ondokewa. *Get rid of*; pata kuokoka katika, jiondolea, epua. **riddance,** *n.* kuokoa, kuokoka *&c.*

ridden, *pf.t.* ya *ride.*

riddle, (1) *n.* kitendawili, fumbo. — *v.i.* sema kwa fumbo.

riddle, (2) *n.* (*sieve*) chekecheke, chungio. — *v.t.* chekecha, chunga, kung'uta; (*pierce*) toboa, chomachoma, zua.

ride, *v.i.* (*p.t.* **rode,** *pf.t.* **ridden**) panda na kuchukuliwa na (enda juu ya) gari (farasi, baisikeli *&c.*); (*of ship*) elea baharini; — *v.t.* panda gari (farasi *&c.*). *It is riding at anchor,* imetia nanga. — *n.* kupanda, kuchukuliwa na, kwenda juu ya (gari, farasi, baisikeli *&c.*), mahali pa kutembea kwa farasi. **rider,** *n.* mpanda farasi (hasa mstadi); (*added clause*) maneno yaliyotiwa baadaye, maneno au sharti iliyotiwa juu au baadaye, nyongeza. **riding,** *a.* -a kupandika (farasi), -a kutumika kwa farasi. — *n.* kupanda (farasi, baisikeli *&c.*), mwendo kwa farasi *&c.*

ridge, *n.* mgongo, kigongo; (*in gardening*) tuta; (*of roof*) utiko, mwamba, juu (ya nyumba); (*of hills*) mgongo, vilele. **ridge-pole,** *n.* mwamba.

ridicule, *n.* cheko, mzaha, dhihaka, masihara. — *v.t.* cheka, fanya mzaha, dhihaki. **ridiculous,** *a.* -a kuchekwa, -a kuchekesha, -a mzaha, -a kudhihaki, -a masihara, -a upuzi.

riding, *a. and n.* taz. *ride.*

rife, *a.* -a kote kote, -a kila mahali, -a kuenea sana. *Be rife,* -wa -ingi, chaga, enea, vumika.

riff-raff, *n.* watu ovyo (wanyonge, wa vivi hivi tu, wasio na cheo).

rifle, *v.t.* teka, nyang'anya, kumba, tafutatafuta (pekuapekua, pinduapindua) ili kuiba; (*a gun &c.*) tia mifuo. — *n.* bunduki (yenye mifuo katika mtutu wake). **rifleman,** *n.* askari mwenye *rifle.* **rifle-range,** *n.* mahali pa kupigia shabaha; (*distance*) mtupo wa risasi ya *rifle.*

rift, *n.* ufa, shimo, bonde, mwatuko, mpasuko. *Rift in the lute,* jambo linaloelekea kuleta matata (kuharibu furaha *&c.*).

rig, *v.t.* pamba (merikebu); (*out*) -pa nguo, visha, valisha; (*up*) tengeneza (hasa kwa vitu vilivyopo tayari). — *n.* pambo (la merikebu); (*clothing*) mavazi, nguo. **rigging,** *n.* pambo (kamba, matanga *&c.* ya merikebu).

right, *a.* (*side*) -a upande wa kuume, -a mkono wa kulia (mlio); (*good*) -a haki, -a adili, -adilifu, -nyofu, -ema, -zuri; (*exact*) sawa, halisi, barabara; (*fitting, true*) -a kweli, -a kufaa, -a heri, wajibu; (*straight*) -a moja kwa moja, -lionyoka. *A right angle,* pembe ya mraba. *All right,* njema, vema. *Be* (*turn out*) *right,* elekea, ongoka, sitawi. — *adv.* vema, njema; (*exactly*) sawa, barabara, hasa; (*very*) sana; (*straight*) kwa mstari ulionyoka, moja kwa moja; (*on*, (*towards the right*) kwa upande wa kuume. *Right reverend*, -a heshima sana. — *n.* (*justice*) haki; (*morality*) adili, uadilifu, unyofu; (*goodness*) wema; (*truth*) kweli; (*correctness*) usawa, uhalisi, usahihi; (*side*) upande wa kuume, mkono wa kulia (wa mlio). *Put to rights*, tengeneza. *On the right*, kuumeni, kwa mkono wa kuume. *A man's rights*, astahiliyo mtu kupewa au kupata, haki. — *v.t.* tengeneza, sahihisha, simamisha, weka sawa (vizuri); (*get justice for*) patia haki; (*place upright*) simamisha sawa (wima). **right-about**, *a.* *right-about turn*, geuka kabisa. **right-angled**, *a.* -enye pembe ya mraba. **right-down**, *a.* kabisa, sana. **righten**, *v.t.* sawazisha, tengeneza, sahihisha. **righteous**, *a.* -nyofu, -ema, -zuri, -a adili, -adilifu. **righteousness**, *n.* wema, unyofu, haki, uadilifu, adili, maadili. **rightful**, *a.* -a haki, -a adili, -adilifu, -ema. **rightfully**, *adv.* kwa haki. **right hand**, *n.* mkono wa kuume (wa kulia, wa mlio); (*helper*) msaidizi mkubwa. **rightly**, *adv.* kwa haki, barabara, sahihi.

rigid, *a.* -siopindikana, -siokunjika, -gumu, -kavu, imara, yabisi, thabiti; (*severe*) -kali, -gumu. *Be rigid*, kazana, kauka, shupaa; (*stern*) -wa kali, -wa -gumu. **rigidity**, *n.* ugumu, ukavu, uthabiti.

rigmarole, *n.* maneno mengi yasiyo na maana, mapayo, upuzi, porojo.

rigor, *n.* (*shivering*) tetemeko, mtetemo (kama kabla ya homa). *Rigor mortis*, ukavu wa maiti, kukauka maiti. **rigorous**, *a.* -kali, -gumu; (*precise, exact*) halisi, sahihi. **rigour**, *n.* ukali, ugumu.

rile, *v.t.* kasirisha, ghadhibisha, nyanyasa, chokoza, kereketa.

rill, *n.* kijito kidogo, mkirizi, kijuto.

rim, *n.* ukingo, kando, mzingo.

rime, *n* umande ulioganda kwa baridi.

rind, *n.* ganda; (*hard*) gome; (*of squeezed fruit &c.*) kaka.

rinderpest, *n.* maradhi ya ng'ombe, sotoka.

ring, (1) *n.* pete; (*circle*) mviringo, duara; (*for races &c.*) uwanja (wa kuchezea mashindano &c.); (*spectators*) jamii ya watu waliohudhuria kutazama; (*society*) shirika la watu wenye shauri moja, hasa wapinganao masharti ya fedha kwa mashindano; (*ferrule*) noleo, pete; (*on sword-sheath*) ukoa. *Nose-ring*, hazama. *Lip-ring*, ndonya. *Ear-ring*, pete ya sikio, bali. *Make a ring*, *Bend into a ring*, peta, petana, petamana, viringanisha; (*gather round*) zunguka kutanika, hudhuria. **ring-dove**, *n.* hua. **ringleader**, *n.* mtangulizi, mkuu (wa jambo au shauri baya, wa watu wabaya). **ringlet**, *n.* songo la nywele, msokoto. **ringworm**, *n.* choa, baka; (*on head*) bato.

ring, (2) *v.t.* (*p.t.* **rang**, *pf.t.* **rung**) (*cause to ring*) piga (kengele); — *v.i.* (*sound*) lia (kama kengele, madini, sauti nyembamba); (*make a noise*) -wa na makelele, vuma sana (habari). *Ring true*, -wa kama ni kweli. *Ring up*, piga simu. — *n.* mlio (wa kengele, madini &c.). **ringer**, *n.* mpiga kengele.

ring-dove, *n.* taz. *ring* (1).

ringleader, *n.*, **ringlet**, *n.*, **ringworm**, *n.* taz. *ring* (1).

rink, *n.* sakafu (au kiwanja cha barafu) ya kuchezea.

rinse, *v.t.* suza, chovyachovya, osha kwa maji; (*the mouth*) sukutua, piga funda.

riot, *n.* ghasia (jeuri, makelele, msukosuko, fitina) ya kuhalifu sheria kufanywa na watu watatu au zaidi; (*dissipation &c.*) upotovu, ufisadi, ufasiki; (*profusion*) wingi. *Run riot*, fanya ufisadi &c.; fuja mali. — *v.i.* fanya ghasia (jeuri, fitina &c.) ya kuhalifu sheria. **rioter**, *n.* mfanya ghasia &c. **riotous**, *a.* -a kuleta ghasia, -potoe.

rip, *v.t.* pasua, rarua, kata, tatua,

tumbua, pangua, kwanua; — *v.i.* pasuka, raruka &c. — *n.* mpasuko. **ripper,** *n.* (*slang*) kitu kizuri sana, mtu mzuri sana. **ripping,** *a.* (*slang*) -zuri sana, -a kupendeza sana.

riparian, *a.* -a kando ya mto.

ripe, *a.* -bivu, -pevu; (*ready*) tayari; (*complete*) kamili, -timilifu. *Of ripe years,* -zima. **ripen,** *v.t.* ivisha, pevusha, komaza; (*perfect*), sitawisha, kamilisha (*prepare*) fanya tayari; — *v.i.* iva, pevuka, komaa, kamilika. **ripeness,** *n.* ubivu, upevu; (*perfection*) ukamilifu, usitawi.

ripper, *n.*, **ripping,** *a.* taz. *rip.*

ripple, *n.* kiwimbi. — *v.i.* -wa na viwimbi, lia kama viwimbi; — *v.t.* fanya viwimbi. **rippling,** *a.* -a viwimbi, -a mlio (-a mfano) wa viwimbi.

rise, *v.i.* (*p.t.* **rose,** *pf.t.* **risen**) enda juu, paa, inuka, panda, kwea, nyanyuka; (*stand up*) simama, ondoka; (*appear*) tokea; (*increase*) ongezeka, zidi; (*advance*) pata cheo, sitawi, tajirika; (*rebel*) asi, fanya fitina (maasi); (*cease sitting*) vunjika (baraza &c.), isha; (*originate*) toka, -wa na asili (na mwanzo), anza, chimbuka; (*as dough*) umuka; (*sun* &c.) chomoza, panda; (*from death*) fufuka; (*from sleep*) amka; (*of tide*) jaa; (*of swelling*) vimba. — *n.* kupanda, kwenda juu, kupaa &c.; (*raised ground*) matuta, mwinuko, kilima, kiduta, mahali pa kupanda; (*degree of elevation*) kadiri ya kupanda; (*increase*) maongezo, nyongeza, kuzidi, ziada; (*advance*) maendeleo; (*origin*) asili, mwanzo, chimbuko; (*flow of tide*) kujaa; (*of sun*) kuchomoza, macheo. mapambazuko. **risen,** *pf.t.* ya *rise.* **rising,** *a.* -a kupanda; (*progressing*) -a kuendelea, hodari, -pasi. *The rising generation,* vijana wa siku hizi. *Rising ground,*. mwinuko, kilima, kiduta. — *n.* (*ascent*) kupanda, mpando, mwinuko; (*revolt*) fitina, kuasi, maasi.

risible, *a.* -a kucheka, -a kuchekesha.

risibility, *n.* kutaka kucheka, kuelekea kucheka.

rising, *a. and n.* taz. *rise.*

risk, *n.* hatari, mashaka, jukumu; (*chance*) bahati. *At the owner's risk,* juu ya mwenyeji. *Insure against risk,* fanya bima, lipa jukumu. *Run a risk,* ingia hatarini, jihatirisha, jasiri, bahatisha. — *v.t.* hatirisha, bahatisha, jasiri. *I will risk it,* hasara juu yangu. **risky,** *a.* -a hatari, -a mashaka.

rissole, *n.* andazi la nyama (samaki) na viazi.

rite, *n.* kanuni (kawaida) ya dini, tendo la ibada. **ritual,** *n.* kawaida za dini, urembo wa ibada, utaratibu wa sala, jamii ya *rites.* **ritualism,** *n.* kupenda na kutumia *ritual*; kutumia *ritual* kupita kiasi. **ritualist,** *n.* ashikaye *ritualism.*

rival, *n.* mshindani. *It has no rival,* haina kifani, haina mwenzi. — *a.* -shindani, -a kushindana. — *v.t.* shindana na, taka kupita (kushinda), jaribu kuwa sawa na, -wa kama sawa na. **rivalry,** *n.* ushindani.

rive, *v.t.* pasua, tatua, rarua, tenga kwa nguvu. **riven,** *a.* -liopasuka, -lioraruka.

river, *n.* mto, mto mkubwa; (*abundance*) wingi. **riverain,** *n.* mkaa kando ya mto. — *a.* -a kando ya mto, -a kukaa kando ya mto. **river-basin,** *n.* nchi inamopita mto ambayo maji yake huingia mto huo. **river-bed,** *n.* chini ya mto. **river-horse,** *n.* kiboko. **riverside,** *n.* kando ya mto, ukingo wa mto. **rivulet,** *n.* kijito.

rivet, *n.* msumari wa kugongomewa ncha zote mbili. — *v.t.* kaza (pigilia, gongomea) kwa *rivet,* kaza. *Rivet the gaze on,* angazia (kazia) macho, tazama sana.

rivulet, *n.* taz. *river*

roach, *n.* namna ya samaki wa maji baridi.

road, *n.* njia; (*main road*) barabara. *On the road,* katika safari, njiani. *Out of the road!* simile, jihadhari!

habedari! **road-hog**, *n.* mwendeshi motakaa asiyejali salama ya wengine. **road-metal**, *n.* kokoto za kutengenezea njia (barabara). **roads, roadstead**, *n.* bandari, maelezi, pa kutia nanga. **roadway**, *n.* njia, barabara.

roam, *v.i.* zunguka, tembea, susurika, zurura, zururika; (*stray*) potea.

roan, (1) *n.* (*colour*) rangi ya farasi (hudhurungi nyeusi).

roan, (2) *n.* (*leather*) ngozi ya kondoo iliyolainishwa na kutiwa dawa na rangi.

roar, *v.i.* nguruma, lia kwa sauti kubwa (kama simba, mzinga, dhoruba, mawimbi &c.), vuma, rindima. — *n.* ngurumo, uvumi, rindimo, shindo kubwa, mlio (wa simba &c.). **roaring**, *a.* -naonguruma, -naovuma &c. — *n.* taz. *roar*.

roast, *v.t.* choma (kwa moto), oka. — *n.* nyama iliyookwa (iliyochomwa).

rob, *v.t.* ibia, nyang'anya, poka, teka, bakwia. **robber**, *n.* mwizi, mwivi, mnyang'anyi, haramia. **robbery**, *n.* wizi, wivi, unyang'anyi, kupoka.

robe, *n.* vazi refu (kama joho) la heshima, (la cheo fulani), vazi la kike. — *v.i.* vaa, valia; — *v.t.* vika, visha.

robin, *n.* ndege mdogo wa Ulaya.

robot, *n.* mashine mfano wa mtu, ifanyayo kazi kama mtu; (*person*) mtu afanyaye kazi kama mashine (bila kutumia akili).

robust, *a.* -enye afya (nguvu, maungo), hodari, -nene. **robustness**, *n.* afya, nguvu, unene, maungo, uthabiti.

rochet, *n.* vazi jeupe refu la askofu.

rock, (1) *v.t.* (*swing*) pembeza, ning'iniza; chuchia; (*shake*) tikisa; — *v.i.* pembea, ning'inia, tikisika; (*of a ship*) sukasuka, fanya mrama; (*stagger*) levya, pepesuka, taka kuanguka, tetereka.

rock, (2) *n.* mwamba, jabali. *Sunken rock*, kipwa. *On the rocks*, pwelewa; (*in money difficulties*) wamba, taiti. *Firm as a rock*, imara (thabiti) kabisa. *Rock bottom*, -a chini kabisa. **rockery**, *n.* chungu ya mawe bustanini ya kupandia maua. **rock-rabbit**, *n.* wibari, pelele, kwanga. **rock-salt**, *n.* chumvi ya mawe. **rocky**, *a.* -a mawe mengi, -enye miamba.

rocket, *n.* fataki kubwa ya kuruka juu.

rock-rabbit, *n.*, **rock-salt**, *n.*, **rocky**, *a.* taz. *rock* (2).

rococo, *a.* -enye mapambo kupita kiasi (hata kuharibu uzuri).

rod, *n.* ufito; (*punishment*) adhabu, pigo; (*authority*) hukumu, mamlaka; (*oppression*) udhalimu, jeuri; (*for fishing*) ufito, mwanzi (wa kuvulia samaki); (*measuring*) chenezo, kigezo; (*measure*) yadi $5\frac{1}{2}$.

rode, *p.t.* ya *ride*.

rodent, *n.* (mnyama) -enye kutafuna (kuguguna), *e.g.* panya, kindi &c.

rodeo, *n.* kukusanya ng'ombe kuwatia alama; (*exhibition*) wonyesho wa wachungaji wapanda farasi wa ng'ombe.

rodomontade, *n.* majivuno, maneno makuu, makeke.

roe, *n.* mayai ya samaki, ng'ofu.

roebuck, *n.* mnyama kama paa.

rogation, Rogation Days, *n.* siku za kuombea, siku tatu kabla ya *Ascension Day*.

rogue, *n.* ayari, mlaghai, mjanja, jambazi, mbaya, mshari, mhuni; (*mischievous child*) mtundu. *Rogue elephant*, tembo mkali aliyejitenga na kundi. **roguery**, *n.* ujanja, hila. ulaghai; (*fun*) ubishi, ucheshi. **roguish**, *a.* -a *roguery*; -cheshi, -tundu.

roister, *v.i.* fanya ghasia (makelele) ya kucheka (ya kufurahi). **roisterer**, *n.* mtu afanyaye ghasia (makelele) ya kufurahi.

role, *n.* daraka la (kazi ya) mtu katika mambo (mchezo).

roll, *v.t.* fingirisha; (*fold*) kunja; (*impel*) sukuma; (*spread*) eneza, toa -ingi (kwa nguvu); (*move by rollers*

&c.) jongeza, kwa magurudumu (kwa nyenzo, kwa magogo, kwa chao); (*revolve*) zungusha; (*coil*) zongomeza; (*cigarettes*) sokota; (*smooth*) lainisha (kwa gogo &c.); (*prolong sound*) fuliza sauti (kama ngurumo), vumisha; — *v.i.* fingirika, bingirika; (*spread*) enea; (*revolve*) zunguka; (*move swiftly*) pita upesi (kwa nguvu); (*of sound*) vuma, rindima, titima, tutuma, nguruma; (*of ship*) sukasuka, fanya mrama; (*of country*) tandaa, tambaa; (*coil*) zongomea. *Roll up*, fingirisha, zongomeza, zonga; (*come in large numbers*) -ja (fika) -ingi. — *n.* kufingirisha, kufingirika &c.; (*anything rolled up*) kikuto; (*of cloth*) jora, taka; (*of paper*) gombo, hati; (*register*) hesabu, tarehe, orodha; (*bread*) mkate; (*sound*) mdundo (wa ngoma), uvumi, ngurumo, rindimo; (*of tobacco*) bumba; (*of ship*) mrama. **roller**, *n.* wenzo, gogo, chao; (*wave*) wimbi kubwa; (*wheel*) gurudumu; (*bandage*) kitambaa cha kuganga; (*broad-billed roller*) jore. **rolling**, *n.* kufingirisha, kufingirika &c., mzunguko, mzingo; (*folding*) mkunjo; (*circular motion*) mwendo wa gurudumu; (*of ship*) mrama, msukosuko. — *a.* -a kufingirika &c.; (*fire*) -a mfululizo; (*stock*) -a kutumika. *He is a rolling stone*), mhamishi huyu, hana kituo. *Rolling prairies* (*country*), nyika pana kubwa (kama bahari na mawimbi yake). **rolling-stock**, *n.* magari ya moshi, behewa na reli zake.

Roman, *a.* -a kirumi, -rumi. — *n.* Mrumi. **Roman Catholic**, *n.* Mkristo wa Kanisa la kirumi. — *a.* -a Kanisa la kirumi. **Romish**, *a.* -a Kanisa la kirumi.

romance, *n.* kisa chenye habari za mambo mengi ya ajabu, hadithi zilizobunika za kupiga chuku; (*fiction*) uwongo, uzushi; (*love story*) hadithi za mahaba. — *a.* -a mfano wa lugha ya Warumi wa kale. *Romance languages*, lugha zilizotokana na *Latin*. — *v.i.* buni hadithi za mambo ya ajabu (ya kupiga chuku), jitungia mambo ya ajabu ya kufurahisha. **romantic**, *a.* -a ajabu, -a kigeni, -a kupiga chuku, -a mahaba.

Romish, *a.* taz. *Roman.*

romp, *v.t.* cheza, rukaruka, randa, chachawa. — *n.* mchezo wa kurukaruka na kufanya kelele.

rood, *n.* sanamu ya Yesu Kristo amekazwa msalabani.

roof, *n.* (*thatched side*) paa; (*end*) kipaa, kisusi; (*stone*) dari, sakafu ya juu; (*in excavation, cave &c.*) juu, upande wa juu. — *v.t.* tia mapaa, tia dari; (*thatch*) ezeka, vimba. **roofing**, *n.* kutia *roof*; vitu vya kufanyizia *roof*, miti, makuti, mabati, matofali. **roofless**, *a.* pasipo *roof*. **roof-tree**, *n.* mwamba.

rook, *n.* namna ya kunguru; (*cheat*) ayari, mlaghai, mdanganyi katika michezo ya karata. — *v.t.* laghai, danganya, ghilibu. **rookery**, *n.* jamii ya miti yenye matundu ya (viota vya) *rooks*.

room, *n.* chumba; (*upper*) orofa; (*front, reception*) sebule, ukumbi; (*store*) ghala; (*space*) nafasi. *Make room for*, ondokea, pisha, ambaza. **roominess**, *n.* nafasi tele, uwazi. **roomy**, *a.* -enye nafasi, -kubwa, -wazi.

roost, *n.* kituo cha ndege, kijiti cha kutulilia, kiota. — *v.i.* jikalia, tulia. **rooster**, *n.* jogoo, jimbi.

root, *n.* shina; (*small*) mzizi; (*origin*) asili, awali, mwanzo; (*cause*) sababu; (*in grammar*) neno la asili, herufi za asili; (*in arithm.*) Taz: *square root.* — *v.t.* panda, kaza chini, penyeza chini; (*establish*) weka imara, kaza, ingiza ndani; — *v.i.* pandika, kazwa; fanyizwa shina, tia mizizi. *Root about*, chimbua. *Root up*, ng'oa, toa. **rootlet**, *n.* mzizi.

rope, *n.* kamba, ukambaa, ugwe; (*large*) jigwe; (*small*) kigwe. — *v.t.* funga kwa kamba; (*enlist services*) shawishi kusaidia. *Know the ropes*, jua desturi na matengenezo. **rope-**

walk, *n.* mahali pa kufanyiza kamba.
rosary, *n.* tasbihi.
rose, (1) *p.t.* ya *rise.*
rose, (2) *n.* waridi. *Rose-water*, marashi mawaridi, maji mawaridi. *Otto of roses*, halwaridi. *Under the rose*, kwa siri. **rose-apple**, *n.* (*fruit*) darabi, pera la kizungu. **roseate**, *a.* -ekundu, -a rangi ya waridi (nyekundu); (*hopeful*) -a furaha, -a kutumaini, -tumainifu. **rosette**, *n.* fundo la utepe, shada. **rose-wood**, namna ya mti mwekundu na mweusi unaotumika kufanyiza vyombo vya nyumbani. **rosy**, *a.* -ekundu, -zuri, -a kutia matumaini, -ema.
rosin, *n.* (sawa na *resin*).
roster, *n.* orodha ya majina ya watu na kazi zao.
rostrum, *n.* mimbara, kitu kilichoinuka cha kusimamia hatibu.
rosy, *a.* taz. *rose* (2).
rot, *v.t.* ozesha, vundisha; — *v.i.* oza, vunda, haribika, pooza; (*talk nonsense*) paya, payuka, bwabwaja, bwata; (*tease &c.*) fanya mzaha (ubishi), nyanyasa. — *n.* kioza; (*nonsense*) upuzi, mapiswa. *What rot!* mawe! upuzi! **rotten**, *a.* -bovu, -liopooza, -baya. **rotter**, *n.* mtu hafifu, mnyonge, mbaya.
rota, *n.* orodha ya majina ya watu na kazi zao, orodha ya zamu za askari.
rotate, *v.t.* zungusha; — *v.i.* zunguka, fuatana kwa kawaida (taratibu). **rotary**, *a.* -a kuzunguka, -nayozunguka. **rotation**, *n.* mzingo, mzunguko; (*turn*) zamu, taratibu, fuatano la taratibu. *Rotation of crops*, mabadilio (mabadiliko) ya mavuno. **rotatory**, *a.* -a kuzunguka.
rote, *n.* *Learn* (*get*) *by rote*, kumbuka kwa akili, jisomesha kwa moyo (kwa ufahamu).
rotten, *a.* **rotter**, *n.* taz. *rot.*
rotund, *a.* -a mviringo (kama sahani); (*plump*) -nene, -lionenepa. **rotundity**, *n.* mviringo, mviringano; (*plumpness*) unene.
rouble, *n.* sarafu ya fedha ya kirusi (*Russia*).
roué, *n.* mpotovu, mpotoe, mwasherati, mfisadi, mfasiki.
rouge, *n.* namna ya unga mwekundu (wa kusafishia fedha), namna ya unga mwekundu unaotumika na wanawake wengine kutia usoni.
rough, *a.* -a kukwaruza, -a kuparuza, si ororo, si laini, si sawa; (*uncivil*) si adabu, si heshima, si makini; (*clumsy*) -gumu, si -pole, -zembe, -a nguvu; (*bitter*) -chungu, si -tamu, -a kukausha ulimi (kinywa), -a kutia ukamvu (ukakasi, ukasasi); (*of sounds*) -a kuchukiza, si -tamu; (*incomplete, unpolished &c.*) -a ovyo, -siotengenezwa vizuri, si kamili; (*not precise*) -a kukisiwa tu, si sahihi. *Rough idea* (*sketch*), dokezo. *Rough sea*, bahari iliyochafuka. *Rough temper*, ukali, kasirani, ugomvi. *Rough tone*, sauti kali. *Rough weather*, pepo na baridi, tufani. *Rough workman*, mparuzi. *Rough and ready*, -a kufaa kwa mara moja, -a kutosha kwa matumizi (haja) ya ghafula, tayari, -elekevu. *A rough diamond*, mzuri ndani (wa moyo) kuliko nje (umbo), mzuri wa moyo si wa uso. — *n.* mfidhuli, msafihi, mjeuri, mshari. — *v.i.* *Rough it*, vumilia hali mbaya na taabu, jivumilisha. **rough-cast**, *n.* chokaa na kokoto za mchanga za kutomelea. **roughen**, *v.t.* fanya *rough*; (*of sea*) chafua; (*of temper*) kasirisha; — *v.i.* fanyika (*rough*), chafuka. **rough-hewn**, *a.* si laini, vivi hivi. **roughness**, *n.* kuwa *rough*, maparuzo, kwaruzo; uchungu *&c.*; (*violence*) jeuri, jefule. **rough-rider**, *n.* mfuga farasi. **rough-shod**, *a.* *Ride rough-shod over* -tojali, dharau, tia uchungu bure.
round, *a.* -a kuviringa, -a duara, -a mviringo, -a kuviringana, -a mviringano (kama duara au kama mpira; (*complete, large*) -zima, -kubwa, -ingi; (*open, plain*) wazi, dhahiri; (*well-finished*) laini, -tamu, -zuri. *All the*

year round, mwaka wote, tangu mwanzo hata mwisho. *Round number*, hesabu iliyo karibu si sawa halisi. *Round game*, mchezo wa watu wengi kucheza kwa zamu. *Round dance*, ngoma ya kuzunguka wawili wawili. *Round hand*, mwandiko wa herufi za mviringo. — *n.* mviringo, mviringano, duara, pete, mzingo; (*in music*) wimbo wa kufukuzana sauti; (*series*) utaratibu, kuandamana, maandamano, mafuatano; (*of ladder*) kipago, kipawa, kipandio, kipande, daraja; (*of soldiers &c.*) kingojo, zamu; (*stage, bout &c.*) sehemu (ya mchezo, kupiga ngumi &c.). *A round of applause*, vifijo, vigelele, makelele ya kuamkia (ya kuonyesha furaha, ya kusifu). *A round of ammunition*, kiasi cha (risasi ya) bunduki (au mzinga). *Go the round of*, maliza. *The whole round of*, -ote, namna zote. *A round of gaieties*, michezo mingi. — *v.t.* viringanisha, petamanisha, fanya kuwa -a mviringo (-a duara); (*complete*) maliza, isha; (*correct*) sahihisha (maneno); (*go round*) zunguka (rasi, pembe &c.), faulu; — *v.i.* petana, petemana, viringana. *Round off*, maliza vizuri. *Round up*, leta pamoja, kusanya. *Round on* (*upon*), geuka ghafula na kushambulia, geuka na kulaumu. — *prep. and adv.* kuzunguka, pande zote (za), mzingo (wa), pote, kwa kila mtu. *Go round*, zunguka, enda kila mahali; (*be given to all*) enea, tosha. *Turn round*, zungusha, pindua; (*go round*) zunguka, geuka, pinduka. *Bring round* (*revive*), huisha, fufua; (*reform*) tuliza, ongoza. *Stand round*, zunguka, hudhuria. *Come* (*get*) *round*, jipendekeza kwa, shawishi, shinda, danganya. *An all-round man*, mtu wa kufaa kwa yote, hodari sana, mwelekevu wa kazi, mjuzi wa kazi zote. **roundabout**, *a.* -a kuzunguka, -a bure, -enye vipengele. **rounded**, *a.* (*composition*) sahili, fasili, -enye ufasihi; (*slightly*) -a bapa. **roundly**, *adv.* sana, wazi. **roundness**, *n.* mviringo, mvringano, kivimbe, kitumbo. **round-robin**, *n.* barua (hati) yenye haja, ya watu wengi waliotia sahihi.

rouse, *v.t.* amsha, shtusha, chomesha, chochea, sukuma, sisimua, sukumiza, harakisha, charakisha, fanya, leta, fufua, huisha; — *v.i.* amka, fufuka, chochewa (chocheka), shtuka, zinduka, zindukana.

rout, *v.t.* shinda, piga, kimbiza, fukuza, furusha. — *n.* kufukuzwa, mafukuzo, makimbizi, kushindwa, maangamizo; (*crowd*) ghasia ya watu.

route, *n.* njia. *En route*, njiani.

routine, *n.* utaratibu, kawaida ya kila siku, desturi.

rove, *v.i.* zunguka mahali mahali, hamahama; (*of affections &c.*) badilibadili; (*of eyes*) tazama huko na huko. **rover**, *n.* mtu wa kuzunguka pote, mhamishi, mtembezi. **roving**, *a.* -kuzunguka pote, -hamishi, -a kubadilibadili, -a kutazama huko na huko.

row, (1) *n.* (*line*) safu, msafa, mstari; (*of things piled up*) rusu; (*of fish &c. on a string*) mtungo, mtanda; (*of plants &c.*) mpando, mstari. *Be in rows*, pangana. *Put in a row*, panga, weka sawasawa, pangisha; (*on a string &c.*) tunga.

row, (2) *n.* (*noise*) makelele, ghasia, zahama, udhia, msukosuko, matata. **rowdy**, *a.* -jeuri, -fidhuli, -a ghasia (makelele, zahama).

row, (3) *v.t.* peleka (endesha) kwa makasia, piga (vuta) makasia. — *n.* kwenda katika mashua. **rower**, *n.* mpiga kasia. **rowing**, *n.* kupiga makasia, mvuto. **rowlock**, *n.* kileti, makosi; (*loop of rope used for oar*) kishwara.

rowdy, *a.* taz. *row* (2).

rowel, *n.* mwiba wa *spur*.

rower, *n.*, **rowing**, *n.*, **rowlock**, *n.* taz. *row* (3).

royal, *a.* -a kifalme, -a kifaume, -a mfalme, -a fahari. **royalism**, *n.* kupenda utawala wa mfalme.

royalist, *n.* ashikaye *royalism.*
royalty, *n.* ufalme, hali ya ufalme, kifalme; (*person*) mfalme, wafalme, watu wa jamaa ya mfalme; (*on books &c.*) sehemu ya bei ya kitabu (au kitu) apewayo mwandishi (au mvumbuzi).
rub, *v.t.* sugua; (*wipe*) pangusa, futa; (*polish*) katua; (*scrape*) paruza; (*bruise*) chubua, chuna; (*grate*) chua; (*to pieces*) fikicha; (*of medicine, oil &c.*) chua, paka, pakaa; (*the body in massage*) singa, sia; (*a child's gums when teething*) nunuza. *Rub up,* tengeneza, amsha; (*irritate*) kasirisha, chomesha, nyanyasa. *Rub out* (*of writing &c.*) futa. — *n.* zuio, shida, pingamizi, mashaka. **rubber,** *n.* mtu au kitu cha kusugulia *&c.*; (*india-rubber*) mpira.
rubber, (1) *n.* (*in cards*) mchezo wa karata, mvumo. — (2), taz. *rub.*
rubbish, *n.* taka, takataka; (*heap of rubbish*) jaa, jalala; (*of demolished house*) kifusi; (*in heaps of a field being cleared or after harvest*) biwi; (*nonsense*) upuzi. *Rubbish!* mawe!
rubble, *n.* kokoto, mawe ya kutomelea; (*remains of demolished house*) kifusi.
rubicund, *a.* -ekundu (uso).
rubric, *n.* amri ya utaratibu wa sala (wa ibada).
ruby, *n.* namna ya kito chekundu cha thamani. — *a.* -ekundu.
ruck, *n.* kikunjo, kunyanzi. — *v.t.* kunjakunja, fanya kunyanzi; — *v.i.* kunjamana, fanyika kunyanzi.
rucksack, *n.* mfuko (bahasha, shanta, kifurushi, mkoba) wa kuchukulia nguo na chakula begani.
ructions, *n.* ghasia, zahama, ugomvi wenye makelele, msukosuko.
rudder, *n.* usukani, mashikio.
ruddle, *n.* ngeu, udongo mwekundu sana. — *v.t.* fanya ngeu, fanya mstari kwa udongo mwekundu.
ruddy, *a.* -ekundu (-a afya).
rude, *a.* fidhuli, -shenzi, -juvi, si adabu, -safihi, -jeuri. **rudely,** *adv.* kwa ufidhuli, *&c.* **rudeness,** *n.* jeuri, ushenzi, ujuvi, usafihi, utovu wa adabu.
rudiment, *n.* (*beginning*) mwanzo, asili, maarifa ya kwanza; (*germ*) uchipuko, mbegu, chanzo. **rudimental, rudimentary,** *a.* -a mwanzo *&c.*
rue, *v.i.* juta, sikitika; — *v.t.* jutia, sikitikia. **rueful,** *a.* -a huzuni, -a majonzi, -a majuto, -a kusikitika.
ruff, *n.* kitambaa chenye vikunjo cha kuvaa shingoni.
ruffian, *n.* mjeuri, mfidhuli, msafihi, mkorofi, mkatili, mtu mbaya (mwovu). **ruffianly,** *a.* -a jeuri, -fidhuli, -korofi, -katili.
ruffle, *v.t.* (*crease*) kunjakunja; (*disturb feathers, hair, water &c.*) chafua, timua; (*disturb, disconcert*) kasirisha, sumbua, udhi; — *v.i.* chafuka, kunjamana, kunjana, timuka. — *n.* vikunjo vya nguo vya kuvaa shingoni (mwisho wa mikono ya vazi *&c.*). **ruffled,** *a.* liokunjamana, -liokunjana, -enye vikunjo; (*of feathers, hair*) -a matimutimu.
rug, *n.* zulia ndogo nene; blanketi nene.
rugged, *a.* -a kuparuza, -a mawe mawe, si sawa, si laini; (*rude*) -shenzi, -kali, si adabu.
ruin, *n.* maangamizi, uharibifu, upotevu, ukumbo, utilifu; (*in business*) ufilisi, kufilisika; (*of buildings &c.*) mavunjiko, maanguko, magofu, mahame, mabaki. *A ruined house,* gofu la nyumba, uhame. — *v.t.* angamiza, vunja, haribu, tilifisha; (*impoverish*) filisi, kumba mali; (*morally*) poteza, potoa, haribu. *Be ruined,* angamia, haribika, hiliki; (*in business*) filisika, tilifika. **ruination,** *n.* kuangamia, kuharibika *&c.*; jambo (kitu) linaloharibu (linaloangamiza *&c.*). **ruinous,** *a.* -haribifu, -nayoharibu *&c.*
rule, *n.* (*regulation*) amri, kanuni, sharti, kawaida, desturi, mila; (*dominion*) utawala, mamlaka, enzi, hukumu, dola; (*for measuring*) rula, chenezo, kigezo, futi. *As a rule,* mara

nyingi, kwa desturi (kawaida), aghalabu — *v.t.* tawala, hukumu; (*control*) ongoza, shurutisha; (*order*) amuru; (*draw a line*) piga (andika) mstari. *Ruled paper*, karatasi ya mistari (ya mifuo). **ruler**, *n.* mtawala, mfalme, mkuu, liwali; (*for measuring*) rula, chenezo, kigezo, futi. **ruling**, *a.* -a kutawala, -a nguvu, -a kuenea, -lio -ingi. — *n.* utawala, amri, hukumu.

rum, (1) *n.* mvinyo inayofanyizwa kwa miwa.

rum, (2) **rummy**, *a.* -a kigeni, -baya.

rumble, *v.i.* nguruma, vuma, tutuma, rindima, nguruma. **rumble**, **rumbling**, *n.* ngurumo, uvumi, tutumo, tetemo, mdundo, rindimo.

ruminate, *v.i.* cheua, tafuna (kama ng'ombe, mbuzi, kondoo); (*consider*) fikirifikiri, waza, tafakari. **ruminant**, *a.* -a kucheua. **rumination**, *n.* kucheua; (*thought*) fikira, mawazo.

rummage, *v.t. and i.* tafuta sana, tafutia kwa kuchafua, fanya fujo au udhia katika kutafuta, dadisi (peleleza, chunguza) ndani ya. *Rummage sale*, kuuza kwa vitu ambako fedha inayopatikana hutumiwa kusaidia maskini (Kanisa &c.).

rumour, *n.* habari, maneno ya watu, kivumo, uvumi, mnong'ono, tetesi, dakizo, udaku. *There is a rumour*, husemwa, huvumishwa, yavumika, iko tetesi ya kuwa.

rump, *n.* tako (la mnyama).

rumple, *v.t.* vungavunga, kunja vibaya, chafua, timua, vuruga.

rumpus, *n.* ghasia, zahama, ugomvi wenye makelele.

run, *v.i.* (*p.t.* **ran**, *pf.t.* **run**) enda mbio, kimbia, pita upesi, pita, enda; (*melt*) yeyuka; (*discharge*) churuza, toka, churuzika, chururika, toka usaha; (*of machines*) enda, fanya kazi; (*of colour*) chujuka; — *v.t.* toa, endesha, pitisha, ingiza, sukuma, sukumiza. *Run a business*, endesha kazi ya duka &c. *Run after*, fuata, mbio, fuatia; (*seek*) tafuta, taka, penda. *Run against*, gonga, gongana na, pambana na. *Run aground*, pweleza; (*of ship*) pwelewa, panda, kwama. *Run away*, toroka, kimbia, enda zake (zao &c.). *Run away with*, iba, nyang'anya. *Run down*, telemka; (*be exhausted*) potewa na nguvu, koma; (*depreciate*) nena, sema, singizia, chongea; (*collide with*) gonga, pambana na, vunja; (*pass, defeat*) patia, pitia (kwa shindano). *Run into*, ingia, jiingiza; (*collide with*) pambana na, gongana na; (*introduce*) ingiza, penyeza. *Run into debt*, jipasha deni. *Run mad*, -wa na wazimu. *Run off* (*trace*), andika, piga (picha, sanamu, mstari &c.). *Run on*, endelea; (*exaggerate*) piga domo, toa maneno mengi; (*reflect on*) kumbuka, waza. *Run over* (*examine lightly*), tazamia upesi; (*overflow*) furika, toka; (*trample on*) kanyaga chini, ponda. *Run out* (*extend*), toa, nyosha; (*complete*) maliza; (*come to an end*) isha. *Run riot*, pita kiasi, fanya upotovu. *Run risk*, pata hatari, jihatirisha, jasiri. *Run short*, punguka, totosha. *Run through* (*money &c.*) poteza, fuja, tapanya; (*examine lightly*) angalia kwa haraka. *Run up*, zidi, ongeza, ongezeka; (*a building*) jenga upesi; (*a flag*) tweka upesi. *Run up to*, kimbilia, patia. *Run with* (*blood &c.*), toka (damu &c.) tele (chapa), churuza, -wa na -ingi, churuzika. — *n.* kwenda mbio, mwendo wa mbio; (*course*) mwendo, njia; (*continuance*) mfulizo, mfululizo, mwendeleo, muda; (*journey*) safari; (*popularity*) kibali, ukubali, kupendeza, kutumika sana, kununuliwa (kusomwa, kuendewa, kutazamwa &c.) sana; (*demand on bank*) kutaka fedha (kwa hofu ya kwamba itakwisha); (*for grazing*) machunga, malisho. *In the long run*, mwisho, hatima. *The common run* (*the ordinary run*) *of mankind*, watu wa vivi hivi (wasio na cheo kikubwa wala wanyonge), walio watu tu. **run-about**, *n.* mtembezi, mtangatanga; (*motor-car*) motakaa ndogo nyepesi.

runnel, *n.* kijito, mlizamu, mrizabu,

chururu. **runner,** *n.* mwenda mbio, mshindani wa mbio; (*messenger*) mjumbe, tarishi; (*surface root*) kitawi (cha mmea utambaao chini); (*plant*) mtambaazi; (*cloth*) kitambaa kirefu, kipambo cha meza. **runner-up,** *n.* mtu wa pili katika shindano la mbio. **running,** *a.* -a kwenda mbio, -a kupita upesi; (*successive*) moja kwa moja, mtawalia, mtawalio, msago; (*accompanying*) -a kufuatana, -a kuandamana; (*discharging*) -a kutoka usaha. *Running fire,* mfululizo wa bunduki (wa mizinga). *Running fight,* vita ya watu wakifukuzana. *Six days running,* siku sita mfululizo (moja kwa moja). — *n.* kwenda mbio, kukimbia, mbio.

rung, (1) *pf.t.* ya *ring.*

rung, (2) *n.* (*of ladder*) kipago, kipandio, kipande (cha ngazi), daraja, kipawa, kidato.

runnel, *n.,* **runner,** *n.,* **runner-up,** *n.,* **running,** *a. and n.* taz. *run.*

rupee, *n.* rupia.

rupture, *v.t.* vunja, pasua, farakanisha, tokeza utumbo; — *v.i.* vunjika, pasuka, farakana. — *n.* kuvunja, kuvunjika, mvunjo; (*discord*) kuvunja urafiki, ugomvi, vita, farakano; (*of bowel &c.*) mshipa, kutokeza utumbo.

rural, *a.* -a shambani, -a mashamba. **ruralize,** *v.i.* shinda shambani.

ruse, *n.* hila, ujanja, werevu, shauri jerevu (la hila).

rush, (1) *n.* (*reed*) nyasi, tete.

rush, (2) *v.i.* enda mbio, timka, titimka, enda kwa kasi, pita kwa nguvu, boboka, kimbia, enda kwa haraka, puruka, bubujika, buguika; — *v.t.* (*bring quickly*) leta upesi; (*bustle along*) himiza, harakisha, peleka kwa haraka; (*capture by rushing*) shambulia, twaa ghafula; (*perform with undue haste*) purukusha. — *n.* mwendo wa nguvu; (*of water*) mkondo, bubujiko; (*sudden abundance*) wingi wa ghafula; (*bustle*) haraka, ghasia, kikaka, kakara, msukosuko.

rusk, *n.* namna ya biskuti (*biscuit*).

russet, *a.* -a rangi kama ya hudhurungi.

rust, *n.* kutu; (*on plants*) maradhi ya mimea kuota kama kutu, kizimwe. — *v.i.* pata (ingia, ota) kutu, liwa, oza. *I am rusty on that subject,* nimesahau habari zake. **rusty,** *a.* -enye kutu, -a kuchakaa.

rustic, *a.* -a mashamba, -a kukaa shambani. — *n.* mkulima, mkaa shambani, mjinga (wa mashamba).

rusticate, *v.i.* shinda shambani; — *v.t.* (*dismiss*) ondosha, hamisha. **rusticity,** *n.* ujinga (wa mashamba), (*bad mannered*) ukosefu wa adabu.

rustle, *v.t.* charakisha, chakarisha, gugurusha; — *v.i.* (*emit sound*) chakacha, fanya sauti kama majani makavu yakipepesuka kwa upepo. **rustle, rustling,** *n.* mchakacho, mchakarisho, uchakacho.

rusty, *a.* taz. *rust.*

rut, (1) *n.* shimo (njiani, palipopita magari), mfuo. *Be in a rut,* fuata taratibu (kawaida, mwendo, desturi) ile ile siku zote bila kubadili wala kufikiri nyingine.

rut (2), *n.* nyege ya wanyama.

ruthless, *a.* pasipo huruma, -kali, -katili, -korofi. **ruthlessly,** *adv.* bila huruma, kwa ukatili.

rye, *n.* nafaka kama ngano.

S

sabbath, *n.* siku takatifu ya kiyahudi, ndiyo Jumamosi; (*Sunday*) Jumapili. **Sabbatarian**, *n.* aadhimishaye Jumamosi kama kwamba ni siku takatifu; aadhimishaye Jumapili kwa kutofanya kazi yo yote wala kutoingia machezoni na mazungumzo *&c.*

sable, *a.* -eusi. — *n.* mnyama mdogo mla nyama mwenye manyoya meusi; (*fur*) manyoya ya *sable. Sable antelope*, palahala.

sabot, *n.* mtalawanda, kiatu cha mti.

sabotage, *n.* kuharibu mashine (mitambo) ya kazi (kuzuia kazi isitendeke)

sabre, *n.* kitara. — *v.t.* kata (chinja) kwa kitara.

sac, *n.* kifuko (cha maji au ute) katika mwili wa mwanadamu au mnyama au katika mmea.

saccharin, *n.* namna ya unga mtamu sana kama sukari. **saccharine**, *a.* -a sukari, kama sukari, -tamu.

sacerdotal, *a.* -a kasisi.

sachet, *n.* kikuba, kifuko (kifurushi) kidogo chenye majani *&c.* yanayonukia vizuri.

sack, (1) *n.* namna ya divai.

sack, (2) *n.* mfuko, gunia. — *v.t.* tia mfukoni (katika gunia); (*dismiss*) ondosha. *Give the sack*, (*slang*) ondoa kazini. **sackcloth, sacking**, *n.* gunia, nguo ya gunia.

sack, (3) *v.t.* teka, kumba, haribu.

sacrament, *n.* siri ya (fumbo la) dini ya kikristo, sakramenti, siri; (*Eucharist*) Ushirika Mtakatifu. **sacramental**, *a.* -a *sacrament.*

sacred, *a.* wakf, -liowekwa wakf, -liowekwa (-liotengwa) kwa ibada ya Mungu, -liowekwa kwa ukumbusho (wa marehemu, tendo jasiri *&c.*), -a Mungu, -a dini, -a heshima sana, -takatifu, -kuu. **sacredness**, *n.* kuwa wakf, utakatifu *&c.* **sacrilege**, *n.* jambo la kumchukiza Mungu, kukufurisha matakatifu, ukufuru, kutumia vibaya kilicho wakf. **sacrilegious**, *a.* -a *sacrilege*, -baya sana, -a kukufuru. **sacristan**, *n.* mngoje wa kanisa atunzaye vyombo vitakatifu *&c.* **sacristy**, *n.* chumba kanisani mlimowekwa vyombo vitakatifu.

sacrifice, *n.* dhabihu, kafara, toleo; (*to spirits of departed*) mizimu tambiko; (*of conciliation*) edaha; (*victim*) madhabuha, mhanga; (*offering*) sadaka, kipaji; (*incurring loss*) kutoa (kuacha, kutupa, kufisha kitu) makusudi; (*self-imposed loss*) kitu kilichotolewa *&c.* makusudi; (*cheap bargain*) kitu kilichouzwa rahisi, kuuza rahisi. — *v.t.* toa dhabihu (kafara *&c.*); (*to spirits of departed* — mizimu) tambika; (*incur loss of*) toa (acha, tupa, fisha kitu) makusudi, jinyima; (*sell cheap*) uza rahisi. **sacrificial**, *a.* -a *sacrifice.*

sacrilege, *n.*, **sacrilegious**, *a.*, **sacristan**, *n.*, **sacristy**, *n.* taz. *sacred.*

sacrosanct, *a.* -takatifu sana, -a kuheshimiwa sana.

sacrum, *n.* kitokono (vifupa vitano vya mwisho wa uti wa mgongo vilivyoungamana).

sad, *a.* -a huzuni, -enye majonzi, -a kuhuzunisha, -a kusikitisha, -zito; (*of colour*) -eusi. **sadden**, *v.t.* huzunisha, sikitisha, tia majonzi, tia uchungu. **sadly**, *adv.* kwa huzuni; (*to a deplorable extent*) sana. **sadness**, *n.* huzuni, majonzi, sikitiko, uzito.

saddle, *n.* tandiko, kiti juu ya farasi, saruji. *Pack-saddle*, shogi. — *v.t.* tandika, tia matandiko. **saddle-bag**, *n.* shogi, horji. **saddler**, *n.* fundi wa kufanyiza matandiko ya farasi, punda *&c.* **saddlery**, *n.* matandiko ya farasi, punda *&c.*

sadism, *n.* namna ya wazimu unaomfanya mtu kuwa mkatili sana.

sadly, *adv.* **sadness**, *n.* taz. *sad.*

safe, *a.* salama, salama salimini, pasipo hatari, -zima; (*certain*) yakini, hakika, bila shaka, sio na mashaka; (*trustworthy*) amini, -aminifu, -a salama; (*sound*) thabiti madhubuti. — *n.* kasha la chuma (la kuwekea fedha &c.), kasha la nguvu sana; (*meat-safe*) kabati la kuwekea vyakula. **safe-conduct**, *n.* hati (ya kusafirisha salama), ruhusa kupita.

safeguard, *n.* (*protection*) himaya; (*security*) kinga, kitu kinachofanya salama, kinacholinda katika hatari. — *v.t.* fanya salama, hakikisha salama, linda, hifadhi, kinga. **safely**, *adv.* salama, kwa salama. **safeness**, *n.* hali ya kuwa salama, pasipo hatari; (*trustworthiness, soundness*) amini, uaminifu, uthabiti, uzima. **safety**, *n.* salama. **safety-lamp**, *n.* taa iliyolindwa isiwashe hewa katika *mine.* **safety-valve**, *n.* kilango cha mvuke katika mashine isipate kupasuka.

saffron, *n.* zafarani; (*colour*) rangi ya manjano.

sag, *v.i.* nepa, inama; (*of spirits*) legea, nyong'onyea.

saga, *n.* hadithi za kale za *Norway.*

sagacious, *n.* -a busara, -a akili, hodari. **sagacity**, *n.* busara, akili, utambuzi.

sage, (1) *n.* (*herb*) namna ya majani yanayotumika kama kiungo cha chakula.

sage, (2) *a.* -a hekima nyingi. — *n.* hakimu, mtaalamu, mwenye hekima nyingi. **sageness**, *n.* hekima nyingi.

sago, *n.* mti kama mtende; moyo wa mti huo, kama wanga, sego.

said, *p.t.* na *pf.t.* ya *say.*

sail, *n.* tanga, shira. *Make* (*set*) *sail,* tweka. *Strike sail,* tua. — *v.t.* endesha kwa tanga, endesha (merikebu, meli, chombo); — *v.i.* safiri (enda) merikebuni (melini, chomboni), pita baharini; (*start on a voyage*) tweka, funga safari chomboni; (*move smoothly*) enda upesi (sawasawa kama kwa mabawa au kwa tanga).

sailcoth, *n.* kitali. **sailing**, *n.* kwenda kwa tanga &c. — *a.* -a kwenda kwa tanga &c. *A sailing vessel,* merikebu ya (chombo cha) matanga. **sailor**, *n.* baharia, mwanamaji.

saint, *n.* mtu mtakatifu aliyekwisha ingia peponi, walii, mtawa, sufii; (*good man*) mtu mwema sana. **sainted**, *a.* -takatifu; (*deceased*) marehemu, hayati. **saintlike**, *a.* kama *saint*, -ema sana. **saintliness**, *n.* utakatifu, utawa, usufii. **saintly**, *a.* -a *saint*, kama *saint*, -ema sana.

sake, *n.* *For the sake of,* kwa ajili (maana, huja, hesabu) ya minajili ya; ili kusaidia au kupendeza. *For my sake,* unipendavyo.

salaam, *n.* salamu. — *v.i.* salimu.

salacious, *a.* -kware, -a ashiki nyingi, -asherati. **salacity**, *n.* ukware, uasherati.

salad, *n.* saladi, namna ya majani yanayolika mabichi.

salamander, *n.* kama chura mwenye kuhadithiwa kwamba anaweza kuishi motoni.

salary, *n.* mshahara, ujira, ijara.

sale, *n.* kuuza, kuchuuza, uchuuzi, kuuzanya, biashara, kutembeza bidhaa, ubazazi; (*auction*) mnada, lilamu. *A sale,* (mwenye duka) kuuza vitu rahisi kuliko kawaida. *Be on sale,* uzanya, tembezwa. *It is not for sale,* haiuzwi. **saleable**, *a.* -a kuuzika, -a kuuzanya. **salesman**, *n.* mwuzaji, mchuuzi; (*auctioneer*) dalali, mnadi.

Salic law, *n.* sheria ya nchi nyingine ya kuwa mwanamke hawezi kutawala nchi.

salient, *a.* -a kutokeza; (*important*) -a maana, -kubwa, -a kuangaliwa. — *n.* pembe inayotokeza mbele.

saline, *a.* -a chumvi.

saliva, *n.* mate, ute, udende, udelele. **salivary**, *a.* -a mate. **salivation**, *n.* kutoka mate mengi.

sallow, *a.* -a rangi ya manjano meupe, -eupe (kama kwa ugonjwa).

sally, *n.* shambulio (tokeo) la ghafula kutoka boma lililozingiwa na adui; (*in speech*) mzaha, ubishi. — *v.i.* shambulia (toka) ghafula nje ya boma linalozingiwa, tokea; (*go for a walk*) tembea. **sally-port,** *n.* kilango cha boma.

salmon, *n.* namna ya samaki mkubwa mwenye nyama nyekundu.

salon, *n.* sebule kubwa, ukumbi mkubwa, chumba cha mazungumzo,

saloon, *n.* sebule kubwa, chumba kikubwa kirefu; (*in ship or train*) chumba cha kulia melini (garini); (*public*) chumba cha kunywea pombe &c.; (*motor-car*) motakaa yenye kifuniko na milango kama chumba kidogo.

salt, *n.* chumvi, munyu. *An old salt,* baharia mstadi. *Salts, Epsom salts,* chumvi ya haluli. *Smelling-salts,* dawa ya kunusa. — *a.* -a chumvi, -a maji ya bahari. — *v.t.* tia chumvi, koleza kwa chumvi. **salt-cellar,** *n.* kidau cha mezani cha kutia chumvi. **salt-lick,** *n.* mahali penye chumvi wanapoendea wanyama kuilamba. **saltness,** *n.* utamu wa (ladha ya) chumvi, chumvi. **salt-pan,** *n.* handaki (shimo) ya kuwekea maji ya chumvi ili yanywee na kubakiza chumvi. **saltpetre,** *n.* shura. **salty,** *a.* -a chumvi.

salubrious, *a.* -a afya (siha, rai), -a kutia afya (uzima, siha, rai), -a kuburudisha, -ema. **salubrity,** *n.* afya, siha, rai, uzima, uzuri (wa kutia afya, siha, rai), hali njema (kwa afya &c.).

salutary, *a.* -a kutia afya (siha, rai), -ema, -a kufaa, -zuri; (*in moral sense*) -a kuonya mema.

salute, *v.t.* salimu, amkia; (*with excessive humility*) kongowea; (*by firing*) piga bunduki (mizinga) ya salamu. — *n.* salamu; (*by firing*) mizinga (bunduki) ya salamu. **salutation,** *n.* salamu, maamkizi.

salvable, *a.* taz. *salvage.*

salvage, *n.* ada (ujira, malipo) ya kuokoa meli (chombo, merikebu) hatarini; kuokoa meli &c. hatarini; bidhaa &c. zilizookolewa katika meli &c. hatarini, pia meli (chombo, merikebu) iliyookolewa. — *v.t.* okoa katika meli (merikebu &c.) iliyovunjika, okoa katika nyumba iliyoshika moto. **salvable,** *a.* -a kuweza kuokolewa katika meli iliyovunjika (katika nyumba iliyoshika moto.)

salvation, *n.* wokovu, wokozi, kuokoa, kuokolewa, kuokoka; (*person, thing*) mwokozi, kitu kinachookoa. **Salvation Army,** *n.* jamii ya Wakristo iliyoanzishwa na *Booth* mwaka 1877 kufanya kazi hasa katika watu maskini na wanyonge.

salve, (1) *v.t.* kama *salvage.*

salve, (2) *n.* dawa ya mafuta ya kupaka, marhamu; (*fig.*) kitulizo. — *v.t.* paka *salve.*

salver, *n.* sinia, kombe.

salvo, *n.* mizinga mingi (bunduki nyingi) ikipigwa pamoja kwa sherehe (ya salamu); (*cheers &c.*) vifijo, vigelele.

same, *a.* -moja, sawa, yule yule (ile ile &c.); (*aforesaid*) huyo (hicho, hiyo &c.). *All the same,* mamoja, haidhuru; (*nevertheless*) lakini. — *adv.* namna ile, kama. **sameness,** *n.* umoja, sawa, mfano mmoja, yale yale, vile vile; (*monotony*) kuchosha, baridi, udufu, uchovu, machovu.

samovar, *n.* buli kubwa la kufanyizia chai, la *Russia.*

sample, *n.* kipande (kidogo, kimoja) cha kuonyesha namna ya kizima (vitu vingi), namna, mfano, -moja katika -ingi, kiolezo. — *v.t.* onja, jaribu. **sampler,** *n.* kiolezo (cha kazi ya ushoni).

sanatorium, *n.* nyumba ya kuugulia wagonjwa na kuburudisha wanaopona. **sanatory,** *a.* -a kutia afya (siha, rai).

sanctify, *v.t.* takasa, fanya -takatifu. **sanctification,** *n.* utakaso, utakatifu, kutakasika. **sanctimonious,** *a.* -a kujifanya mtu wa dini na mtakatifu, -nafiki, -zandiki. **sanctity,** *n.* utakatifu, usufii, utawa, hali ya kuwa wakf. **sanctuary**, *n.* mahali patakatifu, mahali pa ibada, msikiti, kanisa, hekalu; (*in a church*) palipo madhbahu kanisani; (*refuge*) kimbilio. **sanctum**, *n.* chumba cha faragha; (*sanctuary*) mahali patakatifu.

sanction, *n.* idhini, kibali, ukubali, uradhi, usahihi, ruhusa. — *v.t.* tia (toa) idhini, sahihisha, kibali, ridhia, ruhusu.

sanctity, *n.*, **sanctuary**, *n.*, **sanctum**, *n.*, taz. *sanctify*.

sand, *n.* mchanga; (*fine*) ufukwe; (*sandy shore*) ufuko; (*for divining*) ramli. **sand-flea**, *n.* funza, tekenya. **sand-fly**, *n.* usubi. **sand-glass**, *n.* shisha, chupa yenye mchanga ndani ya kupimia saa (wakati). **sandpaper**, *n.* msasa (karatasi yenye mchanga ya kulainishia mbao). **sandpiper**, *n.* kitwitwi. **sandstone**, *n.* jiwe la mchanga uliogandamana. **sandy**, *a.* -a mchanga, -enye mchanga mwingi, -a rangi ya mchanga; (*of soil*) tifutifu.

sandal, *n.* kiatu. *Different kinds are*: ndara, kubazi, makubazi, staka.

sandal-wood, *n.* sandali.

sand-flea, *n.*, **sand-fly**, *n.*, **sand-glass**, *n.*, **sandpaper**, *n.*, **sandpiper**, *n.*, **sandstone**, *n.* taz. *sand.*

sandwich, *n.* vipande vya mkate vyenye nyama &c. kati. — *v.t.* tia (ingiza) kati.

sandy, *a.* taz. *sand.*

sane, *a.* -enye akili zake (zao &c.) timamu (sawasawa), -a akili, -a busara. **sanely**, *adv.* kwa akili, kwa busara. **saneness**, *n.* hali ya kuwa na akili timamu. **sanitary**, *a.* -a kutia afya (siha, rai), -a mambo ya afya, kwa ajili ya afya; safi, pasipo taka (uchafu &c.) zinazodhuru afya. **sanitation**, *n.* kutia afya, maarifa ya mambo ya afya, matendo (mambo, matengenezo) yote yanayaondoa uchafu (taka &c.) unaoweza kudhuru afya, kazi ya kutenda kanuni za afya. **sanity**, *n.* kuwa na akili timamu, akili, busara.

sang, *p.t.* ya *sing.*

sang-froid, *n.* utulivu (katika hatari au shida), ukavu wa macho.

sanguinary, *a.* -kali, -a kufisha watu wengi, -a damu, katili. **sanguine**, *a.* -a tumaini, -tumainifu, -a kutazamia mema tu, -a bidii; (*colour*) -ekundu.

sanitary, *a.*, **sanitation**, *n.*, **sanity**, *n.* taz. *sane.*

sank, *p.t.* ya *sink.*

Sanscrit, *n.* lugha ya kale sana ya kihindi.

sap, (1) *n.* maji (ya miti, majani &c.), utomvu. — *v.t.* (*weaken*) dhoofisha, ondoa nguvu. **sapling**, *n.* mti mdogo, mti mchanga; (*youth*) kijana. **sappy**, *a.* -enye maji mengi, -enye utomvu mwingi, -changa, -a nguvu.

sap, (2) *v.t.* fukua mashimo (handaki) chini ya, tekua, ondoa misingi ya. — *n.* shimo la (handaki ya) kupenyezea watu hata boma la adui. **sapper**, *n.* askari mwenye kazi ya kufanyiza njia, madaraja, maboma, handaki &c.

sapience, *n.* taz. *sapient.*

sapient, *a.* -a busara, -a akili, -juzi; (*aping wisdom*) -a kujifanya kama mwenye akili, -juzi. **sapience**, *n.* busara, akili, ujuzi; (*self-satisfied stupidity*) ukinaifu (wa kujifanya kama mjuzi, kumbe ni mjinga), ujuzi.

sapling, *n.* taz. *sap* (1).

sapodilla, *n.* mratabu.

saponaceous, *a.* -a sabuni, kama sabuni; (*flattering*) -a kujipendekeza, -a kusifusifu bila kustahili.

sapper, *n.* taz. *sap* (2).

sapphire, *n.* johari ya thamani ya rangi ya samawati.

sappy, *a.* taz. *sap* (1).

Saracen, *n.* Mwislamu (wa zamani).

sarcasm, *n.* maneno machungu (ya kuchokoza, ya kuchoma moyo), uchokozi, ubishi, matusi. **sarcastic**, *a.* -chungu, -a kuchoma moyo, -a kuchokoza, -a kutia uchungu, -kali.

sarcophagus, *n.* sanduku kubwa la jiwe la kuwekea maiti.

sardine, *n.* samaki mdogo (hupikwa

na kutiwa katika mafuta ya halzeti ndani ya makopo). *Packed like sardines*, kusongana sana.
sardonic, *a*. *Sardonic smile* (*or laughter*), kucheka kwa uchungu au ukatili (si kwa furaha).
sartorial, *a*. -a kuhusu ushoni wa (nguo za) wanaume.
sash, (1) *n*. mshipi, mahazamu, masombo, ukumbuu, kibwebwe, deuli.
sash, (2) *n*. (*of window*) dirisha la kuinuka na kushuka.
sat, *p.t. and pf.t.* ya *sit*.
Satan, *n*. Shetani, Ibilisi. **satanic**, *a*. -a shetani, -a ibilisi; -ovu, -baya sana, -katili.
satchel, *n*. mkoba, mfuko, bahasha, kifurushi, shanta.
sate, **satiate**, *v.t.* shibisha, kinaisha, vimbisha. **satiated**, *a*. (*be*) shiba, kinai, choka. *I am satiated with this kind of food*, chakula cha namna hii kinaninuka. **satiation**, **satiety**, *n*. kushiba, kujivimbisha, shibe, ukinaifu, kinaya, wingi, ujalivu; (*discomfort caused by over-eating*) vimbizi.
sateen, *n*. kitambaa cha pamba au usufi kinachong'aa kama *satin* (atlasi).
satellite, *n*. (*star*) dunia (nyota inayozunguka dunia (nyota) nyingine, *e.g.* mwezi unaozunguka dunia hii; (*follower*) mfuasi, mwandani (hasa mnyonge anayejipendekeza).
satiate, *v*., **satiation**, *n*., **satiety**, *n*. taz. *sate*.
satin, *n*. atlasi, hariri. — *a*. laini, -a kung'aa, kama atlasi.
satire, *n*. (*ridicule*) dhihaka, mzaha, ubishi; (*invective*) ukali, masuto, masusuiko, matusi, maneno ya kushutumia kwa ukali; (*humour*) kuchekesha, uchekeshi. **satirical**, *a*. -a *satire*. **satirize**, *v.t.* fanyia *satire*, dhihaki, cheka, fanyia mzaha, suta, susuika.
satisfaction, *n*., **satisfactorily**, *adv*., **satisfactory**, *a*., **satisfied**, *a*. taz. *satisfy*.
satisfy, *v.t. and i.* ridhisha, tuliza, tia uradhi, ondolea mashaka, starehesha, tosha, kifu, kidhi, kora; (*with food*) shibisha; (*with money*) lipa. **satisfaction**, *n*., kuridhisha, kuridhika, uradhi, raha mustarehe; (*payment*) malipo, malipizi; (*revenge*) kisasi; (*atonement*) kipatanisho; (*for murder*) dia; (*cause of satisfaction*) kitulizo. **satisfactorily**, *adv*. kwa, kufaa, kwa kutosha &c. **satisfactory**, *a*. -a kuridhisha, -a kufaa, -a kutosha, -a kuthibitisha &c.; (*pleasing*) -a kupendeza, -zuri; (*sound, trustworthy*) amini, -enye sifa njema, -zuri, -aminifu, -a kutumainiwa. **satisfied**, *a*. radhi; (*with food*) -enye kushiba -a kukuta. *Feel quite satisfied*, toshewa, kinai, ridhika. **satisfying**, *a*. -a kuridhisha, -a kupendeza; (*of food*) -a kushibisha.
satrap, *n*. liwali wa kiajemi wa kale.
saturate, *v.t.* nywesha maji mengi, lowesha kabisa, jaliza, nywesha sana. **saturated**, *a*. -a kujaa (-a kulowa) hata haiwezi kuzidi, dabwadabwa, debwedebwe. **saturation**, *n*. hali ya kujaa (kunyweshwa, kulowa, kushiba) maji.
Saturday, *n*. Jumamosi.
Saturn, *n*. jina la sayari moja, zahali. **saturnalia**, *n*. sikukuu kama siku ya mwaka; (*orgy*) siku ya kufanya yo yote: kucheza, kulewa, jeuri &c.
saturnine, *a*. -zito, -kali, -a kasirani.
satyr, *n*. zimwi la mwitu (jini) — nusu mtu nusu mnyama; (*lecherous man*) mkware, mwasherati, mfasiki, mfisadi.
sauce, *n*. mchuzi; (*impudence*) ujuvi, usafihi, ubishi, ufidhuli, ukavu wa macho. **sauce-boat**, *n*. chombo (kibakuli) cha kuwekea *sauce*.
saucepan, *n*. (*metal*) sufuria (ndogo yenye mkono); (*earthen*) chungu, kibia, bunguu. **saucer**, *n*. sahani ndogo, kisahani. **saucily**, *adv*. kwa fidhuli (ujuvi, ukavu wa macho, usafihi). **sauciness**, *n*. ubishi, ujuvi, usafihi, ukavu wa macho, utundu.
saucy, *a*. -juvi, -safihi, -bishi, -cheshi, -fidhuli, -tundu, -kavu wa macho.
saunter, *v.i.* tembea (enda, zunguka,

tanga) polepole (kwa raha), susurika, zurura, zururika. — *n.* matembezi, kujienda.

sausage, *n.* nyama iliyosagwa na kukolewa na kutiwa katika utumbo wa mnyama. **sausage-tree**, *n.* mvongonya, mwegea.

savage, *a.* -kali, katili, -uaji, nduli; (*rude*) -shenzi, -siostaarabika; (*desolate*) pasipo watu, -kiwa; (*angry*) -enye hasira, -a ghadhabu, -a kiruu. — *n.* mshenzi, mtu asiyestaarabika; (*cruel person*) mkali, mkatili, mwuaji &c. **savageness, savagery**, *n.* ushenzi; (*desolation*) ukiwa; (*cruelty*) ukali, ukatili, uuaji.

savanna, savannah, *n.* mbuga, uwanda wenye majani usio na watu, pori, pululu, nyika.

savant, *n.* mwanachuoni, mtaalamu.

save, *v.t.* okoa, ponya, opoa, afua, afu, futusha, gandua, gangua, nafidhi, nusuru; (*reform*) rudisha, tuliza; (*economize*) kabidhi, weka akiba, dunduliza, weka, punguza gharama; (*relieve*) achilia, punguzia kazi; (*guard, preserve*) linda, hifadhi; (*guard against*) kinga, zuia. *Save trouble, expense &c.*, punguza kazi, gharama &c., saidia, faa. **save, saving**, *prep.* ila, isipokuwa, ghairi ya, minghairi. — *n.* kukata gharama, kujiwekea akiba, uwekevu, ukabidhi. — *a.* -a kuokoa &c. **savings**, *n.* akiba ya mali. **savings bank**, *n.* *bank* ya kuwekea akiba ya fedha. **saviour**, *n.* mwokozi.

savoir-faire, *n.* ujuzi wa kujichukua mbele ya watu, malezi mazuri, busara.

savour, *n.* ladha, utamu, harufu. — *v.i.* -wa na ladha ya (utamu wa), harufu ya); (*show signs of*) -wa na dalili ya, onyesha dalili ya. **savourless**, *a.* -chapwa, -dufu, baridi. **savoury**, *a.* -tamu, -a kuchapukia, -a kunukia, -a kutamanisha, -liokolea, -a kupendeza, -zuri. — *n.* chakula kidogo kilichokolewa sana.

saw, (1) *n.* (*maxim*) fumbo la maneno, methali.

saw, (2) *n.* msumeno; (*large, for two men*) jambeni. — *v.t.* (*p.t.* **sawn**) pasua kwa msumeno; — *v.i.* weza kupasuliwa kwa msumeno, tumia msumeno. **sawdust**, *n.* unga (vumbi) wa mbao (wa mti). **sawfish**, *n.* papa upanga, samaki mwenye mdomo kama msumeno. **sawmill**, *n.* kinu (mashine) cha kupasulia mbao, magogo &c. **saw-pit**, *n.* shimo la kupasulia mbao. **sawyer**, *n.* mpasua mbao.

saw, (3) *p.t.* ya *see*.

saxophone, *n.* namna ya tarumbeta.

say, *v.t. and i.* (*p.t. and pf.t.* **said**) sema, nena. *Say to*, ambia. *They say, It is said*, husema, husemwa. *So to say*, kama vile. *Say* (*perhaps*) huenda, labda, kama. *That is to say*, maana yake, yaani. *I don't say, Not to say*, licha, sembuse. *Come along I say*, njoo saa, twende wewe. — *n.* neno. *You have no say in the matter*, huna neno katika jambo hili, humo. *I must have my say*, lazima niseme. **saying**, *n.* neno, fumbo la maneno, methali.

scab, *n.* kigaga. **scabby**, *a.* -a kigaga, -enye vigaga. **scabies**, *n.* upele. **scabious**, *a.* -enye upele, -enye vigaga.

scabbard, *n.* ala, uo.

scabby, *a.*, **scabies**, *n.*, **scabious**, *a.* taz. *scab*.

scaffold, *n.* (*building*) jukwaa, dungu, majengo; (*for execution*) mahali wauaji wanaponyongwa kwa sheria. **scaffolding**, *n.* jukwaa, dungu, majengo.

scald, *v.t.* unguza (choma, washa) kwa maji ya moto; pasha moto mpaka karibu kuchemka. *Scalding hot*, -a moto sana.

scale, (1) *n.* (*of fish &c.*) gamba; (*of metal, mineral*) mavi; (*scurf*) mba. *Scales*, mizani, kapani; (*dish*) kitanga. — *v.t.* paa, magamba, kwangua; — *v.i.* kwanguka, toka. **scaly**, *a.* -enye magamba.

scale, (2) *n.* (*measuring instrument*) kipimio, kipande cha kupimia cheo au kadiri; (*measure, degree*) cheo, kadiri; (*music*) jamii ya sauti nane. *On a large scale*, kwa vikubwa. *On a small scale*, kwa vidogo. — *v.t.* panda, kwea hata juu ya, paramia.

scalene, *a.* (*triangle*) -enye pande zote tatu za urefu mbalimbali.

scallop, *n.* namna ya kombe ya pwani. *Scallops*, marinda, vikunjo.

scallywag, *n.* mtu mvivu, mtu hafifu.

scalp, *n.* ngozi ya kichwa pamoja na nywele zake, ngozi ya kichwa. — *v.t.* chuna ngozi ya kichwa na nywele pamoja.

scalpel, *n.* kisu (cha kazi ya udaktari)

scaly, *a.* taz. *scale* (1).

scamp, (1) *v.t.* fanya (kazi &c.) kwa purukushani, puza, fanya kwa uzembe.

scamp, (2) *n.* mtu hafifu, mtu mvivu; (*mischievous child*) mtoto mtundu. *A handsome young scamp*, kijana mzuri, mcheshi, damisi, mrembo.

scamper, *v.i.* enda mbio mbio, kimbia, puruka.

scan, *v.t.* angalia, chungua, tazamia, tazama sana; (*of verses*) tamka mashairi kulingana na mwendo wake; — *v.i.* fuata mwendo unaolingana.

scandal, *n.* jambo la aibu (linaloaibisha, la kukashifu, linalovunja jina, sifa au heshima), hizaya, tahayuri, taksiri, kashifa, maongezi mabaya, kikwazo, masingizio, machongezi, machongelezo. **scandalize**, *v.t.* aibisha, hizi, chukiza. **scandal-monger**, *n.* mkashifu, mchongelezi, mchongezi, mbukuzi, mbukulia.

scandalous, *a.* -a kuchukiza, -a kuaibisha, -a kuchongeleza, -a kuchongea, -a aibu, -a kuhizi, -a kutahayarisha.

scant, scanty, *a.* -chache, haba, kidogo. **scantiness**, *n.* uchache, ukosefu.

scantling, *n.* boriti inayopungua unene wa inchi 5; kipimo cha kukatiwa mbao, mti au jiwe.

scapegoat, *n.* mtu anayesukumiziwa makosa ya wengine. **scapegrace**, *n.* mtu mbaya, mpotovu, baa.

scapula, *n.* mtulinga.

scar, *n.* kovu, walio, baka. — *v.t.* tia kovu; — *v.i.* duduka, fanyika kovu.

scarce, *a.* haba, -chache, shida, ghali, -adimu, -a kuadimika. *Be scarce*, -wa ghali (haba, -chache &c.), adimika. **scarcely**, *adv.* shida, si sana, kidogo; isipokuwa kwa shida (taabu); si yamkini. **scarceness, scarcity**, *n.* shida, uchache, njaa.

scare, *v.t.* shtusha, gutusha, fadhaisha, ogofya, tisha; (*drive off*) fukuza, winga. — *n.* hofu, fadhaa. **scare-crow**, *n.* sanamu ya mtu kuweka shambani kutisha ndege; mtoto aliyewekwa kufukuza ndege shambani (kuamia shamba).

scarf, *n.* shali, shatoruma; (*for waist* deuli, mahazamu.

scarify, *v.t.* chanjachanja, piga mitai, papura.

scarlet, *n.* rangi nyekundu kama ya damu, wekundu. — *a.* -ekundu.

scarp, *n.* mtelemko wa ghafula, genge, ngome.

scatheless, *a.* pasipo hasara (madhara), -zima. **scathing**, *a.* -chungu, -kali.

scatter, *v.t.* tawanya, tapanya; (*sprinkle*) mwaga, nyunyiza, rasha; (*disperse*) fukuza huko na huko; (*bring to nothing*) batilisha, haribu; (*waste*) tapanya, poteza, fuja; — *v.i.* mwagika, tawanyika, fumukana, kimbia huko na huko; (*be dotted about*) tapakaa. **scatter-brain**, *n.* mtu mwenye wasiwasi, mpuzi.

scavenge, *v.t.* fagia njia za mji, ondoa taka za mji. **scavenger**, *n.* mtu mwenye kazi ya kufagia njia na kuondoa taka za mji, topasi.

scene, *n.* sehemu ya mchezo katika *theatre*; (*place*) mahali (palipofanyika mambo); (*things seen*) mambo yenyewe, mambo yaliyooneka, vitu, hakika ya vitu; (*view*) sura ya nchi, mandhari; (*striking sight*) jambo la kutazamisha, tamasha; (*disturbance*) mambo ya ugomvi (hasira, huzuni), mambo ya kutia kishindo au fadhaa, msukosuko, zahama, ghasia. *Be behind the scenes,* jua siri. **scenery,** *n.* tabia (sura) ya nchi (milima, miti, mwitu &c.) vinavyoonekana, mandhari; (*theatrical*) matengenezo ya mchezo wa *theatre.* **scenic,** *a.* -a *scene.*

scent, *n.* marashi, uturi, manuka, manukato, harufu; (*faculty of smell*) akili ya kunusa, nguvu ya (uwezo wa) kusikia harufu; (*track*) njia, nyayo, dalili. *Scent-bottle* (*for sprinkling*), mrashi. *Be on the scent,* fuata nyayo (kwa kunusa), pata dalili. — *v.t.* tia manukato (uturi &c.) katika, tia marashi; (*as a dog*) nukiza, nusa; (*perceive smell*) sikia harufu; (*perceive in the mind*) ona dalili, shuku, tuhumu.

sceptic, *n.* mwenye mashaka, ashukuye. **sceptical,** *a.* -enye mashaka, -a kushuku. **scepticism,** *n.* mashaka, moyo wa (tabia ya) kuonea mashaka mambo yasiyothibitika kabisa (pia kushuku ya kuwa hayathibitiki).

sceptre, *n.* fimbo ya mfalme, dalili ya enzi; (*sovereignty*) enzi, ufalme.

schedule, *n.* hati, daftari, hesabu, orodha, jedwali, taarifa.

scheme, *n.* shauri, kusudi, nia, azimio, madhumuni; (*systematic arrangement*) taratibu, kawaida, desturi, matengenezo; (*underhand device*) hila. — *v.t.* fanya shauri, waza, kusudia; (*underhand*) tunga (fanya) hila. **schemer,** *n.* mtoa mashauri mengi, mtu wa hila. **scheming,** *a.* -a mashauri mengi, -erevu, -a hila.

schism, *n.* farakano katika watu wenye shauri moja (hasa katika Kanisa au dini). **schismatic,** *a.* -a *schism,* -a kufarakana (kufarakanisha). — *n.* mtu wa *schism.*

schist, *n.* namna ya jiwe gumu linalong'aa na kupasuka upesi tabaka tabaka.

scholar, *n.* (*learner*) mwanafunzi; (*learned man*) mwanachuoni, mwalimu, mtaalamu; (*having a scholarship*) mtu apewaye fedha kwa *University* kumwezesha aendelee katika mafundisho. **scholarship,** *n.* (*learning*) elimu; (*endowment of learner*) malipo ya mwanachuoni, fedha anayopewa mtu apate kuendelea katika mafundisho. **scholastic,** *a.* -a *scholar*; (*learned*) -a elimu nyingi; (*abstruse*) -a fumbo, -gumu kusikia.

school, *n.* chuo, skuli, shule, madarasa, nyumba wanamosomeshwa na kufundishwa watoto (watu); (*pupils*) jamii ya wanafunzi, wana chuoni; (*sect, opinion*) madhehebu, mafundisho; (*followers*) wafuasi; (*of fish*) kundi, wingi. *He has learnt in the school of experience,* anajua mambo ya ulimwengu. — *v.t.* fundisha, ongoza, zuia, tiisha. **schooling,** *n.* elimu, mafundisho, kufundishwa. **schoolmaster,** *n.* mwalimu, mkuu wa *school.* **schoolmistress,** *n.* bibi mwalimu. **schoolroom,** *n.* chumba cha *school,* darasa.

schooner, *n.* jahazi kubwa yenye milingoti miwili au zaidi.

sciatica, *n.* ugonjwa wa kuuma mshipa wa nyuma ya paja.

science, *n.* (*true knowledge*) elimu, maarifa, ujuzi wa hakika, elimu ya kweli; (*physics*) elimu ya ulimwengu na viumbe vyote; maarifa ya jamii ya vitu fulani; (*men of science*) watu wa elimu. *The science of Geology,* maarifa ya mawe. *Science tells us,* walimu wenye maarifa husema. **scientific,** *a.* -a *science,* -juzi. **scientist,** *n.* mtu mwenye maarifa ya *science,* mtaalamu, mwanachuoni wa *science.*

scimitar, *n.* kitara, hanjari.

scintillate, *v.i.* metameta, memeteka.

sciolist, *n.* mjuzi, ajidaiye elimu, jambazi. **sciolism,** *n.* ujuzi, elimu kidogo.

scion, *n.* mtoto, mwana.

scissors, *n. Pair of scissors,* mkasi, makasi.

scoff, *v.i.* dhihaki, fanya mzaha, cheka. — *n.* neno la dhihaka (la kudharau), dharau, mzaha, cheko. **scoffer,** *n.* mtu wa dhihaka, mtu wa dharau (wa mzaha). **scoffing,** *n.* dharau, dhihaka, mzaha.

scold, *v.t.* karipia, kemea, shutumu, laumu. — *n.* mtu (hasa mwanamke mkorofi) mwenye kukaripia *&c.*, mwenye gubu.

sconce, *n.* kipande cha ukutani cha kuwekea mshumaa au taa, mwango.

scone, *n.* mkate mdogo (mtamu).

scoop, *n.* (*metal*) kombe, ukombe, bambo; (*ladle*) kata, upawa; (*spoon*) mwiko, kijiko, mkamshi. — *v.t.* (*hollow out*) komba; (*by digging*) fukua; (*of water*) kumba, vua; (*in small quantities*) chota, danga.

scoot, *v.i.* enda mbio, kimbia. **scooter,** *n.* ubao wenye magurudumu mawili (mfano wa kigari) mchezo wa watoto.

scope, *n.* (*range, room*) enco, upeo, nafasi, mahali; (*power*) nguvu, akili; (*purpose*), shauri, kusudi.

scorbutic, *a.* enye ugonjwa wa *scurvy* (wa kuvimba ufizi na kutoka damu kama kiseyeye). — *n.* dawa ya *scurvy*.

scorch, *v.t.* unguza, choma (kwa moto), umiza kwa moto; (*of sun*) kausha, unguza, choma; (*drive quickly=slang*) enda mbio sana (kupita kadiri); — *v.i.* ungua, choma, umia kwa moto.

score, *n.* (*account*) hesabu (ya gharama, ya mabao *&c.* katika mchezo); (*twenty*) ishirini, korija; (*notch &c.*) mfou, alama, mchoro, pengo, mtai, chale; (*in music*) andiko la (herufi za) muziki. *On the score of,* kwa sababu ya. *Scores,* wingi. *Pay off old scores,* jilipiza kisasi. — *v.t.* chora, tia pengo (mfuo, mtai, alama, chale), kata; (*in games, esp. football*) tia bao; (*make a score*) pata hesabu, pata faida; — *v.i.* (*keep a score*) hesabu; (*make a score*) tia bao. *Score off,* shinda. **scorer,** *b.* mwandishi wa hesabu (za mchezoni).

scoria, *n.* mavi ya chuma, taka za madini, mawe yaliyoyeyuka.

scorn, *v.t.* dharau, beza, dhihaki, tweza, tusha, fanyia mzaha, beja, bekua, mena, turufu, geua, deua, hakiri, jugumu, cheka, nyarafu. — *n.* dharau, bezo, dhihaka, mzaha, twezo, bejo, nyarafu, unyanya, kiburi. **scorner,** *n.* mwenye kudharau (kutweza *&c.*), mtu wa kiburi. **scornful,** *a.* -a kudharau *&c.* *Scornful abuse,* matusi.

scorpion, *n.* nge, kisusuli.

Scot, Scotchman, *n.* mtu wa *Scotland.*

scotch, *v.t.* haribu, zuia, komesha.

scot-free, *a.* pasipo hasara, salama salimini, pasipo kulipa, bure, bilashi.

scoundrel, *n.* mtu mbaya kabisa, mlaghai, baa.

scour, (1) *v.t.* (*pass quickly over*) pitia mbio (hasa katika kutafuta mtu au kitu).

scour, (2) *v.t.* sugua sana, safisha kwa kusugua, paruza, kwaruza.

scourge, *v.t.* piga, rudi, patiliza, adhibu, adhibisha. — *n.* mjeledi, mchapo; (*punishment*) adhabu, malipo, kisasi, rada; (*plague*) pigo, msiba mkuu.

scout, (1) *n.* mpelelezi, mdukizi, doria; (*servant*) mtumishi; (*boy scout*) mwana wa chama kiitwacho *Boy Scouts.* — *v.i.* peleleza nchi, doea, vizia, dukiza. *Scout round,* tafutatafuta.

scout, (2) *v.t.* (*disdain, reject &c.*) dharau, cheka, kataa kabisa.

scow, *n.* tishari.

scowl, *v.i.* kunja (finya) uso, tazama vikali (kwa uchungu). — *n.* uso wa kufinyana (wa kukunjamana), uso mkali (wa uchungu).

scrabble, *v.i.* papasapapasa (kama katika kutafutatafuta kitu), tutusa.

scrag, *n.* mtu (kitu, mti, mmea) aliyevia; (*neck*) sehemu ya shingo (hasa ya kondoo) yenye vifupa. — *v.t.* songa (kaba) koo, nyonga. **scraggy,** *a.* -embamba, -a kimbaombao, -liokonda, -gofu, -chache.

scramble, *v.i.* enda kwa miguu na mikono, paraga, sowera, sombea, enda kwa shida, tambaa; (*struggle*) songana, shindana; — *v.t.* (*eggs &c.*) vuruga. *Scramble for*, buburushana (sukumana) kwa. — *n.* chafuko, fujo, mwendo wa shida, mashindano.

scrap, *n.* kipande kidogo; (*of food*) kombo; (*refuse &c.*) takataka, vitu vikuukuu. — *v.t.* (*discard*) tupa; (*of things which have given long service*) samehe, acha. *Have a scrap*, pigana. **scrappy**, *a.* vivi hivi, ovyo, -siotengenea, shaghalabaghala.

scrape, *v.t.* para, paruza, kwaruza, chubua; (*outside*) puna; (*of fish, vegetables*) paa; (*inside*) kwangua, komba; (*of coco-nut*) kuna. *Scrape along*, kwaruza, enda kwa shida. *Scrape past*, ambaa. *Scrape together*, kusanya kwa shida, pata kwa nguvu, pambanya, dunduliza. *Scrape acquaintance with*, jipendekeza kwa, jidukiza kwa. *Scrape through*, shinda (faulu, fuzu, weza) kwa shida. — *n.* uparuzo *&c.*; (*difficulty*) shida, mashaka, hatari, msiba, matata; (*sound*) sauti ya kukwaruza, kweche. *Be in a scrape*, kwama, -wa matatani.

scraper, *n.* mtu wa (kitu cha) kuparuza *&c.*; kisu, ukombo, mbuzi *&c.*

scrap-heap, *n.* jaa, jalala. **scrapings**, *n.* makombo, takataka, vipande vidogovidogo.

scrappy, *a.* taz. *scrap*.

scratch, *v.t.* kuna, piga mtai, papura, kwakura, peleka (piga) makucha; (*tattoo*) toja, chanja, piga chale; (*with tool, pen &c.*) chora; (*in racing*) toa katika shindano; (*like a horse, fowl &c.*) para. *To scratch oneself*, kujikuna, kujiwasha. *Scratch out*, futa. *Scratch a hole*, fukua. — *n.* mtai, mchoro, choro, chale, mfuo; (*in games*) mstari (wa kuanzia), mwanzo; (*tattoo*) tojo, chanjo, nembo. *Come to the scratch*, jiweka tayari, shika kazi, kaza shauri. — *a.* ovyo, -a watu wo wote, -a bahati. **scratchy**, *a.* kama -mechorwa, -enye sauti ya kukwaruza (ya kweche), -a kuwasha, -a kuchomachoma.

scrawl, *v.t.* andika vibaya, chora. — *n.* mwandiko mbaya, mchoro.

scream, *v.i.* lia kwa nguvu (kwa hofu, maumivu, hasira, kwa kucheka), piga kiyowe. — *n.* kilio cha nguvu; (*for help*) kiyowe; (*for joy*) kigelegele.

screech, *v.i.* lia kwa nguvu (sauti nyembamba, sauti ya kukwaruza). — *n.* kilio (cha sauti nyembamba, cha kukwaruza). **screech-owl**, *n.* bundi.

screed, *n.* barua au maandiko marefu yasiyokolea, yasiyo na mvuto.

screen, *n.* kisetiri, kifuniko, kificho, kinga; (*wall*) kiambaza; (*shield*) ngao, kigao; (*hanging*) pazia; (*something stretched tight*) kiwambo; (*concealment*) kificho, maficho; (*for cinema &c.*) kiwambo cha nguo (kitambaa) cha kutupiwa picha; (*for sifting*) chekecheke. — *v.t.* setiri, funika, ficha; (*protect*) linda, okoa, tunza, hifadhi; (*sieve*) chekecha. **screenings**, *n.* taka zilizosalia baada ya kuchekecha.

screw, *n.* parafujo, msumari wa hesi, skrubu; (*propeller*) majembe, mapanga, rafardha; (*miser*) bahili, mtoza fedha nyingi, kabidhi, mgumu; (*a twist*) msokoto; (*wages*) mshahara. *A screw loose*, kipunguo, kosa; (*mental*) kichaa, akili afkani. *Put the screw on*, lazimisha, kaza. — *v.t.* tia *screw*, kaza kwa *screw*; (*squeeze*) songa; (*twist*) sokota, nyonga; (*the face*) finya, kunja; (*extort*) toza (fedha au kazi kwa nguvu), lazimisha, kalifu. *Screw up courage*, piga moyo konde, kaza moyo. **screw-driver**, *n.* bisibisi, chombo cha kutia au kutoa parafujo *&c.* **screw-pine**, *n.* mkadi. **screw-propeller**, *n.* majembe, mapanga, rafardha. **screw-steamer**, *n.* meli inayoendeshwa na majembe.

scribe, *n.* mwandishi, karani, katibu.

scribble, *v.i.* andika upesi, andika vibaya, chora. — *n.* mwandiko wa haraka, mwandiko mbaya, mchoro.

scribbler, *n.* mwandika ovyo, mwandishi wa habari (hadithi *&c.*)

hafifu, mchorachora. **scrip,** (1) *n.* hati ya fedha (iliyowekwa katika kumpuni ya biashara). **script,** *n.* mwandiko, hati ya mkono. *Script writing,* mwandiko wa chapa. **scriptural,** *a.* -a maandiko matakatifu, -enye kupatana na maneno ya *scripture.* **scripture,** *n.* maandiko matakatifu, jamii ya vitabu vya kanuni vya kikristo, maneno ya *Bible.*

scrimmage, *n.* ghasia ya watu wakibuburashana, mapigano, mashindano yenye ghasia, msukosuko. — *v.i.* buburushana, vutanavutana, shindana kwa ghasia, sukumana, kumbana.

scrip, (1) taz. *scribe.*

scrip, (2) *n.* (*wallet*) kifuko, mkoba, shanta, kifurushi, bahasha.

script, *n.,* **scriptural,** *a.,* **scripture,** *n.* taz. *scribe.*

scrivener, *n.* mwandishi, karani, katibu.

scrofula, *n.* ugonjwa wa kuvimba matezi ya shingoni, maradhi ya mti. **scrofulous,** *a.* -enye *scrofula,* -a *scrofula.*

scroll, *n.* hati ya kuviringisha, hati ndefu.

scrotum, *n.* mfuko wa pumbu, korodani.

scrounge, *v.t.* iba; (*cadge*) doea, randia. **scrounger,** *n.* mnyakuzi, mwizi; (*cadger*) mdoea, mdoya.

scrub, (1) *v.t.* sugua sana (hasa kwa burashi), safisha (kusugua kwa burashi).

scrub, (2) *n.* msitu, koko, makoko, magugu. **scrubby,** *a.* -enye *scrub*; (*slight, paltry*) -nyonge, hafifu, -dogo, -baya.

scruff, *n. Scruff of the neck,* ngozi ya kikosi, kikosi, ukosi.

scrumptious, *a.* -tamu sana, -a kupendeza sana.

scruple, *n.* (*weight*) kipimo kidogo, uzani wa *grain* 20; kidogo sana; (*doubt &c.*) shaka, wasiwasi, shida, hangaiko. — *v.t.* ona wasiwasi, sita, tokubali, toridhia, topenda. *He scruples to go,* hataki kwenda, aenda kwa shida. **scrupulous,** *a.* -a kutaka hakika, -nyofu, -angalifu sana, -a hadhari sana, -a kufanya barabara, -chaguzi.

scrutiny, *n.* kuchunguza, uchunguzi, kuangalia (kutazamia) sana, uangalizi. **scrutinize,** *v.t.* chunguza, angalia (tazamia) sana.

scud, *v.i.* chukuliwa upesi na upepo (kama jahazi, mawingu *&c.*). — *n.* ukungu, umande, kiwingu.

scuffle, *v.i.* buburushana, pigana kwa kusukumana (kukumbana); (*the feet*) tembea kwa kutambaza (kukokoteza) miguu (bila kuinua miguu). — *n.* kububurushana, buburushano, kusukumana, ugomvi wenye ghasia, msukosuko.

scull, *n.* kasia jepesi. — *v.t.* endesha kwa kasia; — *v.i.* piga (vuta) kasia. **sculler,** *n.* mpiga kasia.

scullery, *n.* chumba cha kuoshea sahani na vyombo vya kupikia.

scullion, *n.* mtumishi aoshaye vyombo vya jikoni, boi wa jikoni, chokora.

sculpture, *n.* mchoro, kazi ya kuchora mawe, ubao *&c.*; nakshi, sanamu ya kuchora. **sculptor,** *n.* fundi wa kuchora mawe, mbao *&c.*

scum, *n.* povu, fuo, taka za juu (ya maji *&c.*), kuvu, koga, gaga. *The scum of the earth,* watu wabaya (wanyonge) kabisa.

scupper, *n.* kitundu ubavuni mwa meli cha kuchuruzikia maji, kipenyo.

scurf, *n.* mba, vigaga (vya kichwani katika nywele), ukoga.

scurrilous, *a.* -a kutukana, -a matusi. **scurrility,** *n.* matukano, matusi.

scurry, *v.i.* enda upesi.

scurvy, *n.* ugonjwa wa kuvimba ufizi wa kutoka damu kama kiseyeye. — *a.* -nyonge, -baya. **scurvily,** *adv.* vibaya.

scut, *n.* mkia mfupi wa mnyama, hasa wa sungura.

scuttle, (1) *n.* (*for coals*) ndoo ya kuwekea makaa ya mawe (chumbani).

scuttle, (2) *n.* tundu kama dirisha ubavuni mwa meli. — *v.t.* zamisha meli (merikebu *&c.*) kwa kutoboa chini.

scuttle, (3) *v.i.* kimbia, enda mbio, puruka.

scythe, *n.* mundu mkubwa wa kukatia majani.

sea, *n.* bahari; (*wave*) wimbi; (*abundance*) wingi; (*disturbances*) machafuko. *At sea,* baharini; (*perplexed*) -enye mashaka. *Heavy sea,* mawimbi makubwa. *Go to sea,* -wa baharia. **sea-anemone,** *n.* mnyama kama ua liotalo baharini. **sea-board,** *n.*, **sea-coast,** *n.* nchi karibu ya bahari, mwambao, pwani, nchi za pwani, ukingo wa bahari. **sea-cow,** *n.* nguva. **sea-eagle,** *n.* kwazi, furukombe, koho. **sea-faring,** *a.* -enye kazi chomboni, -a kukaa baharini, -a bahari. *Seafaring men,* mabaharia, wanamaji. **sea-girt,** *a.* -liozungukwa na bahari. **sea-gull,** *n.* shakwe. **sea-kale,** *n.* namna ya mboga ya pwani. **sea-lawyer,** *n.* mbishi ajivuniaye ujuzi wa sheria asio nao. **sea legs,** *n.* *To find* (*get*) *one's sea legs,* kuzoea mrama (mwendo, msukosuko) wa meli (merikebu *&c.*). **sea-level,** *n.* usawa wa bahari. **sea-lion,** *n.* mnyama wa bahari kama *seal* (1). **seaman,** *n.* baharia, mwanamaji. **seamanship,** *n.* maarifa ya kazi ya meli (jahazi, merikebu *&c.*), ufundi wa kuendesha na kusimamia meli (merikebu *&c.*). **sea-mew,** *n.* shakwe. **sea-mile,** *n.* futi 6080. **sea-pig,** *n.* pomboo. **seaport,** *n.* mji wenye bandari. **sea-rover,** *n.* haramia (wa bahari), merikebu ya haramia. **sea-serpent,** *n.* joka kubwa la bahari. **sea-shore,** *n.* ukingo wa bahari, ufuko. *On the sea-shore,* pwani. **sea-sick,** *a.* -enye *sea-sickness.* **sea-sickness,** *n.* ugonjwa wa (taabu ya) bahari, kuchafuka tumbo (kutapika) chomboni, kulewa baharini. **seaside,** *n.* upande wa pwani, ukingo wa bahari, pwani. **sea-urchin,** *n.* mwanamizi. **sea-wall,** *n.* boma la kuzuia nchi isichukuliwe na bahari. **seaward,** *a.* -a upande wa baharini. **sea-water,** *n.* maji ya bahari. **seaweed,** *n.* mwani, maua ya pwani. **seaworthiness,** *n.* kuwa *seaworthy.* **seaworthy,** *a.* (*of ship*) -zima, -ema, -a kwenda baharini. **sea-wrack,** *n.* mwani unaoelea baharini au kutupwa pwani kwa wingi.

seal, (1) *n.* (*animal*) mnyama wa bahari mweye ngozi ya manyoya mazuri sana — *v.t.* winda *seal.* **sealskin,** *n.* ngozi ya *seal.*

seal, (2) *n.* muhuri, chapa, alama; (*sanction*) usahihi, •idhini, ruhusa. — *v.t.* tia muhuri *&c.* *Seal up,* ziba, funga. **sealing-wax,** *n.* lakiri.

sea-lawyer, *n.*, **sea legs,** *n.*, **sea-level,** *n.* taz. *sea.*

sealing-wax, *n.* taz. *seal* (2).

sea-lion, *n.* taz. *sea.*

sealskin, *n.* taz. *seal* (1).

seam, *n.* mshono; (*tacked*) bandi; (*strong*) jongo; (*hemmed*) •upindo; (*of coal, metal*) tabaka ya makaa (madini) katika mwamba; (*in ships*) kiungo, ufa (kati ya mbao); (*wrinkle*) kikunjo, kifinyo, kunyanzi. — *v.t.* shona *seam.* **seamless,** *a.* bila mshono, -liofumwa kipande kimoja. **seamstress,** *n.* mshoni (mwanamke). **seamy,** *a.* -baya. *The seamy side of life.* sehemu ya maisha iliyo mbaya (isiyopendeza, yenye taabu, -a kuchukiza).

seaman, *n.*, **seamanship,** *n.*, **sea-mew,** *n.*, **sea-mile,** *n.* taz. *sea.*

seamless, *a.*, **seamstress,** *n.*, **seamy,** *a.* taz. *seam.*

séance, *n.* mkutano, mkutano wa watu wa kujaribu kuvumbua habari za pepo (mizimu).

sea-pig, *n.*, **seaport,** *n.* taz. *sea.*

sear, *v.t.* unguza, kausha, nyausha, fanya -kavu; (*disfigure*) umbua, rembua.

search, *v.t.* tafuta katika, pekua, peleleza, chakura, duhushi. *Search for,* tafuta, tazamia. — *n.* kutafuta, upelelezi, upekuzi, mchakuro. **searcher,** *n.* mwenye kutafuta, mpelelezi, mpekuzi. **searching,** *a.* -a kujaribia zote, -a kupenya ndani, -kali. **searchlight,** *n.* kurunzi, taa yenye nguvu ya kuangaza usiku. **search-party,** *n.* jamii ya watu waliopelekwa kutafuta mtu (au kitu). **search-warrant,** *n.* hati ya kuruhusu mapolisi kupeleleza (kutafuta, kupekua) ndani ya nyumba.

sea-rover, *n.*, **sea-serpent,** *n.*, **sea-shore,** *n.*, **sea-sick,** *a.*, **seasickness,** *n.*, **seaside,** *n.* taz. *sea.*

season, *n.* wakati, wakati wa mwaka, msimu, majira, muhula; (*suitable time &c.*) wakati ufaao. *The seasons,* pembe za mwaka. *It is in season,* ni wakati (msimu) wake, yapatikana. *The wet season,* masika, siku za mvua. *The hot season,* kaskazi, kiangazi. *The cold season,* kipupwe. — *v.t.* (*food*) koleza, unga, tia kitoweo, tia kiungo; (*fit for use*) tengeneza, tia dawa; (*accustom*) zoeza. **seasonable,** *a.* -a kufaa, kwa wakati wake, sawasawa. **seasoning,** *n.* kukoleza &c., kitoweo, kiungo, mchikicho.

seat, *n.* (*chair, stool &c.*) kiti; (*stool*) kiti, kibago; (*of earth, stone &c.*) baraza, kibaraza; (*stone bench*) ufunga; (*buttocks*) matako; (*on horseback*) kupanda farasi, kikao juu ya farasi; (*residence, place &c.*) nyumba, mahali pa kukalia, kikao, makazi. *Take a seat,* keti, kaa. — *v.t.* ketisha, kalisha, weka, -pa kiti, wekea viti. *Seat oneself,* kaa, keti, starehe. *I am seated,* nimekaa. **seating,** *n.* viti, mahali pa kukaa watu.

sea-urchin, *n.*, **sea-wall,** *n.*, **seaward,** *a.*, **sea-water,** *n.*, **seaweed,** *n.*, **seaworthiness,** *n.*, **seaworthy,** *a.*, **sea-wrack,** *n.* taz. *sea.*

sebaceous, *a.* -enye mafuta, -a mafuta.

secede, *v.i.* jitenga, jiondoa, jitoa, farakana, ondoka, toka katika. **seceder,** *n.* mwenye kujitenga &c. **secession,** *n.* kujitenga, farakano.

seclude, *v.t.* tenga, funga, farakisha tawisha. **secluded,** *a.* -a faragha, -a mbali, pasipo watu, -a utawa. **seclusion,** *n.* faragha, kujitenga, maficho, upweke, utawa; (*of a woman after divorce or death of husband*) eda. *Live in seclusion* (*indoors*), tawa, jitenga.

second, *a.* -a pili, -a baadaye, -a kufuata, -a chini. *On second thought,* baadaye, kisha kufikiri. *It is second to none,* haipitikani kabisa, hakuna bora zaidi. — *n.* (*supporter*) rafiki, msaidia, msaidizi; (*moment*) dakika, nusu dakika, muda mfupi sana; (*sixtieth part of a minute*) nukta, sehemu ya sitini ya *minute* (dakika) moja. *In a second,* ghafula, mara. *Second hand,* mkono (mshale) wa saa unaoonyesha *second.* — *v.t.* saidia, tia moyo, sema mamoja na, taka mamoja na; (*an officer &c.*) toa katika kazi yake hasa ili kumtuma kufanya kazi maalum. **secondary,** *a.* -dogo, hafifu, si bora; (*succeeding*) -a kufuata, -a namna ya pili, -a baadaye. **seconder,** *n.* msaidia, msaidizi, anenaye mamoja na mwingine ili kuthibitisha shauri &c. **second-hand,** *a.* si -pya, -liekwisha kutumika, -a kuuzwa mara ya pili. **secondly,** *adv.* ya pili, tena, baadaye. **second nature,** *n.* desturi, silika, kawaida, mila. **second-rate,** *a.* si -zuri sana, si bora, hafifu, -baya, duni. **second sight,** *n.* utabiri, akili ya kujua yatakayokuja, uaguzi.

secret, *a.* -a siri, -a faragha, -liyofichwa, -a fumbo. — *n.* siri, jambo la siri, fumbo. *In secret,* kwa siri, faraghani. **secrecy,** *n.* siri, faragha, maficho, kusetiri. **secrete,** *v.t.* (*hide*) ficha, setiri; (*physiol.*) fanya (fanyiza) *secretion.* **secretion,** *n.* kitu cho chote (maji, damu, mate, shahamu, nyongo &c.) kilichofanyizwa ndani ya mwili wa mtu (mnyama, mdudu, mmea &c.); kufanya au kufanyiza ndani ya mwili; (*hiding*) kuficha, kusetiri. **secretive,** *a.* -a siri, -fichifichi, -a kufanya *secretion*. **secretly,** *adv.* kwa siri, mang'ungumu. **secretory,** *a.* -a kufanya *secretion*.

secretary, *n.* katibu, karani, mwandishi; (*of committee &c.*) mtunza tarehe. *Secretary of State*, waziri. **secretariat,** *n.* nyumba ya kazi ya *secretary*.

secrete, *v.t.*, **secretion,** *n.*, **secretive,** *a.*, **secretly,** *adv.*, **secretory,** *a.* taz. *secret*.

sect, *n.* madhehebu, jamii ya watu wenye shauri (dini, mwongozi) moja; (*religious*) jamii ya watu waliotengana na Kanisa la kiingereza. **sectarian,** *a.* -a *sect*. — *n.* mtu wa *sect*. **sectarianism,** *n.* ufuasi wa *sect*. **sectary,** *n.* mtu (mfuasi) wa *sect*.

section, *n.* mkato, sehemu, fungu, kipande, baadhi; (*of soldiers*) kikosi (cha askari); (*of book*) juzuu, fungu, gombo. **sectional,** *a.* -a *section*, -enye *section*. **sector,** *n.* kipimo; (*of circle*) sehemu ya duara iliyokatwa kwa mistari miwili inayotoka katikati yake mpaka kizingo; (*military*) sehemu ya nchi inayolindwa na maboma (handaki, askari) vitani.

secular, *a.* -a ulimwengu, -a kidunia (si -a dini, si -a ulimwengu ujao), -a walimwengu, -a matumizi ya siku zote; -a serikali ya nchi (si -a Kanisa); (*of clergy*) -siye *monk*; (*periodical*) -a miaka mingi, -a wakati wake. **secularism,** *n.* tabia na desturi zilizo *secular*, tabia ya ulimwengu. **secularize,** *v.t.* fanya *secular*, tenga na mambo ya dini, twalia Kanisa (mali *&c.*).

secure, *a.* (*safe*) salama, pasipo hofu, pasipo mashaka; (*reliable*) amini, -aminifu; (*certain, sure*) -a hakika, yakini, thabiti. — *v.t.* weka salama, tunza, linda, hifadhi; (*fasten*) funga, kaza; (*get*) pata, jipatia, miliki; (*confirm*) thibitisha, hakikisha; (*confine*) funga. **securable,** *a.* -a kufanyika salama, -a kukazika, -a kupatikana. **security,** salama, raha, mustarehe, kustarehe; (*feeling safe*) kuwa pasipo hofu (mashaka); (*guarantee*) amana, rehani, dhamana, (*personal*) mdhamini; (*bond*) hati, sharti.

sedan-chair, *n.* kiti kinachochukuliwa kama machela.

sedate, *a.* -tulivu, -pole, -a makini. **sedately,** *adv.* kwa utulivu, pole, kwa makini. **sedative,** *a.* -a kutuliza. — *n.* dawa ya kutuliza, kitulizo.

sedentary, *a.* -a kukaa kitako, -a kukaakaa.

sedge, *n.* nyasi (majani) ya mtoni au bwawani, mafunjo, kangaga, njaanjaa.

sediment, *n.* mashapo, takataka za chini, tama, shinda, chenga, chicha, masimbi, mashata, mashudu; (*of river*) matope ya mto. **sedimentary,** *a.* -a *sediment*.

sedition, *n.* maneno na matendo ya kuchochea watu waasi serikali, fitina, maasi. **seditious,** *a.* -a kuchochea watu kuasi serikali,-fitini, -asi.

seduce, *v.t.* vuta (shawishi) kufanya mabaya, potoa, kosesha, bilisi; (*woman*) tongoza; (*with a bribe*) honga. **seducer,** *n.* mdanganyi, mpotezi; (*of women*) mtongozi, mfisadi, mfasiki. **seduction,** *n.* kupotoa, kupoteza, ushawishi, ubilisi, utongozi; (*in innocent sense*) uzuri wa kuvuta, mapendezi. **seductive,** *a.* -zuri, -a kupendeza, -a kuvuta (kwa uzuri, mapendezi *&c*), -a kubembeleza; (*in bad sense*) -a kudanganya, -danganyifu, -a kushawishi (kuvuta) kufanya mabaya, -potoe, -potovu, -a kupoteza, -a kutia bilisi.

sedulous, *a.* -tendaji wa kazi, -a kushika kazi, -angalifu, -a bidii, -a kujitahidi, -a juhudi. **sedulity,** *n.* bidii, juhudi, jitihada, utendaji wa kazi.

see, (1) *v.t.* (*p.t.* **saw,** *pf.t.* **seen**) ona, tazama, angalia; (*understand*) fahamu, hisi, tambua, elewa; (*experience*) -wamo; (*visit*) amkia, zuru, enda kutazama; (*accompany*) sindikiza, peleka; (*meet*) onana na, kuta, ona; (*interview*) onana na, endea kwa shauri (maneno *&c.*); (*take steps to secure that*) angalia, hakikisha. *See off*, sindikiza. *See to, See about, See after*, angalia, tengeneza. *See through, See out*, angalia, linda hata mwisho, saidia, auni, elewa -ote. *See* (*a person*) *off* (*on a journey &c.*), safirisha; (*after a visit*) sindikiza. *Seeing that*, kwa kuwa, kwa maana, maadam. **seeing,** *n.* kuona kwa macho, nguvu ya kuona. **seen,** *a.* (*be*) onekana. **seer,** *n.* mwaguzi, mtabiri, nabii, mnajimu.

see, (2) *n.* jimbo la askofu.

seed, *n.* mbegu; (*one grain*) punje; (*origin*) asili, mwanzo, chimbuko, chanzo; (*offspring*) mzao, mtoto; (*of male animal*) shahawa, manii. *Run to seed*, haribika, chakaa, pooza. — *v.i.* toa mbegu. **seedling,** *n.* mche. **seed-pearl,** *n.* lulu ndogo sana. **seedsman,** *n.* mwuza mbegu. **seed-time,** *n.* majira ya kupanda. **seedy,** *a.* -enye mbegu nyingi; (*shabby*) -kuukuu, -liochakaa, -chakavu; (*indisposed*) -gonjwa.

seeing, *n.* taz. *see* (1).

seek, *v.t.* (*p.t. and pf.t.* **sought**) tafuta, tazamia, riaria; (*ask for*) omba, taka; (*endeavour*) jaribu, jitahidi. **seeker,** *n.* mtafiti, atafutaye, aombaye, mwombi.

seem, *v.i.* onekana, -wa na mfano wa, -wa kama, fanana na. *It seems so*, naona, labda, huenda. **seeming,** *a.* -a kuonekana kama kwamba, -a uwongo, -a kujifanya, si kweli, si halisi. **seemingly,** *adv.* kama, kwa sura, kama kwamba, kwa kuonekana, kwa nje. **seemliness,** *n.* kuwa *seemly*. **seemly,** *a.* -zuri, -a adabu, -a makini, -a kustahili, -a kufaa, wajibu, -a kulaiki.

seen, *pf.t.* ya *see*.

seep, *v.i.* vuja, penya.

seer, *n.* taz. *see* (1).

seesaw, *n.* mchezo wa watoto, pembea. — *v.i.* panda na kushuka; cheza katika pembea.

seethe, *v.t.* tokosa, chemsha; — *v.i.* (*boil up*) chemka, toa povu chacha, chachuka; (*with excitement &c.*) chafuka, vurugika.

segment, *n.* mkato, sehemu (hasa ya asili kama pingili, kiungo cha jongoo *&c.*), sehemu ya duara.

segregate, *v.t.* tenga, weka mbali, farakisha. **segregation,** *n.* kutenga *&c.*

seine, *n.* wavu mkubwa wa kuvulia samaki.

seismic, *a.* -a tetemo (tetemeko) la nchi. **seismology,** *n.* elimu ya matetemo (matetemeko) ya nchi.

seize, *v.t.* (*grasp*) kamata, shika, twaa, dara, shikilia; (*take by force*) twaa kwa nguvu, nyang'anya, pokonya; (*comprehend*) fahamu, elewa; — *v.i.* (*stick, jam &c.*) kwama, shika, shikamana. *Be seized with*, patwa (shikwa, patikana) na. **seizure,** *n.* kukamata, kukamatwa *&c.*; (*attack of illness*) kushikwa na ugonjwa, kipindi; (*fit*) kifafa.

seldom, *adv.* mara chache, shida.

select, *v.t.* chagua, teua, fanidi, hiari, hitiari. — *a.* -a kuchagua, -liochaguliwa, -teule, haba. **selection,** *n.* kuchagua *&c.*; (*portion*) sehemu, baadhi (ya vitu vingi); (*choice bits*) madondoo, mateuzi. **selective,** *a.* -a kuchagua, -enye nguvu ya (uwezo wa) kuchagua. **selectivity,** *n.* nguvu ya (uwezo wa) kuchagua.

self, *n.* (*pl.* **selves**) moyo, nafsi, mwenyewe; (*in verbs*) -ji-. *He killed himself*, alijiua. *It goes by itself*, inajienda. **self-applause,** *n.* kujivuna, majivuno, kujisifu, majisifu. **self-assertion,** *n.* kujitanguliza, kujitokeza mbele. **self-assertive,** *a.* -a kujitanguliza. **self-centred,** *a.* -a kujifikiri mwenyewe. **self-coloured,** *a.* -a rangi moja tu. **self-conceit,** *n.* ukinaifu, kujiona. **self-confidence,** *n.* kujijetea nafsi, kutotaka msaada, kujitegemea nafsi, kujitumainia, ukinaifu, ujasiri. **self-conscious,** *a.* -a kujikumbuka, -enye akili ya kujijua (hali, tabia, nafsi) na kujiongoza; (*shy*) -enye haya (soni). **self-contained,** *a.* (*independent*) -kinaifu; (*reserved*) -nyamavu, makini; (*complete*) -a kujitoshelea, kamili, -enye yote ndani yake, -a kujitosha. **self-control,** *n.* kujiweza, kujitawala (hasira, tamaa, macno). **self-defence,** *n.* kujilinda nafsi (mali, haki &c.), kujipigania. *The art of self-defence,* kupigana ngumi. **self-denial,** *n.* kujihini, kujinyima, kujikania, kujizuia; (*temperance*) kiasi, tawasufi. **self-destruction,** *n.* kujifisha, kujipoteza, kujiangamiza. **self-determination,** *n.* hiari, uchaguo, nguvu ya (uwezo wa, akili ya) kuchagua. **self-devotion,** *n.* kujitoa, kujifunga kwa kazi (kwa ajili ya wengine). **self-display,** *n.* ushaufu, kufanya mikogo, kuranda, kujishaua, majivuno. **self-educated,** *a.* -a kujifunza mwenyewe (bila msaada wa mwalimu au mtu mwingine). **self-esteem,** *n.* kujistahi; (*conceit*) kiburi, kujisifu, kujiona bora, ukinaifu. **self-evident,** *a.* wazi, baini, dhahiri. **self-examination,** *n.* kujitazamia moyo (tabia, mwendo, matendo &c.), kujihoji nafsi, kujitafutia makosa ndani, kujishtaki. **self-existent,** *a.* (*of God*) -sio na mwanzo wala mwisho, -enye kuwa yuko peke yake halisi, azali; (*uncreated*) -sioumbwa, si kiumbe. **self-explanatory,** *a.* -a kujieleza, -enye maelezo yake ndani yake. **self-government,** *n.* kujiweza nafsi, kujitawala -enyewe, utawala wa -enyewe. **self-help,** *n.* kujisaidia mwenyewe, kutumia (matumizi ya) nguvu (akili, uwezo) zako mwenyewe bila msaada. **self-importance,** *n.* kujifikiri mkuu (bora), makuu, majivuno, kiburi, ukinaifu. **self-indulgence,** *n.* anasa, kutimiza tamaa bila kujizuia, ulafi, ulaji &c. **self-interest,** *n.* kujipatia faida, kujipendeza nafsi, choyo. **selfish,** *a.* -a choyo, -a kujiangalia (kujifikiri) nafsi wala si wengine, -a kujipendeza, -a kujipendeza nafsi, -a kushika lake, -a kutojali wengine; (*grasping*) -pasi; (*miserly*) bahili, kabidhi. **selfishness,** *n.* choyo, kuwa *selfish.* **selfishly,** *adv.* kwa choyo, kwa kujifikiri mwenyewe bila kujali wengine. **self-love,** *n.* kujipenda nafsi (kama *selfishness*). **self-made,** *a.* -pasi, -kwasi, -liojipatia utajiri. *A self-made man,* mtu wa vivi hivi tu aliyejipatia utajiri (au ukuu). **self-opinionated,** *a.* -a kushika shauri lake, -kaidi, -shupavu. **self-possessed,** *a.* -a kujiweza nafsi, -a kiasi, -kavu wa macho, -taratibu. **self-possession,** *n.* kuwa *self-possessed,* ukavu wa macho, utulivu. **self-reliance,** *n.* kujijetea nafsi, kutotaka msaada, kujitumainia, ukinaifu, ujasiri. **self-respect,** *n.* kujistahi nafsi, -a kujiheshimu nafsi (kadiri ipasavyo pasipo kiburi), kuchunga cheo. **self-restraint,** *n.* kujitawala, kujizuia. **self-same,** *a.* -moja halisi, sawasawa, yule yule (ile ile, kile kile &c.). **self-satisfaction,** *n.* kujiona, majisifu, ukinaifu. **self-satisfied,** *a.* -a kujiona, -kinaifu, -enye kiburi. **self-sown,** *a.* (*tree*) kimelea; (*plant &c.*) mabotea. **self-sufficiency,** *n.* kinaya, ukinaifu; (*pride*) majivuno, kiburi. **self-sufficient,** *a.* -kinaifu, -a majivuno, -enye kiburi. **self-will,** *n.* ukaidi, ushupavu, maasi. **self-willed,** *a.* -kaidi, -shupavu, -asi, -potovu.

sell, *v.t.* (*p.t. and pf.t.* **sold**) uza, toa kwa fedha; (*deceive*) danganya, ghilibu, punja, kopa; — *v.i.* uzanya, uzika. *Sell up,* filisisha. *Sell out,* uza mali (bidhaa) yote. **seller,** *n.* mwuza; (*article*) kitu kinachouzika (hasa kwa wingi).

selvedge, *n.* upindo.

selves, *pl.* ya *self.*

semantics, *n.* elimu ya lugha inayohusu maana za maneno na jinsi zilivyokua.

semaphore, *n.* mti wenye vipande kama mikono vya kuashiria. — *v.t.*

peleka habari kwa ishara ya *semaphore* au kwa mikono.
semblance, *n.* mfano, sura, umbo.
semen, *n.* shahawa, manii. **seminal**, *a.* -a shahawa (manii), -a mbegu; (*original*) -a asili, -a mwanzo.
semi-, *pref.* nusu, kidogo.
semicircle, *n.* nusu ya duara. **semicircular**, *a.* -a nusu ya duara, kama nusu ya duara.
semicolon, *n.* alama hii (;).
semi-conscious, *a.* -enye hali ya kuwa nusu kujirudia (katika usingizi au kuzimia), ulcoleo.
semi-detached, *a.* (nyumba) -liyoungana na nyingine upande mmoja.
semifluid, *a.* -teketeke (kama maji au mafuta mazito sana).
seminal, *a.* taz. *semen.*
seminary, *n.* chuo, shule, skuli, madarasa (hasa ya dini ya *Roman Catholic*).
Semitic, *a.* -a taifa (au mataifa) lo lote linalosemwa kutokana na Shem, hasa la Kiyahudi, Kiarabu, *Armenian, Phoenician &c.*
semsem, *n.* ufuta; (*oil*) mafuta ya uto.
senate, *n.* baraza kuu ya wazee, halmashauri ya wazee. **senator**, *n.* mtu wa *senate.* **senatorial**, *a.* -a *senator.*
send, *v.t.* (*p.t. and pf.t.* **sent**) peleka, tuma, leta, agiza; (*cause to go*) toa, tupa, rusha, endesha, sukuma, jongeza; (*grant*) jalia; (*dispatch messenger*) tuma (mtu, tarishi, mjumbe). *Send for*, ita, tuma mtu kuita. *He was sent for*, alikwenda kuitwa, aliitwa. *Send back*, rudisha, rejeza. *Send down*, shusha, telemsha. *Send in all directions*, eneza, tapanya, tawanya. *Send on ahead*, tanguliza. *Send out*, toa. **sender**, *n.* mwenye kupeleka *&c.* **send-off**, *n.* *Give a good send-off to*, agana na vizuri (kwa sherehe *&c.*).
seneschal, *n.* msimamizi wa nyumba (zamani za kale).
senile, *a.* -a uzee, -kongwe dhaifu. **senility**, *n.* uzee, ukongwe, udhaifu wa uzee.
senior, *n. and a.* -kubwa (kwa daraja, cheo, umri *&c.*), -a kwanza. **seniority**, *n.* kuwa *senior*; (*rank*) kadiri ya cheo, cheo.
senna, *n.* sanamaki.
sensation, *n.* (*perception by sense*) kuona, maono, kuhisi; (*excited feeling*) kushtuka, kushtusha, shtuko shtusho, fadhaa, kishindo, kichocho; (*exciting object*) kitisho, kituko, kioja, ajabu. **sensational**, *a.* -a kushtusha, -a kutisha, -a ajabu.
sense, *n.* akili, busara; (*meaning*) maana; (*perception*) kuona (kwa macho, masikio, pua, ulimi, kugusa); (*opinion*) shauri; (*lower nature*) mwili. *Have a sense of*, ona. *The sense of smell, hearing, taste &c.*, kusikia, kuonja *&c.* *A man of good sense*, mtu wa akili (busara), hodari. *Pleasures of sense*, anasa za mwili. *In the sense of*, kwa maana, maana yake. *In the same sense*, kwa maana ile ile, maana sawa. *It has a bad sense*, ina maana mbaya. *The senses* (*five senses*), milango ya maarifa (kuona kwa macho, kusikia, kunusa, kuonja, kugusa). *Be out of one's senses, Lose the senses*, potewa na akili, rukwa na akili, fadhaika; (*faint*) zimia, zirai. *Recover the senses*, jirudia, pata akili tena. *Common sense*, busara. *Moral sense*, kupambanua mema na mabaya. — *v.t.* fahamu, tambua, hisi, jua kwa akili, maizi, ng'amua. **senseless**, *a.* -jinga, -pumbavu, pasipo akili, -a upuzi, -puzi. *He fell senseless*, alianguka amezimia. *Be* (*become*) *senseless*, zimia, zirai. **senselessness**, *n.* utovu wa akili, ukosefu wa akili, upumbavu, upuzi, ujinga.
sensibility, *n.* (*sense*) akili; (*sensitiveness*) wepesi wa kuona, kushtuka upesi. **sensible**, *a.* (*prudent*) -enye akili, -a busara, -a maana; (*palpable, perceivable*) -a kuoneka na *senses.* *Be sensible of*, ona, jua, tambua, fahamu, maizi, hisi. *He is sensible*, anazo akili; (*conscious*) amejirudia.
sensitive, *a.* -epesi kuona (kushtuka,

kubadilika, kugeuka, kuwa na hasira au chuki *&c.*), -sioweza kuvumilia maumivu (uchungu, ukali, chukizo, joto, baridi *&c.*). *The sensitive plant,* kifauwongo. **sensitiveness,** *n.* hali (tabia) ya kuwa *sensitive,* wepesi kuona (kushtuka *&c.*), unyeti.

sensual, *a.* -a mwili, -a mambo ya mwili, -a furaha (tamaa) za mwili, -a anasa; (*licentious*) -a ashiki nyingi, -kware, -a asherati, -a ngoa, -fisadi, fasiki; (*appealing to sexual appetite*) -a kutia ashiki (nyege), -a kutamanisha, -a kuamsha (kuchochea) tamaa (ngoa, nyege, ashiki). **sensualist,** *n.* mtu wa anasa, mlafi, mlaji *&c.*, mkware, mwasherati, mwenye ashiki (nyege, ngoa, tamaa) nyingi. **sensuality,** *n.* kuwa *sensual.* **sensualize,** *v.t.* haribu (potoa) kwa anasa za mwili, ongoza vibaya, geuza kinyama. **sensuous,** *a.* kama *sensual.*

sent, *p.t. and pf.t.* ya *send.*

sentence, *n.* (*verdict*) hukumu, maamuzi, neno la mkataa; (*punishment*) adhabu; (*decision*) shauri, usia; (*in Muhammedan law*) fetwa; (*in grammar*) neno au fungu la maneno (linalopasha habari, linalouliza swali, linalojulisha haja au kutoa amri). — *v.t.* (*give, pronounce sentence*) pasisha adhabu, hukumu, amua, kata hukumu. *He was sentenced to death,* alikatiwa hukumu kuuawa. **sententious,** *a.* -enye maneno ya hekima, -a kujivuna (kwa kuwa na maneno ya hekima), -a kujifanya mwenye maarifa.

sentient, *a.* -enye akili ya kuona kwa *senses* (si kama mmea au jiwe). **sentiment,** *n.* nia, shauri, neno, maono, maelekeo ya kuvutwa na upendo (huruma, huba, ashiki *&c.*) kuliko na akili (busara). **sentimental,** *a.* -epesi kuvutwa na upendo (huruma, huba, ashiki *&c.*) kuliko na akili (busara *&c.*), -a kuchukuliwa na fikira. **sentimentalism,** *n.* wepesi wa kuvutwa (kuchukuliwa) na tamaa (ashiki, huruma, upendo *&c.*), kuchukuliwa na fikira (za upendo *&c.*), kuotaota, kujitungia mawazo moyoni.

sentinel, sentry, *n.* askari wa zamu, mngoje zamu, mlinzi. **sentry-box,** *n.* kituo (kibanda) cha *sentry.* **sentry-go,** *n.* zamu ya (kingojo cha) *sentry.*

sepal, *n.* kijani cha shikio la ua.

separate, *v.t.* tenga, gawa, weka mbali, farakisha, bagua, changanua, achanisha, baidisha; (*by sifting*) peta, chekecha, pembua; (*fighters*) amua; (*distinguish between*) pambanua, chagua, teua; (*cut up*) kata, gawa; — *v.i.* tengana, achana, farakana. — *a.* mbali, -liotengwa, peke yake (yao *&c.*), -moja -moja, mbalimbali. **separable,** *a.* -a kutengeka, -a kubaguka, -a kugawanyikana. **separately,** *adv.* mbalimbali, -moja -moja. **separation,** *n.* mtengano, kuachana, mgawo, kufarikiana, farakano, kuwa mbalimbali, kuwa peke yake (yao *&c.*); (*legal &c.*) agano la (amri ya korti ya) kuachana (kukaa mbalimbali).

sepia, *n.* namna ya rangi kama hudhurungi nyeupe.

sepoy, *n.* askari wa kihindi.

September, *n.* mwezi wa tisa wa mwaka wa kizungu, Septemba.

septennial, *a.* -a miaka saba, -a kila mwaka wa saba.

septic, *a.* -a kuoza (kuozesha) kwa sababu ya vijidudu (*bacteria*). **septicaemia,** *n.* hali ya kuoza (kutiwa sumu) damu kwa sababu ya vijidudu. **septic tank,** *n.* tangi (shimo) la kukusanya *sewage; sewage* huyeyuka na kusafishwa na vijidudu vilivyomo.

septuagenarian, *n.* mtu mwenye umri wa miaka sabini.

Septuagesima, *n.* Jumapili ya tatu kabla ya mwanzo wa *Lent.*

Septuagint, *n.* Maandiko matakatifu ya Wayahudi yaliyofasiriwa katika Kiyunani, Agano la Kale kwa Kiyunani.

sepulchre, *n.* kaburi, ziara (hasa

lililofukuliwa katika mwamba au lililojengwa kwa mawe). **sepulchral,** *a.* -a kaburi, -a majonzi (huzuni); (*of sound*) -a kulia wazi, -nene (kama ya majonzi au huzuni). **sepulture,** *n.* kuzika, maziko.

sequel, *n.*. matokeo, mafuatano, mwisho, mambo ya baadaye. **sequent,** *a.* -a kufuata, -a kuandama, -a kutokea. **sequence,** *n.* mwandamano, ufuatano, utaratibu.

sequester, *v.t.* twaa (mali ya mtu kwa muda na kusudi fulani), shika rehani, weka; (*separate*) weka mbali, tenga. **sequestered,** *a.* -a faragha, -a mbali pasipo na watu, -a ukiwa. **sequestrate,** *v.t.* kama *sequester.* **sequestration,** *n.* kutwaa (kutwaliwa) mali (kwa muda na kusudi fulani). **sequestrator,** *n.* afanyaye *sequestration,* mtu mwenye amri ya kutwaa mali mpaka madai yamelipwa.

sequin, *n.* puleki.

seraglio, *n.* nyumba ya wanawake (wake na masuria) wanapotengwa, harimu.

seraph, *n.* (*pl.* **seraphim**) malaika wa daraja ya juu. **seraphic,** *a.* -a *seraph,* kama malaika.

sere, *a.* -liokauka.

serenade, *n.* kuimba nyimbo au kupiga muziki usiku kumsalimia mchumba na kumwita, nyimbo au muziki za kuimba usiku &c. — *v.t.* imbia mchumba nyimbo za *serenade*; piga muziki ya *serenade.*

serene, *a.* eupe, safi, -liotakata, bila mawingu; (*of mind*) -kunjufu, -tulivu. **serenity,** *n.* weupe, ukunjufu, utulivu; (*of weather*) kweupe, kumetakata.

serf, *n.* mtumwa. **serfdom,** *n.* utumwa.

serge, *n.* nguo yenye nguvu ya usufu (manyoya ya kondoo).

sergeant, *n.* askari (polisi) msimamizi, mwenye cheo kati ya *corporal* na *sergeant major,* sajini.

series, *n.* mafuatano, mwandamano, safu, mfululizo. **serial,** *a.* -a kutokea mara kwa mara kwa mara kwa muda wake. *A serial* (*story*) hadithi inayoendelea mwezi baada ya mwezi (juma baada ya juma &c.) katika gazeti.

serious, *a.* (*grave*) -siocheka, -zito, -a kuonya; (*important*) -a maana, -enye habari kubwa (nzito), -kubwa; (*thoughtful* &c.) -a kufikiri, -a fikira; (*dangerous*) -a hatari; (*of illness*) mahututi; (*meaning what one says* &c.) -a kusema (kuonya) yaliyo kweli. *A serious offence,* jambo zito, jambo la maana sana. **seriously,** *adv.* kwa kuonya, kwa fikira, kwa bidii; (*very*) sana. **seriousness,** *n.* uzito.

sermon, *n.* hotuba, mahubiri ya Injili, maneno ya kuonya. **sermonize,** *v.t.* onyaonya, chosha kwa maonyo, huburi ovyo.

serpent, *n.* nyoka. **serpentine,** *a.* -enye mapindi, -a kuzingamana, -a kuzunguka, -a kupindikapindika.

serrated, *a.* -a menomeno, -a mapengo, -liochongoka, kama msumeno.

serried, *a.* -a kusongana, -a kusongamana.

serum, *n.* ute (maji) mweupe wa damu (bila chembe nyekundu zilizo ndani yake); ute (maji) wa mwili wa mtu au mnyama uliotengenezwa kuchanjia kwa dawa ya kuzuia magonjwa.

serval, *n.* ngawa.

serve, *v.t.* tumikia, hudumu, ngojea, tendea kazi; (*treat*) tendea; (*give out*) toa; (*of animal*) panda; — *v.i.* -wa mtumishi, tumika; (*be of use*) faa, saidia, auni. *Serve out,* toa; (*have revenge on*) lipiza kisasi. *Serve up,* pakua, andalia, andika. *Serve for,* faa mahali pa (badala ya). *I will serve you out,* nitakulipa. *It serves you right,* stahili yako. *He has served his time,* amemaliza wakati wake, amewahi. **servant,** *n.* mtumishi, hadimu, mhadimu, boi. **server,** *n.* mngoje, mngojezi. **service,** *n.* huduma, utumishi, kazi, utume; (*use, employment*) matumizi, utumizi, mafaa, manufaa; (*help*) fadhili, msaada, shime; (*of china &c.*) jamii (ya vyombo vya kulia); (*worship*) sala za dini, ibada, hitima, fatiha. *The services, fighting services,* taz. *Army, Navy. Divine service,* ibada ya Mungu, dini. *He is on service,* yuko katika kazi yake. *See service,* tumika vitani. **serviceable,** *a.* (*be*) faa, -wa -a kufaa, tumika, -wa -zima, -enye aushi, -a kudumu siku nyingi. **serviette,** *n.* kitambaa cha kupakatia wakati wa kula. **servile,** *a.* -a kitumwa, -nyonge, dhalili, -a kujipendekeza; (*literal*) -a kufuasa maneno mno. **servility,** *n.* unyonge, kufanya kitumwa, kushika miguu. **servitor,** *n.* mtumishi, mfuasi. **servitude,** *n.* utumwa. *Penal servitude,* kifungo cha muda wa miaka mitatu au zaidi.

sesame, *n.* ufuta.

session, *n.* baraza.

set, *v.t.* (*p.t. and pf.t.* **set**) (*place*) weka, tia mahali, tia; (*fix*) kaza; (*cause*) fanya; (*settle, order*) amrisha, agiza; (*razor &c.*) noa; (*trap*) tega; (*fish trap*) ambika; (*sail*) tweka; (*in line*) panga; (*with jewels*) pamba; (*of fluids*) gandamiza, gandisha; (*plants*) panda, (*from a nursery*) pandikiza, atika; (*a fashion*) anzisha, zua; (*timepiece*) kabilisha vema mikono (ya saa); (*a broken bone*) unga, ungisha, ganga; (*the teeth*) kaza (kama kwa maumivu &c.). — *v.i.* (*of sun*) tua, -chwa, shuka; (*of fluids*) ganda, gandamana; (*current*) enda, pita; (*take root &c.*) toa mizizi, anza kuota. *Set an example to,* weka mfano kwa, -wa (onyesha) mfano (kiolezo) kwa, fuasisha. *Set about,* shika kazi ya, anza, maliki. *Set apart,* weka mbali, tenga, bagua, farakisha, achanisha. *Set aside,* weka, dunduliza, acha, kataa, tangua. *Set at nought,* dharau, beza, tweza, dhihaki, -tojali. *Set at ease,* tuliza, starehesha, teremesha. *Set by,* weka. *Set store by,* tunuka, thamini. *Set down,* weka; (*a load*) tua, panga; (*humiliate*) tweza, dhili, tusha; (*put down in writing*) andika. *Set eyes on,* tazama, tupia jicho, ona. *Set forth* (*explain*), eleza, fafanua, tangaza; (*on a journey &c.*) shika njia, ondoka. *Set forward,* endelea, himiza, endesha. *Set free,* fanya huru, tegua, nasua, namua, achilia. *Set in* (*rain*), anza, shika. *Set going, Set on foot,* endesha, anzisha. *Set on* (*attack*), shambulia, rukia; (*urge to fight*) piganisha, chomesha, chochea. *Set off,* pamba, tia urembo, chukua; (*separate*) tenga; (*on a journey &c.*) ondoka, funga safari. *Set on fire,* choma, tia moto, washa; (*put on the fire*) teleka. *Set out,* andika, rekabisha, panga, weka vizuri; (*on a journey*) ondoka, shika njia. *Set right,* tengeneza, fanyiza, rekabisha. *Set side by side,* ambazana, pambanisha, weka kando kando. *Set teeth on edge,* tia ganzi la meno; (*of acid fruit &c.*) tia ukamvu (ukakasi, ukasasi). *Set to,* tia katika; (*begin*) shika kazi; (*fight*) pigana. *Set to music,* fanyizia (maneno) wimbo, linganisha sauti (ya ngoma, kinanda &c.). *Set up* (*upright*), simamisha, simikisha; (*business*) anza (ingia, shika) kazi (shughuli); (*pretend*) jifanya; (*in type*) panga herufi za chapa. *Set upon,* endea kwa nguvu, shambulia. *Set thinking,* fikirisha, tia fikirani. *Set going,* endesha. — *a.* (*appointed*) -liokazwa. -lioamriwa, -a lazima; (*firm, fixed*) thabiti, madhubuti, -gumu, -siogeuka, imara, -shupavu. *A set speech,* maneno ya utaratibu. — *n.* jamii kikao; (*of a current*) mvuto, mkondo; (*form*) namna, hali; (*pose, position &c.*) kikao; (*friends, relatives &c.*) jamaa, utani; (*in games, dances &c.*) idadi (hesabu) ya watu (michezo &c.) ya kawaida. *Make a set* (*dead set*) *at,* endea, jaribia sana, fanyia bidii nyingi. **set-back,** *n.* mgogoro, kizuizi, jambo liletalo hasara. **set-off,** *n.* malipizi, sawa, kisasi. **set-square,** *n.* kipande chenye umbo la pembetatu, chenye alama za kupimia pembe. **settee,** *n.* kiti kirefu, kitanda. **setter,** *n.* mbwa wa kuwindia. **setting,** *n.* kuweka *&c.*; (*of sun*) kuchwa, machweo, mshuko; (*of a jewel &c.*) kijalizo; (*site, place*) kiweko, kikao, mahali pa kuweka (pa kutia, pa kusimamisha *&c.*).

settle, *v.t.* (*fix*) kaza, fanya imara, weka thabiti, thibitisha; (*quiet*) tuliza, starehesha, ondolea shaka; (*decide*) hukumu, kata jambo (neno), amua, maliza; (*make clear, show*) onyesha, dhihirisha, eleza, thibitisha; (*adjust*) tengeneza, patanisha, suluhisha, fanya suluhu; (*accounts*) fanya safi (barabara), lipa (deni); (*colonize*) kalisha watu katika; — *v.i.* (*reside*) kaa; (*rest*) tua, tulia; (*sink down*) titia, didimia, shuka; (*get clear*) tuama; (*resolve on*) yakinia, azimu, kusudia, nia; (*after war, trouble &c.*) tengemaa, tengemana. **settled,** *a.* imara, thabiti, -tulivu, makini. *A settled country,* nchi inayokaa watu kwa amani, nchi iliyotengemana, nchi yenye amani. **settlement,** *n.* kukaza *&c.*; makazi ya watu waliyohamia, mji mpya, kikao; (*inheritance*) urithi, usia, mali iliyorithiwa; (*agreement*) mapatano, mwafaka, maafikano, suluhu, maagano. **settler,** mhamia mahali, mgeni, mjaji, mlowezi, mja na maji; (*final step*) mwisho. *That's a settler,* basi, imekwisha.

seven, *n. and a.* saba. **sevenfold,** *a.* -a mara saba. **seventeen,** *n. and a.* sabatashara, kumi na saba. **seventh,** *a.* -a saba. **seventeenth,** -a sabatashara. **seventy,** *n. and a.* sabini. **seventieth,** -a sabini.

sever, *v.t.* kata, tenga, vunja, farakisha; — *v.i.* katika, vunjika. **severance,** *n.* kukata, kutenga, kukatika, kutengana.

several, *a.* -ingine, -ingi kidogo, si -ingi, kadha wa kadha; (*some people*) watu; (*separate*) -moja -moja, kila -moja. *Several of the people,* watu wengine, baadhi ya watu. **severally,** *adv.* moja moja, kila mtu.

severance, *n.* taz. *sever.*

severe, *a.* -kali, -zito, -gumu, -a nguvu, bila huruma, -kalifu; (*plain*) -futo, -a mfuto, bila urembo (pambo) **severity,** *n.* ukali, uzito, ugumu, ukalifu.

sew, *v.t.* (*p.t. and pf.t.* **sewed, sewn**) shona. **sewer,** *n.* mshoni. **sewing,** *n.* ushoni, mashono. **sewing-machine,** cherehani.

sewage, *n.* taka zo zote za maji (maji machafu, mkojo, mavi) zilizotoka ndani ya nyumba au mjini katika mifereji (*drains* au *sewers*). **sewer,** *n.* mfereji wa kupeleka *sewage.* **sewerage,** *n.* jumla ya mifereji inayoungana kupeleka *sewage.*

sewing, *n.*, **sewing-machine,** *n.* taz. *sew.*

sex, *n.* hali ya kuwa kiume au kike. *Male sex,* wanaume. *Female sex,* wanawake. **sexless,** *a.* si -a kiume wala -a kike, bila *sex*; (*frigid*) baridi. **sexual,** *a.* -a *sex. Sexual intercourse,* ngono, kulalana, kutwaana. *Sexual passion,* nyege, ashiki, ngoa. *Sexual organs,* (*male*) mboo, uume, dhakari, firaka; (*female*) kuma, uke. **sexuality,** *n.* kuwa na *sex.*

sexagenarian, *n.* mtu mwenye umri wa miaka sitini.

Sexagesima, *n.* Jumapili ya pili kabla ya mwanzo wa *Lent.*

sexless, *a.* taz. *sex.*

sextant, *n.* chombo cha kibaharia cha kutafutia *latitude* na *longitude,* schemu ya sita ya duara.

sexton, *n.* mtunza kanisa na kiwanja chake.

sexual, *a.*, **sexuality,** *n.* taz. *sex.*

shabby, *a.* (*of persons*) -liovaa nguo zilizochakaa (mbovumbovu; (*of behaviour*) -nyonge, -a choyo, bahili. **shabbiness,** *n.* ukuukuu, uchakavu, unyonge, ubahili, uchoyo.

shack, *n.* banda, nyumba ya mfuto.

shackle, *n.* kiungo cha pingu. — *v.t.*

funga kwa pingu, funga pingu; (*hamper &c.*) zuia, wekea mgogoro (kizuizi &c.). *Shackles*, pingu.

shaddock, *n.* furungu, balungi.

shade, *n.* uvuli, kivuli; (*darkness*) giza, utusitusi; (*variation*) tofauti ndogo; (*protection*) kinga, himaya, ulinzi; (*likeness*) mfano; (*of a lamp*) tungi, kisetiri; (*spirit, ghost*) mzimu, kivuli, pepo. *A shade of difference*, tofauti ndogo. *A shade of colour*, rangi, namna ya rangi. *Shade of meaning*, maana, kionyo. *Sunshade*, mwavuli. — *v.t.* tia kivuli, tia giza, kinga jua (joto); — *v.i.* (*shade off, away*) ingiana, fifia, badilika kwa taratibu. **shadow**, *n.* kama *shade, n.* — *v.t.* tia kivuli, tia giza; (*describe dimly*) eleza kidogo, -wa mfano wa; (*follow closely*) fuata karibu karibu, fuatia, vizia. **shadowy**, *a.* -a kivuli, kama kivuli, -a kinyenyezi; (*vague*) si yakini, si hakika, si halisi, si dhahiri. **shady**, *a.* -a *shade*, -enye *shade*; (*mean*) -nyonge, -baya, si -aminifu, si -nyofu, -danganyifu, -a hila, -erevu.

shaft, *n.* kitu cho chote kilicho kirefu chembamba kama mwanzi; (*wooden part*) uti, mti; (*of arrow*) wano; (*missile*) mshale, mkuki; (*of hoe &c.*) mpini, kipini; (*pit*) shimo, tundu, kinywa; (*chimney*) dohani, bomba la kutokea moshi; (*of metal*) ufito (wa chuma &c.); (*of light*) kianga, mwali, mshale, mwonzi.

shag, *n.* tumbako (iliyochambuliwa).

shaggy, *a.* -enye nywele nyingi zilizosokotwa (za matimutimu, zilizotimka, za kimbimbi).

shagreen, *n.* ngozi ya farasi (ngamia, papa &c.) iliyotengenezwa.

Shah, *n.* Sultani wa Uajemi.

shake, *v.t.* (*p.t.* **shook**, *pf.t.* **shaken**) tikisa, tukusa, ning'iniza, tetemesha, shtusha; (*weaken*) dhoofisha, punguzia nguvu, ondolea uthabiti, tia mashaka; — *v.i.* sukasuka, tikisika, titia, tinga, tetema, tetemeka, yumbayumba, ning'inia; (*with fear, cold &c.*) tetemeka, tikisika, gwaya. *Shake off* (*fruit, leaves*) pukusa; (*water &c.*) kukuta, kung'uta. *Shake hands*, pana mikono, shikana mikono amkiana. *Shake out*, futua, kung'uta, kupua. *Shake up*, changanya (kwa kutikisa); (*rouse*) amsha, tia nguvu. — *n.* kutikisa &c. mtikiso, tetemo, tetemeko, msukosuko, mshtusho, kishindo. *In two* (*half a*) *shake*(*s*), sasa hivi. **shakedown**, *n.* malazi yaliyotandikwa chini (badala ya kitanda). **shaker**, *n.* chombo cha kuchanganyia vitu (kwa kukitikisa). **shaking**, *n.* kutikisa, kutikisika &c., mtetemo. **shaky**, *a.* -a kutikisika &c.; (*weak*) dhaifu, -goigoi, hafifu.

shako, *n.* namna ya kikofia kirefu cha askari.

shaky, *a.* taz. *shake*.

shale, *n.* mawe ya tabaka tabaka kama matope yaliyokauka sana.

shall, *v.aux.* (*p.t.* **should**), (*in verbs*) -ta-. *I shall go*, nitakwenda, nakwenda. *You shall go*, huna budi kwenda nenda. *Shall I go?* niende? *Shall you go?* unakwenda? utakwenda. *You shall not go*, huendi, usiende. *If you go, I shall go*, ukienda nitakwenda.

shallot, *n.* namna ya kitunguu kidogo sana.

shallow, *a.* (*of water*) -chache, haba, kidogo; (*foolish*) -a akili chache, hafifu. — *n.* penye maji haba (machache). — *v.i.* punguka urefu (wa maji) taratibu. **shallowness**, *n.* kuwa *shallow*, uchache wa maji (wa akili).

sham, *v.t.* jifanya, jigeuza, iga. *Shamming dead*, kufa uwongo. *Sham sickness*, jisingizia ugonjwa, jigonjweza. — *n.* kujifanya, kujisingizia, mwigo, mfano mtupu; (*hypocrisy*) unafiki, uzandiki, uwongo. — *a.* -a *sham*, -a kuiga, -a uwongo. *Sham fight*, mchezo wa vita.

shamble, *v.i.* enda kama kwamba miguu ni dhaifu (kwa kukokoteza miguu).

shambles, *n.* machinjo, mahali pa kuchinjia wanyama machinjoni.

shame, *n.* (*disgrace*) aibu, fedheha hizaya, ari, izara, jahana, tua; (*modesty*) haya, soni. *It's a shame,* si haki. — *v.t.* aibisha, fedhehesha, hizi, tahayarisha, tia haya, adhiri. **shamefaced,** *a.* -enye haya nyingi. **shamefacedness,** *n.* hali ya kuwa na haya nyingi. **shameful,** -a kutahayarisha, -a kuaibisha, -a kufedhehesha, -a aibu, -baya sana. **shameless,** *a.* pasipo haya, -pujufu, -tovu wa haya, -kavu wa macho, -chafu. *Lead a shameless life, Act shamelessly,* jipujua. **shamelessness,** *n.* kuwa *shameless,* utovu wa haya, upujufu, uchafu.

shampoo, *v.t.* (*massage*) kanda (mwili, maungo); (*head*) osha kichwa na nywele. — *n.* kukanda, mkando; kuosha, (mwosho wa) nywele; sabuni *&c.* ya kuoshea nywele.

shamrock, *n.* mmea ambao vikonyo vyake vina majani matatu matatu, ni ishara ya nchi ya *Ireland.*

shanghai, *v.t.* levya mtu (kwa ulevi au dawa) na kumchukua merikebuni na kumshurutisha afanye kazi ya baharia.

shank, *n.* mguu (hasa muundi wa mguu); (*handle*) mpini, kipini; (*of tool, implement*) kipande kirefu cha kati.

shan't, ufupisho wa *shall not.*

shantung, *n.* (*silk*) lasi.

shanty, *n.* kibanda, kipenu.

shape, *n.* umbo, sura, namna, mfano, mtindo; (*mould*) kalibu; (*for a cap*), faruma. *Take shape,* onekana, pata umbo, tengenea. — *v.t.* fanyiza, tengeneza, umba; (*direct*) ongoza, elekeza; — *v.i.* tengenea, pata umbo, endelea, kua. **shapeless,** *a.* pasipo uzuri, -a vivi hivi, -baya, bila umbo (mzuri), bila sura (nzuri). **shapeliness.** *n.* uzuri (wa umbo). **shapely,** *a.* -zuri, -a kulingana sawasawa, -enye umbo la kupendeza.

shard, *n.* kigae, gae (taz. *potsherd*).

share, *v.t.* gawa, gawanya; — *v.i.* shiriki. — *n.* fungu, sehemu, hisa; (*part of capital*) fungu la rasilmali ya *company. Have shares in,* -wa mshiriki wa. *Go shares in,* shiriki, shirikiana. **shareholder,** *n.* mshiriki mali ya *company.* **sharer,** *n.* mshiriki.

shark, *n.* papa; (*rogue, sharper*) ayari, mlaghai, mdanganyi.

sharp, *a.* -kali, -enye ncha, -liyochongoka; (*vigorous, clever*) -enye akili, hodari, -erevu, -bingwa, -stadi, -a nguvu, -epesi, -elekevu; (*in dealing*) -erevu, -janja, -danganyifu, -laghai, kalamzi; (*quick*) -epesi kuona, -elekevu, hodari; (*bitter*) -chungu, -kali; (*shrill*) -embamba; (*thin*) -embamba, -liokonda, -liogeuka kwa njaa; (*clearly seen, not blurred*) wazi, dhahiri, -a kuonekana vizuri. *A sharp turn,* kugeuka upesi, pindi la mara moja. *Sharp practice,* hila, ujanja, ulaghai, werevu, undaganyifu. *Look sharp!* haya! upesi! hima! chapuchapu! — *n.* (*in music*) sauti iliyokazwa kidogo; alama yake, kipandisho; (*swindler &c.*) ayari mlaghai, mdanganyi, kalamzi. **sharpen,** *v.t.* (*edge*) noa, tia makali; (*point*) chonga, chongoa, fanya -kali; (*arouse*) amsha, tia bidii, tamanisha. **sharpener,** *n.* kitu (chombo) cha kunolea (cha kutia makali, cha kuchongea). **sharper,** *n.* ayari, mjanja, mlaghai, mdanganyifu, kalamzi. **sharpness,** *n.* ukali, uchungu, wepesi, welekevu *&c.* **sharpshooter,** *n.* mwenye shabaha, mstadi wa kupiga shabaha. **sharp-sighted,** *a.* -a macho makali, -a macho ya nguvu, -a kuweza kuona mbali. **sharp-witted,** *a.* -a akili, -a busara, -epesi.

shatter, *v.t.* vunjavunja, pasua, pondaponda, haribu kabisa, angamiza, dhoofisha; — *v.i.* angamia, vunjika, pondeka, haribika, dhoofika.

shave, *v.t.* (*pf.t.* **shaved, shaven**) nyoa, chega; (*smooth*) lainisha (mti kwa kisu, landa *&c.*); (*pass close to*) pita karibu ya, ambaa. — *n.* kunyoa, kuambaa, kuwa karibu

sana. *That was a close shave of being killed*, ilikuwa karibu sana na kuuawa, ilikuwa hatari sana ya kuuawa.
shaving, *n.* (*of wood*) takataka za mbao (kama zile zilizokatwa na landa); (*of hair*) kunyoa, unyozi.
shaving-brush, *n.* burashi ya kunyolea.
shawl, *n.* shali, shatoruma, kashida, mharuma; (*waist*) mahazamu.
she, *pron.* yeye (mwanamke), yule, huyo; (*in verbs*) -a. *She-*, -a kike, jike, *e.g. she-goat*, mbuzi jike (wa kike).
sheaf, *n.*(*pl.* **sheaves**) (*of cut rice &c.*) mganda, tita; (*general*) vitu kadha wa kadha vilivyofungwa pamoja, *e.g.* karatasi, mishale *&c.*
shear, *v.t.* (*pf.t.* **sheared**, **shorn**) kata, kata manyoya, nyoa. **shearer**, *n.* mkata manyoya ya kondoo.
shears, *n.* mkasi mkubwa (taz. *scissors*); (*crane*) winchi, slingi (mtambo wa kuinulia vitu vizito).
sheath, *n.* (*of knife &c.*) ala, uo; (*general*) kifuniko kama mfuko au ala. **sheathe**, *v.t.* futika, weka, funika. **sheathing**, *n.* mabamba ya kubandikiza nje, kifuniko. **sheath-knife**, *n.* kisu chenye ala.
sheave, *n.* (*of pulley*) roda, korodani.
sheaves, *n. pl.* ya *sheaf and sheave.*
shed, (1) *v.t.* (*p.t. and pf.t.* **shed**) (*emit*) toa, toka; (*diffuse*) eneza, tawanya; (*drop*) tonesha, mwaga, -nya; (*of leaves &c.*) pukusa; (*skin*) ambua; (*feathers*) nyonyoa; (*abandon &c.*) acha, tupa.
shed, (2) *n.* banda, kibanda, dungu; (*for cattle &c.*) zizi, tundu.
sheen, *n.* mng'ao, mnang'aniko.
sheep, *n.* (*pl.* **sheep**) kondoo. **sheep-fold**, *n.* zizi. **sheepish**, *a.* -enye haya, -a fadhaa, -a kijinga, -zito, -puzi. **sheep-shearer**, *n.* mkata manyoya ya kondoo. **sheep-shearing**, *n.* kukata manyoya ya kondoo (majira yake). **sheepskin**, *n.* ngozi ya kondoo yenye manyoya yake, ngozi ya kondoo iliyonyonyolewa na kutengenezwa (kwa majalada ya vitabu *&c.*).
sheer, *a.* -a kwenda juu (chini) kiwima sawasawa (ghafula), -a kuchongoka; (*plain*) -tupu, tu; (*of textiles*) -embamba, laini. — *adv.* kabisa, moja kwa moja. — *v.i.* geuka, enda upande. *Sheer off*, geuka (enda) upande; (*depart*) enda, ondoka, toka.
sheet, *n.* (*calico*) shuka; (*of bed*) nguo ya kutandika kitandani, shiti; (*of sail*) demani; (*paper*) ukurasa, laha, sahifa; (*of a book*) gombo, ukurasa; (*of metal*) bamba; (*of water*) eneo la maji, ziwa; (*of rain*) mvua nyingi.
sheet-anchor, *n.* nanga kubwa.
sheeting, *n.* nguo ya *sheet*, nguo pana, nguo, amerikani. **sheet lightning**, *n.* umeme wa kuenea (wa kung'ariza) sana.
sheik, *n.* sheki, sheik.
shekel, *n.* sarafu ya kiyahudi (ya zamani) kama shilingi mbili na senti sabini na tano; kipimo cha kiyahudi (cha zamani kama nusu wakia). *The shekels*, fedha.
shelf, *n.* (*pl.* **shelves**) rafu, kibao (cha kutundikia ukutani, cha ndani ya kabati); (*hanging*) susu; (*sandbank*) fungu; (*rock*) mwamba sawa.
shelve, *v.t.* weka, ahirisha; — *v.i.* (*slope*) inama, telemka, shuka (kwa taratibu). **shelving**, *a.* -a kuinama kwa taratibu.
shell, *n.* (*snail &c.*) konokono, koa; (*flat*) kombe, kome; (*cowry*) kauri, simbi; (*exterior*) nje, upande wa nje, kifuniko; (*of animals*) nyumba, tundu; (*of tortoise, crab &c.*) galili, gome; (*of trees &c.*) gome, ngozi; (*of fruit*) ganda; (*of egg*) kaka, ganda; (*of coco-nut*) kifuu; (*empty*) fuvu, bupuru; (*case*) uo; (*of building*) boma, miti, kiunzi; (*ruin*) gofu; (*cartridge, charge*) risasi, kiasi; (*bomb*) kombora. — *v.t.* toa ganda (gome) la nje, papatua, ambua, menya; (*beans, peas*) pua; (*nuts &c.*) banja, menya; (*coco-nuts*) fua; (*bombard*) pigia risasi (mizinga, makombora). *Shell out* (*slang*), toa fedha, lipa.
shellfish, *n.* wanyama wa bahari

wenye gamba au kombe *&c. e.g.* shaza, kasa, kaa, kamba *&c.* **shell-proof,** *a.* -siovunjika kwa risasi (makombora *&c.*) -a nguvu sana. **shell-shock,** *n.* ugonjwa wa ubongo au kichaa, matokeo ya taabu ya vita. **shelly,** *a.* -a *shells*, -enye *shells* nyingi.

shelter, *n.* (*refuge*) kimbilio, mahali pa salama, kificho, kisetiri, kifuniko, kinga; (*protection*) himaya, ulinzi; (*hut*) kibanda, kipenu, upenu. *Take shelter* (*from rain*), jificha (mvua). — *v.i.* funika, setiri, ficha, linda, hifadhi, kinga, karibisha nyumbani; — *v.i.* jilinda, jikinga, jificha.

shelve, *v.*, **shelves,** *n.pl.*, **shelving,** *a.* taz. *shelf.*

shepherd, *n.* mchunga, mchungaji, mlisha, mlinzi. — *v.t.* chunga; (*guide*) ongoza.

sherbert, *n.* sharabeti.

sherd, *n.* kigae, gae.

sheriff, *n.* mkuu, liwali wa sehemu ya nchi.

sherry, *n.* namna ya divai ya *Spain.*

shew = *show.* **shewn** = *shown.*

shibboleth, *n.* neno la fumbo la kujaribia mtu kuhakikisha kama ni wa jamii au madhehebu ama siyo.

shied, *p.t. and pf.t.* ya *shy.*

shield, *n.* ngao, kigao; (*protection*) himaya, ulinzi, kinga. — *v.t.* linda, hifadhi, funika, setiri. *Shield from,* kingia, zuilia.

shift, *v.t.* (*move*) geuza, sogeza, jongeza, hamisha; (*change clothes*) badili nguo; — *v.i.* sogea, jongea, hama; (*change*) geukageuka. *Shift on to some one else,* sukumizia, kumbishia. *Shift for yourself,* fanya uwezavyo (bila msaada). *Shift one's ground,* ghairi. — *n.* (*device*) hila shauri; (*change*) mageuzi; (*turn*) zamu; (*dress*) nguo ya kike kama kanzu au shati ndefu. *Make shift* (*to*), jaribia uwezavyo, fanya kwa shida, jitahidi, jikalifu. **shifting,** *a.* -a kugeukageuka, -geugeu, -a kigeugeu, -a kughairighairi. **shiftless,** *a.* -zembe, -sio na shauri, -jinga. **shifty,** *a.* -a mashauri mengi, -a hila, -danganyifu; (*changeable*) -a kugeukageuka -a kughairi.

shilling, *n.* shilingi.

shilly-shally, *v.i.* sitasita, chezacheza.

shimmer, *v.i.* metameta, ng'aa, nang'anika. **shimmery,** *a.* -a kumetameta.

shin, *n.* muundi, goko, mguu kati ya goti na kifundo cha chini. *Shin up,* panda, paraga, sombea, paramia.

shindy, *n.* makelele, ghasia, zahama, msukosuko.

shine, *v.i.* (*p.t. and pf.t.* **shone**) ng'aa, nawiri, toa nuru, angaza, mulika, waa, zagaa, metameta; (*as of rubbed with fat, have a sheen &c.*) nang'anika; (*be eminent*) -wa na fahari, tukuka, -wa mashuhuri, tangulia, pata sifa. — *n.* mwanga, nuru, kianga, weupe, mnang'aniko. **shining, shiny,** *a.* -a kung'aa, -eupe, -angavu, -a kunang'anika, -a kumetameta; (*famous*) -adhimu, -a sifa, mashuhuri, maarufu.

shingle, (1) *n.* (*stones*) kokoto za pwani, vijiwe, changarawe. **shingly,** *a.* -a kokoto, -a changarawe.

shingle, (2) *n.* (*of roofing*) ubao mwembamba wa kuezekea nyumba (badala ya mabati, vigae *&c.*). — *v.t.* ezeka kwa *shingles*; (*hair*) kata fupi nywele (mwanamke) za nyuma.

shingles, *n.* ugonjwa wa kutokeza vipele kiunoni.

shingly, *a.* taz. *shingle* (1).

shining, shiny, *a.* taz. *shine.*

ship, *n.* merikebu, jahazi, chombo; (*steamer*) meli; (*of war*) manowari; (*merchantman*) meli ya shehena (ya bidhaa); (*passenger ship, liner*) meli, meli ya abiria; (*brig, schooner*) barakinya; (*full-rigged*) merikebu ya milingoti mitatu. — *v.t.* (*put on board*) pakia, pakiza, shehenesha, sheheni; (*receive on board*) pokea shehena, pokea melini (merikebuni, jahazini; (*of crew*) ajiri (baharia *&c.* kwa kazi ya meli *&c.*). *Ship seas,* pakia mawimbi. *Ship oars,* weka ndani (makasia). **shipboard,** *n.* melini, chomboni, merikebuni. **ship-broker,** *n.* mfanya biashara ya meli (merikebu) na shehena zake. **ship-builder,** *n.* fundi wa kuunda meli (merikebu &c.), mwunzi. **ship-building,** *n.* kuunda meli &c., uunzi wa meli &c. **ship-chandler,** *n.* mwuza zana (pambo na vifaa) za melini &c. **shipmaster,** *n.* mwenyeji wa meli (merikebu &c.), nahodha, kapiteni. **shipmate,** *n.* baharia mwenzi. **shipment,** *n.* mapakizi, kupakia; (*cargo*) shehena. **ship-owner,** *n.* mwenyeji wa meli (merikebu &c.). **shipper,** *n.* mwenye kazi ya kusafirisha vitu (bidhaa, shehena &c.) katika meli, merikebu &c. **shipping,** *n.* meli (merikebu) nyingi, jamii ya meli (merikebu &c.) ya nchi fulani; (*business*) kazi ya kusafirisha bidhaa &c. katika meli, merikebu &c. **shipshape,** *a.* barabara, sawasawa, taratibu. **shipwreck,** *n.* kuvunjika meli (merikebu, jahazi &c.); (*vessel*) meli (merikebu &c.) iliyovunjika; (*ruin*) maangamizi, uharibifu. — *v.t.* angamiza, haribu, poteza. **shipwright,** *n.* fundi wa kuunda au kutengeneza meli &c., mwunzi. **shipyard,** *n.* kiwanda cha kuundia meli (merikebu &c.), karakana, furutile, flotile.

shire, *n.* jimbo, wilaya.

shirk, *v.t.* jitoa katika kazi (madaraka, hatari, shida &c.) ipasayo, epuka, epa, jiepusha na, kimbia, toroka. **shirker,** *n.* mtu ajitoaye katika kazi (madaraka &c.) impasayo.

shirt, *n.* shati, vazi kama kanzu fupi au gwanda. **shirting,** *n.* kitambaa cha shati, amerikani, bafta, nguo &c.

shiver, *v.i.* (*tremble*) tetemeka, gwaya, tapatapa; — *v.t.* (*smash*) vunja vipande vipande, vunja kabisa. — *n.* kitapo, tetemeko, mtetemo; (*small piece*) kipande kidogo, kigereng'enza. **shivering,** *n.* kitapo, tetemeko, mtetemo.

shoal, (1) *n.* (*bank*) fungu. *Shoal water,* maji machache, maji haba.

shoal, (2) *n.* (*of fish*) samaki wengi pamoja, kundi la samaki.

shock, (1) *n.* tita kubwa la ngano &c.; (*of hair*) vunga la nywele. *Shock-headed,* -enye vunga la nywele.

shock, (2) *n.* shindo, kishindo, mshindo, kushtuka, shtuko, mshtuo, kituko, fadhaa; (*great sorrow* &c.) msiba; (*disorder of mind*) wasiwasi (kwa ajili ya maumivu, huzuni, msiba &c.). — *v.t.* tia kishindo, shtua, shtusha, chukiza, fadhaisha, tia haya (wasiwasi). **shocking,** *a.* -a kuchukiza, -a kutia haya; (*of poor quality* &c.) hafifu sana, -baya.

shod, *v. p.t. and pf.t.* ya *shoe. Shod with iron,* -liotiwa chuma chini au katika ncha.

shoddy, *n.* nguo iliyofanyizwa kwa nguo kuukuu iliyochambuliwa na kufanywa tena; kitu cho chote kilicho hafifu (duni). — *a.* -a *shoddy,* -a uwongo, hafifu, duni.

shoe, *n.* kiatu (cha kizungu); (*horse's*) chuma cha chini ya mguu wa farasi, kama kiatu — *v.t.* tia farasi chuma miguuni. **shoeblack,** *n.* msugua viatu. **shoe-buckle,** *n.* bizimu ya kiatu. **shoehorn,** *n.* kipande cha kuvalia viatu. **shoe-lace.** *n.* ukanda (uzi) wa kiatu. **shoe-latchet,** *n.* gidamu. **shoe-leather,** *n.* ngozi iliyotengenezwa ya kufanyizia viatu. **shoemaker,** *n.* mshoni viatu.

shone, *p.t. and pf.t.* ya *shine.*

shook, *p.t.* ya *shake.*

shoot, *v.t.* (*p.t. and pf.t.* **shot**) piga bunduki (mzinga, upindi &c.); (*hit*) tupa, piga, pata; (*send out*) peleka kwa nguvu, rusha, vurumisha, sukuma mbele, toa; — *v.i.* (*sprout*) ota, mea, chipuka; (*dart suddenly* &c.) pita upesi; (*of pain*) choma ghafula. *Shoot at,* pigia, tupia. *Shoot by* (*past*), pitia upesi, ruka, enda mbio. *Shoot up* (*grow*), panda, chipuka, kua, vuvumka. *Shoot the rapids,* telemka mbio mtoni. — *n.* (*plant*) chipukizi.

uchipuko; (*water*) mchirizi, mfereji; (*for logs, coal &c.*) njia ya kutelemshia magogo, makaa &c.; (*jet of water*) bubujiko, foko; (*shooting party*) jamii ya wawinda wanyama, ndege &c. **shooting,** *n.* kutupa, kupiga &c. *Go out shooting,* enda kuwinda. *Good shooting,* mawindo tele; (*aim*) shabaha sana. — *a.* -a kupiga bunduki, -a kuwinda. *Shooting pains,* maumivu ya kuchomachoma, kichomi. **shooting-star,** *n.* kimwondo.

shop, *n.* duka, nyumba ya bidhaa; (*workshop*) kiwanda, karkana. *Set up a shop,* weka duka. *Close a shop,* ondoa (funga) duka. *Keep a small shop,* chuuza. *Talk shop,* ongea (zungumza) habari za kazi. — *v.i.* enda dukani, zunguka kwenye maduka, nunua vitu dukani. *Go shopping,* enda kununua vitu, enda madukani. **shopkeeper,** *n.* mwenyeji wa duka, mchuuzi. **shoplifter,** *n.* mwizi wa vitu dukani, mnyakuzi, mkwepuzi. **shoplifting,** *n.* kuiba dukani. **shopman,** *n.* mwenye duka, mchuuzi, mngoje duka. **shopper,** *n.* aendaye kununua vitu dukani, mnunuzi. **shopping,** *n.* kununua dukani. **shopwalker,** *n.* msimamizi dukani.

shore, (1) *n.* pwani, ukingo wa bahari (wa ziwa), mwambao, kikomo cha bahari; (*beach*) ufuko; (*coast*) upande wa bahari, upande wa pwani. *On (to, at, near) the shore,* pwani. *Go on shore* (*passenger*), shuka pwani, shuka; (*ship*) pwelewa, panda mwambani, kwama. **shoreless,** *a.* pasipo mpaka, -kubwa mno.

shore, (2) *n.* (*prop*) gadi, shiku, makwa. — *v.t.* tegemeza; (*a vessel*) gadimu, shikiza; (*for caulking &c.*) jahabu.

shoreless, *a.* taz. *shore* (1).

shorn, *pf.t.* ya *shear.*

short, *a.* -fupi; (*small*) -dogo; (*deficient*) -pungufu, haba, adimu, -a kuadimika; (*abrupt*) -a maneno machache; (*crumbling*) -a kufikichika. *Be short* (*in growth, stature*), via, kundaa, dumaa. *Short of,* -pungufu -a, pungukiwa na; (*except, unless*) pasipo, isipokuwa. *A short cut,* njia ya kukata. *A short sound,* sauti ndogo. *A short time,* kitambo, kipindi, muda mfupi. *Make short work of,* maliza upesi, (*kill*) ulia mbali. *In short,* jumla, kwa neno moja, kwa ufupi. *Stop short,* katiza, pingamiza; (*come to abrupt stop*) simama (koma) ghafula. *Be short of, Run short of,* zidiwa, pungukiwa, -wa na upunguo wa, -wa na . . . chache, tindikiwa, ishiwa. *Come short of,* pungukia, si patia, -wa si sawa na, tindikia. *The long and short of it,* jambo lenyewe. *Short commons,* chakula haba. **shortage,** *n.* ukosefu, ukosekano, upungufu, uchache. **short-circuit,** *n.* njia fupi (ya kukata) ya umeme (badala ya kufuata njia yake hasa). **shortcoming,** *n.* ukosefu, upungufu, kosa.

shorten, *v.t.* fupisha, punguza, kata, katiza, kusuru; — *v.i.* punguka, pungua, kunjana, nywea. **shortening,** *n.* mafuta (ya kutia katika maandazi &c.). **shorthand,** *n.* namna ya kuandika upesi kwa herufi ndogo chache, mwandiko wa kukata. **short-handed,** *a.* bila watu wa kutosha, -enye watu haba. **short-lived,** *a.* -siokaa sana, -a kupita upesi, -a maisha machache, -epesi kufa, -a muda mfupi. **shortly,** *adv.* (*soon*) mara moja, upesi, ghafula, karibu; (*sharply*) kwa kukata, vikali. **shortness,** *n.* kuwa *short,* ufupi, uchache, ukosefu, upungufu. **shorts,** *n.* suruali fupi (kipande), kaputula. **short-sighted,** *a.* -sioona vema, dhaifu wa macho; (*foolish*) -a akili chache, -jinga, si -a busara, -a kutofikiri mbele. **short-tempered,** *a.* -epesi wa hasira, -epesi wa kupanda hamaki, -a harara. **short-winded,** *a.* -enye pumu, -a kukokota pumzi, -a kutweta.

shot, (1) *p.t.* na *pf.t.* ya *shoot.*

shot, (2) *n.* (*small*) marisaa; (*large*)

risasi; (*discharge*) shindo la (kishindo cha, mshindo wa) bunduki (mzinga, bastola &c.), pigo; (*range*) mfiko wa risasi, mtupo wa risasi; (*marksman*) mtu hodari wa kupiga shabaha; (*target*) shabaha; (*attempt*) jaribio; (*random guess*) kisio. *Within ear-shot,* karibu hata kuweza kusikia (kusikiwa). *Have a shot at it,* jaribu. *Shot-belt,* beti. *Shot-gun,* bunduki ya marisaa. *Shot-proof,* -siopenya marisaa (risasi). *He is a good shot,* ana shabaha sana. — *a. e.g.* (*silk*) (hariri) -enye nyuzi za rangi mbalimbali ndani yake, -a kugeuka rangi.

should, *v.aux. I should love,* imenipasa kupenda, nipende. *I should be glad to play if I could,* ningefurahi kucheza ningeweza.

shoulder, *n.* bega, fuzi, kitu kilichofanana na bega. *Turn a cold shoulder to,* kataa urafiki, dharau, acha. *Put one's shoulder to the wheel,* tia nguvu, tia shime, fanya bidii. *Shoulder to shoulder,* karibu karibu. *Shift the blame &c. on to other shoulders,* sukumiza lawama &c. juu ya mwingine. — *v.t.* twika, chukua begani; — *v.i.* (*thrust*) kumba, songa, sogeza upande. **shoulder-belt,** *n.* ukanda wa begani. **shoulder-blade,** *n.* mtulinga.

shout, *v.i.* piga kelele (yowe), guta, ita, paza sauti, toa sauti kuu. — *n.* ukelele, kelele, mlio mkuu; (*for help*) kiyowe, yowe; (*for joy*) kigelegele, kifijo, shangwe.

shove, *v.t.* sukuma, piga kikumbo, kumba, songa, sogeza, sekua, jongeza. *Push and shove each other,* buburushana, sukumana, kumbana. — *n.* kumbo, kikumbo, sukumo.

shovel, *n.* jembe la kizungu (la kupakulia mchanga &c.) kolego, sepetu. — *v.t.* pakua (ondoa &c.) kwa *shovel.*

show (shew), *v.t.* (*pf.t.* **shown, shewn**) onyesha, weka wazi, tia mbele ya macho, ainisha, angaza; (*disclose*) eleza, funua, bainisha; (*inform*) arifu, aridhia; (*prove, make clear*) dhihirisha, thibitisha, fafanua; (*put out*) toa; (*for sale*) tembeza, tinza; (*guide, conduct*) ongoza; — *v.i.* onekana, tokea. *Show how to do a thing,* fuasisha, oleza. *Show in,* karibisha ndani, peleka ndani. *Show off,* piga umalidadi, koga, piga mikogo, randa, jifahirisha, tamba, jitanibu, belenga. *Show up,* chongea, kashifu. *Show kindness (hospitality &c.) to,* tendea wema, fadhili. *He showed me all possible kindness,* alinitendea kila jambo la wema. — *n.* onyesho; (*spectacle*) tamasha; (*fine appearance*) urembo, fahari, uzuri, umalidadi, usheha, ulimbwende, mangwaji, madaha, madahiro, utanashati; (*likeness*) mfano; (*pretence*) kujifanya, unafiki, uzandiki, uwongo; (*display of goods*) kutembeza, kufanya mwangaza; (*ostentation*) ushaufu, fahari, mikogo, kubelenga; (*trace, vestige*) alama. *Show-bill (-case, -room, -man, -card),* karatasi (sanduku, chumba, mtu, karata) ya kutazamisha watu bidhaa. *Show of hands,* mikono juu. **showiness,** *n.* kuwa *showy,* ushaufu, umalidadi, mangwaji, mashobo &c. **showing,** *n.* wonyesho; (*evidence*) maneno, ushahidi. **showy,** *a.* -shaufu, -a urembo, -a fahari, -a kupiga madaha, -a umalidadi, -a ulimbwende, -a utanashati, -enye mikogo, -a kubelenga, -a makeke.

shower, *n.* (*rain*) manyunyu; (*abundance*) wingi, neema. **showery,** *a.* -a manyunyu, -a kunya (kunyesha) mvua mara kwa mara.

showiness, *n.,* **showing,** *n.,* **showy,** *a.* taz. *show.*

shrank, *p.t.* ya *shrink.*

shrapnel, *n.* risasi ya mzinga yenye marisaa nyingi ndani yake.

shred, *n.* kidogo, kipande, kichane. — *v.t.* chana, pasua.

shrew, *n.* mwanamke mkali mkorofi, mwanamke mzozi (mgomvi) mwenye gubu; (*mouse*) panya mdogo.

shrewish, *a.* -kali, -a kukaripia, -a kukemea, -zozi, -gomvi.

shrewd, *a.* -erevu, -a busara, -a akili. **shrewdness**, *n.* werevu, busara, akili.

shrewish, *a.* taz. *shrew.*

shriek, *v.i.* lia kwa sauti kubwa nyembamba (kama kwa maumivu, hofu, kucheka, hasira &c.). — *n.* mlio wa nguvu (kwa hofu &c.), yowe, unyende.

shrift, *n.* *Give* (*get*) *short shrift*, toa (pewa) muda mfupi sana kwa sala kabla ya kuua (kuuawa), adhibu (pata adhabu) upesi, maliza (malizika) upesi.

shrike, *n.* (*Senegal bush*) kipwe.

shrill, *a.* -embamba (sauti). **shrillness**, *n.* wembamba (wa sauti).

shrimp, *n.* uduvi, ushimbu, kijino, kamba ndogo.

shrine, *n.* mahali patakatifu; pa kuwekea vitakatifu; sanduku lenye vitu vitakatifu; madhabahu, kaburi, ziara.

shrink, *v.i.* (*p.t.* **shrank**, *pf.t.* **shrunk**) nywea, jikunyata, ngwea, jikunja, jitenga (kwa hofu, haya, machukio &c.), rudi nyuma, sinyaa; (*decrease, of cloth &c.*) pungua, punguka, rudi, nywea, (*shrivel*) finyaa, sinyaa, fuwaa, kwajuka, kunjamana, finyana. *Shrink from*, kimbia, kataa, chukiwa na, epukana na, jitenga na. **shrinkage**, *n.* upunguo, kadiri iliyopunguka.

shrive, *v.t.* ghofiri.

shrivel, *v.i.* finyaa, sinyaa, kunjamana, finyana, kauka, nyauka, fuwaa, ungua, kwajuka; — *v.t.* finya, kunja, kausha, nyausha, unguza. **shrivelled**, *a.* -a mafinyo, -a kufinyana, -a kukunjamana, -a makunyanzi.

shroud, *n.* sanda; (*for a woman*) msuani; (*covering*) kifuniko, vazi; (*of ship*) kamba ya mlingoti, ayari. — *v.t.* kafini, funika, gubika.

Shrove Tuesday, *n.* siku inayotangulia majira ya *Lent.*

shrub, *n.* kijiti, gugu. **shrubbery**, *n.* jamii ya vijiti, kichaka. **shrubby**, *a.* -enye *shrub.*

shrug, *v.t.* (*shoulders*) inua (pandisha, kunja) mabega (dalili ya kuonyesha kisito, kusitasita, dharau, kukata tamaa &c.). — *n.* mkunjo wa mabega.

shrunk, *p.t. and pf.t.* ya *shrink.*

shudder, *v.i.* tetema, tetemeka, tapa, gwaya (kwa hofu, baridi, kitisho, machukio). *Shudder at*, chukiwa na, kirihi. — *n.* mtetemo, tetemeko, kitapo.

shuffle, *v.t.* pisha (jongeza) huko na huko, gurugusha, geuzageuza, chafua changa, changanya; (*drag the feet*) kokota (kokoteza) miguu, jikokota; (*cards*) changa (karata); — *v.i.* taataa, furukuta; (*on bullocks*) kweta, sowera, sota; (*equivocate*) geukageuka, fanya hila, danganya, ongopa; (*cards*) changa (karata). — *n.* kupisha (kujongeza, kukokoteza) huko na huko &c.; hila, werevu, madanganyo. **shuffler**, *n.* mjanja, mdanganyifu, si mnyofu.

shun, *v.t.* epuka, epusha, epukana na, jiepusha na, jitenga na, kimbia; (*a blow*) epa.

shunt, *v.t.* sogeza, jongeza (geuza) upande, peleka njia nyingine; (*defer*) weka, ahirisha.

shut, *v.t.* (*p.t. and pf.t.* **shut**) funga, fumba; (*a door, without locking*) shindika, vugaza; — *v.i.* fungika, fumbika. *Shut in*, funga; (*surround*) zunguka, zingia. *Shut off*, katiza, zuia; (*water*) funga; (*electricity, electric light*) zima. *Shut out*, shindisha nje, toa nje; (*preclude*) zuia, kataa, topatana. *Shut up*, funga; (*silence*) nyamazisha, shinda. *Shut up!* basi! kelele! makelele! nyamaza!

shutter, *n.* ubao wa (mbao za) dirisha (kama mlango); kilango kidogo cha kufunga kitundu cha *camera*, kuzuia nuru isipite.

shuttle, *n.* kipande cha kupisha mshindio katika kufuma nguo; (*in sewing machine*) kipande cha kupisha uzi wa chini. **shuttle-cock**, *n.* kipande chenye manyoya cha kuchezea.

shy, (1) *v.t.* (*throw*) tupa, vurumisha.
shy, (2) *a.* -enye haya (soni), -oga, -a hadhari. — *v.i.* (*p.t.* **shied**) (farasi) ruka upande. *Shy at*, epuka, kataa (kwa hofu, machukio *&c.*). **shyly**, *adv.* kwa haya (soni). **shyness**, *n.* haya, soni.
sibilant, *a.* -a kulia kama nyoka, -enye sauti kama s.
sibyl, *n.* nabii mke wa zamani, kizee awezaye kutabiri.
sick, *a.* -gonjwa, -ele. *Sick at heart*, -enye moyo mzito kwa huzuni. *Be sick*, ugua, -wa hawezi (huwezi *&c.*), -wa -gonjwa, -wa na uele, -wa mwele; (*disgusted*) chukizwa, choshwa; (*vomit*) tapika. *Feel sick*, -taka kutapika, chafuka tumbo, ona kichefuchefu (kigagazi). *Be sick of*, kinaika na, choka. *Make sick*, tapisha, chafusha moyo, chafuka. **sicken**, *v.t.* (*cause to vomit*) tapisha; (*disgust*) chukiza, kinaisha, kirihi; — *v.i.* (*be disgusted*) chukizwa; (*become ill*) ugua, shikwa (patwa) na ugonjwa. **sickening**, *a.* -a kutia ugonjwa (uele, maradhi), -a kuchukiza, -a kukinaisha, -a kuchosha. **sickly**, *a.* -gonjwa, kama mgonjwa, dhaifu, -a kufanya ugonjwa, -a kugonjweza, -a kutapisha, -a kuchafuka moyo, -a kigagazi. **sickness**, *n.* ugonjwa, uele, maradhi; (*a sick feeling*) kichefuchefu, kigagazi, kinyaa.
sickle, *n.* mundu.
sickly, *a.*, **sickness**, *n.* taz. *sick.*
side, *n.* upande, janibu; (*of river &c.*) kando, ukingo; (*of body*) ubavu; (*party, faction*) watu wa upande mmoja, jamii, baadhi, wafuasi, wenzi, madhehebu. *Other side of*, upande wa pili wa; (*of river, creek &c.*) ng'ambo ya pili ya, ng'ambo ya. *Side by side*, sawasawa, pamoja, kwa kupambana (kuambaana), kandokando, kuwa sambamba. *On the side of* (*same side as*), hali moja na, shauri moja na. *Be on one side* (*awry, aslant, crooked*), enda mshazari, inama, potoka. *Lay on side*, inika, laza, sinua. *Put on one side* (*set aside*), weka, tenga. *Put on side*, piga makuu, takabari, ringa. — *v.i.* (*with*) chagua upande, fuata. **side-arms**, *n.* silaha za kuvaa ubavuni (upanga, bastola, singe). **sideboard**, *n.* meza ya kuwekea vyombo vya kulia (pengine ni kabati pia). **side-car**, *n.* kigari cha kufungashia ubavuni mwa *motor-cycle*. **side-glance**, *n.* tazamo la kitongotongo. **sidelight**, *n.* taa ya upande; (*fact or knowledge*) jambo (maarifa, habari) lisilofungamana hasa na jambo lenyewe, lakini linaliangazia (linalieleza). **sidelong**, *a.* -a upande, -a kwenda upande. *A sidelong glance*, tazamo la kitongotongo. **side-piece**, *n.* (*of bedstead*) mfumbati; (*of door*) mwimo, mhimili. **side-saddle**, *n.* tandiko la (saruji ya) farasi la kukalia mwanamke miguu yote miwili upande mmoja. **side-slip**, *v.i.* teleza na kwenda upande. — *n.* kuteleza na kwenda upande. **sideways**, *adv.* kwa upande, kwenda upogo, kwenda upande, upogoupogo, si sawa, mshazari. **siding**, *n.* kuchagua upande; (*in railway*) njia ndogo ya gari la moshi, ya upande. **sidle**, *v.i.* enda upande, jipenyeza, jipendekeza.
sidereal, *a.* -a nyota.
side-saddle, *n.*, **sideslip**, *v. and n.*, **sideways**, *adv.*, **siding**, *n.*, **sidle**, *v.* taz. *side.*
siege, *n.* mazingiwa, kuzunguka mji kwa vita.
siesta, *n.* usingizi kidogo wa mchana.
sieve, *n.* chekecheke, chungio; (*basket for sifting*) ungo, tunga. **sieve, sift**, — *v.t.* (*by shaking*) chunga, chekecha; (*by tossing*) peta, pepeta, petua, pembua; (*select carefully*) chaguachagua, teua; (*examine*) hojihoji, tafutia, hakikia, pekua; (*sprinkle*) nyunyiza. **sifter**, *n.* chekecheke, chungio; (*basket*) ungo, tunga.
sigh, *v.i.* piga kite, pumua, hema (kwa taabu, majonzi au baada ya kuondolewa taabu, shaka *&c.*).

Sigh for, tamani sana, onea shauku. — *n.* kite, kupumua, kuhema (kwa taabu *&c.* au kuondolewa taabu *&c.*).

sight, *n.* kuona, kutazama, uwezo wa kuona kwa macho; (*range of*) eneo la jicho, upeo wa macho; (*spectacle*) tamasha, shani, kizushi, kitu kigeni; (*opinion*) macho, akili, maono, nia; (*of gun &c.*) shabaha. *In my sight*, mbele ya macho yangu. *I was in sight of*, niliweza kuona. *Come in sight*, onekana, tokea. *Be out of sight*, toweka, tokomea, toonekana, enda mbali. *At sight*, mara moja, ghafula, kuona tu. *Catch sight of*, ona. *Clear sight*, wangavu wa macho. *Dim sight*, giza la macho, unyenyezi, tandabui. *Within sight of*, karibu. — *v.t.* ona, tazama, angalia; (*aim at*) pigia shabaha, lenga, elekeza. **sightless,** *a.* kipofu. **sightseeing,** *n.* matembezi (kutazama mji, mahali *&c.*). **sightseer,** *n.* mtembezi, mwenendezi, mwenendi.

sign, *n.* dalili, ishara, alama; (*proof*) ushahidi; (*hint, indication*) kionyo, dokezo, konyezo la jicho (la mkono), ukonyezo: (*event*) jambo kubwa; (*miracle*) mwujiza; (*memorial*) ukumbusho, kumbukumbu; (*signboard*) ubao wenye picha (jina, habari); (*likeness, emblem*) mfano. — *v.t.* tia sahihi, sahihisha, andika jina chini, tia mkono; (*make a sign*) ashiria, konyeza, pungia mkono. **signal,** *n.* alama, ishara, dalili, kionyo; (*of boat or train arriving*) selo. — *v.t.* toa ishara, sema (amuru, onya) kwa ishara, ashiria. —*a.* -kuu, mashuhuri. *A signal victory*, kushinda sana. **signalize,** *v.t.* (*celebrate*) tukuza, adhimisha; (*show*) onyesha. *Signalize oneself*, jipatia sifa. **signaller,** *n.* mtu (askari) mwenye kazi ya kupeleka na kupokea habari kwa *signal* (taz. *signal, v.*), **signally,** *adv.* sana. **signalman,** *n.* mtu wa reli (*railway*) mwenye kazi ya kuangalia (kusimamia, kufanya) ishara (vionyo *&c.*) za reli. **signatory,** *n.* mtu atiaye sahihi katika mapatano (maagano, mkataba). **signature,** *n.* sahihi, jina, mkono. **signboard,** *n.* ubao wenye picha dukani ya kuonyesha bidhaa gani inayouzwa, ubao wenye jina au habari. **signet,** *n.* muhuri. *Signet-ring*, pete yenye muhuri. **significance,** *n.* maana. **significant,** *a.* -enye maana, -a kuonya, -kuu. **signification,** *n.* maana, kuonya, kionyo. **signify,** *v.t.* onya, onyesha, kumbusha; (*mean*) -wa na maana ya; (*concern, affect*) pasa, husu, dhuru. *It does not signify*, haidhuru, mamoja, haina maana, si kitu. **sign manual,** *n.* = *signature*, hasa ya mfalme. **sign-post,** *n.* mti wenye mkono (au mikono, au ishara) wa kuonyesha njia.

silent, *a.* -nyamavu, -a kimya, kimya, -stirifu. **silence,** *n.* **kimya,** unyamavu, utulivu. *Silence!* makelele! kelele! nyamaza! —*v.t.* nyamazisha, kataza, tuliza. **silencer,** *n.* kitu (chombo) cha kupunguzia au kuzuilia kelele.

silhouette, *n.* picha ya kivuli (au kama kivuli cheusi) cha mtu au kitu.

silica, *n.* jiwe kama la mchanga au kama kioo.

silk, *n.* hariri; (*tussore*) lasi; (*garment*) vazi la hariri. — *a.* -a hariri. **silken,** *a.* -a hariri, kama hariri, laini. **silkworm,** *n.* mdudu mfanyiza nyuzi za hariri. **silky,** *a.* -a hariri, kama hariri laini; (*of voice, manner &c.*) laini, -a kubembeleza, -bembe.

sill, *n.* ubao wa chini (ya dirisha au mlango), kizingiti.

silly, *a.* -pumbavu, -puzi, -jinga; (*crazy*) -enye kichaa, -enye akili afkani, punguani. **silliness,** *n.* upumbavu, upuzi, ujinga, ukosefu (upungufu) wa akili, puo.

silo, *n.* shimo la (handaki ya, ghala ya) kuwekea majani mabichi kuyahifadhi yawe chakula cha ng'ombe *&c.* wakati majani yanapokosekana.

silt, *n.* matope, mchanga, takataka za mto. — *v.t.* (*up*) jaza matope ziba; — *v.i.* jaa, zibika, fanya mafungu, kauka.

silvan, sylvan, *a.* -a mwituni, -a msitu.

silver, *n.* fedha, sarafu za fedha, rangi ya fedha, vyombo vya fedha. — *v.t.* tia fedha nje, funika kwa fedha, tia rangi ya fedha; — *v.i.* (*become grey*) pata mvi za nywele. — *a.* -a fedha, kama fedha, -a rangi ya fedha. **silver-paper,** *n.* jaribosi yenye rangi ya fedha. **silversmith,** *n.* mfua fedha, sonara (wa vitu vya fedha). **silvery,** *a.* kama fedha, -eupe, -a kung'aa.

simian, *a.* -a jamii ya nyani (kima, tumbili &c.), kama nyani (kima &c.).

similar, *a.* sawa, kama sawa, mfano mmoja, kama hii (ile &c.), -a kufanana. **similarity,** *n.* hali ya kuwa sawa au kufanana, sura moja, mfano, kifani. **similarly,** *adv.* vile vile, vivyo hivyo, kadhalika. **simile,** *n.* mfano wa maneno, methali, fumbo. **similitude,** *n.* hali ya kuwa sawa au kufanana, sura moja, mfano, kifani.

simmer, *v.i.* chemka polepole; (*of feelings &c.*) -wa karibu kuwaka (kwa hasira &c.).

simony, *n* kufanya biashara ya mambo matakatifu ya dini (ya rohoni).

simoom, *n.* upepo wa joto sana wa Uarabu.

simper, *v.i.* chekelea, cheka ovyo (kijinga, kipuzi, kibembe).

simple, *a.* (*single*) -moja, -moja tu; (*indivisible*) -siogawanyikana, -siochanganuka; (*uncomplicated*) si -enye mambo mengi, si -enye matata, si -liotengenezwa sana, -a vivi hivi rahisi kufanya, -epesi kuelea; (*unadorned*) -siopambwa, -a mfuto, si -enye urembo (madoido, mapambo), vivi hivi; (*sincere*) si -enye hila, si -janja, amini, -nyofu; (*unaffected*) si -enye kiburi, makini, -nyenyekevu, kama mtoto; (*intelligible*) wazi, dhahiri, -a kuelea, -a kufahamika bila taabu; (*unwise*) -jinga, -a akili chache; (*unmixed*) -tupu, safi, -siochanganyika, -siodanganywa, pasipo kitu kingine; (*not luxurious*) si -a anasa; (*common*) -a watu wote, -ovyo, vivi hivi. — *n.* dawa ya (namna moja ya) majani, miti maua au mimea. **simpleness,** *n.* hali ya kuwa *simple,* uzuzu, ujinga. **simpleton,** *n.* mjinga, mzuzu, mwenye akili chache, baradhuli, baghami, bozi, daba, juha, jura. **simplicity,** *n.* kuwa *simple,* urahisi, wepesi, utovu wa anasa (wa mapambo mengi, wa matata &c.); unyofu; ujinga, ubaradhuli, ubozi; (*unity*) umoja. **simplification,** *n.* kufanya *simple,* kuondoa shida (matata, mambo magumu &c.). **simplify,** *v.t.* fanya *simple,* fanya rahisi, ondoa shida (matata, mambo magumu &c.), eleza, fumbua, geuza. **simply,** *adv.* pasipo hila, pasipo anasa (matata, mambo magumu &c.); (*only, merely*) tu, peke yake (yao &c.); (*as intens.*) sana.

simulate, *v.t.* iga, fuasa, jifanya, shabihi, jifanya kuwa na, jisingizia, jidai. **simulation,** *n.* kujifanya &c., unafiki, uzandiki.

simultaneous, *a.* -a wakati ule ule, -a dakika ile ile, pale pale, papo hapo, sawa. **simultaneously,** *adv.* sawia, mara hiyo, pale pale, sawasawa.

sin, *n.* dhambi, hatia, uhalifu, kosa, uovu, ubaya. — *v.t.* fanya dhambi, kosa. **sinful,** *a.* -a dhambi &c., -ovu, -baya, -kosefu. **sinfulness,** *n.* hali ya dhambi, kuwa na dhambi, uovu, ubaya, ukosefu. **sinless,** *a.* pasipo dhambi kabisa, bila hatia. **sinlessness,** *n.* kuwa pasipo dhambi, utovu wa dhambi (hatia, uovu &c.). **sinner,** *n.* mwenye dhambi, mfanya dhambi, mkosaji.

since, *adv. prep. and conj.* (*from time of, after*) tangu, baada ya, toka, tokea, baada; (*from then until now*) tangu siku ile (saa ile, wakati ule, hapo) hata (mpaka) sasa; (*in past time*) zamani, kwa wakati uliopita;

(*seeing that, because*) kwa sababu, kwa kuwa, ya kuwa, ya kwamba, maadam. *He came there three days since*, amekuja yapata siku tatu. *It is three days since he came*, tangu alipokuja ni siku tatu, tangu siku tatu alipokuja. *I have not seen him since*, sikumwona tena. *Since last year*, tangu mwaka jana. *Ever since*, tangu siku ile.

sincere, *a.* -a kweli, -enye moyo mweupe, safi, amini, -nyofu. **sincerely**, *adv.* kwa kweli, kwa moyo. **sincerity**, *n.* weupe, unyofu, uaminifu, amini, ukweli, kuwa *sincere*.

sinecure, *n.* uchumi pasipo kazi, faida tupu, kujikalia.

sine qua non, *n.* kanuni hasa, sharti, jambo la lazima.

sinew, *n.* kano, mshipa. *Sinews*, mishipa ya nguvu. *The sinews of war*, zana za vita. **sinewy**, *a.* -a *sinew*, kama *sinew*; (*strong*) -a nguvu, -enye maungo, hodari, -shupavu.

sinful, *a.*, **sinfulness**, *n.* taz. *sin.*

sing, *v.i.* (*p.t.* **sang**, *pf.t.* **sung**) imba, ghani, lia, vuma, simulia kwa utenzi (kwa mashairi); (*rejoice*) shangilia, furahi. **singer**, *n.* mwimbaji; (*professional*) mghani, malenga, manju. **singing**, *n. and a.* kuimba, uimbaji, -a kuimba. **singing-master**, *n.* fundi wa kufundisha nyimbo, mwalimu wa uimbaji. **singsong**, *n.* uvumi, kuimba vibaya, kukokoteza sauti; (*impromtu concert*) jamii ya watu waliokutanika kujiimbia.

singe, *v.t.* unguza, choma; (*become singed*) ungua.

singer, *n.*, **singing**, *n. and a.*, **singing-master**, *n.* taz. *sing.*

single, *a.* -moja, -moja tu, peke yake (yao *&c.*) pasipo mwenzi, -a mtu mmoja tu; (*unmarried man*) siooa, bila mke, -jane, -seja; (*woman*) -sioolewa, bila mume, -jane; (*sincere*) -sio na hila, -eupe, -nyofu, amini. *Single combat*, pigano la watu wawili. *Walk in single file*, fuatana mmoja mmoja (sanjari). — *v.t.* (*out*) chagua, teua, pambanua, twaa -moja, bagua, dhihirisha. **single-handed**, *a.* peke yake (yangu *&c.*). — *adv.* bila msaada, bila kusaidiwa, peke yake (yangu *&c.*). **single-hearted**, **single-minded**, *a.* amini, -nyofu, -eupe, -enye moyo mweupe, -enye nia safi, -a nia moja tu. **singleness**, *n.* kuwa -moja, upweke, umoja; (*sincerity*) unyofu, weupe, amini. **singlestick**, *n.* fimbo ya kupigania, gongo. **singlet**, *n.* fulana. **singly**, *adv.* -moja -moja, kila mtu peke yake, bila mwenzi (msaidizi). pekee.

singsong, *n.* taz. *sing.*

singular, *a.* -a ajabu, -sio -a kawaida, -sio -a desturi, -sio na kifani, -a peke yake, -geni, -a shani, -a kuhusu -moja. — *n.* (*in grammar*) jumla ya umoja. **singularity**, *n.* ajabu, ugeni; (*solitariness*) upweke, umoja. **singularly**, *adv.* kabisa, sana, hasa, ajabu.

sinister, *a.* -baya, -ovu, -a kuogofya, -a kutisha, -a kisirani, -a ndege mbaya, -a shari.

sink, *v.t.* (*p.t.* **sank**, *pf.t.* **sunk**) zamisha, tosa, didimisha; (*in mud*) topeza; (*lessen*) punguza; (*overwhelm*) angamiza, poteza; (*reduce*) shusha, punguza; (*dig*) chimba, fukua; (*conceal &c.*) setiri, ficha, funika; — *v.i.* (*become submerged*) zama, tota, didimia, zizimia, shuka (telemka) chini; (*in mud*) topea; (*of floor*) titia, bonyea; (*be overcome*) lemewa, shindwa; (*lessen*) pungua, punguka, chakaa, legea; (*penetrate*) nywewa, penya, ingia moyoni; (*slope, fall away*) inama, telemka, shuka; (*abate*) tulia, pungua. *Form a sinking fund*, weka mali ya kupunguzia deni. — *n.* mfereji wa (birika la, shimo la) taka; bakuli la kuoshea vyombo vya kupikia na sahani. **sinker**, *n.* chubwi, timazi, bildi.

sinless, *a.*, **sinlessness**, *n.*, **sinner**, *n.* taz. *sin.*

sinuous, *a.* -enye mapindi, -a kuzingazinga, -a mizingo, -a kupindapinda, -a kubetabeta, -a kuzingamana. **sinuosity**, *n.* kuwa na mapindi, mapindi, mizingo, kubetabeta.

sip, *v.t.* konga, -nywa kidogo kidogo, onja (maji, au kitu cha maji). — *n.* kionjo (cha maji au kitu cha maji).

siphon, *n.* kama *pipe* (mrija, neli, bomba, mwanzi) iliyopindika ya kuvutia maji; (*of insects &c.*) pua, mdomo; (*bottle*) chupa (ya *soda &c.*) yenye mrija ndani yake na kipande cha kubonyezea ili kutoa maji yaliyomo.

sir, *n.* bwana, hababi, maulana. **sire**, *n.* bwana, maulana (= *Your Majesty*, taz. *majesty*); (*of animals*) mnyama dume mzazi. **sirrah!** *n.* (zamani) neno la kumtaja mtu kwa ukali (kwa kumshutumu), mbaya wee! mlaghai!

siren, *n.* mwanamke avutaye kwa uzuri (kwa madaha, kwa ujanja), mbembe.; (*hooter*) paipu.

sirloin, *n.* nyama ya ng'ombe ya kiunoni, sarara.

sirocco, *n.* upepo wa hari sana pande za Italia.

sirrah! *n.* taz. *sir*.

sisal, *n.* (*plant*) mkonge, mkatani; (*fibre*) ukonge, katani.

sister, *n.* ndugu mke, dada; (*if addressed or spoken of by brother*) umbu; (*of same kind*) sawa, mwenzi, mfano; (*by profession*) mwanamke mtawa wa chama kitakatifu, sista. *Sister-in-law*, shemeji, wifi. *Foster-sister*, ndugu wa kunyonya. **sisterhood**, *n.* kuwa *sister*; chama kitakatifu cha wanawake watawa. **sisterly**, *a.* -a *sister*, kama *sister*.

sit, *v.i.* (*p.t. and pf.t.* **sat**) kaa kitako, kaa, keti, jilisi; (*perch*) tua, tulia, tenga; (*have seat, position*) -wa na kiti, -wa na mahali; (*hold meeting*) barizi, kutana, fanya mkutano; (*for portrait*) pigwa picha (sanamu); (*on eggs*) atamia; (*suit*) falia, pendeza; (*on horseback*) panda farasi; (*on one's heels*) chutama, chuchumaa; (*astride*) tagaa. *Sit up* (*in bed &c.*) ondoka; (*at night*) kesha; (*as nurse*) uguza usiku. *Sit up for*, kesha, ngojea (mtu) usiku. *To sit on the fence*, kutokuwa upande huu wala huu (wa wagomvi, wenye daawa &c.). *Sit tight*, shikilia shauri (nia, kusudi). *Cause* (*a fowl*) *to sit*, atamisha, wekea mayai. **sitter**, *n.* mwenye kukaa kitako &c. **sitting**, *n.* kikao; (*session*) baraza, mkutano; (*time of business*) muda wa kukalia kazi. **sitting-room**, *n.* sebule, ukumbi, majilisi, chumba cha kukaa na kuzungumza.

site, *n.* mahali (palipochaguliwa, pa kujengea &c.); (*ground*) kiwanja; (*position*) kikao, mahali. **situate**, **situated**, *a.* -liowekwa, -liosimama, -liopo mahali. *It is situated in Egypt*, iko Misri. *I am rather awkwardly situated*, nimo katika shida kidogo. **situation**, *n.* (*place*) mahali, kikao; (*state*) hali, kikao; (*occupation*) kazi. *Grasp the situation*, fahamu (tambua) mambo yalivyo.

sitter, *n.*, **sitting**, *n.*, **sitting-room**, *n.* taz. *sit*.

situate, **situated**, *a.*, **situation**, *n.* taz. *site*.

six, *n. and a.* sita. *At sixes and sevens*, fujofujo, machafuko. *Six of one and half a dozen of the other*, havina tofauti. **sixpence**, *n.* sarafu ya nusushilingi, senti hamsini. **sixteen**, *n. and a.* sitashara, kumi na sita. **sixteenth**, *n.* sehemu ya kumi na sita, $\frac{1}{16}$. — *a.* -a kumi na sita. **sixth**, *n.* sehemu ya sita, $\frac{1}{6}$. — *a.* -a sita. **sixthly**, *adv.* ya sita. **sixtieth**, *a.* -a sitini. — *n.* sehemu ya sitini, $\frac{1}{60}$. **sixty**, *n. and a.* sitini

size, (1) *n.* (*glue*) sherizi.

size, (2) *n.* ukubwa, kiasi, cheo, kadiri, kipimo. — *v.t.* panga kwa kadiri ya ukubwa. *Size up*, kadiri. *Size up the situation*, fahamu sana mambo yalivyo.

sizzle, *v.i.* chachatika, fanya sauti ya mafuta yanayochemka (au chuma cha moto kuchovya majini); (*as of termites when disturbed*) chata.

skate, (1) *n.* (*fish*) taa.
skate, (2) *n.* chuma cha kufungia viatu cha kuteleza juu ya barafu, kitu chenye vigurudumu vinne cha kufungia viatu cha kutembelea upesi. — *v.i.* enda (teleza) kwa *skate.*
skein, *n.* fungu (fundo) la hariri (uzi &c.).
skeleton, *n.* mifupa (yote jamii ya mwili); (*of house &c.*) miti, majengo, boma; (*of ship &c.*) kiunzi; (*outline*) kielezo, habari kidogo. *A mere skeleton,* gofu la mtu, mgofu, mifupa mitupu. **skeleton-key** *n.* kifunguo (ufunguo wa kufungua kufuli nyingi), king'oe.
sketch, *n.* choro, picha (sanamu) iliyoandikwa kwa kalamu (isiyomalizwa); kielezo, habari kidogo, ufupisho wa habari, muhtasari, madokezo. — *v.t.* andika *sketch,* eleza kwa maneno machache, dokeza. **sketchy,** *a.* -a habari chache, -a kudokeza, kidogo kidogo, ovyo, vivi hivi, hafifu.
skew, *a.* -a mshazari, -a kwenda upande, -a kukingama.
skewer, *n.* kibanzi, kibano, mbano, mshikaki. *Fix on skewer,* tunga kijitini (katika mshikaki, kibanzi &c.).
ski, *n.* ubao mwembamba mrefu wa kufungia mguuni wa kwendea mbio juu ya theluji.
skid, *v.i.* teleza (kama motakaa &c. katika njia yenye matope au maji). — *n.* kipande cha kuwekea chini ya gurudumu la gari kulizuia lisizunguke; kuteleza.
skiff, *n.* mashua nyepesi ndogo nyembamba.
skill, *n.* akili, ustadi, ubingwa, umahiri, welekevu, weledi, werevu. **skilled, skilful,** *a.* stadi, -elekevu. *A skilled workman,* fundi, waria, mstadi, bingwa, mahiri.
skim, *v.t.* engua; (*pass close to*) ambaa, pitia upesi; (*hurry over*) soma kwa haraka, onja, angalia kwa haraka (juujuu). *Skim over,* pitia upesi (juujuu); (*become coated over*) tanda, ganda, juu. **skim-milk,** *n.* maziwa yaliyoenguliwa.
skimp, *v.t.* toa vitu (nguo, chakula, majengo, zana &c.) visivyotosha; nyima, toa kwa unyimivu. **skimped,** *a.* -dogo, -chache, -siyotosha, -embamba.
skin, *n.* ngozi; (*of plants, fruit*) ganda, gome; (*on liquids*) utando, ngozi; (*water-skin*) kiriba. *Diseases of the skin,* mba, manawa, mbalanga. — *v.t.* (*peel*) ambua, papua, menya, (*flay*) chuna; (*fleece, swindle*) kumba mali yote; — *v.i.* fanya ngozi, funika kwa ngozi, tanda. **skin-deep,** *a.* -a juujuu, -a kupenya kidogo tu.
skinflint, *n.* bahili, mwenye choyo sana, kabidhi. **skinny,** *a.* -a ngozi tu, -embamba, -liokonda, -gofu, -a kimbaombao.
skip, *v.i.* rukaruka, randa, chachawa, ruka na kupitisha kamba juu ya kichwa na chini ya miguu, pitia upesi; — *v.t.* (*omit*) acha (sehemu ya kazi, kusoma sehemu ya kitabu &c.); (*skip over*) kiuka, chupa. **skipping-rope,** *n.* kamba ya mchezo wa kurukaruka.
skipper, *n.* nahodha; (*of steamer &c.*) kapiteni.
skipping-rope, *n.* taz. *skip.*
skirmish, *n.* vita vidogo, mapigano madogo, mwanzo wa vita, jaribu, shindano. — *v.i.* pigana kidogo, jaribiana. **skirmisher,** *n.* afanyaye *skirmish,* mtangulizi katika vita (mapigano).
skirt, *n.* upande wa chini wa vazi, upindo; (*woman's dress*) vazi la kike la kuvaa kiunoni mpaka miguu chini, marinda; (*border*) mpaka, ukingo, pambizo. — *v.t.* -wa mpakani (ukingoni) pa, pakana na; (*pass near*) pitia nje, ambaa. **skirting-board,** *n.* ubao unaotambaa ukutani chini.
skit, *n.* kiigo cha kuchekesha.
skittish, *a.* -a kuchezacheza.
skittles, *n.* mchezo wa kujaribu kuangusha vipande (kama chupa za mti) kwa tufe. *Skittles!* mawe!

skulk, *v.i.* jificha (ili kuepuka kazi, hatari), jibanza, kimbia kwa haya (woga), toroka, nyatanyata. **skulker**, *n.* ajifichaye (ili kuepuka kazi &c.), mjificha, mtoro.

skull, *n.* kichwa, fuvu (fuu, bupuru) la kichwa. **skull-cap**, *n.* kofia ndogo ya kugandama na kichwa.

skunk, *n.* mnyama mdogo wa *America* atoaye uvundo mbaya sana, kama cheche au nyegere.

sky, *n.* mbingu, anga, hewa, juu. *Clear sky*, kweupe. *Cloudy sky*, mawingu. **sky-blue**, *n.* samawi, rangi ya samawi. **skylark**, *n.* ndege mdogo arukaye juu sana angani mwenye sauti nzuri. — *v.i.* chezacheza kwa makelele. **skylarking**, *n.* kuchezacheza kwa makelele. **skylight**, *n.* dirisha la darini. **skyline**, *n.* upeo wa macho (mbingu na nchi zinapokutana machoni). **skyscraper**, *n.* nyumba ndefu sana yenye orofa nyingi. **skyward(s)**, *adv.* juu sana.

slab, *n.* ubamba *e.g.* wa jiwe, ubao, nyama &c., bamba, kibamba.

slack, *a.* (*idle, lazy*) -legevu, -tepetevu, -zembe, -vivu; (*loose*) -liolegea, -legevu; (*listless, weak*) dhaifu, -nyong'onyevu; (*slow*) si -epesi. *Business is slack*, hakuna kazi, kazi imepungua, hakuna biashara. — *n.* sehemu iliyolegalega. — *v.t.* legeza, punguza, sabili, tuliza; — *v.i.* pungua, punguka, legea, nyong'onyea, ajazi. **slacken**, *v.t. and i.* = *slack*. **slacker**, *n.* mvivu, mzembe. mtepetevu. **slackness**, *n.* ulegevu, utepetevu, uvivu, uzembe, unyong'onyevu, udhaifu, ajizi, uajizi, ukosefu wa kazi (biashara &c.).

slag, *n.* mavi ya chuma (madini &c.).

slain, *p.pt.* ya *slay*.

slake, *v.t.* zima, tuliza, punguza; (*satisfy longing &c.*) ridhisha, timiza; (*of lime &c.*) tia maji.

slam, *v.t.* funga (shindika, vugaza, weka, tupa &c.) kwa kishindo. — *v.i.* fungika kwa kishindo. — *n.* mshindo, kishindo.

slander, *n.* masingizio, chongelezo, uzuzi, uchongezi, uchongelezi. — *v.t.* singizia, amba, sema, chongea, aziri. **slanderer**, *n.* mwambi, mwambaji, msingizia, mchongezi, mchongelezi, mzuzi. **slanderous**, *a.* -a *slander*, -chongezi, -zuzi.

slang, *n.* maneno yanayotumika katika usemi ambayo pengine hayahesabiwi kuwa ya ufasaha wala ya kufaa. — *v.t.* karipia vikali, kemea vikali, tukana.

slant, *v.i.* enda upande, inama; — *v.t.* elekeza upande, inama, inamisha. — *n.* kwenda upande &c.; mwinamo, mainamizi. **slanting**, *a.* (*sideways*) -a kwenda upande, -a upande, mshazari, matemo, -a hanamu; (*down, up*) -a kuinama, -a kupanda.

slap, *v.t.* piga kofi, chapa. *Slap down*, weka kwa kishindo. — *n.* kofi. **slap-dash**, *a.* -zembe, -a harara, -a kupurukusha, -purukushani.

slash, *v.t.* tema, katakata; (*scarify*) toja, chanja; (*lash*) chapa. — *n.* mtemo, tojo, chanjo.

slat, *n.* kipande chembamba cha ubapa cha ubao au madini, ubamba mwembamba.

slate, *n.* jiwe la mbamba; (*for writing on*) kibao; (*for roofing*) kigae cha kuezekea; (*colour*) rangi ya kijivu. — *v.t.* ezeka kwa *slates*; (*scold—slang*) kemea, karipia, laumu. **slate-pencil**, *n.* kalamu ya *slate* (ya jiwe). **slating**, *n slates* za kuezekea nyumba; mwezeko wa *slates*; (*scolding = slang*) mkaripio, kemeo, lawama.

slattern, *n.* mwanamke mkoo asiyetengeneza wala kusafisha nyumba yake wala nguo zake. **slatternly**, *a.* -chafu.

slaughter, *v.t.* chinja, ua -ingi, ua bure. — *n.* (*of animals*) kuchinja, machinjo; (*of men*) mauaji. **slaughterer**, *n.* mchinja wanyama. **slaughter-house**, *n.* machinjoni.

slave, *n.* mtumwa, hadimu, mtwana; (*boy*) kitwana; (*girl*) kijakazi;

(*woman*) mjakazi; (*concubine*) suria; (*raw*) mjinga; (*home-born*) mzalia; (*runaway*) mtoro; (*fellow*) mjoli; (*household*) kijoli; (*taken in war*) mateka; (*weak, slavish*) mtu dhaifu, asiye na neno, hana kalima, kama mtumwa. *A slave to drink*, mlevi mtupu. — *v.i.* -wa kama *slave*; fanya kazi nyingi bure, nyingi mno; jisumbulia kazi. **slaver,** *n.* mwuza watu; (*vessel*) chombo cha kuchukulia watumwa. **slavery,** *n.* utumwa, kazi ya lazima. **slave-stick,** *n.* kongwa. **slave-trade,** *n.* biashara ya watumwa. **slave-trader,** *n.* mwuza watu, mfanyi biashara ya watumwa. **slavish,** *a.* -a kitumwa, -nyonge, dhalili.

slaver, *v.i.* dolola (ute, udende, udelele), tona mate. — *n.* mate, ute, udende, udelele, dovuo.

slavery, *n.*, **slave-stick,** *n.*, **slave-trade,** *n.*, **slave-trader,** *n.*, **slavish,** *a.* taz. *slave.*

slay, *v.t.* (*p.t.* **slew,** *pf.t.* **slain**) ua, fisha, chinja. **slayer,** *n.* mwuaji.

sled, sledge, sleigh, *n.* gari la kuteleza chini kwa vyuma, si kwa magurudumu.

sledge-hammer, *n.* nyundo kubwa nzito.

sleek, *a.* (*of hair*) laini, -a kunang'anika, -a kung'aa; (*of person*) -malidadi sana; (*of manner*) laini, -kinaifu, -a kujikinai.

sleep, *n.* usingizi, kulala, kugona, kusinzia. — *v.i.* (*p.t. and pf.t.* **slept**) sinzia, lala usingizi, lala, gona; (*be unused*) -totumika, lala, -wa kimya; (*of a top &c.*) sinzia; (*be dead*) -fa. *Be fit to sleep in*, lalika. *Things to sleep on*, malazi. **sleeper,** *n.* msinzia, mtu anayelala usingizi; (*of railway*) taruma (mti, gogo au chuma cha kuchukulia *rails*). **sleepiness,** *n.* kuwa *sleep*, -wa na usingizi, macho mazito. **sleeping-place,** *n.* malalo, kilalo, kigono. *Sleeping-bag*, fumba. **sleeping-sickness,** *n.* malale. **sleepless,** *a.* -siopata usingizi, pasipo kusinzia, -a kuwa macho. *I was sleepless*, usingizi uliniparama. **sleepwalker,** *n.* atembeaye katika usingizi. **sleepy,** *a.* -enye usingizi, -zito, -enye kulemewa na usingizi, -a kusinzia, -enye lepe.

sleet, *n.* mvua iliyochangamana na theluji.

sleeve, *n.* mkono wa vazi. *Laugh in (up) one's sleeve*, cheka kindanindani, chekelea kwa siri, furahi kwa siri. **sleeveless,** *a.* -sio na *sleeve*, -a kwapa.

sleigh, *n.* = *sled and sledge.*

sleight, *n.* werevu, hila. *Sleight of hand*, kiinimacho, mazingaombwe, mizungu, mauzauza.

slender, *a.* -embamba, -embamba -refu, -a kimbaombao; (*slight, small*) -dogo, -chache, haba. **slenderness,** *n.* wembamba, hali ya kuwa -embamba -refu; (*smallness*) udogo, uchache, uhaba.

slept, *p.t. and pf.t.* ya *sleep.*

sleuth-hound, *n.* mbwa afuataye nyayo za mtu au mnyama kwa kunusa; (*detective*) mpelelezi (polisi), askari kanzu, jasusi.

slew, *p.t.* ya *slay.*

slice, *n.* cheche, ubale, kipande chembamba, *e.g.* kipande cha mkate *&c.*; (*share*) sehemu, hisa, fungu. — *v.t.* kata vipande vyembamba, lenga, buabua, enga, chanyata, checha; (*slice off*) pangua.

slick, *a.* -erevu, -epesi. *I ran slick into it* (*a tree*), nilipambana nao dafurao.

slid, *p.t.* na *pf.t.* ya *slide.*

slide, *v.i.* (*p.t. and pf.t.* **slid**) teleza, nyinyirika, nyiririka, tiririka, pita upesi (rahisi) sana; (*out of hand &c.*) ponyoka, chopoka. *Let things slide*, jitoa katika, acha, toangalia. — *n.* kuteleza, mahali penye utelezi, kitu kinachoteleza; (*for microscope*) kipande cha kioo cha kuwekea kitu cha kutazamiwa; (*of magic lantern*) kioo chenye picha. **slider,** *n.* mtu au kitu kinachoteleza. **slide-rule,** *n.* rula yenye kipande cha kujongezea cha kufanyia hesabu. **sliding-scale,**

n. taratibu ya kupunguza au kuzidisha kodi, mshahara *&c.*, kupatana na hali ilivyo.

slight, *a.* -dogo, -embamba, kidogo, dhaifu, hafifu. — *v.t.* dharau, tweza, tusha, purukusha, turufu, -tojali, pitia. — *n.* mtwezo, dharau, chukizo, tendo lisilompa mtu heshima iliyo stahili yake. **slightly,** *adv.* kidogo. **slightness,** *n.* udogo *&c.*

slim, *a.* -embamba; (*in degree*) -dogo; (*crafty*) -enye hila, -erevu.

slime, *n.* tope la kunata, ute, utelezi. **slimy,** *a.* -a *slime*, -a kuteleza (kwa matope *&c.*).

sling, *v.t.* (*p.t. and pf.t.* **slung**) tupa, vurumisha; (*with a sling*) piga kombeo, tupa kwa kombeo; (*hoist*) inua na kuhamisha (kujongeza, kupakia *&c.*) kwa kamba (silingi, winchi); (*suspend*) tungika. — *n.* kombeo; (*for arm*) kitambaa cha kuchukulia mkono; (*for hoisting &c.*) kamba na vyango vya kutungikia, tanzi, silingi; (*for a gun*) mweleka.

slink, *v.i.* (*p.t.* **slunk,** *pf.t.* **slunk**) nyatanyata, enda kisirisiri (kwa haya, kwa woga, kwa hila), jikunja.

slip, *v.i.* teleza, ponyoka, chopoka, churupuka; (*pass by, into, out of &c.*) pitia, penya kwa siri, ingia kwa nasibu (kwa hila, kwa kosa), toka (ingia) upesi (kwa urahisi, kwa wepesi); (*err*) kosa; (*become unfastened*) legea, funguka; — *v.t.* (*the memory*) pitia, sahauliwa; (*of dogs &c.*) fungulia; (*insert*) penyeza. *Slip on* (*slip off—clothing*), vaa (vua) upesi. *Slip out* (*off, away*), chopoa. *Slip the cable*, tupa (acha) nanga (kamba). *Let slip*, acha, angusha, fungulia. — *n.* kuteleza, kuponyoka *&c.*; (*error*) kosa; (*garment*) vazi la kupwaya linalovalika upesi; (*cover of pillow &c.*) mfuko, foronya; (*of a tree*) mche, kipandikizi; (*young person*) kijana, mtoto; (*small bit*) kipande chembamba; (*leash*) kitanzi; (*in shipbuilding*) mahali pa kuundia meli, merikebu *&c.*; (*where repairs are done*) jahabu. *Give the slip* (*to*), kimbia, toroka, piga chenga. **slip-knot,** *n.* kitanzi. **slipper,** *n.* sapatu, koshi, kiatu chepesi. **slipperiness,** *n.* utelezi. **slippery,** *a.* -enye utelezi, -a kuteleza; (*cunning*) -janja, -erevu, ayari, -laghai. **slipshod,** *a.* -siotengenea, si taratibu, si halisi, -bayabaya, -a ovyo, -a purukushani. **slipway,** *n.* mahali pa kuundia meli, merikebu *&c.*; jahabu.

slit, *v.t.* (*p.t. and p.ft.* **slit**) pasua, kata, tema, chana, atua, lenga; — *v.i.* pasuka, katika, chanika, atuka. — *n.* mpasuko, ufa mdogo, mtai, mfuo, tundu refu jembamba, mwatuko.

slither, *v.i.* telezateleza, nyinyirika.

sliver, *n.* kipande chembamba.

slobber, *v.i.* toa (toka) mate (ute, udende, udelele), dolola. *Slobber over*, sifusifu kiwongo, rairai, fungia kilemba cha ukoka.

sloe, *n.* tunda la Ulaya kama fuu.

slog, *v.t.* piga kwa nguvu (hasa mpira katika mchezo wa *cricket*). *Slog at, Slog away*, fanya (kazi *&c.*) kwa bidii nyingi.

slogan, *n.* wito wa kutiana shime vitani; neno au maneno yanayoweza kukumbukwa kwa urahisi yanayotumika kuvumisha bidhaa *&c.*

sloop, *n.* chombo cha matanga chenye mlingoti mmoja; manowari ndogo.

slop, *n.* maji yaliyomwagika katika kikombe *&c.* *Slops*, maji yaliyotumika kuoshea vyombo, sahani *&c.*; (*liquid food*) uji, maziwa, mchuzi na chakula chepesi cha wagonjwa. — *v.t.* mwaga kwa kutoangalia; — *v.i.* mwagika. **slop-basin,** *n.* bakuli la kumwagia shinda la chai katika vikombe. **slop-pail,** *n.* ndoo ya kumwagia maji machafu (yaliyotumika). **sloppy,** *a.* -a *slops*, majimaji, -a ovyo, -a purukushani; (*sentiment*) -a juujuu, -a uwongo.

slope, *n.* mtelemko, mwinamo, mainamizi, hanamu, kilima; (*of moun-*

tain, hill &c.) mbavu, mtelemko. — *v.t.* fanyiza *slope*, chongoa, fanya mtelemko (mwinamo); — *v.i.* inama, enda chini. **sloping**, *a.* -enye *slope*, -a kuinama, -a mshazari, -a hanamu.

slop-pail, *n.*, **sloppy**, *a.* taz. *slop*.

slops, *n.* (*pl.*) nguo, blanketi, malazi *&c.* ya kibaharia, nguo za kutungua, mtunguo.

slot, *n.* kuo, mfuo, tundu jembamba. *Slot-machine*, kama sanduku (au kabati) inayotoa paketi za sigareti *&c.* sarafu (*penny, sixpence &c.*) ikitiwa katika tundu lake.

sloth, *n.* uvivu, uzembe, ulegevu; (*animal*) mnyama wa *America* kama dubu akaaye mitini. **slothful**, *a.* -vivu, -zembe, -legevu.

slouch, *v.i.* enda (simama, kaa) hali ya kuinama kichwa na kulegeza mabega. — *n.* mwendo wa (kikao cha) kuinama kichwa na kulegeza mabega, mwendo wa kujikokota. *Slouch-hat*, kofia kama tarai.

slough, (1) *n.* bwawa, ziwa la matope mengi, kinamasi.

slough, (2) *n.* (*cast skin*) mavulio, ngozi kavu (ya kuambuka); (*dead tissue*) ngozi au nyama iliyooza itokayo kidonda kinapopona. — *v.t.* ambua, jigeua ngozi; — *v.i.* ambuka ngozi.

sloven, *n.* mkoo, mtu mzembe, mvivu, mchafu, mpurukushani. **slovenliness**, *n.* ukoo, fujofujo, upurukushani. **slovenly**, *a.* -zembe, -chafu, -koo, -a ovyo ovyo, -purukushani.

slow, *a.* -a kwenda polepole, -a kukawia, -zito, -a nyuma, -a kuchelewa, si -epesi. — *v.t.* (*down, up*) punguza mwendo; — *v.i.* punguka mwendo, enda polepole zaidi. **slow-coach**, *n.* mtu mzito (wa mwendo na akili). **slowly**, *adv.* polepole, taratibu, kinyerenyere. **slowness**, *n.* kwenda polepole *&c.*

sludge, *n.* matope yaliyochanganyika na theluji.

slug, *n.* konokono, koa uchi; (*shot*) marisaa kubwa. **sluggard**, *n.* mvivu, mzito, mtepetevu, msinzia, mzembe. **sluggish**, *a.* -vivu, -zito, -a kwenda pole.

sluice, *n.* mfereji, mlango wa maji. — *v.t.* mwagia maji.

slum(s), *n.* mtaa mchafu wa nyumba mbovu na watu wanyonge maskini.

slumber, *v.i.* sinzia, lala; (*be inactive*) kaakaa, jikalia. — *n.* usingizi; kukaakaa.

slump, *v.i.* anguka (punguka, shuka) ghafula. — *n.* mbwago, mshuko wa ghafula wa bei, upunguo, mpunguko wa ghafula wa tamaa ya bidhaa fulani.

slung, *p.t. and pf.t.* ya *sling*.

slunk, *pf.t.* ya *slink*.

slur, *v.t.* kokoteza maneno, ingizana maneno, sema upesi hata maneno si dhahiri; (*pass hastily*) pitia upesi, setiri; (*disgrace*) aibisha, hizi; — *v.i.* kokoteza maneno. — *n.* aibu, fedheha, hizaya, mtwezo, tahayuri.

slush, *n.* matope mepesi, theluji na maji yaliyochangamana; (*drivel*) upuzi, mapayo.

slut, *n.* mkoo, mwanamke mzembe. **sluttish**, *a.* -koo, -zembe, -vivu.

sly, *a.* -janja, -erevu, -enye hila, -danganyifu, -laghai -kakamavu, kalamzi; (*playful*) -a mzaha, -bishi. *On the sly*, kwa siri, kwa maficho. *A sly person*, ayari. **slyly**, *adv.* kwa hila, kwa siri, kwa werevu. **slyness**, *n.* ujanja, werevu, ulaghai, udanganyifu, uayari.

smack, (1) *n.* (*small boat*) chombo kidogo cha kuvulia samaki.

smack, (2) *n.* (*taste*) utamu, ladha; (*little bit*) kidogo. — *v.i.* (*of*) -wa na ladha ya (utamu wa), fanana kidogo na, onyesha kidogo.

smack, (3) *v.t.* piga kofi; (*the lips*) alisha (midomo), lambitia; (*a whip &c.*) alisha, liza. — *n.* kofi, pigo, mwaliko. — *adv.* kwa kishindo, ghafula. **smacking**, *n.* kupiga (kupigwa).

small, *a.* -dogo, -embamba, -fupi, kidogo, dhaifu, hafifu *Look* (*feel*) *small*, ona haya, fedheheka, tahayari, pumbaa. *Small hours,* usiku wa manane mpaka asubuhi. *Small talk,* maongezi, mazungumzo, soga, porojo. — *n.* sehemu iliyo ndogo au nyembamba, hasa: *small of the back,* juu ya kiuno nyuma. **small-arms,** *n.* silaha (hasa bunduki, bastola *&c.*) zinazochukuliwa na askari. **small fry,** *n.* watu wa vivi hivi (wasio na cheo). **smallness,** *n.* udogo, wembamba, ufupi, udhaifu, uhafifu, unyonge. **small-pox,** *n.* ndui.

smart, *v.i.* washa, choma, chochota, cheneta, chonyota; (*feel hurt &c.*) ona uchungu; (*receive punishment*) tiwa adhabu, adhibika. — *n.* kuchoma, kichomi, mchomo, kuwasha, uchungu, ukali. — *a.* (*quick*) hodari, -epesi, -a nguvu, -kali, -a akili; (*of pain*) -a ghafula, -a kuchoma; (*neat &c.*) nadhifu, -malidadi, marini, -pambi, -enye urembo, -limbwende. *A smart young man,* mmalidadi, mbeja, kijana marini. *The smart set,* jamii ya watu wajidhanio ndio viongozi katika habari za nguo na mavazi; (*slang*) wafua uji. **smarten,** *v.t.* himiza, tia bidii; (*make neat, clean up*) katua, kwatua; — *v.i.* amka; **smartly,** *adv.* upesi, hima; kwa akili, kwa wepesi; kwa unadhifu, vizuri; vikali, kwa nguvu. **smartness,** *n.* unadhifu, umalidadi, mangwaji, ulimbwende, urembo; wepesi, uhodari, welekevu, ustadi.

smash, *v.t.* vunja, ponda, seta, banja; (*defeat*) angamiza, haribu, shinda; (*ruin financially*) filisisha; — *v.i.* vunjika, pondeka; (*collide with*) piga, pambana na; (*be ruined financially*) filisika. — *n.* mavunjiko, maangamizi; (*sound*) kishindo; (*trouble*) matata.

smattering, *n.* kidogo.

smear, *n.* waa, doa, mpako, alama, *e.g.* ya mafuta au rangi *&c.* — *v.t.* paka, tia waa (doa, alama, mpako).

smell, *v.t.* (*p.t. and pf.t.* **smelt**) nusa, sikia harufu; (*suspect*) shuku, tuhumu; — *v.i.* toa harufu; (*sweet*) nukia, firidi; (*nasty*) nuka, nuka vibaya, toa uvundo, vunda. *Smell a rat,* shuku hatari (matata, hila *&c.*). *Smell out,* vumbua, fumbua, gundua. — *n.* harufu, manuka; (*sweet*) manukato, kunukia; (*bad*) harufu mbaya, uvundo, ukuba; (*of the body*) gugumu; (*of perspiration under the armpits*) kikwapa, kutuzi; (*of fish*) vumba. **smelling-salts,** *n.* dawa ya kunusa.

smelt, (1) *n.* namna ya samaki mdogo.

smelt, (2) *v.t.* choma moto mawe kutoa madini, yeyusha mawe yenye madini, yeyusha.

smile, *v.i.* cheka, chekelea (bila kutoa sauti), kunjua uso (kwa furaha *&c.*). *Smile on,* pendelea. — *n.* kicheko, cheko (bila sauti); (*favour*) upendeleo. **smiling,** *a.* -a kuchekelea, -a kukunjua uso, -kunjufu -a uso; (*cheerful, prosperous &c.*) -a neema, -a amani, -tulivu.

smirch, *v.t.* chafua, tia uchafu (waa); (*a person's name*) tusha, haribu jina (sifa). — *n.* waa, doa.

smirk, *v.i.* kunja (finya) midomo kuonyesha ukinaifu (kujitoshelea, kujiridhia), chekelea kipumbavu (kijinga, kiwongo, ovyo). — *n.* kicheko cha kipumbavu (kijinga, kiwongo, cha kuonyesha ukinaifu *&c.*).

smite, *v.t.* (*p.t.* **smote,** *pf.t.* **smitten**) piga sana (kwa nguvu); (defeat) shinda; (*kill*) ua; (*affect the senses*) choma. *Smitten with,* penda sana.

smith, *n.* mfua madini, mhunzi, fundi wa madini. *Blacksmith,* mhunzi. *Silver-, goldsmith,* sonara. **smithy,** *n.* kiwanda cha mhunzi (mfua chuma).

smithereens, *n.* vipande vipande vidogovidogo, vigereng'enza.

smithy, *n.* taz. *smith.*

smitten, *pf.t.* ya *smite.*

smock, smock-frock, *n.* vazi kama kanzu fupi, gwanda.

smoke, *n.* moshi, mvuke; (*with pipe*) kuvuta tumbako. — *v.t.* kausha (samaki, nyama &c.) kwa moshi ili isiharibike; (*disinfect*) fukiza moshi (kiberiti, uvumba &c.) ili kuharibu vijidudu vya ugonjwa (*expel by smoke*) fukuza kwa moshi; (*with pipe*) vuta tumbako (kwa kiko, mtemba, buruma &c.); — *v.i.* (*emit*) toa (foka, toka) moshi; (*a pipe &c.*) vuta tumbako (kiko, sigareti &c.). **smokeless,** *a.* pasipo moshi, -siotoa moshi. **smoker,** *n.* mvuta tumbako; (*compartment*) behewa inamoruhusiwa kuvuta tumbako. **smoke-screen,** *n.* moshi mwingi (wingu la moshi) wa kuficha manowari (askari &c.) vitani. **smoke-stack,** *n.* dohani, bomba la moshi. **smokiness,** *n.* kuwa na moshi. **smoky,** *a.* -a moshi, -enye moshi mwingi, kama moshi.

smooth, *a.* laini, -ororo, sawa (bila mawimbi, matuta, miinuko, mabonde &c.); (*easy, gentle*) rahisi, taratibu, -pole; (*of water*) -tulivu; (*flattering*) -a kujipendekeza, -a kupendeza, -a kurairai; (*glossy*) -a kung'aa; (*of polished or oiled surface*) -a kuteleza, -a kunang'anika; (*of taste*) laini, si -chungu, si -kali. — *v.t.* fanya *smooth,* tandaza, lainisha &c.; (*make easy*) rahisisha, ondoa shida (vizuizi &c.); (*quiet*) tuliza, punguza; (*of wood*) lainisha; (*with a plane*) piga randa; (*with sandpaper &c.*) piga msasa; (*of a mud wall*) rashia, sirima, sisima; (*with a flat iron*) piga pasi. **smoothing-iron,** *n.* pasi. **smoothing-plane,** *n.* randa ya kulainishia. **smoothly,** *adv.* laini, bila kukwaruza, pole, bila shida (taabu, matata, vizuizi &c.), **smoothness,** *n.* ulaini, usawa. urahisi, upole, &c.

smote, *p.t.* ya *smite.*

smother, *v.t.* songa roho, songa, nyonga, kaba koo; (*cover wholly*) funika kabisa, gubika; (*hide*) ficha, setiri; (*fire &c.*) zima kwa kufunika na majivu &c.; — *v.i.* (*feel choked*) songwa roho, songwa.

smoulder, *v.i.* waka na kutoka moshi (si moto); (*be inactive*) sinzia; (*ready to revive*) -wa tayari kuwaka (kuamka, kupata nguvu tena).

smudge, *v.t.* tia waa (doa, alama), chafua (*e.g.* mwandiko wa wino usiokauka bado). — *n.* waa.

smudgy, *a.* -enye waa, -liochafuliwa.

smug, *a.* -a kujikinai, -a kinaya, -a kupendezwa sana na nafsi.

smuggle, *v.t.* ingiza au kutoa bidhaa katika nchi bila kulipa ushuru upasao, ingiza au kutoa kwa siri. **smuggler,** *n.* mtu aingizaye au kutoa bidhaa katika nchi bila kulipa ushuru upasao (au kwa siri). **smuggling,** *n.* kuingiza au kutoa bidhaa &c. taz. *smuggle.*

smut, *n.* masizi, waa la masizi; (*on plants*) maradhi: mimea hufunikwa na vumbi kama masizi; (*obscene writing &c.*) maandiko (maneno, mazungumzo, hadithi) machafu, yenye matusi. **smutty,** *a.* -enye masizi, -enye mawaa ya masizi, -chafu.

snack, *n.* chakula kidogo cha kuliwa kwa haraka, kumbwe.

snaffle, *n.* lijamu ndogo. — *v.t.* tia *snaffle*; (*steal—slang*) iba, kwepua.

snag, *n.* gogo lililoshika mtoni na kufichika, na kuwa hatari kwa mashua, mitumbwi &c.; (*difficulty &c.*) mgogoro, kizuizi, matata (yasiyotazamiwa, ya ghafula).

snail, *n.* koa, konokono.

snake, *n.* nyoka; (*large*) joka.

snap, *v.t.* vunja; (*twigs &c.*) konyoa, kongonyoa; (*with the teeth*) uma, kata kwa meno; (*a whip &c.*) alisha, liza; (*close with a snap*) funga (fumba) ghafula (kwa sauti ya kualika); — *v.i.* vunjika; (*of rope &c.*) katika; (*click*) alika, data; (*bite at*) ng'akia, toa meno; (*close with a click*) fungwa (fungika) ghafula (kwa kishindo), fumba (fumbika) ghafula (kwa kishindo). *Snap at* (*speak crossly*), katiza, dakiza, tolea maneno makali (ya hasira, ya chuki). *Snap one's fingers at*, dharau, tweza, turufu. *Snap up*, shika (twaa, nunua, nyakua *&c.*) upesi. — *n.* kuvunja (kuvunjika, kukatika) ghafula *&c.*; (*sharp click*) mwaliko; (*game*) mchezo wa karata zenye picha, wa watoto. *Take a snap* (*snapshot*) *of*, piga picha (*photograph*) ghafula ya. *A cold snap*, kipindi cha ghafula cha baridi. **snappish,** *a.* -kali, -a hamaki. **snappy,** *a.* -a chuki, -kali, -a hamaki; (*brisk &c.*) -a kukolea. **snapshot,** *n.* mpigo wa ghafula (wa bunduki); (*photograph*) picha ya kupigwa ghafula.

snare, *n.* mtego, tanzi, shabuka; (*spring*) mtambo; (*in moral sense*) kishawishi, jaribu, hila, madanganyo, ubilisi. — *v.t.* tega, kamata, nasa; vuta, shawishi, bilisi.

snarl, *v.i.* (*of dog &c.*) lia na kutoa meno, toa ukali; (*of human beings*) toa maneno makali, toa ukali.

snatch, *v.t.* (*take by force*) nyakua, chopoa, pokonya, bwakua, kwepua, nyang'anya; (*take quickly*) kamatia (jipatia, twaa) upesi. — *n.* kunyakua *&c.*, mnyakuo.

sneak, *v.i.* enda kifichifichi (njongwanjongwa, mang'ungumu), nyatanyata, tambaa; (*tell tales*) chongea. — *n.* mwoga, mnyonge, mchongezi, mbukuzi, mbukulia, sakubimbi. **sneaking,** *a.* fichifichi. -nyonge, -a hila; (*secret*) -a siri. *To have a sneaking regard for him*, kumpenda kwa siri (ingawa hastahili kupendwa).

sneer, *v.i.* cheka kidharau, cheka kwa dhihaka, fanya mzaha, tweza, sema kwa dharau. — *n.* cheko la kudharau, dhihaka, neno la dhihaka (la kumtweza mtu), matusi.

sneeze, *v.i.* piga chafya, chemua. *Not to be sneezed at*, si -baya, si -nyonge. — *n.* chafya.

snick, *v.t.* kata (tia) pengo.

snicker, *v.* taz. *snigger*.

sniff, *v.i.* vuta hewa puani, vuta kamasi; (*smell*) nusa. *Sniff at* dharau. *Sniff up*, vuta puani.

snigger, *v.i.* chekelea kipumbavu, chekelea kifichifichi.

snip, *v.t.* kata kwa mkasi. **snippet,** *n.* kipande kidogo.

snipe, *n.* ndege, jamii ya sululu na kitwitwi. — *v.i.* pigia shabaha (piga) maadui mmoja mmoja kutoka mafichoni (maoteo). **sniper,** *n.* askari mstadi wa shabaha awapigaye maadui mmoja mmoja kutoka mafichoni.

snippet, *n.* taz. *snip*.

snivel, *v.i.* toka kamasi, vutavuta kamasi, lia na huku kutoka kamasi, lialia (kama mtoto mwoga), nung'unika kwa sauti ya kulialia.

snob, *n.* mtu ajipaye makuu, kipenda wakuu (ukuu, utajiri, matajiri), ajipendekezaye kwa wakuu na kutojali wadogo.

snooker, *n.* mchezo wa kugonga tufe katika meza.

snooze, *v.i.* sinzia, lala usingizi muda mfupi. — *n.* usingizi wa muda mfupi.

snore, *v.i.* koroma (usingizini, korota, forota. — *n.* kukoroma, mkoromo, koromo.

snort, *v.i.* koroma (mnyama), fanya sauti kubwa kwa kuvuta (au kutoa) pumzi puani.

snout, *n.* pua (ya mnyama).

snow, *n.* theluji (umande uliogandamana kwa baridi, mvua kama machicha ya nazi). — *v.i.* -nya theluji. **snowball,** *n.* tufe (bonge) la theluji. **snow-blindness,** *n.* kupofuka kwa mng'ao wa theluji. **snow-cap,** *n.* theluji juu ya kilele cha mlima. **snow-drift,** *n.* chungu ya theluji iliyokumbwa na upepo. **snowdrop,** *n.* ua dogo jeupe. **snowflake,** *n.* kidogo cha theluji kama nyoya dogo. **snow-line,** *n.* mahali mlimani ambapo juu yake theluji haiyeyuki daima. **snow-plough,** *n.* gari la kuondoshea theluji njiani. **snowy,** *a.* -a theluji, kama theluji, -eupe sana.

snub, *v.t.* vunja, puza, nyamazisha kwa dharau; (*by interrupting*) katiza, dakiza; (*check*) zuia. — *a. A snub nose*, pua fupi.

snuff, (1) *v.t.* (*a candle*) kata sehemu ya utambi (wa mshumaa) iliyo-ungua; (*extinguish*) zima.

snuff, (2) *n.* tumbako ya kunusa, ugolo. — *v.i.* vuta hewa (tumbako) puani, nusanusa. **snuff-box**, *n.* tabakelo, kijamanda (kijaluba) cha tumbako ya kunusa. **snuffle**, *v.i.* vuta hewa puani, vutavuta kamasi; semea puani. — *n.* kuvutavuta puani (hewa au kamasi); usemi wa puani (wa kipua). **snuffy**, *a.* -enye (kama) tumbako ya kunusa; (*cross*) -a hasira, -a hamaki, -a kasirani.

snug, *a.* -a raha, -a mustarehe, -a kulindwa na baridi (udhia, masumbuo), -a kufichwa; (*neatly arranged &c.*) -a kutengenea, -a kutengeneka, -a kukaa vizuri. **snuggle**, *v.i.* lala karibu sana na (au katika) kwa raha, vamia.

so, *adv. and conj.* (*thus*) hivi, vivi hivi, kadhalika; (*therefore*) kwa hiyo, hivyo, basi; (*very much*) sana. *So that, so . . . that, So . . . as to, So as to* (*of consequence*) hata; (*of purpose*) kwa jinsi, kusudi. *So far as,* kadiri ya, hata. *So-and-so,* fulani. *So so,* vivi hivi, kidogo. *So to speak,* kama hivi, kunradhi nikisema hivi. *Or so,* kadiri ya, kama.

soak, *v.t.* tia maji, nywesha maji, chovya, bambika, lowesha; — *v.i.* lowa, lowama, loweka. *Soak up,* -nywa. **soaked**, *a.* (*soaking wet*) chepechepe, majimaji, -a kulowa.

so-and-so, *n.* taz. *so.*

soap, *n.* sabuni. *Soft soap,* namna ya sabuni nyororo sana; (*flattery*) kusifusifu, kurairai. — *v.t.* tia sabuni. **soap-berry**, *n.* (*tree*) mmwaka, mharita; (*berries*) harita. **soapy**, *a.* -a sabuni, kama sabuni; (*flattering*) -a kujipendekeza, -a kurairai.

soar, *v.i.* ruka juu kwa mabawa, puruka, paa angani; (*of price &c.*) panda upesi.

sob, *v.i.* lia kwa kwikwi (kwa kitefutefu); (*of wind*) vuma kwa sauti ya huzuni. *Sob out,* sema kwa kulia. — *n.* kwikwi ya kulia, kitefutefu, kikwifukwifu.

sober, *a.* -a kiasi, -enye busara, -a makini, -a kujiweza, -tulivu, -taratibu; (*not drunk*) -siolewa, si -levi. — *v.t.* levusha, ondoa ulevi; (*reduce to reasonable state of mind &c.*) tia akili, tuliza. **sobriety**, *n.* kuwa *sober*, kiasi, busara, makini, utulivu, kiasi katika kunywa ulevi (kutolewa).

sobriquet, *n.* msimbo, jina la kupangwa, jina la mzaha; (*assumed name*) jina la kujipa.

soccer, *n.* mchezo wa mpira, futboli.

sociable, *a.* -a utu mwema, -kunjufu, -a kukaribisha watu, -a rafiki wengi, -a kupenda maongezi ya watu, -a maongezi mengi, -a urafiki sana. **social**, *a.* -a watu jamii, -a watu wote, -a watu wao kwa wao; = *sociable*. *Social position,* cheo. *Social interests* (*duties, concerns*) mambo yapasayo watu wote, wanayopasana watu. **socialism**, *n.* kutaka namna zote za kuchuma utajiri, *e.g.* mashamba, viwanda vya kazi, mashimo ya makaa na ya madini *&c.* ziwe mali ya Serikali. **socialist**, *n.* mtu ashikaye shauri la *socialism*. **society**, *n.* watu jamii wakikaa pamoja na kutii sheria na desturi, wakisaidiana na kushirikiana katika mambo ya kusitawisha wote; chama, kikoa, umoja au shirika; kundi la watu wenye shauri moja au hali moja; (*in general*) watu, wanadamu, watu wote; (*intercourse*) kukaa pamoja, kuongea, kuongeana, mazungumzo. *Female society,* mazungumzo ya wanawake. *He is fond of society,* apenda kuongea na watu. **sociology** *n.* elimu ya namna ya na maendeleo ya *society*.

sock, *n.* kama mfuko wa kuvaa mguuni chini, kipande kama wayo cha kutia katika kiatu.

socket, *n.* tundu, kitundu (*e.g.* cha jicho).

sod, *n.* bumba la udongo na majani yake.

soda, *n.* magadi. *Soda-water*, maji yaliyotiwa namna ya hewa.
sodden, *a.* chepechepe, majimaji, -liolowama; (*drunken*) -liokunywa sana, -levi sana.
sodomy, *n.* dhambi ya watu wa *Sodom*; kufira, kufirana, kulawiti. **sodomite**, *n.* mfiraji, mlawiti.
sofa, *n.* kitanda (cha kupumzikia mchana).
soft, *a.* -ororo, -teketeke, laini, dabwadabwa, debwedebwe; (*of clay &c.*) -a kinamo; (*spongy*) yavuyavu; (*pleasant*) -a kupendeza, -tamu; (*gentle*) -pole, -anana; (*feeble*) dhaifu; (*foolish*) -jinga, -a akili afkani. *Feel soft*, bopa. *Soft water*, maji ya mvua. **soften**, *v.t.* fanya *soft*, lainisha; (*mitigate*) punguza, fanya rahisi, punguza; (*palliate*) ombea, tetea; — *v.i.* lainika, tulia. **softly**, *adv.* polepole, kwa utulivu, kimya. **softness**, *n.* wororo, uteketeke, upole.
soggy, *a.* chepechepe, -liolowa maji, -liolowana, dabwadabwa, debwedebwe.
soil, *n.* (*earth*) udongo, ardhi; (*heavy*) udongo mzito; (*light, sandy*) udongo mwepesi, tifutifu; (*country*) nchi. *Owner of the soil*, mwenyeji wa shamba. — *v.t.* tia taka, chafua; — *v.i.* chafuka.
soirée, *n.* mkutano wa watu kuzungumza usiku.
sojourn, *v.i.* kaa, shinda. — *n.* kukaa, muda wa kukaa, kikao. **sojourner**, *n.* mgeni, msafiri, mpitaji, mpita njia, si mkazi.
solace, *v.t.* fariji, tuliza, -pa moyo, tumbuiza, burudisha. — *n.* faraja, tumbuizo, kitulizo.
solar, *a.* -a jua. *The solar system*, jua pamoja na dunia na sayari zinazolizunguka.
solar plexus, *n.* jamii ya mishipa ya fahamu iliyoko nyuma ya mfuko wa tumbo.
sold, *p.t. and pf.t.* ya *sell*.
solder, *v.t.* lehemu, unganisha kwa lehamu. — *n.* lehemu, risasi ya kulehemia.
soldier, *n.* askari. **soldierlike**, **soldierly**, *a.* kama askari, -a kustahili askari. **soldiery**, *n.* askari jamii.
sole, (1) *n.* (*of foot*) wayo, chini ya mguu; (*of shoe*) ngozi ya wayo wa kiatu. — *v.t.* pigilia (shonea) ngozi mpya ya wayo.
sole, (2) *n.* (*fish*) namna ya samaki mwembamba mpana.
sole, (3) *a.* -a peke yake (yao *&c.*), -moja tu, pasipo mwenzi. **solely**, *adv.* tu.
solecism, *n.* usemi mkosefu, usemi usio sahihi (usio safi); (*error*) kosa.
solely, *adv.* taz. *sole* (3).
solemn, *a.* -a dini, -a ibada ya Mungu, -a kukumbuka Mungu, -a kustahili dini; (*orderly, reverently*) -pole, taratibu, zito, -a heshima, -chaji, -a kitawa; (*impressive*) -a kutuliza moyo, -a sherehe, -a kutisha. **solemnity**, *n.* (*ceremonial*) kawaida ya dini, ibada; (*reverence*) heshima, taratibu, uzito, ukumbusho wa Mungu, kicho, uchaji; (*impressiveness*) utulizo, sherehe. **solemnization**, *n.* kufanyika kwa jinsi ya dini, kufanya taratibu. **solemnize**, *v.t.* adhimisha, tukuza, fanya kwa heshima; (*impress, awe*) kumbusha habari ya Mungu, tuliza, tisha. **solemnly**, *adv.* kwa heshima (sherehe, kicho, uchaji, utulivu, makini). **solemness**, *n.* hali ya kuwa *solemn*, heshima, uchaji, kicho, sherehe, utulivu, makini.
sol-fa, *n.* utaratibu wa kutumia *do, re, mi &c.*, kwa sauti katika kuimba.
solicit, *v.t.* omba, taka, sihi, tolea haja; (*of woman*) tongoza, bemba, bembeleza. **solicitation**, *n.* kuomba, maombi, haja; (*immoral*) matongozi. **solicitor**, *n.* mwana sheria. **solicitous**, *a.* -enye kutaka, -a kujisumbulia (neno), -angalifu. **solicitude**, *n.* kujisumbua, moyo wa kutaka, mashaka, tamaa.
solid, *a.* (*firm*) yabisi, -kavu, imara, thabiti, madhubuti, -a nguvu; (*massive, compact*) -nene, si wazi

ndani, -zito, -zima, -gumu, -kavu; (*of character*) -amini, -aminifu, thabiti; (*united*) -a umoja. — *n.* kitu kigumu, kishikikacho (si hewa wala maji). **solidarity,** *n.* umoja, kuwa hali moja, kushirikiana wengi (kama kwamba ni mmoja). **solidification,** *n.* kufanyika *solid.* **solidify,** *v.t.* fanya *solid*; (*set hard*) gandamiza; — *v.i.* gandamana, ganda. **solidity, solidness,** *n.* kuwa *solid,* ugumu &c., kugandamana, kufungamana, kushikamana.

soliloquize, *v.* taz. *soliloquy.*

soliloquy, *n.* kusema na nafsi yake (yako &c.), kunena peke yake (yako &c.) **soliloquize,** *v.i.* jizungumza, nena kwa peke yake, sema na nafsi (yake, yako &c.).

solitariness, *n.* taz. *solitary.*

solitary, *a.* -a peke yake, -moja tu, mbali, pasipo watu, -a kukaa peke yake, -kiwa. **solitariness,** *n.* upweke, ukiwa, kitwea; (*singleness*) umoja. **solitude,** *n.* upekee, upweke, kitwea; (*privacy*) faragha; (*uninhabited place*) ukiwa; (*abandoned place*) mahame.

solo, *n.* wimbo wa mtu mmoja peke yake. **soloist,** *n.* mwenye kuimba peke yake.

solstice, *n.* kituo cha jua kufika kusini au kaskazini, kikomo cha jua.

soluble, *a.* -a kuyeyuka, -a kuweza kuyeyushwa. **solubility,** *n.* uwezo wa kuyeyuka (au kuyeyushwa). **solution,** *n.* (*breaking*) kuvunja, kuchanganua; (*by dissolving*) myeyusho; (*dissolved substance*) kitu kilichoyeyuka (au kuyeyushwa) katika maji; (*explanation*) ufumbuzi, maelezo, kufumbua.

solve, *v.t.* (*explain*) eleza, fumbua; (*put an end to*) ondoa, komesha, shinda. **solvable,** *a.* -a kuweza kufumbuliwa, -a kufumbulika. **solvency,** *n.* kuweza kulipa deni; kuweza kuyeyuka. **solvent,** *a.* -a kuyeyusha; (*of debts*) -a kuweza kulipa deni, -enye mali. — *n.* kiyeyushacho. **solver,** *n.* mwenye kueleza au kufumbua.

sombre, *a.* -a giza, -eusi, -zito, -a huzuni, -a majonzi.

some, *a.* baadhi ya, akali ya, -ingine; (*part*) kidogo; (*about*) kama, karibu; (*a certain amount of*) kadiri, -ingi kidogo. *I want some water,* nataka maji. *Some man, some one, some one or other,* mtu, mtu mmoja, sijui nani. *Some of them go, others do not,* wengine huenda, wengine hawaendi; baadhi yao huenda, wengine hawaendi. *Some day,* pana siku, kwa siku moja, sijui lini. **somebody, some one,** *n.* mtu, mtu mmoja; (*person of importance*) mtu mkuu. **somehow,** *adv. Somehow or other,* kwa njia yo yote, kwa vyo vyote, iwezavyo, sijui kwa nini (kwa namna gani). **something,** *n.* kitu, jambo, neno, kitu kimoja, sijui nini; (*thing of importance*) jambo kubwa, jambo la heri. *He is something of a liar,* hasemi kweli sikuzote. *He's a mason or something,* yu mwashi au fundi wa namna nyingine, sijui. — *adv.* kufanana kidogo, kadiri, kweli kweli. *He is something like his father,* amefanana kidogo na baba yake. *It must be something like six o'clock,* haikosi ni kadiri ya (inapata) saa kumi na mbili. *The King was something like a hero,* mfalme alikuwa shujaa kweli kweli. **sometime,** *adv.* pana siku, siku moja, kwa siku yake, iwezapo, sijui lini, tangu hapo. **sometimes,** *adv.* pana siku, pengine pengine, mara kwa mara. **somewhat,** *adv.* kidogo. **somewhere,** *adv.* pana mahali, iwezapo, po pote, sijui wapi.

somersault, *n.* kitwangomba, kupinduka.

something, *n. and adv.,* **sometime,** *adv.,* **sometimes,** *adv.,* **somewhat,** *adv.,* **somewhere,** *adv.* taz. *some.*

somnambulist, *n.* atembeaye katika usingizi. **somnambulism,** *n.* kutembea katika usingizi.

somnolent, *a.* -a usingizi, -a kusinzia,

lepe, -a kutia (kuleta) usingizi.
somnolence, *n.* usingizi, kusinzia, macho mazito.
son, *n.* mwana, kijana, mtoto mume (wa kiume). *My son*, mwanangu. *Son of*, bin, wa, wadi. *Son-in-law*, mkwe. **sonship**, *n.* kuwa mwana, uana.
sonata, *n.* namna ya muziki yenye sehemu tatu au nne kupigwa kwa ala moja au mbili.
song, *n.* wimbo, ghani. **songster**, *n.* mwimbaji (ndege). **songstress**, *n.* mwimbaji wa kike.
sonnet, *n.* utenzi mfupi.
sonorous, *a.* -a kulia wazi, -a sauti kubwa (nene), -a kuvuma sana. **sonorousness**, *n.* kuvuma sana, mvumo, uvumi.
sonship, *n.* taz. *son.*
soon, *adv.* karibu, halafu kidogo, mara, mara moja, bado kidogo, upesi. *As soon as I can*, upesi niwezavyo, mara niwezapo. *As soon*, sawasawa, zaidi, afadhali. *I would just as soon die*, sawasawa kufa, afadhali nife, mimi tayari kufa. *He arrived too soon*, alifika kabla ya wakati uliopasa(uliowekwa).**sooner**, *adv.* kwanza, upesi, mbele, kabla; (*better*) zaidi, afadhali, bora. *I would as soon go*, nataka kwenda, afadhali niende. *No sooner was it done than ...* mara hiyo ilipofanyika.... *We had no sooner arrived than it rained*, kufika tu na mvua kunyesha sawia. *Sooner or later*, hakuna budi.
soot, *n.* masizi, moshi, kaa moshi. **sooty**, *a.* -a *soot*, -a masizi, -eusi sana.
sooth, *n.* kweli. *In sooth*, kweli. **soothsayer**, *n.* mwaguzi, mtabiri, kahini, mnajimu, nabii; (*diviner*) mpiga ramli, mpiga bao. **soothsaying**, *n.* uaguzi, utabiri, ukahini, unajimu, unabii, ramli, kupiga ramli, kupiga bao.
soothe, *v.t.* tuliza, fariji, tumbuiza, liwaza, rid i ha, burudisha. **soothing**, *a.* -a kutuliza, -a kufariji &c.
soothsayer, *n.*, **soothsaying**, *n.* taz. *sooth.*
sooty, *a.* taz. *soot.*
sop, *n.* kitonge kilichochovywa katika mchuzi; (*to pacify*) kitulizo. — *v.t.* chovya katika mchuzi (maziwa &c.); (*drench*) lowesha. **sopping**, *a.* -a kulowa sana. **soppy**, *a.* chepechepe, -teketeke, dabwadabwa, debwedebwe.
sophism, *n.* neno danganyifu, neno la kupendekeza uwongo, hoja ya ovyo. **sophist**, *n.* .ntumia *sophism.* **sophistic, sophistical**, *a.* -a hila, -danganyifu, -a uwongo. **sophisticate**, *v.t.* haribu tabia, potoa, geuza, ghoshi. **sophisticated**, *a.* si -a asili, si -enye tabia (desturi &c.) ya asili, -a malimwengu, -erevu. **sophistication**, *n.* kuharibu tabia &c. **sophistry**, *n.* kutumia *sophism*, maneno ya hila, madanganyo, werevu, uwongo.
soporific, *a.* -a kutia usingizi.
sopping, *a.*, **soppy**, *a.* taz. *sop.*
soprano, *n.* sauti ya juu ya kuimba ya kike au ya mtoto wa kiume.
sorcerer, *n.* mchawi, mlozi. **sorceress**, *n.* kichawi, mchawi wa kike. **sorcery**, *n.* uchawi, ulozi, usihiri, uramali.
sordid, *a.* -nyonge, -baya, hafifu, dhalili. **sordidness**, *n.* unyonge, ubaya. uhafifu, udhalili.
sore, *n.* kidonda, donda, jeraha; (*large, dirty*) banguzi; (*scrofulous*) mti, nyungunyungu; (*small*) kipele, kijeraha; (*venereal*) sekeneko; (*a grudge*) uchungu, undani; (*cause of scandal*) aibu. — *a.* -a kuwasha, -a kuuma; (*sad*) -a huzuni, -a majonzi; (*affronted*) -a uchungu; (*extreme, severe* &c.) sana. — *adv.* sana. **sorely**, *adv.* kwa jinsi ya kuumiza; (*much*) sana. **soreness**, *n.* kuwasha, kuumiza, maumivu; (*resentment*) uchungu.
sorghum, *n.* mtama.
sorrel, (1) *a.* -a rangi ya hudhurungi nyekundu.
sorrel, (2) *n.* namna ya majani machungu.
sorrow, *n.* huzuni, sikitiko, ghamu,

uzito, kibuhuti; (*for loss*) majonzi; (*for offence*) majuto, toba; (*great*) jitimai, simanzi. **sorrowful,** *a.* -enye *sorrow*.

sorry, *a.* -a huzuni (sikitiko, ghamu, uzito, majonzi, majuto, toba, jitimai, simanzi); (*poor, worthless*) hafifu, -nyonge, maskini. *Be sorry for,* sikitikia, hurumia; (*regret*) tubia, jutia.

sort, *n.* jinsi, namna, aina, **babu,** mtindo; (*rank, position*) cheo, daraja, hali. *Of a sort or kind,* (*like*) ki-, -a ki-, *e.g. of a European sort,* -a kizungu, *A sort of,* -nyangalika. *He is out of sorts,* hawezi kidogo. — *v.t.* (*classify*) tenga, pambanua, ainisha, gawanya, pembua; (*arrange*) andika, panga.

sortie, *n.* shambulio la askari waliozingiwa mjini au bomani juu ya adui walio nje.

SOS wito wa meli (merikebu) wa kutaka msaada.

sot, *n.* mlevi. **sottish,** *a.* -levi.

sotto voce, *adv.* kwa sauti ndogo.

sou, *n.* sarafu ndogo, kadiri ya senti tano. *He hasn't a sou,* hana hata senti moja.

sough, *v.i.* vuma (upepo). — *n.* uvumi, mvumo.

sought, *p.t. and pf.t.* ya *seek.*

soul, *n.* roho, moyo nafsi; (*mind*) akili; (*person*) mtu. *Disembodied soul,* kivuli cha roho, pepo. *Poor soul!* maskini! **soulful,** *a.* -a kuamsha moyo, -a kuamsha (kuleta, kuingiza) maono mema. **soulless,** *a.* baridi, -liopooza, -nyonge, -baya, -kavu.

sound, (1) *n.* (*voice &c.*) sauti, mlio; (*cry*) mlio, lio, kilio; (*report*) mshindo, kishindo; (*roar*) uvumi, mvumo; (*shout*) kelele; (*drum*) ngoma, mdundo. — *v.i.* toa *sound,* tumia *sound,* lia, vuma; — *v.t.* liza; (*of trumpet &c.*) piga; (*spread abroad*) tangaza, vumisha. *Sound a retreat,* amuru (kwa panda au buruji) kurudi. *Sound the praises of,* sifu wazi, tangaza sifa za. *Sound hollow,* lia wazi. *It sounds nice,* tamu kusikia, yavuma. *Sound like,* -wa kama, fanana na. **sounding,** *a.* -a kulia, -a kuvuma, -a fahari.

sound, (2) *a.* (*complete*) -zima, kamili, timamu; (*correct*) halisi, sahihi; (*true*) -a kweli, -a hakika; (*firm*) thabiti, imara, madhubuti; (*trustworthy*) amini, -aminifu, -nyofu; (*strong*) -a nguvu; (*sagacious*) -a akili, -a busara. *He is a man of sound judgement,* ana busara, ana akili njema. *Sound sleep,* usingizi mzito. *A sound beating,* kupiga sana. *Sound in health,* -zima, -enye afya. *Safe and sound,* salama salimini. **soundly,** *adv.* sana, kwa nguvu.

sound, (3) *n.* (*strait*) mlangobahari. — *v.t.* (*ascertain depth*) tia bildi, pima maji kwa bildi; (*test, prove*) jaribia moyo, hakikia shauri, hoji, dadisi, tazamia hali, pima. **sounding,** *n.* *Take soundings,* pima urefu wa maji kwa bildi.

sounding, *a.* taz. *sound* (1), *n.* taz. *sound* (3).

soundly, *adv.* taz. *sound* (2).

soup, *n.* mchuzi.

sour, *a.* -chungu, -kali, -a chachu; (*of temper &c.*) -chungu, -a kasirani, -a chuki, -a kuchacha. — *v.t.* fanya kuwa *sour*; (*spoil*) haribu (tabia &c.) — *v.i.* haribika, chacha, chachuka. **sourly,** *adv.* kwa uchungu (kasirani, chuki). **sourness,** *n.* ukali, uchungu, kasirani, chuki. **sour-sop,** *n.* stafeli, topetope, tomoko.

source, *n.* asili, chimbuko, mwanzo, chanzo, awali; (*of river*) chemchemi.

sourly, *adv.*, **sourness,** *n.*, **soursop,** *n.* taz. *sour.*

souse, *v.t.* chovyachovya, mwagia maji mengi, suza, lowesha, bambika; (*pickle*) loweka katika maji ya chumvi (-siharibike).

south, *n.* kusini, suheli. *South wind,* kusi. *The South,* upande wa kusini, nchi za kusini. — *a.* -a kusini, -a upande wa kusini. — *adv.* kwa kusini. **south-east,** *n.* mashariki ya kusini, akrab matlai. **southerly, southern, southward,** *a.* -a kusini,

-a upande wa kusini. *Southern Cross*, nyota nne za kusini mfano wa msalaba. **south-west**, *a.* magharibi ya kusini, akrab magharibi.

souvenir, *n.* ukumbusho, kumbukumbu; (*of lover*) hiba.

sovereign, *n.* mwenye enzi, mwenye nchi, mfalme; (*coin*) pauni, sarafu ya dhahabu ya kiingereza, thamani yake shilingi ishirini. — *a.* -enye enzi (ezi, hukumu, mamlaka, utawala); (*efficacious &c.*) bora, -a nguvu. **sovereignty**, *n.* enzi, ezi, hukumu, mamlaka, utawala.

sow, (1) *n.* nguruwe jike.

sow, (2) *v.t.* (*pf.t.* **sowed, sown**) panda; (*spread about*) tapanya, eneza; (*rice in holes dibbled*) sia. **sower**, *n.* mpanzi. **sowing**, *n.* mpando, majira ya kupanda.

spa, *n.* chemchemi ya maji yafaayo kama dawa; mji wenye *spa*.

space, *n.* (*room*) nafasi, mahali patupu (pa wazi), mahali; (*open*) uwanda, peupe; (*of time*) muda, muhula, majira; (*interval, distance*) urefu wa kati, mahali pa kati, kitambo, nafasi; (*opportunity*) njia, chimbuko, nafasi. — *v.t.* panga kwa jinsi ya kuacha nafasi kati. **spacing**, *n.* jinsi ya (tendo la) kupanga na kuacha nafasi kati; nafasi kati ya maneno na mistari katika mwandiko, kupiga chapa *&c.* **spacious**, *a.* -kubwa, -pana, -enye nafasi.

spade, *n.* jembe la kizungu, kolego, sepeto; (*in cards*) shupaza. *Call a spade a spade*, sema wazi, sema kweli. **spade-work**, *n.* kazi yenye taabu.

spaghetti, *n.* tambi, unga wa ngano uliofanyizwa kwa mfano wa chango.

spake, (zamani) *p.t.* ya *speak*.

span, (1) *n.* shibiri, futuri; (*short span*) morita; (*period*) muda, kitambo; (*of bridge &c.*) urefu, eneo, upana; (*arch*) tao; (*pair*) jozi, (farasi, ng'ombe *&c.*) wawili. — *v.t.* pima kwa shibiri; (*encircle*) zungushia, ruka, pita juu ya. **spanner**, *n.* koleo, kibano.

span, (2) *p.t.* ya *spin*.

spangle, *n.* puleki. — *v.t.* pamba kwa puleki, metesha.

spaniel, *n.* namna ya mbwa mwenye manyoya marefu na masikio marefu.

spank, *v.t.* piga kofi. *Spank along*, enda mbio. — *n.* kofi, pigo la kofi. **'spanking**, *n.* makofi (ya adhabu). — *a.* -a kwenda mbio.

spanner, *n.* taz. *span* (1).

spar, (1) *n.* boriti, kombamoyo.

spar, (2) *n.* (*mineral*) namna ya jiwe linalong'aa.

spar, (3) *v.i.* pigana ngumi (konde) kwa mchezo, shindana, bishana.

spare, *a.* (*scanty*) haba, -chache; (*moderate*) kiasi; (*reserved*) -a akiba, -a kuweka, -sio na kazi, -a faragha; (*thin*) -embamba, -liokonda, -a kimbaombao; (*in excess*) -a kuzidi. — *v.t.* totumia, nyima, toa (tumia) kwa unyimivu; (*let off, relieve*) achilia, rehemu, samehe, hurumia, pendelea, pumzisha; (*preserve from*) tosumbua, acha; (*give*) -pa; — *v.i.* toa (tumia) haba (-chache), tumia kiasi tu; (*exercise mercy*) -wa na huruma; (*refrain from*) tofanya (todhuru, toumiza *&c.*). *I will spare you* . . ., sitakusumbua kwa (na) . . . . *Please spare me* . . ., usinisumbue kwa (na) . . . . *Spare oneself*, fanya (kazi *&c.*) polepole. *Not to spare oneself*, jitahidi sana, fanya bidii nyingi. *Be enough and to spare*, tosha na kusalia (kusaza). **sparing**, *a.* -a kiasi, -a kujizuia, -a kutoa -chache, kabidhi, -nyimivu, -wekevu. **sparingly**, *adv.* kwa kiasi, kwa uchache.

spark, *n.* cheche, kimeta; (*small quantity*) kidogo. *A gay spark*, mmalidadi, mbeja, damisi. — *v.i.* toa cheche. **sparkle**, *v.i.* metameta, memetuka; (*effervesce*) chemka. **sparkling**, *a.* -a kumetameta, -a kumemetuka; (*of wine &c.*) -navochemka; (*bright*) -angavu, -a kung'aa; (*clever*) -a akili, -zuri sana.

sparrow, *n.* (*Java*) zawaridi; shorewanda; (*Southern grey-headed*) jurawa.

sparse, *a.* haba, -chache, kidogo, mbalimbali, huko na huko. **sparseness**, *n.* uchache, kuwa haba *&c.*

Spartan, *a.* -a nguvu, -a stahimilivu, bila anasa.

spasm, *n.* pindi, kipindi, mpindano, mshtuko, mshindo; (*fit*) kifafa; (*sudden effort*) jaribu la mara moja, bidii ya ghafula, mkazo. **spasmodic**, *a.* -a *spasm*, -a ghafula, -a kukaza.

spat, *p.t.* ya *spit*.

spate, *n.* furiko. *The river is in spate*, mto umefurika.

spatter, *v.t.* tapanya, tupilia (tope *&c.*), nyunyiza; — *v.i.* (*fall*) -nya matone matone.

spatula, *n.* kisu kipana cha kufanyia dawa.

spavin, *n.* ugonjwa wa farasi kuvimba mguuni.

spawn, *n.* mayai ya samaki au chura; (*progeny*) mazao. — *v.t. and i.* toa mayai, zaa.

speak, *v.t.* (*p.t.* **spoke**, *pf.t.* **spoken**) nena; (*say*) sema; (*make known*) tangaza, onyesha, dhihirisha; — *v.i.* sema, nena; (*pronounce*) tamka; (*make a speech*) toa maneno, hubiri wazi, waadhi. *Speak about*, nenea, zungumza habari za, ongea habari za. *Speak against*, amba, sema. *Speak on behalf of* (*against*) tetea. *Speak English*, sema Kiingereza. *Speak badly* (*languages*) goteza maneno; (*with a lisp*) sema kitembe (na kitata); (*with a drawl*) kokoteza maneno; (*with a stutter*) sema kigugumizi, kikisa, gugumia, gugumiza. *Speak distinctly*, pambazua, sema kiada. *Speak haughtily*, deka. *Speak out*, sema sana. *Speak to* (*with*), sema na, zungumza na, ongea na. *Speak volumes*, shuhudia sana. *Speak well for*, shuhudia mazuri. *Speak with energy, excitement*, teta. *Not to speak*, nyamaa, nyamaza. *Nothing to speak of*, kama si kitu, kidogo kidogo. *Not to speak of* (*far from, only, much more than*), licha ya, sembuse. **speaker**, *n.* mnenaji, mwenye kusema; (*in Parliament*) mkuu wa kiti wa *House of Commons*. **speaking**, *n.* kunena, kusema *&c.* *Evil-speaking*, matukano, masingizio. — *a. Speaking acquaintance*, urafiki kidogo. *Be on speaking terms*, juana kidogo. *A speaking likeness*, mfano halisi. *A speaking trumpet*, kama panda (pembe) ya kunenea ya kuongeza sauti. **speech**, *n.* maneno, kunena, uneni; (*mode of speaking*) msemo, usemi; (*language*) lugha, maneno; (*in public*) hotuba, mahubiri, mauidha, malumbo, maneno. *Have the power of speech*, weza kunena. *Make a speech*, toa maneno, hubiri wazi, hutubu, toa hotuba, lumba, waadhi. **speechify**, *v.i.* toa maneno mengi, piga domo. **speechless**, *a.* -sioweza kunena (kwa haya, fadhaa, hofu *&c.*), (*dumb*) bubu. *Be speechless*, (*dumb*) -wa bubu; (*from surprise &c.*) shangaa, pumbaa, duwaa. **spokesman**, *n.* mnenaji, mkuu.

spear, *n.* mkuki, fumo; (*light*) sagai; (*of wood*) mhoro, mrembe; (*shaft*) wano, uti. **spearman**, *n.* askari (mtu) mwenye mkuki.

special, *a.* **specialism**, *n.*, **specialist**, *n.*, **speciality**, *n.*, **specialization**, *n.*, **specialize**, *v.*, **specially**, *adv.* taz. *species*.

specie, *n.* fedha, sarafu (ya shaba, fedha, dhahabu).

species, *n.* aina, namna, jinsi; (*in science*) jamii ya vitu vyenye namna moja. *A species of cloth*, nguo, kama nguo. **special**, *a.* -a peke yake, -a namna, -a mtindo, -a maana, -moja tu, -sio na kifani, bora sana, muhimu, mahsusi, -a kazi moja hasa; (*definite*) maalum. — *n.* mtu wa (kitu cha) kazi moja (kusudi) maalum. **specialism**, *n.* juhudi (kujifunga) kwa kazi moja maalum, uchunguzi wa elimu (maarifa *&c.*) moja maalum. **specialist**, *n.* mchunguzi wa elimu (maarifa *&c.*) maalum, mwenye maarifa hasa wa jambo (ugonjwa, elimu) moja maalum. **speciality**, *n.* kazi hasa (maalum) ya mtu (aiwezayo kabisa), kuwa *special,* bidhaa hasa ya duka fulani. *This is his speciality,* ndiyo kazi (elimu *&c.*) aiwezayo sana. **specialization,** *n.* uchaguzi, upambanuzi, kuchagua na kuchunguza aina moja ya kazi (elimu *&c.*) maalum. **specialize,** *v.t.* chagua, pambanua, chagua na kuchungua (kufanya) aina moja ya kazi (elimu *&c.*) maalum. **specially,** *adv.* zaidi, sana, halisi, makusudi. *He was specially appointed,* aliwekwa kusudi.

specific, *a.* -a namna yake, -a kutofautisha, -a kuonyesha tofauti; (*precise, clear*) dhahiri, -a kusema wazi, -a kuonyesha halisi. *Specific gravity,* uzani wa kitu fulani kuliko maji. — *n.* dawa halisi ya ugonjwa mmoja. **specification,** *n.* kuonyesha halisi; hati au taarifa yenye habari halisi ya kazi (mambo). **specify,** *v.t.* taja, pambanua, eleza, aini, ainisha. **specimen,** *n.* (*sample*) namna, kiolezo, aina; (*part*) kipande, sehemu, -moja (katika vingi vilivyo sawa).

specious, *a.* -enye uzuri (ubora) wa juujuu tu, -a kuonekana kama kwamba ni -zuri lakini sivyo, -a kujipendekeza, -a kujifanya.

speck, *n.* waa, doa, chembe. *Not a speck,* sio hata kidogo. **speckle,** *n.* doa. **speckled,** *a.* -a madoadoa. **speckless,** *a.* bila waa (doa); safi kabisa.

spectacle, *n.* (*beautiful*) tamasha, jambo la urembo (la shangwe, la sherehe), ajabu; (*fearful*) kioja, kitisho; (*wonderful*) kizushi, shani. **spectacles,** *n.* (*a pair of*) miwani. *Put on spectacles,* pachika miwani. **spectacular,** *a.* -a kutazamisha, -a ajabu, -a tamasha, -a sherehe. **spectator,** *n.* mwenye kuona (kutazama, kuwapo, kuhudhuria); (*eyewitness*) shahidi. *There were many spectators,* watu wengi walihudhuria.

spectre, *n.* kivuli, pepo, kizuka, kioja, shetani. **spectral,** *a.* -a kivuli, kama kivuli.

spectrum, *n.* rangi za upindi wa mvua, nuru iliyogeuzwa kwa kioo kuwa rangi mbalimbali. **spectroscope,** *n.* kioo cha kugeuza nuru iwe rangi mbalimbali.

speculate, *v.i.* (*consider*) fikirifikiri, waza, kisia, kisi, bahatisha; (*invest*) hatirisha (bahatisha) fedha kwa ajili ya faida. **speculation,** *n.* (*conjecture*) kukisi, kisio, kubahatisha; (*reflection*) kufikirifikiri, fikira, mawazo mengi; (*risk in trading*) kuhatirisha (kubahatisha) mali kwa ajili ya faida, bahatisho la fedha kwa ajili ya faida. **speculative,** *a.* -a *speculation,* -a hatari, -a bahati; (*fanciful*) si amali, si kweli, -a kukisia. **speculator,** *n.* mtu wa *speculation.*

sped, *p.t. and pf.t.* ya *speed.*

speech, *n.*, **speechify,** *v.*, **speechless,** *a.* taz. *speak.*

speed, *n.* haraka, kwenda mbio, mbio, mwendo mwepesi, wepesi; (*rate of moving*) mwendo, kadiri ya mwendo (ya kwenda). *At full speed,* upesi iwezekanavyo. — *v.t.* (*p.t. and pf.t.* **sped**) himiza, zidisha mwendo, safirisha vema, endesha upesi; (*prosper*) saidia, fanikisha; — *v.i.* enda upesi (mbio), fanya haraka; (*succeed*) fanikiwa; (*fare*) -wa na hali. *How have you sped?* kumekuwaje? **speedily,** *adv.* hima, kwa haraka, mbio, upesi. **speedometer,** *n.* mtambo wa kupimia mwendo wa motakaa *&c.* **speedy,** *a.* -a haraka, -epesi, -a kwenda (-a kuja) upesi (mbio).

spell, (1) *n.* zamu, kingojo, muda, kipindi.

spell, (2) *n.* (*incantation*) maneno ya kunuizia uchawi, uchawi, usihiri, uramali, tego, ulozi; (*fascination*) mvuto, uwezo wa kushinda (kwa uzuri, ufasaha *&c.*). *Be spellbound,* logwa, pagawa, tendewa; (*fascinated*) pumbaa, duwaa, shangaa, shindwa (na uzuri, ufasaha *&c.*). *Remove a spell,* tegua, agua, eua, adua, sukumiza uchawi (usihiri, uramali, ulozi). — *v.t.* (*p.t. and pf.t.* **spelt**) endeleza, nena (andika) herufi za neno fulani. **spelling,** *n.* kuendeleza (neno, herufi moja moja). **spelling-book,** *n.* kitabu cha kufundishia *spelling.*

spend, *v.t.* (*p.t. and pf.t.* **spent**) toa, tumia, lipa, fanya gharama ya, harijia; (*waste*) poteza; (*time*) pisha, pitisha. **spendthrift,** *n.* mpotevu wa mali, mponda mali, mtu wa gharama nyingi, mbadhiri, mbadhirifu. **spent,** *a.* -liochoka, -liotumiliwa mbali, -liokwisha, -liochakaa, -lioishiwa nguvu, -sio ná nguvu.

sperm, *n.* shahawa, manii. *Sperm-whale,* namna ya nyangumi mwenye *spermaceti* ndani ya kichwa chake. **spermaceti,** *n.* kitu kama nta au mafuta ndani ya kichwa cha namna ya nyangumi. **spermatozoa,** *n. pl.* vijidudu vilivyomo katika shahawa, ndivyo vitiavyo mimba. **sperm-oil,** *n.* mafuta ya kichwani mwa *sperm-whale.*

spew, *v.t. and i.* toa katika kutapika, toa kama kwa kutapika, tapika.

sphere, *n.* mviringo, duara; (*globe*) mfano wa dunia; (*environment, range*) eneo, ulimwengu, mazingia, kitendc, ukazi, hali, mambo, manzili; (*province, work*) mahali, hali, cheo, kazi, shughuli. *Sphere of influence,* pa kufanyia hukumu, pa kuweza, milki. **spherical,** *a.* -a mviringo, -a duara. **spheroid,** *n.* kama mviringo wa yai.

sphinx, *n.* mfano wa mnyama mwenye kichwa cha mwanamke na kiwiliwili cha simba mwenye mabawa.

spice, *n.* kitu kitamu cha kukolezea chakula, *e.g.* basibasi, karafuu, dalasini *&c.,* kiungo cha kunukia; (*small bit*) kidogo. — *v.t.* tia *spice,* tia utamu, koleza, unga. **spicy,** *a.* -a *spice.*

spick and span, *a.* safi, nadhifu.

spider, *n.* buibui. *Spiders' web,* utando wa buibui.

spied, *pt. and pf.t.* ya *spy.*

spigot, *n.* kizibo.

spike, *n.* msumari, mwiba, uma, kitu kilichochongoka; (*of corn &c.*) suke; (*of hoe for fixing into the handle*) msuka. — *v.t.* tia (kongomea, choma) kwa *spike;* (*cannon*) haribu kwa kutia msumari tunduni mwa fataki. **spikenard,** *n.* namna ya mafuta yanayonukia sana. **spiky** *a.* -enye ncha kali, -liochongoka, kama *spike.*

spill, (1) *v.t.* (*p.t. and pf.t.* **spilled, spilt**) mwaga, mimina, kupua; (*overthrow*) poteza, angusha, angamiza; — *v.i.* mwagika, miminika. *It is no good crying over spilt milk,* maji yaliyomwagika hayazoleki, *lit. water which has been spilt cannot be gathered up* (*again*). — *n.* anguko, maangamizi. *Have a spill,* anguka, *e.g.* katika baisikeli *&c.*

spill, (2) *n.* kibahaluli, karatasi ya kuwashia taa *&c.*

spin, *v.t.* (*p.t.* **span,** *p.ft.* **spun**) (*twist*) pota, sokota; (*turn quickly*) zungusha upesi (vuru); (*make thread*) pota (sokota, fanyiza) uzi; — *v.i.* fanya kazi ya kupota (kusokota *&c.*) uzi *&c.;* (*revolve*) zunguka upesi (yuru). *Spin out* (*story*), ongeza mno, kokota, endeleza; (*of time*) pisha, kwa shida, endeleza. *Go for a spin,* enda kutembea (kwa gari, motakaa, baisikeli). **spinning,** *n.* kusokota, msokoto, kupota. — *a.* -a kusokotea, -a kupota, -a kuzungukazunguka. *Spinning top,* pia. **spinning-jenny, spinning-wheel,** *n.* mashine ya kupota (ya kusokotea, ya kufanyizia) nyuzi. **spun,** *a.* -liopotwa, -liosokotwa.

spinach, *n.* mboga kama majani ya mfigili, mayugwa, muhogo, viazi, mchicha, mdewere, kunda, ujaka.

spinal, *a.* taz. *spine.*

spindle, *n.* (*in spinning*) pia; (*axle*) mti wa kati (chuma cha kati) ya gurudumu.

spine, *n.* uti wa mgongo; (*prickle*) mwiba; (*of porcupine*) mcheche. **spinal,** *a.* -a *spine. Spinal column,* uti wa mgongo. **spineless,** *a.* -sio na uti wa mgongo, -sio na miiba;

(*weak-willed &c.*) -oga, -a kusitasita, hafifu. **spinose**, *a.* -a miiba mingi. **spiny**, *a.* -enye miiba; (*difficult*) -a mashaka.

spinet, *n.* namna ya kinanda.

spinney, *n.* mwitu mdogo, kichaka.

spinning, *n.* *and* *a.*, **spinning-jenny**, *n.*, **spinning-wheel**, *n.* taz. *spin.*

spinose, *a.* taz. *spine.*

spinster, *n.* mwanamke mzima asiyeslewa, mwanamwali, mjane (asiyeolewa bado).

spiny, *a.* taz. *spine.*

spiracle, *n.* kitundu cha kuvutia pumzi mdudu.

spire, *n.* mnara uliochongoka juu.

spiral, *a.* -a kuzunguka na kuendelea, mfano wa parafujo (msumari wa hesi) au tundu la konokono.

spirillum, *n.* (*tick*) papasi.

spirit, *n.* roho, nafsi; (*breath*) pumzi; (*ghost*) kivuli, mahoka, pepo; (*ancestral*) mzimu; (*fairy*) kizimwi, zimwi; (*evil spirit*) mzuka, pepo mbaya, shetani, afriti; (*temper*) hali ya moyo, tabia; (*person of character*) mtu wa bidii, mwenye nguvu; (*energy*) moyo wa bidii, juhudi, nguvu; (*meaning*) maana, kusudi, kiini; (*immaterial existence*) uzima pasipo mwili, asili ya uzima; (*intoxicating fluid*) mvinyo, kileo, ulevi, taz. *alcohol*. *The world of spirits*, peponi, kuzimu. *The Holy Spirit*, Roho Mtakatifu. *The spirit of the age*, ulimwengu, hali ya ulimwengu. *Good spirits*, furaha, moyo mwepesi, ukunjufu. *Bad spirits*, huzuni, uzito, majonzi. *Ardent spirits*, mvinyo ya nguvu, kileo. *Rectified spirit*, taz. *alcohol*. *Full of spirits*, -enye furaha sana, -epesi. *Out of spirits*, -enye huzuni, -zito. — *v.t.* (*away, off*) ondoa, chukua, twaa (kwa siri, upesi). **spirited**, *a.* -enye moyo mkuu (mwepesi, wa bidii), -a nguvu, -a utendaji, -tendaji, -enye njia, hodari. *Mean-spirited*, -nyonge, -oga, hafifu. *High spirited*, hodari, -changamfu, -kunjufu. **spiritless**, *a.* pasipo furaha (bidii, moyo mkuu), -nyonge, -zito, -oga, baridi, -tepetevu, -nyong'onyevu. **spirit-level**, *n.* pima la maji. **spiritual**, *a.* -enye asili ya roho, -a roho, -a mambo ya roho; (*religious*) -a kuongoka na Roho Mtakatifu, -takatifu; (*ecclesiastical*) -a Kanisa, -a mambo matakatifu, -a wangoje wa Kanisa. *The spiritual world*, mambo ya peponi (ya kuzimu) **spiritualism**, *n.* imani ya kuwa roho (vivuli) za watu waliokufa hurudi na kujionyesha na kuongea na watu. **spiritualist**, *n.* mtu aaminiye *spiritualism*. **spiritualize**, *v.t.* fanya *spiritual*, ongoza (takasa, eleza) kwa elimu ya rohoni. **spirituous**, *a.* -a mvinyo, -a kulevya.

spirt, *v.i.* toka ghafula kwa nguvu, foka, boboka, bubujika. — *v.t.* toa ghafula kwa nguvu, bubujisha. — *n.* tokeo la ghafula (la moto au maji), mruko, mshindo, bubujiko.

spit, (1) *n.* (*metal*) uma; (*wood*) kibanzi, kibano, mshakiki; (*of land*) fungu. *Toast on a spit*, banika. — *v.t.* penyeza uma, choma, tunga kijitini.

spit, (2) *v.i.* (*p.t.* **spat**, *pf.t.* **spit**) tema, tema mate; (*of cat*) toa ukali; (*of boiling liquid &c.*) bubujika, fokafoka. — *n.* mate; (*of rain*) manyunyu. *He is dead spit of his father*, anamlanda kabisa baba yake, amefanana kabisa na baba yake. **spitfire**, *n.* mtu mwenye maneno makali, mtu wa harara (wa hamaki). **spittle**, *n.* mate; (*chewed tobacco &c., red*) utembe. **spittoon**, *n.* kijungu cha kutemea mate, tasa, kitasa.

spite, *n.* chuki, ukorofi, ubaya, mfundo, inadi, inda, unyeti. *He has a spite against me*, anichukia, anikamia. — *v.t.* tolea chuki *&c.* chokoza, sumbua, dhuru (kwa sababu ya uovu au chuki). *In spite of*, ingawa, ijapokuwa, kwa kushindana na, kwa kukataza, kwa kudharau, kwa kutoangalia, kwa kutojali. *He went in spite of me* (*pain, danger*), alikwenda nisipokubali (asizuiwe na maumivu, asione hatari). *In spite of you,* ijapokuwa hutaki mwenyewe. **spiteful,** *a.* -a *spite,* -a chuki, -korofi, -a mfundo, -a inadi *&c.*

spitfire, *n.*, **spittle,** *n.*, **spittoon,** *n.*, taz. *spit* (2).

splash, *v.t.* rusha, rashia, nyunyizia (maji, matope *&c.*), tupia maji; — *v.i.* (*fly about*) ruka, rukaruka. — *n.* kuruka (maji, matope), kishindo (cha maji yakirushwa); (*spot &c.*) doa, waa, alama.

splay, *a.* -a kwenda upande, -a kutanuka, -a mshazari, -a hanamu. *Splay-footed,* -enye nyayo zilizobenuka sana na kwenda upande.

spleen, *n.* wengu, bandama; (*ill-humour*) chuki, hasira, kasirani. **splenetic,** *a.* -sumbufu, -korofi, -kali, -a kasirani. **splenic,** *a.* -a wengu.

splendid, *a.* (*shining*) -a kung'aa, -angavu, -zuri sana; (*glorious*) bora, -tukufu, -a fahari. **splendidly,** *adv.* vizuri sana. **splendour,** *n.* fahari, uzuri, ubora, utukufu, sherehe, wangavu, mng'ao.

splenetic, *a.*, **splenic,** *a.*, taz. *spleen.*

splice, *v.t.* unganisha (kamba) kwa kuzisokota nyuzi zake, fungamanisha, ganga (mti). — *n.* mwungo (wa kamba), mgango.

splint, *n.* gango, banzi, kitata. — *v.t.* ganga (mfupa uliovunjika).

splinter, *n.* kibanzi, kichane, kipande, chenge; (*of glass &c.*) kigeregenja, kigereng'enza. — *v.t.* vunjavunja, pasua vipande vidogo; — *v.i.* vunjikavunjika, pasuka vipande vidogo.

split, *v.t.* (*p.t. and pf.t.* **split**) pasua, tema, kwanua, mamanua, atua, chenga, chanja, chana; (*cassava &c. for cooking or drying*) lenga; — *v.i.* (*become alienated*) farakana, tengana, achana, gombana; (*inform against*) chongea, chongelea, shuhudia; (*become split*) pasuka, kwanuka, chanika, fanya ufa. *Split the difference,* gawa tofauti, katana, fanya suluhu. *Split (one's sides) with laughing,* cheka sana hata kutoweza kujizuia. *Split up,* gawanya, gawanyika, farakisha, farakana. — *n.* mpasuko, ufa, mwatuko; (*disunion*) mtengano, farakano.

splutter, *v.i.* tematema udelele (udende, mate) katika kusema, tatarika (katika kusema); (*of water &c.*) fokafoka, bubujika.

spoil, *n.* (*of war*) mateka, nyara; (*of a hunt*) mawindo. — *v.t.* (*p.t. and pf.t.* **spoiled, spoilt**) (*plunder*) teka, nyang'anya; (*injure, destroy*) haribu, vunja, dhuru, viza; (*a child*) endekeza, enga, dekeza, tundua; — *v.i.* (*go bad*) oza, haribika. **spoiler,** *n.* mnyang'anyi, mtekaji, mharabu.

spoilt-sport, *n.* mtu mchungu (wa chuki), mwenye inadi (inda).

spoliation, *n.* kuteka, kunyang'anya.

spoke, (1) *n.* (*of wheel*) taruma, kipande cha ndani ya gurudumu; (*of bicycle &c.*) uchukuti, tindi; (*rung of ladder*) kipawa, kipandio, kipago. *Put a spoke in his wheel,* pinga (zuia, haribu) shauri lake.

spoke, (2) *p.t.* **spoken,** *pf.t.*, **spokesman,** *n.* taz. *speak.*

spoliation, *n.* taz. *spoil.*

sponge, *n.* sifongo; (*cadger*) mdoya, mpandiaji, mtu arondeaye. *Throw up the sponge,* kushindwa. — *v.t.* safisha (pangusa) kwa *sponge*; — *v.i.* (*cadge*) doya, rondea, dusa, dusia, pandia, chungulia, doea, buga. *Sponge out,* futa, tangua. **spongy,** *a.* -a yavuyavu, kama *sponge,* -enye vitundu vingi, -enye kunywa maji sana, -ororo.

sponsor, *n.* mdhamini.

spontaneous, *a.* (*voluntary*) -a moyo, -a hiari, -a kutaka -enyewe, si kwa lazima wala ushawishi; (*natural*) -a asili, -a kuja peke yake, -a nguvu yake, -enyewe, si kwa kutendeshwa kazi. **spontaneity,** *n.* kuwa *spontaneous.*

spook, *n.* kivuli, pepo, mzuka, taz. *ghost.*

spool, *n.* kipande cha kuzungushia (kutatia, kukunjia) uzi *&c.*

spoon, *n.* mwiko; (*small*) kijiko; (*wooden*) mkamshi; (*ladle*) upawa. *Table-spoon,* kijiko kikubwa; (*as measure*) kadiri ya, *dessert-spoons* mbili, ya *tea-spoons* nne; (*half ounce*) nusu wakia. **spoonful**, *n.* kadiri ya kijiko kimoja, kidogo.

spoor, *n.* nyayo za mnyama. — *v.i.* fuata nyayo za mnyama.

sporadic, *a.* -a kutokea huko na huko (-moja -moja, pengine pengine).

spore, *n.* mbegu; (*bacteria &c.*) kijidudu.

sporran, *n.* mfuko wa ngozi (unaotundikwa mbele katika ukanda kiunoni).

sport, *n.* mchezo, furaha, tafrija; (*jest &c.*) mzaha, masihara, ubishi; (*hunting*) kuwinda, kupiga wanyama (ndege *&c.*), kusaka, uwindaji, usakaji; (*person*) mtu mnyofu (asiyekasirika akishindwa, ashikaye sheria za michezo *&c.*). *Make sport of,* fanya mzaha, dhihaki, cheka, chezea. — *v.i.* cheza, chezacheza, jifurahisha. **sporting**, *a.* -a *sport*; -jasiri, -a kushika sheria za michezo barabara. *A sporting chance,* bahatisho, jambo la kubahatisha. **sportive**, *a.* -a kuchezacheza, purupuru. **sports**, *n.pl.* michezo, mashindano ya michezo. **sportsman**, *n.* mzoevu wa michezo (wa *sport*), mtu mnyofu ashikaye sana sheria za michezo, mjasiri. **sportsmanlike**, *a.* -a kumstahili (-a kumfaa) *sportsman.* **sportsmanship**, *n.* uwindaji, uchezaji, uzoevu wa *sport*; unyofu, ujasiri.

spot, *n.* waa, kipaku, doa, alama, batobato; (*dot*) nukta; (*position*) mahali padogo, mahali penyewe, pale pale, papa hapa; (*blemish, disgrace*) aibu, athari; (*pimple*) upele, kipele, kidudusi, dutu, chunusi, ukurutu; (*small quantity*) kidogo. *Spot cash,* fedha taslimu, nakidi. *Spot goods,* bidhaa ya fedha taslimu. *On the spot,* pale pale, papo hapo, mara hiyo, ghafula, papo kwa papo. — *v.t.* tia waa, doa *&c.*; (*mar*) chafua, haribu; (*identify &c.*) tambua, ona; — *v.i.* (*become discoloured &c.*) pata madoa *&c.* **spotless**, *a.* pasipo mawaa, -eupe, safi. **spotted**, *a.* -a madoadoa, -a marakaraka. **spotty**, *a.* -enye madoadoa (marakaraka); (*pimply*) -a upele, -a chunusi.

spouse, *n.* (*husband*) mume; (*wife*) mke.

spout, *n.* (*from roof*) kopo la nyumba mlizamu, mrizabu; (*of jug &c.*) mdomo; (*of water &c.*) mfoko wa (bubujiko la) maji *&c.* — *v.i.* toka kwa nguvu (maji, moto *&c.*), ruka, foka, bubujika; — *v.t.* toa kwa nguvu, rusha; (*of speech*) piga, domo nena makuu; (*of whale*) toa moshi.

sprain, *v.t.* tegua, shtusha, gutusha. — *n.* kushtuka, mshtuko, kuteguka.

sprang, *p.t.* ya *spring.*

sprat, *n.* namna ya samaki mdogo wa Ulaya.

sprawl, *v.i.* jinyosha, tandawaa; (*be spread out*) eneaenea, tambaa.

spray, (1) *n.* kitawi.

spray, (2) *n.* povu, marasharasha, manyunyu; (*disinfectant &c.*) dawa ya kunyunyizia; (*device*) mrashi, bomba la kupulizia (la kunyunyizia) dawa *&c.* — *v.t.* nyunyizia, pulizia.

spread, *v.t.* (*p.t. and pf.t.* **spread**) (*extend, scatter*) tawanya, eneza, tapanya; (*by smearing*) paka, pakaa; (*unfold, stretch*) kunjua, nyosha, tanda, tandaza, tandika; (*publish*) eneza, tangaza, vumisha, toa; (*disease*) eneza, ambukiza; — *v.i.* tawanyika, eneā, tapanyika, tandaa; (*of a plain*) tambaa, enea. *Spread a table,* andika chakula, andaa. *Spread out,* kunjua, nyosha; (*intrans.*) funuka, funuliwa, tandaa. — *n.* eneo; (*on table*) maandiko ya vyakula, vyakula vingi. **spread-eagle**, *v.t.* funga (mtu) hali mikono na miguu imenyoshwa na kupanuka.

spree, *n.* mchezo, kucheza.

sprig, *n.* kitawi, kichipuko.

sprightly, *a.* -epesi, -changamfu, -a kucheza, -enye furaha. **sprightliness**, *n.* wepesi, uchangamfu, mchezo, furaha.

spring, *v.i.* (*p.t.* **sprang**, *pf.t.* **sprung**) ruka, chupa, enda (rudi) ghafula, toka (tokea) upesi; (*rise, proceed*) onekana, ondoka, chipuka, toka; (*be elastic*) nyumbuka, pindika. *Spring upon*, rukia. *Spring to one's feet*, ondoka ghafula, simama mara. *Spring a leak*, anza kuvuja maji. — *n.* (*metal*) mtambo; (*of watch, clock*) kamani; (*of water*) chemchemi, jicho la maji; (*leap*) ruko, mruko; (*recoil &c.*) kunyumbuka, kurudi ghafula, kuduta; (*season of growth*) majira ya mwaka kati ya *winter* na *summer*; (*source*) asili, mwanzo, chanzo, chimbuko; (*reason*) sababu, kisa; (*moving power*) nguvu. **spring-balance**, *n.* mizani ya mtambo. **springbok**, *n.* mnyama kama paa. **springe**, *n.* kitanzi, tanzi. **spring-tide**, *n.* maji ya kujaa sana maji makuu, bamvua. **springy**, *a.* -a kuruka; (*elastic*) -a kunyumbuka.

sprinkle, *v.t.* nyunyiza, tia kidogo huko na huko, rasha. *Be sprinkled about*, tapakaa. — *n.* manyunyu, marasharasha. **sprinkler**, *n.* kitu cha kunyunyizia; (*for scent*) mrashi. **sprinkling**, *n.* kidogo (-chache) huko na huko; (*of water &c.*) manyunyu, marasharasha.

sprint, *v.i.* enda mbio iwezekanavyo (kwa mwendo mfupi).

sprite, *n.* kizimwi, jini.

sprocket, *n.* jino (la gurudumu). *Sprocket-wheel*, gurudumu lenye meno na mapengo.

sprout, *v.i.* chipuka, chipua, anza kumea, anza kuota, anza kukua. — *n.* chipuko, kichipuko, chipukizi, uchipuko.

spruce, (1) mti kama msunobari.

spruce, (2) *a.* nadhifu, -a urembo, -a malidadi, -a fahari. *Spruce oneself up*, jikwatua.

sprung, *pf.t.* ya *spring*.

spud, *n.* jembe la kupalilia; (*potato = slang*) kiazi. — *v.t.* palia (chimbua) kwa *spud*.

spue, *v.* taz. *spew*.

spume, *n.* povu.

spun, *a. and pf.t.* taz. *spin*.

spunk, *n.* uhodari; (*hot temper*) kasirani, harara, hamaki. **spunky**, *a.* hodari; (*hot tempered*) -a hasira, -a hamaki, -a harara.

spur, *n.* (*of cock*) kipi, kipia, kikwaru; (*of boot*) kichokoo, mwiba, msumari (wa kuchoma farasi mbavuni); (*projection*) kipande kitokezacho; (*of hills*) kilima mbavuni; (*incitement*) kichocheo, kitu cha (jambo la) kuharakisha (kuvuta, kutamanisha, kuchoma). *On the spur of the moment*, mara moja, ghafula, pasipo kufikiri. — *v.t.* choma (farasi kwa *spur*), endesha upesi (kwa nguvu), sukuma mbele, chochea, amsha, tia chonjo (shonga), chonjomoa.

spurious, *a.* -a uwongo, -a kujifanya, si halisi, -a kuiga.

spurn, *v.t.* sukumia mbali, piga teke; (*reject*) kataa kwa dharau, dharau.

spurt, *v.i.* kaza mbio, fanya kipindi cha nguvu; (*rush out &c.*) taz. *spirt*. — *n.* mkazo (wa mbio, nguvu &c.), kipindi cha bidii (nguvu &c.)

sputter, *v.i.* tematema, fokafoka, bubujika; (*in speaking*) tatarika, babaika. Taz. *splutter*.

sputum, *n.* belghamu, kohozi, kohoo, mate.

spy, *v.t.* (*see*) ona; — *v.i.* (*act as a spy*) peleleza, doea, doya, duhushi, dukiza. *Spy into, examine &c.*, chungua, chunguza, fatiisha, dadisi, pekua, chakura. — *n.* mpelelezi, doria, mdoya, mdadisi, mdunzidunzi, mdukizi, duzi, mjasusi. **spy-glass**, *n.* darubini. **spy-hole**, *n.* kitundu cha kuchungulia.

squabble, *n.* ugomvi, mzozo, bishano. — *v.i.* gombana, bishana, zozana, tetana.

squad, *n.* kunci (dogo la askari au watu wanaofanya kazi pamoja).

squadron, *n.* kikosi cha askari

wapanda farasi; (*naval*) kundi dogo la manowari; (*aeroplanes*) kundi la eroplani kumi na mbili; (*of men*) kundi dogo la watu wanaofanya kazi pamoja. **squadron-leader,** *n.* mkuu wa *squadron.*

squalid, *a.* -chafu, -nyonge, -baya, -koo, dhalili. **squalor,** *n.* uchafu, unyonge, ukoo, ubaya, udhalili.

squall, *n.* (*of wind*) dhoruba, tufani ya ghafula, upepo wa mshindo; (*cry*) kilio cha nguvu. — *v.i.* lia kwa nguvu (kama mtoto akipigwa).

squalor, *n.* taz. **squalid.**

squander, *v.t.* poteza (fuja, ponda, badhiri, tapanya) mali, poteza (wakati &c.), toa (tumia) -ingi bure. **squanderer,** *n.* mpotevu wa mali, mfuja (mponda) mali, mbadhiri, mbadhirifu.

square, *n.* mraba, mfano wa mraba; (*in town*) uwanja mkubwa, mahali peupe kati ya nyumba mjini; (*of soldiers*) kikosi, cha askari katika mpango wa mraba; (*carpenter's*) filifili, kipande cha kupimia pembe ya mraba; (*in arithmetic*) jawabu la hesabu iliyozidishwa kwa yenyewe, *e.g.* 144 ni *square* ya 12. *Square root* ya 144 ni 12. — *a.* -a mraba, -a miraba minne, -enye pembe ya mraba; (*exact*) sawasawa, barabara; (*just, fair*) -nyofu, -adili, -adilifu, -a haki. *Square inch* (*foot*), inchi (futi) ya eneo (yaani mraba ambao kila upande wake ni inchi (futi) moja). *Square measure,* kipimo cha eneo. — *v.t.* fanya mraba (jinsi ya mraba); (*in arithmetic*) zidisha hesabu kwa yenyewe, *e.g.* sita mara sita ni thelathini na sita; (*settle account &c.*) lipa, kata neno; (*make agree*) patanisha, sawazisha, linganisha; (*bribe*) lisha rushwa, penyeza fedha, vuta kwa fedha; — *v.i.* (*harmonize*) patana, lingana. **squareness,** *n.* kuwa mfano wa mraba, kuwa sawa; (*honesty &c.*) unyofu, uadilifu.

squash, *v.t.* ponda, seta, songa. — *n.* kusongana watu, msongesonge, msongamano; (*pulp*) mseto; (*drink*) maji ya ndimu (*lime*), chungwa (*orange*), limau (*lemon*) &c. **squashiness,** *n.* uteketeke. **squashy,** *a.* -teketeke, laini, dabwadabwa, debwedebwe.

squat, *v.i.* (*on heels*) chuchumaa, chutama; (*sit*) kaa kitako, keti; (*settle on land*) tua, hamia. — *a.* -fupi -nene. **squatter,** *n.* mtua (mkaa) mahali bila ruhusa.

squaw, *n.* mwanamke *Indian* wa Amerika.

squawk, *n.* kilio kama cha maumivu au hofu.

squeak, *n.* kweche, kilio chembamba (kama cha panya au bawaba isyiyotiwa mafuta). *I had a narrow squeak,* nilipona kwa shida. — *v.i.* toa *squeak,* lia kweche. **squeaky,** *a.* -a kulialia (kama gurudumu &c. lisilotiwa mafuta), -a kulialia kweche kweche.

squeal, *n.* kilio chembamba kirefu (kama cha paka au mtoto mdogo). — *v.i.* toa *squeal.*

squeamish, *a.* (*fastidious*) -chaguzi, -teuzi, -a kuchaguachagua, -kinaifu; (*easily offended*) -a chuki, -a harara; (*sickened &c.*) -a kuchafuka tumbo, -a kichefuchefu, -a kuona kigagazi; (*very scrupulous*) -epesi kuona mashaka. **squeamishness,** *n.* kuwa *squeamish,* uchaguzi, uteuzi, ukinaifu, chuki, harara, kigagazi, kichefuchefu, wepesi kuona mashaka.

squeeze, *v.t.* (*compress with force*) shindilia, songa, kamua, kaba, kanda, bana, songa, minya, shika sana; (*oppress*) onea, kamia; (*pass with pressure*) pita kwa shida, penyeza, pisha; (*make pay*) lipiza, toza; (*as a stone out of fruit &c.*) pujua, bujua. — *n.* kushindilia &c., msongo, msongomano.

squelch, *v.i.* kanyaga na kuponda (na kugandamiza), fanya kelele kama kwa kukanyagia maji au matope laini; (*disconcert*) fadhaisha, nyamazisha kwa dharau.

squib, *n.* fataki ya karatasi yenye

baruti, ya kuchezea; (*lampoon*) mashairi ya kumfanyia mzaha mtu.
squid, *n.* namna ya pweza.
squiffy, *a.* -a kulewa kidogo (na kileo).
squint, *n.* makengeza, kitongo, upogo. *Have a squint at*, tazama. — *v.i.* -wa na macho ya makengeza, tazama kitongotongo. *Squint at*, tazama, tupia jicho. **squint-eyed**, *a.* -enye macho ya makengeza, -a kitongo.
squire, *n.* mwungwana, mtoto wa watu; mwenyeji wa shamba kubwa.
squirm, *v.i.* jinyonganyonga mwili, gaagaa, furukuta; (*be embarrassed*) fadhaika, tahayari, tahayarika; (*feel dislike &c.*) ona (onyesha) uchungu.
squirrel, *n.* kindi, sindi, kidiri, kuchakulo.
squirt, *v.t. and i.* toa (toka) katika tundu dogo kwa nguvu. — *n.* maji yatokayo kwa nguvu katika tundu dogo, kibomba cha kurusha maji.
St., ufupisho wa *street* na *saint*.
stab, *v.t.* choma (kwa kisu, upanga, mkuki *&c.*); (*slander*) singizia, sengenya, chongelea, chongea; — *v.i.* (*hurt, throb &c.*) choma, uma; (*of boil &c.*) pwita. — *n.* mchomo, kichomi.
stability, *n.*, **stabilize**, *v.* taz. *stable* (1).
stable, (1) *a.* thabiti, imara, hodari, -a nguvu, -gumu, madhubuti, -a aushi, -siobadilika. **stability**, *n.* uthabiti, imara, uhodari, nguvu, ugumu, aushi. **stabilize**, *v.t.* imarisha, thibitisha, kaza.
stable, (2) *n.* (*for cattle*) zizi, boma, chaa; (*for horses*) banda la farasi. **stabling**, *n.* mabanda ya farasi.
staccato, *adv.* kwa jinsi sauti zisivyoingiana (kila sauti na kishindo chake halisi).
stack, *n.* chungu ya majani (kuni, boriti, fito, *&c.*); (*smoke-stack*) dohani, bomba la moshi. — *v.t.* weka (panga) chunguchungu, panganya, lundika, omekeza.
stadium, *n.* uwanja wa michezo uliozungunshiwa viti.
staff, *n.* fimbo; (*heavy*) gongo; (*for old or sick person*) mkongojo; (*of spear &c.*) mti, uti; (*flagstaff*) mlingoti; (*support, stay &c.*) tegemeo, nguzo; (*retinue*) wafuasi (wa mtu mkuu, wa jemadari mkuu), jamii ya wadogo; wasaidizi (wa mkuu); (*music*) mistari mitano na nafasi zilizo katikati ya kuandikia alama za sauti; — *v.t.* tia watu wa kazi. **staff-notation**, *n.* mwandiko wa muziki katika mistari mitano na nafasi zilizo katikati. **staff-work**, *n.* matengenezo, kazi ya wasaidizi na wadogo.
stag, *n.* mnyama dume kama paa mkubwa.
stage, *n.* (*platform*) dungu, ulingo, jukwaa; (*in theatre*) mahali palipoinuka pa wachezaji, mahali pa kufanya tamasha; (*acting as profession*) kazi ya *actor*; (*part, division*) sehemu, fungu; (*end of journey*) kikomo; (*part of journey*) kituo, mwendo wa siku, mwendo; (*degree*) daraja; (*condition*) hali. *Last stage* (*end, finish*) mwisho, aheri. — *v.t.* tengeneza mchezo tayari kuonyesha mbele ya watu. **stage-coach**, *n.* gari kubwa (la kuchukulia abiria). **stage-craft**, *n.* ustadi wa kubuni (kutengeneza) michezo ya *theatre* na mambo yanayohusiana nayo. **stage-fright**, *n.* woga (hofu, haya) anaoona mchezaji au mhubiri aonapo watu waliohudhuria kumtazama (kumsikiliza). **staging**, *n.* jukwaa (la watu wajenga nyumba *&c.*); jinsi ya kuonyesha michezo ya *theatre*.
stagger, *v.t.* shangaza, duwaza, tia bumbuazi, pumbaza, fadhaisha; (*walk unsteadily*) pepesuka, pepa, levyalevya, sitasita; (*totter*) tetereka, tikisika, yumbayumba, yonga, yugayuga; (*from old age with aid of stick*) kongoja; (*from weakness*) jikokota; (*be shocked &c.*) shangaa, pumbaa, fadhaika. — *n.* kulewa, kupepa, uleoleo. **staggering**, *a.* -a kupepa, -a kulewalewa; (*shocking &c.*) -a kushangaza, -a kushtua, -a kushtusha, -a kufadhaisha *&c.*

staging, *n.* taz. *stage.*
stagnate, *v.i.* simama, oza, haribika kwa kukaakaa; (*of person*) legea. **stagnant**, *a.* (*of water*) -liosimama, -fu, -bovu; (*inactive*) -legevu, pasipo mwendo, pasipo kazi, -fu. *Trade is stagnant*, biashara haizidi, hakuna tamaa. **stagnation**, *n.* (*of blood &c.*) vilio, kuoza.
staid, *a.* taratibu, -tulivu, -pole, -a kiasi, -zito.
stain *v.t.* tia mawaa (kipaku, taka); (*colour*) tia (paka) rangi; (*disgrace*) aibisha, haribu; — *v.i.* pata rangi (mawaa, kipaku, taka). — *n.* waa, kipaku, taka; (*disgrace*) aibu, fedheha. **stainless**, *a.* pasipo mawaa, -eupe, safi; (*of steel &c.*) -siopata kutu, -siopata alama.
stair, *n.* daraja. *Stairs, flight of stairs*, madaraja, ngazi. *Upstairs*, juu, darini, orofani. *Downstairs*, chini. **staircase**, **stairway**, *n.* = *stairs.*
stake, *n.* mti, nguzo, kiguzo; (*for tethering*) kigingi; (*the stake*) mti wa kufungia watu wa kuchomwa moto; (*martyrdom*) kufa kwa ajili ya imani ya dini; (*wager*) sharti, fedha ya kuchezewa (ya kubahatishwa); (*share*) sehemu, fungu. *Be at stake*, -wa hatarini, hatirishwa. *His life is at stake*, ni kufa au kupona. *Go to the stake*, enda kuchomwa moto (kwa adhabu, kwa ajili ya dini). — *v.t.* (*venture, risk*) tia hatarini, bahatisha; (*wager*) pigiana masharti ya, wekeana masharti; (*mark by stakes, out, off*) weka vijiti (kuwa alama).
stalactite, *n.* maji yaliyogeuka kuwa jiwe na kujitungika juu pangoni. **stalagmite**, *n.* maji yaliyodondoka chini pangoni yakageuka kuwa jiwe.
stale, *a.* -kuukuu, -liochakaa, -bovu, -nayoanza kuchacha (kuvunda, kuoza); (*trite, dull*) baridi, -a ovyo; (*of body, mind*) -a kulegea, -a kunyong'onyea, -a kuchoka. **staleness**, *n.* kuwa kuukuu *&c*;. unyong'onyevu, ulegevu, uchovu, mavundevunde. **stale-mate**, *n.* hali ya kuwa hapana awezaye kushinda, upinzani, mgogoro.
stalk, (1) *n.* (*stem of tree &c.*) shina; (*of rice &c.*) ubua, bua; (*of fruit, flowers*) kikonyo.
stalk, (2) *v.i.* panua miguu (katika kwenda), tagaa, magamaga, ringa; — *v.t. and i.* (*in hunting*) nyatia, nyemelea, fuatia, nyapa, nyendea, winda. **stalking-horse**, *n.* farasi ambaye nyuma yake mwinda ajificha; (*pretext*) hila, mtego.
stall, *n.* (*stable*) zizi, banda; (*for sale of foods*) kiduka, kibanda cha kuuzia vitu, meza ya kuwekea bidhaa; (*official seat*) kiti cha cheo; (*in theatre*) kiti; (*for finger &c.*) kifuko (cha kuwekea kidole *&c.* kilichoumia). —*v.t.* weka (lisha, nenepesha) zizini; — *v.i.* (*of engine &c.*) simama; (*of aeroplane*) punguka mbio hata haiwezekani kuongozwa. *Stall-keeper*, mchuuzi.
stallion, *n.* farasi dume mzima (asiyehasiwa).
stalwart, *a.* -enye maungo, -enye nguvu, -refu -enye maungo, thabiti, -aminifu. — *n.* mtu mwaminifu.
stamen, *n.* sehemu ya ndani ya ua yenye mbelewele (unga).
stamina, *n.* nguvu, uthabiti, ushupavu.
stammer, *v.i.* gugumiza maneno, goteza maneno, babaika, kokoteza maneno, sitasita (katika kusema). — *n.* kigugumizi. **stammering**, *n.* kigugumizi.
stamp, *v.t.* (*imprint*) piga (tia) chapa; (*affix stamp*) bandika tikiti ya posta; (*crush &c.*) ponda, seta, vyoga; (*with feet*) kanyaga, chapa (chapua) miguu; (*make clearly, make clear*) bainisha, thibitisha, dhihirisha; (*impress on mind &c.*) ingiza katika akili (ukumbuko). *Stamp out*, komesha, batilisha, ng'oa -ote. — *n.* chapa, muhuri, alama; kipande cha kupigia chapa; (*postage*) tikiti ya posta; (*kind*) namna, tabia; (*with foot*) kukanyaga, kuchapa miguu,

mchapo wa mguu; (*machine*) kinu cha kupondea (cha kusetea).

stampede, *v.i.* kimbia ghafula (kwa hofu). — *n.* kukimbia ghafula, makimbizi ya ghafula (kwa hofu).

stance, *n.* kikao, jinsi ya kusimama (ya kujiweka) katika michezo mingineyo.

stanch, (1). **staunch,** *v.t.* zuia (damu), viliza.

stanch, (2) *a.* taz. *staunch.*

stanchion, *n.* nguzo.

stand, *v.i.* (*p.t. and pf.t.* **stood**) simama, -wa wima; (*be situated*) kaa, wekwa; (*stop*) tua, koma, simama; (*remain*) kaa, dumu, ishi; (*succeed*) shinda, fanikiwa; (*be in a condition*) -wa na hali; (*be erect*) simama, simika, -wa wima; (*of a ship*) enda. — *v.t.* (*endure*) vumilia, himili, chukua, kubali; (*resist*) zuia, simamia, shindana na, pinza, kinzana na; (*erect*) simamisha, simikisha. *Stand at,* simama kwa, kaa kwa. *Stand by,* -wapo, hudhuria; (*join, assist*) shika, shindania, saidia; (*be deferred*) wekwa, ahiri. *Stand corrected,* kubali kusahihishwa. *Stand fast,* kaa (simama) imara, kita, zinda. *Stand fire,* vumilia bunduki (mzinga &c.), -toshtushwa, -toshindwa. *Stand for,* -wa mahali pa (badala ya, ishara ya); (*be candidate for*) taka kuchaguliwa na watu (kuwa mkubwa). *Stand in need of,* taka, hitaji. *Stand in good stead,* faa. *Stand off,* jitenga, jihadhari. *Stand on ceremony,* ongeza mno heshima, fanya haya. *Do not stand on ceremony,* fanya hapa kama kwako. *Stand one's ground,* simama, shinda. *Stand over,* ahiri, wekwa. *Stand out,* tokeza, fanya nundu (domo, rasi); (*resist*) kataa, kaidi. *Stand security for,* dhamini. *Stand to,* shika, fikiliza, maliza; (*agree with*) patana na. *Stand treat,* lipa gharama. *Stand trial,* thibitika; (*by court*) hukumiwa. *Stand up,* ondoka, simama. *Stand up for,* shindania, tetea, saidia. *Stand upon,* tegemea. — *n.* (*standing*) kusimama; (*halt, place to stop*) kituo, kikomo; (*stage, platform*) mahali pa kusimama, jukwaa, dungu; (*shop*) duka, meza; (*holder of any kind*) kitu cha kuwekea vitu, (kiweko, meza, kinara, kiguzo, kibao, kitegemeo &c.); (*resistance*) ushindani, ukinzani, ukaidi. *Make a stand,* shindana, shika vita. *Come to a stand,* koma, simama, simamishwa. *Be at a stand,* hangaika, shindwa. **standard,** *n.* (*flag*) bendera; (*established test, rule*) kawaida, kanuni, cheo cha kawaida; (*best quality, highest pitch*) kipeo, namna bora; (*upright &c.*) nguzo, mti, mhimili, mwimo. — *a.* -a kawaida, -a kukubaliwa, bora, halisi, hasa. **standardization,** *n.* tendo la *standardize.* **standardize,** *v.t.* fanya kuwa *standard,* sawazisha (kuwa ya kawaida, kuwa ya namna iliyokubaliwa -siobadilika). **stand-by,** *n.* msaada (msaidizi) wa akiba. **standing,** *a.* -a kusimama; (*regular*) -a kanuni; (*permanent*) -a sikuzote; (*of water*) -fu, -tulivu. *Standing army,* askari wa serikali (wa sikuzote). — *n.* kikao, cheo; (*time*) aushi, maisha, muda, wakati. *A man of good standing,* mtu mwenye cheo (mwenye jina, mashuhuri). **stand-offish,** *a.* -a kiburi, si -a urafiki. **standpoint,** *n.* mahali pa kutazama; (*mental*) fikira, maono. **standstill,** *n.* kukoma, kusimama, kukaa. *Work was at a standstill,* kazi ilisimama kabisa.

stank, *p.t.* ya *stink.*

stanza, *n.* fungu la mashairi (manne au zaidi), beti.

staple, *n.* msumari uliopindika kama herufi U wenye ncha mbili, pete, tumbuu; (*chief product*) bidhaa kubwa ya mahali fulani; (*main subject*) jambo lililo kubwa; (*raw cotton*) pamba; (*cotton fibre*) uzi wa pamba. — *a.* -kubwa, -ingi, -a sikuzote.

star, *n.* nyota; (*decoration*) nishani; (*well-known player &c.*) mchezaji &c. mashuhuri. *Falling star,* kimwondo. *Lucky star,* nyota ya jaha. **starfish,** *n.* kiti cha pweza. **star-gazer,** *n.* mnajimu, mpiga falaki. **starless,** *a.* bila nyota. **starlight,** *n.* mwangaza wa nyota. **starred,** *a.* -enye nyota. *Ill-starred,* a bahati mbaya. **starry,** *a.* -enye nyota, kama nyota, -a kung'aa.

starboard, *n.* (chomboni) upande wa kuume.

starch, *n.* wanga, nisha, nishaa, kanji. — *v.t.* tia wanga. **starched,** *a.* -liotiwa wanga, -gumu, si -kunjufu. **starchy,** *a.* -a wanga, kama wanga.

stare, *v.i.* kodoa, kaza macho, ng'ariza macho. *Stare at,* kodolea, kazia (angazia) macho. — *n.* kukodoa, kodolea. **staring,** *a.* -liokazwa, liofumbuliwa sana. *Stark staring mad,* -enye wazimu kabisa.

starfish, *n.,* **star-gazer,** *n.* taz. *star.*

staring, *a.* taz. *stare.*

stark, *a.* (*stiff*) -gumu, -kavu, -siokunjika; (*downright*) -tupu, tu, kabisa. *Stark madness,* wazimu kabisa. **stark-naked,** *a.* -tupu kabisa, uchi, uchi wa nyama.

starless, *a.,* **starlight,** *n.* taz. *star.*

starling, *n.* (*Pemba glossy*) mramba mweusi, kwenzi.

starred, *a.,* **starry,** *a.* taz. *star.*

start, *v.i.* shtuka, gutuka; (*of an animal*) bumburuka; toka mahali pake; (*begin*) anza, amiri, maliki, ondoka, ngo'ka, shika njia, safiri —*v.t.* (*alarm, drive off*) shtusha, shtua, amsha, kimbiza; (*an animal*) bumburusha; (*begin*) anza; (*cause to begin*) anzisha; (*set moving*) endesha, jongeza, sogeza. — *n.* (*fright*) kushtuka, kituko; (*shock*) kishindo, kipindi; (*beginning*) mwanzo, awali, chimbuko; (*departure*) kushika njia, kuondoka; (*in a race*) mwanzo wa shindano. *Get a start of,* tangulia, toka kwanza. *In fits and starts, by starts,* kwa vipindi, kwenda na kusimama. **starter,** *n.* (*person who gives signal*) mshindanishi; (*competitor*) mshindani; (*device*) kitu kinachoanzisha. **starting-point,** *n.* mwanzo, mahali pa kuanza. **startle,** *v.t.* shtusha, hofisha; (*rouse*) amsha, chochea; (*an animal*) bumburusha. **startling,** *a.* -a kushtusha, -a kutisha, -a hofu, -a ajabu.

starve, *v.t.* shindisha (fisha) kwa njaa; — *v.i.* (*abstain from food*) shinda na njaa, jinyima chakula; (*be hungry*) -wa na njaa, umia kwa njaa; (*die of starvation*) -fa kwa njaa. *Starve for,* tamani, onea shauku, taka sana. *Be starved with cold,* ona baridi sana, umia sana kwa baridi. **starvation,** *n.* kuwa na njaa, njaa. **starveling,** *n.* mwenye kukonda kwa njaa.

state, *n.* (*condition*) hali, kikao, manzili; (*rank*) cheo, daraja, kiwango; (*elaborate style*) fahari, heshima, anasa, sherehe; (*political society*) jamii ya watu chini ya mfalme mmoja (chini ya serikali moja). *Chair of state,* kiti cha enzi. *Go in state,* enda kifalme (kwa fahari). — *v.t.* nena, sema, eleza, aridhia. — *a.* -a serikali, -a sherehe (ya serikali). **stated,** *a.* -a kanuni, -a kawaida, -lioamriwa, -a taratibu. **stateliness,** *n.* sherehe, fahari, uzuri, madaha, madahiro. **stately,** *a.* -a fahari, -a sherehe, -zuri, bora, -a madaha. **statement,** *n.* maneno, habari, masimulizi, maelezo, kisa; (*written*) taarifa. **stateroom,** *n.* chumba kikubwa cha kubarizia &c.; (*on ship*) chumba. **statesman,** *n.* mwenye maarifa ya utawala; (*official*) mkubwa wa serikali, mtu wa baraza ya mfalme, waziri, diwani. **statesmanlike,** *a.* -a kumstahili *statesman,* -a akili. **statesmanship,** *n.* akili ya (kazi ya) *statesman,* ustadi katika mambo ya utawala.

statics, *n.* maarifa ya hali ya kusimama vitu, elimu ya usimeme.

station, *n.* (*post*) kingojo, ngojo, lindo; (*resting place*) kituo, kilalo, makao; (*work*) kazi; (*state*) hali, kikao, manzili; (*rank*) cheo, daraja, kiwango; (*on railway &c.*) stesheni, kituo. — *v.t.* weka mahali (kwenye kingojo, zamu &c.). **stationary,** *a.* -a kusimama, -sioondoka, -liokazwa, -a kukaa mahali pamoja (hali moja), -sioondoleka, -siogeuka. **stationer,** *n.* mwuza karatasi ya kuandikia, wino, kalamu &c. **stationery,** *n.* karatasi ya kuandikia, bahasha, kalamu, wino &c.

statistics, *n.* habari zinazoonyeshwa kwa hesabu, *e.g.* za wingi wa watu wanaougua ugonjwa fulani, za watu waliokufa, au kuzaliwa &c. **statistician,** *n.* mtu mwenye maarifa ya *statistics*, awezaye kufanya na kueleza *statistics*.

statue, *n.* sanamu iliyochorwa kwa mawe, madini &c., au kuumbwa kwa udongo. **statuary,** *n.* jamii ya *statues*, mfanyiza *statues*. **statuesque,** *a.* kama sanamu iliyochorwa. **statuette,** *n.* sanamu ndogo iliyochorwa au kuumbwa.

stature, *n.* kimo, urefu.

status, *n.* hali, cheo, kikao, kiwango, daraja. *In statu quo*, kama ilivyokuwa, hali hiyo hiyo.

statute, *n.* sheria, amri ya serikali, sharti la chama &c. **statutable, statutory,** *a.* -a sheria, -liyoamriwa, halali.

staunch, *a.* amini, -aminifu, -a kutumainiwa, thabiti, imara, madhubuti. — *v.* taz. *stanch.*

stave, *n.* kipande au kibao cha pipa; (*of ladder*) kipandio, kipawa, kipago; (*stanza*) fungu la mashairi; (*short pole*) kijiti, gongo; (*in music*) mistari mitano na nafasi zilizo kati yake ya kuandikia muziki. — *v.t.* (*p.t.* **stove**). *Stave in*, bonyeza, vunja. *Stave off*, ahirisha, zuia, kawilisha, kinga.

stay, (1) *v.t.* zuia, simamisha, komesha, ahirisha, kawilisha; — *v.i.* (*remain &c.*) kaa, kawia, ahiri, simama, shinda, kaa nyumbani (kwa). *Stay the course*, -wa na nguvu ya kuendelea mpaka mwisho (wa shindano). — *n.* kukaa, kikao, muda wa kukaa; (*endurance &c.*) nguvu ya kuendelea, ustahimilivu, uvumilivu.

stay, (1) *v.t.* (*prop.*) tegemeza. — *n.* tegemeo, msaada; (*in vessel*) kamba ya mlingoti. *Stays*, vazi la kike la kuwa msaada wa mbavuni.

stead, *n.* *Instead of*, mahali pa, badala ya. *It will stand you in good stead*, itakufaa sana, itakusaidia sana. **steadfast,** *a.* thabiti, madhubuti, imara, amini, -aminifu, -a kutumainiwa, -siosita. **steadfastly,** *adv.* kwa uthabiti, kwa uaminifu, bila kusita. **steadfastness,** *n.* uthabiti, usimeme, uaminifu, unyofu. **steadiness,** *n.* uthabiti, usimeme; (*morality*) adili, uadilifu; (*regularity*) usawa, utaratibu, uaminifu. **steady,** *a.* thabiti, imara, madhubuti, -siosita; (*even*) taratibu, sawa, -siogeuka, -siobadilika, -siotikisika; (*regular*) -a kawaida, -a desturi; (*moral*) -a adili, -adilifu, amini, -aminifu, -nyofu. — *v.t.* weka imara, imarisha, thibitisha, fanya uthabiti; — *v.i.* thibitika, tulia.

steak, *n.* kipande cha nyama ya ng'ombe au ya samaki.

steal, *v.t.* (*p.t.* **stole,** *pf.t.* **stolen**), iba, nyang'anya, poka, pokonya, kwepua, twaa kwa hila (kwa siri, kwa werevu, bila ruhusa); — *v.i.* (*go softly*) enda taratibu pasipo makelele, enda kimya, pita kama mwizi, nyata, enda njongwanjongwa, enda polepole, pita; (*take by degrees*) twaa kidogo kidogo. *Steal upon*, nyemelea, nyatia. *Steal a march on*, tangulia katika shauri, jambo &c., tangulia kufanya. **stealer,** *n.* mwizi, mwivi, mnyang'anyi, mkwepuzi. **stealing,** *n.* wizi, wivi, unyang'anyi, ukwepuzi. **stealth,** *n.* siri; (*trickery*) hila, werevu. *Do good by stealth*, fanya wema kwa siri. **stealthily,** *adv.* kwa siri, kwa hila, kwa werevu, mang'ungumu, njongwanjongwa. **stealthy,** *a.* -a hila, -erevu; (*secret, unnoticed*) -a siri,

-a kwenda polepole, -a kunyemelea, -a kunyatanyata.
steam, *n.* mvuke, moshi. — *v.i.* enda kwa nguvu ya mvuke, enda kwa moshi, enda; — *v.t.* (*apply steam*) tia mvuke; (*cook by steaming*) pika kwa mvuke. **steamboat,** *n.* meli, merikebu ya moshi, mashua ya moshi. **steam-engine,** *n.* mashine ya moshi, kinu cha kazi kinachoendeshwa na mvuke, mtambo; (*locomotive*) gari la moshi. **steamer,** *n.* meli, merekebu ya moshi; (*for cooking*) sufuria ya kupikia kwa mvuke. **steamship,** *n.* meli, merikebu ya moshi. **steamy,** *a.* -a mvuke, kama mvuke.
steed, *n.* farasi.
steel, *n.* chuma cha pua, pua; (*of good quality for swords &c.*) feleji; (*for sharpening knives &c.*) chuma cha kunolea. — *a.* -a chuma cha pua, -a pua, -a feleji. — *v.t.* fanya -gumu, shupaza.
steenbock, *n.* dondoro.
steep, (1) *v.t.* lowesha, loweka, bambika, chovyachovya, jaliza. *Steep in,* nywesha sana; (*teach fully*) fundisha sana.
steep, (2) *a.* -a kuinuka ghafula, -a kusimama sawa, -a wima, -a kwenda juu (chini) ghafula, -a kuchongoka; (*of price &c.*) ghali, -a kupita kiasi. —*n.* mwinuko (mtelemko) wa ghafula mlima. **steepen,** *v.i.* inuka, panda.
steeple, *n.* mnara uliochongoka (hasa wa kanisa). **steeplechase,** *n.* shindano la farasi kwenda moja kwa moja, mwituni, nyikani, kuvuka mito &c.
steer, (1) *n.* ng'ombe dume (hasa maksai).
steer, (2) *v.t.* (*direct*) elekeza njia, ongoza; (*as pilot*) shika usukani, shika shikio, pinga (chombo kwa shikio). **steerage,** *n.* upande wa nyuma melini, upande wa shetri. **steering-wheel,** *n.* usukani, duara ya kupindia meli (motakaa &c.). **steersman,** *n.* mshika usukani, mshika shikio, rubani.
steinbock, *n.* dondoro (*steenbock*).
stellar, *a.* -a nyota.
stem, (1) *n.* (*of tree*) shina; (*of rice &c.*) bua, ubua; (*of fruit, flowers*) kikonyo; (*of ship*) hanamu, kasama; (*of pipe*) mwanzi, mrija, digali, mdakale; (*of wine glass &c.*) mguu; (*of word*) shina.
stem, (2) *v.t.* zuia, pinga, shindana na, ziba, komesha.
stench, *n.* uvundo, harufu mbaya, kunuka.
stencil, *n.* bamba la kupigia chapa. — *v.t.* piga chapa kwa *stencil.*
stenographer, *n.* mwandishi (karani) wa *shorthand.* **stenography,** *n.* = *shorthand.*
stentorian, *a.* -a kusikika mbali, -a nguvu sana, -a kelele.
step, (1) *n.* (*pace, footstep*) hatua; (*small interval*) nafasi ndogo; (*stair*) daraja; (*of a ladder or cut in tree &c.*) kipawa, kipandio, kipago; (*footprint*) wayo; (*gait*) mwendo; (*preceding*) tendo, kitendo, jambo; (*advance*) kiendeleo. *Take steps,* fanya shauri, jiweka tayari, anza. *Take long steps,* tanua miguu. *Pair of steps,* ngazi ya kukunja. — *v.i.* enda, enda polepole, chapa miguu; — *v.t.* (*measure*) pima kwa hatua. *Step over,* kiuka, kia, chupa, dakia. *Step out,* kaza mwendo; (*measure*) pima kwa hatua. *Step in,* ingia; (*intervene*) jitia, jiingiza. **stepping-stone,** *n.* jiwe mtoni la kuvukia; (*fig.*) njia ya kupatia mradi fulani, kazi inayoleta kazi kubwa zaidi.
step-, (2) *pref.* -a kambo. *Stepchild,* mtoto wa kambo. *Stepfather,* baba wa kambo. *Stepmother,* mama wa kambo. *Stepbrother,* ndugu (wa kiume) wa kambo. *Stepsister,* ndugu (wa kike) wa kambo.
steppe, *n.* pori, pululu, nyika, mbuga.
stepping-stone, *n.* taz. *step* (1).
stereoscope, *n.* kama darubini ya kutazamia picha mbili pamoja zikaonekana kuwa moja tu ya kitu chenyewe halisi.
stereotype, *n.* bamba la madini la

kupigia chapa vitabu (herufi zake zimemiminwa wala si mbalimbali). — *v.t.* fanya *stereotype* ya; piga chapa kwa *stereotype*; (*fix*) kaza dumisha; (*repeat unalterably &c.*) fanya namna ile ile tena na tena (siku zote, kila mara).

sterile, *a.* -sioweza kuzaa, tasa, gumba; (*of soil*) kame; (*lifeless*) baridi; (*of food, liquid &c.*) -sio na vijidudu vyo vyote, safi kabisa. **sterility**, *n.* kuwa *sterile*. **sterilize**, *v.t.* fanya kuwa *sterile*; ondoa uwezo wa kuzaa; (*of food &c.*) ondoa (fisha) vijidudu vyote vya ugonjwa.

sterling, *a.* -a fedha ya kiingereza; (*fixed value*) -a thamani isiyobadilika; (*genuine &c.*) safi, halisi, -zuri, -a kutumainiwa.

stern, (1) *a.* -kali, -gumu, bila huruma. **sternly**, *adv.* kwa ukali (ugumu), bila huruma. **sternness**, *n.* ukali, ugumu.

stern, (2) *n.* upande wa nyuma, shetri tezi. **sternmost**, *a.* -a nyuma. **stern-post**, *n.* bumia, fashini.

sternly, *adv.*, **sternness**, *n.* taz. *stern* (1).

sternmost, *a.*, **stern-post**, *n.* taz. *stern* (2).

sternum, *n.* mfupa wa mbele kifuani (wa kidari).

stertorous, *a.* -a kukoroma, -a kukorota, -a kukokota (pumzi).

stethoscope, *n.* kipande cha kusikilizia pumzi au vipigo vya moyo *&c.*

stevedore, *n.* msimamizi wa kupakia na kupakua shehena melini.

stew, *v.t.* tokosa katika maji kidogo; — *v.i.* (*of food stewing*) tokoseka. *Let him stew in his own juice*, mwache bila kumsaidia, mwache afanye awezavyo mwenyewe. — *n.* nyama samaki, mboga *&c.*, iliyotokoswa. *In a great stew*, -enye wasiwasi kabisa, -a kuhangaika sana, katika mashaka mengi.

steward, *n.* mtumishi wa abiria melini; (*of state &c.*) msimamizi, wakili; (*of large household*) mwandishi mkuu; (*at public gathering*) msaidizi, msimamizi. **stewardess**, *n.* mtumishi wa kike melini. **stewardship**, *n.* kazi ya *steward*.

stick, *n.* (*thin*) fimbo, ufito, upao, wasa; (*short stick*) kibarango; (*long thick*) gongo; (*walking*) bakora; (*old man's*) mkongojo; (*knobbed*) rungu; (*slave-stick*) kongwa; (*in general*) kipande, kitu kama *stick*, kijiti, kibanzi, kibano. *Stick of sugar*, gubiti. *Stick of soap*, kinoo (mnara) cha sabuni. — *v.t.* (*p.t. and pf.t.* **stuck**) (*pierce*) choma, penyeza; (*fasten*) kaza, tia; (*tolerate—slang*) vumilia; (*make stick*) bandika, ambisha, ambatisha, gandamiza; — *v.i.* (*be sticky*) nata; (*adhere to*) shikamana na, gandamana na, ganda, ambata; (*remain*) kaa, zinda; (*get fixed*) kwama, sakama, kaza, zuiwa; (*be in difficulties*) -wa na mashaka, kwama, sitasita. *Stick at*, onea mashaka au hofu, zuiwa na; (*persist in*) endelea na, shikilia. *Stick by*, *Stick to*, shikamana na, -wa hali moja na, saidia, gandamia. *Stick* (*in ground*) chomeka, kita; (*in belt, pocket &c.*) futika, tia, pachika. *The meat sticks in my teeth*, nyama inanisakama menoni. *Stick out*, tokeza, futuka, fanya domo, benuka; (*persevere*) dumu, endelea; (*of tongue*) toa. *Stick up*, inuka, nyanyuka, simika, simama. *Stick up for*, shindania, tetea. *He sticks at nothing*, haogopi kitu, hufanya hila au werevu wo wote. **sticking-plaster**, *n.* kibandiko cha dawa, mpakato. **stick-in-the-mud**, *n.* mtu ashikaye ya zamani, asiyeendelea. **sticky**, *a.* -a kunata (kama ute wa yai, embwe, ulimbo *&c.*), -a kinamo.

stickler, *n.* mtu ashikiliaye (desturi, mambo madogodogo ya heshima *&c.*).

sticky, *a.* taz. *stick*.

stiff, *a.* (*hard, unyielding*) -gumu, -nene, -zito; (*rigid*) -gumu, -kavu, -siopindikana; (*constrained*) si -kunjufu, -gumu, baridi; (*difficult*)

-gumu. *Be stiff,* kauka, kazana, shupaa, -wa si laini. *Feel stiff (after hard work &c.)* ona mavune, ona mavundevunde. **stiffen,** *v.t.* fanya *stiff*; *(strengthen)* tia nguvu, imarisha; — *v.i.* *(become stiff)* kauka, kazana, shupana, jikaza; *(of things left exposed)* ng'ang'anaa; *(increase in intensity)* zidi (kupata nguvu &c.). **stiffening,** *n.* kitu cha kuimarishia, cha kufanya kuwa -gumu, *e.g.* dondo katika nguo &c. **stiff-necked,** *a.* shupavu, -kaidi, -gumu. **stiffness,** *n.* kuwa *stiff,* mkazo, kukazana, ugumu, ukavu, ushupavu; *(of muscles after hard work &c.)* mavune, mavundevunde.

stifle, *v.t.* songa; *(restrain, hide)* zuia, fisha, setiri; *(cut short)* katiza, zima, zimisha, komesha; — *v.i.* ona kusongwa, ona kisongo.

stigma, *n.* *(disgrace)* alama ya aibu, aibu, fedheha; *(scar, mark)* waa au kovu mwilini. **stigmatize,** *v.t.* tia alama ya aibu, aibisha, tukana, shutumu, suta, fedhehesha.

stile, *n.* ngazi ya kupita juu ya kitalu au ua.

stiletto, *n.* kisu chembamba cha kuchomea.

still, (1) *n.* chombo cha kupikia tembo, mvinyo &c.

still, (2) *a.* -tulivu, -nyamavu, -kimya. *Still water,* maji matulivu, maji mafu. *Be still,* zizima, tulia, nyamaa. — *v.t.* tuliza, nyamzisha, zizimisha. — *adv.* hata sasa, bado, vile vile, lakini, ingawa hivi, hata hivyo; *(besides)* tena, zaidi. *He was still more frightened,* alizidi kuogopa. **still-born,** *n.* -liozaliwa -fu, -fu tangu uzazi. **stillness,** *n,* kimya, utulivu, raha; *(calm)* shwari.

stilt, *n.* mlonjo. **stilted,** *a.* -a kujivuna, -a kiburi, -a kujifahirisha.

stimulate, *v.t.* amsha, chochea, himiza, harakisha, sukumiza, tamanisha, vuta, chomesha, tia nguvu. **stimulant,** *a.* -a kuamsha, -a kuchochea, &c. — *n.* kichocheo, mvuto, kitamanisho; mvinyo, kileo, dawa ya kuburudisha (ya kutia nguvu). **stimulating,** *n.* -a kuamsha, -a kuchochea, -a kutia nguvu &c. **stimulus,** *n.* kitu cha kuamsha (kuchochea, kuhimiza, kuharakisha, kutamanisha, kutia nguvu), kichocheo, mvuto, kitamanisho, kichokoo.

sting, *n.* uma, mwiba, kisumari; *(pain, smart)* ukali, uchungu, kichomi. — *v.t.* *(p.t. and pf.t.* **stung)** *(of insect &c.)* uma, choma, piga uma; *(of iodine &c.)* washa, choma, chonyota, cheneta, chochota; *(of feeling)* uma, umiza, choma, washa. **stinging,** *a.* -enye uma (mwiba, kisumari), -a kuuma, -kali, -a kuchoma, -a kuwasha. *Stinging-nettle (-caterpillar)* kiwavi.

stingy, *a.* -a choyo, -nyiminyimi, -a kunyima, bahili. **stinginess,** *n.* uchoyo, unyimivu, ubahili.

stink, *v.i.* *(p.t.* **stank,** *pf.t.* **stunk)** nuka, vunda, toa harufu mbaya; *(be offensive)* chukiza. — *n.* uvundo, harufu mbaya, kunuka. **stinking,** *a.* -a kunuka vibaya, -enye harufu mbaya, -a kuvunda.

stint, *v.t.* toa kidogo, toa kwa unyimivu, nyima, kata, zuia, hinisha. — *n.* kizuio, unyimivu. **stintingly,** *adv.* kinyiminyimi, kwa unyimivu, kidogo dogo. **stintless,** *a.* -ingi.

stipend, *n.* mshahara, ujira, ijara. **stipendiary,** *a.* -a mshahara.

stipulate, *v.t.* fanya (weka) masharti, patana. **stipulation,** *n.* sharti, mapatano.

stir, *v.t.* jongeza, sogeza, sukuma, shtua, shtusha; *(food &c.)* koroga, vuruga, buruga; *(of ugali)* songa; *(excite)* chochea, amsha, sukasuka, harakisha, charakisha, chomesha; *(fire)* chochea, chochelea; *(quarrel)* vumbulia, tasliti; *(mud, dust)* tifua; *(mix)* changanya; — *v.i.* enda, jongea, sogea. — *n.* msukosuko, ghasia, makelele, haraka, mambo, zahama. **stirring,** *a.* -tendaji, -epesi, hodari; *(exciting)* -a kuamsha, -a kuchochea, -a mambo mengi, -a kushtusha.

stirrup, *n.* kikuku cha kupandia farasi.

stitch, *v.t.* shonashona, unga (shikiza) kwa kushona. — *n.* (*different kinds are*) ziki, mrera, viboko, vinara; (*in the side*) kichomi. *Without a stitch on,* uchi, uchi wa nyama, -tupu. *A stitch in time saves nine,* usipoziba ufa, utajenga ukuta, *lit. if you don't fill in the crack you will have to build a wall.*

stoat, *n.* mnyama mdogo kama cheche.

stock, *n.* (*root*) shina; (*origin*) asili, nasaba, jadi, kizazi, ukoo, jamaa; (*of gun &c.*) mti, uti, tako; (*store*) akiba, mali; (*live*) mifugo, ng'ombe, kondoo, mbuzi *&c.* (*capital*) rasilmali; (*investment*) mali iliyokopeshwa kwa matumizi ya serikali au ya shirika (*company*); (*quantity*) wingi, kande; (*for soup &c.*) mchuzi; (*for neck*) utepe wa kuvaa shingoni. *Keep in stock,* -wa na . . . tayari. *Make stock of,* faidi. *A laughing-stock,* mzaha (wa watu wote), kichekesho. *Take stock,* hesabu, fanya hesabu, kadirisha; (*watch*) angalia, chungulia. — *v.t.* tia, weka bidhaa katika duka, maarifa katika akili *&c.*); (*keep in stock*) -wa na . . . tayari dukani. — *a.* -a kuwa tayari kwa kawaida, -a kutumika sana. **stock-breeder,** *n.* mfugaji wa ng'ombe, mbuzi, kondoo *&c.* **stock-broker,** *n.* mfanya biashara ya *stocks* (*funds*). **stock exchange,** *n.* nyumba ya biashara ya *stocks* (*funds*) na kazi yake. **stock-farmer,** *n.* mfugaji wa ng'ombe, kondoo, mbuzi *&c.* **stock-holder,** *n.* mwenye *stock* (*investment*). **stock-in-trade,** *n.* vyombo (zana, vifaa, bidhaa *&c.*) vinavyohitajiwa kwa kazi fulani. **stock-jobbing,** *n.* biashara ya *stocks* (*investment*). **stock-market,** *n.* taz. *stock exchange.* **stocks,** *n.* (*for offenders*) mkatale; (*for ships*) jahabu, magadi *&c.* ya kutegemeza chombo (merikebu, meli) kinapoundwa; (*funds*) mali iliyokopeshwa serikali au *company,* rasilmali ya serikali (ya *company*). *It is on the stocks,* inatendwa kazi; iko inatengenezwa, lakini haijawa tayari bado. **stock-still,** *adv.* kimya kabisa, kama jiwe, kama kifu. *Stand stock-still* (*with wonder &c.*) tunduwaa, pumbaa, duwaa, shangaa, pigwa (shikwa) na butaa. **stocky,** *a.* -fupi -nene, -enye maungo, -a mraba, -a miraba minne.

stockade, *n.* boma, ua.

stock-breeder, *n.,* **stock-broker** *n.,* **stock exchange,** *n.,* **stock-farmer,** *n.,* **stock-holder,** *n.* taz. *stock.*

stocking, *n.* soksi ndefu.

stock-in-trade, *n.,* **stock-jobbing,** *n.,* **stock-market,** *n.,* **stocks,** *n.,* **stock-still,** *adv.,* **stocky,** *n.* taz. *stock.*

stodgy, *a.* -zito, -gumu; (*uninteresting &c.*) baridi, -siyokolea.

stoep, *n.* baraza.

stoic, *n.* mtu asiyejali furaha wala huzuni wala maumivu, mtulivu kabisa, mvumilivu kabisa. **stoic, stoical,** *a.* -siyejali furaha wala huzuni wala maumivu, -sio na tamaa, kama jiwe, baridi. **stoicism,** *n.* tabia (hali) ya kuwa *stoical*; utulivu, uvumilivu *&c.*

stoke, *v.t.* tia makaa katika tanuu (moto wa meli, wa mashine *&c.*); chochea, chocheleza. **stokehold,** *n.* mahali melini makaa yanapotiwa motoni. **stoker,** *n.* mchocheaji (moto melini, au katika gari la moshi *&c.*).

stole, (1) *n.* utepe mrefu wa kasisi; utepe wa ngozi wa kuvaa shingoni (vazi la kike).

stole, (2) *p.t.* **stolen,** *pf.t.* ya *steal.*

stolid, *a.* -zito, baridi. **stolidity,** *n.* uzito, ubaridi.

stomach, *n.* tumbo, mfuko wa tumboni; (*inclination*) tamaa ya kula, tamaa, shauku. — *v.t.* vumilia, stahimili, chukua. **stomach-ache,** *n.* kuumwa tumboni, msokoto wa tumboni. **stomacher,** *n.* shali ya kuvaa mwanamke kifuani, kanchiri, sidiria. **stomachic**, *a.* -a tumbo, -a kutuliza tumbo.

stone, *n.* jiwe; (*small*) kokoto, mbwe; (*very small, gravel*) changarawe; (*of fruit*) koko, kokwa; (*precious*) kito, johari; (*hardness*) ugumu, ukali, ushupavu; (*weight*) ratli kumi na nne. — *v.t.* tupia mawe, rujumu; (*of fruit &c.*) toa makokwa; (*squeeze out stone*) bujua, pujua. — *a.* -a jiwe, -a mawe. **stone age**, zamani za kale watu walipofanyiza silaha na vyombo kwa mawe. **stone-blind**, *a.* kipofu kabisa. **stone-cold**, *a.* baridi sana. **stone-cutter**, *n.* mkata mawe. **stoned**, *a.* (*of fruit*) -liotolewa kokwa. **stone-dead**, *a.* -fu kabisa. **stone-deaf**, *a.* kiziwi kabisa. **stone-fruit**, *n.* matunda yenye kokwa. **stoneless**, *a.* pasipo na mawe; (*fruit*) bila kokwa. **stone-mason**, *n.* mwashi. **stone's-cast, stone's throw**, *n.* mtupo wa jiwe. **stone-ware**, *n.* vyombo vya udongo mgumu sana. **stone-work**, *n.* uashi, mawe. **stony**, *a.* -a mawe mengi; (*hard, severe*) -gumu, -kali, bila huruma.

stood, *p.t. and pf.t.* ya *stand*.

stook, *n.* matita yaliyosimamishwa pamoja.

stool, *n.* kiti (kidogo), kibago, kibao cha kukalia; (*excreta*) choo, mavi, kinyesi. *Go to stool*, enda chooni (haja, msalani).

stoop, *v.i.* inama, jikunyata; (*condescend*) jishusha, jidhili. **stooping**, *n.* kiinamizi, kibiongo.

stop, *v.t.* simamisha, komesha, fungisha, zuia, pingia njia; (*close, obstruct*) ziba, funga; — *v.i.* (*discontinue &c.*) acha; (*cease movement*) simama, koma; (*remain*) kaa, shinda; (*rest*) tua, koma, nyamaza, isha. *Stop a tooth*, ziba tundu la jino. *Stop short*, kata (katiza) mwendo. *Stop up*, ziba. — *n.* (*end*) kituo, kikomo, kinga, mwisho; (*obstacle*) kizuizi, kizuio, zuio, mgogoro; (*in writing*) nukta, kituo; (*in machinery &c.*) kipande cha kuzuia au kuziba. *Stop!* basi! tua! ngoja! simama! koma! **stopcock**, *n.* bilula. **stop-gap**, *n.* badala. **stoppage**, *n.* kusimama, kusimamishwa, kupingwa; (*obstruction*) kizuio, kizuizi, mgogoro, kinga. **stopper**, *n.* kizibo, **stop-watch**, *n.* saa inayoweza kuanzishwa na kusimamishwa mara, ya kupimia mbio, mwendo *&c.*

store, *n.* akiba, kande; (*abundance*) wingi, tele; (*supplies*) vifaa, zana; (*room*) ghala, bohari; (*shop*) duka. *In store*, tayari. *Set store by*, penda sana, dhani ya thamani, thamini, chunuka. — *v.t.* weka, kusanya, dunduliza; (*furnish, fill*) pamba, jaliza. **storehouse**, *n.* bohari. **store-keeper**, *n.* mtunza vifaa; (*of shop*) mngoje duka, mchuuzi. **store-room**, *n.* ghala. **stores**, *n.* akiba, vifaa, zana.

storey, story, *n.* orofa. *Third storey*, orofa ya tatu. **storeyed, storied**, *a.* -enye orofa. *Three storeyed*, -enye orofa tatu.

storied, *a.* taz. *story*.

stork, *n.* korongo; (*Africa woolly necked*) kwembe maji.

storm, *n.* dhoruba, tufani, mvua kubwa; (*commotion*) msukosuko, ghasia, zahama, machafuko; (*of applause*) vifijo, makelele; (*of anger*) ghadhabu, kiruu; (*abundance*) wingi. *Take by storm*, twaa ghafula, piga dharuba, pigania sana, twaa kwa nguvu. *A storm in a tea-cup*, ghasia (matata, msukosuko) nyingi juu ya jambo dogo, ghasia *&c.* ya bure. — *v.t.* shambulia, twaa kwa nguvu (ghafulia); (*of wind*) vuma sana; (*show rage*) toa maneno makali, toa ukali, ghadhibika. **storm-bound**, *a.* -a kucheleweshwa na dhoruba (na mawimbi makubwa). **storm-cloud**, *n.* wingu lililo dalili ya dhoruba; (*fig.*) dalili ya msukosuko (matata, ghasia, hatari *&c.*). **stormy**, *a.* -a *storm*, -a tufani, -a dhoruba; (*angry*) -a ghadhabu.

story, *n.* hadithi, kisa, hekaya,

ngano, habari, masimulizi; (*fiction*) hadithi tu, uwongo, maneno. Taz. *storey*. **storied**, *a*. -liohadithiwa vingi.

stoup, *n*. kikombe, kombe.

stout, *a*. -nene, -a nguvu, hodari, thabiti, madhubuti, -stahimilivu. — *n*. namna ya pombe nyeusi. **stoutish**, *a*. -nene kidogo. **stoutness**, *n*. unene, nguvu, uthabiti, ugumu, uhodari; (*of limb*) maungo; (*thickness*) unene, maki.

stove, (1) *p.t.* ya *stave*.

stove, (2) *n*. jiko (la kizungu), chombo chenye moto cha kupikia. **stove-pipe**, *n*. bomba la kutoka moshi wa *stove*.

stow, *v.t.* weka, pakia, tia vizuri. **stowage**, *n*. mapakizi, nafasi ya kupakilia vitu. **stowaway**, *n*. mjificha melini ili kwenda mahali bila kulipa nauli.

straddle, *v.i. and t.* tagaa, magamaga, panua miguu; (*sit astride*) tagaa.

straggle, *v.i.* tawanyika, tapakaa, enea; (*be behindhand*) chelewa, potea, baki nyuma. **straggler**, *n*. aliyepotea, mchelewa. **straggling**, *a*. -liotawanyika, -liotapakaa; (*late*) -liochelewa.

straight, *a*. sawa, -a kunyoka; (*vertical*) -a kusimama, -a wima; (*honest*) -nyofu, amini, adili, adilifu, halisi; (*in order*) -a taratibu; (*direct, frank*) -a dhahiri, -a wazi. *Go straight on*, endelea moja kwa moja. **straighten**, *v.t.* nyosha, kongozoka, fanya sawa, tengeneza; (*a crooked pole*) keua; — *v.i.* nyoka, -wa sawa, tengenea. **straightforward**, *a*. -a kwenda sawa; (*honest*) -nyofu, amini, -aminifu. **straightness**, *n*. kuwa straight, unyofu, usawa, uaminifu. **straightway**, *adv*. mara hiyo, pale pale, papo hapo, ghafula hiyo, bila kukawia.

strain, (1) *n*. (*ancestry &c.*) asili, jadi, nasaba, ukoo, kizazi; (*characteristics*) katiba, tabia; (*manner*) jinsi, mfano· (*of music*) wimbo, sauti.

strain, (2) *v.t.* vuta kwa nguvu, nyosha, kaza; (*over-exert, sprain*) shtusha, shtua, tegua, popotoa, legeza; (*liquid*) kung'uta, chuja; (*meaning*) geuza, haribu; (*principles, point*) kosea kidogo makusudi, vuta; — *v.i.* (*make an effort*) jitahidi, fanya bidii, kakamka; (*as at stool*) jika, kakamua; (*become clarified*) chujika, safika. *Strain to the breast*, kumbatia. — *n*. (*exertion*) juhudi, bidii, kukakamka; (*stretching*) kunyoshwa sana, mkazo; (*nervous fatigue &c.*) uchovu wa akili (kwa kazi nyingi, kuhangaika &c.); (*force of tension*) nguvu za mvuto. **strained**, *a*. -a shida, -a mashaka, -a baridi. **st. ainer**, *n*. (*wicker*) kung'uto, kifumbu; (*general term*) kichujio.

strait, *a*. -embamba, -a mkazo; (*rigid, stern*) -kali, -a shida. **strait, straits**, *n*. (*of sea*) mlangobahari; (*distress*) shida, taabu, dhiki; (*perplexity*) mashaka. *Be in a strait, Be in straits*, kwama, dhikika, pata mashaka, taabika. **straiten**, *v.t.* songa, kaza, dhikisha, taabisha. *Straitened circumstances*, taabu, udhiki, dhiki, ukosefu, uhitaji, utaiti, mwambo, urumo. **strait jacket**, *n*. vazi nene zito la kufungia wenye wazimu. **strait-laced**, *a*. -gumu, -shupavu. **strait waistcoat**, *n*. taz. *strait jacket*.

stramonium, *n*. dawa (ya sumu) iliyofanyizwa kwa maua na mbegu za mrenaha.

strand, (1) *n*. (*in rope*) jino la kamba, ncha. *A rope of three strands*, kamba ya meno matatu.

strand, (2) *n*. ufuko, ukingo wa bahari, pwani. — *v.t.* pweleza, ingiza mwambani, pandisha mwambani (funguni) kwamisha; — *v.i.* pwelea, panda mwambani. **stranded**, *a*. -liopwelewa, -liotupwa mwambani; (*deserted*) -lioachwa katika shida (na rafiki &c.).

strange, *a*. (*foreign*) -geni; (*remarkable*) -zungu, -a ajabu, -a kigeni;

(*new*) -pya, -zushi; (*inexperienced*) -zuzu, -jinga, -siozoea; (*belonging to another*) -a watu, -a mwenyewe. **strangely,** *adv.* kwa jinsi isivyo ya kawaida; (*to a remarkable degree*) sana. **strangeness,** *n.* ugeni, ajabu, upya, uzuzu, ujinga &c. **stranger,** *n.* mgeni. *He is a stranger to me,* simjui. *You are a stranger (rare visitor) nowadays,* umeghalika siku hizi.

strangle, *v.t.* nyonga, songa kwa kamba; (*throttle*) kaba, kaba roho; (*put a stop to*) komesha, zuia. **strangulate,** *v.t* taz. *strangle,* kaba, finya, gandamiza (m.shipa, utumbo, &c.) ili kuziba. **strangulated,** *a.* -liosongwa, -liokabwa. **strangulation,** *n.* msongo wa mshipa, msongo wa roho; (*strangling*) kusonga kwa kamba, kunyonga.

strangury, *n.* kuumiza (kuumia) wakati wa kukojoa; (*caused by bilharzia*) kichocho.

strap, *n.* ukanda, ugwe, kigwe. — *v.t.* funga (piga) kwa ukanda; (*with straps of plaster &c.*) funga (kaza, ganga) kwa ugwe wa mbandiko; (*strop*) noa (kwa ukanda) **strapping,** *a.* -refu, -nene, -enye maungo, -a mraba.

strata, *n.pl.* ya *stratum.*

stratagem, *n.* hila, werevu, madanganyo, ushabaki. **strategic, strategical,** *a.* -a *strategy,* -a hila, -erevu. **strategist,** *a.* mwenye maarifa ya vita na namna ya kudanganya adui. **strategy,** *n.* maarifa ya vita, matengeneo (madaraka) ya vita.

stratum, *n.* (*pl.* **strata**) safu ya mawe (mwamba) yaliyopangilika juu kwa juu, tabaka la mawe, utando wa mawe. **stratification,** *n.* kufanya *stratum,* jinsi ya *stratum.* **stratify,** *v.t.* fanya *stratum.*

straw, *n.* majani makavu (ya ngano, ya shayiri); (*trifle*) si kitu. *The last straw,* kitu kidogo kiletacho maangamizi makuu (chenye hasara kubwa), jambo dogo likomeshalo uvumilivu. *It does not matter a straw,* haidhuru hata kidogo. *A man of straw,* mtu hafifu, asiye thabiti. **strawberry,** *n.* namna ya tunda.

stray, *v.i.* potea, tangatanga, zungukazunguka, yuayua, pita mpaka, toka katika njia; (*err*) kosa. — *a.* -liopotea; (*chance*) -a bahati, -a nasibu, -a vivi hivi. — *n.* mtu (mtoto, mnyama) aliyepotea au asiye na kwao.

streak, *n.* mfuo, mlia, mstari; (*of light*) kianga, mwali; (*of lightning*) umeme. — *v.t.* piga milia. **streaky,** *a.* -enye milia, -enye mistari mistari, -enye mifuo.

stream, *n.* mto mdogo, kijito; (*current*) mkondo; (*tendency*) maelekeo, mvuto; (*continuous series*) mfululizo, watu wengi (magari mengi &c.) wakifuatana, miminiko. *Go up stream,* kata maji. *Go down stream,* fuata maji. — *v.i.* pita (kama maji au mwanga), pita tele, miminika, toka kwa wingi; — *v.t.* toa (mimina) -ingi. **streamer,** *n.* bendera (ndefu nyembamba). **streamlet,** *n.* kijito. **stream-lined,** *a.* -lioumbwa kwa jinsi -sivyozuia hewa.

street, *n.* njia ya mji. *Street arab,* mtoto wa kikopo, mhuni. *On the streets,* kupata uchumi kwa ukahaba. *Not in the same street with,* ni hafifu kuliko, si -zuri kama.

strength, *n.* nguvu, uwezo, uthabiti, ugumu, sulubu, rai, siha; (*large number*) wingi; (*completeness &c.*) hesabu ya kawaida (ipasayo); (*muster roll*) orodha ya majina. *On the strength of,* kwa kutegemea, kwa sababu ya. **strengthen,** *v.t.* tia nguvu, imarisha, thibitisha; (*encourage, help*) -pa moyo, saidia, fariji; — *v.i.* pata moyo, jipa moyo, zidi kupata nguvu, imarika, thibitika. **strengthening,** *a.* -a kutia nguvu, -a kuburudisha.

strenuous, *a.* -a bidii, -a nguvu, -a kujitahidi, -a juhudi. **strenuously,** *adv.* kwa nguvu, kwa bidii.

stress, *n.* (*trouble*) shida, taabu, dhiki; (*strain*) msongo, mkazo; (*emphasis*) mkazo; (*means, force*) maana, nguvu; (*pressure &c.*) sharti. *Lay stress on*, ona -kubwa; (*emphasize*) kaza sauti, tia mkazo. *Stress of weather*, pepo nyingi, taabu ya bahari. — *v.t.* kaza, tia mkazo. onyesha ukubwa wa.

stretch, *v.t.* nyosha, eneza, kunjua, tanda, tanua, wamba; (*knock down*) angusha kirefu (kwa marefu); (*exaggerate*) ongeza mno, piga chuku, pita kiasi cha, vuta, kithiri; — *v.i.* (*stretch oneself*) jinyosha, jibenua, hekemua; (*be elastic*) nyumbuka; (*extend, reach*) enea, tambaa; (*be capable of stretching*) nyoka, tanuka, kunjuka. *Stretch up to*, chuchumia. *Thing stretched over*, kiwambo. — *n.* (*unbroken period*) mfululizo; (*expanse*) eneo; (*act of stretching*) mvuto. **stretcher**, *n.* kitu cha kunyoshea (cha kukunjulia, cha kuongezea urefu au upana); kitanda (cha kuchukulia wagonjwa), machela; (*in boat*) wango, taruma.

strew, *v.t.* (*pf.t.* **strewed, strewn**) tawanya, tapanya, tupa huko na huko, mwaga, nyunyiza.

stricken, *a.* -liojeruhiwa, -liotaabika, -liopigwa.

strict, *a.* halisi, kamili, -a nguvu, -kali, -a kushurutisha utii. **strictly**, *adv.* halisi, kwa kweli. **strictness**, *n.* uhalisi, ukali, nguvu. **stricture**, *n.* shutumu, neno kali, suto; (*medical*) msongo wa mshipa.

stride, *v.i.* (*p.t.* **strode**, *pf.t.* **stridden**) panua miguu, tagaa, enda kwa mashindo, piga hatua ndefu, chapua miguu. — *n.* hatua ndefu, mwendo wa nguvu. *Advance by rapid stride*, endelea upesi. *He will take it in his stride*, ataifanya bila taabu (bila kuhangaika).

strident, *a.* (*of voice*) -a makelele, -a kuchukiza, -a kukwaruza.

strife, *n.* shindano, ushindano; (*war*) vita, pigano, konde; (*quarrel*) ugomvi, kubishana.

strike, *v.t.* (*p.t. and pf.t.* **struck**) piga, chapa; (*knock*) gonga, bisha, gota; (*with knife &c.*) choma; (*collide with*) pambana na, gongana na, piga dafurao; (*reach, come upon*) fikia, pata; (*discover &c.*) vumbua, gundua; (*a match*) paruza; (*coin*) piga chapa; (*a sail &c.*) tua, shusha; (*on rock &c.*) kwama, ingia mwambani; (*leave work*) goma, acha kazi (ili kupata mradi), (*slang*) -nywa maji; (*affect*) ingia moyoni, shtusha, shangaza, choma, tia kishindo; (*of clock*) gonga; (*set, plant*) panda; — *v.i.* piga, chapa; (*of clock*) gonga; (*of match*) waka; (*of plant*) tia mizizi, anza kuota. *It strikes me*, naona, nadhani, nia imeniingia moyoni. *He was struck by fever*, alipatwa (alishikwa, alipatikana na) homa. *Strike a balance*, fanya urari wa hesabu, lipana, katiana. *Strike a bargain*, patana, pigana bei, fanya ubazazi. *Strike a camp*, vunja kambi, ondoka. *Strike a light*, washa taa; (*a match*) paruza (washa) kiberiti. *Strike a tent*, ng'oa (ondoa) hema. *Strike at*, pigia; (*attack*) shambulia. *Strike in*, jitia ghafula, jiingiza katika maneno; (*of disease*) ingia ndani, penya. *Strike off*, futa, ondoa, kata, katia mbali; (*print*) piga chapa; (*diverge*) enda zake (zao &c.) *Strike on*, kuta; (*discover*) vumbua, gundua. *Strike out*, toa, futa; (*invent*) vumbua, gundua, jitungia, jifanyizia. *Strike up* (*music*), anza, anza kuimba (kupiga, kucheza). *Strike a sore place*, tonosha. — *n.* kugoma, kuacha kazi ili kupata nyongeza ya mshahara au mradi mwingine. **striker**, *n.* mtu aachaye kazi ili kupata mradi fulani. **striking**, *a.* -a kushtusha (kushangaza, kustaajabisha, kushinda moyo &c.). *The effect was most striking*, matokeo yake yalikuwa ya ajabu sana.

string, *n.* kitani, uzi, ugwe, kigwe; (*of a bow*) upote; (*series*) mfululizo, mfulizo wingi, moja kwa moja, mwandamano, mfuatano, msago, mtawalia; (*row*) safu; (*of beads*) shada; (*of fish &c.*) mtungo. — *v.t.* (*p.t. and pf.t.* **strung**) fungia kitani, tunga. **string-course,** *n.* ushi. **stringed,** *a.* -enye nyuzi. **stringy,** *a.* -a nyuzinyuzi, kama nyuzi, kama kitani. *Highly strung,* -epesi kuona wasiwasi, -epesi kuhangaika (kufadhaika &c.).

stringent, *a.* -a kushurutisha utii, -sioepukika, -a nguvu, -kali, -a mkazo. **stringency,** *n.* nguvu, ukali, mkazo; (*scarcity of money*) utaiti, mwambo, dhiki.

stringy, *a.* taz. *string.*

strip, *v.t.* vua, vulia; (*skin*) chuna; (*property*) kumba, nyang'anya, teka, fanya -tupu (kame); (*honours &c.*) ondolea, twalia; (*rind &c.*) ambua, babua, bambua, menya; (*leaves &c.*) ponoa, pagua, purura, konyoa, tabua; (*thatch*) ezua, vimbua; (*branches &c.*) kwanua, pogoa; — *v.i.* (*undress*) vua nguo. — *n.* kipande (kirefu chembamba), chane, ubale; (*of wood, lath*) papi, upapi. *Strips of grass, or leaf, for making mats, brushes &c.* miaa, miyaa, mwaa, tabu, tabutabu, chane, ukindu. *Plaited strips* (*fine*) ukili; (*coarse*) shupatu; (*coloured*) nyiza. *Strip of bark, fibre &c.,* upote, ung'ongo, utangule. **stripped,** *a.* -liochanwa; (*naked*) uchi, -tupu. **stripling,** *n.* kijana mwanamume (mwenye umri wa miaka 16 hivi).

stripe, *n.* mlia, mwalamu, uzi, mstari, mfuo, batobato; (*blow*) pigo; (*chevron*) utepe. **striped,** *a.* -a mistari, -enye milia, -a tepe, -enye mifuo.

stripling, *n.* taz. *strip.*

strive, *v.i.* (*p.t.* **strove,** *pf.t.* **striven**) jaribu, jaribia, jitahidi, fanya bidii, fanya juhudi, shindana.

strode, *p.t.* ya *stride.*

stroke, *n.* pigo; (*disaster*) msiba, adhabu; (*sudden effort or effect*) tendo la nguvu, tendo kubwa, mshindo, dhoruba. (*apoplectic*) kifafa. *Give a finishing stroke to,* maliza, kamilisha. *At a stroke,* dharuba moja. — *v.t.* singa (bila mafuta &c.), papasa. *Stroke up the wrong way,* kasirisha. *Stroke down,* tuliza.

stroll, *v.i.* tembea polepole, zungukazunguka, susurika, zurura, zururika, tanga, jienda. — *n.* matembezi, kuzunguka, kutanga. **stroller,** *n.* mpitaji, mtembezi.

strong, *a.* -a nguvu, hodari, -a bidii, thabiti, sulubu, imara, -gumu; (*manly*) -a kiume, -a kinaume, kakawana; (*of tea, tobacco &c.*) msunguti; (*of taste, smell*) -kali, -chungu. **stronghold,** *n.* ngome, boma, gereza, husuni. **strongly,** *adv.* kwa nguvu sana.

strop, *n.* kinoo cha wembe. — *v.t.* noa wembe.

strophanthus, *n.* msunguti, msungululu.

strophe, *n.* sehemu ya wimbo.

strove, *p.t.* ya *strive.*

struck, *p.t. and pf.t.* ya *strike. Be struck all of a heap* (*slang*) fadhaika, shangaa, duwaa, pumbaa.

structure, *n.* muundo, ujenzi, mategeneo; (*natural form*) umbo, jinsi ya kufanyizwa, maumbile, asili. *A structure,* (*building*) jengo; (*wooden*) kiunzi. **structural,** *a.* -a *structure.*

struggle, *v.i.* shindana, jitahidi, fanya bidii, jaribu, jaribia, kakamka; (*in water, move convulsively*) tapatapa; (*offer resistance*) shindana, fanya machachari. — *n.* bidii, mkazo, jaribu, juhudi, kazi ngumu, taabu; (*contest*) shindano, mapigano, vita. **struggling,** *a.* -a kufanya jitihadi &c., -a kushindana.

strum, *v.i.* pigapiga ovyo kwa nguvu (kinanda &c.).

strumpet, *n.* malaya, kahaba.

strung, *p.t. and pf.t.* ya *string.*

strut, *v.i.* enda kwa kujivuna, ringa, tamba, belenga, enda kwa madaha. — *n.* kutamba, mwendo wa maringo (wa madaha, wa kutamba), (*cross-piece*) taruma, gadi, egemezo.

strychnine, *n.* sumu ya mtonga au mtupa.

stub, *n.* (*of a tree*) kishiku, kisiki, kigutu, gutu; (*general*) kidiku, kibutu, kibubutu, kigutu, gutu. — *v.t.* jikwaa (mguu, kidole), piga mdukuo. *Stub up,* ng'oa (chimbua) visiki. **stubby,** *a.* -fupi, -nene.

stubble, *n.* mashina ya majani au mabua yaliyokatika; (*of beard*) ndevu fupi ngumu.

stubborn, *a.* -kaidi, -shupavu, -gumu, -tundu, -kakamzi; (*of courage &c.*) thabiti, imara. **stubbornly,** *adv.* kwa uthabiti, kwa ukaidi. **stubbornness,** *n.* uthabiti, ushupavu, ugumu, ukaidi.

stubby, *a.* taz. *stub.*

stucco, *n.* lipu, chokaa ya kukandikia.

stuck, *p.t. and pf.t.* ya *stick*; *Stuck up,* -a kiburi, -enye majivuno, -a kujivuna, -a kutakabari.

stud, (1) *n.* jamii ya farasi (waliochungwa kusudi kuzaliana au wa kuwinda au wa kushindana mbio &c.).

stud, (2) *n.* (*for collar &c.*) kifungo; (*for decoration*) msumari, kinundu, njumu. — *v.t.* pamba kwa njumu (misumari, vinundu); (*sprinkle &c.*) tapakaza, weka huko na huko. **studded,** *a.* -liopambwa kwa njumu &c.; -liotapakaa . . . .

student, *n.*, **studied,** *a.*, **studio,** *n.*, **studious,** *a.*, **studiousness,** *n.* taz. *study.*

study, *n.* (*mental work*) kujifunza, kusoma kwa bidii, mtaala; (*subjects studied*) kazi za chuoni, vitabu, masomo, kazi; (*careful scrutiny &c.*) uchunguzi, kuchungua; (*in art*) kazi, namna ya kazi, kiolezo; (*room*) chumba cha kusomea; (*endeavour, intention*) mradi, kusudi. — *v.t.* soma, soma sana, jifunza kwa kusoma, taali; (*be concerned with or for &c.*) angalia, shughulikia, fanyia bidii; (*examine &c.*) tafuta habari za, tafiti, chungua, chunguza, peleleza; — *v.i.* soma, taali. **student,** *n.* mwanafunzi, mwana chuoni, mtu wa kusoma, mtu wa mtaala, mtaalamu; (*investigator &c.*) mchunguzi. **studied,** *a.* (*designed*) -a bidii, -a makusudi; (*worked at*) -liofanyiwa kazi nyingi, -liosomwa sana. **studio,** *n.* chumba (kiwanda) cha mchora sanamu (cha mpiga sanamu, cha mwumba sanamu.) **studious,** *a.* -a bidii katika *study*, -a bidii. **studiousness,** *n.* bidii ya kusoma.

stuff, *n.* vitu, vyombo, vifaa, zana, vipambo vya nyumba; (*cloth*) nguo, kitambaa; (*nonsense*) upuzi; (*substance*) asili, kitu cha asili, kitu (cho chote); (*rubbish*) takataka. *Stuff!* mawe! — *v.t.* jaza, jaliza; (*press*) shindilia, songeza; (*gorge*) shibisha, vimbisha, kinaisha; (*fill hole*) ziba; (*cram with learning*) fundisha mambo mengi; — *v.i.* (*eat to excess &c.*) shiba, jishibisha, jivimbisha, -la kwa pupa, lafua. **stuffiness,** *n.* uvuguvugu, ufukuto, jasho, hari. **stuffing,** *n.* kitu cha kujazia (*e.g.* sufi au pamba &c. kwa mito, matakia, magodoro &c.) vitunguu, nyama iliyosagwa na viungo kwa bata &c.). **stuffy,** *a.* -a vuguvugu, pasipopita hewa, -a jasho, -a kusonga; (*of persons*) baridi, -zito.

stultification, *n.* taz. *stultify.*

stultify, *v.t.* pumbaza, onyesha upuzi wa; (*make of no effect &c.*) batili, rahisisha, tangua, vunja. **stultification,** *n.* kupumbaza &c.

stumble, *v.i.* jikwaa, kwaa; (*err*) kosa, kosakosa. *Stumble upon,* kuta, pata kwa bahati, vumbua (gundua) kwa bahati. — *n.* kwao; (*error*) kosa. **stumbling-block,** *n.* kikwazo, jambo la kukosesha, mashaka, mgogoro; (*person*) mtu wa kuchukiza (wa kupingamiza).

stump, *n.* (*of tree*) shina, kishiku, kisiki, kigutu, gutu; (*limb*) gutu, kigutu; (*of arm*) kikono; (*general*) kidiku, kibutu, kibubutu, kigutu, gutu; (*in cricket*) mti, kiguzo. *Go on the stump,* zunguka na kuhubiri. *Draw stumps* (*in cricket*) vunja (mchezo), maliza. *Be completely stumped,* fadhaika kabisa, pumbaa, duwaa, shangaa. *Stir one's stumps,* kaza mwendo. — *v.t.* (*puzzle*) fumba, tatiza, shinda; (*in cricket*) funga; (*tour in*) zunguka na kuhubiri katika; — *v.i.* (*walk heavily*) enda kwa kukanyaga, jikokota, enda kwa vishindo. **stumpy,** *a.* -fupi -nene.

stun, *v.t.* zimisha (poteza akili) kwa kipigo; (*bewilder &c.*) fadhaisha, tia bumbuazi, tia mzumbao, duwaza, shangaza, shtusha, tisha; (*with noise*) ziba masikio, tia uziwi, levya. *Be stunned,* zimia, zirai; (*be bewildered*) fadhaika; pumbaa, duwaa, shangaa. **stunning,** *a.* -a kuzimisha, -a kufadhaisha *&c.*; (*slang*) -a kupendeza sana.

stung, *p.t. and pf.t.* ya *sting.*

stunk, *pf.t.* ya *stink.*

stunning, *a.* taz. *stun.*

stunt, (1) *n.* mkogo, tendo la kuonyesha ustadi mbele ya watu kwa majivuno.

stunt, (2) *v.t.* viza, fupisha, zuia, haribu. *Be stunted,* via, kundaa, dumaa, fuwaa.

stupefy, *v.t.* fadhaisha, tia bumbuazi, duwaza, pumbaza, shangaza, poteza akili; (*intoxicate*) levya. **stupefaction,** *n.* fadhaa, bumbuazi, mzumbao, mshangao, kupotewa akili. **stupefying,** *a.* -a kufadhaisha, -a kutia bumbuazi *&c.*

stupendous, *a.* -kubwa (-ingi) mno ajabu.

stupid, *a.* -pumbavu, -jinga, -zuzu, -zito, pasipo akili; (*intoxicated*) -a kulewa. — *n.* mjinga, mpumbavu, baradhuli, mzuzu. *You stupid! Stupid fool!* mbuzi wee! ng'ombe, ngamia! **stupidity,** *n.* upumbavu ujinga, uzuzu, ubaradhuli, akili chache, uzito, upungufu wa akili. **stupidly,** *adv.* kwa ujinga *&c.* **stupor,** *n.* uzito wa akili, hali ya kuzimia au kupotewa na akili; (*by astonishment*) mzumbao, mshangao, fadhaa, bumbuazi.

sturdy, *a.* -nene, -a nguvu, hodari, -shupavu, -enye maungo. **sturdily,** *adv.* kwa nguvu, hodari. **sturdiness,** *n.* unene, nguvu, uhodari, maungo.

sturgeon, *n.* namna ya samaki mkubwa.

stutter, *v.i.* gugumiza, goteza maneno, babaika, sema kwa kitata. **stutter, stuttering,** *n.* kugugumiza, kigugumizi, kitata.

sty, (1) *n.* (*for pigs*) banda la nguruwe, zizi.

sty(e), (2) *n.* (*in eye*) chokea.

style, *n.* (*kind*) jinsi, namna, mtindo; (*appearance*) sura, umbo; (*good kind*) jinsi bora, namna nzuri; (*mode of writing*) mwandiko; (*temper*) tabia, desturi; (*title*) jina; (*pen, pencil*) kalamu; (*manner, general bearing*) mwendo. *A good* (*literary*) *style,* ufasaha. *In style,* vizuri, kwa fahari, kwa sherehe. — *v.t.* taja, ita. **stylish,** *a.* -zuri, bora, -a siku hizi.

styptic, *a.* -a kuviliza (kukausha, kuzuia) damu (ya kidonda *&c.*).

suasion, *n.* kushawishi, ushawishi.

suave, *a.* laini, -tamu, -a kujipendekeza, -a adabu.

sub- *pref.* chini, -a chini, -dogo kuliko, -a kukaribia.

subaltern, *n.* afisa mdogo (kuliko *captain*).

subaqueous, *a.* -a chini ya maji.

subcommittee, *n.* jamii ya watu waliochaguliwa katika halmashauri (baraza, mkutano) kufanya kazi (shauri) fulani.

subconscious, *a.* -a katika akili lakini -siodhihirika vizuri (-siotambulika vizuri).

subcutaneous, *a.* -a chini ya ngozi.

subdivide, *v.t.* gawa tena (zilizokwisha gawika), zidi kugawa. **subdivision,** *n.* sehemu ya sehemu, kikato.

subdue, *v.t.* tiisha, piga, shinda; (*tame*) fuga; (*quiet*) tuliza, lainisha; (*reduce intensity of*) punguza nguvu (akili). **subdued,** *a.* -a polepole; (*of light &c.*) -siyong'aa sana.

sub-editor, *n.* *editor* mdogo.

subjacent, *a.* -a chini.

subject, *n.* kitu kinachonenwa au kutendewa kazi; (*matter*) jambo, kitu, neno, shughuli, kadhia, kisa, sababu, hoja; (*of king*) raia; (*person*) mtu. — *a*. -a chini, -enye kupasiwa, -enye kuhusiwa, -lio katika hatari ya, -liopatikana na, -lioelekea kupata (kupatwa na). *Subject to*, kwa ruhusa ya, kwa sharti ya, ikiwa. *He is subject to fits*, hushikwa na kifafa. *Subject to your pleasure*, lakini upendavyo wewe. — *v.t.* tiisha, weka chini; (*make liable, affect*) pasisha, pasha. **subjection**, *n*. hali ya kuwa chini. **subjective**, *a*. (*things*) -a nafsi, -a nafsini (-a rohoni, -a moyoni, -a akili, -a mawazo, -a kutungika moyoni tu, si halisi, si hakika); (*person*) -a kujikumbuka nafsi, -enye fikira zake. **subjectivity**, *n*. kuwa *subjective*. **subject-matter**, *n*. yanayonenwa au kutendewa kazi.

subjoin, *v.t.* tia mwishoni, ongeza, tia zaidi.

subjugate, *v.t.* tiisha, piga, shinda. **subjugation**, *n*. kutiisha, kutiishwa &c.

subjunctive, *a*. (*Subjunctive mood*) namna ya *verb* inayoonyesha wazo la moyoni (kusudi, tamaa, tumaini, hofu &c.) si hakika ya jambo lenyewe.

sublet, *v.t.* pangisha nyumba &c. iliyopangwa.

sublimate, *v.t.* (*turn to vapour*) geuza hewa kwa moto; (*refine*) safisha kwa moto, takasa. **sublimation**, *n*. kugeuza, kutakasa, utakaso.

sublime, *a*. -a juu sana, bora sana, aali, adhimu, -kuu, -tukufu mno, -a fahari, -a heri, ajabu, -a kutisha. **sublimity**, *n*. fahari, heri, utukufu, ajabu, adhama.

subluminary, *n*. -a dunia hii, -a ulimwengu; (*unimportant*) -nyonge, hafifu.

submarine, *a*. -a chini ya bahari. — *n*. manowari (chombo) inayoweza kuzama na kwenda chini ya bahari.

submerge, *v.t.* tosa, zamisha, didimisha; — *v.i.* tota, zama, didimia. **submergence, submersion**, *n*. kutota, kutosa, kuzamisha, kuzama, kudidimisha, kudidimia.

submission, *n*., **submissive**, *a*., **submissiveness**, *n*. taz. *submit*.

submit, *v.t.* (*surrender*) shika miguu, jitoa, jiweka chini, tii; (*put forward*) toa, weka; — *v.i.* (*endure*) vumilia, stahimili; (*acquiesce*) kubali, ona radhi, ridhika. **submission**, *n*. kushika miguu, utii; (*meekness*) uvumilivu, uradhi, upole. **submissive**, *a*. -tii, -tiifu, -pole, -nyonge. **submissiveness**, *n*. utii, utiifu, upole, uradhi, uvumilivu, unyonge.

subnormal, *a*. -a kupungua -a kawaida, -baya kuliko -a kawaida.

subordinate, *a*. -a chini, -dogo. — *v.t.* weka chini. — *n*. mdogo. **subordination**, *n*. kuweka (kuwekwa, kujiweka) chini; (*obedience*) utii.

suborn, *v.t.* vuta mtu kufanya mabaya (kushuhudia uwongo &c.) kwa rushwa au njia isiyo ya halali, tumia kushuhudia uwongo, apisha uwongo. **subornation**, *n*. kuapisha uwongo.

subpoena, *n*. hati ya kulazimisha mtu aje mbele ya korti, notisi. —*v.t.* ita kwa notisi kufika mbele ya korti.

subscribe, *v.t.* (*sign*) tia (andika) sahihi, tia mkono, andika jina chini; (*support, approve*) kubali, toa idhini, shuhudia; (*contribute money to*) toa fedha, changa mali. **subscriber**, *n*. mtoa fedha (kwa kusudi fulani) mchanga fedha. **subscription**, *n*. (*approval*) kibali, ukubali; (*signature*) sahihi, mkono, kuandika jina, idhini; (*contribution*) ada (ya gazeti, ya chama &c.), chango.

subsection, *n*. sehemu ya sehemu, kikato.

subsequent, *a*. -a baadaye, -a kufuata, -a kutokea baadaye. **subsequently**, *adv*. baada, baadaye, hatima, hatimaye.

subserve, *v.t.* faa, saidia, auni. **subservience**, *n*. kutii, kufaa. **subservient**, *a*. -a kutii, -a kufaa, -a kusaidia (kusudi fulani).

subside, *v.i.* shuka, pungua, punguka tulia; (*water*) pwa; (*masonry* &c.)

titia. **subsidence,** *n.* kushuka &c., kutitia.

subsidy, *n.* fedha ya msaada. **subsidiary,** *a.* -a kusaidia, -a kuauni; -dogo. **subsidize,** *v.t.* tolea fedha ya kusaidia.

subsist, *v.i.* (*exist, endure*) -wa, kaa, ishi, endelea kuwapo; (*live*) ishi. *Subsist on,* -la, ponea, jilisha. **subsistence,** *n.* chakula, riziki; (*existence*) asili, hakika, kuwapo.

subsoil, *n.* udongo wa chini, tabaka ya udongo chini ya ile ya juu.

substance, *n.* kitu, nyama, mwili; (*matter*) asili ya vitu vyote; (*import*) maana; (*strength*) nguvu, uthabiti; (*wealth*) mali, utajiri. **substantial,** *a.* (*real*) -a hakika, -a kweli; (*strong*) -a nguvu, imara, thabiti, madhubuti; (*wealthy*) -a mali, tajiri; (*important*) -a maana. **substantiate,** *v.t.* thibitisha, hakikia, yakinisha, dhihirisha, shuhudia. **substantive,** *n.* (katika elimu ya sarufi) jina la kitu. — *a.* -a hakika, -a kweli, -a nguvu, -a maana.

substitute, *v.t.* tia mahali pa (badala ya) -ingine, badilisha. — *n.* badala. **substitution,** *n.* kutia (kutiwa) mahali pa au badala ya -ingine, kubadilisha, badilisho.

substratum, *n.* tabaka (safu, rusu) ya chini. *A substratum of truth,* msingi wake (kiini chake) ni kweli bali sehemu nyingine si kweli.

substructure, *n.* majengo ya chini, ujenzi wa chini, msingi.

subtend, *v.t.* enea chini, elekea, elekeana na, kabili.

subterfuge, *n.* hila, werevu, uwongo, kimasomaso, kipengee, upengee.

subterranean, subterraneous, *a.* -a chini ya nchi, -a chini kwa chini.

subtle, *a.* -janja, -erevu, -a hila nyingi; (*delicate fabric*) laini -embamba, -zuri; (*penetrating*) -a kupambanua, -a akili, -a nguvu; (*skilful*) -a ustadi mwingi; (*elusive*) -gumu kueleza (kufahamu), -a kutatiza. **subtlety,** *n.* werevu, busara, hila; (*fineness*) wembamba, ulaini; (*force*) akili, nguvu. **subtly,** *adv.* kwa werevu, kwa hila, kwa akili.

subtract, *v.t.* toa, ondoa, twaa, chukua. **subtraction,** *n.* kutoa, kuondoa &c.; (*in arithmetic*) kutoa.

subtrahend, *n.* kitoleo, hesabu inayotolewa.

suburb, *n.* kiunga, pambizo, kando ya mji. **suburban,** *a.* -a kiungani, -a pambizoni.

subvention, *n.* fedha ya msaada.

subvert, *v.t.* pindua, angamiza, haribu. **subversion,** *n.* kupindua, upinduzi, maangamizi. **subversive,** *a.* -a kupindua, -a kuangamiza, -haribifu.

subway, *n.* njia nayopita chini kwa chini ya nchi.

succeed, *v.t. and i.* (*follow*) fuata, andama; (*take place of*) ingia mahali pa; (*inherit*) rithi; — *v.i.* (*prosper*) fanikiwa, pata, faulu, fuzu, -wa na mwisho mwema, tokea vema, kunjuka, pata mradi (lililokusudiwa, haja); (*in a private matter*) hongera. *Succeed in,* weza, pata, jaliwa, faulu, fuzu. **succeeding,** *a.* -a pili, -a baadaye, -a kufuata, -a kuandama.

success, *n.* (*result*) mwisho; (*good fortune*) mwisho mwema, bahati njema, usitawi, kufanikiwa, njia, heri; (*person*) mtu aliyefaa, aliyefaulu. **successful,** *a.* -a kufanikiwa, -a heri, -a kufuzu, -a bahati, -a kusitawi. **succession,** *n.* kuingia mahali pa, haki ya kushika kazi ya; (*as heir*) kurithi, urithi; (*series*) kufuatana, mafuatano, maandamo, maandamano, mtawalia, msago, mfululizo. *A succession of events,* mambo mengi yakifuatana (yakiandamana, ya mtawalia, ya msago), utaratibu wa mambo. **successively,** *adv.* kwa kufuatana, moja kwa moja, sago, msago, mtawalia, mfululizo.

successor, *n.* afuataye, aingiaye mahali pa mtu, ajaye nyuma, mwandani, badala; (*heir*) mrithi.

succinct, *a.* -a maneno machache (lakini dhahiri). **succinctly,** *adv.* dhahiri kwa maneno machache.

succour, *v.t.* saidia, auni, futusha, leta shime, pigania, tia nguvu, -pa moyo. — *n.* msaada, auni, shime.

succulent, *a.* -enye maji mengi, -a utomvu mwingi.

succumb, *v.i.* (*to*) shindwa, jitoa, patwa; (*die*) -fa, fariki, patwa na faradhi.

such, *a.* hivi, -a jinsi (aina, namna) hii, sawa, -a namna (jinsi, aina) hiyo fulani, kama hiyo (huyo &c.), -liofanana, -a mfano mmoja; (*remarkable*) -kubwa, -ingi ajabu. *Such a thing,* habari hiyo. *Such and such,* fulani. *He is such a fool,* kweli mpumbavu huyu, mpumbavu sana huyu. *Such a business,* jambo kama nini. *Such as,* kama, mithali ya. *Such that,* hata. **suchlike,** *a.* -a mfano huo, -a kama hiyo (hizo, hivyo &c.), -a namna (jinsi, aina) hiyo.

suck, *v.t.* fyonza; (*the breast*) nyonya, amwa; (*dissolve in the mouth*) mumunya, mung'unya; (*absorb*) -nywa; — *v.i.* fyonza, nyonya. *Suck in, Suck up,* -nywa; (*as a pump*) vuta (kwa bomba) *Suck up to* (*slang*), rairai, sifusifu, jipendekeza kwa.

sucker, *n.* (*greenhorn &c.*) baradhuli, mzuzu, mjinga; (*one who sucks*) mnyonya, mfyonza; (*of plant*) mche, chipukizi. **suckle,** *v.t.* nyonyesha. **suckling,** *n.* mtoto anyonyaye, mtoto wa mnyama anyonyaye; (*inexperienced person*) mjinga, mzuzu. **suction,** *n.* kufyonza &c.; kuvuta kwa bomba, mfyonzo, mvuto.

sudd, *n.* matete, majani, magugu &c. yakielea mtoni au ziwani.

sudden, *a.* -a ghafula, -a dharuba moja, -siyotazamiwa. *On a sudden,* ghafula, mara. **suddenly,** *adv.* ghafula. **suddenness,** *n.* ghafula, kuwa ghafula.

sudorific, *a.* (dawa) ya kutoza jasho.

suds, *n.* povu la sabuni.

sue, *v.t. and i.* omba, sihi; (*prosecute*) shtaki, dai.

su de, *n.* namna ya ngozi laini nyembamba.

suet, *n.* shahamu ya nyama, mafuta magumu ya nyama (hasa yanayozunguka mafigo).

suffer, *v.t.* (*endure*) vumilia, stahimili, chukua; (*allow*) acha, kubali, ruhusu; — *v.i.* (*feel pain*) umwa, umizwa, teswa, ona uchungu; (*be damaged*) pata hasara, haribika, dhurika, hasirika; (*be affected*) patwa, tendewa; (*be punished*) patilizwa, rudiwa, adhibishwa. *Suffer from* (*illness &c.*), elekea kupatwa na, patwa na . . . mara kwa mara.

sufferance, *n.* kuachwa, ruhusa; (*endurance*) uvumilivu, ustahimilivu. *He is here on sufferance,* hana haki kuwapo, lakini ameachwa. **sufferer,** *n.* mwenye hasara (taabu, huzuni, maumivu &c.), mteswa, maskini. **suffering,** *n.* umivu, maumivu, kuteswa, mateso, uchungu, taabu.

suffice, *v.t. and i.* tosha, kifu, faa, ridhisha, akidi, weza. **sufficiency,** *n.* kefu, kadiri ya (kiasi cha) kutosha (cha kufaa); (*store, stock*) akiba, mali. **sufficient,** *a.* -a kutosha, -a kufaa, -a kuridhisha. *It is sufficient,* yatosha, basi. **sufficiently,** *adv.* kadiri ya kutosha, kadiri.

suffix, *n.* (*Gram.*) sehemu ya neno inayotiwa mwishoni, baada ya shina (*root*). — *v.t.* tia mwisho wa shina la neno, au mwisho wa neno.

suffocate, *v.t.* songa roho, songa, nyonga, zuia pumzi; — *v.i.* songwa, nyongwa, ona taabu kupumua. **suffocation,** *n.* kusonga (kusongwa) roho &c., msongo wa pumzi (roho).

suffrage, *n.* haki ya kusaidia kuchagua mtu kuwa katika baraza kuu ya serikali (*Parliament*). **suffragan,** *n.* (*bishop*) askofu msaidizi. **suffragette,** *n.* mwanamke aliyedai *suffrage.*

suffuse, *v.t.* funika, jaza, eneza katika. **suffusion,** *n.* kufunika &c.

sugar, *n.* sukari; (*brown, unrefined*) sukari guru. — *v.t.* tia sukari; (*flatter*) sifusifu mno, rairai. **sugar-beet,** *n.* namna ya mboga, kidogo kama kiazi, inayotumika kushindika sukari. **sugar-cane,** *n.* muwa. **sugar-mill,** *n.* kinu cha kushindikia sukari. **sugary,** *a.* -a sukari, kama sukari, -tamu.

suggest, *v.t.* onya, tia moyoni, leta fikira, toa shauri, shauri, penyeza habari; (*give idea of*) dokeza; (*by signs*) ashiria, pungia. **suggestion,** *n.* onyo, shauri, dokezo, ishara, rai. **suggestive,** *a.* -a kuonya, -a maana.

suicide, *n.* kujifisha makusudi, kujiua. *Commit suicide,* jifisha, jiua. **suicidal,** *a.* -a kujifisha, -a kujiua, -a kujiangamiza, -a kujiletea hasara.

suit, *n.* (*of clothes*) kisua (suruali, koti na koti ndogo zote kitambaa namna moja); (*in law*) madai, daawa, mashtaka, maneno, shauri; (*request*) haja, maombi; (*of marriage*) kuposa, maposo; (*of cards*) jamii ya namna moja ya karata, *e.g.* shupaza, pao &c. *Follow suit,* fanya vile vile. — *v.t.* faa, stahili, stahiki, laiki, agia, shimiri, -wa sawa (-zuri), wajibu, pendeza, juzu; (*adapt*) tengeneza, fanya kufaa; — *v.i.* (*agree*) patana, lingana. *Suit oneself,* chagua -enyewe. *Suit yourself,* upendavyo. *Suit each other,* chukuana. **suitability,** *n.* kufaa &c. **suitable,** *a.* -a kufaa, -a kustahili &c., -stahiki. **suit-case,** *n.* kasha jepesi la kuchukulia nguo &c. (la mkononi). **suite,** *n.* jamii ya wafuasi wa mtu mkuu, wafuasi; (*series, set*) jamii ya meza, vitu &c. vya namna moja (vinavyolingana); (*of rooms*) jamii ya vyumba vya kutumika na mtu mmoja (au yeye na watu wake). **suitor,** *n.* mchumba, mwenye kuposa, mposi; (*a law*) mdai.

sulk, *v.i.* nuna, kimwa. **sulkiness,** *n.* uchungu, ukaidi, chuki, kununa, ukimwa. **sulky,** *a.* -enye uchungu, -kaidi, -a kununa, -nuni, -a kukimwa.

sullen, *a.* -enye uchungu, -kaidi, -a chuki; (*gloomy, heavy*) -zito. **sullenness,** *n.* uchungu, ukaidi, chuki, uzito.

sully, *v.t.* chafua, tia uchafu.

sulphur, *n.* kiberiti. **sulphate,** *n.* (*of copper*) mrututu; (*of magnesia*) chumvi ya haluli. **sulphurous,** *a.* -a kiberiti.

sultan, *n.* sultani, mfalme, jumbe, mtawala. **sultana,** *n.* malkia, mkewe sultani. **sultanate, sultanship,** *n.* usultani.

sultry, *a.* -a hari, -a shwari, -a jua kali na jasho; (*oppressive*) -a kusonga; -a hewa nzito. **sultriness,** *n.* hari, shwari, jasho.

sum, *n.* (*total amount*) jumla; (*in arithmetic*) hesabu; (*of money*) fedha; (*meaning*) maana. *A sum of money,* fedha. *Pay a large sum,* lipa fedha nyingi. *Do sums,* fanya hesabu. — *v.t.* hesabu, jumlisha. *Sum up,* jumlisha, fanya muhtasari, sema kwa vichache. **summarily,** *adv.* bila kukawia, bila maneno (matengenezo) mengi. **summarize,** *v.t.* jumlisha, fupisha, sema kwa maneno machache, fanya muhtasari. **summary,** *n.* muhtasari. — *a.* -a mara moja, -a ghafula, bila kukawia, bila maneno (matengenezo) mengi. *In a summary manner,* upesi, kwa haraka, bila kufikiri, mara moja.

summer, *n.* wakati wa jua kali, wakati wa hari; (*in south latitudes*) kiangazi, kaskazi, msimu, chaka. **summer-house,** *n.* banda la kukaa bustanini wakati wa jua kali.

summit, *n.* kilele, kileleta; (*tip*) ncha; (*highest point*) upeo, kipeo, juu. *On the summit of,* juu ya.

summon, *v.t.* ita, alika; (*to court of law*) pelekea notisi, amuru kufika korti (barazani). **summons,** *n.* mwito, mwaliko, jaliko, kuitwa hukumuni (kortini, barazani); (*document*) notisi.

sump, *n.* sehemu ya chini ya mashine mafuta yanapokaa.

sumpter, *a.* (mnyama) -a kazi.

sumptuary, *a.* -a kupunguza gharama, -a kuzuia anasa.

sumptuous, *a.* -a anasa nyingi, -a thamani, -a gharama nyingi, -zuri sana. **sumptuously,** *adv.* kwa anasa. **sumptuousness,** *n.* anasa.

sun, *n.* jua. — *v.t.* anika juani. *Sun oneself,* ota (jiota) jua. **sunbeam,** *n.* mwanga wa jua, kianga. **sunbird,** *n.* chozi. **sunburnt,** *a.* -ekundu (-kavu) kwa jua, -liokauka. **Sunday,** *n.* Jumapili. **sundial,** *n.* ubao wa kujulisha saa ngapi kwa kivuli kinachofanywa na jua. **sunless,** *a.* pasipo jua, -a giza. **sunlight,** *n.* mwangaza wa jua. **sunny,** *a.* -a jua, -a hari; (*joyous*) -a furaha, -kunjufu, -changamfu. **sunproof,** *a.* -siopenyezeka kwa joto la jua. **sunrise,** *n.* kucha, jua lichapo, macheo ya jua, mapambazuko. *From sunrise to sunset,* mchana kutwa. *From sunset to sunrise,* usiku kucha. **sunset,** *n.* magharibi, jua lituapo, machweo, kuchwa. **sunshine,** *n.* jua, mwanga wa jua; (*after rain*) kianga. **sunshade,** *n.* mwavuli wa kukinga jua. **sunstroke,** *n.* kupatwa na jua.

sunder, *v.t.* tenga, pasua, kata; — *v.i.* tengana, tengemana, pasuka, katika.

sundial, *n.* taz. *sun.*

sundry, *a.* -ingine, kadha wa kadha, baadhi. *All and sundry,* kila mtu, watu wote. **sundries,** *n.* takataka, vitu vinginevyo.

sung, *pf.t.* ya *sing.*

sunk, *pf.t.* ya *sink.*

sunless, *a.*, **sunlight,** *n.*, **sunny,** *a.*, **sunproof,** *a.*, **sunrise,** *n.*, **sunset,** *n.*, **sunshine,** *n.*, **sunshade,** *n.*, **sunstroke,** *n.* taz. *sun.*

sup, *v.t. and i.* -la kidogokidogo, konga maji. — *n.* kidogo cha chakula au kinywaji.

superabundance, *n.* taz. *superabundant.*

superabundant, *a.* -ingi mno, -a kusaza, -a kubaki. **superabundance,** *n.* wingi, maziada, masazo, masalio, baki.

superannuate, *v.t.* ondosha katika kazi kwa sababu ya kupita umri wa kanuni. **superannuation,** *n.* kuondosha (kuondoka) katika kazi &c.; (*pension*) mshahara apatao mtu aliyeondoshwa (aliyeondoka) katika kazi kwa sababu amepita umri wa kanuni.

superb, *a.* -zuri sana, bora, -a kipeo cha uzuri (cha ubora).

supercargo, *n.* karani, msimamizi wa shehena melini.

supercilious, *a.* -juvi, -a kiburi, -a kudharau, -a kutakabari, -a kujivuna, sodawi. *A supercilious look,* kutazama kijuvi (kisodawi) macho ya kiburi. **superciliousness,** *n.* ujuvi, kiburi, dharau, majivuno, usodawi.

supererogation, *n.* zaidi ya kadiri ipasayo kwa haki, -a zaidi.

superficies, *n.* upande wa nje (wa juu), sura ya juu, eneo. **superficial** *a.* -a kijuujuu; (*hasty, careless*) -a haraka, -a kutaghafali, -a purukushani, -a kukukusa. *Treat superficially,* purukusha. *A superficial wound,* jeraha dogo (ya nje, ya kijuujuu, ya ngozini tu). **superficially,** *adv.* kwa juujuu tu, kwa haraka, kwa upurukushani.

superfine, *a.* -zuri sana, bora kabisa.

superfluous, *a.* -a bure, -sio na kazi, -siotumika, -a kupita kiasi, -a zaidi. **superfluity,** *n.* usazo, masazo, masalio, baki, mazidio, kisicho na kazi, wingi.

superhuman, *a.* -a kupita uwezo (akili, ukubwa &c.) wa binadamu, -kubwa (-ingi) mno, -a Mungu.

superimpose, *v.t.* weka (tia, jenga &c.) juu (ya kitu kingine).

superincumbent, *a.* -liowekwa juu, -a juu.

superintend, *v.t.* simamia, angalia, amuru kazi, ongoza. **superintendence,** *n.* usimamizi, uongozi, madaraka, matengenezo, maangalizi. **superintendent,** *n.* msimamizi, mwangalizi, mwongozi.

superior, *a.* -a juu, -ema zaidi, -kubwa, bora, aali, aula, -a kupita -ingine, -ingi (-kubwa) zaidi. *Superior to,* -sioshindwa na, kupita, zaidi ya, aali ya, -siovutwa na. — *n.*

mkubwa (kwa cheo, amri *&c.*). **superiority,** *n.* hali ya kuwa *superior,* ukuu, ukubwa (kuliko -ingine).

superlative, *a.* bora mno. *In a superlative degree,* kupita yote.

supernatural, *a.* si -a ulimwengu, si -a jinsi ya viumbe vyote, -a kupita akili, si kwa desturi ya vitu vyote, si -a dunia hii, -a ajabu; (*spiritual*) -a rohoni, -a Mungu; (*miraculous*) -a mwujiza. *The supernatural,* yasiyo-onekana, yapitayo akili zetu.

supernumerary, *a.* -a zaidi kuliko hesabu iliyoamriwa (iliyoruhusiwa).

superpose, *v.t.* weka juu (ya kitu kingine). **superposition,** *n.* ku-weka (kuwekwa) juu.

superscribe, *v.t.* andika juu, tia anwani. **superscription,** *n.* anwani, andiko la juu.

supersede, *v.t.* (*take the place of*) ingia mahali pa, -wa badala ya; (*remove*) ondosha, batilisha, tangua.

superstition, *n.* ushirikina (imani ya mambo ya uchawi, uramali, usihiri, hirizi, kupiga bao, ndege njema na mbaya, majini, mazimwi *&c.*). **superstitious,** *a.* -a ushirikina, -a kuamini mambo ya uchawi, ura-mali *&c.*

superstructure, *n.* ujenzi wa juu, uunzi wa juu.

supervene, *v.i.* tukia baadaye, fuata, tokea, zukia.

supervise, *v.t.* simamia, angalia, amrisha, ongoza. **supervision,** *n.* usimamizi, maangalizi, madaraka, amri, mwongozo. **supervisor,** *n.* msimamizi, mwangalizi.

supine, *a.* (*on the back*) chali, kimgo-ngo; (*slack*) -legevu, -zito, -zembe, -nyogovu, -nyong'onyevu. **supine-ness,** *n.* ulegevu, uzito, uzembe *&c.*

supper, *n.* chakula cha usiku, kijio. **sup,** *v.i.* -la *supper.* **supperless,** *a.* pasipo *supper.*

supplant, *v.t.* twaa mahali pa, ondosha, punguza (poteza) kidogo kidogo kwa siri.

supple, *a.* -a kupindikapindika, -a kunyumbuka, -liopindikana, -epesi, laini; (*yielding*) -a tabia laini, -tii, -tiifu; (*sly*) -a hila, -erevu. **supple-ness,** *n.* ulaini, wepesi, hali (tabia) ya kuweza kupindikapindika *&c.*

supplement, *n.* maongezo, nyongeza, utimizo. — *v.t.* ongeza, timiza.

supplementary, *a.* -a kuongeza, -a kutimiliza, -a zaidi.

suppleness, *n.* taz. *supple.*

supplicate, *v.t.* omba, sihi, taka, lalama. **suppliant,** *a.* -a kuomba, -ombi, -ombaji. **supplication,** *n.* maombi, haja, kuomba, malalamiko. **supplicatory,** *a.* -a kuomba, -omba-ji, -a kulalama.

supply, *v.t.* toa, leta, weka, -pa, auni, jazi, saidia; (*with food &c.*) ruzuku, kimu; (*on credit*) kopesha. *Supply the place of,* -wa mahali pa, -wa badala ya. — *n.* kutoa, kuleta, kuweka; (*store, quantity*) wingi, akiba, jamii, auni, msaada; (*public*) fedha ya serikali. *Supply and demand,* kadiri ya kutaka na ya kupatikana itakwayo, mali na tamaa. **supplies,** *n.* matumizi, akiba, kande, vyakula, riziki, vyombo, vifaa, zana, manufaa.

support, *v.t.* (*bear*) chukua, tegemeza, egemeza, himili; (*endure*) vumilia, stahimili; (*help*) saidia, tegemeza, egemeza, auni, fariji, -pa moyo, pendelea, burudisha; (*maintain*) lisha, chukua, ruzuku, kimu, patia chakula; (*a cause*) shindania, shiki-lia; (*continue*) endeleza, dumisha, fululiza, fuliza; (*attest*) shuhudia, thibitisha; (*attend*) fuatana na, sindikiza. *Support life on,* ponea, -la. *How does he support himself?* anapo-nea nini? apataje riziki? — *n.* kuchukua *&c.* (*prop*) tegemeo, ege-mezo, mwega, nguzo, himili, mwimo, gadi, kitu chenye kazi ya kuchukua *&c., e.g.* mti, kibao, chakula, fedha, riziki *&c.*; (*help*) msaada, auni, shime, upendeleo. *Means of support,* riziki, chakula. **supportable,** *a.* -a kuchukulika, -a kuvumilika, -a kustahimilika. **supporter,** *n.* mtu wa kuchukua *&c.*, msaidizi, mfuasi.

suppose, *v.t.* (*consider*) waza, dhani, ona; (*fancy, guess*) tunga, bahatisha, kisi; (*require*) hitaji, taka. *Suppose that, Supposing,* kama, ikiwa, labda, kwamba, huenda, iwapo. *Suppose they differ,* hata na waachane. **supposable,** -a kuwazikana, yamkini. **supposition,** *n.* wazo, dhana; (*not fact*) hadithi, maneno, uwongo. **supposititious,** *a.* -liotiwa kwa hila, -a hila, -a uwongo, si halisi.

suppress, *v.t.* (*overcome*) shinda, vunja, komesha; (*restrain*) funga, zuia; (*conceal*) ficha, setiri; (*cut out &c.*) kata, futa, toa. **suppressed,** *a.* -liozuia, -liofichwa, -liokomeshwa &c. **suppression,** *n.* kushinda, kuvunja &c. **suppressive,** *a.* -a kushinda, -a kuvunja, -a kukomesha, -a kuzuia &c.

suppurate, *v.i.* tunga usaha. **suppuration,** *n.* kutunga usaha.

supreme, *a.* -kubwa sana, bora, halisi, -zuri kabisa, -a kipeo cha ukubwa (ubora, uzuri &c.). *The Supreme Being,* Mwenyezi Mungu. **supremacy,** *n.* enzi kuu, mamlaka, uwezo, kutawala, nguvu, hukumu, kipeo cha nguvu &c. **supremely,** *adv.* kupita yote, zaidi, hasa.

surcharge, *n.* fedha ya kulipa zaidi ya ile iliyokwisha lipwa. — *v.t.* taka (dai) fedha zaidi kuliko ile iliyokwisha lipwa.

sure *a.* (*certain*) -a hakika, yakini, -a kweli; (*positive*) -a kujua sana; (*trustworthy, safe*) amini, -aminifu, thabiti, madhubuti, salama, -a kutumainiwa, imara; (*confident*) -enye tumaini, pasipo shaka. *You are sure to go,* huna budi utakwenda. *Be sure, Feel sure* (*have no doubt*) yakinia, jua sana, tumaini sána; (*be beyond doubt*) -wa yakini (hakika). *Make sure,* hakiki, hakikisha. *Yes, to be sure,* ndiyo, kweli, naam, kabisa. **surely,** *adv.* hapana shaka, hakuna budi, haikosi; (*safely*) salama, kwa hadhari. **surety,** *n.* dhamana, mdhamini, lazima. **suretyship,** *n.* udhamini.

surf, *n.* mawimbi (yakifanya povu), mawimbi meupe, mawimbi ya kuumuka.

surface, *n.* upande wa nje, upande wa juu, juu, sura, uso. *Surface of the earth,* uso wa dunia, sura ya nchi. — *a.* -a nje, -a juujuu.

surfeit, *n.* shibe, wingi, kinaya. — *v.t.* shibisha, vimbisha, kinaisha.

surge, *v.i.* inuka, fanya mawimbi, umuka, sukasuka. — *n.* mawimbi ya kuumuka, msukosuko.

surgeon, *n.* daktari (hasa mstadi wa kuganga mifupa iliyovunjika na kukata sehemu za mwili zilizoharibika). **surgery,** *n.* udaktari, kazi ya *surgeon*; (*room*) chumba cha kazi ya *surgeon.* **surgical,** *a.* -a daktari, -a udaktari.

surly, *a.* -kali, -chungu, -a chuki, -a kasirani. **surliness,** *n.* ukali, uchungu, chuki, kasirani, hasira.

surmise, *v.i.* (*judge*) dhani, waza; (*guess, fancy*) kisi, bahatisha. — *n.* wazo, dhana, kisio, bahatisho.

surmount, *v.t.* pita juu, pita, shinda, faulu, weza. *Surmounted by . . .,* -enye . . . juu yake. **surmountable,** *a.* -a kupitika, -a kushindika, -a kuwezekana.

surname, *n.* jina la kuonyesha jamaa (jina la ukoo). — *v.t.* tia *surname.*

surpass, *v.t.* pita, shinda, zidi, kulula. *He surpasses him in power,* amemzidi kwa nguvu, amemzidia nguvu. **surpassing,** *a.* -a kupita (kushinda) -ote, -a kipeo.

surplice, *n.* nguo nyeupe kama gwanda inayovaliwa na makasisi, waimbaji &c. kanisani.

surplus, *n.* baki, sazo, salio, ziada, kizidicho kadiri inayotakiwa.

surprise, *n.* (*feeling of wonder*) mshangao, mastaajabu, mzumbao; (*thing*) shani, kizushi, ajabu, kioja; (*bewilderment*) fadhaa, bumbuazi; (*sudden onset*) kugundua, kugunduliwa. *Take by surprise,* jia kwa hila, fumania, gundulia, zukia. *Cause surprise,* shangaza, shtusha, staajabisha, tia kishindo. — *v.t.* staajabisha, ajabisha, shangaza; (*bewilder*) kanganya, fadhaisha, shtusha, tunduwaza, duwaza, pumbaza. **surprising,** *a.* -a ajabu, -a kustaajabisha *&c.*

surrender, *v.t. and i.* (*to*) toa, salimisha, elemea, kiri -meshindwa; (*oneself*) jitoa, jisalimisha. — *n.* kutoa, kutolewa *&c.*

surreptitious, *a.* -a hila, -a siri. **surreptitiously,** *adv.* kwa hila, kwa siri.

surrogate, *n.* naibu, makamu, badala.

surround, *v.t.* (*be, go round*) zunguka, -wa mzingo wa (pande zote za), kando kando ya; (*place round*) zungushia; (*besiege*) zingia, fanyia mazingiwa, husuru. **surrounding,** *a.* -a kuzunguka, -a pande zote. **surroundings,** *n.* mazingia, mahali pa jirani, ujirani, kitende, mastakimu.

surtout, *n.* vazi kama joho, koti refu.

surveillance, *n.* usimamizi, uangalizi, ulinzi, uchunguzi.

survey, *v.t.* (*view &c.*) tazama, kagua, . aua, chungua, angalia; (*measure and describe*) andika ramani ya, pima, kadirisha, andika sura halisi kwa kupima na kuhesabu. — *n.* kutazama *&c.*, tazamo, nadhari. **surveying,** *n.* kutazama *&c.*; (*map-making*) maarifa ya kupima nchi au bahari na kuandika ramani, kupima nchi. **surveyor,** *n.* mwenye kazi ya *surveying*, bwana mpima.

survive, *v.t.* ishi baada ya kufiwa (baada ya hatari, msiba *&c.*), zidi kuishi, zidi kukaa; (*be saved*) okoka, pona katika hatari; — *v.i.* (*remain*) baki, salia. **survival,** *n.* kuishi baada ya kufiwa *&c.*; (*remainder*) baki, masalio, masazo. **survivor,** *n.* mwenye kuokoka, mwenye kuishi baada ya kufiwa.

susceptible, susceptive, *a.* -epesi kuona (kushtuka, kupata, kupatwa *&c.*); (*kind*) -a huruma, -a utu mwema. **susceptibility,** *n.* wepesi wa kuona (kushtuka, kupata, kupatwa *&c.*); (*kindness*) huruma, utu mwema.

suspect, *v.t.* shuku, tuhumu, onea mashaka, dhania viovu; (*fancy*) dhani, kisi, waza. — *a.* -a mashaka, -lioshukiwa. — *n.* mtu anayeshukiwa, mtu anayeonewa mashaka (anayetuhumiwa). **suspicion,** *n.* kudhania viovu, tuhuma, mashaka, dhana, shuku; (*trace, small portion &c.*) kidogo sana, dalili. **suspicious,** *a.* -enye kudhania viovu, -enye mashaka, -a kushuku, -a kutuhumu; (*untrustworthy*) si amini, si wazi, si -nyofu.

suspend, *v.t.* (*hang*) tundika, angika; (*balance*) ning'iniza; (*defer*) weka, ahirisha; (*stop work &c. of*) zuia kazi ya, uzulu, toa, tangua, ondosha kwa muda; (*prohibit*) gombeza, kataza. *Suspend a sitting,* vunja baraza. *Suspend judgement,* ahirisha hukumu. **suspender,** *n.* ukanda wa kuzuia suruali (soksi *&c.*). **suspense,** *n.* mashaka, kusitasita, hangaiko, wasiwasi; (*pause, stop*) kukoma. **suspension,** *n.* kutungika, kuangika, kuondoshwa kwa muda. *Suspension bridge,* daraja lililotundikwa kwa kamba, minyororo *&c.* **suspensory,** *a.* -a kuchukua.

suspicion, *n.*, **suspicious,** *a.* taz. *suspect.*

sustain, *v.t.* chukua, tegemeza, saidia; (*endure*) patwa na, vumilia, stahimili; (*enable to endure*) hifadhi; (*prove*) thibitisha; (*allow*) kubali, toa idhini; (*keep up, maintain*) fululiza, endeleza. **sustenance,** *n.* vyakula, maakuli, riziki. **sustentation,** *n.* kulisha, kusaidia, kuendeleza, kuchukua, kutegemeza.

sutler, *n.* mchuuzi (kwa askari).

suture, *n.* kushona (kwa udaktari), mshono, kiungo.

suzerain, *n.* mfalme, mtawala. **suzerainty,** *n.* ufalme, utawala.

svelte, *a.* (mwanamke) -embamba -enye madaha.

swab, *v.t.* pangusa, safisha (kwa kitambaa au pamba). — *n.* pamba au kitambaa cha kupangusia au cha kupakia dawa.

swaddle, *v.t.* fungafunga katika vitambaa. **swaddling-clothes,** *n.* vitambaa vya kumfungia mtoto, nguo za kitoto.

swagger, *v.i.* tamba, randa, enda kwa kujivuna, nyeta; (*make a show*) piga makuu, piga umalidadi, koga, piga mikogo, fanya fahari, fanya jeuri, takabari. — *n.* majivuno, makuu, umalidadi, mikogo, ufidhuli, jeuri. **swagger-cane,** *n.* kifimbo cha askari.

Swahili, *n. and a.* (*person*) Mswahili; (*language*) Kiswahili.

swain, *n.* mtu wa shamba, mkulima; (*lover*) mchumba (mwanamume).

swallow, (1) *n.* kijumbamshale, kinegwa, mbayuwayu.

swallow, (2) *v.t.* meza, -la -ote, akia; (*put up with*) vumilia, stahimili; (*recant*) jikania, jikatalia, geuza; (*take on trust*) sadiki mara moja pasipo shaka.

swam, *p.t.* ya *swim.*

swamp, *n.* bwawa, ziwa la matope, kinamasi. — *v.t.* jaza maji, tosa majini, pindua; (*ruin*) angamiza, pindua. **swampy,** *a.* -enye mabwawa, -a majimaji, -a kinamasi, -a matope mengi.

swan, *n.* ndege kama bata mkubwa sana.

swank, *v.i. and n.* (*slang*) kama *swagger.*

sward, *n.* mahali penye majani mazuri mafupi.

swarm, (1) *n.* kundi, kundi zima, kundi (bumba) la nyuki &c. — *v.i.* fanya kundi kama nyuki, songamana, -wa -ingi, jaa, zaa sana.

swarm, (2) *v.t.* (*up*) paraga, sombea, paramia.

swarthy, *a.* -eusi (uso, ngozi). **swarthiness,** *n.* weusi.

swashbuckler, *n.* mjeuri, mpiganaji (hasa mjeuri).

swat, *v.t.* piga, ua (inzi, mdudu &c.).

swathe, *v.t.* fungiafungia vitambaa, zungushia (zongomeza) kitambaa.

sway, *v.t.* (*move to and fro*) sukasuka, chuchia; (*swing*) pembeza, ning'iniza; (*influence*) geuza, vuta, ongoza, shawishi, tawala, weza; — *v.i.* (*oscillate* &c.) ning'inia, lewalewa, wayawaya, yonga, konya, yumbayumba, tikisika; (*stagger*) pepesuka, sepetuka, levyalevya, sitasita, tetereka. — *n.* kuning'inia &c.; (*rule*) utawala, uwezo wa mfalme, enzi; (*power, influence*) nguvu, mvuto, mwendo wa nguvu.

swear, *v.t.* (*p.t.* **swore,** *pf.t.* **sworn**) apa, apa yamini; (*cause to swear, administer an oath*), apisha, funga kwa kiapo; (*assert emphatically*) sema kwa uthabiti; — *v.i.* (*curse*) laani, apiza, tukana. *Swear at,* tukana, laani, apiza. *Swear in* (*soldiers* &c.), apisha. *Swear by,* apa kwa; (*trust in*) amini, jetea, tegemea. *Swear eternal friendship* (*by mutual incision*), chanjiana. *Swear mutually* (*to each other*), apiana. *Swear solemnly* (*on the Koran*), apa (piga) yamini (Kurani). *Cause to swear,* apisha, afya. *Swear off,* apa kuacha. *Swear to,* shuhudia kwa kiapo. **swearer,** *n.* (*one who curses*), mtukanaji, mwapizi. **swearing,** *n.* kuapa; (*cursing*) laana, matukano, maapizo.

sweat, *n.* jasho, hari, vukuto. — *v.i.* toa (toka) jasho; (*of objects*) rishai; (*work hard*) fanya kazi kwa bidii, jitahidi; — *v.t.* toza jasho; (*of exaction*) toza (watu) kazi ngumu (ya kumletea mwenyewe faida) kwa mshahara mdogo, onea, dhulumu. **sweated,** *a.* -liofanywa na watu wasiopata mshahara wa kutosha. **sweater,** *n.* namna ya fulana nzito. **sweaty,** *a.* -a jasho, -a hari.

sweep, *v.t.* (*p.t. and pf.t.* **swept**) fagia, pangusa, takasa, zoa, kokoa; (*empty*) fanya -eupe (-tupu); (*remove*) chukua, rusha, ondoa -ote, futia mbali; (*clear out*) kumba; (*survey*) pisha jicho juu ya, tupia jicho, tazama -ote; (*of musical instrument*) pisha mkono juu ya, piga; — *v.i.* fagia; (*move proudly*) pita kwa nguvu (kwa fahari); (*extend &c.*) tambaa, enea, tandaa. *Sweep away*, futia mbali, ondoa -ote, pangusa, kumba. *Sweep up* (*in heaps*), zoa. — *n.* kufagia, mfuto &c. (*of arm, arms*) pigo la ghafula; (*range*) eneo, upeo, pigo; (*direction*) maelekeo; (*current*) mwendo wa nguvu, mkondo, mvuto. *Make a clean sweep*, kumba, futia mbali. **sweepings**, *n.* takataka. **sweepstake**, *n.* mchezo wa kubahatisha fedha katika shindano.

sweet, *a.* -tamu, -a kupendeza, laini, -zuri, -pole; (*to smell*) -a kunukia -a kufiridi; (*water*) baridi. *Of his own sweet will*, apendavyo mwenyewe tu. — *n.* kitu kitamu kama peremende, halua, gubiti, maandazi, vitumbua &c.; (*darling*) mpenzi, kipenzi, tiba. *Sweets* (*enjoyment*), furaha, usitawi. **sweetbread**, *n.* kongosho. **sweeten**, *v.t.* tia utamu, tia sukari, fanya tamu, koleza; — *v.i.* -wa -tamu, geuka -wa -tamu. **sweetheart**, *n.* mchumba. **sweetly**, *adv.* kwa utamu, kwa ulaini, vizuri. **sweetmeat**, *n.* kitu kitamu kama peremende, halua &c. **sweetness**, *n.* utamu. **sweet-oil**, *n.* halzeti, mafuta ya zeituni. **sweet-potato**, *n.* kiazi. **sweets**, *n.* (*pleasures*) utamu, furaha; (*bonbons*) peremende, sukari, vitamu &c. **sweet-sop**, *n.* topetope, tomoko.

swell, *v.i.* (*pf.t.* **swelled, swollen**) vimba, tuna, kubaza, umuka, fura; (*increase*) zidi, ongezeka; (*spread*) tanuka, enea, umuka; (*with rage, anger*) fura, tuna; (*be proud*) jivuna; (*be full of*) ingiwa na . . . ingi; — *v.t.* vimbisha, zidisha, ongeza, panua, furisha. — *n.* kuvimba, kuzidi; (*waves*) mawimbi ya mkoba; (*fop*) mmalidadi, mlimbwende, (*slang*) mfua uji. **swelling**, *n.* uvimbe, kivimbe; (*protuberance*) nundu, kitumbo, rugurugu; (*increase*) maongezo, maziada. — *a.* -a kuvimba, -a kutuna, -a kuzidizidi, -a kuumuka.

swelter, *v.i.* legea (shindwa, nyong'onyea) kwa joto, ona hari.

swept, *p.t. and pf.t.* ya *sweep*.

swerve, *v.i.* geuka, potoka, epa, kwenda upande; (*incline*) inama.

swift, *a.* -epesi, -a mbio, -a mara moja, -a haraka, -a ghafula; (*ready, prompt*) tayari. — *n.* kijumbamshale. **swiftly**, *adv.* upesi, hima, kwa haraka, ghafula. **swiftness**, *n.* wepesi, mbio.

swill, *v.t.* (*rinse*) suza, mwagia maji tele; (*drink*) -nywa kwa pupa; (*mouth*) sukutua.

swim, *v.i.* (*p.t.* **swam**, *pf.t.* **swum**) ogelea, elea, chukuliwa na mkondo; (*move smoothly*) pita upesi; (*be dizzy*) ona kizunguzungu (kisulisuli, gumbizi), sulika, shikwa na gumbizi; — *v.t.* (*cause to swim*) eleza, ogelesha; (*pass by swimming*) vuka kwa kuogelea. **swimmer**, *n.* mwogelea. **swimming**, *n.* kuogelea &c.; (*dizziness*) kizunguzungu, kisulisuli, gumbizi. — *a.* -a kuogelea, -a kuelea; (*dizzy*) -a kizunguzungu, -a kisulisuli, -a gumbizi; (*tearful*) -a machozi. **swimmingly**, *adv.* upesi, vizuri, rahisi.

swindle, *v.t.* punja, kopa, danganya, ghilibu, bilisi, karamkia, laghai. — *n.* kukopa &c. ukopi, ujanja, hila, udhalimu, madanganyo, ulaghai, ubilisi. **swindler**, *n.* mkopi, ayari, mjanja, mdhalimu, mghilibu, mdanganyi, mlaghai.

swine, *n.* nguruwe, jamii ya nguruwe; (*person*) mtu mchafu, mnyonge kabisa, mpujufu. **swinish**, *a.* kama nguruwe, -chafu, -pujufu.

swing, *v.i.* (*p.t. and pf.t.* **swung**) (*rock*) ning'inia, pembea, wayawaya, yumbayumba, lewalewa, cheza, konya, pepesuka; (*be hung*) tundikwa, angikwa, angama; (*move to and fro*) sukasuka, jongea huko na huko; (*move aside or round*) enda upande, enda kuzunguka; — *v.t.* ning'iniza, pembeza, jongeza huko na huko, zungusha kwa nguvu, chezesha. *Swing the lead*, jisingizia kama unafanya kazi. — *n.* kuning'inia *&c.*; (*rope-swing*) pembea; (*sweep, rush, range &c.*) pigo, mwendo wa nguvu, mshindo, mkondo, njia, eneo. *Be in swing* (*in full swing*) -wa katika kufanya (kufanyika) kazi yake, enda, sitawi. *Give full swing to,* endesha, sitawisha, tozuia.

swinish, *a.* taz. *swine.*

swipe, *v.i.* piga kwa nguvu. — *n.* pigo la nguvu.

swirl, *v.i.* zungukazunguka upesi. — *n.* kizingia.

swish, *v.t.* vurumisha; (*make swishing sound*) chakacha, charakisha, chakarisha.

switch, *n.* ufito, mchapo; (*points on railway*) kipindua cha reli; (*of electric light &c.*) mtambo wa kuwashia (kuanzishia) na kuzimia (kufungia); (*of hair*) kishungi; (*made from an animal's tail*) mwengo, mgwisho. — *v.t.* (*strike*) chapa; (*whisk*) sukasuka; (*shift to another track*) geuza njia, geuza upande. *Switch on,* fungua. *Switch off,* funga, zima.

swivel, *n.* pete yenye kuzunguka. — *v.i.* zunguka.

swollen, *pf.t.* ya *swell.*

swoon, *v.i.* zimia, zirai, ghumia. — *n.* kuzimia roho, kuzirai, kughumia.

swoop, *v.i.* ruka chini (kama tai, kipanga *&c.*) — *n.* ruko (la kuja chini), ruko la ghafula. *At one swoop,* dharuba moja.

swop, *v.t.* badilii.

sword, *n.* upanga; (*curved*) kitara; (*short, straight*) sime. **sword-dance,** *n.* hanzua, tari. **sword-fish,** *n.* papa upanga. **swordsman,** *n.* mtu mstadi wa kutumia upanga, askari wa upanga.

swore, sworn, *p.t. and pf.t.* ya *swear.*

swot, *v.i.* soma kwa bidii, fanya kazi kwa bidii sana, jifunza kwa bidii.

swum, *pf.t.* ya *swim.*

swung, *p.t. and pf.t.* ya *swing.*

sybarite, *n.* mtu wa anasa nyingi.

sycamore, *n.* mkuyu.

sycophant, *n.* msifu mbaya, mjipendekeza vibaya. **sycophancy,** *n.* kusifusifu mno, kurairai, kujipendekeza.

syllable, *n.* silabi, herufi au jamii ya herufi zenye kutamkwa kama sauti moja, *e.g.* he-ru-fi ni *syllable* tatu. **syllabic,** *a.* -a *syllable.*

syllabus, *n.* muhtasari ya mafundisho (ya masomo).

syllogism, *n.* hoja yenye sehemu tatu, *e.g.* mdudu ana uhai, jiwe halina uhai, kwa hiyo jiwe si mdudu.

sylph, *n.* kizimwi; (*woman*) kijana mwanamke mwembamba mzuri.

sylvan, *a.* -a mwitu.

symbol, *n.* mfano, alama, dalili, ishara, methali, onyo. **symbolic, symbolical,** *a.* -a mfano *&c.*; (*significant*) -enye maana. **symbolism,** *n.* mifano, kutumia mifano, matumizi ya (utumizi wa) mifano. **symbolize,** *v.t.* onyesha kwa mifano. (dalili *&c.*); fanana na, -wa kama.

symmetry, *n.* ulinganifu, uzuri, kadiri, usawa. **symmetrical,** *a.* -linganifu, -inayolingana, sawa.

sympathy, *n.* huruma, upole, utu mwema, ushirika katika maono ya wengine. **sympathetic,** *a.* -a huruma, -pole, -a moyo mzuri, -enye kushiriki katika (kufahamu) maono (taabu, furaha *&c.*) ya wengine. **sympathetically,** *adv.* kwa huruma, kwa upole, kwa ufahamivu. **sympathize,** *v.i.* -wa na huruma, hurumia, shiriki katika (fahamu) maono (taabu, furaha *&c.*) ya wengine; (*condole*) -pa mkono (kwa msiba *&c.*), -pa pole; (*with a mourner*) -pa makiwa, -pa mbirambi (rambirambi) zake.

symphony, *n.* ulinganifu wa sauti nyingi, wimbo.

symposium, *n.* kula bia, karamu, kikoa, jamii ya watu wakila pamoja; (*writings*) jamii ya maandiko ya watu mbalimbali juu ya jambo (habari, elimu) moja.

symptom, *n.* alama, ishara, dalili, onyo, kionyo, shuku. **symptomatic,** *a.* -a kuonya.

synagogue, *n.* kanisa la kiyahudi.

synchronize, *v.i.* patana, tokea wakati ule ule; — *v.t.* (*regulate*) patanisha, rekabisha. **synchronism,** *n.* wakati mmoja, mwaka mmoja, ulinganifu wa wakati, usawa wa miaka. **synchronous,** *a.* -a wakati ule ule, -a kuwapo (kutokea) wakati ule mmoja.

syncope, *n.* kuzimia, kuzirai, kughumia, kulegea, kama kufa. **syncopate,** *v.t.* fupisha; (*music*) geuza mwendo kwa kukaza sauti isiyokazwa kawaida na kuiingiza katika sauti ya pili ya kukaza.

syndicate, *n.* shirika la watu wenye kazi moja, kumpuni.

synod, *n.* mkutano wa wakubwa wa Kanisa.

synonym, *n.* neno lenye maana ile ile na jingine, maana sawa. **synonymous,** *a.* -enye maana moja, -a kuonyesha kitu kile kile, -a kuhusika na.

synopsis, *n.* muhtasari, ufupisho wa habari, habari nyingi kwa maneno machache, maneno ya kujumlisha maarifa. **synoptic,** *a.* -a muhtasari, -a ufupi, -a maneno machache. **synoptist,** *n.* mwandishi mmojawapo wa vitabu vya Injili, Matayo, Marko, Luka.

syntax, *n.* elimu ya kupanga maneno kwa sarufi.

synthesis, *n.* kutia pamoja, kufanyiza vitu vingi kuwa kimoja, kuunganisha, kuchanganya, kulinganisha, mchanganyiko. **synthetic,** *a.* -a *synthesis*; (*artificial*) -a kufanyizwa (si -a asili).

syphilis, *n.* kaswende, sekeneko. **syphilitic,** *a.* -a kaswende, -a sekeneko.

syphon, *n.* taz. *siphon.*

Syria, *n.* Sham.

syringe, *n.* bomba ndogo (kama ya kutilia dawa ya sindano). — *v.t.* tia kwa *syringe.*

syrup, *n.* asali, kama asali.

system, *n.* (*orderliness*) utaratibu, siasa, ukamilifu, kawaida, desturi; (*series, group*) jamii ya vitu vyenye hali moja au kazi moja ya kuhusiana, jamii nzima; (*entire plan*) mambo yote, habari zote; (*plan, method*) shauri, madaraka, mategeneo, njia; (*body*) mwili, kiwiliwili, maungo. **systematic,** *a.* -a *system*, -a taratibu, -a desturi &c. **systematize,** *v.t.* andika kwa taratibu &c., panga, tengeneza, rekabisha.

T

tab, *n.* kipande (cha karatasi, cha kitambaa, cha utepe).

tabard, *n.* namna ya koti ya rasmi.

tabby, *n.* (*of cat*) -a madoadoa, -a milia myeusi na myeupe. — *n.* paka (hasa jike).

tabernacle, *n.* hema ya ibada au maskani ya Wayahudi; patakatifu; kisanduku kitakatifu. — *v.t.* tua, kaa.

table, *n.* meza, ubamba laini wa mti (madini, jiwe &c.) ulioandikiwa maneno; (*list, index, scheme*) muhtasari, jedwali, orodha, hesabu, daftari, jumla ya habari; (*flat surface*) mahali pa sawa. *Turn the tables*, badilisha hali, pindua mambo. *At table*, chakulani, mezani. *Table of contents*, fahirisi. *Table-cloth*, nguo ya meza. **tableau**, *n.* kama picha lakini ni watu waliojipanga kuigiza picha. **table-d'hote**, *n.* chakula cha hoteli cha bei moja ambacho mlaji aweza kuchagua katika orodha ya vyakula iliyopangwa na mwenyeji. **tableland**, *n.* nchi sawa iliyoinuka. **tablespoon**, *n.* kijiko kikubwa; (*as measure*) nusu wakia. **tablet**, *n.* kibao cha kuandikia, ubamba wa madini *&c.* wenye maandiko; (*of medicine &c.*) kibonge. **tabloid**, *n.* kibonge cha dawa. **tabular**, *a.* kama *table*, -liyopangwa kwa taratibu. **tabulate**, *v.t.* andika wazi (kwa taratibu), panga, fanya muhtasari (hesabu).

taboo, *n.* mwiko, mzio. — *v.t.* zia, harimisha, kataza, gombeza kabisa. — *a.* -a mwiko, -liogombezwa kabisa.

tabor, *n.* namna ya ngoma ndogo.

tabular, *a.*, **tabulate**, *v.* taz. *table*.

tacit, *a.* -a kimya, -liodhihirika pasipo kunena. *He gives a tacit consent*, hakatai. **tacitly**, *adv.* kwa kimya, bila kusema. **taciturn**, *a.* -nyamavu, -a kimya, -a maneno machache, -stirifu. **taciturnity**, *n.* unyamavu, kimya.

tack, *v.t.* (*of ship*) bisha, kisi matanga, pindua demani (goshini); (*in sewing*) shikiza, piga bandi; (*nail*) pigilia kwa misumari midogo. — *n.* msumari mdogo; (*of ship, tacking*) mbisho; (*course*) majira; (*change*) ugeuzi, upinduzi.

tackle, *n.* vyombo (vya jahazi, kamba, ayari *&c.*), zana, vifaa, pambo. — *v.t.* kamata, shikilia, anzisha, anza; (*question*) hoji. **tackling**, *n.* kama *tackle*, *n.*

tacky, *a.* -a kunata.

tact, *n.* busara, akili, ujuzi wa jinsi ya kufanya katika mambo yenye shida *&c.* **tactful**, *a.* -a *tact*, -a busara, -a akili, mahiri. **tactless**, *a.* bila busara, -zito.

tactics, *n.* maarifa ya vita. **tactical**, -a maarifa ya vita. **tactician**, *n.* mjuzi wa maarifa ya vita.

tactile, *a.* -a kugusika, -a kuhusiana na uwezo wa kugusa.

tactless, *a.* taz. *tact*.

tadpole, *n.* mtoto wa chura mara atokapo katika yai, kiluwiluwi.

taffeta, *n.* namna ya nguo ya hariri.

taffrail, *n.* kizuio kinachozunguka ukingo wa meli kuzuia watu wasianguke majini.

tag, *n.* kipande kidogo kilichofungiwa kitu kingine.

tail, *n.* mkia, upande wa mwisho (wa nyuma); (*used as a fly switch &c.*) mgwisho, mwengo; (*feathers*) mleli, msusi. *Put the tail between the legs*, fyata mkia. *Turn tail*, kimbia. *Wag the tail*, sukasuka mkia.

tailor, *n.* mshoni, mshonaji.

taint, *n.* (*blemish*) waa; (*disgrace*) aibu; (*smell*) uvundo, kioza; (*infection*) ugonjwa, kiambukizo. — *v.t.* ambukiza, haribu, ozesha. **tainted**, *a.* -enye waa, -a aibu, -nayovunda, -nayooza.

take, *v.t.* (*p.t.* **took**, *pf.t.* **taken**) twaa, shika, kamata; (*gain, obtain*) pata; (*convey, conduct*) chukua, peleka; (*please*) pendeza; (*choose*) chagua, teua; (*require*) hitaji, taka; (*use*) tumia; (*remove*) toa, ondoa; (*a conveyance*) enda (safiri) katika; (*receive*) pokea; (*endure*) vumilia, stahimili; (*understand*) fahamu, tambua; (*accept*) kubali; — *v.i.* faa, fanya kazi. *Take aback*, shangaza, fadhaisha. *Take a bite*, mega, ambua. *Take a walk*, tembea, enda kutembea. *Take as spoil*, teka. *Take an oath*, apa. *Take across*, vusha, vukisha. *Take aim*, piga shabaha, elekeza bunduki, linga bunduki. *Take after*, fanana na, landa, iga, fuatisha, -wa kama. *Take at one's word*, sadiki, kubali. *Take away*, chukua, ondoa, toa. *Take breath*, pumzika. *Take by force*, nyang'anya, poka, bakwia, bwakua, ghusubu. *Take care,* angalia, tunza, jihadhari. *Take care!* simile! habedari! jihadhari! *Take down,* shusha, telemsha, tweza, tusha, tungua, tundua; (*a building*) bomoa; (*in writing*) andika; (*fruit &c.*) angua. *Take effect,* tenda kazi yake, faa, anza, jiri. *Take the fancy, Take the eye,* vuta, pendeza, tamanisha, tazamisha. *Take fire,* waka, lipuka. *Take fright,* ogopa, shikwa na hofu. *Take heart,* jipa moyo, piga moyo konde. *Take heed,* angalia, jihadhari, jali. *Take hold* (*of*) shika, shikilia, kamata. *Take in* (*understand*) fahamu; (*cheat*) punja, danganya, ghilibu, bilisi, laghai; (*include*) weka, -wa na . . . ndani; (*lessen*) punguza; (*water*) vuja; (*undertake*) jipatia kazi ya; (*buy regularly*) nunua kwa kawaida. *Take in hand,* shika, jitia katika, maliki. *Take into one's head,* azimu, nia, kusudia. *Take in vain,* taja bure, dharau, beza. *Take leave of,* aga, agana na. *Take medicine,* -nywa dawa. *Take notes,* andika makumbusho. *Take notice* (*of*), angalia, jali; (*favour*) pendelea. *Take off* (*clothes, cap &c.*) vua; (*the fire*) ipua, tekua; (*imitate*) iga kwa mzaha, dhihaki; (*remove*) ondoa, toa, kata. *Take oneself off,* ondoka. *Take on oneself,* diriki, tadiriki. *Take orders,* agizwa; (*be ordained*) ingizwa katika uhudumu wa (kazi ya) Kanisa. Taz. (*Holy*) *orders.* *Take out,* toa, ondoa, futua; (*pick out*) chokoa; (*a licence*) kata cheti; (*escort*) fuatana na, peleka. *Take out a tooth,* ng'oa jino. *Take it out of one,* chosha. *Take part,* shiriki. *Take pains with,* angalia sana, sumbukia, fanya kwa bidii, takalifu. *Take place,* -wa, tukia, fanyika, jiri. *Take revenge,* jilipiza kisasi. *Take steps,* anzisha, fanya (shauri &c.). *Take time* (*be slow*) taka (chukua) wakati, -wa jambo la siku nyingi; (*be careful*) enda polepole, jihadhari. *Take the field,* enda kupigana, shika vita, enda kushindana. *Take the ground,* panda, ingia mwambani, kwama, pwelewa. *Take thought,* kumbuka sumbukia. *Take to,* penda, jifunga kwa. *Take to heart,* ona uchungu, tiwa uchungu, sikitikia. *Take to one's bed,* ugua. *Take to one's heels,* kimbia. *Take to task,* kemea, karipia, onya. *Take up* (*in the hand*) zoa, okota; (*in small quantities*) chota, danga; (*lift up*) inua, nyanyua, tweka, twika; (*engage in*) jitia katika, shikilia; (*arrest*) funga, kamata, bamba, dara; (*occupy*) -wa kazi ya, taka, chukua; (*a position*) chagua mahali, tua; (*rebuke*) shutumu, amba. *Take up with,* fanya urafiki na. *Be taken ill* (*worse*), shikia.

taking, *a.* -a kuvuta, -a kupendeza, -a kutamamisha, -zuri. **takings,** *n.* machumo, faida, fedha zilizopokewa (katika kazi, biashara &c.).

talc, *n.* ulanga, namna ya jiwe kama kioo.

tale, *n.* hadithi, kisa, ngano, hekaya; (*fiction*) uwongo, upuzi; (*number, total*) hesabu, jumla. *Tell tales of,* chongea; (*relate*) hadithia, simulia. **talebearer,** *n.* mchongezi, mchongelezi, dukizi, mzuzi, mbukuzi, mbukulia, sakubimbi. **talebearing,** *n.* udukizi, uchongelezi, uchongezi, uzuzi.

talent, *n.* (*money*) hesabu na uzani wa fedha ya zamani ya Wayunani, Warumi &c.; (*faculty &c.*) akili, nguvu, majaliwa, maelekeo ya akili. **talented,** *a.* -elekevu, -enye akili nyingi.

talisman, *n.* talasimu, hirizi, sihiri, kago, azima, fingo, zindiko.

talk, *v.i.* nena, sema, ongea, zungumza. *Talk about,* semea, nena, zungumza (ongea) habari za. *Talk against,* sema, amba, nenea. *Talk down,* pambanya, hinikiza. *Talk in sleep,* weweseka. *Talk loud,* sema sana. *Talk nonsense,* puza, paya, payuka, babaika, bwata, bwabwaja. *Talk over,* semana habari za; (*out, argue*) pambanya, nyenya, shawishi.

Talk through the nose, sema puani, sema kipuani, sema king'ong'o. *Talk to*, sema na, ongea na. — *n.* usemi, maneno, maongezi, mazungumzo, porojo; (*noisy, loud*) mavumi, domo; (*silly*). upuzi, mapayo. **talkative**, *a.* -a maneno mengi, -piga domo, -limi. **talker**, *n.* msemaji, mwenye maneno mengi.

tall, *a.* -refu. *A tall well-made man*, tambo la mtu. *A tall story*, hadithi (habari) yenye shaka. **tallness**, *n.* urefu (wa mtu au kitu), kimo, utambo.

tallow, *n.* mafuta, shahamu.

tally, *n.* kipande cha (kitani ya, alama ya) kuhesabia; (*duplicate*) nakala ya hesabu; (*label*) kipande chenye anwani au maelezo. — *v.i.* -wa sawa, lingana.

tally-ho, *n.* ukelele wa kuitana wawindaji.

Talmud, *n.* kitabu cha mafundisho cha Wayahudi.

talon, *n.* kucha (la ndege), ukucha.

tamable, *a.* taz. *tame*.

tamarind, *n.* (tree) mkwaju; (*fruit*) ukwaju.

tambourine, *n.* kigoma, tari.

tame, *v.t.* fuga; (*subdue*) tiisha, zuia; (*reclaim*) ongoza, ondolea ushenzi. — *a.* -liofugika, -zoevu, -tulivu, -pole; (*mild, dull, feeble*) -legevu, pasipo nguvu, bila akili, dhaifu, baridi. **tamable**, *a.* -a kufugika. **tamely**, *adv.* bila kukaidi. **tamer**, *n.* mfugaji.

tam-o'-shanter, *n.* namna ya kofia.

tamp, *v.t.* shindilia.

tamper, *v.i.* (*with*) haribu, geuza, vuta vibaya (kwa hila, fedha, uwongo &c.).

tan, *v.t.* tia dawa ngozi zisioze; (*make brown*) fanya kuwa -ekundu; (*beat—slang*) piga, chapa; — *v.i.* geuka -ekundu (kwa joto la jua). — *n.* dawa ya kutiwa ngozi zisioze; (*colour*) rangi nyekundu (kama hudhurungi). **tanned**, *a.* (ngozi) -liotiwa dawa isioze; (*with the sun*) -enye rangi nyekundu (kwa joto la jua.) **tanner**, *n.* mtengenezaji wa ngozi zisioze. **tannery**, *n.* kiwanda cha *tanner*. **tanning**, *n.* kazi ya kutia ngozi dawa zisioze.

tandem, *n.* gari linalokokotwa na farasi wawili wamefungiwa mmoja mbele na mwingine nyuma yake; (*bicycle*) baisikeli ya watu wawili, mmoja kukaa mbele na mmoja nyuma yake.

tang, *n.* ladha kali, harufu kali.

tangent, *n.* mstari unaogusa duara (*circle*) bila kuikata. *At a tangent*, mshazari, kwenda upande.

tangerine, *n.* chenza, kangaja.

tangible, *a.* -a kuoneka kwa kugusa, -a kugusika, -a kufumbatika; (*clear*) wazi, dhahiri, hakika. **tangibility**, *n.* kuwa *tangible*.

tangle, *n.* matata, matatizo, mafungamano. — *v.t.* tatanisha, tatiza; (*ensnare*) tega, kamata.

tango, *n.* namna ya ngoma ya kucheza watu wawili.

tank, *n.* birika kubwa (la kuwekea maji akiba, mafuta &c.), hodhi, tangi; (*armoured car*) namna ya motakaa kubwa ya vita yenye mzinga. **tanker**, *n.* meli inayochukua shehena ya mafuta.

tankard, *n.* kopo au kombe kubwa la kunywea.

tanker, *n.* taz *tank*.

tanned, *a.*, **tanner**, *n.*, **tannery**, *n.*; **tanning**, *n.* taz. *tan*.

tantalize, *v.t.* kejeli, shaua, chezea, tamanisha bure.

tantamount, *a.* sawa, mamoja.

tantrum, *n.* hamaki, hasira ya ghafula.

tap, (1) *v.t.* gota, gonga, bisha, chapa, babata, ng'ota. — *n.* kipigo.

tap, (2) *v.t.* (*broach*) zibua pipa, toa (maji, mvinyo &c.). **tap-room**, *n.* duka la kunywea pombe, tembo &c. **tap-root**, *n.* mzizi mkuu wa mti au mmea.

tape, *n.* utepe, kigwe, ugwe. **tape-measure**, *n.* utepe wa kupimia. **tapeworm**, *n.* tegu, namna ya chango.

taper, *n.* mshumaa mwembamba sana. — *v.t.* chongoa; — *v.i.* chongoka. **tapering,** *a.* -a kuchongoka, -a kupunguka unene taratibu (mpaka kufanya ncha).

tapestry, *n.* nguo nene yenye sanamu ya kutundika ukutani, zulia ya ukutani.

tapeworm, *n.* taz. *tape.*

tapioca, *n.* wanga wa muhogo.

tapir, *n.* mnyama wa Hindi na Amerika, kidogo kama nguruwe mkubwa.

tappet, *n.* kipande kitokezacho katika gurudumu la mashine cha kugeuzia mwendo wa kuzunguka uwe wa juu na chini.

tap-room, *n.*, **tap-root,** *n.* taz. *tap* (2.)

tar, (1) *n.* lami. — *v.t.* paka lami. *Tarred with the same brush,* -enye tabia (hitilafu, mawaa &c.) zile zile. **tarry,** *a.* -a lami, kama lami, -enye lami.

tar, (2) *n.* (*sailor*) baharia.

tarantula, *n.* buibui, mkubwa mwenye sumu.

tardy, *a.* -zembe, -vivu, -legevu, -a kuchelewa, -a kusita, -a usiri, -a kulimatia, ajizi. **tardily,** *adv.* kwa uzembe, kwa kukawia. **tardiness,** *n.* kuwa *tardy,* uzembe, uvivu, ulegevu, usiri, kuchelewa, uajizi.

tare, (1) *n.* kigugu mwitu.

tare, (2) *n.* turuhani (uzani wa kasha bila vitu vilivyomo, au gari bila mizigo yake).

target, *n.* shabaha.

tariff, *n.* (*of custom's duties*) orodha ya ushuru wa forodhani; (*of food*) orodha ya bei ya vyakula.

tarn, *n.* ziwa dogo (la maji).

tarnish, *v.t.* haribu kwa kutu (ukuvu, ukungu); fifisha nuru; (*disgrace*) aibisha, patia aibu; — *v.i.* geuka rangi kwa kutu, otà kutu (ukuvu, ukungu), acha kung'aa (kwa sababu ya ukuvu, ukungu, kutu), fifia nuru, potewa na uzuri. — *n.* kutu, ukuvu, ukungu; (*disgrace*) aibu.

taro, *n.* myugwa; (*root*) jimbi.

tarpaulin, *n.* turubali, nguo nene iliyopakwa lami.

tarry, (1) *a.* taz. *tar* (1).

tarry, (2) *v.i.* kawia, chelewa, limatia, kaa nyuma, usiri, kaakaa; (*wait*) ngoja.

tart, (1) *a.* -chungu, -kali.

tart, (2) *n.* maandazi ya matunda.

tartan, *n.* nguo nene ya watu wa *Scotland,* yenye mirabaraba.

tartar, (1) *n.* mtu wa *Tartary;* (*difficult person*) mtu mkali sana, mtu mkaidi sana.

tartar, (2) *n.* (*of teeth*) ukoga, ugaga, ugwagwa.

task, *n.* kazi. *Take to task,* kemea, karipia, laumu, shutumu, taradhia. — *v.t.* amria kazi; (*put to strain*) bidiisha, jitahidisha, jaribisha, taabisha, chosha, kalifu. **taskmaster,** *n.* msimamizi.

tassel, *n.* kishada, kifundo. **tasselled,** *a.* -enye vishada.

taste, *v.t. and i* onja dhuku; (*test*) jaribu; (*take a little*) twaa kidogo; — *v.i.* (*have flavour*) -wa na ladha, kolea; (*be savoury*) chapukia. *It tastes nice,* ni tamu, inachapukia. — *n.* utamu, ladha; (*act of tasting*) kuonja, maonji, kionjo, kumbwe; (*liking*) tamaa, upendo, shauku, akili; (*perception of beauty*) akili za kupambanua mazuri hasa; (*judgement*) akili za kuchagua vema; (*style*) namna nzuri, jinsi nzuri. *A man of taste,* mtu wa akili, mchaguzi, mteuzi, msaanifu. *Have a taste for,* jua, weza, penda. *Give a nice taste to* (*food*), koleza, chapukiza, unga. **tasteful,** *a.* -a akili, -zuri, -fasihi. **tasteless,** *a.* pasipo ladha; (*dull, flat*) dufu, chapwa, baridi. *It is tasteless,* ni baridi, ni chapwa. **tasty,** *a.* -tamu, -a kuchapukia, -a kukolea, -zuri.

tatters, *n.* nguo mbovumbovu, matambaa. **tattered,** *a.* (*clothes*) -bovubovu, -liotatukatatuka. **tatterdemalion,** *n.* mtu aliyevaa nguo mbovumbovu, chafuchafu.

tattle, *n.* mapayo, vijineno, upuzi.

— *v.i.* payapaya, payuka, bwata, tatarika, bwabwaja. **tattler,** *n.* mpayukaji.

tattoo, (1) *n.* (*of drum*) mdundo wa ngoma ya kuita askari; tamasha ya michezo ya kiaskari, hasa usiku.

tattoo, (2) *v.t.* chanja, piga chale, chora, toja. — *n.* nembo, chanjo, chale, mchoro, tojo.

taught, *p.t. and pf.t.* ya *teach.*

taunt, *v.t.* suta, tusha, dhihaki, cheka, fanyia mzaha. — *n.* mzaha, suto, tayo, shutumu, tusi, dhihaka. **taunting,** *a.* -a kusuta *&c.*

taut, *a.* -a kukaza, -liokazwa, -a kudinda.

tautology, *n.* kutumia maneno yayo kwa yayo, kusema yale yale tu.

tavern, *n.* duka la mvinyo, pombe *&c.*; mkahawa, hoteli.

tawdry, *a.* -a kimalidadi (lakini hafifu), -shaufu, -a fahari (lakini duni).

tawny, *a.* -a rangi ya hudhurungi, -a rangi ya mchanga (wa pwani).

tax, *n.* kodi, ushuru; (*strain*) mzigo, taabu. — *v.t.* toza kodi, lipiza ushuru; (*put strain on*) kaza, lemeza, lemea, kalifu; (*accuse*) shtaki, laumu. *Tax strength* (*resources*), tia juhudi (gharama). **taxable,** *a.* -a kulipa kodi, -a kupasiwa ushuru. **taxation,** *n.* kutoza kodi, kodi, ushuru. *Heavy taxation,* ushuru mwingi. **tax-gatherer,** *n.* mtoza kodi.

taxi, *n.* motakaa ya abiria (ya kupanga). — *v.i.* enda katika *taxi*; (*of aeroplane*) tambaa chini (or majini).

taxidermy, *n.* maarifa ya kutengeneza ngozi ya wanyama, ndege *&c.* ziwe kama kwamba ni hai. **taxidermist,** *n.* fundi wa *taxidermy.*

tea, *n.* chai; (*evening meal*) chakula cha jioni. *Tea-caddy,* mkebe wa chai. *Tea-cloth,* kitambaa cha kufutia vikombe *&c.* *Tea-cup,* kikombe cha kunywea chai. *Tea-pot,* buli. *Tea-party,* chakula cha jioni, jamii ya watu wakinywa chai pamoja. *Tea-spoon,* kijiko cha chai.

teach, *v.t.* (*p.t. and pf.t.* **taught**) (*knowledge*) funda, funza, fundisha; (*manners*) tia adabu, adibisha; (*generally*) ongoza, lea, onya, zoeza. **teachable,** *a.* -epesi kujifunza, -elekevu, -sikivu, -sikilivu. **teachableness,** *n.* wepesi wa kujifunza, welekevu, usikizi, usikivu. **teacher,** *n.* mwalimu, mkufunzi, mfunzi, mfundishi, fundi. **teaching,** *n.* mafundisho, elimu, masomo, madhehebu.

teak, *n.* msaji; (*East African*) mvule.

teal, *n.* ndege kama bata mdogo.

team, *n.* jamii ya farasi, ya ng'ombe *&c.* waliofunganishwa na gari; (*of players &c.*) kikoa, kundi la watu wakicheza (wakifanya kazi) pamoja, timu.

tear, (1) *v.t.* (*p.t.* **tore,** *pf.t.* **torn**), pasua, rarua, tatua, papura; (*agitate*) hangaisha, tia wasiwasi; (*divide*) tenga, gawanya, farakisha; (*wrest*) ondoa kwa nguvu, chukua kwa jeuri; (*the hair*) ng'oa; — *v.i.* pasuka, raruka *&c.* *Tear away,* gandua; (*move, go quickly*) puruka, enda mbio (kwa kasi). *Tear in strips,* chana. *Tear in pieces,* nyambua, chambua, chamvua. *Tear a piece off,* kwanua, nyakua; (*of meat with the teeth*) ng'wafua. *Tear off* (*skin &c.*), ambua; (*clothes*) vua upesi; (*boughs &c.*) kwanua, konyoa, kongonyoa; (*run*) ondoka mbio. *Tear down,* angusha, bomoa, angamiza. *Tear up,* pasua; (*uproot*) ng'oa; (*destroy*) angamiza. — *n.* mpasuo, mpasuko, mtatuko; (*split &c.*) ufa.

tear, (2) *n.* chozi. *Shed tears, Burst into tears,* bubujika (toa, toka) machozi. *Affect to tears,* toa (toza) machozi. *In tears,* kwa machozi, kwa kulia. **tearful,** *a.* -enye machozi, -a kulia. **tearless,** *a.* pasipo machozi, -kavu.

tease, *v.t.* (*fibres &c.*) chamvua, chambua, chana; (*annoy &c.*) chokoza, sumbua, udhi, tesa, nyeta, kejeli, tashtiti, sunza, kefyakefya, kera, nyanyasa. (*importune*) chagiza.

teasel, teazel, teazle, *n.* namna ya

ua lenye miiba linalotumika kuchania na kulainisha nguo. **teaser,** *n.* mchokozi, mwudhi; (*problem &c.*) fumbo, tatizo.

teat, *n.* titi, chuchu ya ziwa, cho chote kinachofanana na chuchu.

technical, *a.* -a ufundi, -a fundi mwenyewe, -a kazi fulani, -a mtambo (mashine). **technicality,** *n.* kuwa *technical*, kitu kilicho (neno lililo) *technical*. **technique,** *n.* ufundi, ustadi, jinsi ya kufanya kazi fulani. **technology,** *n.* elimu na habari za ufundi (kuipambanua na ile ya sanaa).

Te Deum, *n.* wimbo wa kikristo wa kumshukuru Mwenyezi Mungu.

tedious, *a.* -a kuchosha, -chovu, -a taabu, -a kutaabisha, -kokotevu, baridi, dufu. **tediousness,** *n.* ukokotevu, machovu, taabu. **tedium,** *n.* uchovu, taabu, ubaridi, udufu.

tee, *n.* kichungu kidogo cha kuwekea tufe (katika mchezo wa *golf*).

teem, (1) *v.t.* mimina (madini iliyoyeyuka katika kalibu).

teem, (2) *v.i.* jaa tele, zaa sana. **teeming,** *a.* -ingi sana.

teens, *n.* umri wa kati ya miaka kumi na ishirini.

teeth, *n.pl.* ya *tooth*. *Cast in one's teeth,* shutumu. *Hold in the teeth,* vuata. *In the teeth of,* kwa kushindana na, (= *In spite of*). **teethe,** *v.i.* ota meno. **teething,** *n.* kuota meno. *Rub a child's gums when teething,* nunuza.

teetotal, *a.* -siyekunywa vileo vya namna yo yote. **teetotaler,** *n.* mtu asiyekunywa namna yo yote ya kileo. **teetotalism,** *n.* kutokunywa namna yo yote ya kileo.

teetotum, *n.* namna ya pia ya mraba yenye hesabu kila upande, ya kuchezea kama kura.

telegram, *n.* simu, habari kwa simu. **telegraph,** *n.* simu. — *v.t.* peleka habari kwa simu, piga simu. **telegraphic,** *a.* -a simu. **telegraphist,** *n.* mtu wa simu. **telegraphy,** *n.* maarifa (ufundi) wa simu.

teleology, *n.* kusadiki (mafundisho, mawazo) ya kuwa viumbe vyote viliumbwa na Mungu kwa kusudi maalum.

telepathy, *n.* uwezo wa ajabu wa kupisha (kupeleka) mawazo (fikira) bila kusema wala kuashiria, uwezo wa kushirikiana mawazo.

telephone, *n.* simu ya kupelekea sauti mbali.

telescope, *n.* darubini. — *v.i.* ingiana (kama sehemu za mtutu wa darubini); (*be forced one into the other*) vunjika kwa kuingizana. **telescopic,** *a.* -a darubini, -a kutazama mbali, -a kuonekana kwa darubini.

television, *n.* kupeleka (kupokea) picha kwa simu (au simu ya hewani).

tell, *v.t.* (*p.t. and pf.t.* **told**) nena; (*relate*) simulia, hubiri, toa habari, ambia, aridhia; (*count*) hesabu; (*make known*) eleza, tangaza, hubiri; (*discover*) fahamu, ona; (*order*) amuru, agiza; — *v.i.* (*have effect*) -wa na nguvu (na njia), endeleza kazi. *Tell of, Tell tales,* chongea, kashifu. *Tell on,* chosha, legeza, vuta, geuza. *I tell you, it is so,* ndiyo ati. **teller,** *n.* mnenaji, msimulizi; (*counter*) mwenye kuhesabu. **telling,** *a.* -a nguvu, -enye njia, -a kuchoma moyo. **telltale,** *n.* mdukizi, mchongezi, mchongelezi, mkashifu. — *a.* -a kutoa habari, -a kushuhudia, -a kuvumbua siri; -a kufunulia.

temerity, *n.* ujasiri mwingi, kuthubutu; (*audacity &c.*) ukavu wa macho, ushupavu, ujuvi.

temper, *v.t.* (*compound*) changanya; (*moderate*) geuza; (*mitigate*) tuliza, lainisha, zimua, zizimua, punguza ukali (nguvu &c.); (*metal*) tia matiko, chovya; (*clay*) kanda, finyanga; — *v.i.* lainika. — *n.* (*disposition*) tabia, hali, moyo; (*good temper*) upole, ukunjufu, kiasi; (*bad temper*) chuki, hasira, harara, hamaki; (*of metals*) ugumu, matiko. *Be out of temper, Be in a temper,* -wa na hasira (chuki), kasirika, hamaki, panda hamaki. *Keep one's temper,* tulia, jiweza, jizuia. *Lose one's temper*, kasirika, hamaki, panda hamaki, ingiwa na hasira. *Be in a good temper*, kunjuka, changamka. *Hot-tempered*, -a harara, -a hamaki. **temperament**, *n.* tabia, moyo, hali, mwenendo. **temperamental**, *a.* -epesi wa kukasirika (wa kuona furaha, chuki, hasira &c.).

temperate, *a.* -a kiasi, -a kadiri, -a kujiweza. *Temperate zone*, sehemu ya dunia pasipo jua kali wala baridi kali. **temperance**, *n.* kiasi, kadiri, tawasufi, kujiweza (hasa katika kunywa vileo); (*total abstinence*) kutokunywa kileo cha namna yo yote. **temperature**, *n.* kadiri au hali ya kuwa na joto au baridi. *High temperature*, joto, hari. *Low temperature*, baridi. *Have a temperature*, -wa na homa.

tempest, *n.* tufani, dhoruba, upepo mwingi, kimbunga. **tempestuous**, *a.* -a tufani, -a dhoruba; (*sea*) -enye, kuchafuka sana; (*debate &c.*) -a ugomvi mwingi, -a kubishana.

temple, (1) *n.* hekalu, kanisa; (*Mohammedan*) msikiti.

temple, (2) *n.* panja; (*forehead*) kipaji cha uso.

templet, *n.* kiolezo (cha ubamba wa ubao au madini) cha kukatia ubao au jiwe &c.

tempo, *n.* mwendo (mpigo) wa muziki.

temporal, *a.* -a maisha (si -a milele), -a kupita, -a dunia hii; (*power &c.*) -a mambo ya dunia hii, si ya Mungu. **temporality**, *n.* mali hasa ya Kanisa, mali zilizo wakf. **temporally**, *adv.* kwa wakiti, kwa kitambo, kwa muhula. **temporary**, *a.* -a wakati, -a kitambo (si -a siku zote), **temporize**, *v.i.* sitasita, geuka-geuka, kawia (katika kutenda jambo kuu).

tempt, *v.t.* (*test*) jaribu, jaribia; (*mislead*) vuta kwa mabaya, shawishi, bilisi; (*excite desire* tamanisha; (*seduce*) tongoza. **temptation**, *n.* (*trial*) jaribu; (*enticement*) kishawishi, ushawishi, ubilisi, mvuto (kwa mabaya). **tempter**, *n.* mwenye kuvuta (kwa mabaya, kwa kukosesha), mshawishi. *The tempter*, shetani, ibilisi. **tempting**, *a.* -a kuvuta,-a kutumanisha. **temptress**, *n.* *tempter* wa kike.

ten, *n.* *and a.* kumi; (*decade*) mwongo. *The upper ten*, watu wakuu. *Ten to one*, kumi kwa moja. **tenfold**, *adv.* mara kumi. **tenth**, *a.* -a kumi. — *n.* sehemu ya kumi. **tenthly**, *a.* -a kumi.

tenable, *a.* -a kushika, -a kulindika, -a kuthibitika, -a nguvu.

tenacious, *a.* -a kushika, -a kunata, -a kuambata, -a kushikamana; (*obstinate*) -shupavu, -gumu, -a kushikilia kauli yake. **tenacity**, *n.* nguvu ya kushika (ya kushikamana, ya kunata, ya kuambata); ushupavu, ugumu, uthabiti.

tenant, *n.* mwenye kupanga (nyumba au shamba), mpangaji. **tenancy**, *n.* upangaji, wakati (muda) wa kupanga. **tenantry**, *n.* jamii ya wapangaji.

tend, (1) *v.t.* (*take care of*) tunza, chunga, linda. **tender**, *n.* mtunzaji, mchungaji, mlinzi; (*small ship*) meli ndogo (stima) ya kupeleka abiria, chakula, vifaa &c. mpaka meli kubwa; (*of railway engine*) gari la kuchukulia maji na makaa ya gari la moshi.

tend, (2) *v.i.* elekea, taka kwenda, vutwa, enda; (*be of use*) saidia, faa. **tendency**, *n.* maelekeo, maelekezo, kutaka kwenda, utashi; (*movement attraction*) mwendo, mvuto.

tender, (1) *n.* taz. *tend* (1).

tender, (2) *v.t.* toa, taka kupa, tolea. — *n.* kutoa, toleo, malipo. *Legal tender*, fedha (sarafu) inayoruhusiwa na serikali.

tender, (3) *a.* (*soft, delicate*) -ororo, -embamba; (*weak, fragile*) dhaifu, -epesi kuvunjika (kuharibika, kudhurika); (*sensitive*) -epesi kuumia, -a kuuma; (*soft-hearted, gentle*) -a huruma, -ema, -pole, -a upendo, -a utu mwema. *Of tender age*, -changa, -toto. **tenderfoot,** *n.* asiyejua desturi, mjinga, mzuzu. **tender-hearted,** *a.* -a huruma, -a upendo, -pole. **tenderly,** *adv.* polepole, kwa huruma, kwa upendo, kwa upole. **tenderness,** *n.* kuwa *tender*, wororo, wembamba, wepesi kuona huruma (maumivu &c.), utu mwema.

tendon, *n.* ukano, mshipa.

tendril, *n.* ukono, kikonyo.

tenement, *n.* nyumba, makao.

tenet, *n.* madhehebu, mafundisho, itikadi.

tennis, *n.* mchezo wa tufe na vibao.

tenon, *n.* ulimi (wa ubao).

tenor, *n.* (*meaning*) maana; (*course, tendency*) mwendo, maelekeo; (*in music*) sauti nyembamba ya utu uzima; (*singer*) mwimbaji mwenye sauti nyembamba ya utu uzima.

tense, (1) *n.* (*in grammar*) namna ya *verb* inayoonyesha wakati wa tendo au wa hali.

tense, (2) *a.* -liyokazana, -liokazwa, -a liyonyoshwa sana, -liyoshupana, -a mkazo, -a kudinda. — *v.t.* kaza, shupaza, kita. **tensile,** *a.* -a kutanuka, -a kunyosheka. **tension,** *n.* kunyosha, kutanuka, mkazo, mvuto; (*excitement*) hangaiko, wasiwasi.

tent, *n.* hema. *Strike a tent*, ng'oa (ondoa) hema. *Pitch a tent*, simikisha (piga) hema. *Tent-pegs*, mambo, vigingi.

tentacle, *n.* mkono, kikono.

tentative, *a.* -a kujaribia.

tenter-hooks, *n.* *Be on tenter-hooks*, hangaika, ona wasiwasi, fadhaika, hamanika.

tenth, *a.*, **tenthly,** *a.* taz. *ten*.

tenuous, *a.* -embamba. **tenuity,** *n.* wembamba.

tenure, *n.* kumiliki, kuwa bwana, uenyeji; (*period*) wakati (muda) wa kumiliki; (*conditions*) masharti ya kumiliki.

tepid, *a.* -a uvuguvugu, fufutende; (*of feelings*) baridi. *Be tepid*, vuvuwaa. **tepidity,** *n.* uvuguvugu.

teraphim, *n.* sanamu ndogo za kiyahudi zamani zilizotumika katika kuagulia.

tercentenary, *n.* mwaka wa mia tatu (wa thelatha mia) na sikukuu yake.

tergiversate, *v.i.* ghairighairi, badilibadili nia (shauri). **tergiversation,** *n.* kugeukageuka, kuwa na hila nyingi, werevu, uayari.

term, *n.* (*limit, end*) mpaka, kikomo, kipeo, mwisho; (*period*) muda, muhula, majira; (*in schools*) muda wa chuo (kutoka ruhusa, mpaka, ruhusa); (*word*) neno; (*condition*) sharti. *Be on good terms*, -wa na urafiki, patana, chukuana. *Make terms, come to terms*, patana. *Bring to terms*, patanisha, afikanisha. *In terms*, dhahiri, halisi. —*v.t.* taja, ita. **terminable,** *a.* -enye mwisho, -a kutiwa mwisho. **terminal,** *n.* ncha, mwisho. — *a.* -a mwishoni, -a kwenye ncha; -a kila *term* (*period*). **terminate,** *v.t.* zuia, komesha, kata; — *v.i.* isha, koma. **termination,** *n.* kikomo, mwisho, mpaka, kipeo, ncha; (*end of word*) *syllable*, ya mwisho wa neno. **terminology,** *n.* maneno na majina yatumikayo kwa mambo ya kazi fulani au ya elimu fulani; maarifa ya kutaja majina. **terminus,** *n.* kikomo cha njia ya magari ya moshi, kituo.

termagant, *n.* mwanamke mwenye jeuri na makelele, mwanamke mkorofi.

terminable, *a.*, **terminal,** *n.*, **terminate,** *v.*, **termination,** *n.*, **terminology,** *n.*, **terminus,** *n.* taz. *term*.

termite, *n.* mchwā; (*winged*) kumbikumbi. *Ant-hill*, kichuguu, chuguu.

tern, *n.* shakwe.

ternary, *a.* tatu tatu, -a tatu tatu.

terpischorean, *a.* -a ngoma (ya kucheza).

terrace, *n.* mahali palipoinuka pa kutembelea au penye nyumba; (*on hill*) palipochimbiwa na kusawazishwa katika mtelemko wa mlima, au palipozuiwa na boma. — *v.t.* fanya *terrace*, chimba na kusawazisha au kuzuia kwa boma.

terra-cotta, *n*. udongo mwekundu mzuri wa ufinyanzi. **terra-firma**, *n*. nchi kavu.

terrapin, *n*. kasa.

terrestial, *a*. -a dunia, -a mfano wa dunia.

terrible, *a*. -a kuogofya, -a kutisha, -a hofu; (*excessive*) sana. **terribleness**, *n*. kuwa *terrible*, wogofya, tisho. **terribly**, *adv*. sana. **terrific**, *a*. -a kuogofya, -a kutisha, -a hofu. **terrify**, *v.t.* ogofya, tisha, tia hofu, hofisha. **terror**, *n*. hofu kuu, tisho, maogofya. **terrorize**, *v.t.* tisha, tiisha kwa ukatili (udhalimu &c.), ogofya.

terrier, *n*. namna ya mbwa mdogo mwenye manyoya mafupi.

terrific, *a*., **terrify**, *v*. taz. *terrible*.

territory, *n*. nchi, jimbo, ardhi. **territorial**, *a*. -a nchi fulani, -a ardhi.

terror, *n*., **terrorize**, *v.t.* taz. *terrible*.

terse, *a*. -a maneno machache. **tersely**, *adv*. kwa maneno machache. **terseness**, *n*. kutumia maneno machache, uchache wa maneno.

tertian, *a*. -a kila siku ya tatu. **tertiary**, *a*. -a tatu.

tesselated, *a*. -a vijiwe (vidogo vya mraba vyenye rangi).

test, *v.t.* jaribu, jaribia, angalia, chungua, chunguza, hakikia, onja. — *n*. jaribu, jaribio, maonji; (*standard*) kanuni; (*proof*) mathubutu; (*criterion*) tofauti, alama, dalili. *Test-tube*, kama chupa cha kujaribia dawa &c. **tested**, *a*. -liojaribiwa, -thabiti, -liyothibitika, jarabati.

testament, *n*. hati ya kurithisha mali, hati ya wosia, wosia. *Old Testament*, torati, maandiko ya Agano la Kale. *New Testament*, Injili, maandiko ya Agano Jipya. **testamentary**, *a*. -a wosia. **testator**, *n*. mwenye kuandika wasia, mwusia.

testicle, *n*. pumbu, kokwa ya (yai la) pumbu, korodani, kende.

testify, *v.t.* *and* *i*. shuhudia, sema kwa kiapo, toa mathubutu. **testimonial**, *n*. hati (barua) au zawadi ya kusifu, ya kushuhudia kazi njema, ya kushukuru, barua ya sifa, barua. **testimony**, *n*. ushahidi, ushuhuda, maneno ya kuhakikisha, mathubutu.

testily, *adv*. taz. *testy*.

testimonial, *n*., **testimony**, *n*. taz. *testify*.

testy, *a*. -a harara, -epesi kuona hasira, -a hamaki, -a chuki, -kali. **testily**, *adv*. kwa harara, vikali, kwa hasira.

tetanus, *n*. pepo punda.

tête-à-tête, *n*. maongezi ya faraghani ya watu wawili tu.

tether, *v.t.* fungasha (mnyama) kwa kamba na kigingi. — *n*. kamba ya kufungashia mnyama kwa kigingi. *I am at the end of my tether*, nimeishiwa nguvu (mali, uwezo &c.).

tetragon, *n*. umbo lenye pembe nne, kama mraba &c. **tetragonal**, *a*. -enye pembe nne.

tetrarch, *n*. jumbe mdogo zamani za Warumi.

tetter, *n*. ugonjwa wa ngozi kama choa, ukurutu &c.

Teutonic, *a*. -a Wadachi wa kale, -a asili ya Wadachi.

text, *n*. maneno yenyewe (ya andiko lo lote); (*verse*) fungu dogo la maneno la *Bible*, aya; (*subject*) jambo, neno, jawabu, kiini. **text-book**, *n*. kitabu cha mafundisho. **text-hand**, *n*. mwandiko wa herufi kubwa. **textual**, *a*. -a *text*, -a maneno yenyewe. *Textual criticism*, kuchungua maneno yenyewe yalivyopata kuandikwa hivi au hivi, si maana yake.

textile, *a*. -a kusokotwa, -a kufumwa, -a nyuzi, -a kufanya nguo (kitambaa). *Textiles*, namna zote za nguo, vitambaa. **texture**, *n*. jinsi ya kusokotwa au kufumwa, jinsi ya kufanyizwa, asili, matengeneo, umbo, namna (*e.g.* laini, kukwaruza, -nene, -embamba &c.).

textual, *a.* taz. *text.*
texture, *n.* taz. *textile.*
than, *conj.* kuliko, kama, wala si. *More than,* zaidi ya, fauka ya, kupita, kushinda, kuliko.
thane, *n.* sheki (wa Uingereza zamani kabla ya A.D. 1066).
thank, *v.t.* shukuru, tolea asante, itika marahaba; (*feel grateful*) ona shukrani, -wa na shukrani moyoni. *Thank you!* asante! marahaba! *I will thank you to,* utafadhali. *Thanks to the rain,* kwa sababu ya kunyesha mvua. **thankful,** *a.* -enye shukrani, -a kushukuru. **thankless,** *a.* pasipo shukrani; (*fruitless*) pasipo faida, -a bure. **thankoffering,** *n.* sadaka ya kushukuru (ya kutolea shukrani). **thanks,** *n.* shukrani, asante, marahaba. **thanksgiving,** *n.* kushukuru, sikukuu ya kushukuru, shukrani. **thankworthy,** *a.* -a kushukuru, -a kustahili shukrani.
that, *a. and pron.* yule (ule, ile &c.); (*the afore-mentioned*) huyo (huo, hiyo &c.); (*relative*) -o (-ye, -yo, -vyo &c.). — *conj.* kama, ya kwamba, ya kuwa, kwa sababu, kwa kusudi, ili. *That, so that* (*purpose*), *In order that, To the end that,* ili, makusudi, kwa jinsi (pamoja na *subjunctive*). *Oh that, Would that,* laiti. *So that, So . . . that,* (*result*) hata, kwa jinsi. *All that, All that sort of thing,* mambo kama haya. *For that, In that,* kwa kuwa, kwa maana. *That is to say,* ndiyo maana yake, yaani.
thatch, *v.t.* ezeka, vimba (nyumba kwa makuti, nyasi &c.). — *n.* maezeko; (*coco-nut leaves*) makuti; (*grass*) majani. *Put on thatch,* ezeka, vimba. *Strip off thatch,* ezua, vimbua. **thatched,** *a.* -lioezekwa makuti (majani &c.). **thatching,** *n.* maezeko, makuti, majani &c.
thaw, *v.t.* (barafu na theluji) yeyusha; — *v.i.* yeyuka.
the, *def. art.* (*particular*) yule (ule, ile &c.; wale, ile, zile &c.); (*generic: not translated*) *The lion killed him,* yule simba alimwua. *The lion is a fierce animal,* simba ni mnyama mkali. *The horse and dog are faithful servants,* farasi na mbwa ni watumishi waaminifu.
theatre, *n.* jumba la kuchezea michezo (ya kuigiza mambo ya hadithi &c.) mbele ya watu; (*scene of important events*) mahali palipotokea jambo kuu (jambo la sifa). *Operating theatre,* chumba cha udaktari wa kukata sehemu za mwili zilizoharibika. **theatrical,** *a.* -a *theatre,* -a kujifanya, -a kuigiza, -a fahari.
thee, *pron.* wewe, = *you*; (*in comp.*) -ku-, *e.g. I see thee,* nakuona.
theft, *n.* (*thieving*) wizi, wivi, wibaji, kuiba.
their, theirs, *a.* -ao (wao, yao &c.).
theism, *n.* kumwamini Mungu mmoja. **theist,** *n.* mtu amwaminiye Mungu mmoja.
them, *pron.* wao, hao, wale (yale, hayo &c.); (*in comp.*) -wa- (-i-, -ya- &c.). **themselves,** *pron.* -enyewe (zenyewe &c.) nafsi; (*reflexive*) -ji-. *They hurt themselves,* walijiumiza. *They went themselves,* walikwenda wenyewe.
theme, *n.* jambo au kitu kinachofikiriwa au kuandikiwa maneno, jambo, neno, hoja, kisa, kiini.
themselves, *pron.* taz. *them.*
then, *adv.* (*time*) siku ile, wakati ule, zamani zile, pale, ndipo, hapo; (*next, after*) baadaye, halafu, kisha, aidha, tena; (*cause*) basi, kwa hiyo, kwa sababu hii; (*condition*) ikiwa hivi, ingawa hivi. *Now and then,* pengine pengine, pana wakati, mara kwa mara. *Then and there,* papo hapo, pale pale. *Till then,* hata (mpaka) wakati fulani.
thence, *adv.* toka huko, huko. **thenceforth, thenceforward,** *adv.* toka huko, tokea hapo.
theocracy, *n.* kutawala kwa Mungu peke yake (au kwa makuhani au makasisi) wanaodai kutawala kwa maongozi ya Mungu. **theocratic,** *a.* -a *theocracy.*

theodolite, *n.* chombo (kama darubini) cha kupimia nchi, urefu wa kwenda juu au kwenda mbali *&c.*, katika kuandika ramani.

theologian, *n.*, **theological,** *a.* taz. *theology.*

theology, *n.* elimu ya tabia na sifa za Mungu na dini. **theologian,** *n.* mwanafunzi (mwalimu, mchunguzi) wa *theology.* **theological,** *a.* -a elimu ya *theology.*

theophany, *n.* tokeo la Mungu waziwazi, kuonekana Mungu.

theorem, *n.*, **theoretical,** *a.*, **theorist,** *n.*, **theorize,** *v.* taz. *theory.*

theory, *n.* maelezo (mafafanusi) ya akili, shauri la akili bila amali, elimu tupu; (*guesswork*) makisio, habari ya bahati, kubahatisha, shauri, nia. **theorem,** *n.* neno litakalo kuthibitika au liwezalo kuhakikishwa. **theoretic,** *a.* -a *theory.* **theorist,** *n.* mtu hodari wa *theory,* mtu mwenye elimu tupu, si mtu wa amali, mtu wa mashauri mengi. **theorize,** *v.i.* toa *theories* nyingi, eleza kwa akili bila amali, bahatisha, kisia.

theosophy, *n.* imani ya kuwa wanadamu wanaweza kupata elimu (habari) za Mungu kwa kuwa safi kabisa na kumwaza Mungu kwa bidii.

therapeutic, *a.* -a kuponya (magonjwa, maradhi). **therapeutics,** *n.* maarifa ya kuponya magonjwa, utabibu.

there, *adv.* (*local*) pale, hapo, kule, huko, mle, humo; (*in comp.*) pa-, ku-, m-, -po, -ko, -mo; (*general*) katika haya, kwa hiyo. *There was a man,* palikuwa na mtu. *He was there,* alikuwako. *It was there I saw him,* ndipo nilipomwona. *There!* tazama! ah! *Thereabouts,* karibu, kama hivi. *Thereafter,* baadaye, halafu. *There at,* pale, kwa hiyo. *Thereby,* kwa hiyo, kwa sababu hii. *Therefore,* kwa sababu hii, kwa hii. *Therefrom,* kutoka huko, katika hii, humo. *Therein,* katika hii, humo. *Thereof,* -a hii, -a hiyo. *Thereon, Thereupon,* kwa sababu hii, kwa hiyo, pale, mara. *Thereto,* kwa hii, kwa hiyo. *Therewith,* kwa hii, na hii.

therm, *n.* kipimo cha kadiri ya joto.

thermal, *a.* -a moto, -a joto.

thermometer, *n.* kipimo cha kupimia joto na baridi. **thermos flask,** *n.* chupa inayodumisha yaliyomo kuwa na joto au baridi. **thermostat,** *n.* chombo kinachodumisha kadiri ile ile ya joto.

thesaurus, *n.* hazina, kusanyiko; (*dictionary*) kamusi.

these, *a. and pron. pl.* ya *this* (hawa, haya, hii *&c.*).

thesis, *n.* jambo la kuandikiwa habari, jambo la kubishaniwa maneno; (*for purposes of a degree*) insha (kitabu, maandiko) iliyoandikwa kusudi kupata cheo (*degree*) cha *University.*

thews, *n.* kano, maungo, nguvu.

they, *pron.* wao (wale, ile, zile *&c*); (*in verbs*) wa- (i-, zi-, ya- *&c.*).

thick, *a.* -nene, -zito; (*crowded*) -a kusongana, -a kusongamana, -ingi pamoja; (*cloth*) -nene, maradufu; (*sound*) -zito, si wazi; (*liquid*) rojorojo, -zito. *Through thick and thin,* kwa heri na kwa shari, kwa vyo vyote, kwa kila hali. *Thick with* (*abounding in*) -enye . . . -ingi, -enye kujaa; (*friendly with*) -enye urafiki na. *In the thick of it,* katikati yake.

thicken, *v.t.* fanya kuwa *thick.* gandamiza, songanisha, zidisha; — *v.i.* -wa -zito (-nene); zidi, gandamana, songamana. *The plot thickens* mambo yaendelea (yaiva, yasitawi). **thicket,** *n.* kichaka, chaka; (*of mangroves*) koko. **thickhead,** *n.* mbaradhuli, mzuzu, mtu mzito (wa akili), mgumu, mpumbavu. **thickly,** *adv.* kwa wingi; (*indistinctly*) kwa kugugumiza. **thickness,** *n.* unene, kuwa *thick,* maki. **thick-skinned,** *a.* -siyejali wengine, -gumu kutambua maono ya wengine.

thief, *n.* (*pl. thieves*) mwivi, mwizi, mwibaji, mkwepuzi. **thieve,** *v.i.* iba. **thievish,** *a.* (*person*) kijivi, -ibaji.

thigh, *n.* upaja, paja, kiga, kiweo.
thimble, *n.* kastabini, kustabuni, subana, subano, tondoo.
thin, *a.* -embamba, -dogo; (*emaciated*) -gofu, -liokonda, -a kimbaombao; (*poor, weak*) hafifu, dhaifu, -goigoi; (*deficient*) -chache, si -ingi; (*liquid*) -a majimaji, -liochujuka. — *v.t.* fanya kuwa *thin*, punguza; — *v.i.* lainika, -wa -embamba, punguka; (*of persons*) konda, nyorora, dhoofu.
thine, *a.* -ako, = *yours*.
thing, *n.* kitu, jambo, neno, dude, kidude. *Poor thing*, (*person*) mtu maskini, mnyonge. *Things*, vyombo, mali, takataka, nguo, vikorokoro. *Be the thing*, faa, -wa -zima, -wa halisi (sawa).
think, *v.i.* (*p.t. and pf.t.* **thought**) (*reflect*) fikiri, tafakari, waza, kumbuka; (*suppose*) dhani, ona; (*purpose*) azimu, nia, kusudia, dhamiri; — *v.t.* fikiri, dhani. *Think better of*, ghairi, geuza, shauri. *Think well of*, onea mema, penda, sifu. *Think much of*, kumbuka sana, angalia, jali. *Think little of*, dharau, toangalia. *I think so*, naona, nadhani. **thinker**, *n.* mtu wa kufikiri (wa fikira nyingi, wa akili). **thinking**, *n.* kufikiri, kutafakari, fikira, mawazo. — *a.* -a kufikiri &c.
third, *n. and a.* theluthu, fungu la (sehemu ya) tatu, -a tatu. **thirdly**, *adv.* ya tatu. **third-rate**, *a.* -a tatu, -a cheo cha (namba ya) tatu, hafifu. **thirteen**, *n. and a.* thelatashara, kumi na tatu. **thirteenth**, *a.* -a kumi na tatu. **thirtieth**, *a.* -a thelathini. **thirty**, *n. and a.* thelathini.
thirst, *n.* kiu; (*yearning*) shauku, tamaa. — *v.i.* ona kiu, -wa na kiu. *Thirst for*, onea shauku, tamani, taka sana. **thirsty**, *a.* -enye kiu; (*dry*) -kavu. *I am thirsty*, nina kiu.
thirteen, *n. and a.*, **thirteenth**, *a.*, **thirtieth**, *n. and a.*, **thirty**, *n. and a.* taz. *third*.
this, *a.* huyu (huu, hii &c.).
thistle, *n.* gugu la Ulaya lenye miiba, mbaruti.
thither, *adv.* huko, kule.
thong, *n.* ugwe, kigwe, ukanda.
thorax, *n.* kifua; (*of animals and birds*) kidari.
thorn, *n.* mwiba; (*thorny shrub*) mchongoma, mkwamba. *Be on thorns*, ona wasiwasi, hangaika, fadhaika sana, sumbuka mno. **thorny**, *a.* -enye miiba; (*difficult*) -a taabu, -a mashaka.
thorough, *a.* kamili, -kamilifu, -zima, -a kweli, halisi. *A thorough rascal*, ayari wa kupindukia. **thoroughbred**, *a.* -a mbegu njema, -a asili bora. **thoroughfare**, *n.* njia wazi kwa watu wote, njia ya kupitika sana, barabara, njia kuu. **thoroughgoing**, *a.* -a kwelikweli, hasa, halisi, hodari, -nyofu. **thoroughly**, *adv.* kabisa, kwa bidii sana, kamili, kwelikweli. **thoroughness**, *n.* ukamilifu, bidii nyingi, uhalisi. **thorough-paced**, *a.* halisi, -a kweli, kamili.
those, *pl.* ya *that*, wao, wale, ile, zile &c.
thou, *pron.* = *you*, wewe.
though, *conj.* ingawa, ikiwa, ijapo, ijapokuwa, kwamba. *As though*, kama kwamba. *Even though*, ingawa, ijapokuwa. — *adv.* lakini, basi.
thought, (1) *p.t. and pf.t.* ya *think*.
thought, (2) *n.* wazo, nia, fikira, dhana, taamuli; (*caution*) hadhari, tunza, uangalifu; (*anxiety*) mashaka shughuli. *Take thought for*, angalia, tunza, tazamia, kumbuka, zingatia, jisumbulia. **thoughtful**, *a.* -a kufikiri, -a mawazo, -zingativu; (*careful*) -a hadhari, -angalifu. **thoughtless**, *a.* si -angalifu, -zembe, -a haraka, -pumbavu, -epesi, jasiri. **thoughtlessness**, *n.* uzembe, upurukushani, kutoangalia, haraka.
thousand, *n. and a.* elfu. *A thousand* (*in poetry*), kikwi. *A hundred thousand*, laki. *Two thousand*, elfeen. **thousandth**, *a.* -a elfu.
thrall, *n.* mtumwa; utumwa. **thraldom**, *n.* utumwa.

thrash, *v.t.* (*grain*) pura, piga, kafua, puta; (*by rubbing*) fikicha; (*beat*) pigapiga sana, shinda, twanga. *Thrash out a question,* fanyia maneno mpaka kudhihirisha (mpaka kueleza wazi). **thrashing,** *n.* kupura, kupiga &c., mapigo mengi; (*defeat*) ushinde. **thrashing-floor,** *n.* sakafu (ya kupuria &c., nafaka), uga.

threshold, *n.* kizingiti (cha ehini); (*opening*) mwanzo. *Cross the threshold,* ingia nyumbani.

thread, *n.* uzi, kitani; (*course*) mwendo, njia, kufululiza, mfululizo, mfulizo; (*of screw*) ukali uzungukao mpaka mwisho (wa msumari wa hesi, wa parafujo, wa skrubu). *Take up the thread of,* rudia, rejea. *Hang by a thread,* -wa katika hatari kubwa. — *v.t.* tunga uzi (katika tundu la sindano), tungia; (*pass through*) pita, penya. *The needle is threaded,* uzi umetungia sindano. **threadbare,** *a.* -kuukuu, -bovu; (*uninteresting*) baridi. **threadworm,** *n.* uchango mdogo wa tumboni. **thready,** *a.* kama uzi, -a nyuzinyuzi.

threat, *n.* kamio, ogofya, tisho, neno la kutia hofu; **threaten,** *v.t. and i.* kamia, ogofya, tisha, tia hofu; (*indicate*) onya, julisha, toa ishara ya; (*impend*) taka kuja, taka kuumiza (kuleta hasara) -wa karibu kuja, karibia. *Be threatened with,* ona karibu, -wa karibu kupatwa na, -wa na hofu ya. **threatening,** *a.* -a kutisha, -a kuogofya; (*warning*) -enye dalili ya hatari (shida &c.)

three, *n. and a.* tatu, -tatu. **threefold,** *a.* -a mara tatu. **three-ply,** *a.* -enye tabaka (nyuzi, kamba &c.) tatu. **threescore,** *n. and a.* sitini.

thrice, *adv.* mara tatu.

thresh, *v.*, **threshing,** *n.*, **threshing-floor,** *n.*, **threshold,** *n.* taz. *thrash.*

threw, *p.t.* ya *throw.*

thrice, *adv.* taz. *three.*

thrift, *n.* uwekevu, ikitisadi, kiasi katika kutumia fedha, uangalifu katika kutumia mali &c., kusimamia uzuri, usimamizi mzuri, kufanikiwa, upasi, ukabidhi. **thriftless,** *a.* -potevu -a mali, -tapanyaji, -a mali, -fujaji -a mali, -a kuponda mali, -jinga. **thrifty,** *a.* -a kiasi, -wekevu, -a kusimamia vizuri, -a pasi, -angalizi (kwa mambo ya mali), -kabidhi.

thrill, *v.t.* sisimua, tetemesha, tia furaha (hofu, maumivu &c.) kuu; (*affect, shock*) choma, penya, shtusha; — *v.i.* shtuka, sisimka, tetema, ona furaha (hofu &c.) kuu. — *n.* kituko, kitetemo, msisimko, kitapo, kipindi, kishindo, mshindo. **thrilling,** *a.* -a kusisimua, -a kustusha, -a kutetemesha.

thrive, *v.i.* (*p.t.* **throve,** *p.t.* **thriven**) (*prosper*) pata mali, fanikiwa, sitawi, ondokea; (*plants*) sitawi; (*grow fat*) nenepa, pata maungo, tonoka, tononeka. **thriving,** *a.* -pasi, -kuza, -enye hali njema, -a kufanikiwa.

throat, *n.* koo, umio, roho.

throb, *v.i.* puma, pwita, pigapiga, papa, papatika, tetema, tuta, furukuta. — *n.* pigo, tetemo, kipapo. **throbbing,** *n.* mpumo, kupapa, kupigapiga, tetemo, kupwita. — *a.* -a kutetema, -a kupigapiga, -a kupapa, -a kupwita.

throe, *n.* maumivu makuu, uchungu, taabu, juhudi; (*of birth*) uchungu (utungu) wa kuzaa.

throne, *n.* kiti cha enzi, kiti cha fahari, kiti kikuu; (*royal power*) ufalme; (*king*) mfalme. — *v.t.* weka katikwa kiti cha enzi.

throng, *n.* msongamano wa watu, ghasia ya watu, msukosuko, zahama, makutano, wingi. — *v.i.* songa, songamana, songana, jaa tele; — *v.t.* sumbua kwa kusonga, jaza tele.

throttle, *v.t.* songa roho, kaba; (*machine &c.*) punguza mvuke (petroli, nguvu). — *n.* kilango cha mashine kinachopitisha na kuzuia mvuke (petroli &c.); (*throat*) koo, umio, roho.

through, *prep.* kwa, katika; (*throughout, from end to end of*) toka upande huu hata upande wa pili wa, pote katika, tangu mwanzo hata mwisho wa; (*within*) ndani ya, katika ya; (*because of, by means of*) kwa sababu ya, kwa njia ya, kwa kutumia, kwa mkono wa. — *adv.* hata mwisho, hata upande wa pili, katikati. *Go through with*, maliza. *Pass through* (*to other side*) tumbuza, penya. *Fall through*, isha, -fa. *Through* (*ticket, train &c.*) -a kwenda njia yote, -a safari nzima. *Through and through*, kote, sana, kabisa. **throughout**, *prep.* pote pote, kote kote, katika. — *adv.* pote pote, pia, kabisa, kwa wakati wote, mpaka mwisho.

throve, *p.t.* ya *thrive*.

throw, *v.t.* (*p.t.* **threw**, *pf. t.* **thrown**) tupa, gea, rusha, vurumisha, pisha, peleka, piga. (*a rider*) angusha, rusha; — *v.i* tupa, peleka. *Throw about*, tapanya. *Throw away*, tupa, kataza, poteza, tumia bure, fuja. *Throw back*, rejeza, rudisha; (*reject*) kataza; (*check progress*) poteza kazi, sahaulisha mafundisho. *Throw down*, angusha, angua; (*a load*) bwaga; (*into a hole, water &c.*) tumbukiza; (*break, destroy*) vunja, bomoa, haribu angamiza. *Throw in*, ongeza, tia bure, toa mara kwa mara. *Throw in one's teeth*, simanga. *Throw off*, ondoa, jiondolea, tupa, kupua, acha; (*a load*) bwaga; (*illness*) pona katika. *Throw oneself on*, jitoa kwa, kimbilia, tegemea. *Throw out*, toa; (*reject*) kataa, (*confuse*) fadhaisha, pumbaza, duwaza; (*construct*) fanyiza. *Throw over*, tupa, acha, tenga. *Throw up* (*resign*) acha, toka, jitoa; (*vomit*) tapika; (*construct*) fanyiza (jenga) upesi. — *n.* pigo, mrusho; (*range*) mtupo.

thrush, (1) *n.* namna ya ndege wa Ulaya aimbaye vizuri.

thrush, (2) *n.* ugonjwa wa kuvimba ulimi na ufizi, wa watoto wachanga.

thrust, *v.t.* (*p.t. and pf.t.* **thrust**) sukuma (jongeza, sogeza, toa) kwa nguvu, kumba, songa. *Thrust aside* (*in scorn &c.*), deua, geua. *Thrust in*, ingiza, penyeza, choma. *Thrust out*, fukuza, ondoa, toa; (*the lower lip as a sign of derision &c.*) bibidia. — *n.* pigo, kumbo, chomo, mdukuo.

thud, *n.* mshindo.

thug, *n.* mwizi mwuaji (wa kihindi).

thumb, *n.* kidole cha gumba. *Under the thumb of*, chini ya, katika utumwa wa. — *v.t.* haribu (chafua) kwa kugusagusa.

thump, *n.* ngumi, pigo la ngumi (au la rungu &c.). — *v.t.* piga, piga ngumi.

thunder, *n.* (*clap*) radi, mshindo wa ngurumo; (*distant*) ngurumo. — *v.i.* piga ngurumo. *It thundered yesterday*, jana kulipiga ngurumo. **thunderbolt**, *n.* radi; (*great surprise*) jambo la kushtusha sana. **thunder-clap**, *n.* radi, ngurumo. **thunderstorm**, *n.* mvua na ngurumo, mvua ya radi. **thunder-struck**, *a.* (*be*) kushangaa sana, kufadhaika, kushtushwa sana, shikwa na bumbuazi, kupumbaa, kuduwaa.

thurible, *n.* chetezo. **thurifer**, *n.* mchukua chetezo.

Thursday, *n.* Alhamisi.

thus, *adv.* hivi, hivyo, vivi hivi, ndivyo.

thwack, *v.t.* piga kwa nguvu. — *n.* pigo la nguvu, kikumbo.

thwart, *v.t.* zuia, pinga, pinza, shinda. — *n.* kiti cha mvuta kasia. **athwart**, *adv.* kwa upande, kwa kupinga, kwa kukingama.

thy, *a.* = *your*, -ako. **thyself**, *pron.* (= *yourself*) wewe mwenyewe, nafsi yako; (*in comp.*) -ji-.

thyroid, *n.* kikoromeo, dundumio.

thyself, *pron.* taz. *thy*.

tiara, *n.* taji.

tibia, *n.* muundi wa mguu, goko.

tic, *n.* mtetemo wa uso.

tick, (1) *n.* (*cattle*) kupe; (*spirillum*) papasi.

tick, (2) *n.* (*cover*) nguo ya (mfuko wa) godoro. **ticking**, *n.* nguo ya godoro.

tick, (3) *v.i.* piga ta-ta-ta (kama saa). — *n.* pigo la saa, ta-ta-ta-.

ticket, *n.* cheti, kibarua, kipande, tikiti.

ticking, *n.* taz. *tick* (2).

tickle, *v.t.* tekenya, nyegeresha, nyea; (*amuse*) chekesha, furahisha; — *v.i.* tekenya, nyegeresha, washa. **tickling**, *n.* mnyeo, kutekenya. **ticklish**, *a.* -a kuona kutekenya upesi; (*difficult*) -a mashaka, -a kutaka uangalifu mwingi; (*quarrelsome*) -epesi kukasirika (kuudhika), -a chuki.

tide, *n.* maji kujaa na kupwa; (*course*) mwendo, mkondo. *Spring tides*, bamvua, maji makuu. *Neap tides*, maji mafu. *High tide*, maji kujaa. *Low tide*, maji kupwa. — *v.i. Tide over a difficulty*, faulu, jiponya katika shida. **tidal**, *a.* -a *tide*, penye *tide*. **tideless**, *a.* pasipo *tide*.

tidiness, *n.* taz. *tidy*.

tidings, *n.* habari, taarifa.

tidy, *a.* -liotengenea, -a taratibu, nadhifu, -safi, -zuri. — *v.i.* nadhifisha; tengeneza, weka sawa, takasa, kwatua, safidi. **tidiness**, *n.* kutengeneka, unadhifu, utaratibu, utengemano.

tie, *v.t.* funga (kwa kamba, kitani, uzi &c.), boba, piga fundo; (*join*) unganisha, fungasha fungasa; (*obstruct*) funga zuia; (*impose obligation upon*) tia sharti, amrisha; (*in a faggot*) tita; — *v.i.* (*in games &c.*) -wa sawasawa, enda sare. — *n.* kifungo, kiungo, fundo; (*necktie*) kitambaa cha (utepe wa) shingoni; (*obligation*) mtu anayekuhusu; (*in games &c.*) usawa, suluhu.

tier, *n.* tabaka, safu, rusu, daraja.

tiff, *n.* ugomvi kidogo.

tiffin, *n.* chakula cha adhuhuri.

tiger, *n.* mnyama wa kihindi kama chui mkubwa. **tigress**, *n. tiger* jike.

tight, *a.* -a kukaza, -liokazwa, -kazo; (*water-tight*) -siovuja; (*air-tight*) -siopisha hewa; (*stretched*) -lionyoshwa sana, -liokazana, -liowambwa, (*of money*) adimu, -a kuadimika, ghali; (*of persons*) -a choyo, bahili, -nyimivu; (*of clothing &c.*) -a kubana, -a kufinya. *A tight corner*, jambo lenye hatari (shida, dhiki). *Be tight*, dhiki, kaza, bana, finya; (*be drunk*) lewa. **tighten**, *v.t.* kaza; — *v.i.* kazana, kazika. **tightly**, *adv.* kikiki, kwa kukaza. **tightness**, *n.* kukaza, kufinya.

tigress, *n.* taz. *tiger*.

tike, tyke, *n.* mbwa wa vivi hivi tu.

tile, *n.* kigae (cha kuezekea, cha kubandikiza ukutani au sakafuni). — *v.t.* ezeka nyumba kwa vigae.

till, (1) *n.* kikasha (cha mezani), mtoto wa meza, mtoto wa kasha.

till, (2) *conj.* hata, mpaka.

till, (3) *v.t.* lima. **tillage**, *n.* kilimo, ulimaji, ukulima, zaraa. **tiller**, *n.* mkulima, mlimaji.

tiller, *n.* kana. *Tiller rope*, mjiari, ujari.

tilt, *v.t.* (*cause to slope*) inamisha, tusha upande; — *v.i.* inama, lala upande; (*take part in tournament*) pigana kwa farasi na mikuki mirefu. — *n.* mainamizi.

timber, *n.* miti, mbao. — *a.* -a miti, -a mbao.

timbre, *n.* tabia ya (uzuri wa, utamu wa) sauti. **timbrel**, *n.* kigoma, tari.

time, *n.* wakati, majira; (*duration*) maisha, aushi; (*opportunity*) nafasi, wasaa; (*period, space of*) muda, muhula, kipindi; (*short*) kitambo; (*leisure*) faragha; (*hour*) saa; (*life*) maisha; (*time of life, age*) umri; (*moment, chance*) saa; (*age, epoch*) zamani, wakati, siku. *First* (*second &c.*) *time*, mara ya kwanza (ya pili &c.). *Time out of mind*, tangu zamani sana. *Time!* basi! koma! *Times* (*ages*) zamani. *Times past*, zamani za kale. *Present time*, zamani hizi, siku hizi. (*In arithmetic*) *three times two*, tatu mara mbili. *In time*, halafu. *Be in time*, wahi, diriki. *Be in time!* usichelewe! *What is the time?* saa ngapi? *At times*, pana siku, pengine. *At the times of*, mwenye. *For some time*, tangu hapo. *For the time being*, kwa muda, kwa kitambo, kwa wakati. *From time immemorial*, tangu zamani za kwanza. *From time to time*, pengine, mara kwa mara. *In no time*, mara moja. *Keep time*, enda sawa, piga sawasawa, shika mwendo. *Mark time* (*military*) simama na kuchapua miguu; (*pause*) ngoja. *Once upon a time*, hapo kale. *Pass the time of day*, amkiana, ulizana habari. *Some time ago*, hapo kale. *Take time*, taka (chukua) wakati. *It takes time*, si jambo la mara moja. *Take your time*, usifanye haraka. — *v.t.* (*settle time of*) chagua vema saa ya, amuru saa ya; (*observe time of*) angalia wakati wa. *Well timed*, -a wakati unaofaa, heri, -a bahati. **time-honoured,** *a.* -enye sifa kwa kukaa sana, -enye aushi ya heshima, -lioadhimishwa kwa muda mrefu. **time-keeper,** *n.* mwenye kuangalia (kuamuru, kuandika) wakati (muda wa kazi, saa &c.); (*clock*) saa. **timely,** *a.* -a wakati wa kufaa, -a kuja sawa, -a kufaa, -lipofaa. **time-piece,** *n.* saa. **time-server,** *n.* mgeugeu, mjipendekeza kwa wakuu. **time-table,** *n.* orodha ya saa au wakati. **time-worn,** *a.* -kuukuu, -liochakaa.

timid, *a.* -oga, -pesi kushtushwa, -enye haya. **timidity,** *n.* woga, haya. **timorous,** *a.* -oga.

tin, *n.* bati. *A tin, Tin vessel*, kopo, kikopo, mkebe. — *v.t.* tia bati, rasisi; (*pack in tins*) tia katika kopo (mkebe). — *a.* -a bati. **tin-foil,** *n.* jaribosi. **tinned,** *a.* (*milk, fruit &c.*) -a kopo, -a mkebe.

tincture, *n.* dawa ya maji; (*small quantity*) kidogo, alama, dalili. — *v.t.* tia rangi kidogo, tia kidogo, changanya kidogo.

tinder, *n.* vitu vikavu vya kuchochea moto.

tin-foil, *n.* taz. *tin.*

tinea, *n.* ugonjwa wa ngozi, hasa choa na bato.

tinge, *v.t.* tia rangi kidogo, geuza kidogo. — *n.* (*colour*) rangi; (*small quantity*) kidogo, alama, dalili.

tingle, *v.i.* ona mnyeo, washa, chatika damu, sisimka. **tingling,** *n.* mnyeo, msisimko.

tinker, *n.* mfua bati, mtengenezaji vyombo vya bati. — *v.t.* tengeneza ovyo ovyo.

tinkle, *v.i.* lia kama njuga au kengele ndogo. — *n.* mlio wa njuga (wa kengele ndogo).

tinned, *a.* taz. *tin.*

tinsel, *n.* zari, nguo ya kumetameta. — *a.* -a *tinsel*; (*showy*) -a urembo, -shaufu; (*unreal*) -a ovyo.

tint, *n.* rangi. — *v.t.* tia rangi (kidogo).

tiny, *a.* -dogo mno, kadogo.

tip, (1) *n.* (*end*) ncha, kipande cha ncha, kilembwa; (*of a mountain, hill &c.*) kilele, kileleta; (*pointed part*) ncha, sehemu iliyochongoka, mchonge; (*touch*) mguso. — *v.* tia katika ncha. **tiptoe,** *adv.* kwa ncha za vidole vya miguu, njongwanjongwa, mzofafa. *Stand on tiptoe*, chuchumia. *Be on tiptoe* (*of expectation*) kodolea, tazamia kwa juhudi sana. — *v.i.* enda njongwanjongwa, enda (nyatia) kwa ncha za vidole vya miguu, enda kwa kuchuchumia, enda kwa mzofafa. **tiptop,** *a.* bora, -a upeo, -zuri kabisa. — *n.* upeo, ukomo, ncha, kilele.

tip, (2) *v.t.* (*set on side*) inamisha upande mmoja, weka upande (mshazari); —*v.i.* inama. *Tip-cat*, geli. *Tip out*, mwaga (kwa kuinamisha chombo, gari, &c.). *Tip over*, pindua, pindukiza, pinduka. *Tip up*, inamisha. *Tip-up seat*, kiti cha kukunja (kwa kuinua au kuinamisha tako lake). — *n.* jaa, mahali pa kutupia taka.

tip, (3) *n.* (*present*) bakshishi, zawadi, ada; (*hint*) kionyo, kidokezi, shauri. —*v.t.* -pa bakshishi (zawadi &c). **tipster,** *n.* mtu apataye uchumi kwa kushauri watu farasi wanaoelekea kushinda katika mashindano.

tippet, *n.* vazi la mabegani.

tipple, *v.i.* -nywa sana (ulevi). **tippler,** *n.* mlevi. **tipsy,** *a.* *Be tipsy*, lewa (hasa kulewa kidogo).

tipster, *n.* taz. *tip* (3).

tipsy, *a.* taz. *tipple.*

tiptoe, *adv.*, **tiptop**, *n.* & *a.* taz. *tip* (1).

tirade, *n.* maneno mengi ya juhudi (ya kukaripia, ya kushutumu, ya kulaumu).

tire, (1), **tyre**, *n.* duara ya (kizingo cha) chuma -nje ya gurudumu; (*rubber*) mpira (wa baisikeli, motakaa &c.).

tire, (2) *v.t.* chosha, legeza, taabisha; —*v.i.* (*become tired*) choka, legea, nyong'onyea. *I am tired of this food*, chakula hiki kinaninuka (kimenichosa, kimenikinaisha). *They are tired of each other*, wananukana. **tired**, *a.* -chovu, -legevu, -nyong'onyevu, -tepetevu. *Become tired*, choka, nyong'onyea, sakara, sakarika. **tiredness**, *n.* uchovu, kuchoka, mavundevunde, unyong'onyevu, unyogovu, taabu. **tireless**, *a.* -siochoka, -enye bidii (nguvu, juhudi) nyingi (isiyokwisha). **tiresome**, *a.* -a kuchosha, -a kutaabisha, -a kusumbua, -tiriri, -tukutu. **tiring**, *a.* -a kuchosha, -a kutaabisha.

tiro, **tyro**, *n.* mtu mpya (wa kazi &c.), mjinga, mwanafunzi.

tissue, *n.* nguo nyembamba sana, shashi, melimeli; nguo nyembamba ya hariri yenye zari; (*collection, series*) jamii, mafuatano; (*substance*) kitu, nyama, mwili. *A tissue of lies*, mawongo matupu. **tissue-paper**, *n.* karatasi ya shashi.

tit, (1) *n.* taz. *teat.*

tit, (2) *n.* namna ya ndege mdogo mwenye rangi.

tit-for-tat, pigo kwa pigo, yaani kumfanyia mtu kama alivyokufanyia wewe.

titanic, *a.* -kubwa mno.

titbit, *n.* kipande kidogo kizuri (cha chakula, cha habari).

tithe, *n.* zaka, sehemu ya kumi; (*ecclesiastical*) sehemu ya mavuno iliyotolewa kwa Kanisa; (*small portion*) kipande kidogo, sehemu ndogo, fungu dogo, kidogo.

titilate, *v.t.* tekenya, nyegeresha, chochea, amsha, sisimua. **titilation**, *n.* mnyeo, msisimko.

titivate, *v.t.* kwatua, fanya nadhifu, nadhifisha, tengeneza, safisha, safidi.

title, *n.* (*address*) anwani; (*name*) jina la heshima (la cheo); (*claim, right*) haki. **titled**, *a.* -enye jina la heshima (*e.g. Sir, Lord &c.*). **title-deed**, *n.* hati ya kuthibitisha uenyeji. **title-page**, *n.* ukurasa wa kwanza wa kitabu, wenye jina lake. **titular**, *a.* kwa jina tu.

titter, *v.i.* jichekea, fanya kicheko, chekelea. — *n.* kicheko.

title-tattle, *n.* vijineno, maongezi, porojo, soga.

titular, *a.* taz. *title.*

to, *prep. and conj.* kwa, katika, -ni, hata, mpaka, hadi; (*of purpose*) ili, kusudi, (*or subjunctive*); (*in verbs*) -ia, -ea; (*infin.*) ku-. *A place to run to, to fly to*, mahali pa kukimbilia, kimbilio. *To love*, kupenda. *To a man*, -ote pia, kila mtu. *To and fro*, huko na huko, kwenda na kurudi. *A man to carry*, mtu wa kuchukua. *He went to buy*, alikwenda anunue (kununua, ili anunue).

toad, *n.* chura. **toadstool**, *n.* uyoga, kiyoga. **toady**, *n.* mjipendekeza, msifusifu mno, ajinyenyekeaye mno. — *v.t.* jipendekeza kwa, rairai, sifusifu mno; jinyenyekea mno.

toast, *v.t.* choma (moto); (*on a spit*) banika; (*drink health of*) ombea salama (takia heri, afya &c.) karamuni pamoja na kunywa divai. *Toast a person*, -nywa divai na kumtakia heri &c. — *n.* mkate uliochomwa (nje); (*of honour*) mtu, kitu au jambo linalotajwa, kisha watu hunywa divai kama kwamba kuliheshimu au kulitakia heri. salamu ya karamuni.

tobacco, *n.* tumbako. **tobacconist**, *n.* mwuza tumbako. **tobacco-pipe**, *n.* kiko, mtemba; (*hookah*) buruma.

tobacco-pouch, *n.* mkoba (mfuko) wa kutilia tumbako.

toboggan, *n.* gari lisilo na magurudumu la kutelemkia milima yenye theluji.

tocsin, *n.* kamsa, kengele ya kuonya hatari.

to-day, *n. and adv.* leo, leo hivi, siku hii; (*the present time*) siku hizi.

toddle, *v.i.* batabata (kama mtoto ndiyo kwanza aweze kwenda).

toddy, *n.* mvinyo pamoja na maji ya moto, sukari, maji ya limau *&c.*

to-do, *n.* ghasia, zahama, fujo, msukosuko, matata.

toe, *n.* kidole cha mguu. *Toe the line*, fanya ilivyoamriwa (iliyo desturi). **toed**, *a.* -enye *toes*. **toe-nail**, *n.* ukucha wa kidole cha mguu.

toff, *n.* (*slang*) mmalidadi, mlimbwende, mmbuji, mbeja, damisi; (*slang*) mfua uji.

toffee, toffy, *n.* sukari iliyochanganywa na siagi na kuchemshwa.

together, *adv.* pamoja, -ote, jamii, jumla; (*with verbs, often*) -ana. *Fight together*, pigana. *Meet together*, kutana. *Talk together*, semezana.

toil, (1) *n.* wavu, mtego. *In the toils*, naswa, tegwa.

toil, (2) *n.* kazi, kazi ya taabu, kazi ngumu. — *v.i.* jitahidi, fanya kazi kwa bidii; (*go painfully &c.*) enda kwa taabu, jikokota. **toiler**, *n.* mfanya kazi ngumu, mfanya bidii. **toilsome**, *a.* -a kazi, -a taabu.

toilet, *n.* kunawa na kuvaa nguo *&c.*, kivao, kujikwatua.

toilsome, *a.* taz. *toil* (2).

token, *n.* (*sign*) dalili, ishara, alama; (*pledge*) amana; (*of love*) huba.

told, *p.t. and pf.t.* ya *tell*.

tolerate, *v.t.* vumilia, stahimili, chukuana na. **tolerable**, *a.* -a kuvumilika, -a kustahimilika, -a kuchukulika; (*in moderate degree*) -a kadiri, -a wastani. **tolerably**, *adv.* kadiri, si sana. **tolerance**, *n.* kuchukuliana, kuvumiliana, kuachiliana, uvumilivu, ustahimilivu. **tolerant**, *a.* -a kuvumilia, -a kuchukuana, -vumilivu, -stahimilivu. **toleration**, *n.* kuchukuliana *&c.* taz. *tolerance*; (*in religion*) kuchukuana watu wa dini mbalimbali.

toll, (1) *v.t.* (mtu) piga au gonga (kengele) moja moja (polepole); (kengele) lia (piga, gonga) moja moja (polepole). — *n.* mlio wa kengele inyopigwa moja moja polepole.

toll, (2) *n.* ushuru, kodi, ada (hasa ya kupita barabara au kuvuka daraja). **toll-bar, toll-gate**, *n.* mlango pa kulipa kodi, ada *&c.*

Tom, *n.* ufupisho wa *Thomas*. *Tom, Dick and Harry*, watu wote, watu wa namna zote, mtu ye yote. **tomboy**, *n.* mtoto wa kike mwenye mwendo (tabia) wa mtoto wa kiume. **tom-cat**, *n.* paka dume. **tomfool**, *n.* mpumbavu. **tomfoolery**, *n.* upumbavu. **tommy**, *n.* ufupisho wa *Tommy Atkins*, = askari wa kiingereza. *Tommy rot*, upuzi kabisa.

tomahawk, *n.* shoka la vita (kama la wenyeji wa Amerika ya kaskazini).

tomato, *n.* (*plant*) mnyanya, mtunguja; (*fruit*) nyanya, tunguja.

tomb, *n.* kaburi, ziara. **tombstone**, *n.* jiwe la kaburi, jiwe la ukumbusho wa marehemu.

tomboy, *n.* taz. *tom*.

tombstone, *n.* taz. *tomb*.

tom-cat, *n.* taz. *tom*.

tome, *n.* chuo, kitabu, hasa kikubwa; gombo la kitabu.

tomfool, *n.*, **tomfoolery**, *n.*, **tommy**, *n.* taz. *tom*.

to-morrow, *n. and adv.* kesho. *Day after to-morrow*, kesho kutwa. (*Third day after*, mtondo. *Fourth day after*, mtondogoo.)

ton, *n.* frasila 64, ratli 2,240. *Tons of*, wingi wa. **tonnage**, *n.* ukubwa wa tumbo la (ngama ya) meli (jahazi, chombo), kadiri ya shehena; (*total shipping*) jamii zote za meli, merikebu *&c.* za nchi fulani.

tone, *n.* (*sound*) sauti, namna ya (tabia ya) sauti; (*manner, style*) namna, jinsi, tabia, hali. — *v.t.* geuza (rangi, sauti *&c.*). *Tone down*, zimua, punguza, tuliza; — *v.i.* (*become quiet, less intense*), pungua, tulia. *Tone up*, zidisha (rangi &c.). **toneless**, *a.* kimya; (*spiritless*) baridi. **tonic**, *a.* (*musical*) -a sauti, -a kuimba. — *n.* dawa ya kutia afya na nguvu, mkuyati. **tonic sol-fa**, *n.* namna ya kuandika wimbo &c. kwa herufi, do, re mi &c.

tongs, *n.* koleo.

tongue, *n.* ulimi; (*speech*) usemi, kunena; (*language*) lugha, maneno, ki-, *e.g. the Swahili tongue*, Kiswahili; (*of land*) rasi; (*general*) kitu kitokezacho kama ulimi. *Hold the tongue*, nyamaza. *Give tongue*, lia. **tongue-tied**, *a.* bubu, -nyamavu.

tonic, *a. and n.*, **tonic sol-fa**, *n.* taz. *tone.*

to-night, *n. and adv.* usiku huu, usiku ujao.

tonnage, *n.* taz. *ton.*

tonsil, *n.* kitu cha kooni, kama kinundu. **tonsillitis**, *n.* tezi la kooni.

tonsure, *n.* kipara cha utosini. **tonsorial**, *a.* -a kinyozi.

too, *adv.* mno kabisa, kupita kiasi, kupita ipaswavyo, kadiri isiyofaa; (*in addition*) na, tena, juu, zaidi. *Be too much for*, kulia, lemea, shinda, zidi.

took, *p.t.* ya *take.*

tool, *n.* chombo, samani, ala, kipande, zana; (*slave*) mtumwa, kitumwa.

tooth, *n.* (*pl.* **teeth**) jino; (*incisor*) jino la mbele; (*molar*) gego, chego; (*eye tooth*) chonge. *Show the teeth*, toa meno. *Got to have a tooth out*, enda kung'oa jino. *Having lost a front tooth*, -enye pengo. *Tooth and nail*, kwa juhudi sana, kwa nguvu zote. *A sweet tooth*, kupenda vitamu. *In the teeth of*, pasipo hofu ya, bila kuogopa, pasipo kuangalia, kwa kudharau. **toothache**, *n.* kuuma jino. **tooth-brush**, *n.* (*stick*) mswaki. **toothed**, *a.* -enye meno. **toothless**, *a.* -siye na meno; (*person*) kibogoyo. **tooth-paste**, *n.* dawa ya kusugulia meno. **toothsome**, *a.* -tamu, -zuri, -a kuchapukia, -a kukolea.

top, (1) *n.* (*child's toy*) pia.

top, (2) *n.* (*highest part*) upande wa juu, palipo juu, juu; (*summit*) kilele, kileleta, ncha ya juu; (*highest degree*) kipeo, upeo, kikomo cha juu; (*chief person*) mtu wa kwanza, mkuu, mtangulizi; (*cover*) kifuniko, kipande cha juu. *Top of the head*, utosi. *On the top* (*of*), juu (ya). *At the top of his voice*, kwa kupaaza sauti sana. *Top-boots*, viatu virefu. — *a.* -a juu, -a kipeo, -nayozidi. — *v.t.* (*cover*) funika juu; (*surmount*) fika juu; (*surpass*) pita; (*rise above*) inuka juu, nyanyuka; (*cut off top*) kata juu. **topcoat**, *n.* koti kubwa la kuvaa nje (kama joho). **top-dressing**, *n.* mbolea (samadi) ya kutawanyia juu ya ardhi. **top-heavy**, *a.* -zito kwa juu (kuliko chini). **top-hole**, *a.* (*slang*) -zuri kabisa, bora sana. **topknot**, *n.* kishungi. **topmost**, *a.* -a juu kabisa. **topping**, *a.* -zuri sana, -a kupendeza sana.

topaz, *n.* kito cha thamani kama yakuti ya manjano.

topcoat, *n.*, **top-dressing**, *n.* taz. *top* (2).

toper, *n.* mlevi.

top-heavy, *a.*, **top-hole**, *a.* taz. *top* (2).

topic, *n.* jambo la kuzungumziwa (la kufikiriwa, la kuandikiwa habari au la kubishaniwa maneno), kiini cha habari. **topical**, *a.* -a jambo linalofikiriwa na watu (linaloshughulisha fikira za watu, linalozungumzwa na watu).

topknot, *n.*, **topmost**, *a.* taz. *top* (2).

topography, *n.* maarifa ya hali (tabia, milima &c.) ya mahali, habari na tabia za mahali. **topographer**, *n.* mtungaji (mjuzi) wa *topography.* **topographical**, *a.* -a kueleza (kuonyesha) tabia na habari za mahali.

topping, *a.* taz. *top* (2).

topple, *v.i.* tikisika, tetereka, taka kuanguka. *Topple over*, pinduka, anguka.

topsy-turvy, *adv.* and *a.* kichwa

chini, kwa kupinduka, -a fujo, -liofujika, -liochafuka, -liovurugika.

toque, *n.* kofia ndogo (hasa ya kike).

tor, *n.* mlima uliochongoka wenye majabali.

torch, *n.* mwenge; (*electric*) kurunzi. **torchlight**, *n.* mwanga wa mienge.

tore, *p.t.* ya *tear.*

toreador, *n.* mpanda farasi apiganaye na ng'ombe (katika michezo).

torment, *n.* (*pain*) maumivu mabaya, adhabu, mateso, uchungu; (*trouble*) udhia, sumbuo, hangaiko, wasiwasi. — *v.t.* tesa, tia maumivu makali, tia uchungu mwingi, umiza vibaya, adhibu, adhibisha; (*worry &c.*) sumbua, udhi, hangaisha, ifya, tia wasiwasi, chagiza; (*tease*) chokoza, sumbua, udhi, tashtiti, sunza, kefyakefya, kera, nyanyasa, nyeta, kejeli. **tormenting**, *a.* -a kutia *torment.* **tormentor**, *n.* mtesi, mwadhibisha, mwudhi, msumbuaji, atiaye *torment.*

torn, *p.t.* ya *tear.*

tornado, *n.* tufani kuu, kimbunga.

torpedo, *n.* risasi kubwa (kombora kubwa) inayopigwa na manowari kwenda chini ya maji. — *v.t.* piga kwa *torpedo.* **torpedo-boat**, *n.* manowari ndogo iendayo upesi sana, ya kupigia *torpedo.*

torpid, *a.* -zito, -legevu, -vivu, kama -enye usingizi, -tepetevu, kama -fu, -a lepe; (*of the mind*) -zito, baridi. **torpidity, torpor**, *n.* uzito, lepe, ufu, usingizi, ubaridi, ulegevu, utepetevu.

torque, *n.* mkufu (wa kuvaa shingoni).

torrent, *n.* mvo, maji ya ghafula, maji mengi yakipita kwa kasi; (*quantity*) wingi; (*sudden rush*) bubujiko, mfoko. **torrential**, *a.* -a wingi sana, -a nguvu nyingi.

torrid, *a.* -a hari sana, -a joto jingi, -liokauka kwa joto la jua. *Torrid zone*, sehemu ya dunia papitapo jua kichwani hasa.

torsion, *n.* msokoto; nguvu ya mtambo au kitu kilichosokotwa ya kujinyosha tena.

torso, *n.* kiwiliwili (yaani mwili bila kichwa na miguu na mikono).

tort, *n.* daawa.

tortoise, *n.* kobe; (*marine*) ng'amba, kasa. **tortoise-shell**, *n.* ng'amba.

tortuous, *a.* -a vizingo vingi, -a kubetabeṭa, -a kupindapinda, -a mapindi, -a kuzunguka, -enye vipengee; (*of character &c.*) -enye hila, -erevu, -enye vipengee, -laghai.

torture, *n.* mateso, adhabu kali, maumivu makali, uchungu mwingi. — *v.t.* tesa, adhibu, adhibisha, umiza vibaya, tia maumivu makali, tia uchungu mwingi; (*mental*) sumbua, udhi, hangaisha, tia shaka (wasiwasi).

tory, *n.* jamii ya watu wa serikali ya Uingereza wanaotaka kudumisha mambo yalivyo au kuyabadili kwa taratibu sana.

toss, *v.t.* rusha juu, tupa, sukasuka, chafua; (*of the head*) deua, geua, inua ghafula (kwa kiburi, kwa dharau *&c.*); — *v.i.* (*of a ship*) fanya mrama, sukasuka; (*of the sea*) chafuka. *Toss about* (*as a sick man*), gaagaa, furukuta, taataa. *Toss up*, bahatisha. — *n.* kurusha, mrusho. **tossing**, *n.* kurusha, mrusho, msukosuko, kugaagaa *&c.*

tot, (1) *n.* mtoto mdogo; (*of liquor*) kidogo.

tot, (2) *v.t.* (*up*) jumlisha. — *n.* jumla.

total, *n.* jumla, jamii. — *a.* -ote pia, jumla, jamii. — *v.t.* jumlisha. **totality**, *n.* (*sum*) jumla; (*completeness*) kuwa kamili, utimilivu. **totalizator**, *n.* mashine inayotumika katika kubahatisha fedha katika mashindano ya farasi. **totally**, *adv.* kabisa, pia.

totem, *n.* kitu (mnyama, ndege, mti *&c.*) kinachoheshimiwa na ukoo *&c.*, tambiko. **totemism**, *n.* imani ya *totem*, utambikaji.

totter, *v.i.* tikisika, titia, tetereka, tetemeka, pepa, pepesuka, sesetuka, levyalevya; (*like an old man*) kongoja, jikokota. **tottering**, *a.* -a kutikisika *&c.*

touch, *v.t.* gusa; (*lightly*) papasa, (*reach*) fikia; (*concern*) pasa, husu; (*affect*) pendeza, sikitikisha, huzunisha, tia huruma (majuto, uradhi &c.), vuta; (*test*) jaribia, onja; (*eat*) -la (*equal, rival in merit*) faa, shinda. *Touch on,* nena katika kupita, eleza kidogo. *Touch up,* (*improve*) tengeneza; (*rouse*) amsha, chochea. *Touch at,* wasilia, tia nanga penye, tua kwa. — *n.* kugusa &c. mguso; (*small amount*) kidogo; (*mode of handling*) mkono. *A touch of fever,* homa kidogo. *Sense of touch,* kuona kwa kugusa. *Touch and go,* hatari kubwa, shida sana. *Be in touch with,* jua sana mambo ya. **touching,** *a.* -a kutia huruma, -a kuhuzunisha. — *prep.* juu ya, kwa habari ya. **touch-stone,** *n.* kitu cha kujaribia (cha kuhakikishia, cha kuthibitishia). **touchwood,** *n.* kidondo, mti mkavu wa kuwashia moto. **touchy,** *a.* -epesi kuona hasira (chuki, uchungu), -a harara, -a chukichuki.

tough, *a.* -gumu, -siotatuka, -lioshikamana, thabiti, -shupavu; (*of humans* &c.) -enye nguvu nyingi, -shupavu; (*of task* &c.) -gumu, -a taabu. **toughen,** *v.t. and i.* fanya (fanyika) *tough.* **toughness,** *n.* kuwa *tough,* ugumu, uthabiti, ushupavu, nguvu.

toupee, *n.* kishungi.

tour, *n.* utalii, safari ya kutalii (kutazama, kuaua) nchi, safari ya kuzunguka na kutazama nchi. —*v.i.* talii, safiri (zunguka) kutazama nchi, aua nchi. **tourist,** *n.* msafiri wa kutalii (kuzunguka na kutazama) nchi.

tournament, *n.* jamii ya michezo ya kushindana; mchezo wa vita.

tourniquet, *n.* kikazo, kisongo (cha kuzuilia damu).

tousle, *v.t.* chafua, fuja. *Tousled hair,* matimutimu ya nywele.

tout, *v.i.* sapa, sapasapa. — *n.* msapaji, mwangazi, mtembezi.

tout ensemble, *n.* jinsi inavyoonekana jumla (yote pamoja).

tow, (1) *n.* kitani; (*coco-nut fibre*) usumba.

tow, (2) *v.t.* (chombo) vuta kwa kamba, fungasha, fungasa. *Take in tow,* fungasha, fungasa. **towage,** *n.* kuvuta kwa kamba; (*fee*) ada (malipo) ya kuvuta (chombo &c.) kwa kamba. **tow-line, tow-rope,** *n.* kamba ya kufungashia (chombo), fungashia, dakawa.

toward, towards, *prep.* kwa, kwenda kwa (upande wa); (*in respect of*) juu ya; (*near*) karibu ya. — *a.* (*docile* &c.) -sikivu, -epesi, -elekevu; (*fortunate*) -a kufaa, -a bahati.

towel, *n.* kitambaa (cha kufutia uso, mikono &c.).

tower, *n.* mnara; (*fortified*) ngome, boma, husuni. *A tower of strength,* tegemeo kuu, mtu awezaye kutumainiwa kwa msaada. — *v.i.* enda juu sana, simama. *Tower above,* zidi kwa urefu (kwa kimo, kwa akili). **towering,** *a.* -a kwenda juu sana, -refu sana. *A towering rage,* hasira kali, kiruu.

tow-line, *n.* taz. *tow* (2).

town, *n.* mji. *Go up to town,* enda mji wa *London.* — *a.* -a mji. **town clerk,** *n.* mwandishi (karani) wa baraza ya mji. **town council,** *n.* baraza ya mji. **town councillor,** *n.* mtu wa baraza ya mji. **town crier,** *n.* mpiga mbiu wa mji. **town hall,** *n.* jumba la *town council.* **townsfolk,** *n.* watu wa mji, wakaa mjini, wenyeji. **township,** *n.* mji na pambizo zake. **townsman,** *n.* mtu wa mji, mkaa mjini. *My fellow townsman,* mwenzi wangu, wa mji mmoja nami.

tow-rope, *n.* taz. *tow* (2).

toxic, *a.* -a sumu. **toxicology,** *n.* maarifa ya sumu. **toxin,** *n.* sumu.

toy, *n.* kitu cha kuchezea watoto, kipuzi, kitu hafifu, takataka. — *v.i.* chezacheza.

trace, (1) *n.* (*of harness*) ukanda (ugwe) mnene wa kuvutia gari. *Kick over the traces,* asi, halifu.

trace, (2) *n.* dalili, alama; (*track*)

nyayo; (*of thing crawling*) utambazi; (*of thing dragged*) mkokoto, maburuzo, mbuuzo. — *v.t.* fuatia kwa kuangalia nyayo (alama), tafuta; (*copy*) fuatisha kwa kuandika katika karatasi nyembamba iliyowekwa juu ya picha *&c.*; (*draw*) andika, andika picha ya. **traceable**, *a.* -a kuonekana, -a kutafutikana. **tracery**, *n.* pambo la mistari mistari. (ya milia milia); (*of window*) pambo la mawe dirishani. **tracing**, *n.* kufuatisha, kufuata, kunakili; nakili, nakala, mfano.

trachea, *n.* koo, umio wa pumzi.

tracing, *n.* taz. *trace* (2).

track, *n.* njia, mwendo; (*through grass or water*) mkondo; (*footsteps*) nyayo, utambaazi; (*of dragging*), mkokoto, maburuzo, mburuzo. *The beaten track*, jinsi (namna, njia) ya kawaida. —*v.t.* fuatia kwa nyayo (alama za). **trackless**, pasipo njia, -sioendeka.

tract, *n.* (*booklet*) kitabu (*chuo*) kidogo (hasa chenye habari za dini au serikali); (*of country*) eneo, nchi, jimbo; (*of time*) muda, muhula. **tractability**, *n.* utii, usikivu, usikizi, welekevu, utulivu. **tractable**, *a.* -a kutii, -tiifu, -sikivu, -elekevu, -tulivu. **traction**, *n.* kukokota, namna ya nguvu ya kuendesha (*e.g.* ya motakaa, ya gari la moshi *&c.*). **traction-engine**, *n.* gari la moshi la kukokota magari makubwa barabarani. **tractor**, *n.* taz. *traction-engine*; motakaa ya kukokota magari.

trade, *n.* biashara; (*employment*) kazi, uchumi, shughuli; (*men of the same trade*) watu wenye namna ile ile ya kazi. — *v.i.* fanya biashara, tafuta faida. **trade-mark**, *n.* chapa (ya bidhaa). **trader**, *n.* mfanyi biashara, mchuuzi, mbazazi. **tradesman**, *n.* = *trader*. **tradespeople**, *n.* watu na biashara (na watu wa nyumba zao). **trade union**, *n.* chama cha watu wenye kazi ile ile. **trade-wind**, *n.* upepo unaovuma sawasawa daima (mmoja kutoka mashariki ya kaskazini ya ikweta, mwingine kutoka mashariki ya kusini ya ikweta). **trading**, *n.* biashara. — *a.* -a biashara.

tradition, *n.* mapokeo, mazoeo, mafundisho yaliyotokea zamani; (*handing on*) kupokezanya. **traditional**, *a.* -a *tradition*.

traduce, *v.t.* singizia, tusha, nenea, umbua.

traffic, *n.* biashara, ubazazi, uchuuzi, kupeleka bidhaa huko na huko, kubadilishana mali; (*of vehicles &c.*) kupitapita magari (motakaa, watu) barabarani na njiani, au meli na merikebu baharini. — *v.i.* fanya biashara, chuuza, badilishana mali.

tragedy, *n.* mchezo wa *theatre* wa kuhuzunisha (unaoigiza msiba, hatari, huzuni *&c.*); (*disaster*) msiba, sikitiko, jambo liletalo huzuni. **tragedian**, *n.* mcheza (mwandikaji) wa *tragedy*. **tragic**, **tragical**, *a.* -a msiba, -a huzuni, -a mauti, -a majonzi.

trail, *n.* nyayo, utambaazi, mkokoto, maburuzo, mburuzo; (*through grass*) mkondo; (*sign*) alama, dalili; (*path*) njia. — *v.t.* kokota, buruta, burura, tambaza; — *v.i.* kokoteka, tambaa. **trailer**, *n.* (*of plant*) mkono; (*vehicle*) gari la kufungashia nyuma ya gari jingine.

train, *v.t.* fundisha, lea, ongoza, zoeza; (*animals*) fuga; (*plants*) otesha, tengeneza; (*direct upon*) elekeza; — *v.i.* (*practise &c.*) jifunza, jizoeza. — *n.* (*attendants*) wafuasi, waandami; (*procession, file &c.*) mafuatano, maandamano, mfulizo, msago, mtawalio; (*of dress*) sehemu ya vazi inayotambaa (inayokokotezwa); (*of railway*) jamii ya behewa (majani) ikikokotwa na gari la moshi; (*process*) mwendo, kazi, njia. **trainer**, *n.* mkufunzi, mzoezi; (*of animals*) mfugaji. **training**, *n.* (*of mind*) malezi, mafundisho; (*study*) mtaala, kusoma; (*of body*) kuzoea (kuzoeza) kazi ngumu au mchezo wa bidii; (*of animals*) mfugo, ufugaji. **training-college,** *n.* chuo kinamofundishwa ualimu.

train-oil, *n.* mafuta ya nyangumi.

trait, *n.* tofauti, dalili, onyo; (*character*) tabia.

traitor, *n.* msaliti, haini, mpenyezi, mdanganyi. **traitorous,** *a.* -a kusaliti, haini, -danganyifu. **traitress,** *n.* *traitor* wa kike.

trajectory, *n.* njia ya kitu kitupwacho kipitavyo hewani, njia ya mviringo.

tram, tram-car, *n.* gari linalopita njiani juu ya vyuma (reli), hasa la kuchukulia abiria. **tramway,** *n.* reli (njia ya vyuma) ya kupitia gari.

trammel, *n.* kizuio, kizuizi, mgogoro, kifungo. — *v.t.* zuia, tatiza, tatanisha.

tramp, *v.i.* safiri (kwa miguu), enda kwa miguu, tembeatembea, zungukazunguka, susurika, zurura, zururika; (*walk heavily*) enda kwa kishindo. — *n.* mshindo (wa kukanyagisha miguu); (*journey*) safari; (*beggar*) mtu asiye na makao, atembeaye huko na huko akiomba riziki.

trample, *v.t.* (*down*) kanyaga, vyoga, gandamiza (ponda, shindisha, vunja, haribu) kwa miguu; (*despise*) dharau, beza; (*oppress*) onea, dhulumu.

tramway, *n.* taz. *tram.*

trance, *n.* hali kama ya usingizi mzito sana; hali kama ya usingizi mzito pamoja na kuona njozi (ruya, ndoto).

tranquil, *a.* -tulivu, -a raha, -starehefu; (*sea*) shwari. **tranquillity,** *n.* utulivu, raha, ustarehe, mustarehe. **tranquillize,** *v.t.* tuliza, starehesha, ridhisha, poza; — *v.i.* tulia, starehe.

transact, *v.t.* tenda (shuguli), fanya, maliza. **transaction,** *n.* jambo (la kufanyika), shughuli, tendo. *Transactions,* matendo; (*record*) taarifa, habari.

transatlantic, *a.* -a ng'ambo ya pili ya *Atlantic Ocean,* -a kupita katika *Atlantic Ocean.*

transcend, *v.t.* (*over-step*) ruka mpaka; (*surpass*) pitilia mbali, shinda, -wa bora kuliko. **transcendent,** *a.* bora sana, aali. **transcendental,** *a.* -a kupita akili, -a fumbo. **transcendentalism,** *n.* kujua kwa akili tu pasipo kuona wala kujaribia, fikira ngumu, fumbo la mawazo.

transcribe, *v.t* fuatisha, nakili. **transcript,** *n.* nakili, nakala, mfano. **transcription,** *n.* kufuatisha, kunakili; (*a copy*) nakili, nakala, mfano.

transept, *n.* upande wa kanisa utokezapo kuume na kushoto, pande la kanisa.

transfer, *v.t.* pisha, hamisha, jongeza pengine, geuza, toa; (*money, shares &c.*) hamili; (*property*) sihia. — *n.* kupisha, kutoa *&c.*; mtu au kitu kilichohamishwa *&c.*; (*document*) hawala, hati ya kubadilisha jina (mwenyewe), hati ya kusihia mali; (*picture, design &c.*) picha (urembo) iliyopigwa chapa katika karatasi nyembamba ambayo ikitiwa maji na kugandamizwa katika karatasi nyingine au kitambaa *&c.* picha hiyo inapigwa chapa humo. **transferable,** *a.* -a kubadilishwa. **transference,** *n.* kupisha, kupita, kusihia *&c.*

transfigure, *v.t.* geuza, badili, badilisha (hasa kuwa -zuri zaidi). **transfiguration,** *n.* kugeuza, kugeuka, ugeuzi, ugeuko.

transfix, *v.t.* choma (kwa mkuki, mshale *&c.*); (*with terror &c.*) shangaza, pumbaza, duwaza, fadhaisha, shtusha, tia bumbuazi (kwa hofu *&c.*).

transform, *v.t.* geuza, badili. **transformation,** *n.* ugeuzi, kugeuka, kubadili, kubadilika, badiliko. **transformer,** *n.* kitu (mtu) kinachogeuza au kubadili, hasa kitu kinachobadili namna va nguvu ya umeme.

transfuse, *v.t.* mimina, pisha, penyeza, nywesha; (*of blood*) toa (damu) katika, mishipa ya mtu na kutia katika mishipa ya mtu mwingine. **transfusion,** *n.* kumimina, kumimi.

nika *&c.*; (*of blood*) kutoa damu katika mishipa ya mtu na kuitia katika mishipa ya mtu mwingine.

transgress, *v.t.* kosa, kosea, halifu, asi, vunja; (*overstep*) ruka mpaka. **transgression,** *n.* kosa, dhambi, uhalifu, uasi. **transgressor,** *n.* mkosaji, mhalifu, mwasi, mvunja sheria (sharti, desturi).

transient, *a.* -a kupita, -siodumu, -sioishi, -a mara moja tu, -a muda mfupi tu. **transit,** *n.* kupita, kupisha, kupeleka, kuchukua. *Goods in transit,* bidhaa (mizigo *&c.*) iliyo katika kuchukuliwa toka mahali mpaka pengine; (*of stars &c.*) kupitana nyota. **transition,** *n.* kupita, kugeuka. *Transition period,* wakati ulio baina hali mbili maalum, wakati hali au mambo yanapobadilika. **transitional,** *a.* -a katika kupita (kubadilika, kupelekwa *&c.*). **transitive,** *a.* (*in gram.*) *verb* isiyotumika ila pamoja na *object.* **transitory,** *a.* -a kupita, -a kitambo, -a muda mfupi tu, -siodumu.

translate, *v.t.* fasiri, tafsiri, geuza lugha nyingine; (*transfer*) weka, pengine, hamisha. **translation,** *n.* kufasiri, fasiri, tafsiri *&c.* **translator,** *n.* mfasiri.

transliterate, *v.t.* andika kwa herufi nyingine (zisizo za lugha yenyewe). **transliteration,** *n.* kuandika kwa (mwandiko wa, maandiko ya) herufi nyingine (zisizo za lugha yenyewe).

translucent, *a.* -a kupenya (kupenyeka) nuru, -a kupenyezeka kwa nuru, -angavu, -a kuonya.

transmigrate, *v.i.* hama, hajiri, gura; (*of the soul*) (roho) ingia katika mwili mwingine baada ya kufa. **transmigration,** *n.* kuhama, mhamo, kugeuka hali nyingine. *Transmigration of souls,* roho ya mtu kuingia katika mwili mwingine mtu afapo. **transmigratory,** *a.* -a kuhama.

transmit, *v.t.* pisha, peleka. **transmission,** *n.* kupisha, mpisho.

transmute, *v.t.* geuza. **transmutable,** *a.* -a kugeuka, -a kubadilika. **transmutation,** *n.* ugeuzi, badiliko.

transom, *n.* kizingiti cha juu.

transparent, *a.* -a kuonya, -a kupenya (kupenyeka) nuru, -angavu; (*clear, obvious*) -a kuelea wazi, bayana, dhahiri. **transparency,** *n.* hali ya kuwa *transparent,* uangavu.

transpire, *v.i.* julikana, tangaa, bainika.

transplant, *v.t.* atika, pandikia, pandikiza, panda pengine; (*remove*) hamisha. **transplantation,** *n.* kuatika, mwatiko *&c.*

transport, *v.t.* chukua, pagaza, safirisha, peleka; (*of criminals &c.*) hamisha nchi nyingine; (*excite violently*) choma (shinda) moyo, fadhaisha, poteza akili. — *n.* uchukuzi, uhamali; (*by porter*) upagazi; (*excess of joy &c.*) furaha kubwa, kipindi (cha furaha, hofu, ajabu *&c.*); (*transfer*) kusafirisha (mali au watu); (*ship*) meli ya kuchukulia askari na vitu vyao. **transportation,** *n.* kuchukua, kuchukulika *&c.*, uchukuzi, uhamali, upagazi, uhamisho.

transpose, *v.t.* badilisha mahali (herufi *&c.*); (*in music*) badili sauti (*e.g.* kuipandisha au kuitelemsha). **transposition,** *n.* kubadilisha, kubadilika.

trans-ship, *v.t.* badili meli (merikebu), badilisha shehena.

transubstantiation, *n.* kugeuka asili ya mwili na damu ya Yesu Kristo, katika Ushirika Mtakatifu (*Holy Communion*).

transverse, *a.* -a kukingana, -a kukingamana.

trap, *n.* mtego, shabaki; (*spring*) mtambo; (*trick, device*) hila, shabaki, ushabiki; (*bend in pipe*) kombo (pindi, kuruba) la bomba la kuwekea maji kidogo ili kuzuia harufu isirudi; (*carriage*) gari lenye magurudumu mawili la kukokotwa na farasi. —*v.t.* tega, nasa; (*deceive*) danganya, laghai, ghilibu. **trap-door,** *n.* mlango wa sakafuni au darini wa kuinuliwa juu si wa kwenda upande.

trapeze, *n*. pembea.

trappings, *n*. matandiko (ya farasi *&c.*), mapambo ya farasi, mavalio.

trash, *n*. takataka, upuzi, vitu hafifu visivyo na thamani. **trashy**, *a*. -a ovyo, hafifu, -sio na thamani, -siofaa kitu.

travail, *n*. uchungu (utungu) wa kuzaa. — *v.i.* shikwa na (ona) uchungu wa kuzaa; (*toil painfully*) taabika.

travel, *v.i.* safiri, pita, enda, abiri. — *n*. safari mwendo. **traveller**, *n*. msafiri, abiria.

traverse, *v.t.* (*cross*) kingama; (*travel over*) pitia; (*oppose*) kaidi, kanusha, kinza. — *n*. kitu kinachokingama.

travesty, *v.t.* iga kwa dhihaka, iga kwa jinsi ya kuleta dharau. — *n*. mwigo, dhihaka, kiigo.

trawl, *v.t.* vua samaki kwa kukokota wavu chini chini. **trawler**, *n*. chombo cha kuvulia samaki kwa *trawl*.

tray, *n*. sinia, kombe, sahani, chano, hero.

treachery, *n*. udanganyifu, hila usaliti. **treacherous**, *a*. -danganyifu, -janja, -a haini, -a hila.

treacle, *n*. asali ya miwa.

tread, *v.t.* (*p.t.* **trod**, *pf.t.* **trodden**) kanyaga, vyoga, gandamiza (shindilia, angusha) kwa kukanyaga, enda, liwata. — *n*. kukanyaga, mshindo wa mguu; (*of wheel, tyre*) sehemu ya gurudumu (mpira) inayogusa chini. **treadle, treadmill**, *n*. shinikizo la kukanyaga; (*of loom &c.*) mdoshi.

treason, *n*. uhalifu, maasi, fitina (hasa juu ya mfalme au serikali). *High treason*, kujaribu kumdhuru mfalme (au malkia, au mwana atakayemrithi). **treasonable**, *a*. -halifu, -asi, -a fitina.

treasure, *n*. hazina, tunu, azizi, mali; (*beloved*) mpenzi, kipenzi; (*useful servant*) mtumishi mwaminifu mweza kazi zote. — *v.t.* tunuka, thamini; (*hoard up*) weka (fedha, vito *&c.*). **treasurer**, *n*. mtunza hazina, karani wa kulinda (wa kutunza hesabu ya) fedha, bwana fedha. **treasure-trove**, *n*. mali (vitu vya fedha na dhahabu na sarafu) iliyovumbulika chini, dafina.

treasury, *n*. nyumba ya hazina, afisi ya bwana fedha ya serikali, (*Arabic*) beit al mal; (*public funds*) mali ya serikali.

treat, *v.t.* tendea; (*explain*) eleza; (*entertain*) karibisha, lisha, lipia gharama; (*attend as doctor*) tia dawa, uguza, tibu, ganga. *Treat with*, fanya shauri na. *Be (medically) treated*, alikwa, gangwa, tibiwa. — *n*. (*feast*) karamu, tafrija; (*pleasure*) jambo la furaha, mapendezi. **treatment**, *n*. jinsi ya kutenda, jinsi ya kutendewa; (*medical*) dawa, uganga, udaktari, utabibu. *Be under treatment*, alikwa. **treaty**, *n*. mapatano, mkataba, maafikano, mwafikano.

treatise, *n*. kitabu kidogo, maandiko, makala.

treatment, *n*., **treaty**, *n*. taz. *treat*.

treble, *n*. sauti nyembamba ya kuimba ya watoto au wanawake. — *a*. -a mara tatu. — *v.t.* zidisha kwa tatu; — *v.i.* zidi mara tatu.

tree, *n*. mti. *Family tree*, nasaba. *Up a tree (in doubt)*, katika mashaka. — *a*. -a miti, -a kupanda (-a kukaa) juu ya mti.

trek, *v.i.* safiri katika gari linalokokotwa na ng'ombe, hama.

trellis, *n*. papi au fito zilizokingamana, kama wavu, kama kimia. *Trellis-work screen (indoor)* kiambaza cha papi (fito); (*outdoor*) ua wa papi (fito).

tremble, *v.i.* tetema, tetemeka, tikisika, titia, tukutika, vinyavinya, gwaya; (*be anxious or perturbed*) ona wasiwasi, hangaika, ona mashaka. — *n*. mtetemo, tetemeko, mtikisiko. **trembling**, *n*. kutetema, kutetemeka *&c.*; hali ya kuona hofu nyingi (mashaka mengi), mang'ang'amu, mang'amung'amu. **tremor**, *n*. tetemo, tetemeko, utukuto, tukutiko. **tremulous,** *a.* -a kutetema, -a kuvinyavinya *&c.*; (*timid*) -oga, -enye hofu, -a kusitasita.

tremendous, *a.* -a hofu, -a kutisha, -kubwa mno, -ingi ajabu.

tremor, *n.*, **tremulous,** *a.* taz. *tremble.*

trench, *n.* handaki, ufuo, mfereji; (*for foundation*) msingi. — *v.t.* chimba handaki (mfereji, ufuo); — *v.i.* (*on, upon*) jitwalia sehemu, katia, punguza, iba mpaka wa.

trenchant, *a.* -kali; (*incisive &c.*) -a kukata maneno, -a tama, mkataa, -erevu -a kutia uchungu. **trencher,** *n.* (*for mortar*) chano; (*large plate*) kombe, sahani. *A good trencher-man,* mlaji sana. **trench mortar,** *n.* kombora ya kutumia katika handaki.

trend, *v.i.* pinda, beta, elekea. — *n.* maelekeo, mwendo.

trepan, trephine, *v.t.* kata na kuondoa (sehemu ya fuvu la kichwa katika utabibu).

trepidation, *n.* tetemo, tetemeko, tukutiko, utukuto; (*alarm &c.*) fadhaa, hofu, hangaiko, wasiwasi, kiherehere, kiwewe, mang'ang'amu, mang'amung'amu.

trespass, *v.i.* ingia shamba (bustani, kiwanja *&c.*) la mtu bila ruhusa (palipogombezwa); (*pass bounds, annoy*) ruka mpaka, pita kiasi, sumbua, udhi; (*ask too much*) takia -ingi; (*sin, commit an offence*) kosa, halifu sheria, fanya dhambi. — *n.* kosa, uhalifu, mwingilio wa shamba *&c.* la watu bila ruhusa.

tress, *n.* ushungi, kishungi, bwenzi, msongo, msokoto wa nywele.

trestle, *n.* tegemeo la meza au mbao (lenye matendegu matatu au manne), farasi ya kuwekea mbao (katika kujenga *&c.*).

triad, *n.* vitu vitatu pamoja (kama kwamba ni kitu kimoja tu).

trial, *n.* kujaribu, majaribu, maonji, jaribio; (*legal*) hukumu; (*competition*) mashindano; (*trouble*) taabu, shida, pingamizi, udhia.

triangle, *n.* umbo lenye pembe tatu, pembetatu. **triangular,** *a.* -enye pembe tatu. **triangulate,** *v.t.* kata (eneo *&c.*) kuwa *triangle* ili kupima. **triangulation,** *n.* kupima kwa kutumia *triangle.*

tribe, *n.* kabila; (*large*) taifa; (*kind*) aina, jinsi, namna. *Of what tribe are you?* mtu gani wewe? **tribal,** *a.* -a kabila. *Tribal mark,* nembo, mpororo.

tribulation, *n.* taabu, huzuni, majonzi, mateso, shida, msiba.

tribune, *n.* (*officer*) mtu mkubwa wa serikali ya kirumi zamani; (*raised dais &c.*) mimbara, dungu, ulingo, jukwaa. **tribunal,** *n.* baraza ya hukumu, korti.

tribute, *n.* ushuru, kodi. *Pay tribute to a person,* sifu, taja sifa za mtu. **tributary,** *a.* -a kulipa kodi, -a chini, -a kuleta msaada. — *n.* mkuu wa serikali au serikali iliyo chini ya serikali nyingine; (*stream*) kijito (kinachoingia mto), mtoto wa mto.

trice, *n.* *In a trice,* mara moja, kufumba na kufumbua, ukope wa juu na wa chini.

trick, *n.* hila, kitimbi, madanganyo; (*habit*) mazoea, desturi; (*conjuring*) kiinimacho, mazingaombwe, mizungu, miujiza, mauzauza; (*in cards*) sehemu moja ya mchezo. *This will do the trick,* hiki kitafaa. *The whole bag of tricks,* yote pia. — *v.t.* punja, danganya, laghai, ghilibu, hadaa, kopa, kalamkia. *Trick out,* pamba. **trickery,** *n.* taz. *trick, n.*, werevu, udanganyifu, ulaghai, uayari. **trickish,** *a.* -a hila *&c.* **trickster,** *n.* mwenye hila, mdanganyi, mlaghai, mwerevu, mghilibu, ayari.

trickle, *v.i.* tiririka, chururu, chururika, nyinyirika, tambaa. — *n.* chururu, mtiririko, mchuruziko, mchuruzo.

trickster, *n.* taz. *trick.*

tricolour, *n.* bendera yenye rangi tatu, hasa ya kifaransa.

tricycle, *n.* gari kama baisikeli lenye magurudumu matatu.

trident, *n.* chusa chenye ncha tatu, mkuki wa vyembe vitatu.

tried, *a. p.t. and pf.t.* ya *try.*
triennial, *a.* -a kila mwaka wa tatu.
trier, *n.* taz. *try.*
trifle, *n.* jambo hafifu, kitu kisicho na thamani, kama si kitu, kidogo, takataka; (*sweet*) namna ya maandazi. — *v.i.* chezacheza, puza. **trifler,** *n.* mpuzi, kijoyojoyo, mpurukushani. **trifling,** *a.* hafifu, -pumbavu, -dogo.
trigger, *n.* mtambo wa bunduki (bastola).
trigonometry, *n.* elimu ihusuyo *triangles.*
trilateral, *a.* -a mistari mitatu.
trilingual, *a.* -a lugha tatu.
trill, *v.i.* tetemesha sauti katika kuimba, piga vigelegele, tia madoido au madende (katika kuimba). — *n.* mtetemo wa sauti, madende, madoido (katika kuimba), kigelegele.
trim, *v.t.* tengeneza; (*adjust balance*) sawazisha; (*decorate*) pamba, remba; (*cut*) kata; (*plants*) chenga; (*vegetables*) chambua. — *a.* -liotengeneka, -zuri, taratibu, nadhifu, -liokwatuliwa. — *n.* matengeneo, mapambo; (*condition*) hali. **trimmer,** *n.* mtengenezaji &c.; (*time-server*) mgeuzi. **trimming,** *n.* (*ornament*) mapambo; (*time-serving*) kugeuka, ugeuzi, ugeugeu.
trinity, *n.* utatu, tatu pamoja; (*God*) Mungu aliye na asili moja na nafsi tatu, Utatu Mtakatifu. **Trinitarian,** *n.* aaminiye ukweli wa *Trinity.*
trinket, *n.* kipambo kidogo kizuri (*e.g.* kishaufu, pete, kipini &c.).
trio, *n.* watatu pamoja; (*music*) wimbo wa kuimbwa na watu watatu, au kupigwa kwa ala tatu.
trip, *v.i.* enda mbio kwa hatua fupi; (*dance*) cheza; (*stumble*) kwaa, kwaza; (*err*) kosa. *Trip up,* kwaza, piga ugoe; (*oneself*) jikwaza. — *n.* safari ndogo, matembezi. **tripper,** *n.* msafiri (wa safari ndogo ya kujifurahisha).
tripartite, *a.* -a sehemu tatu.
tripe, *n.* matumbo (yanayopikwa kwa kula); (*slang*) upuzi, maandiko hafifu.
triple, *a.* -a mara tatu, -a tatu pamoja. — *v.t.* zidisha kwa tatu. **triplet,** *n.* vitu vitatu pamoja; (*child*) mmoja wa watoto watatu waliozaliwa pamoja (na mama mmoja).
triplex, *a.* -a tabaka tatu, -a mara tatu. **triplicate,** *v.t.* fanya nakili tatu. — *n.* nakili ya tatu.
tripod, *n.* kiti (meza, kiweko &c.) chenye miguu mitatu.
tripper, *n.* taz. *trip.*
trireme, *n.* chombo cha zamani sana chenye makasia mengi yaliyopigwa na safu tatu za watu.
trisect, *v.t.* kata vipande vitatu vilivyo sawa.
trisyllable, *n.* neno lenye *syllables* tatu, *e.g.* ma-ne-no.
trite, *a.* -liojulikana sana, baridi, -dufu, -ovyo.
triturate, *v.t.* fikicha, chua, saga, ponda, funda. **trituration,** *n.* kufikicha &c.
triumph, *n.* shangwe, shangilio, furaha kuu; (*success*) kushinda, kufaulu, kufanikiwa, kusitawi, kushangilia. *Shouts of triumph,* makelele ya furaha, vigelegele, shangwe, vifijo. *Have* (*enjoy*) *a triumph,* shangiliwa, pokewa kwa shangwe na vigelegele baada ya vita (baada ya kufaulu katika jambo kuu). — *v.i.* shangilia; (*succeed*) shinda; (*boast*) jivuna (juu ya adui), simanga. **triumphal,** *a.* -a shangwe. **triumphant,** *a.* -a shangwe, -a kushinda, -lioshinda, -a furaha (kwa sababu ya kushinda).
triune, *a.* (Mungu) mmoja mwenye nafsi tatu.
trivet, *n.* kipande chenye miguu mitatu (chenye vishikio vitatu). *Right as a trivet,* vizuri kabisa, sijambo (hajambo &c.) kabisa.
trivial, *a.* -a sikuzote, -siyo na maana sana, hafifu, duni. **triviality,** *n.* uhafifu, upuzi; jambo lisilo na maana sana, jambo hafifu.
trod, *p.t.* **trodden,** *pf.t.* ya *tread.*
troglodyte, *n.* mkaa pangoni (wa zamani sana).

troll, (1) *v.t.* imba (ovyo ovyo); (*in fishing*) vua samaki (kwa kutupa na kuvuta chambo).

troll, (2) *n.* zimwi.

trolley, *n.* gari lenye magurudumu mawili la kusukumwa na mtu; gari lenye magurudumu manne la kwenda juu ya reli (vyuma).

trollop, *n.* mwanamke mkoo (mzembe, mchafu), malaya, kahaba.

trombone, *n.* tarumbeta yenye sauti nene sana.

troop, *n.* kundi, jeshi, kikosi (cha askari wapanda farasi). — *v.i.* enda -ingi pamoja, songa mbele pamoja, enda kwa kusongana. **trooper,** *n.* askari mpanda farasi. **troop-ship,** *n.* meli ya kuabirishia askari.

trophy, *n.* ukumbusho wa kushinda, kumbukumbu.

tropics, *n.* sehemu ya dunia papitapo jua kichwani hasa, nchi zilizo chini ya jua, nchi za joto jingi. **tropical,** *a.* -a *tropics*, -a joto jingi, -a hari nyingi.

trot, *v.i.* enda kwa matiti, enda shoti, enda upesi (bila kukimbia hasa). — *n.* mwendo wa matiti (wa shoti, wa mashindo); (*of persons*) mwendo wa mbio (bila kukimbia hasa). **trotter,** *n.* mguu (wa chini mpaka kisingino) wa nguruwe.

troth, *n.* *Plight one's troth,* toa ahadi, ahidi (hasa kuoa).

trotter, *n.* taz. *trot.*

troubadour, *n.* mtunga mashairi mwimbaji wa zamani katika nchi ya Ufaransa na nchi nyinginezo.

trouble, *v.t.* udhi, taabisha, sumbua, chokoza, pekecha, janga, hangaisha, kalifu; — *v.i.* jikalifu, jisumbua. — *n.* adha, udhia, taabu, mashaka, janga, masumbuko, kayaya, gubu.

troublesome, *a.* -a udhia, -sumbufu, -a taabu, -chokozi, -a shida; (*unruly*) -tukutu, -kaidi. **troublous,** *a.* -a msukosuko, -liochafuka, -a taabu.

trough, *n.* kihori, chombo kirefu cha kuwekea maji na chakula cha farasi na mifugo; (*between waves*) bonde (katikati ya mawimbi), mshuko wa wimbi.

trounce, *v.t.* piga sana, chapa sana.

troupe, *n.* kundi la wachezaji (waimbaji &c.).

trousers, *n.* suruali.

trousseau, *n.* vipambo na nguo &c., za bibi arusi.

trout, *n.* namna ya samaki wa mitoni, Ulaya.

trove, *a.* taz. *treasure-trove.*

trow, *v.i.* sadiki, ona.

trowel, *n.* (*mason's*) mwiko.

troy weight, *n.* kipimo cha kupimia dhahabu na fedha.

truant, *n.* mtoro. *Play truant,* toroka (kazi, chuoni).

truce, *n.* mapatano ya kitambo, amani kwa muda.

truck, (1) *n.* kubadilishana (bidhaa); bidhaa ndogo ndogo (zisizo na thamani nyingi); (*nonsense*) upuzi. *Truck system,* kulipa nguo, bidhaa &c., kwa mshahara badala ya fedha. *Don't have any truck with him,* usishughulike naye, usiandamane naye.

truck, (2) *n.* gari dogo (la kuchukulia mizigo).

truckle, *v.i.* (*to*) jidhili kwa, jitusha mbele ya, jipendekeza kwa, shika miguu ya, jinyenyekea sana kwa, rairai.

truckle-bed, *n.* kitanda kidogo (hasa chenye vigurudumu katika matendegu yake).

truculent, *a.* -kali, -gomvi, -juvi, -shupavu, -fidhuli, -safihi. **truculence,** *n.* ukali, ugomvi, ufidhuli, usafihi.

trudge, *v.i.* enda kwa kukokota miguu, jikokoteza miguu, enda kwa taabu.

true, *a.* kweli, -a hakika; (*trusty*) amini, -aminifu; (*exact*) halisi, sahihi; (*equal*) sawa; (*just*) -a haki, -nyofu, -adilifu. *Be true to,* shikilia, fuata, gandama na, ambatana na, toacha. — *v.t.* sahihisha, sawazisha. **truism,** *n.* neno la kweli lisilo na shaka (lisilohitajiwa kutajwa). **truly,** *adv.*

kweli, kwa kweli, hakika. **truth,** *n.* (*fact*) kweli, hakika, yakini; (*statement*) kanuni yenye hakika, maneno ya kweli; (*deed*) haki. **truthful,** *a.* kweli, amini, -sema kweli. **truthfulness,** *n.* ukweli.

trump, (1) *n.* taz. *trumpet.*

trump, (2) *n.* turufu, karata inayoshinda (katika mchezo wa karata; (*generous person*) mtu mzuri, mhisani. — *v.t.* shinda kwa turufu.

trump, (3) *v.t.* (*up*) fanya kwa uwongo, tunga, zua. **trumpery,** *n.* mambo ya kishaufu (ya ovyo), upuzi. — *a.* -shaufu, hafifu, ovyo.

trumpet, *n.* tarumbeta, baragumu, panda. — *v.t.* eneza, tangaza, vumisha. **trump,** *n.* mlio wa tarumbeta, **trumpeter,** *n.* mpiga tarumbeta (baragumu, panda). **trumpeting,** *n.* mlio wa tarumbeta; (*of elephant*) mlio wa tembo (ndovu).

truncate, *v.t.* kata, fupisha.

truncheon, *n.* kirungu, rungu, kigongo, kibarango.

trundle, *v.t.* fingirisha; — *v.i.* fingirika.

trunk, *n.* (*of a tree*) shina, jiti; (*stump*) siki, kisiki, kishiku, jiti; (*cut down*) gogo; (*body*) kiwiliwili (bila kichwa, miguu na mikono); (*of elephant*) mkono, mkonga, mwiro; (*box*) kasha, sanduku; (*main part*) sehemu kuu, asili. *A trunk-line, Trunk railway,* njia kuu ya gari la moshi. *Trunk road,* barabara, njia kuu.

truss, *n.* (*bundle*) fungu, mzigo, robota, mtumba; (*surgical*) mshipi wa kukazia utumbo; (*of roof*) mkingiko. — *v.t.* kunja, funga.

trust, *n.* (*faith, belief*) tumaini, imani, itibari; (*faithfulness*) haki, amini; (*pledge, deposit*) amana, agizo, dhamana, rehani; (*combination of firms*) ushirika wa makumpuni. — *v.t.* amini, aminia, tawakali; (*entrust*) aminisha; (*be confident*) tumaini, jetea, tumai. **trustee,** *n.* mdhamini. *Act as trustee for,* shika (tunza) mali ya. **trustful,** *a.* -a kuamini, -tumainifu. **trustworthy, trusty,** *a.* amini, -aminifu, thabiti, madhubuti, hodari.

truth, *n.,* **truthful,** *a.,* **truthfulness,** *n.* taz. *true.*

try, *v.t.* (*p.t. and pf.t.* **tried**) jaribu, jaribia, jitahidi, fanya bidii; (*judge by law*) hukumu; (*test, examine*) hakikia, angalia, tafutia, hoji, onja, (*afflict*) taabisha, chosha, sumbua, kalifu. *Try on* (*clothes &c.*) linga. — *n.* jaribu. **tried,** *a.* -liojaribiwa, mjarabati. **trying,** *a.* -a kujaribia; (*oppressive*) -a kulemea, -zito, -a kutaabisha, -a taabu, -sumbufu, -a kusumbua, -kali, -kalifu.

trypansomiasis, *n.* malale, ugonjwa uletwao na mbung'o (chafuo).

tryst, *n.* miadi ya kuonana, mahali palipotajwa katika miadi ya kuonana.

tsetse-fly, *n.* mbung'o, chafuo, ndorobo.

T-square, *n.* kipande chenye umbo la herufi T kinachotumika katika kuandika picha *&c.*

tub, *n.* pipa. **tubby,** *a.* -fupi, -nene.

tube, *n.* bomba, mwanzi, neli, mrija. **tubing,** *n.* kama *tube.* **tubular,** *a.* -a *tube,* kama *tube.*

tuber, *n.* kinundu katika mzizi wa mmea, kama kiazi. **tubercle,** *n.* kinundu (mwilini), kipele. **tuberculosis,** *n.* ugonjwa fulani, hasa wa kifua, kifua kikuu.

tubing, *n.,* **tubular,** *a.* taz. *tube.*

tuck, *v.t.* kunja, finya, fyata; (*fold up*) futika, weka. *Tuck up a loin-cloth,* piga ubinda (winda). *Tuck up dress* (*trousers, sleeves &c.*) sega, pania kanzu (suruali, mikono *&c.*) — *n.* finyo, kunjo, pindo, kunyanzi.

Tuesday, *n.* Jumanne.

tuft, *n.* kishungi, ushungi, kishada, bwenzi. *A tuft of grass,* kichungu.

tug, *v.t.* vuta (kokota) kwa nguvu, vutavuta, vuta ghafula au kwa kishindo. — *n.* bidii ya kuvuta, mvuto, kishindo; (*steamer*) stima (meli ndogo) yenye nguvu nyingi yenye kazi ya kuvuta meli kubwa.

tug-of-war, *n.* mchezo wa kushindana kwa kuvutana kamba.
tuition, *n.* malezi, mafundisho.
tulip, *n.* namna ya ua; (*yellow tulip tree*) mtakawa.
tumble, *v.i.* (*down*) anguka; (*into*) tumbukia; (*over*) pinduka; (*about*) jifingirisha, jitapatapa, gaagaa; (*over*) jikwaa na kuanguka; (*turn somersault*) piga kichwangomba; — *v.t.* (*disarrange*) chafua, fuja, vuruga; (*cause to fall*) angusha, tumbukiza, pindua. **tumbled,** *a.* -liovurugika, -liochafuka, -liofujika. *Tumbled hair,* matimutimu ya nywele. **tumble-down,** *a.* -bovu.
tumbler, *n.* (*glass*) bilauri; (*small moving part*) kipande (ndani ya kufuli au kitasa); (*acrobat*) mpiga kichwangomba, mpiga pindu.
tumbrel, *n.* gari, hasa lenye magurudumu mawili la kuchukulia vyombo vya kiaskari, risasi &c.
tumefaction, *n.*, **tumescent,** *a.* taz. *tumid.*
tumid, *a.* -liovimba. **tumefaction,** *n.* kuvimba, uvimbe, kivimbe. **tumescent,** *a.* -liyovimba. **tumour,** *n.* kivimbe, uvimbe, tezi.
tumult, *n.* makelele, ghasia, zahama, msukosuko, machafuko. **tumultuous,** *a.* -a *tumult,* -liochafuka.
tumulus, *n.* fungu, chungu; (*of white ant*) kichuguu.
tun, *n.* pipa kubwa.
tune, *n.* wimbo, sauti, mafuatano ya sauti katika kuimba au kupiga ngoma, ulinganifu wa sauti, utaratibu. — *v.t.* linganya (linganisha) sauti (kinanda &c.). *Tune up,* anza kulinganisha sauti; (*begin to play*) anza kupiga (muziki). **tuneful,** *a.* -a kutoa sauti nzuri (ya kupendeza). **tuning-fork,** *n.* kipande cha chuma kinachotoa sauti fulani kipigwapo.
tungsten, *n.* namna ya madini ngumu sana ya thamani nyingi.
tunic, *n.* koti (*e.g.* la kiaskari), kanzu fupi, gwanda.
tuning-fork, *n.* taz. *tune.*
tunnel, *n.* shimo refu la kupenya ndani au la kupita chini, shimo, tundu. — *v.t.* fanya *tunnel,* fukua chini.
turban, *n.* kilemba.
turbid, *a.* -liyotibuliwa, -liovurugika, -enye matope, -enye takataka, -liyochafuka, -liyofujika.
turbine, *n.* gurudumu linaloendeshwa na nguvu za maji, za mvuke &c.
turbot, *n.* samaki mkubwa mpana.
turbulent, *a.* -a makelele, -a ghasia, -a jeuri, -a msukosuko, -siyozuiwa, -siyotawaliwa. **turbulence,** *n.* makelele, ghasia, zahama, jeuri, msukosuko, ukaidi, maasi, utukutu.
tureen, *n.* kombe (bakuli) la kutilia mchuzi.
turf, *n.* majani mororo na udongo wake; (*race-course*) mahali pa kushindania farasi; (*racing affairs*) mashindano ya farasi na watu na mambo yanayohusiana nayo.
turgid, *a.* -liovimba, -liotutuka, -liotutumka; (*boastful* &c.) -a kujivuna, -a kiburi, -a kutakabari. **turgidity,** *n.* uvimbe, kuvimba &c.; kiburi, majivuno.
turkey, *n.* bata mzinga; (*country*) Uturuki. *The Sultan of Turkey,* Sultani Rum. **Turkish,** *a.* -a Turuki, -a kituruki. — *n.* (*language*) kituruki **Turkish delight,** *n.* halua.
turmeric, *n.* manjano.
turmoil, *n.* makelele, msukosuko, ghasia, zahama, machafuko, udhia, fujo.
turn, *v.t.* (*revolve*) zungusha, gugurusha; (*over, aside*) geuza, pindua; (*shape &c. on a lathe*) kereza, fanya kwa kerezo; (*sour* &c.) chachisha, ozesha; (*stomach*) chafua, tia kigagazi; (*of age*) pita kwa umri; — *v.i.* zunguka, geuka, pinduka, betabeta; (*sour* &c.) chacha, vunda. *Turn a cold shoulder to, Turn the back on,* dharau, beza, geua, deua, geukia, -pa mgongo, -pa kisogo. *Turn the edge of,* ondoa (haribu) makali ya, tia ubutu, seneza. *Turn the flank of,* zunguka nyuma ya. *Turn the head* (*make crazy*) poteza (rusha) akili,

tia wazimu (kichaa). *Turn a corner,* zunguka, geuka; (*pass a critical point*) -wa hajambo, pona, faulu. *Turn adrift,* tupa, acha. *Turn against,* geuka adui wa. *Turn a penny by,* faidia kidogo. *Turn aside,* kengeua. *Turn away,* geuka, enda zake (zao &c.); (*dismiss*) ondosha; (*avert*) kinga, geuzia mbali, epa. *Turn back,* rudi, rejea. *Turn down,* (*refuse*) kataa. *Turn down a lamp,* shusha utambi. *Turn in* (*to bed*), enda kulala. *Turn inside out,* fidua, fudua, fudikiza. *Turn off* (*water &c.*) zuia, funga, ziba; (*dismiss*) ondosha. *Turn on* (*steam &c.*) fungulia, zibua. *Turn one's hand to,* shika kazi ya. *Turn over,* pindua, fudikiza; (*in the mind*) fikiri. *Turn over and over* (*somersaults*), pinduka. *Turn over a new leaf,* tulia, jirudia. *Turn out,* (*happen*) tekelea, tokea, jiri; (*dismiss*) ondosha; (*of manufactures*) fanyiza. *Turn out well,* fanikia, sitawi. *Turn round,* zungusha, fingirisha, guguru-sha; (*intrans.*) geuka, zunguka, zinga, fingirika, guguruka. *Turn the tables,* geuza (pindua) mambo pia. *Turn tail,* kimbia. *Turn to* (*rely on*), tumaini, tegemea, kimbilia. *Turn to advantage or account,* tumia kwa faida, faidi, chuma. *Turn turtle,* pinduka; (*trans.*) pindua. *Turn up,* tokea, tukia, zuka; (*a wick*) chochea, pandisha, panza; (*soil &c.*) fukua; (*dress, sleeves, trousers &c.*) sega, pania. *Turn upon,* rudia, rudishia; (*attack*) shambulia. *Turn upside down,* fudikiza, pindua; (*confuse &c.*) pindua, chafua, buruga, fuja. — *n.* kuzunguka, kuzungusha &c.; (*curve, bend*) pindi, kizingo, mzingo, kuruba; (*revolution*) mzunguko, mabadili, mageuzi, mapinduzi; (*succession*) zamu; (*in games*) mchezo; (*in drinking*) duru; (*mode of expression &c.*) namna, jinsi; (*of illness &c.*) kipindi. *It is his turn to play,* zamu yake kucheza, mchezo wake. *By turns,* kwa zamu, kwa kupokezana, kipokee. *In turns,* kwa zamu, taratibu. *Do a good* (*bad*) *turn to,* tendea mema (mabaya). *Take* (*go for*) *a turn,* enda kutembea. *Serve a turn,* faa. *It gave me quite a turn,* ilinishtusha, iliniduwaza, ilinifadhaisha. *It is done to a turn,* kimeiva barabara, kimepikwa barabara. **turncoat,** *n.* mgeuzi mkufuru, mkimbizi (kwa ajili ya kupata faida au nafuu). **turner,** *n.* mkereza. **turnery** *n.* vitu vilivyofanyizwa kwa kerezo. **turning,** *n.* kuzunguka, mzunguko, pindi, mzingo, kuruba; (*using lathe*) ukerezo. **turning-point,** *n.* (*highest, furthest*) upeo, kipeo, kikomo; (*place of turning*) pa kugeuka; (*decisive point*) neno la kukata jambo, jambo kuu. **turnkey,** *n.* bawabu wa gereza. **turn-out,** *n.* jumla ya watu waliohudhuria kwenye mkutano (mchezo &c.). **turnover,** *n.* (*pie*) namna ya maandazi yaliyokunjika; (*in business*) jumla ya fedha iliyopokewa na kulipwa katika muda maalum. **turnpike,** *n.* mlango njiani patolewapo kodi. **turnstile,** *n.* mlango mwembamba wa kupishia watu mmoja mmoja.

turnip, *n.* mboga kidogo kama muhogo.

turnkey, *n.,* **turn-out,** *n.,* **turnover,** *n.,* **turnpike,** *n.,* **turnstile,** *n.* taz. *turn.*

turpentine, *n.* terafini (namna ya mafuta).

turpitude, *n.* uovu, ubaya, ufisadi, ufasiki, upotovu, aibu, unyonge.

turquoise, *n.* feruzi.

turret, *n.* mnara, kinara; (*in man-of-war*) banda la chuma lenye mizinga.

turtle, (1) *n.* kasa; (*hawkshead*) ng'amba. *Turn turtle,* pinduka.

turtle, (2) *n.* (*dove*) hua.

tusk, *n.* jino; (*elephants*) pembe; (*large*) pembe ya mtao; (*middle-sized*) buri; (*small*) kalasha; (*of boar*) upamba; (*small, of rhinoceros*) kipusa.

tussle, *v.i.* pigana sana, pigana kwa ghasia, buburushana. — *n.* ghasia, msukosuko, pigano la ghasia. (*strenuous effort*) juhudi, jitihadi.

tussore, *n.* lasi.

tutor, *n.* mwalimu, mkufunzi, mfunzi. **tutelage,** *n.* mafundisho, malezi, maongozi, ulinzi. **tutelar,** *a.* -a kulinda. **tutorial,** *a.* -a mwalimu.

twaddle, *n.* upuzi, mapayo, mapayuko, mabwato, maneno matupu. — *v.i.* payapaya, payuka, bwata, bwabwaja, tatarika.

twain, *n.* and *a.* vitu vyo vyote viwili pamoja, wawili, viwili, -wili. *Cut in twain,* kata sehemu mbili.

twang, *n.* mlio (wa uzi wa zeze au upindi &c. ukipigwa); (*nasal*) usemi wa puani (wa king'ong'o). — *v.t.* liza (zeze &c.) kwa kunyakua nyuzi zake.

tweak, *v.t.* nyakua, binya, finya.

tweed, *n.* nguo ya manyoya ya kondoo.

tweezers, *n.* kikoleo, kibano; (*for depilation*) mentari.

twelve, *n.* and *a.* thenashara, kumi na mbili. *The Twelve,* mitume thenashara wa Yesu Kristo. **twelfth,** *a.* -a thenashara. **twelvemonth,** *n.* mwaka mmoja.

twenty, *n.* and *a.* ishirini. **twentieth,** *a.* -a ishirini.

twice, *adv.* mara mbili.

twiddle, *v.t.* sokotasokota. *Twiddle one's thumbs,* kaa kivivu.

twig, *n.* kitawi, kijiti.

twilight, *n.* majilio ya nuru asubuhi na maondokeo yake jioni, ukungu; (*dawn*) ukungu wa alfajiri, mapambazuko, mchana mdogo; (*evening*) kiusikusiku, gizagiza, ukungu wa jioni.

twin, *n.* pacha; (*equal*) sawa, mwenzi, mfano mmoja. *Twin houses,* nyumba pacha.

twine, *n.* kitani, uzi. — *v.t.* songa, sokota; (*twist*) sokotasokota.

twinge, *n.* mchomo (wa maumivu), kichomi. — *v.i.* choma, pwita, umiza ghafula.

twinkle, *v.i.* metameta, meremeta; (*brighten*) angaza. — *n.* kumetameta, kimeta, wangavu. **twinkling,** *n.* kama *twinkle, n.*; (*moment*) dakika moja. *In the twinkling of an eye,* kwa ukope wa juu na wa chini, kufumba na kufumbua, mara moja, kwa kupepesa macho.

twirl, *v.t.* zungusha upesi kwa vidole, zungusha, vuruvuru, gugurusha; (*in the air*) vurumisha; (*between the palms*) pekecha; (*twist*) sokotasokota; — *v.i.* zunguka upesi (vuruvuru).

twist, *v.t.* (*string, rope*) pota, sokota; (*plait*) sokota, suka; (*distort*) geuza, potoa, vuta; (*strain*) popotoa, shtusha, tegua; — *v.i.* (*write*) songa, nyonga, nyeng'enya, finginyika; (*be twisted*) songamana, potoka, sokoteka &c. (*of road*) betabeta. *Twist off,* kongonyoa, konyoa. — *n.* pindi, kuruba, mageuzi; (*of rope &c.*) mkunjo; (*mental*) kinyongo. **twister,** *n.* matatizo, fumbo; (*dishonest person*) mwerevu, mtu mwenye hila, mlaghai.

twit, *v.t.* kumbusha makosa, simbulia, simanga, tusha, chokoza, shutumu, suta.

twitch, *v.t.* (*jerk*) shtusha, gutusha; (*off*) nyakua, twaa ghafula; — *v.i.* (*move spasmodically*) shtuka, gutuka, tetema. — *n.* mvuto (finyo) la ghafula, kituko, kipindi, mshtuko, mtetemo.

twitter, *v.i.* lia (kama ndege mdogo). **twitter, twittering,** *n.* mlio wa ndege mdogo. *Be in a twitter,* ona wasiwasi, hangaika, fadhaika.

two, *n.* and *a.* mbili, -wili, -bili, pili. *Two and two,* wawili wawili (mbili mbili &c.). *A pair,* jozi. *Put two and two together,* enenza mambo. **two-edged,** *a.* -kali kuwili. **two-faced,** *a.* -enye nyuso mbili; (*person*) kauleni, -a uwongo. **twofold,** *a.* -a mara mbili, maradufu.

tympanum, *n.* kiwambo cha sikio.

type, *n.* (*printing*) herufi za chapa, chapa; (*emblem*) kiolezo, mfano, kifani, methali, ishara; (*kind*) aina, jinsi, namna; (*ideal*) kitu kamili, kipeo, kitu cha namna hasa. — *v.t.* andika (piga chapa) kwa *typewriter*. **typewriter,** *n.* chombo cha kuandikia kwa chapa. **typewriting,** *n.* mwandiko wa *typewriter*. **typical,** *a.* -a mfano hasa, -a kufanana sana na asili, -a mfano mmoja. **typify,** *v.t.* -wa mfano wa. **typist,** *n.* karani wa kupiga *typewriter*. **typographical,** *a.* -a chapa, -a kupiga chapa. **typography,** *n.* maarifa ya kupiga chapa, matumizi ya chapa.

typhoid, *n.* homa mbaya matumboni. **typhus,** *n.* homa kali iletwayo na chawa.

typhoon, *n.* tufani, kimbunga.

typhus, *n.* taz. *typhoid.*

typical, *a.*, **typify,** *v.*, **typist,** *n.*, **typographical,** *a.*, **typography,** *n.* taz. *type.*

tyrant, *n.* mdhalimu, mjeuri, mshari; (*despot*) sultani (mwenye nguvu yote peke yake), sultani mkorofi. **tyrannical,** *a.* -a kudhulumu, -dhalimu, -onevu, -a jeuri, -a shari. **tyrannize,** *v.i.* dhulumu, onea, fanyia jeuri **tyrannous,** *a.* -dhalimu, -onevu, jeuri, -korofi. **tyranny,** *n.* kuonea watu bure pasipo haki, udhalimu, kupiga ubwana, ukali, ukorofi, jeuri, ujuba, jefule; (*despotism*) utawala wa mtu mmoja peke yake, utawala wa sultani mkorofi.

tyro, *n.* mwanafunzi, mjinga.

U

ubiquitous, *a.* -a kuwapo kote kote, -a kuwapo pote pote, -a kuwapo (kuenea) kila mahali. **ubiquity,** *n.* kuwapo mahali pote au mahali pengi sana, kuenea pote.

udder, *n.* kiwele.

ugly, *a.* -baya, -a kuchukiza. *He is ugly,* hana uso. **ugliness,** *n.* ubaya (wa uso, umbo, sura), -a kuchukiza macho.

ukelele, *n.* namna ya zeze.

ulcer, *n.* donda, kidonda; (*large, dirty*) banguzi; (*slow, creeping*) tambaazi. **ulcerate,** *v.t. and i.* fanya (fanyika) vidonda. **ulceration,** *n.* kidonda. **ulcerous,** *a.* -a vidonda.

ulna, *n.* mfupa mkubwa wa mkono kati ya kiko na kiwiko.

ulster, *n.* koti kubwa la nje lenye ukanda.

ulterior, *a.* -a nyuma, -a baadaye, -a zaidi; (*undisclosed*) -a siri, -a moyoni.

ultimate, *a.* -a mwisho, -a kwanza, -a asili. *Ultimate cause,* chanzo, asili. **ultimately,** *adv.* baadaye, mwisho. **ultimatum,** *n.* mwisho, neno la mwisho (la tama), mkataa, kukata maneno. **ultimo,** *adv.* mwezi uliopita.

ultra, *pref.* -a kupita kiasi, mno, sana.

ultramarine, *n.* rangi ya samawi. — *a.* -a rangi ya samawi.

umbilical, *a.* -a kitovu.

umbrage, *n.* wivu, chuki, uchungu.

umbrella, *n.* mwavuli.

umpire, *n.* mwamuzi.

un-, (1) *pref.* (mwanzoni pa maneno mengi, maana yake) si.

un-, (2) *pref.* (mwanzoni pa maneno

mengi, maana yake ni kama kubadili mwisho wa *verb* ya Kiswahili kuwa -ua, *e.g. tie*, funga; *untie*, fungua).

unabashed, *a*. -siye na haya, -enye macho makavu, -shupavu.

unabated, *a*. -siopungua, -a kudumu (kuendelea kwa nguvu zote).

unable, *a*. (*be*) toweza, tokuwa na nguvu. *I am unable to go*, siwezi kwenda.

unaccountable, *a*. -siotambulikana, -siofahamikana, -a ajabu sana. **unaccountably**, *adv*. kwa jinsi isivyotambulika (isivyoelezeka).

unaccustomed, *a*. -siozoea, -siyo -a kawaida, -sio -a desturi, -a kigeni.

unadorned, *a*. bila mapambo, -a vivi hivi, -sio na urembo.

unaffected, *a*. (*sincere*) -a kweli, -nyofu; (*unchanged*) -siogeuzwa, -siona, -siovutwa.

unaided, *a*. bila msaada, peke yake (yao &c.).

unalloyed, *a*. safi, -a kweli, halisi, -sioghoshiwa, -siochanganyika (na kitu kingine, na maono mengine).

unalterable, *a*. -siobadilika, -sioweza kugeuzwa, thabiti, imara, madhubuti.

unanimous, *a*. -enye shauri moja, -liokubaliwa na wote, -a wote pamoja. **unanimity**, *n*. umoja. **unanimously**, *adv*. kwa umoja.

unanswerable, *a*. -siokanikana, -sioweza kukanushwa.

unappreciated, *a*. -siohesabiwa kuwa na thamani, -siothaminiwa.

unapproachable, *a*. -siofikika, -sioambilika, -gumu.

unarmed, *a*. -sio na silaha, -sio na njia ya kujilinda.

unashamed, *a*. -sioona haya, -sio na haya, -juvi, -enye macho makavu, -shupavu.

unasked, *a*. bila kuombwa (kuulizwa, kualikwa, kukaribishwa, kutafutwa).

unassailable, *a*. -sioweza kukanushwa, -siokanikana, thabiti, imara, -sioshambulikana.

unassayed, *a*. -siojaribiwa.

unassignable, *a*. -sioandikiwa, -siohesabiwa, -sioweza kupakizwa, -sioweza kudhaniwa.

unassisted, *a*. -siosaidiwa, bila msaada, peke yake (yao &c.).

unassuming, *a*. -nyenyekevu, -siotaka makuu, -siojitanguliza, -enye haya.

unattached, *a*. -siofungwa, -siofungamana na, -siotwaliwa.

unattainable, *a*. -siopatikana, -siofikika.

unauthorized, *a*. bila amri, bila idhini, bila ruhusa.

unavailing, *a*. -siofaa, si -enye njia, -a bure.

unavoidable, *a*. -sioepukika, -a faradhi, -a lazima, -siopitishika.

unawares, *adv*. ghafula, bila kutazamiwa, kwa siri.

unbalanced, *a*. (*of mind*) -enye wazimu, -enye kichaa.

unbar, *v.t.* fungua, komoa.

unbearable, *a*. -siovumilika, -siostahimilika.

unbecoming, *a*. -sio desturi, -siofaa, si -zuri, -baya.

unbelief, *n*. kutoamini, kutokuwa na imani, ukafiri. **unbeliever**, *n*. asiyesadiki, mwenye mashaka mengi. kafiri.

unbend, *v.t.* (*p.t. and pf.t.* **unbent**) kunjua, pindua, legeza, nyosha, fungua; — *v.i.* kunjuka, legea, nyoka, funguka; (*be genial*) kunjuka, changamka. **unbending**, *a*. -siokunjuka, -siopindika; (*resolute*) -gumu, -shupavu.

unbiased, unbiassed, *a*. -a haki, -adilifu, sawa, -siopendelea.

unbidden, *a*. -sioitwa, -sioalikwa, -siokaribishwa, pasipo kuamriwa.

unbind, *v.t.* (*p.t. and pf.t.* **unbound**) fungua.

unblemished, *a*. pasipo mawaa, -eupe, safi, kamili.

unblushing, *a*. -sioona haya, -kavu wa macho, -shupavu, -fidhuli, -pujufu.

unbolt, *v.t.* fungua, komoa, chopoa.

unborn, *a*. -siozaliwa bado, -a kutokea baadaye.

unbosom, *v.t.* funua, ungama.
unbound, *a.* -liofunguliwa; (*of books*) pasipo jalada. **unbounded,** *a.* pasipo kiasi, pasipo mpaka, -ingi sana.
unbridled, *a.* -siozuiwa, -a jeuri, -kali sana.
unbroken, *a.* -zima, kamili, -siovunjika, -siokatika; (*of horses*) -siofugwa; (*of soil*) -siolimwa.
unburden, *v.t.* fungulia mzigo, fariji, pumzisha.
unbutton, *v.t.* fungua.
uncage, *v.t.* fungua, toa kitunduni.
uncanny, *a.* -sio -a kawaida, -sio a desturi, -a kutisha, -a kuogofya, -a kigeni, -a kioja.
uncared-for, *a.* -lioachwa, -liotupwa, -siotunzwa, -sioangaliwa, -siolelewa.
unceasing, *a.* -a daima, -siokwisha, -a kuendelea bila kukoma. **unceasingly,** *adv.* daima, sikuzote, bila kukoma, mfululizo.
uncertain, *a.* -sio hakika, si amini, -a mashaka, -a kubadilibadili, -geugeu. **uncertainty,** *n.* mashaka, mabadili.
uncertified, *a.* -siohakikishwa, -siothibitishwa.
unchain, *v.t.* fungulia minyororo.
unchallenged, *a.* -siokanushwa, -siokaidiwa.
unchangeable, *a.* -siobadilika, thabiti, hali moja, imara, madhubuti, -a kuendelea bila kubadilika.
uncharitable, *a.* -gumu, -siohurumia, -sioonea huruma. **uncharitableness,** *n.* ugumu wa moyo, utovu wa huruma.
unchaste, *a.* -zinifu, -asherati.
unchecked, *a.* -siozuiwa; (*untested*) -siotazamwa, -siojaribiwa.
uncivilized, *a.* -siostaarabika, -shenzi, -sio na adabu.
unclasp, *v.t.* fungua, fumbua.
unclassified, *a.* -siopangwa taratibu, -siowekwa kila namna mbalimbali, -a ovyo, shelabela, shaghalabaghala.
uncle, *n.* (*mother's brother*) mjomba; (*father's brother*) amu; (*older than father*) baba mkubwa; (*if younger*) baba mdogo.
unclean, *a.* -chafu, -sio safi, -najisi, -koo, -a taka; (*unchaste*) -zinifu, -asherati. **uncleanness,** *n.* uchafu, unajisi, janaba, ukoo, ujusi, uzinifu, uasherati.
uncloak, *v.t.* funua, onyesha wazi.
unclose, *v.t.* fumbua, funua, fungua.
unclothe, *v.t.* vua, vulia nguo. **unclothed,** *a.* -siovaa nguo, uchi, -tupu.
uncoil, *v.t.* legeza mapindi; (*straighten*) nyosha, kunjua, fundua; — *v.i.* nyoka, kunjuka, pinduka.
uncomfortable, *a.* -siofaa, si -zuri, -siotengenea, -siotulia, -sio na raha, -siostarehesha, -a kutia wasiwasi, -a kuhangaisha, -sumbufu.
uncommon, *a.* -a kigeni, ajabu, si -a kawaida, si -a sikuzote, si -a desturi, -a shida, bora, -a peke yake.
uncommunicative, *a.* -a siri, -tulivu, -siotoa habari.
uncomplaining, *a.* -sionung'unika, -vumilivu, -stahimilivu.
uncomplimentary, *a.* -sio -a adabu, -fidhuli, -safihi, -a kuchukiza, -a kutia uchungu.
uncompromising, *a.* -gumu, -a kushikilia shauri, -siobadili shauri.
unconcern, *n.* ukavu wa macho, utovu wa haya, uzembe. **unconcerned,** *a.* -kavu wa macho, -zembe.
unconditional, *a.* halisi, kabisa, pasipo neno la zaidi, bila masharti.
uncongenial, *a.* -siopatana, -siofaa, -a kuchukiza, -siopendeza, -sio na raha.
unconnected, *a.* -a mbalimbali, -siohusiana, -siofungamana, -sioungamana.
unconquerable, *a.* -sioshindika, -sioweza kushindwa. **unconquered,** *a.* -sioshindwa.
unconscionable, *a.* -a kupita kiasi, mno kabisa.
unconscious, *a.* bila kufahamu, bila kuwa na habari, -siofahamika (asione mwenyewe, asijue mwenyewe). **unconsciousness,** *n.* (*ignorance*) kuto-

fahamu, ujinga, kutojua; (*absence of mind*) kusinzia akili; (*fainting condition*) kuzimia roho, kughumia, kuzirai. **unconsciously,** *adv.* bila kufahamu, bila kujua.

unconstitutional, *a.* si kwa sheria ya nchi, si kwa kawaida ya serikali, -a kuasi, -a kuhalifu, sio haki.

unconstrained, *a.* -siozuiwa, -sioshurutishwa, -a hiari.

uncontrollable, *a.* -siozuilika.

unconventional, *a.* -siofuata desturi (kawaida).

unconverted, *a.* -siobadilika, -sioongoka.

unconvincing, *a.* -siosadikisha, -siothibitisha.

uncork, *v.t.* zibua.

uncorrected, *a.* -siosahihishwa, -siotolewa makosa.

uncorroborated, *a.* -sioshuhudiwa, -siothibitika.

uncouple, *v.t.* fungulia, achanisha.

uncouth, *a.* -jinga, -zuzu, -baya, -geni, -shenzi.

uncover, *v.t.* funua, weka wazi, fichua, gubua.

unction, *n.* kupaka mafuta; (*in speech*) usemaji wa bidii na nguvu. **unctious,** *a.* -a mafuta, laini, -ororo.

uncultivated, *a.* -siolimwa, -siotengenezwa; (*mind*) -sio na elimu, -jinga, -sio na malezi mema.

uncurl, *v.t.* legeza; (*straighten*) nyosha, toa mapindi; — *v.i.* legea, nyoka, toka mapindi.

undated, *a.* -siotiwa (-sioandikiwa) tarehe.

undaunted, *a.* pasipo hofu, -kavu wa macho, hodari, -jasiri.

undeceive, *v.t.* fumbua (mtu) macho, eleza, bainisha.

undecided, *a.* (shauri, maneno) -siokatika, -siothibitishwa; (*irresolute*) -a kusitasita, -a kuhangaika, -sio imara.

undefiled, *a.* safi, -siochanganyika (na kitu duni), -sioghoshiwa.

undefined, *a.* -sio dhahiri, -siodhihirika, -sio waziwazi, -siopambanuka, -sioelezwa.

undeniable, *a.* -siokanikana, -sioweza kukanushwa, pasipo mashaka.

under, *adv. and prep.* chini (ya); (*less than*) -dogo (-chache, -pungufu) kuliko; (*in state of*) kwa, katika, -enye; (*on condition of*) kwa sharti ya. *Under arms*, -enye silaha, tayari kwa vita. *Under fire*, katika kupigana, vitani mwenyewe. *Under foot*, chini. *Under repair*, katika kutengenezwa. *Under sail*, kwa matanga. *Under sentence*, katika adhabu. *Be under weigh* (*of ship*), enda. *Get under weigh*, ng'oa nanga, tweka.

underbred, *a.* si -enye malezi mazuri, -siojua desturi, -jinga, -shenzi, -a kimashamba.

underclothes, *n.* nguo za kuvaa ndani (ya nguo nyingine).

undercurrent, *n.* mkondo wa chini; (*tendency*) maelekeo, maono ya siri.

underdog, *n.* mtu asiye na bahati, asiyesitawi.

underdone, *a.* (*not well cooked*) -bichi, -sioiva vizuri.

under-estimate, *v.t.* hesabu (kisia, dhania) kuwa kidogo kuliko kilivyo.

undergo, *v.t.* (*p.t.* **underwent,** *pf.t.* **undergone** (*be treated with*) (tendewa, pasishwa; (*endure*) vumilia, stahimili, pata, patwa na.

undergraduate, *n.* mwanafunzi wa *University*.

underground, *a. n. and adv.* chini ya nchi, chini.

undergrowth, *n.* magugu, msitu; (*in mangrove swamp*) makoko.

underhand, *a.* -a hila, -danganyifu, -janja. *Underhand dealings*, madanganyo, mafamba.

underlie, *v.t.* -wa chini ya, -wa msingi wa (mwanzo wa, asili ya, maana ya).

underline, *v.t.* andikia (pigia) mstari chini.

underling, *n.* mdogo (wa cheo, kazi).

undermine, *v.t.* fukua chini (makusudi kubomoa), ekua; (*influence &c.*) haribu, dhoofisha.

underneath, *adv. and prep.* chini (ya).

underpin, *v.t.* tegemeza (imarisha) kwa miti, nguzo &c.; gadimu, tia magadi.

underrate, *v.t.* rahisisha, dhani hafifu, tusha, hesabu (dhania, kisia) kuwa kidogo kuliko kilivyo.

undersell, *v.t.* uza rahisi kuliko.

under-shirt, *n.* fulana.

undersized, *a.* -dogo, -liovia, -liodumaa.

understand, *v.t.* (*p.t.* *and* *pf.t.* **understood**) fahamu, tambua, sikia, ng'amua, maizi, komanya, atikali, tanabahi; (*take for granted*) fahamu pasipo kuambiwa, sikia maana pasipo neno; — *v.i.* fahamu, tambua, ambiwa. *I do not understand you*, sisikii vema, sifahamu, sielewi maana, umenifumba maneno. *It is understood* (*assumed*), ndiyo maana halisi, imekubalika. **understanding**, *n.* akili; (*agreement*) mapatano, shauri moja.

understate, *v.t.* punguza, rahisisha.

understood, *p.t.* *and* *pf.t.* ya *understand*.

undertake, *v.t.* (*p.t.* **undertook**, *pf.t.* **undertaken**) diriki, tadariki, jifunga kwa, jaribia; (*promise*) ahidi, toa ahadi; (*begin*) anza, shika, ingia. **undertaker**, *n.* mwenye kutengeneza maziko, mzishi, mpambaji. **undertaking**, *n.* shughuli, jambo, kazi; (*pledge, engagement*) sharti, daraka, ahadi. *Give an undertaking for*, jifunga kwa, fanyia daraka (sharti), dhaminisha.

undertone, *n.* sauti ndogo.

undertook, *p.t.* ya *undertake*.

undervalue, *v.t.* = *underrate*.

underwear, *n.* nguo za kuvaa ndani (ya nguo nyingine).

underwent, *p.t.* ya *undergo*.

underwood, *n.* magugu, msitu.

underworld, *n.* jehanamu; (*of a city*) jamii ya watu waovu, wevi *&c.* wa mji.

underwrite, *v.t.* kubali jukumu (hasa ya meli ya shehena). **underwriter**, *n.* mwenye kukubali jukumu (hasa ya meli ya shehena).

undeserved, *a.* -siostahili, -sio haki.

undesirable, *a.* -siotakiwa, -siofaa, -baya.

undeveloped, *a.* -viza, -liovia, -lio dumaa, -siositawi, -siokua vema, -siokomaa, -changa.

undid, *p.t.* ya *undo*.

undignified, *a.* -sio adabu, -siofaa, -sio heshima.

undisciplined, *a.* -sioamrishwa vizuri, -siozoezwa kutii amri, -a ovyo.

undisguised, *a.* -siofichwa, -siofunikwa, -siogeuzwa, wazi, dhahiri, bayana.

undivided, *a.* -siogawanyika, -moja, -zima, -ote.

undo, *v.t.* (*p.t.* **undid**, *pf.t.* **undone**) tangua, fundua, funua, fungua, feleti; (*a bundle &c.*) futua; (*stitches*) fumua, shonoa; (*plaits of hair*) funguza; (*ruin*) angamiza, poteza, haribu.

undoubted, *a.* -a hakika, halisi, bila shaka. **undoubtedly**, *adv.* pasipo shaka, hapana budi.

undress, *v.t.* vua (vulia) nguo, vusha nguo; — *v.i.* vua, vulia. **undressed**, *a.* (*naked*) bila nguo, uchi, -tupu; (*in night attire*) -liovaa nguo za kulalia; (*of leather &c.*) -siotengenezwa.

undue, *a.* -a kadiri isiyofaa, si kadiri. **unduly**, *adv.* mno, si sawa, si kwa haki.

undulate, *v.i.* -wa na miinuko na mabonde, -wa na umbo kama mawimbi, inuka na kushuka. **undulation**, *n.* mwendo wa wimbi, hali ya kuinuka na kushuka kama mawimbi, vilima na mabonde; (*rising ground*) kiduta, kilima, mwinuko. **undulatory, undulating**, *a.* -a kuinuka na kushuka, -enye vilima na mabonde.

unduly, *adv.* taz. *undue*.

undying, *a.* -siokufa, -sioisha, -a aushi, -a milele.

unearth, *v.t.* fukua, funua, vumbua, gundua. **unearthly**, *a.* si -a dunia hii, -a peponi, -a shetani, -zuri sana, -baya sana.

uneasiness, *n.* taz. *uneasy*.

uneasy, *a.* si -a raha, si -tulivu, -tukutu, -a mashaka, -enye fadhaa, -a wasiwasi. **uneasiness**, *n.* mashaka, wasiwasi, fadhaa, hangaiko, utukutu, udhia, machugachuga, mang'amung'amu, mang'ang'amu.

uneatable, *a.* -siolika, -siofaa kwa chakula.

unedifying, *a.* -siofaa (kwa kuwa ya aibu, ya kupotosha *&c.*).

uneducated, *a.* -siofundishwa, -sio na elimu, -sioelimishwa, -jinga.

unemployed, *a.* -sio na kazi, -sioajiriwa. — *n.* jamii ya watu wasio na kazi.

unending, *a.* -sioisha, -a kuendelea bila kikomo.

unenlightened, *a.* -siofundishwa, -siojulishwa, -siostaarabishwa, -jinga, -a gizani, -shenzi.

unenterprising, *a.* si -jasiri, -a moyo mchache, baridi, -oga.

unequal, *a.* si sawa, -siolingana, -a kuhitilafiana; (*to*) -sioweza. **unequalled**, *a.* -sio na kifani.

unerring, *a.* -siokosa, -a hakika.

unessential, *a.* si -a lazima, si kanuni, si -a maana sana.

uneven, *a.* si sawa.

uneventful, *a.* bila jambo la maana sana, -a vivi hivi.

unexampled, *a.* -sio na kifani, -a peke yake.

unexceptionable, *a.* -zuri, -eupe, safi, -sio na lawama, kamili.

unexpected, *a.* -a ghafula, -siotazamiwa. **unexpectedly**, *adv.* ghafula.

unfading, *a.* -siofifia, -sioharibika, -siopooza, -siosahaulika.

unfailing, *a.* -a daima, -siokwisha.

unfair, *a.* si sawa, si -a haki, si -adilifu, -a hila, -danganyifu.

unfaithful, *a.* si amini, si -aminifu; (*adulterous*) -zinifu, -zinzi; (*untrue*) si -a kweli, -a uwongo.

unfaltering, *a.* imara, thabiti, madhubuti, -siosita.

unfashionable, *a.* si -a namna ya siku hizi, -a zamani.

unfasten, *v.t.* fungua, komoa, fundua, gandua.

unfathomable, *a.* -siofikika chini, -a kwenda chini sana; (*inexplicable*) -siofahamika, -siotambulikana, -gumu sana, -a fumbo.

unfavourable, *a.* -siofaa.

unfeeling, *a.* -sio na huruma, -a moyo mgumu.

unfeigned, *a.* -a kweli, halisi.

unfetter, *v.t.* fungua (pingu).

unfinished, *a.* -siokwisha, si kamili, -siomalizwa.

unfit, *a.* -siofaa, dhaifu, -baya. — *v.t.* fanya *unfit*, dhoofisha, ondolea nguvu (uwezo *&c.*).

unfix, *v.t.* fungua, legeza, toa, bandua.

unflagging, *a.* -siochoka, -a bidii nyingi, -a juhudi.

unflinching, *a.* -siosita, -siolegea, -siokimbia, -sioshindwa, thabiti, imara, -gumu.

unfold, *v.t.* kunjua, funua, nyosha, tandua; (*reveal*) funua, eleza, fahamisha, simulia, hadithia.

unforeseen, *a.* -siotazamiwa, -a ghafula, -siofikiriwa.

unforgiving, *a.* -siosamehe, -siohurumia, -gumu.

unformed, *a.* -changa, -siokomaa, -bichi, -sio kamili.

unfortunate, *a.* -a bahati mbaya, -a msiba, -a shari, maskini.

unfounded, *a.* -siothibitishwa, -sio na msingi.

unfrequented, *a.* pasipopita watu wengi, -kiwa.

unfriendly, *a.* -a adui, si -a rafiki, -kali.

unfrock, *v.t.* ondolea cheo cha upadre (ukasisi).

unfruitful, *a.* -siozaa sana, -a bure; (*barren*) -siozaa, tasa, -gumba.

unfurl, *v.t.* fungua, kunjua; (*of sail, flag &c.*) tweka; — *v.i.* funguka, kunjuka.

unfurnished, *a.* (*house, apartments*) -tupu, -siopambwa, -sio na vyombo.

ungainly, *a.* si -zuri, -zito.

ungarbled, *a.* -siogeuzwa, -a kweli, -nyofu, -a hakika.

ungenerous, *a.* si -karimu, -nyimivu, si -nyofu.

ungodly, *a.* si -cha Mungu, -ovu, -baya.

ungraceful, *a.* si -zuri, si -a madaha, -zito.

ungracious, *a.* si -ema, si -zuri, si -a adabu, si jamala, -gumu, -chungu.

ungrateful, *a.* -sio na shukrani.

ungrounded, *a.* bila kisa (sababu, hoja), -siothibitishwa.

unguarded, *a.* -siolindwa, bila hadhari. *In an unguarded moment,* bila kufikiri, ghafula. **unguardedly**, *adv.* kwa ujinga.

unguent, *n.* mafuta (ya dawa).

unhallowed, *a.* -ovu, -baya, -a shetani, -najisi.

unhappy, *a.* -a huzuni, -a majonzi, -a msiba, -a moyo mzito. **unhappiness**, *n.* huzuni, majonzi, uzito, uchungu.

unharness, *v.t.* tandua, fungulia.

unhealthy, *a.* -sio na afya, dhaifu, -a kuleta ugonjwa.

unheeded, *a.* -siosikilizwa, -sioangaliwa, -siofuatwa, -a kudharauliwa. **unheedful**, *a.* -zembe, -siyeangalia, -siyejali.

unhesitatingly, *adv.* bila kusita, mara hiyo, papo hapo.

unhinge, *v.t.* ondoa mahali pake; (*cause madness*) rusha akili, tia wazimu.

unholy, *a.* -ovu, -a shetani, -chafu, -najisi.

unhook, *v.t.* fungua, toa katika ndoana, tungua.

unhorse, *v.t.* rusha (angusha) juu ya farasi.

unhurt, *a.* bila kuumia, bila kuumizwa, bila kupata madhara, -siodhurika, -sioharibika, -zima.

unicorn, *n.* mnyama (wa hadithi) kama farasi mwenye pembe moja.

unification, *n.* taz. *unify.*

uniform, *a.* -a mfano mmoja, sawasawa, -a kulingana. — *n.* kivao cha askari, mapolisi *&c.*, nguo za rasmi. **uniformity**, *n.* kuwa sawa, kuwa mfano mmoja, umoja, ulinganifu.

unify, *v.t.* fanya kuwa -moja, fanya kuwa mfano mmoja, sawazisha. **unification**, *n.* kufanya (kufanyika) -moja, kuungamanisha.

unilateral, *a.* -a kuhusu (kupasa, kujuzu) upande (baadhi, mtu, taifa) mmoja tu.

unimpaired, *a.* -sioharibika, -siodhurika, -zima, kamili.

unimpeachable, *a.* -eupe, safi, -sio na shaka, -siolaumika.

unimportant, *a.* -sio na maana sana, hafifu, -dogo.

uninhabitable, *a.* -sioweza kukaa watu, -sipokalika na watu. **uninhabited**, *a.* -sipokaa watu, -kiwa.

uninitiated, *a.* -siofundishwa, -sioingizwa (katika chama, madhehebu *&c.*).

unintelligible, *a.* -sio na maana, -siotambulikana, -a fumbo.

unintentional, *a.* si -a kusudi, si makusudi, -siokusudiwa.

uninterrupted, *a.* -a mfululizo, -a mfulizo -a kufululiza, -a moja kwa moja, bila kuzuiwa.

union, *n.* umoja, kuwa -moja, kufungamana; fungamano, mwungano; (*concord*) urafiki, hali moja, shauri moja; (*society*) jamii, chama. *Union Jack*, bendera ya Waingereza wote.

unique, *a.* -a namna ya peke yake, -sio na kifani.

unison, *n.* kuimba sauti moja, kuimba wote sawasawa, sauti moja.

unit, *n.* kitu kimoja, jamii ya vitu au watu (inayofikiriwa kama kwamba ni kitu kimoja), kitu kinachotumika kupimia, *e.g.* yadi ni *unit* ya kupimia urefu.

Unitarian, *n.* taz. *unite.*

unite, *v.t.* unga, unganisha, ungamanisha; — *v.i.* ungana, ungamana, unganika, -wa shauri moja, patana. *United States*, nchi ya Amerika. **Unitarian**, *n.* mtu aaminiye ya kuwa Mungu ni mmoja, hamna nafsi tatu. **united**, *a.* -liounganа, -liounganishwa, -a umoja, -enye shauri moja. **unity**, *n.* umoja, kuwa -moja, kupatana, upendano, ulinganifu, upatanifu.

universal, *a.* taz. *universe.*

universe, *n.* ulimwengu, vitu vyote. **universal**, *a.* -a watu wote, a-kuenea pote, -a wakati wote, -a mahali pote, -a kazi zote. **university**, *n.* chuo cha elimu kubwa na walimu wakubwa wanaofundisha humo.

unjust, *a.* -sio na haki, -dhalimu, -onevu. **unjustly**, *adv.* bila haki, kwa udhalimu, kwa jeuri. **unjustifiable**, *a.* bila sababu ya haki (kisa, hoja).

unkempt, *a.* -liochafuka, -liotimka, -a matimutimu.

unkind, unkindly, *a.* si -enye huruma, si -a upole, -a uadui, si -ema, -kali. **unkindness**, *n.* ukali.

unknit, *v.t.* fumua, fungua.

unknot, *v.t.* fundua, fungua.

unknown, *a.* -siojulika, -siojulikana, -siobainika, -siotambulikana. **unknowingly**, *adv.* bila kuwa na habari, bila kujua, si makusudi, kwa ujinga.

unlace, *v.t.* fumua, fungua.

unlade, *v.t.* shusha (toa, telemsha) shehena, pakua shehena.

unlatch, *v.t.* fungua, komoa.

unlawful, *a.* -liokatazwa na sheria, -sio sheria, -liogombezwa na sheria, haramu.

unlearned, *a.* -sioelimishwa, -siofundishwa, -sio na elimu (maarifa), -jinga.

unleavened, *a.* -siotiwa chachu (hamira).

unless, *conj.* ila, isipokuwa.

unlicensed, *a.* bila ruhusa (cheti, hati).

unlike, *a.* si sawa, mbalimbali, -siofanana, -naoachana, -siopatana, -a kuhitilafiana, -enye tofauti. **unlikelihood**, *n.* kuwa *unlikely*. **unlikely**, *a.* -sioonekana kuwa kweli, kama si yamkini. *It is unlikely*, naona sivyo.

unlimber, *v.t.* weka mzinga tayari kupiga.

unlimited, *a.* pasipo kiasi, -ingi mno, -siozuiwa, -sio na mpaka.

unload, *v.t.* shusha, tua, ondolea mzigo, pakua shehena.

unlock, *v.t.* fungua.

unlooked-for, *a.* -siotazamiwa.

unloose, *v.t.* fungua.

unloved, *a.* -siopendwa. **unlovely**, *a.* si -zuri, si -a kupendeza, -baya, -a kuchukiza.

unluckily, *adv.* taz. *unlucky.*

unlucky, *a.* -a bahati, -a kisirani, -a ndege mbaya, -a shari. **unluckily**, *adv.* kwa bahati mbaya.

unmake, *v.t.* haribu umbo la, umbua.

unman, *v.t.* legeza moyo, fadhaisha, tisha.

unmanageable, *a.* -sioweza kuongozwa, -sioweza kuzuiwa.

unmannerliness, *n.* taz. *unmannerly.*

unmannerly, *a.* si -a adabu, -fidhuli, -safihi. **unmannerliness**, *n.* ufidhuli, usafihi.

unmarried, *a.* (*of man*) -siooa, -jane, kapera -seja; (*woman*) -sioolewa, -jane.

unmask, *v.t.* funua, ondolea kificho, toa wazi, dhihirisha.

unmeaning, *a.* -puzi, -sio na maana.

unmeant, *a.* -siokusudiwa, -a bahati, -a nasibu.

unmeet, *a.* -siofaa, si wajibu.

unmentionable, *a.* -siofaa kutajwa.

unmerciful, *a.* -sio na huruma, -kali, -korofi, katili.

unmethodical, *a.* -sio na taratibu, -a ovyo, -a fujo, -liochafuka, -liofujika.

unmindful, *a.* -siokumbuka, -sahaulifu, -zembe, -siozingatia, -siojali, -sioangalia.

unmistakable, *a.* dhahiri, wazi, bayana sana.

unmitigated, *a.* sana, kabisa.

unmixed, *a.* -tupu, safi, -sioghoshiwa.

unmolested, *a.* bila kusumbuliwa, -a raha.

unmoor, *v.t.* fungua amari, fungua.

unnatural, *a.* si -a asili, si -a kawaida ya asili, -baya sana, -potovu, -potoe, -liopotoka.

unnecessary, *a.* si kanuni, -siohitajika, -a bure.

unnerve, *v.t.* ogofya, tisha, fadhaisha, shtusha, legeza moyo.

unnoticed, *a.* bila kuonwa, -sioonwa, -siosikiwa, -sioangaliwa; (*unmentioned*) -siotajwa, -sionenwa.

unobtainable, *a.* -siopatikana, ghaibu, -lioadimika, adimu.

unobtrusive, *a.* -nyenyekevu, -enye haya, -siyejitanguliza.
unoccupied, *a.* (*house*) -siyo na mkaaji; (*person*) -siye na kazi, -enye faragha.
unorganized, *a.* -siotengenezwa, si -a taratibu.
unpack, *v.t.* fungua mizigo (vyombo).
unpalatable, *a.* -a kuchukiza, chapwa, -chungu.
unparalleled, *a.* -sio na kifani, -a peke yake.
unpardonable, *a.* -siosameheka, -baya sana.
unperturbed, *a.* -tulivu, -sioshtuka.
unpick, *v.t.* fumua, shonoa.
unpleasant, *a.* -baya, -siopendeza, chapwa, -a kuchukiza, -sumbufu. **unpleasantness**, *n.* ubaya, machukizo; (*quarrel*) ugomvi.
unpolluted, *a.* safi.
unpopular, *a.* -siopendwa (na wengi).
unpractical, *a.* si -a amali, si -tendaji.
unprecedented, *a.* -sio na kifani, -a peke yake.
unprejudiced, *a.* -siopendelea, adili, -adilifu, sawa, -a haki.
unpremeditated, *a.* -siotengenezwa tayari, -siofikiriwa (kabla ya kutenda).
unprepared, *a.* si tayari, -siotengenezwa tayari.
unprincipled, *a.* -potovu, -a tabia mbaya.
unproductive, *a.* -siozaa, -sioleta faida, -a bure.
unprofitable, *a.* -sioleta faida, -a kuleta hasara, -a bure.
unpropitious, *a.* ndege mbaya, -a kisirani, -a shari, -a bahati mbaya.
unprotected, *a.* -siolindwa, -siohifadhiwa.
unqualified, *a.* -sioweza, -siostahili, -sio na hati (idhini, ruhusa); (*not modified*) thabiti, halisi; (*downright*) kabisa, sana.
unquenchable, *a.* -siozimika, -siotulizika.
unquestionable, *a.* pasipo shaka, hakika, halisi, kanuni, -siokanikana, -sioweza kukanushwa.
unquiet, *a.* -si tulivu, -tukutu, -a msukosuko.
unravel, *v.t.* fungua, fumua, tatanua; (*explain*) fafanua, eleza, fumbua.
unready, *a.* si tayari; (*slow &c.*) -zito, si -elekvu.
unreal, *a.* si -a hakika, kama ndoto, kama njozi, kama kivuli. **unreality**, *n.* kuwa *unreal*.
unreasonable, *a.* si kwa akili, -pumbavu, muhali.
unrecognizable, *a.* siyotambulikana.
unregenerate, *a.* -sioongoka, -siozaliwa mara ya pili kwa *baptism*.
unrelenting, *a.* -siotubu, -sioachilia, sio na huruma, -siohurumia, -kali, -gumu sana.
unreliable, *a.* si amini, si -aminifu, -zembe, -janja, si yakini, si thabiti, -sioweza kutumainiwa.
unremitting, *a.* -siolegea, -siochoka, -enye bidii (juhudi, jitihadi), -a kufululiza, -a kufuliza, -a kudumu, -a kushikilia, -a kuendelea.
unremunerative, *a.* -sioleta faida, -a bure.
unrepentant, *a.* -siotubu, -siojuta, -siosikitika, -gumu, -shupavu.
unreserved, *a.* wazi, -kunjufu; (*free from reservations*) bila sharti; (*not allotted*) -siowekwa (mtu, kazi *&c.*), -sioandikiwa (mtu, kazi *&c.*). **unreservedly**, *adv.* bila sharti.
unrest, *n.* wasiwasi, hangaiko, msukosuko.
unrestrained, *a.* -siozuiwa.
unrestricted, *a.* -siozuiwa, bila kizuizi, -sio na mpaka, -sio na sharti, -siofungwa.
unrighteous, *a.* -baya, -ovu, dhalimu, -a dhambi, si -a haki. **unrighteousness**, *n.* ubaya, uovu, udhalimu, dhambi.
unripe, *a.* -bichi, -changa. **unripeness**, *n.* ubichi, uchanga.
unrivalled, *a.* -siopitika, -sio na kifani, bora peke yake, -a kupita -ote, -a kushinda -ote.
unrobe, *v.t. and i.* vua (vulia) nguo.
unroll, *v.t.* fumua, kunjua, zingua.
unruffled, *a.* -tulivu, -a shwari, -a raha.

unruly, *a.* -kaidi, -tundu, -tukutu, -asi.
unsaddle, *v.t.* tandua, ondoa matandiko (ya farasi &c.)
unsafe, *a.* si salama, -a hatari.
unsaleable, *a.* -siouzika, -siouzanya, -siopata mnunuzi.
unsatisfactory, *a.* -sioridhisha, -siofaa.
unsavoury, *a.* -a kuchukiza, -siopendeza; (*of food*) chapwa, -siokolea, si -tamu, -sio na ladha.
unsay, *v.t.* (*p.t. and pf.t.* **unsaid**) geuza maneno, rudisha maneno.
unscathed, *a.* -siodhurika, -sioumizwa, salama, -zima.
unscrew, *v.t.* toa parafujo (msumari wa hesi, skrubu), kongoa.
unscrupulous, *a.* -baya, si -nyofu, potoe, -a tabia mbaya.
unseal, *v.t.* vunja muhuri ya, fungua, funua.
unsearchable, *a.* -siotafutikana, -siovumbulika, -a siri, -a fumbo.
unseasonable, *a.* -a wakati usiofaa, si wakati wake.
unseat, *v.t.* ondosha katika mahali pake, rusha juu ya farasi.
unseaworthy, *a.* (meli, chombo) -bovu, -siofaa kusafiri baharini.
unseemly, *a.* -siofaa, si -a adabu, si -zuri, -baya, -chafu.
unseen, *a.* -sioonekana.
unselfish, *a.* -a kufikiri wengine kuliko mwenyewe, -a hisani, -a kupendelea wengine kuliko mwenyewe.
unserviceable, *a.* -siotumikana, -liochakaa, -bovu.
unsettle, *v.t.* taharakisha, tia wasiwasi, fadhaisha, sumbua, hangaisha. **unsettled,** *a.* -a wasiwasi, -a kuhangaika, -tukutu, pasipo kituo, -geugeu, -geuzi.
unshaken, *a.* thabiti, imara, -siotikisika.
unsheathe, *v.t.* chomoa, futa, vuta, toa.
unship, *v.t.* shusha chomboni, ondosha katika mahali pake.
unsightly, *a.* -siopendeza macho, -a kuchukiza, -baya.
unskilful, *a.* si- -bingwa, si -stadi, si -elekevu, -zito, si hodari, -siojua kazi. **unskilfulness,** *n.* uzito, ujinga, utovu wa ustadi (ufundi, ubingwa).
unslaked, *a.* (*lime*) -siotiwa maji; (*thirst &c.*) -siozimwa, -siotulizwa, -sioridhika.
unsociable, *a.* -siopenda mazungumzo na watu; (*person*) mkaa peke yake, mkataa urafiki.
unsolicited, *a.* -sioombwa.
unsophisticated, *a.* -sioharibika, -zima, halisi.
unsought, *a.* -siotafutwa, -sioombwa.
unsound, *a.* si -zima, si amini, -pungufu, -baya, -bovu.
unsparing, *a.* (*generous*) -karimu, -paji; (*cruel*) -katili, -sio na huruma, -sioachilia, -kali, -gumu.
unspeakable, *a.* -sionenekana, -sioelezeka; (*in good sense*) -a kipeo, bora, -zuri kabisa; (*in bad sense*) -baya sana, -a kuchukiza.
unspecified, *a.* -siotajwa, -siosemwa.
unspotted, *a.* pasipo mawaa, -eupe, safi.
unstable, *a.* si thabiti, si imara, -geugeu, -geuzi, -a kusitasita, goigoi, -a kutetereka, -a kutitia.
unstained, *a.* pasipo mawaa, -eupe, safi.
unsteady, *a.* si thabiti, si mara, -geuzi, -geugeu, -a kusitasita, -a kutikisika, -a kutetereka, -a kutitia.
unstinted, *a.* -ingi.
unstop, *v.t.* zibua, ondoa kizuizi (kizibo).
unstrung, *a.* (*mentally*) -a wasiwasi.
unstudied, *a.* -sio makusudi, -siokusudiwa, -a ujinga, -a asili.
unsubstantial, *a.* -epesi, -embamba; si hakika, kama ndoto, kama kivuli, hafifu, ovyo. **unsubstantiated,** *a.* -siothibitika.
unsuccessful, *a.* -siofanikiwa, -siositawi, -siofaulu, si -a heri.
unsuitable, *a.* -siofaa.
unsullied, *a.* pasipo mawaa, safi, -eupe.
unswerving, *a.* thabiti, imara, -siosita.

unsymmetrical, *a.* -siolingana, si -linganifu.
untamed, *a.* -siofugwa, -siozuiwa, -kali.
untenable, *a.* -siothibitika, -sioshikika.
unthatch, *v.t.* ezua, vimbua, ondoa makuti (nyasi, majani) ya paa.
unthinking, *a.* -a haraka, -zembe, -siofikiri, -sioangalia, -pumbavu, -ovyo.
untidy, *a.* -siotengenea, si taratibu, -koo, ovyo, -liochafuka, -liofujika.
untie, *v.t.* fungua, fundua.
until, *con. and prep.* hata, mpaka, hadi.
untimely, *a.* -a wakati usiofaa, si wakati wake.
untiring, *a.* -siochoka, -siolegea, -enye bidii (juhudi, jitihadi).
unto, *prep.* = *to*, kwenda kwa, hata, mpaka, hadi.
untold, *a.* siosimuliwa, -siohadithiwa, -siofunuliwa; (*beyond counting*) -ingi sana hata haihesabiki.
untouchable, *a.* -siogusika. — *n.* mtu wa jamii ya Wahindi wa cheo cha chini sana hata wa vyeo vya juu wakimgusa huhesabiwa kuwa na najisi.
untoward, *a.* (*perverse*) -kaidi, -potoe; (*unfortunate*) -siofaa, -sumbufu.
untraceable, *a.* -siopatikana, -sioonekana.
untrained, *a.* -siofundishwa, -jinga; (*of animals*) -siofugwa.
untrammelled, *a.* -siozuiwa, -siopingwa, -a huru.
untrue, *a.* si kweli, si hakika, -a uwongo, -mbea. **untruth**, *n.* uwongo. **untruthful**, *a.* -a kusema uwongo, si amini.
unturned, *a.* *Leave no stone unturned*, jaribia njia zote.
untwine, **untwist**, *v.t.* fumua, tatanua, sokotoa.
unusual, *a.* si -a kawaida, si -a desturi, si -a sikuzote, -a kigeni, -geni.
unutterable, *a.* -sionenekana, -sioelezeka; (*bad*) -baya kabisa.
unvarnished, *a.* -siopakwa *varnish*; (*plain, simple*) -sioongezewa, -a kweli tupu, -siotiwa chuku.
unvarying, *a.* -siobadilika, sawasawa sikuzote, -a kudumu, -a kuendelea vivyo hivyo.
unveil, *v.t.* funua.
unwarily, *adv.* taz. *unwary*.
unwarrantable, *a.* si -enye sababu (kisa, hoja), si -a akili, si -a haki.
unwary, *a.* si -enye hadhari, -jinga, -zembe. **unwarily**, *adv.* bila hadhari kwa uzembe.
unwavering, *a.* bila kusita, thabiti, imara, madhubuti.
unwearied, *a.* si -legevu, -siochoka, -a kudumu, -enye bidii (juhudi).
unwelcome, *a.* -siopendeza, -siotakiwa, -baya.
unwell, *a.* -gonjwa. *I am unwell*, siwezi.
unwholesome, *a.* -a kudhuru afya, -a kuleta ugonjwa, -sio na afya, -baya.
unwieldy, *a.* -kubwa -zito.
unwilling, *a.* -siotaka, -siopenda, si -epesi, -kokotevu, -a kujikalifu, -a kujishurutisha.
unwind, *v.t.* (*p.t. and pf.t.* **unwound**) fumua, fungua, sokotoa, zongoa.
unwise, *a.* si -a akili, si -a busara, si -a maarifa, -pumbavu.
unwitting, *a.* pasipo kujua, -siokusudiwa, si -a kusudi. **unwittingly**, *adv.* bila kujua, bila kukusudia, kwa ujinga.
unwonted, *a.* -a desturi, si -a kawaida, si -a mazoea, -a kigeni, -geni.
unworthy, *a.* -siostahili, -siofaa.
unwound, *p.t. and pf.t.* ya *unwind*.
unwritten, *a.* -sioandikwa, -a kufahamika kwa akili tu, -a desturi (si sheria).
unyoke, *v.t.* fungulia.
up, *adv.* juu; (*increased*) zaidi; (*equal*) sawa; (*wholly*) pia; (*aside*) mbali. *Be up*, (*awake*) amka; (*on horseback*) panda farasi; (*erect*) simama; (*of liquids*) toa povu. *It is all up with ...* -meangamia, -mekwisha. *Time is up*, saa imekwisha. *Be up in*, jua

sana. *Be up to, (work)* faa kwa; *(time)* wahi; *(tricks)* si shindwa. *Blow up,* vunja (pasua) kwa baruti; *(rebuke)* kemea sana, karipia. *Come up with,* patia, fikia. *Cut up,* kata-kata. *Draw up, (write)* andika; *(stop)* tua, simama. *Eat up,* -la -ote. *Grow up,* kua, pevuka, komaa. *Give up,* toa, acha, shindwa. *Ups and downs,* mageuzi ya hali, heri na shari, mapinduzi. *What is up?* kuna nini? *Go up, (ascend)* panda; *(increase)* zidi, panda, kwea. *Lay up,* weka akiba. *Knock up,* chosha sana, legeza nguvu, tia ugonjwa. *Get up, (learn)* jifunza; *(rise)* ondoka. *Up in arms,* -enye hasira, hamaki, panda hamaki, tayari kupigana. — *prep.* juu ya. *Up a tree (in difficulties)* katika mashaka. *Up to the eyes,* pia, kabisa. *Be up to the eyes in,* jaa, songwa na. *Up to the mark,* -zima, tayari. *Up to anything,* hodari sana, -jasiri, -gumu. *Go up to the country,* enda bara, enda safari, enda nchi za juu. *Go up a river,* kata maji, pita mtoni.

upbraid, *v.t.* karipia, kemea, laumu, shutumu.

up-country, *n.* bara (mbali na pwani). *Go up-country,* enda (panda) bara.

upheaval, *n.* mapinduzi, mageuzi, mabadiliko.

uphill, *a.* -a shida, -gumu, -zito, -a taabu; *(sloping)* -a kupanda.

uphold, *v.t.* (*p.t. and pf.t.* **upheld**) tegemeza, imarisha, zuia; *(morally)* tetea, shindania, saidia; *(confirm)* thibitisha.

upholster, *v.t.* pamba nyumba (kwa zulia, vyombo *&c.*); *(a chair &c.)* tia matakia, funika kwa nguo (ngozi *&c.*). **upholsterer,** *n.* mwuza zulia, matakia, vyombo vya nyumba *&c.*; mtengenezaji wa viti *&c.* **upholstery,** *n.* pambo la nyumba (zulia, matakia, vyombo *&c.*).

upkeep, *n.* gharama, matumizi, haraja.

upland, *n.* nchi iliyoinuka, vilima.

uplift, *v.t.* inua, pandisha, kweza; *(spirits)* changamsha, burudisha.

upon, *prep.* juu ya = *on.*

upper, *a.* -a juu, bora. *The upper classes,* waungwana, matajiri. *Get the upper hand,* shinda, weza, pata amri juu ya, shinda nguvu. — *n.* sehemu ya juu ya kiatu. *Be down on one's uppers,* dhikika, -wa maskini, fukarika. **uppermost,** *a.* -a juu kabisa, bora. **uppish,** *a.* -juvi, -fidhuli, -safihi, -kavu wa macho, -shupavu.

upright, *a.* -a kusimama wima, -a kiwimawima; *(honest)* -a haki, amini, -aminifu, -nyofu, adili, -adilifu. — *n.* mhimili, mwimo, nguzo. **uprightness,** *n.* unyofu, uaminifu.

uprising, *n.* kuondoka (kuamka) kitandani; *(revolt)* maasi, uhalifu, machafuko.

uproar, *n.* makelele, fujo, zahama, ghasia, msukosuko, mchafuko. **uproarious,** *a.* -a makelele (fujo, zahama, ghasia *&c.*).

uproot, *v.t.* ng'oa, ondosha pia, haribu kabisa.

upset, *v.t.* (*p.t. and pf.t.* **upset**) pindua, pindukiza; *(defeat)* shinda; *(disturb)* tia wasiwasi, hangaisha, fadhaisha; *(health)* chafua. — *n.* machafuko, fujo, matata.

upshot, *n.* mwisho, matokeo.

upside, *n.* upande wa juu. *Turn upside-down,* pindua, fudikiza, chafua, fuja, vuruga. *Upside-down,* juu chini, fudifudi, shelabela.

upstart, *n.* mtu aliyetajirika (aliyepata cheo kikubwa) ghafula; *(insolent person)* mfidhuli, msafihi.

upstream, *adv.* kwa kukata maji.

up-to-date, *a.* -a siku zizi hizi, -pya.

upward, *a.* -a kwenda juu, -a kuelekea juu; *(aspiring)* -a kutaka mema. **upwards,** *adv.* juu. *Upwards of,* zaidi ya.

urban, *a.* -a mji, -a mjini, -a biladia. **urbane,** *a.* -a adabu sana, -enye malezi mazuri, -a makini, -a madaha. **urbanity,** *n.* adabu, utu mwema, makini, madaha.

urchin, *n.* mtoto (mwanamume) mtundu, mhuni.

urethra, *n.* mshipa wa kupitia mkojo.
urge, *v.t.* sihi sana, ombaomba, chagiza, shurutisha, nyenya, sisitiza; (*press forward*) endesha mbele, sukuma, sukumiza. **urgency**, *n.* bidii, lazima, jambo muhimu. **urgent**, *a.* -a lazima, muhimu, -a maana, -a juhudi, -a haraka.
urine, *n.* mkojo. **urinal**, *n.* pa kukojolea, pa kutabawali. **urinary**, *a.* -a mkojo. **urinate**, *v.i.* kojoa, tabawali.
urn, *n.* chombo kirefu cha udongo au bati, cha kutilia maji, chai, kahawa *&c.*
us, *pron.* sisi; (*in comp.*) -tu-.
use, *v.t.* tumia; (*treat*) tendea. *Use up*, maliza, isha -ote, poteza, tumilia mbali. *It is used up*, imetumikana, imekwisha. *Used to work*, -zoevu (zoelevu) -a kazi. — *n.* matumizi, utumi, tumio, utumishi, kazi; (*advantage*) faida, manufaa; (*custom*) mazoea, desturi, kawaida, ada; (*need*) uhitaji. *Make use of*, tumia, tuma. *Be of use*, faa, -wa na manufaa. *Lose the use of* (*limb &c.*), potewa na nguvu ya. **used**, *a* (*be*) zoea, zoelea. *I used to go*, nilizoea kwenda, ilikuwa desturi yangu kwenda, huenda. *It used to be so*, ilikuwa hivyo zamani. *I am used to him*, nina mazoea naye, ni mzoevu naye. **useful**, *a.* -a kufaa, -a manufaa, -a kutumika. *Useful things*, vifaa, mafao. **usefulness**, *n.* kuwa *useful*, utumizi, ufao, ufanisi, mafaa. **useless**, *a.* -siofaa, -sio na kazi, -bovu, -a bure. **uselessness**, *n.* kuwa *useless*, ufefe. **user**, *n.* atumiaye. **usual**, *a.* -a desturi, -a kawaida, -a kutumikana. **usually**, *adv.* desturi, kwa kawaida, aghalabu. *In verbs*, hu-, *e.g. he usually comes*, huja.
usher, *n.* bawabu; (*under-master*) mwalimu mdogo.
usual, *a.*, **usually**, *adv.* taz. *use.*
usufruct, *n.* haki ya kutumia shamba *&c.* la mwingine, kwa sharti kutokuliharibu.
usurer, *n.* **usurious**, *a.* taz. *usury.*
usurp, *v.t.* jitwalia bila haki, nyang'anya (usultani, ufalme, nguvu *&c.*). **usurpation**, *n.* kunyang'anya, unyang'anyi. **usurper**, *n.* mnyang'anyi ufalme (usultani *&c.*).
usury, *n.* riba. **usurer**, *n.* mla riba. **usurious**, *a.* -a riba, -a kula riba.
utensil, *n.* chombo, ala, samani.
uterus, *n.* mji wa mimba. **uterine**, *a.* -a mama mmoja (baba mbalimbali).
utility, *n.* kufaa, faida, matumizi, manufaa, mafaa. **utilitarian**, *a.* -a kutafuta faida, -a kufaa, -enye manufaa. **utilize**, *v.t.* tumia, chumia, tumia kuleta faida, faidia.
utmost, *a.* -a kwisha, -a mbali sana, -a juu sana; (*entire, whole*) kabisa, halisi, hasa. *Utmost limit*, kipeo, upeo, kikomo, mpaka, ncha, pembe. *To the utmost*, mpaka (hata, hadi) mwisho, iwezavyo, sana.
Utopia, *n.* kipeo cha hali nzuri ya serikali na watu (cha kuwazika tu). **Utopian**, *a.* bora mno, -a heri mno, -a ndoto, -a ukamilifu wa kuwazika tu.
utter, (1) *a.* kabisa, pia, halisi, -tupu. **utterly**, *adv.* kabisa, pia. **uttermost**, *a.* -a kwisha, taz. *utmost.* *Uttermost part*, pembe, ncha.
utter, (2) *v.t.* toa, eneza, nena, tamka. **utterance**, *n.* usemi, maneno.
utterly, *adv.*, **uttermost**, *a.* taz. *utter* (1).
uvula, *n.* kidakatonge, kimio.
uxorious, *a.* -a kupenda sana mkewe, -enye shauku sana ya mkewe.

V

V. herufi ya Kirumi, maana yake tano.
vacant, *a.* -tupu, pasipo kitu (mtu, kazi, mawazo), -jinga, -a kijinga. **vacancy**, *n.* kuwa -tupu, pasipo kazi; (*leisure*) kujikalia, faragha; (*interval*) nafasi wazi, nafasi kati; (*post unfilled*) patakwapo mtu, (kazi) isiyo na mtu; (*of mind &c.*) ujinga, upumbavu. **vacate**, *v.t.* acha, ondoka katika; (*annul*) tangua, batili, futa. **vacation**, *n.* kuacha, kutangua, kufuta; (*holiday*) muda wa kucheza (wa kupumzika, wa kuachwa kazi), likizo, livu, ruhusa.
vaccine, *n.* dawa ya kuchanjia (hasa ndui). **vaccinate**, *v.t.* chanja ndui. vaccination, *n.* kuchanjia ndui.
vacillate, *v.i.* sitasita, tangatanga, badilibadili, geukageuka, ghairighairi. **vacillation**, *n.* kusitasita &c.
vacuity, *n.* taz. *vacuous.*
vacuous, *a.* -tupu, -jinga, sio na maana, -vivu. **vacuity**, *n.* uwazi, kuwa -tupu, utupu, mahali pasipo na kitu, patupu, nafasi wazi; (*folly*) ujinga. **vacuum**, *n.* mahali pasipo na kitu, hali ya chombo kilichotolewa hewa ya ndani, hali ya kuwa hamna kitu cho chote, uwazi.
vagabond, *n.* asiye na kwao wala kazi ila hutembea ovyo tu, mhuni. **vagabondage**, *n.* hali ya (tabia ya) *vagabond*, uhuni.
vagary, *n.* kinyongo, upumbavu, upuzi, mchezo, mabadili.
agina, *n.* kuma, uke.
vagrant, *n.* = *vagabond.* **vagrancy**, *n.* = *vagabondage.*
vague, *a.* -siofahamika vizuri, -sioelezwa vizuri, -a mashaka, si dhahiri, si hakika, si yakini. **vagueness**, *n.* kuwa *vague.*
vain, *a.* (*useless*) -tupu, -a bure, -siofaa; (*foolish, fanciful*) kama ndoto, -pumbavu; (*ostentatious &c.*) -shaufu, -a nje tu, hafifu; (*conceited*) -a kujiona, -a umalidadi, -a fahari, -kinaifu, -a kujikinai, -a kiburi. **vainglorious**, *a.* -a kujiona, -a kuona makuu, -a kujisifu. **vainglory**, *n.* kiburi, kujiona, kuona makuu, majivuno, majisifu, fahari. **vainly**, *adv.* bure, bila kuweza; (*conceitedly*) kwa kiburi. **vanity**, *n.* (*futility*) ubatili, matupu, upuzi; (*conceit*) kujivuna, majivuno, majisifu, umalidadi, ushaufu, kiburi.
vale, *n.* bonde.
valediction, *n.* kuaga, kusema, 'kwa heri', kuagana; (*final*) buriani. **valedictory**, *a.* -a kuaga, -a kuagana.
valet, *n.* mtumishi (wa kiume), boi (hasa wa kutunza nguo za bwana wake).
valetudinarian, *n.* mgonjwa, mwele.
valiant, valorous, *a.* shujaa, -jasiri, hodari. **valour**, *n.* ushujaa, ujasiri, uhodari.
valid, *a.* -a sheria, thabiti, -a nguvu, -enye sababu, -a akili. **validate**, *v.t.* patanisha na sheria, thibitisha, halalisha. **validity**, *n.* nguvu, uthabiti.
valise, *n.* mfuko, bahasha kubwa, furushi (la kutilia nguo).
valley, *n.* bonde.
valorous, *a.*, **valour**, *n.* taz. *valiant.*
valse, *n.* taz. *waltz.*
valuable, *a.*, **valuation**, *n.* taz. *value.*
value, *n.* thamani, bei, kima, saari, kiasi, kadiri, upataji, uzani. *Set a value on*, thamini &c. taz. *value, v. Be of value*, faa, saidia, auni. — *v.t.* thamini, tia bei, kadirisha, hesabu thamani ya; (*esteem*) thamini, heshimu, ona kuwa -a tunu, tunuka, dhani bora. **valuable**, *a.* -a thamani, -a tunu, bora sana, -a heshima, -a

kufaa, -a kusaidia. **valuation,** *n.* kukadirisha, kuthamini, hesabu ya thamani. **valueless,** *a.* hafifu, -siofaa, ovyo, -a bure.

valve, *n.* kilango; (*of door*) ubao mmoja (upande mmoja) wa mlango; (*shell*) kombe; (*wireless*) chombo kama taa ya umeme kinachotumika kupokea mawimbi ya umeme yenye habari &c. **valvular,** *a.* -enye *valve.*

vamp, *n.* kiraka cha kutengenezea kiatu. — *v.t.* tia kiatu kiraka; (*in music*) fuatisha mwimbaji kwa kupiga kinanda &c. vivi hivi tu.

vampire, *n.* kizuu kinachodhaniwa na wengine kufyonza damu ya watu walalapo usingizi; namna ya popo mfyonza damu.

van, (1) *n.* gari kubwa la mizigo.

van, (2) *n.* (*front*) upande wa mbele, sehemu ya mbele. **vanguard,** *n.* watangulizi (wa jeshi la askari), askari wa mbele.

vandal, *n.* mtu aharibuye vitu vya sanaa kwa ujinga wake, mharabu. **vandalism,** *n.* kuharibu kwa ujinga.

vane, *n.* kipande juu ya mnara cha kuonyesha upepo unakotoka.

vanguard, *n.* taz. *van* (2).

vanilla, *n.* lavani, namna ya kiungo cha vitu vitamu.

vanish, *v.i.* toweka, tokomea, enda zake (zao &c.), fifia; (*be absorbed*) nywewa, liwa; (*end*) isha.

vanity, *n.* taz. *vain.*

vanquish, *v.t.* shinda, piga, tiisha. **vanquisher,** *n.* mshindaji, mshindi.

vantage, *n.* *Point of vantage,* mahali pafaapo (pa kushambulia au kukinga shambulio).

vapid, *a.* chapwa, dufu, -zito, baridi, -siokolea. **vapidity,** *n.* uchapwa, udufu, uzito, ubaridi.

vaporize, *v.* taz. *vapour.*

vapour, *n.* (*as steam*) mvuke; (*smoke*) moshi; (*exhalation*) mvukuto, mfukuto; (*mist*) umande, ukungu. *Vapour bath,* mafusho, mafukizo, buhuri. **vaporize,** *v.t.* fanya mvuke (moshi), fukiza, geuza mvuke; — *v.i.* fanyika (geuka) mvuke (moshi).

variability, *n.*, **variable,** *a.*, **variance,** *n.*, **variant,** *n.*, **variation,** *n.* taz. *vary.*

varicose, *a.* -liovimba (mishipa ya damu). **varicocele,** *n.* kipumbu.

varied, *a.*, **variegated,** *a.*, **variety** *n.*, **various,** *a.* taz. *vary.*

varlet, *n.* mtumishi (mwanamume); mtwana.

varnish, *n.* rangi ya sandarusi. — *v.t.* paka *varnish.*

vary, *v.t.* geuza, badili (badilisha); — *v.i.* geuka, badilika, -wa mbalimbali, -wa pengine hivi pengine hivi. **variability,** *n.* maelekeo ya kubadilibadili, ugeuzi, ubadilifu. **variable,** *a.* -a kugeuka, -a kubadilika, -enye mageuzi, -geugeu. **variance,** *n.* badiliko, tofauti; (*between persons*) ugomvi, fitina, ubishi, mabishano, mzozo. *At variance* (*with*), si sawa (na), -siopatana (na), mbali (na), hitilafiana. **variant,** *n.* namna nyingine (lakini kiini chake ni sawasawa). **variation,** *n.* ugeuzi, kubadilika, badiliko, tofauti. **varied,** *a.* -a namna nyingi, mbalimbali, -ingine -ingine. **variegated,** *a.* -a rangi nyingi mbalimbali, -a rangi rangi, -a namna nyingi mbalimbali. **variety,** *n.* (*difference*) tofauti, kuwa mbalimbali; (*collection*) jamii (ya vitu mbalimbali); (*species*) kitu kinachohitilafiana na vitu vingine vya namna yake, namna; (*many kinds*) namna nyingi. **various,** *a.* mbalimbali, -ingine -ingine, -ingi.

vascular, *a.* -enye mishipa (ya damu &c.), -a mishipa (ya damu, &c.).

vase, *n.* chombo cha kutilia maji, maua ya mapambo &c.

vaseline, *n.* mafuta ya kusingia ngozi &c.

vassal, *n.* raia, mtumwa, mtu.

vast, *a.* -kubwa mno, -ingi mno. **vastly,** *adv.* sana, mno.

vat, *n.* pipa kubwa.

vaticinate, *v.t.* bashiri, agua, tabiri.

vaudeville, *n.* mchezo wa *theatre* wa kuimba, kucheza &c.

vault, (1) *v.i.* ruka. — *n.* ruko, mruko.

vault, (2) *n.* (*roof*), kuba, zege; (*cellar*) chumba kilichofukuliwa chini; (*grave*) kaburi. — *v.t.* fanya kuba (zege) juu ya. **vaulted,** *a.* -enye kuba, kama zege.

vaunt, *v.t.* jivuna, jisifu, jigamba, jibodoa, takabari, faragua, jitanibu. — *n.* majisifu, majivuno, maneno makuu. **vaunter,** *n.* mjisifu, ajivunaye.

V.C., ufupisho wa *Victoria Cross.*

veal, *n.* nyama ya ndama wa ng'ombe.

Veda, *n.* vitabu vitakatifu vya kale vya Wahindi.

vedette, *n.* mlinzi mpanda farasi, mpelelezi.

veer, *v.i.* geuka, badili, zinga; (*tack*) fanya mbisho.

vegetable, *n.* mboga. *Vegetable marrow,* mumunye, mung'unye. *The vegetable kingdom,* jamii ya mimea na miti. **vegetarian,** *n.* mla mboga tu (asiyekula nyama wala samaki ye yote). **vegetate,** *v.i.* ota, mea; (*be idle*) -la na kulala tu, jikalia. **vegetation,** *n.* uoto, oto, kimeacho, yameayo, jamii ya miti, mimea, maua; (*idle life*) maisha ya kula na kulala tu.

vehement, *a.* -kali, -a nguvu, -a juhudi, -a bidii. **vehemence,** *n.* ukali, harara, juhudi, bidii, nguvu.

vehicle, *n.* gari; (*instrument, means*) kitu cha kupelekea (cha kuenezea), njia, chombo. **vehicular,** *a.* -a magari.

veil, *n.* utaji, shela, barakoa; (*covering*) kifuniko. — *v.t.* funika, ficha, setiri. **veiled,** *a.* -enye kuvaa utaji (shela, barakoa); (*concealed*) -liofichwa, -a kindani.

vein, *n.* mshipa wa damu, vena; (*in leaf*) uzi, chelewa; (*in rock*) bamba la jiwe, ufa mwambani, mila; (*kind, quality*) namna, tabia, moyo, maana; (*strain &c.*) dalili, kidogo. *In comic vein,* kwa mzaha, kwa mchezo. **venous,** *a.* -a *vein.*

veldt, *n.* mbuga, tambarare, uwanda.

vellum, *n.* ngozi nyembamba nyeupe ya mnyama iliyotengenezwa kama karatasi ya kuandikia.

velocity, *n.* mwendo, mwendo wa mbio, mbio.

velvet, *n.* mahameli, kiludhu. — *a.* -a mahameli, laini (kama mahameli). **velveteen,** *n.* nguo kama mahameli. **velvety,** *a.* laini (kama mahameli).

venal, *a.* -a kupatikana kwa fedha, -a kufanya vyo vyote kwa fedha, -a kula rushwa.

vend, *v.t.* uza, chuuza, tembeza (ili kuuza). **vendee,** *n.* mnunuzi. **vendor,** *n.* mchuuzi, mtembezi bidhaa, auzaye.

vendetta, *n.* kisasi baina jamaa na jamaa (cha kurithi).

vendor, *n.* taz. *vend.*

veneer, *n.* ubao mwembamba sana wa mti mzuri wa kubandikia ubao usio mzuri; (*show*) uzuri wa nje, urembo. — *v.t.* bandika *veneer.*

venerable, *a.* taz. *venerate.*

venerate, *v.t.* heshimu, tukuza, jali, stahi; (*God*) -cha. **venerable,** *a.* -a heshima, -tukufu, -a kuheshimiwa, -a kustahiwa. **veneration,** *n.* heshima, ustahifu, ustahi, kicho.

venereal, *a.* -a mambo ya uasherati (uzinzi). *Venereal disease,* (*syphilis*) kaswende, sekeneko; (*gonorrhoea*) kisonono.

vengeance, *n.* kisasi. *Take vengeance,* lipiza kisasi, jilipiza. *With a vengeance,* kwa nguvu, bila shaka. **vengeful,** *a.* -a kisasi, -a kutaka kisasi, -kali.

venial, *a.* -a kusameheka, -dogo, -epesi, -a kuachilika.

venison, *n.* nyama ya *deer.*

venom, *n.* sumu (ya nyoka, ya mdudu); (*spite*) ukali, chuki, uchungu. **venomous,** *a.* -a sumu, -kali, -a chuki, -chungu.

venous, *a.* taz. *vein.*

vent, *n.* tundu, kitundu, pa kutokea. *Give vent to,* toa, onyesha. — *v.t.* toa nje, toa wazi. **vent-hole,** *n.* tundu la (bomba la) kutokeza harufu (moshi, mvuke &c.).

ventilate, *v.t.* pisha hewa safi, burudisha hewa; (*spread abroad*) eneza, tangaza, toa nje. **ventilation**, *n.* kupisha hewa safi, kuburudisha hewa, chombo cha kuburudisha hewa; kutangaa, kujulikana sana. **ventilator**, *n.* tundu la (chombo cha) kupitisha au kuburudisha hewa.

ventral, *a.* -a tumbo.

ventricle, *n.* kama kifuko mwilini, hasa cha moyoni.

ventriloquist, *n.* mtu awezaye kutoa sauti, kama kwamba inatoka kwa mwingine mbali kidogo. **ventriloquism**, *n.* kutoa sauti kama kwamba inatoka kwa mtu mwingine mbali kidogo.

venture, *v.t.* thubutu, diriki, tadiriki, jasiri, jipa moyo, jihatirisha, bahatisha; (*risk*) hatirisha. — *n.* bahati, hatari, jambo la bahati (la hatari). **venturesome**, *a.* -jasiri, hodari, -a hatari, -a kubahatisha.

venue, *n.* mahali pa kukutanika.

Venus, *n.* (*planet*) ng'andu, zuhura; (*goddess*) mungu wa kike wa ashiki (wa kirumi zamani).

veracious, *a.* -a kusema kweli, -a kweli. **veracity**, *n.* kweli, ukweli.

verandah, *n*, baraza ya nyumba.

verb, *n.* neno linaloarifu tendo au hali, kiarifa. **verbal**, *a.* -a *verb*, -a maneno tu (si kuandika), -a maneno yenyewe halisi, -a maneno tu (si ya maana yake). **verbally**, *adv.* kwa maneno (si kwa maandiko), kwa kuambiwa hasa. **verbatim**, *adv.* kwa maneno yenyewe hasa. **verbiage**, *n.* maneno mengi ya bure (ya ovyo), domo. **verbose**, *a.* -a maneno mengi. **verbosity**, *n.* kutoa maneno mengi, kupiga domo, wingi wa maneno, domo.

verdant, *a.* -a majani mazuri (mabichi, ya chanikiwiti), -a kusitawi; (*inexperienced*) -jinga, -siojua mambo. **verdure**, *n.* majani mabichi ya chanikiwiti, majani, mimea, miti.

verdict, *n.* hukumu, hukumu ya kukata maneno, maamuzi; (*decision*) neno mkataa, jibu shauri, neno, wosia, usia.

verdigris, *n.* kutu ya shaba.

verdure, *n.* taz. *verdant.*

verge, *n.* ukingo, kando; (*limit*) mpaka, mwisho, upeo. *On the verge of* (*near*), karibu ya, katika. — *v.i.* inamia, elekea, karibia. **verger**, *n.* mngoje wa kanisa awaonyeshaye watu mahali pa kukaa, na kutunza vitu vya kanisa.

verifiable, *a.*, **verification**, *n.* taz. *verify.*

verify, *v.t.* hakiki, hakikisha, thibitisha. **verifiable**, *a.* -a kuhakiki, -a kuthibitika. **verification**, *n.* kuhakiki, kuthibitisha, thibitisho.

verily, *adv.* kweli.

verisimilitude, *n.* kuonekana kama kwamba ni kweli.

verity, *n.* hakika, kanuni, kuwa kweli, kweli. **veritable**, *a.* -a kweli, -a hakika, halisi.

vermicelli, *n.* tambi, unga uliofanyizwa kuwa kama nyuzi.

vermicide, *n.* dawa ya kutoa michango tumboni. **vermicular**, *a.* -a funza, -a mchango, -a kujinyonganyonga kama funza. **vermiform**, *a.* -enye umbo kama la funza. **vermifuge**, *n.* dawa ya kutoa michango tumboni.

vermilion, *n.* rangi nyekundu kama damu. — *a.* -a rangi ya damu, -ekundu.

vermin, *n.* wanyama, wadudu na ndege wanaohasiri mali au kuleta (hasara) madhara, *e.g.* panya, simba, fungo, mwewe, kunguni, chawa, viroboto &c. **verminous**, *a.* -a *vermin*, -enye chawa (viroboto, kunguni).

vermouth, *n.* namna ya divai.

vernacular, *n.* lugha ya (msemo wa) watu wenyewe (ya wenyeji, ya nchi). — *a.* -a lugha ya (msemo wa) wenyeji.

vernal, *a.* -a wakati wa *Spring.*

vernier, *n.* kipande kidogo cha kupimia urefu wa vitu vidogodogo.

versatile, *a.* hodari kwa kazi yo yote, -enye akili nyepesi, -elekevu sana: (*changeful*) -geuzi, geugeu,

-badilifu, si thabiti. **versatility**, *n.* uwezo wa kufanya kazi za namna nyingi (wa kushughulikia mambo ya namna nyingi).

verse, *n.* shairi, mashairi, mstari mmoja wa utenzi, fungu la mashairi mawili, manne, sita *&c.*; (*of Koran &c.*) aya. **versify**, *v.t.* tunga mashairi, geuza (kuwa) mashairi.

versed, *a.* (*in*) -juzi -a, -enye maarifa ya, -zoevu -a.

versify, *v.* taz. *verse.*

version, *n.* tafsiri; (*account*) maneno, masimulizi, habari. *That is his version of it,* ndivyo anavyosema yeye.

versus, *prep.* kwa kushindana na.

vertebra, *n.* fundo (pingili) la uti wa mgongo. **vertebral**, *a.* -a uti wa mgongo. *Vertebral column,* uti wa mgongo. **vertebrate**, *a.* -enye uti wa mgongo. — *n.* mnyama mwenye uti wa mgongo.

vertex, *n.* ncha ya juu, kilele, kipeo.

vertical, *a.* -a kwenda juu (au chini) sawasawa, -a kusimama wima, -a wima, -a kiwimawima; (*overhead*) kichwani, juu.

vertigo, *n.* kizunguzungu, kisusuli, kisulisuli, kisunzi, gumbizi.

verve, *n.* nguvu, bidii, moyo.

very, *a.* halisi. — *adv.* sana, kabisa, chakari. *The very same,* yule yule (kile kile, ile ile *&c.*).

vesicle, *n.* kilengelenge.

vespers, *n.* sala za jioni.

vessel, *n.* chombo; (*ship &c.*) chombo jahazi, meli, merikebu; (*vein &c.*) mshipa.

vest, *n.* fulana; (*waistcoat*) kisibau cha kwapa kizungu. — *v.t.* (*dress*) vika; (*entrust*) weka, wekea, kabidhi, kabidhisha, -pa. **vested**, *a.* *Vested right,* haki imara, haki ya daima. **vestment**, *n.* vazi la kasisi, vazi, nguo. **vestry**, *n.* chumba cha kuvalia nguo kanisani; (*parish council*) baraza ya watu watunzao mambo ya kanisa. **vesture**, *n.* vazi, nguo.

vestibule, *n.* ukumbi, sebule.

vestige, *n.* alama, dalili, baki, sazo.

vestment, *n.*, **vestry**, *n.*, **vesture**, *n.* taz. *vest.*

veteran, *n.* mzee mwenye maarifa, hasa askari. — *a.* -zee -enye maarifa ya kazi fulani.

veterinary, *a.* -enye elimu ya maradhi za wanyama. *Veterinary surgeon,* mganga wa wanyama.

veto, *v.t.* kataza, gombeza, piga marufuku. — *n.* katazo, neno la kugombeza; (*right*) haki ya (uwezo wa) mfalme (mkubwa) kukataza sheria isifanyike.

vex, *v.t.* chokoza, sumbua, udhi, taabisha, hangaisha, kasirisha, tia uchungu, chukiza, chusha, ifya, kera, nyanyasa. **vexation**, *n.* uchokozi, masumbuo, wasiwasi, hangaiko, uchungu, chukizo, gubu, kasirani, kero. **vexatious**, *a.* -chokozi, -sumbufu, -a kuudhi, -a kukasirisha, -a kutia uchungu. **vexed**, *a.* -a kushindaniwa, -a kubishaniwa maneno, -enye matata. **vexing**, *a.* -chokozi, -sumbufu *&c.* taz. *vexatious.*

via, *prep.* kupita katika, kupitia, kwa njia ya.

viaduct, *n.* daraja refu (ulalo mrefu) linalovuka genge au korongo la kupisha watu au reli ya gari la moshi.

vial, *n.* chupa ndogo.

viands, *n.* chakula, vyakula, maakuli.

viaticum, *n.* Ushirika Mtakatifu wa kufani.

vibrate, *v.i.* tikisika, tetemeka, tinga, chezacheza; (*sway, swing*) ning'inia, yumbayumba, wayawaya; (*hesitate*) sita. **vibrant**, *a.* -a kutetemeka, -a kutikisika *&c.* **vibration**, *n.* mtetemo, kutetemeka, mtikisiko, kutikisika. **vibratory**, *a.* -a kutetemeka *&c.*

vicar, *n.* kasisi (*padre*) mkubwa wa mtaa au mji. **vicarage**, *n.* nyumba ya *vicar.* **vicariate**, *n.* kazi ya *vicar.*

vicarious, *a.* -a mahali pa -ingine, -a kuwa badala, -a mjumbe.

vice, (1) *n.* (*defect*) kosa, upungufu; (*wickedness*) uovu, ubaya, ufisadi, ufasiki; (*fornication*) uasherati; (*in* *animals*) ukali. **vicious,** *a.* -baya, -ovu, -asherati; -fisadi, -fasiki; (*animal*) -kali, -kaidi, -baya. *A vicious life, Vicious living,* maisha ya upotovu (ya uovu, ya ufasiki &c.) *A vicious circle,* mambo mabaya yanayotendana hata kuzidisha ubaya wake, *e.g.* hofu huleta ugonjwa na ugonjwa huzidisha hofu &c. **viciously,** *adv.* kwa ukali, kwa uovu &c.

vice, (2) *n.* (*carpenter's*) jiliwa.

vice-, (3) *pref.* -dogo, -a chini, mahali pa. *E.g. Vice-admiral, Admiral* mdogo. *Vicegerent,* kaimu, mjumbe. *Vice-president,* kaimu wa *president.*

viceroy, *n.* mjumbe atawalaye badala ya mfalme, kaimu.

vice versa, *adv.* na . . . kadhalika, na . . . vivyo, *e.g. I hate him and he vice versa,* namchukia na yeye kadhalika (na yeye vivyo).

vicinity, *n.* ujirani, kuwa karibu.

vicious, *a.,* **viciously,** *adv.* taz. *vice* (1).

vicissitudes, *n.* mabadili, mageuzi.

victim, *n.* (*sacrificial*) madhabuha, kafara, mhanga; (*who suffers from another's persecution* &c.) mtu (au mnyama) anayesumbuka au kuuawa au kupatwa na mabaya asiyostahili (bure, bila kukosa) kwa ajili ya mwingine; (*sufferer*) mtu ateswaye (asumbuliwaye) na tabia yake mbaya (msiba, ugonjwa &c.); (*dupe*) baradhuli, mzuzu, mjinga. **victimize,** *v.t.* danganya, ghilibu, laghai, dhulumu, onea, tendea mabaya bure, sumbua.

victor, *n.* mshindi, mshindaji. **victorious,** *a.* -a kushinda, -a kufaulu, -a shangwe. **victory,** *a.* -a kushinda, ushindi, kufaulu.

Victoria Cross, *n.* nishani yenye heshima kupita zote anazoweza kupata askari au baharia kwa ushujaa vitani, ufupisho ni V.C.

victorious, *a.,* **victory,** *n.* taz. *victor.*

victual, *v.t.* wekea akiba ya vyakula, tolea vyakula (meli &c.). **victuals,** *n.* vyakula, maakuli, riziki.

vicuna, *n.* namna ya nguo nzuri za manyoya ya *vicuna* (mnyama kidogo kama kondoo).

vide, *v.* tazama, *e.g. vide page 100,* tazama ukurasa wa 100.

vie, *v.i.* (*with*) shindana (na), -wa karibu sawa (na).

view, *v.t.* (*inspect, look at*) tazama, angalia, aua, kagua; (*see, hold opinion concerning*) ona; (*contemplate*) fikiri, tafakari. —*n.* kutazama, kuangalia &c.; (*range*) upeo wa macho; (*scene*) mandhari, jamii ya vitu vilivyo mbele ya macho, sura ya ulimwengu, kuonekana vitu; (*picture*) sanamu, picha; (*opinion*) maono, nia, rai, shauri; (*mental range*) ufahamu. *Come into view,* onekana. *Be in view, Be in full view,* onekana, fafanuka, -wa waziwazi, -wa mbele ya macho. *Have in view,* kumbuka, kusudia, azimu. *In* (*within*) *view,* mbele ya macho. *In view of,* kwa sababu (maana, habari) ya. *With a view to,* kwa maana ya, kwa kusudi la, makusudi, ili. **view-finder,** *n.* kioo kidogo katika *camera* kinachoonyesha picha itakayopigwa. **viewless,** *a.* -sioonekana. **views,** *n.* maono, nia, shauri.

vigil, *n.* kesha; (*eve*) siku inayotangulia sikukuu. **vigilance,** *n.* kuwa macho, hadhari, uangalifu. **vigilant,** *a.* macho, -angalifu, -enye hadhari.

vignette, *n.* sanamu (picha) ndogo nzuri.

vigorous, *a.* taz. *vigour.*

vigour, *n.* nguvu, wepesi, bidii, juhudi, sulubu, utendaji. **vigorous,** *a.* -a nguvu, hodari, -tendaji, -epesi, -a juhudi.

viking, *n.* mmoja wa maharamia wa meli za kaskazini walioshambulia na kuteka nyara pwani za Uingereza, Ufaransa &c.

vile, *a.* -ovu, -potovu, -baya sana, -nyonge kabisa. **vileness,** *n.* uovu, upotovu, ubaya, unyonge. **vilify,** *v.t.* tusha, tukana, singizia, chongeleza, sutasuta.

villa, *n.* nyumba yenye bustani, nyumba ya shambani.

village, *n.* mji mdogo kondeni, kijiji, kitongoji, chengo, kiambo. **villager**, *n.* mtu akaaye kondeni (katika mji mdogo), mtu wa shamba.

villain, *n.* mtu mbaya sana, mlaghai, jeuri, mshari, baa. **villainous**, *a.* -baya sana, -a jeuri, -a shari. **villainy**, *n.* ubaya, jeuri, uovu, ulaghai, shari.

vim, *n.* nguvu, juhudi, utendaji.

vinaigrette, *n.* chupa ndogo ya marashi.

vindicate, *v.t.* thibitisha haki ya, thibitisha, tetea, shuhudia. **vindication**, *n.* kutetea, utetesi, thibitisho, mathubutu, ushuhuda.

vindictive, *a.* -a kutaka kisasi, -a kulipiza kisasi, -kali, -korofi, -enye uchungu, -a shari.

vine, *n.* mzabibu. **vine-dresser**, *n.* mlimaji (mtunza) wa mizabibu. **vinegar**, *n.* siki. **vinery**, *n.* nyumba inamomea mizabibu. **vineyard**, *n.* shamba la mizabibu. **vinous**, *a.* -a divai, kama divai. **vintage**, *n.* mavuno ya mizabibu. **vintner**, *n.* mfanya biashara ya divai.

viola, *n.* namna ya zeze la kizungu, fidla.

violate, *v.t.* tendea jeuri (ufidhuli), usafihi, unajisi, ghusubu, vunja, haribu, aibisha. **violation**, *n.* kutendea jeuri &c., mvunjo.

violent, *a.* -a nguvu nyingi, -kali sana, -a juhudi, jabari, -a jeuri. **violence**, *n.* nguvu, ukali, juhudi, mshindo, jeuri, kani, ujuba, jefule.

violet, *n.* ua dogo la kunukia la rangi ya urujuani; (*colour*) rangi ya urujuani.

violin, *n.* zeze la kizungu, fidla. **violinist**, *n.* mpiga *violin*. **violoncello**, *n.* namna ya zeze kubwa lenye sauti nene.

viper, *n.* namna ya nyoka mwenye sumu.

virago, *n.* mwanamke mgomvi mwenye makelele.

virgin, *n.* bikira, mwanamwali. — *a.* -safi kabisa, -siyoguswa. *Virgin soil*, nchi isyolimwa bado. *Virgin gold*, dhahabu safi. *Virgin forest*, mwitu pasipokanyaga mtu. **virginity**, *n.* ubikira.

virile, *a.* -a kiume, -enye nguvu na tabia za kiume, (mwanamume) -zazi, -a nguvu, -tendaji. **virility**, *n.* utu ume, kiume, nguvu, utendaji, nguvu za (mwanamume) kuzaa.

virtue, *n.* (*strength*) nguvu, uwezo; (*goodness*) wema, maadili; (*chastity*) usafi; (*specific*) wema *plur.* njema. *All the virtues*, njema zote. *The virtues of faith, hope and charity*, njema za imani, tumaini na upendano. *He has all the virtues*, kila namna ya *virtue* anayo, anazo njema zote. *By virtue of*, kwa nguvu ya. **virtual**, *a.* -a kweli lakini si kwa jina. *He is the virtual head*, yeye ni mkubwa wa kweli (lakini mwingine anatajwa kuwa mkubwa); (*in effect*) -enye kuwa pasipo kuonekana; (*in appearance*) -a kuonekana pasipo kuwa. **virtually**, *adv.* kwa kweli (ingawa haionekani kuwa), karibu. *It is virtually finished*, inakaribia kwisha. **virtuous**, *a.* -enye *virtue*, -ema, -adilifu, -nyofu; (*chaste*) safi. **virtuousness**, *n.* wema, uadilifu, unyofu, usafi.

virtuoso, *n.* mtu mstadi wa elimu, hasa ya *music*; mwenye maarifa ya vitu vya tunu na sanaa.

virtuous, *a.*, **virtuousness**, *n.* taz. *virtue*.

virus, *n.* sumu, sumu ya kuambukiza. **virulence**, *n.* nguvu ya kuambukiza, nguvu mbaya (kama ya sumu), ubaya mwingi. **virulent**, *a.* -enye sumu kali, -a kudhuru sana, -kali sana.

visa, *n.* taz. *visé*.

visage, *n.* uso, sura.

vis-à-vis, *adv.* uso kuelekea uso, -a kuelekea.

viscera, *n.* matumbo, moyo, maini, mapafu &c. ya mnyama.

viscid, **viscous**, *a.* -a kunata, kama ulimbo, kama ute wa yai. **viscidity**, **viscosity**, *n.* kunata, unato, mnato.

viscount, *n.* jina la daraja ya heshima Kiingereza chini ya *earl.*

visé, *n.* sahihi (chapa) inayotiwa katika *passport* kuonyesha ya kuwa imetazamwa na kuthibitishwa.

visible, *a.* -lioonekana, -a kuonekana wazi. **visibility,** *n.* kuwa *visible,* mwangaza. *Visibility is bad,* mwangaza hautoshi. **visibly,** *adv.* kwa jinsi ya kuonekana. **vision,** *n.* kuona; (*apparition*) tokeo, njozi; (*fancy, phantom*) kivuli, ndoto; (*insight*) akili, busara. **visionary,** *a.* -a kutungika tu, si hakika, -a njozi, -a ndoto. — *n.* mtu wa mawazo mengi, si wa amali. **vista,** *n.* sura ya nchi (miti, milima &c.) inayoonekana mbali katika nafasi nyembamba, *e.g.* baina ya safu mbili za miti; kama sura katika ufahamu ya mambo mengi yakifuatana. **visual,** *a.* -a kuona, -a macho. **visualize,** *v.t. and i.* leta (ona) katika ufahamu kama kwamba ni picha.

visit, *v.t.* zuru, enda kuamkia (kutazama, kuangalia); (*in morning*) amkia, sabahi; (*in evening*) tuesha; (*for congratulation*) hongeza, pongeza; (*punish*) patiliza. *Visit a grave,* zuru kaburi. *Visit to inspect,* kagua. — *n.* kuzuru, maamkizi. (*congratulatory*) mahongezo; (*business*) majilio, maangalizi. *Pay a visit,* = *visit. Go for a visit in the country,* enda kushinda shamba. **visitant,** *n.* = *visitor.* **visitation,** *n.* kuzuru &c.; (*penal*) hukumu, mapatilizo; (*accidental*) msiba; (*divine*) Mungu. *A terrible visitation,* msiba mkuu. *Visitation of sick,* (*Mohammedan service for*) buruda. **visitor,** *n.* -enye kuzuru, mgeni.

visor, *n.* kipande cha mbele cha kofia ya chuma.

vista, *n.,* **visual,** *a.,* **visualize,** *v.* taz. *vision.*

vital, *a.* -a uzima, -a uhai, -a lazima kwa uzima (kwa uhai), -a kiini hasa, -a maana sana, -a kupasa mno, -a lazima. *Vital parts,* moyo, kichwa, mapafu, maini &c. **vitality,** *n.* kuwa na uzima (uhai), nguvu, utendaji, juhudi, wepesi. **vitalize,** *v.t.* tia uzima (uhai), huisha, tia nguvu, fufua. **vitals,** *n.* viungo vya mwili vilivyo lazima kwa uhai, *e.g.* moyo, kichwa, maini, mapafu &c.; (*essence*) kiini. **vitamin,** *n.* kitu kilichomo ndani ya matunda, maziwa, majani &c. kilicho cha lazima kwa afya.

vitiate, *v.t.* haribu, punguza nguvu, rahisisha; (*air*) chafua; (*annul*) tangua, batili, futa. **vitiation,** *n.* kuharibu, kuharibika, mtanguo, uchafuko.

vitreous, *a.* -a kioo, kama kioo.

vitriol, *n.* mrututu, dawa ya mrututu; (*of expression*) uchungu, ukali. **vitriolic,** *a.* -a mrututu; (*of expression &c.*) -chungu, -kali.

vituperate, *v.t.* kemea vikali, karipia, shutumu, laumu, tukana. **vituperation,** *n.* kemeo, karipio, matukano, matusi. **vituperative,** *a.* -a kukemea vikali, -a kutukana &c.

vivacious, *a.* -epesi -changamfu, -kunjufu, -a furaha, -a kuchezacheza, purupuru. **vivacity,** *n.* wepesi, uchangamfu, ukunjufu, uchezaji.

viva voce, *adv.* kwa mdomo (sauti, maneno).

vivid, *a.* kama kweli, kama ni hai, mfano halisi; (*of colour &c.*) -angavu, -a kung'aa sana, dhahiri. **vividly,** *adv.* kwa dhahiri, kama kwamba ni kweli (ni hai &c.). **vividness,** *n.* udhahiri, kama *vivid.*

vivify, *v.t.* amsha, huisha, tia uzima, chochea, changamsha.

viviparous, *a.* -a kuzaa watoto wazima (si mayai).

vivisection, *n.* (daktari) kukata mnyama aliye hai kusudi kuvumbua habari za ugonjwa, za viungo vya ndani &c.

vixen, *n.* mbweha jike; (*woman*) mwanamke mkali (mchuki, mgomvi, mchungu).

vizier, *n.* waziri.

vocable, *n.* neno. **vocabulary,** *n.* jumla ya maneno yanayotumiwa na mtu (mwandishi); (*list*) orodha ya maneno na maelezo yake, kamusi.

vocal, *a.* -a sauti, -a kusemwa (kuimbwa) na sauti. **vocalist,** *n.* mwimbaji. **vocalize,** *v.t.* sema kwa sauti, toa sauti ya kusikilika; (*point, supply vowel signs to*) tia (andika) irabu. **vocally,** *adv.* kwa sauti, kwa maneno.

vocation, *n.* kazi, shughuli, uchumi, maishilio; (*special aptitude*) welekevu, moyo, uwezo. *Have a vocation,* itwa na Mungu kushika kazi fulani.

vocative, *a.* (*case*) -a kuita au kusema na mtu, *e.g.* Ee Mungu, Enyi watu.

vociferate, *v.i.* toa sauti kubwa, piga makelele. **vociferation,** *n.* sauti kubwa, makelele. **vociferous,** *a.* -a makelele.

vodka, *n.* namna ya kileo cha nguvu cha *Russia.*

vogue, *n.* mtindo (jinsi, desturi, mazoea) ya sasa (ya wakati unaotajwa au kufikiriwa). *In vogue,* desturi, kawaida. *Be in vogue,* chaga, tumika, enea.

voice, *n.* sauti, mlio; (*speech*) usemi; (*words* maneno); (*in grammar*) namna ya *verb* inayoonyesha kutenda au kutendwa; (*choice*) hiari, uchaguo; (*opinion*) maono, shauri. — *v.t.* sema, taja, eleza. **voiceless,** *a.* pasipo sauti, bubu, -liopwewa sauti.

void, *a.* -tupu, pasipo mtu (kitu); (*useless*) -a bure; (*null*) -liotanguka, -liobatilika, -liofutwa, -lioondolewa; (*void of, lacking, deficient in*) -tovu, bila, -sio na . . . , pasipo. — *n.* nafasi, wazi, peupe, pasipo kitu, utupu, patupu, uwazi, ukiwa. — *v.t.* toa, -nya; (*annul*) tangua, batili, futa. **voidable,** *a.* -a kubatilika, -a kufutika.

volatile, *a.* -a kufukizwa, -a kugeuka hewa (mvuke); (*person*) -enye moyo mwepesi, -a kuchezacheza, -badilifu, -geugeu. **volatilize,** *v.t.* fukiza, geuza kuwa hewa (mvuke); — *v.i.* fukizika, geuka kuwa hewa (mvuke).

volcano, *n.* mlima wenye shimo mnamotoka moshi, moto na mawe yaliyoyeyuka, volkeno. **volcanic,** *a.* -a *volcano.*

vole, *n.* mnyama mdogo kama panya.

volition, *n.* hiari, hitiari, uchaguo, akili ya kuchagua, moyo, akili.

volley, *n.* mshindo wa bunduki nyingi zikipigwa pamoja, vitu vingi vikitokea pamoja, wingi. *A volley of abuse,* tapishi (la matukano, matusi).

volt, *n.* kipimo cha nguvu ya umeme (*electricity*). **voltage,** *n.* hesabu (kadiri) ya *volts.*

voluble, *a.* -a kutoa maneno mengi, -semaji, -a kupiga domo. **volubility,** *n.* tabia ya kutoa maneno mengi, usemaji, domo.

volume, *n.* kitabu, chuo; (*part of a book*) gombo, sehemu; (*size, quantity*) cheo, ukubwa; (*great quantity*) wingi. *Speak volumes,* shuhudia sana. **voluminous,** *a.* -kubwa, -ingi.

voluntary, *a.* pasipo lazima, bila kulazimishwa, bila kushurutishwa, -a hiari, -a kuchagua (kupenda) mwenyewe, -a kutawaliwa (kujongezwa, kuendeshwa, kufanyiwa) na akili (ufahamu, hiari); (*unpaid*) pasipo mshahara, -a bure. *It is quite voluntary,* kila mtu apendavyo; (*for you*) upendavyo, hiari yako, juu yako. — *n.* wimbo unaopigwa na kinanda kanisani (hasa kabla ya au baada ya ibada). **volunteer,** *n.* mchagua, mtu ajitoaye kwa hiari yake kufanya jambo (hasa la taabu, la hatari); mtu ajiandikaye askari. — *v.i.* jitoa (kwa kazi fulani), jitia kazini kwa moyo (bila mshahara); (*as a soldier*) jiandika askari; (*offer freely*) toa kwa hiari (bila kushurutishwa, bila kulazimishwa).

voluptuary, *n.* taz. *voluptuous.*

voluptuous, *n.* -a anasa nyingi, -a ashiki, -a kutia ashiki. **voluptuary,** *n.* mtu wa anasa nyingi, mwenye ashiki nyingi.

vomit, *v.t.* tapika; (*emit*) toa nje, foka, bubujisha. — *n.* matapika, matapishi. **vomiting,** kutapika, mtapiko, kukokomoka. **vomitive,** *a.* -a kutapisha. — *n.* tapisho.

voodoo, *n.* uchawi, ulozi. — *v.t.* loga, fanyia uchawi.

voracious, *a.* -a kula sana, -lafi, -enye pupa. **voraciously,** *adv.* kwa pupa, kwa roho, kwa kulafua. **voracity,** *n.* kula sana, ulafi, pupa ya kula, roho.

vortex, *n.* kizingia, mzunguko wa maji au hewa; (*fig.*) mvuto.

votary, *n.* mtu aliyejifunga kwa kazi (shauri, madhehebu); (*devotee*) mtawa; (*of sport &c.*) mfuasi.

vote, *v.i.* (*express opinion*) toa shauri, taka, chagua; (*attest opinion*) shuhudia kwa hati (kwa mwandiko, kwa kipande, kwa ishara); — *v.t.* (*assign, allot*) toa, tenga; (*regard as &c.*) hesabia, dhani; (*suggest*) toa shauri. — *n.* (*wish*) shauri, nia; (*in election*) kipande (hati, mwandiko, ishara) cha kushuhudia matakwa; (*choice*) chaguo; (*right to vote*) haki ya kushuhudia matakwa (nia, shauri) katika *election*. **voter,** *n.* mwenye *vote,* mwenye haki ya kushuhudia matakwa katika *election &c.* **voting,** *n.* kutoa shauri, kushuhudia matakwa. **votive,** *a.* -a kushuhudia nadhiri, wakf.

vouch, *v.i.* (*for*) shuhudia, thibitisha. **voucher,** *n.* hati ya ushuhuda (hasa ya kushuhudia ya kuwa fedha imelipwa). **vouchsafe,** *v.t.* jalia, kubali.

vow, *n.* nadhiri. *Make a vow,* weka nadhiri. *Perform a vow,* ondoa nadhiri. — *v.t.* weka nadhiri, ahidi kwa kiapo; (*assert &c.*) sema kwa uthabiti.

vowel, *n.* herufi (sauti) iwezayo kutamkwa peke yake, kama *a, e, i, o, u*; vokali. *Vowel points,* irabu.

voyage, *n.* safari (ya baharini). — *v.i.* safiri (kwa chombo, katika jahazi, melini). **voyager,** *n.* abiria, msafiri (melini, chomboni).

vulcanite, *n.* kitu kidogo kama mpingo kilicho mchanganyiko wa mpira na kiberiti. **vulcanize,** *v.t.* changanya mpira na kiberiti kuufanya mgumu zaidi; (*a patch &c.*) tengeneza kwa mpira na kupasha moto ili iwe na nguvu zaidi.

vulgar, *a.* -a watu wote, -a wingi wa watu; (*rude*) -a kishenzi, -sio na adabu, -tovu -a adabu, -sio -a malezi mazuri. **vulgarism,** *n.* usemi wa (neno la) kimashamba. **vulgarity,** *n.* ukosefu wa adabu, utovu wa adabu, ushenzi; ufidhuli, ujuvi, usafihi. **vulgarize,** *v.t.* eneza kwa watu wote, fanya -a watu wote, rahisisha, tweza.

Vulgate, *n.* *Bible* kwa maneno ya Kirumi (*Latin*).

vulnerable, *a.* -naoweza kupatwa (kushindwa, kudhuriwa, kuharibiwa), -naoelekea kujeruhiwa, -naoweza kujeruhiwa, -siolindwa vizuri, si salama, si thabiti.

vulpine, *a.* kama mbweha; (*cunning*) -erevu, -janja.

vulture, *n.* tai. **vulturine,** *a.* -a tai, kama tai. *Vulturine fish-eagle,* koho.

W

wabble, *v.* taz. *wobble.*

wad, *n.* busha, fusha, kibonge cha kitu cho chote (*e.g.* pamba) cha kukazia (cha kushindilia); (*of notes*) kibunda cha noti (za fedha). **wadding,** *n.* pamba, kitu chororo cha kushindilia kuzuia vitu visicheze (visilegelege).

waddle, *v.i.* batabata, bata, batua, magamaga, enda kama bata, tagaa. — *n.* mwendo wa bata (wa kutagaa, wa kumagamaga).

wade, *v.i.* enda (pita) kwa shida kwa miguu (kama majini, matopeni, mchangani), vuka (mto) kwa miguu (si kwa kuogelea); (*do with effort*) tenda kazi (soma *&c.*) kwa shida; (*intervene &c.*) ingia, jiingiza, jidukiza. **wader,** *n.* ndege atembeaye majini, kama kitwitwi *&c.* **waders,** *n.* viatu virefu vya kufika juu ya magoti, vya kuendea majini (matopeni).

wafer, *n.* mkate mdogo mwembamba; kipande kidogo chembamba cha lakiri au karatasi yenye gundi cha kufungia bahasha. *As thin as a wafer,* -embamba sana.

waft, *v.t.* peperusha, chukua (kama maji au upepo unavyochukua).

wag, *v.t.* tikisa, yumbisha, punga, suka, ning'iniza; — *v.i.* sukasuka, yumbayumba, wayawaya, ning'inia, tikisika. — *n.* mtikiso, mtikisiko, msukosuko; (*person*) mcheshi, mchekeshi, mbishi. **waggery,** *n.* ucheshi, uchekeshi, ubishi, mzaha. **waggish,** *a.* -cheshi, -chekeshi, -bishi. **waggle,** *v.t. and i.* tikisatikisa. **wagtail,** *n.* jamii ya ndege kama kitwitwi.

wage, *v.t.* (*war*) pigana, fanya vita. **wage, wages,** *n.* ujira, ijara; (*monthly*) mshahara; (*sailor's—rare*) halasa. *A living wage,* mshahara wa kumtosha mtu. **wager,** *n.* sharti, fedha ya kubahatisha. *Lay a wager,* = **wager,** *v.t.* pinga, piga masharti, bahatisha fedha, au kitu.

waggery, *n.,* **waggish,** *a.* taz. *wag.*

wag(g)on, *n.* gari kubwa (lenye magurudumu manne). **wag(g)onner,** *n.* msimamizi (mwendeshi) wa *wagon.*

wagtail, *n.* taz. *wag.*

waif, *n.* mkiwa, mtu aliyepotea au kutupwa (hasa mtoto).

wail, *v.i.* lia kwa huzuni, omboleza. **wail, wailing,** *n.* maombolezo, vilio, mlio.

wainscoat, wainscoating, *n.* mbao za ukutani ndani ya nyumba.

waist, *n.* kiunoni, sehemu nyembamba ya mwili katikati ya nyonga na mbavu; sehemu ya katikati. **waistband, waistbelt,** *n.* mshipi wa kiunoni, ukanda. **waist-cloth,** *n.* shuka, kikoi *&c.* **waistcoat,** *n.* kisibau; (*sleeved*) kisibau cha mikono; (*sleeveless*) kisibau cha kwapa. **waist-deep, waist-high,** *a. and adv.* -a kufika kiunoni, -a kiunoni.

wait, *v.i.* ngoja, ngojea, kaa. *Wait for* (*something to happen, give time for*), limbika, kalia. *Wait on* (*upon, for*), ngojea; (*at table*) andikia, tumikia; (*remain with*) dumia. *Lie in wait,* ota, vizia, otea. — *n.* muda wa kungojea (wa kungoja). **waiter,** *n.* mtumishi, mwandikaji, mwandishi, boi; (*tray*) sinia, kombe. **waiting,** *n.* utumishi. **waiting-room,** *n.* chumba cha kukaa kungojea. **waitress,** *n.* mwandishi wa kike wa hoteli au mkahawa. **waits,** *n.* kundi la watu waendao kuzuru nyumba na kuimba sikukuu ya *Christmas.*

waive, *v.t.* acha kudai (fedha, haki *&c.*), samehe (deni *&c.*), bihi; (*dowry*) burai (mahari).

wake, (1) *n.* (*of ship*) mkondo (wa nyuma ya meli, jahazi *&c.*). *In the wake of,* nyuma ya, kufuata.

wake, (2) *v.t.* (*p.t.* **waked, woke**) amsha; (*with a start*) zindua; (*rouse*) chochea, sukuma, harakisha, shtua, shtusha; — *v.i.* amka, zinduka, zindukana; (*be, remain awake*) kesha, kaa macho. — *n.* (*festival*) sikukuu; (*vigil beside a corpse*) kukesha usiku kuangalia maiti. **wakeful**, *a.* macho, -a kukesha, bila usingizi. *I spent a wakeful night*, usingizi uliniparama, sikuweza kupata usingizi. **waken**, *v.t. and i.* = *wake*.

wale, *n.* alama ya pigo, walio, mtai, kovu.

walk, *v.i.* enda kwa miguu, enda, tembea; (*behave*) -wa na mwenendo, fanya. *Walk about*, zunguka, tembea, tanga, susurika, zurura, zururika. *Walk stealthily*, nyata, tambaa, nyapanyapa, enda njongwanjongwa. *Walk away with*, shinda bila taabu. *Walk off with*, iba. — *n.* mwendo wa polepole kwa miguu, kwenda kwa miguu, mwendo; (*for exercise*) matembezi, matembeleo; (*excursion*) matembezi, safari; (*road*) njia; (*conduct, life*) mwendo, mwenendo, maisha, maishilio, uchumi, hali ya maisha. *Go for a walk*, enda kutembea, jienda. *A walk-over*, tendo la kushinda bila taabu. **walker**, *n.* aendaye kwa miguu, mtu hodari wa kwenda. **walking**, *n.* mwendo wa miguu, kwenda kwa miguu, matembezi. **walking-stick**, *n.* bakora, fimbo.

wall, *n.* (*of stone*) ukuta; (*of enclosure*) kitalu, ua; (*of mud and sticks*) kiambaza; (*fortification*) boma. *Go to the wall*, shindwa, onewa. — *v.t.* jengea boma, zungushia ukuta. **wall-plate**, *n.* mbati, mwamba.

wallet, *n.* mkoba, shanta, kifurushi, bahasha.

wall-eyed, *a.* -a makengeza.

wallop, *v.t.* piga sana.

wallow, *v.i.* gaagaa (fingirika) matopeni (majini), tapatapa; (*indulge to excess*) ingia sana, shiriki sana, jifunga sana na.

wall-plate, *n.* taz. *wall*.

walnut, *n.* jozi.

walrus, *n.* mnyama mkubwa wa bahari kama kiboko.

waltz, *n.* ngoma ya kizungu ya watu wawili wawili kuzunguka pamoja.

wan, *a.* -eupe (kwa ugonjwa, taabu, wasiwasi &c.).

wand, *n.* ufito, fimbo nyembamba.

wander, *v.i.* zunguka, tanga, yuayua, zurura, zururika, susurika; (*stray*) potea, potoka; (*be crazy*) potewa na akili, shikwa na kichaa; (*be delirious*) weweseka, payuka (kwa homa, ugonjwa &c.). **wanderer**, *n.* mtembezi, mhamaji, mwenye kupotea. **wandering**, *n.* mzunguko, zunguko, kupotea, safari ndefu; (*mental*) kupotewa na akili; (*delirium*) kupayuka, upayukaji. — *a.* kuzunguka, -a kutangatanga, -a kubetabeta, -liopotea; (*mental*) -enye kichaa, -liopotewa na akili; (*delirious*) -enye kupayuka (kwa ugonjwa &c.).

wane, *v.i.* pungua, fifia, punguka, legea.

wangle, *v.t.* (*slang*) pata kwa hila (kwa werevu, kwa kujipendekeza).

want, *n.* (*lack, deficiency*) upungufu, kipunguo, ukosefu, utovu, shida, uchache, kuwa haba; (*felt need*) uhitaji, haja, udhuru, matakwa; (*poverty*) umaskini, ufukara, shida, kuwa haba, utaiti, dhiki. *Be in want*, -wa maskini (fukara), zidiwa, dhikika, taiti, wamba. *Be in want of*, hitaji, taka, -wa na -chache, -wa pasipo. — *v.t.* (*need*) taka, hitaji; (*be without*) pungukiwa na, -wa pasipo; (*desire*) taka, tamani; (*deserve*) stahili, *e.g. you want thrashing*, wastahili kupigwa. **wanting**, *a.* -pungufu, -kosefu, -chache, haba. *It is wanting*, haipo, imetindika.

wanton, *a.* (*uncontrolled*) -siozuiwa, -tundu, -tukutu, -a kuchezacheza; (*licentious &c.*) -potovu, -a asherati, -zinifu, -shaufu, -pujufu, -kware, -fasiki, -fisadi, -potoe. — *n.* mtembezi, mwasherati, mzinzi, mkware, mfisadi, mfasiki, kahaba, malaya (hasa mwanamke). — *v.i.* chezacheza, kuwa *wanton*.

war, *n.* vita, kondo. *A war of words*, ugomvi, kubishana maneno, mzozo. *War to the knife*, pigana mpaka mmoja ameshindwa kabisa. — *v.i.* fanya vita, pigana. **war-cloud**, *n.* dalili ya vita kukaribia (kuwa karibu). **war-cry,** *n.* ukelele wa kutiana shime vitani. **warfare,** *n.* vita, kondo, mambo ya vita. **war-like,** *n.* -a vita, -epesi kwa vita, hodari kwa vita, -a kufaa kwa vita, -a kuelekea kuleta vita. **war office,** *n.* afisi za Uingereza zinazoangalia mashauri na habari za vita. **warrior,** *n.* askari, mtu wa vita, shujaa. **war-ship,** *n.* manowari.

warble, *v.i.* imba, hasa kwa kutia madende (madoido) kama ndege waimbavyo. **warbler,** *n.* ndege mwimbaji; mwimbaji.

war-cloud, *n.*, **war-cry,** *n.* taz. *war.*

ward, *v.t.* (*off*) kinga, epusha, bekua. — *n.* (*guard*) ulinzi, himaya, mlindo, uhifadhi; (*guardian*) mlinzi, mhifadhi; (*orphan*) yatima; (*minor under guardian*) mtoto wa kulea; (*of town*) mtaa; (*of hospital*) chumba; (*of lock, key*) mtoto, jino. **warden,** *n.* mlinzi; mkuu wa mtaa (wa chuo kikubwa). **warder,** *n.* mlinzi, bawabu, askari alindaye wafungwa. **wardrobe,** *n.* chumba, sanduku au kabati ya kuwekea nguo (mavazi); jamii ya mavazi. **ward-room,** *n.* chumba cha mazungumzo cha maofisa manowarini.

ware! (1) *int.* angalia! jihadhari! habedari!

ware, (2) *n.* kitu kilichofanyizwa cha biashara, *e.g. ironware,* kitu cha chuma; *earthenware,* kitu cha udongo &c. **warehouse,** *n.* ghala, bohari. **wares,** *n. pl.* bidhaa, vitu vya biashara.

warfare, *n.* taz. *war.*

warily, *adv.*, **wariness,** *n.* taz. *wary.*

warlike, *a.* taz. *war.*

warlock, *n.* mchawi, mlozi.

warm, *a.* -a moto (lakini si sana) -enye joto la kadiri, -a uvuguvugu, fufutende; (*hearty*) -a moyo, -a bidii; (*angry*) -a hasira, -a uchungu, -a harara; (*cordial*) -kunjufu, -ema sana. *You are getting warm,* unakaribia (kitu unachotafuta). — *v.t.* pasha moto; (*stir up*) amsha, harakisha, chochea; (*stimulate*) tia moyo (bidii, shauku). **warm-blooded,** *a.* -epesi wa hasira (ashiki, harara &c.). **warm-hearted,** *a.* -paji, -karimu, -ema, -kunjufu, -a huruma, -a upendo. **warmth,** *n.* moto, joto, uharara, hari; (*anger*) ukali, hasira, uchungu; (*cordiality*) wema mwingi, ukunjufu, ukarimu.

warn, *v.t.* onya, hadharisha, asa, shauri; (*signal*) ashiria, pungia, konyeza. **warning,** *n.* onyo, shauri; (*signal*) ishara, konyezo.

war office, *n.* taz. *war.*

warp, *v.t.* (*bend*) pinda, tia kombo; (*twist*) potoa, potosha, benua; (*move by ropes*) vuta chombo kwa kukifungashia nguzo (mwamba, jiwe &c.); — *v.i.* potoka, pindika, kunjika. — *n.* (*of weaver*) mtande; (*of ship*) kamba ya kufungashia; (*twist*) kombo.

warrant, *v.t.* -wa dhamini ya, shuhudia, thibitisha, sema kwa uthabiti. — *n.* (*justification*) haki, sababu; (*authority*) hati au alama ya kupa amri ya kufanya jambo (*e.g.* kukamata mtu, kufunga mtu, kushika mali &.); (*pledge guarantee*) sharti, amana, madhubuti, ushuhuda, dhamana. **warrantable,** *a.* -a haki, -ema, -naothibitika. **warrant officer,** *n.* askari &c. mwenye cheo baina ya *Commissioned officer* na *non-commissioned officer, e.g. sergeant major.* **warranty,** *n.* sababu, haki, thibitisho.

warren, *n.* shamba lenye sungura wengi.

warrior, *n.*, **war-ship,** *n.* taz. *war.*

wart, *n.* chunjua, sugu, dutu. **wart-hog,** *n.* ngiri, mbango, nguruwe mwitu, gwase.

wary, *a.* -a hadhari, -angalifu, -a macho. **warily,** *adv.* kwa hadhari, kwa uangalifu. **wariness,** *n.* hadhari, uangalifu, macho.

was, *p.t.* ya *be, am.*

wash, *v.t.* osha; (*bathe*) ogesha; (*clothes*) fua; (*gently by dabbing*) chachaga, chanyata; (*hands and face*) nawa; (*feet*) tawadha; (*private* *parts*) chamba; (*ceremonially*) toharisha, eua; (*extend to, of water*) tia maji, fikishia maji, fikia (maji); (*in mining*) toa udongo, mchanga *&c.* kwa maji; — *v.i.* nawa, tawadha, fua nguo; (*stand water, of clothes*) fulika. *Wash off* (*away, out*), futa, ondoa, chukua, chimbua, haribu (kwa maji). *Wash with*, (*apply*) tia, paka. *Wash out* (*of colours*), chujua; (*intrans.*) chujuka. *Wash one's hands of*, jitoa (jiondoa) kabisa (katika jambo, shauri *&c.*), acha, tupa. *Wash mouth out*, sukutua. *Be washed out*, choka, legea, nyong'onyea. — *n.* josho; (*of sea*) mawimbi, mfuo wa bahari; (*of boat and current*) mkondo; (*liquid application*) dawa ya maji ya kupaka, ya kuoshea; (*sea marsh*) wangwa; (*sediment &c.*) udongo, mchanga, taka; (*laundry*) dobi; (*coat of paint, line &c.*) pako la rangi, chokaa *&c.* *Send to the wash*, peleka kwa dobi. **washable**, *a.* -a kufulika. **wash-basin, wash-bowl, wash-hand-basin**, *n.* bakuli la kunawia. **washer**, *n.* pete ya chuma, mpira *&c.* ya kukazia parafujo *&c.* **washerman**, *n.* dobi, mfua nguo. **wash-house**, *n.* chumba cha (banda la) kufulia nguo. **washing**, *n.* kazi ya dobi, mwosho, nguo zinazofuliwa. **wash-leather**, *n.* ngozi laini inayotumika kusugulia na kusafishia vitu. **wash-out**, *n.* kuchukuliwa udongo na furiko la maji. *It was a complete wash-out*, ilipooza kabisa. **wash-stand**, *n.* meza ya kuwekea bakuli la kunawia, sabuni *&c.* **washy**, *a.* -a majimaji, hafifu, dhaifu, ovyo.

wasp, *n.* mdudu aumaye kama nyuki, namna ya nyigu. **waspish**, *a.* -kali, -a chukuchuki.

wassail, *n.* karamu ya ulevi.

waste, *a.* -a takataka, -ovyo, -siofaa, -liotupwa, -sio na faida, -a bure; (*desert*) -a ukiwa, -a jangwa, pasipo na watu wala shamba. *Lay waste*, haribu, teka, poteza. — *v.t.* (*squander &c.*) poteza, tapanya, fuja, tumia bure, badhiri, ponda mali, tupatupa, avya, tumia vibaya; (*lay waste*) angamiza, teka, fanya ukiwa; (*spoil*) haribu, vunja; (*weaken*) dhoofisha, punguza. — *v.i.* (*decay*) chakaa, dhoofika, lika. — *n.* upotevu, uharibifu, ufujaji; (*desert*) jangwa, ukiwa, mahali pasipolimwa wala kukaa watu; (*rubbish*) takataka, kisichofaa tena, kilichochakaa, kilichotupwa. **wastage**, *n.* hasara ijayo kwa kutumika au kuchakaa. **wasteful**, *a.* -potevu, -fujaji, -a kupoteza bure, -a kutumia vibaya, -a kutoa au kutumia -ingi kupita kiasi (kupita kilichopasa), -a kutapanya ovyo, -badhirifu. **wastefulness**, *n.* upotevu, ubadhirifu, budhara. **wastefully**, *adv.* kwa fujo, kwa upotevu *&c.* **waste-pipe**, *n.* bomba la kuondoa maji yanayozidi au maji machafu. **waster**, *n.* mpotevu, mharibifu, mfujaji, mponda mali, mtu hafifu, mvivu. **wasting**, *a.* -a kuchakaa, -a kudhoofika, -a kukonda, -gofu; -a kudhoofisha, -a kukondesha, -a kuharibu kidogo kidogo. **wastrel**, *n.* taz. *waster.*

watch, *n.* (*timepiece*) saa (ya mfukoni au mkononi); (*at night*) kesha; (*guard*) lindo, ulinzi; (*sentry*) mlinzi, mshika zamu, mngoje; (*post*) kingojo, zamu; (*on board ship*) kingojo, zamu ya saa nne (isipokuwa *dog watches* ambazo ni saa mbili mbili). *Be on the watch for*, tazamia, hadhari; (*in ambush*) otea, vizia. *Keep watch*, shika zamu, ngoja kwa zamu; (*at night*) kesha. *Keep watch over*, linda, chunga, tunza, chungulia, peleleza; (*of sick*) uguza. — *v.i.* (*night*) kesha; (*be vigilant*) -wa macho, angalia sana; (*guard*) linda, ngojea; (*observe closely*) tazamia, chungulia; (*be wary*) hadhari. *Watch over*, tunza, linda; (*sick person*) uguza. **watch-dog**, *n.* mbwa wa kulinda nyumba *&c.* **watcher**, *n.* mwangalizi, mpelelezi. **watchful**, *a.* macho, -a hadhari, -angalifu, -chunguzi. **watchmaker,** *n.* fundi wa kufanyiza au kutengeneza saa. **watchman,** *n.* mngoje, mlinzi (hasa alindaye duka, nyumba *&c.* usiku). **watchspring,** *n.* mtambo wa saa, kamani. **watchword,** *n.* neno la siri la kujulishia, neno la fumbo la kutaka shime *&c.*

water, *n.* maji; (*salt*) maji ya chumvi; (*fresh*) maji matamu, (*cold*) maji baridi; (*hard*) maji ya kisimani; (*soft*) maji ya mvua. *Of the first water,* safi kabisa, bora (-zuri) kabisa. *Get into hot water,* pata matata. *Throw cold water on,* vunja moyo, pooza; (*oppose*) zuia, pinga. *Spend money like water,* fuja (ponda, tapanya) mali, tumia fedha kwa wingi. *Make* (*pass*) *water,* kojoa, tabawali. *Oil on the troubled waters,* kitulizo. — *v.t.* nywesha, tia maji; (*sprinkle*) nyunyizia; (*dilute with water*) zimua. *Water down,* (*dilute*) zimua kwa maji; (*weaken force*) legeza, badili. *Make the mouth water,* tamanisha sana. *My mouth waters,* ninatona mate, nalambitia. *My eyes water,* machozi yanitoka. *Take in water,* pakia maji. **water-bottle,** *n.* chupa ya maji, kiriba. **water-carrier,** *n.* mchukuzi wa maji, mzegazega, maharasi. **water-cart,** *n.* gari lenye tangi la kunyunyizia maji barabarani. **water-closet,** *n.* choo cha maji, chooni, msalani. **water-cooler,** *n.* gudulia, rishai. **water-course,** *n.* mfereji wa maji, kijito, korongo. **waterfall,** *n.* poromoko la maji, anguko la maji. **waterfowl,** *n.* ndege wa maji. **water-hole,** *n.* kisima. **wateriness,** *n.* hali ya kuwa majimaji. **watering-place,** *n.* kituo penye maji, mahali pa kujiburudisha, mahali penye afya nyingi. **water-jar,** *n.* mtungi, gudulia; (*large*) kasiki; (*large stone*) baläsi. **waterless,** *a.* pasipo maji, -kàvu, -kame. **water-level,** *n.* kipimo cha maji. **water-lily,** *n.* yungiyungi. **water-line,** *n.* mstari mbavuni pa meli panapofikiwa na maji. **water-logged,** *a.* (*of boat, ship*) -liojaa maji. **water-main,** *n.* bomba kubwa la kuleta maji. **waterman,** *n.* mwanamaji, mvushaji, baharia. **water-mark,** *n.* alama ya kuonyesha palipofikiwa na maji; mahali pwani panapofikiwa na maji makuu; (*on paper*) alama kuonyesha namna. **water-melon,** *n.* tikiti (maji). **water-mill,** *n.* kinu kiendeshwacho kwa gurudumu linalozungushwa na maji. **water-pipe,** *n.* bomba la kuchukulia maji. **water-plane,** *n.* eropleni inayoweza kutua majini. **water-power,** *n.* nguvu ya maji (ya kuendeshea mashine *&c.*). **waterproof,** *a.* -siovuja maji, -siopenya maji, -siyopapa; (*india rubber*) -a nguo ya mpira. — *n.* nguo (koti) iliyotengenezwa isipenye maji. **watershed,** *n.* milima katikati ya mito, inayogawa mito ya nchi kwenda huko na huko. **water-skin,** *n.* kiriba. **waterspout,** *n.* nguzo ya maji kama chamchela ya maji (hasa baharini), (*of roof*) kopo, mlizamu. **water-sprite,** *n.* zimwi la maji. **water-supply,** *n.* akiba ya maji, matengenezo yote ya kukusanya maji na kuyapeleka kwa wenyeji wa mji. **water-tank,** *n.* tangi au birika kubwa la kuwekea maji. **water-tap,** *n.* bilula. **watertight,** *a.* -siovuja maji. **water-wheel,** *n.* gurudumu lizungushwalo na nguvu ya maji ya mto (la kuendesha kinu *&c.*). **waterworks,** *n.* matengenezo, viwanda, mabomba *&c.* ya kuvutia maji na kuyapeleka kote mjini. **watery,** *a.* -a majimaji; (*moist*) -chepechepe, chege, chelema, -a rutuba; (*tearful*) -a machozi; (*insipid*) -dufu, baridi, ovyo.

watt, *n.* kipimo cha nguvu ya umeme (*electricity*).

wattle, *n.* ufito; (*of birds*) ndevu. *Wattle-and-daub hut,* kibanda cha fito kilichokandikwa.

wave, *v.t.* (*as a flag*) pepea; (*as a signal*) punga; (*shake*) tikisa, konya, ning'iniza; — *v.i.* (*flag*) pepea; (*undulate*) -wa kama mawimbi, -wa kama matuta, -wa na migongo migongo, inuka na kushuka; (*shake*) tikisika, wayawaya, yumbayumba, ning'inia. — *n.* wimbi, cho chote kifananacho na wimbi; (*in particles*) tikisiko la vipande vipande vya hewa &c.; (*rush, impulse*) mjio; (*gesture*) mpungo, ishara, konyezo. *Wave of heat* (*passion* &c.) mjio wa joto (hasira &c.). **wave-length,** *n.* urefu baina ya vilele vya mawimbi. **wavelet,** *n.* kiwimbi. **waver,** *v.i.* tikisa, sitasita, yumbayumba, pepesuka, tetereka, titia, -wa na mashaka, -wa katika hatari ya kuanguka. **waverer,** *n.* mwenye kusitasita, mwenye wasiwasi au mashaka. **wavy,** *a.* -enye mawimbi, -a matao, -a kuinuka na kushuka.

wax, (1) *v.i.* zidi, kua, ongezeka, -wa. *Wax and wane,* kuzidi na kupungua. *Wax merry,* -wa na furaha, furahi.

wax, (2) *n.* nta. — *v.t.* tia nta. **waxen,** *a.* -a nta. **waxwork,** *n.* kilichofanyika kwa nta, hasa sanamu ya mtu. **waxy,** *a.* kama nta, laini.

way, *n.* njia, kipito; (*distance*) mwendo, hatua; (*method*) jinsi, namna, njia, shauri; (*habit*) mwenendo, desturi, mazoea; (*condition*) hali; (*will*) nia. *A long way,* mbali. *A short way,* karibu. *In a way,* kidogo, kama. *In the way,* njiani. *By the way,* jambo dogo, si ya maana sana, kwa kupitia; (*conj.*) walakini. *By way of,* kwa, kwa kusudi la, kwa kuwa, mahali pa. *Out of the way,* -a kigeni, -geni, -ajabu, -a shida, -a tunu, -sio -a kawaida. *Out of the way! Clear the way!* simile! jihadhari! jitenge! habedari! *Be out of the way,* -wa mbali. *Be in the way,* zuia, pinga, udhi, sumbua, pingamiza, kinza, kingamia. *Give way,* shindwa, legea, vunjika, poromoka, anguka; (*acquiesce*) ridhika, kubali. *Get* (*have*) *one's way,* pata haja, fikiliza shauri, faulu, shinda. *Make way for,* ondoka, pisha. *Make one's way,* endelea, fanikiwa, sitawi. *Ways and means,* namna na matengenezo ya kufanya jambo, namna za kupata fedha kwa ajili ya kuendesha kazi ya serikali. *Be under way,* (meli, merikebu &c.) -wa katika kwenda. *Lead the way,* tangulia, ongoza. *Put one's self out of the way,* jisumbua, jikalifu. **waybill,** *n.* orodha ya majina ya abiria na shehena. **wayfarer,** *n.* msafiri, mgeni, mpita njia. **wayfaring,** *a.* -a kusafiri, -a kupita. **waylay,** *v.t.* otea, vizia. **wayside,** *n.* kando ya njia. **wayward,** *a.* -kaidi, -potovu, -badilifu, -tundu, -tukutu. **waywardness,** *n.* ukaidi, upotovu &c. **wayworn,** *a.* -a kuchoka kwa safari.

we, *pron.* sisi; (*in comp.*) tu-.

weak, *a.* dhaifu, hafifu, -legevu, -goigoi, -sio na nguvu, -sio na afya, -epesi kushindwa. *Weak in will,* -enye moyo mchache. **weaken,** *v.t.* dhoofisha, legeza, punguza nguvu (uwezo, amri, afya), viza; — *v.i.* dhoofu, dhoofika, legea, pungua au pungukiwa na nguvu (uwezo &c.). **weak-kneed,** *a.* -enye woga, -a kusitasita, -sio thabiti, -nyonge. **weakling,** *n.* mtu dhaifu, mwoga. **weakly,** *a.* dhaifu, hafifu, -legevu, -goigoi, -sio na (nguvu). **weak-minded,** *a.* -enye akili chache, -enye akili afkani. **weakness,** *n.* udhaifu, uhafifu, ufefe, uajizi. *He has a weakness for sweet things,* apenda sana vitu vitamu.

weal, (1) *n.* alama ya pigo, walio, mtai, kovu.

weal, (2) *n.* hali njema, usitawi, neema. *For the public* (*general, or common*) *weal,* kwa ajili ya hali (usitawi, neema) ya watu wote. **wealth,** *n.* utajiri, mali nyingi, ukwasi; (*abundance*) wingi, neema, nafasi. **wealthiness,** *n.* utajiri, ukwasi, hali ya kuwa na mali nyingi. **wealthy,** *a.* tajiri, -kwasi, -enye mali nyingi, -enye wingi wa neema (mali &c.).

wean, *v.t.* achisha maziwa ya mama, achisha kunyonya, achisha, likiza.

weapon, *n.* silaha, cho chote cha kupigania au kujitetea, *e.g.* mkuki, bunduki, rungu, upanga *&c.* **weaponed,** *a.* -enye silaha. **weaponless,** *a.* bila silaha.

wear, (1) *v.t.* bisha, pindua demani.

wear, (2) *v.t. and i.* (*p.t.* **wore,** *pf.t.* **worn**) vaa; (*grand or special clothing, dress up*) valia; (*appear as*) -wa na sura ya, -wa kama kwamba; (*consume by use*) maliza, punguza, chakaza, -la, haribu kwa kutumia (kwa kusugua, kwa kuchua); (*of time*) pita kama kwamba haupiti, pita polepole sana; (*consume slowly*) maliza (punguza) taratibu; — *v.i.* (*last*) tumika siku nyingi, -wa na aushi, kaa sana bila kuchakaa. *Wear away, Wear off,* punguza, maliza, -la; (*intrans.*) pita, isha, nyamaza, pungua, tulia taratibu. *Wear on,* pita. *Wear and tear,* hasara (uharibifu, ukuukuu *&c.*) iliyopatwa kwa kutumia (kutumika). *Wear out,* chakaa, lika, isha kabisa; (*exhaust*) choka, taabika, sumbuka mno. — *n.* kuchakaa, kutumika sana, kupunguka; (*use*) matumizi; (*duration*) aushi, maisha; (*process of wasting &c.*) utumilifu, uharibifu; (*things worn*) mavao, mavazi, mavalio, libasi, nguo. **wearable,** *a.* -a kuvalika, -a kufaa kuvaliwa. **wearing,** *a.* -a kula, -a kupunguza, -a kutumia *&c.*; (*exhausting*) -a kuchosha, -a taabu, -a kusumbua mno. **wearing-apparel,** *n.* mavazi, mavao, mavalio, nguo, libasi. **worn, worn-out,** *a.* -kuukuu, -a kuchakaa kwa kutumika, -lioishiwa nguvu; (*of persons*) -a kuchoka sana, dhaifu kwa kazi au bidii nyingi, -a mavundevunde, -a kusakarika; (*with age*) -kongwe.

weariless, *a.*, **wearily,** *adv.*, **weariness,** *n.* taz. *weary.*

wearing, *a.*, **wearing-apparel,** *n.* taz. *wear* (2).

weary, *a.* -liochoka, -a kuchoka, -a taabu, -a kutaabisha. — *v.t.* (*tire*) chosha, legeza, taabisha; (*harass*) sumbua, chosha; — *v.i.* choka, legea, sumbuka, taabika; (*weary for*) tamani. **weariless,** *a.* -siyochoka, -a bidii nyingi. **wearily,** *adv.* kwa taabu, katika hali ya kuchoka. **weariness,** *n.* kuchoka, uchovu, ulegevu, unyong'onyevu, unyogovu, mavundevunde, utakalifu. **wearisome,** *a.* -a kuchosha, -a taabu, -sumbufu.

weasel, *n.* mnyama mdogo kama cheche.

weather, *n.* hali au tabia ya hewa (joto, baridi, mvua, unyevu, mawingu, upepo *&c.*). *What sort of weather?* kumekuwaje? *Cold weather,* baridi. *Hot weather,* jua kali, joto, jasho, hari. *Cloudy weather,* mawingu, kumetanda, ukungu. *Fine weather,* kuzuri, kweupe, kumetakata. *Wet weather,* mvua. *Keep one's weather eye open,* -wa macho, -wa tayari kwa mambo. — *v.t.* faulu, pita (toka) salama. **weather-beaten,** *a.* -enye a lama ya kupigwa na jua (upepo, baridi, mvua). **weather-boarding, -boards,** *n.* mbao za bapa zinazopitana ili kuzuia mvua isiingie. **weather-bound,** *a.* -liozuiwa na upepo (dhoruba). **weathercock,** *n.* kipande juu ya mnara (mlingoti *&c.*) kuonyesha upepo utokako (mara nyingi ni mfano wa jogoo au mshale). **weather-forecast,** *n.* maaguzi ya upepo (baridi, mvua *&c.*). **weather-proof,** *a.* imara, -siyoingilika kwa upepo (mvua, baridi *&c.*). **weather-prophet,** *n.* mwaguzi mvua (baridi, upepo *&c.*). **weather-side,** *n.* upande wa joshini.

weave, *v.t.* (*p.t.* **wove,** *pf.t.* **woven**) fuma; (*invent*) tunga, zua. **weaver,** *n.* mfuma, mfumaji. **weaver-bird,** *n.* mzingi; (*Grosbeak*) yombiyombi, katadole; (*Orange-yellow*) mnana.

web, *n.* kilichofumwa; (*woven cloths*) nguo; (*of spider*) utando; (*of water-bird's feet &c.*) utando wa ngozi kati ya vidole; (*plot, scheme*) matata, shauri la hila. **webbed,** *a.* -enye utando **wa** ngozi kati ya vidole. **webbing,** *n.* utepe wa nguo. **web-footed, web-toed,** *a.* -enye utando wa ngozi kati ya vidole vya miguu.

wed, *v.t.* (*man*) oa; (*woman*) olewa; (*parents, minister, guardian &c.*) oza; (*man and woman*) oana; (*unite closely*) ungisha, unganisha; — *v.i.* oa, olewa. **wedded,** *a.* (*people*) -a waliooana; (*united closely*) -liounganishwa imara. **wedding,** *n.* arusi, ndoa, nikahi. **wedding-dower,** *n.* mahari. **wedding-feast,** *n.* lima, lima ya wali. **wedding-ring,** *n.* pete inayovishwa bibi arusi katika ndoa. **wedlock,** *n.* hali na maisha ya watu waliooana.

wedge, *n.* kabari. *The thin end of the wedge,* jambo dogo au hafifu linaloelekea kuleta jambo kubwa halafu. — *v.t.* kaza kwa kabari; (*jam, fix*) kwamisha, kwaza, sakisha. *Be wedged together,* songana, kazana.

wedlock, *n.* taz. *wed.*

Wednesday, *n.* Jumatano.

wee, *a.* -dogo sana.

weed, *n.* gugu, majani, kwekwe; (*person*) mtu mrefu mwembamba dhaifu, mtu hafifu (dhaifu); (*cigar*) sigara, biri. — *v.t.* palia magugu; (*weed out*) ondoa vitu hafifu visivyofaa kitu, pembua, chagua. **weedy,** *a.* -enye magugu; (*of persons*) -embamba dhaifu, dhaifu, -liovia, -liokonda, -goigoi.

weeds, *n.* nguo za mjane (mwanamke) anayehani.

weedy, *a.* taz. *weed.*

week, *n.* juma, muda wa siku saba (hasa tangu Jumapili mpaka Jumapili). **week-day,** *n.* siku yo yote ya juma isipokuwa Jumapili. **week-end,** *n.* Jumamosi, Jumapili na asubuhi ya Jumatatu. **weekly,** *a.* -a kila juma, -a kila siku saba.

ween, *v.t.* dhani, ona, sadiki.

weep, *v.i.* (*p.t. and pf.t.* **wept**) lia, toa (toka) machozi; (*drip*) tona, nya dondoka. **weeping,** *n.* kilio, machozi.

weevil, *n.* kidudu (funza) kilacho nafaka, matumba ya pamba *&c.*

weft, *n.* mshindio (wa kitu kilichofumwa).

weigh, *v.t.* pima uzito, pima kwa mizani, hesabu uzani; (*raise anchor*) ng'oa (nanga); (*consider*) fikiri, hakiki, enenza; — *v.i.* (*have specified weight*) -wa na uzani wa . . .; (*be of influence*) -wa na maana, -wa na nguvu, -wa na uwezo, vuta, shawishi. *Weigh on,* lemea, sumbua, udhi. *Weigh down,* topeza, lemeza, inikiza. *Weigh out,* pima na kugawia. *It weighs five pounds,* uzito (uzani) wake ni ratli tano. — *n.* *Get under weigh,* ng'oa nanga, tweka. *Be under weigh,* enda, pita. **weighing-machine,** *n.* mizani kubwa. **weight,** *n.* uzito, uzani; (*gross*) ghafi; (*heavy thing*) kitu kizito, kiinikizo; (*pressure, power*) nguvu, sharti; (*importance*) nguvu, maana; (*trouble*) taabu, udhia; (*thing for measuring weight, weight of scales*) jiwe (la mizani), kipande cha kupimia uzani. — *v.t.* tia uzito, lemeza, inikiza. **weighty,** *a.* -zito; (*important*) -kubwa, -a maana, -a nguvu.

weir, *n.* boma la kuzuia maji, kikinga mto.

weird, *n.* (*fate*) ajali, mambo yatokeayo. — *a.* (*uncanny*) -a kutisha, -a kufadhaisha, -a kuogofya; (*unearthly*) -a uchawi, -a shetani.

welcome, *a.* -a kupewa (kupokewa, kukaribishwa) kwa furaha, -a kufurahia, -a furaha, -a kufurahisha, -a kupendeza. *Be welcome to,* (*be gladly received*) pewa (pokewa) kwa furaha; (*be given free use of*) pewa ruhusa ya kutumia bure, pewa bure. — *n.* kukaribisha (kukaribishwa) kwa furaha, makaribisho, karibisho lenye furaha, salamu, maamkizi, furaha. — *v.t.* karibisha vizuri, pokea kwa furaha, salimu, hongeza, amkia; (*go out to welcome*) laki.

weld, *v.t.* tambúza, gandamiza, unga, tia weko, unganisha imara (chuma, madini) kwa kufua.

welfare, *n.* hali njema, hali, usitawi,

neema, afya. *Child welfare*, utunzaji wa watoto, mambo yanayofanyika kutunza na kukuza hali ya watoto, wawe na afya na malezi mema.

welkin, *n.* mbingu.

well, (1) *n.* kisima, chemchemi, shimo la kutekea maji, shimo. — *v.i.* bubujika, foka, chemka fura, toka kama maji ya chemchemi.

well, (2) *adv.* vema, vizuri, sana, kabisa, barabara, kwa kufaa; (*interrog.*) je? nini basi? kuna nini? sema! — *a.* -ema, -a hali njema, heri, bahati njema; (*in health*) -zima, -enye afya, *It is well*, vema, heri, yafaa. *Well, how are you?* je, u hali gani? *He is well* (*doing well*), hajambo. *Get well*, pona, pata nafuu (ashekali, afueni). *Do well*, sitawi, fanikiwa. *Well done!* njema! vema! vizuri sana! *Well off, Well to do*, -enye mali, tajiri, -enye neema. *Be* (*turn out*) *well*, elekea, ongokea. **well-advised**, *a.* -a busara. **well-appointed**, *a.* -zuri, -enye manufaa, -a kufaa. **well-balanced**, *a.* -a kutengenezwa (kurekebishwa) vizuri; (*sane &c.*) -enye busara. **well-behaved**, *a.* -enye malezi mema, -enye adabu, -a mwenendo mzuri. **well-being**, *n.* hali njema, usitawi, afya, raha. **well-beloved**, *a.* -penzi, -a kupendwa sana. **well-born**, *a.* -a jamaa (ukoo, mbegu, nasaba, jadi) bora, -ungwana, -a kiungwana. **well-bred**, *a.* -enye malezi mazuri, -enye adabu, -ungwana, -a kiungwana. **well-conditioned**, *a.* -enye hali njema, -a adabu, -enye malezi mazuri. **well-conducted**, *a.* -enye mwenendo mzuri, -enye adabu. **well-disposed**, *a.* -fadhili, -a hisani, -ema; -a kupendelea. **well-doer**, *n.* mtu mtenda mema, mfadhili. **well-doing**, *n.* kutenda mema, ufadhili. **well-favoured**, *a.* -zuri, -a kupendeza, -enye sura (umbo) nzuri. **well-founded, well-grounded**, *a.* imara, -a kuelekea kuwa kweli, -liothibitika. **well-knit**, *a.* -kakamavu, -shupavu (maungo), kakawana. **well-known**, *a.* maarufu, mashuhuri, bayana. **well-nigh**, *adv.* karibu. **well-off**, *a.* tajiri, -enye neema. **well-proportioned**, *a.* -enye sehemu (viungo) zinazolingana vizuri. **well-read**, *a.* -a maarifa (elimu) nyingi. **well-timed**, *a.* -a wakati wa kufaa. **well-to-do**, *a.* tajiri, -enye neema. **well-worn**, *a.* -liotumika sana, -a zamani.

welt, *n.* mshono wa kunjo za viatu; (*weal*) alama ya pigo, walio, kovu. — *v.t.* piga sana.

welter, *v.i.* gaagaa, fingirika, jinyonganyonga. — *n.* msukosuko, ghasia, machafuko.

wen, *n.* kivimbe, tezi.

wench, *n.* mwanamke, mwanamke mtumishi.

wend, *v.t.* enda.

went, *p.t.* ya *go.*

wept, *p.t. and pf.t.* ya *weep.*

were, *v.* = *was p.t.* ya *be, am.*

Wesleyan, *a.* -a ufuasi wa mtu aliyeitwa jina lake *Wesley*. — *n.* mfuasi wa *Wesley*. **Wesleyanism**, *n.* madhehebu ya Wakristo, wafuasi wa mafundisho ya *Wesley*.

west, *n.* magharibi, machweo ya jua. *The West*, nchi za magharibi. **westerly, western, westward**, *a.* -a magharibi, -a upande wa magharibi.

wet, *a.* majimaji, chepechepe, -a rutuba, -nyevu, -a mvua nyingi, -liolowa maji, -liolowana. *Get wet*, pata maji, lowa, lowana. *A wet blanket*, mtu au jambo linaloharibu furaha (linalopoozesha). — *v.t.* tia maji, lowesha, nyunyiza maji, chovya majini, bambika. **wet-nurse**, *n.* mama wa kunyonya.

wether, *n.* kondoo maksai.

wet-nurse, *n.* taz. *wet.*

whack, *v.t.* piga kwa kishindo. — *n.* pigo, dharuba.

whale, *n.* nyangumi. **whalebone**, *n.* ufupa wa kinywani mwa nyangumi. **whaler**, *n.* mwinda nyangumi; (*vessel*) chombo cha kuwindia nyangumi. **whale-oil,** *n.* mafuta yapatikanayo katika shahamu ya nyangumi. **whaling,** *n.* mwindo (kuwinda) wa nyangumi.

wharf, *n.* mahali pwani au kando ya mto pa kupakia na kupakua shehena ya meli, gati. **wharfage,** *n.* ada inayotozwa kwa kutumia *wharf.* **wharfinger,** *n.* mwenye *wharf.*

what, *pron.* (*relat.* = *that which*) -yo-, -cho-, -zo-, &c.; (*interr.*) -pi? *e.g.* yupi? upi? zipi? &c.; (*what sort?*) gani? (*what like?*) kama nini? jinsi gani? (*how much, how great*) kadiri gani? (*interj.*) jinsi -livyo, *e.g. What a wonderful thing!* jinsi kilivyo ajabu. *A what-do-you-call-it,* nini hii, dude, nyangalika, kinyangalika. *What if,* ikiwa, kama. *What of,* waonaje juu ya? *What for?* kwa nini? *What though,* ijapokuwa, ingawa, hata kama. *What time?* wakati ule ule. *What with,* kwa kuwa, kwa ajili (sababu) ya.

wheat, *n.* ngano. **wheaten,** *a.* -a ngano, -a unga wa ngano.

wheedle, *v.t.* bemba, bembeleza, shawishi, vuta kwa maneno matamu (kwa kujipendekeza, kwa kurairai). **wheedling,** *a.* -bembe, -a kubembeleza, -a kujipendekeza, -a kurairai.

wheel, *n.* gurudumu; (*in ships*) usukani, duara ya usukani. *Wheels within wheels,* matata mengi, mambo ya kindani yakileteana matata. *Put a spoke in one's wheel,* zuia, pinga, komesha. *Put one's shoulder to the wheel,* fanya bidii, tia shime. — *v.t.* zungusha, geuza; (*convey by carriage*) peleka kwa magurudumu (kwa gari); — *v.i.* zunguka, geuka. **wheelbarrow,** *n.* gari dogo lenye gurudumu moja tu. **wheeled,** *a.* -enye magurudumu. **wheelwright,** *n.* fundi wa kufanyiza magurudumu ya gari.

wheeze, *v.i.* korota, forota, kokota pumzi, pumua kwa shida.

whelk, *n.* namna ya konokono wa pwani.

whelm, *v.t.* (*cover completely*) funika kabisa, gharikisha; (*plunge deep*) tosa, zamisha; (*ruin*) angamiza, haribu.

whelp, *n.* mtoto wa mbwa na wa jamii ya wanyama wa mwitu kama simba, chui &c.; (*ill-bred youth*) kijana mfidhuli (msafihi, mshupavu, mtundu). — *v.t.* zaa (kwa mbwa, simba &c.).

when, *adv.* lini? wakati gani? — *conj.* (*time*) -po, wakati wa. *When I went,* nilipokwenda. *When you go,* uendapo, utakapokwenda. **whence,** *adv. and rel. pron.* -ko, -mo, -po; (*interrog.*) wapi? kutoka wapi? *I know whence he comes,* nakujua atokako. *Whence does he come?* atoka wapi? **whenever, whensoever,** *adv.* kila mara, pindi, -po, po pote. *Whenever, Whensoever, I go,* kila mara nikienda (niendapo), pindi niendapo. *Whenever he likes,* po pote apendapo, apendapo.

where, *adv. and conj.* -ko, -mo, -po; (*interrog.*) wapi? mahali gani? *Where are you going?* unakwenda wapi. *We must go where we can get food,* hatuna budi kwenda mahali tunapoweza kupata chakula. **whereabouts,** *adv.* wapi? karibu na wapi? — *n.* makao. *His whereabouts,* mahali alipo sasa. **whereas,** *conj.* kwa maana, kwa kuwa, kwa sababu; (*where in fact*) lakini. **whereat,** *adv.* hapo, kwa hiyo. **whereby,** *adv.* ambayo kwayo (ambacho kwacho &c.), kwa hiyo, hivyo. **wherefore,** *adv.* kwa nini? kwa sababu hii. — *n.* sababu, kisa. **wherefrom,** *adv.* -po, -mo, -ko, kutoka huko; (*interrog.*) kutoka wapi? **wherein,** *adv.* -ko, -mo, -po, katika hii; (*interrog.*) katika nini? kwa namna gani? jinsi gani? **whereon,** *adv.* baadaye, kwa sababu hii, kwa hiyo; (*interrog.*) katika nini? kwa nini? **wheresoever,** *adv.* = *wherever.* **whereupon,** *adv.* baadaye, hapo, ndipo, kwa sababu hii, kwa hiyo; (*interrog.*) katika nini? kwa nini?

wherever, *adv.* -lipo pote, mahali pote, -po, po pote, *Sit wherever you like,* keti mahali upendapo (po pote upendapo). *Wherever he goes,* po pote aendapo. **wherewith,** *adv.* kwa hii, na hii, enye hii; (*interrog.*) kwa nini? na nini? **wherewithal,** *adv.* = *wherewith.* — *n.* mali, njia, uwezo, nafasi.

wherry, *n.* mashua ndogo nyepesi.

whet, *v.t.* noa; (*excite*) tamanisha, chochea, amsha, zidisha, washa (tamaa ya chakula, kinywaji &c.). **whetstone,** *n.* kinoo; (*coarse*) suguo.

whether, *conj.* kama, (kwamba). *Whether he likes this or this,* kama (kwamba) anapenda hii au hii. *Whether or no,* kwa vyo vyote, ukipenda usipende.

whetstone, *n.* taz. *whet.*

whey, *n.* maziwa yaliyo nguliwa, mtindi.

which, *pron.* (*relat.*) -o- (-ye-, -yo-, -zo- &c.). *All the books which I have read,* vitabu vyote nilivyosoma; amba-, *e.g.* vitabu vyote ambavyo nilivisoma; (*interrog.*) -pi? (yapi? upi? vipi? &c.). **whichever, whichsoever,** *pron.* -o -ote, (ye yote, cho chote &c.).

whiff, *n.* pulizo la ghafula la pumzi au moshi kinywani, kishindo cha ghafula cha upepo; (*smell*) harufu.

whig, *n.* (zamani Kiingereza) mtu wa jamii ya watu waliotaka kupunguza uwezo wa mfalme, watu wawe na nguvu zaidi katika mashauri ya serikali.

while, *n.* muda, wakati, muhula. *A long while,* muda mrefu, wakati nwingi, sana. *After a while,* halafu, baadaye. *All the while,* wakati huo wote, wakati ule ule, pale pale; (*in surprise*) kumbe! tahamaki! *A little while,* muda kidogo. *Be worth while,* faa, -wa heri, afadhali, stahili. — *v.t. While away the time,* pisha wakati. — *conj.* wakati wa, wakati ule ule, huku, wakati -po, -ki-. *He sang while climbing,* alipanda na huku anaimba. *It was raining while we were out,* tulipokuwa nje, mvua ilikunya. **whilst,** *conj.* = *while, conj.*

whim, *n.* nia wazo (hasa ya kigeni au kinyongo). **whimsical,** *a.* -enye mawazo ya kigeni (ya kinyongo), -a kigeni, -badilifu.

whimbrel, *n.* membe.

whimper, *v.i.* lialia (kwa sauti ndogo —kama mtoto mgonjwa).

whimsical, *a.* taz. *whim.*

whine, *v.i.* lia (kama mbwa anayeogopa); (*of person*) lalamika kinyonge, nung'unikia mambo madogodogo. — *n.* mlio (wa mbwa anayeogopa), lalamiko, nung'uniko, mnung'uniko.

whinny, *v.i.* lialia (kwa farasi kwa furaha, kumwamkia bwana wake).

whip, *v.t.* chapa, piga mjeledi, piga; (*conquer*) shinda, piga; (*eggs &c.*) pigapiga; (*in sewing*) minika, pinda na kushikiza. *Whip off,* pokonya upesi, twaa (ondoa) ghafula. *Whip out,* chomoa, chopoa; (*make hasty exit*) toka ghafula. *Whip round,* geuka upesi. *Whip up* (*people*) kusanya; (*of money*) changa. — *n.* mchapo, kikoto, mjeledi; (*driver*) saisi; (*parliament*) mtu mwenye kazi ya kuhudhurisha watu wa *parliament* wanapotakiwa. **whip-cord,** *n.* kigwe cha nguvu; (*fabric*) namna ya nguo nzito. **whip-hand,** *n.* uwezo, nguvu za kushinda (za kutiisha, za kutawala). **whipper-in,** *n.* msimamizi wa mbwa katika kuwinda. **whipper-snapper,** *n.* mtu mnyonge ajivunaye (ajitokezaye mbele). **whipping,** *n.* kupiga (kupigwa) mjeledi; kushinda (kushindwa), adhabu ya kupigwa. **whipping-post,** *n.* mti wa kufungia watu wachapwe au kupigwa mijeledi.

whippet, *n.* mbwa wa kushindania mbio.

whipping, *n.,* **whipping-post,** *n.* taz. *whip.*

whir(r), *v.i.* zunguka vuruvuru, vuma (kama kitu kinachozunguka vuruvuru au kinachovurumishwa). — *n.* uvumi (wa kitu kinachozu-

nguka vuruvuru au kinachovurumishwa).
whirl, *v.t.* zungusha vuruvuru, zungusha upesi, vurumisha; — *v.i.* zunguka vuruvuru (upesi); (*of brain*) ona kizunguzungu, pumbaa, fadhaika. — *n.* mwendo wa kuzunguka vuruvuru; (*confession of mind*) fadhaa, wasiwasi. **whirligig**, *n.* kitu cha kuchezea cha watoto kinachozungukazunguka. **whirlpool**, *n.* kizingia cha maji, mzunguko (mzingo) wa maji. **whirlwind**, *n.* pepo za chamchela, kimbunga, kinyamkela.
whirr, *v. and n.* taz. *whir*.
whisk, *n.* pigo (mguso, tendo, mwendo) jepesi la upesi, panguso; (*brush*) kifagio; (*for beating eggs &c.*) chombo cha kupigapiga, mayai &c. — *v.t.* tikisa (endesha, rusha, pangusa) upesi; (*stir*) pigapiga, buruga upesi, suka; — *v.i.* sukasuka, tikisika (enda, ruka) upesi. *Whisk off*, pangusa, rusha upesi; (*carry off*) chukua (twaa) upesi.
whiskers, *n.* ndevu za mashavuni, sharafa. **whiskered**, *a.* -enye *whiskers*.
whisky, *n.* namna ya kileo kifanyizwacho kwa nafaka.
whisper, *v.i.* nong'ona. *Whisper to*, nong'oneza. — *n.* mnong'ono, manong'onezo.
whist, (1) *n.* namna ya mchezo wa karata.
whist, (2) **whisht**! *int.* usu! shi! buu! — *v.i.* nyamaa.
whistle, *v.i.* piga mwunzi (mluzi, msonyo, miunzi, mbinja, ubinja); (*of engine &c.*) piga paipu. *Whistle a tune*, endeleza ubinja. — *n.* mluzi, uluzi, msonyo, mwunzi; (*instrument*) filimbi, kipenga; (*of engine, ship &c.*) paipu.
whit, *n.* kidogo sana, chembe. *Not a whit*, hapana hata kidogo, hata chembe.
white, *a.* -eupe, safi. *White lie*, uwongo kama si uwongo, werevu, ujanja. *White hair*, mvi. — *n.* weupe, rangi nyeupe; (*of egg*) ute wa yai. **white ant**, *n.* mchwa. **whitebait**, *n.* samaki mdogo kama dagaa. **white elephant**, *n.* kitu kilicho mali yako (yake &c.) kisichotakiwa kiletacho masumbuko tu. **white-eye**, *n.* (*Pemba*) shige la manjano. **white ensign**, *n.* bendera nyeupe yenye msalaba mwekundu, ni bendera ya manowari za Kiingereza. **white feather**, *n.* alama ya woga. **white flag**, *n.* bendera nyeupe, alama ya kutaka amani au kukiri kushindwa. **white heat**, *n.* joto sana la kutosha kufanya chuma (madini) kuwa cheupe; (*passion &c.*) harara. **white-lead**, *n.* kama unga wa kufanyizia rangi nyeupe. **white-livered**, *a.* -oga, -nyonge. **whiten**, *v.t.* fanya -eupe, paka (tia) rangi nyeupe; — *v.i.* geuka kuwa -eupe. **whiteness**, *n.* weupe. **whitening**, *n.* chokaa, chaki. **white paper**, *n.* taarifa ya serikali ya habari maalum. **whitewash**, *n.* chokaa ya kupaka. — *v.t.* paka chokaa; (*a person*) setiri au rahisisha (tabia mbaya, matendo mabaya) yake. **whiting**, *n.* chokaa, chaki; (*fish*) namna ya samaki. **whitish**, *a.* -eupe kidogo.
whither, *adv.* -ko, -mo, -po, kwenda huko; (*interrog.*) wapi? kwenda wapi? *Whither did they go?* walikwenda wapi? *Let him go whither he will*, aende apendapo &c. — *n.* mahali -po (-ko, -mo). *We know not the whither of our destinies*, hatujui mahali tulipoandikiwa. **whithersoever**, *adv.* po pote, ko kote.
whiting, *n.*, **whitish**, *a.* taz. *white*.
whitlow, *n.* mdudu wa kidoleni.
Whitsunday, *n.* sikukuu ya *Pentecost*.
Whitsuntide, *n.* juma linaloanziwa na *Whitsunday*.
whittle, *v.t.* katakata (chongachonga) mti vipande vyembamba; (*down*) punguza kidogo kidogo.
whiz(z), *n.* uvumi (wa kitu kilichovurumishwa kama mshale &c.). — *v.i.* pita upesi hewani kwa uvumi.
who, *pron.* -o-, -ye-; (*interrog.*) nani?

yupi? **whoever, whosoever,** *pron.* ye yote, -o -ote.
whole, *a.* (*sound*) -zima, -enye afya kamili, kamili, -timilifu; (*all*) -ote pia; (*perfect*) kamili, kamilifu, timilifu, bila upungufu. *On the whole,* mwisho, basi, kisha kufikiri. — *n.* kitu kizima, jamii yote, jumla, kitu kimoja chenye sehemu nyingi. **wholeness,** *n.* hali ya kuwa *whole,* uzima, umoja, ukamilifu. **wholesale,** *a.* (*trade*) -a biashara nyingi, -a jumla. — *adv.* jumla, shelabela. **wholesome,** *a.* -a kufaa kwa afya, -enye afya, -zima, -zuri, safi. **wholly,** *adv.* pia, kabisa, hasa.
whom, *pron.* = *who.* **whomsoever,** *pron.* = *whosoever.*
whoop, *v.i.* piga ukelele (wa shangwe, wa kudharau &c., lakini hasa wa mtoto ashikwapo na kifaduro). — *n.* ukelele wa kukohoa wa mtoto mwenye kifaduro; ukelele wa shangwe (wa kudharau &c.). **whooping-cough,** *n.* kifaduro.
whop, *v.t.* (*slang*) piga; (*defeat*) shinda, piga. **whopper,** *n.* (*slang*) kitu cho chote kilicho kikubwa au bora; (*a lie*) uwongo. **whopping,** *n.* (*slang*) kupiga (kupigwa), kushinda (kushindwa). — *a.* (*slang*) -kubwa sana, -zuri sana.
whore, *n.* kahaba, malaya, danguro. — *v.i.* fanya ukahaba (umalaya &c.). **whore-monger,** *n.* mwasherati.
whorl, *n.* mzingo, duara au kama duara. **whorled,** *a.* -enye mzingo, -a mzingo, *e.g.* kama alama zilizo katika ngozi ya ncha za vidole.
whose, *pron.* -a huyo (wao &c.), -ake; (*interrog.*) -a nani? **whosoever,** *pron.* ye yote.
why, *adv.* kwa nini? mbona? kwa sababu gani? sababu, hata. *I will tell you why,* nitakuambia sababu. *Tell us the reason why you came,* utueleze sababu hata uje. — *n.* sababu, kisa, hoja. — *int.* kumbe! je! ati! *Why look at that!* kumbe! (je! ati!) tazama kule!
whydah, *n.* (*pin-tailed*) msese.
wick, *n.* (*of lamp*) utambi, ujali, mjali; (*of candle*) kope.
wicked, *a.* -ovu, -baya, -a dhambi, -korofi, -potoe, -potovu, habithi. **wickedly,** *adv.* kwa uovu. **wickedness,** *n.* uovu, ubaya, dhambi, ukorofi, upotovu, ufasiki, ufisadi, maovu, mabaya.
wicker, *n.* -a fito (henzerani, matete) zilizosukwa.
wicket, *n.* kilango; (*at cricket*) vijiti vitatu vinavyolindwa na mwenye kushika bao.
wide, *a.* -pana, -liotanuka, -a kuenea mbali, -a kufika mbali, -enye nafasi kubwa katikati; (*broad, thick*) -nene; (*wise*) -a maarifa mengi, -a akili; (*erroneous*) -a kuepea, -a kukosa, -a kwenda upande. — *adv.* mbali, kwa upande. **wide-awake,** *a.* macho, -epesi, tayari. — *n.* namna ya kofia kama tarai. **widely,** *adv.* sana, mahali pengi. **widen,** *v.t.* tanua, panua, zidisha, eneza; (*draw apart*) nanua; — *v.i.* tanuka, panuka, zidi, enea. **widespread,** *a.* -a kuenea sana, -a mahali pengi, -a kuchaga. **width,** *n.* upana, mapana, eneo. *Width of view,* maarifa mengi, ujuzi.
widow, *n.* mjane (mwanamke aliyefiwa na mume). **widower,** *n.* mjane (mwanamume aliyefiwa na mke). **widowhood,** *n.* ujane (wa mke).
width, *n.* taz. *wide.*
wield, *v.t.* (*control*) tawala, ongoza, simamia; (*use*) tumia kwa mkono; (*brandish*) punga, tikisa mkononi.
wife, *n.* (*pl.* **wives**) mke, ahali. **wifeless,** *a.* -siye na mke. **wifely,** *a.* -a mke, -a kuhusu mke.
wig, *n.* kifuniko cha kichwa kilichofanyizwa kwa nywele.
wiggle, *v.t.* jongeza (shtua) kidogo; — *v.i.* shtuka, furukuta, jongea kidogo.
wight, *n.* mtu.
wigwam, *n.* namna ya hema ya wenyeji wa Amerika ya Kaskazini, ya ngozi.
wild, *a.* (*animals*) -a mwitu, -sio-

fugwa; (*plants*) -a gugu, -siopandwa ila hujiotea; (*uncivilized*) -shenzi; (*desert*) -a ukiwa, -a jangwa, pasipo watu; (*violent*) -a nguvu, -a jeuri; (*ungoverned, vicious*) -potovu, -kaidi, -shupavu, -korofi, -a kufanya vyo vyote; (*wide of the mark*) -a kwenda upande, -a kukosa; (*eager, keen*) -enye bidii, -a juhudi; (*disordered*) -liochafuka, -liovurugika; (*random*) -a ovyo. — *n*. mwitu, nyika, pori, jangwa. **wild-cat**, *n*. paka mwitu. **wildebeest**, *n*. nyumbu. **wilderness**, *n*. jangwa, nyika, pori, pululu, mahali pakame. **wildfire**, *n*. *spread like wildfire*, enea upesi mno. **wildly**, *adv*. ovyo, bure, pasipo akili, kwa nguvu, kama kwa wazimu. **wildness**, *n*. kuwa *wild*.

wile, *n*. hila, ujanja, werevu. — *v.t.* danganya, laghai, bembeleza. *Wile away the time*, pisha wakati kwa kujipendeza. **wily**, *a*. -erevu, -janja, -a hila, -danganyifu.

will, *n*. nguvu ya mtu kuchagua au kukataa neno, nia, kusudi, moyo, mapenzi; (*legal*) wosia; (*free will*) hiari, hitiari, kuchagua, uchaguo, akili; (*command*) amri, hukumu; (*energy &c.*) bidii, juhudi, moyo; (*purpose*) mapenzi, kusudi, nia., *At will, At his will*, apendavyo, hiari yake. — *v.t.* (*p.t.* **would**) taka, penda, chagua, azimu, kusudia, nia, nuia, hiari; (*order*) amuru; (*bequeath*) usia; (*in comp.*) -ta-. *I will go*, nitakwenda. *You will go*, sharti uende. *I will not*, sitaki, sikubali. — *aux*. (haina mkazo:—katika usemi hutamkwa *l* na katika kuandika *'ll*, *e.g. I'll*, nita . . .; *he'll*, ata . . .; *she'll*, ata . . .; *you'll*, uta; *we'll*, tuta . . .; *they'll*, wata . . .). *He'll come*, atakuja. *I'll go*, nitakwenda. **wilful**, *a*. -kaidi, -tundu, -potovu, -gumu; (*of action*) -a kusudi, -liokusudiwa. **wilfully**, *adv*. kwa kusudi, makusudi, kwa kutaka. **wilfulness**, *n*. ukaidi, utundu, upotovu, ugumu, ushupavu. **willing**, *a*. -enye nia ya kufanya jambo, -a kutaka, tayari, -epesi, -a moyo, pasipo lazima. *Be willing*, kubali, -wa radhi, taka, -wa tayari. **willingly**, *adv*. kwa nia (kutaka, moyo, kupenda, hiari). **willingness**, *n*. wepesi, hiari, nia ya kufanya. **will-power**, *n*. uwezo wa kutawala (wa kuvumilia, wa kuvuta wengine kutii), uthabiti wa moyo na nia. **willy-nilly**, *adv*. sharti, bila hiari, -kitaka, -sitake.

willow, *n*. namna ya mti umeao karibu na maji. **willowy**, *a*. (*of figure*) -refu, -embamba -enye madaha.

will-power, *n*., **willy-nilly**, *adv*. taz. *will*.

wilt, *v.i.* fifia, dhoofu, kwajuka, pungukiwa na nguvu (uzuri).

wily, *a*. taz. *wile*.

wimple, *n*. utaji.

win, *v.t.* (*p.t. and pf.t.* **won**) (*get*) pata, jipatia (kwa jitihadi); (*conquer*) shinda, tia fora; (*persuade*) vuta, shawishi, ongoa, bembeleza. *Win back* (*again*), jirudishia, jipatia tena, patanisha. — *n*. kushinda. **winner**, *n*. mshindi, mshindaji. **winning**, *a*. -a kushinda, -shindaji; (*attractive*) -a kuvuta, -a kutamanisha, -a kupendeza; (*graceful*) -a madaha, -zuri. **winning-post**, *n*. mlingoti (nguzo, mti) mwisho wa mwendo wa kushindania. **winnings**, *n*. faida, mapato.

wince, *v.i.* nywea, shtuka, jikunja (kama mtu aliyeumizwa sana kwa kitu au maneno).

winch, *n*. winchi, slingi, mtambo wa kuvutia kamba ya nanga *&c*.

wind, (1) *n*. upepo; (*cold wind*) baridi; (*breath*) pumzi; (*flatulence*) riahi, rihi. *Light wind*, mpepea. *Head wind*, pepo za mbele. *Fair wind*, pepo za omo. *Wind on the beam*, pepo za ubavu, matanga kisi. *Adverse* (*contrary*) *wind*, mbisho, tanga mbili. *Wind instruments*, (*trumpet*) paanda, tarumbeta, baragumu; (*pipe*) zomari, filimbi. *Get wind of*, sikia habari za. *Be in the* *wind*, vumika, -ja. — *v.t.* (*scent*) sikia harufu ya; (*exhaust*) katisha pumzi; (*rest*) pumzisha. **wind-bound,** *a.* (*of a ship*) -liozuiwa na upepo. **windfall,** *n.* pato la bahati (la heri, lisilotazamiwa); (*of fruit*) pooza. **wind-gauge,** *n.* kipande cha kupimia nguvu za upepo. **wind-jammer,** *n.* merikebu kubwa ya matanga yenye mbio sana. **wind-mill,** *n.* kinu chenye gurudumu linaloendeshwa na upepo; (*child's toy*) kititia, kibaramwezi. **window,** *n.* dirisha; (*small*) mwangaza. **wind-pipe,** *n.* koo, umio (wa pumzi). **wind-screen,** *n.* kioo cha mbele cha motakaa. **wind-swept,** *a.* -a kuvumiwa na upepo mwingi. **wind-ward,** *a.* -a upande wa upepo (wa goshini, wa juu). **windy,** *a.* -a upepo mwingi; (*lengthy, useless*) -a maneno — mengi, -tupu, -a ovyo; (*afraid* = *slang*) -a kuogopa, -oga.

wind, (2) *v.t.* (*p.t. and pf.t.* **wound**) pinda, zungusha, zonga, zongomeza; (*wool &c.*) kunja, tatiza; — *v.i.* (*go*) pita, enda; (*follow tortuous course*) zunguka, pindika, betabeta, fanya mapindi, potoka, fanya kuruba. *Wind up*, (*a clock*) tia ufunguo, kaza; (*thread &c.*) kunja; (*finish*) maliza, kata, komesha; (*conclude speech*) fanya mwisho wa maneno. **winding,** *n.* kizingo, pindi, kuruba; (*folding*) mkunjo. **winding-sheet,** *n.* sanda, kipindo; (*for woman*) msuani. **wind-ing-up,** *n.* kumaliza, mwisho; (*liquidation*) kufunga hesabu. **wind-lass,** *n.* mtambo wa kuinulia vitu, winchi, slingi.

wind-bound, *a.*, **windfall,** *n.*, **wind-gauge,** *n.* taz. *wind* (1).

winding-, *n.*, **winding-sheet,** *n.*, **winding-up,** *n.*, **windlass,** *n.* taz. *wind* (2).

windmill, *n.*, **window,** *n.*, **wind-pipe,** *n.*, **wind-screen,** *n.*, **wind-swept,** *a.*, **windward,** *a.*, **windy,** *a.* taz. *wind* (1).

wine, *n.* divai. **winebibber,** *n.* mnywaji sana wa divai. **wine-bottle,** *n.* chupa ya kutilia divai. **wineglass,** *n.* bilauri ya kunywea divai. **winepress,** *n.* kishinikizo cha kushindikia zabibu kufanya divai.

wing, *n.* bawa, ubawa; (*of building, army &c.*) upande, pembe, sehemu; (*protection*) himaya, utunzo, uangalizi. *Wing feather*, ubawa. *Be on the wing, Take wing*, ruka, puruka, ondoka. *On the wings of the wind*, upesi iwezekanavyo. *Take under one's wing*, tunza, -pa himaya, linda. *Clip the wings of*, zuia. — *v.t.* himiza; weka (tia) mabawa (pande); (*wound*) piga (vunja) bawa; jeruhi mkono au bega. **winged,** *a.* -enye mabawa; (*wounded in wing or arm &c.*) -liovunjika (liojeruhiwa) bawa (mkono, bega).

wink, *v.i.* pesa, pepesa, kupia, konyeza jicho. *Wink at* (*overlook*), achilia, samehe, pisha, fanya kama kwamba huoni. — *n.* kope la juu na chini, konyezo la macho. *Give a wink to*, pigia ukope, konyezea. *Forty winks*, usingizi kidogo.

winkle, *n.* namna ya konokono la pwani.

winner, *n.*, **winning,** *a.*, **winning-post,** *n.*, **winnings,** *n.* taz. *win.*

winnow, *v.t.* pepeta, pembua.

winsome, *a.* -a kufurahisha, -a kupendeza, -zuri, -a furaha.

winter, *n.* majira ya baridi (Desemba, Januari na Februari kizungu), kipupwe. — *v.i.* kaa (majira ya *winter*). *Winter in France*, kaa Ufaransa majira ya *winter*. **wintry,** *a.* -a majira ya *winter*, -a baridi kali.

wipe, *v.t.* safisha kwa kufuta, pangusa, sugua, futa. *Wipe the floor with* (*slang*), shinda kabisa. *Wipe out*, futa, tangua, batili.

wire, *n.* uzi wa madini, masango (ya chuma, shaba, fedha &c.), seng'enge, masoka; (*telegraph*) simu. — *v.t.* funga (kaza) kwa *wire*; (*telegraph*) piga simu, arifu kwa simu; (*a house &c.*) tia (pigilia) nyuzi za taa za umeme &c. **wireless,** *n.* simu ya hewani. **wireless station,** *n.* mahali simu za hewani zinapopelekwa na kupokewa. **wire-netting,** *n.* wavu wa nyuzi za chuma (shaba &c.). **wire-puller,** *n.* mtu avutaye mambo kwa siri. **wire-rope,** *n.* namna ya kamba iliyofanyizwa kwa nyuzi za chuma (shaba &c.) zilizosokotwa. **wiring,** *n.* nyuzi (za nyumbani &c.) za taa za umeme (simu &c.). **wiry,** *a.* kama uzi wa chuma (shaba &c.) (*person*) -embamba -enye nguvu.

wise, (1) *n.* namna, jinsi. *In any wise,* kwa jinsi yo yote. *In no wise,* sivyo kabisa, sivyo kwa jinsi yo yote.

wise, (2) *a.* -a busara (akili, hekima), -enye elimu (maarifa), -enye kujua. **wisdom,** *n.* hekima; (*learning*) elimu, maarifa; (*sagacity*) busara, akili; (*in a sly way*) werevu; (*intellect*) akili nyingi. **wiseacre,** *n.* mtu ajifanyaye mjuzi, mjuvi.

wish, *v.t.* taka, penda, tamani, nuia. *I wish you would go,* tafadhali uende (nenda). — *n.* tamaa, matakwa, mapenzi, matilaba, itakiwavyo, maombi. **wishful,** *a.* -enye kutaka, -tamanifu, -enye bidii.

wishy-washy, *a.* dufu, chapwa, -siokolea, baridi, hafifu.

wisp, *n.* kichopa, kitita (cha majani, nyasi &c.); (*of hair*) nywele kidogo.

wistful, *a.* (*pensive*) -nyamavu, -enye fikira nyingi; (*eager*) -enye bidii, -a kutaka, -a kutamani. **wistfully,** *adv.* kwa kutaka sana, kwa kuomba kimya.

wit, (1) *v. To wit,* yaani, ndiyo.

wit, (2) *n.* akili; (*humour*) uchekeshi, mzaha, uwezo wa kusema maneno ya maana ya kuchekesha. — *n.* mchekeshi, mtu asemaye maneno ya maana ya kuchekesha. **witless,** *a.* pasipo akili, -jinga, -baradhuli, -zito. **witticism,** *n.* ubishi, mzaha neno la akili, neno jerevu. **wittingly,** *adv.* makusudi, kwa moyo, **kwa akili.** **witty,** *a.* -a akili na kuchekesha, -enye *wit.*

witch, *n.* mwanamke mchawi, kichawi, mlozi. **witchcraft,** *n.* uchawi, ulozi, usihiri, uramali. *Remove witchcraft,* adua, eua, zingua, zindua, tegua. **witchery,** *n.* = *witchcraft*; (*fascination, charm*) ushawishi wa kushinda moyo, uzuri wa kupoteza akili, mvuto, maliwazo. **witch-doctor,** *n.* mchawi, mlozi.

with, *prep.* (*persons*) na; (*things*) kwa; (*together with*) pamoja na, upande wa; (*near*) karibu ya; (*among*) kati ya; (*as to*) juu ya. *Compared with,* kuliko. **withal,** *adv.* pamoja na yote, zaidi, juu ya hayo, tena.

withdraw, *v.t.* (*p.t.* **withdrew,** *p.pt.* **withdrawn**) ondoa, toa, chukua; (*recall*) rudisha, tangua; — *v.i.* (*leave &c.*) ondoka, toka, enda zake (zao &c.), rudi nyuma. **withdrawal,** *n.* kuondoa, kuondoka.

withe, withy, *n.* ufito, ubugu.

wither, *v.i.* chakaa, nyauka, pooza, -fa, dhoofu, kutaa; — *v.t.* fifisha, nyausha, dhoofisha, poozesha; (*disconcert, &c.*) fadhaisha, nyamazisha. **withered,** *a.* -liokauka, -liofifia, -liopooza.

withers, *n.* kigongo katikati ya mabega ya farasi.

withhold, *v.t.* (*p.t. and pf.t.* **withheld**) nyima, zuia, hini. *Withhold consent,* kataa. *Withhold help,* kataa kusaidia, nyima msaada.

within, *adv. and prep.* ndani (ya); (*of limit*) -dogo kuliko. *Within an hour,* haipati saa. *Within my power,* (*strength*) kadiri yangu; (*authority*) chini yangu, juu yangu, amri yangu. *Within call,* karibu hata kuweza kusikia kuitwa.

without, *adv. and prep.* (*outside*) nje (ya); (*not with*) pasipo, bila, ghairi ya, minghairi. *He tried without success,* alijaribu asipate (asiweze, asishinde, asifaulu).

withstand, *v.t.* (*p.t. and p.t.* **withstood**) simamia, zuia, pingia njia, shindana na.

withy, *n.* taz. *withe.*

witless, *a.* taz. *wit* (2).

witness, *n.* shahidi; (*evidence*) ushuhuda, ushahidi, mathubutu. — *v.t.* ona -enyewe, tazama, angalia; (*attest*) shuhudia, thibitisha.
witticism, *n.*, **wittingly**, *adv.*, **witty**, *a.* taz. *wit.*
wives, *n. pl.* ya *wife.*
wizard, *n.* mchawi, mlozi. **wizardry**, *n.* uchawi, ulozi, usihiri, uramali.
wizen(**ed**), *a.* -liosinyaa, -liokauka, -kavu.
woad, *n.* namna ya rangi ya buluu.
wobble, *v.i.* yumbayumba, wayawaya, ning'inia, tikisika, yua, tetereka, titia; (*hesitate &c.*) sitasita, badilibadili, ghairighairi.
woe, *n.* (*calamity &c.*) msiba, tukio baya, taabu; (*grief*) majonzi, huzuni, ghamu. *Woe is me!* ole wangu! **woebegone**, **woful**, *a.* -a huzuni nyingi, -a hali nyonge kabisa.
woke, *p.t.* ya *wake.*
wold, *n.* pori, pululu, mbuga.
wolf, *n.* (*pl.* **wolves**) mbwa mwitu. *Keep the wolf from the door*, epusha njaa. — *v.t.* -la kwa pupa, lafua. **wolf-cub**, *n.* mtoto wa mbwa mwitu. **wolf-hound**, *n.* mbwa wa kuwindia *wolf.* **wolfish**, *a.* kama mbwa wa mwitu, -kali, -lafi.
woman, *n.* (*pl.* **women**) mwanamke; (*young, unmarried*) mwanamwali, msichana; (*old*) kizee, shaibu; (*slave*) mjakazi, kijakazi. **woman-hater**, *n.* mwanamume achukiaye wanawake. **womanhood**, *n.* utu uke, tabia na mambo yampasayo mwanamke. **womanish**, *a.* -a kike, -enye tabia ya mwanamke, dhaifu, -oga. **womankind**, *n.* akina wanawake, wanawake wote. **womanlike**, **womanly**, *a.* -a mwanamke, kama mwanamke, -a kike, -a kustahili mwanamke, -a namna ya kike. **womenfolk**, *n.* akina wanawake.
womb, *n.* tumbo la uzazi, mji wa uzazi.
women, *n. pl.*, **womenfolk**, *n.* taz. *woman.*
won, *p.t. and pf.t.* ya *win.*
wonder, *n.* ajabu, mzungu, kioja, mwujiza, shani; (*as felt*) ajabu, mshangao. *No wonder*, si shani. *A nine days' wonder*, jambo au kitu kinachostaajabisha watu kwa muda kidogo. — *v.i.* staajabu, ona ajabu, staajabika, roja, shangaa. *I wonder . . .*, sijui . . ., *e.g. I wonder who he is*, sijui huyu ni nani. *I wonder if he will come*, sijui kama atakuja. *I wonder that*, naona ajabu ya kuwa. **wonderful**, *a.* -a ajabu, -a shani, -a kustaajabisha, -zuri sana. **wondering**, *n.* mshangao, ajabu. **wonder-struck**, *a.* (*be*) tunduwaa, shangaa mno, pigwa bumbuazi, ona mshangao, staajabika. **wonder-worker**, *n.* mfanya miujiza. **wondrous**, *a.* -a ajabu sana, -a shani, -a kustaajabisha, -a kushangaza.
won't, = *will not.*
wont, *n.* mazoea, desturi, ada. — *a.* -zoefu. *Be wont to*, zoea. *He is wont to go*, huenda, desturi yake kwenda, mara kwa mara aenda. **wonted**, *a.* -a desturi, -a kawaida.
woo, *v.t.* posa (mwanamke); bembeleza. **wooer**, *n.* mposi, mchumba.
wood, *n.* mti; (*plank*) ubao. *A piece of wood*, kijiti, kipande, kibao. *Firewood*, kuni; (*one piece*) ukuni. *A wood*, mwitu. *Underwood*, msitu, vichaka, makoko. *Be out of the wood*, okoka, pona, toka hatarini (mashakani). **wood-carving**, *n.* nakshi ya mti. **wood-craft**, *n.* maarifa ya mambo ya mwituni. **woodcut**, *n.* chapa ya mti iliyochorwa picha (sanamu). **wooded**, *a.* -a mwitu, -a msitu, -enye miti. **wooden**, *a.* -a mti, -a mbao, -a miti; (*of character*) -zito -a akili, -gumu. **wooden-headed**, *a.* -jinga, -zito, -gumu. **wood-fibre**, nyuzinyuzi za mti (hutumika kufanyizia karatasi &c.). **woodland**, *n.* nchi yenye miti, mwitu, msitu. **woodman**, *n.* mlinzi wa mwitu, mkata miti mwituni. **woodpecker**, *n.* gogota, kigogota, gogonola. **wood-pigeon**, *n.* hua. **wood-pulp**, *n.* nyuzinyuzi za miti

zilizopondwa za kufanyizia karatasi &c. **woodwork,** *n.* sehemu ya jengo (nyumba &c.) ya miti au mbao. **woody,** *a.* kama mti, -enye asili ya mti; (*containing trees &c.*) -a msitu, -a miti mingi.

wooer, *n.* taz. *woo.*

wool, *n.* (*of animals*) manyoya; (*in trade*) sufu. *Pull wool over the ears,* hadaa, ghilibu, danganya. **wool-gathering,** *n.* usahaulivu, chechele, kuwaza mambo ya kivivu, uvivu wa akili, utepetevu. **woollen,** *a.* -a sufu; (*cloth*) joho, (*thick*) bushuti. **woolly,** *a.* -enye manyoya mengi, kama sufu. *Woolly haired,* -enye nywele kama sufu. **woolsack,** *n.* kiti cha mkuu wa *House of Lords,* Uingereza. **wool-staple,** *n.* namna ya manyoya, hasa kwa urefu wa nyuzi zake.

word, *n.* neno; (*promise*) ahadi; (*news*) habari; (*order*) amri; (*Divine*) Yesu Kristo, Mwana wa Mungu. *Scriptures,* maandiko matakatifu. — *v.t.* sema, eleza, panga (maneno). *Have words,* gombana, bishana, zozana. *In a word, In one word,* kwa neno moja, kwa ufupi, kwa machache, jumla, mwisho. *In word,* kwa maneno tu. *Word for word,* maneno yote halisi. *Upon my word,* kweli, nasema kweli. *Break one's word,* vunja ahadi. *Keep one's word,* shika (fikiliza, tekeleza, timiza) ahadi, timiza maneno. *Give one's word,* toa ahadi, jifunga. *Eat one's word,* rudisha maneno, ungama uwongo, kiri uwongo. *Have the last word,* shinda. **wordily,** *adv.* kwa maneno mengi. **wording,** *n.* jinsi (namna, tabia, nahau) ya maneno; maneno yenyewe. **wordless,** *a.* kimya. **word-picture,** *n.* maelezo (mafafanusi) stadi yamfanyayo mtu kama kwamba aona picha. **wordy,** *a.* -a maneno mengi.

wore, *p.t.* ya *wear.*

work, *n.* kazi, amali, bidii, juhudi, uchumi, maishilio; cho chote kilichofanyizwa au kutengenezwa; (*literary*) kitabu, chuo, maandiko; (*sewing*) ushoni. *Works,* (*factory*) uwanda wa kufanyia kazi fulani, kiwanda cha fundi; (*of mechanism*) mitambo, matengenezo, mashine; (*acts*) matendo. *Set to work,* (*begin*) anza, shika kazi; (*appoint work*) agiza kazi. *Work of art,* kazi ya sanaa, sanaa, kazi sanifu. — *v.t.* fanya kazi, toa bidii, jitahidi; (*be successful*) faa, faulu; (*machine*) tenda kazi, enda, endelea, tumika; (*be effected*) fanyika polepole (kwa shida, kwa taabu); (*result*) tokea punde kwa punde; (*sew*) shona; (*cause to work*) tendesha kazi, endesha, tumikisha; (*produce by labour*) fanya kwa shida (kwa taabu). *Work in,* ingiza, changanya. *Work into,* ingia taratibu, badili, geuza. *Work at,* tendea kazi. *Work out,* fanyiza kwa kujitahidi sana (kwa kufikiri sana), maliza, fumbua. *Work up,* jifunza sana; (*incite*) amsha, harakisha, sukuma, chochea, himiza; (*create by slow degrees*) fanya (jenga, umba) kwa taratibu; (*use*) tumia. **workable,** *a.* -a kuweza kufanyika (kutendeka, kuendeshwa, kulimika &c.), -a amali. **worker,** *n.* mfanya kazi, mtu mwenye bidii ya kazi, mtendaji. **workhouse,** *n.* nyumba ya kukaa na kutunzwa maskini. **working,** *n.* tendo la (jinsi ya) kufanya kazi, kazi, matengenezo, sehemu zinazofanya kazi. **workingman, workman,** *n.* mtendaji kazi, kibarua; (*skilled*) fundi, mstadi. **workmanlike,** *a.* -ema, kazi njema, -stadi, -a ufundi. **workmanship,** *n.* jinsi ya kufanyiza, kazi, ustadi wa mfanya kazi. **workshop,** *n.* kiwanda cha kufanyia kazi; (*containing machines &c.*) karakana, furutile, flotile.

world, *n.* ulimwengu, dunia; (*people*) walimwengu; (*affairs*) malimwengu, mambo; (*total, sum*) jamii; (*evil*) watu waovu. *All the world,* kila mtu, kila kitu. *A world of . . .,* -ingi sana. *A man of the world,* mtu mwenye maarifa ya malimwengu, mjuzi, mtu wa anasa, ajuaye mambo. *For all the world like,* sawa kabisa, mfano mmoja. *The Old World = Europe, Asia, Africa. The New World = America. The vegetable world,* jamii ya mimea yote. *The animal world,* jamii ya wanyama wote. *The heathen world,* jamii ya watu wasiomwamini Mungu. *The religious world,* jamii ya watu wa dini na mambo ya dini. *The world to come,* ahera. *What in the world will you do?* utafanyaje basi? **worldliness,** *n.* tabia ya kupenda mambo na anasa za dunia. **worldling,** *n.* mtu apendaye mambo na anasa za dunia. **worldly,** *a.* -a dunia, -a kusahau Mungu, -a kupenda mambo ya anasa za dunia. **worldly-wise,** *a.* -enye maarifa mengi ya mambo ya dunia. **world-wide,** *a.* -a kuenea pote pote.

worm, *n.* (*earth*) nyungunyungu; (*in bowels*), chango, -mnyoo, nangonango; mchango; (*for bait*) daa; (*maggot*) funza, buu; (*tapeworm*) tegu; (*person*) mtu mnyonge kabisa; (*of screw*) nyuzi za parafujo (msumari wa hesi, skrubu) zinazozunguka. — *v.t. Worm one's way in,* ingia kwa siri taratibu. *Worm out,* vumbua kisirisiri. **worm-eaten,** *a.* -liotobolewa na funza, -liochakaa, -a zamani.

wormwood, *n.* pakanga; (*bitterness*) uchungu.

worn, *a. and pt.,* **worn-out,** *a.* taz. *wear* (1).

worry, *v.t.* udhi, sumbua, chokoza, harakisha, kera, hangaisha, hamanisha; (*tear*) rarua; (*importune*) chagiza; — *v.i.* jisumbua, fadhaika, hangaika, ona wasiwasi, hamanika, kereka. — *n.* taabu, udhia, kero, wasiwasi, mashaka, hamaniko. **worrying,** *a.* -sumbufu, -a kufadhaisha, -a mashaka, -a kutia wasiwasi.

worse, *a.* -baya zaidi. *He is worse of sickness),* ugonjwa umemzidi.

worst, *a.* -baya kuliko -ote, -baya sana. *Get the worst,* shindwa. *At the worst,* iwayo yote, kwa vyo vyote. — *adv.* vibaya kuliko -ote. — *v.t.* shinda.

worship, *n.* ibada, sala; (*fervent esteem*) heshima nyingi; (*as title*) jina la heshima, hasa la jaji (hakimu). *His worship,* (*judge, Mayor*). — *v.t.* abudu, sujudu; (*honour much*) heshimu (stahi, penda) mno. *House or place of worship,* kanisa, msikiti. **worshipful,** *a.* -a kustahili heshima. **worshipper,** *n.* mwabudu.

worst, *a. and v.* taz. *worse.*

worsted, *n.* sufu, uzi wa sufu. — *a.* -a sufu.

wort, *n.* togwa, pombe tamu isiyochachwa.

worth, *n.* (*value*) thamani; (*price*) bei, kima; (*excellence*) wema, uzuri, ustahiki; (*amount*) kiasi. — *a.* -enye thamani sawa na, -a kupata, -a kustahili, -stahifu. *What is it worth?* kiasi gani? chapatajе? *Be worth while,* faa. *It is not worth while,* haidhuru, mamoja, haina maana. **worthily,** *adv.* kwa ustahifu, kwa haki, kweli. **worthiness,** *n.* ustahabu, ustahilivu, haki, kustahili, ustahiki. **worthless,** *a.* -sio na thamani, hafifu, dhaifu, -bovu, ovyo, -siyofaa kitu, duni, dufu. **worthlessness,** *n.* uhafifu, udhaifu, ubovu, kutofaa kitu, ufefe. **worthy,** *a.* -a kufaa, -a kustahili, -ema, bora, -a kustahiki, -a kupasisha, -a kujuzia. *Make worthy, Think worthy,* stahilisha. — *n.* mtu mkuu (mwema, mwenye sifa, mashuhuri &c.).

would, *p.t.* ya *will. In contingent tenses,* -nge-, -ngali-. *Would that,* laiti. **would-be,** *a.* -enye kutaka, -enye nia ya, -a kujifanya, -a uwongo.

wound, (1) *p.t. and pf.t.* ya *wind* (2).

wound, (2) *n.* jeraha, kidonda; (*injury*) hasara; (*of feelings*) uchungu. — *v.t.* jeruhi, tia jeraha, umiza; (*vex*) udhi, tia uchungu, choma moyo, sikitisha.

wove, *p.t.,* **woven,** *p.f.t.* ya *weave.*

wrack, *n.* mwani (majani) wa baharini uliotupwa ufukoni bisibisi.

wraith, *n.* mzuka, pepo, kivuli.

wrangle, *v.i.* gombana, zozana, bishana kwa makelele. — *n.* ugomvi, mzozo, bishano lenye makelele. **wrangler**, *n.* mgomvi; (*mathematician*) mtu ashindaye katika mtihani fulani wa *Cambridge University*.

wrap, *v.t.* kunja, viringisha, zongomeza, funika, setiri. *Be wrapped up in*, fungamana na, jifunga kwa, jitia katika. **wrap, wrapper**, *n.* nguo ya kujifunika, shali, karatasi ya kufungia kitu, *e.g.* kifurushi.

wrath, *n.* ghadhabu, hasira, uchungu, hari, harara, ghaidi, kiruu, hamaki, kasirani, mfundo, kinyongo, undani. **wrathful**, *a.* -a ghadhabu (hasira &c.).

wreak, *v.t.* lipiza, pasisha, fikiliza, timiliza, patiliza.

wreath, *n.* (*flowers*) maua yaliyosokotwa kama kata au mnyororo, masongo; (*of smoke &c.*) mzingo, pindi, songo. **wreathe**, *v.t.* zungusha, zungushia; — *v.i.* zunguka, fanya *wreath* au kitu kama *wreath*. *His face was wreathed in smiles*, uso wake ulikunjuka sana kwa kuchekelea.

wreck, *n.* kuvunjika chombo (merikebu, jahazi, meli), mavunjiko ya merikebu &c.; (*ruin*) mwangamizo, maangamizi, mvunjiko, mavunjiko, maboromoko, mabaki ya kitu kilichoharibika. — *v.t.* haribu, angamiza, bomoa; (*of ships*) vunja chombo, *e.g.* kwa kukipweleza mwambani &c. **wreckage**, *n.* mabaki ya chombo (au kitu) kilichovunjika). **wrecker**, *n.* mharibu, mwangamizi, mtu avunjaye au kuharibu meli &c., kwa kukipweleza mwambani &c., kusudi.

wren, *n.* namna ya ndege mdogo.

wrench, *v.t.* vuta ghafula kwa nguvu, ng'oa kwa nguvu; (*twist &c.*) nyonga, songoa, songonyoa; (*strain*) tegua, shtusha, gutusha, popotoa. — *n.* shtuo, teguo; (*painful emotion*) maumivu, uchungu; (*tool*) chombo cha kukazia misumari mikubwa ya hesi (parafujo, skrubu), bisibisi.

wrest, *v.t.* pokonya, nyang'anya, twaa (bila) kwa nguvu; (*distort*) vuta, geuza, potoa. **wrestle**, *v.i.* shindana mweleka. shindana mbavu, shindana kwa nguvu, jitahidi sana. **wrestler**, *n.* mshindani mweleka.

wretch, *n.* maskini, fukara, mtu mnyonge; (*scoundrel*) mtu mbaya sana, mtu mwovu sana, mshari, baa. **wretched**, *a.* -enye hali mbaya (hafifu), -a taabu, -a huzuni, -a maumivu, -baya, duni, hafifu, dhalili.

wrick, *v.t.* shtusha, tegua. — *n.* shtuo, teguko.

wriggle, *v.i.* jinyonganyonga, nyekenya, pindapinda, vinginyika, enda kwa kujipindapinda, gaagaa, furukuta. *Wriggle out*, okoka kwa hila (kwa werevu). — *n.* tendo la kujinyonganyonga &c. **wriggler**, *n.* ajipindapindaye &c.; mtu mwerevu, mwenye hila, mgeugeu.

wring, *v.t.* (*p.t. and pf.t.* **wrung**) (*clothes*) kamua, songoa, songonyoa, guruta; (*hands*) tukusa; (*neck*) songa, nyonga, kongonyoa, konyoa, popotoa; (*cause pain*) umiza, tia uchungu; (*strain*) popotoa, shtusha; (*extort*) toza kwa nguvu. **wringer**, *n.* *wringing-machine*, guruto.

wrinkle, (1) *n.* shauri la kufaa (la kusaidia).

wrinkle, (2) *n.* kifinyo, kikunjo, kunyanzi. — *v.t.* fanya vifinyo (vikunjo, makunyanzi). **wrinkly**, *a.* -enye vifinyo (vikunjo, makunyanzi) vingi.

wrist, *n.* kiwiko, kifundo (cha mkono), kilimbili.

write, *v.i.* (*p.t.* **wrote**, *pf.t.* **written**) andika; (*a book*) buni, tunga; (*poetry*) tunga; (*engrave*) chora; (*correspond*) andika barua; (*badly*) chorachora. *Write down*, andika. *Write off*, futa. **writ**, *n.* hati. *Holy writ*, Maandiko Matakatifu. *Serve* *a writ on*, mpe mtu hati (notisi) ya kumwita mbele ya korti. **writer,** *n.* mwandishi, katibu, karani. **writing,** *n.* mwandiko, mkono; (*cursive*) mwandiko wa michoro; (*script*) mwandiko wa chapa; (*style*) maandishi. **writings,** *n. pl.* maandiko, vitabu, vyuo. **writing-desk,** *n.* dawati. **writing-ink,** *n.* wino. **writing-paper,** *n.* karatasi ya kuandikia. **written,** *a.* -lioandikwa.

writhe, *v.i.* jinyonga, jitapa, nyekenya, furukuta, gaagaa, tukutiza, vinginyika.

writing, *n.*, **writings,** *n.*, **writing-desk,** *n.*, **writing-ink,** *n.*, **writing-paper,** *n.*, **written,** *a.* taz. *write.*

wrong, *a.* -baya, -ovu, -a dhambi; (*mistaken*) -kosefu, si sawa, si haki, si saḥihi; (*unsuited*) -siofaa. *That is wrong* (*mistaken*), sivyo, haifai, ni kosa. *Go wrong,* enda upande, potoka, pooza. *You are wrong,* umekosa. — *adv.* kwa jinsi isivyo sahihi, vibaya. — *n.* mabaya, maovu, ubaya, uovu, kosa, dhambi; (*injustice*) udhalimu, dhuluma, madhara. — *v.t.* dhulumu, dhalimu, tendea mabaya, dhuru, hasiri. **wrongdoer,** *n.* mtenda mabaya, mwovu, mdhalimu. **wrongful,** *a.* si haki, -a kudhuru, -dhalimu, -baya, -onevu, si sawa. **wrong-headed,** *a.* -tundu, -kaidi, -potovu, -baya.

wrote, *p.t.* ya *write.*

wroth, *a.* (*be*) ghadhibika, kasirika, -wa na hasira.

wrought, *p.t. and pf.t.* ya *work. He wrought,* alitenda, alifanyiza, alitenda kazi. **wrought-iron,** *n.* chuma kilichofuliwa.

wrung, *p.t. and pf.t.* ya *wring.*

wry, *a.* -a upande, -a kitongo, -a upogo, -liopotoka. *Make a wry face* (*mouth*), kunja (finya) uso (kwa kuona machukizo au maumivu &c.).

X

X, herufi ya Kirumi, maana yake kumi.

Xmas, *n* = *Christmas.*

X-rays, *n.* namna ya nuru ya umeme inayoweza kupenya vitu visivyopenyeka kwa nuru ya vivi hivi, *e.g.* mwili wa mtu &c.

xylonite, *n.* = *celluloid.*

xylophone, *n.* marimba; (*large*) chondo.

Y

yacht, *n.* chombo cha anasa cha kutembelea baharini au cha kushindania mbio kwa matanga. — *v.i.* tembelea katika *yacht*. **yachting**, *n.* matumizi au mashindano ya *yacht*.

yak, *n.* mnyama wa *Tibet* kama ng'ombe mwenye manyoya marefu.

yam, *n.* kiazi kikuu.

yank, *v.t.* vuta kwa nguvu (ghafula), shtua.

Yankee, *n.* mtu wa Amerika.

yap, *v.i.* lialia kwa sauti nyembamba (kama mbwa waliavyo pengine).

yard, (1) *n.* (*measure*) yadi, wari, kipimo cha urefu cha inchi 36 au futi 3; (*of ship*) foromali.

yard, (2) *n.* (*enclosure*) ua, uga, kitalu, uwanja; (*work-yard*) kiwanda, karakana, flotile, furutile.

yarn, *n.* kitani, nyuzi zilizosokotwa; (*story*) hadithi, kisa, masimulizi; (*exaggerated report &c.*) kupiga chuku; (*conversation*) maongezi, mazungumzo, porojo, soga. — *v.i.* simulia hadithi, ongea, zungumza.

yashmak, *n.* barakoa, shela.

yawl, *n.* mashua ya jahazi au meli; chombo kidogo chenye matanga.

yawn, *v.i.* piga miayo, fumbua sana kinywa, kama kwa mshangao *&c.* (*lie open*) fumbuka, -wa wazi (kama pango, shimo *&c.*). — *n.* mwayo. **yawning**, *a.* -liofumbuka, wazi; (*drowsy*) -enye kusinziasinzia.

yaws, *n.* buba.

ye, *pron.* = *you*, ninyi; (*in comp.*) m-, -wa-.

yea, *int.* ndiyo, naam, kweli.

year, *n.* mwaka, siku 365. *Leap year*, mwaka mrefu, yaani wa siku 366. *Attain years of discretion*, pata akili, -wa mtu mzima. *Last year*, mwaka jana. *Year before last*, mwaka wa juzi. *Years ago*, tangu zamani, zamani sana. **yearling**, *n.* mnyama wa mwaka mmoja. **yearly**, *a.* -a kila mwaka.

yearn, *v.i.* taka sana, tamani sana, onea shauku. **yearning**, *n.* upendo, huruma, hamu, tamaa, uchu, shauku, hawa, jadi, kwiu. **yearningly**, *adv.* kwa kutamani sana, kwa upendo (hamu, huruma, shauku).

yeast, *n.* chachu, hamira. **yeasty**, *a.* -enye povu, -lioumuka, kama chachu.

yell, *v.i.* piga yowe, piga kelele (ya hofu, ya umivu, ya vita *&c.*). — *n.* kelele (ya hofu, ya vita, ya umivu *&c.*).

yellow, *a.* -a kimanjano, -a rangi ya majano. *Yellow-fever*, namna ya homa kali sana iletwayo na aina ya mbu (*stegomyia*).

yelp, *v.i.* lia (kama mbwa akipigwa). — *n.* mlio (kama wa mbwa akipigwa).

yeoman, *n.* mkulima. *Yeoman's service*, msaada mkuu, utumishi ulio bora. **yeomanry**, *n.* wakulima; (*military*) askari wapanda farasi.

yes, *adv.* ndiyo, naam, vema, vyema, ehee, ewaa, eewala.

yesterday, *n.* jana. *Yesternight*, usiku wa leo. *Yesteryear*, mwaka jana.

yet, *adv.* (*until now &c.*) hata sasa, bado, -ja-, *e.g. he has not come yet*, hajaja bado; (*at this present time*) sasa; (*still*) hata sasa; (*in addition &c.*) tena; (*but*) lakini, walakini.

yew, *n.* mti kama mvinje.

Yiddish, *n.* mchanganyiko wa lugha ya Kiyahudi na kidachi unaotumika sasa na *Jews* (Wayahudi wa siku hizi).

yield, *v.t.* (*give up*) toa, acha; (*produce*) zaa; — *v.i.* (*submit*) jitoa, shindwa, ridhika, kubali; (*of material objects*) topea, bonyea, nepa, napukia. — *n.* uzao, mazao, mavuno, chumo, mapato, faida. **yielding**, *a.* laini, -ororo, teketeke, -a kubonyea; (*compliant*) -tiifu, -sikivu, -epesi kushawishika (wa kuvutika).

ylang-ylang, *n.* (*tree*) mlangilangi; (*flower*) langilangi.

yodel, *v.i.* imba (kwa madoido, kwa madende).

yoke, *n.* (*for cattle*) nira; (*slave's*) kongwa, mkatale; (*pair*) jozi; (*bondage*) utumwa; (*authority, power*) nguvu, uwezo, mkono. — *v.t.* fungia nira, fungasa, fungasha, fungashia (ng'ombe) na gari; (*bind, tie together*) funga, funganisha. **yoke-fellow,** *n.* mwenzi wa kazi.

yokel, *n.* mtu wa kimashamba, mjinga, mzuzu.

yolk, *n.* kiini cha yai.

yon, *a.* yule, huyo (ule, huo, ile, hilo *&c.*). — *adv.* kule, huko. **yonder,** *a. and adv.* kule, huko.

yore, *n.* *Of yore,* -a kale, hapo kale, -a zamani.

you, *pron.* wewe; (*in comp.*) u-, -ku-; (*plur.*) ninyi; (*in comp.*) m-, -wa-.

young, *a.* -dogo, -changa, -toto; (*inexperienced*) -jinga. *A young man,* kijana, mvulana. *A young woman,* kijana, mwanamwali, msichana. — *n.* mtoto; (*bird*) kinda; (*animal*) mtoto, mwana. *With young,* -enye mimba, -zito. **youngster,** *n.* mtoto, kijana.

your, yours, *a.* -ako; (*plur.*) -enu. **yourself,** (*plur.* **yourselves,**) *pron.* wewe mwenyewe; (*plur.*) ninyi wenyewe; (*reflex.*) -ji-.

youth, *n.* ujana, uvulana, usichana, shababi, udogo. — *n.* kijana; (*young man*) kijana mwanamume, mvulana, ghulamu. **youthful,** *a.* -a ujana, -a nguvu.

yule, yuletide, *n.* sikukuu ya *Christmas.*

Z

zany, *n.* mcheshi, mchekeshi, mpuzi.

Zanzibar, *n.* (*town and island*) Unguja. *A Zanzibar man,* mtu wa Unguja. *The Zanzibar dialect of Swahili,* Kiunguja.

zariba, *n.* boma, hasa la miiba.

zeal, *n.* juhudi, bidii, ujitihadi, uharara, moyo, nguvu, ghera, jadi. **zealot,** *n.* mwenye bidii mno (kupita kiasi), mwenye uharara; (*devotee*) mtawa, sufii. **zealous,** *a.* -enye bidii (juhudi, moyo, uharara). **zealously,** *adv.* kwa bidii, kwa moyo *&c.*

zebra, *n.* punda milia.

zebu, *n.* ng'ombe (mwenye nundu).

zenana, *n.* sehemu ya nyumba ya kihindi ya wanawake.

Zend-Avesta, *n.* kitabu kitakatifu cha kale cha Waajemi (cha Maparisi).

zenith, *n.* mbinguni sawasawa juu kichwani; (*height*) upeo, kipeo, usitawi.

zephyr, *n.* upepo mwanana (wa magharibi).

zeppelin, *n.* namna ya eropleni kama *balloon* kubwa sana inayoendeshwa na mashine.

zero, *n.* si kitu (*cipher*) sifuri; (*starting-point*) mwanzo; (*lowest stage*) mwisho.

zest, *n.* bidii, pupa; (*relish*) utamu, ladha, kiungo cha kukolea.

zigzag, *a.* -a kupindukapinduka, -a kipengee, -a kupotokapotoka, upogoupogo.

zinc, *n.* namna ya madini nyeupe; hutumiwa sana kupaka juu ya chuma kufanyiza mabati *&c.*, zinki.

zither, *n.* namna ya zeze.

zodiac, *n.* sehemu ya uwingu juu kama ukanda inayoelekeana na *tropics* chini, yenye mafungu makuu kumi na mawili ya nyota yaitwayo *Signs of the zodiac.*

zone, *n.* mshipi, ukanda; (*stripe, band*) mlia; (*in geography*) sehemu maalum ya dunia au nchi.

zoology, *n.* elimu na maarifa ya vitu vyenye uhai, *e.g.* wanyama, ndege, samaki *&c.* **zoo, zoological gardens**, *n.* bustani kubwa mlimowekwa jamii ya wanyama, ndege *&c.* wa namna zote, wamefungwa katika vitundu au mahali wasipoweza kutoka. **zoological**, *a.* -a *zoology.* **zoologist**, *n.* mwenye elimu ya *zoology.*

zoophyte, *n.* mnyama au mdudu kama mmea, yaani nusu mnyama nusu mmea.

zymotic, *a.* *Zymotic diseases*, magonjwa mengineyo ya kuambukiza, *e.g.* ndui, surua, kifaduro, kuhara damu *&c.*